D1587061

THE MANUAL OF
CULTIVATED
ORCHID SPECIES

Helmut Bechtel • Phillip Cribb • Edmund Launert

THE MANUAL OF CULTIVATED ORCHID SPECIES

Third Edition

BLANDFORD

A BLANDFORD BOOK

This edition published in the UK 1992 by Blandford
Reprinted 1998

Cassell Imprint
Wellington House
125 Strand
London WC2R 0BB

First edition 1981
Second edition 1986

English language text copyright © 1981, 1986 & 1992 Blandford Press.

Originally published in Germany as *Orchideenatlas*
World copyright © 1980 Eugen Ulmer GmbH, Stuttgart

British Library Cataloguing in Publication Data
Bechtel, Helmut
The manual of cultivated orchid species.
1. Cultivated orchids
I. Title, II. Cribb, Phillip III. Launert, Edmund IV.
[Orchideenatlas. *English*]
635.93415
ISBN 0-7137-2104-9

Printed and bound in Great Britain by The Bath Press, Bath.

Contents

Acknowledgments

The text authors wish to thank Professor G. Prance, Director of the Royal Botanic Gardens, Kew, for his permission to use the resources of both the library and the Orchid Herbarium. Thanks are also due to Professor G. Lucas, Keeper of the Herbarium, and Mr P. Taylor, formerly Curator of the Orchid Herbarium at Kew. Special thanks are due to David Menzies, formerly Orchid Grower at the Royal Botanic Gardens, Kew, for his valuable assistance in writing the cultivation instructions. Valuable advice was also received from Mark Wood of Great Bardfield, Essex (*Paphiopedilum*) and C.J. Seth of Bromsgrove, Worcestershire (*Cymbidium*).

The line drawings were executed by Miss Victoria Goaman, Miss Christabel King, Mrs Ann Davies and Mrs Mair Swann.

Photographic Credits

The majority of the colour photographs are by Helmut Bechtel but others are from the following collections:

Kew Collection: *Acoridium saccolabium, Aeranthes henricii, Armodorum sulingii, Brachycorythis henryi, Brassia caudata, Calopogon tuberosus, Campylocentrum micranthum, Catasetum saccatum* var. *christyanum, Cattleya rex, Chrysocycnis schlimii, Cleistes rosea, Coelogyne asperata, Coelogyne rochussenii, Cryptopus elatus, Cymbidiella pardalina, Dendrobium harveyanum, Dilochia cantleyi, Dimorphorchis rossii, Dipodium pictum, Disa stolzii, Dyakia hendersoniana, Encyclia guatemalensis, Epidendrum coronatum, Eulophia cucullata, Eurychone rothschildiana, Goodyera maximowicziana, Lacaena bicolor, Laelia jongheana, Maxillaria desvauxiana, Ondicium hookeri, Oncidium marshallianum, Oncidium obryzatum, Panisea uniflora, Paphinia cristata, Paphiopedilum armeniacum, Paphiopedilum kolopakingii, Paphiopedilum malipoense, Paphiopedilum micranthum, Paphiopedilum superbiens, Paraphalaenopsis denevei, Paraphalaenopsis laycockii, Phalaenopsis sumatrana, Phragmipedium besseae, Phragmipedium klotzschianum, Platanthera psycodes, Pleione aurita, Podangis dactyloceras, Satyrium nepalense, Schlimmia trifida, Sunipia paleacea, Teuscheria wageneri, Trichotosia ferox, Tridactyle gentilii, Trigonidium egertonianum, Zygosepalum labiosum, Zygosepalum lindeniae*

Mark Clements: *Dendrobium spectabile*

Phillip Cribb: *Acianthus caudatus, Ascoglossum calopterum, Bromheadia finlaysoniana, Caladenia menziesii, Calypso bulbosa, Chiloglottis gunnii, Corybas diemenicus, Cremastra appendiculata, Cryptostylis arachnites, Cymbidiella pardalina, Cypripedium reginae, Dactylorhiza foliosa, Dactylostalix ringens, Dendrobium bellatulum, Dendrobium devonianum, Dendrobium gouldii, Dendrobium scabrilingue, Dendrobium speciosum, Dendrobium taurinum, Diplocaulobium regale, Diuris punctata, Dracula robledorum, Flickingeria comata, Geodorum purpureum, Grammatophyllum speciosum, Habenaria splendens, Lepanthes calodictyon, Lepanthopsis floripecten, Masdevallia mendozae, Mischobulbum cordifolium, Paphiopedilum emersonii, Paphiopedilum lowii, Paphiopedilum supardii, Paraphalaenopsis labukensis, Phymatidium tillansioides, Pleione forrestii, Plocoglottis acuminata, Pterostylis baptistii, Renantherella histrionica* var. *auyongii, Spathoglottis petri, Thecopus maingayi, Thecostele alata, Thelymitra antennifera, Thelymitra variegata, Warmingia eugenii, Zeuxine strateumatica*

Paul and Jenne Davies: *Bothriochilus bellus, Chelonistele sulphurea, Coelogyne pandurata, Dendrobium discolor, Dimerandra emarginata, Encyclia polybulbon, Epidendrum latifolium, Maxillaria rufescens, Mediocalcar decoratum, Mormolyca ringens, Oncidium baueri, Platystele stenostachya, Pleurothallis octomerioides, Pterostylis curta*

Trudi Marsh: *Sobennikoffia robusta*

David Menzies: *Ancistrochilus rothschildianus, Angraecum infundibulare, Angraecum sesquipedale, Bulbophyllum barbigerum, Bulbophyllum lasiochilum, Bulbophyllum medusae, Catasetum discolor* var. *roseoalbum, Cattleya bowringiana, Cattleya guttata, Cattleya leopoldii, Cattleya violacea, Ceratostylis retisquama, Coelia triptera, Coelogyne dayana, Coelogyne lentiginosa, Cryptarrhena lunata, Cryptochilus sanguineus, Cymbidium hookerianum, Dendrobium jonesii, Dendrobium kingianum, Dendrobium lindleyi, Dendrobium lituiflorum, Dendrobium pulchellum, Dendrochilum filiforme, Disperis fanniniae, Dracula bella, Dryadella simula, Earina autumnalis, Epidendrum secundum, Eriopsis biloba, Grobya amherstiae, Isabelia virginalis, Isochilus major, Lembloglossum rossii, Leptotes bicolor, Lycaste aromatica, Myrmecophila tibicinis, Odontoglossum harryanum, Oncidium luridum, Oncidium nubigenum, Paphiopedilum argus, Paphiopedilum barbatum, Paphiopedilum druryi, Paphiopedilum rothschildianum, Pecteilis sagarikii, Phragmipedium longifolium, Pleione hookeriana, Polystachya paniculata, Psychopsis papilio, Solendium racemosum, Spiranthes cernua* var. *odorata, Stanhopea ecornuta, Stanhopea hernandezii, Stelis argentata, Stolzia repens, Trichoceros antennifer, Vanilla planifolia, Warrea warreana*

Otto Sebeseri: *Myrmecophila brysiana, Neogardneria murrayana, Ponerorchis graminifolia, Prescottia plantaginea, Sedirea japonica, Thrixspermum centipeda*

Introduction

The popularity of orchid growing as a hobby has steadily increased since Victorian times despite temporary setbacks brought about by the two World Wars. The heyday of the cultivation of orchid species was undoubtedly in the latter half of the last century whilst, in this century, we have seen the introduction of tens of thousands of orchid hybrids, and the apparently unlimited variety of new forms and colours available has ensured their continuing popularity. However, the species which, as can be seen here, exhibit an incredible range of variability in shape, colour and size have continued to attract admirers amongst orchid growers. In the last twenty years or so a resurgence of interest in the species has occurred and most collections now have at least a few pans or pots of them.

Many thousands of species have been or are still in cultivation and more continue to be introduced each year. The sheer number of species involved has meant that identification has always been a great problem. Competent floristic accounts exist for the orchids of some areas of the world such as Peru, Thailand, West Africa and Brazil but these are often expensive and rare or even unobtainable works. Other areas rich in orchids, such as Colombia and New Guinea, lack comprehensive floristic accounts and yet large numbers of their species are cultivated. Therefore, the need for a relatively comprehensive survey, such as is provided here, of orchid genera and species commonly found in cultivation is obvious.

We hope this work will make it easier for the orchid grower to identify his plants and will also enable him to develop his interest in any particular genus by suggesting further reading on the subject.

Phillip Cribb
Edmund Launert
Kew

7

Preface to the Third Edition

The family Orchidaceae is the largest family of flowering plants and still one of the least known. This may surprise readers but the reasons are clear: first, the sheer number of orchids is daunting, even the most conservative estimate putting it at more than 15,000 species in nearly a thousand genera; second, the majority of orchids are found in the tropics, which are still relatively understudied (even today the number of orchid species new to science being described each year runs into hundreds) and third, orchids make poor herbarium specimens that are difficult to interpret even given access to comparable living material. In truth, many botanists avoid the family altogether because of its size and inaccessibility, there being many easier groups of plants to study.

Nevertheless, the science of orchid taxonomy progresses rapidly and, in the eleven years since the first edition of the *Manual of Cultivated Orchid Species*, a considerable volume of literature has appeared on the family. While much of this is of more interest to the horticulturalist, several major taxonomic treatments have added a great deal to our knowledge of orchids. First among these is the work of Robert Dressler (1981, 1983) which has brought to a far wider audience the intricacies of orchid biology, diversity and classification. His treatment of the family is more or less followed here.

Monographs and revisions have appeared on a wide range of genera and have lead to the description of several spectacular new species of horticultural merit, notably in *Paphiopedilum* and *Phragmipedium*. Carlyle Luer's monumental publications on *Masdevallia*, *Pleurothallis* and their allies deserve special mention. Not only has he described hundreds of new species but he has memorably founded the genus *Dracula* and has given *Dracula vampira* to orchid lovers with a taste for the lurid and dramatic. Major revisions of several other garden-worthy genera have also appeared, including *Odontoglossum* (Bockemuhl, 1989), *Cattleya* and *Laelia* (Withner, 1989, 1990), *Paphiopedilum* (Karasawa, 1982 and Cribb, 1987), *Aerangis* (Stewart, 1979), *Cymbidium* (Du Puy and Cribb, 1988), *Pleione* (Cribb and Butterfield, 1988), *Chelonistele* (de Vogel, 1986) and African *Bulbophyllum* (Vermeulen, 1987).

Several major floristic treatments have also been published or have been completed in the last decade. The detailed and careful work of Gunnar Seidenfaden (1975–1988) on the rich Thai orchid flora, which has provided so much to brighten orchid collections around the world, must take pride of place. His meticulous and well-illustrated accounts are useful throughout the region.

The first generic accounts of south-east Asian orchids of the *Flora Malesiana* region are beginning to appear in the new series *Orchid Monographs* (1985–). In tropical Africa, the orchid account for the *Flora of Tropical East Africa* is now complete in three volumes (Summerhayes, 1968, and Cribb, 1984 and 1989), while the first of the two volumes of Orchidaceae for the *Flore d'Afrique Centrale* (Geerinck, 1984) has also appeared. A fully illustrated account of South African orchids by J. Stewart *et al.* (1984) was published recently.

The unique Australian orchid flora have recently received detailed examination from Jones (1988) and Clements (1989), and many new taxa are being described as a result of their studies. In the Pacific, the first accounts of the orchids of Vanuatu, the Solomon Islands and Bougainville (Lewis and Cribb, 1989, 1991) have recently been published, as has been the precursor to an account of Fijian orchids by Kores (1989).

In the New World, the *Icones Plantarum Tropicarum* (1980 onwards) series, initiated by the Marie Selby Botanical Gardens and continued by the Missouri Botanical Garden, has maintained the tradition of Dunsterville and Garay's seminal *Venezuelan Orchids Illustrated* (1959–1976). In the *Icones* we now have a first account of the orchids of Nicaragua (Hamer, 1982–1984), and incomplete but growing access to the orchids of Ecuador (Dodson and Dodson, 1980–1984), Peru (Dodson and Bennett, 1989) and Bolivia (Vasquez and Dodson, 1982, Dodson and Vasquez, 1989). Hamer's account of the orchids of El Salvador (1974–1981) is now complete in three volumes while the first part of an orchid flora of Central America (Hamer, 1989) has recently appeared.

Inevitably, these and the many other taxonomic publications on orchids have led to a number of name changes, even in well-known orchids. No one enjoys discovering that the famous *Odontoglossum pescatorei* should now be called *O. nobile* or that *Dendrobium ruppianum* is now correctly *D. jonesii*. Similarly, understanding of generic concepts has changed where detailed studies have been made of particular groups. The large heterogeneous genus *Odontoglossum*, for example, has been the subject of intensive morphological studies leading to the recognition of segregates such as *Rossioglossum*, *Lemboglossum* and *Ticoglossum*. Such reassessments are by no means complete and current and future studies on other aspects, such as biochemistry and anatomy, will undoubtedly clarify relationships – and may lead to even further changes in our perception of the genera. However, that is the price of progress. Knowledge of the family Orchidaceae increases by the day and the name changes that result reflect that fact. Many of these are the result of changes of taxonomic opinion leading, for example, to names previously considered to belong to distinct species to be considered synonymous. However, an equal number of names have changed because names have been resurrected from synonymy or been previously misapplied.

The contents of the present edition represent a considerable expansion over that of the previous two. Almost 140 genera have been added and more than twice that number of species. In doing so, we have attempted to include at least one representative species of all of those genera that are commonly in cultivation. In addition, we have added a selection of the many genera that can be considered rare in collections. However, we have not attempted to be comprehensive, realising that perhaps three-quarters of all the tropical orchid species and genera have been in cultivation at some time in the past century and a half. To attempt completeness would require a team of botanists, many volumes and several years of work. We have, instead, attempted to deal with the understandable desire of growers to identify all their specimens by providing references to the latest taxonomic treatments of orchid genera of which we are aware. The sheer scale of publications on orchids means that we may have missed a few and we would be grateful to readers if they could point out such ommissions.

We would like to give our particular thanks to the many botanists and growers who have commented on the previous editions and have helped us in the preparation of this one.

Some additional and replacement photographs for this edition have been kindly provided by David Menzies, Otto Sebeseri, Paul Davies and Phillip Cribb. The additional line illustrations have been drawn by Cherry Ann Lavrih.

We would, in conclusion, like to thank our wives Marianne and Jean for their help and fortitude.

Phillip Cribb
Edmund Launert
Kew

PART I

The Morphology of Orchids

The diversity of form found in the orchid family is amazing. The smallest orchids are possibly some of the tiny *Bulbophyllum* species which are no more than a few millimetres tall while the liana-like *Vanilla* species that climb up into the tallest forest trees may reach 30 m or more long. Vanillas are by no means the bulkiest orchids because some of the giant specimens of *Grammatophyllum speciosum* may weigh many tens of kilogrammes. What then unites these diverse species into the family called the Orchidaceae? The distinctive features of orchids which separate them from other flowering plants lie primarily in their flowers.

The Orchid Flower

Three major evolutionary trends may be discerned in the orchid flower when compared with other families, namely: reduction in the number of parts, fusion of those parts, and the elaboration of one of the petals to form a lip. Each of these is closely associated with the pollination mechanism of the orchid whose flowers function to permit species-specific pollination, thus preventing all potential pollinators other than the right one from gaining access to the pollen and stigmatic surface.

All orchids are monocotyledons, having many vegetative and other features in common with less advanced families such as the Liliaceae, Iridaceae and Amaryllidaceae. This is true also of orchid flowers which typically have their parts in whorls of three or modifications of a basically trimerous pattern.

In order to discuss these trends in more detail let us first look at the flower of a typical orchid such as *Cymbidium* or *Cattleya*. Starting at the base, the typical orchid flower emerges from the axil of a floral bract on a flower stalk known as the **pedicel**. All orchids have an **inferior ovary** borne at the apex of the pedicel and below the place of attachment of the other floral segments. The ovary is often distinguishable from the pedicel by being longitudinally 3- to 6-ribbed. After pollination, the ovary swells into a much more obvious, more or less ellipsoidal or cylindrical seed pod.

The lowermost whorl of floral segments consists of a **calyx** of three **sepals.** The upper or dorsal sepal often differs from the other two lateral sepals in shape and size. In many orchids the sepals are rather dully coloured but frequently they cannot be distinguished from the petals and, infrequently, as in *Masdevallia* they are the largest and most colourful segments. In *Masdevallia*, the sepals are fused in their basal part to form a short tube enclosing the other floral parts. This fusion of parts is also seen in the slipper orchids where the later-

Structure of orchid flowers
1 – *Cypripedium* flower, longitudinal section (× 1⅓)
a – Pedicel
b – Ovary
c – Anther
d – Staminode
e – Lip

2 – *Cattleya aclandiae* flower (× ⅔)
a – Lip
b – Lateral sepal
c – Dorsal sepal
d – Petal
e – Column

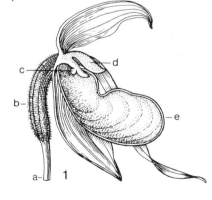

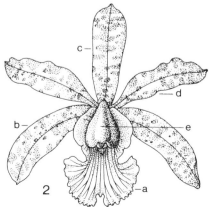

al sepals are fused to the apex; nearly all slipper orchids thus apparently have only two sepals. The fusion has progressed further still in *Zootrophion* where only an operculum is left on each side of the flower between the upper or dorsal sepal and each lateral sepal, which are themselves fused to the apex.

Within the calyx is found the **corolla** which again consists of three segments. Two of these are the **petals** placed on each side of the dorsal sepal. In most orchids such as *Cattleya* or *Oncidium*, these are showy and brightly coloured, presumably to fulfil their role in attracting pollinators. The third segment of the corolla is a highly modified petal known as the **lip** (or **labellum**) of the orchid. The lip in most orchids is larger than the other petals and is often three-lobed or even more complex and tripartite as in *Coryanthes* and *Stanhopea*. The lip is often furnished with a central **callus** or calli and may also be pubescent. The calli or hairs are often arranged longitudinally to direct a pollinator towards the back of the lip where a **spur** or **saccate nectary** may be found. In some species the spur is a prominent feature of the flower and may be very long, as in *Angraecum sesquipedale* whose spur may reach 30 cm in length.

The lip is frequently lowermost in the flower acting as a landing platform for potential pollinating insects. Since the lip lies uppermost in the flower bud, it can only attain a ventral position if the flower or inflorescence turns through 180°. In many species with erect inflorescences the pedicel twists through 180° as the flower opens and this feature is termed **resupination**. Thus, all *Cattleya* and *Laelia* species have resupinate flowers. Fewer orchids have **non-resupinate** flowers but these are found in the European saprophytic orchid *Epipogium aphyllum* and also in *Polystachya*, *Malaxis* and some *Catasetum* species.

In a few orchid genera, the lip is an insignificant feature of the flower, such as in *Masdevallia*, *Stelis* and *Pleurothallis*, yet even here the lip bears longitudinal calli and differs in shape from the petals. Rarely, orchid flowers are found in which the lip and petals are indistinguishable. Generally these are abnormal or monstrous forms and are said to have **peloric** flowers. Even more rarely the petals may re-

Lip terminology
a – Claw   c – Mid-lobe
b – Side lobe   d – Disc

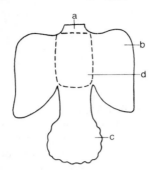

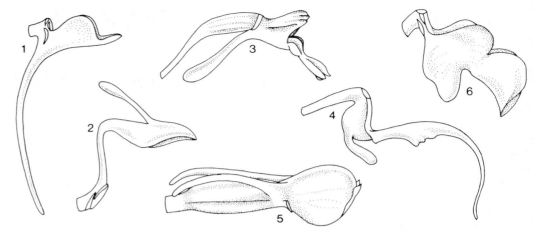

Spur formation and form
1 – Spur formed from base of lip, *Amesiella philippinensis* ($\times 1\frac{1}{2}$)
2 – Spur formed from dorsal sepal, *Disa erubescens* ($\times 1\frac{1}{2}$)
3 – Spur formed from lip, *Calanthe aureiflora* ($\times 1\frac{1}{2}$)
4 – Spur formed from column-foot, *Aeranthes caudata* ($\times 1\frac{1}{2}$)
5 – Spurs formed from lip, *Satyrium nepalense* ($\times 2\frac{1}{5}$)
6 – Spur formed from lip, *Eulophia cucullata* ($\times 1\frac{1}{2}$)

Lip lobing
1 – Lobed at apex, *Anguloa*
2 – Lobed in middle, *Ansellia*
3 – Lobed at base, *Leptotes*

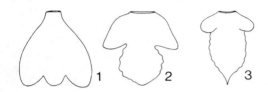

Callus types
1 – Complex, *Oncidium citrinum*
2 – Simple, *Maxillaria ringens*
3 – Lamellate, *Coelogyne suaveolens*

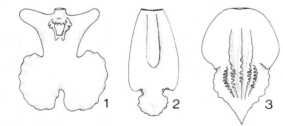

Non-resupinate and resupinate flowers
1 – Non-resupinate, *Epipogium aphyllum* ($\times 1\frac{4}{5}$)
2 – Resupinate, *Oeceoclades saundersiana* ($\times 1$)

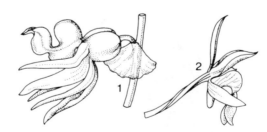

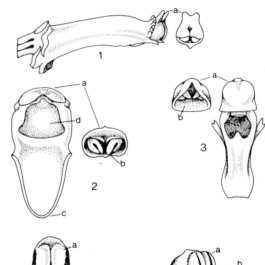

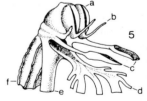

Column types
1 – *Eulophia leachii* ($\times 4$). a Anther-cap.
2 – *Angraecum erectum* ($\times 4$). a Anther-cap, b Pollinium, c Base of lip, d Stigmatic cavity.
3 – *Cyrtochilum falcipetalum* ($\times 2$). a Anther-cap, b Pollinia
4 – *Orchis morio* ($\times 6\frac{1}{5}$). a Anther, b Rostellum, c Stigmatic cavity, d Base of lip.
5 – *Habenaria occlusa* ($\times 2$). a Anther, b Rostellar arms, c Stigmatic arms, d Base of lip, e Base of spur, f Ovary.

semble the lip and again these are abnormal peloric flowers.

The major differences between orchid flowers and those of other monocotyledons are found in their innermost fertile parts. Here, the orchid flowers have undergone great reduction in the number of anthers and stigmatic surfaces and also great fusion to unite both the male and female reproductive organs into a single structure called the **column.**

In the vast majority of orchids, the column bears but a single **anther** held either at its apex or dorsally. The anther consists of a short **filament** attaching an **anther-cap** to the column and within the anther-cap the pollen is concealed. Unlike the dust-like pollen of lilies, orchids hold their pollen in a number of discrete pollen masses called **pollinia.** The num-

ber of pollinia commonly varies from two to eight depending upon the orchid species. The texture of the pollinia is also of taxonomic interest with genera such as *Orchis* and *Ophrys* having sectile mealy pollinia but others such as *Angraecum* and *Vanda* having waxy solid pollinia. In the former, the pollinia often taper below into a stalk (**caudicle**) which attaches each pollinium to a sticky gland called the **viscidium.** In the latter group, the pollinia are attached to one or two straps of tissue of stigmatic origin each called a **stipe** (plural **stipites**). Each stipe ends again in a sticky viscidium. The structure comprising pollinia, stipe and viscidium is called the **pollinarium.**

The column also bears the female reproductive surface known as the **stigma**, which is usually a shallow hollow on the innerside of the

Variation in number of pollinia
1 – Two, *Eulophia*
2 – Four, *Bulbophyllum*
3 – Eight, *Phaius*

1   2   3

Variation in caudicle structure
1 – *Habenaria*   5 – *Habenaria*
2 – *Orchis*   6 – *Satyrium*
3 – *Orchis*   7 – *Disa*
4 – *Disa*

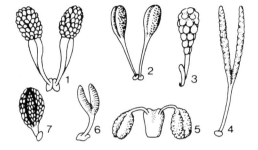

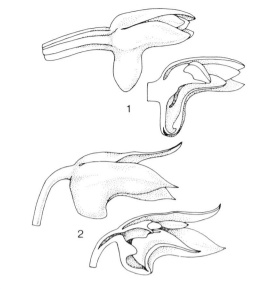

Mentum types
1 – *Appendicula angustifolia* (× 6½)
2 – *Bulbophyllum gibbosum* (× 4⅓)

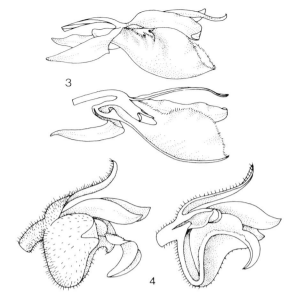

3 – *Dendrobium primulinum* (× 1)
4 – *Polystachya affinis* (× 3⅓)

column. In some species, its monocotyledonous trimerous nature can be seen, as it is divided faintly into three parts. The stigma produces a sticky sugary liquid in which pollen grains can germinate. In *Habenaria, Bonatea* and related terrestrial genera the two stigmatic surfaces are borne on the end of stalks. In most orchid species, part of one of the three stigma lobes is modified to form a **rostellum.** The rostellum lies between the anther and stigma in the form of an entire, lobed or pointed flap. On the end of this flap is the sticky viscidium which is thus placed in a position in which it and the attached pollinia can be picked up by a visiting pollinator.

In two groups of orchids, the reproductive parts differ from the plan outlined above. Firstly, in the slipper orchids (which gain their name from their deeply saccate lip) the column bears two rather than a single anther. Each anther lies ventrally on the column just behind a shield-shaped sterile anther called the **staminode.** The slipper orchids are thought to be an evolutionary primitive group of orchids because of this feature and have been placed therefore in their own subfamily Cypripedioideae.

Similar, but thought to be even more primitive, are the genera *Apostasia* and *Neuwiedia* both from South East Asia. These have either two or three fertile anthers which are partially free from the central column in a more or less regular flower. These two genera comprise the subfamily of the orchids known as the Apostasioideae.

Other features of the column of some genera are outgrowths and projections such as side flaps in *Oncidium*, apical extensions (**stelidia** of *Bulbophyllum)* and basal protuberances as in *Solenidium*. An extension of the column at its base into a **column-foot** is also found, which, in some genera such as *Polystachya* and *Dendrobium*, is fused to the lateral sepals at their base to form a more or less spur-like hood or **mentum.** The lip is then inserted at the apex of the column-foot.

Heteranthy of flowers is known in several quite unrelated genera of orchids. Thus, in some species of *Oncidium* such as *O. heteranthum* and *O. abortivum*, we find in the basal part of each branch of the inflorescence, small, sterile flowers whilst fertile, larger flowers are confined to the terminal parts of the inflorescence. Indeed, in *O. heteranthum* only the terminal flower is fertile.

Grammatophyllum speciosum, noted for its enormous size, is another species which has some sterile flowers on the lower parts of the inflorescence. These flowers are larger than the fertile ones and their lateral sepals are fused and the lip quite absent. In the Asiatic species, *Dimorphorchis lowii,* two distinct types of flowers are also found but in this case both are fertile. The lower flowers are odourless and the upper flowers are differently coloured and slightly scented.

Floral dimorphism related to sex is also known in orchids in some species of *Catasetum, Cycnoches* and *Mormodes* of the subtribe Cata-

setinae. Both male and female flowers may be produced by the same plant but on separate inflorescences and often temporally separated so that cross-pollination will occur. The different function of the sexually distinct flowers is expressed in differences in flower shape and position. Thus, in *Catasetum*, female flowers have the column placed ventrally whilst, in most species, the male flowers have the column

1   2   3   4

Variation in stipe structure
1   *Saccolabium*
2   *Ypsilopus*
3   *Chamaeangis*
4   *Diaphananthe*

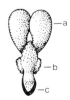

Pollinarium, *Brassia* (× 8½)
a   Pollinia
b   Stipe
c   Viscidium

Column-foot structure
Dendrobium hildebrandtii, longitudinal section
of column and lip (× 3⅘)

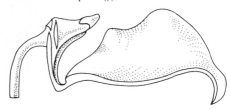

placed dorsally. Not only are male and female flowers morphologically distinct but the size of male and female flowers can be quite different. For example, the female flowers of *Cycnoches egertonianum* are about 20 times as heavy as the male flowers. The male flowers do, however, make up in numbers what they lack in weight, for the usual ratio of male to female flowers is 25:1. The proportion of male to female flowers seems to be controlled by the amount of sunlight received by the plant, with female flowers only being produced in optimum light conditions (Dodson, *Annals of the Missouri Botanic Gardens*, 1962).

The ovary of orchids lies beneath the point of insertion of the sepals and is termed an inferior ovary. After fertilisation of the ovule, development occurs to produce the seed inside the fruit which is generally formed by the growth of the trilocular ovary. The **seeds** of orchids are extremely light, generally fusiform in shape and contain little other than the few-celled embryo. Certainly, a single fruit of some orchid species can contain many thousands of seeds; R.A. Rolfe estimated that a single pod of *Cycnoches chlorochilon* contained about 3,751,000 seeds. When the fruit is ripe and the seeds are mature they are released by the longitudinal splitting of the fruit, generally along three lines of weakness. The seeds are so light that they are dispersed by breezes.

All orchid flowers are borne on a short to elongated **pedicel** or flower stalk continuous with the ovary, subtended by a floral **bract** which is often green and resembles a small leaf.

Each floral axis and the flowers borne on it is termed an **inflorescence**. In genera such as *Paphiopedilum*, *Masdevallia* and *Angraecum* some species have in each inflorescence only a single flower borne at the apex of an axis called the **peduncle**. However, most orchids have many flowers in each inflorescence. In most terrestrial orchids and in epiphytic genera such as *Bulbophyllum* and *Dendrobium* many species have their flowers borne in a **raceme**, spaced out along an unbranched elongated axis called the **rhachis**. The rhachis is an extension of the peduncle which ends below the lowermost flower. Less frequently, the rhachis is reduced

so much that the flowers emerge from the same point at the apex of the peduncle in an **umbel**. This is the common form of inflorescence in *Bulbophyllum* sect. *Cirrhopetalum*. Branching inflorescences or **panicles** are also commonly found in some genera such as *Oncidium*. Rarely, the inflorescence is condensed to form a head, as in members of the daisy family (Compositae) and this unusual situation is found in the subterranean orchid *Rhizanthella gardneri*.

Vegetative Morphology

Although it is for their often exquisite flowers that orchids are justifiably valued, the diversity of their vegetative organs is no less remarkable. This diversity in vegetative morphology may best be understood by relating it to the major environments that orchids have succeeded in colonising.

Types of habit
1 – Terrestrial, *Disa erubescens*
2 – Saprophytic, *Epipogium aphyllum*
3 – Subterranean, *Rhizanthella gardneri*
4 – Epiphytic, lacking leaves, *Microcoelia microglossa*
5 – Epiphytic, with leaves, *Coelogyne salmonicolor*

The first is on the ground and orchids which live with their roots in soil are called **terrestrial**. Terrestrial species predominate in the temperate regions of the earth's surface such as Europe, North America, Argentina and the southern half of Australia. Even in the tropics, terrestrial species may be quite numerous and conspicuous, for example, the jewel orchids of South East Asia, and *Calanthe* species of Africa, Asia and Australasia. Some species, such as *Vanilla planifolia*, which are essentially terrestrial in nature, have developed a liana form of growth, so that with their base in the soil they can scramble up the surrounding vegetation and into the crown of a tree where they can flower in epiphytic conditions.

The second area that orchids have succeeded in colonising is the relatively competition-free but physiologically demanding environment provided in the canopy and on the branches and trunks of forest trees. Species which live on other plants without harming them are called **epiphytes** and by far the larger number of orchids may be regarded as **epiphytic** species. Most epiphytic orchids are confined to the tropics of Asia, America, Australasia and Africa and it is in these regions that evolution has produced such an explosion of species, from the pea-sized plants of *Bulbophyllum minutissimum* to the 2-ton giant *Grammatophyllum speciosum*.

A modification of the epiphytic habit is seen in a few species such as *Pleurothallis teres* and *Laelia flava* where the substrate on which they exist is rock. Such species are conveniently termed **rupicolous** or **lithophytic** species.

Many terrestrial orchids have to survive a period of adverse conditions annually, e.g. winter in temperate zones or drought in the tropics. This is accomplished by the orchid having a dormant phase. Although some species, such as *Cypripedium* and *Epipactis*, survive winter conditions by storing reserves in their rhizomes, most temperate terrestrial orchids survive by storing reserves underground in **tubers**. (The word *Orchis* derives from the Greek word referring to the testicular nature of the paired tubers of European species.) Tuber shape may vary from round or elliptic as in some *Habenaria* species, to long and root-like in the South American species of *Cyclopogon* and *Sarcoglottis*. In the spring, the tuber sends out a shoot from its apex. Often the shoot is abbreviated and the leaves form a rosette at ground level. The flowering spike is sent up from the apex of the stem and, once flowering is over and sufficient stocks are gathered for new tubers to be formed, the parts of the orchid above ground level die back.

Two growth forms occur amongst epiphytic orchids: firstly, **sympodial growth** and, secondly, **monopodial growth**. Sympodial

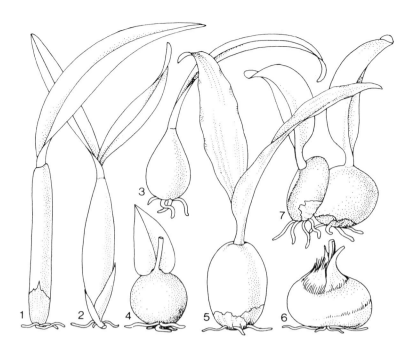

Pseudobulb shapes
1 – Cylindrical, *Macradenia*
2 – Fusiform, *Encyclia*
3 – Ovoid, *Encyclia*
4 – Globose, *Pinelia*
5 – Ellipsoid, *Coelogyne*
6 – Dorsoventrally compressed, *Bletia*
7 – Bilaterally compressed, *Trichopilia*

Variation in vegetative habit within a single genus (*Dendrobium*)
1 – *D. bellatulum*
2 – *D. williamsonii*
3 – *D. leonis*
4 – *D. cucumerinum*
5 – *D. striolatum*
6 – *D. cuthbertsonii*

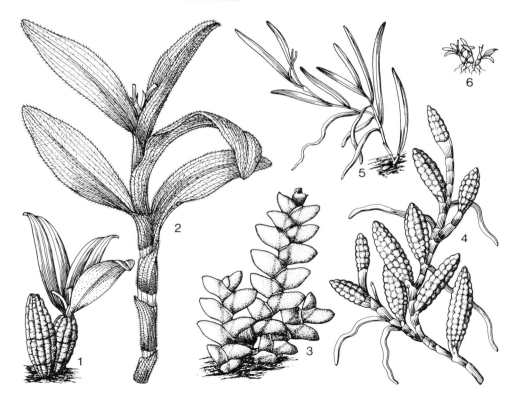

growth occurs in plants in which successive new growths each originate from the base of the preceding one. Two kinds of sympodia are recognised: firstly, the **acranthous** type in which the main axis is composed of annual sections each of which begins in scale leaves and ends in an inflorescence, and secondly, the **pleuranthous** type where the shoot which continues the main axis for the current year, stops short at the end of its growing period and the inflorescences are borne on lateral axes. The sympodial growth habit is thought to be the primitive condition.

The epiphytic species living in the tree canopy may be subject to extreme climatic conditions, such as drought, and have developed characteristic features to enable them to survive in what can be an inhospitable environment. The most remarkable of these features is the development of **pseudobulbs** in some species. Pseudobulbs are water storage organs formed by swelling of one to many internodes of the stem and are found in great variety in many orchid genera. The diversity of shape and size found in pseudobulbs of different orchid species even of a single genus are illustrated here (right).

Although the life of each shoot in sympodial orchids is determinate (of limited duration), the life of a plant may be unlimited, and many sympodial orchids grown at Kew are around 100 years old and are still growing healthily.

The pattern of growth which is characteristic of many epiphytic orchids is monopodial growth where the leaves and stem are produced from an apical growing point in an indeterminate fashion (of unlimited duration). Most commonly, monopodial orchids bear their flowers in axillary inflorescences and adventitious roots are given out at the nodes.

Typically, monopodial orchids have an elongated stem and may even reach many feet in length as in *Vanda suavis* and *Angraecum erectum*, but the stem may be abbreviated as in *Phalaenopsis* and *Aerangis* where new growths are formed from side shoots of the main stem. The commercially important *Vanilla* grows in a monopodial fashion and forms a liana many metres long. Some *Gastrodia* species may also grow to over 18 m long but scramble over surrounding vegetation rather than forming a liana.

In all plants, the function of **roots** is twofold: firstly, to secure the plant in its habitat much like an anchor, and, secondly, to provide the plant with an adequate supply of water and dissolved mineral salts. With terrestrial species of orchid, the structure of the roots and their function is relatively straightforward. In species as diverse as *Ophrys holoserica* and *Arundina graminifolia* the roots are long, thin and fibrous,

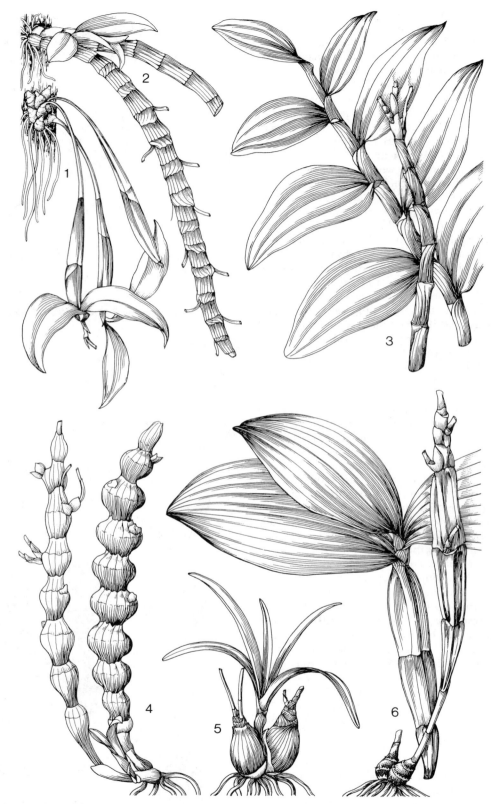

Variation in vegetative habit within a single genus (*Dendrobium*) continued.

1 – *D. tetragonum*
2 – *D. cretaceum*
3 – *D. secundum*
4 – *D. crassinode*
5 – *D. canaliculatum*
6 – *D. farmeri*

given off from the base of the erect stem. Such roots branch rarely and are often quite densely hairy (tomentose), so that moisture can be absorbed even from between the minutest particles in the soil.

The roots of epiphytic orchids also perform the functions of support and supply. However, these epiphytes live in a relatively inhospitable environment, for, in the crowns of trees or on their branches, water supply may be highly erratic and, furthermore, rainwater contains only very limited amounts of dissolved mineral salts.

Morphologically, the roots of epiphytic orchids are often among their most distinctive features. In sympodial orchids the roots are given off from the rhizome often clustered beneath the pseudobulbs whilst, in monopodial orchids, adventitious roots are emitted opposite the leaves. The long, often bootlace-thick roots may hang from the plant in festoons and Forget, one of Sander's collectors in South America, calculated that on one plant he found, the roots constituted some two-thirds of the total mass of the plant.

The most distinctive feature of the roots of epiphytic orchids is their shiny, silvery-grey covering, called the **velamen**. The velamen consists of one to several layers of epidermal cells whose silvery appearance results from the loss of their protoplasts at an early stage (a few millimetres from the root tip). These cells, which cover the whole root apart from a few millimetres at the root tip, function in the absorption of moisture from the atmosphere and possibly as a protective layer in cold or dry conditions. Where a root touches the bark of a tree it forms a close union with the bark so that the roots are extremely difficult to prize away and the plant is thus anchored in its precarious position. Only where the roots can penetrate mossy areas on the branches will a more regular water supply be available and even here the water is relatively nutrient poor. To combat the poor nutrient and irregular water supply, epiphytic orchids can grow very slowly and even survive through apparently dormant periods.

A remarkable feature of the roots of many epiphytic orchids is that they are photosynthetic. In many species, such as *Aerangis* and *Phalaenopsis*, the only clue to this is the green root tip, but in some leafless orchid genera, e.g. *Microcoelia*, *Polyradicion*, *Campylocentrum* and *Taeniophyllum*, the roots have completely taken over the role of the leaves as photosynthetic organs. Indeed, in *Taeniophyllum* the roots may become quite flattened and even leaf-like and green.

A velamen has been reported in some terrestrial species such as *Cypripedium irapeanum*, but it is very thin and not apparent to the naked eye.

In sympodial orchids, the **leaves** are borne along the stem but may appear to form a rosette if the stem is abbreviated or if the stem is pseudobulbous, in which case the leaves are characteristically borne towards the apex of the pseudobulb. The number of leaves borne at the apex of a pseudobulb may be important in classifying a species or group of species. For example, *Polystachya cultriformis* and its allies bear a single leaf at the apex of the pseudobulb, whilst the genus *Cattleya* may be divided into those species bearing one leaf per pseudobulb and those bearing two (or occasionally more).

It is convenient to consider orchid leaves as falling into one of two groups: either **plicate** or **conduplicate**. Plicate leaves are thin and membranous in texture and are ribbed parallel to the course of the vascular bundles. They often last only one season, as in *Lycaste* species and *Cypripedium reginae*, and do not function in water retention. The plicate leaves of orchids are very similar to those borne by members of the lily family (Liliaceae) and possibly indicate an origin for the Orchidaceae from lily-like ancestors. Indeed, some of the supposedly most primitive members of the Orchidaceae, such as *Apostasia* and *Cypripedium*, have such plicate leaves.

Many orchids, particularly epiphytic species, have fleshy or leathery, conduplicate leaves, V-shaped in cross section, strengthened by thickening of the cell walls and often by sclerenchyma fibres. The stomata are virtually confined to the lower leaf surface and the epidermis may be extremely thick. Thus, the leaf can effectively control water loss from the plant which may be subjected to intense radiation in an exposed position in the crown of a tree.

In some genera, such as *Cymbidium*, some species have conduplicate and some plicate leaves. The separation of *Cypripedium* and *Paphiopedilum* into distinct genera, is based to some extent on their distinctive leaf morphology.

Conclusion

An appreciation of the vegetative structure of orchids can provide the grower with the clues he needs to give his orchids optimal conditions for growth. If the seasonal nature of the growth that can be found in many orchids is ignored, then they will perish rapidly. A knowledge of the floral morphology is just as critical for naming orchids because they are classified into genera and species on the finer details of the structure of their sepals, petals, lip and column. The floral dissections supplied with each illustrated plate in this volume provide the essential information for identification. For most species the shape of the sepals, petals and especially the lip will provide all of the information the reader needs. However, for the more critical taxa, details of the column, anther, pollinia and rostellum may be needed before accurate identification is possible.

The Life of Orchids

Fundamental to any consideration of orchid germination, growth and development is the orchid seed. Orchids have probably the smallest seeds of all flowering plants, approached in size only by those by the Burmanniaceae, the Begoniaceae and some parasitic plants. Orchid seeds are dust-like, closest in size to fungus and fern spores. To see their shape and surface structure, highpowered light and electron microscopes are required. The range of weight of mature seed has been calculated by H. Burgeff (1936) to be between 0.3 and 14 μg per seed. This leaves the seed little opportunity to include any food store, such as is found in many larger seeds, to nourish the germinating seedling.

Each seed consists of an embryo of between 8 and 100 cells. This is attached to a suspensor and generally lacks a seedling leaf (cotyledon). The embryo and suspensor are enclosed in a loose, thickened covering (the testa) which may vary greatly in form, form spherical to spindle-shaped, and in ornamentation.

The number of seeds produced by each plant more than compensates for their minute size. R.A. Rolfe estimated that a single capsule of the swan orchid, *Cycnoches chlorochilon*, contained 3,751,000 and Burgeff estimated an average of 3,932,948 seeds in each capsule. Typically, each plant produces several capsules per inflorescence each season and thus seed production per plant may be immense!

The Mycorrhizal Association

Orchid seed will not germinate and grow successfully without the seedling being infected before or soon after germination by fungal threads, termed hyphae. This association of orchid and fungus is called mycorrhizal and was first noted, and its nature established, by the French botanist Noel Bernard at the turn of the century. His work, and subsequently that of Hans Burgeff from 1909 onwards, has elucidated many of the details of this extraordinary association.

All orchids are infected by a fungus for part or all of their life under natural conditions. The relationship between the mycorrhizal fungus and orchid is generally beneficial to both

organisms: the fungus provides nutrients for orchid growth while the orchid provides a home for the fungus. Such a relationship is termed symbiotic and differs from a parasitic association where one organism (the parasite) harms the other (the host).

The fungus obtains nutrient from organic material in the substrate by breaking down complex organic substances, such as cellulose,

Fruit and seed types
1 – *Masdevallia* fruit
2 – *Dendrobium* fruit
3 – *Paphiopedilum* fruit
4 – *Coelia* fruit
5 – *Vanilla* fruit
6 – *Epidendrum elongatum* seed (× 35)
7 – *Pterygodium atratum* seed (× 70)
8 – *Vanilla planifolia* seed (× 140)

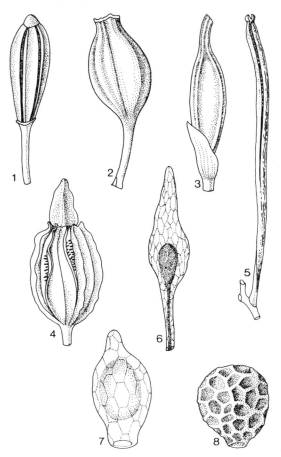

starch or lignin, to simple chemicals by means of excreted enzymes (catalysts). The simple chemicals such as the energy-rich sugars glucose and fructose, are reabsorbed and transported by the fungal hyphae to the orchid where they are used for growth and development. Organisms such as these fungi, which live by decomposing organic material are called saprophytes. Most orchids, by virtue of their mycorrhizal fungi, are for at least some part of their lives secondarily saprophytic, and for some species their whole life cycle is spent in this state.

Sooner or later, however, most species develop the green pigment, chlorophyll, in the cells of their leaves and often in their stems, pseudobulbs and roots. Chlorophyll is a pigment which traps the energy of sunlight to convert water and carbon dioxide to energy-rich carbohydrates. This process is called photosynthesis and organisms which photosynthesise are said to have an autotrophic method of nutrition.

Many fungi have now been successfully isolated from orchids and have been cultivated on an artificial culture medium. The species of fungi isolated so far have fallen into two distinct groups. Firstly, Basidiomycetes (cap fungi) which have hyphae with clamp connections, have been isolated from some orchids, whilst Fungi Imperfecti, which lack known fruiting bodies, have been found in others. Examples of the former are *Marasmius coniatus* isolated from *Didymoplexis*, *Xerotus javanicus* from *Gastrodia* and, rather surprisingly, the honey fungus (*Armillaria mellea*), a parasite of trees, from *Gastrodia elata* and also from *Galeola septrionalis*. In the latter group, many *Rhizoctonia* species have been isolated from a variety of photosynthetic orchid species. Interestingly, some of the *Rhizoctonia* mycelia have produced fruiting bodies of typical Basidiomycetes (*Corticum*) in culture. Nearly all of the mycorrhizal fungi isolated so far have proved to be common species, many being widespread in a variety of soil types and habitats.

Controversy still exists on the question of orchid-fungus specificity. The early results of Bernard indicated that, in *Phalaenopsis*, a high degree of specificity existed, but later work by Burgeff (1936) and J.T. Curtis (1939) tends to

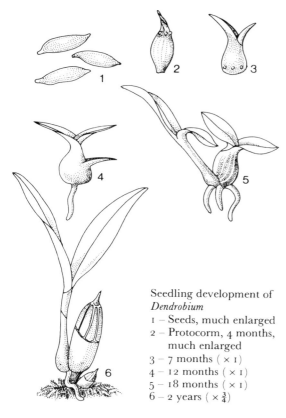

Seedling development of
Dendrobium
1 – Seeds, much enlarged
2 – Protocorm, 4 months,
     much enlarged
3 – 7 months (× 1)
4 – 12 months (× 1)
5 – 18 months (× 1)
6 – 2 years (× ¾)

contradict this. Amongst photosynthetic and partially saprophytic orchids, they detected a tendency for certain fungi to be associated with certain taxonomic or ecological groupings of orchids but were unable to generalise, because a fungal strain isolated from one species of orchid often proved more effective in mycelial formation with seeds of another species than with those of the original host. The fungi associated with wholly saprophytic species are apparently more species-specific. However, this may merely reflect the lack of research on these species rather than a real specificity. Thus *Armillaria mellea* forms mycorrhizal associations with both *Gastrodia* and *Galeola* species so it apparently has a wide host range both as an orchid symbiont and as a parasite of trees.

Life Cycle

The life cycles of many orchids have now been studied by Bernard, Irmisch, Burgeff and others. Many of these are summarised by Burgeff (1936, 1959). J.L. Harley (1959) has usefully considered the life cycle of orchids to consist of five stages which may be summarised as follows:

1. The embryo absorbs water, swells, and ruptures the testa.

2. The food material of the seed is utilised and some growth occurs.
3. Organic matter is absorbed from the substrate and organs are differentiated.
4. Chlorophyll formation occurs in the leaves or other photosynthetic organs and the embryo becomes gradually autotropic.
5. The plant matures and produces an inflorescence.

All orchids pass through the first three stages during their life cycle. Most also pass through a more or less extended period in stage 4 before moving to stage 5, but the wholly saprophytic species pass straight from stage 3 to 5.

The mycorrhizal association in nature occurs very early in the life cycle. In the first or second stages outlined above, the fungal hyphae penetrate the embryonic tissue of the orchid. The sequence was first described by Bernard (1909) for *Phalaenopsis amabilis*. The fungus enters the embryo through its suspensor and the growth of the embryo is immediately stimulated. The central area of the embryo is soon entirely colonised and at this stage differentiation begins with the formation of epidermal hairs and an apical meristem leading to **protocorm** formation. The protocorm is either radial or asymmetric in structure depending on the orchid species. It soon develops a central conducting strand, an apical series of leaves and roots from the axis near the leaf bases. The fungus becomes restricted to the outer (cortical region) of the protocorm and is connected to the substrate by the many hyphae passing through the epidermal hairs. The fungus does not remain uniformly healthy within the protocorm tissues: in the central region the coiled hyphae within the cells become disorganised, lose their regular form and are digested. The digested matter is utilised for growth by the orchid. With the division of cells in the young orchid meristem, the hyphae rapidly penetrate the new cells formed and the process of colonisation and digestion quickly follows that of growth. As the orchid embryo differentiates, the area infected by fungal hyphae progressively becomes restricted so that finally it occupies only that part of the protocorm in contact with the substrate. Young roots as they are formed, are infected from the substrate and in the orchid cells colonisation and digestion continues in regions behind the apical meristem.

Not infrequently in these early stages, the fungus may adopt a more aggressive parasitic role, especially if the embryo is at all sickly, and the latter is swiftly killed. Alternatively, if the orchid cells digest the fungus too quickly they may completely eliminate it from the protocorm.

The period of time an orchid exists in stage 3 as a saprophyte varies widely from species to

species and with environmental conditions. Thus, some species of *Vanda*, *Angraecum* and *Phalaenopsis* are reported to have a very short saprophytic phase whereas species of *Cymbidium*, *Cypripedium*, *Orchis* and *Listera* are all reported to have a long saprophytic period. Complete saprophytism is widespread among orchid genera, being recorded in genera as diverse as *Cymbidium*, *Eulophia*, *Neottia*, *Epipogium*, *Galeola*, *Gastrodia* and *Didymoplexis*. The efficacy of the saprophytic existence is demonstrated dramatically by the 16 m-long liana-like *Galeola hydra* and also by the extraordinary subterranean *Rhizanthella gardneri* and *R. slateri*. Both these Australian orchids spend their whole existence underground even to the extent of flowering and fruiting there!

Pollination and Seed Production

Survival and growth are only two aspects of the life of an orchid, the third, vital to the continuation of the species, is successful reproduction. Seeds are prolifically produced in orchids and their minute size makes them ideally suited to dispersal by air currents. Seed, however, can only be produced by successful pollination of orchid flowers. In their pollination, orchids reach a degree of complexity seldom rivalled elsewhere in the Plant Kingdom. This aspect of orchid life is dealt with in greater detail on page 21. An overall picture emerges of orchid pollination that is highly species-specific, each orchid species being pollinated by one specific organism (most frequently an insect). The orchid flowers are modified to attract only their own pollinator and sufficient pollen is transferred in the pollinia to ensure high seed set in the next flower visited by the pollinator.

The Success of Orchids

One might suppose that the absolute dependence of orchids upon the mycorrhizal association would be disadvantageous to the survival of the family. The necessity for an orchid seed to germinate in the presence of a fungal spore or hypha might be expected to reduce dramatically the proportion of orchids that successfully survive to adulthood. Why then are orchids so successful?

No simple answer can be provided but undoubtedly several factors merit attention. Firstly, orchids generally favour habitats where interplant competition is low and the epiphytic life undoubtedly offers an enormous number of micro-habitats from the ground to tree trunk or branch tip where few other plants can exist.

The mycorrhizal relationship may itself be less of a sieve than it at first appears. The relationship is apparently not highly specific and the fungi so far indentified are common and widespread species. Thus, where orchid seed lands, the chances are high that suitable fungal spores will be present. Oakes Ames noted that on Krakatoa, which had been effectively sterilised when it was formed by a gigantic eruption, some of the first colonisers were orchids. He suggested that the colonising seeds brought the necessary fungal spores with them.

Ames' example of orchids colonising Krakatoa emphasises the importance of small size, lightness and high seed production for orchids. They are ideally suited to wind dispersal and the widespread distribution of many species confirms that long-distance dispersal does occur. Thus, *Polystachya concreta* is almost pantropical, *Bulbophyllum longiflorum* is found from Africa across to the Pacific Islands and *Eulophia alta* and *Oeceoclades maculata* are both recorded from South America and Africa. Undoubtedly large quantities of orchid seed must fall on 'stony ground' unsuitable for germination, but the success of the orchids numerically and in distribution demonstrates the success of their life style.

The Ecology of Orchids

It appears a contradiction that the orchids, which have a reputation for being so difficult to cultivate, should be the largest family of flowering plants and be found in almost every environment on the earth's surface.

Calypso bulbosa flowers in the short arctic summer and survives through the ferocious winter in a dormant state. Most temperate orchids also have to survive a more or less severe winter season where snow is often frequent and frosts can freeze the ground to a depth of several centimetres. In the tropics conditions can be equally severe for, in the deciduous forests, the dry season can last for several months and epiphytic species survive only by virtue of the water stored in their thick leathery leaves and fleshy pseudobulbs. Some orchids such as *Eulophia petersii* in Africa and Arabia survive on the edges of deserts whilst others survive long droughts perched on exposed rocks. Even in tropical rain forests epiphytic species growing on exposed branches have to endure dry spells often hours long inbetween rain showers.

At the other extreme, orchids such as *Liparis loeselii* and *Hammarbya paludosa* in Europe and the *Disa, Satyrium* and *Habenaria* species of the perennially wet grasslands of tropical Africa may be almost aquatic with the roots, tubers and stems permanently submerged.

Surely though, the most remarkable orchids of all are the Australian species *Rhizanthella gardneri* and *R. slateri* whose truffle-like existence is wholly subterranean. These have been found less than a dozen times and little is known of their ecology other than that flowering apparently occurs when the inflorescence is below the soil surface and the flowers are pollinated by small flies that reach the flowers through the gap made by the bracts around the flowers parting the surface leaf litter.

Despite the vast range of habitats occupied by orchids, individual species are often exacting in their cultural requirements and will fail to survive if conditions are at all unfavourable. Several factors affect orchid growth, and climatic factors, altitude, substrate type and competition from other plants may all be critical. Similarly, for successful reproduction the presence of a suitable pollinating organism is also essential.

Climatic Factors

Logically one would expect that orchids from tropical countries would require higher average temperatures than those from temperate zones. The term 'tropical', however, covers a multitude of diverse climates from that of the rain forest where temperatures never drop below 15°C throughout the year to that of the tropical mountains where orchids have been recorded up to 4000 m or more and frosts are a regular occurrence.

Thus, whereas a rain forest species from the Amazon basin could not be expected to survive an average European winter without protection and added heat, some of the higher altitude Himalayan species such as *Pleione bulbocodioides* and *Bletilla striata* thrive when left out in the milder winters in western Europe.

It is, of course, difficult for any grower to provide a large number of distinct temperature regimes for his orchids and most compromise by having two or three houses ranging from a hothouse where temperatures are not allowed to fall below about 15°C, to a cool house where lower temperatures are permitted although 10°C is generally thought to be a suitable minimum.

Other important climatic factors are rainfall and humidity. The two are often not equatable in natural habitats, for even heavy rainfall may have only a temporary effect if run-off is swift. For orchids in an exposed situation such as on rocks or outer branches of a tree, the ability to absorb water swiftly is important and the special structure of the roots where the absorbing power of the velamen is great, is critical. Organic debris which accumulates between the roots and pseudobulbs may also be important acting as a sponge to hold on to rainwater for an extended period.

Rainfall, especially if heavy, will, of course, raise the humidity swiftly in most habitats as it moistens the surrounding vegetation and soil. However, the tropical sun quickly lowers the humidity especially in the forest canopy and many orchids have adapted by evolving tough leathery leaves and thick fleshy pseudobulbs both of which are specially adapted to reduce water loss in a similar manner to cacti in the American deserts.

High humidity is not necessarily a product of rainfall and on many tropical mountains rainfall may be relatively low even where forest survives. These mountain forests often rely for moisture on being constantly enveloped in mist or cloud which keeps the humidity at 100%. Misting devices are often employed in orchid houses to mimic the effect. The high humidity of mountain (montane) forests produces a wealth of epiphytic growth besides orchids with mosses, liverworts, and filmy ferns being particularly important members of these floras. These can absorb large amounts of water and, as they often cover the orchid roots, serve to keep the orchids supplied with water even when the mist clears.

The third climatic factor which affects orchids is the amount of radiation or sunlight incident on their foliage. Many tropical epiphytes in the forest canopy live for a large part of their lives in full sunlight and the same is true of many terrestrial orchids living in the tropical and temperate mountains where irradiation may be very intense during the day. It is extremely difficult to mimic in the greenhouse the condition of high irradiation and high temperature experienced by montane orchids during the day, and the often low temperatures and high humidity experienced during the night. Artificial illumination is often used in cultivation but the quality of the light from such lamps seldom approaches that of sunlight. However, in many plants daylength may be critical in triggering flowering and then artificial light sources are useful to control the daylength requirements of any particular species.

Many orchids, however, shun direct sunlight and some, especially the saprophytic and other forest floor species, do not apparently need direct sunlight at all to survive and grow. Terrestrial orchids of the forest floor often live in deep shade and if placed in the sunlight in cultivation will soon perish. Adequate shading can thus be critical if some species of *Paphiopedilum, Calanthe, Liparis,* etc. are to be grown successfully in cultivation.

Altitude

Altitude has been touched upon briefly in the consideration of climate above. As the altitude increases, the mean temperature decreases so that, for example, on Mt Kilimanjaro in Tanzania, forest gives way to scrub, and eventually to subalpine grassland and alpine conditions at about 3400 m. The situation is similar in the Andes, in the Himalayas and on other tropical mountains. On such mountains, species are often confined to a narrow altitudinal band, mostly controlled by the minimum temperature. Species found at altitude in the equatorial regions are also often found at lower levels further away from the Equator. Conversely, most tropical orchids from lower levels near the Equator are more restricted in their latitudinal distribution.

Besides the drop in temperature with increase of altitude, other factors such as pressure and the quality of the sunlight also change. At higher altitudes the amount of ultraviolet light increases because the atmosphere is thinner and thus less is screened out. How this affects the orchids and other higher altitudes plants is unknown, but it has been suggested that such a change in the radiation could result in a higher mutation rate and possibly lead to greater speciation at high altitudes.

Substrate Factors

Soil conditions and soil types can affect orchids in several ways either directly, in the case of terrestrial species, or indirectly with epiphytes.

Many terrestrial species are confined to a particular type of habitat, for example, in South East Asia *Paphiopedilum niveum* and allied species are restricted to limestone outcrops, many species in Europe are also confined to chalk or limestone localities and, in Africa, many *Disa* and *Satyrium* species are only found in marshes and swamps.

Terrestrial orchids live with their roots and tubers or rhizomes in direct contact with the soil. The mineral and nutrient content of the soil can then directly influence the orchid, for any water absorbed by the plant will contain dissolved nutrients and mineral ions. The effect of such substances on the orchid and its associated mycorrhizal fungus will depend upon their requirements for these substances. Those orchids confined to limestone areas may actively require high levels of calcium ions or may tolerate high concentrations of these ions. Alternatively, the alkaline environment produced by water containing high levels of dissolved calcium may be critical. The effect of the mineral content of the soil may, however, be less direct as, by excluding intolerant species, the interplant competition may be reduced to a level where the orchid can survive satisfactorily in a more open environment.

For epiphytic species, the effect of soil type is less direct but nevertheless important because the soil type often dictates the vegetation type. Rain forest will not grow on some nutrient-deficient tropical soils and thus the associated epiphytes of that forest will be absent.

More critically, in tropical forests, certain species of tree seem to be favoured by epiphytic orchids whilst neighbouring trees will be devoid of epiphytes. Tropical orchids do seem to prefer rough-barked tree species to their smooth-barked neighbours. Presumably, the rough bark allows the orchid roots to grasp the host more easily and the crevices may also allow detritus to collect more easily around the roots. The exudates of the bark may also be critical, particularly for the survival of the mycorrhizal fungi associated with the orchids. The precipitation in an area is critical here, for in wetter areas these preferences are less marked and may disappear altogether.

Competition

Several terrestrial orchids such as *Spiranthes spiralis*, *Ophrys apifera* and *Epipactis helleborine* are well known as primary colonisers of bare soil, whilst *Spiranthes sinensis* and *Cynorkis fasciata* are common weeds in orchid greenhouses. Orchids are also amongst the earliest colonisers of disturbed soils such as the banks of road cuttings in the tropics. It serves to illustrate that many orchids are early colonisers of disturbed areas and their light, highly mobile seeds must be a critical factor for this role.

It is also true that many terrestrial orchids are intolerant of competition from other plants. Thus, in Europe, orchids will disappear from chalk grassland which is invaded by scrub or by a vigorous grass, or from a marsh which is invaded by reeds or shrubs. Conversely, many species will survive and flourish in the absence of competition, as is impressively illustrated in East Africa, where *Disperis*, *Habenaria* and *Nervilia* species form almost the only ground cover in cypress plantations.

Two factors are important in interplant competition: firstly, competition for soil space and nutrients and, secondly, competition above the ground for light. Both certainly may be important for grassland species whereas the former is more likely to affect forest floor species.

The success in terms of number of species of tropical epiphytic orchids is no doubt in large part due to competition or, to be more exact, the lack of competition from other plants. Epiphytic (and lithophytic) orchids occupy a habitat in which there are relatively few potential competitors and a variety of ecological niches from which to choose, ranging from ver-

tical main trunks and stout horizontal boughs to the finest twigs. Epiphytic orchids are also well adapted to gather and retain water in what is in many ways a xerophytic environment for much of the time.

Pollination Ecology

In orchids, reproduction is a delicate balance. On the one hand, it is advantageous for an orchid thriving in a stable environment to maintain the *status quo*, but on the other hand, many habitats are far from stable and, where the environment is in a state of flux, it may be an advantage for an orchid to produce highly variable progeny so that at least some will survive any changes that may occur.

Self-conservation in orchids
Orchids preserve the *status quo* in a number of ways. Many species undergo a period of dormancy as tubers and may increase their population slowly, as plants will occasionally produce two or more tubers in a year. Similarly, rhizomatous species may produce two or more shoots in a season and, as the older growths die off, so the new shoots detach to form new plants. Exceptionally, orchids may reproduce asexually by bulbils. *Hammarbya paludosa*, the European bog orchid, produces bulbils on its leaves whilst *Cynorkis uncata* from East Africa produces bulbils in the leaf axils. In all cases outlined above the progeny will be identical to the parent plant and a genetically uniform population will result.

Sexual reproduction may also lead to the same result but only when inbreeding replaces outbreeding as the norm. *Ophrys apifera*, the common European bee orchid, is a species which reproduces entirely by self-pollination. Charles Darwin first noticed that insects apparently played no role in its pollination. The pollen masses curl out of the anther loculi in the newly opened flower and eventually enter the stigmatic cavity of the same flower. Seed set is correspondingly high in this species and this process leads to populations which are genetically rather uniform. In many situations of environmental stability the result may be highly desirable and the widespread and common bee orchid seems to thrive on it.

Self-preservation in orchids
Self-pollination is, however, an exception among orchids. Most species are highly adapted to outbreeding in the wild. As a result, the progeny of orchids are genetically rather variable. The variability observed between several individuals of the same species is well known to the orchid grower who will often

select the form with the best-coloured or best-shaped flowers for future breeding. The variability observed in the flowers is paralleled throughout the plant in its morphology, physiology and biochemistry. This variability is the base material for the future evolution of the species. Plants like the bee orchid which are self-pollinated are at an evolutionary full stop!

Darwin (1862) was the first to study closely the pollination biology of orchid flowers and his detailed and accurate observations have fascinated generations of biologists, leading many on to similar studies. Good summaries of orchid pollination biology are to be found in L. van der Pijl and C. Dodson's *Orchid Flowers – their Pollination and Evolution* (1966) and M. Procter and P. Yeo's *The Pollination of Flowers* (1973).

Orchids are pollinated by an enormous variety of insects and less commonly by birds and bats. Specificity is high, with each orchid species usually being pollinated by its own particular associated organism. Observation of the shape, structure and colour of an orchid flower can often suggests the pollinator. White flowers of simple structure which emit a scent at dusk or at night will probably be visited and pollinated by moths. Red flowers with deep nectaries might be butterfly or even hummingbird pollinated. Bees do not see the red end of the spectrum and are attracted to blue, yellow, or white flowers and to those which reflect ultraviolet light, which is in their visible spectrum. Beetles, flies, and wasps are all important orchid pollinators. It is scarcely surprising that so many different animals pollinate orchids when one remembers the enormous size of the family.

Pollinators are attracted to orchid flowers by a variety of stimuli, the most obvious being visual. However, tactile and olfactory stimuli are also of great importance. Of the visual stimuli the most important are flower colour and patterning and flower shape. These are most often concentrated on the lip which frequently is far larger and more brightly coloured than the other floral segments. In addition the lip often bears honey guides leading the pollinator to a source of nectar but also bringing it into contact with the sexual parts of the flower.

The promise of food is a major attractant to potential pollinators and many orchids possess nectaries in the form of a spur or a pouch at the base of the lip. Strangely, many orchids do not secrete any nectar so the visiting pollinator will not gain from its visit. The orchids are also parsimonious where potential pollinators such as beetles and bees are attracted. The lip indumentum in many orchids consists of pollen-like farinaceous hairs which are chewed by the pollinator. Thus, the pollen itself, which is vulnerable because it is concentrated in a limited number of pollen masses, is protected.

Many orchids are fragrant, and the scents attract pollinators. However, not all species are pleasantly scented. In a genus such as *Bulbophyllum* the flowers are often dully coloured and emit a strong unpleasant smell of rotting flesh. The insects visiting these flowers are carrion flies and beetles which prove to be just as efficient pollinators as the more flamboyant insects such as bees and butterflies.

In contrast with self-pollinating species, outcrossing species depend for a reasonable level of seed production upon the frequency of visits by potential pollinators. Orchids have adapted in many ways to increase the likelihood of pollination. As van der Pijl and Dodson (1966) state: 'We do believe that the pollinators of orchids have played a major role in their evolution.' Many species have long-lasting flowers with scents emitted only when the pollinator is active. Thus, African *Angraecum* species pollinated by moths only produce a scent at dusk or at night.

Another adaptation to ensure that high seed production will result from pollination is that pollen is aggregated into a number of discrete masses (pollinia) in each anther. Enough pollen is then removed by a pollinating organism to ensure that all ovules in an ovary of the next receptive flower can be fertilised as a result of a single visit. Visits by pollinating insects need not necessarily be frequent to ensure that an orchid has a high reproductive capability.

Resupination is one of the most frequent floral adaptions to pollination in orchids. Flowers are resupinate when the lip which in the bud is in the upper (dorsal) position comes by various means to occupy a lower (ventral) position in the open flower. The lip, often enlarged and more elaborate than the petals, is an ideal landing platform for a visiting insect in this lower position. Most commonly in erect inflorescences the flower stalk (either pedicel or ovary) twists through 180° as the bud opens. However, in pendulous inflorescences the lip lies naturally in the lowermost position without any twisting of the flower stalk. The variations, are great and in some flowers a twist of 360° has been noted.

Twisting of the floral organs is not confined to the flower stalk alone. In *Mormodes*, for example, the delivery of the forcibly ejected pollinia onto the back of the pollinating bee is ensured by twisting of the column to one side and by a corresponding twisting of the lip. The lip rests near its apex on the tip of the column. When a bee lands on the lip the column-tip is stimulated and the pollinia are forcibly ejected to land on the bee's back.

Perhaps the most remarkable adaptations found in orchid flowers are those associated with pollination by bees and wasps. Of these, the extraordinary pseudocopulation by male

bees and wasps of orchids in genera as diverse as *Ophrys*, *Cryptostylis*, *Trichoceros* and *Telipogon* must rank among the most remarkable. In *Ophrys*, males of the pollinating species emerging well before their females are attracted to the orchid flowers by a scent which imitates that secreted by the abdominal glands of the female bees or wasps. As the male approaches the flower, visual stimuli of colour and shape come into action, for the flowers of *Ophrys* species closely resemble insects. Their vernacular names of 'bee', 'fly', 'wasp', and 'spider' orchid note this mimicry. Finally, when the insect alights on the orchid lip further tactile stimuli from hairs on the lip elicit strong copulatory motions in the male bringing it into contact with the sticky tips (viscidia) of the pollinia. These are then borne away by the insect on its visits to other flowers. After a few minutes the stalks of the pollen masses curve and the pollen masses are positioned to enter the stigmatic cavity of the next orchid flower visited.

Studies on tropical orchid pollination have revealed a wealth of unusual mechanisms (e.g. those outlined for *Coryanthes* and *Cycnoches*). The work of C. Dodson and R. Dressler in the tropical Americas deserves special mention here. They have elucidated the mechanisms by which many tropical species are pollinated and they have concentrated particularly on studying genera in the *Stanhopea* alliance which are pollinated by Euglossine bees. They have progressed to the point where they have extracted and analysed the floral fragrances which attract the pollinating bees. Furthermore, they have attracted bees to gel impregnated by these scents thereby confirming which species pollinates which orchid, the orchids being identified from pollinia attached to attracted bees.

Indeed, the diversity of orchids seems to be directly linked to the availability of pollinators: as the insects have the largest number of species of all animals, so those plants, the orchids, which rely on them for pollination have a corresponding and overwhelming diversity.

In a few genera of orchids, the prevention of self-fertilisation has progressed to the ultimate step of separating the male from the female sexual organs in the flower. In *Catasetum*, which Darwin called 'the most remarkable of all Orchids', the male and female flowers are borne in separate inflorescences and are so distinct that John Lindley placed them originally in separate genera! Furthermore the trigger mechanism which fires the pollinia onto the bee in the male flowers must rank as one of the most sophisticated of all pollinating mechanisms. As Darwin so accurately stated 'the contrivances by which Orchids are fertilised, are as varied and almost as perfect as any of the most beautiful adaptations in the Animal Kingdom.'

The History of Orchids in Cultivation

For over 150 years the main source of orchid species for trade has been the importation into Europe and more recently into North America, Australia, etc. of native plants, often in large quantities, from their natural habitats in the tropical regions of the world. In the nineteenth century, the whole orchid trade was run by enterprising firms such as Messrs Loddiges, Low & Co., Veitch & Sons, and Sander & Co. who sent their collectors to all parts of the world in the quest for novel species. One of the features of the trade was the sales of their exotic discoveries which took place at regular intervals at Protheroe and Morris and Stevens' Sales Rooms in London where rare plants exchanged hands, often for astonishingly high prices.

Despite many setbacks, the cultivation of orchid species was gradually mastered, so that by the turn of the century the more meticulous growers were obtaining a high percentage success rate in growing and flowering species from many different habitats all over the world. Indeed, the longevity of orchid plants in cultivation is still something of a mystery, but several plants in the orchid greenhouses at Kew are over 100 years old and are still thriving and flowering regularly.

However, the early attempts to grow orchids had been far from successful and many tens of thousands of plants must have perished in the early years of their popularity up until the mid-nineteenth century. Indeed, Sir Joseph Hooker described England at that time as 'the grave of tropical orchids'.

The earliest record we have of the introduction of a tropical orchid into cultivation is that by Peter Collinson in 1731 who sent a plant of *Bletia verecunda* to Mr Wager in England, but no record exists of its survival to flowering. The first orchids which we know to have survived, albeit for only a short time, in cultivation are a *Vanilla* species possibly *Vanilla planifolia* and several *Epidendrum* species recorded by Phillip Miller in the second edition of his *Dictionary of Gardening* (1768). In 1778, Dr John Fothergill introduced from China *Phaius tankervilleae* and *Cymbidium ensifolium* and the latter was flowered the same year by Mrs Hird of Apperley Bridge, Yorkshire.

Records at the Royal Botanic Gardens, Kew show that, in 1787, *Epidendrum (Encyclia) cochleatum* and the closely related *E. fragrans* flowered for the first time in cultivation. By 1794, 15 tropical species were in cultivation at Kew, mostly brought there from the West Indies by Admiral Bligh of 'Bounty' fame.

From that time onwards, tropical and especially epiphytic orchids continued to be introduced into Europe, particularly into England, in ever-increasing numbers. Unfortunately, several factors meant that the necessary knowledge and skills required to grow these plants successfully, lagged far behind. In particular, a misunderstanding of the true nature of epiphytic orchids prevailed for many years because orchids were considered to be parasitic on their supporting trees. The *Botanical Register* t. 17 (1815) states 'the cultivation of tropical parasites was long regarded as hopeless; it appeared a vain attempt to find substitutes for the various trees each species might affect within the limits of a hot house'. A further problem was the general lack of appreciation of the habitat and environmental conditions experienced by orchids in their natural state. John Lindley, when secretary of the Horticultural Society of London, looked into the vexed problem of growing tropical orchids and suggested in 1830 a regime which, although successful for those species of hot, low altitude, tropical forests, was totally unsuitable for growing the far more numerous species of tropical montane forest areas.

However, improvements in cultivation methods, although slow in surfacing and the subject of great resistance in many quarters, began to gain acceptance. In 1812 a plant of *Oncidium bifolium* received by Messrs Loddiges survived and flowered throughout the long sea journey from Monte Video to England by being hung up in the cabin without its roots being placed in earth. The following year Mr Fairbairn, the gardener at Claremont, flowered *Aerides odorata* which he had grown in a hanging basket full of old tar and moss, the whole plant and basket being plunged several times a day into a tub of water to keep it moist. A similar hanging basket method was adopted by that most influential botanist Sir Joseph Banks in his glasshouses at Isleworth. His baskets were of interwoven twigs secured by twine and the plant was placed inside on a thin vegetable mould compost covered by enough moss to retain moisture (*Botanical Register*, t. 220).

At about the same time, Dean Herbert was experimenting, with some success, with an idea suggested to him by Dr Wallich, Director of the Calcutta Botanic Garden, in attaching *Epidendrum* species to the stems of trees by cutting a notch in the bark, inserting the plant like a graft and tying moss about it to support the young roots until they had become securely attached to the bark.

Similar improvements in the environmental conditions under which most orchids were grown were slower to surface, for the influence of Messrs Loddiges and of John Lindley's early advice on orchid culture could not be lightly ignored. However, the information sent to Lindley by the many collectors with whom he had contact soon began to make its mark in his writings in the *Botanical Register* and later in the *Gardeners' Chronicle* which he founded in 1845. Alan Cunningham in Australia, George Ure Skinner in Guatemala, John Gibson in the Khasia Hills of India, William Lobb in Peru, and George Gardner in the Organ Mountains of Brazil all sent back sound advice on the environment in which the orchids they sent back to England survived in nature. Such advice was not before time either, for the fascination of the orchids was rapidly being appreciated by horticulturists and many collections both large and small were being formed. Unfortunately, Sir Joseph Hooker's remark that during this time England was 'the grave of tropical orchids' was near the mark.

A few gardeners had also begun to experiment with growing conditions at this time in the hope of growing these beautiful plants more successfully. Probably the earliest of these was Joseph Cooper, the gardener to Earl Fitzwilliam at Wentworth in Yorkshire. By 1835 he was in charge of a thriving orchid collection, his main deviation from standard growing practice being the maintenance of a lower mean temperature in the houses and the better ventilation. He also initiated the damping down of orchid houses, that is, the maintenance of a moist atmosphere by regular watering of the staging and floors in the houses.

Many further innovations, often of a simple

nature such as the syringing of plants to imitate fine misty showers by Donald Beaton and the introduction by Anthony Bacon of Glamorganshire of heating houses by piped hot water, all contributed to the improved lot of the cultivated epiphytic orchid.

The knowledge acquired over the previous 75 years or so since orchids first appeared in cultivation was summarised by B.S. Williams in the first edition of *The Orchid Grower's Manual* (1851), and yet orchids continued to be lost in cultivation mainly because growers were reluctant to depart from the early views of Lindley and grew orchids in a uniformly hot climate. Only after Lindley in the *Gardeners' Chronicle* (1859) and James Bateman in his *Monograph of Odontoglossum* (1874) condemned these practices was the hold of these early ideas on orchid cultivation finally broken.

By the 1880s orchid cultivation had assumed an essentially modern aspect and although plants were still lost, most, once established, survived happily in the greenhouses of temperate lands far from their tropical homes.

Nowadays, the efforts of horticulturists in growing mature plants are centred on computer-controlled greenhouses, improvement of the growing medium, with osmunda fibre largely replaced by chopped pine bark or synthetic substrates, on improved-formula fertilisers and on pest control by chemical spraying.

In October 1856, John Dominy, who was the orchid grower for the firm of Veitch & Sons of Chelsea, flowered the first artificially produced hybrid orchid, *Calanthe* Dominyi. It was an event that presaged two major developments: the popularity of orchid hybrids and the improvement of orchid propagation from seed. Other growers such as Seden and Watson rapidly followed Dominy's lead and interspecific and intergeneric hybrids of many kinds were raised and flowered. The appeal of producing novel flowers which were often showier than their parents and allowed unlimited scope for growers to exercise their inventiveness gradually came to take precedence over the cultivation of species in many collections. The need to keep track of the large numbers of hybrids produced was instrumental in the pub-

lication of the influential *Orchid Stud Book* (1909) by R.A. Rolfe and C. Hurst, and F. Sander's *Orchid Guide* (1901) which later developed into Sander's *List of Orchid Hybrids* which continues to the present day.

The production of hybrid seed is relatively easy providing, as is often the case, the parents are interfertile. The pollinia are removed from the flower of the male parent and are transferred to the stigma of the flower of the female parent. After fertilisation, seed development can be gauged by the swelling and ripening of the developing ovary (the capsule) which may take a few weeks or occasionally as long as a year. However, in the early years of orchid hybridisation the difficulties began once the seed was harvested because in orchids, although a great deal of seed is produced, it is minute and generally lacks a food store to assist the seedling in its early stages of development.

The methods of seed sowing and germination recommended, for example, by J. Veitch's *A Manual of Orchidaceous Plants* (1894) are unreliable to say the least. It was recommended that seed be sprinkled around the base of an established orchid on the old compost and that the seedlings be removed when large enough to survive handling. Needless to say, this method and others recommended by other contemporary authors met with only limited success.

The first breakthrough which eventually led to reliable seed germination was made by the Frenchman Noel Bernard who, between 1903 and 1909 isolated the mycorrhizal fungi from orchids and published a series of papers which elucidated the symbiotic relationship of orchids and their associated mycorrhizal fungi (see Chapter 2), and he also established that orchid seed would only germinate and grow normally if the fungus was present.

Bernard's work and that of Hans Burgeff (1909 onwards) enables orchid seed to be germinated and grown successfully *in vitro* on an agar medium containing ground salep (*Ophrys* tuber extract) which on analysis proved to contain 27% starch, 5% protein and traces of sugar and minerals, providing the fungus was present.

However, the work of L. Knudsen (1922 onwards) really opened up the field for the horticultural exploitation of *in vitro* orchid culture. Knudsen pointed out that the fungus would convert carbohydrates, such as starch, and complex sugars such as sucrose, into simple sugars, such as fructose and glucose, and in doing so made these simple sugars available to the orchid. By 1930, he had successfully germinated seed on an artificial medium by adding simple sugars which thus eliminated the need for fungal infection of the medium, and had grown plants to flowering *in vitro*. From this time onwards most of the research has centred around the influence of asymbiotic methods (i.e. those lacking a fungus) on seedling growth, with little or no attention paid to conditions of germination as they exist in nature.

The development of efficient seed germination and seedling production in the laboratory is now an established part of many orchid growing establishments and it has done much to reduce the cost of orchids to the public and to increase the availability of many species which had previously been rare and unavailable to most growers. Undoubtedly though, the major development which has resulted from the improvement of *in vitro* culture since the technique was first developed, has been the possibility of multiplying desirable hybrids and species by meristem culture. Although the first attempts at meristem culture were made by Robbins in 1922, success was not obtained until 1946 when E. Ball successfully cultured meristems of *Tropaeolum majus* and *Lupinus albus*.

By 1960 G. Morel had adapted the technique successfully to grow *Cymbidium* and subsequent work by a number of researchers has shown that the technique may be used in nearly all the commercially important orchid genera and hybrid genera, although *Paphiopedilum* has proved to be somewhat intransigent. Excellent accounts of the present state of meristem culture techniques are provided by Morel (1974) and J. Arditti (1977), the latter giving in addition detailed instructions on all the techniques and solutions used to date.

The Cultivation of Orchids

Literature

The literature on orchid cultivation is extensive, at times it seems almost overwhelmingly so, particularly to the beginner. Many books are devoted to the subject and these are supplemented by regular articles in nearly all of the journals published by orchid societies throughout the world. The advice is generally provided by experienced growers, with first-hand knowledge of the techniques they are advocating but, unfortunately, this is not always the case. For convenience, the literature on orchid-growing can be considered under three headings.

Classical texts

Several manuals written it the nineteenth century or early in this century have stood the test of time. Notable amongst these are *A Manual of Orchidaceous Plants* (J. Veitch, 1887–1894), *The Orchid Grower's Manual* (B.S. Williams, 1894, 7th ed.) and *Sander's Orchid Guide* (F. Sanders, 1901). The first is particularly useful for its comprehensive descriptions of species and varieties and for its habitat notes. Williams' classic work is probably the most comprehensive account of orchids and their cultivation ever published and is widely used at the present day. Its recent reprinting testifies to its continuing popularity. It could truly be considered the Mrs Beeton's Cookbook of the orchid world.

Die Orchideen, the encyclopaedic work of Schlechter (1927), also deserves mention but is more concerned with identification and describing the diversity of the family than with their cultivation.

Modern texts

With the advent of good and reasonably cheap colour printing, we have seen an explosion of orchid books published in recent years. Unfortunately, the majority are little more than picture books, often covering a selection of frequently misidentified orchids. A few, however, are valuable additions to any grower's library. Richter's *Orchid Care* (1972), Northern's *Home Orchid Growing* (4th ed., 1990), B. Williams' *Orchids for Everyone* (1980) and G. Fast's

Orchideenkultur (1980) are among the most useful of these. Each is well illustrated and written by authors with a wealth of practical experience.

Orchid journals

Since the last decade of the nineteenth century, orchid journals have played an increasingly important role in teaching growers good cultural techniques. At present, such journals are produced by societies or groups in over eighteen countries throughout the world. Indeed in some countries, notably the USA and Great Britain, several are published.

Not surprisingly perhaps, the *American Orchid Society Bulletin* has by far the largest circulation of around 25,000. It is by no means, however, the oldest journal. The first magazine devoted to orchids was *L'Orchidophile*, published between 1881 and 1893 in Paris. As it died, *Orchid Review* was founded in London by Robert Allen Rolfe, the Kew orchid botanist. It has continued until the present day and remains one of the most influential journals with a world-wide circulation.

Of the other journals, few approach the West German Orchid Society (D.O.G.) publication, *Die Orchidee,* in quality and scope and it is highly recommended.

One of the major problems confronting the orchid grower can be the inaccessibility of the literature and this is especially true of the classic texts and the older volumes or orchid journals, some of which are virtually unobtainable outside specialist libraries. Fortunately, many of the orchid societies possess excellent libraries and will lend books to members.

We would strongly recommend readers to join their local orchid society, not only to gain access to literature sources and plants but also to benefit from the advice and experience of other members.

Initial Thoughts

Growing orchids can be compared to cooking. Providing the instructions are followed you will not go far wrong but, like cooking, experience and sensible experimentation will often produce results little short of spectacular.

Knowing a little about the orchids you are

trying to grow is of the utmost importance for successful cultivation. Questions such as – Is it correctly named? Where does it come from? What altitude does it grow at? What climatic regime does it tolerate there? How does it grow? – should all be asked before attempting to grow a plant. The wrong answers can swiftly produce fatal results whereas a sound knowledge of habitat and growth requirements will enable sound judgements to be made on how a particular species should be grown. The older manuals often contain such useful information and another fertile source are the floristic accounts written for many countries of the world (see Bibliography at end).

Temperature Regimes

Although by far the greatest number of orchids grow in the tropics, they extend from the Arctic in the north to the southernmost tip of South America. Even in the tropics, they can be found from sea level to over 4000 m on the mountains. In attempting to grow orchids from such a wide range of different environments, growers have generally compromised by using three regimes – warm, intermediate and cool – for their glasshouses. For many plants, these are only a rough approximation to their natural conditions but experience has shown that most orchids can be satisfactorily grown in one of them.

In the warm house, the night temperature is not allowed to fall below 18°C with a minimum day lift of about 5–6°C. Such a house is suitable for orchids from the tropical lowlands, such as *Phalaenopsis*, many *Paphiopedilum* species, *Vanda*, cane *Dendrobium* and the leathery-leaved *Cymbidium* species.

The minimum night temperature of the intermediate house is 15°C. Here can be grown the higher altitude *Paphiopedilum* species, such as *P. insigne* and *P. spicerianum*, as well as many species of *Dendrobium, Cattleya, Maxillaria, Coelogyne* and *Oncidium*.

Finally, in the cool house, a night minimum of about 12°C is maintained. Orchids that can be grown under this regime include *Cymbidium, Pleione* (during the summer), high-altitude and temperate (Australian) *Dendrobium, Odontoglos-*

sum, Masdevallia, Pleurothallis and *Lycaste*. The surprisingly large number of orchids that can tolerate such a regime is a reflection of the large number of species found at relatively high altitudes on the tropical mountains. Indeed the regions with the largest number of orchid species, such as Colombia, Ecuador, New Guinea and Borneo, are all mountainous areas.

Light

The above regimes may also be divided by the light requirements of the orchids. An excellent guide to the likely tolerance of a species can be gained from a knowledge of where it grows in the wild and in what situation. Thus, many *Vanda* and cane and temperate (Australian) *Dendrobium* species grow in full sunlight and are tolerant of high light intensities and the consequent high temperatures generated in a lightly shaded glasshouse. In contrast, most *Phalaenopsis* and *Paphiopedilum* species grow in deep shade, either low down in the forest canopy or on the forest floor and should be well shaded in summer.

Humidity and Air Movement

Most orchids benefit during the growing season from high relative humidity in the glasshouse. Damping down by spraying the floor with water both morning and night is the best method for achieving this.

Air movement is beneficial to most orchids and can usually be achieved by good side ventilation in a small glass house or by an electric fan. Care, however, must be taken to ensure that a high relative humidity is maintained throughout the day.

Nutrition

Many epiphytic species appear to survive and grow quite happily in nature with little evidence of nutrition. However, in cultivation, all species thrive and grow far more rapidly if fertiliser is regularly applied during the growing season. A standard balanced N:P:K fertiliser, obtainable from most nurseries, is usually all that is required. More exotic liquid fertilisers obtained by steeping elephant or buffalo dung in water have been reported from the more remote areas of Africa and Asia.

Composts

Orchids are relatively versatile plants and will tolerate a wide variety of growing media. Often local conditions and the availability of various constituents will dictate the composition of the growing medium used. Thus, in all the older books, *Osmunda* fibre is the recommended basic ingredient for epiphytic mixes. Nowadays, it is too expensive, or even unobtainable, and is replaced by the more mundane chopped conifer bark or an artificial coarse composite medium.

It is true that the epiphytic orchids are more tolerant than the terrestrial ones. A few epiphytes will grow quite happily suspended in the air on a piece of string while others will grow well when attached by thread or wire to a slab of cork bark. In contrast, some terrestrials, such as the saprophytic species, are almost impossible to cultivate while others, such as the European *Ophrys* and *Cypripedium calceolus*, are notoriously tricky. All the successful growing media have one feature in common and that is free drainage. Without this, an orchid will quickly succumb to the various rots to which they are prone.

Ingredients

While appreciating the difficulty growers may experience in obtaining some of the ingredients mentioned in the three composts recommended here, we would emphasise that, with a little thought, an effective local substitute can usually be found for each. If in doubt, then some simple experimenting will usually solve the problem!

Compost A: 6 parts of coniferous bark; 1 part of perlag or pumice; 1 part of coarse peat; 1 part of charcoal.

This is the basic mix suitable for all epiphytes and some terrestrials. In most countries, the preferred bark is pine. Compost A is made up in three grades, to suit different pot and plant sizes, with bark particle sizes of 1–3 mm, 4–6 mm and 7–12 mm. Even coarser mixes may be used for large *Vanda* and *Angraecum* species.

The coarse grade of Irish sphagnum peat, widely available in Europe, is recommended for compost A. After sieving, pieces of a similar size to those of the bark and perlite are left. While peat is a useful water retainer in the compost, its presence is not essential.

Chopped green *Sphagnum* moss is also a useful ingredient when available and when soft water is used. It is particularly good for fine-rooted genera, such as *Masdevallia, Pleurothallis* and *Odontoglossum*.

Other inert substrates such as Rockwool have proved popular in recent years, degrading less rapidly than conifer bark.

Compost B: Equal parts of peat, loam and sand. This is used for most terrestrial orchids.

Compost C: A fine version of compost A with added peat and live *Sphagnum* moss (when available). A ratio of 3 parts of peat to 6 parts of bark is preferred.

Pests and Diseases

Healthy orchids are far more resistant to pests and diseases than weak plants. Therefore, good cultivation methods are essential if such problems are to be kept to a minimum.

Orchids are, however, susceptible to a variety of pests, such as aphids, red spider mite, mealy bug and scale, and to various bacterial, fungal and viral diseases. An excellent account for the identification and treatment of such problems is provided by Williams (1980).

Artificial Hybridisation

'Cross breeding among Orchidaceous plants would perhaps lead to very startling results; but, unfortunately, they are not easily raised by seed. I have, however, raised *Bletia, Cattleya, Orchis (Herminium) monorchis* and *Ophrys aranifera* from seed; and if I were not, during the greater part of the year, absent from my place where my plants are deposited, I could succeed in obtaining crosses in that order. I had well-formed pods last spring of Orchid by pollen of *Ophrys* as well as of other species of *Orchis* which had been forced; and if I had remained on the spot I think I should have obtained some cross-bred Orchidaceous seed. An intelligent garden-er may do much for science by attempts of this kind, if he keeps accurate notes of what he attempts and does not jump at immature con-clusions.'

When the Reverend W. Herbert wrote these words in the *Journal of the Horticultural Society* in 1847, he little realised how prophetic they

A chronological list of some of the most important early developments in the hybridisation of orchids

Date	Hybrid	Parentage	Comments
1853	Cattleya	C. guttata x C. loddigesii	John Dominy's first cross
1856	Calanthe Dominyi	C. furcata x C. masuca	First flowered and named hybrid orchid, flowered by Dominy
1856	Cattleya Hybrida	C. guttata x C. loddigesii	Flowered by Dominy
1863	First Laeliocattleya	Cattleya mossiae x Laelia crispa	First intergeneric hybrid
1864	Laelia Pilcheri	L. crispa x L. perrinii	First hybrid Laelia
1869	Paphiopedilum Harrisianum	P. villosum x P. barbatum	Named after Dr Harris of Exeter who suggested the idea of hybridising orchids to John Dominy
1871	Paphiopedilum Ashburtoniae	P. barbatum x P. insigne	Made by Mr Cross, the second successful orchid hybridiser
1873	Paphiopedilum Crossianum	P. insigne x P. venustum	Mr Cross's second Paphiopedilum hybrid
	Phragmipedium Sedenii	P. longifolium x P. schlimii	First hybrid flowered by Seden who succeeded Dominy as Veitch's orchid grower
	Cattleya Fausta	C. loddigesii x C. Exoniensis	First secondary hybrid
1874	Dendrobium Ainsworthii	D. aureum x D. nobile	First described Dendrobium hybrid
1878	Lycaste Hybrida	L. skinneri x L. deppei	Produced by W. Marshall of Enfield
1880	Masdevallia Chelsonii	M. amabilis x M. veitchiana	First Masdevallia hybrid
1881	Cattleya Calumnalta	C. intermedia x C. aclandiae	First hybrid produced on the Continent, by M. Bleu of Paris
1886	Sophrocattleya Batemaniana	Sophronitis grandiflora x Cattleya intermedia	First bigeneric hybrid
1886	Phalaenopsis x intermedia	P. aphrodite x P. rosea	Parentage of wild plant predicted by Lindley in 1853
1888	Epidendrum Obrienianum	E. erectum x E. radicans	Raised by Seden
1889	Miltonia Bleuana	M. vexillaria x M. roezlii	Raised by M. Bleu of Paris
	Cymbidium Veitchii	C. lowianum x C. eburneum	First hybrid Cymbidium raised by Seden
1890	Odontoglossum Wilckeanum	O. crispum x O. luteo-purpureum	Raised by Baron E. de Rothschild of Armanvilliers, nr Paris
	Epiphronitis Veitchii	Sophronitis grandiflora x Epidendrum radicans	Raised by Seden
1891	Odontoglossum x excellens	O. pescatorii x O. triumphans	The raising of the artificial hybrid confirmed Reichenbach's hypothesis of the origin of wild O. excellens
1892	Sophrolaeliocattleya Veitchiana	Sophronitis grandiflora x Laeliocattleya Schilleriana	First trigeneric hybrid
1893	Vanda Miss Joaquim	V. hookeriana x V. teres	Birth of the Singapore cut flower trade in Vandaceous orchids
1894	Epilaelia Hardyana	Epidendrum ciliare x Laelia anceps	Third intergeneric hybrid
1897	Epicattleya Matutina	Cattleya bowringiana x E. radicans	Raised at Veitch's
1899	Angraecum Veitchii	A. sesquipedale x A. superbum	First Madagascan orchids used in hybridisation
1901	The rediscovery of Mendel's work on inheritance of characters		
1904	Odontioda Vuylstekeae	Cochlioda noetzliana x Odontoglossum pescatorei	Raised by Charles Vuylsteke of Ghent, Belgium
1906	Coelogyne Brymeriana	C. dayana x C. asperata	Raised by Col. Brymer of Doncaster, England
1906	Sander's List of Orchid Hybrids published		List of hybrids and their parentage to 1906
1909	Rolfe and Hurst's Orchid Stud Book published		A survey of hybridisation to 1908 and lists of orchid hybrids, parentage, hybridisers, etc.

would turn out to be. Although he never found the time himself to successfully grow orchid hybrids from seed, less than ten years afterwards in 1856, John Dominy had a spectacular success when he flowered a hybrid plant he had raised from seed obtained by crossing *Calanthe furcata* with *Calanthe masuca*. Dominy was the orchid grower for the firm of J. Veitch & Sons of Exeter and his breakthrough not only gave Veitch's firm a ten year start in the field but also opened the way for the massive production of hybrids which has come to dominate orchid cultivation at the present day. John Lindley, who named the first hybrid *Calanthe* Dominyi after its raiser, realised immediately the nomenclatural problems that would result when hybridising became widespread. He is said to have exclaimed to Dominy, 'Why you will drive botanists mad!' Certainly those botanists involved at the present day with the classification, nomenclature and registration of orchid species and hybrids would be the first to agree with Lindley's sentiments.

It has never ceased to surprise orchid growers how easy it is to hybridise orchids. Not only are interspecific crosses often easily made but intergeneric hybrids have also been produced in great numbers. Why, we may ask, are orchids so easily hybridised? In most other plants, hybridisation seems to be an exception rather than the rule. Indeed, experimental systematists have even considered the definition of a species to rest on the criteria of crossability and high seedling viability of members within the specific group, whilst with individuals of other species crossability is either not possible or reduced and the offspring have a lower viability.

Several considerations must be taken into account when considering orchid hybridisation. Orchids are a highly evolved group of plants still undergoing evolution. The theory is that morphological adaptation to insect pollinators has run ahead of the build-up of incompatibility factors between style tissue and pollen of closely related species. Indeed, such incompatibility is scarcely needed, for the insect-orchid species relationships seem to be highly specific (see van der Pijl and Dodson, 1966). A further factor that may explain the lack of interspecific pollen-style incompatibility would be the geographical or ecological isolation of species which would reduce the chances of hybridisation in nature. That ecological barriers do exist was demonstrated by C. Dodson (1966) who found that in the disturbed habitat provided by the pruning of guava trees in Ecuador, hybrid swarms of *Oncidium pumilio* and *Oncidium pusillum* were found on the pruned trees. *Oncidium pusillum* normally grows in shady locations on lianas overhanging streams, and *O. pumilio* grows in direct sunlight in the tops of guava trees, but the hybrids named by H.G. Reichenbach *Oncidium x glossomystax*, have found ideal conditions to survive on the semishaded lower parts of the trees. Until the disturbance caused by pruning the trees, no such ecological site was available for the hybrid.

Finally, the multitude of artificial hybrids (upwards of 70,000 have been registered to date) represent hybrids of relatively few of the ± 800 genera of orchids recognised at the present day. Indeed, the majority of commercially important genera involved in hybridisation can almost be counted on two hands, such as, *Dendrobium*, *Paphiopedilum*, *Cymbidium*, *Odontoglossum*, *Oncidium*, *Vanda*, *Miltonia*, *Cattleya*, *Laelia*, *Epidendrum*, and *Phalaenopsis*. Of course, many other genera have been involved in hybridisation programmes, but it would be true to say that only with relatively closely related genera are hybrids easily obtained, e.g. no one has succeeded in crossing *Paphiopedilum* with *Cattleya* whereas *Cattleya* and *Laelia* species cross fairly easily.

A brief list of some of the more important events in the development of orchid hybridisation are given in the table on p. 28.

Endangered Orchids and Their Conservation

R. Melville (1970) estimated that 5–10% of the quarter of a million flowering plants in the world are in imminent danger of extinction. Applied to orchids this would mean that between 850 and 3000 species would fall into this category (as estimates of the number of orchids vary between 17,000 and 30,000 species). Indeed, these figures may be on the low side, for most orchids grow in the tropical forests which are probably the most vulnerable of all habitats in this overpopulated world.

Few figures are available on the number of orchids which are endangered in any tropical country, but U.C. Pradhan in the *American Orchid Society Bulletin* (1977) listed 63 species (8%) of Indian orchids as endangered, threatened or possibly already extinct. This agrees well with Melville's estimate for flowering plants in general. However, Kataki (1976) in the same journal listed 35 species as scarce or near extinction in India, and only 14 species were common to both his and Pradhan's lists. Thus it seems more likely that the number of endangered orchids in India may be well over 10% and this situation is probably paralleled in many other countries, in the tropics and subtropics.

Despite the staggering size of the problem, it is only recently that efforts have been made to protect orchids other than on a local level. Indeed, the need to conserve plants at all has taken a minor place in conservationists' priorities. Plants lack the general appeal of birds and mammals and money is far more readily available from the public for animal conservation projects. The irony is that all animal life ultimately relies upon plants for its existence and hence the first priority should be the preservation of the habitat and flora to provide a healthy environment in which the animals can survive and increase. Of course, many reserves set up specifically for animals do provide equivalent protection for the plants therein, although this is not always the case as Tsavo National Park in Kenya has disturbingly shown where the elephants have destroyed most of their savanna woodland habitat.

The Vulnerability of Orchids

Although the largest family of flowering plants, the orchids are also probably among the most seriously threatened. Their vulnerability stems from two sources: the first being their highly specialised life cycle, growing in association with a mycorrhizal fungus, and the second being the decorative nature and beauty of many species when in flower which has made them so sought after by man.

Each orchid species is adapted to life in a specialised environment. The difficulties experienced by horticulturists in successfully growing and flowering many species can leave little doubt of their often fastidious requirements for light, water, shade and nutrients. Because of their specialised requirements many orchids are very restricted in distribution and endemism is high in many areas. In Papua-New Guinea, the majority of the 2600 species, and 29 of the 128 genera are endemic, often being found in only one or a few areas on the island. The same is true of the orchids of other areas, particularly islands such as New Caledonia (66% endemicity) and Madagascar (over 90%).

Where orchids are so restricted in distribution they are particularly vulnerable to both natural and man-made changes in the environment. Natural changes in the world's climate over the past few thousand years have undoubtedly led to the extinction of many species. Others may be on the very verge of extinction in relict habitats, such as *Paphiopedilum druryi* in southern India and *Cattleya dormaniana* in eastern Brazil.

However, such losses and the time-scale involved are minute compared to the destruction attributable directly to man's activities. In recent times and particularly in the last thirty years, environmental change on a massive scale has accompanied man's inroads into the tropical forests of the world. In the Americas, Africa and Asia, forests are being clear-felled for lumber, paper pulp, agriculture and a variety of other reasons at the astonishing rate of about 12 hectares a minute. In most cases, the process is irreversible, for the delicate ecological balance of the forest, once upset, cannot be reconstituted. When the forest goes, so too do the orchids. The epiphytes lose their means of support and the terrestrials lose their shade, nutrients and their water supply, for forests generate rainfall and once felled the area may quickly become a semidesert.

In Costa Rica, over one million hectares of forest disappeared between 1950 and 1973. Elsewhere the same story can be told, and in many countries, especially those that are overpopulated, forest exists now only in inaccessible spots unsuitable for cultivation. How many species have already become extinct can only be guessed at, but *Laelia milleri* first described less than 20 years ago is already extinct in the wild as its habitat has been destroyed by mining. Similarly, *Oncidium macranthum* may also be gone, for the area in the Ecuadorean forests where it was found has been almost completely destroyed for charcoal production.

Although only one species, cultivated vanilla (*Vanilla planifolia*), has ever attained importance as a crop plant, orchids have nevertheless in some areas been of economic importance since the earliest times. The ancient Greeks following the 'Doctrine of Signatures' used orchid tubers, which are shaped like human testicles, as an aphrodisiac. In the eastern Mediterranean and Middle East, these tubers are still collected in large numbers and sold as 'salep' for the same purpose. In Africa, similar properties are prescribed to *Ansellia* pseudobulbs in Zululand and in parts of East Africa. Such uses could undoubtedly affect local orchid populations adversely although it is doubtful if any species has been brought to extinction by them.

From the late eighteenth century, the leisure time brought about by the increasing wealth generated by the British Empire undoubtedly led to the rapid increase in the growing of exotic plants in England. Orchids from the tropics were noted for their beautiful flowers, their great diversity of form and for the difficulty of their successful cultivation.

It is ironical that the unique beauty and exotic flowers of some orchids have led some species to the verge of extinction, for many would consider these the best reasons for protecting orchids! Orchids, often in considerable quantities, have been and still are being collected from the wild for sale to growers. Frederick Sander, founder of the famous orchid nursery at St Albans, had, at one time in the late nineteenth century, thirty-nine collectors active in the tropics. They often collected thousands of plants of a single desirable species, destroying large tracts of forest to reach these epiphytic plants. The area where *Miltoniopsis vexillaria* was found was said to have been cleared 'as if by forest fires'. Sometimes, the forest was destroyed to ensure the failure of a rival firm in obtaining the same species.

All too often the orchids when collected, failed to survive the long sea journeys to Europe. For example, the thousands of plants of *Dendrobium phalaenopsis* var. *schroederianum* collected by W. Micholitz in New Guinea perished *en route* to Sander at Macassar in the Celebes. Sander when he learnt of the loss cabled his collector to 'return re-collect'. Roebelin's first collection of 21,000 *Vanda (Euanthe) sanderiana* was similarly lost during an earthquake in port in the Philippines.

Other collectors were more successful. Forstermann spent months in Assam and had to kill a tiger before he returned with 40,000 plants of *Paphiopedilum fairrieanum*. The rewards available to the successful collector are summed up by Sir Joseph Hooker, who commented in his journals that a collector in the Khasia Hills might clear between £2000 and £3000 in a year, and that in the mid-nineteenth century! His own efforts to send seven men's loads of *Vanda coerulea* to Kew were less rewarding as due to 'unavoidable accidents and difficulties' few plants reached Kew alive.

The First World War (1914–18) spelt the end of collecting activities by the large European orchid firms of Sander, Low, Veitch, and Linden. Even prior to the outbreak of war it had become obvious that the days of the European professional orchid collector were almost over, for the most productive areas in the tropics had been comprehensively collected over by a succession of intrepid men. With most of the dazzling orchid species seriously depleted in the wild, collectors could no longer find sufficient quantities of plants to satisfy the nurseries, and furthermore the supply of novelties, which in the nineteenth century seemed endless, began to dry up.

Although the days of the professional European collectors are long past, collecting is still prevalent in many tropical areas. Firms have sprung up in many countries which specialise in exporting native species. Although a few grow these from seed or propagate from stock plants, the main source of supply is still wild-collected material. Such specimens are seldom established before they are exported and the consequent loss of plants in the importing country is often high.

National and Local Controls

In many parts of the world orchids are completely protected in the wild. The protection operates either at the national level by the promulgation of laws preventing the collection of orchids in the wild, or locally by the establishment of National Parks or native reserves where the habitat is totally protected and the collection of all animals and plants is forbidden.

The universal appeal of orchids has ensured their protection from being picked or dug up in several countries. In Britain, complete protection is given to *Cypripedium calceolus*, *Cephalanthera rubra*, *Orchis militaris* and *Epipogium aphyllum* whilst all other species are protected somewhat by the law which forbids picking or digging of wild flowers without the permission of the landowner. In Germany, total protection is afforded to all species. Strangely though, where most orchids grow, protection is often totally lacking at the national level. This is true of many tropical countries where the showier species are found and, even in Mediterranean Europe, orchids are almost unprotected in most countries.

One of the smallest nature reserves in the world at Mildenhall in England was set up to protect *Orchis militaris*. Not all orchids are as fortunate but many gain considerable protection inside National Parks and other native reserves. Even in reserves set up for other wildlife, such as for birds, orchids and other plants will often be totally protected. Occasionally such reserves can have the opposite effect and lead to the extinction, at least locally, of a species. This can often occur where a reserve is set aside but no management programme is undertaken. This has often occurred where a traditional land management treatment is neglected and a vegetation type previously encouraged is thereby superseded by a more natural climax vegetation type, e.g. where a marsh eventually dries out and is replaced by woodland.

However, the most dangerous threat to both national and local protection of wildlife arises through ignorance of the laws by local people who have most access to the endangered species. Only widespread education programmes can solve this problem.

International Laws

A landmark in wildlife conservation occurred in March 1973 with the foundation of the Convention on *International Trade in Endangered Species of Wild Fauna and Flora* (C.I.T.E.S.), often called the 'Washington Convention', by the International Union for Conservation of Nature and Natural Resources (I.U.C.N.). Conscious of the growing threat to much of the world's wildlife the Convention, recognising that international co-operation is essential for the protection of certain species against overexploitation through international trade, listed threatened species of animals and plants in a series of appendices.

In Appendix 1 are listed species considered to be threatened by extinction and included are the following orchids: *Cattleya skinneri*, *C. trianaei*, *Didiciea cunninghamii*, *Laelia jongheana*, *L. lobata*, *Lycaste virginalis* var. *alba*, *Peristeria elata*, *Renanthera imschootiana* and *Vanda coerulea*, all *Paphiopedilum* and all *Phragmipedium* species.

All Appendix 1 species are stringently protected under the Convention and only in exceptional circumstances may licences be granted for their export and import. Since 1985, all European orchids are treated as Appendix 1 species within the European Common Market.

Although a few orchids appear in the first appendix it is the second appendix and the articles relating to species contained therein which most affects orchid trade, because all the remaining orchid species are included there! Trade in Appendix 2 species is subject to strict regulations to prevent their overexploitation. This takes the form of documentation requirements for all international trade in these orchids. Thus an importer in a country which has endorsed the Convention must usually obtain an import permit which is given under strict scientific control and also an export permit from the country of origin of the orchids.

Over one hundred countries have so far adopted the Convention. Therefore, theoretically, the international trade in orchid species is now regulated in many countries so that any endangered species can be protected if necessary by the exporting or importing country refusing to issue the necessary permits.

At present, permits are readily obtained in most of the signatory countries where the issuing authorities are mostly engaged in determining the volume of trade and the nature of the trade. Thus, information is being gathered on which species are actually endangered by overexploitation. Inevitably, some species and genera are more susceptible to indiscriminate collection in the wild than others. In particular, species in the most popularly cultivated genera such as *Cattleya*, *Laelia*, *Paphiopedilum*, *Cypripedium*, *Dendrobium*, *Cymbidium*, and *Odontoglossum* are probably in the greatest danger.

A major and, some consider, insurmountable

problem in controlling the trade in orchid species is that most species are exported in the non-flowering state. It would tax the ability and knowledge of most experienced orchid growers and botanists to identify such plants so that it is unreasonable to expect customs officials to do so. Similarly it is often difficult to distinguish orchid species from hybrids in the sterile state while most customs officials would still be lost if the same plants were in flower. For this reason all orchids, rather than just rare and endangered species, are included in Appendix 2 of the Convention.

A possible solution to the problem of identification mentioned above may lie in restricting international trade eventually to flasked seedlings and mericlones. This would benefit orchid species in nature by removing the incentive for their collection as mature plants. It would also encourage the development of a nursery trade in the exporting countries where the flasking of the orchid seed or meristems would be undertaken. In many tropical countries such industries are already being developed.

The Future

Man is the principal agent that endangers orchids. Legal curbs on his activities to prevent excessive habitat destruction and overcollecting may slow down his destructive activities. Unfortunately, the laws erected to protect wildlife are least likely to be enforced in many areas of the world where plants are most endangered. Possibly the problem may only be resolved when conservation and the care of the environment is taught in schools and colleges as a subject like mathematics and chemistry. Certainly, the success of such education, for example, in parts of East Africa and southern Mexico is producing an awareness of the need for conservation not only amongst children but in their parents as well.

Orchids have now been cultivated, often on a grand scale, in Europe and North America for well over 100 years. Many thousands of species must have been in cultivation during that time. Undoubtedly many hundreds still survive in cultivation, for example M. Hofmann (1975) indicated that over 4000 species were being grown in a number of major German collections in 1975. This represents a source of germplasm which might indirectly be used to protect these species in the wild, as many species can now be satisfactorily raised from seed or meristem culture. Inevitably, if many hundreds of well grown seedlings reached the market and at a moderate cost, it would take pressure off the wild populations by undercutting the price at which wild-collected and unestablished plants could be sold. Furthermore many orchids survive in cultivation for many years (some plants at Kew are about 100 years old) and these could continue to supply seed over a considerable period of time.

Sadly the beauty which has led to orchids being prized so greatly may have led many to the brink of extinction. Some species may only be remembered by future generations of orchid lovers as fading illustrations in ageing books. Nowhere is the situation more aptly expressed than in the title of a New York Botanical Garden Symposium entitled 'Extinction is Forever'.

Orchid Nomenclature

Whilst scientific (Latin) names are undoubtedly difficult to learn and, for many, difficult to pronounce, they do perform an essential function in providing each orchid with a tag by which it may be known and recognised without confusion throughout the botanical and horticultural world. Many orchid enthusiasts loudly proclaim their love of vernacular names but the confusion that can result from their use is easily demonstrated by, for example, the fact that the English 'butterfly orchid' *Platanthera bifolia* is not the same species as the Continental one, *Orchis papilionacea* and again in the United States the 'lady's slipper orchid' might refer to any of a dozen native and many more exotic species. Scientific names are universal and mean the same to a Chinese as to a European or South American.

However, there is more to scientific names than that, for contained within each binomial name is a wealth of information. If we take the names *Oncidium nanum* and *Oncidium longipes* both having the same generic name, we can accurately state that these two orchids have certain characteristics in common, so that if we know the characteristics of the first species we can deduce with some degree of accuracy many of the characters of the second. The difference between these names lies in the specific epithet of each and from this we can state that, although some characters may be held in common, the two species differ to a greater or lesser extent but at least enough for the two to be recognisably distinct. Again the generic name *Oncidium* allows us to obtain further information, because scientists such as John Lindley, George Bentham, Rudolf Schlechter and Robert Dressler have arranged the genera in classification systems which also provide information such as morphological similarity or dissimilarity, putative relationships and even possible evolution.

Names also reflect the state of our knowledge of orchids. Thus, the genus *Paphiopedilum* was established by E. Pfitzer in 1888 to include some of the species previously included in the genus *Cypripedium*. As the tropical Asiatic species are distinct in several ways from the temperate species, he established for the former a new genus which has subsequently met with unanimous approval from other botanists.

The Naming of Wild Orchids

The naming of orchids is governed by two codes: firstly, the *International Code of Botanical Nomenclature* (I.C.B.N.) and, secondly, the *International Code of Nomenclature of Cultivated Plants* (I.C.N.C.P.). Orchid names are merely conventional symbols which serve as a means of reference and avoid the need to use cumbersome descriptive phrases in referring to these plants. They can only effectively be used if they are understood by all who use the system. Thus the names, however communicated, should call to mind the concepts intended by the transmitter and receiver of the names. To avoid confusions that would exist if, for example, each nation used its own system and language, the two codes mentioned above have been introduced to standardise plant names.

Each code consists of a number of **rules** or **articles**, some supplemented by **recommendations**. The provisions of the rules are mandatory and must be followed. Recommendations indicate the best procedure to be followed, but names which are contrary to a recommendation cannot be rejected on that account.

The enforcement of the rules depends solely on the voluntary agreement of systematists to follow their provisions, Nevertheless, the flouting of the rules can only lead to nomenclatural instability and confusion.

The following arguments, applicable to the nomenclature of wild orchids, are given within the framework of the I.C.B.N.

Names of taxa above the rank of genus

The names of taxa above the rank of genus, such as family, tribe and order, consist of a single term only (uninomial). They are plural nouns or adjectives used as nouns and are written with a capital initial letter. To enable the rank of any of these taxa to be recognised, the Code has standardised the ending for the names of all taxa of a given rank. Thus, the names of plant families must end in *-aceae*.

Taxa above the rank of genus and their endings

Category	Botanical ending	Example
Division	-phyta*	Spermatophyta
Subdivision	-phytina*	
Class	-phyceae*	
Subclass	-phycidae*	
Order	-ales	Orchidales
Suborder	-ineae	
Family	-aceae	Orchidaceae
Subfamily	-oideae	Apostasioideae
Tribe	-eae	Neottieae
Subtribe	-inae	Spiranthinae

* Recommended but not mandatory.

The use of the categories above is strictly hierarchical.

Names of genera

Generic names are also uninomial and are singular nouns written with an initial capital letter and italicised e.g. *Pleurothallis*, *Rudolfiella*, *Sirhookera*, etc.

Names of intermediate rank between genus and species

The Code allows several categories of taxa between the levels of genus and species. The name of such a taxon is not a uninomial but is a combination of the name of the genus in which the taxon is classified with another term peculiar to the taxon and preceded by a word indicating its rank, e.g.

Paphiopedilum   subg.   *Brachypetalum*
generic name   subgenus   name of subgenus

This last term may be a singular noun or plural adjective and must be written with a capital letter.

Categories between genus and species

Category	Abbreviation	Example
Subgenus	subg.	*Paphiopedilum* subg. *Anotopetalum*
Section	sect.	*Polystachya* sect. *Affines*
Series	series	Seldom used in Orchidaceae
Subseries	subseries	Seldom used in Orchidaceae

Names of species

All described orchid species possess a two-word (binomial) latinised name. The first term of the name is the name of the **genus** (plural – genera) to which the species belongs. The generic name is always written with a capital initial letter. The second term is the **specific** epithet which agrees in gender with the generic name if adjectival and is written with a lower case initial letter, even if a proper noun or personal name. Together the generic name and specific epithet form the specific name, e.g.

Paphiopedilum appletonianum
Generic   Specific
name   epithet

Specific name

In the genus *Paphiopedilum* there are many other species and in these the specific epithet differentiates each species, e.g. *Paphiopedilum praestans*, *P. insigne*, *P. charlesworthii* etc.

In use, the specific epithet in the binomial cannot be used alone e.g. *Coelogyne macdonaldii* cannot be referred to as *macdonaldii*. However, once the name has been used in full in a written text then the generic name can be abbreviated to the initial letter, e.g. *Coelogyne macdonaldii* would become *C. macdonaldii* providing this does not lead to any ambiguity.

The latin binomial name of an orchid species when cited should also be followed by the name of the author who described the species, e.g. *Paphiopedilum delenatii* Guillamin indicates that *P. delenatii* was described by A. Guillamin and *Cattleya luteola* Lindl. indicates that *C. luteola* was described by John Lindley (if a date follows the author's name this indicates the year in which the species was described). Often the author's name may be abbreviated, thus Lindley is abbreviated to Lindl.; H.G. Reichenbach to Rchb.f. (the f. standing for *filius* as his father was also a botanist who described many plants); and Schlechter to Schltr.

Often a species described originally in one genus may be transferred to another genus when further work elucidates its true taxonomic position. Such was the case with *Paphiopedilum insigne* which was originally described by Lindley as *Cypripedium insigne* but was later transferred by E. Pfitzer to the genus *Paphiopedilum*. The correct citation of the species is now:

Paphiopedilum insigne (Lindl.) Pfitz.

Occasionally even more elaborate authority citations are given, such as *Epidendrum skinneri* Batem. ex Lindl. which indicates that Lindley described *E. skinneri* from a name proposed but not published by James Bateman.

Names below the rank of species

Several categories of taxa below the species rank are recognised in the I.C.B.N. These are the subspecies (abbreviated to subsp.); variety (abbreviated to var.) and the form. The categories, subvariety and subform are allowed but are only infrequently used. The name of a taxon at this level consists of the specific name followed by a term peculiar to the taxon preceded by a word indicative of rank (this is obligatory in the Botanical Code), e.g. *Paphiopedilum insigne* var. *sanderae*; *Disa rungweënsis* subsp. *rhodesiaca*.

As with taxa above the rank of species, so are those below that rank strictly hierarchical in the descending order: subspecies, variety, form. Thus, a variety of a subspecies or species and a form of a subspecies or species are allowed, whilst a variety of a form or a subspecies of a variety are not.

As with specific and generic names, those below the specific level consist of a latinised term, most commonly, a descriptive adjective or possessive noun.

The Stability of Taxonomic Names

The most frequent cause of aggravation between orchid growers and orchid taxonomists may be found when the taxonomists replace a well-known name of long standing by an apparently new name. Such conflicts often lead to the old and the new names being used side by side for many years with each group appearing intransigent in its determination to stick to the name it champions. Invariably, such situations arise from growers misunderstanding the role of taxonomists following the rules of the codes and of taxonomists failing to appreciate the problems growers face when names are changed.

Name changes may arise from several causes. Taxonomy attempts to reflect the relationships between plants in the names given, e.g. if we grow *Cattleya mossiae* and are offered *Cattleya labiata* then we know that the latter will resemble the former in many ways. As new research on orchids is completed, our information increases and our understanding of these relationships also improves. This often leads to the reformulation of our ideas and consequently may lead to name changes which better reflect relationships. Such was the case when the genus *Aerangis* in Africa and Madagascar was removed from the genus *Angraecum*.

A second major cause of name changes also results from our better understanding of orchids at the present day. Often a species was described several times either because authors were unaware of the previously published names or because the geographical extent of a species was unknown. Thus, *Dendrobium purpureum* was described under several different names from various island groups in South East Asia before P.F. Hunt realised that all these were assignable to *D. purpureum*. Several names referring to the same species are called synonyms and, according to the I.C.B.N., the earliest validly published name is the correct name for the species. The mass of name changes of the last few years have often been the result of botanists studying old literature and unearthing earlier names for species known to horticulture under a later synonym. Jeffrey (1973) has suggested that the majority of such name-changing is past. No doubt most orchid growers and taxonomists hope that he is right.

A further cause of name changes results from the original misidentification of a plant when brought into cultivation. The incorrect name may become well-known until the misidentification is recognised.

The Naming of New Species

For validity, a new species' description must be published in a journal or book or similar publication and not in a manuscript or in a single document. Furthermore, the description of the species, or a diagnosis which gives the salient features of the new species distinguishing it from similar species, must accompany the specific name. Commonly both a diagnosis and a description are given and one at least must be in Latin.

A further requirement is for a type herbarium specimen to be cited with the description. The description should be of the type specimen and the location of the type (i.e. the herbarium where it is deposited) should also be noted. The process of typification allows for maximum fixity, for anyone may refer back to the type specimen to see exactly what the author was describing. A corollary of the type concept is that the type may fall within the range of variation of a species and may indeed be somewhat unrepresentative of the species as a whole.

The terminology associated with the concept of type specimens is often misused. The terms most frequently used are as follows:

1. Holotype – either the sole specimen used by the author of a name or the one specimen designated by him as the type.
2. Isotype – another specimen of the same collection as that designated as the holotype by the author.
3. Syntype – either any one of two or more specimens used by the author of a name who did not designate a holotype *or* any one of two or more specimens designated by him simultaneously as types.
4. Lectotype – a specimen selected subsequently from amongst syntypes to serve as the nomenclatural type.
5. Neotype – a specimen selected to serve as the nomenclatural type when, through loss or destruction, no holotype, lectotype or syntype exists.

When a name is published validly within the rules of the code it is termed legitimate. Thus the terms type, valid and legitimate have strict definitions in taxonomy and should not be used in a general sense.

If two or more names (synonyms) have been applied to a single taxon then it is the first given that is the correct name. At specific level and below, the term of the name peculiar to the taxon dates from the place of its original publication irrespective of the combination in which it was originally published. Furthermore, no name has priority outside the rank in which it was given. For plants, the starting date, before which publications can be ignored, is 1753, the publication of Linnaeus' *Species Plantarum*.

Names which are excluded from the rule of priority include:

1. Homonyms – Names spelt in an identical manner based on different types, are homonyms. Of two or more homonyms, all except the oldest are excluded.
2. Superfluous names – A name is nomenclaturally superfluous, and thus excluded when published, if the taxon to which it was applied, as circumscribed by the author, included the type of another name which ought to have been adopted under the rules.
3. Tautonyms – When the name of a species has the second term exactly repeating the generic name, then it is excluded as a tautonym.
4. Ambiguous names – Names which have been used for so long by different authors in different senses that they are persistent sources of error or confusion, are excluded.
5. Dubious names – When the typification and application of a name are uncertain, it is termed dubious and is excluded.

Finally, we would like to mention the problem of the conservation and rejection of names. In plants, the conservation or rejection of specific names has until recently been inadmissible and is, even now, restricted to certain important crop and horticultural plants. Names from generic to family levels may be conserved and then only by submitting written and documented proposals to the General Committee of the International Commission for Botanical Nomenclature, who in turn may submit them to the International Botanical Congress for adoption.

The Naming of Cultivated Orchids

The naming of cultivated orchids is also guided by the *International Code of Botanical Nomenclature* (I.C.B.N.) and the *International Code of Nomenclature for Cultivated Plants* (I.C.N.C.P.). However, the naming and publication of lists of cultivated orchids dates back to Bohnhof's *Dictionnaire des Orchidées Hybrides* in 1895 and the more influential Sander's *List of Orchid Hybrids* (1906) and thus the practices evolved for naming cultivated orchids predated and differed, at that time, in details from those outlined in the two codes. The Second World Orchid Conference in Hawaii in 1957 constituted the International Orchid Commission on Classification, Nomenclature and Registration and one of their main functions was to make the provisions of the two codes as widely known as possible among orchidists. In 1969, the Commission published a *Handbook on Orchid Nomenclature and Registration* (3rd edition, 1985) which outlines the general principles of plant nomenclature; the rules (from I.C.B.N. and I.C.N.C.P.) as they affect the nomenclature of both wild and cultivated orchids; and gives a complete list of all orchid hybrid generic names.

The purpose of both codes is to promote uniformity, accuracy and fixity in the naming of plants, and for this reason the rules of the codes function retroactively. The necessity for these features in the naming of orchids need not be emphasised when it is realised that there may be as many as 30,000 species of orchids and already more than double that number of registered hybrids in about 600 hybrid genera to date. Furthermore, the number of hybrids increases each year and shows no sign of slowing down.

The majority of cultivated orchids fall into the category of artificial hybrids and, for this account, we would like to consider these hybrids as either **intrageneric** (hybrids between two species or hybrids of the same genus) or **intergeneric** (hybrids between species or hybrids of different genera). Such artificially produced hybrid orchids are named at three levels, having a generic name, a grex epithet and a cultivar epithet, e.g.

Cymbidium	Babylon	'Castle Hill'
Generic name	Grex epithet	Cultivar epithet

Grex name (spanning Generic name and Grex epithet)

Cultivar name (spanning all three)

Generic level names

In print, all generic names are italicised and have their first letter capitalised.

(a) Ordinary generic names are used when a hybrid is formed by the crossing of two species (or hybrids) of the same genus (intrageneric). e.g. *Cymbidium* Ballianum is a hybrid of *Cymbidium eburneum* with *Cymbidium mastersii*.

(b) An up-to-date list of all intergeneric hybrid names is given in the 1985–90 supplement to Sander's *List of Orchid Hybrids* (1991). Intergeneric hybrid names fall into two categories depending on the number of genera involved in the ancestry of the hybrid. All intergeneric hybrid names should be preceded by a multiplication sign ×, although this is often omitted.

(i) Bigeneric hybrid names are composed of a part or all of each of the parent generic names united to form a single new hybrid generic name, e.g. a hybrid between a *Schomburgkia* species and a *Cattleya* species is called a × *Schombocattleya;* hybrids between *Epidendrum* and *Sophronitis* species are known as × *Epiphronitis.* It does not matter which genus is the seed and which the pollen parent of the cross, the generic name remains the same.

(ii) Trigeneric names may follow a similar form to bigeneric names, being composition names of the three parent genera: thus × *Schombolaeliocattleya* is the generic name of a hybrid whose parentage involves the three genera *Schomburgkia*, *Laelia* and *Cattleya*. Alternatively, trigeneric hybrid names (and also hybrids involving four or more genera) may be formed by adding the suffix -*ara* to a root which is, most frequently, the surname of an orchidist, e.g. × *Vuylstekeara*, named after M. Vuylsteke, is the name of a hybrid genus whose parentage involved the genera *Cochlioda*, *Miltonia* and *Odontoglossum;* × *Holttumara*, named after Professor R. Holttum, is a hybrid involving the genera *Arachnis*, *Vanda* and *Renanthera*.

Grex names

In orchids, the term **grex** denotes a group of individual plants of an artificial hybrid all bearing the same grex name. The **grex name** is applied to all the progeny directly raised from two parent plants which bear the same pair of specific or collective or grex names, regardless of parental cultivars and regardless of which was used as a seed parent and which as a pollen parent. The term grex name is used in connection with orchids only and is covered by the term **collective name** in the I.C.N.C.P.

Grex names may consist either of a formula in which the parental names are linked by a multiplication sign, e.g. *Cattleya* Edithiae × *C.* Suzanne Hye or *Cymbidium lowianum* × *C. giganteum*, or of a generic name followed by a grex epithet. This epithet must be a fancy name (i.e. in modern language) if registered after 1 January 1959, consisting of from one to three words and should not be italicised, e.g. *Cattleya* Bow Bells in which *Cattleya* is the generic name and Bow Bells is the grex epithet.

Cultivar names

A cultivar in orchids is a clone, that is, a genetically uniform assemblage of individuals derived originally from a single seedling individual by vegetative propagation. Cultivar names are combinations formed from the generic name, specific or grex name, specific or grex epithet followed by a cultivar epithet.

Cultivar epithets must be fancy (modern language) names consisting of from one to three words, each of which is capitalised (unless convention decrees otherwise). The cultivar epithet is never italicised and should be placed within single inverted commas, e.g. *Cymbidium* Babylon 'Castle Hill' is a cultivar name of which *Cymbidium* is the generic name; Babylon is the grex epithet and 'Castle Hill' is the cultivar name. Similarly, we can have *Odontoglossum crispum* 'Everest' where the first two terms constitute the specific name and 'Everest' the cultivar epithet.

The legitimacy of grex and cultivar names

For legitimacy, a new name at the grex or cultivar level must have been validly published and new grex names must (after 1 January 1967) also be accepted by the International Registration Authority (now the Royal Horticultural Society). Rule 5 of the Rules for Nomenclature and Registration for Cultivated Orchids as laid out in the *Handbook* (1985), states that 'Registration of grex names of orchids is of the greatest importance for nomenclatural stability'. For valid publication of a grex name, a statement of the names of the parents of the grex and publication in an accepted form, e.g. printed for distribution to the public in a reputable journal, are required. A cultivar name is valid if it is published in an accepted manner, e.g. printed for distribution to the public and it should be accompanied by a description if published after 1 January 1959 (Article 26 of I.C.N.C.P). This provision has unfortunately been widely ignored in the case of orchid cultivars but the International Orchid Commission in their handbook strongly recommend that in future Article 26 should be adhered to.

Valid publication of registered grex names of orchids is treated as beginning from Sander's *Complete List of Orchid Hybrids* (to 1 January 1946), as supplemented by Sander's *One-Table List of Orchid Hybrids* vols. I & II (1946–60).

The correct name of an orchid grex or cultivar, where more than one name is available, is based on the following priorities: (1) for grex names: on priority of registration or, in the case of grexes named before 1 January 1967 on priority of registration or publication; (2) for cultivar names: on priority of publication. Contrary to the rule of priority which invariably holds for specific, subspecific, varietal and form epithets, a grex or cultivar name if generally used may be retained instead of an earlier legitimate name for the same taxon if the use of the latter would lead to confusion. Such action may only be taken with the approval of the International Registration Authority.

The Classification of the Orchid Family

The orchid family is one of the three largest families of flowering plants. Estimates of the number of species vary between 15,000 and 30,000 in over 800 genera. The great disparity in estimating the number of species probably arises from botanists taking a narrow or broader concept of specific variability. However, what cannot be denied is the sheer richness of the family in both species and genera and the consequent need to order the genera into groups in an ascending hierarchy (subtribe, tribe, subfamily) within the family.

Carl von Linné (Linnaeus) the father of modern botany and, more specifically, of taxonomy, included some 69 species of orchid of eight genera in the first edition of his profoundly influential work *Species Plantarum* (1753). Most of these were European orchids and his descriptions were based on those in earlier works such as those of L. Fuchs (1542), Dodoneus (1583) and Caspar Bauhin (1620) or on specimens in his herbarium collection. In the following half century the number of known species rapidly increased as the plant riches of the Old and New World tropics and of Australia were collected and described.

Three landmarks presaged the first attempt by John Lindley to classify the whole of the orchid family into groups above the level of genus. Firstly, O. Swartz who described many species and several genera of tropical American orchids in the period 1788–1800 was the first botanist to recognise the difference between those species with one anther (the Monandrae of later authors) and those with two anthers (the Diandrae of later authors).

The second significant event was the recognition by Robert Brown in 1810 in his *Prodromus Florae Novae Hollandiae* of four groups within the Monandreae determined by form, position and degree of persistence of the anther; by the character of the pollen masses, and by the habit. Recognition of the importance of the characters of the anther and pollinia has formed the basis of all subsequent attempts to classify the Orchidaceae.

The third landmark was the detailed explanation of the parts of the orchid flower given by L.C. Richard in his account of European orchids in *Mémoires du Muséum d'Histoire Naturelle, Paris* (1812). His terminology persists to the present day.

The early attempts of Linnaeus, Olof Swartz, Robert Brown and C.L. Blume to classify orchids above the species' level dealt with relatively few species from limited geographical areas, mostly with a markedly temperate bias. However, the early nineteenth century saw the start, not only of improved techniques and great success in the growing of tropical epiphytic orchids, but also the initiation of the importation on a large scale of tropical orchids into Europe, which exploded in the latter part of the century into one of the most colourful and extravagant of all the Victorian crazes. The man at the centre of the naming and classifying of these was John Lindley, the Professor of Botany at London University, and a man of immense learning and prodigious output on many aspects of botany, horticulture and agriculture. His major interest lay in orchids and his studies mark the start of modern orchidology, when he produced between 1830 and 1840 *Genera and Species of Orchidaceous Plants,* the most comprehensive treatment of orchid classification at that time and a work which is still often consulted by modern taxonomists.

Nearly 2000 species, which is probably only 10% of presently known species, are described and classified in the work but unlike previous accounts these orchids dealt with were sent to Lindley from all parts of the world and included a good proportion of tropical forms. The species are arranged in Lindley's treatment by genus and the genera in turn are arranged in tribes. He divided the family Orchidaceae into a total of seven tribes as follows:

I. Anther, one only
  A. Pollen masses waxy
    (a) No caudicula or separable stigma gland
        Tribe I. Malaxeae (or Malaxideae)
    (b) A distinct caudicula, but no separable stigmatic gland
        Tribe II. Epidendreae
    (c) A distinct caudicula, united to a deciduous stigmatic gland
        Tribe III. Vandeae
  B. Pollen powdery, granular or sectile
    (a) Anther terminal, erect
        Tribe IV. Ophreae (or Ophrydeae)
    (b) Anther terminal, opercular (lying over rostellum)
        Tribe V. Arethuseae
    (c) Anther dorsal (behind the rostellum)
        Tribe VI. Neottieae
II. Anthers, two
        Tribe VII. Cypripedieae

The remarkable feature of Lindley's system is that despite rank and name changes, the uniting of some of Lindley's tribes and the rearrangement of his tribes into a pattern supposedly reflecting more closely the evolutionary advancement of the tribes, the basic pattern and plan of the system can still be easily detected in most modern-day classifications of the family. It is true to say that John Lindley has exercised on the orchid world a greater influence than any other botanist, the more so when it is remembered that his *Genera and Species of Orchidaceous Plants* was only one of a series of influential orchid books that he produced which included also *Sertum Orchidacearum* (1837–42), *Illustrations of Orchidaceous Plants* (1830–38) with F. Bauer and *Folia Orchidacea* (1852–59).

The latter half of the nineteenth century was the most active period in orchid taxonomy with H.G. Reichenbach, F. Kraenzlin, R.A. Rolfe and others all describing new species, and writing orchid monographs, revisions and floras. However, no major attempt to improve upon Lindley's classification of the family was made until 1881 when George Bentham published, in the *Journal of the Linnean Society,* a system which was later amplified in his and Joseph Hooker's *Genera Plantarum* (1883). Essentially, his system differed from that of Lindley in that only five tribes were recognised with the Malaxideae and Epidendreae being united into a single tribe, the Epidendreae, and the Arethuseae being included in the Neottieae. Furthermore, Bentham outlined the characters and limits of each tribe in great detail. Other features of Bentham's system included the subdivision of the five tribes into a number of subtribes and the inclusion of *Apostasia* and *Neuwiedia* (previously placed in a separate family Apostasiaceae) in the tribe Cypripedieae.

One of the most interesting attempts at classifying the Orchidaceae and the most radical departure from the basic Lindley scheme was the system proposed by Ernst Pfitzer in A. Engler and K.A. Prantl's *Die Natürlichen Pflanzenfamilien* (1889). The major differences from Bentham's system were that, firstly, following the classical work of Darwin, the group of orchids characterised by two anthers (the Cypripedilinae of Pfitzer) were placed first in the scheme by Pfitzer reflecting the now widely held view that these are the most primitive of the orchids, and, secondly, after the initial division of the orchids upon anther and pollen characters, the chief emphasis was placed on vegetative rather than floral characters.

Following the comprehensive systems outlined by Bentham and Pfitzer no further major improvements or changes were proposed until the system used by Rudolf Schlechter was posthumously published in *Notizblatt des Botanischen Gartens und Museums zu Berlin-Dahlem* (1926). Schlechter's knowledge of the family as a whole was probably unsurpassed in this century, and his floristic work on New Guinea, African and South and Central American orchids are major references for botanists working on those floras.

A useful and updated version of Schlechter's system which keys out the subfamilies, tribes and subtribes and lists the genera in each subtribe has been given by C. Schweinfurth in C. Withner's *The Orchids* (1959). Schlechter's system has been widely used and still is used in a modified form, for example, in the Kew Herbarium. It combines the main features of Bentham's system which relied upon reproductive structures and Pfitzer's system which placed greater emphasis on vegetative characters. More important from the practical point of view is the arrangement of the system, which is set out as a highly usable dichotomous key.

The main systems used to classify the Orchidaceae have been compared in tabular form by L. van der Pijl and C. Dodson (1966) and by Leslie Garay (1972). Articles by Garay (1960) and R. Dressler and Dodson (1960) were the first of several recent attempts to reassess the classification of the Orchidaceae above the level of genus. These most interesting papers and several other recent papers which deal with aspects of the subject have been enlarged upon and critically discussed by van der Pijl and Dodson (1966), Garay (1972) and by Dressler (1974).

Despite disagreement over the rank of some groups and the relationships between genera, subtribes, etc. these recent accounts have incorporated a great deal of information on orchids which was unavailable to Schlechter

and also have brought the nomenclature of the subfamilies, tribes and subtribes into line with the *International Code of Botanical Nomenclature*. This has resulted in many name changes but will undoubtedly assist in the future stabilisation of the nomenclature.

The most recent fully published classification of the orchids is that of Dressler (1981). He modified it somewhat in 1983 and his treatment will be followed here. Dressler and his predecessors have attempted to group similar orchids together and to show how these groups are related to one another. The theory of evolution has provided a rationale for most authors who have attempted to construct classifications of related groups and most recent classifications have attempted to suggest evolutionary relationships.

In addition to the floral and vegetative features used by previous authorities, Dressler has added much additional information from anatomy, cytology and micromorphology to improve and substantiate his classification. He divides the orchids into five subfamilies; Apostasioideae, Cypripedioideae, Spiranthoideae, Orchidoideae and Epidendroideae.

The Apostasioideae, comprising the genera *Apostasia* and *Neuwiedia*, are usually considered to be the most primitive orchids, or, by some, a distinct family, the Apostasiaceae. Both genera are Asiatic. They are terrestrials with plicate leaves, an erect spicate many-flowered inflorescence and flowers that are in many ways more like those of lilies than orchids. The flowers have three similar sepals and three more or less similar petals, one of which, the lip, may be slightly larger. The column bears a style to which two or three stamens are only partially fused at the base. They do, however, have tubers, an endomycorrhizal association and dust-like seeds. On balance, we prefer to include them within the Orchidaceae.

The Cypripedioideae have also, at times, been treated as a separate family. The are mainly terrestrial but a few are epiphytic. The stems may be short or long and the leaves either plicate or conduplicate. The flowers are quite distinctive with a large dorsal sepal and usually fused lateral sepals. The lateral petals are spreading or pendulous and range from subcircular to elongate and ribbon-like. The lip is always calceolate or slipper-shaped, hence their popular name of 'slipper orchids'. The column is short with 2 lateral ventral fertile anthers and a large sterile, usually shield-shaped, anther or staminode. The stigma is stalked and ventral. The Cypripedioideae do, however, have dust-like seeds, a mycorrhizal association, and a column with fused stamens and style. On balance, therefore, we include them in the orchid family.

All of the other orchid subfamilies have a column with a single anther and pollen massed into discrete pollinia. The Spiranthinae are well represented in cultivation and include the pretty jewel orchids that are such a feature of the flora of the forest floor. Genera such as *Macodes*, *Goodyera*, *Anoectochilus*, *Ludisia*, *Zeuxine* and *Cryptostylis* are all included in this subfamily which is characterised by the dorsal erect anther which is subequal to the rostellum, the mealy pollinia being attached to a viscidium at the apex of the rostellum, and usually by the creeping fleshy rhizome.

Members of the Orchidoideae have become more popular in cultivation in recent years. This subfamily includes genera such as *Disa*, *Orchis*, *Ophrys*, *Habenaria*, *Corybas* and *Satyrium*. They possess root-stem tuberoids (often referred to as tubers), sectile pollinia and an anther firmly attached by its base to the column.

The remaining and majority of orchids in cultivation are placed in the fifth family, the Epidendroideae, characterised by hard discrete pollinia in an apically attached anther. It is not only the largest subfamily but also the most diverse, and has been divided into two subfamilies by some authors. Those genera with lateral inflorescences, and an anther with reduced partitions, superposed pollinia, viscidia and stipes have been included in the Vandoideae. Their distinction is, however, far from clear-cut and Dressler (1983) has concluded that the Vandoideae should therefore be included in the Epidendroideae.

Genera in all of the subfamilies are included in the Manual. We list below these genera in their appropriate subfamilies and tribes and encourage readers to study their orchids closely. A knowledge of orchid classification can give some insight into the identity of an unknown orchid and how to grow it.

SUBFAMILY **Apostasioideae**

Apostasia, Neuwiedia

SUBFAMILY **Cypripedioideae**

Cypripedium, Paphiopedilum, Phragmipedium, Selenipedium

SUBFAMILY **Spiranthoideae**

Tribe Tropidieae
  Corymborchis, Tropidia

Tribe Erythrodeae
  Anoectochilus, Dossinia, Goodyera, Hetaeria, Ludisia, Macodes, Zeuxine

Tribe Cranichideae
  Subtribe Spiranthinae *Cyclopogon, Pelexia, Sarcoglottis, Spiranthes, Stenorrhynchus*
  Subtribe Cryptostylidinae *Cryptostylis*

Subtribe Cranichidinae *Prescottia, Cranichis, Ponthieva*

SUBFAMILY **Orchidoideae**

Tribe Neottieae
  Subtribe Limodorinae *Epipactis*
Tribe Diurideae
  Subtribe Diuridinae *Diuris, Thelymitra*
  Subtribe Acianthinae *Corybas, Acianthus*
  Subtribe Chloraeinae *Chloraea*
  Subtribe Caladeniinae *Caladenia, Chiloglottis*
  Subtribe Pterostylidinae *Pterostylis*

Tribe Orchideae
  Subtribe Habenariinae *Bonatea, Cynorkis, Habenaria, Pecteilis, Stenoglottis*
  Subtribe Orchidinae *Anacamptis, Barlia, Bartholina, Brachycorythis, Dactylorhiza, Gymnadenia, Himantoglossum, Ophrys, Orchis, Platanthera, Ponerorchis, Serapias*

Tribe Diseae
  Subtribe Coryciinae *Disperis*
  Subtribe Disinae *Disa*
  Subtribe Satyriinae *Satyrium*

SUBFAMILY **Epidendroideae**

Tribe Vanilleae
  Subtribe Vanillinae *Vanilla*
  Subtribe Pogoniinae *Cleistes, Pogonia*

Tribe Gastrodieae
  Subtribe Nerviliinae *Nervilia*

Tribe Arethuseae
  Subtribe Arethusinae *Arethusa*
  Subtribe Bletiinae *Acanthephippium, Ancistrochilus, Arundina, Bletia, Bletilla, Calanthe, Calopogon, Cephalantheropsis, Chysis, Coelia, Dilochia, Ipsea, Mischobulbum, Nephelaphyllum, Phaius, Plocoglottis, Spathoglottis, Tainia*
  Subtribe Sobraliinae *Arpophyllum, Elleanthus, Sobralia*

Tribe Epidendreae
  Subtribe Eriinae *Ceratostylis, Cryptochilus, Epiblastus, Eria, Mediocalcar, Porpax*
  Subtribe Podochilinae *Agrostophyllum, Appendicula*
  Subtribe Thelasiinae *Phreatia, Thelasis*
  Subtribe Laeliinae *Alamania, Amblostoma, Barkeria, Brassavola, Broughtonia, Cattleya, Cattleyopsis, Caularthron, Dimerandra, Diothonaea, Domingoa, Encyclia, Epidanthus, Epidendrum, Hagsatera, Hexadesmia, Hexisea, Isabelia, Isochilus, Jacquiniella, Laelia, Laeliopsis, Lanium, Leptotes, Myrmecophila, Nageliella, Neocogniauxia, Nidema, Oerstedella, Ponera, Psychilis, Rhyncholaelia, Scaphyglottis, Schomburgkia, Sophronitella, Sophronitis, Tetramicra*
  Subtribe Meiracylliinae *Meiracyllium*
  Subtribe Pleurothallidinae *Barbosella, Dracula, Dresslerella, Dryadella, Lepanthes, Lepanthopsis, Masdevallia, Myoxanthus, Octomeria, Physosiphon, Platystele, Porroglossum, Restrepia, Restrepiella, Scaphosepalum, Stelis, Trisetella, Zootrophion*

Tribe Malaxideae
  Liparis, Malaxis, Oberonia

Tribe Dendrobieae
  Subtribe Thuniinae *Thunia*
  Subtribe Coelogyninae *Acoridium, Chelonistele, Coelogyne, Dendrochilum, Otochilus, Panisea, Pholidota, Pleione*
  Subtribe Glomerinae *Earina*
  Subtribe Dendrobiinae *Cadetia, Dendrobium, Diplocaulobium, Epigeneium, Flickingeria*
  Subtribe Bulbophyllinae *Bulbophyllum, Trias*
  Subtribe Sunipiinae *Sunipia*

Tribe Cryptarrheneae
  Cryptarrhena

Tribe Calypsoeae
  Subtribe Calypsoinae *Calypso*
  Subtribe Corallorhizinae *Aplectrum, Cremastra, Dactylostalix, Govenia, Oreorchis*

Tribe Cymbidieae
  Subtribe Cyrtopodiinae *Ansellia, Bromheadia, Cymbidiella, Cymbidium, Cyrtopodium, Dipodium, Eriopsis, Eulophia, Eulophiella, Galeandra, Geodorum, Grammangis, Grammatophyllum, Graphorkis, Grobya, Oeceoclades, Porphyroglottis*
  Subtribe Genyorchidinae *Genyorchis*
  Subtribe Thecostelinae *Thecostele, Thecopus*
  Subtribe Acriopsidinae *Acriopsis*

Tribe Polystachyeae
  Polystachya

Tribe Vandeae
  Subtribe Sarcanthinae *Acampe, Aerides, Amesiella, Arachnis, Armodorum, Ascoglossum, Camarotis, Chiloschista, Cleisostoma, Dimorphorchis, Diploprora, Doritis, Esmeralda, Gastrochilus, Haraella, Holcoglossum, Hygrochilus, Kingidium, Luisia, Neofinetia, Ornithochilus, Papilionanthe, Paraphalaenopsis, Pelatantheria, Phalaenopsis, Pomatocalpa, Pteroceras, Renanthera, Renantherella, Rhynchostylis, Robiquetia, Sarcochilus, Schoenorchis, Sedirea, Seidenfadenia, Smitinandia, Staurochilus, Taeniophyllum, Thrixspermum, Trichoglottis, Vanda, Vandopsis*
  Subtribe Angraecinae *Aeranthes, Angraecum, Campylocentrum, Cryptopus, Dendrophylax, Jumellea, Neobathiea, Oeonia, Oeoniella, Polyradicion, Sobennikoffia*
  Subtribe Aerangidinae *Aerangis, Ancistrorhynchus, Angraecopsis, Bolusiella, Calyptrochilum, Chamaeangis, Cyrtorchis, Diaphananthe, Eurychone, Listrostachys, Microcoelia, Mystacidium, Plectrelminthus, Podangis, Rangaeris, Solenangis, Sphyrarhynchus, Tridactyle, Ypsilopus*

Tribe Maxillarieae
  Subtribe Zygopetalinae *Acacallis, Aganisia, Batemannia, Bollea, Chaubardia, Chaubardiella, Chondrorhyncha, Cochleanthes, Huntleya, Kefersteinia, Koellensteinia, Mendoncella, Neogardneria, Pabstia, Pescatorea, Promenaea, Stenia, Warrea, Wareella, Zygopetalum, Zygosepalum*
  Subtribe Bifrenariinae *Bifrenaria, Rudolfiella, Teuscheria, Xylobium*
  Subtribe Lycastinae *Anguloa, Lycaste, Neomoorea*
  Subtribe Maxillariinae *Chrysocycnis, Maxillaria, Mormolyca, Scuticaria, Trigonidium*
  Subtribe Dichaeinae *Dichaea*
  Subtribe Telipogoninae *Telipogon, Trichoceros*
  Subtribe Ornithocephalinae *Ornithocephalus, Phymatidium, Zygostates*

Tribe Gongoreae
  Subtribe Catasetinae *Catasetum, Clowesia, Cycnoches, Dressleria, Mormodes*
  Subtribe Stanhopeinae *Acineta, Cirrhaea, Coryanthes, Embreea, Gongora, Houlletia, Kegeliella, Lacaena, Lueddemannia, Lycomormium, Paphinia, Peristeria, Polycycnis, Schlimmia, Sievekingia, Stanhopea, Trevoria*

Tribe Oncidieae
  Ada, Anneliesia, Aspasia, Brachtia, Brassia, Capanemia, Caucaea, Cischweinfia, Cochlioda, Comparettia, Erycina, Gomesa, Helcia, Hispaniella, Ionopsis, Lemboglossum, Leochilus, Lockhartia, Macradenia, Mexicoa, Miltonia, Miltonioides, Miltoniopsis, Notylia, Odontoglossum, Oncidium, Ornithophora, Osmoglossum, Otoglossum, Palumbina, Psychopsis, Psychopsiella, Psygmorchis, Rodriguezia, Rossioglossum, Scelochilus, Sigmatostalix, Solenidium, Symphyglossum, Ticoglossum, Tolumnia, Trichopilia, Warmingia

The genus

Most authorities currently accept between 750 and 1000 genera in the family Orchidaceae. There is a general consensus on the delimitation of many genera but a considerable proportion remain the subject of disagreement. As botanists have learned more about orchids it has been inevitable that ideas have changed about generic concepts. In particular, the major trend of recent years has been for the larger genera such as *Epidendrum, Pleurothallis, Odontoglossum, Oncidium* and *Dendrobium* to be more narrowly defined and groups previously incorporated within the broader definition of the genus to be segregated off as distinct genera. The philosophical justification behind such division is the attempt to make genera monophyletic, that is for a genus to include all species derived from a common ancestor. In reality much of the splitting up of orchid genera has been done for the pragmatic reason that large genera are difficult to deal with and that smaller genera are a convenience. Sir Joseph Hooker expressed the opinion over a century ago that orchid genera were by and large categories of convenience and we would not disagree that this is still a fair assessment. Many authors have based their attempts to subdivide large genera on an incomplete knowledge of the species, examining only a part of a large genus. A few treatments of genera such as those by Luer of *Pleurothallis* and *Masdevallia*, in the sense of the 1st edition of the 'Manual of cultivated orchid species', are honourable exceptions.

It is not surprising, therefore, if many of the segregate genera have yet to receive wide acceptance amongst botanists. Furthermore, the horticultural use of generic names such as *Psychopsis*, *Tolumnia* and *Cyrtochilum* (*Oncidium* segregates) and *Rossioglossum*, *Lemboglossum* and *Ticoglossum* (*Odontoglossum* segregates) has not been widely accepted because these orchids are used in hybridising and their progeny are still registered under *Oncidium* and *Odontoglossum* respectively.

In the current edition of the Manual, users will see that we have accepted a number of segregate genera, some of which have yet to be at all widely used in horticulture. We have examined each case on its merits and have only accepted those new generic segregates which we think deserve recognition for sound scientific reasons. We do, however, recognise that rigorous analyses by modern techniques such as cladistic analysis are needed and that these may lead us to change some of our decisions when such evidence is available.

The species

One of the most difficult and contentious problems facing botanists is the judgement of where specific boundaries can be drawn. Plant species are sometimes very variable and this can lead to disagreement, even amongst experienced botanists, as to what to consider as a species and how to treat any infraspecific variability. Botanists generally look for marked discontinuities in morphological and micromorphological variation and some degree of breeding barrier to help them with the somewhat artificial preoccupation of tidily dividing the plants of the world into species. In temperate areas of the world where the plants are often well known, it is sometimes possible to demonstrate discontinuities between closely allied species and even the breeding barriers that keep them distinct. Variable species can also be readily identified when the variability between populations can be seen to be continuous. In other species, it may be possible to show that there are minor disjunctions in one or two char-

acters that allow infraspecific variants to be formally recognised. In such cases the botanist usually has copious material to study and often access to living populations allowing detailed examination not only of the gross morphology but also of cytology, anatomy, biochemistry and breeding systems to help him arrive at a sound decision.

The position in the tropics is seldom as clear-cut because the botanist is usually working with little material ranging from a few specimens to even a single specimen. The study material, usually herbarium specimens, is often incomplete, lacking fruit, flowers or leaves. This can make the task of the orchid taxonomist difficult especially where the critical differences are small or obscure. He must then extrapolate from his experience of other better known groups of orchids and other plants to arrive at a satisfactory judgement. Often, therefore, such decisions may have to be revised when further material becomes available.

The classification of tropical orchids is still incomplete and dozens of new species are being described every year. Few genera have been the subject of a recent systematic revision and the variation of their constituent species assessed and analysed. Where this has happened, as in *Paphiopedilum* and *Cymbidium*, it has been possible to reduce some names to synonymy. For example, we now know that *Cypripedium elliottianum* is the same as *Paphiopedilum rothschildianum* and, as a later name, is a synonym of the latter. It has also been possible to recognise some infraspecific taxa within variable species. The taxon known in much of the horticultural literature as *Paphiopedilum virens* has been shown to be a variant, with more horizontal petals, of the widespread species *Paphiopedilum javanicum* from Java, Sumatra, Bali and Flores. The Bornean plants from Mt Kinabalu are now treated as *P. javanicum* var. *virens*.

As more of the tropical hinterland is explored and plants are discovered from previously inaccessible areas, we are beginning to understand the orchids better. This will inevitably lead to reassessments of the species and consequent name changes that most of us find so irritating.

Key to Subfamilies and Tribes

(after Dressler, 1981)

1. Flowers normally with 2 or 3 fertile anthers
   2

   Flowers with a single fertile anther 3

2. Lip deeply saccate; fertile anthers 2; sterile anther (staminode) shield-shaped at the apex of the column ....
   .... Subfamily Cypripedioideae

Lip petal-like, not saccate; fertile anthers 2 or 3, joined at the base only to the column
.... Subfamily Apostasioideae

3. Pollen masses 2, soft, mealy, sectile or not; leaves usually spirally arranged, convolute, not basally jointed 4
   Pollen masses 2, 4 or 8, usually hard, waxy; leaves distichous, usually joined at the base
   11
   (Subfamily Epidendroideae)

4. Anther erect in the bud, bending down over apex of column to become more or less operculate at the apex of the column
   10

   Anther remaining erect or bending back, not short and operculate at the end of the column 5

5. Rostellum equalling the anther; viscidium at the apex of the anther and attached to the apex of the pollen masses or caudicles; plants lacking root-stem tuberoids 6
   (Subfamily Spiranthoideae)

   Rostellum usually shorter than the anther; anther usually projecting beyond rostellum; viscidium, if present, usually at the base or in middle of pollen masses; plants often with root-stem tuberoids 8
   (Subfamily Orchidoideae)

6. Roots usually scattered on rhizome; pollinia sectile 7

   Roots usually clustered; pollinia not sectile
   .... Tribe Cranichideae

7. Stems woody; leaves plicate; inflorescences terminal or lateral .... Tribe Tropidieae

   Stems fleshy, herbaceous; leaves conduplicate; inflorescence terminal ....
   .... Tribe Erythrodeae

8. Plants lacking root-stem tuberoids; leaves plicate or conduplicate; anther generally oblong .... Tribe Neottieae

   Plants usually with root-stem tuberoids; leaves conduplicate; anther often conical
   9

9. Viscidium usually double; pollinia sectile, usually with prominent caudicles; anther firmly attached to the column 10

   Viscidium single or absent; pollinia sectile or not, usually lacking caudicles; column with a restriction below the anther ....
   .... Tribe Diurideae

10. Anther erect; lip with a single basal spur or lacking one .... Tribe Orchideae

Anther bent back from the column or recumbent; spurs various, double if formed from the lip . . . . Tribe Diseae

11. Anther erect in early bud, bending downwards over apex of column to become operculate on apex of column; pollinia 2, 4, 6 or 8, usually flattened or club-shaped, with or without caudicles and viscidia, usually lacking a stipe 12

Anther usually operculate at apex of column but not bending downwards during development; pollinia 2 or 4, usually dorso-ventrally flattened, with reduced caudicles; stipe or stipes usually present 22

12. Pollinia mealy or sectile, 2 or 4, lacking caudicles; leaves, if present, non-articulate 13

Pollinia either mealy or hard, if soft, usually 8 and with caudicles; leaves usually articulated 15

13. Pollinia soft and mealy; plants often liana-like . . . . Tribe Vanilleae

Pollinia sectile 14

14. Leaves narrow, plicate . . . . Tribe Arethuseae

Leaves broad, more or less fan-shaped, or abent . . . . Tribe Gastrodieae

15. Pollinia 2 or 4, quite naked, without caudicles, rarely with viscidia or stipes 16

Pollinia 2 to 8, with distinct caudicles 17

16. Flowers lacking a distinct column-foot; leaves plicate or conduplicate; pollinia often clavate . . . . Tribe Malaxideae

Flowers with a distinct column-foot; leaves always conduplicate . . . . Tribe Dendrobieae (in part)

17. Pollinia usually 8 and rather soft; plants usually cormous; leaves usually plicate; inflorescences lateral . . . . Tribe Arethuseae

Pollinia 2 to 8, usually rather hard; plants with pseudobulbs, corms or slender stems; leaves usually conduplicate; inflorescence usually terminal 18

18. Pollinia 4, soft and mealy; plants with elongate, leafy pseudobulbs and terminal inflorescences . . . . Tribe Dendrobieae (in part)

Pollinia not as above 19

19. Pollinia superposed, with cylindrical, translucent caudicles or with a well-developed stipe 20

Pollinia superposed or not, with mealy caudicles 21

20. Pollinia with cylindrical translucent caudicles . . . . Tribe Cryptarrheneae

Pollinia with a definite broad stipe . . . . Tribe Calypsoeae

21. Pollinia 4, superposed or ovoid; plants usually with pseudobulbs of one internode; inflorescences terminal . . . . Tribe Coelogyneae

Pollinia various but not superposed; plants usually with pseudobulbs of several nodes, or lacking . . . . Tribe Epidendreae

22. Plants always monopodial . . . . Tribe Vandeae

Plants usually sympodial 23

23. Pollinia 4 24

Pollinia 2 and often cleft 25

24. Plants with pseudobulbs of several internodes or elongate stems; inflorescence usually terminal . . . . Tribe Polystachyeae

Plants various; inflorescences usually lateral . . . . Tribe Maxillarieae

25. Plants usually with corms or pseudobulbs of several internodes; leaves usually plicate 26

Plants usually with pseudobulbs of one internode, or lacking pseudobulbs; leaves plicate or conduplicate 28

26. Pollinia laterally flattened . . . . Tribe Cymbidieae (in part)

Pollinia thick and dorso-ventrally flattened 27

27. Plants with a sensitive rostellum which discharges the viscidia when triggered; flowers bisexual or unisexual . . . . Tribe Gongoreae (in part)

Plants lacking a sensitive rostellum; flowers bisexual . . . . . Tribe Cymbidieae (in part)

28. Leaves plicate   Tribe Gongoreae (in part)

Leaves conduplicate 29

29. Old World Plants . . Tribe Cymbidieae (in part)

New World plants . . . . . Tribe Oncidieae

PART II

Cultivated Orchid Genera and Species

Generic Accounts

The genera are arranged alphabetically in the text. Under each generic heading, the subfamily, tribe and, if appropriate, the subtribe to which it belongs are provided. The classification system outlined by R. Dressler in his *The Orchids. Natural History and Classification* (1981) and modified by him in *Telopea* (pp. 413–424) in 1983 is followed here. The generic description includes a synopsis of those features which serve to distinguish the genus from other allied genera. Notes on the distribution and number of species in the genus are also provided. Figures for the number of species in a genus are often approximate especially where the genus has not recently been revised or where specific limits are the cause of controversy between botanists. A short account of the history of the classification of the genus from its first description then follows, and the major taxonomic treatments of the genus are mentioned so that the reader can, if he wishes, refer to those works for a more detailed treatment. The type species, which is that species upon which the genus was founded, is indicated. Where several species are given under this heading none has yet been chosen to be the type species but those listed were described by the author at the same time as he established the genus.

Species Accounts

Where more than a single species is described in a genus, the species accounts are arranged alphabetically.

For each species, a description of its characteristic features is given. Measurements and shapes indicated here are taken from typical specimens and data available to the authors at the time of publication. Plants are variable, often remarkably so, and the reader must bear this in mind when comparing his specimen with the description.

The limits of distribution as presently understood follow the specific description. The brief history of the discovery and taxonomy of each species should be read in conjunction with the lists of synonyms which follows it. The

synonyms are those names, other than the correct name, which have been applied to the species. It must be remembered when using this book, that a degree of conservatism persists in horticultural circles and that many species and also genera are far better known under a synonymous name than under the correct name presently accepted by botanists.

Acacallis Lindl.

Subfamily Epidendroideae
Tribe Maxillarieae
Subtribe Zygopetalinae

Medium-sized epiphytic herbs with a creeping, scandent rhizome. **Pseudobulbs** produced at intervals of 2–5 cm, ovoid, compressed, 1- or 2-leaved. **Leaves** oblong-lanceolate, shortly petiolate. **Inflorescences** longer than the leaves, racemose, 3- to 7-flowered. **Flowers** large, showy, of a distinctive colour, non-resupinate. **Sepals** and **petals** subsimilar. **Lip** with a somewhat long and narrow fringed claw and reniform limb which is concave and undulate on the margins. **Column** triquetral, with 2 subquadrate wings; foot long, slender; pollinia 4, superposed; stipe rectangular.
DISTRIBUTION   A monotypic genus in tropical S. America.
DERIVATION OF NAME   From the Greek Akakallis, who was a nymph and the lover of Apollo.
TAXONOMY   A monotypic genus founded by John Lindley in 1853 in *Folia Orchidacea* (*Acacallis*) based on a species discovered by the intrepid collector Richard Spruce near Manaus in Brazil.

Lindley states its affinities lie with *Huntleya*, *Warrea* etc. but it may be clearly distinguished from those by its 'long narrow lip hypochil[e] with a deep bag at the point, surrounded by a five-lobed reflexed border, and furnished in front with three projecting processes arising from the very base of the mesochil[e] and its junction with the hypochil[e] and just above the concave ribbed base of the epichil[e].' *Acacallis* is most closely allied to *Aganisia* and other genera allied to *Zygopetalum*. Its taxonomic position has been recently discussed by L. Garay in

Orquideologia (1973). He concludes that it is distinct from *Aganisia*, with which it has been united by some botanists, such as H.G. Reichenbach, Rudolf Schlechter and R.E. Schultes, on account of its scandent habit, non-resupinate flowers, the cochleate epichile to the lip, the column with a long, slender, free foot and the pollinia which are borne on a short, subquadrate stipe.
TYPE SPECIES   *A. cyanea* Lindl.
SYNONYM   *Kochiophyton* Cogn.
CULTURE   Compost A. Temp. Winter min. 15°C. These plants should be grown in a basket, or mounted on a slab of fern-fibre or cork. They require humid conditions under moderate shade and should be carefully watered throughout the year.

Acacallis cyanea Lindl. [Colour Plate]
A climbing, epiphytic plant with a somewhat compressed rhizome covered in shredded, light brown sheaths. **Pseudobulbs** subfusiform, wrinkled, covered in light brown sheaths, up to 5 cm long, 1.5 cm across, 1–2-leaved at apex. **Leaves** elliptic, obtuse, petiolate, articulated half way along the petiole, up to 25 cm long, 7.5 cm broad, very shiny green on upper surface. **Inflorescence** arcuate, basal, laxly several-flowered. **Flowers** showy; sepals and petals bluish-mauve on outer surface, pink-flushed within; lip goldy-bronze with a reddish-mauve or bluish-purple centre, veins paler; callus orange-pink yellowish at back; column-wings streaked red-mauve. **Sepals** and **petals** subsimilar, elliptic, acute or apiculate, slightly concave, 3.5–4 cm long, 2.5 cm broad. **Lip** clawed, flabellate, apiculate at the broadly rounded apex, auriculate at the base, 2.7 cm long, 3.2 cm broad, sides of lamina upcurved, margins undulate-serrate; callus fleshy, erect, divided into fleshy finger-like projections above. **Column** erect, 2-winged at apex; wings subquadrate-rounded.
DISTRIBUTION   Brazil, Venezuela and Colombia.
HISTORY   Discovered by Richard Spruce on the Rio Negro in Brazil in July 1851 and described by John Lindley in 1853 in *Folia Orchidacea* (*Acacallis*). It was introduced into cultivation many years later and flowered in cultivation for the first time in 1882 in the

collection of the Hon. Erasmus Corning of Albany, New York.

SYNONYMS *Acacallis hoehnei* Schltr.; *Aganisia tricolor* Batem.; *Aganisia coerulea* Rchb.f.; *Kochiophyton negrense* Schltr.; *K. coerulens* Hoehne

Acampe Lindl.

Subfamily Epidendroideae
Tribe Vandeae
Subtribe Sarcanthinae

Medium-sized epiphytic plants with ± elongate monopodial stems. **Leaves** distichous, coriaceous, obliquely 2-lobed at apex, articulated below to a persistent leaf-sheath. **Inflorescence** densely few- to many-flowered, racemose to subcorymbose, simple or branched. **Flowers** small to medium-sized, fleshy, brittle. **Sepals** and **petals** spreading, free, subsimilar; lateral sepals somewhat adnate to the lip on either side of the spur. **Lip** saccate or spurred, firmly attached to the column-base, entire, auriculate, often with elevated lamellae or hairs running into the spur or saccate base. **Column** fleshy, small, lacking a foot; rostellum short, obscure; pollinia 4 in two appressed unequal pairs, waxy, with a long subulate stipe; viscidium very small.

DISTRIBUTION About ten species in India, China, S.E. Asia, the islands of the Indian Ocean and in tropical Africa.

DERIVATION OF NAME From the Greek *akampes* (rigid), in reference to the small brittle flowers and probably in allusion to Rheede's 'rigid air flower'.

TAXONOMY Described in 1853 by John Lindley in *Folia Orchidacea* (*Acampe*). Lindley transferred eight species previously referred to *Vanda* and *Saccolabium*, on account of 'their small brittle flowers, in which there is no flexibility, their lip adnate to the edges of the column, the slender caudicle, and very small gland'.

Nomenclature in the genus is extremely confused for two reasons: first, *Acampe rigida* was among the earliest known of Asiatic orchids, being described as 'Thalia Maravara' in Rheede's *Hortus Indicus Malabaricus* (1703). This name has not been taken up as it is pre-Linnaean, but several post-Linnaean names have subsequently been attached to Rheede's species. Secondly, *Acampe* is a very widespread genus and many superfluous names exist, some of which have already been sunk in synonymy. The full confusion surrounding *Acampe* has recently been summarised by G. Seidenfaden in 1977 in the *Botanical Museum Leaflets of Harvard University,* in an article entitled 'Thalia Maravara and the rigid air blossom'.

TYPE SPECIES *A. multiflora* (Lindl.) Lindl. [= *A. rigida* (Buch.-Ham. ex J.E. Smith) P.F. Hunt].

CULTURE Compost A or mounted. Temp. Winter min. 13–15°C. As for Vanda. The plants grow well in baskets, or mounted on cork or fern-fibre slabs.

Acampe papillosa (Lindl.) Lindl.
[Colour Plate]

A large epiphytic plant, up to 90 cm high. **Stem** elongate, branched, scandent, 60–90 cm long, up to 0.5 cm broad. **Leaves** oblong-ligulate, rounded and obliquely notched at apex, 7.5–15 cm long, 1–2.2 cm broad. **Inflorescences** short, up to 2.5 cm long, densely many-flowered; bracts semi-circular. **Flowers** 1.8 cm across; ovary very short; sepals and petals yellow blotched with brown; lip whitish. **Sepals** oblong-elliptic or oblong, obtuse, 0.6–0.9 cm long, 0.2–0.3 cm broad. **Petals** narrowly linear-elliptic, obtuse, similar to sepals. **Lip** 3-lobed, somewhat subsaccate at base, pubescent in lower half, papillose above; side lobes obscurely triangular, erect; mid-lobe ovate, erose on margins; spur conical, pubescent within.

DISTRIBUTION N.W. India and Burma to Thailand, Laos and Vietnam; in lower montane forest.

HISTORY Described in 1832 in the *Botanical Register* (t. 1552) by John Lindley as *Saccolabium papillosum* based on a collection made by Dr N. Wallich at Prome in India. Lindley transferred it to *Acampe* in *Folia Orchidacea* (*Acampe*: p. 2). Lindley considered this species conspecific with Rheede's 'Thalia Maravara' (a pre-Linnaean name), *Cymbidium praemorsum* Sw. and *Aerides undulatum* J.E. Smith but this treatment is no longer followed.

SYNONYMS *Saccolabium papillosum* Lindl.; *S. carinatum* Griff.

Acampe rigida (Buch.-Ham. ex J.E. Smith) P.F. Hunt

An erect epiphytic plant. **Stem** stout, unbranched or rarely branched, entirely covered by distichous, overlapping leaf-bases, 30 or more cm long. **Leaves** distichous, fleshy-coriaceous, conduplicate, arcuate, linear-lorate, unequally 2-lobed at apex, 15–45 cm long, 3–5 cm broad. **Inflorescences** axillary, mostly shorter than the leaves, densely many-flowered, subcapitate, ± branching, up to 20 cm long. **Flowers** fleshy, 1.8 cm across; sepals and petals yellow, spotted or marked with crimson or red-brown; lip white spotted with red. **Sepals** and **petals** subsimilar, free, subspreading, obovate-elliptic, rounded at the apex, up to 0.9 cm long, 0.5 cm broad. **Lip** porrect, obscurely 3-lobed, 0.5–0.8 cm long, 0.3 cm broad; side

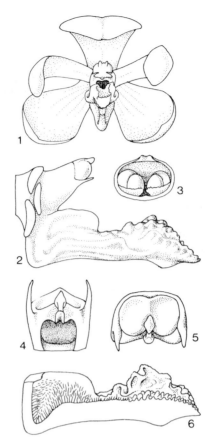

Acampe rigida
1 – Flower (× 2)
2 – Column and lip, side view (× 7)
3 – Anther (× 15)
4 – Column from below (× 15)
5 – Column, front view (× 15)
6 – Lip, longitudinal section (× 7)

lobes rounded, erect, short; mid-lobe bullate, ovate, rounded at apex; callus a fleshy pubescent ridge. **Column** short, stout, 0.2–0.3 cm long.

DISTRIBUTION Tropical Asia across to E. Africa; in lowland woodland and forest.

HISTORY The full confused taxonomic history of this widespread species has been discussed at length by G. Seidenfaden in the *Botanical Museum Leaflets of Harvard University* (1977). It was originally described in 1819 by J.E. Smith in Rees's *Cyclopedia* (p. 39) as *Aerides rigida* based on a Dr F. Buchanan-Hamilton collection and name. P.F. Hunt transferred it to *Acampe* in 1970 in the *Kew Bulletin* (p. 98).

SYNONYMS include *Aerides rigida* J.E. Smith; *Vanda multiflora* Lindl.; *V. longifolia* Lindl.; *Acampe multiflora* (Lindl.) Lindl.; *A. longifolia* (Lindl.) Lindl.; *A. pachyglossa* Rchb.f.; *A. renschiana* Rchb.f.

Acanthephippium Blume

Subfamily Epidendroideae
Tribe Arethuseae
Subtribe Bletiinae

Terrestrial herbs with epiphytic-type roots. **Pseudobulbs** rather long, 2- to several-leaved towards apex. **Leaves** large, plicate. **Inflorescence** lateral, few-flowered, racemose; peduncle short and fleshy; bracts more or less prominent. **Flowers** few, urn-shaped or campanulate, suberect, rather large, showy. **Sepals** fleshy, connate to form a large swollen tube, enclosing the petals and lip. **Petals** much narrower than the sepals. **Lip** ± 3-lobed, saddle-shaped, hinged at apex of column-foot. **Column** short, stout, fleshy with a long foot; foot adnate to lateral sepals forming a broad mentum; pollinia 8, cohering by means of a granular mass; viscidium absent.

DISTRIBUTION   About 15 species in tropical Asia, Malaysia and across to Fiji.
DERIVATION OF NAME   From the Greek *akantha* (thorn) and *ephippion* (saddle), probably referring to the shape of the blade of the lip which has 2 parallel, toothed crests which fancifully resemble a saddle.
TAXONOMY   This genus was described in 1825 by C.L. Blume in his *Bijdragen* (p. 353) as *Acanthophippium* and is still occasionally met with under this spelling. Blume corrected his own orthographic error in 1828 in his *Flora Javae*. The swollen sepal-tube, with its mentum, and the saddle-shaped lip, are distinctive features of this genus which is allied to *Phaius*.
TYPE SPECIES   *A. javanicum* Blume
CULTURE   Compost C. Temp. Winter min. 12°C. As for *Phaius*. The plants grow well in pans, and during growth should be given humid, shady conditions with plenty of water. After the pseudobulbs are fully grown, the plants should be kept almost dry and in a cooler place.

Acanthephippium javanicum Blume

A large terrestrial herb. **Pseudobulbs** large, subcylindric, slightly tapering to apex, several-noded, up to 25 cm long, 5 cm in diameter, about 3- to 4-leaved near apex. **Leaves** shortly stalked, elliptic, acute or acuminate, up to 50 cm long, 15 cm broad. **Inflorescences** 1 or 2, from the middle nodes of the pseudobulb, racemose, few-flowered, 25 or more cm long; bracts large, ovate, acute, 3 cm long. **Flowers** campanulate, pale or dull yellow, lined and mottled rose-purple or pink; lip white and pale yellow, spotted red on side lobes, with a purple apex to the mid-lobe. **Sepals** united to form a subcylindric tube, 4.5 cm long, 3.3 cm broad; free apices of sepals 1.8 cm long, obtuse; mentum large, 2-lobed at apex, about 2 cm long. **Petals** projecting slightly between sepals at mouth of tube. **Lip** deeply 3-lobed above the middle, almost concealed by sepals, about 2 cm long, 2 cm broad; side lobes erect, oblong, with a dilated truncate apex, 0.8 cm long, 0.4 cm broad; mid-lobe convex, recurved, somewhat pandurate, obtuse; callus basal, of toothed keels. **Column** fleshy; 1.5 cm long; foot long, curved slightly, over 1 cm long.
DISTRIBUTION   Malaya, Sumatra, Java and Borneo.
HISTORY   Described by C.L. Blume in 1825 in *Bijdragen* (p. 354) based on a plant he collected on Mt Salak in Java. Messrs Loddiges introduced it into cultivation in 1844.

Acianthus R. Br.

Subfamily Orchidoideae
Tribe Diurideae
Subtribe Acianthinae

Dwarf terrestrial unifoliate herbs, often colony-forming, growing from underground tubers (root-stem tuberoids). **Leaf** solitary, apical on short erect stem, entire to palmately lobed, sometimes with contrasting veins. **Inflorescence** terminal, laxly few- to many-flowered. **Flowers** subsessile, rather spidery, green to purple. **Sepals** free, with short to long acuminate tails; dorsal sepal hooded over the column; lateral sepals narrower and spreading or pendent. **Petals** free, spreading. **Lip** conspicuous, entire, often cordate, lacking a spur but with two basal nectaries. **Column** terete, strongly incurved in apical half, dilated at base, winged at apex; pollinia 2 or 4 and bipartite, clavate, attached by caudicles to a broad viscidium.
DISTRIBUTION   A genus of about 20 species in Australia, New Zealand, New Caledonia and the Solomon Islands. Only the Australian species are to be found in cultivation.
DERIVATION OF NAME   From the Greek *akis* (needle or barb) and *anthos* (flower), from the slender acuminate sepals and petals of some of the species.
TAXONOMY   The genus was established in 1810 by Robert Brown in his *Prodromus Florae Novae Hollandiae* (p. 321). *Acianthus* is allied to *Corybas* but is readily distinguished by its several-flowered inflorescences and flowers which lack spurs to the lip. An account of the Australian species and their cultivation is given by David Jones (1988) in his *Native Orchids of Australia* (p. 384).
TYPE SPECIES   *A. fornicatus* R. Br., *A. exsertus* R. Br. and *A. caudatus* R. Br.
CULTURE   Temp. Winter min. 5°C. Compost 35% loam, 35% sand, 15% peat, 15% leaf mould. Repot annually during summer dormancy, with tuber 2 cm below the surface. Water lightly until autumn, when new growths appear, then gradually increase. Dry off in spring as the leaves die back.

Acianthus caudatus R. Br. [Colour Plate]

A dwarf terrestrial, 5–22 cm tall, often forming colonies and growing from small underground tubers. **Leaf** solitary, borne on a stalk above the ground but horizontal to surface, cordate, rarely somewhat 3-lobed, apiculate, 1.2–4 cm long, 1–3.5 cm wide, with reticulate venation above, purplish below. **Inflorescence** 1- to 9-flowered; peduncle slender, erect, glabrous; bracts lanceolate, acuminate, 3–5 mm long. **Flowers** plum-purple or rarely green. **Dorsal sepal** erect, ovate at base but with a long filiform apex, 1.6–3.5 cm long, 1.5–2.5 mm wide; **lateral sepals** similar but smaller and dependent. **Petals** flaccate, ovate, acuminate, 4–5 mm long. **Lip** recurved, lanceolate, acute, 2.5 mm long; callus of 2 triangular teeth at base. **Column** curved, clavate, 3–4 mm long.
DISTRIBUTION   Australia: Tasmania, Victoria, eastern S. Australia and New South Wales; growing in sandy loams in dry sclerophyllous forests of *Eucalyptus*.
HISTORY   Originally collected by F. Bauer near Port Jackson and described by Robert Brown in 1810 in his *Prodromus Florae Novae Hollandiae* (p. 321).

Acanthephippium javanicum
1 - Habit ($\times \frac{1}{3}$)
2 - Flower ($\times \frac{2}{3}$)
3 - Lip ($\times 1$)
4 - Column and column-foot ($\times 1$)

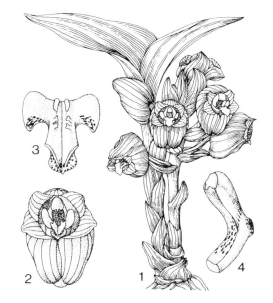

Acianthus exsertus R. Br.

A colony-forming species 10–20(–30) cm tall. **Leaf** borne horizontal to ground, heart-shaped, shortly apiculate, 2–4 cm long, 1.5–3.5 cm wide, green above, purple beneath. **Inflorescence** 5- to 20-flowered, up to 20 cm long; peduncle slender, wiry, 2.5–3.5 cm long; bracts broadly ovate, apiculate, 3–4 mm long. **Flowers** green to purplish maroon, about 5 mm across. **Dorsal sepal** ovate, longly apiculate, 6–10 mm long, 1.5–3 mm wide; **lateral sepals** pendent, linear, apiculate, 6–10 mm long, 1 mm wide. **Petals** reflexed, ovate-lanceolate, acuminate. 4–5 mm long, 1 mm wide. **Lip** entire, ovate, deflexed, shortly apiculate, 4–5 mm long, 3.5–4 mm wide; callus narrow, central, a roughened band from base to apex of lip. **Column** 2–3 mm long.

DISTRIBUTION Australia; from central and southern Queensland south to Tasmania and west to southern S. Australia; in forest and woodland in sandy soils.

HISTORY Originally collected at Port Jackson (now Sydney) by Robert Brown and described by him in 1810 in his *Prodromus Florae Novae Hollandiae* (p. 321).

CLOSELY RELATED SPECIES *A. fornicatus* R. Br., also from eastern Australia, is another colony-forming species that is easy to cultivate. It differs in having much broader dorsal sepals and lip and lateral sepals that are parallel below but spread at the apex.

Acineta Lindl.

Subfamily Epidendroideae
Tribe Gongoreae
Subtribe Stanhopeinae

Stout epiphytic herbs. **Pseudobulbs** ovoid or subcylindric, often laterally compressed or furrowed, 1- to 4-leaved at apex. **Leaves** plicate. **Inflorescences** elongate, pendulous or erect, racemose, from the base of the pseudobulb. **Flowers** usually many, fleshy, relatively large and conspicuous. **Sepals** subequal, broadly concave; dorsal sepal free; lateral sepals usually connate at the base. **Petals** similar to sepals but smaller. **Lip** 3-lobed, fleshy, concave to subsaccate on the hypochile; side lobes large, erect, triangular or subreniform; midlobe keeled, concave or spreading; disc fleshy, with variously-shaped appendages. **Column** erect, usually pubescent, somewhat arcuate, subclavate or narrowly winged, lacking a foot; pollinia 2, waxy.

DISTRIBUTION About 15 species, ranging from S. Mexico to Venezuela, Ecuador and Peru.

DERIVATION OF NAME From the Greek *akinetos* (immovable), describing the rigid jointless condition of the lip.

TAXONOMY John Lindley described this genus in 1843 in the *Botanical Register* (misc. p. 67). Vegetatively *Acineta* species most nearly resemble *Stanhopea* but they are most closely allied to *Peristeria* differing in that the side lobes of the lip are joined by a large central callus, and that the lip hypochile is long, being at least as long as the side lobes. The most recent revision of the genus was published by Rudolf Schlechter in 1917 in *Orchis*. Of the 13 species covered in his account, *A. chrysantha* and *A. sella-turcica* would now appear to be conspecific.

TYPE SPECIES *A. humboldtii* (Lindl.) Lindl. [= *A. superba* (H.B.K.) Rchb.f.]

SYNONYM *Neippergia* C. Morren

CULTURE Compost A. Temp. Winter min. 12°–15°C. Warmer while growing. As for *Stanhopea*. Because the flower spikes often grow straight downwards, the plants should be grown in hanging baskets. During growth, they require humid conditions under moderate shade, and with plenty of water at the roots. When growth is complete, a cooler dry period should be given.

Acineta chrysantha (C. Morr.) Lindl. & Paxt.
[Colour Plate]

A robust epiphytic plant. **Pseudobulbs** ovoid to subconical, somewhat compressed, ± sulcate, 8–10 cm long, 6–8 cm broad, 3- to 4-leaved at apex. **Leaves** oblanceolate, acute, plicate, 30–45 cm long. **Inflorescences** basal, pendulous, many-flowered. **Flowers** fleshy, subglobose, large, showy; sepals yellow; petals yellow, ± spotted red on margins and towards base; lip yellow, spotted red-brown. **Sepals** free, concave, 2.5–3.5 cm long, 2–2.7 cm broad; dorsal sepal oblong-ovate, obtuse; lateral sepals elliptic-ovate, acute. **Petals** membranaceous, obovate, acute, 3–3.2 cm long, 1.8–2 cm broad. **Lip** very fleshy, 3-lobed, clawed, 2.5–3 cm long and broad; claw concave, with a terminal erect fleshy horn; side lobes erect, subreniform; mid-lobe short, slightly concave, spreading, rhombic-obovate, acute, 0.8–1.2 cm long and broad; callus prominent, erect, with 2 lateral subfalcate wings, apical margin projecting and fleshy-dentate. **Column** stout, pubescent, 2–2.2 cm long, apex narrowly winged.

DISTRIBUTION Costa Rica and Panama.

HISTORY This species first flowered in the collection of A. Michelynck of Ghent, Belgium, and was described in 1849 as *Neippergia chrysantha* by C. Morren in the *Annales de la Société Royale, Gand* (p. 375). It was later transferred in 1850 by John Lindley and Joseph Paxton in their *Flower Garden* (p. 31) to the genus *Acineta*. This species is still grown under the later synonymous name *A. densa* Lindl. & Paxt.

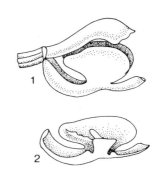

Acineta gymnostele
1 – Column and lip, side view (× ⁴⁄₅)
2 – Lip, longitudinal section (× ⁴⁄₅)

SYNONYMS *Neippergia chrysantha* C. Morr.; *Acineta densa* Lindl. & Paxt.; *A. sella-turcica* Rchb.f.; *A. warscewiczii* Klotzsch

Acineta gymnostele Schltr.

An epiphytic herb. **Pseudobulbs** long, ovoid, 8–10 cm long, 4–5 cm broad, 3- or 4-leaved at apex. **Leaves** oblanceolate, acute, 30–45 cm long, 5–7 cm broad. **Inflorescences** basal, pendulous, 30–70 cm long, many-flowered. **Flowers** showy, golden-yellow; lip purple-spotted. **Dorsal sepal** oblong, obtuse or apiculate, concave, 3 cm long; **lateral sepals** obliquely oblong-elliptic, obtuse, keeled on reverse, 3 cm long. **Petals** obliquely ovate from a narrow base, obtuse or obtusely apiculate, 2.8 cm long. **Lip** curved, longly clawed, 3-lobed in the apical half, 2.7 cm long, 1.8 cm broad; claw with incurved sides, fleshy towards base of mid-lobe; side lobes erect, elliptic, basal margin ornamented with a crenate lamella; mid-lobe oblovate-oblong, small; callus at base of mid-lobe subquadrate, fleshy, obtusely 3-lobed in front. **Column** clavate, arcuate towards apex, 2.6 cm long.

DISTRIBUTION Unknown.

HISTORY Described by Rudolf Schlechter in 1917 in *Orchis* (p. 45) based on a plant of unknown provenance.

Acineta superba (H.B.K.) Rchb.f.
[Colour Plate]

A stout epiphytic plant. **Pseudobulbs** ovoid, slightly angular, 7–10 cm long, 4–6 cm across, 2- to 3-leaved at apex. **Leaves** lanceolate, acute, plicate, 25–45 cm long, 4–7 cm broad. **Inflorescences** elongate, basal, pendent, racemose, 5- to many-flowered. **Flowers** fleshy, large, not opening widely, variable in colour from pale yellow to reddish-brown, spotted red to brownish-purple. **Sepals** concave; dorsal sepal oblanceolate, acute, 3.5–4 cm long, 2–2.2 cm broad; lateral sepals oblique, elliptic-lanceolate, acute, 3.5–4 cm long, 2–2.5 cm broad. **Petals** membranaceous, oblanceolate, obtuse to subacute, 3–3.5 cm long, 1.8–2 cm broad. **Lip** very fleshy, clawed, gibbous, 3-lobed, 1.8–2 cm long and broad; side lobes erect, broadly triangular; mid-lobe elongate, obovate, obtuse; disc with a conspicuous, erect, oblong, fleshy callus with 2 divergent forked processes arising from a narrow common base. **Column** stout, pubescent, 1.8–2 cm long, narrowly winged above, apex hooded.

DISTRIBUTION   Colombia,   Venezuela, Ecuador and possibly Panama.

HISTORY   This showy species was first discovered by A. von Humboldt and A.J.A. Bonpland in the Catacocha valley near Zaruma, Ecuador. They described it with C.S. Kunth in 1815 in their *Nova Genera et Species Plantarum* (p. 343) as *Anguloa superba* and H.G. Reichenbach transferred it to *Acineta* in 1863 in *Walpers, Annales Botanices* (p. 609).

SYNONYMS   *Anguloa superba* H.B.K.; *Peristeria humboldtii* Lindl.; *Acineta humboldtii* (Lindl.) Lindl.; *Acineta fulva* Klotzsch; *Acineta colmanii* Hort.

Acoridium Nees & Meyen
Subfamily Epidendroideae
Tribe Coelogyneae
Subtribe Coelogyninae

Small to medium-sized epiphytic herbs with clustered to spaced one-noded, unifoliate, ovoid to fusiform pseudobulbs on short rhizomes. **Leaf** fleshy-coriaceous to thinly coriaceous, subplicate, erect or suberect, linear to lanceolate, acute to obtuse. **Inflorescence** apical, simple, racemose, densely many-flowered, with the flowers in two ranks; peduncle slender, wiry; bracts conspicuous. **Flowers** small. **Sepals** free, the laterals often broader than the dorsal. **Petals** free, smaller than the sepals. **Lip** rigidly attached to the column base, very small, saccate or concave at the base, 3-lobed, often obscurely so, lacking a spur. **Column** slender, lacking wings or arms; rostellum prominent; pollinia 4, waxy, adhering to a small viscidium.

DISTRIBUTION   A genus of perhaps 60 to 70 species in the Philippines.

DERIVATION OF NAME   The diminutive of *acorun*, the Sweet Flag, because the leaves somewhat resemble those of *Acorus* in the Araceae.

HISTORY   C. Nees and Meyen established this genus in 1843 in *Nova Acta Academiae Caesarea Leopoldino-Carolinae Germanicae Naturae Curiosorum* (Suppl. 1: p. 131). *Acoridium* is closely allied to *Dendrochilum* but is readily distinguished by its lack of arms or wings to the column, and by the saccate or concave lip that is firmly attached to the column base. Many authors such as Valmayor, in her *Orchidiana*

Philippiniana (1984), have considered *Acoridium* to be congeneric with *Dendrochilum* but we have followed Oakes Ames (1925), in his *Enumeration of Philippine Apostasiaceae and Orchidaceae* (p. 284), in keeping them separate.

TYPE SPECIES   *Acoridium tenellum* Nees & Meyen

CULTURE   Temp. Winter min. 12°C. Cultivation as for *Dendrochilum*.

Acoridium saccolabium (Kraenzl.) Ames
[Colour Plate]
Small epiphytic plants with clustered slender pseudobulbs 2–6.5 cm long, enclosed when young by brownish sheaths. **Leaf** fleshy-coriaceous, linear, acuminate, 19–30 cm long, 0.6–0.9 cm wide; petiole slender 7–10 cm long. **Inflorescence** longer than the subtending leaf, densely many-flowered, with the flowers in two ranks; petiole slender, wiry; rhachis up to about 11 cm long; bracts broadly ovate, spotted, as long as the flowers. **Flowers** cinnabar-red, small. **Dorsal sepal** oblong-lanceolate, obtusely acute, 2–3 mm long, 1 mm wide; **lateral sepals** almost circular, 3–3.5 mm long and broad. **Lip** deeply saccate at the base, 3-lobed in front, 1 mm long, 0.5 mm wide; side lobes inconspicuous, linear-lanceolate; mid-lobe triangular.

DISTRIBUTION   Philippines: Luzon only.

HISTORY   The original collection of this pretty orchid was made by Loher and it was described as *Dendrochilum saccolabium* by F. Kraenzlin in 1916 in the *Annalen des K.K. Naturhistorischen Hofmuseums, Wien* (p. 56). Oakes Ames transferred it to *Acoridium* in 1922 in the seventh fascicle of his *Orchidaceae* (p. 80).

SYNONYM   *Dendrochilum saccolabium* Kraenzl.

Acriopsis Reinw. ex Blume
Subfamily Epidendroideae
Tribe Cymbidieae
Subtribe Acriopsidinae

Small epiphytic herbs with clustered pseudobulbs of several nodes; roots branching, often with many tapering erect branches. **Leaves** 2–4, from upper nodes of pseudobulb, conduplicate, with sheathing petioles. **Inflorescences** basal, laxly few- to many-flowered, racemose or paniculate; peduncle elongate; bracts small, persistent. **Flowers** small, more or less twisted but not resupinate, cruciform. **Dorsal sepal** free, lanceolate; **lateral sepals** fused to the apex. **Petals** spreading, oblong to obovate. **Lip** 3-lobed pandurate or entire, adnate at the base to the base of the column to form a tubular cavity, with a 2-ridged callus on the disc. **Column** elongate, straight or slightly sigmoid, with 2 long lateral arms and a prominent apical

hood over the anther; pollinia 4, connate in 2 pairs, attached by a linear stipe to a small viscidium.

DISTRIBUTION   A small genus of six species centred on Malaya and Borneo but extending to Nepal in the north-west and eastwards to Australia and the Solomon Islands.

DERIVATION OF NAME   From the Greek *akros* (locust), based on the supposed resemblance of the auriculate column to a locust.

TAXONOMY   This distinctive genus was described by C.L. Blume in his *Bijdragen* (p. 376) in 1825 using a name coined by Reinwart. It is probably most closely allied to *Thecostele* and *Thecopus* but differs in having several-noded pseudobulbs, connate lateral sepals, a non-articulated apical part to the lip, a hooded apex to the lip and a distinctive pollinarium.

The genus has recently been revised by Minderhoud and de Vogel (1986) in the first volume of *Orchid Monographs* (pp. 1–16) They recognise six species and five varieties.

TYPE SPECIES   *Acriopsis javanica* Reinw. ex Bl.

CULTURE   Temp. Winter min. 12°C. Best grown mounted under conditions of moderate shade and humidity. Water well while growing but give a nearly dry rest period when growth is complete.

Acriopsis javanica Reinw. ex Bl.
A small to medium-sized plant. **Pseudobulbs** clustered, ovoid, 5–7-noded, 3–4-leaved at the apex. **Leaves** coriaceous, linear, obtuse, 5–28 cm long, 0.3–2.2 cm wide. **Inflorescence** erect, paniculate, up to 90 cm long, up to 200-flowered; peduncle 8.5–55 cm long; branches up to 7, up to 25 cm long; bracts triangular, 1.5–3 mm long. **Flowers** small, the sepals and petals greenish white to cream-coloured marked with purple, the lip cream-coloured marked with purple; pedicel and ovary 3–6.5 mm long. **Dorsal sepal** oblong-lanceolate, acute, cucullate, 4.5–7 mm long, 1–3 mm wide; synsepalum similar but slightly wider. **Petals** oblong to obovate, rounded at the apex, 4.5–7 mm long, 1.5–3 mm wide. **Lip** 3-lobed, papillose, adnate to the column for 2–3 mm at the base, 4–8 mm long; side lobes spreading, obliquely elliptic, obtuse, erose on margin; mid-lobe linear to obovate, emarginate, 3.5–6 mm long, 2–5 mm wide; callus of two ridges at the base of the mid-lobe. **Column** 4–6 mm long, with linear lateral arms and a deflexed hooded apex.

DISTRIBUTION   Widespread from Indo-China and Thailand to the Philippines, N.E. Australia and the Solomon Islands; common in a variety of lowland and montane forests and swampy forests up to 1600 m.

HISTORY   The original collections of this

widespread orchid were made on Mt Salak in western Java by C.L. Blume, who described it in 1825 in his *Bijdragen* (p. 377). Minderhoud and de Vogel (1986) in *Orchid Monographs* (p. 10) recognise three varieties: the typical one is widespread throughout the range; var. *floribunda*, known only from Bucas Grande Island in the Philippines, has a much narrower lip with narrower side lobes; var. *auriculata*, widespread from Burma to Borneo, is distinguished by the auricles found at the base of the lip and the short spathulate mid-lobe.

SYNONYMS include *Acriopsis picta* Rchb.f.; *A. nelsoniana* Bailey; *A. papuana* Schltr.; *A. philippinensis* Ames

---

Ada Lindl.
Subfamily Epidendroideae
Tribe Oncidieae

Medium-sized epiphytic or rarely lithophytic plants. **Pseudobulbs** lacking, reduced or well-developed, 1- or 2-leaved at apex, usually hidden by leaf-bearing sheaths. **Leaves** linear-lanceolate to ovate-lanceolate or ovate-elliptic, asymmetric at the apex, acuminate. **Inflorescences** 1 to many, axillary, shorter or longer than the subtending leaf; bracts long, navicular, papery. **Flowers** green, brown, yellow-brown or red-orange, often showy. **Sepals** and **petals** subsimilar, free, mostly spreading, linear-lanceolate, acuminate. **Lip** oblong-lanceolate, linear-lanceolate or pandurate, acuminate; callus of 2 parallel lamellae, often terminating in 2 tooth-like mounds. **Column** short, inflated below; pollinia 2, reniform or obovoid, slightly flattened, grooved; stipe obovate to rectangular; viscidium ovate.

DISTRIBUTION About 10 species from Costa Rica and Panama, south to Venezuela and Peru.

DERIVATION OF NAME Named after Ada, the sister of Artemisia, from Caria in Greek mythology.

TAXONOMY Described in 1853 by John Lindley in *Folia Orchidacea* (*Ada*), Ada has until recently been considered a monotypic genus. However, N.H. Williams in *Brittonia* (1972) has shown that several other species previously referred to *Brassia* sect. *Glumaceae* should be included in *Ada*. *Ada* may be distinguished from *Brassia* in having numerous distichous leaves and often reduced development of the pseudobulb; numerous inflorescences per plant; sepals and petals that are subsimilar; and a reflexed lip bearing a bilamellate basal callus often terminating in 2 tooth-like mounds.

TYPE SPECIES *A. aurantiaca* Lindl.
CULTURE Compost A. Temp. Winter min.

10°–12°C. As for *Odontoglossum*. The plants need ample water while growing, with less given after growth is complete.

Ada aurantiaca Lindl. [Colour Plate]
Pseudobulbs elliptic-pyriform, compressed, 7.5–10 cm long, 1- or 2-leaved at apex, dark green, subtended by leaf-bearing sheaths. **Leaves** linear-lanceolate, acuminate, 10–30 cm long, 1–2.5 cm broad. **Inflorescence** up to 35 cm long, 7- to 12-flowered (or more); bracts large, 0.6–2.5 cm long, acute. **Flowers** clustered, not opening widely, brilliant orange-red or cinnabar-red. **Sepals** linear-lanceolate, 2–3.8 cm long, 0.3–0.8 cm broad, acuminate. **Petals** linear-lanceolate, 1.5–2.5 cm long, 0.3–0.7 cm broad, acuminate. **Lip** linear-lanceolate to oblanceolate, parallel to column, apiculate, 1–1.6 cm long, 0.2–0.6 cm broad; callus of 2 parallel lamellae with an erect recurved tooth towards the apex of each, pubescent at base. **Column** short, stout, 0.4–0.5 cm long.

DISTRIBUTION Colombia and Venezuela.
HISTORY Discovered by L. Schlim in 1851 near Pamplona in Colombia at an altitude of 2500 m. The first living plants arrived in Europe in 1853 and one of the first to flower was in the collection of James Bateman at Biddulph Grange near Congleton in England. This was described by John Lindley in 1854 in *Folia Orchidacea* (*Ada*) as the type of the genus.
SYNONYMS *Ada lehmannii* Rolfe; *Mesospinidium aurantiacum* (Lindl.) Rchb.f.; *Brassia cinnabarina* Linden ex Lindl.; *Oncidium cinnabarinum* (Linden ex Lindl.) Rchb.f.; *Mesospinidium aurantiacum* (Linden ex Lindl.) Rchb.f.

Ada glumacea (Lindl.) N.H. Williams [Colour Plate]
An epiphytic plant. **Pseudobulbs** elliptic-pyriform, up to 6 cm long, 2 cm across, pale green, 1-leafed at apex. **Leaves** lanceolate, 7–50 cm long, 2.1–3.6 cm broad, acute. **Inflorescence** as long as or longer than the leaves, spreading, few-flowered; bracts large, papery, 2.5–3.5 cm long. **Flowers** spaced on rhachis; sepals and petals light yellow-green with chocolate-brown markings in basal half; lip cream-coloured marked with brown; column dark green-brown. **Sepals** linear-lanceolate, 2–2.5 cm long, 0.3–0.4 cm broad, acuminate; lateral sepals somewhat falcate. **Petals** lanceolate, reflexed at apex, 1–1.9 cm long, 0.4–0.7 cm broad. **Lip** ovate-elliptic, acute or acuminate, 1.1 cm long, 0.7 cm broad; callus of 2 parallel pubescent lamellae with a tooth-like mound at or beyond the middle of each lamella. **Column** 0.4–0.5 cm high, suberect.

DISTRIBUTION Colombia, Ecuador and Venezuela.
HISTORY Originally collected for Messrs

Linden of Brussels, near Merida in Venezuela and described in 1846 by John Lindley in *Orchidaceae Lindenianae* (p. 17). Recently, N.H. Williams (1972) in *Brittonia* (p. 107) transferred this species to the genus *Ada*.
SYNONYMS *Brassia glumacea* Lindl.; *Oncidium glumaceum* (Lindl.) Rchb.f.; *Brassia imbricata* Lindl.; *Oncidium imbricatum* (Lindl.) Rchb.f.

Ada keiliana (Rchb.f. ex Lindl.) N.H. Williams [Colour Plate]
An epiphytic plant. **Pseudobulbs** pyriform, smooth, up to 8 cm long, 2 cm across, compressed, subtended by several leaf-bearing sheaths. **Leaves** linear-lanceolate, thin-textured, 18–60 cm long, 2–4 cm broad, acute. **Inflorescence** spreading-suberect, up to 30 cm long, few-flowered; bracts papery, pale green, lanceolate, 1.4–3.6 cm long. **Flowers** with sepals and petals pale yellow-green havily spotted with dark brown or deep maroon; lip creamy-white grading to yellow at margins and apex. **Dorsal sepal** lanceolate, 4–6 cm long, 0.3–0.7 cm broad, long-acuminate; **lateral sepals** falcate-lanceolate, 3.5–8 cm long, 0.2–0.6 cm broad, long-acuminate. **Petals** falcate, linear-lanceolate, 2.2–5.5 cm long, 0.3–0.7 cm broad, acuminate. **Lip** ovate-oblong, 1.6–3.3 cm long, 0.7–1.5 cm broad, long-acuminate; callus of 2 arching basal lamellae with a terminal tooth-like projection on each side at apex. **Column** 0.4–0.6 cm long, obscurely winged at apex.

DISTRIBUTION Venezuela and Colombia.
HISTORY Discovered in La Guaira in Venezuela and sent as an herbarium specimen to H.G. Reichenbach. However, it was eventually described as *Brassia keiliana* by John Lindley in 1852 in Paxton's *Flower Garden* (p. 108).
SYNONYMS *Brassia keiliana* Rchb.f. ex Lindl.; *Oncidium keilianum* (Rchb.f. ex Lindl.) Rchb.f.; *Brassia cinnamomea* Linden ex Lindl.; *B. havanensis* Hort. ex Lindl.

Aerangis Rchb.f.
Subfamily Epidendroideae
Tribe Vandeae
Subtribe Aerangidinae

Small to medium-sized epiphytic or rarely lithophytic plants. **Stems** very short or less commonly longer. **Leaves** several, arranged fanwise to distichously, mostly obovate, obcuneate or oblanceolate, often twisted above sheath so that they all lie in one plane, unequally 2-lobed at apex, coriaceous or rarely fleshy. **Inflorescences** racemose or rarely 1-flowered; rhachis often zig-zag; bracts small to large. **Flowers** medium-sized to large, white, ± flushed pink or green especially on the spur, or yellow, alternate; column white or rarely red. **Sepals** and **petals** subsimilar, often lanceolate, less commonly elliptic, ± acuminate. **Lip** ± similar to the petals, spurred at the base; spur often long and slender. **Column** short to medium-sized; pollinia 2, ovoid; stipe linear or oblanceolate; viscidium 1, circular to elliptic.

DISTRIBUTION About 50 species, widespread in tropical Africa and Madagascar with a single species in Sri Lanka; in lowland riverine or montane forests or savanna woodlands.

DERIVATION OF NAME From the Greek *aer* (air) and *angos* (vessel), possibly alluding to the very long spur on the lip in the type species.

TAXONOMY H.G. Reichenbach described this genus in 1865 in *Flora* (p. 190). Many *Aerangis* species were originally described in the genus *Angraecum* but have subsequently been transferred, notably by Rudolf Schlechter and V.S. Summerhayes.

Aerangis is easily distinguished from *Angraecum* by its simple, elongated rostellum and associated linear or oblanceolate stipe. In most *Aerangis* species, the attractive white flowers are borne in a spreading or pendulous raceme and the genus is further characterised by its 2 pollinia on a single stipe and a reflexed lip which is shorter than the spur. J. Stewart has recently revised the African species of *Aerangis* in the *Kew Bulletin* (1979) and the Madagascan species in the *American Orchid Society Bulletin* (pp. 792–802, 903, 909, 1008–1015 & 1117–1124) in 1986.

TYPE SPECIES *A. flabellifolia* Rchb.f. [= *A. brachycarpa* (A. Rich.) Dur. & Schinz].

SYNONYM *Barombia* Schltr.

CULTURE Compost A or mounted. Temp. Winter min. mostly 12–15°C. The plants need shady humid conditions, but the roots must never remain wet. They may be grown in hanging baskets, or mounted on fern-fibre or cork slabs. In either case, the roots dry rapidly between waterings, which should be quite frequent, especially in warm weather. Species such as *A. friesiorum* or *A. coriacea* benefit from a short dry spell when new leaves are fully grown.

Aerangis articulata (Rchb.f.) Schltr
[Colour Plate]

A small epiphytic plant. **Stem** short, stout, 7.5 –12.5 cm long, several-leaved. **Leaves** obovate or oblong-obovate, coriaceous, obliquely 2-lobed at apex, 7.5–12.5 cm long, 2.5–3.7 cm broad. **Inflorescence** 22–38 cm long, pendulous, racemose, several-flowered; peduncle green, stout. **Flowers** pure white, up to 5 cm across; pedicels pale orange-red. **Sepals** elliptic-oblong, acute, 2.3 cm long, 0.5 cm broad. **Petals** similar to sepals. **Lip** broadly oblong-ovate, acute, 2.2 cm long.

DISTRIBUTION Madagascar.

HISTORY Discovered by the Rev. W. Ellis in Madagascar. He brought three plants to England where they flowered in 1871. H.G. Reichenbach described it in the following year in the *Gardeners' Chronicle* (p. 73) as *Angraecum articulatum* and Rudolf Schlechter (1914) subsequently transferred it to *Aerangis* in *Die Orchideen* (p. 597). H. Perrier de la Bâthie, in the *Flore de Madagascar* (1941), considers *A. articulata* to be possibly a hybrid of *A. stylosa* with a related species, but he gives no evidence for this theory other than that *A. articulata* is somewhat variable.

SYNONYMS *Angraecum articulatum* Rchb.f.; *Angraecum descendens* Rchb.f.

Aerangis brachycarpa (A. Rich.) Dur. & Schinz [Colour Plate]

A small to medium-sized epiphytic plant. **Stem** short, often pendulous or spreading, covered by leaf-bases. **Leaves** obovate or obcordate, coriaceous, more or less equally, obtusely, roundly 2-lobed at apex, 10–25 cm long, 3–6 cm broad, brown-spotted, venation obvious. **Inflorescences** arching or pendulous, ± axillary, up to 35 cm long, laxly 8- to 12-flowered. **Flowers** stellate, 5–5.6 cm across, fragrant; sepals, petals and lip white, tipped with pink; spur pinkish; column white. **Sepals** and **petals** lanceolate, acuminate, 1.6–2.8 cm long, 0.4–0.6 cm broad. **Lip** similar to sepals, recurved, 1.9 cm long, 0.5 cm broad; spur slender, down-curved, cylindric, up to 16.5 cm long, pinkish-brown, apex blunt. **Column** fleshy, 0.5 cm long.

DISTRIBUTION Ethiopia and Uganda, south to Zambia and Angola; 1500–2300 m altitude; in dense shade in montane forest.

HISTORY This species was first collected by Schimper in Ethiopia in the mid-nineteenth century. It was described as *Dendrobium? brachycarpum* by A. Richard in *Voyage au Abyssinie* (p. 282). In 1850, it was transferred in 1895 to *Aerangis* by Th. Durand and Schinz in *Conspectus Florae Africanae* (p. 50). J. Stewart has recently pointed out in the *Kew Bulletin* (1979) that this species has been frequently cultivated under the later synonym *A. flabellifolia* Rchb.f., and less often as *A. rohlfsiana* (Kraenzl.) Schltr., another later synonym.

SYNONYMS include *Dendrobium? brachycarpum* A. Rich.; *Aerangis flabellifolia* Rchb.f.; *Angraecum rohlfsianum* Kraenzl.; *Aerangis rohlfsiana* (Kraenzl.) Schltr.

CLOSELY RELATED SPECIES *Aerangis confusa* J. Stewart [Colour Plate] has, until recently, been consistently misidentified as *A. brachycarpa*, but is distinguished by its much smaller flowers and shorter spur. Although known for many years in cultivation, *A. confusa*

has only recently been described by J. Stewart in the *Kew Bulletin* (1979), based on a specimen collected by Smart on the escarpment forest 48 km west of Nairobi.

Aerangis confusa J. Stewart [Colour Plate]
See under *Aerangis brachycarpa*.

Aerangis fastuosa (Rchb.f.) Schltr.
[Colour Plate]

A small epiphytic plant. **Stem** very short. **Leaves** obovate to oblong-cuneiform, 1.8–7.5 cm long, 1.2–2 cm broad, unequally obscurely 2-lobed at apex. **Inflorescence** 1- to 3-flowered, up to 5 cm long; bracts large, cucullate, a quarter of the length of the ovary and pedicel. **Sepals** sub-similar, oblong-ligulate to oblong-ovate, 1.6–3 cm long, 0.6–1.1 cm broad. **Petals** similar to sepals, rather oblanceolate. **Lip** narrowly elliptic-rhombic, 2–2.5 cm long, 0.4–0.8 cm broad; spur filiform, 7–8 cm long. **Column** short.

DISTRIBUTION Madagascar.

HISTORY Originally sent from Madagascar by Leon Humblot to Fred Sander, this species was described by H.G. Reichenbach in 1881 in the *Gardeners' Chronicle* (pp. 748 & 844) as *Angraecum fastuosum*. However, Rudolf Schlechter transferred it to *Aerangis* in 1914 in *Die Orchideen* (p. 598).

SYNONYMS *Angraecum fastuosum* Rchb.f.; *Rhaphidorhynchus fastuosus* (Rchb.f.) Finet; *Angorchis fastuosa* (Rchb.f.) O. Ktze.

Aerangis gracillima (Kraenzl.) J. Stewart & Arends

An epiphyte with a short leafy stem up to 3 cm long. **Leaves** falcate, oblanceolate to obovate, unequally acutely or subacutely bilobed at the apex, 12–18 cm long, 2.6–5.5 cm wide, articulated and twisted at the base to lie in one plane. **Inflorescences** pendent, 35–80 cm long, laxly 3–11-flowered; peduncle wiry, terete; bracts elliptic, obtuse, 5–7 mm long, dark brown. **Flowers** white with a pale brown spur and reddish tips to the segments; pedicel and ovary long. **Sepals** linear, acuminate, 4–5.5 cm long, 2–3.5 mm wide. **Petals** linear, acuminate, 4–5.3 cm long, 2–3.5 mm wide. **Lip** linear, acuminate, 4–4.6 cm long, 4–5 mm wide; spur filiform, pendent, 17–22 cm long. **Column** slenderly clavate, 3–3.4 cm long.

DISTRIBUTION Cameroon and Gabon only.

HISTORY Originally collected by Preuss at Barombi in Cameroon and described as *Angraecum gracillimum* by Kraenzlin in 1893 in Engler's *Botanische Jahrbuch* (p. 59). Schlechter made it the type of his new genus *Barombia* in 1914 in the first edition of his book *Die Orchideen* (p. 600). However, J. Stewart and C. Arends

(1988) have recently shown that *Barombia* should be considered a synonym of *Aerangis*.

SYNONYM *Angraecum gracillimum* Kraenzl.; *Barombia gracillima* (Kraenzl.) Schltr.

Aerangis kirkii (Rolfe) Schltr. [Colour Plate]

A small epiphytic plant. **Stem** short, concealed amongst leaf-bases. **Leaves** distichous, radiating, closely set, coriaceous, cuneate-lanceolate, deeply notched at apex, apical lobes rounded, up to 15 cm long, 1.5 cm broad. **Inflorescences** longer than the leaves, 2- to 5-flowered. **Flowers** stellate, faintly scented, pure- or creamy-white; spur brownish. **Sepals** lanceolate, acuminate, 1.6–3 cm long, 0.5 cm broad. **Petals** similar to sepals but shorter. **Lip** lanceolate, long-acuminate, shorter than the sepals; spur curved, narrowly cylindric, 6–7 cm long. **Column** short, subterete, 0.4 cm long.

DISTRIBUTION Kenya and Tanzania; mainly in coastal and riverine forest.

HISTORY This species was first flowered in cultivation by B.S. Williams of the Victoria and Paradise Nurseries, Upper Holloway, London, having been sent to him by Dr John Kirk of Zanzibar. H.G. Reichenbach described it as *Angraecum bilobum* var. *kirkii* in the *Gardeners' Chronicle* (n.s. 18: p. 488) in 1882, but R.A. Rolfe raised it to specific status as *Angraecum kirkii* in 1897 in the *Flora of Tropical Africa* (p. 136). Rudolf Schlechter transferred it to *Aerangis* in 1914 in his *Die Orchideen* (p. 599).

SYNONYMS *Angraecum kirkii* (Rchb.f.) Rolfe; *Angraecum bilobum* Lindl. var. *kirkii* Rchb.f.

Aerangis kotschyana (Rchb.f.) Schltr.
[Colour Plate]

A large, showy epiphytic plant. **Stem** short, stout, up to 7 cm long, 1.5–2.5 cm broad, 3- to 6-leaved. **Roots** thick, fleshy, grey-brown, with a green or orange apex. **Leaves** distichous, oblong to obovate, coriaceous, broad and unequally roundly 2-lobed at apex, margins undulate, 12–20 cm long, 4–6 cm broad, dark green, often mottled. **Inflorescences** 2–4, spreading to pendulous, 22–32 cm long, 8- to 12-flowered; bracts black, ovate, acute. **Flowers** very showy, white, with a pinkish-brown spur; pedicel and ovary green. **Dorsal sepal** erect, elliptic or elliptic-lanceolate, subacute, 2–2.5 cm long; **lateral sepals** reflexed, elliptic-lanceolate to oblanceolate, obtuse, 2–2.8 cm long. **Petals** reflexed, oblanceolate, obtuse, 1–2.3 cm long. **Lip** dependent, pandurate to ovate-elliptic, apiculate or acuminate, 1.5–2 cm long, 0.8–1.5 cm broad; spur pendulous, spirally twisted, up to 22 cm long. **Column** short, stout.

DISTRIBUTION Tropical and S. Africa, south to the Transvaal.

HISTORY Discovered in the Sudan by Theodore Kotschy in 1839. *A. kotschyana* is one of the most spectacular of the African epiphytic orchids. It was described by H.G. Reichenbach as *Angraecum kotschyanum* in *Oesterreichische Botanische Zeitschrift* (p. 338) in 1864, and was transferred to the genus *Aerangis* by Rudolf Schlechter in 1918 in *Beihefte zum Botanischen Zentralblatt* (p. 118).

SYNONYMS *Angraecum kotschyanum* Rchb.f.; *A. kotschyi* Rchb.f.

Aerangis luteoalba (Kraenzl.) Schltr.
[Colour Plate]

A small, almost stemless epiphytic plant with flattened roots. **Leaves** spreading, more or less distichous, 6–10, linear, curved, fleshy, unequally roundly 2-lobed at apex, all set in same plant, up to 12 cm long, 0.6–1 cm broad. **Inorescences** 2–3 or more, spreading, arcuate or pendulous, racemose, laxly 6- to 25-flowered, 7–25 cm long; rhachis fractiflex; bracts small, sheathing. **Flowers** showy, up to 3 cm across; segments all in the same plane, pure white, creamy or yellowish with a white or scarlet column. **Sepals** elliptic, obtuse or apiculate, 1.4 cm long, 0.4 cm broad. **Petals** elliptic, apiculate, 1.4 cm long, 0.6 cm broad. **Lip** with a short narrow claw, elliptic above, apiculate, 1.9 cm long, 1.2 cm broad; spur at base of lip curved, narrowly cylindric, attenuate, 2.5–4 cm long. **Column** short, rather small, 0.2 cm long.

DISTRIBUTION Cameroon, Zaïre, Uganda, Ethiopia, Somalia, Kenya and Tanzania; mostly in riverine or lower montane forests, below 1700 m altitude.

HISTORY Originally described as *Angraecum luteo-album* in 1895 by Fritz Kraenzlin in Engler's, *Die Pflanzenwelt Ost-Afrikas* (C: p. 158) based on a collection from Zaire by Stuhlmann. It was transferred by Rudolf Schlechter to *Aerangis* in 1918 in *Beihefte zum Botanisches Zentralblatt* (p. 118).

Var. *rhodosticta* (Kraenzl.) J. Stewart [Colour Plate] (syn. *Aerangis rhodosticta* (Kraenzl.) Schltr., which has a red or orange column, is by far the commoner variety and is frequently found in collections.

SYNONYMS *Angraecum rhodostictum* Kraenzl.; *Angraecum mirabile* Hort.; *Angraecum albido-rubrum* De Wild.; *Aerangis albido-rubra* (De Wild.) Schltr.

Aerangis stylosa (Rolfe) Schltr.

A small epiphytic plant. **Stem** short, 2- to 4-leaved. **Leaves** fleshy, oblong-obovate or elliptic, narrowing gradually towards the base, coriaceous, 6.5–12.5 cm long, up to 6 cm broad, greyish green. **Inflorescences** of 6–15 flowers, more or less pendent, up to 60 cm long; bracts cucullate, 1 cm long, 1.2 cm broad. **Flowers** white; pedicel and ovary 2.5–4 cm long. **Sepals** reflexed, lanceolate, subacute, 1.2–2 cm long, 0.4 cm broad. **Petals** similar to sepals. **Lip** lanceolate, reflexed, 9- to 11-nerved, 1.2–2 cm long, 0.4 cm broad; spur 10–15 cm long. **Column** glabrous, 0.5–0.7 cm long.

DISTRIBUTION Madagascar and the Comoros; sea level to 1400 m altitude.

HISTORY Originally described by R.A. Rolfe in 1895 as *Angraecum stylosum* in the *Kew Bulletin* (p. 194) and transferred to the genus *Aerangis* by Rudolf Schlechter in 1915 in *Beihefte zum Botanischen Zentalblatt* (p. 427).

SYNONYMS *Angraecum stylosum* Rolfe; *Angraecum fournierae* André; *Aerangis venusta* Schltr.; *Aerangis crassipes* Schltr.

CLOSELY RELATED SPECIES Very closely related to *Aerangis modesta* (Hooker f.) Schltr., also from Madagascar, from which it may be distinguished by its larger flowers.

Aerangis ugandensis Summerh.
[Colour Plate]

A small epiphytic plant. **Stem** short, up to 8 cm long. **Leaves** 6–8, distichous, cuneate or cuneate-oblanceolate, unequally obtusely 2-lobed at apex, 5–20 cm long, 1.5–2.5 cm broad, marked above with numerous parallel veins. **Inflorescences** 2 or more, pendulous, basal, 10- to 15-flowered; bracts truncate, 0.2 cm long. **Flowers** spreading or subreflexed, stellate, white, **Sepals** oblong-lanceolate, acute,

Aerangis stylosa
1 Flower, front view (× ¾)
2 Flower, side view (× ¾)
3 Column from below (× 4)

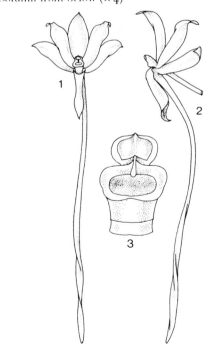

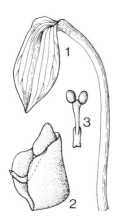

Aerangis calantha
1 – Lip and spur, side view (× 3)
2 – Column, side view (× 10)
3 – Pollinia, stipe and viscidium (× 10)

0.6–0.8 cm long, 0.3 cm broad. **Petals** similar, 0.6–0.7 cm long, 0.3 cm broad. **Lip** oblong, shortly acute, side margins reflexed, 0.6–0.7 cm long, 0.3–0.4 cm broad; spur narrowly cylindric, straight, 1–2 cm long, pointed. **Column** short, 0.2 cm long.
DISTRIBUTION Zaïre, Burundi, Uganda and W. Kenya; in riverine forests.
HISTORY Discovered by J.D. Snowden on Mt Elgon in Uganda at an altitude of 1500 m in May 1925, and described in 1931 by V.S. Summerhayes in the *Kew Bulletin* (p. 390).
CLOSELY RELATED SPECIES *Aerangis calantha* (Schltr.) Schltr. is widespread in tropical Africa from Ghana across to Uganda and south to Angola and Tanzania. In flower size it most closely approaches *A. ugandensis*, but it has a longer spur, shorter segments and is vegetatively quite distinct, resembling a small plant of *A. luteoalba* with short, linear or linear-oblanceolate leaves on a short stem.

Aeranthes Lindl.

Subfamily Epidendroideae
Tribe Vandeae
Subtribe Angraecinae

Epiphytic herbs with a short stem or lacking a stem. **Leaves** distichous, ± fleshy-coriaceous. **Inflorescence** 1- to several-flowered, racemose or rarely branching, mostly pendulous; peduncle ± wiry. **Flowers** small to large, often hyaline, green, yellow or rarely white. **Sepals** subsimilar often long-attenuate above; lateral sepals attached to column-foot. **Petals** similar to dorsal sepal but smaller. **Lip** subarticulate to

column-foot, entire, often long-attenuate in front. **Column** short; rostellum 2-lobed; pollinia 2, porate; stipites 2; viscidia 2; column-foot inflated, spurred; spur often forward pointing, cylindric or inflated in apical half, often porrect.
DISTRIBUTION 30 species in Madagascar, the Comoros and the Mascarene Islands and two species in tropical Africa.
DERIVATION OF NAME From the Greek *aer* (air, mist) and *anthos* (flower), either in allusion to the epiphytic habit or delicate flowers ('air-flowers') or to the damp habitats favoured by the species of this genus ('mist flowers').
TAXONOMY *Aeranthes* was established by John Lindley in 1824 in the *Botanical Register* (t. 817). It is characterised by its short stems, wiry scapes and translucent flowers with 2 porate pollinia each attached to its own viscidium, a lip borne at right-angles to the column, a short column which is dilated towards the base, and the forward-pointing spur.
Aeranthes is allied to *Angraecum* but is readily distinguished by the expanded column-foot which is spurred, and the hyaline flowers.
The most recent survey of the genus is that of H. Perrier de la Bâthie in *Flore de Madagascar* (1941), in which the species are described and keyed out. Since then several new species have been described and new collections have emphasised the inadequacy of Perrier's key. A few species are included in F. Hillerman & A. Holst's *An Introduction to Cultivated Angraecoid Orchids* (1986).
TYPE SPECIES *A. grandiflora* Lindl.
CULTURE Compost A. Temp. Winter min. 15°C. Shady and very humid conditions are required by these plants and they should never be allowed to become very dry. As long as the compost remains fresh and well-drained, water may be freely given, especially when the roots are active. Those species such as *A. caudata*, which have long inflorescences, should be hung up when flowering.

Aeranthes grandiflora Lindl.

[Colour Plate]
An epiphytic plant with a very short stem. **Leaves** distichous, 5–7, narrowly oblong, coriaceous, unequally roundly 2-lobed above, 15–25 cm long, 3–3.5 cm broad. **Inflorescences** pendulous, 10–30 cm long, 1- or 2-flowered; peduncle entirely covered by sheaths. **Flowers** large, showy, white or greenish-white; acumens and spur yellowish. **Dorsal sepal** oblong-ovate, longly acuminate-apiculate above, 5 cm long, 1.4 cm broad below; **lateral sepals** obliquely ovate below, longly acuminate above, 5 cm long, basal part adnate to the column-foot to form saccate mentum. **Petals** free, ovate, long-acuminate, 4 cm long. **Lip** auriculate at base, oblong-elliptic,

acuminate, 4 cm long, 2 cm broad. **Column** 0.3–0.4 cm long; foot long, cucullate, 2 cm long, 0.9 cm broad; spur from base of column-foot cylindrical, narrowing before apex then abruptly dilated at apex.
DISTRIBUTION Central and E. Madagascar; sea level to 1200 m in humid forests.
HISTORY First collected by Forbes on Mt Ambre, Madagascar and described in 1824 in the *Botanical Register* (t. 817) by John Lindley.
CLOSELY RELATED SPECIES *Aeranthes caudata* Rolfe is similar to *A. grandiflora* in its habit and pendulous inflorescences but is readily distinguished by its smaller, pendulous, translucent green flowers and many-flowered inflorescences. *Aeranthes ramosa* Rolfe is also allied to *A. grandiflora* but is distinguished by its smaller yellow-green flowers with shortly caudate segments and a cylindric spur which is not dilated above nor bent forward beneath the lip.

Aeranthes henricii Schltr.

[Colour Plate]
A large epiphytic plant with a very short stem. **Leaves** distichous, suberect-spreading, 4–6, ligulate, unequally 2-lobed at apex, coriaceous, 9–24 cm long, 1.6–5.5 cm broad, margins

Aeranthes caudata
1 Plant (× ⅕)
2 Lip (× 1)
3 Column from below with anther-cap raised (× 4)
4 Column, side view (× 4)

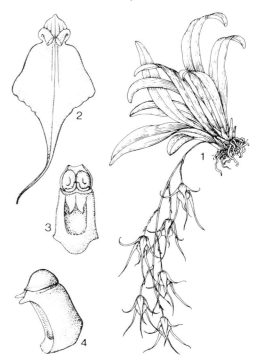

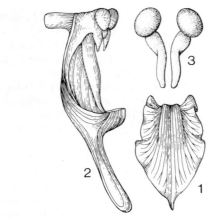

Aeranthes ramosa
1 Lip (× 1)
2 - Column, column-foot and spur (× 2)
3 Pollinia, stipites and viscidia (× 8)

Aeranthes henrici
1 – Flower (× 2/5)
2 - Lip (× 3/4)
3 – Column, column-foot and spur, side view (× 3/4)
4 – Dorsal sepal (× 3/4)
5 – Lateral sepal (× 3/4)
6 – Petal (× 3/4)

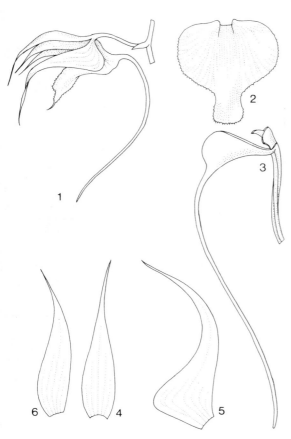

slightly undulate. **Inflorescence** pendent, 12–40 cm long, 3- to 6-flowered; peduncle, 6–15 cm long; bracts oval-obtuse, 1.5 cm long. **Flowers** pure white, showy and very large. **Sepals** lanceolate, long-acuminate-filamentous at apex, up to 11 cm long, up to 2 cm broad; lateral sepals oblique. **Petals** similar to sepals, up to 9 cm long. **Lip** obscurely 3-lobed, very broad, margins ciliate-fimbriate, apex long-apiculate; lamina 4 cm long, 3.8 cm broad; apicule up to 6 cm long. **Column** short, 0.8 cm long; foot cucullate, obovate when spread, prolonged at base into a filiform spur, 16 cm long.

DISTRIBUTION Central Madagascar; sea level to 1000 m altitude, in humid forests.

HISTORY The largest flowered species in the genus. *A. henricii* was discovered in 1919 in the Sambirano Mts by Henri Perrier de la Bâthie. Rudolf Schlechter named it in his honour in 1925 in *Fedde, Repertorium, Beihefte* (p. 278).

Aerides Lour.
Subfamily Epidendroideae
Tribe Vandeae
Subtribe Sarcanthinae

Epiphytic herbs with leafy, monopodial stems, lacking pseudobulbs. **Leaves** distichous, linear, coriaceous. **Flowers** usually many and showy, in dense or lax decurved racemes. **Sepals** broad, spreading; laterals adnate at the base to the column-foot. **Petals** broad and spreading. **Lip** ± 3-lobed, spurred at base; side lobes obscure to large; mid-lobe larger than side lobes or smaller and incurved between side lobes. **Column** short, with a short or long foot; rostellum short or long, bifid; anther 2-celled, ± beaked; pollinia 2, globose, sulcate, attached by a linear or oblong stipe to a small semicircular viscidium.

DISTRIBUTION About 20 species in S.E. Asia.

DERIVATION OF NAME This name alludes to the epiphytic habit of the plants and derives from the Greek *aer* (air) and *eides* (resembling). It is a patronymic meaning literally 'children of the air'.

TAXONOMY First described in the *Flora Cochinchinensis* (p. 525) in 1790 by Juan Loureiro. A small genus of attractive and fragrantly flowered species, most, if not all, of which have been or are in cultivation. Nearly all have white or off-white flowers variously marked with mauve or purple. R. Holttum in the *Orchids of Malaya* (1964) gives a key to the Malayan, as well as the commonly cultivated extra-Malayan, species. The Thai species are considered by G. Seidenfaden (1988) in *Opera Botanica*.

Aerides is allied to *Trichoglottis* but is distinguished by its lip, which is jointed onto the mostly long column-foot and has an ascending or recurved spur.

The genus is further characterised by the lateral sepals being decurrent on the column-foot, the well developed, porrect rostellum, the 2 unequally cleft pollinia on a single slender stipe and the 3-lobed lip which is variously ornamented within.

The species with leaves that are cylindric, fleshy and grooved above have now been transferred to other genera. *A. mitrata* Rchb.f. has recently been placed by L. Garay in the *Botanical Museum Leaflets of Harvard University* (1972), in a genus of its own, *Seidenfadenia* Garay. *A. vandarum* has been placed in *Papilionanthe*. Fourteen species of *Aerides* have recently been illustrated in colour by J. Wood and G. Kennedy in the *Orchid Digest* (1979).

TYPE SPECIES *A. odorata* Lour.

CULTURE Compost A. Temp. Winter min. 15°C. *Aerides* are probably best grown in hanging baskets, where their numerous long roots can grow and hang freely. They should be disturbed as infrequently as possible. Moderately shady and very humid conditions are required, but stagnant air should be avoided. The plants may be watered freely in warm weather and more moderately in winter.

Aerides jarckiana Shcltr. [Colour Plate]
An epiphytic plant, up to 40 cm tall. **Stems** curved or recurved, 30–35 cm long. **Leaves** lorate, leathery, 12–20 cm long, 2–3 cm broad, unequally 2-lobed at apex, slightly dorsally carinate. **Inflorescences** subpendulous, densely many-flowered, 40–65 cm long; peduncles 30–50 cm long, clothed with remote, tubular, ovate sheaths up to 1.3 cm long; bracts ovate, acute, reflexed, up to 0.6 cm long. **Flowers** odourless, 1.2–1.3 cm across, 1.8–1.9 cm long; sepals and petals rose or white spotted with light pink; mid-lobe of lip purple to magenta; side lobes pink spotted with magenta; spur magenta; pedicel and ovary white to pink. **Dorsal sepal** suborbicular-oblong, 0.7 cm long, 0.4–0.5 cm broad; **lateral sepals** convex, suborbicular, subtruncate to rounded, 0.7 cm long, 0.6 cm broad. **Petals** oblong-suborbicular or ovate, rounded, 0.65 cm long, 0.4 cm broad. **Lip** fleshy, 3-lobed; side lobes incurved and overlapping, falcate-oblong, obtuse and denticulate at the apex, 0.3 cm long, 0.2 cm broad; mid-lobe lanceolate, strongly incurved and apiculate at apex, 0.5–0.6 cm long, 0.3 cm broad; spur conical, somewhat incurved, obtuse, 0.9–1.0 cm long. **Column** erect, very short, fleshy, 0.8 cm long including the slightly convex foot.

DISTRIBUTION The Philippines (Luzon).

HISTORY Described by Rudolf Schlechter in 1915 in *Orchis* (p. 53), based on a plant which flowered in the collection of Schmidt in Dresden. Schmidt received the plant from Jarck, after whom it is named, who collected it near the lagoon of Manila.

Aerides maculosa Lindl. [Colour Plate]

A medium-sized epiphytic plant with a short stem, 4–6 cm long. **Leaves** flat, ligulate, ± curved, roundly lobed at apex, 15–23 cm long, 3–4.5 cm broad. **Inflorescences** mostly branched, longer than the leaves, up to 40 cm long, laxly many-flowered. **Flowers** variable in size, white, flushed rose and spotted with purple, apex bright rose or amethystine; lip amethyst-purple with a paler margin, claw and auricles white streaked with purple, spur-apex green; column white, anther yellow. **Sepals** elliptic-oblong, obtuse, 1.2 cm long, 0.5 cm broad. **Petals** similar to the sepals, 1.1 cm long. **Lip** 3-lobed, shortly clawed, with 2 small white tubercles at the base, 1.8 cm long, 1.2 cm broad; side lobes auriculate; mid-lobe ovate or ovate-oblong, flat, apex broad, obtuse or retuse, margins undulate; spur slender, with a broad mouth, uncinately incurved, 0.6 cm long.
DISTRIBUTION India (Western Ghats).
HISTORY Introduced by Messrs Loddiges of Hackney, London and Messrs Rollisson of Tooting, London, it flowered for the first time in England in their nurseries in July 1844. John Lindley described it the following year in the *Botanical Register* (t. 58).
SYNONYM *Saccolabium speciosum* Wight
CLOSELY RELATED SPECIES Somewhat intermediate between *Aerides crispa* Lindl. and *A. multiflora* but with smaller flowers than the latter species.

Aerides multiflora Roxb. [Colour Plate]

A large, erect to pendulous, epiphytic plant with fleshy, fibrous roots. **Stem** stout, 10–25 cm long, many-leaved. **Leaves** ligulate, distichous, deeply channelled and keeled, curved, 2-lobed, 15–34 cm long, 1.3–1.9 cm broad. **Inflorescences** racemose or rarely branched, 15–34 cm long, densely many-flowered. **Flowers** 2–3.2 cm across, fragrant, white or rose-purple sometimes spotted darker amethyst-purple at the apex; lip light amethyst-purple. **Sepals** and **petals** subsimilar, oblong, elliptic-oblong or orbicular, rounded, 0.8–1.6 cm long, 0.6–1 cm broad. **Lip** clawed, geniculate, 3-lobed, convex, margins recurved, 1.5 cm long, 1.1 cm broad; mid-lobe cordate or hastate-ovate, rounded, slightly convex above; callus fleshy, incurved, 2-lobed on the base of the midlobe; spur pointing forwards, short, straight, compressed, 0.4–0.5 cm long. **Col-**

umn beaked, with 2 rounded auricles on the foot.
DISTRIBUTION Tropical Himalayas, India, south to Thailand, Tenasserim and Indo-China.
HISTORY Originally described by W. Roxburgh in 1795 in his *Plants of the Coast of Coromandel* (p. 63), who discovered it in Sylhet.

Several varieties are, or have been, in cultivation, the showiest and most popular of which is var. *lobbii* Veitch with more numerous and richly coloured flowers than the typical form. Var. *lobbii* was introduced by Thomas Lobb from Moulmein in Burma in 1851.
SYNONYMS *Aerides affinis* Wall.; *A. lobbii* Hort.; *A. veitchii* Hort.; *A. trigona* Klotzsch
CLOSELY RELATED SPECIES See *A. fieldingii* and *A. maculosum*.

Aerides odorata Lour. [Colour Plate]

A very variable epiphytic plant, up to 1 m long. **Stem** very stout, drooping, branching, mostly 10–30 cm long. **Leaves** fleshy, incurved, oblong-ligulate, roundly lobed at apex, 15–30 cm long, 1.8–5 cm broad, pale green. **Inflorescences** many, pendulous, 25–35 cm long, densely up to 30-flowered; peduncle and rhachis stout, sticky when young; bracts 0.5 cm long, acute. **Flowers** sweet-smelling, purple or nearly white, often purple-spotted and tipped; spur greenish or yellowish at the apex. **Dorsal sepal** oblong, obtuse, 1.2 cm long, 0.8 cm broad; **lateral sepals** longer than the dorsal sepal, narrowly triangular-lanceolate, 1 cm broad. **Petals** narrowly oblong, obtuse, 1.2 cm long, 0.7 cm broad. **Lip** 3-lobed, almost enclosing the column, 1 cm long, 0.4 cm broad; side lobes subcuneate-subquadrate, erect, margins entire or toothed; mid-lobe short, incurved, oblong-lanceolate, acute, entire to erose; disc with small keels around the nectary and 2 curved appendages in the mouth; spur large, horn-like, incurved. **Column** short; anther obtuse.
DISTRIBUTION Tropical Himalayas of India (Sikkim) and Nepal, the Khasia Hills south to Tenasserim, S.E. Asia, Java, S. China, the Malay Archipelago and the Philippines.
HISTORY *A. odorata* is the type species of the genus and was introduced by Sir Joseph Banks to the Royal Botanic Gardens at Kew in 1800 from China where Juan Loureiro discovered it several years previously. Loureiro described it in 1790 in his *Flora Cochinchinensis* (p. 525). This species was subsequently collected in India by W. Roxburgh and in Nepal by N. Wallich who sent plants to the Horticultural Society of London where it flowered in the summer of 1831.

The variety *lawrenceae* (Rchb.f.) Hort. [Colour Plate] of *A. odorata* from the Philippines, differs in having longer racemes bearing larger

flowers in which the purple spots are much brighter.
SYNONYM *Aerides cornuta* Roxb.

Aerides rosea Lodd. ex Lindl. [Colour Plate]

A robust epiphytic plant. **Stems** stout, 10–25 cm long. **Leaves** deeply channelled, keeled, curved, ligulate, 2-lobed at apex, 15–35 cm long, 2.5–4.3 cm broad. **Inflorescences** 45–60 cm long or more, racemose or rarely branched near the base, densely many-flowered. **Flowers** up to 3.7 cm across; dorsal sepal and petals amethyst-purple suffused with white, sometimes with basal half white dotted with purple; lateral sepals white with a pale apical spot; lip amethyst-purple mottled white, spur whitish. **Dorsal sepal** and **petals** obovate, obtuse, 1.2–1.8 cm long, 0.6 cm broad; **lateral sepals** broadly elliptic, 1.2–1.9 cm long, 0.7 cm broad. **Lip** 3-lobed, deltoid or trullate, acute, very slightly laterally compressed, 1.6 cm long, 1.1 cm broad; side lobes small, incurved over mouth of spur; mid-lobe hastate, acute; spur 4 mm long, funnel-shaped. **Column** 5 mm long.
DISTRIBUTION India (Sikkim Himalayas and Assam), Burma, S. China, Thailand, Vietnam and Laos.
HISTORY Introduced into cultivation in 1850 by Thomas Lobb for the firm of Messrs Veitch & Sons. The type was flowered by Messrs Loddiges and was described by John Lindley in Paxton's *Flower Garden* (p. 109) in 1852.

It is still commonly found in cultivation as *Aerides fieldingii*, a later synonym.
SYNONYMS *A. fieldingii* Williams; *A. williamsii* Warner
CLOSELY RELATED SPECIES Very closely allied to *A. multiflora*, but distinguished by its different habit and the very acute mid-lobe of its differently coloured flowers.

Aganisia Lindl.

Subfamily Epidendroideae
Tribe Maxillarieae
Subtribe Zygopetalinae

Creeping epiphytes with elongated scandent rhizomes with widely separated pseudobulbs. **Pseudobulbs** obscure, unifoliate at apex. **Leaves** plicate, slenderly petiolate. **Inflorescence** few- to many-flowered, emerging from the base of the pseudobulb or laterally. **Flowers** blue or white and yellow. **Sepals** and **petals** free, subsimilar, spreading. **Lip** 3-lobed or bipartite, callose, not spurred; side lobes broad and rounded; midlobe entire. **Column** short, winged at apex, lacking a foot; pollinia 4, superposed, hard, yellow, on an oblong elongate stipe.

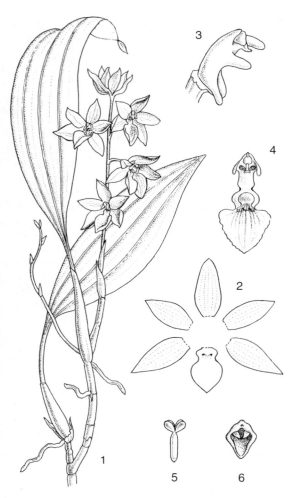

1. *Aganisia pulchella*
   1 – Habit ($\times \frac{1}{4}$)
   2 – Sepals, petals and lip ($\times$ 1)
   3 – Column, side view ($\times$ 3)
   4 – Column and lip ($\times$ 1)
   5 – Pollinarium ($\times$ 6)
   6 – Anther-cap ($\times$ 7)

DISTRIBUTION Two species only in lowland northern S. America and Trinidad.
DERIVATION OF NAME From the Greek *aganos* (gentle, mild), given in allusion to the pretty, neat appearance of the plant.
TAXONOMY This genus was established by John Lindley in 1839 in the *Botanical Register* (misc. p. 45). It is allied to *Acacallis*.
TYPE SPECIES *A. pulchella* Lindl.
CULTURE Temp. Winter min. 15°C. Because of its climbing habit, should be mounted. Requires good humidity and air movement with moderate shade. Water carefully throughout the year.

Aganisia pulchella **Lindl.**
A scandent epiphyte with an elongated many-noded rhizome 2–3 mm in diameter. **Pseudobulbs** obscure, covered with papery sheaths, 2–3 cm long, 3–5 mm in diameter, unifoliate at apex. **Leaf** erect, plicate, prominently 3-nerved, lanceolate, acuminate, 10–25 cm long, 2.5–4.5 cm wide, articulated in the middle of the slender 4–7 cm-long petiole. **Inflorescences** lateral, 4.5–9 cm long, laxly 2- to 8-flowered; peduncle short; bracts triangular-ovate, 3–4.5 mm long. **Flowers** 0.3 cm across, white with a yellow mark on the lip and a yellow callus marked with purple. **Sepals** subsimilar, oblong or oblong-ovate, acute, 16–17 mm long, 7 mm wide. **Petals** similar, 14–15 mm long, 6–7 mm wide. **Lip** bipartite, 12–13 mm long, 9–12 mm wide; epichile concave; hypochile ovate to subcircular, obtuse or acute; callus at the base of the lip, a transverse 3-ridged rugulose raised disc. **Column** 5 mm long, with 2 apical falcate wings.
DISTRIBUTION Venezuela, Guyana, Amazonian Brazil and Trinidad; up to 1000 m.
HISTORY Originally described in 1839 in the *Botanical Register* (misc. p. 45) by John Lindley based on a plant collected in Guyana by Brotherton for Messrs Loddiges.
SYNONYM *A. brachypoda* Schltr.

Alamania **La Llave & Lex.**
Subfamily Epidendroideae
Tribe Epidendreae
Subtribe Laeliinae

Small epiphytic plants with a creeping rhizome. **Stems** small, slightly fleshy, pseudobulbous, 2- to 3-leaved at apex. **Inflorescence** terminal from leafless pseudobulb, covered below by umbricate membranous-scarious bracts, racemose, densely few-flowered above. **Flowers** medium-sized, fairly showy, red. **Sepals** and **petals** subequal, erect-spreading, narrow. **Lip** connate with base of column, erect, similar to sepals, with small basal teeth at sides. **Column** erect, semiterete, lacking wings: pollinia 4, broadly ovoid-compressed. lacking appendages.
DISTRIBUTION Mexico, one species only.
DERIVATION OF NAME Named in honour of Don Lucas Alaman, a Mexican public official and friend of the authors.
TAXONOMY Described in 1825 by P. La Llave and J. Lexarza in their *Novorum Vegetabilium Descriptiones* (p. 31).

Alamania is a distinctive orchid with flowers almost the colour of *Sophronitis coccinea*. It is most closely allied to *Hexisea*, from which it differs in lacking a saccate or gibbous base to the lip, and to *Epidendrum. Cattleya* and *Nageliella* from which it may be distinguished by its lip which is geniculate at the junction with the column.

TYPE SPECIES *A punicea* La Llave & Lex.
CULTURE Compost A. Temp. Winter min. 10–12°C. This species should be grown in a small pan. It requires humid, shady conditions. Water should be carefully given throughout the year.

Alamania punicea **La Llave & Lex.**
[Colour Plate]
A dwarf epiphytic plant. **Pseudobulbs** clustered, ovoid, 0.8 cm long, 0.7 cm in diameter, 2- or 3-leaved above. **Leaves** coriaceous, oblong-elliptic, obtuse, slightly conduplicate, up to 2.5 cm long, 1 cm broad. **Inflorescence** erect, terminal on leafless pseudobulbs, racemose, equal to or slightly shorter than the leaves, 1- to several-flowered. **Flowers** medium-sized, showy, scarlet with a yellow base to the lip; column white or yellow, pollinia red. **Sepals** and **petals** free, spreading, oblong-elliptic, acute, 1.2–1.4 cm long, 0.3–0.4 cm broad, subsimilar. **Lip** similar to other segments, obscurely angled on each side in the middle, auriculate at the base, acute, 1.3 cm long, 0.3–0.4 cm broad; callus of 3 low rounded ridges, the central one extending well down the lamina. **Column** short, stout: pollinia 4.
DISTRIBUTION Mexico only; on oaks at about 1800 m.
HISTORY Originally described by P. La Llave and J. Lexarza in 1825 in their *Novorum Vegetabilium Descriptiones* (p. 31) based on their own collection from Mt Quinzeo near Vallisolet.

Amblostoma **Scheidw.**
Subfamily Epidendroideae
Tribe Epidendreae
Subtribe Laeliinae

Erect epiphytic plants with leafy, articulated stems. **Leaves** sessile, subcoriaceous, subcarinate. **Inflorescence** apical, racemose, simple or poorly branched; bracts minute. **Flowers** small, alternate, pedicellate: perianth subconnivent. **Sepals** concave, equal, connate at the base. **Petals** narrower, reflexed. **Lip** cuneiform, bicristate within, connate at the base with the column, free part trifid, **Column** truncate; anther applanate, broadly cordate, 4-locular; pollinia 4, waxy, spherical, joined in pairs.
DISTRIBUTION A small genus of some nine species from tropical S. and Central America.
DERIVATION OF NAME From the Greek *amblys* (blunt) and *stoma* (mouth), an allusion to the flat appearance of the flower due to the lip being firmly adnate to the column.
TAXONOMY *Amblostoma* was established in 1838 by M.J. Scheidweiler in F. Otto and A.

Dietrich's *Allgemeine Gartenzeitung* (p. 383). It is allied to *Cladobium*, *Nanodes* and *Neolehmannia*, being distinguished by its tall erect stems which are not superposed but are sometimes branched. From the typical section of *Epidendrum* which it superficially resembles closely, it may be readily distinguished by its subglobose unappendaged pollinia.

TYPE SPECIES   *A. cernuum* Scheidw.

CULTURE   Compost A Temp. Winter min. 12–15°C. As for *Epidendrum*. The plants need good humidity and moderate shade, with plenty of water while growing, and a drier period when the pseudobulbs are fully grown.

Amblostoma tridactylum (Lindl.) Rchb.f.
[Colour Plate]

An erect epiphytic plant with a short creeping rhizome. **Stems** narrowly fusiform-terete, 20–30 cm long, 0.8–1.5 cm thick in the middle, clothed with numerous scarious sheaths along the length. **Leaves** 4–5, in the apical half of the stem, erect or suberect, rigid, linear-ligulate, rounded at apex, 12–18 cm long, 0.8–1.4 cm broad, conduplicate below, articulated to a sheathing leaf-base. **Inflorescence** paniculate, erect-spreading, often densely many-flowered, 15–20 cm long. **Flowers** very small, fragrant, pale yellow, brownish-yellow or yellowish-green; column green, **Sepals** slightly concave, fleshy, oblong to obovate, obtuse or slightly apiculate, 0.3 cm long, 0.15–0.2 cm broad. **Petals** fleshy, oblong-spathulate, obtuse, incurved, 0.35–0.4 cm long, 0.1 cm broad. **Lip** fused to column below, saccate at base, 3-lobed in apical part; side lobes fleshy, linear, obtuse, incurved-spreading; mid-lobe much smaller than the side lobes, linear, obtuse; callus depressed, trifid. **Column** fleshy, obconical 0.2 cm long.

DISTRIBUTION   Brazil.

HISTORY   Originally described by John Lindley in 1838 in the *Botanical Register* (misc. 81) as *Epidendrum tridactylum* based on a plant collected by George Gardner in the Organ Mts in Brazil and given to Lindley by Stephen Cannon of Stratford Green, London. H.G. Reichenbach transferred it to the genus *Amblostoma* in 1864 in *Walpers, Annales Botanices* (p. 485).

Amesiella Garay
Subfamily Epidendroideae
Tribe Vandeae
Subtribe Sarcanthinae

Small epiphytic herbs with short stems. **Leaves** distichous, fleshy. **Inflorescences** shortly pedunculate, racemose, few-flowered; bracts rigid. **Flowers** large, white. **Sepals** and **petals** similar, spreading; lateral sepals adnate to the column-foot. **Lip** inserted at the apex of the column-foot, 3-lobed; spur long and narrow. **Column** terete, erect, puberulent, with a distinct foot; rostellum 3-lobed; pollinia 2, entire; stipe oblong-linear; viscidium suborbicular.

DISTRIBUTION   A monotypic genus confined to the Philippines.

DERIVATION OF NAME   Named in honour of Professor Oakes Ames (1874–1950) founder of the Orchid Herbarium of Oakes Ames at Harvard University and author of numerous works on Philippine and American orchids.

TAXONOMY   For many years the type species of this genus has been cultivated under the name *Angraecum philippinense* but many years ago Rudolf Schlechter had intended to remove it from the predominantly African and Madagascan genus *Angraecum*, and indeed his name *Amesiella* for the new genus was published posthumously in 1926 in *Notizblatt des Botanischen Gartens und Museums zu Berlin-Dahlem*. Unfortunately, the name lacked an accompanying description to validate it. L. Garay eventually validated the genus in 1972 in *Botanical Museum Leaflets of Harvard University* (p. 159).

Amesiella is allied to *Neofinetia*, differing in having a distinct column-foot with a free apex and in having a prominent 3-lobed rostellum. In these features it is also quite distinct from *Angraecum*.

TYPE SPECIES   *A. philippinensis* (Ames) Garay

CULTURE   Compost A. Temp. Winter min. 10–12°C. *Amesiella* may be grown in a small pot or basket under humid conditions and moderate shade. While the roots are active, plenty of water is required but, on completion of growth, less should be given.

Amesiella philippinensis (Ames) Garay
[Colour Plate]

Small epiphytic plants, 3–6 cm high with fleshy roots. **Stem** very short. **Leaves** elliptic-oblong, obtuse, 2–5.5 cm long, 0.6–1.4 cm broad. **Inflorescence** about 4 cm long, few-flowered; peduncle fleshy, stout, conspicuously winged; bracts rigid, fleshy, 0.5 cm long, triangular, acute. **Flowers** large, not fragrant, pure white. **Dorsal sepal** elliptic, cuneate at base, rounded or obtuse above, about 2.2 cm long, 1.4–1.5 cm broad; **lateral sepals** similar to dorsal sepal. **Petals** broadly spathulate, very obtuse, about 2.2 cm long, 1.5 cm broad. **Lip** 3-lobed; side lobes somewhat oblong, 0.4–0.5 cm long, 0.65 cm broad at base; mid-lobe oblong, rounded at apex, 0.9 cm long, about 0.75 cm broad; spur slender, 3.5 cm long. **Column** rather stout, about 0.7 cm long.

DISTRIBUTION   The Philippines; epiphytic in montane forests at about 800 m altitude.

HISTORY   Discovered by E.D. Merrill on the forested slopes of Mt Halcon and described by Oakes Ames in 1907 as *Angraecum philippinense* in the *Philippines Journal of Science (Botany)* (p. 336). Recently L. Garay has transferred it to the genus *Amesiella* in 1972 in the *Botanical Museum Leaflets of Harvard University* (p. 160).

SYNONYM   *Angraecum philippinense* Ames

Anacamptis L.C. Rich.
Subfamily Orchidoideae
Tribe Orchideae
Subtribe Orchidinae

Small to medium-sized terrestrial herbs growing from ovoid or subglobose underground tuberoids. **Stem** erect, leafy. **Leaves** rather fleshy, arranged in a spiral. **Inflorescence** spicate, densely many-flowered, pyramidal to shortly cylindrical; bracts lanceolate. **Flowers** small, sweetly scented, purple, pink or rarely white. **Sepals** and **petals** free, subsimilar; dorsal sepal and petals connivent to form a hood over the column; lateral sepals spreading. **Lip** 3-lobed, spurred at the base; callus of 2 short ridges either side of the mouth of the slender elongate

Amesiella philippinensis
1 – Flower (× 1)
2 – Column and lip, side view (× 1½)
3 – Anther (× 6)

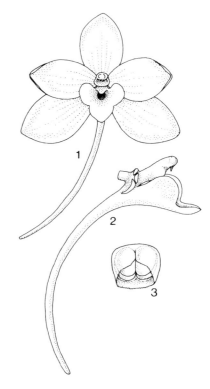

spur. **Column** short; pollinia 2, clavate, mealy attached to a solitary transversely elongate viscidium.

DISTRIBUTION A small genus of two species only, widespread in Europe, Asia Minor and N.W. Africa.

DERIVATION OF NAME From the Greek *anakamptein* (bend back), possibly a reference to either the reflexed bracts or the reflexed pollinia.

HISTORY *Anacamptis* was established as a distinct genus by the French botanist L.C. Richard in 1818 in the journal *Mémoires du Muséum National d'Histoire Naturelle, Paris* (pp. 47, 55). It is superficially not unlike *Gymnadenia* but can be easily distinguished by the characteristic 2-ridged callus on the lip and by its spherical or ovoid, rather than palmate, tuberoids.

TYPE SPECIES *A. pyramidalis* (L.) L.C. Rich.

CULTURE Temp Winter min. 5°C Compost 35% loam, 35% sharp sand, 20% leaf mould, 10% fine grade bark. Repot annually in spring, incorporating a third of the old compost in the new mix. Summer flowering, after which plants die down and should be much drier until the new shoot starts into growth.

Anacamptis pyramidalis (L.) L.C. Rich.
[Colour Plate]

A terrestrial plant 20–60 cm tall. **Leaves** linear to oblong-lanceolate, acute, canaliculate, 8–25 cm long, 0.5–1.5 cm wide. **Inflorescence** erect, densely many-flowered, pyramidal at first becoming cylindrical with age, 2–8 cm long; bracts linear-lanceolate, acuminate, 0.8–1.5 cm long. **Flowers** purple, pink or white, fragrant; ovary 6–10 mm long. **Dorsal sepal** narrowly elliptic, acute, 4–6 mm long, 2 mm wide; **lateral sepals** obliquely broadly lanceolate, acute, 4–6 mm long, 2–3 mm wide. **Petals** broadly lanceolate, acute, 4–6 mm long, 2 mm wide. **Lip** strongly 3-lobed, 6–9 mm long and wide; lobes oblong, subequal, c. 4 mm long; spur slender, filiform, slightly incurved, 12–14 mm long.

DISTRIBUTION Throughout Europe, the Middle East and N.W. Africa; a calcicole usually found in grassland or scrub on chalk, limestone or in dune slacks, usually in full sun.

HISTORY Linnaeus described this common European orchid in 1753 in the first edition of his seminal work *Species Plantarum* (p. 940) as *Orchis pyramidalis*. L.C. Richard made it the type of his new genus *Anacamptis* in 1818.

SYNONYM *Orchis pyramidalis* L.

CLOSELY RELATED SPECIES The Fragrant Orchid, *Gymnadenia conopsea*, found throughout Europe and temperate Asia, is similar but differs in being a larger plant with a cylindrical inflorescence of pinkish-purple, sweetly scented flowers with a lip that lacks the fleshy callus lobes at the base and has a longer spur.

Ancistrochilus Rolfe
Subfamily Epidendroideae
Tribe Arethuseae
Subtribe Bletiinae

Small to medium-sized epiphytic herbs. **Pseudobulbs** orbicular, conical or pyriform, ± flattened, 2-leaved at apex. **Leaves** plicate, thin-textured, narrowly lanceolate to elliptic-lanceolate, petiolate below. **Inflorescences** basal, suberect-arcuate, 1- to few-flowered, pubescent on axis, bracts, ovaries and outside of sepals. **Flowers** showy; sepals and petals white to rose-purple; lip purple with green and brown side lobes. **Sepals** and **petals** free, spreading; petals narrower than sepals. **Lip** 3-lobed; side lobes erect, rounded; mid-lobe narrowly triangular-lanceolate, recurved. **Column** porrect, slender, almost as long as the lip, dilated slightly at apex; pollinia 8, equal, elongate, attached to a sticky appendage.

DISTRIBUTION Two species in W. Africa across to Uganda and Tanzania.

DERIVATION OF NAME From the Greek *ankistron* (hook) and *cheilos* (lip), referring to the hook-like mid-lobe of the lip.

TAXONOMY *Ancistrochilus* was described by R.A. Rolfe in 1897 in Dyer's *Flora of Tropical Africa* (p. 44). It is one of the most striking of the African epiphytic orchid genera and resembles more closely Asiatic orchids such as *Pachystoma*, and in its vegetative habit *Pleione*, than any of the African orchids.

TYPE SPECIES *A. thomsonianus* (Rchb.f.) Rolfe

CULTURE Compost A. Temp. Min. 15°C while growing, 12°C while resting. *Ancistrochilus* species grow well in small pans. While growing they require plenty of water, and moderate shade, but after the leaves have dropped, they should be kept almost dry until new growth begins. The inflorescences appear from the base of mature pseudobulbs, usually as the leaves begin to fall.

Ancistrochilus rothschildianus O'Brien
[Colour Plate]

A small epiphytic herb, 15–35 cm high. **Pseudobulbs** clustered, conical or pyriform, often appearing rather dried up, up to 5 cm in diameter, 2-leaved at apex. **Leaves** lanceolate to elliptic-lanceolate or oblanceolate, acute or acuminate, suberect to arching, 10–40 cm long, 2–7.5 cm broad, thin and soft-textured. **In-**

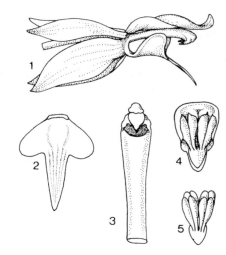

Ancistrochilus rothschildianus
1 – Flower, side view (× 1)
2 – Lip (× 1)
3 – Column (× 2)
4 – Anther (× 6)
5 – Pollinia (× 6)

florescence from the base of the pseudobulb, 2- to 5-flowered, arcuate; peduncle pubescent; bracts ovate-lanceolate, acuminate, erect, pubescent. **Flowers** large and showy for size of plant; sepals and petals white, lilac or rose-pink; lip mid-lobe rich purple with a yellow apex; side lobes and column greenish mottled with brown. **Sepals** narrowly elliptic, obtuse or subacute, 2–3 cm long, 0.6–1 cm broad. **Petals** oblanceolate, acute, up to 2.5 cm long, 0.3 cm broad. **Lip** 3-lobed, 0.8–1.2 cm long; side lobes erect, rounded; mid-lobe ligulate, recurved, acute. **Column** slightly arcuate, up to 1.2 cm long.

DISTRIBUTION Tropical Africa from Guinea and Sierra Leone across to Uganda; in forests often growing on bare trunks and larger branches of forest trees.

HISTORY Described in 1907 by James O'Brien in the *Gardeners' Chronicle* (ser. 3, 41, 51) based on a plant from Nigeria flowered by the Hon. Walter Rothschild after whom it was named.

CLOSELY RELATED SPECIES One of the showiest of the African epiphytic orchids, which, vegetatively, closely resembles *Pleione*. The only other species in the genus is *Ancistrochilus thomsonianus* (Rchb.f.) Rolfe, which has narrower pseudobulbs and larger flowers with longer, more acuminate white sepals.

Ancistrorhynchus Finet

Subfamily Epidendroideae
Tribe Vandeae
Subtribe Aerangidinae

Small to quite large epiphytic plants, with very short or elongate stems. **Leaves** distichous, several, canaliculate or twisted at the base to lie in one plane, linear or tapering above, unequally 2- lobed and ± dentate or serrate at apex. **Inflorescences** axillary, very dense, almost spherical, subsessile; bracts large, as long as flowers, chaffy. **Flowers** small, white, ± marked with green or yellow. **Sepals** and **petals** free, subsimilar. **Lip** entire to obscurely 3-lobed, larger than other segments, spurred; spur with a wide mouth, swollen at apex. **Column** very short, fleshy; rostellum pointed downwards and then sharply reflexed so that the apex points upwards; stipe linear; viscidium long and narrow.

DISTRIBUTION About 14 species in tropical Africa.

DERIVATION OF NAME From the Greek *ankistron* (hook), and *rhynchos* (beak), in allusion to the hook-like rostellum which is curved back on itself.

TAXONOMY Established by Achille Finet in 1907 in *Mémoires Société Botanique, France* (p. 44). *Ancistrorhynchus* is one the angraecoid genera so typical of Africa and is distinguished by its almost capitate, subsessile inflorescence and small flowers in which the rostellum is dependent at first but then is curved back on itself so that the apex points upwards.

V.S. Summerhayes (1944) revised the genus in the *Botanical Museum Leaflets of Harvard University* (p. 205).

TYPE SPECIES *A. recurvus* Finet
SYNONYM *Cephalangraecum* Schltr.

CULTURE Compost A. Temp. Winter min. 12–15°C. These plants may be grown in pots or baskets. Larger specimens tend to hang downwards, with their roots in the air. They require shady, humid conditions, with plenty of water while growing and less after growth is complete.

Ancistrorhynchus cephalotes (Rchb.f.) Summerh. [Colour Plate]

A medium-sized epiphytic plant lacking pseudobulbs. **Stems** erect, 5–20 cm long, distichously several-leaved, often curved. **Leaves** linear, somewhat conduplicate especially below, 2-lobed at apex, 7–40 cm long, 0.8–1.9 cm broad. **Inflorescence** ± fasciculate, many-flowered; bracts large, chaffy. **Flowers** white with green or yellow blotches on the lip. **Sepals** narrowly oblong, obtuse, 0.4–0.7 cm long, 0.2–

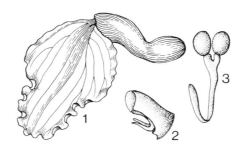

Ancistrorhynchus clandestinus
1 – Lip and spur (× 6)
2 – Column, side view (× 6)
3 – Pollinia, stipe and viscidium (× 13)

0.3 cm broad. **Petals** elliptic-obovate, obtuse, 0.6 cm long, 0.3 cm broad. **Lip** indistinctly 3-lobed ±, cordate, as broad as long or broader, 0.4–0.7 cm long, 0.4–0.9 cm broad; spur straight or only slightly curved, somewhat inflated towards apex, 0.6–1 cm long. **Column** very short, 0.1 cm long.

DISTRIBUTION Guinea and Sierra Leone, east to Nigeria.

HISTORY Originally described in 1872 by H.G. Reichenbach as *Listrostachys cephalotes* in the *Gardeners' Chronicle* (p. 1687) based on a plant grown by George Green in the collection of W. Saunders at Hillfield House, Reigate, England. V.S. Summerhayes transferred it to *Ancistrorhynchus* in 1944 in the *Botanical Museum Leaflets of Harvard University* (p. 206).

SYNONYMS *Angraecum cephalotes* (Rchb.f.) Kraenzl.; *Listrostachys cephalotes* Rchb.f.

CLOSELY RELATED SPECIES *Ancistrorhynchus clandestinus* (Lindl.) Schltr. is allied to *A. cephalotes* but is readily distinguished by its much longer leaves which are markedly unequally 2-lobed at the apex, its shorter bracts and flower in which the lip is markedly 3-lobed and the pollinia are borne on a single stipe. *A. clandestinus* is widely distributed from Sierra Leone to Zaïre.

Angraecopsis Kraenzl.

Subfamily Epidendroideae
Tribe Vandeae
Subtribe Aerangidinae

Small epiphytic plants with short, or very short stems. **Leaves** distichous, often twisted at the base to lie in one plane, linear, ± falcate, unequally 2-lobed at apex. **Inflorescences** axillary, long-racemose, laxly to densely several-flowered. **Flowers** small, often diaphanous, white, yellow or pale green. **Sepals** subsimilar, free. **Petals** ± deltoid, anticous margin rounded and projecting a long way forwards.

Lip deeply 3-lobed (rarely entire), spurred at the base; spur mostly cylindric, slender, often much longer than the lip and curved. **Column** short, fleshy; rostellum short, bifid; pollinia 2, waxy; stipites 2; viscidium 1.

DISTRIBUTION About 16 species widespread in tropical Africa and Madagascar.

DERIVATION OF NAME From *Angraecum*, a genus of African epiphytic orchids and the Greek *opsis* (looking like), from their resemblance to some *Angraecum* species.

TAXONOMY *Angraecopsis* was established by F. Kraenzlin in A. Engler's *Botanische Jahrbücher* (p. 171) in 1900. The genus is characterised by its short rostellum with a viscidium as long as it is wide, by its deeply 3-lobed lip (in most cases) and by its more or less deltoid petals which project a long way forwards. It is most closely allied to *Diaphananthe*, where the lip is nearly always entire often with a tooth in the mouth of the spur and the petals are never deltoid. V.S. Summerhayes revised *Angraecopsis* in 1951 in the *Botanical Museum Leaflets of Harvard University* recognising 14 species in two sections (*Eu*) *Angraecopsis* of 10 species with a more or less 3-lobed lip and *Cardiochilus* with an entire lip, cordate at the base.

TYPE SPECIES *A. tenerrima* Kraenzl.
CULTURE As for small *Angraecum* species.

Angraecopsis breviloba Summerh.

A tiny epiphytic plant. **Stem** very short, about 1 cm long. 4-leaved. **Roots** numerous, flattened onto substrate, greenish-grey, 0.15–0.3 cm broad. **Leaves** deciduous, ligulate, shortly unequally 2-lobed at apex, up to 3 cm long, 0.5 cm broad. **Inflorescence** spreading or ascending, up to 7 cm long, densely many-flowered; rhachis flexuose, angled; bracts sheathing, obtuse or acute, 0.1–0.25 cm long. **Flowers**

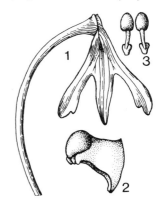

Angraecopsis tenerrima
1 – Lip and spur (× 3)
2 – Column, side view (× 6)
3 – Pollinia, stipites and viscidia (× 6)

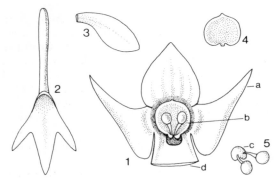

Angraecopsis elliptica
1 – Dorsal sepal, petals and column (× 7½)
   a Petal, b Column, anther-cap removed, c Viscidium, d Lip base
2 – Lip and spur (× 4)
3 – Lateral sepal (× 4)
4 – Anther-cap (× 7½)
5 – Pollinia (× 7)

secund, pale green. **Dorsal sepal** recurved, oblong-lanceolate, subacute or obtuse, 0.4 cm long, 0.15 cm broad; **lateral sepals** porrect, curvate, subspathulate, lanceolate, acute, 0.5 cm long, 0.15 cm broad. **Petals** oblique, triangular-lanceolate, acute, 0.4 cm long, 0.15 cm broad. **Lip** incurved slightly, 3-lobed in basal half, 0.4 cm long; side lobes tooth-like; mid-lobe fleshy-subulate, 0.3 cm long; spur dependent or slightly incurved, swollen somewhat, 0.4–0.5 cm long, 0.1 cm in diameter. **Column** truncate, 0.1 cm long.

DISTRIBUTION   Kenya and Tanzania.

HISTORY   Discovered by Mrs W. Moreau on Mondul Mt, west of Arusha in Tanzania in 1942 and described by V.S. Summerhayes in 1945 in the *Botanical Museum Leaflets of Harvard University* (p. 256).

CLOSELY RELATED SPECIES   *Angraecopsis tenerrima* Kraenzl. is a much larger plant than *A. breviloba* and has the largest flowers in the genus with the spur reaching 5 cm or more long, its lip is deeply 3-lobed in the middle and the side lobes are oblanceolate and often bilobulate towards the apex. This species, which has only been found in Tanzania so far, has white flowers. *Angraecopsis elliptica* Summerh. from Nigeria and Cameroon, is distinguished by its pale green flowers, more or less tinged with orange on the deeply 3-lobed lip and by its elliptic-oblong or oblanceolate leaves. *Angraecopsis amaniensis* Summerh. and *A. tenuicalcar* Summerh. are allied to *A. breviloba* but have a longer spur which is never inflated.

Angraecum Bory
Subfamily Epidendroideae
Tribe Vandeae
Subtribe Angraecinae

Very small to large epiphytic, lithophytic or terrestrial herbs. **Stems** non-pseudobulbous, very short to long, very rarely branching, covered by leaf-bases, leafy throughout length. **Leaves** distichous, often fleshy or coriaceous, unequally 2-lobed at apex. **Inflorescences** lateral, axillary, 1- to many-flowered and racemose, rarely branched. **Flowers** very small and insignificant to large and showy, ± fleshy, white, green, yellow or ochre. **Sepals** and **petals** subsimilar, linear-lanceolate. **Lip** often much larger than the other segments, concave, entire or obscurely lobed, spurred at the base, with a central linear ± tapering callus; spur with a broad mouth. **Column** short, deeply cleft in front; rostellum bifid; pollinia 2, waxy; stipes 2, short; viscidia 2.

DISTRIBUTION   Some 200 species widespread in tropical and S. Africa, Madagascar and the adjacent islands.

DERIVATION OF NAME   Derived from the Malayan word *angurek*, for epiphytic orchids resembling *Aerides*, *Vanda*, etc.

TAXONOMY   The name was given by Col. Bory de St Vincent in 1804 in his *Voyages* (p. 359). As *Angraecum* was the earliest genus of Madagascan and African sarcanthoid orchid described, many species no longer considered to be in the genus were originally described there, much as in the way that American epiphytic species were placed in *Epidendrum* in the early days.

The genus *Angraecum* caused many difficulties to botanists in the past because of the differing circumscriptions given to the genus by different botanists. However, the work of Rudolf Schlechter and, latterly, V.S. Summerhayes on the African Angraecoid genera has resulted in the reduction in the size of *Angraecum* into a fairly natural genus and the removal of many aberrant species into different genera such as *Aerangis*, *Rangaeris*, *Tridactyle*, *Jumellea* and *Ypsilopus*. *Angraecum* is now restricted for those species in which the column apex is deeply divided in front, the lip is usually very concave and entire with the base more or less enveloping the column.

L. Garay (1973) in the *Kew Bulletin* revised *Angraecum* at sectional level, in all, accepting 19 sections. This account also gives a useful key to the sections and lists all the specific epithets in the genus. Those still accepted in the genus are placed in their appropriate section or, if now considered synonymous, the accepted specific epithet is given. Many of the species originally described in *Angraecum* are now considered to belong to other genera and the correct name for these species is also given.

TYPE SPECIES   *A. eburneum* Bory
CULTURE   Compost A or mounted. Temp. Winter min. 10–12°C, for montane species, 15°C, for lowland species. All *Angraecum* species require humid conditions, with more or less shade, according to natural habitat. The cooler growing species generally require more shade than the large tropical ones such as *A. eburneum*. These large plants grow well in pots, baskets or even beds, so long as the drainage is good. Small species are usually better grown mounted on slabs of fern-fibre or cork. They all require to be well-watered, especially during active growth.

Angraecum calceolus Thou. [Colour Plate]
A small epiphytic plant. **Stem** very short to short, 3- to 10-leaved. **Leaves** narrowly lanceolate or ligulate, 10–20 cm long, 0.8–1.8 cm broad, borne distichously. **Inflorescences** a little shorter than the leaves, often branched; branches short, 4- to 6-flowered; bracts oval, acute or apiculate. **Flowers** greenish-white. **Sepals** lanceolate, acute or acuminate, 0.8 cm long; lateral sepals keeled on reverse. **Petals** shorter and narrower than the sepals. **Lip** cucullate, ovate-lanceolate, 0.7–1 cm long, 0.4–0.5 cm broad, acuminate; spur cylindrical, 1.5 cm long. **Column** 0.2 cm long.

DISTRIBUTION   Madagascar, the Mascarene Islands, Comoros and the Seychelles.

HISTORY   Originally collected by Aubert du Petit Thouars on Mauritius and figured by him in 1822 in *Orchidées des Iles Australes de l'Afrique* (t. 78).

SYNONYMS   *Aeranthus calceolus* (Thou.) S. Moore; *Epidorchis calceolus* (Thou.) O. Ktze.; *Mystacidium calceolus* (Thou.) Cord.; *Macroplectrum calceolus* (Thou.) Finet; *Angraecum rhopaloceras* Schltr.

Angraecum chevalieri Summerh.
A small epiphytic plant. **Stem** erect, leafy throughout, 6–11 cm long, 0.3 cm in diameter. **Leaves** linear-ligulate or narrowly oblong, imbricate at the base, obtusely 2-lobed at apex, 4–7 cm long, 0.6–1 cm broad. **Inflorescence** suberect, 3–4 cm long; rhachis slender; bracts broadly ovate, acute or shortly acuminate. **Flowers** green. **Sepals** lanceolate, acute, 1 cm long, 0.2 cm broad; lateral sepals oblique. **Petals** narrowly lanceolate, acuminate, 1 cm long, 0.12 cm broad. **Lip** elliptic, acuminate, 0.75 cm long, 0.3 cm broad; spur filiform, slightly S-shaped and clavate-inflated above the middle, 1.6–2 cm long. **Column** short, 0.2 cm long.

DISTRIBUTION   W. Africa, Zaïre and Uganda.

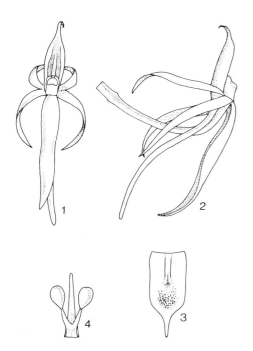

Angraecum chevalieri
1 – Flower (×2)
2 – Flower, side view (×2)
3 – Lip (×3)
4 – Pollinia, stipites and viscidium (×8)

HISTORY Discovered in Sassandra, Ivory Coast, between Sogni and Koualé in 1909 by Auguste Chevalier and described by V.S. Summerhayes in 1936 in the *Kew Bulletin* (p. 230).
CLOSELY RELATED SPECIES Allied to *Angraecum multinominatum* Rendle

Angraecum cultriforme Summerh.

A small epiphytic herb, up to about 15 cm long. **Leaves** distichous, horizontal, narrowly oblong or linear-oblong to ligulate, unequally 2-lobed at apex, up to 6 cm long, 0.5–1 cm broad, articulated below to a pluricostate sheathing base. **Inflorescences** axillary, spreading, shorter than the leaves, 1-flowered; bracts

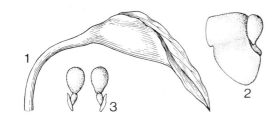

Angraecum cultriforme
1 – Lip and base of spur (×4)
2 – Column, side view (×6)
3 – Pollinia, stipites and viscidia (×13)

ovate, acute, 2–4 cm long. **Flowers** yellow-green or pale ochre to orange-yellow. **Dorsal sepal** reflexed, lanceolate, acute or acuminate, 1.1–1.9 cm long, 0.2–0.3 cm broad; **lateral sepals** similar but oblique and slightly broader. **Petals** reflexed, obliquely lanceolate, acuminate, 1.0–1.5 cm long, 0.15–0.3 cm broad. **Lip** porrect, strongly concave, lanceolate-ovate, acuminate and recurved at the apex, 0.8–1.5 cm long, 0.45–0.6 cm broad, with a central longitudinal ridge-like callus; spur often straight, narrowly cylindrical, slightly inflated towards the apex, 1.7–2.6 cm long. **Column** short, fleshy, 0.1–0.2 cm long, truncate.
DISTRIBUTION Kenya. Tanzania and Zambia.
HISTORY *A. cultriforme* is one of a number of smaller *Angraecum* species with yellowish or greenish flowers found in E. and Central Africa. It was described in 1958 by V.S. Summerhayes in the *Kew Bulletin* (p. 272) based on a specimen collected near Handeni in N.E. Tanzania and flowered in cultivation by Helen Faulkner.

Angraecum dasycarpum Schltr. [Colour Plate]
A small epiphytic plant with cylindrical stems, up to 10 cm long, 0.25–0.3 cm in diameter. **Leaves** dense, oblong, obtuse or shortly apiculate, fleshy with a thinner margin, 7–10 cm long, 0.4–0.7 cm broad. **Inflorescences** very short, covered by sheaths. **Flowers** white. **Sepals** oblong, obtuse, 0.65 cm long. **Petals** oblong-ligulate, obtuse, 0.6 cm long. **Lip** oblong-ligulate, obtuse, slightly attenuate below the middle, concave, 0.55 cm long; spur cylindric-oblong, obtuse, slightly attenuate above the middle, set against the ovary, 0.4 cm long. **Column** very short.
DISTRIBUTION Madagascar, in eastern forests.
HISTORY Described by Rudolf Schlechter in 1918 in *Fedde, Repertorium Specierum Novarum* (p. 337) from a plant lacking exact provenance data but collected by Laggiara in Madagascar.

Angraecum distichum Lindl. [Colour Plate]
A small epiphytic plant with slender leafy stems, often forming large clumps. **Leaves** distichous, falcately oblong-elliptic, bilaterally compressed, sulcate on upper margin, 0.5–1 cm long, 0.3–0.7 cm broad. **Inflorescences** axillary, 1-flowered. **Flower** small, white. **Sepals** spreading, elliptic, obtuse, 0.3–0.4 cm long, 0.15–0.2 cm broad. **Petals** spreading, elliptic-oblong, obtuse, 0.3–0.4 cm long, 0.15 cm broad. **Lip** obscurely 3-lobed, concave, obtuse to apiculate, 0.3 cm long, 0.3 cm broad; side lobes erect around column; spur straight, tapering in apical part, 0.4–0.7 cm long. **Column** very short, 0.1 cm long.

DISTRIBUTION Guinea and Sierra Leone, east to Uganda and south to Angola.
HISTORY This strange little plant which vegetatively resembles *Dendrobium leonis* and some *Lockhartia* species was discovered in Sierra Leone and imported from there by Messrs Loddiges of Hackney, London. John Lindley described it in 1836 in the *Botanical Register* (t. 1781).
CLOSELY RELATED SPECIES See *A. gabonense*.

Angraecum eburneum Bory [Colour Plate]
A large, erect, epiphytic, terrestrial or lithophytic plant, up to 1.3 m tall. **Stem** stout, branched, 10- to 15-leaved. **Roots** stout, long, arising adventitiously along the stem. **Leaves** rigid, coriaceous, ligulate, unequally roundly bilobed at apex, 30 cm or more long, 3 cm broad. **Inflorescence** suberect to horizontal, 15- to 30-flowered; peduncle stout, green; bracts sheathing, dark brown or black. **Flowers** large, showy, white with green or yellow-green sepals, segments fleshy. **Sepals** lanceolate, acute, reflexed, 4–5 cm long, 0.9–1.1 cm broad. **Petals** lanceolate, acute, 3.5–4.5 cm long, 0.9 cm broad. **Lip** broadly ovate to cordate, concave, apiculate in front, 3.5 cm long, 3 cm broad; disc with a central tapering raised callus; spur narrowing gradually to the apex, 6–7 cm long. **Column** very thick and fleshy.
DISTRIBUTION Madagascar, Mascarene Islands, Comoros and E. Africa.
HISTORY Originally discovered by Col. Bory de St Vincent on Réunion and described by him in 1804 in his *Voyages* (p. 359). The typical variety (or subspecies according to some authorities) is confined to the Mascarene Islands. Two further varieties, *superbum* (*Angraecum superbum* Thou.) and *xerophilum*, are found in Madagascar with the former also being found in the Comoros. Var. *superbum* has much larger flowers with the lip reaching 4 cm in length and 4.7 cm in breadth; var. *xerophilum* has smaller flowers and a relatively longer spur. The E. African *Angraecum giryamae* has been reduced to varietal rank by A.B. Rendle with some justification for it differs from the typical form only in minor details of tepal size.
SYNONYMS include *Limodorum eburneum* (Bory) Willd.; *Angraecum virens* Lindl.; *Angorchis eburnea* (Bory) O. Ktze.; *Angraecum superbum* Thou.; *Angraecum brongniartianum* Rchb.f.; *Angraecum comorense* Kraenzl.; *Angraecum voeltzkowianum* Kraenzl.; *Angraecum giryamae* Rchb.f.

Angraecum eichlerianum Kraenzl.
[Colour Plate]
A large epiphytic plant, 60 cm or more high; adventitious roots prominent. **Stems** erect,

covered with leaf-bases, 30–60 or more cm long, 0.8 cm in diameter, distichously many-leaved. **Leaves** narrowly elliptic-oblong, unequally roundly 2-lobed at the apex, 7–10 cm long, 1.5–4 cm broad. **Inflorescences** arising opposite the leaves, spreading-deflexed. 1-flowered, up to 8 cm long. **Flowers** showy; sepals and petals pale green; lip white. **Sepals** lanceolate, acuminate, 3.5–6 cm long, 0.7–1.1 cm broad. **Petals** linear-lanceolate, acute, up to 5 cm long, 0.8 cm broad. **Lip** ± cordate, obscurely 3-lobed in front, broadest in front, up to 5 cm long, 4–5 cm broad; side lobes projecting forwards beyond the base of the mid-lobe; mid-lobe shortly triangular, acute; spur with a broad conical mouth abruptly constricted in the middle, 3–4 cm long. **Column** short, stout fleshy, deeply bifid in front, 0.5 cm long.

DISTRIBUTION S. Nigeria. Cameroon. Gabon, Zaïre and Angola.

HISTORY Described by F. Kraenzlin in 1882 in *Wittmack, Garten-Zeitung* (p. 434) based on a specimen collected near Kassambra.

CLOSELY RELATED SPECIES Very closely allied to *Angraecum birrimense* Rolfe which has a narrower, almost orbicular lip and shorter sepals. See also *A. infundibulare*.

Angraecum gabonense Summerh.
[Colour Plate]

A small epiphytic herb. **Stems** tufted, slender, branching, dependent but upcurved at the apex, leafy throughout, up to 35 cm long. **Leaves** distichous, fleshy, linear-lanceolate to oblong-lanceolate, subulate-acuminate at apex, 1–2 cm long, 0.2–0.4 cm broad. **Inflorescences** short, 1-flowered. **Flowers** white. **Sepals** spreading, ligulate-oblanceolate, obtuse, 0.6 cm long, 0.2 cm broad. **Petals** similar to sepals. **Lip** concave, orbicular-ovate, apiculate-acuminate, 0.35–0.4 cm long, 0.5 cm broad; spur straight or slightly incurved, slightly inflated towards the apex, 0.25–0.35 cm long. **Column** short, truncate, 0.2 cm long.

DISTRIBUTION Gabon only.

HISTORY Described by V.S. Summerhayes in 1954 in the *Kew Bulletin* (p. 587) based on a specimen collected by Le Testu in 1927 on the Upper N'Gounié River, N.E. of Les Echiras in Gabon.

CLOSELY RELATED SPECIES *A. gabonense* is allied to *A. distichum* but is readily distinguished by its narrower linear-lanceolate and acuminate leaves.

Angraecum infundibulare Lindl.
[Colour Plate]

A large epiphytic plant, 60 cm or more tall. **Stem** elongated, leafy, terete, somewhat zig-zag, rarely branching, covered by sheathing leaf-bases, rooting along length. **Leaves** re-

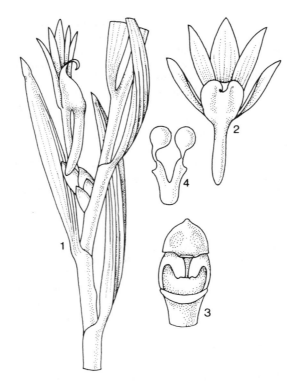

Angraecum gabonense
1 – Stem, leaves and flower (× 4)
2 – Flower (× 4)
3 – Column (× 13)
4 – Pollinia, stipites and viscidium (× 18)

latively thin-textured, narrowly oblong-elliptic or oblanceolate, unequally 2-lobed at apex, up to 20 cm long, 4 cm broad, with a compressed sheathing leaf-base up to 3.5 cm long. **Inflorescences** 1-flowered, emerging through base of leaf-sheaths; peduncle terete, 2–5.5 cm long; bract ovate, acute, 0.6 cm long. **Flowers** very large, showy; sepals, petals and spur pale green; lip white with a green mark in the throat. **Sepals** linear, acuminate, 6–7.5 cm long, 0.5–0.6 cm broad. **Petals** similar but shorter, 5.5–6.5 cm long. **Lip** oval, apiculate, tubular at base, 7.5 cm long, 5 cm broad; spur with a broad mouth, funnel-shaped and erect at base, filiform and decurved in apical two-thirds, up to 18 cm long. **Column** fleshy, 0.5 cm long.

DISTRIBUTION S. Nigeria, Cameroon, Principe, Zaïre, Ethiopia and Uganda; sea level to 1350 m altitude, in rain forest.

HISTORY This is probably the largest-flowered African *Angraecum*. It was described in 1862 by John Lindley in the *Journal of the Linnean Society* (p. 136) based on a specimen collected on the Brass River in S. Nigeria by Barter.

SYNONYM *Mystacidium infundibulare* (Lindl.) Rolfe

CLOSELY RELATED SPECIES *A. infundibulare* is closely related to *A. eichlerianum* and *Angraecum birrimense* Rolfe but differs in its far larger flower with a longer spur always over 10 cm long.

Angraecum leonis (Rchb.f.) Veitch
[Colour Plate]

A medium-sized epiphytic plant. **Stem** short, stout, 4- or 5-leaved. **Leaves** distichous, narrowly ensiform, spreading, falcate, fleshy-coriaceous, 5–25 cm long, 1.6–2.2 cm broad. **Inflorescences** erect or suberect, 1 or 2 from below the leaves, 1- to 7-flowered; peduncle short, 1.5–2 cm long; bracts scarious, very broad. **Flowers** white; segments spreading, fleshy; pedicels compressed, narrowly winged. **Sepals** lanceolate, acuminate, dorsally keeled, 2 cm long, 0.5 cm broad. **Petals** narrowly ovate-lanceolate, attenuate, acute, 2 cm long, 0.6 cm broad. **Lip** concave, broadly ovate-orbicular or cordate, acuminate, 2.4 cm long, 2 cm broad; disc with a short, attenuate, fleshy central ridge; spur filiform below a dilated base, twisted-undulate, 7–9 cm long. **Column** stout, 0.4 cm long, 0.5 cm broad.

DISTRIBUTION Madagascar and the Comoros.

HISTORY Discovered by Leon Humblot in the Comoros, *A. leonis* was first described by H.G. Reichenbach in 1885 in the *Gardeners' Chronicle* (p. 80) as *Aeranthus leonis*. In 1894 J. Veitch transferred it to the genus *Angraecum* in the *Manual of Orchidaceous Plants*.

SYNONYMS *Aeranthus leonis* Rchb.f.; *Angraecum humblotii* Rchb.f.; *Mystacidium leonis* (Rchb.f.) Rolfe; *Macroplectrum leonis* (Rchb.f.) Finet

CLOSELY RELATED SPECIES *A. magdalenae*.

Angraecum magdalenae Schltr. & H. Perr.
[Colour Plate]

A medium-sized lithophytic plant. **Stem** short, 6- to 8-leaved, up to 15 cm long. **Leaves** distichous, fleshy-coriaceous, oblong-ligulate, unequally obtusely 2-lobed at apex, 13–36 cm long, 2.5–4.5 cm broad. **Inflorescence** from below the leaves, 1- to 5-flowered; peduncle stout, 2–3 cm long; bracts yellow, rigid, triangular, rounded at apex. **Flowers** white, very fleshy, large; pedicellate ovary 8 cm long, green. **Sepals** elliptic-lanceolate, attenuate at base, obtusely pointed above, 4–6 cm long, 1.8 cm broad. **Petals** ovate, broader but shorter than the sepals. **Lip** concave, suborbicular-obovate, shortly acuminate, 6 cm long, the acumen extending in a keel; spur with a wide mouth, attenuate-filiform, 10–11 cm long. **Column** 0.5–0.6 cm long, stout.

DISTRIBUTION Madagascar; growing on

unshaded or lightly shaded quartzite boulders at about 2000 m altitude.
HISTORY Discovered by Madeleine Durchud on Mt Ibity to the south of Antsirabe in Madagascar and described by Rudolf Schlechter and Henri Perrier de la Bâthie in 1925 in *Fedde, Repertorium Specierum Novarum* (p. 354).
CLOSELY RELATED SPECIES *A. magdalenae* is closely related to *A. leonis*.

Angraecum ochraceum (Ridley) Schltr.
A small epiphytic plant. **Stem** short, several-leaved. **Leaves** narrowly linear-lanceolate, unequally 2-lobed at apex, 10 cm long, 0.4–0.6 cm broad. **Inflorescences** shorter than the leaves, 1-flowered, up to 7.5 cm long; peduncle slender; bracts ovate. **Flowers** small, ochre-coloured. **Sepals** narrowly lanceolate, acute, 0.4 cm long, 0.2 cm broad. **Petals** similar to sepals but shorter and narrower. **Lip** concave, cymbiform, acute; spur filiform, slightly inflated at apex, 1.9 cm long. **Column** very short.
DISTRIBUTION Madagascar.
HISTORY Discovered by the Rev. Deans Cowan at Ankafina in Madagascar and described in 1885 by H.N. Ridley as *Mystacidium ochraceum* in the *Journal of the Linnean Society* (p. 488). Rudolf Schlechter transferred it to the genus *Angraecum* in 1915 in *Beihefte zum Botanischen Zentralblatt* (p. 436).
SYNONYMS *Mystacidium ochraceum* Ridley; *Macroplectrum ochraceum* (Ridley) Finet

Angraecum reygaertii De Wild. [Colour Plate]
An erect or pendulous epiphytic plant. **Stems** long, fairly slender, leafy, covered by leaf-sheaths. **Leaves** oblong, obscurely unequally 2-lobed at rounded apex, 10–15 cm long, 2–3.2 cm broad. **Inflorescences** arising opposite the leaves, suberect or spreading, 1-flowered, about 6 cm long. **Flower** non-resupinate, fairly showy, pure white; lip-base green. **Sepals** lanceolate, acuminate, 2.8–3.2 cm long, 0.4–0.6 cm broad; dorsal sepal reflexed. **Petals** narrowly elliptic-lanceolate, acute, 2.6 cm long, 0.4 cm broad. **Lip** lanceolate to oblong-lanceolate, acute or acuminate, 2.5 cm long, 0.4 cm broad; callus basal, short, a fleshy ridge; spur almost straight, 5–6 cm long. **Column** short, stout, 0.4 cm long.
DISTRIBUTION Cameroon, Zaïre and Uganda.
HISTORY F. Reygaert discovered this pretty species in 1913 at Mobwasa in Zaïre and it was described in 1916 by E. de Wildeman in the *Bulletin du Jardin Botanique, Bruxelles* (p. 190).

Angraecum scottianum Rchb.f. [Colour Plate]
A small epiphytic plant, with a tufted habit. **Stems** erect or pendent, elongated, cylindrical,

10–15 cm long, 6- to 8-leaved. **Leaves** subcylindrical or terete, subulate, bicarinate, canaliculate, 9 cm long, 0.3 cm broad. **Inflorescence** 1-flowered (rarely more opening in succession); peduncle 7–8 cm long, thickened towards the apex; bracts scarious, tubular, 0.8 cm long. **Flowers** non-resupinate, white. **Sepals** ligulate, acute, 2.7 cm long, 0.4 cm broad. **Petals** similar but narrower. **Lip** uppermost in flower, concave, orbicular-reniform, shortly acuminate in front, auricles curved up on either side of column, 2.5–2.7 cm long, 2.5–4 cm broad; spur pendent, filiform-attenuate, 9–10 cm long. **Column** short, stout.
DISTRIBUTION Comoros; growing in exposed positions, 350–600 m altitude.
HISTORY *A. scottianum* was introduced into cultivation by R. Scott who received it from the Comoros. H.G. Reichenbach named it after him in 1878 in the *Gardeners' Chronicle*. (n.s. 10: p. 556).
SYNONYMS *Angraecum reichenbachianum* Kraenzl.: *Angorchis scottiana* (Rchb.f.) O. Ktze.
CLOSELY RELATED SPECIES *A. scottianum* is closely allied to *Angraecum pseudofilicornu* H. Perr., but has cylindrical leaves.

Angraecum sesquipedale Thou. [Colour Plate]
An epiphytic or more rarely lithophytic plant, often growing in dense tufts, up to 1 m high. **Stems** rarely straight, shorter than the leaves, many-leaved. **Roots** stout, greyish, adventitious. **Leaves** distichous, ligulate, coriaceous, unequally roundly 2-lobed at the apex, 22–30 cm long, 3 cm broad. **Inflorescences** shorter than the leaves, 2- to 6-flowered; peduncle stout, 10–12 cm long; bracts one-quarter the length of the pedicel and ovary. **Flowers** large, showy, white or creamy-white, star-shaped; segments spreading, fleshy. **Sepals** ovate-lanceolate, 7–9 cm long, 2 cm broad. **Petals** similar to sepals, 7–8 cm long, 2.5–2.8 cm broad. **Lip** concave, ovate-subpandurate, obtusely-acuminate at apex, 6.5–8 cm long, 3.5–4 cm broad; callus of 2 bosses at mouth of spur running into a central raised ridge in front; spur pendent, 30–35 cm long. **Column** stout, 1 cm long.
DISTRIBUTION E. Madagascar; sea level to 100 m altitude.
HISTORY Discovered by Aubert du Petit Thouars in E. Madagascar and described by him in 1822 in *Orchidées des Iles Australes de l'Afrique* (tt. 66, 67). This species is commonly cultivated and is colloquially known as the 'comet orchid'. It achieved fame when Charles Darwin predicted that it would be pollinated by a long-tongued hawk-moth. His prediction was corroborated when it was indeed found

to be pollinated by a hawk-moth which was named *Xanthopan morganii praedicta* in honour of Darwin's foresight.
SYNONYMS *Aeranthus sesquipedale* (Thou.) Lindl.; *Angorchis sesquipedalis* (Thou.) O. Ktze.; *Macroplectrum sesquipedale* (Thou.) Pfitz.; *Mystacidium sesquipedale* (Thou.) Rolfe

Anguloa Ruiz & Pavon
Subfamily Epidendroideae
Tribe Maxillarieae
Subtribe Zygopetalinae

Large epiphytic or terrestrial herbs with short stems sheathed at the base and few-leaved above, developing into fleshy pseudobulbs. **Leaves** imbricate, large, plicate. **Inflorescences** lateral, basal, erect, 1-flowered, clothed with several loose sheaths. **Flowers** large, showy, almost cup-shaped, rather fleshy, ± nodding. **Sepals** broad, subequal; lateral sepals oblique, cucullate-rounded at the base. **Petals** similar to dorsal sepal but smaller. **Lip** 3-lobed, erect, parallel to column; side lobes large, often rounded in front; mid-lobe small; disc with a central longitudinal callus. **Column** erect, stout, wingless, with a stout foot, apex of column with a pair of triangular-lanceolate appendages in front; pollinia 4.
DISTRIBUTION A small genus of about ten species in Venezuela, Colombia, Ecuador and Peru.
DERIVATION OF NAME Named in honour of Don Francisco de Angulo who was Director-General of Mines in Peru and a keen student of the local flora at that time.
TAXONOMY Described in 1794 by Hipolito Ruiz and José Pavon in *Prodromus Florae Peruvianae et Chilensis* (p. 118, t. 26) based on *Anguloa uniflora*. *Anguloa* is allied to *Lycaste*, with which it has been hybridised, but is easily distinguished by its tulip-like subglobose flowers.
  Rudolf Schlechter revised the genus in 1916 in *Orchis*, dividing the species into two sections: *(Eu)Anguloa* with a glabrous lip and prominent side lobes to the rostellum and *Guloanga* with a pubescent lip and a less deeply-lobed rostellum.
TYPE SPECIES *A. uniflora* Ruiz & Pavon
CULTURE Compost A. Temp. Winter min. 12–15°C. As for *Lycaste*. The flowers appear with the new growths from the base of mature pseudobulbs. Water must be very carefully given until after root growth is well established. It is important to keep the new shoots dry. During growth, the plants need moist humid conditions with good shade, but after leaf-fall, much less water should be given and a cooler, lighter place chosen.

Anguloa cliftonii Rolfe [Colour Plate]

A large terrestrial plant, 30–40 cm tall. **Pseudo-bulbs** clustered, ovoid-oblong, 11–15 cm long, 4.5–6.5 cm in diameter, 2- to 3-leaved. **Leaves** elliptic-oblong, acuminate, subundulate, attenuate at the base, 15–30 cm long, 7–9 cm broad. **Inflorescences** erect, 20–26 cm long, covered with imbricating sheaths; bracts elliptic-lanceolate, acute, 5–6 cm long. **Flower** large, campanulate, suberect; sepals and petals lemon-yellow; petals lined purple at the base and transversely lined and reticulated above; lip brownish-yellow, spotted with brown on the limb of the front lobe. **Dorsal sepal** elliptic-oblong, subobtuse, about 10 cm long, 5 cm broad; **lateral sepals** orbicular-elliptic, falcate-incurved at the subobtuse apex, 7.5 cm long, 4 cm broad. **Petals** orbicular-ovate, subobtuse, 7.5 cm long, 4.5 cm broad. **Lip** erect, clawed, 4 cm long; claw ligulate, 1 cm long; lamina 3-lobed, saccate at the base; side lobes falcate-incurved, obtuse, 0.8 cm long; mid-lobe broadly clawed, triangular, pubescent, acuminate, with a 2-lobed or obcordate basal callus. **Column** fleshy, 3.5 cm long.

DISTRIBUTION Colombia.
HISTORY Introduced into cultivation by Messrs Charlesworth of Hayward's Heath, Sussex, England. It was first flowered by J. Talbot Clifton of Lytham Hall, Lancashire, England, after whom it was named by R.A. Rolfe in 1910 in the *Kew Bulletin* (p. 160).
CLOSELY RELATED SPECIES *A. cliftonii* is superficially similar to *A. clowesii* which, however, has a distinct lip with narrowly oblong side lobes, acute in front, a pubescent mid-lobe to the lip which lacks a distinct claw and is acutely 3-lobed near the apex, and a pubescent apex to the oblong, central callus. The side lobes of the lip in *A. cliftonii* are streaked with purplish-brown whereas in *A. clowesii* they are uniformly orange-yellow.

Anguloa clowesii Lindl. [Colour Plate]

A large terrestrial plant. **Pseudobulbs** clustered, conical-pyriform, sulcate, slightly compressed, up to 13 cm long, 7 cm in diameter, several-leaved. **Leaves** plicate, obovate, obtuse, 45–80 cm long, 26 cm broad. **Inflorescences** erect, up to 30 cm long, 1-flowered; peduncles stout, covered with large, slightly inflated sheaths. **Flower** large, showy; sepals and petals thick, rigid, lemon-yellow; lip fleshy-rigid, pale creamy-green or yellow with a waxy shine; column white. **Sepals** elliptic, subacute or apiculate, concave, 6.5–7 cm long, 5 cm broad. **Petals** elliptic, similar to sepals but slightly smaller. **Lip** concave, elliptic in outline, 3-lobed towards the apex, hinged to column-foot, 4 cm long, 2.5 cm broad; side lobes erect, obliquely triangular, acute in front; mid-lobe

fleshy, subrhombic, shortly glandular-pubescent; callus at base of mid-lobe, porrect, shortly bifurcate, glandular-pubescent. **Column** stout, 2.5 cm long.

DISTRIBUTION Venezuela and Colombia.
HISTORY Discovered by J. Linden near Jaji in Mérida province in 1842 and shortly afterwards by L. Schlim near Ocaña. It first flowered in cultivation for the Rev. John Clowes of Manchester and was described by John Lindley in 1844 in the *Botanical Register* (misc. 29).
CLOSELY RELATED SPECIES See *A. cliftonii*.

Anguloa uniflora Ruiz & Pavon
[Colour Plate]

A large terrestrial or epiphytic plant. **Pseudobulbs** clustered oblong-conical, with several longitudinal grooves, up to 15 cm long. 6 cm broad, covered when young with several imbricate, leaf-bearing sheaths, 1- or 2-leaved at apex. **Leaves** obovate, subobtuse, erect-spreading, plicate, up to 45 cm long, 16 cm broad. **Inflorescence** erect, from the base of the pseudobulb, 1-flowered, up to 25 cm long. **Flower** showy, fleshy; sepals and petals white with small red spots on inner surface; lip white marked with pale chestnut-brown on the dorsal surface, callus yellow; column white, yellow at the base. **Sepals** ovate, concave, subacute or apiculate, 5–6.6 cm long, 3.2–3.6 cm broad; lateral sepals forming a mentum with the column-foot. **Petals** elliptic, subacute, 5 cm long, 2.4 cm broad. **Lip** subquadrate-obcordate, 3-lobed at the apex, 3 cm long, 2.9 cm broad; side lobes erect, rounded in front, larger than the mid-lobe; mid-lobe shortly triangular, decurved; callus porrect, fleshy, at base of mid-lobe. **Column** stout, subterete, 3 cm long.

DISTRIBUTION Colombia and Venezuela south to Peru.
HISTORY Collected for the first time by H. Ruiz and J. Pavon at Muña in Peru and described by them in 1798 in their *Systema Vegeta-*

Anguloa lips
1 – *A. uniflora* (× $\frac{4}{5}$)
2 – *A. clowesii* (× $\frac{4}{5}$)

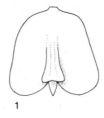

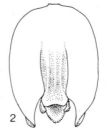

bilium Florae Peruvianae et Chilensis (p. 228). It first flowered in cultivation in 1842 in the collection of G. Barker of Birmingham.
SYNONYMS *Anguloa eburnea* B.S. Williams; *A. turneri* B.S. Williams

---

Anneliesia Brieger & Lueckel
Subfamily Epidendroideae
Tribe Oncidieae

Large epiphytic herbs. **Stems** pseudobulbous, ovoid, subtended by leaf-bearing sheaths and 2-leaved at the apex. **Leaves** thinly coriaceous. **Inflorescences** axillary from basal leaf sheaths, erect or spreading, laxly few-flowered, simply racemose. **Flowers** large, showy, opening widely. **Sepals** and **petals** subsimilar, spreading, free, yellow or greenish-yellow blotched with purple-brown. **Lip** sessile, tubular or funnel-shaped, inserted at the base at 45° to the column, lacking a spur, with a callus of 5–7 raised ridges in basal part of lip. **Column** short, fleshy, with 2 lateral auricles or wings and a terminal erose margin overtopping the anther; pollinia 2, ovoid, deeply cleft, attached by an oblanceolate stipe to a small circular viscidium.

DISTRIBUTION A monotypic genus.
DERIVATION OF NAME Named in honour of Frau Anneliese Brieger Kaiser, the wife of the geneticist and orchidologist Professor F.G. Brieger of the University of São Paulo, Brazil.
TAXONOMY *Anneliesia* is a segregate from *Miltonia* that was established in 1983 in the journal *Die Orchideen* (p. 130) by F.G. Brieger and Emil Lueckel. It differs from *Miltonia*, in which genus it was previously included, because of its distinctive callus of 5–7 ridges which emerge from a pubescent swelling at the base of the lip, and the funnel-shaped lip which is inserted at 45° to the base of the column.

The generic delimitation of this genus and its close allies is problematic and remains the subject of much debate at the present time. Undoubtedly a survey of this group of genera is needed to clarify relationships that are still unclear.
TYPE SPECIES *Miltonia candida* Lindl.
CULTURE Temp. Winter min. 12°C. Grown as Brazilian miltonias in a medium epiphyte compost. Flowers from summer to autumn.

Anneliesia candida (Lindl.) Brieger & Lueckel [Colour Plate]

A large epiphyte with ovoid somewhat compressed pseudobulbs up to 10 cm long, 3 cm in diameter, 2-leaved at the apex and subtended by 2 or more foliaceous sheaths. **Leaves** narrowly elliptic to oblanceolate, acute, 8–20 cm long, 2.8–3.4 cm wide. **Inflorescences** erect, 3- to 7-flowered, 23–40 cm long; peduncle and rhachis terete; bracts lanceolate, acute, 8–18 mm long. **Flowers** large, up to 9 cm across; sepals and petals yellow or greenish-yellow with large red-brown blotches; lip white, with purplish veins, or less commonly pink; pedicel and ovary 2.5–3.7 cm long. **Sepals** oblong-elliptic, acute, 3.7–4.7 cm long, 0.8–1.4 cm wide. **Petals** elliptic, obtuse or subacute, 3.5–4.5 cm long, 0.8–1.6 cm wide. **Lip** funnel-shaped, obovate-subcircular, very obscurely 3-lobed in the apical half, 3–3.7 cm long, 2.5–3.7 cm wide, the apical margin erose; callus of 5–7 raised veins in the basal part of the lip. **Column** erect, 10–14 mm long, with lateral tooth-like wings in the middle and an erose apical margin.

DISTRIBUTION   E. Brazil only.
HISTORY John Lindley described this attractive orchid in 1838 as *Miltonia candida* in the *Botanical Register* (misc. no. 29) based on a collection flowered by Messrs Loddiges. It was transferred as the type of the new genus *Anneliesia* in 1983 by Brieger and Lueckel in the journal *Die Orchideen* (p. 130).
SYNONYMS *Miltonia candida* Lindl.; *Oncidium candidum* (Lindl.) Rchb.f. non Lindl.

Anoectochilus **Blume**
Subfamily Spiranthoideae
Tribe Cranichideae
Subtribe Goodyerinae

Small terrestrial herbs with creeping horizontal stems. **Leaves** petiolate, ovate or lanceolate, often prettily marked on the veins with gold, purple or white. **Inflorescence** terminal, erect, spicate, glandular-pubescent. **Flowers** small. **Sepals** free; dorsal sepal forming a hood with the petals. **Petals** small, narrowly acuminate. **Lip** erect, adnate to the base of the column, contracted into an entire, toothed or pectinate claw beyond the saccate, spurred base and with 2 or rarely 4 terminal, wing-like lobes; spur exserted beyond the bases of the sepals and bicallose within. **Column** short, appendaged in front; stigmatic lobes lateral; pollinia narrowed into short or long caudicles.
DISTRIBUTION   About 25–40 species from India and S.E. Asia to Australia, Polynesia and adjacent islands; growing in moist humus in the deep shade in forests.
DERIVATION OF NAME   From the Greek *anoektos* (open) and *cheilos* (lip) in reference to the open appearance of the lip achieved by a sharp bend on the isthmus which directs the apical part of the lip downwards.
TAXONOMY   Described in 1828 by C.L.

Blume in *Flora Javae* (praef. vi), *Anoectochilus* has been conserved as a generic name over *Anecochilus* Blume published in 1825 in *Bijdragen* (p. 411). The treatment of this genus by R. Holttum (1964) in the *Orchids of Malaya* is followed here. He included *Odontochilus* within his interpretation of the genus *Anoectochilus*, thus broadening the genus to include about 40 species. Species of *Odontochilus* have green leaves and a saccate base to the lip whilst those of *Anoectochilus* have coloured leaves and a distinct spur. However, *A. calcaratus* (Hooker f.) Ridley is intermediate between the two and species in both have the characteristic flanges on the edges of the claw of the lip. This amalgamation still leaves us with a very natural genus.
TYPE SPECIES   *A. setaceus* Blume Lindl. [= *Anecochilus setaceus* Blume].
SYNONYM   *Odontochilus* Blume
CULTURE   Compost C + chopped live *Sphagnum* moss. Temp. Winter min. 15°C. These plants, although sometimes temperamental, grow quite rapidly under the correct conditions. They require high humidity and good shade at all times, with evenly moist compost. They should be grown in well-drained shallow pans, and may need the extra shelter of a glass frame to succed.

Anoectochilus sikkimensis **King & Pantling**
A small terrestrial plant with a creeping stem, 0.6 cm in diameter. **Leaves** 4–5, elliptic-ovate, acute, narrowed to a broad sheathing petiole, 5–7 cm long, 2.5–3.5 cm broad, upper surface very dark red, with a velvety sheen, veined with golden yellow. **Inflorescence** erect, 15–23 cm long, several-flowered; bracts lanceolate; ovary glandular-pubescent. **Flowers** 1.5 cm long; sepals olive-green and white; lip white with green teeth on the claw. **Dorsal sepal** oblong, obtuse, concave; **lateral sepals** oblong, acute, spreading. **Petals** oblanceolate, beaked near the apex. **Lip** with 2 divergent cuneate lobes, the claw with 4 pairs of short, forward-pointing teeth; spur pouch-like short, bifid, with ovoid calli within; **Column** with 2 parallel, raised lines below large, ovate rostellum resting on a

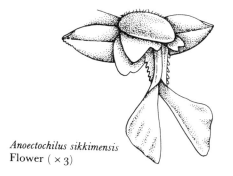

Anoectochilus sikkimensis
Flower (× 3)

large, forcipate process beneath which are 2 flat, converging calli.
DISTRIBUTION   India (Sikkim); 900–1500 m altitude.
HISTORY   Discovered in Sikkim by R. Pantling and described by him and Sir George King in 1896 in the *Journal of the Asiatic Society of Bengal* (p. 124).
CLOSELY RELATED SPECIES Differs from *Anoectochilus roxburghii* Lindl, which it resembles in its leaves, in its smaller flowers, differently-shaped petals and pollinia and in the terminal lobes of the lip and in the teeth of the claw which are much smaller.

Ansellia **Lindl.**
Subfamily Epidendroideae
Tribe Cymbidieae
Subtribe Cymbidiinae

Large epiphytic or rarely terrestrial herbs. **Pseudobulbs** tall, tufted, fusiform, several-noded, leafy, with many aerial roots given off from the base. **Leaves** plicate, petiolate, articulate, fairly thin-textured; leaf-base persistent. **Inflorescences** paniculate, erect, spreading, many flowered. **Flowers** resupinate, medium-sized, showy, yellow, ± marked with pale or deep maroon-brown. **Sepals** and **petals** free, subsimilar spreading. **Lip** 3-lobed, porrect, lacking a spur, 2- or 3-keeled along disc. **Column** porrect, somewhat arcuate, semiterete, auriculate at base; pollinia 4 in 2 closely appressed pairs, waxy; stipe 1; viscidium 1, lunate.
DISTRIBUTION   Probably only two very variable species widespread in tropical Africa and eastern S. Africa.
DERIVATION OF NAME   Named by John Lindley in honour of John Ansell who collected the type species on Fernando Po (now Macias Nguema) in 1841.
TAXONOMY   Described by Lindley in 1844 in the *Botanical Register* (sub t. 12), *Ansellia* is superficially similar to *Cymbidium* in many characteristics, although quite different in its manner of growth. The auricles at the base of the column, the 4 pollinia and the very narrow viscidium firming away to each side, serve to distinguish it as well.
Only *Ansellia* and *Graphorkis* of the African orchid genera have erect white roots around the base of the pseudobulbs.
The genus was revised by V.S. Summerhayes in the *Kew Bulletin of Miscellaneous Information* (1937).
TYPE SPECIES   *A. africana* Lindl.
CULTURE   Compost A. Temp. Winter min. 15°C. When the new growths appear, the

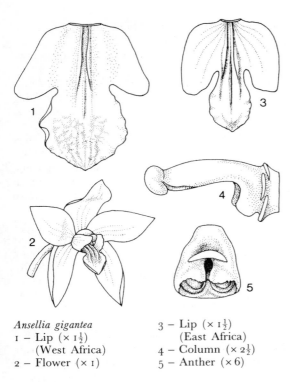

Ansellia gigantea
1 – Lip (× 1½)
   (West Africa)
2 – Flower (× 1)
3 – Lip (× 1½)
   (East Africa)
4 – Column (× 2½)
5 – Anther (× 6)

plants may be repotted if necessary, using relatively large containers, as root growth is vigorous. Water must be given carefully until the roots are well-developed, after which plenty of water is required. During growth, shade should be applied, but only enough to prevent scorching of the leaves. When the pseudobulbs are fully grown, the plants should remain almost dry.

Ansellia africana Lindl. [Colour Plate]

A robust epiphytic plant forming large clumps. **Pseudobulbs** cane-like, fusiform-cylindrical, many-noded, yellow, 25–50 cm or more long, 2–3 cm broad, 6- to 7-leaved. **Roots** white, forming dense masses around the base of the plant. **Leaves** narrowly ligulate-lanceolate, acute, plicate. 20–30 cm long, 2.5–4.0 cm broad. **Inflorescence** mostly produced from near apex of the pseudobulbs, paniculate, up to 50 cm long, many flowered; branches 5–6, spreading. **Flowers** variable in shape, 3–5 cm across; pure yellow or yellow, spotted with maroon or brown on sepals and petals; lip orange-yellow, lined with red-brown on side lobes, callus orange-yellow or yellow. **Sepals** oblong-ligulate to narrowly elliptic, rounded or acute. **Petals** ligulate to narrowly elliptic, acute or rounded. **Lip** 3-lobed in basal half; side lobes erect, narrowly oblong; mid-lobe oblong-oblanceolate, subacute; callus of 3 longitudinal ridges along length of disc. **Column** arcuate, slender 1 cm long.

DISTRIBUTION Tropical and S. Africa; in drier warmer areas along river valleys and by the coast.

HISTORY *Ansellia africana*, the well-known Leopard orchid, was described by John Lindley in 1844 in the *Botanical Register* (sub t. 12) based on a collection made by Ansell on the island of Fernando Po. It is a wide-ranging species, especially variable in its flower size, colouration and lip shape. Summerhayes (1937) considered this variation and concluded that two species should be recognised: *A. africana* from W. and C. Africa, with a broad lip with 3 prominent ridges to the callus, and *A. gigantea*, ranging from the Sudan south to S. Africa, with narrower segments and only 2 prominent ridges on the lip. With more material at hand, recent authors (e.g. Cribb, 1984, in *Flora of Tropical East Africa*) have considered that the variation is such that only one species, *A. africana*, can be recognised, albeit with many recognisable and often geographically based forms.

Two plants are illustrated here: the former specimen agrees well with W. African *A. africana*, while the latter is a S. African plant that is typical of *A. gigantea* var. *gigantea* [Colour plate]. The E. African forms referable to *A. gigantea* var. *nilotica* are in many ways intermediate.

SYNONYMS *Ansellia gigantea* Rchb.f.; *A. nilotica* (Baker) N.E. Brown; *A. congolensis* Rodigas; *A. confusa* N.E. Brown; *A. humilis* Bulliard

Arachnis Blume
Subfamily Epidendroideae
Tribe Vandeae
Subtribe Sarcanthinae

Scandent, usually terrestrial herbs with long, branching stems (rarely short and stout). **Leaves** distichous, complanate, oblong or gradually narrowing towards the apex, sheathing at the base. **Inflorescence** rigid, short or long, simple or branched, few- to many-flowered. **Flowers** often showy, fragrant. **Sepals** and **petals** subsimilar, spreading, narrow, broader towards the apex. **Lip** articulated to the column-foot by a short flexible strap, 3-lobed; side lobes broad, quadrangular to triangular, erect, porrect; mid-lobe fleshy, with a raised mid-ridge, and a fleshy, blunt to attenuate protuberance below the apex. **Column** short; thick; pollinia 4; stipe broad, short; viscidium broadly ovate.

DISTRIBUTION S.E. Asia, Indonesia, the Philippines, New Guinea and the Solomon Islands; about six species.

DERIVATION OF NAME From the Greek *arachne* (spider), from the fancied resemblance of the flowers to a spider.

TAXONOMY The treatment of the genus has varied greatly since it was first described by C.L. Blume in 1825 in *Bijdragen* (p. 365). Since that time species included in *Arachnis* have also been variously placed in the following genera: *Aerides*, *Arachnanthe*, *Armodorum*, *Arrhynchium*, *Dimorphorchis*, *Esmeralda*, *Renanthera*, *Stauropsis*, *Trichoglottis*, *Vanda* and *Vandopsis*. The taxonomy of *Arachnis* has been discussed by many botanists in the last 150 years, including John Lindley, H.G. Reichenbach, E. Pfitzer, Rudolf Schlechter, J.J. Smith and R. Holttum. Their ideas have been discussed by Kiat Tan in *Selbyana* in 1975 and his treatment of *Arachnis* and the allied genera, *Esmeralda*, *Armodorum* and *Dimorphorchis* is followed here.

Arachnis can be distinguished from *Vandopsis* and *Renanthera* by the structure of the lip and its relation to the column; from *Esmeralda* and *Armodorum* by the structure of the lip; and from *Dimorphorchis* by the lack of floral dimorphism exhibited by *Arachnis*.

TYPE SPECIES *A. moschifera* Blume [= *A. flosaëris* (L.) Rchb.f.].

CULTURE Compost A. Temp. Winter min. 15°C. The smaller growing species may be grown in baskets, but the remainder should be grown in pots, with some support provided for the tall, climbing stems. The plants require plenty of water at all times and as much light as possible, short of burning the leaves when grown under glass. They are often reluctant to flower until they have grown to a considerable size.

Arachnis flosaëris (L.) Rchb.f. [Colour Plate]

A large plant with terete stems, 120–250 cm tall. **Leaves** ligulate or linear-oblong, notched at the apex, 10–18 cm long, up to 5 cm broad. **Inflorescences** simple or paniculate, ascending or drooping, 60–160 cm long; branches short, divaricate, 2- to 3-flowered. **Flowers** showy, 7.5–10 cm across, musk-scented, dark green or yellow, barred with maroon; lip with several orange lamellae, end of side lobes maroon. **Dorsal sepal** erect, linear, up to 7 cm long, 1.6 cm broad; **lateral sepals** and **petals** narrowly linear-spathulate, falcate, shorter and broader than the dorsal sepal. **Lip** 3-lobed, 1.5–2 cm long, 1.4–2.2 cm broad; side lobes quadrate, recurved on upper surface; mid-lobe obovate, fleshy, acuminate, shortly spurred below, 1.3 cm long. **Column** broad, truncate, 1.3 cm long.

DISTRIBUTION Malaya, Sumatra, Java, Borneo and the Philippines.

HISTORY This, the type species of the genus *Arachnis*, was originally described by Carl von Linné as *Epidendrum flosaëris* in 1753 in *Species Plantarum* (p. 952). It was transferred to the genus *Arachnis* by H.G. Reichenbach in 1886 in *Botanischen Zentralblatt* (p. 343).

SYNONYMS *Aerides arachnites* Sw.; *Renanthera arachnitis* (Sw.) Lindl.; *R. flosaëris* (L.) Rchb.f.; *Limodorum flosaëris* (L.) Sw.; *Epidendrum flosaëris* L.; *Arachnis moschifera* Blume; *Arachnanthe moschifera* Blume

Armodorum Breda

Subfamily Epidendroideae
Tribe Vandeae
Subtribe Sarcanthinae

Scandent, epiphytic or terrestrial plants with monopodial stems sometimes branching near the base. **Leaves** distichous, coriaceous, linear. **Inflorescences** rigid, short or long, simple or branching, few- to many-flowered. **Flowers** fleshy. **Sepals** and **petals** free, subsimilar, spreading, narrowly spathulate. **Lip** articulated to the base of the column by a short strap of flexible tissue, fleshy, 3-lobed; side lobes erect, small; mid-lobe fleshy, dependent, ligulate or ovate, usually with 2 basal callus lobes almost obscuring the mouth of the spur; spur prominent. **Column** short, fleshy; pollinia 4 in 2 pairs, flattened, subequal; stipe short, broad; viscidium broadly ovate to elliptic.
DISTRIBUTION   Four species from S. China and S.E. Asia to the Malay Archipelago.
DERIVATION OF NAME   From the Greek *harmos* (crack in the wall), and *doron* (gift), in possible allusion to its supposed habit of growing in cracks or crevices of rock.
TAXONOMY   A small genus allied to *Aerides* and *Arachnis* and at various times included in both. The recent revision by Kiat Tan (1975) in *Selbyana* has delimited *Armodorum* clearly and clarified its relationships. The genus was originally established by Breda in 1827 in *Genera et Species Orchidearum . . . colligerunt H. Kuhl et J.C. van Hasselt* (t. 6). The four species are readily distinguished from *Arachnis* by the presence of a distinct spur and their distinct flower colour.
TYPE SPECIES   *A. distichum* Breda (= *A. sulingii* (Bl.) Schltr.)
SYNONYM   *Arrhynchium* Lindl.
CULTURE   Temp. Winter min. 15°C. Probably best grown as mounted or hanging specimens. Conditions as for strap-leaved vandas, with plenty of water while growing, and a drier period for dormant, established plants.

Armodorum sulingii (Bl.) Schltr.
[Colour Plate]
A large lithophyte or epiphyte with long branching stems, usually rooting near the base. **Leaves** linear, cyurved, bilobed at apex, 13–30 cm long, 1.2–2.5 cm wide. **Inflorescences** unbranched, shorter or somewhat longer than the leaves, 4- to 7-flowered; bracts scarious,

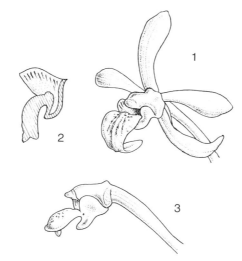

2. *Armodorum sulingii*
    1 – Flower (× 1)
    2 – Lip, longitudinal section (× 3)
    3 – Column, lip, ovary and pedicel (× 1¾)

broadly triangular, 5 mm long. **Flowers** c. 5 cm across; sepals and petals glossy brown; lip light yellow with brown stripes; pedicel and ovary 2.6–2.8 cm long. **Sepals** narrowly oblanceolate, obtuse, 2.2–2.5 cm long, 5–6 mm wide. **Petals** oblanceolate, obtuse, 2 cm long, 7 mm wide. **Lip** 3-lobed, 8–9 mm long, 7 mm wide; side lobes erect, triangular, 4 mm wide; mid-lobe deflexed, convex, elliptic, obtuse, with a raised grooved white callus at the base and 3 verrucose ridges in front; spur short, thick, parallel to the lip mid-lobe, 3–4 mm long. **Column** short, thick, 4–6 mm long.
DISTRIBUTION   Sumatra, Java and Bali; 450–600 m in primary forest.
HISTORY   Originally collected on Mt Suling in Java by Carl Blume and described by him as *Aerides sulingii* in 1825 in his *Bijdragen* (p. 367).
  It was transferred to the genus *Armodorum* by Rudolf Schlechter in 1911 in *Fedde, Repertorium Specierum Novarum* (p. 197).
SYNONYMS   *Aerides sulingii* Bl.; *Armodorum distichum* Breda; *Renanthera sulingii* (Bl.) Lindl.; *Vanda sulingii* (Bl.) Bl.; *Arachnanthe sulingii* (Bl.) Bentham; *Arachnis sulingii* (Bl.) Rchb.f.

Arpophyllum La Llave & Lex.

Subfamily Epidendroideae
Tribe Arethuseae
Subtribe Sobraliinae

Epiphytic or terrestrial herbs with a stout, simple or branching rhizome. **Stems** indurated to slightly pseudobulbous, ± covered by scarious sheaths, 1-leafed at apex. **Leaf** fleshy-coriaceous, articulate. **Inflorescence** terminal, erect, a showy, cylindrical raceme, densely many-flowered, subtended by a large spathaceous bract. **Flowers** small, purple. **Sepals** spreading: lateral sepals gibbous at the base, adnate to the column. **Petals** smaller than the sepals. **Lip** uppermost, saccate at the base. **Column** erect, slightly arcuate, wingless: pollinia 8, waxy, pyriform.
DISTRIBUTION   Five species widespread in Central America.
DERIVATION OF NAME   From the Greek *harpe* (sickle) and *phyllon* (leaf) a reference to the leaf shape of the type species, *A. spicatum*.
TAXONOMY   Described in 1825 by P. La Llave and J. Lexarza in their *Nova Genera et Species* (p. 19).
  Arpophyllum is allied to *Isochilus* and *Elleanthus* but is easily distinguished by its 8 pollinia, the solitary leaf borne at the apex of a stout stem and the inflorescence which is subtended by a single large spathe.
  The genus has been revised by D. Correll in *Lloydia* (1947) and by L. Garay in *Orquideologia* (1970) reprinted, and somewhat modified, in *Orquidea (Mexico)* in 1974. Correll reduced the number of species to two, namely *A. alpinum* Lindl. and *A. spicatum* La Llave & Lex. However, Garay has shown that, in all, five species may be separated which are best identified by their vegetative characteristics. All species are illustrated by Garay in his articles.
TYPE SPECIES   *A. spicatum* La Llave & Lex.
CULTURE   Compost A. Temp. Winter min. 12–15°C. As for *Cattleya*. While growing, the plants need plenty of water and only moderate shade. When growth is complete, a cooler and drier rest is required, but shrivelling should be avoided.

Arpophyllum giganteum Lindl. [Colour Plate]
A medium to large epiphytic plant, up to about 1 m tall. **Stems** erect, up to about 22 cm long, covered by several sheaths, 1-leafed at apex, arising several cm apart from a stout creeping rhizome. **Leaf** arched, coriaceous, linear-ligulate, acute, up to 46 cm long, 4 cm broad, conduplicate at the base. **Inflorescence** erect, a cylindrical raceme up to 18 cm long, 3 cm in diameter; peduncle about 20 cm long, red-violet, enclosed partly by a flattened sheath. **Flowers** small, pink-purple, non-resupinate; column rose-violet. **Sepals** elliptic or oblong-elliptic, obtuse, 0.6 cm long, 0.25–0.3 cm broad. **Petals** oblanceolate, rounded, 0.6 cm long, 0.2 cm broad. **Lip** obovate, rounded and denticulate at apex, saccate at base, 0.65 cm long, 0.4 cm broad. **Column** 0.3–0.4 cm long.
DISTRIBUTION   Common and widely distributed from Mexico south to Costa Rica and

also in Colombia and in Jamaica: 1400–1500 m altitude.

HISTORY John Lindley described this species in the *Annals and Magazine of Natural History* (p. 384) in 1840 based on a collection made by Th. Hartweg between Tanetza and Talea in Mexico.

SYNONYMS *Arpophyllum cardinale* Linden & Rchb.f.; *A. squarrosum* Hort.: *A. jamaicense* Schltr.; *A. stenostachyum* Schltr.

CLOSELY RELATED SPECIES *A. giganteum* is allied to *A. spicatum* which is, however, a smaller plant with falcate-fleshy leaves which are conduplicate throughout and apparently subequitant.

Arpophyllum spicatum La Llave & Lex.

An epiphytic or lithophytic plant, up to 75 cm tall. **Stems** compressed, several-jointed, emitted from a creeping rhizome, up to 16 cm long, covered by tabular sheaths, 1-leafed at apex. **Leaf** ligulate, obtuse, keeled below, conduplicate, fleshy-coriaceous, up to 50 cm long, 4 cm broad. **Inflorescence** erect, up to 40 cm long, densely many-flowered in a cylindrical head, basal sheath compressed, up to 15 cm long. **Flowers** purplish-pink. **Sepals** oblong or elliptic-oblong, 0.5–0.6 cm long, 0.2–0.3 cm broad. **Petals** linear-oblanceolate, rounded or obtuse, margins erose, 0.5 cm long, 0.2 cm broad. **Lip** saccate at base, constricted above, expanded above into an obovate lamina, forming a hood over the column, 0.6 cm long, 0.35 cm broad. **Column** arcuate, 0.4 cm long.

DISTRIBUTION Mexico to Costa Rica, mostly below 1500 m altitude.

HISTORY *A. spicatum* was first collected near Arumbaro in Mexico by P. La Llave and J. Lexarza who described it in 1825 in their *Orchidianum Opusculum* (p. 20).

CLOSELY RELATED SPECIES *A. giganteum* is very closely allied to *A. spicatum* but is a larger plant with a leathery, flattened rather than conduplicate, lorate leaf. Florally, the two species are practically inseparable and many authors consider them to be conspecific.

Arundina Blume
Subfamily Epidendroideae
Tribe Arethuseae
Subtribe Thuniinae

Large terrestrial herbs with rigid, terete, sheathed, unbranched stems. **Leaves** narrow, distichous, grass-like. **Inflorescences** terminal, erect, single or branched. **Flowers** large, showy, purple to white. **Sepals** free, spreading, lanceolate, acuminate. **Petals** broader but similar. **Lip** large, broad, sessile on the base of the

column and embracing it. **Column** long, slender, narrowly winged, lacking a foot: pollinia 8, in compressed, superposed pairs. cohering to a sticky viscidium.

DISTRIBUTION Possibly up to eight species in Sri Lanka, India, China, S.E. Asia and Malaysia across to Tahiti and adjacent islands but excluding the Philippines.

DERIVATION OF NAME The reed-like stems of the species of the genus inspired Blume to base the generic name on the Greek word *arundo* (reed).

TAXONOMY Described in 1825 by C.L. Blume in *Bijdragen* (p. 401). Several species have been distinguished in this genus by various authors and it seems likely that many, if not all of these names, may be reduced to synonymy in one very variable species. R. Holttum discusses the variability of *A. graminifolia* in some detail in the *Orchids of Malaya* (1964).

TYPE SPECIES *A. speciosa* Blume

CULTURE Compost B or C. Temp. Winter min. 15°C. As for *Sobralia*, but somewhat warmer. *Arundina* species often grow better in well-drained beds, but may be grown in large pots. During growth, they need plenty of water and light, with only moderate shade. When growth is complete, after flowering, less water is required.

Arundina graminifolia (D. Don) Hochr.
[Colour Plate]

A large terrestrial herb with erect stems, 1.5–2.5 m long, up to 1.5 cm in diameter. **Leaves** distichous, narrowly oblong-lanceolate, grass-like, 12–30 cm long, 1.6–2.5 cm broad. **Inflorescence** terminal, erect, simple or branched, 15–30 cm long; bracts broad, coriaceous, subacute, 0.6 cm long. **Flowers** large, purple-red, flesh-coloured or white; lip darker-coloured than other segments. **Sepals** narrowly elliptic-lanceolate, acute, up to 3.8 cm long, 1.1 cm broad. **Petals** orbicular-obovate, obtuse, margins undulate, up to 3.9 cm long, 2.2 cm broad. **Lip** ± obscurely 3-lobed, 4 cm long, 3.5 cm broad; side lobes incurved around column, rounded; mid-lobe subquadrate, margins crisped, deeply emarginate at the apex; disc with 3 lamellate nerves. **Column** clavate, 1.5 cm long, narrowly winged.

DISTRIBUTION Java, Indo-China, Thailand, Malaya, the Malay Archipelago, north to the tropical Himalayas of Nepal.

HISTORY Originally described as *Bletia graminifolia* by David Don in his *Prodromus Florae Nepalensis* (p. 29) in 1825 based on a F. Buchanan-Hamilton collection from Suembu in Nepal. B. Hochreutiner transferred it to *Arundina* in 1910 in the *Bulletin of New York Botanic Garden* (p. 270).

SYNONYMS *Arundina bambusifolia* (Roxb.)

Lindl.; *Cymbidium bambusifolium* Roxb.; *Bletia graminifolia* D. Don: *Limodorum graminifolium* (D. Don) Buch.-Ham.

Ascocentrum Schltr.
Subfamily Epidendroideae
Tribe Vandeae
Subtribe Sarcanthinae

Small epiphytic plants resembling *Vanda* in habit. **Inflorescence** erect or spreading, many-flowered. **Flowers** small, often showy, facing all ways, wide opening. **Sepals** and **petals** similar. **Lip** 3-lobed, immovable, fixed to the base of the column and slightly joined to it at the base of the side lobes; mid-lobe tongue-shaped, porrect or decurved; spur shorter than the ovary and pedicel, lacking keels or septa, with a small thickening in the mouth at the base of the mid-lobe. **Column** short, lacking a column-foot; pollinia 2, cleft, on a short stipe which is narrow or widened from a narrow base.

DISTRIBUTION Five species from the Himalayas to S.E. Asia, Java. S. China, Taiwan and the Philippines.

DERIVATION OF NAME From the Greek *ascos* (bag) and *kentron* (spur), alluding to the large spur of the lip.

TAXONOMY Rudolf Schlechter described *Ascocentrum* in 1913 in *Fedde, Repertorium Specierum Novarum, Beihefte* (p. 975) based on *Saccolabium miniatum* Lindl. which he removed from *Saccolabium* because of its distinct lip. *Ascocentrum* is allied to *Vanda* but is distinguished by the smaller distinctively coloured flowers and the narrow stipe and from *Saccolabium* it may be distinguished by its elongate, nearly flat mid-lobe to the lip and the posterior margins of the side lobes of the lip almost touching the column. All of the species are illustrated in the account of the genus by G. Seidenfaden (1988) in *Opera Botanica* (95: 310–318).

TYPE SPECIES *A. miniatum* (Lindl.) Schltr.

CULTURE Compost A. Temp. Winter min. 15°C. As for *Vanda. Ascocentrum* species are small plants and are best grown in baskets or pans. They require a humid atmosphere at all times, with good light and plenty of water while in active growth. At other times, less water should be given.

Ascocentrum ampullaceum (Roxb.) Schltr.
[Colour Plate]

Stem short, simple, several-leaved, with fleshy, cord-like roots. **Leaves** suberect, distichous, ligulate, acutely bifid or truncate and toothed at apex, thick, up to 14 cm long, 1.3 cm broad, keeled below, grooved above. **Inflorescence** subsessile, shorter than the leaves, erect, axillary, up to 8 cm long; bracts minute. **Flowers** 1.8 cm across, deep rose-red; anther purplish. **Sepals** elliptic-obovate, obtuse or rounded, spreading, up to 0.9 cm long, 0.5 cm broad. **Petals** similar to the sepals but slightly longer. **Lip** ligulate, deflexed, rounded at the apex, 0.6–0.7 cm long, 0.3 cm broad; spur straight, longer than the lip, slightly inflated towards the apex, 0.8 cm long. **Column** short.

DISTRIBUTION Tropical Himalayas, Burma and Thailand: 300–900 m altitude.

HISTORY Originally found in Sylhet by M.R. Smith, Dr Roxburgh's correspondent, but later discovered by Dr N. Wallich near Bemphedy. It was described by W. Roxburgh in 1832 in *Flora Indica* (p. 476) as *Aerides ampullaceum*. Rudolf Schlechter transferred it to *Ascocentrum* in 1913 in *Fedde, Repertorium Specierum Novarum, Beihefte* (p. 975).

SYNONYMS *Saccolabium ampullaceum* (Roxb.) Lindl.; *Aerides ampullaceum* Roxb.

Ascocentrum curvifolium (Lindl.) Schltr.
[Colour Plate]

An epiphytic herb, up to 25 cm high. **Stems** short, often bifurcate, stout, woody below, covered by leaf-bases, up to 1 cm in diameter. **Leaves** distichous. narrowly linear, strongly decurved, praemorse or bidentate at apex, 10–30 cm long, 1–1.6 cm broad. **Inflorescence** axillary, much shorter than the leaves, up to 26 cm long, erect, densely many-flowered in the upper two-thirds. **Flowers** 2–2.7 cm across, showy, scarlet with a golden-yellow lip; spur orange; column cinnabar-red, anther-cap purple. **Sepals** obovate-oblong, obtuse or rounded at the apex, 1–1.4 cm long, 0.5–0.75 cm broad. **Petals** obovate, obtuse, 1–1.2 cm long, 0.5–0.6 cm broad. **Lip** obscurely 3-lobed, 0.6 cm long, 0.2 cm broad, truncate, bituberculate at base; side lobes triangular, erect; mid-lobe linear-oblong: spur straight, cylindric, slightly swollen towards apex, 0.6 cm long. **Column** short, stout, 0.15 cm long.

DISTRIBUTION Nepal, India (Assam), Burma, Thailand and Indo-China.

HISTORY Discovered in Nepal by Dr N. Wallich and also by J. Macrae who flowered it in Sri Lanka, this species was described as *Saccolabium curvifolium* by John Lindley in his *Genera and Species of Orchidaceous Plants* (p. 222) in 1833. Rudolf Schlechter transferred it to *Ascocentrum* in 1913 in *Fedde, Repertorium Specierum Novarum, Beihefte* (p. 975).

Some confusion existed when this plant first became known, when it was mixed up with the widespread species *A. miniatum* (Lindl.) Schltr. Even Lindley confused it in his herbarium, for a single sheet bears plants of both species on it.

Furthermore, the plant figured as *Saccolabium miniatum* Lindl. in the *Botanical Magazine* (t. 5326) is in reality *A. curvifolium*.

SYNONYMS *Saccolabium curvifolium* Lindl.; *S. rubrum* Lindl.; *S. miniatum* Hooker non Lindl.

CLOSELY RELATED SPECIES *A. curvifolium* may be readily distinguished from *A. miniatum* by its longer, light-green leaves, larger inflorescences and flowers, and by the details of the lip.

Ascocentrum miniatum (Lindl.) Schltr.
[Colour Plate]

An erect epiphytic herb, up to 25 cm or so tall. **Stem** erect, stout, covered by persistent distichous leaf-bases, up to about 20 cm long. **Leaves** distichous, ligulate, conduplicate, toothed at apex, 5–25 cm long, 1–1.4 cm broad. **Inflorescences** erect, up to 24 cm long, densely many-flowered in a more or less cylindrical raceme. **Flowers** small, showy, about 1 cm long, orange or scarlet. **Sepals** elliptic-obovate, obtuse, up to 0.8 cm long, 0.3 cm broad. **Petals** similar to sepals but shorter. **Lip** ligulate, subacute, deflexed, 0.4 cm long, 0.15 cm broad; spur cylindric, straight, dependent, 0.7–0.9 cm long. **Column** short, terete.

DISTRIBUTION Himalayas to Thailand, Malaya and Java.

HISTORY Originally imported to England by Messrs Veitch from Java and flowered by both C. Warner and Rucker before it was described by John Lindley in 1847 in *Botanical Register* (sub t. 26) as *Saccolabium miniatum*. Rudolf Schlechter transferred it to *Ascocentrum* in 1913 in *Fedde, Repertorium Specierum Novarum, Beihefte* (p. 975).

SYNONYMS *Saccolabium miniatum* Lindl.; *Gastrochilus miniatus* (Lindl.) O. Ktze.

CLOSELY RELATED SPECIES See *A. curvifolium*.

Ascoglossum Schltr.
Subfamily Epidendroideae
Tribe Vandeae
Subtribe Sarcanthinae

Epiphytic plants with elongate leafy rarely branching stems; roots in the basal part, flexuous, densely sublepidote-rugulose. **Leaves** coriaceous, distichous, linear, unequally bilobed. **Inflorescences** lateral, emerging through the sheathing leaf bases, branching, laxly many-flowered; peduncle long, terete. **Flowers** showy, rose-purple; pedicel and ovary glabrous. **Sepals** and **petals** subsimilar, reflexed, free; lateral sepals clawed. **Lip** 3-lobed, saccately spurred; side lobes erect; mid-lobe small, ovate-lanceolate; spur clavate to subglobose. **Column**

short, fleshy; pollinia 4 in 2 pairs; stipe linear; viscidium large, subquadrate.

DISTRIBUTION A small genus of one or possibly two species in the Moluccas, New Guinea and the Solomon Islands.

DERIVATION OF NAME From the Greek *askos* (bag) and *glossa* (tongue), in allusion to the saccate lip.

TAXONOMY A genus erected by Rudolf Schlechter in 1913 in his definitive account of the orchids of German New Guinea in *Fedde, Repertorium Specierum Novarum, Beihefte* (p. 974). The genus is a segregate of *Saccolabium* in the sense used before Schlechter's work. It is most closely allied to *Ascocentrum* but differs in having a branching inflorescence, clawed lateral sepals, a shorter column and distinct pollinarium.

T.YPE SPECIES *A. calopterum* (Rchb.f.) Schltr.

CULTURE Temp. Winter min. 15°C. May be grown mounted or in baskets like vandas. Water well when actively growing.

Ascoglossum calopterum (Rchb.f.) Schltr.
[Colour Plate]

A large epiphyte with ascending or arcuate stems 40–50 cm long, 8–15 mm in diameter; roots stout 4–6 mm in diameter. **Leaves** arcuate-spreading, strap-like, unequally bilobed at the apex, obtuse, 10–25 cm long, 2–2.5 cm wide; sheathing bases up to 2.5 cm long. **Inflorescences** branching, 30–60 cm long; peduncle 20–30 cm long, purple; branches about 6-flowered; bracts triangular-ovate, 2–3 mm long. **Flowers** deep rose-purple, lip suffused with orange, bilaterally flattened; pedicel and ovary purple, 13–18 mm long. **Dorsal sepal** reflexed, oblong-spathulate, obtuse, 14 mm long, 5 mm wide; **lateral sepals** reflexed, narrowly spathulate, obtuse or acute, 15–16 mm long, 6–9 mm wide. **Petals** reflexed, narrowly elliptic, acute or obtuse, 11–12 mm long, 4 mm wide. **Lip** 3-lobed, 12 mm long; side lobes erect, attached to the column, 4 mm long, 2.5 mm wide; mid-lobe ligulate, acute, 2 mm long, 1 mm wide; spur clavate, 5–9 mm long. **Column** 5–6 mm long.

DISTRIBUTION The Moluccas, New Guinea, the Philippines and the Solomon Islands; sea level to 300 m.

HISTORY This attractive orchid was first described as *Saccolabium calopterum* by H.G. Reichenbach in 1882 in the *Gardeners' Chronicle* (n.s. 18: p. 520). It was transferred to *Ascoglossum* by Schlechter in 1913 in *Fedde, Repertorium Specierum Novarum Beihefte* (p. 975).

SYNONYMS *Saccolabium calopterum* Rchb.f.; *S. schleinitzianum* Kraenzl.; *S. purpureum* J.J. Sm.; *Cleisostoma cryptochilum* Muell.

Aspasia Lindl.
Subfamily Epidendroideae
Tribe Oncidieae

Epiphytic herbs with short, erect pseudobulbs. **Pseudobulbs** concealed by imbricate ± leaf-bearing sheaths below, compressed, 1- or 2-leaved at apex. **Leaves** subcoriaceous, spreading. **Inflorescence** basal, erect, 1- to few-flowered, racemose. **Flowers** showy, large. **Sepals** similar, free, spreading. **Petals** shorter but broader than sepals, free from sepals, spreading. **Lip** adnate at base to column, free lamina deflexed-spreading. **Column** at right-angles to the lip, erect, subterete; pollinia 2, pyriform.

DISTRIBUTION About 10 species, widespread in tropical Central and S. America from Nicaragua to Brazil; sea level to 1000 m, often epiphytic on trees overhanging rivers.

DERIVATION OF NAME Possibly from the Greek *aspasios* (glad, delightful) in allusion to its pretty flowers or, more probably, in honour of Aspasia, the Athenian wife of Pericles.

TAXONOMY Described in 1832 by John Lindley in his *Genera and Species of Orchidaceous Plants* (p. 139), *Aspasia* is allied to *Brassia*, *Miltonia*, *Helcia* and *Trichopilia*, but differs in that the margins of the lip are united to the column near the middle of the column and the lip then bends to become perpendicular to the column; the clinandrium is not hooded; the anther-cap is large and fleshy; and the petals are often adnate to the column for a short distance.

Rudolf Schlechter revised the genus in 1922 in *Gartenflora*, recognising eight species, one of which he described as new, and listed two obscure species as well, but N.H. Williams, who has recently revised *Aspasia* in *Brittonia* (1974), accepts only five species and lists one obscure species. In both the above accounts a key is given to identify the species.

TYPE SPECIES *A. epidendroides* Lindl.

SYNONYM *Tropianthus* Scheidw.

CULTURE Compost A. Temp. Winter min. 12–15°C. *Aspasia* species may be grown in pots, or mounted on slabs of fern-fibre or cork. They require humid, shady conditions while growing, with plenty of water, but when growth is complete, much less water should be given.

Aspasia epidendroides Lindl. [Colour Plate]
An epiphytic plant, up to 40 cm or more tall. **Pseudobulbs** terminating a short, stalk-like stem, oblong-ovoid to elliptic-oblong, compressed, 5.5–12 cm long, 1.5–4.5 cm broad. 2-leaved at apex, subtended by 2–3 distichous leaf-bearing sheaths. **Leaves** linear-oblong to narrowly lanceolate, acute or acuminate, subcoriaceous, 15–30 cm long, 1.7–4 cm broad.

Inflorescence erect, 10–25 cm long, racemose, few-flowered; bracts scarious, appressed, acuminate. **Flowers** distichously arranged, variable in colour; sepals greenish, spotted or blotched bronze or brown: petals greenish-brown, dull white or reddish: lip dull white or cream, marked with pink or purple blotches: column white. **Dorsal sepal** obovate-elliptic, adnate to column-base, erect, concave, obtuse, 2–2.5 cm long, 0.7–1 cm broad: **lateral sepals** obliquely oblanceolate, reflexed, concave, obtuse, up to 2.5 cm long, 1 cm broad. **Petals** obovate-spathulate, obtuse, 1.9–2.2 cm long, 1 cm broad. **Lip** clawed, claw united to column-base, lamina at right-angles to the column, subquadrate-pandurate, retuse, constricted in the middle to appear 3-lobed, 1.7 cm long and broad; side lobules convex; small mid-lobe concave; disc with 2 or 3 elevated radiating ridges. **Column** fleshy, 1.4–1.8 cm long.

DISTRIBUTION Guatemala to Panama and northern S. America; up to 700 m altitude.

HISTORY Discovered in both Panama and W. Colombia by Hugh Cuming and described in 1834 by John Lindley in Hooker's *Journal of Botany* (p. 6).

Baptistonia Barb. Rodr.
Subfamily Epidendroideae
Tribe Oncidieae

Epiphytic plants with clustered subcylindric pseudobulbs, 1–2-leaved, subtended by basal sheaths. **Leaves** coriaceous, conduplicate at the base. **Inflorescences** basal from the axils of the sheaths, pendent, simple or few-branched, subdensely 6- to many-flowered; branches short; peduncle wiry. **Flowers** medium-sized, attractive, not opening widely. **Dorsal sepal** and **petals** subsimilar, free. **Lateral sepals** united almost to apex. **Lip** 3-lobed, more or less parallel to the column, with a complex tuberculate callus. **Column** pointing forwards, decurved at apex, shortly hirsute; anther hirsute; pollinia 2, attached by an oblanceolate stipe to a small viscidium.

DISTRIBUTION A monotypic genus endemic to Brazil.

DERIVATION OF NAME Named for Dr Baptista Caetano d'A Nogueira, an eminent ninetenth-century Brazilian philologist and ethnologist.

TAXONOMY *Baptistonia* was described by the Brazilian botanist Barbosa Rodrigues in 1877 in his *Genera et Species Orchidearum Novarum* (p. 95). It is closely allied to *Oncidium* but differs in the flowers which do not open widely and in the distinctive 3-lobed porrect lip and hirsute column.

TYPE SPECIES *Baptistonia echinata* Barb. Rodr.

CULTURE Temp. Winter min. 15°C. Prefers to grow mounted rather than in pots, so should be tied to a piece of tree fern or cork. Requires moderate shade and humidity with less water given when the pseudobulbs are fully developed. Flowers from late winter to spring.

Baptistonia echinata Barb. Rodr.
[Colour Plate]
A small epiphyte with narrowly ellipsoidal or subcylindric, somewhat compressed, 1- to 2-leaved pseudobulbs, 3–10 cm long, 1–1.5 cm in diameter. **Leaves** oblong-lanceolate, narrowly elliptic or obovate, acute, 10–15 cm long, 1.5–2.1 cm wide. **Inflorescences** 1–2, pendulous, unbranched or with up to 5 branches, subdensely few- to many-flowered; branches up to 2 cm long, 2- to 6-flowered; peduncle elongate, wiry; bracts papery, elliptic, obtuse, 3–6 mm long. **Flowers** attractive, nutant; sepals pale brownish yellow to greenish white with a pale brownish margin; petals whitish with transverse maroon bars; lip yellow with a purple mid-lobe and purple bars between side lobes; pedicel and ovary 7–14 mm long. **Dorsal sepal** hooded over column, obovate-elliptic, obtuse or subacute, 12–13 mm long, 5–6 mm wide; **lateral sepals** porrect, united almost to apex, spathulate, bidentate, 9–12 mm long, 5–7 mm wide. **Petals** recurved-spreading, oblong-obovate, obtuse, 9–12 mm long, 5–6 mm wide. **Lip** 3-lobed, 13–16 mm long, 10–15 mm wide; side lobes erect, elliptic, rounded in front; mid-lobe broadly ovate, mucronate; callus fleshy, tuberculate with 2 large white fleshy erect teeth in the centre. **Column** 6–7 mm long, hirsute, with an obtuse fleshy wing on each side and a denticulately winged apex.

DISTRIBUTION Brazil only.

HISTORY Originally described by João Barbosa Rodrigues in the first volume of his *Genera et Species Orchidearum Novarum* (p. 95) in 1877 based on his own collection from the Serra da Tijuca in the province of Rio de Janeiro.

SYNONYM *Oncidium brunleesianum* Rchb.f.

Barbosella Schltr.
Subfamily Epidendroideae
Tribe Epidendreae
Subtribe Pleurothallidinae

Dwarf epiphytic plants with clustered, very short stems, 1-leafed at apex. **Leaf** coriaceous-fleshy, narrow, almost cylindric. **Inflorescence** 1- or rarely 2-flowered, erect in front of leaf. **Dorsal sepal** and **petals** free, slender with long drawn out apices; **lateral sepals** connate almost to apex. **Lip** much smaller than the sepals, entire, excavate at base. **Column** porrect, short; pollinia 4.

DISTRIBUTION About 20 species from Costa Rica, south to Brazil and Argentina.

DERIVATION OF NAME Named in honour of Dr João Barbosa Rodrigues (1842–1909), the eminent Brazilian orchid taxonomist and Director of the Jardim Botânico in Rio de Janeiro from 1889 onwards.

TAXONOMY Described in 1918 in *Fedde, Repertorium Specierum Novarum* (p. 259) by Rudolf Schlechter. *Barbosella* has been included by some authors in *Pleurothallis* but may be distinguished by its 4, rather than 2 pollinia. Superficially *Barbosella* closely resembles *Restrepia* but it is distinguished by its shorter stems, narrow, fleshy subcylindric leaves, the thinly drawn out dorsal sepal and petals which never have club-shaped apical swellings, and the comparatively short lip which lacks side lobes and has a basal cavity.

TYPE SPECIES *Barbosella gardneri* (Lindl.) Schltr.

CULTURE Compost A or mounted. Temp. Winter min. 12–15°C. As for the small *Pleurothallis*. These tiny creeping plants need humid, shady conditions, and must never remain dry for long. They may be grown in shallow pans, or tied to slabs of fern-fibre or cork, with a little moss to retain moisture. When established, they form a dense mat, and flower more than once annually.

Barbosella cucullata (Lindl.) Schltr.
[Colour Plate]

A very small epiphytic plant, up to 8 cm tall, with a short, creeping rhizome. **Stem** very short, approximate, 1-leafed. **Leaf** erect, fleshy, oblanceolate, minutely tridenticulate at apex, up to 5 cm long, 0.6 cm broad, margins incurved below, surface rough-textured. **Inflorescence** erect, 1-flowered, up to 8 cm long. **Flowers** large for size of plant, narrow, pale yellow-green. **Dorsal sepal** linear, erect, acuminate, 2 cm long, 0.15 cm broad; **lateral sepals** united to the apex, lamina lanceolate, bidenticulate at the apex, 2 cm long, 0.6 cm broad. **Petals** linear, acuminate, 1 cm long, 0.1 cm broad. **Lip** articulated to the column-foot, ovate-subrhombic, fleshy, with a deep cavity at the base, 0.3 cm long, 0.2 cm broad, apex recurved. **Column** very short, curved above, 0.3 cm long; column-foot fleshy, rounded.

DISTRIBUTION Colombia, Venezuela. Ecuador and Peru.

HISTORY First collected in Ecuador by Th. Hartweg and originally described in 1845 by John Lindley as *Restrepia cucullata* in the *Annals and Magazine of Natural History* (p. 108). Rudolf Schlechter transferred it to the genus *Barbosella*

in 1918 in *Fedde, Repertorium Specierum Novarum* (p. 259).

Barkeria Knowles & Westcott
Subfamily Epidendroideae
Tribe Epidendreae
Subtribe Laeliinae

Medium-sized epiphytic or lithophytic plants, erect, often tufted. **Pseudobulbs** slender, fusiform, bearing leaf-sheaths. **Leaves** 2–7, linear-lanceolate to broadly ovate. **Inflorescence** a terminal raceme, sometimes branched, with closely clasping scarious bracts along the peduncle. **Flowers** mostly showy, segments reflexed to porrect. **Sepals** and **petals** similar, free, petals sometimes wider. **Lip** free or adnate to the column for half the column's length, simple; callus absent or of 3 thickened ridges. **Column** short to long with widely spreading, membranaceous wings, appressed against lip or divergent; rostellum tongue-shaped; pollinia 4, waxy, sometimes united in pairs by caudicles; viscidium absent.

DISTRIBUTION Central America, about 10 species.

DERIVATION OF NAME Named in honour of George Barker of Spingfield, England, an eminent orchid grower who died in 1845. He was the first to import and grow the type species of the genus.

TAXONOMY *Barkeria* was established in 1838 in the *Floral Cabinet* (p. 7, t. 49) by G. Knowles and F. Westcott. They stated that *Barkeria* lies intermediately between *Epidendrum* and *Cattleya*, resembling the latter more particularly in its anther-case and pollen masses.

More recently, *Barkeria* has been placed by many botanists within *Epidendrum* as it is considered that the distinguishing characters are of little taxonomic importance. However, the species of *Barkeria* are easy to recognise from most other *Epidendrum* species and as they are relatively frequently found in cultivation, the genus is maintained as distinct here.

The genus has recently been reinstated by L. Thien and R. Dressler in *Brittonia* (1970) who distinguish it from *Epidendrum* on the structure of the rostellum and column in the flower and on the shape of the pseudobulbs. The five species and seven subspecies they recognised have been keyed out and are described by them.

Since their article, several others have appeared in the journal *Orquidea* (*Mexico*) and in the *American Orchid Society Bulletin* 1973 on *Barkeria* by F. Halbinger. In particular, several taxa treated at subspecific rank by Thien and Dressler have been raised to specific rank and two new species have been described (*B. halbingeri* and *B. dorotheae*). A key to all the species recognised by Halbinger is given by him in

Orquidea (1977).

TYPE SPECIES *B. elegans* Knowles & Westcott

CULTURE Compost A. Temp. Winter min. 10–12°C. These slender plants should be grown in small pots or pans. During active growth they require plenty of water and only moderate shade, but when growth is complete, some, or all of the leaves fall off and the plants must then be kept almost dry and given light, cool, conditions.

Barkeria cyclotella Rchb.f. [Colour Plate]
See under *Barkeria lindleyana*.

Barkeria lindleyana Batem. ex Lindl.
[Colour Plate]

An erect, caespitose or repent, epiphytic or lithophytic plant, up to 90 cm tall. **Stems** fusiform-cylindric, 4–15 cm long, 0.6 cm in diameter, concealed by whitish scarious leaf-sheaths. **Leaves** articulate below, distichous, linear-lanceolate or ovate to oblong-lanceolate, acute or acuminate, subcoriaceous, spreading-recurved, 4–15 cm long, 1.5–4 cm broad, ± purple-striate. **Inflorescence** racemose, laxly few- to many-flowered; bracts linear-lanceolate, acuminate, up to 3.5 cm long. **Flowers** showy, rather variable in colour but mostly lilac; lip with red lines below column. **Sepals** elliptic to linear-lanceolate, subacute to acuminate, 1.8–3.7 cm long, 0.5–1 cm broad. **Petals** shortly clawed, suborbicular-ovate, obtuse to acuminate, margins undulate, 1.5–3.7 cm long, 0.7–2 broad. **Lip** suborbicular-ovate or elliptic-lanceolate to oblong-quadrate, retuse or apiculate, margins undulate or subserrate, 1.8–3.5 cm long, 1–2.5 cm broad; disc 3- to 5-ridged in the central part. **Column** appressed to lip, 1–1.4 cm long.

DISTRIBUTION Mexico, south to Costa Rica; up to 2500 m altitude.

HISTORY Discovered in Guatemala by George Ure Skinner and named by James Bateman after John Lindley who described it in the *Botanical Register* (misc. 2) in 1842.

Two subspecies are recognised: subsp. *lindleyana*, which is an epiphytic caespitose plant and subsp. *vanneriana*, which is repent and lithophytic.

SYNONYM *Epidendrum lindleyanum* (Batem. ex Lindl.) Rchb.f.

CLOSELY RELATED SPECIES *Barkeria cyclotella* Rchb.f. [Colour Plate] is closely allied to *B. lindleyana* and has been treated by some authors as a variety of that species, or even as conspecific. It differs from *B. lindleyana*, however, in its generally shorter, erect scape, smaller flowers, shorter column and the obovate to subquadrate lip which frequently has a small mucro at its apex. Furthermore, the lip is flatter and has less prominent keels. *B. cyclotella* is found only in Mexico in the states of Guerrero, Oaxaca, Mexico and Michoacan, growing as an epiphyte or lithophyte at between 1300 and 1900 m. *B. spectabilis* Batem. ex Lindl. [Colour Plate], from S. Mexico, Guatemala and El Salvador, has larger, paler flower with an ovate lip that lacks a purple mark at the apex.

Barkeria skinneri (Batem. ex Lindl.) Paxt.
[Colour Plate]
A slender epiphytic plant, 50 cm high. **Stems** clustered, fusiform-cylindric, 5–14 cm long, 0.4–0.5 cm in diameter, concealed by scarious leaf-sheaths. **Leaves** several, elliptic or elliptic-lanceolate, acute to acuminate, distichous, fleshy, 2.5–15 cm long, 1–2 cm broad. **Inflorescence** terminal, racemose or paniculate, few- to many-flowered, up to 15 cm long; peduncle concealed by long, imbricate scarious sheaths. **Flowers** showy, lilac-purple, rose-purple or reddish-magenta with yellow keels; pedicellate-ovary slender, reddish. **Sepals** spreading, elliptic or elliptic-lanceolate, acute to acuminate, 1.5–2.2 cm long, 0.4–0.8 cm broad. **Petals** broadly elliptic or ovate, acute to shortly acuminate, 1.3–2.2 cm long, 0.6–1 cm broad. **Lip** adnate to column for basal 0.3 cm; lamina broadly ovate to elliptic, obtuse to acuminate, 1.3–1.8 cm long, 0.7–1.5 cm broad; disc with 3 central yellowish ridges, ± thickened and raised towards the base. **Column** slightly clavate, 0.6–0.8 cm long.
DISTRIBUTION Guatemala; up to 1900 m altitude.
HISTORY Discovered by George Ure Skinner in Guatemala and named in his honour by James Bateman, it was described by John Lindley as *Epidendrum skinneri* in the *Botanical Register* (t. 1881). O. Ames and D. Correll (1952) in the *Orchids of Guatemala* still treated this species in that genus, but nowadays most authors follow J. Paxton who, in 1849 in the *Magazine of Botany* (p. 1), transferred it to the genus *Barkeria*.
SYNONYMS *Epidendrum skinneri* Batem. ex Lindl.; *E. fuchsii* Regel
CLOSELY RELATED SPECIES See *B. lindleyana*.

Barkeria spectabilis Batem. ex Lindl.
[Colour Plate]
See under *Barkeria lindleyana*.

Barlia Parlatore
Subfamily Orchidoideae
Tribe Orchidieae
Subtribe Orchidiinae

Medium-sized terrestrial herbs growing from underground tubers (root-stem tuberoids).

Leaves succulent, suberect or spreading, several, basal and sometimes cauline, glossy green. **Inflorescence** erect, densely many-flowered, spicate; peduncle stout; bracts prominent, foliose. **Flowers** resupinate, showy, sweetly scented. **Sepals** and **petals** forming a hood over the column, the sepals similar, the petals smaller and narrower. **Lip** pendent, 3-lobed, the lobes short, spurred at the base; spur tapering, shorter than the lip. **Column** erect; pollinia 2, mealy, attached by slender stalks to a circular small viscidium enclosed in a bursicle.
DISTRIBUTION A small genus of two species in Mediterranean Europe and N.W. Africa and the Canary Islands.
DERIVATION OF NAME Commemorating Sr Barla, an Italian botanist who collected the original material for Parlatore.
TAXONOMY *Barlia* was described in 1858 in *Nuovi generi e nuovi specie plantarum monocotyledoni* (p. 5) by the Italian botanist Parlatore. It is very closely related to *Himantoglossum* and was formerly considered congeneric with it. However, its lip lacks the long tail-like mid-lobe and slender linear side-lobes of *Himantoglossum*.
TYPE SPECIES *B. longibracteata* (Biv.) Parl.
CULTURE Temp. Winter min. 5°C. Compost as for *Anacamptis* but winter growing and spring flowering. Water during growth and repot in the autumn. Much less water during summer dormancy.

Barlia robertiana (Loisel.) W. Greuter
[Colour Plate]
A robust terrestrial plant, 25–80 cm tall, with large ovoid or ellipsoid tubers. **Leaves** 5–10, oblong-elliptic, acute or obtuse, 10–30 cm long, 3–10 cm wide, glossy green. **Inflorescence** conical to cylindrical, erect, densely many-flowered; peduncle 6–23 cm long, bearing several sheaths; bracts lanceolate, acuminate, 10–15 mm long. **Flowers** 3–4.5 cm long, with green, brown, yellowish or purple sepals and a whitish lip with a greenish, greyish, brown or purple marginal band, and similarly flecked in the middle; ovary 7–9 mm long. **Sepals** concave, elliptic-ovate, obtuse, 7–11 mm long, 1.5–3 mm wide. **Petals** similar but smaller. **Lip** pendent, 3-lobed, 13–20 mm long; side lobes incurved oblong-elliptic, obtuse; mid-lobe much longer, flabellate, bilobulate with each lobe oblong; spur incurved conical, 4–6 mm long. **Column** 7–8 mm long.
DISTRIBUTION Mediterranean and sub-mediterranean Europe and N.W. Africa; in pine woods, scrub and grassy places on well-drained neutral and alkaline soils; sea level to 1000 m.
HISTORY Originally described by Jean Loiseleur-Deslongchamps in 1828 as *Orchis robertiana* in his *Flora Gallica* (p. 606), based on

a French collection by D. Robert. It was subsequently transferred to the present genus by W. Greuter in 1967 in the journal *Boissiera* (p. 192).
SYNONYMS *Orchis robertiana* Loisel.; *O. longibracteata* Biv.; *Barlia longibracteata* (Biv.) Parl.; *Himantoglossum longibracteatum* (Biv.) Schltr.

Bartholina R. Br.
Subfamily Orchidoideae
Tribe Orchidieae
Subtribe Orchidiinae

Small terrestrial plants perennating by root-stem tuberoids. Leaf solitary, basal, appressed to the ground, pilose. **Inflorescence** erect, 1-flowered; peduncle slender, pilose. **Flower** large for the plant, hydra-like, showy, resupinate, becoming erect. **Sepals** erect, similar, shortly connate at the base and with the lip forming a tube, pubescent on the outside, petals free, lanceolate. **Lip** spreading, obscurely 3-lobed, the lobes deeply pectinate, spurred at the base. **Column** with an erect acute anther; pollinia 2, mealy, oblong, each attached by a rigid linear stalk to a small viscidium.
DISTRIBUTION A genus of two species endemic to Cape Province of South Africa.
DERIVATION OF NAME Commemorating the Danish anatomist and physiologist, Thomas Bartholin.
TAXONOMY This small genus was founded by Robert Brown in 1813 in the 2nd edition of Aiton's *Hortus Kewensis* (p. 194). It is closely allied to the African terrestrial genus *Holothrix* which has its pollinia attached by short stalks to a single viscidium
CULTURE Temp. Winter min. 10°C. Compost as for *Acianthus*. Grows in autumn and all winter, with summer dormancy. In natural habitat tends to flower after fires.

Bartholina burmanniana (L.) Ker
[Colour Plate]
An erect slender terrestrial plant 7.5–20 cm tall, hairy all over except for the petals and lip. **Leaf** flat on the ground, somewhat convex, orbicular, cordate at the base, obtuse, 1.6–2.5 cm long and wide, pilose. **Inflorescence** 1-flowered; peduncle pilose; bract erect, ovate, acute, as long as the pedicel, pilose. **Flower** with green sepals, white petals and a creamy lip; pedicel and ovary 1.4–1.7 cm long, pubescent. **Sepals** linear-lanceolate, 1–1.2 cm long, shortly connate at the base. **Petals** falcate-lanceolate, acute or acuminate, 1.5–1.8 cm long, 3–4 mm wide. **Lip** obscurely 3-lobed, with each lobe deeply lacerate, 2.3–3.5 cm long, the segments linear-acuminate; spur cylindrical-decurved, 6 mm long. **Column** 7–9 mm long.

DISTRIBUTION S. Africa: Cape Province only; sea level to 900 m in sandy places in scrub.

HISTORY Linnaeus described this strange orchid, one of the first South African orchids to be seen in Europe, as *Orchis burmanniana* in 1763 in the 2nd edition of his *Species Plantarum* (p. 1334). The type had been collected by his pupil Johannes Burmann in the Cape. It was transferred to the present genus by Ker in 1818 in the *Journal of Science of the Royal Institute* (p. 204).

SYNONYMS *Orchis burmanniana* L.; *O. pectinata* Thunb.; *Arethusa ciliaris* L.f.; *Bartholina pectinata* (Thunb.) R. Br.

Batemannia Lindl.

Subfamily Epidendroideae
Tribe Maxillarieae
Subtribe Zygopetalinae

Epiphytes with clustered one-noded pseudobulbs. **Leaves** apical on pseudobulb, plicate. **Inflorescences** lateral, few- to many-flowered, shorter than the leaves, arcuate to pendent. **Flowers** medium-sized, showy. **Sepals** and **petals** free; lateral sepals dissimilar from dorsal, attached at the apex of the column-foot; petals often adnate to the dorsal sepal. **Lip** 3-lobed, ecalcarate; callus a transverse flattened ridge. **Column** clavate; pollinia 4, pyriform, flattened, superposed, attached by a short wide stipe to a flattened viscidium that is wider than long.

DISTRIBUTION Five species in the Amazon basin.

DERIVATION OF NAME Named in honour of the nineteenth-century orchid grower James Bateman of Knypersley Hall, Cheshire, an avid collector and cultivator of orchids and the author of the monumental *Orchidaceae of Mexico and Guatemala*.

TAXONOMY John Lindley established this genus in 1834 in the *Botanical Register* (t. 1714). It is allied to *Zygopetalum* and *Pabstia*.

TYPE SPECIES *B. colleyi* Lindl.

CULTURE Temp. Winter min. 15°C. Grows well in pots, much as *Bifrenaria*. Inflorescences arise from the base of the pseudobulbs.

Batemannia colleyi Lindl.

A medium-sized epiphyte. **Pseudobulbs** ovoid or ellipsoidal, 1.5–6 cm long, 0.8–2 cm wide, compressed-tetragonal, subtended by ephemeral sheaths, 2-leaved at apex. **Leaves** lanceolate or narrowly elliptic, acute or acuminate, 15–30 cm long, 3–4.5 cm wide, shortly petiolate. **Inflorescences** basal, 2- to 5-flowered, 6–15 cm long; peduncle and rhachis, flexuous; bracts

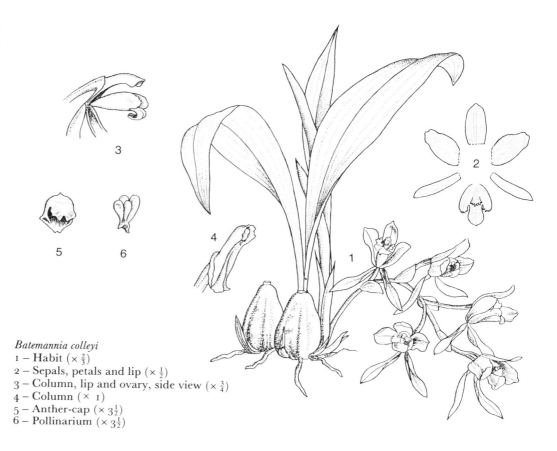

Batemannia colleyi
1 – Habit ($\times \frac{2}{3}$)
2 – Sepals, petals and lip ($\times \frac{1}{2}$)
3 – Column, lip and ovary, side view ($\times \frac{3}{4}$)
4 – Column ($\times$ 1)
5 – Anther-cap ($\times 3\frac{1}{2}$)
6 – Pollinarium ($\times 3\frac{1}{2}$)

elliptic to obovate, 1.5–2 cm long. **Flowers** somewhat fleshy; sepals and petals pale green strongly flushed with purple or bronzy brown; lip white or cream with a yellowish tinge; pedicel and ovary 2–3.5 cm long. **Dorsal sepal** elliptic to lanceolate, obtuse to acute, 1.6–2.7 cm long, 4–9 mm wide; **lateral sepals** oblanceolate, rounded, deflexed and spreading, 2.1–3.6 cm long, 0.4–0.7 cm wide. **Petals** porrect but recurved towards apex, oblong-elliptic to oblanceolate, obtuse, 2.2–3.3 cm long, 0.6–0.7 cm wide. **Lip** 3-lobed, 2–2.2 cm long, 1.2–1.6 cm wide; side lobes erect, narrowly oblong, rounded and erose on front margins; midlobe recurved, obovate, obtuse, erose; callus a transverse erose flap at the base of the mid-lobe. **Column** 11–16 mm long; foot 6–7 mm long.

DISTRIBUTION Colombia, Venezuela and Guyana south to Bolivia and Brazil; lowland rain and riverine forest.

HISTORY Originally described by John Lindley in 1835 in the *Botanical Register* (t. 1714) based on a plant collected in Guyana by Mr Colley who collected there for James Bateman.

SYNONYMS *Lycaste colleyi* (Lindl.) Hort. ex Planchon; *Maxillaria colleyi* (Lindl.) Hort. ex Planchon; *Petronia regia* Barb. Rodr.; *Batemannia petronia* Barb. Rodr.; *B. yauaperyensis* Barb. Rodr.; *B. peruviana* Rolfe

---

Bifrenaria Lindl.

Subfamily Epidendroideae
Tribe Maxillarieae
Subtribe Zygopetalinae

Epiphytic or terrestrial herbs with 1- or 2-leaved pseudobulbs. **Leaves** thinly papyraceous, plicate, erect or suberect. **Inflorescence** racemose, basal, erect to arcuate, laxly few-flowered. **Flowers** showy. **Sepals** subsimilar, free, spreading; lateral sepals adnate to the column-foot, forming an obscure spur-like mentum. **Petals** free, suberect, smaller than sepals. **Lip** articulated to apex of column-foot, clawed 3-lobed in the middle; side lobes erect; callus lobed, central. **Column** erect, fleshy, auriculate at apex; pollinia 4, or 2 and sulcate, waxy; stipites 2, very short or elongate; viscidium 1.

DISTRIBUTION About 30 or so species from Panama, Trinidad and northern S. America south to Peru and Brazil.

DERIVATION OF NAME Derived from the Latin *bi* (two) and *frenum* (rein, strap) alluding to the 2 strap-like stipites joining the pollinia and the viscidium. This character distinguishes the genus from *Maxillaria*.

TAXONOMY John Lindley described this genus in 1833 in his *Genera and Species of Orchidaceous Plants* (p. 152). *Bifrenaria* is allied to

Pabstia (*Colax*) and *Maxillaria*, but is distinguished by its 2 stipites and obscure viscidium.

In *Orchidaceae Brasilienses* (1977), G. Pabst and F. Dungs have considered *Stenocoryne* Lindl. to be a synonym of *Bifrenaria* and have subdivided 22 Brazilian species of the latter into three groups as follows:

1. *B. harrisoniae* alliance – 12 species with large flowers, 4 cm or more across when flattened out.
2. *B. racemosa* alliance – 7 species with smaller flowers, 2–3 cm across when flattened out; lip entire of obscurely 3-lobed.
3. *B. longicornis* alliance – 3 species; as group 2 but lip clearly 3-lobed. Groups 2 and 3 correspond to *Stenocoryne*.

TYPE SPECIES *B. atropurpurea* (Lodd.) Lindl.
SYNONYM *Stenocoryne* Lindl.; *Adipe* Raf.; *Lindleyella* Schltr.
CULTURE Compost A. Temp. Winter min. 12–16°C. During growth, *Bifrenaria* species should be given warm, humid conditions and moderate shade, with plenty of water at the roots. When the pseudobulbs are fully formed, the plants require less warmth and much less water.

Bifrenaria atropurpurea (Lodd.) Lindl.
[Colour Plate]
A medium-sized epiphytic plant. **Pseudobulbs** ovoid-subconical, obtusely 4-angled, 5–7 cm long, 1-leafed at apex. **Leaf** oblong-lanceolate, acute, plicate, 20–25 cm long, 7 cm broad. **Inflorescence** erect or slightly arcuate, 3- to 5-flowered, 6–8 cm long; bracts subappressed, rigid, somewhat multistriate, 2–2.5 cm long. **Flowers** erect or erect-spreading, large, showy, fragrant; sepals and petals dark purplish-brown with a yellow centre; lip rose-coloured and white; anther white. **Sepals** coriaceous, broadly oblong, abruptly acute, 2.6–2.7 cm long, 1.2–1.3 cm broad; lateral sepals forming with the column-foot a rectangular, acute-angled mentum. **Petals** broadly rhombic-oblong, obtuse, 1.7 cm long, 0.8 cm broad. **Lip** erect, slightly concave, fleshy, shortly clawed, 3-lobed above, 1.6–1.7 cm long, 0.9–1 cm broad; side lobes short, broadly triangular, obtuse, spreading; mid-lobe transverse, revolute, obscurely tri-lobulate, suberose; disc somewhat puberulent, with a central 3-lobed callus. **Column** short, terete, incurved, 0.8–0.9 cm long.
DISTRIBUTION Brazil.
HISTORY *B. atropurpurea* is the type species of the genus and was discovered by F. Warre in the Organ Mts near Rio de Janeiro in 1828 for Messrs Loddiges. It was described by George Loddiges (1832) in the *Botanical Cabinet* (t. 1877) as *Maxillaria atropurpurea* and transferred to *Bifrenaria* by John Lindley in 1832 in his *Genera and Species of Orchidaceous Plants* (p. 152).
SYNONYM *Maxillaria atropurpurea* Lodd.

Bifrenaria harrisoniae (Hooker) Rchb.f.
[Colour Plate]
A medium-sized epiphytic plant with clustered pseudobulbs. **Pseudobulbs** broadly ovoid-pyriform, angled, deeply sulcate, 5–7.5 cm long, up to 3 cm in diameter, 1-leafed at apex. **Leaf** elliptic-oblong, suberect, subacute or obtuse, thin-textured, 22–30 cm long, 7.5–10 cm broad. **Inflorescence** basal, 1-flowered, shorter than the leaves, up to 15 cm long; peduncle pale green, terete; bracts cucullate, acute, papery, up to 1.5 cm long. **Flowers** 7.5 cm broad, showy, fragrant, suberect; segments spreading; sepals and petals ivory-white to yellow; lip white or yellow, lined rich purple; callus and mentum yellow; column white. **Dorsal sepal** concave, oblong-obovate, rounded at apex, 4 cm long, 2.4 cm broad; **lateral sepals** obliquely oblong, rounded, 4.5 cm long, 2.8 cm broad, prolonged at base to form a spur-like mentum, 2 cm long. **Petals** elliptic, rounded, 3.5 cm long, 2.2 cm broad. **Lip** shortly narrowly clawed, 3-lobed in apical half, densely pubescent, 4.8 cm long, 3.8 cm broad; side lobes oblong, rounded, erect on either side of column; mid-lobe reflexed, orbicular, margins undulate; callus a central fleshy knob. **Column** 2.2 cm long; foot slender, pubescent 2.5 cm long.
DISTRIBUTION Brazil.
HISTORY Sent in 1821 or 1822 from Rio de Janeiro by William Harrison, a British merchant, to his brother Richard in Liverpool. Sir William Hooker named it in 1825 in his *Exotic Flora* (t. 210) as *Dendrobium harrisoniae* in honour of Mrs Arnold Harrison, a relative of William and Richard and owner of a fine collection of orchids. H.G. Reichenbach transferred it to the genus *Bifrenaria* in 1855 in *Bonplandia* (p. 217).
SYNONYMS *Dendrobium harrisoniae* Hooker; *Maxillaria harrisoniae* (Hooker) Lindl.; *Lycaste harrisoniae* (Hooker) B.S. Williams

---

Bletia Ruiz & Pavon
Subfamily Epidendroideae
Tribe Arethuseae
Subtribe Bletiinae

Erect terrestrial plants with subglobose pseudobulbs. **Leaves** few, deciduous, plicate, thickly membranaceous, petiolate below. **Inflorescence** erect, lateral, racemose or sometimes paniculate, laxly many-flowered, up to 1 m high. **Flowers** often showy. **Sepals** and **petals** subsimilar, free, spreading. **Lip** attached to the column-base, free, entire to 3-lobed; side lobes erect; mid-lobe broad, erect or recurved, spreading, often crisped, ± emarginate or bilobulate; disc lamellate or with 5–7 denticulate crests. **Column** elongate, arcuate, auriculate above; pollinia 8, in 2 sets of 4, yellow, hard, compressed.
DISTRIBUTION About 26 species widely distributed in the American tropics and subtropics from Florida south to Argentina.
DERIVATION OF NAME Given in honour of Don Luis Blet, a Spanish pharmacist and botanist of the eighteenth century.
TAXONOMY Described in 1794 by H. Ruiz and J. Pavon in their *Prodromus Florae Peruvianae et Chilensis* (p. 119, t. 26), *Bletia* closely resembles *Spathoglottis* in its habit, but most species of the former are deciduous and their inflorescences are erect rather than nodding.

P.H. Allen in the *Flora of Panama* (1949) stated that careful comparison of the available material on the 40–50 described species in the genus would probably reduce the number of valid species to about a dozen, some of which would be widespread.

R. Dressler in *Brittonia* (1968), recognises 26 species in his key to the genus. Dressler's key is based mainly on size of flowers and on details of lip structure, and especially on the form and proportions of the lobes when flattened. He points out that the lamellae on the lip are very variable and thus have not been used by him in constructing the key except as a present or absent character.
TYPE SPECIES *B. catenulata* Ruiz & Pavon
SYNONYM *Crybe* Lindl.
CULTURE Compost B. or C. Temp. Winter min. 12°C. While the leaves are growing, the plants need plenty of water and moderate shade but after leaf-fall, very little water should be given until the flower buds begin to form; unlike *Bletilla*, these arise from the bare pseudobulbs.

Bletia catenulata Ruiz & Pavon
[Colour Plate]
A large, rather variable, terrestrial plant. **Pseudobulbs** ovoid to depressed-subglobose, up to 6 cm long, 1- to several-leaved above. **Leaves** distichous, deciduous, linear-elliptic or elliptic-lanceolate, acuminate, 20–90 cm long, 0.5–8 cm broad. **Inflorescences** lateral, erect, racemose or rarely 1-branched, 60–200 cm long. **Flowers** large and showy, pink purple or red, with a central yellow or white streak on the lip. **Sepals** oblong-elliptic, subacute or acute, 3.4 cm long, 0.7–1.2 cm broad. **Petals** ovate, rounded to subacute, 3 cm long, 2 cm broad, margins, ± lobulate or irregular. **Lip** suborbicular in outline, deeply 3-lobed in the middle, 3.5 cm long; side lobes erect-incurved, suborbicular-ovate; midlobe transversely obovate-reniform; disc with 3–5

thickened nerves to above the middle. **Column** subclavate, arcuate, winged above, about 2 cm long.

DISTRIBUTION Colombia south to Bolivia and also in Brazil.

HISTORY Discovered by J. Pavon at Pozuzu and Chaclla, towards S. Domingo and Llanamapanaui growing in woods and clearings and described by H. Ruiz and J. Pavon in their *Systema Vegetabilium Florae Peruvianae et Chilensis* (p. 229) in 1798.

SYNONYMS *Bletia sanguinea* Poepp. & Endl.; *B. sherrattiana* Batem. ex. Lindl; *Regnellia purpurea* Barb. Rodr.; *Bletia watsonii* Hooker; *B. rodriguesii* Cogn.

Bletilla Rchb.f.

Subfamily Epidendroideae
Tribe Arethuseae
Subtribe Bletiinae

Terrestrial herbs with plicate leaves. Base of stem swollen into a distinct corm. **Inflorescence** terminal, racemose, laxly several-flowered. **Flowers** medium-sized, showy. **Sepals** and **petals** subsimilar, free, ringent. **Lip** 3-lobed; side lobes enfolding column; mid-lobe porrect or recurved; disc lamellate or papillose. **Column** slender, lacking a foot, narrowly winged on each side; anther 2-celled; pollinia 8; stigma transverse under rostellum.

DISTRIBUTION Some nine species in E. Asia, Taiwan and the adjacent islands.

DERIVATION OF NAME The generic name is a diminutive of *Bletia*, a genus of American orchids to which their flowers bear a resemblance.

TAXONOMY Described by H.G. Reichenbach in 1853 in *Flore des Serres* (p. 246), *Bletilla* has been conserved over *Jimensia* Raf. (1838). Rudolf Schlechter reviewed the genus in 1911 in *Fedde, Repertorium Specierum Novarum*, listing six species, one of which is now considered to be in the genus *Arethusa*, as *A. japonica* A. Gray.

Kiat Tan in *Brittonia* (1969) has discussed the taxonomic affinities of *Bletilla* in the Orchidaceae and concludes that it shows more affinities with *Bletia* in the subtribe *Bletiinae* than with *Arethusa* in the subtribe *Arethusinae* where it has previously been placed by most authorities, including Schlechter.

TYPE SPECIES *Bletilla gebina* (Lindl.) Rchb.f. [= *Bletilla striata* (Thunb.) Rchb.f.].

CULTURE Compost B or C in pots, may be grown in beds outdoors. Temp. Hardy outdoors, protect from severe frosts. The corm-like pseudobulbs should be planted and covered with about 2–5 cm of compost. When the new shoots are growing, the plants may be carefully watered and, as the flower stems appear inside the young shoots, water should be freely given. When the leaves have fallen, the plants need a cool, dry rest, but those in pots must not be allowed to shrivel. Some shade is required for leafy plants under glass.

Bletilla striata (Thunb.) Rchb.f.
[Colour Plate]

A terrestrial plant, up to 60 cm tall. **Tuber** compressed, subrotund. **Stem** erect, enclosed below by imbricating sheaths, leafy above. **Leaves** plicate, oblong-lanceolate, acuminate, often rather narrow, up to 45 cm long, 5 cm broad. **Inflorescence** slender, erect, laxly several-flowered; bracts inconspicuous, ovate-triangular, up to 0.3 cm long. **Flowers** rose-pink or rarely white. **Sepals** and **petals** subsimilar, oblong-lanceolate or obovate-oblanceolate, acute, up to 3.5 cm long, 0.8 cm broad. **Lip** 3-lobed, up to 3.5 cm long, 2 cm broad; side lobes erect, semiovate; mid-lobe recurved, subquadrate, somewhat emarginate; disc with 5 parallel, flexuose lamellae.

DISTRIBUTION Japan, China, E. Tibet and Okinawa.

HISTORY Discovered in Japan by Carl Thunberg and described by him in 1784 in *Flora Japonica* (p. 28) as *Limodorum striatum*. H.G. Reichenbach transferred it to *Bletilla* in 1878 in the *Botanische Zeitung* (p. 75).

SYNONYMS include *Limodorum striatum* Thunb.: *Epidendrum tuberosum* Lour.; *Cymbidium striatum* (Thunb.) Sw.; *Cymbidium hyacinthinum* J.E. Smith; *Gyas humilis* Salisb.; *Bletia gebina* Lindl.; *Bletilla gebina* (Lindl.) Rchb.f.; *Bletia striata* (Thunb.) Druce; *Jimensia striata* (Thunb.) Garay & Schultes

---

Bollea Rchb.f.

Subfamily Epidendroideae
Tribe Maxillarieae
Subtribe Zygopetalinae

Medium-sized epiphytic plants with a very short stem, lacking pseudobulbs. **Leaves** distichous, imbricate, long, narrowly ligulate, erect or erect-spreading, conduplicate and articulate below, chartaceous. **Inflorescence** 1-flowered, arcuate or pendulous; bracts broadly ovate-triangular. **Flowers** large, showy, shortly pedicellate, fleshy. **Sepals** and **petals** subsimilar, free, spreading; lateral sepals attached to the column-foot, forming with it a short distinct mentum. **Lip** articulated with apex of column-foot; claw linear, ecallose; limb broad, entire, transversely callose below; callus multi-costate above and fleshy. **Column** short, fleshy, navicular, strongly excavate in front, produced into a short foot below; pollinia 4, waxy, obovoid, compressed, paired; stipe ligulate; viscidium large.

DISTRIBUTION About six species in Brazil, Colombia and Ecuador.

DERIVATION OF NAME Named in honour of Dr Carl Boll, a patron of horticulture in Germany.

TAXONOMY First described in 1852 in the *Botanische Zeitung* (p. 667) by H.G. Reichenbach, *Bollea* is readily identifiable by its hooded column which protrudes over the fleshy, semicircular callus of the lip, and by the lip being firmly adnate to the column-foot.

It is most closely allied to *Pescatorea*, *Huntleya* and *Stenia*, and in nature *Bollea* species hybridise freely with certain species of *Pescatorea*. The genus has been reviewed most recently by J.A. Fowlie in the *Orchid Digest* (1969).

TYPE SPECIES *B. violacea* (Lindl.) Rchb.f.

CULTURE Compost. A. Temp. Winter min. 12–15°C. As for *Chondrorhyncha*, *Warscewiczella* etc. The plants grow well in baskets, under humid, shady conditions. They should be carefully watered at all times and never allowed to become dry.

Bollea coelestis (Rchb.f.)

A tufted epiphytic plant lacking any pseudobulbs. **Leaves** 6–10 per growth, oblong-lanceolate, acuminate, 15–30 cm long, 3–5 cm broad. **Inflorescences** several at a time, suberect or nodding, shorter than the leaves, with a small sheathing bract at each node, 1-flowered. **Flowers** 7.5–12 cm across, showy; sepals and petals bluish-violet, paler at margins and base, yellowish at the spices; lip bluish-violet with a buff-yellow crest; column bluish-violet above, yellow in front, spotted red towards base. **Dorsal sepal** broadly obovate, curved forwards, 4.5 cm long, 2 cm broad; **lateral sepals** ovate-oblong. **Petals** similar to dorsal sepal, spreading. **Lip** with a large semicircular crest occupying the basal three-quarters, deeply grooved longitudinally into numerous rounded ridges, 2.5 cm long; lamina ovate, with recurved margins and apex. **Column** broad, arching, convex, hairy towards the base, 2.3 cm long.

DISTRIBUTION Colombia and Ecuador.

HISTORY Introduced into cultivation by Messrs Backhouse of York, England, in 1876 and described the same year by H.G. Reichenbach in the *Gardeners' Chronicle* (n.s. 5: p. 756). He transferred it the following year to the genus *Bollea* in the same journal.

Little was known of the provenance of this orchid until Benedict Roezl wrote to Godefroy's *Orchidophile* stating that it was found by his nephew Edward Klaboch on the way from

Buenaventura to Cali over the Cordillera Occidental of Colombia at an altitude of 1900 m.

SYNONYMS *Zygopetalum coeleste* (Rchb.f.) Rchb.f.; *Bollea pulvinaris* Rchb.f.

CLOSELY RELATED SPECIES *Bollea violacea* (Lindl.) Rchb.f. [Colour Plate], from Colombia, differs in having a violet flower with a purple callus, narrower apex to the lip and narrower sepals and petals.

Bolusiella Schltr.
Subfamily Epidendroideae
Tribe Vandeae
Subtribe Aerangidinae

Very small epiphytic herbs with a very short stem. **Leaves** few to several, arranged fanwise on the stem, equitant, fleshy. **Inflorescence** few- to many-flowered, racemose, axillary. **Flowers** minute to very small, with a very short pedicel, mostly white. **Sepals** and **petals** subequal. **Lip** spurred at base, entire or more commonly 3-lobed, acute; spur equal to, or shorter than, the limb of the lip, ± curved forwards below the lip. **Column** very short with a pointed rostellum; pollinia 2, waxy; stipites 2, short; viscidium disc-like.

DISTRIBUTION About ten species, widespread in tropical Africa and south to Natal.

DERIVATION OF NAME Named in honour of that pioneer South African botanist Sir Harry Bolus (1834–1911) who wrote *Icones Orchidearum Austro-Africanum*.

TAXONOMY Described by Rudolf Schlechter in 1918 in *Beihefte zum Botanischen Zentralblatt* (p. 105), *Bolusiella* is a very distinct genus of African Sarcanthoid orchids. Many of the species were originally described in the genera *Listrostachys* and *Angraecum* before the generic limits of those had been properly delimited.

Bolusiella is superficially similar to *Podangis* and *Oberonia* in its vegetative habit in that all have bilaterally compressed leaves. However, it differs from the former in its much smaller flowers borne in fairly long inflorescences and from the latter in having a much shorter stem and lateral white-flowered inflorescences.

TYPE SPECIES Several species were mentioned when the genus was established.

CULTURE Compost A or mounted. Temp. Winter min. 12–15°C. These little plants are often difficult to establish, but grow well when tied to small pieces of fern-fibre or cork, and hung in moderately shady, humid conditions. They should be misted several times daily when the roots are active, but much less frequently when growth is completed.

Bolusiella iridifolia (Rolfe) Schltr.

A very small epiphytic plant lacking any pseudobulbs. **Leaves** distichous, arranged fanwise, very fleshy, more or less compressed and triangular in cross-section, sulcate, recurved, 1.5–4 cm long. **Inflorescences** axillary, suberect-spreading, usually overtopping the leaves, up to 5.5 cm long, many-flowered; bracts shorter than the flowers. **Flowers** minute, white. **Sepals** oblong, subacute, 0.2–0.3 cm long, 0.1 cm broad. **Petals** oblong, obtuse, 0.2 cm long, 0.1 cm broad. **Lip** oblong, rounded, 0.25–0.5 cm long; spur at right-angles to the lip, slightly inflated to ellipsoid, a little shorter than the lip, up to 0.2 cm long. **Column** short, stout, 0.5 cm long.

DISTRIBUTION Ivory Coast to Cameroon in W. Africa, Zaire, Uganda, Kenya and Angola.

HISTORY Originally described in 1897 as *Listrostachys iridifolia* by R.A. Rolfe in the *Flora of Tropical Africa* (p. 167), based on a specimen collected at Golungo Alto, Angola, by F. Welwitsch. Rudolf Schlechter transferred it to *Bolusiella* in 1918 in *Beihefte zum Botanischen Zentralblatt* (p. 105).

SYNONYM *Listrostachys iridifolia* Rolfe

CLOSELY RELATED SPECIES *B. iridifolia* differs from *B. imbricata* in having leaves with a deep V-shaped dorsal groove and in its shorter sepals and petals and ellipsoidal spur.

Bolusiella maudiae (H. Bolus) Schltr.
[Colour Plate]
A dwarf epiphytic plant with a very short stem. **Leaves** 5–10, arranged distichously in a fan on the stem, bilaterally flattened and fleshy, surfaces convex, 1–3.5 cm long, 0.3–0.9 cm broad. **Inflorescences** axillary, racemose, up to 7 cm long, densely many-flowered; bracts distichous, as large as or larger than flowers, overlapping at the base. **Flowers** minute, white; spur pale olive-green. **Sepals** and **petals** elliptic, obtuse, subsimilar, 0.3–0.4 cm long. **Lip** narrowly oblong, 0.2–0.3 cm long; spur shorter than the lip, not inflated. **Column** very short, fleshy.

DISTRIBUTION Ghana to Uganda and Kenya and south to Natal.

HISTORY Discovered in Zululand by Mrs Charles Saunders and described by Harry Bolus as *Angraecum maudiae* in the first volume of his *Icones Orchidearum Austro-Africanarum* (t. 9) in 1896. Rudolf Schlechter transferred it to *Bolusiella* in 1918 in *Beihefte zum Botanischen Zentralblatt* (p. 106).

SYNONYMS *Angraecum maudiae* Bolus; *Listrostachys imbricata* Rolfe; *Bolusiella imbricata* (Rolfe) Schltr.

CLOSELY RELATED SPECIES See *B. iridifolia*.

Bonatea Willd.
Subfamily Orchidoideae
Tribe Orchideae
Subtribe Orchidinae

Medium-sized to large terrestrial herbs with thick, elongated, fleshy tubers. **Stems** erect, leafy throughout length, stout. **Leaves** fairly thin-textured, ovate or ovate-lanceolate, lowermost sheath-like. **Inflorescence** terminal, racemose, many-flowered. **Flowers** large, green and white, fairly showy. **Dorsal sepal** cucullate; **lateral sepals** deflexed, larger than dorsal sepal, fused to the column. **Petals** erect, linear, adnate to the dorsal sepal, forming a hood over the anther. **Lip** long-clawed, 3-lobed; spur long, cylindrical, with a tooth in the mouth. **Column** large; anther erect, stigmatic arms long, porrect; rostellum mid-lobe hooded and side lobes porrect or upcurved, slender.

DISTRIBUTION Fewer than ten species, widespread in tropical Africa and south to S. Africa, also in the N. Yemen.

DERIVATION OF NAME This genus was named in honour of M. Bonat, Professor of Botany at Padua in Italy.

TAXONOMY Named by C.L. Willdenow in 1805 in the 4th edition of *Species Plantarum* (p. 43), *Bonatea* closely resembles many of the larger-flowered *Habenaria* species in vegetative and floral morphology. It is, however, distinct in having a tooth in the mouth of the spur and in having a hooded mid-lobe to the rostellum.

TYPE SPECIES *B. speciosa* (L.f.) Willd.

CULTURE Compost C. Temp. Winter min. 15°C. As for the tropical *Habenaria* species. During growth the plants need plenty of water and moderate shade, but when the stems have died down after flowering, little or no water should be given until new growth commences.

Bonatea antennifera Rolfe
A large terrestrial plant, up to 1 m high with a stout, somewhat glaucous, leafy stem. **Leaves** sessile, amplexicaul, oblong, subacute, spreading, 7.5–15 cm long, 2.5–5 cm broad, decreasing upwards into the bracts. **Inflorescences** terminal, racemose, above 23 cm long, laxly many-flowered. **Flowers** large, green and white; bracts lanceolate, acuminate, 2.5–5 cm long. **Dorsal sepal** cucullate, elliptic, acuminate, 2–2.5 cm long; **lateral sepals** oblique, oblong, acuminate, recurved at the apex, 2–2.5 cm long, with an acute tooth on the inner margin. **Petals** bipartite; upper lobe linear, acute, up to 2.5 cm long; lower lobe filiform, curved, up to 4.5 cm long. **Lip** 3-lobed; side lobes filiform, 5 or more cm long; mid-lobe linear, recurved, sharply bent in the middle, 3 cm

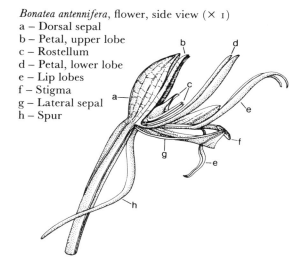

Bonatea antennifera, flower, side view (× 1)
a – Dorsal sepal
b – Petal, upper lobe
c – Rostellum
d – Petal, lower lobe
e – Lip lobes
f – Stigma
g – Lateral sepal
h – Spur

long; spur cylindrical, somewhat clavate towards the apex, 4–4.5 cm long. **Column** 0.8 cm high, apiculate; rostellum cucullate; stigmas clavate, 2 cm long, united to the combined base of the lip, petals and lateral sepals.
DISTRIBUTION   Zimbabwe and S. Africa.
HISTORY   Described in 1905 by R.A. Rolfe in the *Gardeners' Chronicle* (ser. 3, 38: p. 450) based on a specimen collected by C.F.M. Munro in Rhodesia.

Bothriochilus Lemaire
Subfamily Epidendroideae
Tribe Arethuseae
Subtribe Bletiinae

Epiphytic, lithophytic or terrestrial herbs with a creeping rhizome. **Pseudobulbs** ovoid or pyriform, several-leaved above. **Leaves** subcoriaceous, plicate, linear-lanceolate, articulated to their tubular sheaths. **Inflorescence** lateral, from the base of the pseudobulbs. **Flowers** ± showy. **Dorsal sepal** free; **lateral sepals** decurrent on the column-foot to form a conspicuous spur-like mentum. **Petals** similar to dorsal sepal. **Lip** ± saccate below, ± 3-lobed at apex. **Column** erect, long and slender, wingless, with a long foot; pollinia 8, waxy.
DISTRIBUTION   Four species, Mexico to Panama.
DERIVATION OF NAME   From the Greek *bothrion* (small hollow) and *chilus* (lip) in reference to the saccate base of the lip.
TAXONOMY   Described in 1852 by C. Lemaire in *Le Jardin Fleuriste* (t. 325). H.G. Reichenbach considered *Bothriochilus* to be a synonym of *Coelia*. Currently the two genera are considered distinct, similar in having 8 pollinia and 2- or more-leaved pseudobulbs but with *Bothriochilus* having a conspicuous mentum

and a much longer column-foot as long as the column itself.
TYPE SPECIES   *B. bellus* Lemaire
CULTURE   Compost A. Temp. Winter min. 12–15°C. During the winter months when the plants are resting, very little water is required; only enough to prevent shrivelling of the pseudobulbs. The inflorescences grow from the side of the new shoots in the spring, and after flowering, the plants should be given increasing amounts of water, as the growths expand. Moderate shade should be given during growth.

Bothriochilus bellus (Lemaire) Lemaire
[Colour Plate]
A slender terrestrial plant, 30–80 cm tall. **Pseudobulbs** ovoid-globose, slightly compressed, smooth, 3–5 cm long, 1.5–2.5 cm broad, 3-leaved. **Leaves** clustered, erect-spreading, linear-lanceolate, long-acuminate, membranaceous, 15–60 cm long, 1–2 cm broad, articulated at base to a tubular sheath. **Inflorescence** 2- to several-flowered, up to 15 cm long, clothed by distichous, imbricate, ovate-lanceolate, glossy brown sheaths. **Flowers** large, tubular below, funnel-shaped above, yellowish-white, rose-purple at the apices of the segments, fragrant; lip mid-lobe orange. **Dorsal sepal** oblong-elliptic, obtuse, 3.5 cm long, 1 cm broad; **lateral sepals** obliquely oblong, obtuse, 5 cm long, 1 cm broad, long-decurrent at base to form a conspicuous mentum with the column-foot, 2 cm long. **Petals** obliquely oblong-spathulate, rounded, 3.5 cm long, 1 cm broad. **Lip** saccate at base; lamina narrowly cuneate, 3-lobed near the apex, 4.5 cm long, 1.2 cm broad; side lobes rounded; mid-lobe oblong-triangular, acute, upper surface granulose-thickened. **Column** slender, minutely toothed at the apex, 1.5 cm long.
DISTRIBUTION   Mexico, Guatemala and Honduras; in rain forests up to 1500 m altitude.
HISTORY   This, the type species of the genus *Bothriochilus*, was described in 1853 as *Bifrenaria bella* by C. Lemaire in the *Jardin Fleuriste* (t. 325). It was transferred to *Bothriochilus* also by Lemaire in 1856 in *L'Illustration Horticole* (misc. 30, 31) from a plant collected by M.F. Devros on the island of Ste Catherine.
B. bellus is a distinctive species, readily recognised by its erect few-flowered inflorescences arising from the base of the 3-leaved pseudobulbs and its fairly large showy flowers with white sepals tipped with purple and a yellow lip.
SYNONYM   *Coelia bella* (Lemaire) Rchb.f.

Brachtia Rchb.f.
Subfamily Epidendroideae
Tribe Oncidieae

Small epiphytes with stout ascending rhizomes covered by papery sheaths. **Pseudobulbs** compressed, narrowly oblong-ovate, ancipitous, 1- to 2-leaved, completely enclosed by imbricate leaf-bearing sheaths. **Leaves** fleshy to chartaceous. **Inflorescences** lateral, erect or arcuate, many-flowered; peduncle with a few sheaths; bracts either secund or distichous, prominent, glumaceous. **Flowers** fleshy, small. **Dorsal sepal** free, cucullate, dorsally carinate; **lateral sepals** similar but decurrent on the cuniculate ovary. **Petals** broader than the sepals, somewhat concave, apiculate. **Lip** firmly adnate to and confluent with the nectary, very fleshy, saccate at the base; calli 2-ridged, papillate and pubescent at the base. Column very short, winged, with a foot; pollinia 2, sulcate, on a subquadrate stipe with a small viscidium.
DISTRIBUTION   A small genus of some six species from the Andes of Venezuela to Ecuador.
DERIVATION OF NAME   Named after Captain Albert Bracht, an Austro-Hungarian army officer who collected plants in N.E. Italy.
TAXONOMY   *Brachtia* was established in 1850 by H.G. Reichenbach in the journal *Linnaea* (p. 853). It is allied to *Brassia* but is readily distinguished by the cuniculate ovary.
TYPE SPECIES   *B. glumacea* Rchb.f.
CULTURE   Temp. Winter min. 10°C. As with many high-altitude epiphytes these may be difficult to maintain. Probably best grown mounted and hung in a shady, humid atmosphere, such as is suitable for cool-growing masdevallias.

Brachtia andina Rchb.f.
An epiphyte with a stout ascending rhizome covered in sheathing bracts. **Pseudobulbs** ancipitous, narrowly oblong-ovate, up to 4 cm long, unifoliate. **Leaf** erect, narrowly oblong-elliptic, obtuse, 10–16 cm long, 0.3 cm wide. **Inflorescence** erect, more or less equalling leaf, up to 22 cm long, densely many-flowered, secund; bracts glumaceous, cupuliform, acute, up to 2 cm long, overtopping flowers. **Flowers** fleshy, yellow; pedicel and ovary prominently cuniculate, 6–8 mm long. **Dorsal** sepal narrowly oblong-elliptic, acute, 8 mm long, 2–3 mm wide; **lateral sepals** linear-oblong, acute, 8 mm long, 1.5–2 mm wide. **Petals** elliptic, obtuse, mucronate, 8 mm long, 3.5 mm wide. **Lip** cuneate-flabellate, subtruncate to slightly emarginate, 6 mm long, 5 mm wide; calli 2, parallel, fleshy, with a hirsute cushion behind. **Column**

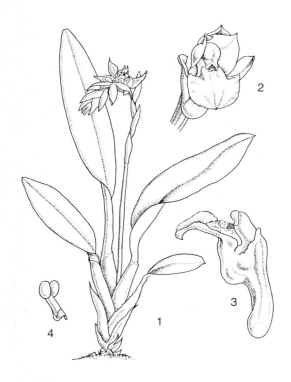

Brachtia andina
1 – Habit (× ½)
2 – Flower (× 3)
3 – Column, lip and ovary, side view (× 3)
4 – Pollinarium (× 7)

short, winged, with wings decurrent on the nectary; foot short.

DISTRIBUTION Colombia and Ecuador; 200–2500 m.

HISTORY The type specimen of *B. andina* was collected by Jameson near Quito in Ecuador and was described by Reichenbach in 1856 in *Bonplandia* (p. 322).

SYNONYM *B. verruculifera* Schltr.

Brachycorythis Lindl.
Subfamily Orchidoideae
Tribe Orchideae
Subtribe Orchidinae

Small to medium-sized terrestrial plants with ellipsoidal to fusiform tuberous roots and leafy erect stems. **Leaves** numerous, overlapping, sheathing at the base. **Inflorescence** terminal, laxly to densely many-flowered, often cylindrical; bracts leafy. **Flowers** small to large, often showy, white, yellow, pink or purple. **Sepals** free; lateral sepals spreading, oblique, falcate. **Petals** usually adnate to the dorsal sepal. **Lip** porrect, bipartite; hypochile saccate or spurred; epichile flattened, entire or trilobed. **Column**

erect, rather slender; anther loculi parallel, lacking canals; pollinia 2, mealy, with caudicles; rostellum 3-lobed, with a small erect folded mid-lobe and fleshy side lobes.

DISTRIBUTION A genus of some 35 species in tropical and S. Africa and tropical Asia.

DERIVATION OF NAME From the Greek *brachys* (short) and *korys* (helmet), referring to the strongly cucullate perianth that resembles a helmet.

TAXONOMY *Brachycorythis* is allied to the European genera *Orchis* and *Dactylorhiza* but is distinguished by its characteristically bipartite lip. It was established by John Lindley in 1838 in his *Genera and Species of Orchidaceous Plants* (p. 363) and has been most recently revised by Victor Summerhayes in the *Kew Bulletin* (p. 221) in 1955.

TYPE SPECIES *B. ovata* Lindl.

CULTURE Temp. Winter min. 10°C. As for *Habenaria* and many *Disa* species. A typical grassland or woodland terrestrial.

Brachycorythis helferi (Rchb.f.) Summerhayes

A terrestrial plant 15–60 cm tall. **Leaves** lanceolate or ovate-lanceolate, acuminate, 5.5–14 cm long, 1.5–3.5 cm wide. **Inflorescence** 6–20 cm long; bracts lanceolate, acuminate, overtopping flowers, 3–9 cm long. **Flowers** variable in colour; sepals and petals pale green variously edged or flushed with purple; lip white, with a yellow mark on disc and sometimes spotted with purple, to mauve; pedicel and ovary c.1 cm long. **Dorsal sepal** lanceolate, acuminate, 13–22 mm long, 3.7–6.5 mm wide; **lateral sepals** falcate, lanceolate, acuminate, 15–22 mm long, 3–6.5 mm wide. **Petals** lanceolate, acuminate, 11–19 mm long, 3–5 mm wide. **Lip** orbicular-ovate, obtuse, 12–33 mm long, 12–30 mm wide, erose; spur conical, deflexed and cylindrical towards apex, 6.5–10.5 mm long. **Column** 4–6 mm high.

DISTRIBUTION N.E. India (Assam), Burma, Thailand and Laos; up to 1600 m in deciduous mixed forest, bamboo forest and grassland.

HISTORY Helfer collected the type material in Tenasserim in Burma and Reichenbach named it after him as *Gymnadenia helferi* in 1872 in *Flora* (p. 270). Summerhayes transferred it to the present genus in the *Kew Bulletin* (p. 235) in 1955.

SYNONYMS *Gymnadenia helferi* Rchb.f.; *Habenaria helferi* (Rchb.f.) Hook.f.; *Platanthera helferi* (Rchb.f.) Kraenzl.; *Phyllompax helferi* (Rchb.f.) Schltr.

CLOSELY RELATED SPECIES *Brachycorythis henryi* (Schltr.) Summerhayes [Colour Plate] from Burma, China and N. Thailand, is very closely allied to *B. helferi* and may be no

more than a large-flowered variant of it. It differs in having shorter leaves, less than 7.5 cm long, and larger flowers that overtop the bracts.

Brassavola R. Br.
Subfamily Epidendroideae
Tribe Epidendreae
Subtribe Laeliinae

Epiphytic or lithophytic plants with slender or somewhat thickened stems, 1- or rarely 2-leaved at apex. **Leaves** terete to flattened-coriaceous. **Inflorescence** 1- to several-flowered, terminal or lateral, racemose. **Flowers** large, fairly showy. **Sepals** and **petals** subsimilar, spreading, linear to linear-lanceolate. **Lip** clawed, tubular around the column below, spreading above, margins fimbriate or entire. **Column** erect, short, mostly 2-winged; anther aperculate; pollinia 8.

DISTRIBUTION A small genus of about 15 species, all tropical American from Mexico through Central America and the W. Indies to Brazil and Argentina.

DERIVATION OF NAME Named for Sr Antonio Musa Brassavola, a Venetian nobleman and botanist. He was Professor of Logic, Physics and Medicine at Ferrara in Italy.

TAXONOMY R. Brown described the genus in 1813 in the 2nd edition of William Aiton's *Hortus Kewensis* (p. 216). Unfortunately, M. Adanson had already used *Brassavola* as a generic name in the Compositae but *Brassavola* R. Br. has now been conserved as a generic name in the Orchidaceae. *Brassavola* is allied to *Laelia* being similar in having 8 pollinia in pairs each joined by parallel caudicles. *Brassavola* is distinct, however, in that the lip broadens abruptly into the lamina and the pollinia are of two unequal sizes.

Both R.A. Rolfe in the *Orchid Review* (1902) and Rudolf Schlechter in *Orchis* (1919) have revised *Brassavola*.

More recently the sectional limits in the genus have been discussed by H.G. Jones in a series of articles culminating in a revision of the genus in *Annales des Naturhistorischen Museums in Wien* (1975) where he accepts five sections in the genus as follows:

1. sect. *Grandiflorae* in which the leaves are flat and broad. This corresponds to *Rhyncholaelia* Schltr. and was excluded by Schlechter from his revision and by us here.

2. sect. *Brassavola* in which the leaves are narrow, terete or semiterete and the lip apex is attenuated into a long slender point.

3. sect. *Sessililabia*. as above but lip apex not

attenuate and lip sessile. This section includes both sect. *Conchoglossum* and sect. *Prionoglossum* of Schlechter's revision.

4. sect. *Cuneilabia* in which the lip is cuneiform and the inflorescence is terminal.
5. sect. *Lateraliflorae*, similar to the above section but with a lateral inflorescence. This was included by Schlechter in the above section.

Jones also provides in this article a key to the sections, species and varieties of *Brassavola*.

TYPE SPECIES *Epidendrum cucullatum* L. [= B. *cucullata* (L.) R. Br.].

CULTURE Compost A. Temp. Winter min. 15°C. Summer max. 30°C. May be grown in pots but as most are pendulous to some degree, hanging baskets are better. *Brassavola* species like good light and, when growing, high humidity. Water may be freely given during the growing season, but less is required after flowering. Care must be taken not to allow shrivelling of the leaves during the rest period. Normal flowering time, early or late summer.

Brassavola cebolleta Rchb.f.

A small epiphytic plant. **Stems** slender, erect or ascending, slightly arcuate and flexuose, 1- or 2-articulated, 1-leafed a apex. **Leaf** erect, spreading or arcuate, subcylindric, sulcate above, long-attenuate at apex, 12–15 cm long, 0.3–0.4 cm in diameter. **Inflorescence** erect or slightly arcuate. 1- or 2-flowered, shorter than the leaves; bracts spreading, coriaceous, narrowly triangular, 0.3 cm long. **Flowers** rather small, pale green with a white lip; disc green; column white with a green base; pedicel 4–7 cm long. **Sepals** spreading, subsimilar, linear-lanceolate, acuminate, 2–2.5 cm long, 0.4 cm broad; lateral sepals subfalcate. **Petals** linear, long-acuminate, 2–2.5 cm long, 0.25 cm broad. **Lip** membranaceous, connate to the column at the base, ovate or obovate, acute and recurved above, 1.5–2 cm long, 1.2–1.5 cm broad. **Column** erect, slightly incurved, attenuate above, 0.8–1 cm long, minutely auriculate.

DISTRIBUTION E. Brazil and Paraguay.

Brassavola lips
1 – *B. cebolleta* (× ⅘)
2 – *B. cordata* (× ⅘)

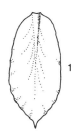 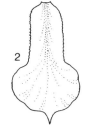

HISTORY Introduced into cultivation from Brazil by Consul Schiller and described by H.G. Reichenbach in 1855 in *Bonplandia* (p. 221).

SYNONYM *B. chacoensis* Kraenzl.

CLOSELY RELATED SPECIES See *B. tuberculata.*

Brassavola cordata Lindl.

A medium-sized epiphytic plant. **Stems** robust, terete, clavate, 2- to 3-noded, erect or ascending, 2–6 cm long, 0.5 cm broad above, 1-leafed at apex. **Leaf** erect, often slightly arcuate, shiny, deep green, thickly fleshy, almost semi-cylindric, linear-lanceolate, acute, deeply channelled above, 12–15 cm long, 1–1.2 cm broad, 0.5 cm thick. **Inflorescence** erect to slightly arcuate, 7–8 cm long, 3- to 5-flowered, subtended by a basal spathaceous bract; bracts narrowly triangular, membranaceous, concave, 0.3–0.4 cm long. **Flowers** medium-sized, shortly pedicellate, pale green spotted with red; lip white with a green base; column pale green. **Sepals** submembranaceous, linear, acuminate, 3 cm long, 0.4 cm broad; lateral sepals subfalcate. **Petals** narrowly linear, very acute, slightly oblique, 3 cm long, 0.3 cm broad. **Lip** erect-spreading, submembranaceous, free at the base, clawed, broadly ovate, cordate or cucullate at the base, abruptly shortly acuminate and recurved at the apex, 2.5 cm long, 1.2–1.3 cm broad. **Column** erect, 0.4–0.5 cm long.

DISTRIBUTION Brazil.

HISTORY Imported to England from Brazil by Messrs Loddiges in about 1835 and figured and described in the *Botanical Register* (t. 1913) the following year by John Lindley.

CLOSELY RELATED SPECIES Allied to B. *nodosa* but its flowers are only half as large and the lip and apex of the column are quite distinct.

Brassavola cucullata (L.) R. Br.

[Colour Plate]

An epiphytic plant, up to 40 cm high, often growing in large clumps. **Stems** erect-ascending, slender, terete, jointed, up to 21 cm long, concealed by white, scarious, tubular sheaths, 1-leafed at apex. **Leaf** linear-subulate, almost terete, fleshy-coriaceous, 18–35 cm long, 0.7 cm broad. **Inflorescence** short, 1- to 3-flowered; peduncle terete, 1–1.5 cm long; bracts tubular, scarious, 1 cm long. **Flowers** showy, fragrant at night; sepals and petals yellowish or white, ± tinged with red-brown on outer surface; lip white; pedicellate-ovary up to 23 cm long. **Sepals** linear-lanceolate, long-attenuate, 7–12.5 cm long, 0.6–0.9 cm broad. **Petal** similar to sepals but less than 0.5 cm broad. **Lip** shortly clawed, broadly cordate or suborbicular-ovate above, tubular at base, side

margins entire, ± denticulate or lacerate, long-acuminate at apex, 6–9.5 cm long, 1.5–2.5 cm broad. **Column** clavate, toothed at the apex, winged in front, 1.5–2 cm long.

DISTRIBUTION Mexico to Honduras, the W. Indies and northern S. America; in rain forests up to 1800 m altitude.

HISTORY Described by Carl von Linné in 1763 as *Epidendrum cucullatum* in the 2nd edition of *Species Plantarum* (p. 1350). R. Brown made it the type species of his new genus *Brassavola* in 1813 in the 2nd edition of William Aiton's *Hortus Kewensis* (p. 216).

SYNONYMS *Epidendrum cucullatum* L.; *Brassavola cuspidata* Hooker.

CLOSELY RELATED SPECIES Distinguished from *B. nodosa* by its narrower, longer leaves and the longer peduncle.

Brassavola flagellaris Barb. Rodr.

[Colour Plate]

A creeping epiphytic or lithophytic plant. **Stem** elongate, robust, cylindric, 4- to 5-noded, erect or ascending, 20–22 cm long, 0.5 cm in diameter above, 1-leafed at apex. **Leaf** reflexed above, rigid, slender, terete, deeply sulcate above, longly subulate and acute at apex, 40–50 cm long, 0.4 cm in diameter. **Inflorescence** erect-spreading, arcuate, 12–15 cm long, 5- to 15-flowered, subtended by an elongate spathe with a subulate acuminate apex; bracts concave, triangular, acute, 0.4 cm long. **Flowers** large, longly pedicellate, straw-coloured with a white lip spotted with golden-yellow at the base; column white. **Sepals** spreading, linear-lanceolate, long-acuminate, 3.5–4 cm long, 0.5–0.6 cm broad; lateral sepals oblique. **Petals** linear, long-acuminate, 3–3.5 cm long, 0.2 cm broad. **Lip** erect, membranaceous, shortly narrowly clawed, broadly obovate-subpanduriform above, subcordate at the base, 3 cm long, 2.2 cm broad; disc unicostate. **Column** erect, clavate, 3-angled in cross-section, 1 cm long, tridentate at the apex.

DISTRIBUTION E. Brazil only.

HISTORY Discovered by João Barbosa Rodrigues growing on trees and rocks by the River Parahybuna in Minas Gerais, Brazil. He described it in 1882 in his *Genera et Species Orchidearum Novarum* (p. 161).

Brassavola nodosa (L.) Lindl. [Colour Plate]

An epiphytic or lithophytic plant, up to 45 cm tall. **Stem** short, terete, 4–15 cm long, covered by scarious tubular sheaths, 1-leafed at apex. **Leaf** very fleshy-coriaceous, linear, acute or acuminate, sulcate above, up to 32 cm long, 2–3 cm broad. **Inflorescence** terminal, up to 20 cm long, 1- to several-flowered; peduncle terete; bracts triangular-lanceolate, acute, scarious, 0.5–1 cm long. **Flowers** showy, 7–8 cm across, fragrant at night; sepals and petals pale green; lip white, purple-spotted at base. **Sepals** linear, attenuate, 5–9.5 cm long, 0.3–0.5 cm broad. **Petals** similar to sepals. **Lip** with a tubular claw, spreading, ovate-orbicular above, apiculate-acuminate at apex, ± conspicuously venose, 2.5–5.5 cm long, 2.2–4.5 cm broad. **Column** small, 0.8 cm long.

DISTRIBUTION Mexico to Panama and Venezuela; sea level to 500 m altitude, often growing in xerophytic conditions on cacti and on the roots of mangroves by the sea shore.

HISTORY Originally described in 1735 by Carl von Linné in *Species Plantarum* as *Epidendrum nodosum* (p. 953) but transferred to *Brassavola* in 1831 in *Genera and Species of Orchidaceous Plants* (p. 114) by John Lindley.

SYNONYMS *Epidendrum nodosum* L.; *Brassavola venosa* Lindl.; *B.rhopalorrhachis* Rchb.f.

CLOSELY RELATED SPECIES *See B. cordata and B. cucullata.*

Brassavola tuberculata Hooker
[Colour Plate]

A large epiphytic or lithophytic plant. **Stems** short, clustered, robust, cylindric, 2- to 4-noded, erect or ascending, 6–15 cm long, 0.4–0.7 cm in diameter, 1-leafed at apex. **Leaf** erect, often arcuate, rigid, subcylindric, deeply trisulcate above, acute or attenuate at apex, 12–22 cm long, 0.6–0.8 cm broad. **Inflorescence** erect or arcuate, 1- to 2-flowered; peduncle 2–6 cm long; bracts erect-spreading, narrowly triangular, acuminate, 0.6 cm long. **Flowers** with sepals yellow or yellow-green, spotted red below; petals yellow or yellow-green; lip yellowish in the basal half. **Sepals** spreading, broadly linear, long-acuminate, 3.5–4 cm long, 0.4–0.6 cm broad; lateral sepals falcate. **Petals** subfalcate, linear, acute, 3.5–4 cm broad. **Lip** erect, shortly connate to the column-base, broadly elliptic-ovate above, obtuse or retuse and minutely apiculate, margins entire or more or less undulate, 3–3.5 cm long, 2.5–3 cm broad; disc keeled at the base. **Column** clavate, slightly incurved, triquetrous, 1.1–1.2 cm long.

DISTRIBUTION Brazil and Bolivia.

HISTORY First found by William Harrison growing on tree trunks near the sea at Botafoga Bay in Brazil. He sent plants to his brother Richard of Aigburgh near Liverpool, England, where it first flowered in cultivation in 1828. Sir William Hooker described it in the following year in the *Botanical Magazine* (t. 2878).

SYNONYMS *Brassavola fragrans* Lemaire; *B. gibbiana* Hort.; *B. perrinii* Lindl.

CLOSELY RELATED SPECIES *B. cebolleta* from Brazil is allied to *B. tuberculata* but differs in having slenderer 1- or 2-noded stems, a slen-

der leaf and smaller flowers with narrow sepals and petals and an acute apex to the lip.

Brassia R. Br.
Subfamily Epidendroideae
Tribe Oncidieae

Epiphytic or rarely terrestrial plants small to very large, with a stout rhizome. **Pseudobulbs** subglobose-ovoid to oblong-cylindrical, 1- or 2-leaved (rarely more), subtended by 2 or more pairs of imbricating sheaths. **Leaves** linear, oblong-oblanceolate or elliptic-oblong. **Inflorescences** lateral, basal, axillary, ± equalling the leaves in length, racemose or rarely paniculate, few to many-flowered. **Flowers** small to large, often showy. **Sepals** similar, free, linear-lanceolate, long-acuminate. **Petals** similar to sepals but shorter. **Lip** sessile, spreading, simple or pandurate, shorter than sepals and petals, with 2 or more ridges or calli at base. **Column** short, stout, wingless, without a foot; pollinia 2, obovoid, attached by a short stipe to a viscidium.

DISTRIBUTION Tropical Americas, about 25 species.

DERIVATION OF NAME Named in honour of William Brass, a botanist and illustrator who collected plants in Guinea and South Africa for Sir Joseph Banks.

TAXONOMY Robert Brown described the genus in 1813 in the 2nd edition of William Aiton's *Hortus Kewensis* (p. 215). John Lindley divided the species of the genus into two sections; *Eubrassia* with short inconspicuous bracts, and *Glumaceae* with long herbaceous bracts. However, N.H. Williams has recently shown in *Brittonia* (1972) that the species of sect. *Glumaceae* should be separated from the other *Brassia* species at the generic level. Furthermore, he placed the glumaceous *Brassia* species in the genus *Ada* which had hitherto been considered monospecific (*Ada aurantiaca* Lindl.).

Species of *Brassia* can be distinguished by their larger, distinct pseudobulbs, which are from 1- to 3-leaved, (as opposed to the indistinct 1-leafed pseudobulbs of *Ada*); their leaves have 1 main vein below; the bracts are small and are not papery and each growth has a maximum of 2 inflorescences.

Recently in *Orchidaceae Brasilienses* (1977), G. Pabst and F. Dungs have treated the 13 Brazilian species in four groups as follows:

1. *B. bidens* alliance – lip verrucose; rhizome long.
2. *B. candida* alliance – lip smooth; pseudobulbs approximate; lateral sepals very long, at least twice as long as the dorsal sepal. This group includes *B. caudata*.
3. *B. lawrenceana* alliance – lateral sepals short, equal or only a little longer than the dorsal sepal; petals only half the length of the dorsal sepal. This group includes *B. lawrenceana* and *B. lanceana*.
4. *B. arachnoidea* alliance – as group 3 but the petals almost as long as the dorsal sepals.

These groupings do not necessarily reflect the affinities of each species but are useful in identifying the species.

TYPE SPECIES *B. maculata* R. Br.

CULTURE Compost A. Temp. Winter min. 15–18°C. As for *Cattleya* but with a little more shade. Water freely during the growing season and keep drier when at rest, but avoiding undue shrivelling. The plants prefer to remain undisturbed for several years, as long as the compost remains sound. The roots will frequently leave the pot or container but this is generally a sign of good health. Flowering at various times, sometimes more than once in a year.

Brassia arcuigera Rchb.f. [Colour Plate]

A very variable plant with a stout creeping rhizome. **Pseudobulbs** ovoid, compressed, 5–18 cm long, 1-leafed at apex, subtended at base by 2–3 imbricating sheaths. **Leaf** oblong or oblong-elliptic, 15–56 cm long, 4–7 cm broad, acute. **Inflorescence** lateral, 30–60 cm long, laxly 4- to 15-flowered; bracts triangular-ovate, small. **Flowers** large, with orange or yellow-green sepals and petals, marked with large maroon blotches in the basal quarter; lip pale cream, spotted purple at base. **Dorsal sepal** linear-lanceolate, long-acuminate, 7–12 cm long, 0.5–0.7 m broad; **lateral sepals** similar to dorsal sepal but 24 cm long. **Petals** obliquely linear-lanceolate, 4–7.6 cm long, 0.4–0.5 cm broad, long-acuminate. **Lip** oblong-lanceolate, long-acuminate, 4–7.6 cm long, up to 1.5 cm broad; disc with 2 maroon, pubescent, fleshy ridges at base, ending in erect tubercles. **Column** short, stout, 0.6 cm long.

DISTRIBUTION Costa Rica, Panama and Peru.

HISTORY This species first flowered in cultivation in 1868 in the collection of Wentworth Butler of Strete Raleigh near Exeter, England. It was originally described by H.G. Reichenbach in the *Gardeners' Chronicle* (p. 388) in 1869 based on a specimen imported from Peru by Messrs Veitch. It is still frequently grown under the later synonym *B. longissima* (Rchb.f.) Nash.

SYNONYMS *Brassia lawrenceana* Lindl. var. *longissima* Rchb.f.; *Brassia longissima* (Rchb.f.) Nash

CLOSELY RELATED SPECIES Similar to *B. lawrenceana* but the flowers are much larger.

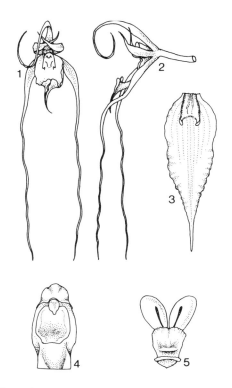

Brassia caudata
1 – Flower, front view (× ¾)
2 – Flower, side view (× ¾)
3 – Lip (× 1⅔)
4 – Column from below (× 3)
5 – Pollinia, stipe and viscidium (× 6)

Brassia caudata (L.) Lindl. [Colour Plate]

An epiphytic plant, up to 50 cm tall. **Pseudobulbs** oblong-elliptic, compressed, 6–15.5 cm long, 2–3.5 cm in diameter, 2- or 3-leaved at apex. **Leaves** oblong-elliptic, oblong-lanceolate or oblanceolate, coriaceous, 13–35 cm long, 2–6 cm broad, acute or obtuse. **Inflorescence** suberect to spreading, up to 40 cm long, laxly few-flowered; bracts distichous, triangular, concave, scarious, 0.5–1.0 cm long, acute. **Flowers** showy; sepals and petals orange-yellow, marked red-brown; lip yellow or greenish, spotted red-brown near base. **Dorsal sepal** linear-lanceolate, 3.5–7.5 cm long, 0.3–0.5 cm broad, long-acuminate; **lateral sepals** linear-lanceolate, long-attenuate, up to 13 cm long, 0.5–0.7 cm broad, dorsally keeled. **Petals** narrowly lanceolate, long-attenuate, falcate, incurving, 2–3 cm long, 0.3–0.4 cm broad. **Lip** sessile, obovate-elliptic, margins undulate, apex long-acuminate, 1.5–4 cm long, 0.7–1.3 cm broad; disc with 2 pubescent lamellae contiguous at base, broken up into teeth in front. **Column** erect, stout, 0.4 cm long.
DISTRIBUTION Florida, the W. Indies, Mexico south to Panama; in humid forests, to 1200 m altitude.

HISTORY One of the earliest American orchids to be described. Carl von Linné described it as *Epidendrum caudatum* based on a C. Plumier name in 1759 in *Systema Naturae* (p. 1246) and it was transferred by John Lindley to the genus *Brassia* in 1824 in the *Botanical Register* (t. 832).
SYNONYMS *Epidendrum caudatum* L.; *Oncidium caudatum* (L.) Rchb.f.; *Brassia lewisii* Rolfe; *Malaxis caudata* (L.) Willd.
CLOSELY RELATED SPECIES Similar to *B. maculata* but distinguished by its distinct lip with its dissected callus. See also *B. verrucosa*.

Brassia gireoudeana Rchb.f. & Warsc.
[Colour Plate]
See under *Brassia maculata*.

Brassia lawrenceana Lindl. [Colour Plate]

An epiphytic plant. **Pseudobulbs** ovate-oblong, compressed, pale green, up to 10 cm long, 3 cm broad, mostly 2-leaved at apex, subtended by old grey leaf-bases. **Leaves** oblong-oblanceolate, thin-textured, up to 40 cm long, 5 cm broad, acute. **Inflorescence** spreading-arcuate, fairly densely 7- to 10-flowered, racemose, as long or longer than the leaves. **Flowers** pale green, spotted at base of segments with chocolate-red markings; lip very pale green, yellow between the callus lamellae; column white at base, green above. **Sepals** linear-lanceolate, twisted, 6–7 cm long, 0.5–0.6 cm broad, long-acuminate. **Petals** similar to sepals but falcate, 3.5 cm long, 0.5 cm broad, long-acuminate. **Lip** obovate-pandurate, long-acuminate, up to 4.5 cm long, 2 cm broad, side margins revolute, apical margins undulate; disc with an oblong pubescent callus at base, concave in centre. **Column** erect.
DISTRIBUTION Guyana, Venezuela, Surinam and Brazil.
HISTORY Originally described by John Lindley in 1841 in the *Botanical Register* (t. 1754) from a plant of doubtful provenance. Plants introduced under the name *B. cochleata* were sent to Messrs Low & Co. of Clapton, London, by their collector John Henchman from Demerara (now Georgetown), Guyana.
SYNONYMS *Brassia cochleata* Knowles & Westcott; *B. angusta* Lindl.; *Oncidium lawrenceanum* (Lind.) Rchb.f.
CLOSELY RELATED SPECIES See *B. arcuigera*.

Brassia maculata R. Br.

A large epiphytic or rarely lithophytic plant, up to 1 m tall, with a stout creeping rhizome. **Pseudobulbs** ovoid to oblong-elliptic, compressed, 6–15 cm long, 2–4.5 cm broad, 1- or 2-leaved at apex. **Leaves** oblong-ligulate, coriaceous, 13–45 cm long, 3.5–5.5 cm broad, acute or obtuse. **Inflorescence** basal, subtended by a leaf-base, up to 90 cm long, laxly few- to many-flowered; bracts distichous, ovate, concave, scarious, 0.5–1 cm long. **Flowers** showy, 5–7 cm across, greenish-yellow, marked with purple; lip yellowish and purple-spotted; column bright green, speckled brown. **Sepals** linear-lanceolate, concave below, 3.5–6.5 cm long, 0.4–0.6 cm broad, acuminate. **Petals** linear-lanceolate, 2.2–3.5 cm long, 0.35–0.45 cm broad, acuminate. **Lip** sessile, subpandurate, lateral margins recurved, undulate apex rounded to obtuse, mucronate, 2.2–3.2 cm long, 1.8–2.5 cm broad; disc with a yellow or orange pubescent bilamellate callus, 0.6 cm long. **Column** short, stout, 0.5 cm long.
DISTRIBUTION The W. Indies, Belize, Guatemala and Honduras; rare, up to 750 m altitude.
HISTORY Introduced from Jamaica by Sir Joseph Banks and described by Robert Brown in William Aiton's *Hortus Kewensis* (p. 215) in 1813. One of Banks' plants flowered at the Royal Botanic Gardens, Kew in 1814.
SYNONYMS *Brassia wrayae* Skinner; *B. guttata* Lindl.; *Oncidium brassia* Rchb.f.
CLOSELY RELATED SPECIES *B. maculata* may be distinguished from *B. caudata* by its more evenly spotted lip which is conspicuously

Brassia maculata
1 – Flower, front view (× ¾)
2 – Flower, side view (× ¾)
3 – Lip (× 1)
4 – Column from below (× 3)
5 – Pollinia, stipe and viscidium (× 6)

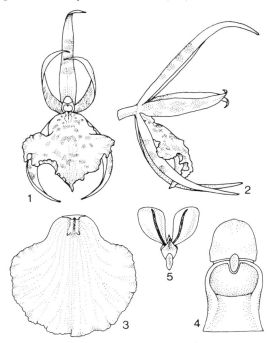

dilated in the middle and rounded or obtuse at the apex and by its callus of entire lamellae. *Brassia gireoudeana* Rchb.f. & Warsc. [Colour Plate] from Costa Rica is allied to *B. maculata* but is readily distinguished by its much longer sepals and by its light yellow apiculate lip which is spotted with brown in the central part only.

Brassia verrucosa Lindl. [Colour Plate]

A large epiphytic plant, 80 cm or more high. **Pseudobulbs** narrowly ovoid, compressed, clustered, 6–10 cm long, 2.5–4 cm in diameter, 2-leaved at apex, subtended by several scarious, ± leaf-bearing sheaths. **Leaves** oblong-elliptic, lanceolate or oblanceolate, coriaceous, 13–45 cm long, 3–4.5 cm broad, acute. **Inflorescence** basal, subtended by a leaf, up to 75 cm long, laxly many-flowered; bracts triangular, concave, distichous, acute, 0.5–1 cm long. **Flowers** showy, pale green spotted with dark brown; lip whitish, with green warts in lower half and reddish spots at the base; column green. **Sepals** linear-lanceolate, ± undulate, 5–12 cm long, 0.3–0.7 cm broad, long-acuminate; lateral sepals oblique and longer than the dorsal sepal. **Petals** linear-lanceolate, falcate, 3.5–5.5 cm long, 0.3–0.7 cm broad, long-acuminate. **Lip** sessile, subpanduriform, lateral margins recurved, apex broadly rounded to acuminate, 1.8–5 cm long, 1.3–2.5 cm broad; disc with a yellow bilamellate callus. **Column** small, minutely papillose, 0.5 cm long.

DISTRIBUTION Mexico, Guatemala, Honduras and Venezuela; rare in humid forests up to 1600 m altitude.

HISTORY The type specimen was collected by George Barker in Guatemala and was described in 1840 by John Lindley in the *Botanical Register* (misc. 36). The specific epithet refers to the warts on the lip.

SYNONYMS *Brassia brachiata* Lindl.; *B. aristata* Lindl.; *B. ophioglossoides* Klotzsch & Karst.; *B. coryandra* C. Morr.; *B. longiloba* DC.; *Oncidium verrucosum* (Lindl.) Rchb.f.; *O. brachiatum* (Lindl.) Rchb.f.

CLOSELY RELATED SPECIES *B. caudata* may be readily distinguished from *B. verrucosa* by its lack of greenish warts or excrescences on the lip, by its more acuminate lip and sepals, and by its longer sepals. *B. maculata*, like *B. caudata*, lacks any warts on the disc of the lip.

Bromheadia Lindl.
Subfamily Epidendroideae
Tribe Cymbideae
Subtribe Cyrtopodiinae

Small to large terrestrial or, less commonly, epiphytic plants. **Stems** cane-like, not pseudobulbous, elongate, leafy. **Leaves** distichous, coriaceous, flat or bilaterally compressed, articulated to sheathing leaf bases. **Inflorescence** terminal, simple or branched, with the flowers in opposite ranks; bracts stiff, persistent. **Flowers** resupinate, medium-sized, sometimes showy, produced one or a few at a time. **Sepals** and **petals** similar, free. **Lip** 3-lobed, lacking a spur, with a bipartite callus of a longitudinal basal ridge and a more complex swelling on the mid-lobe. **Column** elongate, terete, 2-winged, lacking a foot; pollinia 2, porate, sessile, attached directly to a large triangular or saddle-shaped viscidium; rostellum of 2 flaps meeting at a point.

DISTRIBUTION A genus of about 20 species ranging from Thailand and the Malay Peninsula to the Philippines and N.E. Australia. Borneo is probably the centre of diversity with about 12 species.

DERIVATION OF NAME Named in honour of Sir Edward French Bromhead F.R.S., a keen student of botany and friend of John Lindley.

HISTORY John Lindley established the genus in 1841 in the *Botanical Register* (misc. 184). It is allied to *Eulophia* and *Cymbidium* but is readily distinguished by cane-like stems, distichously arranged flowers produced in succession, and the sessile pollinia.

TYPE SPECIES *B. palustris* Lindl. (= *B. finlaysoniana* (Lindl.) Miq.)

CULTURE Temp. Winter min. 12–15°C. Epiphytic species may be grown in pots in a well-drained epiphyte mix., while the terrestrials require a more retentive combination such as fibrous peat (40%), bark (40%), perlite (20%). Water should be given carefully throughout the year.

Bromheadia finlaysoniana (Lindl.) Miq.
[Colour Plate]

A large terrestrial often forming large clumps. **Stems** cane-like, slender, erect, 75–275 cm tall. **Leaves** distichous, flat, coriaceous, oblong or oblong-elliptic, obtuse, 4–15 cm long, 1–2.8 cm wide, articulated to a tubular sheathing leaf base. **Inflorescence** terminal, simple or branched; each branch zig-zag, 2–40 cm long; bracts alternate, ovate-triangular, obtuse, 4–5 mm long. **Flowers** produced successively one at a time, faintly scented, white or pale pink

with a yellow patch on the lip at the base of the mid-lobe and purple veins on the lip lobes; pedicel and ovary 1.5–1.8 cm long. **Dorsal sepal** lanceolate or elliptic-lanceolate, acute to acuminate, 3.5–4 cm long, 0.8–1 cm wide; **lateral sepals** similar but oblique. **Petals** lanceolate or elliptic-lanceolate, acute or acuminate, 3.2–3.6 cm long, 1.4–1.8 cm wide. **Lip** 3-lobed in apical half, 2.5–2.8 cm long, 1.9–2.5 cm wide; side lobes erect, narrowly elliptic, rounded in front; mid-lobe ovate, acute or apiculate, erose-papillose on the margins; callus a linear and raised ridge in the basal half of the lip, with several verrucose ridges on the mid-lobe. **Column** 1.8–2 cm long.

DISTRIBUTION Thailand, Laos, Cambodia and Malaya to Sumatra, Borneo, New Guinea, the Philippines and N.E. Australia; in swamps, forest on sandy soils and in scrubby forest; sea level to 1300 m.

HISTORY John Lindley described this species as *Grammatophyllum finlaysonianum* in 1833 in his *Genera and Species of Orchidaceous Plants* (p. 173) based on specimens collected in Singapore by Finlayson and Wallich. F. Miquel transferred it to *Bromheadia* in his *Florae Indiae Bataviae* (vol. 3: p. 709) in 1859.

SYNONYMS *Grammatophyllum finlaysonianum* Lindl.; *Bromheadia palustris* Lindl.; *B. sylvestris* Ridl.

Broughtonia R. Br.
Subfamily Epidendroideae
Tribe Epidendreae
Subtribe Laeliinae

Medium-sized epiphytic plants. **Pseudobulbs** clustered, flattened, subcircular, 1- or 2-leaved at apex. **Leaves** conduplicate, coriaceous. **Inflorescence** terminal, several- to many-flowered. **Flowers** showy, medium-sized. **Sepals** and **petals** free from each other, spreading, subsimilar; petals slightly broader than the sepals; sepaline spur long, adnate to the ovary. **Lip** entire or somewhat 3-lobed, tubular, convolute below, enclosing the column, pilose on the upper surface. **Column** short; pollinia 4, flattened, attached to caudicles.

DISTRIBUTION Two species in Jamaica and Cuba.

DERIVATION OF NAME *Broughtonia* was named in honour of Arthur Broughton, an English botanist who collected in Jamaica in the early part of the nineteenth century.

TAXONOMY *Broughtonia* was proposed by R. Brown in 1813 in the 2nd edition of William Aiton's *Hortus Kewensis* (p. 217). It is closely allied to *Laeliopsis* Lindl. and to *Cattleyopsis* Lemaire from which it may be distinguished by the long proximally swollen sepaline tube which is adnate to the ovary and its coriaceous leaves with entire margins and short column with its 4 pollinia.

Many authors have indeed considered these last two congeneric with *Broughtonia*, but D. Correll in the *Botanical Museum Leaflets of Harvard University* (1941) has kept both separate as they have leaves which are fleshy, rigid and have serrate edges. In addition *Cattleyopsis* like *Laelia* has 8 rather than 4 pollinia although these are of two distinct sizes in the former. The most recent revision of this genus, *Laeliopsis* and *Cattleyopsis* is that of R. Sauleda and R. Adams in *Rhodora* in 1984 (pp. 445–467).
TYPE SPECIES   *B. sanguinea* (Sw.) R. Br.
CULTURE   Compost A or mounted. Temp. Winter min. 15°C. *Broughtonia* plants are probably best grown mounted on cork-bark or fern-fibre, but may also be grown in pans. They require good light and humidity with plenty of water while growing, and much less when growth is completed.

Broughtonia sanguinea (Sw.) R. Br.
[Colour Plate]
A medium-sized epiphytic plant, 30–45 cm high. **Pseudobulbs** globular to almost cylindric, clustered, 2.5–5 cm in diameter, 2-leaved. **Leaves** coriaceous, oblong, somewhat acute, 8–20 cm long, 1.5–4.5 cm broad. **Inflorescence** long, 20–48 cm long, simple or branched, 5- to 12-flowered in apical few cm; bracts minute. **Flowers** showy, 1.3–2.5 cm across, crimson; lip yellow at base with purplish veins. **Sepals** oblong-lanceolate, acute, 1.5–2.4 cm long, 0.4–0.6 cm broad; lateral sepals broader than dorsal, falcate. **Petals** roundish-elliptic, tapering to base and acute or obtuse at apex, 1.5–2.4 cm long, 0.7 cm broad. **Lip** up to 2.2 cm long, 2.4 cm broad, roundish, truncate, margins erose. **Column** about 0.9 cm long, slightly curved, thicker and winged above.
DISTRIBUTION Jamaica and Cuba; sea level to 800 m.
HISTORY Originally described by O. Swartz in 1788 in his *Prodromus Descriptionem Vegetabilium*, (p. 124) as *Epidendrum sanguineum* based on a collection made by R. Brown in Jamaica and an illustration of Sir Hans Sloane.

R. Brown transferred it to *Broughtonia* in 1813 in the 2nd edition of William Aiton's *Hortus Kewensis* (p. 217).
SYNONYMS   *Epidendrum sanguineum* Sw.; *Dendrobium sanguineum* (Sw.) Sw.; *Broughtonia coccinea* Lindl.

Bulbophyllum Thou.
Subfamily Epidendroideae
Tribe Dendrobieae
Subtribe Bulbophyllinae

Small to large epiphytic herbs. **Rhizome** short to long, creeping or hanging, ± covered by scarious sheaths. **Pseudobulbs** stout, sessile, often angled, spaced to clustered on rhizome, 1- to 2 (or rarely more)-leaved at apex. **Leaves** thin-textured to coriaceous, erect, suberect, spreading or pendulous. **Inflorescences** lateral from the base of the pseudobulbs, racemose to capitate, 1- to many-flowered; rhachis sometimes flattened. **Flowers** minute to large, mostly not very showy. **Dorsal sepal** free; **lateral sepals** connate at base to column-foot forming a saccate mentum, sometimes connate above. **Petals** free, smaller than sepals. **Lip** simple to 3-lobed, ± fleshy, often ciliate or pubescent, often recurved. **Column** short, erect with ± aristate terminal teeth or wings; anther terminal; pollinia 4, waxy.
DISTRIBUTION   One of the largest genera with possibly as many as 1000 species reaching their greatest diversity in S.E. Asia and adjacent regions but also widespread through Africa, Australasia and tropical America.
DERIVATION OF NAME   From the Greek *bulbos* (bulb) and *phyllon* (leaf), referring to the prominent leafy pseudobulbs of most species.
TAXONOMY   *Bulbophyllum* was established by Aubert du Petit Thouars in 1822 in *Orchidées des Iles Australes de l'Afrique* (tt. 93–97). The name has been conserved over Thouars' earlier generic name *Phyllorkis* (1809).

Most species in this large genus have a distinctive appearance in which the pseudobulb, which is mostly fairly prominent, appears to rest on the continuous rhizome. Nevertheless the plants are truly sympodial, each new growth arising from a bud at the base of the previous pseudobulb. The characteristic pseudobulbs and basal inflorescence serve to distinguish it from other genera such as *Dendrobium* in which the flowers have a distinct mentum.

In such a large genus it is possible to subdivide the species into sections but, as intermediate species are common, these are generally less distinct than the sections in some other genera such as *Dendrobium* and *Eria*. A full survey of the genus at sectional level has still to be made, but R. Holttum in *Orchids of Malaya* (1964) has distinguished 12 sections and over 100 species. The Thai and S.E. Asia species have also been considered by G. Seidenfaden in *Dansk Botanisk Arkiv* (1980). Many African species have previously been considered in the genus *Megaclinium* Lindl., characterised by a broad, flat

rhachis to the inflorescence, but these are now included in *Bulbophyllum* as many intermediate species are known. Indeed, in a single species such as *B. congolanum* Schltr. all variations are known from plants with a terete rhachis to those with a rhachis over 1 cm broad. The African species have recently been revised by J.J. Vermeulen (1987) in the second volume of *Orchid Monographs*.

Again, the genus *Cirrhopetalum* Thou. is considered by most recent authorities such as G. Seidenfaden in *Dansk Botanisk Arkiv* (1974, 1980) and A. Dockrill in *Australian Indigenous Orchids* (1969) to intergrade with *Bulbophyllum* to such an extent that it must be considered synonymous. Whilst agreeing that this is a sound judgement from the taxonomic point of view, *Cirrhopetalum* has been maintained by many growers as the majority of its cultivated species can be fairly readily distinguished from most *Bulbophyllum* species by their umbellate inflorescences. *Bulbophyllum* is such an unwieldy genus in terms of the number of species, that any attempt to subdivide it based on sound principles will be welcomed.
SYNONYMS   *Megaclinium* Lindl.; *Cirrhopetalum* Thou.; *Ephippium* Bl.; *Zygoglossum* Reinw.
TYPE SPECIES   *B. nutans* Thou. typ. cons.
CULTURE   Compost A. Temp. Tropical species, winter min. 15–18°C. Other species from higher altitudes, min. 10–15°C. The majority of *Bulbophyllum* species, being creeping plants, are best grown in shallow pans or baskets. They all require high humidity during growth, and moderate shade. When the new pseudobulbs are fully grown, much less water can be given, although mist forest plants should not remain dry for long. The exceptions are some species from India and Burma, which are adapted to a severe dry season. Species such as *B. auricomum* are deciduous and must remain dry for several weeks. *Bulbophyllum* plants should be allowed to grow undisturbed for as long as possible, especially the small species.

Bulbophyllum barbigerum Lindl.
[Colour Plate]
A small epiphytic plant with a fairly stout, creeping rhizome. **Pseudobulbs** much flattened, elliptic or circular in outline, 1.5–3 cm long, 1.5–2.7 broad, 1-leafed at apex. **Leaf** oblong or elliptic, rounded and emarginate at the apex, coriaceous, 2.5–11 cm long, 1–2.8 cm broad. **Inflorescence** erect or spreading, racemose, 9–20 cm long, laxly several-flowered; bracts narrowly ovate, acuminate, spreading, 0.9 cm long. **Flowers** small, deep red or wine-coloured; sepals tinged greenish. **Sepals** linear-lanceolate, attenuate to acute at apex, 1 cm long, 0.3 cm broad. **Petals** minutely triangular, 0.1 cm long and broad. **Lip** linear-ligulate,

ciliate on margins, with an apical tuft of long, radiating, clavate hairs, 1 cm long, 0.15 cm broad. **Column** short, erect with long, tapering deflexed stelidia and a short foot.

DISTRIBUTION Sierra Leone, east to Cameroon and Zaïre.

HISTORY This delightful species was introduced into cultivation from Sierra Leone by Messrs Loddiges, for whom it flowered in June 1836. John Lindley described it in 1837 in the *Botanical Register* (t. 1942).

CLOSELY RELATED SPECIES *B. barbigerum* is allied to *B. distans* but is a much smaller plant with flattened pseudobulbs and spreading bracts, and the hairs on the lip are clavate at the apex.

Bulbophyllum careyanum (Hooker) Sprengel
[Colour Plate]

A medium-sized epiphytic plant with a stout rhizome. **Pseudobulbs** globose-ovoid or oblong-ovoid, lightly grooved, 1-leafed, 1.5–5 cm long, 1.5–2.5 cm broad. **Leaf** erect or suberect, subpetiolate, oblong or linear-oblong, obtuse, 10–25 cm long, 2.5–5 cm broad. **Inflorescence** 12–23 cm long, decurved; raceme cylindric, densely many-flowered; bracts equally or exceeding the flowers. **Flowers** densely imbricating, 0.6–0.8 cm long, orange-yellow or greenish, more or less spotted and suffused with red-brown or purple; lip violet; column orange-yellow. **Sepals** oblong-ovate, acute; dorsal sepal 0.5 cm long, 0.25 cm broad; lateral sepals 0.6–0.8 cm long. **Petals** broadly ovate, aristate, very small. **Lip** auriculate at base, subentire, shortly stipitate, recurved, 0.5 cm long, 0.2 cm broad. **Column** stelidia long-aristate from a broad base.

DISTRIBUTION Nepal, India (the Khasia Hills) and Burma.

HISTORY Discovered in Nepal and sent to the Liverpool Botanic Garden in England by Dr Carey of Serampore after whom it was named. It first flowered in October 1824 and was described as *Anisopetalum careyanum* in the same year by Sir William Hooker in his *Exotic Flora* (t. 149). Kurt Sprengel transferred it to *Bulbophyllum* in 1826 in the 16th edition of Linnaeus' *Systema Vegetabilium* (p. 732).

Var. *ochracea* from Arracan has unspotted ochre-coloured flowers and a red-brown lip.

SYNONYMS *Anisopetalum careyanum* Hooker; *Pleurothallis purpurea* D. Don; *Tribrachia purpurea* (D. Don) Lindl.

CLOSELY RELATED SPECIES See *B. crassipes* and *B. neilgherrense*.

Bulbophyllum cocoinum Batem. ex Lindl.
[Colour Plate]

A small, epiphytic plant, 10–50 cm long. **Pseudobulbs** ovoid, biconvex or 3- or 4-angled, 1.5–4 cm long, 1-leafed at apex. **Leaf** lanceolate or oblong-lanceolate, acute, 8–27 cm long, 1–3 cm broad. **Inflorescences** pendulous, 14–45 cm long, racemose, many-flowered. **Flowers** white, greenish or cream-coloured, often flushed pink or purple. **Sepals** lanceolate, long-acuminate, 0.8–1.4 cm long. **Petals** oblanceolate, denticulate, 0.25–0.35 cm long. **Lip** entire or with rounded, obscure side lobes, margins ciliolate or denticulate, 0.25–0.3 long, 0.1 cm broad. **Column** short, stout, 0.15 cm long; stelidia porrect, over 0.1 cm long; acute; foot curved.

DISTRIBUTION Sierra Leone to Ghana and Pagulu, possible also in Uganda.

HISTORY Imported from Sierra Leone by Messrs Loddiges for whom it flowered at Hackney, London, in January 1835. John Lindley received a plant from them and also from James Bateman at about the same time and described it in the *Botanical Register* (t. 1964) in 1836.

Bulbophyllum crassipes Hooker f.

A creeping epiphytic herb with a robust rhizome, 0.4–0.5 cm thick. **Pseudobulbs** conical, 5–7 cm apart on the rhizome, 5 cm long, 1.5–2 cm broad, angled when dry, concealed by a ventricose sheath, 1-leafed at apex. **Leaf** oblong, obtuse or shortly mucronate, shortly petiolate, thickly coriaceous, 6–12 cm long, 1.5–2 cm broad. **Inflorescence** 15–20 cm long; bracts oblong, obtuse, 0.7–1 cm long. **Flowers** yellowish-gold, small. **Dorsal sepal** obovate to elliptic, rounded at the apex, 0.5 cm long, 0.3 cm broad; **lateral sepals** ovate, acuminate, oblique, 0.75 cm long, 0.4 cm broad; mentum 0.2 cm high. **Petals** narrowly elliptic, 0.3 m long, 0.1 cm broad. **Lip** linguiform, grooved above, 0.3 cm long. **Column** 0.3 cm long; stelidia triangular.

DISTRIBUTION India, Burma and Indo-China.

Bulbophyllum crassipes
1 – Flower (× 4⅓)
2 – Column (× 6½)
 a Column
 b Anther-cap
 c Stelidium
 d Column-foot

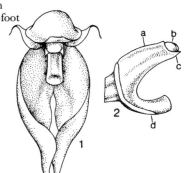

HISTORY Collected by Dr N. Wallich at Martaban and by C.B. Clarke in Sikkim, and described by Sir Joseph Hooker (1890) in the *Flora of British India* (p. 760).

SYNONYM *B. careyanum* Wall. non Sprengel

CLOSELY RELATED SPECIES Similar in vegetative habit to *B. careyanum* but differing in its longer column with short erect stelidia.

Bulbophyllum dearei (Hort.) Rchb.f.
[Colour Plate]

Pseudobulbs clustered or slightly spread, narrowly conical, up to 3 cm long, 1 cm broad, 1-leafed at apex. **Leaf** elliptic-oblong, acute, or obtuse, 10–17 cm long, up to 5 cm broad; petiole 3 cm long, slender. **Inflorescences** erect, about as long as the leaves, 1-flowered. **Flowers** large, showy; dorsal sepal tawny-yellow, spotted with red, lateral sepals with purple markings on both sides; petals tawny-yellow, with deeper venation and some reddish-purple spots; lip whitish, mottled with purple; column deep tawny-yellow, margined with red. **Dorsal sepal** ovate-lanceolate, acute, curved forwards, 3.5–4.6 cm long, 1.4–1.7 cm broad; **lateral sepals** lanceolate-falcate, dilated and saccate at the base, 2.5 cm long, 0.8–1 cm broad. **Petals** linear-lanceolate, acute or acuminate, reflexed, 3–3.5 cm long, 0.8 cm broad. **Lip** highly mobile with a flexible claw, triangular with upturned sides and reflexed at apex, 1.3 cm long, 0.7 cm broad; crest U-shaped. **Column** very short.

DISTRIBUTION The Philippines (Palawan and Mindanao) and Borneo; at low altitudes.

Bulbophyllum dearei
1 – Flower (× ¾)
2 – Column, column-foot and lip (× 2)
3 – Anther (× 6½)
4 – Pollinia (× 6½)

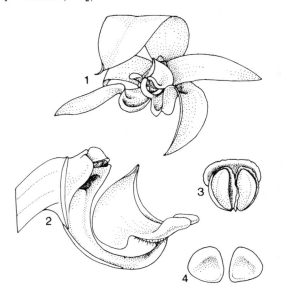

HISTORY Introduced from the Philippines by Col. Deare after whom it was named as *Sarcopodium dearei* in the *Gardeners' Chronicle* of 1883. H.G. Reichenbach transferred it to *Bulbophyllum* in 1888 in *Flora* (p. 156). This species is still occasionally cultivated under the later synonym *B. godseffianum*.
SYNONYMS *Bulbophyllum godseffianum* Weathers; *Sacropodium dearei* Hort.; *Phyllorchis dearei* (Hort.) O. Ktze.

Bulbophyllum distans Lindl. [Colour Plate]
A medium-sized epiphytic plant with a creeping rhizome. **Pseudobulbs** conical or ovoid, 3- to 4-angled, 1–4 cm long, 1–2.5 cm in diameter, 1-leafed at apex. **Leaf** oblong, rounded, shortly petiolate, coriaceous, 9–15 cm long, 1.6–3.5 cm broad. **Inflorescences** erect, 15–60 cm long, laxly many-flowered; bracts 0.4–1.5 cm long, greenish. **Flowers** opening in succession; sepals yellowish-green or variously tinged maroon or purplish; lip maroon or purplish. **Sepals** lanceolate or linear-lanceolate, acuminate or attenuate, 0.9–1.1 cm long, 0.2–0.3 cm broad. **Petals** slender, falcate, linear-attenuate, acuminate, 0.4 cm long. **Lip** linear, somewhat fleshy, with 2 reflexed, papillose, ± hyaline auricles on the fleshy base, about 0.8 cm long, longer hairs on lip arising from above and below on margins and on surface of lip. **Column** short, truncate; stelidia tapering, deflexed; foot short, curved inwards.
DISTRIBUTION W. Africa across to Uganda; in rain forest and lower montane forest.
HISTORY Discovered in 1860 on the banks of the River Nun in W. Africa by G. Mann and described two years later by John Lindley in the *Journal of the Linnean Society, Botany* (p. 125).
CLOSELY RELATED SPECIES Closely allied to *Bulbophyllum calamarium* Lindl. which may be distinguished by its ligulate fleshy lip from which the longer hairs arise only from the ventral margins. See also *B. barbigerum*.

Bulbophyllum falcatum (Lindl.) Rchb.f. [Colour Plate]
A small, erect, epiphytic plant, up to 35 cm high. **Pseubobulbs** ovoid or elongate-ovoid, 3- to 4-angled, 2–6 cm long, 2-leaved at apex. **Leaves** oblong-lanceolate or oblanceolate, 4–16 cm long, 0.6–2.3 cm broad. **Inflorescences** up to 35 cm long; rhachis thin, flattened, with sinuate margins, up to 1.4 cm broad, green or purple. **Flowers** erect, inturned, green or variously marked purple to entirely red or purple, apex of petals yellow. **Dorsal sepal** more or less spathulate or widened above the middle, thick and fleshy on apical margins, rounded at the apex, 0.4–0.7 cm long; **lateral sepals** falcate, acute. **Petals** linear or oblong, falcate, obtuse to rounded and somewhat thickened

at apex, 0.2–0.3 cm long. **Lip** relatively thin and flat, curvate, 0.2 cm long, 0.15 cm broad, glabrous. **Column** short, 0.1 cm long; wings rounded.
DISTRIBUTION Guinea and Sierra Leone, east to Zaïre and Uganda.
HISTORY Originally described as *Megaclinium falcatum* by John Lindley in the *Botanical Register* (t. 989) in 1826. H.G. Reichenbach transferred it to *Bulbophyllum* in 1864 in *Walpers, Annales Botanices* (p. 258).
SYNONYMS *Megaclinium falcatum* Lindl.; *M. endotrachys* Kraenzl.; *Bulbophyllum leptorhachis* Schltr.

Bulbophyllum gracillimum (Rolfe) Rolfe [Colour Plate]
See under *Bulbophyllum longissimum*.

Bulbophyllum lasiochilum Parish & Rchb.f. [Colour Plate]
A small epiphytic plant with a large slender rhizome bearing pseudobulbs at intervals of about 3 cm. **Pseudobulbs** ovoid-pyriform, 2–3 cm long, 1.5–2 cm broad, 1-leafed at apex. **Leaf** erect, oblong-elliptic, minutely bifid at the apex, coriaceous, 4–7 cm long, 2 cm broad. **Inflorescence** erect, 1-flowered, 7 cm long; scape purple-spotted. **Flower** large; dorsal sepal and petals purple; lateral sepals yellowish with large crimson spots; lip purple with long purple marginal hairs. **Dorsal sepal** curved forward, linear-lanceolate, up to 1.5 cm long, 0.4 cm broad; **lateral sepals** free except near base, falcate, inrolled, ovate, subacute, 2–3 cm

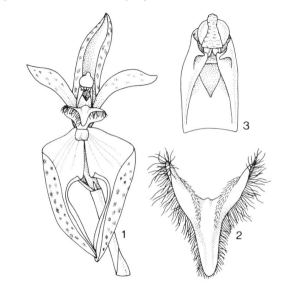

Bulbophyllum lasiochilum
1 – Flower (× 2)
2 – Lip (× 4)
3 – Column from below (× 6)

long, 0.8 cm broad. **Petals** falcate, narrowly linear-oblanceolate, acute, 1.2 cm long, 0.3 cm broad, margins minutely denticulate. **Lip** 3-lobed, 0.5–1 cm long, 0.4 cm broad, deeply cleft at base; side lobes slightly down-curved, pubescent; mid-lobe fleshy, ligulate, rounded at the apex. **Column** short, stout, 0.4 cm long; stelidia short, pointed, deflexed; column-foot 0.6 cm long.
DISTRIBUTION S. Burma, Thailand and Malaya.
HISTORY Discovered by Charles Parish in Burma and described by him and H.G. Reichenbach in 1874 in the *Transactions of the Linnean Society* (p. 153).
SYNONYMS *Cirrhopetalum breviscapum* Rolfe; *B. breviscapum* (Rolfe) Ridley

Bulbophyllum leopardinum (Wall.) Lindl. [Colour Plate]
A medium-sized epiphytic plant. **Pseudobulbs** clustered, ovoid-oblong to cylindric-ovoid, slightly compressed, smooth or with indistinct rounded ridges, 2–5 cm long, 1–2.5 cm in diameter, 1-leafed at apex. **Leaf** coriaceous, rigid, oblong, petiolate, 7.5–20 cm long, 2.5–6 cm broad; petiole 2.5–7 cm long. **Inflorescence** very short, 1- to 3-flowered; bracts large, broadly ovate, acute. **Flowers** fasciculate, globose-campanulate, 2–3 cm across, pale yellowish-brown or greenish, closely spotted with purple; lip deep purple; column pale yellow. **Dorsal sepal** ovate-lanceolate, acute, 2 cm long, 0.8 cm broad; **lateral sepals** obliquely ovate, acuminate, 2.3 cm long, 1 cm broad. **Petals** small, broadly ovate, acute or acuminate, 1.5 cm long. **Lip** fleshy, ovate, obtuse, entire, decurved, denticulate on the basal auricles, with 2 pronounced, smooth longitudinal ridges on each side of mid-line, 1.5 cm long, 1 cm broad. **Column** thick, 0.3–0.4 cm long; stelidia stout, triangular, 0.1 cm long.
DISTRIBUTION Nepal and India (Sikkim and Assam); in forests between 900 and 1900 m altitude.
HISTORY First collected in 1821 on Mt Chandaghiry in the Nepalese Himalayas by Dr N. Wallich and described by John Lindley in his *Genera and Species of Orchidaceous Plants* (p. 48).
SYNONYMS *Sarcopodium leopardinum* Lindl.; *Dendrobium leopardinum* Wall.
CLOSELY RELATED SPECIES Similar to *Bulbophyllum griffithii* (Lindl.) Rchb.f., which differs in having 1-flowered inflorescences and is a smaller plant with narrowly oblong leaves.

Bulbophyllum lobbii Lindl. [Colour Plate]
An epiphytic plant with a stout rhizome. **Pseudobulbs** ovoid, 3–8 cm apart on rhizome, smooth when young, 3–5 cm long, 2–3 cm

broad, unifoliate, with dark-green reticulations on a lighter background. **Leaf** linear-oblong, petiolate, coriaceous, obtuse, 10–25 cm long, up to 7 cm broad; petiole 3 cm long. **Inflorescences** 1-flowered; peduncle 10–15 cm long, speckled. **Flowers** wide-opening, 6–10 cm across, very variable in colour, pale yellow, ochreous or reddish-yellow with red nerves or with yellow and pink speckles and lined with brown. **Dorsal sepal** erect, lanceolate, acuminate, up to 5 cm long, 1.2 cm broad; **lateral sepals** ovate-lanceolate, falcate, concave below, apices curved. **Petals** narrow, spreading, almost horizontal, 3.7 cm long, much narrower than sepals. **Lip** broadly ovate, recurved, acute, up to 0.9 cm long, 0.7 cm broad. **Column** short, broad; stelidia very short.

DISTRIBUTION Java, Sumatra, Borneo, Malaya, Thailand and Burma (Tenasserim).

HISTORY *B. lobbii* was considered by John Lindley to be the finest species of this large genus. He named it in 1847 in the *Botanical Register* (sub t. 29) after Thomas Lobb who discovered it in Java whilst collecting for Messrs Veitch.

Bulbophyllum longiflorum Thou.

A small epiphytic plant. **Pseudobulbs** borne at 2–4 cm intervals on a creeping rhizome, conical or ovoid, obscurely angled, 2.2–4.6 cm long, 1.2–1.6 cm broad, 1-leafed at apex. **Leaf** suberect, elliptic to oblong-elliptic, coriaceous, rounded and slightly notched at apex, 12–18 cm long, 3–4 cm broad. **Inflorescence** erect or arcuate, ± equal to leaf in length, umbellate, 3- to 7-flowered; peduncle terete, long. **Flowers** all facing outwards, up to 4.5 cm long; sepals yellow or orange-yellow, densely spotted red with dark reddish-black apices; lip and petals dark red; column yellowish-white. **Dorsal sepal** ovate, concave, with an apical bristle-like extension, 1.5 cm long; **lateral sepals** connate in apical two-thirds except at apex, lanceolate, 2–4 cm long, outer margins reflexed. **Petals** 0.4–1 cm long, triangular, margins fringed, with a bristle-like extension at the apex. **Lip** small, motile, strongly curved, keeled on upper surface, 0.5 cm long, 0.2 cm broad. **Column** small; stelidia sharply pointed, porrect, 0.4 cm long.

DISTRIBUTION Tropical Africa, Madagascar, the islands of the Indian Ocean, S.E. Asia, Indonesia, the Pacific Islands and N.E. Australia; in forest up to 1200 m.

HISTORY Originally described in 1786 by George Forster in *Florulae Insularum Australium Prodromus* (p. 60) as *Epidendrum umbellatum* from a plant collected in the Society Islands. Sir William Hooker and G. Arnott transferred it to *Cirrhopetalum* in 1832 in the Botany of Capt. Beechey's *Voyage in the 'Blossom'*.

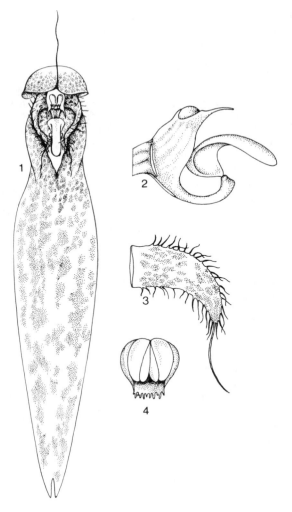

Bulbophyllum longiflorum
1 – Flower (× 2)
2 – Column, column-foot and lip, side view (× 4)
3 – Petal (× 4)
4 – Anther (× 11)

If *Cirrhopetalum* is considered a synonym of *Bulbophyllum* (as we do here following G. Seidenfaden in *Dansk Botanisk Arkiv*, 1973), then the name for this species must be *Bulbophyllum longiflorum* Thou. because the epithet *umbellatum* had already been used in *Bulbophyllum* for another species. Aubert du Petit Thouars published his *B. longiflorum* in 1822 in his *Orchidées des Iles Australes de l'Afrique* (t. 98).

SYNONYMS include *Epidendrum umbellatum* Forst.f.; *Cymbidium umbellatum* (Forst.f.) Sprengel; *Cirrhopetalum thouarsii* Lindl.; *Bulbophyllum clavigerum* Fitzg.; *Cirrhopetalum umbellatum* (Forst.) Hooker & Arn., *Cirrhopetalum longiflorum* (Thou.) Schltr.

Bulbophyllum longissimum (Ridley) Ridley
[Colour Plate]

A creeping epiphytic plant with a stout rhizome. **Pseudobulbs** borne 3–7 cm apart, ovoid, 2.5–4 cm long, 1.5–7.5 cm broad, 1-leafed at apex. **Leaf** erect, recurved above, oblong, subacute, coriaceous, attenuate below, 9–15 cm long, 2.5–4.5 cm broad. **Inflorescence** arcuate or pendulous, about 20 cm long, with 4–7 flowers in a terminal umbel; bracts oblong-lanceolate, acuminate, 1–1.5 cm long. **Flowers** very long; dorsal sepal greenish-white; lateral sepals pink or off-white, all sepals longitudinally striped with purple; petals and lip green tinged with purple. **Dorsal sepal** lanceolate or oblong-lanceolate, ciliate, concave, 1.5–1.8 cm long, 0.5 cm broad; **lateral sepals** connate except at base, ligulate, longly caudate, 20–30 cm long, 1 cm broad. **Petals** falcate, oblong or oblong-lanceolate, subacute, ciliate, 0.8–1 cm long. **Lip** recurved, oblong-ovate, subacute, fleshy, grooved, 0.8 cm long. **Column** oblong, 0.8 cm long; stelidia falcate-incurved, filiform, acute.

DISTRIBUTION Peninsular Thailand and Malaya.

HISTORY This extraordinary plant was discovered near Panga in Thailand by Charles Curtis for whom it flowered in October 1893 in the Penang Botanic Garden. H.N. Ridley described it in 1896 as *Cirrhopetalum longissimum* in the *Journal of the Linnean Society* (p. 280). It was transferred to *Bulbophyllum* by him in 1911 in the *Journal of the Straits Branch of the Royal Asiatic Society* (p. 194).

SYNONYM *Cirrhopetalum longissimum* Ridley

CLOSELY RELATED SPECIES *Bulbophyllum rothschildianum* (O'Brien) J.J. Smith [Colour Plate] is closely allied but differs in having shorter, broader lateral sepals, and terete or flattened movable appendages on the margins of the dorsal sepal and petals. *Bulbophyllum gracillimum* (Rolfe) Rolfe [Colour Plate] from Thailand, Malaya and Sumatra across to New Guinea and the Pacific Islands is very variable in flower colour and lateral sepal length. It is allied to *B. longissimum* but has a shorter dorsal sepal up to 1 cm long and the apex of the dorsal sepal and petals are drawn out into long threads as long as or longer than the laminae proper.

Bulbophyllum mastersianum (Rolfe) J.J. Smith [Colour Plate]

An erect epiphytic plant. **Pseudobulbs** clustered, ovoid, obscurely angled, 2.5–3.5 cm long, 1.5–2 cm in diameter, 1-leafed at apex. **Leaf** erect or suberect, arcuate, oblong, subobtuse, attenuate below, coriaceous, 10–12 cm long, 2–3 cm broad. **Inflorescence** basal, erect, 12–15 cm long, with 6–8 flowers in a terminal umbel; peduncle slender, terete, purple; bracts linear-lanceolate, acute, 0.6–0.7 cm long. **Flowers** yellow suffused with brown, up to 4 cm long. **Dorsal sepal** elliptic-ovate, cucullate, subacute, margins shortly ciliate, 0.6 cm long, 0.3 cm broad; **lateral sepals** connate almost to apex, linear-oblong, emarginate, 3–3.5 cm long, 1–1.2 cm broad. **Petals** falcate-oblong, acute, 0.6 cm long, margin minutely ciliate. **Lip** recurved, fleshy, linear-oblong, 0.3–0.4 cm long. **Column** fleshy, 0.2 cm long; stelidia short.

DISTRIBUTION   Borneo and the Moluccas.
HISTORY   First introduced into cultivation by Messrs Linden of Brussels for whom it flowered in June 1890. R.A. Rolfe described it as *Cirrhopetalum mastersianum* in 1890 in *Lindenia* (p. 33, t. 255) naming it in honour of Dr Masters, then editor of the *Gardeners' Chronicle*.

J.J. Smith (1912) transferred it to *Bulbophyllum* in the *Bulletin du Jardin Botanique, Buitenzorg* (p. 26).
SYNONYM   *Cirrhopetalum mastersianum* Rolfe

Bulbophyllum medusae (Lindl.) Rchb.f.
[Colour Plate]
A small epiphytic herb with a stout rhizome. **Pseudobulbs** ovoid-conical to pyriform, often curved, ribbed, 2–5 cm long, 2 cm in diameter, unifoliate. **Leaf** linear-oblong or elliptic-oblong, very coriaceous, 12.5–15 cm long, 1.5–2 cm broad; petiole short, somewhat obscure. **Inflorescences** curved, 15–20 cm long with flowers in a dense globose head; peduncle stout, loosely sheathed. **Flowers** 7.5 cm long, yellow, spotted red. **Dorsal sepal** lanceolate, long-acuminate, with a long capillary apex, 2.5 cm long, 0.3 cm broad; **lateral sepals** lanceolate, similar to but longer than the dorsal sepal. **Petals** ovate-lanceolate, apices capillary, long-acuminate, 0.5 cm long, 0.2 cm broad. **Lip** nearly straight, ovate, fleshy below, erosely ridged above, 0.15 cm long. **Column** with long stelidia, 0.3 cm long.

DISTRIBUTION   Malaya, Thailand, Sumatra, Borneo and the Philippines.
HISTORY   Introduced into cultivation from Singapore by Messrs Loddiges and described as *Cirrhopetalum medusae* by John Lindley in 1842 in the *Botanical Register* (t. 12).

It was transferred to the present genus by H.G. Reichenbach in 1861 in *Walpers, Annales Botanices* (p. 262). *B. medusae* is readily distinguished by its tightly clustered, almost globular heads of strongly scented creamy flowers from which the lateral sepals hang in a weeping manner, and by its slender dorsal sepal and petals which have entire margins.

SYNONYMS   *Cirrhopetalum medusae* Lindl.; *Phyllorchis medusae* (Lindl.) O. Ktze.

Bulbophyllum neilgherrense Wight
Pseudobulbs ovoid-conical, smooth, slightly compressed, distant on a creeping rhizome, 3.5–5 cm long, 2–3 cm in diameter, 1-leafed at apex. **Leaf** suberect, elliptic-oblong or oblong, fleshy-coriaceous, 10–15 cm long, 3.5–4 cm broad, very shortly petiolate. **Inflorescences** erect or suberect, 7.5–18 cm long, fairly densely many-flowered; peduncle terete, jointed, sheathed at the joint with a membranaceous sterile bract; bracts acute, shorter than the flowers. **Flowers** largish, dull brownish-yellow to purplish-green; lip greenish-brown to purple. **Dorsal sepal** broadly ovate, 0.4–0.5 cm long, 0.2 cm broad; **lateral sepals** oblong, connivent at the base, 2–3 times larger than dorsal sepal. **Petals** triangular-ovate, acuminate, 0.3 cm long, up to 0.1 cm broad. **Lip** auriculate, recurved, 0.4–0.6 cm broad; auricles entire or denticulate; mid-lobe ligulate, entire, grooved dorsally. **Column** with lanceolate stelidia.
DISTRIBUTION   S. India (Malabar, in the Nilghiri Hills).
HISTORY   Discovered in 1849 in S. India in the Nilghiri Hills (Neilgherries) by McIvor, and at Malabar by Robert Wight who described it in 1851 in *Icones Plantarum Indiae Orientalis* (t. 1650).
CLOSELY RELATED SPECIES   *B. neilgherrense* is allied to *B. careyanum* but differs in having a longer, more erect, fewer-flowered and less dense inflorescence and rather larger distinctively coloured flowers.

Bulbophyllum ornatissimum (Rchb.f.)
J.J. Smith [Colour Plate]
Pseudobulbs ovoid to oblong-conical, 3- or 4-angled, 2.5–5 cm long, 1.2 cm broad, 1-leafed. **Leaf** erect, linear-oblong, obtuse, shortly petiolate, 10–16 cm long, up to 3.7 cm broad; petiole 2 cm long. **Inflorescence** erect, with a robust peduncle, subumbellate, 15 cm or more long, 4- to 5-flowered. **Flower** up to 10 cm long; sepals and petals pale yellow or yellow-green streaked and stained with purple. **Dorsal sepal** cymbiform, ovate, acuminate, longly ciliate, 1.5 cm long, 0.8 cm broad; **lateral sepals** linear-lanceolate, connate above the middle, acuminate, apices filiform, 5–10 cm long, 0.9 cm broad at base. **Petals** subulate-lanceolate, falcate, slightly ciliate on lower margins, with a tuft of narrowly obpyriform hairs at the apex, 1–1.4 cm long, 0.4 cm broad. **Lip** strigose, recurved, fleshy, ovate, 2-ridged on upper surface, shortly ciliate, rounded at the apex, 0.6 cm long, 0.3 cm broad. **Column** with decurved stelidia, 0.5 cm long.
DISTRIBUTION   India (Sikkim Himalayas and Assam).
HISTORY   Described by H.G. Reichenbach in 1882 in the *Gardeners' Chronicle* (n.s. 18, p.

424) from specimens of unknown provenance sent to him first by W. Bull and later by C.W. Strickland, James O'Brien and Messrs Veitch. J.J. Smith transferred this species to *Bulbophyllum* in 1912 in the *Bulletin du Jardin Botanique de Buitenzorg* (p. 26) and G. Seidenfaden has recently followed this treatment.
SYNONYMS   *Cirrhopetalum ornatissimum* Rchb.f.; *Phyllorchis ornatissimum* (Rchb.f.) O. Ktze.

Bulbophyllum patens King ex Hooker f.
[Colour Plate]
A medium-sized epiphytic plant with a stout rhizome. **Pseudobulbs** ellipsoid, 2–3.8 cm long, 1–2 cm in diameter, 1–8 cm apart on the rhizomes, 1-leafed at apex. **Leaf** fleshy, elliptic-oblong, acute, shortly petiolate, 15–20 cm long, 5–6.5 cm broad; petiole 1–2 cm long. **Inflorescence** arcuate, short, 1-flowered, 0.6–5.2 cm long; peduncle clothed with short, imbricate scales, yellow, speckled with red. **Flower** wide-opening, with pale yellow or white sepals and petals suffused and densely spotted with reddish purple; lip purple. **Dorsal sepal** erect, incurved, linear-lanceolate, 2–2.5 cm long, 0.7–0.8 cm broad; **lateral sepals** ovate-lanceolate, falcately decurved, broader than the dorsal sepal. **Petals** linear-oblanceolate, acute, 2 cm long, 0.4–0.5 cm broad. **Lip** shortly stipitate, linear-oblong, straight, fleshy, 0.8–1 cm long, 0.3 cm broad. **Column** short, truncate, lacking stelidia, 0.5 cm long.
DISTRIBUTION   Malaya and Sumatra; in the lowlands, possible also in Java and Borneo.
HISTORY   First collected by Kunstler in Perak and described by Sir Joseph Hooker (based on an unpublished description by George King) in 1891 in Hooker's *Icones Plantarum* (t. 2054). This species was first brought into cultivation in 1913 by the Hon. C.M. Rothschild of Ashton Wold, Northamptonshire, England.

Bulbophyllum rothschildianum (O'Brien)
J.J. Smith [Colour Plate]
See under *Cirrhopetalum longissimum*.

Bulbophyllum roxburghii (Lindl.) Rchb.f.
[Colour Plate]
Pseudobulbs small, subglobose, 1.2 cm long, 1-leafed at apex. **Leaf** linear-oblong, rounded at apex, 7.5–10 cm long, 1.5–2 cm broad. **Inflorescence** longer than the leaf, umbellate, many-flowered, up to 15 cm long. **Flowers** with dorsal sepal and petals yellow, striped with red; lateral sepals yellow; lip red-purple. **Dorsal sepal** broadly ovate, aristate, ciliate, 0.3–0.4 cm long, 0.2 cm broad; **lateral sepals** subfalcate, connate in the middle, obtuse, 1–1.6 cm long, 0.4 cm broad. **Petals** similar to dorsal

sepal. **Lip** smooth, strongly recurved, ovate, 0.2 cm long. **Column** lacking stelidia, stout, 0.15 cm long.

DISTRIBUTION   India (Ganges Delta).

HISTORY   Described by John Lindley (1830) in his *Genera and Species of Orchidaceous Plants* (p. 58) as *Cirrhopetalum roxburghii* based on a specimen collected by Carey in the Gangetic Plain and communicated by W. Roxburgh.

It was transferred to *Bulbophyllum* by H.G. Reichenbach in *Walpers, Annales Botanices* (p. 263) in 1861.

SYNONYMS   *Cirrhopetalum roxburghii* Lindl.; *Aerides radiatum* Roxb. ex Lindl.

Cadetia Gaud.

Subfamily Epidendroideae
Tribe Dendrobieae
Subtribe Dendrobiinae

Small epiphytic herbs with stems either tufted or spaced along a rhizome. **Stems** short to medium, several-noded, fleshy and dilated above, 1-leafed at apex. **Leaf** flat, fleshy or rarely thinner-textured. **Flowers** on slender pedicels, small, borne singly or a few at a time in succession from a bract at the apex ofter stem. **Sepals** rather broad; mentum large but not long. **Petals** narrower than sepals. **Lip** joined to apex of column-foot and the side to form a distinct mentum, 3-lobed; side lobes small, erect, embracing the column; mid-lobe usually decurved, pubescent. **Column** toothed at apex, pubescent ventrally. with a column-foot; pollinia 4, in 2 closely appressed pairs; lacking caudicles.

DISTRIBUTION   About 50 species, mostly in New Guinea, but extending to Indonesia and Australasia.

DERIVATION OF NAME   Named in memory of Cadet de Gassicourt, the author of a dictionary of chemical terms and of a formulary in France.

TAXONOMY   Named in 1826 in the Botany of Louis de Freycinet's *Voyage sur L'Uranie et La Physicienne* (p. 422, t. 23) by Charles Gaudichaud.

Cadetia is allied to *Ephemerantha* P. F. Hunt & Summerh, and *Diplocaulobium* (Rchb.f.) Kraenzl, but is easily distinguished from either by its longer lasting white flowers and the lip which is joined to the column-foot at the sides as well as at the apex to form a distinct spur.

Cadetia has been divided into three readily distinguishable sections by Rudolf Schlechter in *Fedde, Repertorium Specierum Novarum, Beihefte* (1914) as follows:

1. *Sarcocadetia* has the stems spaced along the rhizome.

2. *Pterocadetia* has tufted stems which are ± cylindric and fleshy for most of their length and the ovaries are smooth.

3. *Cadetia* also with tufted stems which are slender and terete, broadening towards the apex, and the ovaries which are rounded and densely covered with soft, fleshy hairs.

TYPE SPECIES   *C. umbellata* Gaud.

CULTURE   Compost A. Temp. Winter min. 12–15°C. As for tropical *Dendrobium* species. During growth *Cadetia* species require moderate shade and plenty of water, with a drier period after growth is completed. Being small plants they should never be allowed to become too dry at this time. Flowers may appear more than once annually.

Cadetia taylori (F. Muell.) Schltr.

A small, densely-tufted epiphytic plant. **Pseudobulbs** cylindric, shallowly sulcate, 2.5–10 cm long, 0.3–0.5 cm in diameter, covered below when young by a tightly sheathing bract, 1-leafed at apex. **Leaf** oblong, suberect, emarginate, 1.5–5 cm long, 0.7–1.2 cm broad. **Inflorescence** axillary, 1-flowered, suberect-arcuate, shorter than the leaf. **Flower** 1–1.2 cm in diameter, white with a yellow and pink lip. **Dorsal sepal** oblong, curving forward over column, obtuse or subacute, 0.4–0.6 cm long, 0.2 cm broad; **lateral sepals** spreading, broadly oblong or ovate, obtuse, 0.5–0.6 cm, 0.4–0.5 cm broad, forming with the column-foot a sub-

Cadetia taylori
1 – Flower (× 4)
2 – Lip from above (× 4)
3 – Column from below (× 8)
4 – Pollinia (× 18)

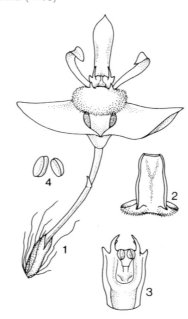

cylindric mentum 0.4–0.5 cm long. **Petals** linear, arcuate, acute, 0.4–0.6 cm long, 0.05 cm broad. **Lip** 3-lobed in middle, clawed, pubescent on disc and mid-lobe, 0.6–0.8 cm long, 0.4–0.5 cm broad; side lobes erect, obovate, smaller than mid-lobe; mid-lobe transversely elliptic or oblong-elliptic, recurved, fleshy. **Column** porrect, 0.4 cm long, with 5 apical teeth, tomentose below stigma: column-foot 0.3 cm long.

DISTRIBUTION   E. Australia (Queensland) and New Guinea; sea level to 1200 m in tropical rain forests.

HISTORY   Baron F. von Mueller originally described this species as *Bulbophyllum taylori* in 1874 in *Fragmenta Phytographiae Australiae* (p. 150) based on a plant collected in riverine forest near Bloomfield's River by Norman Taylor.

Rudolf Schlechter transferred it to *Cadetia* in *Fedde, Repertorium, Beihefte* (p. 424) in 1912.

SYNONYMS   *Bulbophyllum taylori* F. Muell.; *Dendrobium uniflos* F. Muell.; *D. hispidum* F. Muell. non A. Rich.; *D. taylori* (F. Muell.) Fitzg.

Caladenia R. Br.

Subfamily Orchidoideae
Tribe Diurideae
Subtribe Caladeniinae

Small to medium-sized terrestrial herbs growing from subterranean tubers (root-stem tuberoids). **Leaf** solitary, basal, convolute, conduplicate, sometimes pubescent. **Inflorescence** erect, 1- to several-flowered, simple; peduncle wiry, often pubescent. **Flowers** small to relatively large, sometimes showy, resupinate. **Sepals** and **petals** spreading, free, often subsimilar. **Lip** free, smaller than the other segments, usually 3-lobed, adorned with a callus of warts or papillae or hairs. **Column** arcuate, often winged above; pollinia 4, soft, mealy; stigma entire.

DISTRIBUTION   A genus of some 80 or more species that are predominantly Australian with outlying species reaching New Zealand, New Caledonia and Java.

DERIVATION OF NAME   From the Greek *kalos* (beautiful) and *aden* (gland), from the glandular disc of the lip.

TAXONOMY   *Caladenia* was established by Robert Brown in his *Prodromus Florae Novae Hollandiae* (p. 323) in 1810. It is one of the largest genera of Australian terrestrial orchids and contains some of the most beautiful of the native species. The deep cobalt blue *C. deformis* and *C. sericea*, the primrose yellow *C. flava* from Western Australia, and the large spider orchids such as *C. patersonii* and *C. dilatata* are some of the most striking. However, many of the species have proved to be difficult to propagate in cultivation. A summary of those in cultivation is provided by Elliot and Jones (1982) in their *Encyclopedia of Australian Plants* (p. 402).

TYPE SPECIES   Not designated.

CULTURE   More or less as for *Acianthus*.

Caladenia menziesii R. Br. [Colour Plate]

A terrestrial colony-forming plant growing from small ovoid or globose underground tubers. **Leaf** basal solitary, ovate-lanceolate, acute, 3–13 cm long, 0.9–2.6 cm wide, bright green, glabrous. **Inflorescence** erect, 5–20 cm tall, 1- to 2-flowered at the apex; bracts 3–5 mm long. Flowers erect, 1.5–2.5 cm long, white and deep red or maroon; pedicel and ovary c. 10 mm long. **Dorsal sepal** hooded, oblong-lanceolate, acute, 12–15 mm long, 4–5 mm wide; **lateral sepals** deflexed, obliquely lanceolate, acute, 15–18 mm long, 4–5 mm wide. **Petals** erect like rabbit's ears, spathulate, acute, 15–20 mm long, 2 mm wide, glandular hairy. **Lip** recurved, obscurely 3-lobed, ovate, acuminate, 9–11 mm long, 6–7 mm wide; callus stalked, in 2–4 rows. **Column** 6–7 mm long.

DISTRIBUTION   Australia: Victoria, Tasmania, S. Australia and W. Australia; common in sandy soils in open woodland in coastal areas.

HISTORY   Although not the showiest species in the genus, *C. menziesii* is one of the easiest to grow and it will multiply in cultivation. In the wild it flowers well only after fire but it can be induced to flower in cultivation by putting the dormant tubers in a plastic bag with a ripe banana for a few days before replanting.

C. menziesii was first collected by D. Menzies, after whom it was named by Robert Brown in his *Prodromus Florae Novae Hollandiae* (p. 325) in 1810.

SYNONYMS   include *Caladenia macrophylla* R. Br.; *Leptoceras menziesii* (R. Br.) Lindl.; *L. oblonga* Lindl.

Calanthe R. Br.

Subfamily Epidendroideae
Tribe Arethuseae
Subtribe Bletiinae

Medium-sized to large terrestrial or rarely epiphytic herbs, ± pseudobulbous. **Stems** short or long, 2- to several-leaved. **Leaves** plicate, petiolate, often large, ± deciduous. **Inflorescence** axillary, terminal or from the side of the leafy pseudobulb, laxly to densely few- to many-flowered, racemose. **Flowers** small to medium-sized, often showy. **Sepals** subequal, spreading, rarely connivent. **Petals** similar, broad or narrow. **Lip** adnate at the base to the column, 3-lobed; mid-lobe often deeply bifid; disc lamellate or verrucose at the base. **Column** fleshy, long or short, truncate; pollinia 8, waxy, cohering in pairs to a granular viscidium.

DISTRIBUTION   About 150 or so species throughout the tropics but mostly in tropical Asia.

DERIVATION OF NAME   Derived from the Greek *kalos* (beautiful) and *anthe* (flower), in allusion to the pretty flowers of many *Calanthe* species.

TAXONOMY   *Calanthe* was described by R. Brown in 1821 in the *Botanical Register* (sub t. 573). This name has been conserved as a generic name over *Alismorkis* Thou. (1809).

The genus is allied to *Phaius* but is characterised by the fusion of the underside of the column to the lip base. John Lindley divided *Calanthe* into two sections according to whether 'the spur of the labellum (is) elongated, or short or quite obsolete'. However, this distinction is far from natural and a better division was that suggested by George Bentham who divided the genus into two sections, *Vestitae* and *Veratrifoliae*. The former is characterised by the pseudobulbs being more or less elongate-angulate and covered with a grey-green reticulated membranous sheath, by the large plicate deciduous leaves and by the laxly racemose, hairy inflorescence with large inflated bracts; the latter section is characterised by the small or obsolete pseudobulbs, the broad spreading persistent leaves and the densely racemose inflorescence with small appressed bracts. Species within each section hybridise with other species in the same section but not with species of the other section.

These sections correspond to sections *Preptanthe* and (*Eu*) *Calanthe* respectively of recent authors such as R. Holttum and G. Seidenfaden.

Although many species of *Calanthe* are of restricted distribution, some, such as *C. triplicata* and *C. sylvatica* are remarkably widespread. The recognition of such widespread species has led to several familiar names being relegated to synonymy. A revision of *Calanthe* on a worldwide scale is undoubtedly required. The only recent accounts of *Calanthe* have been those of R. Holttum in the *Orchids of Malaya* (1964) and G. Seidenfaden in *Dansk Botanisk Arkiv* (1975) both of which confine their attentions to S.E. Asian species.

TYPE SPECIES   *Limodorum veratrifolium* Willd., (= *C. triplicata* (Willem.) Ames)

SYNONYMS   *Alismorkis* Thou.; *Ghiesbrechtia* A. Rich. & Galeotti

CULTURE   Compost C. Temp. Winter min.

Calanthe lips
1 – *C. vestita* (× 1)
2 – *C. plantaginea* (× 1)
3 – *C. reflexa* (× 1)
4 – *C. ceciliae* (× 1)
5 – *C. tricarinata* (× 1)
6 – *C. angustifolia* (× 1)
7 – *C. brevicornu* (× 1)
8 – *C. cardioglossa* (× 2)
9a – *C. pulchra*, side view (× 1)
9b – *C. pulchra*, front view (× 1)
10 – *C. discolor* (× 1)
11 – *C. masuca* (× 1)
12 – *C. triplicata* (× 1)
13 – *C. rubens* (× 1)
14 – *C. masuca*, pollinia (× 6)

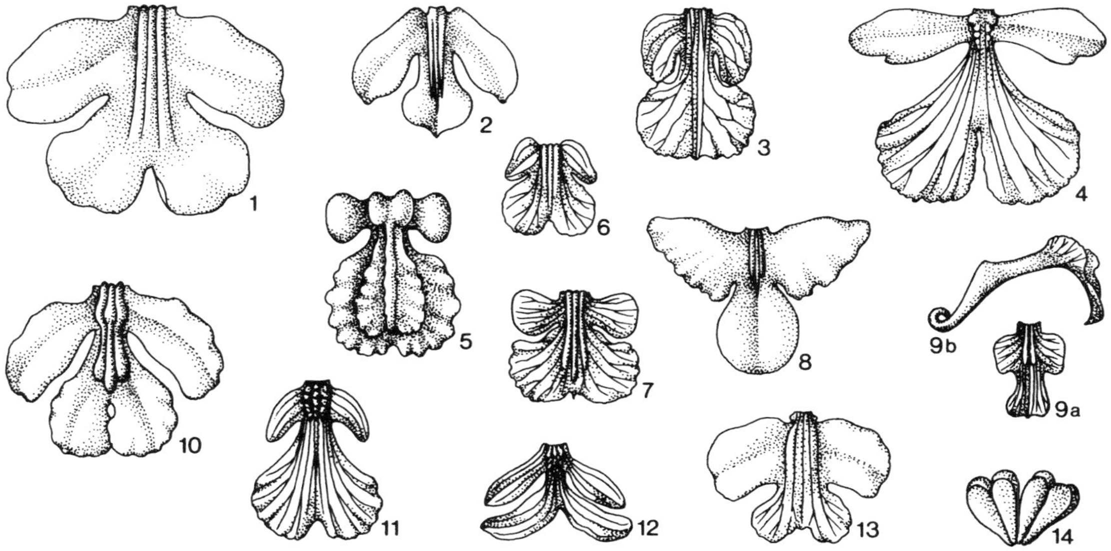

12–15°C. A little higher for evergreens. *Calanthe* species divide naturally into two types; deciduous and evergreen. The deciduous species should be given moderate shade, with plenty of warmth and moisture while growing, but after leaf-fall must be kept cool and completely dry. The flower stems appear from the bare pseudobulbs. Evergreen species should be given more shade, and must never become really dry, although less water is required when the current growth is complete.

Calanthe angustifolia (Bl.) Lindl.

A terrestrial plant up to about 35 cm tall, with pseudobulbs borne 5–6.5 cm apart on a subterranean, creeping rhizome. **Leaves** 3–6, linear-lanceolate, acute, 24–50 cm long, 1.5–4.5 cm wide; petiole up to 15 cm long. **Inflorescence** densely 6- to 18-flowered, 18–35 cm long; bracts lanceolate, up to 1.5 cm long, white, deciduous. **Flowers** pure white, sometimes with yellow side lobes to the lip, about 1.5 cm across. **Sepals** and **petals** oblong-ovate to elliptic, apiculate, 11–12 mm long, 5–6 mm wide. **Lip** 3-lobed, 7–9 mm long and wide; side lobes spreading, rounded; mid-lobe transversely oblong, emarginate or shortly apiculate; spur short, clavate, 7–9 mm long. **Column** 4 mm long.

DISTRIBUTION Malaya, Java, Sumatra and the Philippines; in montane forest, 1200–2300 m.

HISTORY Originallly described as *Amblyglottis angustifolia* by Carl Blume in his *Bijdragen* (p. 369, t. 368) in 1825, based on his own collection from Java. John Lindley transferred it to *Calanthe* in 1833 in *Genera and Species of Orchidaceous Plants* (p. 250).

SYNONYMS *Amblyglottis angustifolia* Bl.; *Calanthe phajoides* Rchb.f.

Calanthe brevicornu Lindl.

A terrestrial herb with clustered, ovoid, pointed pseudobulbs, 2–3 cm long. **Leaves** 2–4, suberect, lanceolate, acute, 25–30 cm long, 7–10 cm wide, pale green, subtended by two cylindrical sheaths. **Inflorescences** 1–2, erect, laxly 15- to 30-flowered, much longer than the leaves; rhachis 15–30 cm long, puberulous; bracts lanceolate, acuminate, 1–2.5 cm long, **Flowers** 3.5–4 cm across, fragrant, with sepals and petals green tinged with pink or reddish brown on the inside and whitish or yellow on the outside, the lip and column dull purple edged with white; pedicel and ovary 1.3–2.5 cm long, puberulous. **Sepals** lanceolate, acute, 1.9–2.5 cm long, 04–0.7 cm wide. **Petals** similar but smaller. **Lip** 3-lobed, 1–1.5 cm long and 0.9–1.2 cm wide; side lobes spreading oblong-falcate; mid-lobe transversely oblong-reniform to obovate, shortly apiculate;

callus of three short lamellae on basal part of mid-lobe; spur shortly cylindrical, 1–2 mm long. **Column** 4–6 mm long.

DISTRIBUTION N. India, Nepal and Sikkim across to S.W. China; in temperate rain forest and wet places; 1500–2700 m.

HISTORY Described in 1833 by John Lindley in his *Genera and Species of Orchidaceous Plants* (p. 251), based on a Wallich collection from Nepal.

Calanthe cardioglossa Schltr.

A medium-sized terrestrial herb, 30–35 cm tall. **Pseudobulbs** ovoid, pyramidal, 3.5–6 cm long, 1.5 cm in diameter 5- to 6-ridged when dry, 1- to 3-leaved. **Leaves** elliptic-lanceolate, acuminate, petiolate, 20–25 cm long, 4–5 cm broad; petiole 3–4 cm long. **Inflorescence** basal, erect, 15–30 cm long; peduncle softly pubescent; bracts ovate-lanceolate, narrow, 1.2 cm long. **Flowers** showy; sepals and petals white to rose-pink; lip white, heavily striped purple, spur white. **Dorsal sepal** narrowly elliptic-lanceolate, acute or acuminate, 1.2 cm long, 0.5 cm broad; **lateral sepals** oblique at base, lanceolate, acuminate, a little larger than the dorsal. **Petals** narrowly elliptic, acute, 1.2 cm long, 0.5 cm broad. **Lip** 3-lobed, cordate when spread, 1.3 cm long, 1.6 cm broad; side lobes obovate, erect-incurved; mid-lobe subrhombic, obtuse; spur terete, almost straight to somewhat sigmoid, pubescent, 1.4–1.8 cm long.

DISTRIBUTION Vietnam, Laos, Kampuchea and Thailand.

HISTORY Discovered by Hosseus on Doi Suthep in Thailand at an altitude of 1500 m and described by Rudolf Schlechter in 1906 in *Fedde, Repertorium Specierum Novarum* (p. 85).

SYNONYMS *Calanthe hosseusiana* Kraenzl.; *C. succedanea* Gagn.

Calanthe ceciliae Rchb.f.

A terrestrial plant with clustered growths. **Leaves** 4–5, lanceolate to elliptic, acuminate, up to 85 cm long, 6–16 cm wide, dark green; petiole up to 12 cm long. **Inflorescence** 40 cm to 1 m tall, laxly to subdensely up to 30-flowered; peduncle and rhachis shortly pubescent; bracts lanceolate, acuminate, small, up to 1.5 cm long. **Flowers** about 3 cm across, white to lilac, turning brownish orange with age. **Sepals** spreading, ovate-lanceolate, acuminate, 1.2–1.6 cm long, 0.4–1 cm wide. **Petals** similar but slightly smaller. **Lip** 3-lobed, 1.3–2 cm long, 1.3–2.3 cm wide; side lobes spreading, ovate; mid-lobe deeply bilobulate, each lobule broader than the side lobes; callus of two short verrucose ridges; spur straight, ascending, slenderly cylindrical, 2.5–5 cm long. **Column** 5 mm long.

DISTRIBUTION Malaya, Sumatra and

Java; in lowland and montane forest, 400–2000 m.

HISTORY H.G. Reichenbach described this pretty orchid in the *Gardeners' Chronicle* (n.s. 19: p. 432) in 1883, based on a specimen flowered by Messrs. Low of Clapton and collected by Sir Hugh Low in Perak. It was named for Cecily, daughter of Sir F.A. Weld, then Governor of the Straits Settlements.

SYNONYMS *Calanthe wrayi* Hook.f.; *C. sumatrana* Boerl.

Calanthe discolor Lindl. [Colour Plate]

A medium-sized terrestrial herb with a short horizontal rhizome. **Pseudobulbs** small, enveloped by leaf-bases, about 3 cm long, 2- to 4-leaved. **Leaves** elliptic-lanceolate to obovate-oblong, acute, 15–25 cm long, 6 cm broad, narrowed below into a long, grooved petiole, minutely puberulent on lower surface. **Inflorescence** erect, 37–50 cm long, racemose, laxly 10- to 15-flowered; peduncle stout; rhachis minutely puberulent; bracts narrowly lanceolate, up to 1 cm long. **Flowers** 3.7–5 cm across; sepals and petals maroon or purplish; lip clear, pale pink; column pale pinkish. **Dorsal sepal** elliptic-oblong, acute or subacuminate, 2–2.5 cm long, 0.8–1 cm broad; **lateral sepals** similar. **Petals** linear-spathulate, acute, up to 2.3 cm long, 0.8 cm broad. **Lip** cuneate-flabellate at base, 3-lobed; side lobes semiovate or oblong-obovate; mid-lobe obcordate, emarginate, smaller than side lobes; disc with 3 raised lamellae running onto mid-lobe; spur incurved, puberulent, up to 1 cm long. **Column** stout, terete, short, 0.5 cm long.

DISTRIBUTION Japan and the Ryukyu Islands; growing in forests.

HISTORY *Calanthe discolor* was described by John Lindley in 1838 in *Sertum Orchidacearum* (sub t. 9) based on a plant sent to him by Auguste Mechelynck of Ghent, Belgium, and was erroneously thought to have originated in Java.

SYNONYMS *Alismorkis discolor* (Lindl.) O. Ktze.; *Calanthe lurida* Decne.; *C. amamiana* Fukuyama; *C. tokunoshimensis* Hatusima & Ida

CLOSELY RELATED SPECIES *C. striata* (Thunb.) R. Br. (syn. *C. sieboldii* Decne) [Colour Plate] differs from *C. discolor* in having larger yellow flowers with a lip in which the mid-lobe is relatively small and entire (rather than deeply emarginate).

Calanthe plantaginea Lindl.

A terrestrial herb. **Leaves** 2, elliptic or lanceolate, 30–50 cm long, 5–13 cm wide, developing with the flowers, subtended by 3 tubular sheaths. **Inflorescence** erect, 30–50 cm long, laxly many-flowered; raceme 20–30 cm long; bracts lanceolate, acute, 5–6 mm long. **Flowers** extremely fragrant, nutant, 3 cm across, white, whitish violet or mauve with an orange callus; pedicel and ovary 1.7–2.5 cm long, pubescent. **Sepals** oblanceolate, acute, 1.5–2 cm long, 0.5–0.6 cm wide. **Petals** similar but smaller. **Lip** 3-lobed, 1.2–1.6 cm long and wide; side lobes spreading, falcate-obovate; mid-lobe obovate, shortly apiculate, slightly broader than the side lobes; callus of 3 slender ridges onto base of mid-lobe; spur slenderly cylindrical-filiform, 2–2.4 cm long, parallel with the ovary. **Column** 5–7 mm long.

DISTRIBUTION Nepal and Bhutan to N. E. India; on steep slopes and in rocky places in and on the edge of forest and bamboo thickets, 1500–2800 m.

HISTORY John Lindley described this species in 1833 in his *Genera and Species of Orchidaceous Plants* (p. 250), based on two of Nathaniel Wallich's collections from Kumaon and Nepal.

Calanthe pulchra (Bl.) Lindl.

A terrestrial plant with clustered growths, up to about 65 cm tall. **Pseudobulbs** obscure, hidden by leaf-bases. **Leaves** 5–6, plicate, lanceolate, acute, up to 65 cm long, 8.5 cm wide. **Inflorescences** erect, densely 40- to 60-flowered in a cylindrical head; peduncle slightly longer than the fully developed rhachis; bracts deciduous, lanceolate, acuminate, up to 2.5 cm long. **Flowers** about 11 mm across, orange-yellow with a darker lip, not opening widely. **Sepals** lanceolate, acuminate, 10–18 mm long, 4–6 mm wide. **Petals** oblong-obovate, 10–12 mm long, 5–6 mm wide. **Lip** 3-lobed, 9 mm long, 5–6 mm wide; side lobes erect, rounded; mid-lobe linear-oblong, acute or shortly pointed 6–7 mm long, 3–4 mm wide; spur cylindrical, hooked at recurved apex, 7–9 mm long.

DISTRIBUTION Malaya, Java, Sumatra, Borneo and the Philippines; in primary forest, 500–1000 m.

HISTORY Originally described by Carl Blume in 1825 in his *Bijdragen* (p. 371) as *Amblyglottis pulchra*, based on his own collection from Java. It was transferred to *Calanthe* by John Lindley in *Genera and Species of Orchidaceous Plants* (p. 250) in 1833.

SYNONYMS *Amblyglottis pulchra* Bl.; *Calanthe curculigoides* Lindl.

Calanthe reflexa Maxim.

A terrestrial herb with a very short stem. **Leaves** 3–5, the lowermost two sheathing, the rest plicate, elliptic-lanceolate, acuminate, 6.5–3.2 cm long, 2–7 cm wide, sparsely puberulous above. **Inflorescence** erect, 20–60 cm long, laxly to subdensely many-flowered; peduncle and rhachis puberulous; bracts lanceolate, acu-

minate, 1–1.5 cm long. **Flowers** lilac with paler sepals and petals, puberulous on outside of sepals; pedicel and ovary puberulous. **Sepals** reflexed, lanceolate, acuminate, 0.9–1.6 cm long, 0.4–0.6 cm wide. **Petals** reflexed, linear-tapering, 0.9–1.2 cm long, 0.15–0.2 cm wide. **Lip** 3-lobed, 1.2–1.8 cm long, 0.7–1.1 cm wide; side lobes spreading-incurved, obliquely elliptic; mid-lobe clawed, fan-shaped-reniform, retuse and shortly apiculate, with undulate margins; callus of two short indistinct basal ridges; spur absent. **Column** 5–6 mm long.

DISTRIBUTION S. Japan, W. China and Taiwan; in montane woodland, moist grassland and thickets, up to 2750 m.

HISTORY This delicately flowered orchid was described in 1873 by the Russian botanist C.J. Maximowicz in the *Bulletin de l'Academie Imperiale des Sciences, St Petersbourg* (p. 68), based on his own collections from near Nagasaki and on Mts Wunzen and Naga in southern Japan.

Calanthe rubens Ridley [Colour Plate]

Pseudobulbs ovoid or conical, angled and sulcate, 6–15 cm long, 4 cm in diameter, silvery-coloured. **Leaves** shortly petiolate, elliptic, acuminate, up to 40 cm long, 15 cm broad. **Inflorescence** produced before the leaves, many-flowered, up to 50 cm long; scape pubescent; bracts broad, ovate, acuminate, 2 cm long, 0.5 cm broad. **Flowers** pink or rarely white, with a central crimson median stripe on the lip, pubescent on outer surface. **Sepals** narrowly elliptic, acute or acuminate, 1.5–1.8 cm long, 0.7 cm broad. **Petals** obovate, obtuse, 1.5 cm long, 0.8 cm broad. **Lip** 3-lobed in basal half, 1.6 cm long, 2 cm broad; side lobes oblong, truncate, 1 cm long; mid-lobe cuneate, bilobulate, larger than side lobes, each lobule oblong, truncate; spur slender, dependent, 1.5–1.7 cm long, pubescent, mouth broad.

DISTRIBUTION Thailand and N. Malaya; found on limestone.

HISTORY Described by H.N. Ridley in 1890 in the *Gardeners' Chronicle* (ser. 3, 7: p. 576), based on a plant collected by Charles Curtis in the Langkawi Islands off the west coast of Malaya.

SYNONYM *Preptanthe rubens* Ridley

Calanthe sylvatica (Thou.) Lindl.
[Colour Plate]

A medium-sized to large epiphytic plant. **Pseudobulbs** small, 2- to 4-noded, concealed by leaf-bases. **Leaves** elliptic-lanceolate, acuminate, 20–30 cm long, 7.5–12.5 cm broad, narrowed below into a petiole. **Inflorescence** erect, longer than the leaves, up to 70 cm or more long, racemose, few- to many-flowered. **Flowers** showy, 2.5–5 cm across, white to lilac with a white or dark reddish-purple lip,

callus white or yellow-orange. **Sepals** ovate-lanceolate, acuminate, 1.5–3 cm long, 0.7–1.2 cm broad. **Petals** narrowly elliptic-lanceolate, acuminate, slightly smaller than the sepals. **Lip** 3-lobed, fused at the base to the column, 1–2 cm long, 1–1.7 cm broad, spreading; side lobes auriculate to oblong, spreading; mid-lobe cuneate-flabellate to obcordate, emarginate; disc with a cluster of tubercles in 3 rows at the base; spur slender, incurved to S-shaped, 1–3.5 cm long.

DISTRIBUTION The Mascarene Islands and Madagascar, Africa and possibly India; in rain and montane forests, sea level to 2000 m altitude.

HISTORY Discovered in the Mascarene Islands by Aubert du Petit Thouars, who named it *Centrosis sylvatica* in 1822 in his *Orchidées des Iles Australes de l'Afrique* (tt. 35, 36).

John Lindley transferred it to *Calanthe* in 1833 in his *Genera and Species of Orchidaceous Plants* (p. 250).

SYNONYMS *Calanthe natalensis* Rchb.f.; *C. corymbosa* Lindl.; *C. volkensii* Rolfe; *C. warpurii* Rolfe; *Centrosis sylvatica* Thou.; *Centrosis aubertii* A. Rich.

CLOSELY RELATED SPECIES *C. sylvatica* is closely allied to or possibly conspecific with *C. masuca* Lindl. and *C. emarginata* Bl. from N. India, China and S.E. Asia. They differ from *C. sylvatica* in minor details of spur length, flower size, and lip lobe length but these differences may not be enough to consider each a distinct species.

Calanthe tricarinata Lindl.

A terrestrial herb up to 50 cm tall with ovoid pseudobulbs, 2–2.5 cm long. **Leaves** 2–4, plicate, oblanceolate, acute, 25–35 cm long, 5–7.5 cm wide. **Inflorescence** erect, up to 50 cm long, densely 8- to 12-flowered; peduncle and rhachis shortly pubescent; bracts lanceolate, half as long as the ovary. **Flowers** 1.8–2.5 cm across, with yellow or green sepals and petals, edged with white, and a blood-red or orange-yellow lip; pedicel and ovary shortly pubescent. **Sepals** lanceolate, acute, 1.2–1.5 cm long, 0.4–0.6 cm wide. **Petals** clawed, lanceolate, acuminate, shorter than the sepals. **Lip** 3-lobed, 0.8–1 cm long and wide, saccate at the base; side lobes short, erect, obtuse; mid-lobe flat, circular-oblong, with undulate-crispate margins, callus of 3–5 longitudinal lamellae. **Column** 5 mm long, only fused to lip in basal part, puberulent.

DISTRIBUTION Nepal and N.E. India across China to Taiwan and Japan; in montane forest in shade, 1700–3300 m.

HISTORY This distinctive species was described in 1833 by John Lindley in his *Genera and Species of Orchidaceous Plants* (p. 252), based on a Wallich collection (no. 7339) from Nepal. It is almost hardy in the British Isles and will survive with only a little protection from winter cold and rain.

Calanthe triplicata (Willem.) Ames
[Colour Plate]
A large, very variable terrestrial plant up to 1 m tall with a stout, short rhizome. **Pseudobulbs** ovoid, 3- to 6-leaved. **Leaves** large, plicate, ovate-lanceolate to narrowly elliptic-lanceolate, acute or acuminate, long-petiolate, strongly ribbed, 45–60 cm long, 12 cm broad, puberulent beneath. **Inflorescence** erect, racemose, densely many-flowered towards the apex, much longer than the leaves; peduncle puberulent. **Flowers** 5 cm long, white with pale green tips to the sepals; callus yellow or orange. **Sepals** elliptic-obovate, with a small green apiculus, 1.2–1.5 cm long, 0.6–0.7 cm broad. **Petals** broadly oblong or oblanceolate, apiculate, 1.3 cm long, 0.5–0.7 cm broad. **Lip** adnate to column at base, 3-lobed, 1.3–1.8 cm long, up to 1.3 cm broad; side lobes oblong, obtuse, spreading; mid-lobe deeply divided into 2 linear-oblong, falcately recurved segments, sinus acute; disc tuberculate; spur slender, arcuate, 1.5–2.5 cm long. **Column** somewhat pubescent.

DISTRIBUTION S. India, Sri Lanka, S.E. Asia, Indonesia and Japan, south to Australia and Fiji.

HISTORY C. *triplicata*, which is better known under its synonym C. *veratrifolia* (Willd.) R. Br., is the type species of the genus. It was described in 1796 as *Orchis triplicata* by Willemet in *Usteri, Annalen der Botanik* (p. 52) based on Rumphius' '*Flos triplicatus*...' in *Herbarium Amboinense* (1750). This name was ignored until Oakes Ames transferred it to the genus *Calanthe* in 1907 in *Philippine Journal of Science, Botany* (p. 326).

It was also discovered in Australia by Alan Cunningham who sent it to J. Colvill's nursery in Chelsea, London, where it flowered in 1823.

This plant was figured as C. *veratrifolia* in Curtis' *Botanical Magazine* (t. 2615).

SYNONYMS Include *Orchis triplicata* Willem.; *Calanthe veratrifolia* (Willd.) R. Br.; *Limodorum veratrifolium* Willd.; *Calanthe comosa* Rchb.f.; *C. perrottetii* A. Rich.; *C. furcata* Batem. ex Lindl.

Calanthe vestita Wall. ex Lindl.
Pseudobulbs subconical, bluntly angled, 8–12.5 cm long, pale greenish-grey-striated. **Leaves** appearing after the flowers, broadly lanceolate, acuminate, 45–60 cm long, 10–12 cm broad, narrowed below into a channelled and winged petiole, prominently ribbed below. **Inflorescences** suberect or nodding, 60–80 cm

long, racemose from near the base, many-flowered; peduncle very pubescent; bracts large, conspicuous, ovate-lanceolate, acuminate. **Flowers** 5–7.5 cm high, milky-white with a yellow-striate blotch on the lip in front of the column; spur greenish. **Sepals** spreading elliptic-oblong, apiculate, 2 cm long, 0.7 cm broad; lateral sepals oblique. **Petals** obovate-oblong, obtuse, 1.8 cm long, 1 cm broad. **Lip** flat, 3-lobed, obovate, 1.5–2 cm long, 2 cm broad; side lobes obliquely oblong, obtuse, 1 cm long; mid-lobe broadly obcordate, 1.2 cm long, 1.8 cm broad, deeply cleft; spur slender, decurved, 2 cm long. **Column** stout, 0.6 cm long.

DISTRIBUTION Burma, Thailand, Indo-China, Malaya, Borneo and the Celebes.

HISTORY This beautiful *Calanthe* was discovered by Dr N. Wallich at Tavoy in Tenasserim, Burma, in 1826 and later by William Griffith at Mergui nearby. John Lindley described it in 1833 in his *Genera and Species of Orchidaceous Plants* (p. 250).

Several varieties of this species have been described including var. *rubro-maculata* Paxt. in which the blotch on the lip is red-purple; var. *regnieri* (Rchb.f.) Veitch [Colour Plate] which has more elongate pseudobulbs and a rose-coloured lip with a crimson-purple blotch at the base.

Calopogon R. Br.
Subfamily Epidendroideae
Tribe Arethuseae
Subtribe Bletiinae

Terrestrial plants growing from small pearly underground corms. **Leaves** 1- to few, grass-like. **Inflorescence** erect, terminal, few-flowered. **Flowers** non-resupinate, showy, white or pink, rather flat. **Sepals** and **petals** subsimilar, free, widely spreading. **Lip** erect, hinged, obscurely 3-lobed at the base, the side lobes small and fleshy, the mid-lobe spathulate, with a callus of long glandular hairs in the middle. **Column** slender, arcuate, winged above; pollinia 4 in two pairs, mealy.

DISTRIBUTION A genus of four species only in N. America and the W. Indies.

DERIVATION OF NAME From the Greek *kalos* (beautiful) and *pogon* (beard), in reference to the tuft of hairs on the lip.

TAXONOMY A distinctive genus that was described by Robert Brown in the 2nd edition of Aiton's *Hortus Kewensis* (p. 204) in 1813. Its non-resupinate flowers and bearded lip make it unlikely to be mistaken for other members of the the subtribe.

TYPE SPECIES C. *pulchellus* (Salisb.) R. Br.
CULTURE Temp. Winter min. 5°C. Com-

post as for *Anacamptis*. Repot in spring and water carefully during growing period. Flowering in late spring or summer. Keep much drier during the winter dormancy.

Calopogon tuberosus (L.) Britton, Sterns & Pogg. [Colour Plate]
A terrestrial herb, up to 120 cm tall, growing from an ovoid, subterranean, cormous pseudobulb, 1–2 cm in diameter. **Leaves** 1–5, linear-lanceolate, acuminate, 20–50 cm long, 1–4 cm wide, ribbed. **Inflorescence** erect, laxly 3- to 25-flowered; peduncle stout, greenish purple; bracts ovate, acute, 4–6 mm long. **Flowers** non-resupinate, pink or white with a yellow or brown blotch at the apex of the callus on the lip; pedicel and ovary stout, 7–10 mm long. **Dorsal sepal** obovate or oblong-elliptic, acute, 2–2.3 cm long, 0.7–0.8 cm wide; **lateral sepals** obliquely oblong-elliptic or ovate, subacute or apiculate, 1.5–1.7 cm long, 1–1.1 cm wide. **Petals** falcate, narrowly oblong, obtuse, 2–2.2 cm long, 0.6–0.8 cm wide. **Lip** erect, obscurely 3-lobed at the base, 1.3–1.6 cm long, 1–1.2 cm wide; side lobes small, rounded; mid-lobe obovate-spathulate, truncate to emarginate; callus of many clavate hairs on the claw of the mid-lobe. Column 1.7–1.8 cm long, with auriculate wings near the apex.

DISTRIBUTION Widespread in eastern and central N. America from Canada south to Florida, also in the Bahamas and Cuba; in marshy areas and swamps.

HISTORY This is one of the first of the North American orchids to be given a binomial name when Linnaeus named it as *Limodorum tuberosum* in the 1st edition of his *Species Plantarum* (p. 950) in 1753. It was transferred to the present genus in 1888 by Britton, Sterns and Poggenburg in their *Preliminary Catalog of New York Plants* (p. 52).

Calopogon tuberosus
Flower (× 1½)

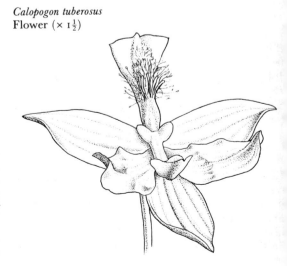

SYNONYMS *Limodorum tuberosum* L.; *L. pulchellum* Salisb.; *Calopogon pulchellus* (Salisb.) R. Br.

Calypso Salisbury
Subfamily Epidendroideae
Tribe Calypsoeae

Dwarf terrestrial herbs with solitary pseudobulbs subtended by membranous sheaths at the base and bearing a single petiolate leaf at the apex. **Leaf** elliptic to oblong, plicate. **Inflorescence** erect, 1-flowered, longer than the leaf, axillary from basal sheaths. **Flower** showy. **Sepals** and **petals** erect or spreading, free, similar, lanceolate, acute. **Lip** resupinate, calceolate, porrect, bearing 2 spurs at the back. **Column** broad, hooded, fleshy; pollinia 4, in 2 superposed pairs, borne on a prominent viscidium; stigma entire.
DISTRIBUTION A monotypic genus, circumboreal in distribution.
DERIVATION OF NAME From *Kalypso*, a Greek sea nymph whose name means hiding or concealment, probably given in allusion to the rarity of this orchid in Europe or to its isolated and secluded habitat.
TAXONOMY The English botanist R. Salisbury named this delightful orchid in 1807 in his *Paradisus Londinensis* (t. 89). It is readily recognised by its characteristic and pretty flower which has a slipper-shaped lip with 2 spurs at the back. It is, however, not related to the true slipper orchids but occupies a rather isolated position in the subfamily Epidendroideae.
TYPE SPECIES *C. borealis* (Sw.) Salisb.
CULTURE Temp. Winter min. 5°C. Appears to grow best in coniferous leaf litter which also sustains the mycorrhizal fungus. Keep shaded and watered throughout the year, with an annual top-dressing of fresh leafmould.

Calypso bulbosa (L.) Oakes [Colour Plate]
A dwarf terrestrial, 8–20 cm tall, with a small slender unifoliate subterranean ovoid pseudobulb, 0.6–1.2 cm long, 0.5–1 mm in diameter. **Leaf** ovate to elliptic, acute, 2–6 cm long, 1–5 cm wide, sometimes undulate, dark green above, purple beneath. **Inflorescence** erect, 1-flowered, 7–19 cm long; bract linear-lanceolate, acute, longer than the pedicel and ovary, 15–30 mm long. **Flower** showy, relatively large for the plant, the sepals and petals pink, the lip white or pink with pink or yellow markings, the column white or pink; pedicel and ovary 15–25 mm long. **Sepals** and **petals** lanceolate, acute, 12–20 mm long, 2.5–4 mm wide. **Lip** calceolate, pandurate, obtuse, 15–23 mm long,

7–10 mm wide, pubescent on the front margins of the mouth, the apical part spreading and broadly ovate; spurs 2, appressed to lip, as long as or longer than the lip. **Column** petaloid, 7–9 mm long and wide.
DISTRIBUTION Northern N. America, N. Europe and N. Asia across to Japan; sea level to 3000 m, in damp mossy places in coniferous woods and in bogs, flowering after the snow has melted in the spring.
HISTORY *Calypso* was known to Linnaeus who described it in *Cypripedium bulbosum* in *Species Plantarum* (p. 951) in 1753. It was transferred to the present genus by Oakes (1842) in Thompson's *History of Vermont* (p. 200).
   C. bulbosa is a variable species with three distinct varieties recognised. The typical one is found in Scandinavia and northern Asia. The other two are North American: var. *americana* is the prettier with a large yellow tuft of hairs on the front margin of the mouth and a weakly spotted front lobe to the lip; var. *occidentalis* has a duller flower with a white tuft of hairs and an irregularly blotched apical lobe to the lip.
SYNONYMS *Cypripedium bulbosum* L.; *Calypso borealis* (Sw.) Salisb.; *C. occidentalis* (Holz.) A.A. Heller

Calyptrochilum Kraenzl.
Subfamily Epidendroideae
Tribe Vandeae
Subtribe Aerangidinae

Medium-sized epiphytic plants with long pendulous or spreading stems. **Leaves** distichous, twisted at base to lie in 1 plane, fleshy, oblong, unequally 2-lobed at the apex. **Inflorescences** emerging below leaves from leaf axils, densely racemose, few- to many-flowered; rhachis often zig-zag. **Flowers** white or cream, with green or orange on the lip. **Sepals** and **petals** free, subsimilar, acuminate. **Lip** spreading, ± 3-lobed, spurred at the base; spur abruptly recurved near apex, with a broad mouth, swollen at apex. **Column** short, fleshy; pollinia 2, waxy; stipe linear, slightly dilated above; viscidium 1.
DISTRIBUTION Two species widespread in tropical Africa from Guinea to Sierra Leone across to E. Africa and south to Zambia.
DERIVATION OF NAME From the Greek *kalyptra* (veil or covering) and *cheilos* (lip), in reference to the calyptrate condition of the lip.
TAXONOMY Originally established in 1895 by F. Kraenzlin in A. Engler's *Botanische Jahrbücher* (p. 30). The species in this genus were originally included in *Angraecum* but differ in having an elongated rostellum, a spur which is abruptly recurved and is swollen near the apex.
TYPE SPECIES *C. preussii* Kraenzl. [= *C. emarginatum* (Sw.) Schltr.].

CULTURE Compost A or mounted. Temp. Winter min. 15°C. As they have pendent stems, these plants are most easily grown when tied to long pieces of fern-fibre or cork. Their roots are then free to hang, or to grow back on to the support. They require shady, humid conditions, but when the roots have stopped growing, less water is required.

Calyptrochilum christyanum (Rchb.f.) Summerh. [Colour Plate]
A pendulous epiphytic or rarely lithophytic species. **Stems** pendent, woody, sheathed at base with dark-brown, persistent leaf-bases, up to 60 cm long, 12- to 26-leaved. **Roots** numerous, adventitious, pale grey, up to 23 cm long. **Leaves** ligulate, unequally 2-lobed at apex, margins slightly recurved, coriaceous, 7–11 cm long, 2.2–2.4 cm broad, dull olive-green. **Inflorescences** short, borne beneath the leaves, 4- to 6-flowered; rhachis short, zig-zag, 1–3.5 cm long; bracts ovate, acute, dark brown. **Flowers** translucent, white, dull orange near the spur; column green. **Sepals** ovate, acute, 1 cm long, 0.5 cm broad. **Petals** similar but ovate-elliptic. **Lip** 3-lobed, 1.2 cm long and broad; side lobes orbicular; mid-lobe subquadrate, emarginate, margin undulate; spur saccate at base, narrowing towards apex, with an ellipsoid terminal swelling. **Column** short, stout.
DISTRIBUTION Tropical Africa; common in riparian forest, 400–1000 m altitude.
HISTORY H.G. Reichenbach described this species in 1880 in the *Gardeners' Chronicle* (pt. 1: p. 806) as *Angraecum christyanum* from a plant which flowered in the collection of Thomas Christy of Sydenham, England. V.S. Summerhayes transferred it to the genus *Calyptrochilum* in the *Flora of West Tropical Africa* (p. 450) in 1936.
SYNONYM *Angraecum christyanum* Rchb.f.

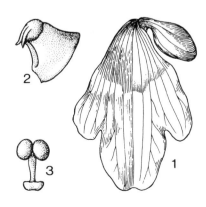

Calyptrochilum christyanum
1 – Lip and spur (× 3)
2 – Column, side view (× 3)
3 – Pollinia, stipe and viscidium (× 6)

Camarotis Lindl.

Subfamily Epidendroideae
Tribe Vandeae
Subtribe Sarcanthinae

Epiphytic or lithophytic herbs with long, erect or climbing stems. **Leaves** well-spaced, distichous, ligulate or ovate. **Inflorescences** axillary, racemose, erect or drooping, few-to many-flowered. **Flowers** non-resupinate, small-to medium-sized, fleshy. **Sepals** and **petals** subsimilar, free, narrow, spreading or deflexed. **Lip** immovably attached to apex of column-foot, saccate, 3-lobed, spurred in front; side lobes erect, broad, short, ± adnate to column-base; mid-lobe very small, closely appressed to the front margins of the side lobes; spur ± conical, hollow and with a septum at the apex and a bidentate, fleshy or valvate callus arising from the base of the anterior wall. **Column** short, with a very short foot; rostellum elongate; pollinia 4, in 2 closely appressed pairs; stipe long, slender; viscidium small.

DISTRIBUTION About 20 species from S.E. Asia to the Philippines and south through Indonesia to Australia.

DERIVATION OF NAME From the Greek *kamarotis* (arched), probably in allusion to the chambered structure of the lip.

TAXONOMY *Camarotis* was established by John Lindley in 1833 in his *Genera and Species of Orchidaceous Plants* (p. 219). It was reduced to synonymy in *Sarcochilus* sect. *Micropera* Lindl. by G. Bentham and J. Hooker in *Genera Plantarum* (1883) but many subsequent authors have resurrected it as distinct, based mainly upon its lip which is uppermost in the flower and has an appendage attached to the top of the anterior wall of the spur which is directed towards the apex of the spur.

TYPE SPECIES *C. purpurea* Lindl.

CULTURE Compost A. Temp. Winter min. 15°C. As for *Arachnis*. The plants need good light and high humidity at all times. As they grow quite tall, they should be given the support of a piece of fern-fibre or cork, over which the roots can grow. Plenty of water should be given when the roots are active.

Camarotis obtusa Lindl.

An erect or pendulous epiphytic plant. **Stem** terete, elongate, covered with persistent leaf-bases, 0.4–0.5 cm in diameter. **Leaves** distichous, ligulate, obtuse, spreading-suberect, coriaceous, 6–12 cm long, 0.7–1 cm broad. **Inflorescence** very shortly peduncled, erect, laxly-flowered. **Flowers** 1.2 cm across, pale rose-coloured; lip yellowish. **Sepals** and **petals** linear-oblong or oblong-elliptic, obtuse, 0.5 cm long, 0.25 cm broad. **Lip** 3-lobed above, glo-

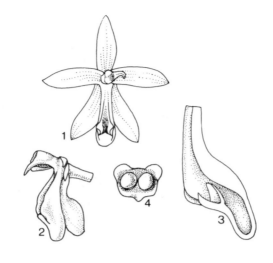

Camarotis obtusa
1 – Flower (× 2)
2 – Column, lip and lateral sepal, side view (× 3)
3 – Lip, longitudinal section (× 4)
4 – Anther (× 8)

bose below, obtuse and decurved at the apex, 0.4 cm long, 0.4 cm broad; side lobes incurved, erect; mid-lobe minutely 3-toothed and fleshy in front, mouth with an exserted anticous lamella. **Column** with a long beak, obliquely incurved.

DISTRIBUTION India (Sikkim), Burma and Thailand.

HISTORY A plant of Indian origin was originally given by James Bateman to Messrs Loddiges and described by John Lindley in 1844 in the *Botanical Register* (misc. 73).

SYNONYM *Sarcochilus obtusus* (Lindl.) Benth. ex Hooker f.

Campylocentrum Bentham

Subfamily Epidendroideae
Tribe Vandeae
Subtribe Angraecinae

Small leafless or leafy epiphytic herbs with short to elongate stems, the leafless species with many elongate chlorophyllous roots. **Leaves**, if present, coriaceous, distichous, oblong-elliptic to linear, unequally bilobed at the apex. **Inflorescences** short, lateral, simple, racemose, laxly to densely few- to many-flowered. **Flowers** distichous, small, white or greenish. **Sepals** and **petals** not spreading widely, free, subsimilar. **Lip** sessile, entire or 3-lobed, with a prominent elongate often recurved spur at the base, ecallose. **Column** short, fleshy, lacking a foot; rostellum short, bilobed; pollinia 2, ovoid, each attached by a stipe to a viscidium.

DISTRIBUTION A genus of perhaps 30 species widespread in tropical and subtropical America from southern Florida, the W. Indies and Mexico south to Brazil.

DERIVATION OF NAME From the Greek *kampylos* (crooked) and *kentron* (spur), from the shape of the spur of the type species.

HISTORY A. Richard and Galeotti originally established this genus as *Todaroa* in 1845 but, unfortunately, that name had already been used two years previously for another genus by Parlatore. George Bentham, therefore, renamed the orchid genus as *Campylocentrum* in 1881 in the *Journal of the Linnean Society* (p. 337). It is the largest vandoid genus in the New World but not much seen in cultivation as none of the species has particularly pretty or showy flowers.

Campylocentrum is allied to the African genus *Angraecum* but lacks a callus on the lip and includes leafless and leaf-bearing species.

TYPE SPECIES *Todaroa micrantha* A. Rich. & Gal.

SYNONYM *Todaroa* A. Rich & Gal. non Parl.

CULTURE Temp. Winter min. 12°C. Species divide into two groups: leafy and leafless. Both require shade and humidity throughout the year, but the leafy species benefit from mounting with a mossy substrate, the leafless species are better maintained on bare wood or cork.

Campylocentrum micranthum (Lindl.) Rolfe
[Colour Plate]

An epiphyte with an elongate, leafy stem, up to 35 cm long, enclosed by imbricate leaf-bases. **Leaves** coriaceous, narrowly elliptic, obtuse, 4–9 cm long, 1.2–2 cm wide, articulated to persistent sheathing leaf bases. **Inflorescences** lateral, 3–4 cm long, densely many-flowered in 2 ranks; bracts ovate, obtuse, 1–2 mm long. **Flowers** small, erect, white or yellowish-white; pedicel and ovary 1–2 mm long. **Sepals** lanceolate, acute or acuminate, 4–4.5 mm long, 0.7–1 mm wide. **Petals** similar, 4 mm long, 0.7–1 mm wide. **Lip** 3-lobed at the base, 4–5 mm long, 1–1.5 mm wide; side lobes erect, narrowly elliptic, rounded in front; mid-lobe lanceolate, acuminate; spur incurved, clavate, 4–5 mm long. **Column** 1 mm long.

DISTRIBUTION Cuba, Hispaniola, Jamaica, Trinidad, Central and S. America from Mexico to Brazil.

HISTORY Originally described as *Angraecum micranthum* by John Lindley (1836) in the *Botanical Register* (t. 1772). It was transferred to *Campylocentrum* by Robert Rolfe (1903) in the *Orchid Review* (p. 245).

SYNONYMS *Angraecum micranthum* Lindl.; *A. brevifolium* Lindl.; *A. lansbergii* Rchb.f.; *Aeran-

thus micranthus (Lindl.) Rchb.f.; *A. lansbergii* (Rchb.f.) Rchb.f.; *Campylocentrum panamense* Ames; *C. peniculus* Schltr.

Capanemia Barb. Rodr.
Subfamily Epidendroideae
Tribe Oncidieae

Dwarf epiphytic plants with very short pseudobulbous stems. **Pseudobulbs** covered by 2–3 sheaths, 1-leafed at apex. **Leaf** small, fleshy, linear or terete. **Inflorescence** few- to many-flowered; peduncle filiform; bracts scarious, very small. **Flowers** small to minute. **Sepals** and **petals** subequal, erect, narrow, free or rarely with the lateral sepals united. **Lip** erect from the base of the column, free, sessile, entire, slightly excavate at the base, with 1 or 2 calli on the fleshy disc. **Column** erect, short, fleshy, lacking a foot, with 2 elongate spreading or recurved auricles at apex; pollinia 2, waxy, ovoid-subglobose, sulcate attached by a linear stipe to a minute viscidium.
DISTRIBUTION   About 15 species in Brazil, Paraguay and Argentina.
DERIVATION OF NAME   Named in honour of Dr Guillemo Schuch de Capanema, a Brazilian naturalist of that time.
TAXONOMY   Described by João Barbosa Rodrigues in 1877 in his *Genera et Species Orchidearum Novarum* (p. 137), *Capenemia* was treated as congeneric in part with *Quekettia* and in part with *Rodriguezia* by A. Cogniaux in Martius's *Flora Brasiliensis* (1906). More recently, Rudolf Schlechter, in 'Die Orchideenflora von Rio Grande do Sul' in *Fedde, Repertorium Specierum Novarum, Beihefte* (1925), reinstated the genus *Capanemia* and this treatment was followed by F.C. Hoehne (1949) in his *Iconografía de Orchidaceas do Brasil*. A detailed account of the genus is given by G. Pabst in *Orquideologia* (1972) where a key to all the known species is provided. He has divided the genus into two sections: sect. *Planifolia* in which the species have flat leaves, and sect. *Capanemia* in which the species have subulate or needle-shaped leaves.
G. Pabst and F. Dungs in *Orchidaceae Brasilienses* (1977) have further separated the 15 Brazilian species into five groupings as follows:
1. *C. thereziae* alliance – three species with normal flat or fleshy leaves.
2. *C. superflua* alliance – three species with terete leaves more than 0.2 cm across; plants large, 5 cm or more high.
3. *C. micromera* alliance – two species with terete leaves of 0.1 cm in diameter; plants small, up to 3 cm high; lip with only 1 lenghty callus in the middle of the disc.

4. *C. angustilabia* alliance – three species as group 3 but lip with 2 calli and a 0.3–0.5 cm long lip.
5. *C. pygmaea* alliance – four species as group 4 but lip only 0.15–0.2 cm long.
Capanemia is closely allied to *Quekettia* Lindl. but may be distinguished by its short thick column prolonged at the apex into spreading wings, whilst in the latter genus the column is slender and has unciform auricles on either side of the stigmatic cavity.
TYPE SPECIES   *C. micromera* Barb. Rodr. (lectotype chosen by Pabst in 1972).
CULTURE   Compost A. Temp. Winter min. 15°C. These small plants require moist, shady conditions while growing, and a slightly drier period when growth is complete. Shallow pots or pans are the most suitable containers.

Capanemia micromera Barb. Rodr.
A small epiphytic plant. **Pseudobulbs** minute, obovoid, 2-bracted and 2-leaved at apex. **Leaves** subterete, very small, fleshy, narowly linear, sulcate above, very acute, 1.5–2.5 cm long, 0.1 cm thick. **Inflorescence** ascending, 1- or 2-flowered, 1–1.5 cm long. **Flowers** white with a yellow callus. **Dorsal sepal** oblong-lanceolate, acute or shortly acuminate, 2 mm long, 0.8 mm broad; **lateral sepals** larger, spreading. **Petals** oblong-lanceolate, acute, 2–2.3 mm long, 0.8 mm broad. **Lip** oblong-panduriform, acute, 2.5 mm long, 1 mm broad; callus fleshy, excavated at the base, bidentate at apex. **Column** auriculate and recurved at apex, 0.5 mm long.
DISTRIBUTION   Brazil.
HSITORY   J. Barbosa Rodrigues collected *C. micromera* on the banks of the River Dourado, a tributary of the River Sapucahy, in Minas Gerais State. He described it in 1877 in his *Genera et Species Orchidearum Novarum* (p. 137).
SYNONYM   *Quekettia micromera* (Barb. Rodr.) Cogn.

Capanemia micromera
Floral dissection (× 6)

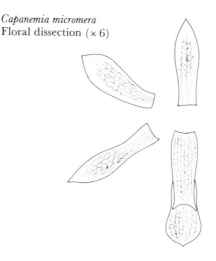

CLOSELY RELATED SPECIES   See *C. superflua*.

Capanemia superflua (Rchb.f.) Garay
[Colour Plate]
A small epiphytic plant. **Pseudobulbs** small, elongate, attenuate, clustered. **Leaves** cylindrical, acute, fleshy, sulcate above, 5–7 cm long, 2.5–3 cm broad. **Inflorescence** suberect or pendulous, densely few- to many-flowered, 4–7 cm long. **Flowers** minute, white with yellow calli and a lilac anther-cap. **Dorsal sepal** oblong, incurved, 3.5 mm long, 1.5–2 mm broad; **lateral sepals** subspreading, oblong, acute, 5 mm long, 2.5 mm broad. **Petals** erect, ovate-subrhombic, acute, 3.5–4 mm long, 2.5 mm broad. **Lip** subpanduriform to broadly triangular-obovate, retuse, pubescent and saccate below, 6 mm long, 4 mm broad; calli 2, basal, elevated. **Column** short, stout, minutely biauriculate above; rostellum bidentate; stigma pubescent.
DISTRIBUTION   Brazil and Argentina.
HISTORY   Originally described in 1864 by H.G. Reichenbach in *Walpers, Annales Botanices* (p. 721) as *Oncidium superfluum* based on a Widgren collection from Minas Gerais. L. Garay transferred it to the genus *Capanemia* in the *Botanical Museum Leaflets of Harvard University* (p. 261) in 1967.
This species is sometimes cultivated under the synonym *C. uliginosa* Barb. Rodr.
SYNONYMS   *Oncidium superfluum* Rchb.f.; *Capanemia uliginosa* Barb. Rodr.; *C. juergensenii* (Kraenzl.) Schltr.; *Rodriguezia anomala* Rolfe
CLOSELY RELATED SPECIES   *C. micromera* is distinguished from *C. superflua* by its minute size, being less than 3 cm high, its slender terete leaves less than 0.1 cm in diameter and by its lip which has only 1 long callus in the middle.

Catasetum Kunth
Subfamily Epidendroideae
Tribe Gongoreae
Subtribe Catasetinae

Usually epiphytic herbs with very short stems. **Pseudobulbs** fleshy, ovoid, conical or fusiform, several-noded, covered with leaf-sheaths when young. **Leaves** large, plicate, narrow in basal part and articulated to a leaf-sheath, deciduous. **Inflorescence** lateral from the base of a pseudobulb, erect or arching to pendulous, racemose. **Flowers** few to many, mostly unisexual, rarely hermaphroditic, di- or rarely trimorphic. **Sepals** and **petals** free. **Lip** fleshy, ridged, sessile at base of column. **Column** erect, fleshy.

Male flowers with a fleshy lip, concave, saccate or helmet-shaped, with entire, fimbriate, crenulate or dentate margins to the orifice. **Column** mostly with 2 antennae at base which are sensitive to touch, releasing the pollinia explosively.

Female flowers less numerous than male flowers. **Lip** mostly saccate or helmet-shaped, ± dorsally flattened. **Column** short, stout, anther- and antenna-less.

DISTRIBUTION Tropical Central and S. America and the W. Indies, about 50 species.

DERIVATION OF NAME From the Greek *kata* (down) and the Latin *seta* (bristle), referring to the 2 antenna-like appendages at the base of the column in male flowers.

TAXONOMY *Catasetum* was described by C.S. Kunth in his *Synopsis Plantarum* (p. 330) in 1822 using a name suggested by L.C. Richard.

Taxonomically, it is an extremely difficult genus mainly because of the dimorphic flowers of many species and also because of the morphological variability of the flowers of many species. By the mid-19th century various reports were beginning to be received of the flowers of two genera, *Myanthus* and *Monachanthus* which had been described by John Lindley being found on the same plant as the flowers of *Catasetum*. It was left for Charles Darwin in the *Journal of the Linnean Society* (1862) to collate all the evidence and conclude that *Monachanthus viridis* represented the female flowers, *Myanthus barbatus* the hermaphrodite flowers and *Catasetum tridentatum* the male flowers all of one species. Thus *Myanthus* and *Monachanthus* were reduced to synonymy in the earlier *Catasetum*.

However, even Darwin had erred somewhat for R.A. Rolfe in the same journal in 1891 showed that *Myanthus barbatus* and *Catasetum tridentatum* were in fact both male flowers and *Monachanthus viridis* was the female flower of the former only. In the same article, Rolfe revised *Catasetum*, dividing the genus into four sections: (*Eu*) *Catasetum* with 10 species; *Myanthus* with 15 species; *Ecirrhosae* with 8 species and *Pseudocatasetum* with 3 species.

In the most recent revision of the whole genus by R. Mansfeld, in *Fedde, Repertorium Specierum Novarum* (1932), the genus was divided into two subgenera: *Clowesia* in which the flowers are hermaphrodite and monomorphic and lack antennae on the column (corresponding to Rolfe's sect. *Ecirrhosae*), and *Orthocatasetum* in which the flowers are unisexual and dimorphic or rarely trimorphic. He further divided the latter into two sections: *Pseudocatasetum* in which the male flowers lack antennae on the column, and *Meizocatasetum* where the columns of the male flowers are antenniferous (this latter corresponds to Rolfe's two sections (*Eu*) *Catasetum* and *Myanthus*). *Meizocatasetum* was

again divided by Mansfeld into two subsections: *Isoceras* in which the antennae are symmetrical, and *Anisoceras* where the antennae are asymmetrical.

Recently, C. Dodson in *Selbyana* (1975) has transferred the species of sect. *Pseudocatasetum* to a new genus, *Dressleria*, and has raised Mansfeld's subgenus *Clowesia* to generic rank. In *Dressleria*, the pollinial trigger-release mechanism is at the apex of the column; in *Clowesia* they are released by pressure on the stipe; and in *Catasetum* by pressure on the basal antennae of the column.

Bees of the genera *Eulaema*, *Euplusia* and *Euglossa* are mainly responsible for the pollination of *Catasetum* (see L. van der Pijl and C. Dodson in *Orchid Flowers*, 1966). In most *Catasetum* species the male flowers begin to emit a strong musky odour 2–3 days after opening. Male bees are attracted by this, enter the flower and proceed to scratch at the source of the odour which is normally directly beneath the antennae at the base of the column. The bees touch an antenna and this moves the rostellum which holds the viscidium in place. The viscidium is released and is thrown by the tension-bound stipe onto the back of the bee. The sticky secretion on the viscidium sets rapidly and the stipe hangs down along the dorsal midline of the bee's abdomen. By the time the bee enters a female flowers, the anther-cap has dropped off revealing the large pollinia which then hang in the correct position to be placed on the stigmatic surface of the non-resupinate female flower.

TYPE SPECIES *C. macrocarpum* Kunth

SYNONYMS *Monachanthus* Lindl.; *Myanthus* Lindl.

CULTURE Compost A or B Temp. Resting 12–15°C, growing 15–18°C. *Catasetum* species seem to grow well in a variety of composts, so long as the containers are well-drained. During growth, they should be given ample water and humidity, with only moderate shade. While the new shoots are small, water must be given with great caution to avoid sudden rotting. After the leaves have fallen, cooler, and drier conditions should be given, little water being needed.

Catasetum barbatum (Lindl.) Lindl.
[Colour Plate]

A large epiphytic plant with 2 sexual forms. **Pseudobulbs** oblong-fusiform, 10–15 cm long, concealed by several leaf-bearing sheaths when young. **Leaves** distichous, oblong-lanceolate to elliptic-oblanceolate, 20–45 cm long, 3–8 cm broad, acute, smaller towards base, prominently 3-nerved. **Inflorescences** male and female on same or different plants; male inflorescence basal, stout, more or less arcuate, longer than the leaves, densely many-flowered above.

Male flowers large, membranaceous, dark

green with transverse brown spots; lip rose-coloured. **Sepals** narrowly elliptic-lanceolate, up to 2.6 cm long, 0.6 cm broad, acuminate. **Petals** narrowly lanceolate. connivent with the dorsal sepal, long-acuminate. **Lip** flat, linear, 1.5 cm long, 0.4 cm broad, inflexed in the middle with a conical sac-like depression, margin lacerate or fimbriate; disc with a large conical basal tooth. **Column** long and stout, rostrate at apex, 2 cm long, with 2 slender, parallel antennae.

Female flowers smaller, fleshy and green. **Sepals** and **petals** similar, reflexed, oblong-lanceolate up to 2.4 cm long, 0.7 cm broad, acute or acuminate. **Lip** deeply saccate, subrotund, mouth narrow, margins revolute, 2 cm long, 1.2 cm deep. **Column** fleshy, 1.3 cm long.

DISTRIBUTION Guyana, Brazil and Peru.

HISTORY Discovered in Guyana at the Wapopekai Falls on the Massarony River by John Henchman who sent plants to Messrs Low & Co. of Clapton, London, where they flowered in 1835. John Lindley originally described male flowers from these plants as *Myanthus barbatus* in 1836 in the *Botanical Register* (t. 1778) but when he realised that *Catasetum* species had dimorphic flowers he transferred it to that genus in 1844 in the *Botanical Register* (misc. 34).

SYNONYMS *Myanthus barbatus* Lindl.; *Catasetum proboscideum* Lindl.; *C. spinosum* Lindl.; *Myanthus spinosus* (Lindl.) Hooker; *Catasetum crinitum* Linden; *C. garnettianum* Rolfe; *C. macrocarpum* Stein; *C. polydactylon* Schltr.

Catasetum discolor (Lindl.) Lindl.

A medium-sized terrestrial or epiphytic plant. **Pseudobulbs** ovoid to narrowly ovoid-fusiform, 2- to 3-noded, up to 20 cm long, heavily ribbed with age. **Leaves** 6–7, plicate, petiolate, linear-lanceolate, acute, 20–40 cm long, 2.5–4.5 cm broad, articulated above base, often absent at time of flowering. **Inflorescences** erect or arcuate, laxly 12- to 25-flowered; bracts ovate, acute, up to 1 cm long. **Flowers** male and female similar, but male flowers smaller.

Male flowers with lip uppermost or lowermost, green, ± flushed with pink or purple; column off-white. **Sepals** spreading, oblong-lanceolate, obtuse or subacute, 1.2–1.5 cm long, 0.5–0.6 cm broad. **Petals** oblong, obtuse, 1.4 cm long, 0.5 cm broad. **Lip** saccate, acute or apiculate, side margins long-fringed, 1.5 cm deep, 2 cm broad, inside of lip velvety pubescent. **Column** lacking noticeable basal antennae.

DISTRIBUTION Venezuela, Guyana, Surinam, Brazil and Colombia; in light, open forest often in sandy soil or on palm trees.

HISTORY Lindley described this species in

1834 in the *Botanical Register* (t. 1735) as *Monachanthus discolor* based on a specimen flowered by Messrs Loddiges, but he later transferred it to *Catasetum* in the same journal (misc. 34) in 1841.

It occurs in a variety of colour forms some of which have varietal names, e.g. *C. discolor* var. *roseo-album* [Colour Plate].
SYNONYMS include *Monachanthus discolor* Lindl.; *Catasetum roseo-album* Lindl.; *C. ciliatum* Barb. Rodr.; *C. claesianum* Cogn.; *C. gardneri* Schltr.

Catasetum fimbriatum (C. Morr.) Lindl.
[Colour Plate]
A large epiphytic plant. **Pseudobulbs** conical-fusiform, several-noded, multisulcate when old, 12–20 cm long, 3–5 cm in diameter. **Leaves** submembranaceous, erect-spreading, oblong-ligulate, acute, 30–55 cm long, 6–10 cm broad. **Inflorescence** arching, racemose, many-flowered.

Male-flowers resupinate, pale green, suffused and barred with pink with a greenish-yellow lip; column white. **Sepals** narrowly elliptic-oblanceolate, acute, 2.8–3.8 cm long, 0.9–1.4 cm broad; lateral sepals spreading. **Petals** erect with dorsal sepal, oblanceolate, elliptic, acute, up to 3.6 cm long, 1.4 cm broad. **Lip** cordate-saccate, margins erose-fimbriate, 3 cm long, 4 cm broad. **Column** short, 2.5 cm long; antennae short, parallel or slightly incurved only, 1.1 cm long.

Female flowers resupinate, borne on same inflorescence as male flowers, dull yellow-green. **Sepals** and **petals** reflexed, oblong, subacute. **Lip** deeply pouched, margins entire, slightly reflexed, apiculate.
DISTRIBUTION Tropical S. America.
HISTORY This species was introduced into cultivation in 1847 by J. de Jonghe, having been discovered in Brazil near Villa Franca in São Paulo State. The male plant was first described as *Myanthus fimbriatus* by C. Morren in 1848 in *Annales Société Anonyme, Gand* (p. 453, t. 231) but was later transferred by John Lindley in 1850 in Paxton's *Flower Garden* (p. 124) to the genus *Catasetum*.
SYNONYMS *Myanthus fimbriatus* C. Morr.; *Catasetum cogniauxii* Linden; *C. ornithorrhynchum* Porsch; *C. pflanzii* Schltr.; *C. wredeanum* Schltr.

Catasetum gnomus Linden & Rchb.f.
[Colour Plate]
A medium-sized epiphytic plant. **Pseudobulbs** robust, conical-fusiform, slightly compressed, plurisulcate when older, 11–16 cm long, 3–4 cm in diameter, 3-leaved. **Leaves** erect, spreading or recurved, lanceolate, acute or shortly acuminate, 20–25 cm long, 3–4 cm broad. **Inflorescence** erect or ascending, up to

60 cm long, laxly many-flowered above; bracts short, fleshy, appressed, narrowly triangular, acute, 4–6 cm long. **Flowers** nodding or pendulous, slightly fragrant, 3 forms of flower: male, female and hermaphrodite.

Male flowers green, spotted purple, with a whitish lip also spotted purple; column greenish-white, spotted purple. **Sepals** fleshy, broadly oblong, acute or shortly acuminate, 5 cm long, 1.5–1.8 cm broad. **Petals** lanceolate, acute, 4.5 cm long, 1.2 cm broad. **Lip** uppermost, fleshy, rigid, obtusely conical, deeply saccate, shortly acuminate at apex, margins undulate-denticulate or serrate, 2 cm long; antennae 1.8–2 cm long, 1 straight, the other incurved towards apex.

Female flowers green, spotted with purple on sepals and petals; lip pale green with a pale yellow margin. **Sepals** and **petals** as in male flower. **Lip** uppermost, deeply saccate, margin dentate.
DISTRIBUTION Brazil (Amazonas State).
HISTORY Discovered on the Rio Negro in Brazil by Gustav Wallis who sent it to Jean Linden. It was described in *Xenia Orchidacea* (vol. 2, p. 171) by Linden and H.G. Reichenbach in 1874.
SYNONYMS *Catasetum heteranthum* Barb. Rodr.; *C. gnomus* Hort.

Catasetum integerrimum Hooker
[Colour Plate]
Pseudobulbs conical-fusiform, covered with scarious imbricating leaf-sheaths when growing, 8–15 cm long, 4–5 cm in diameter. **Leaves** 6–7, oblanceolate, suberect, subacute, membranous, up to 65 cm long, 10 cm broad. **Inflorescence** erect or suberect, racemose, 3- to 10-flowered, up to 40 cm long; bracts ovate-lanceolate, acute, 1 cm long.

Male flowers non-resupinate, yellow-green marked and suffused with purple on base of segments: pedicel geniculate. **Sepals** ovate-lanceolate, concave, acuminate or apiculate, 3.2–4.8 cm long, 1.5–2.3 cm broad. **Petals** similar to sepals, 3–4 cm long, 1.8–2.6 cm broad. **Lip** uppermost, fleshy, conical, saccate, obtuse below, margins ciliate or dentate towards base, mouth circular, 3 cm long, 2–2.5 cm broad. **Column** large, up to 3.5 cm long: antennae terete, curved.

Female flowers non-resupinate. **Sepals** and **petals** concave-incurved over column; sepals oblong-subquadrate, rounded or apiculate at apex, 2.8–3.5 cm long, 2 cm broad; petals suborbicular-quadrate, acute, 2.7 cm long, 2 cm broad. **Lip** broadly calceolate, dorsally compressed, rigid, fleshy, 4 cm long and broad, 2.5 cm deep. **Column** 2 cm long, stout, long-rostrate at apex.

DISTRIBUTION Mexico, Guatemala, Belize and Nicaragua; up to 1850 m.
HISTORY Discovered in Guatemala by George Ure Skinner who sent a plant to the Duke of Bedford at Woburn Abbey, England. It was described by Sir William Hooker in 1841 in Curtis' *Botanical Magazine* (t. 3823).
SYNONYM *Catasetum maculatum* auct. non Kunth
CLOSELY RELATED SPECIES Similar to *C. maculatum* but with a broader conical lip and rather less heavily marked with maroon.

Catasetum macrocarpum Kunth
[Colour Plate]
A large epiphytic plant. **Pseudobulbs** conical-fusiform, 10–30 cm long, 6 cm broad, clothed in numerous distichous leaf-bases. **Leaves** 5–7 towards apex of pseudobulb, oblong-lanceolate, acuminate, 25–60 cm long, 4–12 cm broad. **Inflorescence** erect, robust, 15–30 cm long, 5- to 10-flowered above; bracts narrowly triangular, acute, 0.6–1.0 cm long.

Male flowers variable in colour, fragrant, non-resupinate, green or yellow-green, spotted with purple; column white with maroon markings and a pale-green or yellow central cavity. **Sepals** lanceolate, concave, incurved, acuminate, 4.2–4.5 cm long, 0.9–1.4 cm broad. **Petals** obovate or oblong-ovate, acuminate, concave, 4 cm long, 2.4 cm broad. **Lip** very fleshy, uppermost, deeply cucullate, almost calceiform, 2 cm long, tridentate at apex; side lobes large, rounded; mid-lobe small, tongue-shaped. **Column** 2.5–3 cm long, with a long, incurved apical beak; antennae 2 cm long, 1 porrect, the other incurved strongly towards the apex.

Female flowers non-resupinate, borne on same plant as male flowers; sepals green ± spotted maroon; petals yellow-green, spotted or suffused crimson; lip green outside, yellow within. **Sepals** oblong-obovate. **Petals** obovate. **Lip** helmet-shaped, broad across apex, 3 cm high, 2.5 cm broad.
DISTRIBUTION Brazil, Guyana, Venezuela and Trinidad; sea level to 1200 m altitude.
HISTORY Described by C.S. Kunth in 1822 in *Synopsis Plantarum* (p. 331) based on a manuscript name given by L.C. Richard.
SYNONYMS *Catasetum tridentatum* Hooker; *C. floribundum* Hooker; *C. claveringii* Lindl. ex Van Jeel; *Monachanthus viridis* Lindl.; *Catasetum tricolor* Hort. ex Planchon; *C. linguiferum* Schltr.
CLOSELY RELATED SPECIES Allied to *C. maculatum* but distinguished by the entire revolute margins to the lip which is yellower and has a raised fleshy apicule.

Catasetum maculatum Kunth [Colour Plate]
A large epiphytic plant. **Pseudobulbs** conical-

fusiform, clustered, many-noded, up to 20 cm long, covered when young by several distichous greyish sheaths and leaf-bases. **Leaves** 3–5 per growth, oblanceolate, suberect-spreading, acute, up to 50 cm long, 9 cm broad. **Inflorescence** arcuate, up to 40 cm long, 9- or more-flowered towards apex; bracts ovate, pale green, 1 cm long. **Flowers** non-resupinate; sepals and petals greenish-brown marked and suffused with maroon; lip greenish-yellow, ± heavily suffused with maroon; column pale creamy-green, spotted maroon; pedicel arcuate.

Male flowers non-resupinate. **Sepals** elliptic to obovate, acute, margins inrolled somewhat, 4–4.5 cm long, 1.7–1.8 cm broad. **Petals** ovate-elliptic, acute, margins ciliate, 4 cm long, 1.7 cm broad. **Lip** deeply cucullate, somewhat conical very fleshy-coriaceous, 2.2 cm deep, margins fimbriate, ± with maroon marginal hairs. **Column** 2.2 cm long; 1 antennae porrect, the other strongly curved.

Female flowers non-resupinate. **Sepals** and **petals** oblong-elliptic, subacute to obtuse, all deflexed, about 2 cm long, 1 cm broad. **Lip** deeply saccate with a broad apex, margins shortly fimbriate, about 3 cm long, 1.8 cm across. **Column** short, stout, very fleshy.

DISTRIBUTION Panama, Costa Rica, Colombia, Ecuador and Venezuela; a common lowland species.

HISTORY This species was discovered by F.H.A. von Humboldt and A. Bonpland near Turbaco in Colombia and it was described by C.S. Kunth in 1822 in *Synopsis Plantarum* (p. 331) of Humboldt and Bonpland's collections.

SYNONYM *Catasetum oerstedii* Rchb.f.

CLOSELY RELATED SPECIES Allied to *C. macrocarpum* and *C. integerrimum*.

Catasetum microglossum Rolfe [Colour Plate]

A large epiphytic plant. **Pseudobulbs** ellipsoid-fusiform, concealed by imbricating distichous leaf-bases, up to 10 cm long. **Leaves** oblong-elliptic or oblanceolate, up to 28 cm long, 6.5 cm broad, acute, or acuminate. **Inflorescence** lateral, arcuate to pendulous, up to 65 cm long, racemose above, loosely many-flowered.

Male flowers dull purple or maroon with a yellow lip. **Dorsal sepal** narrowly oblong-lanceolate, cucullate, up to 2.5 cm long, 0.6 cm broad, acute; **lateral sepals** almost parallel, similar but broader. **Petals** erect, connivent with the dorsal sepal, similar to but shorter than the dorsal sepal. **Lip** very small, reflexed, saccate, margins erect, subentire, 0.5–0.8 cm long; disc covered with many lacerate crests. **Column** clavate, 1.7 cm long, with 2 subparallel incurved antennae.

Female flowers dissimilar to male, galeate, lacking antennae, green.

DISTRIBUTION Peru.

HISTORY Described by R.A. Rolfe in the *Botanical Magazine* (t. 8514) in 1913 from a specimen found by Fox on the Rio Igaraparana, a tributary of the Rio Putumayo in Peru.

CLOSELY RELATED SPECIES Allied to *Catasetum tenebrosum* Kraenzl, which, however, has a larger lip which lacks any lacerate crests.

Catasetum pileatum Rchb.f. [Colour Plate]

A large epiphytic plant. **Pseudobulbs** clustered, fusiform-ovoid, several-noded, plurisulcate when old, covered with distichous leaf-bases when young, 15–25 cm long. **Leaves** several, distichous, lanceolate, suberect, 20–35 cm long, 4–7 cm broad, acute. **Male inflorescence** pendent, basal, racemose, up to 40 cm long, many-flowered; bracts oblong, acute, 0.7–1.0 cm long.

Male flowers very variable in colour, mostly waxy-white, pale creamy-yellow or yellowish-green tinged, ± shaded or spotted with purple; column white; **sepals** lanceolate, acute, with inrolled margins, 4–7 cm long, 1.4–1.7 cm broad. **Petals** suberect, elliptic-lanceolate, acute, thin-textured, 4–7 cm long, 1.5–2.5 cm broad. **Lip** cordate-cucullate, with a sac-like pouch in centre, 4–5 cm long, 6–7 cm broad, obtuse. **Column** 4 cm long, with a long beak; antennae in male flower crossing over, 1 porrect, the other strongly incurved at tip.

Female flower non-resupinate; sepals and petals creamy; lip rich yolk-yellow to pale yellow. **Sepals** and **petals** similar to those of male flower. **Lip** conically saccate, margins reflexed somewhat.

DISTRIBUTION Venezuela (national flower), Trinidad and Brazil.

HISTORY Introduced into cultivation by Messrs Linden from Venezuela and described by H.G. Reichenbach in 1882 in the *Gardeners' Chronicle* (n.s. 18: p. 616).

SYNONYM *Catasetum bungerothii* N.E.Br.

CLOSELY RELATED SPECIES See *C. platyglossum*.

Catasetum platyglossum Schltr. [Colour Plate]

A robust epiphytic plant with the habit of *C. pileatum* Rchb.f. **Pseudobulbs** conical-fusiform, covered with scarious imbricating leaf-sheaths when young, 15–25 cm long, 5 cm broad. **Leaves** 4–6, elliptic, acuminate, 30–35 cm long, 9–11 cm broad. **Inflorescence** pendulous or arcuate, laxly 4- or 5-flowered, about 30 cm long.

Male flowers large, showy, creamy-yellow, ± suffused with vinous red; callus ± purple. **Sepals** oblong or oblong-elliptic, concave, apiculate, 4 cm long, 1.8 cm broad. **Petals** obliquely and broadly elliptic, obtuse, erect, 4 cm long, 2.2–2.3 cm broad. **Lip** broadly elliptic

at base, 3-lobed above, saccate in basal half, margins undulate, 2–3.8 cm long, 3.5–4.5 cm broad; callus lunate, fleshy, above saccate base to lip. **Column** slightly curvate, 3.5 cm long; antennae subulate, decurved, crossing over.

Female flowers somewhat similar to male, galeate, lacking antennae.

DISTRIBUTION Ecuador and Colombia.

HISTORY The exact locality of the original collection is unknown, but it possibly came from Colombia. The species was first flowered in 1915 in the Marburg Botanic Garden, Germany, and it was described by Rudolf Schlechter in 1916 in the journal *Orchis* (p. 186).

SYNONYM *Catasetum sodiroi* Schltr.

CLOSELY RELATED SPECIES Allied to *C. pileatum* but distinguished by its broader concave sepals, stouter column and the callus above the saccate base to the lip.

Catasetum saccatum Lindl.

A large variable epiphytic plant. **Pseudobulbs** robust, subconical, slightly compressed, 2- to 5-noded, at first covered by sheaths, later plurisulcate, 7–20 cm long, 2.5–4.5 cm in diameter. **Leaves** erect or spreading, lanceolate-subspathulate, shortly acuminate, 20–40 cm long, 4–6 cm broad. **Inflorescence** robust, erect or subnodding, 25–40 cm long, laxly 5- to 8-flowered; peduncle deep purple-brown; bracts triangular-lanceolate, concave, acuminate, 0.8–1.3 cm long.

Male flowers spreading or slightly nodding, fragrant, variable but in typical form olive-brown with green marmorations; lip disc and mid-lobe purple-brown, side lobes greenish. **Sepals** slightly concave, linear-lanceolate, long-acuminate, 6.5 cm long, 0.6–0.9 cm broad. **Petals** membranous, erect, linear-lanceolate, long-acuminate, 5.8 cm long, 0.8 cm broad. **Lip** reflexed, 2.5–3 cm long, lowermost, fleshy, 3-lobed, with a conical saccate depression near base, margins long-fimbriate, shortly acuminate at the apex. **Column** very long, fleshy, apex longly rostrate, 5–6 cm long; antennae 1.5 cm long, 1 straight and the other strongly incurved.

Female flowers non-resupinate yellow-green, ± spotted red-brown. **Sepals** and **petals** smaller than in male flower; sepals elliptic-lanceolate, acute, 2.9 cm long, 0.75 cm broad, petals oblong-elliptic, acuminate, 2.9 cm long, 1.2 cm broad. **Lip** deeply saccate, 2.9 cm long, slightly laterally compressed, margins fimbriate, decurved. **Column** stout, 1 cm long.

DISTRIBUTION Peru, Brazil and Guyana; up to 1700 m elevation.

HISTORY Introduced into cultivation from Guyana by Messrs Loddiges and described in 1840 in the *Botanical Register* (misc. 76) by John Lindley.

Var. *christyanum* [Colour Plate] was introduced from Brazil by Thomas Christy of Sydenham, England. H.G. Reichenbach named it *C. christyanum* in his honour but it is undoubtedly only a variety of *C. saccatum*, differing in its coloration but no more.

SYNONYMS *Catasetum incurvum* Klotzsch; *C. baraquinianum* Lemaire; *C. secundum* Klotzsch ex Rchb.f.; *C. histrio* Klotzsch ex Rchb.f.; *C. stupendum* Cogn.; *C. cruciatum* Schltr.

Cattleya Lindl.
Subfamily Epidendroideae
Tribe Epidendreae
Subtribe Laeliinae

Epiphytic or lithophytic plants with ± thickened, pseudobulbous stems, with 1 or 2 leaves at apex of each. **Leaves** coriaceous or fleshy, usually thick. **Inflorescence** terminal, 1-flowered or racemose; peduncle usually subtended by a large spathaceous sheath. **Flowers** 1- to few, ± large, showy. **Sepals** free, more or less equal, fleshy. **Petals** mostly much broader than sepals and less fleshy. **Lip** sessile, erect, free or rarely adnate to column-base, entire to deeply 3-lobed, sides or side lobes enfolding column. **Column** usually long, ± wingless, semiterete, ± arcuate; anther terminal; pollinia 4, waxy, somewhat compressed. **Capsule** ellipsoidal.

DISTRIBUTION The tropics of Central and S. America, about 50 species.

Cattleya lips (all × ½)
1 – *C. violacea*
2 – *C. iricolor*
3 – *C. deckeri*
4 – *C. rex*
5 – *C. bowringiana*

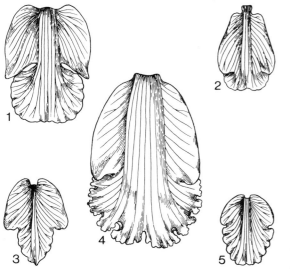

DERIVATION OF NAME John Lindley named the genus after William Cattley (1788–1835), who was one of the first horticulturalists to grow epiphytic orchids successfully in England.

TAXONOMY John Lindley described *Cattleya* in 1821 in *Collectanea Botanica* (t. 33). The genus is closely allied to *Laelia* which has 8 pollinia and many species are morphologically so similar that they could easily be confused. Despite the difference in number of pollinia, *Cattleya* hybridises freely with *Laelia* and a number of other allied genera such as *Epidendrum* and *Brassavola*. As with *Laelia*, the species may be conveniently divided into those that have 1-leafed pseudobulbs and those that have 2-leaved pseudobulbs. From a botanical point of view *Cattleya* is scarcely distinguishable morphologically from *Encyclia* other than that *Cattleya* species have larger, showier flowers. Indeed, H.G. Reichenbach and some other botanists have placed all the *Cattleya* species into *Epidendrum* (which then also contained *Encyclia*). However, it is generally felt that *Cattleya* should be retained as a distinct genus containing a few showy species of horticultural merit rather than sink it in the anonymity of the overlarge genera *Encyclia* or *Epidendrum*. The genus has been revised most recently by Carl Withner (1988) in the first volume of his *The Cattleyas and their relatives*.

TYPE SPECIES *C. labiata* Lindl.
CULTURE Compost A. Temp. Winter min. 12–15°C. *Cattleya* species should be grown in pots. They require conditions of good light and humidity, with plenty of water during growth. Some shade will be needed in summer to avoid leaf-scorch. When pseudobulbs are fully formed, less water should be given.

Cattleya aclandiae Lindl. [Colour Plate]
A rather dwarf, epiphytic plant. **Pseudobulbs** slender, jointed, furrowed, 7.5–12.5 cm long, 2-leaved at apex. **Leaves** spreading, elliptic, 5–7.5 cm long, thick and fleshy, ± red-spotted. **Inflorescence** 1- or 2 (rarely more)-flowered, terminal. **Flowers** 7.5–10 cm across; petals and sepals yellowish-green to brown covered with transverse dark purple blotches and spots; lip bright rose-purple lined deep purple on veins, paler at base and on side lobes, with a yellow spot in centre; column amethyst-purple. **Sepals** elliptic-oblong, fleshy, 5 cm long, 1.8 cm broad, obtuse, undulate. **Petals** similar to sepals, 4.5 cm long, 1.8 cm broad, obtuse or rounded, undulate. **Lip** 3-lobed, 5 cm long, 3.7 cm broad; side lobes suberect, rather obscure, scarcely embracing the column; mid-lobe broadly oblong or reniform, emarginate, undulate. **Column** clavate, with 2 wing-like margins, 2.5 cm long.

DISTRIBUTION Brazil (confined to Bahia State); an epiphyte on trees in rather dry areas near the coast.
HISTORY This pretty species was named by John Lindley in 1840 in the *Botanical Register* (t. 48) after Lady Acland of Killerton, near Exeter, England, whose husband introduced it into cultivation in Europe, Lt James of H.M.S. *Spey* having discovered it in Brazil in October 1839. This species is sparingly but successfully used in hybridisation, as it breeds easily with other members of the genus *Cattleya* and the multifarious hybrids of *Cattleya* affinity.
CLOSELY RELATED SPECIES *Cattleya velutina* Rchb.f. [Colour Plate] is similar to this species. It is found in the states of Espiritu Santo, Rio de Janeiro and São Paulo in Brazil and is similar to *C. aclandiae* and *C. bicolor* in that it bears flowers on well-developed pseudobulbs and in that the side lobes of the lip embrace the column. It differs from both in having larger flowers with a distinctly coloured lip which is predominantly white marked with yellow and lined with crimson-purple.

Cattleya amethystoglossa Linden & Rchb.f.
[Colour Plate]
See under *Cattleya guttata*.

Cattleya aurantiaca (Batem. ex Lindl.) P.N. Don [Colour Plate]
A stout epiphytic plant, up to 55 cm tall often forming clumps over 25 cm in diameter. **Pseudobulbs** fusiform-clavate, up to 33 cm long, 2-leaved near apex. **Leaves** broadly ovate to oblong-elliptic, 5–18 cm long, 2.5–5.5 cm broad, notched at apex. **Inflorescence** few- to many-flowered, subtended by a compressed sheath. **Flowers** 3–4 cm in diameter, orange, orange-yellow or orange-red, with brownish spots and streaks; lip ± marked with maroon or blackish stripes. **Sepals** linear-elliptic to lanceolate, 1.8–2.7 cm long, 0.4–0.6 cm broad, acute; lateral sepals somewhat oblique. **Petals** elliptic-oblanceolate, 1.8–2.5 cm long, 0.4–0.5 cm broad, acute or subacute. **Lip** broadly ovate to oblong-elliptic, somewhat dilated below middle, rounded or acute, 1.7–2.2 cm long, 0.8–1 cm broad. **Column** cylindrical, ± arcuate, 0.8 cm long.
DISTRIBUTION This species forms a link between the closely allied genera *Cattleya* and *Epidendrum* and has been placed in both genera. It was originally described by John Lindley as *Epidendrum aurantiacum* in 1838 in the *Botanical Register* (misc. p. 8) based on a Guatemalan collection made by George Ure Skinner. It was transferred to *Cattleya* by P.N. Don in the *Florist's Journal* (p. 185) in 1840.

This species has been widely used in cultivation to introduce the colours red and orange

into hybrids of the predominantly purple-coloured *Catttleya* alliance.
SYNONYMS *Epidendrum aurantiacum* Batem. ex Lindl.

Cattleya bicolor Lindl. [Colour Plate]

Pseudobulbs long and slender, up to 30 cm or more long, clustered, swollen and rooting at the base, jointed, grooved, 2-leaved at apex. **Leaves** spreading, oblong-lorate, coriaceous, 16 cm long, 25 cm broad, obtuse, faintly streaked. **Inflorescence** 2- to 7-flowered, 20 cm long, subtended by a green- and purple-mottled spathe at base. **Flowers** slightly fragrant, up to 9 cm across; sepals and petals coppery-brown or tawny-yellow; lip side lobes pink, mid-lobe crimson edged pink, margin white. **Sepals** oblong-lanceolate, 4.5 cm long, 1 cm broad, acute; lateral sepals slightly deflexed, falcate. **Petals** similar, somewhat obovate or broadly spathulate, 4.5 cm long, 1.6 cm broad; apiculate. **Lip** long, oblong-cuneate, arcuate, reflexed, broad and 2-lobed at apex, 3.5 cm long, 1.7 cm broad, margin recurved. **Column** very large, exposed, 3 cm long.
DISTRIBUTION Brazil.
HISTORY Known originally only from a painting by M.E. Descourtilz which John Lindley published, this plant was first imported in 1838 by Messrs Loddiges. Lindley described the species based on Descourtilz's drawing in the *Botanical Register* (sub t. 1919) in 1836.
CLOSELY RELATED SPECIES Easily recognised and distinguished from the other two-coloured *Cattleya* species from Brazil by the lack of spotting on the sepals and petals. See also *C. aclandiae*.

Cattleya bowringiana O'Brien [Colour Plate]

A very floriferous lithophytic plant, up to 60 cm high, or rarely higher. **Pseudobulbs** club-shaped, 20–60 cm long, rarely more, 0.7 cm in diameter, swollen at base, 2 (rarely 3)-leaved at apex. **Leaves** narrowly oblong, leathery, 15–20 cm long, 5–6 cm broad, obtuse, dark green. **Inflorescence** 5- to 15 (rarely 47)-flowered, up to 25 cm long or more, subtended by 2 compressed sheaths at base. **Flowers** up to 7 cm across; sepals and petals magenta with deeper coloured veins; lip pale rose-purple at base, deep purple around margin with white blotches edged with pale yellow in the throat; column white, tinged pink at base. **Sepals** oblong or narrowly elliptic, 3.9–4.9 cm long, 1–1.2 cm broad, acute. **Petals** broader than the sepals, ovate-oblong, 4.1–4.9 cm long, 2.4–2.8 cm broad, obtuse, margins undulate. **Lip** ovate-oblong, 3.6–4 cm long, 2.7–3.4 cm broad, basal half curved up around column to form a tube, apical margin undulate. **Column** 1–1.2 cm long, narrowly winged on either side.

DISTRIBUTION A rare species in Guatemala and Belize; growing on rocks and cliffs, exposed to the sun, in ravines along streams.
HISTORY Described in the *Gardeners' Chronicle* (n.s. 24: p. 683) by James O'Brien in 1885, it had been imported the previous year from Belize by the firm of Messrs Veitch & Sons of Exeter, England. The species was dedicated to J.C. Bowring of Windsor, England who was a keen amateur grower of orchids at that time.
SYNONYMS *C. autumnalis* O'Brien; *C. skinneri* var. *bowringiana* Kraenzl.
CLOSELY RELATED SPECIES Closely related to *C. skinneri* from which it differs in its more vigorous habit, longer and more slender stems and leaves, smaller flowers and rather differently shaped flowers. *C. deckeri* is also closely related but it has a uniformly coloured lip. See also *C. lawrenceana*.

Cattleya deckeri Klotzsch

A stout plant, up to 30 cm tall. **Pseudobulbs** clustered, club-shaped, flattened, up to 30 cm long, 2-leaved at apex. **Leaves** ovate-oblong, 10–15 cm long, 3.5–5 cm broad. **Inflorescence** 2- to 8-flowered, up to 15 cm long, subtended by a large basal sheath. **Flowers** up to 8 cm across, pale purplish-rose with a dark purple lip. **Sepals** lanceolate-elliptic, 2.5 cm long, 1 cm broad, acute or apiculate. **Petals** ovate-oblong, 2.5 cm long, 1.8 cm broad, acute, margins undulate. **Lip** obscurely 3-lobed, elliptic-obovate, 2.3 cm long, 2 cm broad; side lobes forming a tube over column; mid-lobe acute. **Column** short, 1 cm long, dilated towards apex.
DISTRIBUTION Guatemala to Panama, Colombia and Trinidad; on rocks and trees, up to 1000 m.
HISTORY Described in 1855 by O. Klotzsch in F. Otto and A. Dietrich's *Allgemeine Gartenzeitung* (p. 81).
SYNONYMS *Cattleya skinneri* var. *parviflora* Hooker; *C. patinii* Cogn.
CLOSELY RELATED SPECIES Readily distinguished from *C. skinneri* by the absence of any white markings on the lip. See also *C. bowringiana*.

Cattleya dormaniana Rchb.f. [Colour Plate]

See under *Cattleya guttata*.

Cattleya dowiana Batem. [Colour Plate]

Pseudobulbs clavate, ridged, 12 cm long, 3 cm broad, arising from a short, stout rhizome, 1-leafed at apex. **Leaf** broadly oblong, leathery, 16–29 cm long, 4–7 cm broad, rounded, notched at apex. **Inflorescence** 2- to 6-flowered, subtended by a broad spathe at base. **Flowers** up to 15 cm across, very showy; petals and sepals rich yellow; petals ± veined magenta; lip rich crimson-purple, veined golden-yellow with

3 prominent golden streaks in the centre, velvety; column yellow. **Sepals** lanceolate, 8.7 cm long, 1.7 cm broad. **Petals** oblong-elliptic, 8 cm long, 5 cm broad, obtuse, margins very undulate. **Lip** obscurely 3-lobed, oblong, 9 cm long, 7 cm broad, emarginate; side lobes erect, almost enclosing the column; mid-lobe spreading widely. **Column** subarcuate, 3.5 cm long.
DISTRIBUTION Costa Rica and Colombia.
HISTORY This superb species was discovered by J. Warscewicz in Costa Rica but the plants he sent to Europe died on arrival. Fortunately, it was rediscovered some 10 years later in 1864 by M. Arce who collected plants for George Ure Skinner. Plants of this collection were sent to Messrs Veitch & Sons of Exeter, England, who flowered it for the first time in 1865. James Bateman named it in the *Gardeners' Chronicle* (p. 922) in 1866 after Capt. J. Dow of the American Packet Service who had frequently assisted naturalists in bringing home their many discoveries.
   Var. *aurea* (Linden) B.S. Williams from Colombia has more copious and irrregularly distributed markings on the lip and is of paler colour. It is considered by Withner (1988) in his *The Cattleyas and their relatives* to warrant recognition as a distinct species.
CLOSELY RELATED SPECIES Vegetatively similar to *C. labiata* but distinguished by its beautiful golden-yellow and crimson flower. Some authorities consider it to be a variety or subspecies of *C. labiata*.

Cattleya eldorado Linden [Colour Plate]

Pseudobulbs smooth, ± cylindrical, up to 15 cm long, 1.5 cm in diameter, 1-leafed at apex. **Leaf** rigid, leathery, erect, up to 24 cm long, 5 cm broad. **Inflorescence** 1- to 3-flowered, on a short scape. **Flowers** up to 14 cm across; sepals and petals pale pink; lip creamy-white with an orange-yellow throat edged with white and purple with a wide purple area on front of mid-lobe and a deeper mauve spot at apex; column white or pink with brown scurf at apex. **Dorsal sepal** narrowly oblong-elliptic, 7 cm long, 2.6 cm broad, acute; **lateral sepals** deflexed. **Petals** elliptic, 6.6 cm long, 4.4 cm broad, obtuse to subacute, with undulate margins. **Lip** very obscurely 3-lobed, 7 cm long, 5 cm broad, emarginate; side lobes forming tube around column; mid-lobe spreading, erose. **Column** 3 cm long.
DISTRIBUTION Brazil (states of Amazonas and Para).
HISTORY First imported by Messrs Linden in 1866 from the Rio Negro region of Brazil. It was described by Jean Linden in 1869 in van Houtte's *Flore des Serres* (t. 1826). It remained scarce until 1876 when a further importation was made by M. Binot.

SYNONYMS include *Cattleya mcmorlandii* Nichols; *C. virginalis* Linden & André

CLOSELY RELATED SPECIES Similar to *C. labiata*, of which it may prove to be a variety or subspecies, but with smaller paler flowers, a more tubular lip, more rounded and smooth stems and more rigid leathery, erect leaves.

Cattleya forbesii Lindl. [Colour Plate]

An epiphytic plant of medium size. **Pseudobulbs** 15–20 cm tall, slightly swollen, covered with membranous sheaths, 2-leaved at apex. **Leaves** oblong, coriaceous, spreading, 9–11 cm long, 2.5–5 cm broad, rounded, notched at apex. **Inflorescence** 2- to 5-flowered, 10–12.5 cm long, subtended by a basal sheath. **Flowers** 6–10 cm across; sepals and petals pale green, ± tinged purple-brown; lip pink on side lobes, yellow in centre, striped purple and with a white margin to mid-lobe; column white. **Dorsal sepal** linear-lanceolate, spreading, 5 cm long, 1 cm broad, subacute; **lateral sepals** similar but falcate-deflexed. **Petals** similar to sepals but falcate, 4.5 cm long, 0.9 cm broad, acute. **Lip** 3-lobed, 4.5 cm long, 3.6 cm broad; side lobes oblong, rounded, curved over column to form a tube; mid-lobe short, rotund, spreading, margin undulate-crisped. **Column** clavate, semiterete, 2.5 cm long.

DISTRIBUTION Brazil (Rio de Janeiro, São Paulo, Parana and Santa Catarina States); growing on rocks, trees and shrubs near streams and on the seashore.

HISTORY Introduced into cultivation by H.O. Forbes who collected it for the Horticultural Society of London. John Lindley named it in 1823 in honour of its discoverer in *Collectanea Botanica* (sub t. 33).

SYNONYMS *Cattleya pauper* (Vell.) Stellfeld.; *C. vestalis* Hoffmannsegg; *C. fulva* Beer; *C. isopetala* Beer

Cattleya gaskelliana Sander ex Rchb.f. [Colour Plate]

An epiphytic plant. **Pseudobulbs** clavate, compressed, grooved, up to 20 cm long, 2 cm broad, 1-leafed at apex, clothed in greyish sheaths. **Leaf** elliptic-ovate, 23 cm long, 7 cm broad, thick and coriaceous. **Flowers** up to 17 cm across, variable in colour; sepals and petals white to pale amethyst-purple, suffused with white but sometimes deeper coloured with a central white band; lip side lobes pale purple, mid-lobe rosy-mauve, throat orange or tawny-yellow with a white spot on either side and a rich purple spot in front; column cream at base, pink above, anther-cap pink. **Sepals** oblanceolate, up to 9 cm long, 2 cm broad, subacute. **Petals** elliptic to ovate, 9 cm long, 6 cm broad, obtuse. **Lip** oblong-elliptic, 8 cm long, 6 cm broad, margins crisped.

DISTRIBUTION Venezuela and Colombia; 750–1000 m altitude.

HISTORY The first plants in Europe were sold in England at Stevens' Sales Rooms to Messrs Sander & Co. of St Albans in 1883. Sander named the plant in his catalogue after Holbrook Gaskell of Liverpool who then possessed one of the finest collections of orchids in the British Isles. It was described by H.G. Reichenbach in the same year in the *Gardeners' Chronicle* (n.s. 19: 243).

Var. *alba*, a white flowered variety, is known.

CLOSELY RELATED SPECIES Closely related to *C. labiata*, *C. mossiae* and *C. lueddemanniana* and it is considered by some to be a variety or subspecies of *C. labiata*. May be distinguished from *C. mossiae* by its growth habit, the shape of the pseudobulbs and the presence of a white area between the yellow and purple of the lip.

Cattleya granulosa Lindl. [Colour Plate]

An erect, stout epiphytic plant. **Pseudobulbs** elongate, cylindrical-compressed, 30–50 cm long, 1–2 cm broad, 2-leaved at apex. **Leaves** oblong-lanceolate or elliptic-ovate, coriaceous, 12–24 cm long, 3.5–7.6 cm broad, obtuse. **Inflorescence** racemose, 3- to 8-flowered, terminal and rather short. **Flowers** large and showy, 8–11 cm across; sepals and petals olive-green or green, spotted with maroon; lip white on sides and at apex, yellow with crimson-orange spots in the middle. **Sepals** fleshy, oblong-elliptic, 6–8.5 cm long, 1.2–2.3 cm broad, acute or obtuse; lateral sepals falcate and slightly narrower than dorsal sepal. **Petals** obliquely obovate-oblong, submembranous, 5.5–7.5 cm long, 2.5–3.5 cm broad, obtuse or rounded, margins crisped-undulate. **Lip** deeply 3-lobed, 4.5–5.5 cm broad; side lobes triangular-semiovate, erect over column, acute or obtuse; mid-lobe broadly clawed at base, dilated above into a flabellate-subreniform lamina, margins crisped to frilled; disc and base of mid-lobe covered with granulose papillae. **Column** clavate, thick, 2.5–3 cm long.

DISTRIBUTION Brazil, on trees in hills near the coast; up to 900 m.

HISTORY The type collection of this species was supposedly made by Th. Hartweg in 1840 in Guatemala. However, it is probable that this information was spread by horticulturalists to mislead their competitors and that it came from Brazil via Guatemala. John Lindley described the species in the *Botanical Register* (t. 1) in 1842 naming it for its granulose lip.

Var. *schofieldiana*, which flowered for the first time in the collection of C.W. Law-Schofield of Manchester, England in 1882, originated in Brazil and is the variety most frequently used in hybridisation. Withner (1988) considers this to be a distinct species *C. schofieldiana* Rchb.f. in his *The Cattleyas and Their Relatives*. *C. granulosa* has been used to introduce the colours green and yellow into the hybrid complex.

CLOSELY RELATED SPECIES Similar to *C. guttata* but with larger flowers and a longer claw to the mid-lobe of the lip.

Cattleya guttata Lindl. [Colour Plate]

An erect, lithophytic or epiphytic plant. **Pseudobulbs** cylindrical, elongate, 50–100 cm long, 2-leaved at apex. **Leaves** spreading, elliptic-oblong, very coriaceous, 15–22 cm long. **Inflorescence** 5- to 10-flowered, up to 15 cm long, subtended by a broad sheath. **Flowers** 5–8 cm across; sepals and petals yellowish-green to olive, spotted dark purple; lip pale pink or white in basal half, rose-purple above. **Sepals** oblong-lanceolate, 3.7 cm long, 0.8 cm broad, obtuse; lateral sepals subfalcate. **Petals** oblong to elliptic-oblong, 3.5 cm long, 1.3 cm broad, obtuse, margins undulate. **Lip** 3-lobed, 2.8 cm long, 2.4 cm broad; side lobes erect, enclosing column, acute; mid-lobe obcordate, papillate, clawed, with a shallow apical sinus. **Column** 3-angled in cross-section.

DISTRIBUTION Brazil (Minas Gerais, Rio de Janeiro and São Paulo States).

HISTORY *C. guttata* was described by John Lindley in the *Botanical Register* (t. 1406) in 1831. It was introduced into cultivation by the Rt Hon. Robert Gordon who sent plants from Rio de Janeiro to the Horticultural Society of London in 1827.

SYNONYM *Cattleya elatior* Lindl.; *C. tigrina* A.Rich.; *C. sphenophora* Morr.

CLOSELY RELATED SPECIES *C. guttata* is very closely allied to *C. leopoldii*, the latter being considered by some a variety of the former, although the two species are geographically isolated. *C. guttata* may be distinguished by its few-flowered inflorescences, by its slightly smaller flowers with acute apices to the sepals and petals, and by its lip which has a narrower clawed mid-lobe less deeply incised at the apex. *Cattleya dormaniana* Rchb.f. [Colour Plate] is allied to *C. guttata* and *C. leopoldii* but its sepals lack any spotting and its flower is smaller with narrower segments. *Cattleya amethystoglossa* Linden & Rchb.f. [Colour Plate] is allied to *C. guttata* and *C. leopoldii* but it is readily distinguished by its pale pink sepals and petals spotted with darker pinkish-purple. See also *C. granulosa*.

Cattleya intermedia Graham [Colour Plate]

An epiphytic or lithophytic plant, growing in tufts. **Pseudobulbs** cylindrical, 25–40 cm long, 1.5 cm in diameter, 2-leaved at apex. **Leaves** ovate-oblong, fleshy, spreading, 7–15 cm long,

4–7 cm broad, obtuse, notched at apex. **Inflorescence** 3- to 5-flowered, occasionally more, up to 25 cm tall, subtended by a basal sheath. **Flowers** 10–12.5 cm across, pale purple to white with mid-lobe of lip usually rich purple; sepals and petals occasionally spotted purple; column stained pale purple. **Sepals** oblong-lanceolate, 6.5 cm long, 1.4 cm broad, acute, margins reflexed; lateral sepals falcate. **Petals** falcate, narrowly lanceolate, 5.5 cm long, 1.5 cm broad, acute, undulate. **Lip** oval-oblong, 3-lobed, 5 cm long, 4 cm broad; side lobes curved over column to form a tube, rounded at apex; mid-lobe spreading, rotund, margin undulate-crisped, erose. **Column** clavate, arcuate, 2.5 cm long.

DISTRIBUTION Brazil (Rio de Janeiro, São Paulo, Parana, Santa Catarina and Rio Grande do Sul States); growing on small trees or rocks by streams or by the sea. Over-collection and habitat destruction are rapidly leading to its extermination.

HISTORY First introduced in 1824 by R. Graham who brought it from William Harrison of Rio de Janeiro to the Glasgow Botanic Gardens where it flowered for the first time in 1826. Graham described it in the *Botanical Magazine* (t. 2851) in 1828. It was named *intermedia* for the medium-size of its flowers in the genus.

SYNONYMS *Cattleya ovata* Lindl.; *C. maritima* Lindl.; *C. amethystina* C. Morr.; *C. amabilis* Hort.

Cattleya iricolor Rchb.f. [Colour Plate]

An erect epiphytic plant. **Pseudobulbs** clavate, compressed, 10–12.5 cm long, 1-leafed. **Leaves** ligulate, up to 30 cm long, emarginate at apex. **Inflorescence** 2- to 3-flowered, up to 15 cm long. **Flowers** small in genus, up to 7.5 cm across; ivory-white to creamy-white sepals and petals; lip white with an orange central area and purple stripes; column white. **Sepals** elliptic-lanceolate, 5 cm long, 0.7 cm broad, acute; lateral sepals, subfalcate-deflexed. **Petals** similar to sepals, 4.7 cm long, 0.8 cm broad, obtuse. **Lip** obscurely 3-lobed, 3.5 cm long, 2.8 cm broad; side lobes forming a tube around the column, purple-striped; mid-lobe reflexed, acute. **Column** 1.8 cm long, clavate, slightly winged, arcuate.

DISTRIBUTION Ecuador (in valleys near the towns of Puyo and Tena); at about 1000 m, very rare.

HISTORY A great rarity from Ecuador which H.G. Reichenbach described in the *Gardeners' Chronicle* (n.s. 2: 162) of 1874 from a plant bought by Messrs Veitch & Sons at Stevens' Sale Rooms, England. The single plant in cultivation completely disappeared around the turn of the century until 1962 when Padre Angel M. Andreeti, a Salesian mission-ary, rediscovered it in Ecuador (see P. Taylor in *Orchid Review*, 1974).

Cattleya labiata Lindl. [Colour Plate]

A very variable epiphytic species. **Pseudobulbs** club-shaped, 12–30 cm long, slightly compressed, clothed with greenish, thin-textured sheaths, furrowed with age, 1-leafed at apex. **Rhizome** thick, about 1 cm in diameter. **Leaf** oblong, 15–25 cm long, 6 cm broad, obtuse, coriaceous and long-lived. **Inflorescence** 2- to 5-flowered, subtended by 2 sheaths. **Flowers** 12.5–15 cm across; petals and sepals pale to bright rose; lip rich magenta-purple, bordered rose-lilac, throat with a pale yellow blotch ± streaked purple; column yellow. **Sepals** lanceolate, 8 cm long, 2.2 cm broad, acute, recurved at apex; lateral sepals slightly falcate. **Petals** ovate, 7.5 cm long, 5.5 cm broad, obtuse, margins undulate. **Lip** ovate-oblong, obscurely 3-lobed; side lobes curved over column to form a tube; mid-lobe spreading, deeply emarginate, with a crisped or frilled margin. **Column** club-shaped, semiterete, grooved ventrally, expanded into 2 wing-like margins.

DISTRIBUTION E. Brazil.

HISTORY Introduced into cultivation by W. Swainson from Brazil in 1818 and said to have been collected in the Organ Mts. It is no longer found there but is not uncommon in the eastern states of Brazil. *C. labiata* was described by John Lindley in *Collectanea Botanica* (t. 33) in 1821 and is the type of the genus.

C. labiata was the first of the showy, larger-flowered, 1-leafed *Cattleya* species to be discovered. This and other species such as *C. mossiae*, *C. warscewiczii*, *C. trianaei* and *C. dowiana* are very closely related and have been considered by some botanists intraspecific variants of a single species, *C. labiata*. Because of the horticultural importance of these taxa, they are treated here at specific rank.

SYNONYM *Cattleya lemoniana* Lindl.

CLOSELY RELATED SPECIES *Cattleya warneri* S. Moore [Colour Plate] from S. Brazil is very closely allied to *C. labiata* and has been considered a variety of it. It differs mainly in its larger flower size and in its flower colour, having delicate rose-coloured sepals and petals shaded with amethyst-purple and a lip which is richly veined with purple within, with a tawny or orange-yellow disc striated with pale lilac or white, a pale rosy amethyst-purple margin and a deep purple central spot on the mid-lobe. See also *C. dowiana*, *C. eldorado*, *C. gaskelliana*, *C. mendelii*, *C. mossiae*, *C. trianaei*, *C. warscewiczii*.

Cattleya lawrenceana Rchb.f. [Colour Plate]

An epiphytic plant, up to 40 cm high. **Pseudobulbs** erect, gradually widening towards the apex, sulcate, compressed, 2- to 3-noded, up to 39 cm long, green or purplish-green, ± covered with persistent white sheaths, 1-leafed at apex. **Leaf** oblong-ligulate, thick, rigid, up to 20 cm long, 4.5 cm broad, obtuse, green, ± purple spotted. **Inflorescence** racemose, terminal, up to 7-flowered, subtended at base by a broad sheath up to 10 cm long. **Flowers** showy, 10–13 cm across, light to fairly dark rosy-purple, rarely pure white; lip with a light rosy-purple throat, white in centre with purple veins and velvety dark purple at apex; column white. **Dorsal sepal** narrowly elliptic, 7 cm long, 1.6 cm broad, mucronate; **lateral sepals** falcately narrowly oblong, 7 cm long, 1.6 cm broad, acute. **Petals** oblong to subrhombic, 7 cm long, 2.7–4.3 cm broad, obtuse, margin undulate especially in apical half. **Lip** more or less oblong, slightly wider in apical half, 6 cm long, 4 cm broad, notched at apex, sides erect around column forming a trumpet. **Column** fleshy, dilated in apical half, 2 cm long.

DISTRIBUTION Venezuela and Guyana; 1200–1400 m altitude.

HISTORY H.G. Reichenbach described this species in honour of Sir Trevor Lawrence in the *Gardeners' Chronicle* (n.s. 23: p. 338) of 1885. The plant had, however, been discovered many years before in 1842 by Sir Robert Schomburgk at the foot of Mt Roraima in Guyana. Reichenbach's specimens were collected by Seidel, one of the collectors from Sander & Co., also on Roraima.

Several varieties have been introduced into cultivation which differ mainly in flower size and coloration.

CLOSELY RELATED SPECIES Similar in flower to *C. skinneri* and *C. bowringiana* but it may be readily distinguished from these as it has 1-leafed and not 2-leaved pseudobulbs.

Cattleya leopoldii Verschaff. ex Lemaire [Colour Plate]

Pseudobulbs cylindrical, slightly thickened above, 30–120 cm long, covered with white sheaths, 2-leaved at apex. **Leaves** oblong-elliptic, leathery, up to 22 cm long, 6 cm broad, with sharp often serrated edges. **Inflorescence** 3- to 10-(or more) flowered, subtended by a large, broad sheath. Flowers 7–11 cm across, fragrant; sepals and petals olive-green to bronzy-green, heavily spotted maroon; lip pale pink at base and side lobes, mid-lobe rich rose-purple with darker veins; column white with a rich purple mark at apex. **Sepals** narrowly oblanceolate, about 5 cm long, 1.2 cm broad, acute; lateral sepals slightly falcate, deflexed. **Petals** narrowly obovate, 5 cm long, 1.8 cm broad, obtuse. **Lip** 3-lobed, 4.5 cm long, 4 cm broad; side lobes triangular, acute, erect over column; mid-lobe transversely oblong, clawed with a broad apical sinus. **Column** up to 3.5 cm long, arcuate, clavate.

DISTRIBUTION S. Brazil (Santa Catarina and Rio Grande do Sul States); in coastal forests up to 100 m.

HISTORY First collected by F. Devros for Alex Verschaffelt of Ghent. Verschaffelt dedicated it to King Leopold I of Belgium and it was described by C. Lemaire in *L'Illustration Horticole* (misc. p. 68) in 1854.

Var. *pernambucensis* is a smaller plant, known from Bahia and Pernambuco States in N.E. Brazil.

SYNONYMS *Cattleya guttata* var. *leopoldii* (Verschaff. ex Lemaire) Rolfe

Cattleya loddigesii Lindl. [Colour Plate]

An epiphytic or lithophytic plant. **Stems** cylindrical, narrowing below, 20–30 cm long, 2-leaved at apex. **Leaves** elliptic-oblong, leathery, 10–12.5 cm long, 4–5.5 cm broad, obtuse. **Inflorescence** 2- to 9-flowered, up to 30 cm long, subtended by a broad basal sheath. **Flowers** 8–11 cm across; sepals and petals pale rose-lilac; lip as sepals and petals below, mid-lobe pale amethyst-purple, disc whitish passing to yellow below; column white. **Sepals** elliptic-oblong, 4.5–6.5 cm long, 2 cm broad, obtuse; lateral sepals subfalcate-deflexed. **Petals** obliquely oblong-elliptic, 5.5–6 cm long, 2–2.5 cm broad, obtuse, undulate. **Lip** suborbicular, 3-lobed; side lobes erect incurved, subrectangular, front margin dentate; mid-lobe spreading, crisped at margin. **Column** clavate, arcuate, with a wing on each side, 3 cm long.

DISTRIBUTION S. Brazil (Parana and Minas Gerais States).

HISTORY The first *Cattleya* to be introduced into Europe. Messrs Loddiges of Hackney, London, introduced it from Rio de Janeiro and described it in the *Botanical Cabinet* (t. 337) of 1819 as *Epidendrum violaceum*. When John Lindley founded the genus *Cattleya* based on *C. labiata* in *Collectanea Botanica* (sub t. 33) in 1823 he described the plant as *C. loddigesii* in honour of the firm that introduced it because the Loddiges name was a later homonym of *E. violaceum* Jacq. (1760).

CLOSELY RELATED SPECIES *Cattleya harrisoniana* Batem. ex Lindl., from swampy areas in Rio de Janeiro and Minas Gerais States of Brazil, is considered by some a variety of *C. loddigesii* but it differs in having slenderer, longer pseudobulbs and leaves and a yellower lip with more reflexed side lobes.

Cattleya luteola Lindl. [Colour Plate]

A dwarf epiphytic plant, up to 18 cm tall, with a slender creeping rhizome. **Pseudobulbs** clavate, ellipsoid or clavate-cylindrical, sulcate with age, up to 15 cm long, 1-leafed at apex. **Leaf** oblong or oblong-elliptic, 6–17 cm long, 3.8 cm broad, obtuse or notched at apex. **Inflorescence** terminal, racemose, several-flowered, shorter than leaf, at base covered with a large scarious sheath. **Flowers** rather small, 4.5–5 cm across, green or yellow; lip spotted or streaked crimson. **Sepals** oblong or narrowly-oblong, to 4.5 cm long, acute; lateral sepals obliquely oblong-elliptic. **Petals** narrowly elliptic-oblong, slightly falcate, as broad as dorsal sepal. **Lip** suborbicular, up to 2.8 cm long and broad, obscurely 3-lobed in front, anterior margin crenulate; disc densely shortly pubescent above middle. **Column** short, arcuate, 2-winged, half length of lip.

DISTRIBUTION Brazil, Peru, Ecuador and Bolivia.

HISTORY Originally described by John Lindley in 1852 in the *Gardeners' Chronicle* (p. 774). The first record of its cultivation in Europe was by Messrs Backhouse of York, England, who successfully flowered plants collected in the Amazonas area of Brazil.

SYNONYMS include *Cattleya flavida* Klotzsch; *C. meyeri* Regel; *C. flavida* Klotzsch; *Epidendrum luteolum* (Lindl.) Rchb.f.; *C. sulphurea* Hort.

Cattleya maxima Lindl. [Colour Plate]

An erect, tufted plant, up to 40 cm tall. **Pseudobulbs** club-shaped, stout, 10–39 cm long, compressed, sulcate with age, 1-leafed at apex, almost covered with large membranous sheaths. **Leaf** oblong to oblong-ligulate, up to 25 cm long, 7.5 cm broad, rounded or obtuse, notched at apex. **Inflorescence** terminal, laxly few- to 15-flowered, base covered with a large sheath up to 12 cm long. **Flowers** large and showy, 12.5 cm across; petals and sepals rose to lilac; lip pale pink, veined purple with a central yellow band; column white. **Sepals** lanceolate, up to 8.5 cm long, acuminate; lateral sepals rather shorter than dorsal. **Petals** oblong-ovate or oblong-elliptic, up to 8.5 cm long, twice as broad as sepals. **Lip** ovate-oblong, obscurely 3-lobed, 5–7 cm long, 4 cm broad; side lobes forming a tube over column; mid-lobe spreading, margin crisped-undulate. **Column** slender, obscurely angled, up to 2.5 cm long.

DISTRIBUTION Ecuador, Colombia and Peru.

HISTORY Originally collected by the Spanish botanists H. Ruiz and J. Pavon from near Guayaquil in Ecuador and described from this collection by John Lindley in his *Genera and Species of Orchidaceous Plants* (p. 116) in 1831. The species was introduced into cultivation in 1824 by Th. Hartweg but his plants lasted only a season or two before they died. In 1855 W. Farmer of Cheam in Surrey, England,

acquired a further batch and from that time *C. maxima* has remained in cultivation.

A white-flowered form of *C. maxima* is known together with a slender pale-flowered variety.

SYNONYMS *Epidendrum maximum* (Lindl). Rchb.f.; *Cattleya malouana* Lindl. & Rodr.

CLOSELY RELATED SPECIES See *C. rex*.

Cattleya mendelii Hort. [Colour Plate]

Pseudobulbs cylindrical, 6–18 cm long, 2 cm broad, grooved, shiny, 1-leafed at apex. **Leaf** oblong, up to 23 cm long, 6 cm broad, very leathery, rounded at apex. **Inflorescence** 2- to 3-flowered. **Flowers** 17–20 cm across, rarely more, showy; sepals and petals white, ± tinted pale rose; side lobes of lip white or lilac, mid-lobe rich crimson-purple, sharply separated from yellow disc which is marked with purple streaks. **Sepals** narrowly elliptic-lanceolate, 9.5 cm long, 2.3 cm broad, acute. **Petals** elliptic to ovate, 9 cm long, 6 cm broad, obtuse to sub-acute, margins undulate. **Lip** oblong, very obscurely 3-lobed, 8.5 cm long, 5 cm broad, deeply notched at apex; side lobes erect around column; mid-lobe spreading. **Column** 3.5 cm long, arcuate, clavate; mid-tooth at apex truncate.

DISTRIBUTION Eastern Cordillera slopes in Colombia; growing on rocks and precipices.

HISTORY Introduced in 1870 by Messrs Low & Co. of Clapton, London, and shortly afterwards by Messrs Backhouse of York who named it after Samuel Mendel of Manchester in the 6th edition of B.S. Williams's *Orchid Grower's Manual* (p. 190) in the same year. It was flowered for the first time in cultivation by John Day of Tottenham, London, in 1871.

SYNONYM *Cattleya labiata* var. *mendelii* Rchb.f.

CLOSELY RELATED SPECIES May be distinguished from *C. labiata* and its relatives by the contrasting deeply coloured lip and white or pale sepals and petals. Morphologically it can scarcely be distinguished from *C. labiata* and it may prove to be only a variety or subspecies of that species as some botanists have suggested.

Cattleya mossiae Hooker [Colour Plate]

A very variable species particularly in flower colour. **Pseudobulb** fusiform, ridged, green, 1-leafed at apex. **Leaf** oblong to narrowly ovate-oblong, up to 28 cm long, 4.5 cm broad, rounded at apex. **Inflorescence** 2- to 4-flowered, 30 cm high. **Flowers** very variable, 14–18 across; sepals and petals pale to dark pink or lilac or rarely white; lip pink or lilac with a central orange-yellow area in throat lined deep purple-magenta and a rich purple area on the mid-lobe. **Dorsal sepal** lanceolate, 8.5 cm long, 1.7 cm broad, acute; **lateral** sepals slightly obliquely oblanceolate. **Petals** ovate-elliptic, 8.5 cm long, 5 cm broad, obtuse, margin erose, very undulate. **Lip** oblong, obscurely 3-lobed, 7 cm long, 4.6 cm broad; side lobes erect forming a tube over column; mid-lobe rounded, notched at apex, spreading, margin very crisped-undulate. **Column** apex with a spathulate appendage, clavate, arcuate, up to 3.5 cm long.

DISTRIBUTION Venezuela; in north coastal mountain range.

HISTORY First introduced into cultivation by George Green of Liverpool, England, who received it from La Guaira, Venezuela in 1836. It flowered for the first time in the collection of Mrs Moss of Liverpool, after whom Sir William Hooker named it in the *Botanical Magazine* (t. 3669) in 1838.

SYNONYM *Cattleya labiata* var. *mossiae* Lindl.

CLOSELY RELATED SPECIES Another of the *C. labiata* alliance which many consider to be but a very variable species with several geographical varieties or subspecies recognisable mainly on flower colour. The coloration of the lip is particularly characteristic of this species. See also *C. gaskelliana*.

Cattleya percivaliana (Rchb.f.) O'Brien [Colour Plate]

An epiphytic or lithophytic plant, up to 50 cm tall. **Pseudobulbs** up to 15 cm long, 2 cm broad, broadest in middle, compressed, green, clothed in white sheaths when young, 1-leafed at apex. **Leaf** narrowly oblong-elliptic, rigid, suberect, up to 25 cm long, 5 cm broad, obtuse. **Inflorescence** terminal, 2- to 4-flowered, up to 25 cm long, subtended at base by a compressed green sheath. **Flowers** very showy, 10–13 cm across, musty smelling; sepals and petals rosy-purple and very finely veined; lip maroon with yellow veins at base, disc golden yellow, with maroon veins in centre, richly velvety-magenta at apex; column white, apical projection purple. **Dorsal sepal** narrowly oblanceolate-elliptic, 7.5 cm long, 2.5 cm broad, acute; **lateral sepals** decurved, obliquely narrowly elliptic, 7 cm long, 2.3 cm broad, acute. **Petals** ovate to subrhombic, 7.5 cm long, 6 cm broad, obtuse, margin in apical half undulate and erose. **Lip** oblong to broadly elliptic, truncate, notched at apex, sides forming a trumpet over column.

DISTRIBUTION Venezuela; from 1300–1900 m altitude, growing on rocks in full sun near rivers.

HISTORY A very variable species particularly in the extent to which the lip is marked with golden-yellow. This species was originally described in 1882 by H.G. Reichenbach as a variety of *C. labiata* in the *Gardeners' Chronicle* (n.s. 17: 796), but James O'Brien raised it to the rank of species in the same journal (n.s. 20:

404) the next year. It was discovered by J. Arnold, one of Sander's collectors, in the cordillera of Venezuela. Reichenbach named it in honour of R.P. Percival of Birkdale, Southport.

SYNONYM *Cattleya labiata* var. *percivaliana* Rchb.f.

Cattleya rex O'Brien [Colour Plate]

An epiphytic plant, up to 50 cm tall, growing in tufts. **Pseudobulbs** clustered, cylindrical-clavate, somewhat compressed, up to 35 cm long, 1-leafed at apex. **Leaf** oblong or oblong-elliptic, coriaceous, up to 35 cm long, 6 cm broad, obtuse. **Inflorescence** shorter than leaf, up to 20 cm long, laxly 3- to 10-flowered, subtended by a long sheath up to 13 cm long. **Flowers** very large and showy; sepals and petals creamy-white or ivory-white, lip with yellow side lobes and a rose-coloured anterior part, throat yellow, veined red. **Dorsal sepal** narrowly elliptic-lanceolate, up to 8 cm long, subacute; **lateral sepals** similar, slightly oblique and shorter. **Petals** elliptic or rhombic-elliptic, 8 cm long, 3 times broader than sepals, obtuse, margins undulate. **Lip** obovate to oval-oblong, 8 cm long, 4–5 cm broad, forming a tube around the column, entire or obscurely 3-lobed above the middle, anterior margins crenulate-undulate. **Column** stout, clavate, up to 3.5 cm long.

DISTRIBUTION Peru and Colombia.

HISTORY Described by James O'Brien in 1890 in the *Gardeners' Chronicle* (ser. 3, 8: 684), based on a plant introduced into Belgium. F. Sander introduced it into England two years later.

CLOSELY RELATED SPECIES Closely related to *C. maxima* but distinguished by its differently coloured flowers.

Cattleya schilleriana Rchb.f. [Colour Plate]

A small epiphytic plant. **Pseudobulbs** club-shaped, 10–15 cm high, sulcate, often tinged reddish-purple, 2-leaved at apex. **Leaves** elliptic-oblong, spreading, deep green above, reddish-purple below. **Inflorescence** 1- or 2-flowered, but rarely more. **Flowers** 7.6–10 cm across; sepals and petals olive-brown to mahogany-brown, spotted dark maroon; lip whitish, heavily veined purple and with a central yellow area; column white, streaked and spotted purple. **Sepals** oblong-lanceolate, 6 cm long, 2 cm broad, obtuse, margins slightly wavy; lateral sepals similar to dorsal sepal but slightly falcate. **Petals** ligulate, 5.5 cm long, 1.6 cm broad, obtuse, margins undulate. **Lip** 3-lobed, 5.5 cm long, 4.2 cm broad; side lobes curved above column almost forming a tube, apex recurved, subacute; mid-lobe broadly flabellate, margin fimbriate. **Column** clavate, concave below, 3 cm long, winged.

DISTRIBUTION Brazil (in Espiritu Santo and Bahia States).

HISTORY The first record of this distinct species was from Consul Schiller who flowered a plant in Hamburg in 1857 and H.G. Reichenbach named the plant after him when he described it in the *Berliner Allgemeine Gartenzeitung* (p. 325) in the same year.

It is rarely used in hybridisation.

CLOSELY RELATED SPECIES Somewhat intermediate in its flowers between *C. guttata* and *C. aclandiae*.

Cattleya schroederae Hort. [Colour Plate]

See under *Cattleya trianaei*.

Cattleya skinneri Batem. [Colour Plate]

A stout, erect, epiphytic or terrestrial plant, up to 50 cm tall, often growing in dense clumps. **Pseudobulbs** clavate, compressed, aculeate, up to 35 cm long, 2–3 cm broad, covered by tubular sheaths when young, 2-leaved at apex. **Leaves** oblong-elliptic or oblong, fleshy-coriaceous, 10–20 cm long, 2.5–6 cm broad, obtuse. **Inflorescence** racemose, short, 4- to 12-flowered, subtended by a large sheath, up to 12 cm long. **Flowers** medium-sized up to 7.6 cm across, showy, rose- to vivid-purple, rarely white; lip with a white or creamy throat, disc whitish. **Sepals** linear-lanceolate or elliptic-lanceolate, 4–6.5 cm long, 1–1.8 cm broad, obtuse or acute. **Petals** broadly ovate, 4–6.7 cm long, 1.8–3.5 cm broad, rounded or apiculate, margins undulate. **Lip** oblong-elliptic, entire, forming a funnel around the column, 3–5 cm long, 2–3.5 cm broad, emarginate; disc keeled to apex. **Column** small, slender, 0.8–1.2 cm long.

DISTRIBUTION Mexico, Belize, Guatemala, Honduras, Costa Rica and possibly Panama; an uncommon epiphyte on trees in humid forests and also found as a terrestrial on granite slopes, up to 1250 m altitude.

HISTORY Discovered in Guatemala by George Ure Skinner. He sent plants to James Bateman who named it in honour of its discoverer in his *Orchidaceae of Mexico and Guatemala* (1838).

C. skinneri is the national flower of Costa Rica where it is most commonly found.

A white-flowered variety is also known which was introduced from Costa Rica by A.R. Endres who sent plants to Messrs Veitch & Sons of Exeter, England.

CLOSELY RELATED SPECIES See *C. bowringiana*, *C. deckeri* and *C. lawrenceana*.

Cattleya trianaei Linden & Rchb.f. [Colour Plate]

An epiphytic plant. **Pseudobulbs** narrowly clavate, grooved, up to 30 cm long, 2 cm broad,

1-leafed at apex, shiny yellow-orange. **Leaf** oblong to elliptic-oblong, up to 28 cm long, 7 cm broad, rounded, notched at apex. **Inflorescence** 3- to 14-flowered, up to 30 cm long. **Flowers** up to 15–23 cm across, very showy; sepals and petals variable in colour, white, delicate rose or purple; lip side lobes as petals and sepals, mid-lobe rich crimson-purple or paler, disc orange-yellow, ± striated purple, pink or white. **Sepals** oblanceolate, 8.7 cm long, 2 cm broad, subacute. **Petals** ovate-elliptic, 8.5 cm long, 6 cm broad, obtuse, with undulate-crispate margins. **Lip** elliptic to oblong-ovate, obscurely 3-lobed, up to 8 cm long, 6 cm broad, notched at apex, side lobes forming a tube around column, apical margins undulate-crispate. **Column** 3.5 cm long.

DISTRIBUTION Colombia; widespread in all three Cordilleras but now rare as it has been grossly over-collected.

HISTORY Introduced in 1856 by Rucker of Wandsworth, London, who received a specimen from Colombia. However, no valid name for it was published until Jean Linden and H.G. Reichenbach described it in *Botanische Zeitung* (p. 74) in 1864 naming it after Dr Triana, a botanist from Bogotá, Colombia.

SYNONYMS *Cattleya quadricolor* Lindl.; *C. bogotensis* Linden ex C. Morr.; *C. labiata* var. *trianaei* (Linden & Rchb.f.) Duchartre

CLOSELY RELATED SPECIES This is distinguished from other species of the *labiata* group by its rich coloration and lip which has a less crisped and spreading mid-lobe. *Cattleya schroederae* Hort. [Colour Plate] is very closely allied to *C. trianaei* and is considered by some to be a variety of the latter. They possess a similar flower shape but *C. schroederae* is readily distinguished by its very fragrant flowers, by the extraordinary crispation of the petals and lip margin and by the extensive orange area of the lip. The overall flower colour of *C. schroederae* varies from pure white through various shades of rose-pink to light purple.

Cattleya velutina Rchb.f. [Colour Plate]
See under *Cattleya aclandiae*.

Cattleya violacea (H.B.K.) Rolfe
[Colour Plate]
A medium to large epiphytic plant, up to about 60 cm tall. **Pseudobulbs** clavate, up to 30 cm long, 1.7 cm in diameter, concealed by green or purple-green sheaths when young, 2-leaved at apex. **Leaves** spreading, rigid, coriaceous, elliptic or elliptic-ovate, rounded or obtuse at apex, up to 15 cm long, 6–8 cm broad, margins recurved. **Inflorescences** erect, up to 30 cm long, 2- to 5-flowered; peduncle enclosed at base by 1 or 2 compressed sheaths; bracts broadly ovate, obtuse, 0.4 cm long. **Flowers**

very showy, clear rose-purple, 7.6–10 cm across; lip deep purple with a white base, marked with yellow. **Dorsal sepal** spreading, linear-lanceolate, acute, up to 6.7 cm long, 1 cm broad; **lateral sepals** similar but falcate, up to 6.5 cm long, 2 cm broad. **Petals** spreading, subrhombic, obtuse, up to 6.5 cm long, 3.5 cm broad, margins slightly undulate. **Lip** 3-lobed, up to 5.5 cm long, 5 cm broad; side lobes erect, incurved over column, triangular and subacute in front; mid-lobe transversely oblong, shallowly emarginate, with erose margins. **Column** slightly arcuate, subclavate, 2.6 cm long.

DISTRIBUTION Brazil, Peru, Venezuela and Guyana; in exposed situations on trees along rivers, between 300 and 700 m.

HISTORY Another of the many new orchids collected by F.H.A. von Humboldt and A. Bonpland in Venezuela on the Orinoco River near San Fernando de Atabape.

It was described by them and C.S. Kunth in 1815 in *Nova Genera et Species Plantarum* (p. 341) as *Cymbidium violaceum* but was later transferred to *Cattleya* by R.A. Rolfe in the *Gardeners' Chronicle* (ser. 3, 5: 802) of 1889.

SYNONYMS *Cymbidium violaceum* H.B.K.; *Catleya superba* Schomb. ex Lindl.; *Epidendrum violaceum* (H.B.K.) Rchb.f.; *E. superbum* (Schomb. ex Lindl.) Rchb.f.

Cattleya walkeriana Gardn. [Colour Plate]
A small, creeping epiphytic or lithophytic plant. **Pseudobulbs** jointed, bulbous or shortly fusiform, up to 15 cm long, 2 cm broad, shiny yellow, 1- or rarely 2-leaved at apex. **Leaves** elliptic or ovate, leathery, 5–10 cm long, 3–5 cm broad, rounded at apex. **Inflorescence** up to 20 cm long, 1- to 3-flowered, borne on slender shoots. **Flowers** up to 10 cm across, bright rose-purple to pale pink-lilac; lip with a white or pale yellow disc striated with purple and with a broad anterior border of amethyst-purple. **Sepals** oblong-lanceolate, 5 cm long, 1.2 cm broad, acute. **Petals** subrhombic-elliptic, 5 cm long, 2.4 cm broad, obtuse, margins undulate. **Lip** entire or obscurely 3-lobed, ± shovel-shaped, cucullate, 4 cm long, 3.2 cm broad; side lobes rounded erect over column-base; mid-lobe transversely ovate or reniform, spreading, margin deflexed. **Column** winged, clavate, 2.5 cm long.

DISTRIBUTION Brazil (Bahia and Minas Gerais States) on moist rocks or small trees by streams.

HISTORY Discovered in 1839 or 1840 by George Gardner in Bahia State. He named this species after his friend Edward Walker in the *London Journal of Botany* (p. 662) in 1843. Rucker first flowered it in cultivation in 1947 and John Lindley named it as *C. bulbosa*, which name was

commonly used for cultivated plants for many years.

SYNONYMS *Cattleya bulbosa* Lindl.; *Epidendrum walkerianum* (Gardn.) Rchb.f.

CLOSELY RELATED SPECIES *Cattleya nobilior* Rchb.f. is very closely related but has rather larger flowers, 10–12 cm across.

Cattleya warneri S. Moore [Colour Plate]
See under *Cattleya labiata*.

Cattleya warscewiczii Rchb.f. [Colour Plate]
An epiphytic plant. **Pseudobulbs** thick, shiny, cigar-shaped, 10 cm long, 2 cm broad, grooved deeply, 1-leafed at apex. **Leaf** oblong, 20 cm long, 5 cm broad, very thick, leathery, rounded at apex. **Inflorescence** 4- to 7-flowered, up to 45 cm long. **Flowers** 17–23 cm across, very large and showy; sepals and petals rich rose-pink; lip carmine or rich purple with yellow in throat. **Dorsal sepal** narrowly oblanceolate, 10 cm long, 2.5 cm broad, acute; **lateral sepals** similar but slightly obliquely falcate. **Petals** ovate-elliptic, 9.5 cm long, 5.0 cm broad, obtuse, margins undulate. **Lip** oblong, emarginate, very obscurely 3-lobed, 8 cm long, 5.5 cm broad; side lobes forming tube over column, mid-lobe spreading widely, margin crisped-undulate and reflexed somewhat in front. **Column** clavate, 3 cm long, arcuate.

DISTRIBUTION Colombia; 500–1500 m altitude, on trees by streams, often growing in full sunlight.

HISTORY Discovered by Josef Warscewicz in 1848 or 1849 in the province of Medellin in Colombia. H.G. Reichenbach described it from Warscewicz's herbarium specimens in *Bonplandia* (p. 112) in 1854. It did not become common in collections until 1870 when Roezl collected it in quantity in Medellin.

SYNONYMS *Cattleya gigas* Linden & André; *C. labiata* var. *warscewiczii* Rchb.f.

CLOSELY RELATED SPECIES Closely related to *C. labiata* of which it may prove to be a variety or subspecies. It has the largest flowers of any of the *labiata* group.

Cattleyopsis Lindl.
Subfamily Epidendroideae
Tribe Epidendreae
Subtribe Laeliinae

Small to medium-sized epiphytes. **Pseudobulbs** small, ovoid-cylindrical to ellipsoidal, 1- to 2-leaved at the apex, few-noded. **Leaves** fleshy-rigid, with erose margins. **Inflorescence** erect, terminal, few-flowered, simple; bracts small. **Flowers** small to medium-sized, showy. **Sepals** and **petals** spreading or not spreading widely, free, subsimilar or with the petals broader. **Lip** entire, tubular at the base, spreading in front, with hairs or papillae on the central veins, lacking a spur. **Column** slender, elongate, clavate, with 2 basal appendages; pollinia 8, unequal.

DISTRIBUTION A small genus of three species in the Caribbean islands of Cuba, Jamaica and the Bahamas.

DERIVATION OF THE NAME From the resemblance of the flowers of the type species to those of a *Cattleya*.

TAXONOMY The genus *Cattleyopsis* was established by Lemaire in *Le Jardin Fleuriste* (misc. p. 59) in 1853.

It is closely allied to *Laeliopsis* and *Broughtonia*; it differs from the former in having basal appendages to the column and 8 rather than 4 pollinia; and from the latter in having fleshy-rigid erose leaves, a longer column with basal appendages but lacking a swollen nectary at the base of the lip. Sauleda and Adams (1989) have recently produced keys to distinguish these genera in the *Orchid Digest* (p. 39).

TYPE SPECIES *C. delicatula* Lem. (= *C. lindenii* (Lindl.) Cogn.)

CULTURE Temp. Winter min. 15°C. Probably best grown mounted, where the roots can dry out quickly after watering, as for *Broughtonia*. Requires good light and humidity.

Cattleyopsis lindenii (Lindl.) Cogn.

An epiphyte with ovoid-cylindric pseudobulbs, 1–7 cm long, 0.5–0.9 cm long, 1- to 2-leaved at the apex. **Leaves** linear-oblong, obtuse, 7–14 cm long, 1.3–2 cm wide. **Inflorescences** erect to arcuate, 25–70 cm long, rather densely few- to 15-flowered at the apex; peduncle elongate, slender, terete; bracts ovate, acute, c. 2 mm long. **Flowers** showy, rose-pink to purple, with the lip with a white throat, a yellow mark at the base and purple radiating veins; pedicel and ovary 1.5–2.8 cm long. **Sepals** and **petals** lanceolate, acute, 2.5–3 cm long, 0.5–1 cm wide, the petals broader than the sepals. **Lip** broadly obovate, emarginate, 3–4 cm long, 2–2.3 cm wide, the veins pubescent almost to the apex. **Column** 1.1–1.3 cm long.

DISTRIBUTION Cuba and Bermuda only; on trees and shrubs in coastal copses and pine woods; sea level to 200 m.

HISTORY This pretty orchid was discovered by Jean Linden in 1844 in Cuba between San Andres and le Saltaderol. Lindley described it as *Laelia lindenii* in his *Orchidaceae Lindenianae* (p. 10) in 1846. Cogniaux transferred it to the present genus in 1910 in Urban's *Symbolae Antillanae* (p. 544).

SYNONYMS *Laelia lindenii* Lindl.; *Broughtonia lilacina* Henfr.; *Cattleyopsis delicatula* Lem.; *C. northropiana* Cogn.

CLOSELY RELATED SPECIES *C. ortegesiana* (Rchb.f.) Cogn., from Cuba, resembles closely the Jamaican *Broughtonia sanguinea* (Sw.) R. Br. in its flower shape but it differs in having a distinctive slenderer column and petals with entire margins.

Caucaea Schltr.
Subfamily Epidendroideae
Tribe Oncidieae

Small epiphytic herbs with clustered, narrowly ovoid, compressed pseudobulbs, unifoliate at the apex and subtended by several rarely leaf-bearing, imbricate, acuminate sheaths. **Leaves** coriaceous, oblanceolate, erect to spreading. **Inflorescences** erect, axillary, basal, unbranched or rarely 1-branched, laxly few- to 15-flowered. **Flowers** small; pedicel and ovary relatively long. **Dorsal sepal** and **petals** free, subsimilar, spreading; **lateral sepals** united almost to apex, parallel to lip. **Lip** obscurely 3-lobed at base, porrect, straight, with a basal callus, lacking a spur. **Column** short, fleshy, basally winged but lacking a foot; pollinia 2, cleft; stipe small, oblong; viscidium small, circular.

DISTRIBUTION A monotypic genus in Venezuela, Colombia and Ecuador.

DERIVATION OF NAME A name derived from the Colombian Department of Cauca, where the type was originally collected.

TAXONOMY A genus established by Rudolf Schlechter in *Fedde, Repertorium Specierum Novar-*

Cattleyopsis lindenii
1 – Habit ($\times \frac{1}{3}$)
1 – Dorsal sepal ($\times$ 1)
3 – Lateral sepal ($\times$ 1)
4 – Petal ($\times$ 1)
5 – Lip ($\times$ 1)
6 – Column ($\times \frac{1}{2}$)

Caucaea radiata
1 – Habit ($\times \frac{4}{5}$)
2 – Sepals and petals ($\times$ 3)
3 – Lip ($\times$ 4)
4 – Column and lip, side view ($\times 4\frac{3}{4}$)
5 – Column, ventral view ($\times$ 5)
6 – Polinarium and anther-cap ($\times$ 11)

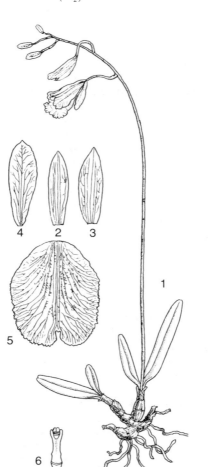

um, Beihefte (p. 189) in 1920. It is most closely related to *Brassia* but is readily distinguished by its much smaller habit and flowers.
TYPE SPECIES *C. obscura* (Lehm. & Kraenzl.) Schltr. (= *C. radiata* (Lindl.) Mansf.)
CULTURE Temp. Winter min. 10°C. Cultivation generally as for *Brachtia*.

Caucaea radiata (Lindl.) Mansf.

A small epiphyte with narrowly ovoid pseudobulbs, 1.5–3.5 cm long, 5–10 mm wide, unifoliate at the apex. **Leaf** oblanceolate to linear-lanceolate, acute, 5–12 cm long, 4–10 mm wide. **Inflorescences** erect, 6–22 cm long, laxly 3- to 15-flowered; peduncle wiry; bracts ovate-triangular, acuminate, sheathing at the base, 2.5–5 mm long. **Flowers** small, fleshy; sepals light brown with a maroon flush, warty on outside; petals white, warty on outside; lip white with pink spots and a yellow callus; pedicel and ovary 10–14 mm long. **Dorsal sepal** narrowly elliptic, ovate, acute, 6–7 mm long, 2–3 mm wide; **lateral sepals** united almost to apex, elliptic-ovate, with tips divergent, 6–7 mm long, 3–3.5 mm wide. **Petals** oblong-ovate, acute, 4–5 mm long, 2–2.5 mm wide. **Lip** rigidly adnate to base of column, obscurely 3-lobed, 5 mm long, 3 mm wide; side lobes narrowly elliptic; mid-lobe oblong, obtuse; callus a subquadrate raised fleshy knob. **Column** strongly roundly winged, 2 mm long; anther red.
DISTRIBUTION Venezuela, Colombia and Ecuador, in cloud forest, up to 3200 m elevation.
HISTORY John Lindley originally described this rather insignificant orchid as *Abola radiata* in 1853 in his *Folia Orchidacea* (Abola) based on a specimen collected in Pamplona Province in Colombia by L. Schlim, collecting for the orchid firm of Messrs Linden. It was transferred to the present genus by Mansfeld in *Fedde, Repertorium Specierum Novarum* in 1934.
SYNONYMS *Abola radiata* Lindl.; *Mesospinidium radiatum* (Lindl). Reichb.f.; *Rodriguesia obscura* Lehm. & Kraenzl.; *Caucaea obscura* (Lehm. & Kraenzl.) Schltr.; *Leochilus lehmannianus* Kraenzl.; *L. radiatus* (Lindl.) Kraenzl.; *Gomesa erectiflora* A.D. Hawkes

Caularthron Raf.
Subfamily Epidendroideae
Tribe Epidendreae
Subtribe Laeliinae

Medium-sized epiphytic plants. **Pseudobulbs**, fleshy, elongate, with several leaves at apex. **Inflorescence** racemose or paniculate, few- to many-flowered; peduncle elongate. **Flowers** medium-sized, ± showy. **Sepals** and **petals** free, spreading, ovate to elliptic. **Lip** ± 3-lobed; side lobes dentate or lobulate, ± reflexed; mid-lobe triangular to lanceolate; disc with a pair of raised fleshy calli. **Column** short, winged, slightly curved; anther terminal; pollinia 4, waxy.
DISTRIBUTION Two or possibly three species in S. America and Trinidad.
DERIVATION OF NAME The name of this genus refers to the persistent leaf-bases on the pseudobulbs and derives from the Greek *kaulos* (stem) and *arthron* (joint).
TAXONOMY Still referred by some botanists to the genus *Diacrium* Lindl. which is a later synonym. *Caularthron* is closely allied to *Epidendrum* and was described in 1836 by S. Rafinesque in *Flora Telluriana* (p. 40). From *Epidendrum* it is easily distinguished by the hollow horn-like processes on the lip.

In *Caularthron* the stems of some species, e.g. *C. bilamellatum* (Rchb.f.) R.E. Schultes, are thickened into pseudobulbs which are hollow and lodge ants.
TYPE SPECIES *C. bicornutum* (Hooker) Raf.
SYNONYM *Diacrium* Lindl.
CULTURE Compost A. Temp. Winter min. 15°C, higher when growing. Generally as for *Cattleya*, but a more severe dry rest period is required after flowering. When in active growth, water should be freely given, and only moderate shade is required. The plants grow well in hanging baskets, where the additional light is an advantage.

Caularthron bicornutum (Hooker) Raf.
[Colour Plate]
Pseudobulbs long-cylindrical, 10–30 cm long, 2–6 cm in diameter, 3- to 4-leaved towards apex. **Leaves** oblong or elliptic-oblong, fleshy-coriaceous, 6–20 cm long, 2–5 cm broad, obtuse. **Inflorescence** racemose, erect, up to 40 cm long, few- to 20-flowered. **Flowers** showy, up to 6 cm across, white with a yellow callus and purple-spotted lip. **Sepals** broadly ovate-lanceolate, up to 3 cm long, 1.8 cm broad, shortly acuminate or obtuse. **Petals** broadly ovate, up to 2.8 cm long, 2.3 cm broad, acute, upper margin notched. **Lip** 3-lobed, fleshy, 2 cm long; side lobes elliptic, rounded, much shorter than mid-lobe; mid-lobe ligulate to lanceolate, acute; callus 2-lobed, each lobe erect. **Column** 1.5 cm long, broader towards apex.
DISTRIBUTION Brazil, Colombia, Venezuela, Guyana, Trinidad and Tobago; often grows on trees by the seashore or by rivers.
HISTORY Described originally in 1834 by Sir William Hooker in the *Botanical Magazine* (t. 3332) as *Epidendrum bicornutum*, it was transferred by S. Rafinesque to *Caularthron* in 1836 in *Flora Telluriana* (p. 41).

SYNONYMS *Epidendrum bicornutum* Hooker; *Diacrium bicornutum* (Hooker) Benth.
CLOSELY RELATED SPECIES *Caularthron bilamellatum* (Rchb.f.) R.E. Schultes may be distinguished from *C. bicornutum* by its entire or obscurely 3-lobed lip and much smaller flowers.

Cephalatheropsis Guill.
Subfamily Epidendroideae
Tribe Arethuseae
Subtribe Bletiinae

Medium-sized terrestrial plants with bamboo-like leafy stems and creeping slender rhizomes. **Leaves** plicate, spreading-arcuate, chartaceous, articulate. **Inflorescences** axillary, laxly few- to many-flowered. **Flowers** showy, medium-sized. **Sepals** and **petals** free, subsimilar, spreading to reflexed. **Lip** 3-lobed, attached to the base of the column, ecallose and lacking a spur; side lobes erect, recurved at apex; mid-lobe transverse, bilobed. **Column** short, fleshy, pubescent, winged on sides; rostellum ovate, acute; pollinia 8, pyriform.
DISTRIBUTION A small genus of perhaps six or seven species widespread in E. and S.E. Asia from Japan, China and Taiwan south to Thailand, peninsular Malaysia and Indonesia.
DERIVATION OF NAME From the supposed resemblance of these plants to the orchid genus *Cephalanthera*.
TAXONOMY *Cephalantheropsis* was described by the French botanist Guillaumin in 1960 in *Bulletin du Muséum d'Histoire Naturelle, Paris* (p. 188). It is a segregate genus of *Phaius* distinguished by the lack of a spur or saccate base to the lip and by the rather distinctive lip. It also lies close to *Calanthe* but lacks the fusion of the column to the base of the lip that is typical of that genus.
TYPE SPECIES *C. lateriscapa* Guill.
CULTURE Temp. Winter min. 12°C. Cultivation as for the tropical calanthes or terrestrial bromheadias. The plants should be given shaded conditions and not allowed to dry out.

Cephalantheropsis gracilis (Lindl.) S.Y. Hu
A slender terrestrial plant with leafy stems, 20–50 cm tall. **Leaves** lanceolate to narrowly elliptic, acuminate or acute, 15–26 cm long, 3–8 cm wide, sheathing at the base. **Inflorescences** lateral, axillary, laxly to densely few- to many-flowered, up to 50 cm long, erect or suberect; peduncle terete, slender, up to 20 cm long; bracts deciduous, linear, setose, 2–3 mm long. **Flowers** white with yellow callus-ridges, hairy on the outside; pedicel and ovary pubescent, 16–20 mm long. **Sepals** lanceolate, acute, 1–1.7 cm long, 0.3–0.4 cm wide. **Petals** narrowly oblong to lanceolate, acute, 1–1.5 cm long, 0.2–

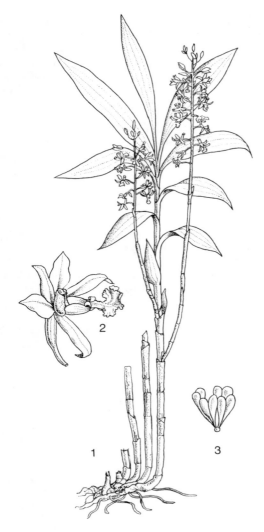

Cephalantheropsis gracilis
1 – Habit ($\times \frac{1}{4}$)
2 – Flower ($\times \frac{1}{2}$)
3 – Pollinarium ($\times 6$)

0.3 cm wide. **Lip** 3-lobed in the middle, 9–14 mm long, 6–8 mm wide; side lobes erect, oblong, acute at the front; mid-lobe shortly clawed, transversely oblong, emarginate, with strongly undulate-crisped margins; callus of 2 parallel ridges in basal half of lip. **Column** fleshy, 4–5 mm long, densely pubescent, with a short foot.

DISTRIBUTION N.E. India and Sikkim across to Japan and south to Malaya, in forest up to 1500 m.

HISTORY This species was first described as *Calanthe gracilis* in 1833 by John Lindley in his *Genera and Species of Orchidaceous Plants* (p. 251) based on a collection made by Nathaniel Wallich in Sylhet. It was transferred to the present genus by S.Y. Hu in 1972 in the *Quarterly Journal of the Taiwan Museum* (p. 213).

SYNONYMS *C. gracilis* Lindl.; *C. longipes* Hook.f.; *Phaius gracilis* (Lindl.) Hay.

Ceratostylis Blume
Subfamily Epidendroideae
Tribe Epidendreae
Subtribe Eriinae

Small epiphytic herbs with fibrous roots and simple or branched tufted stems, rarely leafless and rush-like. **Leaves** solitary, narrow, coriaceous, fleshy or subterete, rarely thin-textured. **Flowers** small, solitary or a few in a small cluster of bracts. **Sepals** erect, connivent; lateral sepals broader, forming a saccate or spur-like mentum with the column-foot. **Petals** narrower than the sepals. **Lip** adnate to the column-foot by a long incumbent claw; lamina short, erect-spreading, fleshy, entire. **Column** short, dilated above, 2-lobed or with 2 spathulate erect arms; foot long; anther 2-celled; pollinia 8, small, in fours or all together attached to a small viscidium.

DISTRIBUTION Some 60 species in India, S.E. Asia, the Philippines and Pacific Islands.

DERIVATION OF NAME From the Greek *keras* or *kerato* (horn) and *stylis* (style), from the fleshy horn-like appearance of the column.

TAXONOMY C.L. Blume described it in 1825 in *Bijdragen* (p. 304, t. 56). *Ceratostylis* is allied to *Agrostophyllum* and *Sarcostoma*, differing from the former in having unifoliate stems, 1-flowered inflorescences, and 8 rather than 4 pollinia.

TYPE SPECIES Several species were mentioned by Blume when the genus was described.

CULTURE Compost A. Temp. Winter min. 15°C. The more pendent species, such as *C. retisquama*, are best grown in shallow baskets, while pots are suitable for the remainder. They all require moderately shady, humid conditions while growing, and plenty of water. When growth is complete, less water should be given, but the plants should never remain dry for very long. They often produce flowers more than once annually.

Ceratostylis retisquama Rchb.f. [Colour Plate]
An epiphytic herb with short roots. **Rhizomes** pendulous, up to 25 cm long, loosely tufted, sparingly branched above, terete, 0.4–0.6 cm thick, covered with persistent, reticulate, chestnut-brown, chaffy sheaths. **Leaves** solitary on very short, free stems arising 2–3 cm apart on the rhizome, narrowly linear-lanceolate, very thick and fleshy, semiterete, upper surface deeply grooved, shortly petiolate below, obtuse and shortly and obliquely bifid at the apex, 9–12 cm long, 1.2–1.5 cm broad. **Inflorescence** terminal, but apparently axillary, bearing 1 to several flowers in succession; bracts similar to stem scales but smaller. **Flowers** brick-red with a whitish lip. **Dorsal sepal** oblong-elliptic, 2 cm long, 0.9 cm broad; **lateral sepals** similar to dorsal but connate for basal 1 cm, forming a short mentum 0.3 cm long. **Petals** narrowly obovate, 2 cm long, 0.8 cm broad. **Lip** fleshy, shortly clawed, ovate below and broadly cuneate-obtuse above, 0.7 cm long; side margins erect around the column; disc bicarinate,

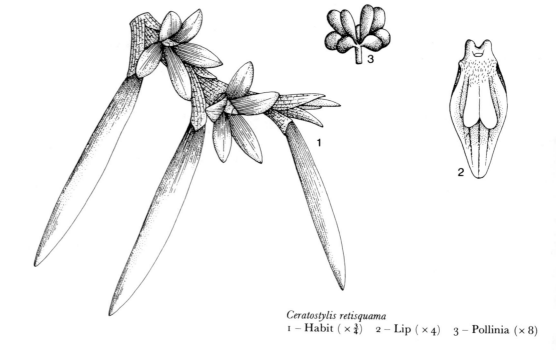

Ceratostylis retisquama
1 – Habit ($\times \frac{3}{4}$)   2 – Lip ($\times 4$)   3 – Pollinia ($\times 8$)

with a basal pubescent cushion. **Column** 0.4 cm long; side arms erect, rounded at the apex; pollinia 8, joined to a small elongate viscidium.

DISTRIBUTION Philippines (Luzon and Mindanao).

HISTORY Discovered in the Philippines by Hugh Cuming and described by H.G. Reichenbach in *Bonplandia* (p. 53) in 1857. This species is better known in cultivation under the name *C. rubra* Ames, but P. Taylor in the *Botanical Magazine* (1973) has recently shown this to be a later synonym.

SYNONYMS *Ceratostylis rubra* Ames; *C. latipetala* Ames

Chamaeangis Schltr.

Subfamily Epidendroideae
Tribe Vandeae
Subtribe Aerangidinae

Small to medium-sized epiphytic plants with short or very short leafy stems. **Leaves** erect spreading or spreading, commonly fleshy, linear-ligulate or ligulate. **Inflorescence** laxly to densely many-flowered, 1- to several-flowered at each node. **Flowers** very small or small, greenish-yellow, greenish-white or orange-ochre; bracts minute, very much shorter than the ovary. **Sepals** and **petals** subsimilar, free, spreading. **Lip** similar to petals but slightly broader, fleshy; spur cylindric, decurved, often ± dilated at the apex. **Column** very short, fleshy, footless; rostellum distinctly produced; pollinia globose or subglobose, 2, attached by a single linear stipe or 2 stipites to a circular or ovate viscidium.

DISTRIBUTION About 15 species in tropical Africa, Madagascar, the Mascarene Islands and Comoros.

DERIVATION OF NAME From the Greek *chamai* (lowly) and *angos* (vessel), in reference to the swollen vessel-like spur of the small flowers of many species in the genus.

TAXONOMY *Chamaeangis* was established by Rudolf Schlechter in 1915 in Engler's *Botonische Jahrbucher* (p. 597) based on a number of species previously referred to *Angraecum* and *Listrostachys* but differing from those genera in flower structure.

Schlechter recognised two sections in the genus:

(*Eu*) *Chamaeangis* species have separate stipites and a single viscidium, and all the African species fall in this section.

Microterangis species have a single stipe and viscidium to the pollinia, and all of the Madagascan species except *C. gracilis* (Thou.) Schltr. fall here.

Chamaeangis is characterised by its small

flowers which are often borne in whorls at the nodes, by its often swollen spur apex, by its short, thin, rather than fleshy, rostellum and by its pollinial apparatus with 1 or 2 stipites borne on a single viscidium.

TYPE SPECIES Several species were mentioned by Schlechter when he established the genus.

CULTURE Compost A or mounted. Temp. Winter min. 12–15°C. As for *Diaphananthe* and *Tridactyle*.

Chamaeangis odoratissima (Rchb.f.) Schltr.

An erect epiphytic herb with a stout elongate stem up to 50 cm long. **Roots** stout, arising along stem, emerging through the leaf-sheaths opposite the leaves. **Leaves** distichous, articulated to a sheathing base, spaced along stem, spreading, falcate twisted to lie in 1 plane, narrowly oblong-ligulate to oblanceolate, obtuse or rounded at the unequally 2-lobed apex, 10–25 cm long, 2–3.5 cm broad. **Inflorescence** spreading-arcuate, cylindric, racemose, densely many-flowered, up to 30 cm long, 2- to 6-flowered at each node. **Flowers** pale green, yellow or greenish-brown, very small. **Dorsal sepal** elliptic to subcircular, obtuse, 0.15–0.2 cm long, 0.15 cm broad; **lateral sepals** oblong-elliptic, obtuse, 0.2 cm long, 0.13 cm broad. **Petals** elliptic to circular, obtuse, 0.14 cm long. **Lip** deflexed, broadly ovate to elliptic, obtuse

Chamaeangis odoratissima
1 – Flower, front view (× 6)
2 – Flower, side view (× 6)
3 – Column, front view (× 13)
4 – Pollinia, stipites and viscidium (× 18)

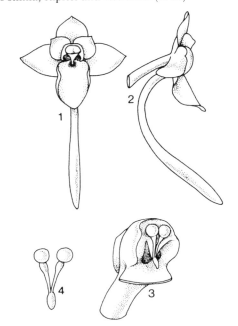

or rounded, 0.2 cm long, 0.14 cm broad; spur dependent, cylindric, slightly apically dilated, 0.8–1.3 cm long. **Column** short, stout, 0.1 cm long.

DISTRIBUTION Sierra Leone east to Uganda and Kenya.

HISTORY This species was first described by H.G. Reichenbach in 1856 in *Bonplandia* (p. 326) as *Angraecum odoratissimum* based on a cultivated plant of unknown origin. Rudolf Schlechter transferred it to *Chamaeangis* in 1915 in Engler's *Botanische Jahrbucher* (p. 597).

SYNONYMS *Angraecum odoratissimum* Rchb.f.; *Listrostachys odoratissima* (Rchb.f.) Rchb.f.

Chaubardia Reichb.f.

Subfamily Epidendroideae
Tribe Maxillarieae
Subtribe Zygopetalinae

Small to medium-sized caespitose epiphytic plants with small 1-leafed pseudobulbs subtended by leaf-bearing sheaths. **Leaves** thinly coriaceous, flexible. **Inflorescences** axillary, 1-flowered, erect or arcuate; peduncle terete. **Flowers** small to medium-sized, with spreading segments. **Sepals** and **petals** subsimilar, free. **Lip** attached to apex of column-foot, entire, callose, lacking a spur. **Column** elongate, pubescent on ventral side, with a short foot; pollinia 4 in unequal pairs, ovoid, compressed, with a short stipe and small viscidium.

DISTRIBUTION A small genus of about four species in tropical S. America and Trinidad.

DERIVATION OF NAME Dedicated by Reichenbach to his friend M. Chaubard, who worked on the European flora.

TAXONOMY H.G. Reichenbach established this genus in 1852 in the *Botanische Zeitung* (p. 671).

TYPE SPECIES *C. surinamensis* Reichb.f.

SYNONYM *Hoehneella* Ruschi

CULTURE Temp. Winter min. 12°C. With very small, obscure pseudobulbs, these are plants which require humid, shady conditions, with even moisture throughout the year. May be grown in pots, or mounted under suitable conditions.

Chaubardia surinamensis Reichb.f.

A small epiphyte with small ovoid, compressed, unifoliate pseudobulbs, subtended by leaf-bearing sheaths. **Leaves** oblanceolate, acute, 8–15 cm long, 1–1.5 cm wide. **Inflorescences** 1-flowered, up to 7 cm long; peduncle terete; bracts. **Flowers** pale green to white with violet-blue to pink edges to the callus on the lip, column yellow on lower side; pedicel and ovary

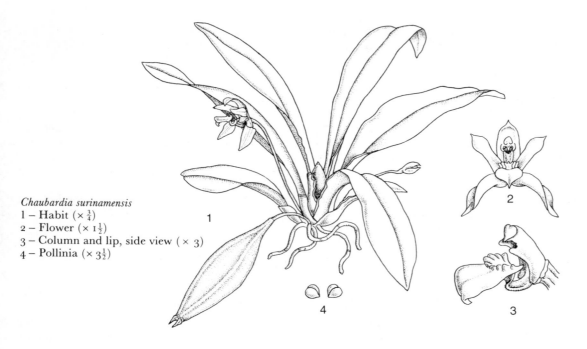

Chaubardia surinamensis
1 – Habit (× ¾)
2 – Flower (× 1½)
3 – Column and lip, side view (× 3)
4 – Pollinia (× 3½)

1–1.5 cm long. **Dorsal sepal** elliptic, shortly apiculate, hooded over the column, 9–10 mm long, 4–8 mm wide; **lateral sepals** obliquely lanceolate, acuminate, incurved, 9–10 mm long, 5–8 mm wide. **Petals** lanceolate, acute or acuminate, 9–10 mm long, 3–6 mm wide. **Lip** shortly clawed, ovate to oblong-ovate, acute or acuminate, 7.5–12 mm long, 6 mm wide; callus in basal part of lip, fleshy, raised, 9-costate, toothed in front. **Column** 5 mm long, pubescent beneath; foot geniculate, 4–5 mm long.
DISTRIBUTION Trinidad and the Guianas to Bolivia and Peru, on low trees by creeks and rivers, up to 500 m.
HISTORY This widely distributed orchid was originally described in 1852 by H.G. Reichenbach in the *Botanische Zeitung* (p. 672).
SYNONYMS *Zygopetalum trinitatis* Ames; *Cochleanthes trinitatis* (Ames) Schultes; *Hoehneella santos-nevesii* Ruschi; *H. trinitatis* (Ames) Fowlie

Chaubardiella Garay
Subfamily Epidendroideae
Tribe Maxillarieae
Subfamily Zygopetalinae

Small to medium-sized epiphytes with short leafy stems but lacking pseudobulbs. **Leaves** thinly coriacous, distichous. **Inflorescences** axillary, 1-flowered. **Flowers** small to medium-sized, opening widely, somewhat showy. **Sepals** and **petals** free, subsimilar; lateral sepals oblique. **Lip** strongly concave, entire, articulated to the column-foot, with a callus, lacking a spur. **Column** elongate, fleshy, with a foot; rostellum filiform or acicular; pollinia 4, pyriform,

attached by a short stipe to an ovate viscidium.
DISTRIBUTION A small genus of some five species in tropical Central and S. America.
DERIVATION OF NAME From the suggested resemblance of the flowers to those of a little *Chaubardia*. Chaubard was a French botanist and friend of H.G. Reichenbach.
TAXONOMY *Chaubardiella* is a segregate genus of *Chaubardia* distinguished by the absence of pseudobulbs and by its distinctive slender rostellum. It was established in 1969 by Leslie Garay in the journal *Orquideologia* (p. 146).
TYPE SPECIES *Chaubardia tigrina* Garay & Dunsterville
CULTURE As for *Chaubardia*.

Chaubardiella calceolaris Garay
A small epiphyte with a very short, clustered, leafy stem. **Leaves** in a fan, distichous, thin, oblanceolate to obovate, acute or acuminate, 6–10 cm long, 1.3–2 cm wide, grey-green. **Inflorescences** arcuate-suberect, axillary, 1-flowered; peduncle slender; bracts hyaline, ovate-cucullate, 5–6 mm long. **Flowers** conspicuously spreading, pale straw-yellow to yellow-green, with purple or red spotting on the lip; pedicel and ovary 5–6 mm long. **Dorsal sepal** ovate, subacute to obtuse, concave, 15–18 mm long, 8–10 mm wide; **lateral sepals** obliquely ovate to elliptic, obtuse, 20–24 mm long, 9–12 mm wide. **Petals** broadly elliptic, obtuse, 15–18 mm long, 8–11 mm wide. **Lip** entire, concave, calceiform-subglobose, shortly apiculate, 15 mm long and broad when flattened, shortly narrowly clawed at the base; callus in middle of lip, subquadrate and tricostate, with a slender

elongate tooth on each side. **Column** 10 mm long; foot short, pubescent.
DISTRIBUTION Peru and Ecuador, in cloud forest, 1900–2200 m.
HISTORY The type collection was collected by P. Hutchison and J. Wright in Bongara Province of Peru and was described by Leslie Garay in 1969 in *Orquideologia* (p. 148).

Chelonistele Pfitzer
Subfamily Epidendroideae
Tribe Coelogyneae
Subtribe Coelogyniinae

Small to medium-sized epiphytes or lithophtes with a creeping rhizome. **Pseudobulbs** clustered or spaced on rhizome, short and swollen to slender, terete or bilaterally flattened, 1- or 2-leaved at apex. **Leaves** deciduous, plicate, elliptic to linear, petiolate, articulated at the apex of the pseudobulb. **Inflorescences** erect to spreading, racemose, emerging with the leaves or before the leaves develop, few- to many-flowered; bracts distichous, caducous, papery to membranous. **Flowers** small to

Chaubardiella calceolaris
1 – Habit (× ¾)
2 – Lip (× 1½)
3 – Column and lip, side view (× 1½)
4 – Pollinarium (× 3½)

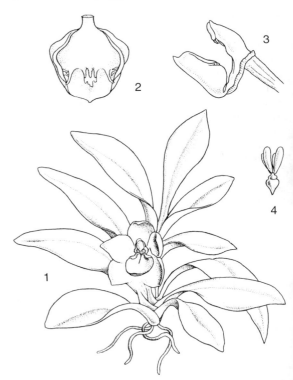

108

medium-sized, resembling a *Coelogyne*-flower, distichous or secund. **Sepals** subsimilar, free. **Petals** linear to ovate-lanceolate, spreading to recurved-rolled up. **Lip** deflexed, 3-lobed, sometimes obscurely so, concave or saccate at the base, with a callus of 2 more or less parallel keels on the upper surface. **Column** elongate, spathulate, winged towards apex; pollinia 4, each attached to a small caudicle.

DISTRIBUTION   A small genus of about 11 species in S.E. Asia and the Malay Archipelago, 10 being endemic to Borneo.

DERIVATION OF NAME   From the Greek *chelone* (turtle or tortoise shell) and *stele* (column), in allusion to winged column.

TAXONOMY   *Chelonistele* is closely allied to *Coelogyne* but is readily distinguished by its characteristic lip which is saccate at the base, has more or less prominent side lobes that emerge above the base of the lip, and has a callus usually of 2 raised keels on the upper surface. The winged column of *Chelonistele* is also distinctive.

Chelonistele was established in 1907 by Pfitzer in Engler's *Pflanzenreich Orchidaceae, Coelogyneae* (p. 136). The genus has recently been monographed by Ed. de Vogel (1986) in the first volume of *Orchid Monographs* (pp. 23–40). A key is provided to the 11 species he recognises.

TYPE SPECIES   *C. sulphurea* (Bl.) Pfitzer (lectotype).

CULTURE   Temp. Winter min. 12°C. Very like *Dendrochilum* and some *Coelogyne* in requirements, as flowers come from centre of new growth.

Chelonistele sulphurea (Bl.) Pfitzer
[Colour Plate]

An epiphyte with swollen to slender pseudobulbs, 3–8 cm long, 1- to 2-leaved at the apex. **Leaves** narrowly lanceolate to obovate-lanceolate, acute, 6–30 cm long, 0.8–3.5 cm wide; petiole 2.5–10 cm long. **Inflorescence** emerging just before or with the young leaves at the apex of the new growth, usually 4- to 10-flowered; peduncle 3–6 cm long but elongating after anthesis; rhachis 3.5–12 cm long; bracts ovate-oblong to ovate, 1.7–2.5 cm long. **Flowers** more or less secund, rather translucent, white, greenish, buff or pale pink with a large yellow or orange-yellow mark in the middle of the lip; pedicel and ovary 10–16 mm long, triangular in cross-section. **Dorsal sepal** ovate-oblong, acute, 10–15.5 mm long, 4–5.5 mm wide; **lateral sepals** oblique at base, ovate-lanceolate to oblong, acute, 10–16 mm long, 3.5–6 mm wide. **Petals** linear, truncate to acute, strongly rolled back. **Lip** 3-lobed in basal half, saccate at base, 11–17 mm long, 8–11 mm wide; side lobes triangular to oblong; midlobe broadly clawed, transversely oblong to reniform, emarginate; callus of 2 raised keels in

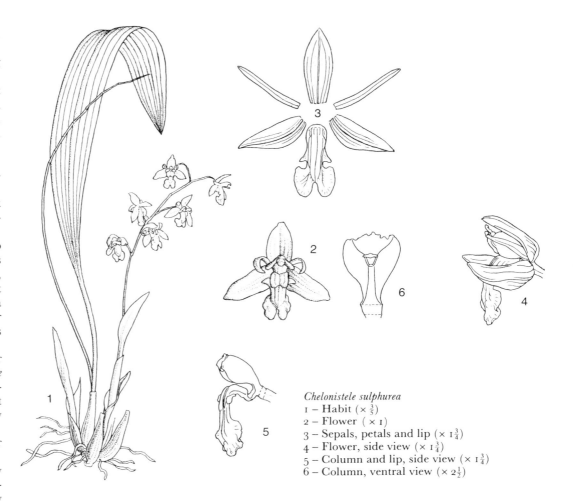

Chelonistele sulphurea
1 – Habit (× $\frac{3}{5}$)
2 – Flower (× 1)
3 – Sepals, petals and lip (× $1\frac{3}{4}$)
4 – Flower, side view (× $1\frac{3}{4}$)
5 – Column and lip, side view (× $1\frac{3}{4}$)
6 – Column, ventral view (× $2\frac{1}{2}$)

basal half or central part of lip. **Column** spathulate, 7–12 mm long, winged and hooded at apex.

DISTRIBUTION   Peninsular Malaya, Sumatra, Borneo, Java and the S. Philippines, growing in shade often near ground in forest, 600–2700 m.

HISTORY   This pretty orchid was first collected by Blume in Java and was described by him as *Chelonanthera sulphurea* in 1825 in his *Bijdragen* (p. 383). Pfitzer made it the type of *Chelonistele* in 1907 in Engler's *Pflanzenreich Orchidaceae, Coelogyneae* (p. 137).

SYNONYMS   include *Chelonanthera sulphurea* Bl.; *Chelonistele pusilla* (Ridley) Ridley; *C. perakensis* (Rolfe) Ridley; *C. cuneata* (J.J. Sm.) Carr; *Coelogyne decipiens* Sander; *C. beyrodtiana* Schltr.

Chiloglottis R. Br.
Subfamily Orchidoideae
Tribe Diurideae
Subtribe Caladeniinae

Small colony-forming terrestrial herbs, perennating by root-stem tuberoids. **Stems** short,

2-leaved. **Leaves** subopposite, prostrate or suberect, elliptic. **Inflorescence** terminal, 1-flowered; peduncle slender. **Flowers** erect or suberect, dull maroon and green; pedicel elongating rapidly after pollination. **Dorsal sepal** free, hooded over column; **lateral sepals** free, spreading or decurved, smaller than the dorsal sepal. **Petals** free, spreading. **Lip** large, entire, tremulous and moving in the wind or fixed and immovable; callus of few to many stalked or unstalked, glossy knobs and warts mainly at base of lip. **Column** incurved, elongate, narrowly or broadly winged; pollinia 4, mealy.

DISTRIBUTION   A genus of about 15 species in Australia and New Zealand.

DERIVATION OF NAME   Derived from the Greek *cheilos* (lip) and *glottis* (gullet), in allusion to resemblance of the lip and callus to a human throat.

TAXONOMY   This genus was established by Robert Brown in 1810 in his *Prodromus Florae Novae Hollandiae* (p. 322). It is allied to *Caladenia* but is readily distinguished by its 1-flowered inflorescences and characteristic entire lip. An excellent account of the Australian species and their cultivation is given by David Jones (1988) in his *Native Orchids of Australia* (p. 143).

TYPE SPECIES   *C. diphylla* R. Br.
CULTURE   As for *Acianthus.*

Chiloglottis gunnii Lindl. [Colour Plate]

Small colony-forming plants up to 40 cm tall. **Leaves** 2, suberect-spreading, elliptic-ovate, 3–10 cm long, 1–3.5 cm wide, petiolate, dark green. **Inflorescence** 4–40 cm tall, 1- or rarely 2-flowered; bracts narrowly elliptic or lanceolate, acuminate, 1.4–3.2 cm long. **Flowers** 3–4 cm across, dark reddish-brown to purplish-green; pedicel and ovary 1.8–2.5 cm long, pedicel elongating to 4 cm long after fertilisation. **Dorsal sepal** obovate, acute, 1.5–2.2 cm long, 1–1.2 cm wide; **lateral sepals** linear-lanceolate, acuminate, 1.5–2 cm long, 1–2 mm wide. **Petals** incurved, lanceolate, acute, 1.5–2.2 cm long, 5–6 mm wide. **Lip** shortly clawed, broadly ovate, subacute to acute, 12–16 mm long, 11–15 mm wide; callus of several clavate, dark red to black knobs in basal part of lip. **Column** incurved, narrowly winged above, 1.2–1.5 cm long.
DISTRIBUTION   Australia, from New South Wales to Victoria and Tasmania, and New Zealand, common in high rainfall forest and also in woodland in leaf litter, up to 1600 m.
HISTORY   First collected by Ronald Campbell Gunn in 1837 at Circular Head in Tasmania and described by John Lindley in 1840 in his *Genera and Species of Orchidaceous Plants* (p. 387).

Chiloschista Lindl.

Subfamily Epidendroideae
Tribe Vandeae
Subtribe Sarcanthinae

Small epiphytic plants lacking, or rarely with a few small leaves and with long, flattened, greenish roots. **Inflorescences** erect or suberect with a pubescent axis, several-flowered, racemose. **Flowers** subspreading, white to yellow, ± spotted crimson, fragrant. **Petals** ± larger than the sepals; lateral sepals adnate to column below. **Lip** ± clawed, articulated to column, 3-lobed, pouched or spurred in front with an erect finger-like callus which arises near the base of the back wall and is ± hirsute or papillose, anterior wall thick and hirsute. **Column** small, erect, semiterete, with foot at ± right-angles to the column; anther-cap with two lateral filiform appendages; pollinia 4 in 2 pairs, with a subulate slender stipe and a small viscidium.
DISTRIBUTION   About 17 species in India, S. China, S.E. Asia, Indonesia and Australia.

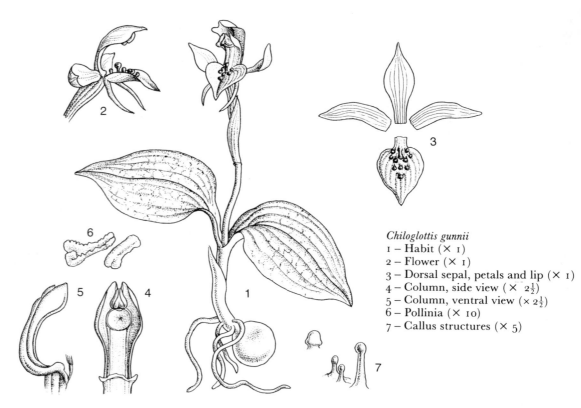

Chiloglottis gunnii
1 – Habit (× 1)
2 – Flower (× 1)
3 – Dorsal sepal, petals and lip (× 1)
4 – Column, side view (× 2½)
5 – Column, ventral view (× 2½)
6 – Pollinia (× 10)
7 – Callus structures (× 5)

DERIVATION OF NAME   From the Greek *cheilos* (lip), and *schistos* (cleft), referring to the bipartite or cleft lip in the type species.
TAXONOMY   *Chiloschista* was described by John Lindley in 1832 in the *Botanical Register* (sub t. 1522). It is allied to *Sarcochilus* and the two genera have been treated as congeneric by some authors such as George Bentham and J.D. Hooker (1883). However, *Chiloschista* is readily distinguished by its leafless habit and lip structure.

The account of the genus by Seidenfaden (1988) in *Opera Botanica* (p. 168) is recommended.
TYPE SPECIES   *C. usneoides* (D. Don) Lindl.
CULTURE   Best mounted. Temp. Winter min. 12–15°C. As with other leafless epiphytes, these plants require high humidity and moderate shade. While actively growing, they need plenty of water, but should be allowed to dry between waterings. For this reason, they can be tied to pieces of cork-bark or other material, so that the roots may flow over the surface.

Chiloschista lunifera (Rchb.f.) J.J. Smith

A small, leafless epiphytic plant with long, greenish roots. **Stem** very short. **Inflorescence** erect or suberect to arching or pendulous, up to about 20 cm long, 12- (or more)-flowered; peduncle green, spotted purple, pubescent, terete; bracts small, ovate, acute. **Flowers** 1.1–1.6 cm across; sepals and petals yellow or greenish-yellow, red-brown in central area; lip white, yellowish on side lobes and below, lined with crimson on side lobes; column green. **Sepals** and **petals** subsimilar, elliptic to ovate, rounded or obtuse, 0.7–0.9 cm long, 0.6 cm broad; petals ciliate. **Lip** 3-lobed, saccate at base, 0.8 cm long and broad when spread; side lobes subquadrate, erect-incurved; mid-lobe smaller, blunt, emarginate; disc with an erect, fleshy, pubescent callus. **Column** fleshy, 0.4 cm long; foot spotted with red, 0.4 cm long.
DISTRIBUTION   Burma, Thailand and Laos.
HISTORY   Originally introduced into cultivation by Messrs Veitch in 1868 and described by H.G. Reichenbach in the same year as *Thrixspermum luniferum* in the *Gardeners' Chronicle* (p. 786) based on a plant collected by Charles Parish at Moulmein in Burma. J.J. Smith transferred it to *Chiloschista* in 1905 in his *Die Orchideen von Java* (p. 553).
SYNONYMS   *Thrixspermum luniferum* Rchb.f.; *Sarochilus luniferus* (Rchb.f.) Hooker f.
CLOSELY RELATED SPECIES   *Chiloschista parishii* Seidenf. [Colour Plate], from Nepal across to S. China and Thailand, is often confused with *C. lunifera* but differs in having sepals and petals spotted with chestnut-brown and densely shortly pubescent on the outer surface.

Chloraea Lindl.

Subfamily Orchidoideae
Tribe Diurideae
Subtribe Chloraeinae

Small to medium-sized, glabrous, terrestrial plants with numerous, fasciculate, fleshy, cylindrical, hairy roots. **Leaves** several, in a basal rosette or scattered along the stem, flat, lanceolate to ovate, sessile, green. **Inflorescence** erect, terminal, few- to many-flowered; bracts leafy. **Flowers** white, green, yellow, orange or red. **Sepals** free, subsimilar; lateral sepals with short to long, attenuate, swollen tips. **Petals** free, shorter but broader than the sepals, often adnate to the dorsal sepal. **Lip** entire or 3-lobed, membranaceous to fleshy, with or without a callus of crests, lacking a spur. **Column** elongate, incurved, with 2 nectaries at the base; pollinia 2 deeply divided, mealy.

DISTRIBUTION A genus of about 50 species in Chile, Argentina, S. Brazil, Uruguay, Peru and Bolivia.

DERIVATION OF NAME From the Greek *chloraia* (pale green) in reference to the flower colour of the type species.

TAXONOMY *Chloraea* was established by John Lindley in 1827 in the *Brand. Quarterly Journal of the Royal Institute* (p. 47). It has most recently been revised in 1969 by Maeve Correa in the journal *Darwinia* (p. 374).

TYPE SPECIES *C. galeata* Lindl.

SYNONYMS *Ulantha* Hook.; *Bieneria* Reichb.f.

CULTURE Temp. Winter min. 12°C. Compost as for *Acianthus*. As with *Cryptostylis*, the plants have fleshy roots rather than tubers and therefore should not be allowed to dry out while dormant.

Chloraea crispa Lindl.

A terrestrial herb 40–90 cm tall. **Leaves** basal in a rosette, lanceolate or oblanceolate, acute to subacute, 10–18 cm long, 2–3 cm wide; stem covered with lanceolate, membranaceous sheaths. **Inflorescence** densely few-flowered; bracts papery, lanceolate, acuminate, 3–4 cm long. **Flowers** showy, white, not opening widely; pedicel and ovary 1.5–2.4 cm long. **Dorsal sepal** lanceolate, acute, 2.5–3.5 cm long, 6–9 mm wide; **lateral sepals** narrowly oblong-lanceolate, shortly acuminate, 2.2–3.3 cm long, 5–7 mm wide. **Petals** oblong-ovate, obtuse, 1.8–3 cm long, 6–10 cm wide. **Lip** 3-lobed, recurved in apical half, membranaceous, 2–3 cm long and wide; side lobes obliquely rounded; mid-lobe transversely oblong, shallowly emarginate, with a serrate margin; callus of several rows of elongate papillae in centre of lip. **Column** slenderly clavate, incurved, 2–2.3 cm long.

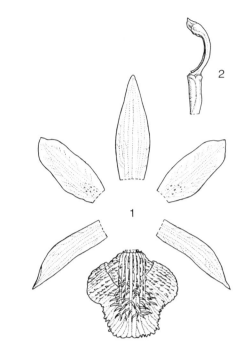

Chloraea crispa
1 – Sepals, petals and lip (× 1)
2 – Column and ovary (× 1)

DISTRIBUTION Chile; sea level–300 m, in sandly soils amongst grass and shrubs.

HISTORY The type was collected by Lord Colchester near Conception and was described in 1840 by John Lindley in his *Genera and Species of Orchidaceous Plants* (p. 453).

SYNONYMS *C. pogonata* Phil.; *C. dasypogon* Phil.; *Asarca pogonata* (Phil.) O. Kuntze; *A. dasypogon* (Phil.) O. Kuntze

Chondrorhyncha Lindl.

Subfamily Epidendroideae
Tribe Oncidieae

Small epiphytic plants lacking pseudobulbs. **Stems** rhizomatous, leafy, short. **Leaves** oblong-oblanceolate, plicate-nervose, petiolate, articulated to the leaf-sheaths. **Inflorescence** borne directly on the rhizome, 1-flowered. **Sepals** subsimilar, oblong-elliptic to lanceolate; **dorsal sepal** adnate to the column at the base; **lateral sepals** oblique, adnate to the column-foot. **Petals** obovate-elliptic. **Lip** sessile, erect, concave, entire; callus basal, toothed. **Column** semiterete, with a short foot; rostellum elongate; pollinia 4, waxy.

DISTRIBUTION A small genus of only a few species confined to the tropics of Central and S. America.

DERIVATION OF NAME From the Greek *chondros* (cartilage) and *rhynchos* (beak) referring to the beak-like rostellum.

TAXONOMY *Chondrorhyncha* was described by John Lindley in 1846 in *Orchidaceae Lindenianae* (p. 12) where he stated that it was allied to *Helcia* and *Trichopilia* but differd in 'the extremely oblique insertion of the sepals' and 'the long cartilaginous bristle-like rostellum, which is covered by a broad, soft acuminate gland'. However, *Chondrorhyncha* is more closely allied to *Cochleanthes*, *Huntleya* and *Kefersteinia* but is characterised by the cartilaginous 3-parted rostellum in which the mid-tooth is longest and by the rather prominent column-foot and the position of the callus on the lip.

L. Garay (1969, 1973) in *Orquideologia* has reviewed the generic limits of *Chondrorhyncha* and its allied genera which he distinguishes clearly from those genera allied to *Zygopetalum* because the latter always have prominent leaf-bearing pseudobulbs.

TYPE SPECIES *C. rosea* Lindl.

SYNONYM *Warscewiczella* Rchb.f.

CULTURE Compost A. Temp. Winter min. 12–15°C. The plants are best grown in baskets, under conditions of good shade and high humidity. The roots should never become very dry, so good drainage is essential.

Chondrorhyncha rosea Lindl.

A medium-sized epiphyte with a short stem and lacking pseudobulbs. **Leaves** clustered, 4–5, oblanceolate, acute, 10–26 cm long, 1.5.–2.5 cm wide, sheathing at the base. **Inflorescences** basal, erect or spreading, one-flowered; peduncle slender, 6–8 cm long, bearing 3–4 sheaths; bract sheathing, elliptical, 7–9 mm long. **Flower** with yellowish or pale green sepals, white petals and a white lip grading to pale green at the base and spotted with rosy red; pedicel and ovary 1.5 cm long, grooved. **Sepals** concave, spathulate, obtuse; dorsal sepal erect, 2.2–2.4 cm long, 1 cm wide; lateral sepals upcurved, 3–3.3 cm long, 0.8–0.9 cm wide; mentum short but acute. **Petals** pointing forwards but with spreading tips, obovate, obtuse, 2.5–2.7 cm long, 1.2–1.3 cm wide. **Lip** tubular with a spreading apical margin, obovate, sometimes bilobed at retuse apex, 3 cm long, 2 cm wide; callus central on lip, a raised three-ridged flap. **Column** clavate, 2 cm long, with a short foot.

DISTRIBUTION Venezuela only; in montane forest 1800–2000 m.

HISTORY Described in 1846 by John Lindley in his *Orchidaceae Lindenianae* (p. 13) based on a collection made by Linden in the province of Merida.

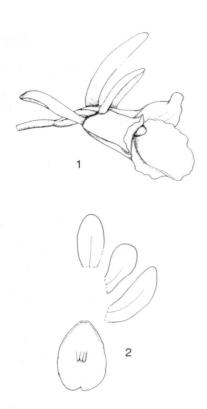

Chondrorhyncha rosea

1 – Flower (× ¾)
2 – Dorsal sepal, lateral sepal and lip (× ½)

Chrysocycnis Linden & Rchb.f.

Subfamily Epidendroideae
Tribe Maxillarieae
Subfamily Maxillariinae

Scandent plants starting as terrestrials but becoming epiphytic above, with elongate ascending branching rhizomes, rooting from the base of the pseudobulbs. **Pseudobulbs** well spaced on the rhizomes, ovoid-elliptic, unifoliate, subtended by imbricate often leaf-bearing sheaths. **Leaves** coriaceous, erect, shortly petiolate, large. **Inflorescences** basal, 1-flowered, much shorter than the leaf. **Flower** flat. **Sepals** and **petals** free, subsimilar, spreading widely. **Lip** 3-lobed, convex, pubescent. **Column** strongly incurved, swollen at the base, pubescent; pollinia 4, in 2 unequal pairs, attached to a saddle-shaped viscidium.

DISTRIBUTION A genus of about five species in Central and Andean S. America.
DERIVATION OF NAME From the Greek *chrysous* (golden) and *kyknos* (swan), from the fancied resemblance of the flowers to a golden swan because of the elegant slender curved column.
TAXONOMY Jean Linden and Reichenbach described this genus in 1854 in the journal *Bon-*

plandia (p. 280). It is allied to *Maxillaria* and *Mormolyca* but is readily distinguished by its flat flowers with their distinctive small hairy lip and strongly incurved column.
TYPE SPECIES *C. schlimii* Linden & Rchb.f.
CULTURE Temp. Winter min. 10°C. High altitude plants with a tendency to grow upwards, hence the need to mount them. Keep shaded in summer, in a humid atmosphere, and never let them dry out.

Chrysocycnis schlimii Linden & Rchb.f.
[Colour Plate]
A scandent terrestrial plant with a stout, mostly naked, branching rhizome, 4–5 mm in diameter. **Pseudobulbs** up to 20 cm apart, narrowly ovoid, slightly compressed, 2–10 cm long, 0.8–3 cm across. **Leaves** elliptic-ovate or elliptic-lanceolate, acute, 10–45 cm long, 3–11 cm wide, shortly petiolate at the base. **Inflorescences** 1-flowered, up to 7 cm long; bract lanceolate, acuminate, sheathing at the base, 1.5–2.5 cm long. **Flowers** 5–6 cm long; sepals and petals orange-brown, spotted with chestnut towards the apex of sepals and barred with chestnut on the upper edge of the petals; lip yellow or brown in apical part, white with dark maroon at the base; pedicel and ovary 3–4 cm long. **Dorsal sepal** narrowly elliptic, acute, 3–3.3 cm long, 1–1.2 cm wide; **lateral sepals** obliquely elliptic-ovate, 1.9–2.7 cm long, 1.2–1.4 cm wide. **Petals** obliquely lanceolate, acute, 2.5–2.7 cm long, 1–1.1 cm wide. **Lip** 3-lobed, convex, 1–1.2 cm long and wide, pubescent; side lobes oblong, spreading; mid-lobe larger, oblong, obtuse; callus a swollen mound at the base.
DISTRIBUTION Venezuela to Ecuador, in cloud forest 1700–2700 m.
HISTORY This strange orchid was first described by Jean Linden and Reichenbach in 1854 in *Bonplandia* (p. 280) based on a collection made by L. Schlim in Ocana Province in Colombia.
SYNONYM *C. trigonidii* Linden & Rchb.f.

Chysis Lindl.

Subfamily Epidendroideae
Tribe Arethuseae
Subtribe Bletiinae

Epiphytic or lithophytic herbs. **Pseudobulbs** clustered, fleshy, fusiform, ± covered by scarious sheaths, several-leaved. **Leaves** spaced or crowded near apex, distichous, plicate, articulated to leaf-bases. **Inflorescences** lateral, from nodes of old pseudobulbs, laxly racemose. **Flowers** several, showy. **Sepals** subequal, free, spreading; lateral sepals connate to the column-foot, forming a short mentum. **Lip** erect, 3-

lobed; disc nervose, lamellate below. **Column** erect, incurved, broadly 2-winged above, with a short fooot; pollinia 8, waxy.
DISTRIBUTION About six species from Mexico through Central America and the Andes of S. America to Venezuela and Peru.
DERIVATION OF NAME From the Greek *chysis* (melting) in allusion to the fused appearance of the pollinia when the flower opens resulting from self-fertilisation.
TAXONOMY Described by John Lindley in 1837 in the *Botanical Register* (t. 1937) who commented that although similar to *Dendrobium* and *Cyrtopodium* and their allies in its habit it is more closely related to *Epidendrum*. Its pollinia consist of 'two yellow plates, placed side by side in the bed of the anther, united at the back and slightly notched on the outer edge, so that it is in reality 4-lobed, the lobes being extremely unequal; each lobe has a thickened margin, and rising up, overlies and conceals 4 other lobes of a thicker texture and smaller size, 2 of which arise from the back and 2 from the front of the inner edge of the principal lobes of the plate above described. This remarkable structure may be theoretically described as being equivalent to eight pollen masses, of which the straps of connection, such as exist in all Epidendreae, are run together into two plates, from an expansion of the edges of which the pollen masses appear to spring.'

P.H. Allen in the *Flora of Panama* (1949) and in the *American Orchid Society Bulletin* (1955) considered that, upon examination of all the herbaria material at the Ames Herbarium and the Missouri Botanic Garden, the genus consisted of two very variable species, *C. aurea* and *C. laevis* Lindl., differing fundamentally in the number of fleshy crests of the disc and in the frontal margins of the lip mid-lobe. He further divided the former into one variety and three forms.

However, J.A. Fowlie in *Orchid Digest* (1971) disagreed with Allen in reducing the several described taxa to two species and resurrected *C. tricostata* Schltr, whilst elevating *C. aurea* var. *maculata* Hooker to specific rank as *C. maculata* (Hooker) Fowlie. The various taxa are keyed out by Allen but not by Fowlie whose article is instead accompanied by photographs of each species.
TYPE SPECIES *C. aurea* Lindl.
CULTURE Compost A. Temp. Winter min. 12–15°C. These plants grow well in baskets, but may also be grown in pots. During growth they need a humid atmosphere, warmth and moderate shade, with plenty of water. When growth is complete, the leaves fall, and the plants should be kept cooler and almost dry. The flowers appear from the side of the new shoots.

Chysis aurea Lindl. [Colour Plate]

A coarse, pendulous epiphytic plant, 75 cm or more long. **Pseudobulbs** elongate, fusiform-clavate, many-noded, compressed, up to 45 cm long, many-leaved towards apex. **Leaves** distichous, oblong-lanceolate, acuminate, undulate, membranous, up to 45 cm long, 6 cm broad. **Inflorescence** racemose, up to about 45 cm long, 6- to 12-flowered; bracts ovate, acuminate, concave, up to 2.5 cm long **Flowers** lemon-yellow; petals marked with brown; lip whitish, marked with maroon or dull brown. **Dorsal sepal** linear-oblong or oblong-elliptic, obtuse, 3–4.5 cm long, 0.8–1.5 cm broad; **lateral sepals** triangular-lanceolate, falcate, obtuse, 2.5–3.5 cm long, 1.2–2 cm broad, forming with the column-foot a short mentum. **Petals** obovate, rounded at apex, falcate, margins undulate-crisped, 3–4 cm long, 0.7–1.5 cm broad, **Lip** arcuate, deeply 3-lobed, concave below, obovate-cuneate in outline, 2–2.5 cm long. 2.5–3.5 cm broad; side lobes oblong, erect; mid-lobe suborbicular to transversely elliptic, emarginate, margins undulate-crisped; disc with 5 velvety-pubescent ridges. **Column** incurved, 1.5 cm long with a prominent foot.
DISTRIBUTION Mexico to Panama, Colombia and Venezuela; up to 1700 m altitude.
HISTORY Discovered by John Henchman in 1834 in the Cumanacoa Valley in Venezuela. He sent plants to Messrs Low of Clapton, London, who flowered it in the following year. It was described in 1837 by John Lindley in the *Botanical Register* (t. 1937) from a plant sent to him by Low.
CLOSELY RELATED SPECIES *C. aurea* is closely allied to *C. bractescens*. *Chysis tricostata* Schltr. [Colour Plate] from Costa Rica and Nicaragua is allied to *C. aurea* but differs in having only 3 longitudinal keels on the lip.

Chysis bractescens Lindl. [Colour Plate]

A coarse epiphytic plant, up to 50 cm or more tall. **Pseudobulbs** fusiform, up to 30 cm long, 4 cm in diameter, concealed by white scarious sheaths, several-leaved towards apex. **Leaves** linear or oblong-lanceolate, acuminate, undulate, up to 40 cm long, 6 cm broad. **Inflorescence** borne from the lower nodes of the old pseudobulbs, racemose, 4- to 8-flowered; bracts foliaceous, ovate or acuminate, concave, up to 4.5 cm long. **Flowers** ivory-white, with a yellow lip, marked with reddish-purple. **Dorsal sepal** oblong, obtuse, 3.8–4.5 cm long, 1.5–2.3 cm broad; **lateral sepals** ovate-triangular, oblique, obtuse, 3.5–4 cm long, 2 cm broad, forming with the column-foot a prominent mentum. **Petals** oblique oblong-spathulate, obtuse or rounded, 3.5–4.6 cm long, 1.6–2.3 cm broad. **Lip** suborbicular-flabellate, deeply 3-lobed, up to 3.5 cm long, 4 cm broad; side lobes oblong-

falcate, erect; mid-lobe obovate, emarginate; disc with 5–7 velvety-pubescent ridges to base of mid-lobe. **Column** fleshy, incurved, 1.5 cm long with a long foot.
DISTRIBUTION Mexico, Guatemala and Belize: up to 850 m altitude.
HISTORY Introduced into cultivation by George Barker, probably from Mexico, and described by John Lindley in 1840 in the *Botanical Register* (misc. 61).
SYNONYMS *Thowaldsenia speciosa* Liebm.; *Chysis aurea* var. *bractescens* (Lindl.) P.H. Allen
CLOSELY RELATED SPECIES *C. bractescens* is closely allied to *C. aurea*.

Chysis tricostata Schltr. [Colour Plate]
See under *Chysis aurea*.

Cirrhaea Lindl.
Subfamily Epidendroideae
Tribe Gongoreae
Subtribe Stanhopeinae

Medium-sized epiphytic herbs with ovoid, ribbed, sometimes quadrangular, unifoliate pseudobulbs. **Leaf** erect or arcuate, plicate, petiolate. **Inflorescences** basal, pendent, laxly to densely many-flowered, racemose. **Flowers** medium-sized, with lip uppermost. **Sepals** free, oblong, acute or obtuse. **Petals** free, linear-lanceolate, acute to obtuse. **Lip** clawed, 3-lobed, attached to the short column-foot. **Column** slender-clavate, incurved, with a short foot; rostellum setose, porrect; pollinia 2, pyriform, sulcate, attached by a short stipe to an obovate or circular viscidium.
DISTRIBUTION Some six species in Brazil.
DERIVATION OF NAME From the Latin *cirrus* (tendril), descriptive of the slender porrect rostellum.
TAXONOMY *Cirrhaea* was described by John Lindley in 1825 in the *Botanical Register* (sub t. 930) and in greater detail in the same journal (t. 1538) in 1832.
    This genus is allied to *Gongora* and *Polycycnis* but is readily distinguished by its distictive 3-lobed lip and column.
TYPE SPECIES *Cymbidium dependens* Lodd.
CULTURE Temp. Winter min. 12–15°C. Grown as for *Gongora*.

Cirrhaea dependens (Lodd.) G. Don [Colour Plate]

An erect or spreading epiphyte with clustered, ovoid, somewhat 4-angled, unifoliate pseudobulbs, 4–5.5 cm long, 1.5–3.5 cm in diameter; roots 1.5 mm in diameter, white. **Leaf** suberect-arcuate, lanceolate or oblanceolate, acuminate, 20–50 cm long, 3–5 cm wide; petiole slender, 4.5–9 cm long. **Inflorescences** pen-

dent, 20–35 cm long, densely 6- to 20-flowered; bracts triangular-lanceolate, up to 10 mm long. **Flowers** fragrant, the sepals and petals green more or less marked with purple, the lip purplish or cream marked with purple; pedicel and ovary geniculate, 1.7–2.7 cm long. **Dorsal sepal** linear-lanceolate, subacute, 2.2–2.5 cm long, 0.5 cm wide; **lateral sepals** lanceolate, acute, 2.1–2.4 cm long, 0.5–0.6 cm wide. **Petals** linear-lanceolate, acute, curved at the base, 2–2.4 cm long, 0.3 cm wide. **Lip** fleshy, long-clawed, 3-lobed in the middle, 1.8–2 cm long, 0.6–0.8 cm wide; side lobes retrorse, lanceolate, acute, parallel to the claw; mid-lobe triangular-lanceolate, acute, 0.8 cm long; callus a raised fleshy bump at the apex of the claw. **Column** 1.1–1.2 cm long.
DISTRIBUTION Brazil only.
HISTORY Originally introduced by George Loddiges and described by him in 1825 as *Cymbidium dependens* in the *Botanical Cabinet* (t. 936). It was transferred to *Cirrhaea* by George Don in Loudon's *Hortus Britannicus* (p. 370) in 1830.
SYNONYMS *Cymbidium dependens* Lodd.; *Cirrhaea warreana* Lodd.; *C. loddigesii* Lindl.; *Gongora viridifusca* Hook.; *Cirrhaea viridipurpurea* (Hook.) Lindl.; *C. tristis* Lindl.

Cischweinfia Dressler & L.O. Williams
Subfamily Epidendroideae
Tribe Oncidieae

Small epiphytes with clustered monophyllous ellipsoidal or ovoid-ellipsoidal somewhat flattened pseudobulbs, subtended by several distichous leaf-bearing sheaths. **Leaves** relatively thin-textured, articulated at base. **Inflorescences** shorter than the leaves, few-flowered, axillary from basal sheaths. **Flowers** small to medium-sized. **Sepals** and **petals** free, subsimilar. **Lip** basally adnate to the column by the margins of the claw, pubescent within; spur adnate to the ovary for entire length. **Column** with 2 auricles borne beneath the stigmatic cavity; clinandrium petaloid, hooded over the anther; pollinia 2; stipe slender, elongate; viscidium small.
DISTRIBUTION Four species only, from Panama and Costa Rica south to Ecuador.
DERIVATION OF NAME Named in honour of the American orchid taxonomist C.S. Schweinfurth, co-author of the *Orchids of Guatemala* and author of the *Orchids of Peru*. He succeeded Oakes Ames as curator of the Oakes Ames Herbarium at Harvard.
TAXONOMY This small genus was erected in 1970 by Robert Dressler and L.O. Williams in the *American Orchid Society Bulletin* (p. 991). It is closely related to *Trichopilia* but is readily

distinguished by its lip which is fused at its margins to the column to form a nectary which is fused below to the ovary.

TYPE SPECIES *Aspasia pusilla* C. Schweinf. (= *Cischweinfia pusilla* (C. Schweinf.) Dressler & L.O. Williams).

CULTURE Temp. Winter min. 15°C. Grow under conditions of moderate shade and humidity, either mounted or in well-drained pots. Give less water when the growths are completed.

Cischweinfia dasyandra (Rchb.f.) Dressler & L.O. Williams

A small epiphyte with clustered clavate to elliptic bilaterally compressed pseudobulbs, 2–2.6 cm long, 0.4–0.7 cm wide, unifoliate at the apex; roots slender, 0.5 mm in diameter. **Leaves** erect, linear to linear-lanceolate, acuminate, 6.5–17.5 cm long, 0.4–0.7 cm wide. **Inflorescences** 2- to 5-flowered, 3.5–6 cm long; peduncle wiry, 1–2.5 cm long; bracts ovate, acute, sheathing at base, 3 mm long. **Flowers** small; sepals and petals green or yellow-green; lip cream with pale pink spots and yellow-orange to brownish yellow in the throat; pedicel and ovary verrucose, 1–1.5 cm long. **Sepals** linear-oblanceolate, acute, 10–13 mm long, 2.5–3 mm wide. **Petals** oblanceolate, acute, 10–12 mm long, 2 mm wide. **Lip** tubular, obscurely 3-lobed in apical half, ovate, obtuse, 9 mm long and wide; callus in basal half of lip, a ridge which is bifid in front. **Column** 5 mm long, wih 2 prominent forward projecting pegs at base of stigma.

DISTRIBUTION Panama, Costa Rica and Colombia; 300–1500 m.

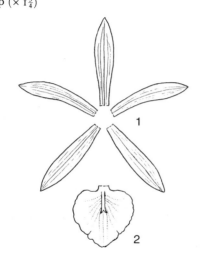

Cischweinfia dasyandra
1 – Sepals and petals (× 1¾)
2 – Lip (× 1¾)

HISTORY Originally described and illustrated by Reichenbach as *Trichopilia dasyandra* in 1878 in the third volume of his *Xenia Orchidacea* (p. 64, t. 230) based on a collection by Endres from Costa Rica. Dressler and L.O. Williams transferred it to *Cischweinfia* in 1970 in the *American Orchid Society Bulletin* (p. 991).

SYNONYMS *Trichopilia dasyandra* Rchb.f.; *Leucohyle dasyandra* (Rchb.f.) Schltr.

Cleisostoma Blume
Subfamily Epidendroideae
Tribe Vandeae
Subtribe Sarcanthinae

Small to medium-sized epiphytic plants. **Stems** short or long, erect or hanging. **Leaves** flat or terete. **Inflorescences** short or long, simple or more commonly more or less branched, erect or pendulous, many-flowered. **Flowers** rather small and fleshy. **Sepals** and **petals** subequal, usually spreading. **Lip** 3-lobed, spurred, joined a little to the foot of the column by the back margins of the side lobes, with a conspicuous callus of various form at the entrance of the spur on its back wall, and often also on the front wall at the base of the mid-lobe; side lobes more or less erect, triangular; mid-lobe straight or sometimes curved upwards, mostly triangular-hastate, with small spreading barbs at the base; spur conical or cylindrical rarely saccate, often longitudinally septate. **Column** short, with a short foot; pollinia 4, united into 2 round bodies; stipe usually narrow but widened near apex; viscidium small or large, sometimes horseshoe-shaped.

DISTRIBUTION One of the largest genera of small-flowered orchids in the subtribe Sarcanthinae, probably 80–100 species widely distributed in India, S.E. Asia, Indonesia, New Guinea, the Philippines and Pacific Islands to Australia.

DERIVATION OF NAME From the Greek *kleistos* (closed) and *stoma* (mouth), in allusion to the calli which almost block the mouth of the spur.

TAXONOMY C.L. Blume (1825) published *Cleisostoma* in the key to genera of Javanese orchids in his *Bijdragen* (p. 362), based on *Cleisostoma sagittatum*. It is characterised by the possession of the large callus at the back of the spur just in the entrance which often has a groove in its lower surface, the groove resting on the top edge of the septum which divides the bottom of the spur. Often the front callus interlocks with the back callus effectively blocking the entrance to the spur.

A few species of *Cleisostoma* are widespread and have been commonly collected, but many species have been collected infrequently and

often are known from only a few herbarium specimens. The species from Thailand and adjacent areas have been revised by Seidenfaden (1975) in *Dansk Botanisk Arkiv* (vol. 29(3)).

Until recently this genus has been known under the name *Sarcanthus* Lindl. However, L. Garay (1972) in *Botanical Museum Leaflets of Harvard University* has shown that *Sarcanthus* is a later homonym and is also predated by *Cleisostoma*. The confusion has arisen because John Lindley described *Sarcanthus* twice, based on a different type species each time. First in 1824 he described it based on *Epidendrum praemorsum* Roxb. which is now included in the genus *Acampe*; then in 1826, he published it again typifying it this time with *S. rostratus* Lindl.

TYPE SPECIES *C. sagittatum* Blume
SYNONYM *Sarcanthus* Lindl.

CULTURE Compost A. Temp. Winter min 12–15°C. The species may be grown in pans or baskets or mounted on slabs according to habit. They require humid conditions at all times and moderate shade during the summer months. Water is needed during growth but less should be given when the plants are not active.

Cleisostoma filiforme (Lindl.) Garay
[Colour Plate]

Stem pendulous, terete, 15–25 cm long, internodes 1.5–5 cm long. **Leaves** distant, elongate, filiform, cylindric, acuminate, 5–15 cm long, 0.5–0.3 cm broad. **Inflorescences** curved, racemose, laxly-flowered; bracts minute, lanceolate. **Flowers** 0.6–0.8 cm across; sepals and petals orange to chocolate-brown, margins and mid-rib green; lip white, yellow at base and with a white mid-lobe; column yellow. **Sepals** oblong, obtuse, 0.4 cm long, 0.15 cm broad. **Petals** linear, obtuse, 0.3 cm long, 0.05 cm broad. **Lip** broadly conical, fleshy, 3-lobed, 0.4 cm long; side lobes triangular, acute, incurved; mid-lobe short, broad, toothed on each side at the base; spur saccate or shortly cylindrical, 0.2 cm long, with a narrow lamina from the base of mid-lobe downwards and a very large callus below the column on the back wall of the spur. **Column** very broad, stout; stipe broad.

DISTRIBUTION India (Sikkim Himalayas and the Khasia Hills), Burma, Thailand and Laos.

HISTORY Discovered in India by Dr N. Wallich who sent it to Col. Fielding. John Lindley described it as *Sarcanthus filiformis* in 1842 in the *Botanical Register* (misc. p. 61) but L. Garay transferred it to *Cleisostoma* in 1972 in the *Botanical Museum Leaflets of Harvard University* (p. 171).

SYNONYMS *Sarcanthus filiformis* Lindl.; *Saccolabium filiforme* (Lindl.) Lindl.

Cleisostoma racemiferum (Lindl.) Garay

Stem stout, up to 1.2 cm broad, roots very robust. **Leaves** ligulate, spreading, coriaceous, keeled on reverse, unequally roundly 2-lobed at apex, 25–36 cm long, 3.5 cm broad. **Inflorescence** lateral, paniculate, conspicuously branched, laxly many-flowered, longer than the leaves; peduncle 15–25 cm long; bracts elliptic-lanceolate, 0.3 cm long. **Flowers** small, 0.8 cm across, brownish-black edged with yellow; lip yellowish; column white. **Dorsal sepal** elliptic, rounded at the apex, 0.5 cm long, 0.25 cm broad; **lateral sepals** oblique, obtuse. **Petals** similar to the dorsal sepal but a little smaller, rounded at the apex. **Lip** 3-lobed; side lobes obliquely triangular, prolonged into an acumen, incurved; mid-lobe very fleshy, triangular, narrow incurved, longitudinally hollowed in the middle; posterior callus roundly 2-lobed, papillose; spur slightly incurved, nearly cylindric, 0.4 cm long, semiseptate. **Column** short, stout.

DISTRIBUTION India, Nepal, Bhutan, S. China, Thailand, Burma, Laos and Vietnam; 1300–1800 m.

HISTORY Discovered by Dr N. Wallich and described as *Saccolabium racemiferum* by John Lindley in 1833 in his *Genera and Species of Orchidaceous Plants* (p. 224). H.G. Reichenbach transferred it in 1864 to *Sarcanthus* in Walpers, *Annales Botanices* (p. 68), but more recently L. Garay (1972) transferred it to *Cleisostoma* in *Botanical Museum Leaflets of Harvard University* (p. 173).

SYNONYMS *Sacanthus pallidus* Lindl.; *S. tricolor* Rchb.f.; *Saccolabium racemiferum* Lindl.; *Sarcanthus racemifer* (Lindl.) Rchb.f.

Cleisostoma scortechinii (Hooker f.) Garay

[Colour Plate]

Stem elongate, robust, 0.5–0.6 cm thick, with internodes 2.3 cm long. **Leaves** very thick, oblong-lanceolate, flat, acute, 5–15 cm long, 2.2 cm broad. **Inflorescences** stiffly pendulous, as long as the leaves, many-flowered; peduncle very stout. **Flowers** 0.8 cm across; sepals and petals lurid purple with a green mid-rib and margins; lip yellowish, ± with a pale mauve mid-lobe, dorsal callus pale greenish. **Sepals** oblong, rounded to acute, 0.45–0.55 cm long, 0.25–0.3 cm broad. **Petals** narrowly oblong, rounded at the apex, 0.4 cm long, 0.1 cm broad. **Lip** 3-lobed, 0.5 cm long, 0.3–0.4 cm broad; side lobes obsolete; mid-lobe hastately deltoid; spur 2-celled, 0.4–0.5 cm long, narrowed at apex; dorsal callus large, rectangular and emarginate from the front. **Column** short, 0.25 cm long; anther obtusely beaked.

DISTRIBUTION Thailand and Malaya.

HISTORY Discovered by Scortechini in Perak and described as *Sarcanthus scortechinii* in his honour by Sir Joseph Hooker in 1890 in the

Flora of British India (p. 68). L. Garay transferred it to *Cleisostoma* in the *Botanical Museum Leaflets of Harvard University* (p. 174) in 1972.

SYNONYM *Sarcanthus scortechinii* Hooker f.

Cleistes L.C. Rich. ex Lindl.

Subfamily Epidendroideae
Tribe Vanilleae
Subtribe Pogoniinae

Medium-sized terrestrial plants producing slender erect stems growing from underground nodular or fibrous tubers. **Leaf** solitary, cauline, conduplicate, lanceolate sessile, ovate or lanceolate, acute or acuminate. **Inflorescence** terminal, laxly few-flowered; bracts conspicuous, leafy. **Flowers** showy, not opening widely, large, yellow, pink or purple; ovary with an abscission point at the base of the perianth. **Sepals** and **petals** free, subsimilar. **Lip** entire or obscurely 3-lobed, lacking a spur, with a central longitudinal callus. **Column** elongate, subclavate; pollinia 2, mealy, lacking a viscidium.

DISTRIBUTION A genus of about 40 species in the tropical Americas from Florida south to Brazil.

DERIVATION OF NAME From the Greek *kleistos* (closed), in reference to the flowers which do not open at all widely.

TAXONOMY The name of this genus was coined by L.C. Richard in *Mémoires du Muséum d'Histoire Naturelle, Paris* (p. 31) in 1818 but it was left to John Lindley to validly publish it in 1840 in his *Genera and Species of Orchidaceous Plants* (p. 409). It is closely allied to *Pogonia* but generally can be distinguished by its different rootstock, larger size and larger campanulate flowers.

TYPE SPECIES *C. lutea* Lindl.

CULTURE Temp. Winter min. 5–7°C. Notoriously difficult to maintain in cultivation, but worth trying in a mix as for *Anacamptis*. As a bog plant, should not be allowed to become too dry during dormancy.

Cleistes rosea Lindl. [Colour Plate]

A large terrestrial plant 30–140 cm tall. **Stem** slender bearing a single leaf in the middle. **Leaf** ovate-lanceolate, acute, sessile and amplexicaul at the base, 3–12 cm long, 0.8–2.5 cm wide, glaucous. **Inflorescence** 1- to 3-flowered; bracts leafy, ovate-lanceolate, acuminate, 4–13 cm long. **Flowers** large, with the sepals greenish on the outside, rose-purple within, the petals and lip rose-pink or rose-purple, not opening widely; pedicel and ovary 1–3 cm long. **Sepals** linear-oblanceolate, acuminate, 5–7.5 cm long, 0.4–0.7 cm wide. **Petals** oblanceolate, acute, 4–6 cm long, 0.8–1.2 cm wide. **Lip**

rather tubular, obovate, acute, obscurely 3-lobed near the apex, 5–6 cm long, 1.5–3.5 cm wide, with 2 stalked glands at the base; callus of several retrorse barbate ridges. **Column** clavate, 2.5–3 cm long.

DISTRIBUTION Costa Rica and Panama to Colombia, Venezuela and Guyana; in savannas and marshes; up to 1600 m.

HISTORY This was first collected by Richard Schomburgk in Guyana and was described in 1840 by John Lindley in his *Genera and Species of Orchidaceous Plants* (p. 410).

SYNONYM *Pogonia rosea* (Lindl.) Hemsl.

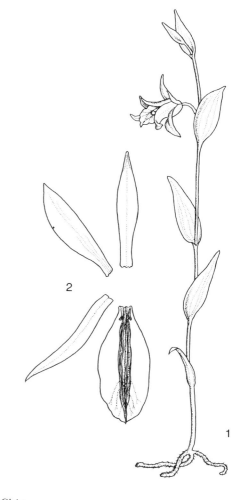

Cleistes rosea

1 – Habit ($\times \frac{1}{3}$)

2 – Dorsal sepal, lateral sepal, petal and lip ($\times \frac{3}{4}$)

Clowesia Lindl.

Subfamily Epidendroideae
Tribe Gongoreae
Subtribe Catasetinae

Vegetatively similar to *Catasetum*. **Inflorescence** from the basal nodes of the pseudobulb, pendent, racemose, several-flowered. **Flowers** complex, fairly showy, membranous, bisexual, anther and stigma both functional. **Sepals** and **petals** free, petals often broader and ± fringed. **Lip** free from column, saccate or spurred, apex fringed, denticulate or entire. **Column** short to fairly long, lacking antennae at the base; pollinia 2, large, sulcate; stipe 1, tensioned; viscidium large, released explosively by pressure on the stipe.

DISTRIBUTION   Five species from Mexico south to Venezuela.

DERIVATION OF NAME   Named in honour of the Rev. John Clowes of Broughton Hall, Manchester, England, who was a keen orchid grower and the first to flower the type species of the genus.

TAXONOMY   The genus. *Clowesia* was established by John Lindley in the *Botanical Register* (t. 39, misc. 25) in 1843. Most subsequent authors have treated *Clowesia* as a section of *Catasetum* with a total of five species of mainly Central American origin.

Recently C. Dodson, in *Selbyana* (1975), has resurrected *Clowesia* and has transferred the other four species allied to *C. rosea* to that genus. *Clowesia* is distinguished readily from *Catasetum* by its bisexual flowers and by its pollination mechanism, for its pollinia are discharged by pressure being applied to the stipe of the pollinarium. From *Dressleria* it may be distinguished by its pendulous inflorescence, membranous flower parts, free lip and by its distinct method for releasing the pollinia.

TYPE SPECIES   *C. rosea* Lindl.

CULTURE   Compost A or B. Temp. and general culture as for *Catasetum*.

Clowesia russelliana (Hooker) Dodson

A fairly large epiphytic plant. **Pseudobulbs** ovoid, several-noded, grooved when old, up to 7 cm long, 3.5 cm broad, 6- to 8-leaved. **Leaves** plicate, suberect, oblanceolate to oblong-oblanceolate, acute, up to 40 cm long, 7 cm broad. **Inflorescence** basal, pendulous, up to 30 cm long, racemose, up to 25-flowered; rhachis stout, somewhat angular; bracts ovate, acute, purplish, small. **Flowers** large, 5–6 cm across, rather sickly sweetly scented; sepals and petals very pale green, lined with darker green veins; lip green at base, whitish in front, with a raised white callus; column green above, white below; anther white. **Dorsal sepal** concave, in-

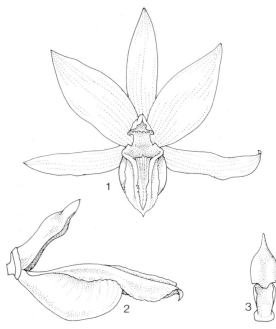

Clowesia russelliana
1 – Flower (× ¾)
2 – Column and lip, side view (× 2)
3 – Column from below (× 2)

curved, oblong-elliptic, apiculate, 3.5 cm long, 1.2 cm broad. **Lateral sepals** spreading, narrowly oblong, falcate below, obtuse, 3.7 cm long, 1.2 cm broad. **Petals** elliptic-ovate, acute, margins obscurely erose, 3.7 cm long, 1.7 cm broad. **Lip** saccate-calceolate below, margins outrolled, 3 cm long, 1.4 cm broad; front lobe oblong-obovate, porrect, with thin-fringed margins; callus on front lobe with irregular toothed margins. **Column** erect, slightly arcuate, 2.2 cm long.

DISTRIBUTION   Mexico, south to Panama and Venezuela.

HISTORY   Discovered in Guatemala by George Ure Skinner in 1838 who sent plants to the Duke of Bedford at Woburn, England, for whom it first flowered in 1840. Sir William Hooker described it as *Catasetum russellianum* in the Duke's honour in the *Botanical Magazine* (t. 3777) in 1840. C. Dodson (1975) transferred it to *Clowesia* in *Selbyana* (p. 136)

SYNONYM   *Catasetum russellianum* Hooker

Cochleanthes Raf.

Subfamily Epidendroideae
Tribe Maxillarieae
Subtribe Zygopetalinae

Medium-sized epiphytic plants with a short leafy stem, lacking pseudobulbs. **Leaves** numerous, distichous, borne in a fan, thinly membranous, articulated to conduplicate sheaths near the base. **Inflorescence** axillary, 1-flowered, much shorter than the leaves. **Flowers** large, rather fleshy, showy, whitish with a bluish or violet-marked lip, fragrant. **Sepals** subequal, free, spreading; lateral sepals attached to the column-foot. **Petals** similar to sepals. **Lips** articulated to column-foot, 3-lobed or entire, shortly clawed, with a basal transverse fleshy ridged callus; sides of lip embracing colum. **Column** fleshy, incurved, with a short foot, wingless or with 2 short wings; pollinia 4, pyriform, on an ovate to elliptic, broad viscidium.

DISTRIBUTION   Some nine species widely distributed in the American tropics.

DERIVATION OF NAME   The name derives from the Greek *kochlias* (spiral shell), and *anthos* (flower), descriptive of the appearance of the flower.

TAXONOMY   *Cochleanthes* was established in 1836 by C.S. Rafinesque in his *Flora Telluriana* (p. 45).

Cochleanthes species have often been placed in other genera such a *Zygopetalum* and *Warscewiczella*; however, *Cochleanthes* is much more closely allied to *Chondrorhyncha* and related genera (see L. Garay in *Orquideologia* 1969). It is readily distinguished from *Chondrorhyncha* by its short column-foot which forms an obtuse mentum and the transverse semicircular plate-like or gyrose callus near the base of the lip. The genus has recently been revised by Senghas (1990) in *Die Orchideen* (pp. 89–96).

TYPE SPECIES   *C. fragrans* Raf. [= *C. flabelliformis* (Sw.) R.E. Schultes & Garay].

CULTURE   Compost A. Temp. Winter min. 12–15°C. As for *Chondrorhyncha* and *Huntleya*.

Cochleanthes aromatica (Rchb.f.) Schultes & Garay

An erect epiphytic herb lacking any pseudobulbs. **Leaves** plicate, linear-ligulate to elliptic-lanceolate, acute to shortly acuminate, 15–30 cm long, 1.5–2.5 broad. **Inflorescence** erect or arcuate, axillary, 7–9 cm long, 1-flowered. **Flowers** relatively large, showy; sepals and petals pale or yellowish-green; lip lavender or violet with white margins, the callus violet-blue. **Dorsal sepal** elliptic-lanceolate, acuminate, 2.5–3 cm long, 0.6–0.8 cm broad; **lateral sepals** lanceolate, acuminate. **Petals** lanceolate, acuminate, 2.5–3 cm long, 0.5–0.6 cm broad. **Lip** subpandurate, obscurely lobed at the base, abruptly contracted into a short claw, 2.2–2.5 cm long, 1.5–1.7 cm broad, divided into a basal, rectangular half and a broader, undulate, reflexed apex; callus lunate, radiate or rhombic, plurisulcate. **Column** short, erect, clavate, narrowly winged.

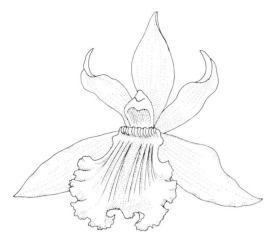

Cochleanthes aromatica
Flower ($\times \frac{3}{4}$)

DISTRIBUTION Costa Rica and Panama.
HISTORY Originally described as *Zygopetalum aromaticum* by H.G. Reichenbach in 1852 in the *Botanische Zeitung* (p. 668) from a Central American specimen flowered in cultivation. P.H. Allen transferred it to *Chondrorhyncha* in 1949 in the *Flora of Panama* (Orchidaceae, p. 421). Richard Schultes and Leslie Garay (1954) transferred it to *Cochleanthes* in the *Botanical Museum Leaflets of Harvard University* (p. 323).
SYNONYMS *Zygopetalum aromaticum* Rchb.f.; *Z. wendlandii* Rchb.f.; *Warscewiczella aromatica* (Rchb.f.) Rchb.f.; *Bollea wendlandiana* Rchb.f.; *Warscewiczella wendlandii* (Rchb.f.) Schltr.; *Chondrorhyncha aromatica* (Rchb.f.) P.H. Allen

Cochleanthes discolor (Lindl.) R.E. Schultes & Garay [Colour Plate]

An epiphytic plant with clustered, very short, leafy stems. **Leaves** distichous, about 5, suberect-spreading, ligulate-oblanceolate, acute, up to 20 cm long, 2–5 cm broad. **Inflorescence** erect, basal, subtended by a basal sheath, 1-flowered; peduncle terete, up to 10 cm long; bract pale green; thin-textured, 1.2 cm long. **Flower** showy; sepals pale green; petals creamy-green, tinged pale violet in the apical two-thirds; lip dark violet-purple with darker nervation, margins pale; callus shiny yellow; column white. **Sepals** elliptic, obtuse or rounded, 3.3–3.6 cm long, 1.4–1.6 cm broad. **Petals** porrect, recurved at the apex, elliptic, rounded, 3.2 cm long, 1.7 cm broad. **Lip** involute below, shortly clawed, subquadrate-ovate, emarginate, 3.6 cm long, 4.2 cm broad, apical margins reflexed; callus fleshy, porrect, of several ridges spreading fanwise in front. **Column** densely pubescent beneath; foot very short, bearing a small retrorse pubescent hook.
DISTRIBUTION Cuba, Honduras, Costa Rica, Panama and Venezuela.

HISTORY Originally described by John Lindley as *Warrea discolor* in 1849 in the *Journal of the Horticultural Society of London* (p. 265) from a plant collected by J. Warscewicz in Costa Rica. R.E. Schultes and L. Garay transferred it to the genus *Cochleanthes* in 1959 in the *Botanical Museum Leaflets of Harvard University* (p. 322).
SYNONYMS *Warrea discolor* Lindl.; *Warscewiczella discolor* (Lindl.) Rchb.f.; *Zygopetalum discolor* (Lindl.) Rchb.f.; *Chondrorhyncha discolor* (Lindl.) P.H. Allen
CLOSELY RELATED SPECIES *Cochleanthes flabelliformis* (Sw.) R.E. Schultes & Garay is distinguished from *C. discolor* by its flower colour, entire, ovoid (rather than 3-lobed) lip and by its more regularly incised basal callus on the lip.

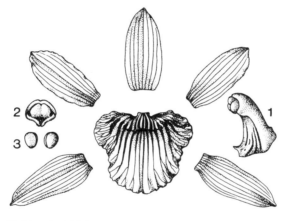

Cochleanthes flabelliformis
Floral dissection ($\times \frac{4}{5}$)
1 – Column ($\times 1\frac{1}{2}$)
2 – Anther-cap ($\times 1\frac{1}{2}$)
3 – Pollinia ($\times 2\frac{1}{2}$)

Cochlioda Lindl.
Subfamily Epidendroideae
Tribe Oncidieae

Small to medium-sized epiphytic plants. **Pseudobulbs** short, compressed, 1- or 2-leaved at apex. **Leaves** linear to oblong or lorate. **Inflorescences** 1 or 2, basal, erect to arcuate or pendent, laxly racemose or rarely paniculate above; bracts large or ± small. **Flowers** small to medium-sized, scarlet to rose-red, with spreading segments. **Sepals** subequal, free. **Petals** broader than sepals, somewhat oblique. **Lip** with an erect claw, ± adnate to column; lamina spreading, 3-lobed; side lobe rounded or oblong ± reflexed; mid-lobe erect, entire to bilobulate. **Column** erect, ± incurved, slender, winged above; pollinia 2; stigmatic cavities 2.
DISTRIBUTION Ecuador, Peru and Bolivia; a small genus of about six species.
DERIVATION OF NAME From the Greek *kochlioides* (spiral; snail-shell) alluding to the snail-shell appearance of the calli of the lip as described by Lindley in the type species.
TAXONOMY *Cochlioda* was established in 1853 by John Lindley in *Folia Orchidacea* (Cochlioda) based on *C. densiflora* collected by A. Mathews in Peru.

It is characterised by its lip which is partially adnate to the column at its base and by its 2 stigmatic cavities. This latter character serves to distinguish it from the allied genera *Odontoglossum* and *Symphyglossum* Schltr. The genus was revised by R. Schlechter in *Orchis* in 1919.
TYPE SPECIES *C. densiflora* Lindl.
CULTURE Compost A. Temp. Winter min. 12°C. Max. below 25°C in summer. As for cool-growing *Odontoglossum* species. The plants require cool, shady conditions in summer, with moderate humidity and fresh air when possible. Water must be carefully given when the new shoots are developing, and less water is required when growth is complete.

Cochlioda rosea (Lindl.) Benth.
[Colour Plate]

A small or medium-sized epiphytic plant with an abbreviated rhizome. **Pseudobulbs** clustered, ovoid, compressed, 3–5 cm long, 1- or 2-leaved at apex, subtended by 2 pairs of distichous, ± leaf-bearing sheaths. **Leaves** elliptic-oblong to linear, obtuse to acute, sub-petiolate at base, 6–20 cm long, 1–2.5 cm broad. **Inflorescences** lateral, erect to flexuose and arcuate, racemose or paniculate, laxly 5- to 20-flowered. 13–40 cm long. **Flowers** rose-red, segments spreading. **Sepals** subsimilar, elliptic-lanceolate, acute, 1.1–1.3 cm long, 0.2–0.4 cm broad. **Petals** elliptic-lanceolate, acute, 1.1 cm long, 0.6 cm broad. **Lip** adnate to the lower third of the column, 3-lobed at or below the middle, 1–1.6 cm long; side lobes short, obliquely ovate; mid-lobe porrect, linear-oblong to cuneate, obtuse or truncate; disc with 1 or 2 pairs of basal, short, fleshy keels. **Column** stout, 3-lobed at the apex, 0.7 cm long.
DISTRIBUTION Ecuador and Peru.
HISTORY Discovered by Theodore Hartweg at the Quebrada de las Juntas near Loxa (now Loja) in Ecuador and originally described by John Lindley as *Odontoglossum roseum* in 1844 in G. Bentham's *Plantae Hartwegianae* (p. 151). Bentham later transferred it to *Cochlioda* in 1881 in the *Journal of the Linnean Society* (p. 327).
SYNONYMS *Odontoglossum roseum* Lindl.; *Mesopinidium roseum* (Lindl.) Rchb.f.

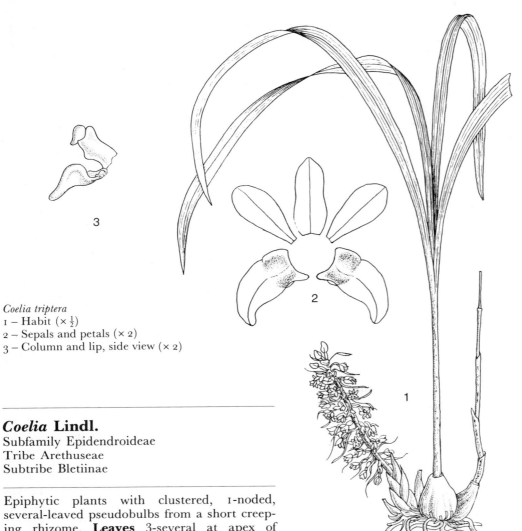

Coelia triptera
1 – Habit (× ½)
2 – Sepals and petals (× 2)
3 – Column and lip, side view (× 2)

Coelia Lindl.

Subfamily Epidendroideae
Tribe Arethuseae
Subtribe Bletiinae

Epiphytic plants with clustered, 1-noded, several-leaved pseudobulbs from a short creeping rhizome. **Leaves** 3-several at apex of pseudobulb, plicate, suberect, sheathing below to simulate a stem. **Inflorescence** lateral, basal from pseudobulb, laxly several-flowered, racemose, subtended by several distichous, imbricate sheaths. **Flowers** small, fleshy, not opening widely; ovary conspicuously erosely winged. **Sepals** and **petals** subsimilar, free. **Lip** sagittate, shorter than the sepals and petals. **Column** erect, stout, lacking wings and with an almost obsolete foot; pollinia 8, waxy.
DISTRIBUTION A monotypic genus from Mexico, Guatemala and the W. Indies.
DERIVATION OF NAME From the Greek *koilos* (hollow), in allusion to the supposed hollow body formed by each pair of pollen masses as illustrated by Bauer. This appearance was later shown to be an artifact of preservation.
TAXONOMY *Coelia* was established by John Lindley in 1830 in his *Genera and Species of Orchidaceous Plants* (p. 36). The genus is closely allied to *Bothriochilus* but distinguished by the virtual absence of a column-foot and mentum. A discussion of the relationships of these genera is

given by Pridgeon in 1978 in *Orquidea* (*Mex.*) (p. 81).
TYPE SPECIES *C. triptera* (J.E. Smith) G. Don ex Steud.
CULTURE Temp. Winter min. 12°C. Grows well in pots in epiphyte mix, under moderate shade. Give a drier period when growth is finished. Flowers in spring with new growths.

Coelia triptera (J.E. Smith) G. Don ex Steud.
[Colour Plate]
An epiphyte or lithophyte up to 60 cm tall with ovoid to ellipsoidal pseudobulbs 2.5–6.5 cm long, 1.5–2.5 cm in diameter and extended above into a narrow stem formed by the leaf bases. **Leaves** 4–5, erect-spreading, linear-lanceolate, long-acuminate, 12–50 cm long, 1–2.3 cm wide, articulate to leaf bases. **Inflorescence** 12–18 cm long, densely several- to many-flowered; bracts prominent, longer than the flowers, linear-lanceolate, 2–4 cm long.

Flowers white, strongly sweetly scented; pedicel and ovary 1–1.2 cm long, ovary erosely ridged. **Dorsal sepal** ovate-elliptic to elliptic-oblong, obtuse, 7–9 mm long, 3.5–5 mm wide; **lateral sepals** obliquely ovate, slightly connate at base, 8–9 mm long, 4–5 mm wide. **Petals** oblong-spathulate to oblong-obovate, rounded at the apex, 7–9 mm long, 3.5–5 mm wide. **Lip** erect, sagittate above, acute, recurved and with convex thickened margins in apical half, 6–7 mm long, 5 mm wide. **Column** about 2 mm long, stout.
DISTRIBUTION Mexico, Guatemala and the W. Indies, 500–1200 m.
HISTORY First described in the genus *Epidendrum* by J.E. Smith (1793) in his *Icones Pictae Plantarum Rariorum* (t. 14), based on a Jamaican introduction flowered by the Hon. Daines Barrington. It was subsequently transferred to the genus *Coelia* by Steudel in his *Nomenclator Botanicus* (p. 394) of 1840.
SYNONYM *Epidendrum tripterum* J.E. Smith; *Cymbidium tripterum* (J.E. Smith) Sw.; *Coelia baueriana* Lindl.; *C. glacialis* Houtte ex Heynh.

Coeliopsis Rchb.f.

Subfamily Epidendroideae
Tribe Cymbideae
Subtribe Stanhopeinae

Epiphytic plants with stout ovoid or subcylindrical pseudobulbs with 2–4 leaves at the apex. **Leaves** plicate, prominently veined, oblanceolate, acuminate. **Inflorescences** short, pendent, densely 5- to 15-flowered in a subcapitate head. **Flowers** very fleshy, waxy, white. **Sepals** subsimilar but the laterals connate and forming a conspicuous saccate mentum at the base. **Petals** free, narrower than the sepals. **Lip** 3-lobed, ecallose. Column short, clavate, winged; pollinia 2, waxy, sessile on a reniform viscidium.
DISTRIBUTION A monotypic genus from Colombia, Costa Rica and Panama.
DERIVATION OF NAME From the Greek *koilos* (hollow) and *opsis* (appearance), in allusion to its resemblance to the orchid genus *Coelia*.
TAXONOMY H.G. Reichenbach established this genus in 1872 in the *Gardeners' Chronicle* (p. 9). It is not, as its name suggests, closely related to *Coelia* but its affinities lie rather with *Houlletia* and *Lacaena*.
TYPE SPECIES *C. hyacinthosma* Rchb.f.
CULTURE Temp. Winter min. 15°C. Grown as *Stanhopea* in baskets, as inflorescences show the same tendency to burrow.

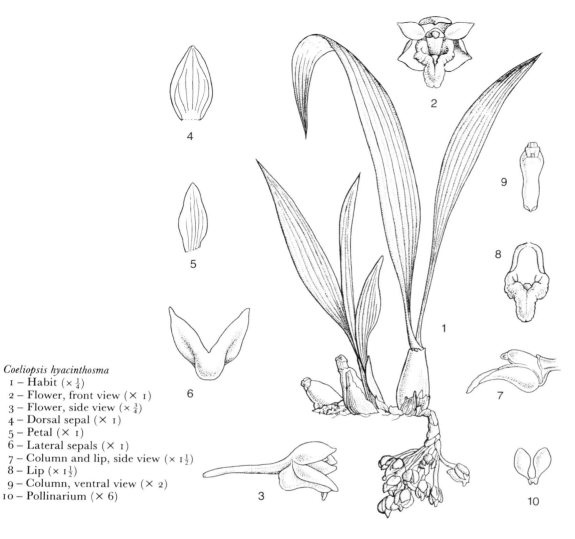

Coeliopsis hyacinthosma
1 – Habit (× ¼)
2 – Flower, front view (× 1)
3 – Flower, side view (× ¾)
4 – Dorsal sepal (× 1)
5 – Petal (× 1)
6 – Lateral sepals (× 1)
7 – Column and lip, side view (× 1½)
8 – Lip (× 1½)
9 – Column, ventral view (× 2)
10 – Pollinarium (× 6)

Coeliopsis hyacinthosma Rchb.f.
[Colour Plate]

An epiphyte with ovoid or subcylindrical pseudobulbs 6.5–8.5 cm long, 2.5–4 cm in diameter, enveloped in papery sheaths at the base. **Leaves** 2–4, oblanceolate, acuminate, 30–50 cm long, 2–7 cm wide. **Inflorescences** 4–5 cm long, pendent, subcapitate, 5- to 15-flowered; bracts chartaceous, lanceolate, acuminate, 1–1.5 cm long. **Flowers** very fleshy, smelling of hyacinths, white with an orange spot on the lip and a purple blotch on the column-foot; pedicel and ovary 1.5–1.8 cm long. **Dorsal sepal** lanceolate, acute, 1.8–2.2 cm long, 0.9–1.2 cm wide; **lateral sepals** obliquely ovate, acute; mentum saccate, 4 mm long. **Petals** lanceolate, acute, 1.5–1.6 cm long, 0.5–0.6 cm wide. **Lip** 3-lobed, 1.6–1.8 cm long, 1.2–1.4 cm wide, papillose; side lobes erect, with spreading fimbriate apical margins; mid-lobe rectangular or ovate, truncate or obtuse, strongly reflexed, with fimbriate margins. **Column** 0.9–1.1 cm long, subclavate, winged.

DISTRIBUTION Colombia, Costa Rica and Panama only, in lower montane wet forest from 300–1000 m.
HISTORY *C. hyacinthosma* was described by H.G. Reichenbach in the *Gardeners' Chronicle* (p. 9) of 1872 based on a specimen from Panama flowered in England in the collection of W. Wilson Saunders.

Coelogyne Lindl.
Subfamily Epidendroideae
Tribe Coelogyeae
Subtribe Coelogyninae

Epiphytic herbs. **Pseudobulbs** ovoid, conical or cylindrical, close or distant, 1- or 2-leaved at apex. **Leaves** narrow to broad, elliptic, plicate. **Inflorescences** erect or pendulous, 1- to many-flowered. **Flowers** small to large and showy, opening simultaneously or 1 at a time. **Sepals** free, often strongly concave. **Petals** free, often narrower than sepals. **Lip** 3-lobed, somewhat concave at base; side lobes erect on either side of column; mid-lobe spreading; disc keeled with keels often spreading onto mid-lobe of lip. **Column** long, anther ventral at apex of column; rostellum large; pollinia 2.
DISTRIBUTION A large genus of over 100 species found in S.E. Asia, India, Indonesia, China and the Pacific Islands.
DERIVATION OF NAME From the Greek *koilos* (hollow) and *gyne* (female), probably referring to the deeply set stigmatic cavity found in the genus.
TAXONOMY The genus *Coelogyne* was founded by John Lindley in 1821 in his *Collectanea Botanica* (sub t. 33).

E. Pfitzer and F. Kraenzlin revised the genus in A. Engler's *Das Pflanzenreich* (1907). They divided the 103 species in the genus into two series: *Succedaneae* in which the flowers open in succession in the inflorescence and *Simultaneae* in which the flowers open simultaneously. The former was then divided into two subseries with a total of four sections whilst in the latter, three subseries were recognised with a total of ten sections.

Since the revision of Pfitzer and Kraenzlin was published, a further 140 or so new species have been described and it is obvious, as stated by G. Seidenfaden in *Dansk Botanisk Arkiv* (1975), that the genus is in need of a new revision. Seidenfaden has also produced a somewhat modified key to ten of the 14 sections recognised in *Das Pflanzenreich* and, in treating the 32 species of *Coelogyne* found in Thailand, has added much information to and has elucidated the identity of, several obscure taxa by consulting H.G. Reichenbach's herbarium which was unavailable to Pfitzer and Kraenzlin.

F. Butzin has recently published a key to the cultivated species of *Coelogyne* (over 80 in all) in *Willdenowia* (1974). He has divided the genus into five subgenera: *Coelogyne* (with 14 sections), *Chelonistele*, *Hologyne*, *Ptychogyne* and *Cyathogyne*. The last four have all been treated at various times by other botanists as distinct genera.

Several features should be looked for when attempting to identify a species apart from flower colour and lip ornamentation. In particular, the characters of the inflorescence are of importance such as the presence or absence of basal sheathing bracts and whether the flowers open one at a time or simultaneously. One feature often overlooked is the development of the inflorescence which may be: (a) after the pseudobulb has finished growing (*hysteranthous* development of inflorescence); (b) simultaneous with the growth of the pseudobulb (*synanthous*); (c) before the pseudobulb with the leaves develops (*proteranthous*); or (d) when the

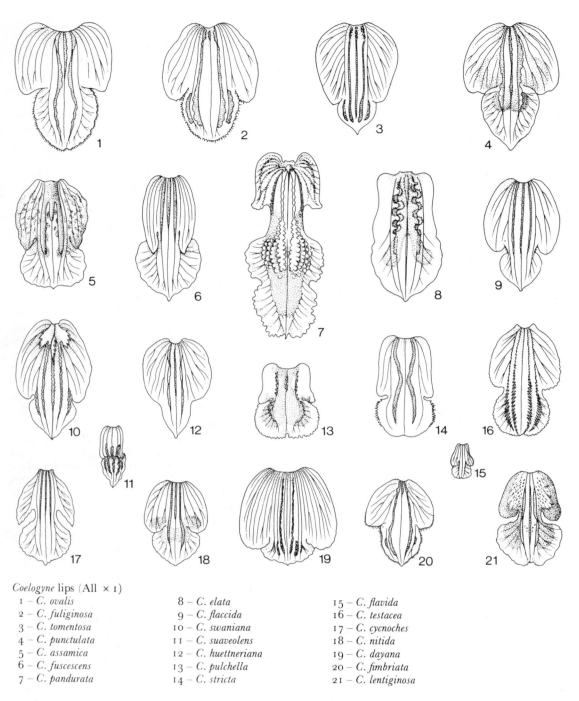

Coelogyne lips (All × 1)

CULTURE The species of *Coelogyne* vary greatly in their temperature requirements as would be expected from the great variety of habitats and altitudinal range in which they are found in the wild. Most species from New Guinea, Borneo and the Far East, where they grow at low altitudes, require a warm house with a minimum night temperature in the winter of 15°C. Most of the Indian, Burmese and many Malayan species grow at higher altitudes in the mountains and may be grown in a cool house where the temperature is not allowed to fall below 10°C in winter.

As many species produce pendulous inflorescences they are best grown in baskets or pans which can be suspended. *Coelogyne* species thrive on a compost of three parts bark to one part sphagnum moss with a little added charcoal. Care should be taken when watering young shoots but when actively growing the plants should be kept well watered.

***Coelogyne asperata* Lindl.** [Colour Plate]
Pseudobulbs somewhat compressed, ribbed, broadly conical, up to 15 cm long. **Leaves** oblanceolate, up to 60 cm long, 12 cm broad, long-petiolate. **Inflorescence** up to 30 cm long, curvate, many-flowered; 1 sheath on scape below basal flower; bracts ovate, large, dry, concave, 3 cm long. **Flowers** fragrant, creamy-white; lip side lobes veined light brown; verrucose keels rich brown. **Sepals** lanceolate, 3.5–4 cm long, 1 cm broad, acute. **Petals** narrowly lanceolate, 3.5 cm long, 0.5 cm broad, acute. **Lip** 3-lobed; side lobes rounded, erect; mid-lobe deflexed, ovate, acute; verrucose; disc 2-keeled. **Column** arcuate, 1.5 cm long.
DISTRIBUTION Malaysia and Sumatra to New Guinea and the islands of the S.W. Pacific; a lowland species on trees and rocks by streams in primary forest.
HISTORY Described in the *Journal of the Horticultural Society* (p. 221) in 1849 by John Lindley, who received a flowering plant collected in Borneo from T. Twisden Hodges in May of that year. This species is probably best known as one of the parents of the green-flowered hybrid *C.* × Burfordiensis.

***Coelogyne corymbosa* Lindl.** [Colour Plate]
A creeping epiphytic herb, up to 17 cm high. **Pseudobulbs** short, clustered, ovoid to sub-rhomboidal, 2.5–4 cm long, 2-leaved at apex. **Leaves** elliptic-lanceolate, suberect, 10–20 cm long, 2–3.5 cm broad, acute. **Inflorescence** erect or drooping, 2- to 4-flowered, 20 cm long; scape covered in sheaths to first flower. **Flowers** fragrant. up to 7 cm across, white with 4 large yellow eyes bordered with orange-red on lip. **Sepals** lanceolate, 2.5–3.8 cm long, 0.9 cm broad, acute. **Petals** narrowly lanceolate, up to

inflorescence is borne on a separate shoot which produces only rudimentary pseudobulbs and leaves (termed *heteranthous* by R. Holttum in the *Orchids of Malaya*, 1964.) These variations in inflorescence development are found throughout the group of genera related to *Coelogyne* such as *Pholidota*, *Dendrochilum* and *Pleione* the terms may be used for those genera as well as for *Coelogyne*.

The species of *Coelogyne* are justly popular for their free-flowering and delicately-coloured, but often showy blooms. Few hybrid *Coelogynes* have captured the imagination but the spectacular green-flowered *C.* × Burfordiensis , which is a cross of *C. pandurata* and *C. asperata*, is justifiably popular.
TYPE SPECIES Several species were mentioned by Lindley when he established the genus.
SYNONYMS *Acanthoglossum* Blume; *Gomphostylis* Wall. ex Lindl.; *Chelonanthera* Blume; *Hologyne* Pfitz.; *Ptychogyne* Pfitz.

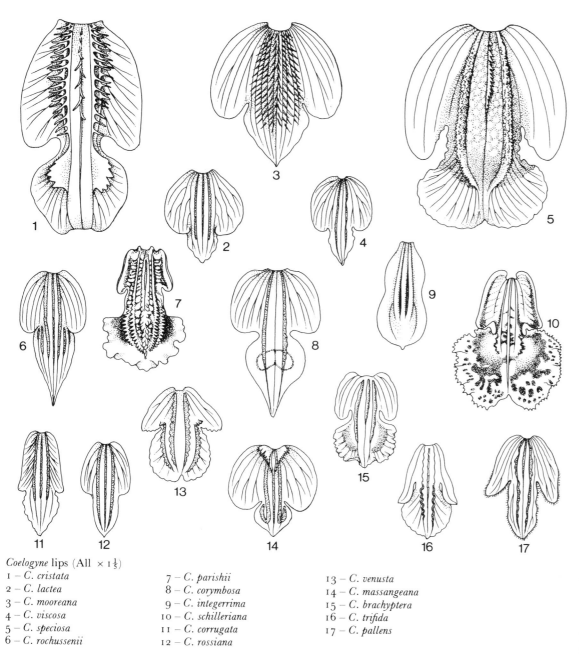

Coelogyne lips (All × 1⅓)

1 – *C. cristata*
2 – *C. lactea*
3 – *C. mooreana*
4 – *C. viscosa*
5 – *C. speciosa*
6 – *C. rochussenii*
7 – *C. parishii*
8 – *C. corymbosa*
9 – *C. integerrima*
10 – *C. schilleriana*
11 – *C. corrugata*
12 – *C. rossiana*
13 – *C. venusta*
14 – *C. massangeana*
15 – *C. brachyptera*
16 – *C. trifida*
17 – *C. pallens*

late yellow plates on mid-lobe. **Sepals** narrowly elliptic-oblong, undulate, 3.7–5 cm long. 1.7 cm broad, subacute. **Petals** similar to sepals, 4.5 cm long, 1.7 cm broad, acute. **Lip** 3-lobed, up to 4 cm long, 3.5 cm broad; side lobes large, rounded; mid-lobe suborbicular: disc bearing fimbriate keels onto mid-lobe. **Column** arcuate, 2.7 cm long.

DISTRIBUTION   E. Himalayas; 1500–2100 m altitude.

HISTORY   John Lindley described *C. cristata* in his *Collectanea Botanica* (sub t. 33) in 1822 based on a specimen from Nepal collected by Dr N. Wallich. Many colour varieties of this species are known.

Coelogyne dayana (Rchb.f.) Rolfe
[Colour Plate] See under *Coelogyne massangeana*.

Coelogyne fimbriata Lindl.
A creeping epiphytic herb, up to 10 cm high. Pseudobulbs given off from a creeping rhizome, 3–4 cm apart, ovoid to ellipsoid, 2.5 cm long, 1.2 cm broad, 2-leaved at apex. **Leaves** oblong-elliptic, up to 9 cm long, 1.4 cm broad, acute. **Inflorescence** 1- to few-flowered, 5 cm high, subtended at base by a narrow sheath. **Flowers** 3–3.5 cm across, segments spreading little; sepals and petals pale yellow; lip whitish or pale yellow marked with dark brown. **Sepals** lanceolate, 2 cm long, 0.6 cm broad, acute. **Petals** linear-filiform, 2 cm long, acute or subacute. **Lip** 3-lobed, 1.6–2 cm long, 1.2 cm broad, margins ciliate; side lobes oblong-elliptic, obtuse or acute; mid-lobe sub-quadrate to oblong, 1 cm long, 0.7–1 cm broad, obtuse or emarginate; disc 3-keeled at base, 2 outer undulate keels reaching middle of mid-lobe where they are flanked by 2 short keels. **Column** slightly arcuate, widening towards apex. 1.2 cm long.

DISTRIBUTION   Widespread from India (the Khasia Hills, Manipur), Laos, Kampuchea, Vietnam, Thailand, Malaya and China, across to Hong Kong.

HISTORY   Described by John Lindley in 1825 in the *Botanical Register* (t. 868), *C. fimbriata* was first introduced from China by J.D. Parks who sent plants from Macau to the Horticultural Society in London in 1823.

SYNONYMS   *Coelogyne ovalis* auct.; *C. leungiana* Hu; *C. laotica* Gagn.

CLOSELY RELATED SPECIES   Closely related to other species of sect. *Fuliginosae* such as *Coelogyne pallens* Ridley, *C. fuliginosa* and *C. ovalis*. It may be distinguished from *C. pallens* by its obtuse, truncate side lobes to the lip and from the other species by its smaller flowers.

Coelogyne flaccida Lindl. [Colour Plate]
Pseudobulbs conical, up to 12 cm long   2.5

3.3 cm long, 0.8 cm broad, acute. **Lip** 3-lobed, 3 cm long, 1.7 cm broad; side lobes erose, rounded; mid-lobe ovate to ovate-lanceolate, acute to acuminate; disc with 3 low ridges onto mid-lobe.

DISTRIBUTION   Himalayas from Sikkim eastwards and the Khasia Hills; 1800–2700 m altitude.

HISTORY   Described by John Lindley in *Folia Orchidacea* (*Coelogyne*: p. 7) in 1854 based on a collection made by Sir Joseph Hooker in Sikkim.

CLOSELY RELATED SPECIES   Often con-

fused with *C. nitida* which, however, flowers from its mature pseudobulbs.

Coelogyne cristata Lindl. [Colour Plate]
Pseudobulbs oblong, closely spaced on rhizome, 5–7.5 cm long, up to 4 cm in diameter, 2-leaved at apex. **Leaves** narrowly lanceolate, sessile, 15–30 cm long, up to 2.7 cm broad, acute. **Inflorescence** pendulous, 15–30 cm long, 3- to 10-flowered; bracts up to 5 cm long, persistent. **Flowers** very large, about 8 cm across; sepals and petals white; lip white with yellow lamellae between side lobes and 2 crenu-

cm broad, 2-leaved at apex. **Leaves** lanceolate, 19 cm long 2–3 cm broad, acuminate; petiole about 4 cm long. **Inflorescence** pendulous, about 9-flowered, up to 20 cm long. **Flowers** up to 3–5 cm across, white with yellow on middle of lip, striped red on side lobes and spotted red at base of mid-lobe; column white. **Sepals** lanceolate, 2–4 cm long, 0.4 cm broad, acute. **Petals** linear, reflexed, 2 cm long, 0.2 cm broad, subacute. **Lip** 3-lobed, 1.7 cm long, 1.2 cm broad; side lobes oblong, erect, rounded; mid-lobe reflexed, ovate-lanceolate, acute; disc bearing 3 undulate keels from base onto base of mid-lobe. **Column** 1.5 cm long.

DISTRIBUTION E. Himalayas including Nepal, Sikkim, Burma, S.W. China & Laos.
HISTORY Collected by N. Wallich in Nepal and mentioned by him in his Catalogue (no. 1961), this species was formally described by John Lindley in *Genera and Species of Orchidaceous Plants* (p. 39) in 1830.
CLOSELY RELATED SPECIES Very closely related to *C. lactea*.

Coelogyne fuliginosa Hooker [Colour Plate]

Pseudobulbs fusiform, distant on a slender rhizome, 5–7.5 cm long, 2-leaved. **Leaves** lanceolate, 14 cm long, 3 cm broad, membranous to coriaceous. **Inflorescence** 3- to 4-flowered. **Flowers** orange-yellow; lip dark brown. **Sepals** oblong-lanceolate, 3 cm long or more, acute. **Petals** filiform. **Lip** 3-lobed, 2.1 cm long, 1.5 cm broad, side lobes oblong, rounded, inner margins ciliate; mid-lobe ovate, 1 cm long and broad, margin ciliate; 3-keeled at base, 2 outer keels running onto mid-lobe where they are flanked by 2 shorter keels. **Column** clavate, 1.3 cm long, winged on each side above.

DISTRIBUTION Burma, Thailand and Java(?).
HISTORY Although the name *C. fuliginosa* was proposed in Loddiges' catalogue probably by John Lindley as early as 1844, it remained for Sir William Hooker to describe it validly in the *Botanical Magazine* (t. 4440) in 1849.
SYNONYMS *Coelogyne ovalis* auct. non Lindl.; *C. fimbriata* auct. non Lindl.
CLOSELY RELATED SPECIES A species often confused with *C. fimbriata* and *C. ovalis*. However, it has larger flowers than the former and the keels on the lip are less wavy and lower than in *C. ovalis*. *C. fuliginosa* always has an extra pair of keels on the mid-lobe.

Coelogyne fuscescens Lindl.

A creeping herb, up to 30 cm high. **Pseudobulbs** erect, closely spaced on rhizome, fusiform, 8–10 cm long, 1–2 cm broad, 2-leaved at apex. **Leaves** oblanceolate to oblong-elliptic, acute, up to 28 cm long, 6 cm broad. **Inflorescence** 2- to 7-flowered, 16 cm long, erect or

suberect; scape subtended by 4–5 short sheaths. **Flowers** 3.5–5 cm across; sepals and petals pale yellow or pale yellow-green. ± flushed brown towards the apex; lip whitish with a pale yellow-green central stripe and marked with brown. **Sepals** oblong-lanceolate, 3–4 cm long, 0.9 cm broad, acute. **Petals** linear, 2.7–3.5 cm long, 0.3 cm broad, acute. **Lip** narrowly elliptic-oblong in outline, 3-lobed, 3–4 cm long, 1.5 broad; side lobes narrowly oblong, narrower than mid-lobe; mid-lobe broadly ovate to cordate, 2.0 cm long and broad, acute; disc with 3 fleshy keels running from base onto base of mid-lobe. **Column** curved towards apex, 1.3–2 cm long.

DISTRIBUTION Nepal, India (Sikkim, the Khasia and Lushai Hills) and Bhutan.
HISTORY The name *C. fuscescens* was first used by N. Wallich in the Catalogue of his collection in Nepal but the name was validly published by John Lindley in 1830 in *Genera and Species of Orchidaceous Plants* (p. 41).

Var. *brunnea* (Lindl.) Lindl. with a brown-marked lip with an acute mid-lobe is found in Burma, Thailand, Laos and Vietnam.
SYNONYM *Coelogyne brunnea* Lindl.
CLOSELY RELATED SPECIES *C. fuscescens* may be distinguished from *Coelogyne assamica* Linden & Rchb.f. by its longer lip and by its caducous bracts.

Coelogyne lactea Rchb.f.

Pseudobulbs closely-spaced, ovoid-conical, 6–12 cm long, 1.5–4 cm broad, lightly sulcate, 2-leaved at apex. **Leaves** oblong, 20 cm long, 3–5 cm broad, acute, petiolate; petiole 2.5 cm long, fleshy. **Inflorescence** about 10-flowered, up to 18 cm long, ± horizontal. **Flowers** 4 cm across, creamy-white; side lobes of lip brown. **Sepals** subsimilar, oblong, 2.3 cm long, 0.8 cm broad, obtuse. **Petals** linear, 2 cm long, 0.3 cm broad, obtuse or subacute. **Lip** 3-lobed, 2 cm long, 1.4 cm broad; side lobes ovate, curved up either side of column; mid-lobe much longer, ovate, acute; disc bearing 3 undulate keels from base to base of mid-lobe. **Column** 1.6 cm long, slightly broader towards apex, apex erose but not 3-lobed.

DISTRIBUTION Burma, Thailand, Laos and Vietnam.
HISTORY Described by H.G. Reichenbach in the *Gardeners' Chronicle* (n.s. 23: p. 692) of 1885 from a plant grown by John Day of Tottenham, London in 1884.
SYNONYM *Coelogyne huettneriana* auct. non Rchb.f.
CLOSELY RELATED SPECIES *Coelogyne huettneriana* Rchb.f. has much broader, fleshier petals and the column-apex is trifid. G. Seidenfaden in *Dansk Botanisk Arkiv* (1975) has pointed out that plants grown under the name *C. huett-*

neriana almost invariably should be called *C. lactea* Rchb.f.. Seidenfaden also considers that *C. flaccida* may prove to be merely a variety of *C. lactea* differing only in having a thinner pendulous inflorescence with more flowers on it.

Coelogyne lawrenceana Rolfe [Colour Plate]

See under *Coelogyne speciosa*.

Coelogyne lentiginosa Lindl. [Colour Plate]

A medium-sized epiphytic herb with a stout creeping rhizome 0.4–0.6 cm in diameter. **Pseudobulbs** ovoid, narrowly ellipsoidal or narrowly cylindrical, 3.5–9.5 cm long, 1.2–2 cm in diameter, glossy light green when young, yellow with age, 2-leaved at apex. **Leaves** arcuate to suberect, very narrowly elliptic to oblanceolate, acute, 8–20 cm long, 1.6–2.5 cm broad, shortly petiolate below. **Inflorescence** proteranthous, 6–16 cm long, erect, 4- to 5-flowered; bract chartaceous, lanceolate, acute, spreading, 1.2–2 cm long. **Flowers** erect; sepals and petals pale green; lip white, marked with red-brown or dark brown and with a broad orange area in centre of mid-lobe. **Sepals** and **petals** subsimilar, narrowly lanceolate, acute, 1.7–2.2 cm long, 0.3–0.5 cm broad. **Lip** 3-lobed in the middle, slightly arcuate, 1.8 cm long, 1.2 cm broad, with 3 low, rather undulate keels running from the base onto the mid-lobe; side lobes suberect, narrowly oblong, shortly rounded in front; mid-lobe spreading, broadly clawed below, broadly ovate and subacute above. **Column** arcuate, 1–1.2 cm long.

DISTRIBUTION Burma, Thailand and Vietnam; 800–1400 m altitude.
HISTORY First collected by T. Lobb, one of Veitch's collectors, at Moulmein in Burma, this attractive orchid was described in 1854 by John Lindley in his *Folia Orchidacea, Coelogyne* (p. 3). It was later figured in the *Botanical Magazine* (t. 5958) in 1872.

Coelogyne massangeana Rchb.f. [Colour Plate]

Pseudobulbs elongate-conical with 2 opposite longitudinal ridges when young, 5–10 cm long, 2.5 cm broad at base, somewhat angled, 1-leafed at apex. **Leaf** elliptic-obovate, 10–50 cm long, 3.5–8 cm broad, long-petiolate. **Inflorescence** heteranthous, pendulous, about 30-flowered; rhachis zig-zag, very flexuous, wiry, up to 45 cm long; bracts short, broad, persistent. **Flowers** 6 cm across, pale yellowish; lip side lobes blue-grey or browny-maroon, veined white or yellow, mid-lobe brown and pale yellow. **Sepals** oblong-lanceolate, 3 cm long, 0.6 cm broad, subacute. **Petals** narrowly oblong-lanceolate, 2.8 cm long, 0.4 cm broad, obtuse. **Lip** 3-lobed, 2 cm long, 1.9 cm broad; side lobes narrowly elliptic-oblong or rounded, broadest at base, erect over column; mid-lobe pendent, oblong, obtuse; disc 3-keeled, verrucose and fimbriate at base, becoming lower quickly and running onto mid-lobe where they are contiguous with 2 additional outer keels.

DISTRIBUTION Malaya, Sumatra, Borneo and Java; growing in mountainous regions.

HISTORY Described by H.G. Reichenbach in the *Gardeners' Chronicle* (n.s. 10: p. 684) of 1878 and named in honour of M.D. Massange of the Château de Baillonville near Marche, France, who sent the type specimen to Reichenbach.

SYNONYMS *Coelogyne dayana* var. *massangeana* Ridley; *C. tomentosa* var. *massangeana* Ridley; *C. densiflora* Ridley

CLOSELY RELATED SPECIES Closely related to *Coelogyne dayana* (Rchb.f.) Rolfe [Colour Plate] which is proteranthous and has a 2-keeled lip; to *C. tomentosa* which has orange or salmon flowers; and to *C. rochussenii* which has a triangular mid-lobe to the lip.

Coelogyne mooreana Rolfe [Colour Plate]

Pseudobulbs clustered, ovoid, bluntly angulate, slightly furrowed. **Leaves** narrowly linear-oblanceolate, up to 40 cm long, 3.5 cm broad, acute, petiolate. **Inflorescence** erect, about 4- to 8-flowered, up to 50 cm long, erect, proteranthous. **Flowers** about 10 cm across; sepals and petals pure white; lip white with a dark orange or ochreous disc; column pale yellow. **Sepals** broadly lanceolate, 5 cm long, 1.3 cm broad, acute to acuminate, slightly keeled. **Petals** similar to sepals. **Lip** 3-lobed, 4 cm long, 3 cm broad; side lobes erect around column, broadly rounded; mid-lobe ovate, acute; disc bearing 3 long fimbriate lamellae from base to base of mid-lobe. **Column** 2.5 cm long, dilated towards apex.

DISTRIBUTION Vietnam; 1300 m altitude.

HISTORY First introduced in 1906 by Messrs Sander & Sons of St Albans, England, who were sent plants of this spectacular species by W. Micholitz from the Lang Bian range in Annam. Fred Sander named it after F.W. Moore of the Glasnevin Botanic Gardens, Dublin. It received a First Class Certificate from the Royal Horticultural Society, London, in December 1906. R.A. Rolfe formally described it in 1907 in the *Kew Bulletin* (p. 129).

Coelogyne nitida Lindl. [Colour Plate]

Pseudobulbs ovoid to conical, 3–8 cm long, 1.3 cm in diameter, 1- or 2-leaved at apex. **Leaves** narrowly elliptic-lanceolate, 8–25 cm long, 2–6 cm broad, acute. **Inflorescence** 3- to 6-flowered, proteranthous, erect or drooping, about 20 cm long. **Flowers** 4 cm across, white with yellow eye-marks on side lobes and a yellow disc bordered with red. **Sepals** narrowly

oblong, up to 3.5 cm long, 0.7 cm broad, subacute to obtuse. **Petals** narrowly oblong-lanceolate, 2.5 cm long, 0.5 cm broad, subacute. **Lip** 3-lobed, almost ovate, 1.9 cm long, 1.6 cm broad; side lobes oblong to rounded; mid-lobe rotund to cordate, rounded to subacute; disc 3-keeled at base, 2 outer keels running onto base of mid-lobe. **Column** 1.2 cm long, slightly wider towards apex.

DISTRIBUTION Very widespread from N.W. Himalayas, Nepal, India (Sikkim), Bhutan, Bangladesh (Sylhet), China (Yunnan), Burma, Thailand and Laos.

HISTORY Described by John Lindley in *Collectanea Botanica* (sub t. 33) in 1822 based on a specimen collected from Nepal by N. Wallich.

SYNONYMS *Coelogyne ochracea* Lindl.; not *C. nitida* of some authors.

CLOSELY RELATED SPECIES Closely related and often confused with *Coelogyne punctulata* Lindl. which is a hysteranthous species with flowers that are somewhat larger with the 3 keels on the lip reaching onto the mid-lobe. See also *C. corymbosa*.

Coelogyne ovalis Lindl. [Colour Plate]

A creeping epiphytic herb, up to 25 cm high. **Pseudobulbs** ovoid-fusiform to fusiform, 3–6 cm long, 1.5 cm broad, borne somewhat distant on a creeping rhizome, 2-leaved at apex. **Leaves** narrowly elliptic, 9–15 cm long, 2.5–4 cm broad, acute to acuminate. **Inflorescence** few-flowered, 12 cm long, subtended at base by 3 sheaths. **Flowers** 3 cm or more across, pale buff-brown; lip marked darker brown. **Sepals** ovate-lanceolate, 3 cm or more long, 1.3 cm broad, acute. **Petals** linear, 2.7 cm long, 0.1 cm broad, acute. **Lip** 3-lobed in middle, 2.5 cm long, 1.8 cm across; side lobes oblong or triangular, ± somewhat truncate, ciliate; mid-lobe ovate, shortly ciliate; disc 3-keeled at base, 2 outer keels undulate onto mid-lobe. **Column** 1.5 cm long, clavate.

DISTRIBUTION W. Himalayas, Nepal, Tibet, China (Yunnan), India (Sikkim, Assam, Manipur, the Khasia Hills), Burma (Tenasserim) and Thailand.

HISTORY Described by John Lindley in the *Botanical Register* (misc. 171) of 1838 based on a plant collected by N. Wallich in Nepal and sent by him to Messrs Loddiges.

SYNONYMS *Coelogyne triplicatula* Rchb.f.; *C. pilosissima* Planchon

CLOSELY RELATED SPECIES Often confused with *C. fimbriata* and *C. fuliginosa*, but the lack of additional lamellae outside the main lamellae on the lip mid-lobe allows it to be distinguished from these species.

Coelogyne pandurata Lindl. [Colour Plate]

A large epiphytic plant, up to 50 cm high.

Pseudobulbs well-spaced, strongly compressed, oblong or suborbicular, sulcate, 7.5–12.5 cm long, 2–3 cm broad, borne on a short rhizome. **Leaves** elliptic-lanceolate, rigid, 20–45 cm long, 7 cm broad; petiole stout. **Inflorescence** arcuate 15–30 cm long, few-flowered; scape very stout, 1 or 2 sheaths below basal flowers. **Flowers** 7–10 cm across, fragrant, clear bright green; lip appearing black-mottled. **Sepals** linear-oblong, 3.5–5 cm long, 1.3 cm broad, acute; dorsal sepal larger than lateral sepals, keeled on reverse. **Petals** subspathulate, clawed, 4.5 cm long, 1.2 cm broad; acute. **Lip** 3-lobed, panduriform, cordate at base, 4 cm long, 1.5 cm broad; side lobes small, upcurved; mid-lobe broad, crisped-undulate; disc bilamellate, verrucose on mid-lobe. **Column** apex winged.

DISTRIBUTION Malaya to Borneo; growing on large trees by lowland rivers.

HISTORY Named for its panduriform (fiddle-shaped) lip by John Lindley in the *Gardeners' Chronicle* (p. 791) of 1853. The type specimen was sent to Lindley in 1853 by the firm of Loddiges who received it from Borneo. *C. pandurata* was crossed with *C. asperata* to produce the popular hybrid *C.* × Burfordiensis which can be easily distinguished by the brown rather than blackish markings on the lip.

CLOSELY RELATED SPECIES Similar to *Coelogyne mayeriana* Rchb.f. which, however, has less compressed pseudobulbs, smaller flowers and a lip whose mid-lobe widens only gradually at the base rather than abruptly as in *C. pandurata*.

C. pandurata is also closely allied to *C. parishii* but is readily distinguished by its larger, more boldly marked flowers and much longer terminal lobe to the lip.

Coelogyne parishii Hooker [Colour Plate]

Pseudobulbs very narrowly conical, yellowish, angled, 10–15 cm long, 0.7 cm in diameter, 2-leaved at apex. **Leaves** elliptic or lanceolate, 18 cm long, 3.5 cm broad, subacute. **Inflorescence** 3- to 5-flowered, drooping or erect. **Flowers** large, 7–7.5 cm across, green to yellow-green; lip bluish-green, blotched with dark purplish-black. **Sepals** lanceolate, 3 cm long, 0.8 cm broad, acute. **Petals** linear-lanceolate, 2.7 cm long, 0.3 cm broad, acute. **Lip** panduriform, 2.3 cm long, 1.6 cm broad; side lobes auriculate; mid-lobe truncate at base, broadly clawed, broader than long, undulate; disc with 4 pectinate ridges on mid-lobe, verrucose on mid-line. **Column** arcuate, 1.5 cm long.

DISTRIBUTION Burma.

HISTORY Described by Sir William Hooker in the *Botanical Magazine* (t. 5323) in 1846. He named it after the Rev. Charles Parish who collected it in Burma and sent the first living plants to Messrs Low of Clapton, England.

CLOSELY RELATED SPECIES This species strikingly resembles *C. pandurata* but is much smaller in all its parts and has narrower lanceolate bracts and distinctive lip ornamentation.

C. brachyptera Rchb.f., from Burma, Thailand and Indo-China, is closely allied but has a quite distinct callus on the lip.

Coelogyne rochussenii De Vries
[Colour Plate]

Pseudobulbs narrowly cylindrical, up to 20 cm long, sulcate, well-spaced on rhizome. **Leaves** oblanceolate to obovate, up to 30 cm long, 11 cm broad, acute or acuminate; petiole 6 cm long. **Inflorescence** heteranthous, slender, pendent, up to 70 cm long, about 40-flowered, with several spaced bracts below lowermost flower. **Flowers** fragrant, lemon-yellow, rather small, up to 3.7 cm across. **Sepals** narrowly lanceolate, 2.5 cm long, 0.5 cm broad, acute. **Petals** narrower than sepals, oblanceolate, 2.5 cm long, 0.3 cm broad, acute. **Lip** 3-lobed, 3 cm long, 1.4 cm broad; side lobes narrowly elliptic, rounded in front, erect; mid-lobe lanceolate, decurved, acuminate; disc bearing 3 toothed rounded keels, the outer 2 reaching the middle of the mid-lobe where they are flanked by additional shorter keels.

DISTRIBUTION Malaya, Sumatra and Borneo, east to the Philippines.

HISTORY Described by Willem De Vries in *Illustrationes des Orchidées des Indes Néerlandaises* (t. 2 & 11) in 1854.

CLOSELY RELATED SPECIES Allied to *C. massangeana* and *C. dayana* but easily distinguished by the shape of its leaves and pseudobulbs, the heteranthous inflorescence and the lanceolate mid-lobe to the lip.

Coelogyne speciosa (Blume) Lindl.
[Colour Plate]

Pseudobulbs ovoid, 2.5–8 cm long, 1-leafed at apex. **Leaf** elliptic or lanceolate, 10–30 cm long, 3–9 cm broad, acute, petiolate. **Inflorescence** drooping, 1- to 3-flowered, proteranthous; bracts deciduous. **Flowers** large, greenish-yellow to pale salmon; lip red-brown or dark brown with a white apex; column white. **Sepals** oblong-lanceolate, 6 cm long, 0.9 cm broad, acute. **Petals** narrowly linear, reflexed, 5 cm long, 0.3 cm broad, acute. **Lip** 3-lobed, 5 cm long, 3 cm broad; side lobes obtuse, toothed; mid-lobe broadly clawed, rounded, erose; disc with 3 compound muricate ridges. **Column** arcuate, 3.5 cm long, dilated at apex.

DISTRIBUTION Java, Malaya, Borneo and Sumatra.

HISTORY Originally described in 1825 in his *Bijdragen* (p. 384, t. 51) by C.L. Blume as *Chelonanthera speciosa* but transferred to *Coelogyne* by John Lindley in *Genera and Species of Orchidaceous Plants* (p. 39) in 1830.

SYNONYM *Chelonanthera speciosa* Blume

CLOSELY RELATED SPECIES Allied to *Coelogyne xyrekes* Ridley, a common plant of mountain forests in Malaya and also found in Thailand. *Coelogyne lawrenceana* Rolfe [Colour Plate] is also allied to *C. speciosa*, being distinguished by its slenderer pseudobulbs, longer inflorescence and larger, distinctly-coloured flowers in which the lip bears 3 or more longitudinal toothed parallel lamellae onto the base of the mid-lobe.

Coelogyne tomentosa Lindl.

Pseudobulbs ovoid to narrowly ovoid, 6 cm long, 3 cm broad. **Leaves** rigid, lanceolate, 30–50 cm long, 2.5–10 cm broad; petiole 8 cm long. **Inflorescence** heteranthous, pendent, 30–45 cm long, many-flowered; basal sheaths loose-fitting; bracts pubescent and persistent. **Flowers** light orange or salmon; lip yellow with brown-streaked side lobes; ovary pubescent. **Sepals** narrowly oblong, 2.5–3.5 cm long, 0.7 cm broad, subacute to acute. **Petals** narrowly oblong-lanceolate, 2.5 cm long, 0.8 cm broad, acute. **Lip** 3-lobed, 2.5 cm long, 1.7 cm broad; side lobes rounded, much shorter than mid-lobe, erect on either side of column; mid-lobe pendent, ovate, acute; disc with 3 papillate keels at base and onto mid-lobe, mid-lobe with 2 additional outer keels.

DISTRIBUTION Malaya, Thailand, Java, Borneo and possibly Sumatra.

HISTORY Described by John Lindley in *Folia Orchidacea* (*Coelogyne*: p. 3) of 1854, based on a specimen collected by Thomas Lobb in Borneo.

CLOSELY RELATED SPECIES Similar to *C. massangeana* but with ovoid rather than elongated pseudobulbs and with deeper coloured flowers.

Comparettia Poepp. & Endl.
Subfamily Epidendroideae
Tribe Oncidieae

Epiphytic plants with slender short rhizomes. **Pseudobulbs** small, 1-leafed. **Leaf** coriaceous. **Inflorescences** basal, simple or branching. **Flowers** small, showy, distant. **Dorsal sepal** free, erect; **lateral sepals** united, forming at the base a long spur-like mentum. **Petals** similar to dorsal sepal but broader. **Lip** clawed, spreading, larger than the other segments, bearing 2 long terete tails at the base which are enclosed within the mentum. **Column** erect, lacking wings or a foot; pollinia 2, waxy, sulcate.

DISTRIBUTION Fewer than 12 species in the American tropics but best represented in the Andes of S. America.

DERIVATION OF NAME Named in honour of Andreo Comparetti, the Professor of Botany at Padua University in Italy. He was an eminent botanist and physiologist and was the first to explain the nature of spirally thickened vessels in wood.

TAXONOMY Described by E.F. Poeppig and S. L. Endlicher in 1835 in *Nova Genera ac Species Plantarum* (p. 42, t. 73).

Comparettia is allied to *Scelochilus* which differs in lacking lamellae on the base of the lip; and to *Ionopsis* differing in its possession of 2 filiform appendages at the base of the lip.

TYPE SPECIES *C. falcata* Poepp. & Endl.

CULTURE Compost A. Winter min. 12–15°C. *Comparettia* species may be grown either in small pots, or mounted on slabs of fern-fibre or cork. They require shady, humid conditions, and should never be allowed to dry out for any length of time.

Comparettia coccinea Lindl. [Colour Plate]

A small lithophytic or epiphytic plant. **Pseudobulbs** oblong-fusiform, compressed, covered by ovate-triangular sheaths at first, 1.5–3 cm long, 0.4–0.8 cm across, 1-leafed at apex. **Leaf** coriaceous, narrowly lanceolate-ligulate, obliquely acute at the apex, attenuate below, 5–9 cm long, 1–1.5 cm broad, dark green above, purple below. **Inflorescence** slender, nodding, simple or rarely somewhat branched, laxly 5- to 10-flowered, 15–20 cm long. **Flowers** showy, spreading or nodding; sepals and petals pale yellow and red with an orange-red margin; lip scarlet. **Dorsal sepal** membranaceous, ovate, acute, 0.8–0.9 cm long, 0.5–0.6 cm broad; **lateral sepals** connate, 0.9 cm long, 0.5 cm broad, produced at the base into an elongate, acute, somewhat arcuate spur, 1.2–1.5 cm long. **Petals** ovate, acute or minutely apiculate, 0.7–0.8 cm long, 0.4–0.5 cm broad. **Lip** deflexed, broadly obcordate, distinctly 3-lobed, 1.5–1.6 cm long, 1.3–1.4 cm broad; side lobes auriculate, subrotund; mid-lobe subquadrate or transversely oblong, emarginate; disc at the base shortly bilamellate; spurs at base of lip arcuate, 0.8 cm long, ciliate. **Column** short, 0.3 cm long, glabrous.

DISTRIBUTION Brazil.

HISTORY *C. coccinea* was first imported from Brazil by Messrs Loddiges in 1837 and was described the following year by John Lindley in the *Botanical Register* (t. 68). It was, however, lost to cultivation for many years until 1865 when it was reintroduced from near Rio de

Janeiro by Ambroise Verschaffelt of Ghent through his correspondent, J. Pinelle.

Comparettia falcata Poepp. & Endl.
[Colour Plate]

A medium-sized, rather variable plant with a very short rhizome. **Pseudobulbs** clustered, oblong-cylindric, compressed somewhat, 1–4 cm long, 1-leafed at apex, covered by 1 to several pairs of distichous ± leaf-bearing sheaths. **Leaf** elliptic to oblong, acute to rounded, 3–18 cm long, 1–5 cm broad. **Inflorescence** basal, much longer than the leaves, arcuate or nodding. 6–90 cm long, racemose or rarely paniculate, laxly 2- to many-flowered. **Flowers** deep rose-pink to pink, marked with white. **Dorsal sepal** elliptic or oblong-ovate, acute, concave, up to 1 cm long, 0.5 cm broad; **lateral sepals** connate, lamina oblong-ovate, concave, bidentate or entire at the apex, extended at the base into a slender decurved spur 1.5 cm long. **Petals** spreading, elliptic, subacute, 1.1 cm long, 0.7 cm broad. **Lip** obscurely 3-lobed, 1.1–1.7 cm long, 1.1 cm broad, with 2 slender capillary spurs at the base within the sepaline spur; side lobes auriculate; mid-lobe broadly oblong, spreading, emarginate. **Column** small, clavate, 0.5 cm long.

DISTRIBUTION   Mexico, south to Bolivia and Brazil and the W. Indies.

HISTORY   Discovered by E.F. Poeppig near Cuchero and between Cassapi and Pampayacu in Peru and described by him and S.L. Endlicher in their *Nova Genera ac Species Plantarum* (1: p. 42, t. 73) in 1836.

SYNONYM   *Comparettia rosea* Lindl.

Comparettia macroplectron Rchb.f. & Triana
[Colour Plate]

A medium-sized epiphytic plant. **Pseudobulbs** very short, 2- to 3-leaved. **Leaves** oblong or oblong-ligulate, obtuse, 10 cm long, 2.3 cm broad. **Inflorescence** racemose, secund, up to about 35 cm long, 4- to about 8-flowered. **Flowers** medium-sized, membranaceous, rose-pink, spotted with rose-purple with a white spur. **Dorsal sepal** ligulate, acute, erect, 1.4 cm long, 0.3 cm broad; **lateral sepals** connate, ligulate, acute, 1.2–1.5 cm long; spur straight, slender-attenuate, up to 5 cm long. **Petals** ovate, apiculate, suberect, 1.3 cm long, 0.7 cm broad. **Lip** clawed, auriculate at base, flabellate-cuneate above, bilobulate, 2.6–3.5 cm long, 2–2.5 cm broad; callus bilamellate at the base of claw. **Column** erect, 0.8 cm long.

DISTRIBUTION   Colombia

HISTORY   Discovered in Colombia by M. Triana and described by him and H.G. Reichenbach in the *Gardeners' Chronicle* (n.s. 10: p. 524) of 1878.

Comparettia speciosa Rchb.f. [Colour Plate]

An epiphytic plant with very short, subcylindric stems sheathed with pale, membranous, acute scales. **Leaves** oblong-lanceolate, acute, 10–25 cm long, up to 4.2 cm broad. **Inflorescences** up to 50 cm long, racemose or branching, laxly 7- to many-flowered towards apex. **Flowers** about 3.5 cm high, bright orange-scarlet; column-wings green, anther white. **Dorsal sepal** ovate, acuminate, 1.4 cm long, 04. cm broad; **lateral sepals** connate, concave, acute; spur slender, obscurely pubescent, up to 3.5 cm long, longer than the pedicel and ovary. **Petals** ovate, acuminate, 1.2 cm long, 0.6 cm broad. **Lip** shortly, narrowly clawed, 3-lobed, up to 2.4 cm long, 3 cm broad; side lobes auriculate; mid-lobe subquadrate to transversely oblong, emarginate, 1.7 cm long. **Column** short, winged, 0.8 cm long; anther beaked.

DISTRIBUTION   Ecuador.

HISTORY   Discovered on the Eastern Cordillera of Ecuador in 1877 by Edward Klaboch who introduced it into cultivation in Europe. H.G. Reichenbach described it the following year in the *Gardeners' Chronicle* (n.s. 10; p. 524).

Coryanthes Hooker
Subfamily Epidendroideae
Tribe Gongoreae
Substribe Stannopeinae

Large epiphytic plants. **Pseudobulbs** short to elongated, fleshy, 2-leaved. **Leaves** large, plicate, prominently nerved. **Inflorescence** lateral, from the base of the pseudobulb, reflexed, racemose, laxly few-flowered. **Flowers** large, complex, showy. **Sepals** free, spreading, large, undulate-flexuous; dorsal sepal shorter than the lateral sepals. **Petals** erect, twisted, smaller than the sepals. **Lip** fleshy, tripartite, longly clawed, spreading; hypochile formed from side lobes, cup-shaped; mesochile elongate, sometimes fluted; epichile large, galeate. **Column** long, terete, apex inflexed-clavate or shortly 2-winged, 2-winged or 2-horned at the base; pollinia 2, waxy.

DISTRIBUTION   Some 15 to 20 species confined to Central and S. America from Guatemala to Peru and Brazil.

DERIVATION OF NAME   From the Greek *korys* (helmet) and *anthos* (flower), in allusion to the shape of the lip epichile.

TAXONOMY   The genus was first described by Sir William Hooker in 1831 in the *Botanical Magazine* (t. 3102).

The complex flowers of *Coryanthes* species are remarkably adapted to pollination by insects. Charles Darwin studied their pollination mechanism obtaining much information from

Dr Crueger's observation of plants in Trinidad. These initial observations have been supplemented by those of P.H. Allen (1951) in the *American Orchid Society Bulletin* and those of C. Dodson summarised in van der Pijl and Dodson, *Orchid Flowers – Their Pollination and Evolution* (1966).

Briefly, in the complex, even grotesque flower of *Coryanthes*, the lip is divided into 3 parts: a globular or hood-shaped hypochile above, an elongate and sometimes fluted mesochile and a bucket-shaped epichile. The epichile is partially filled with a sugary exudate during the last few hours before anthesis by two organs at the base of the column which exude the liquid in drips.

Bees of the genera *Euglossa*, *Euplusia* or *Eulaema* are attracted by the strong odour emitted by the hypochile where they scratch. They soon fall from the hypochile into the water-filled bucket of the epichile from where, because their wings are wetted, they cannot escape by flight. Their only exit is by way of a narrow tunnel between the epichile lip and the column-apex. As they squeeze through this gap they come into contact with and remove the pollinia. When they visit the next flower the process is then repeated and the pollinia are transferred to the stigma of the second flower.

Apparently each species produces a distinctive odour from the lip hypochile thus attracting a different pollinating species of bee and maintaining the specific integrity of each species.

The genus was first revised by R. Schlechter in *Orchis* (1917). He accepted 14 species in two sections and listed an additional three obscure species. Sect. (*Eu*) *Coryanthes* contained those species with a smooth mesochile to the lip including *C. speciosa* Hooker; *C. albertinae* Karst.; whilst in sect. *Lamellunguis* the species such as *C. biflora* Barb. Rodr. and *C. macrantha* (Hooker) Hooker have a mesochile flanked by lamellar outgrowths.

G. Pabst and F. Dungs in *Orchidaceae Brasilienses* (1977) have divided the eight or nine Brazilian species into two groups as follows:

1. *C. maculata* alliance – 6 species having a lip with a smooth mesochile. This corresponds to Schlechter's sect. *Coryanthes*.
2. *C. biflora* alliance – 2 or 3 species having a lip with transverse lamellae on the mesochile. This corresponds to Schlechter's sect. *Lamellunguis*.

Coryanthes species often occur as a conspicuous element in the unique arboreal ant gardens, in the nests of ants of the genera *Camponotus* and *Azteca*, often along with a tufted orange- or purple-flowered *Epidendrum* species, *Peperomia* and Gesneriad species.

TYPE SPECIES   *C. maculata* Hooker

CULTURE Compost A. Temp. Winter min. 15°C. As for *Stanhopea*, but rather warmer. While the plants are growing, they need good humidity and evenly moist roots, with moderate shade. When growth is complete, less water should be given, but plants should not be kept as dry as *Stanhopea* during the resting period.

Coryanthes macrantha (Hooker) Hooker

A medium-sized epiphytic plant. **Pseudobulbs** ± clustered, narrowly ovoid to pyriform-cylindric, 10 cm or more long, 2-leaved at apex. **Leaves** erect-spreading, petiolate, elliptic or oblong-elliptic, acute, plicate, chartaceous, up to 45 cm long, 8 cm broad. **Inflorescence** spreading or pendent, from the base of the pseudobulb, shorter or longer than the leaves, 1-to 3-flowered; bracts large, concave, scarious. **Flowers** large, yellow to orange or red, spotted with red-violet on sepals, petals and epichile of

Coryanthes macrantha
1 – Habit ($\times \frac{1}{10}$)
2 – Flower ($\times \frac{4}{5}$)
3 – Column-apex ($\times 1\frac{1}{3}$)
4 – Pollinia, stipe and viscidium ($\times 2$)

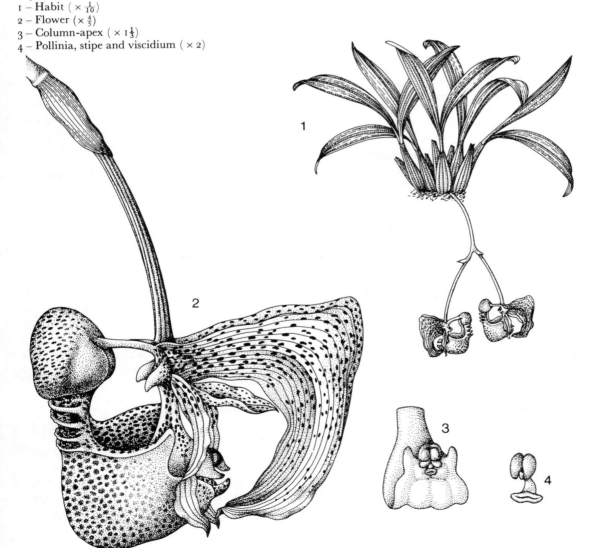

lip. **Sepals** thinly membranaceous; dorsal sepal more or less ovate, obtuse, 5 cm long, 4.5 cm broad; lateral sepals reflexed, ± ovate, acute or acuminate, up to 10 cm long, 5 cm broad. **Petals** thinly membranaceous, linear-oblong, falcate, twisted, acute or obtuse, up to 5.5 cm long. **Lip** complex, divided into a clawed concave hypochile, a semitubular mesochile and a large bucket-like epichile; hypochile 2.5–3.8 cm broad and deep, pubescent in front; mesochile stout, with 3–6 transverse lobulate fleshy lamellae on outside, 2.5 cm long; epichile about 5 cm long and almost as deep, trilobulate in front, almost filled with liquid. **Column** stout, about 4.5 cm long, dilated towards apex, 2-winged at summit, with a pair of oblique glands or horns at the base.

DISTRIBUTION Peru, Venezuela, Trinidad and Guyana: in lowland forest.

HISTORY Discovered near Caracas in Venezuela, by D. Lockhart in 1828 and soon afterwards by James Ankers in the same country. A plant sent by the latter to C.S. Parker flowered in the Liverpool Botanic Garden in 1831. Sir William Hooker described it in 1831 in his *Botanical Miscellany* (t. 80) as *Gongora macrantha* but later that year in the *Botanical Magazine* (t. 3102) transferred it to the genus *Coryanthes*.

SYNONYM *Gongora macrantha* Hooker

Corybas Salisb.

Subfamily Orchidoideae
Tribe Diurideae
Subtribe Acianthinae

Dwarf terrestrial colony-forming herbs growing from ovoid or ellipsoid tubers (root-stem tuberoids). **Leaf** solitary, usually heart-shaped, prostrate, sometimes with white or pink venation. **Inflorescence** 1-flowered, sessile. **Flower** resupinate, small, sitting on the leaf surface, purple or pink and white. **Dorsal sepal** hooded over the column; **lateral sepals** and **petals** often reduced or vestigial, linear. **Lip** larger than the other segments, recurved, entire, tubular at the base, expanded above, often with an erose or lacerate margin, sometimes 2-spurred at the base. **Column** short, fleshy; pollinia 4, in 2 pairs, with a viscidium; stigma entire.

DISTRIBUTION A genus of perhaps 100 species widespread from the Himalayas through S.E. Asia to the Pacific Islands and Australia. The centre of diversity is the island of New Guinea.

DERIVATION OF NAME From *Korybas*, a priest of the goddess Cybele or a drunken man, from the fanciful resemblance of the flower to the head of either.

TAXONOMY The genus was described by R. Salisbury in 1807 in his *Paradisus Londinensis* (t. 83). However, for the next century it was better known by the later Robert Brown name of *Corysanthes* (1810). *Corybas* is most closely allied to *Acianthus* but is distinguished by its solitary helmet-shaped sessile flowers.

The S.E. Asian species of *Corybas* have recently been revised by John Dransfield *et al.* (1985) in the *Kew Bulletin* (p. 575); the species from New Guinea and adjacent islands by P. van Royen (1983) in *The Genus Corybas in its Eastern Areas;* and the Australian species by David Jones (1988) in his *Native Orchids of Australia* (pp. 314–322). Only the Australian and New Zealand species are at all likely to be seen in cultivation.

TYPE SPECIES *C. aconitiflorus* Salisb.

SYNONYM *Corysanthes* Lindl.

CULTURE As for *Acianthus*. Keep moist and

shady during the growing season and avoid severe drying when dormant.

Corybas diemenicus (Lindl.) Rupp
[Colour Plate]

A tiny colony-forming terrestrial. **Leaf** prostrate, fleshy, heart-shaped or ovate, acute to obtuse, 1.5–2.5 cm long, 1–2 cm wide, green. **Flower** up to 1.6 cm tall, purple with a white throat; ovary 6–7 mm long. **Dorsal sepal** strongly hooded, porrect, obovate, obtuse, 2–2.4 cm long, 1.2–1.5 cm wide; **lateral sepals** and **petals** filiform, acuminate, 3–5 mm long, 1 mm wide. **Lip** strongly recurved, almost circular, emarginate, strongly dentate on the margins, 1.5–1.6 cm long and wide, glabrous, basal auricles tubular, open at the apex.

DISTRIBUTION Australia: southern New South Wales to S. Australia and Tasmania; in fern gullies, sheltered slopes, and other moist protected sites in woodland and heathland; sea level to 1000 m.

HISTORY John Lindley described this pretty miniature in 1840 as *Corysanthes diemenica* in his *Genera and Species of Orchidaceous Plants* (p. 393) based on a Gunn collection from Tasmania. It was transferred to the present genus by the Rev. Rupp in 1928 in the *Proceedings of the Linnean Society of New South Wales* (p. 55). This is one of the easiest species to grow and flower.

SYNONYMS *Corysanthes diemenica* Lindl.; *C. dilatatus* Rupp & Nicholls; *Corybas dilatatus* (Rupp & Nicholls) Rupp

Corymborkis Thou.
Subfamily Spiranthoideae
Tribe Erythrodeae
Subtribe Tropidiinae

Terrestrial herbs with short, sympodial, creeping, subterranean rhizomes: roots fasciculate, wiry. **Stems** erect, terete, unbranched, leafy, rather woody, bamboo-like. **Leaves** plicate, distichous or apparently spirally arranged, sessile or shortly petiolate, sheathing at the base. **Inflorescences** axillary, paniculate, few- to many-flowered. **Flowers** distichously arranged, often not opening widely, white, pale green or yellow, fragrant, sometimes quite showy; pedicels short, twisted to make flowers appear secundly arranged. **Sepals** and **petals** subsimilar, narrow, clawed, basally connivent. **Lip** spathulate, with 2 longitudinal keels, embracing the column below. **Column** elongate, slender, straight, more or less terete, with 2 apical auricles; rostellum erect, bifid; pollinia 2, sectile, obovoid, with slender caudicles and a peltate viscidium.

DISTRIBUTION A small pantropical genus of about five species.

DERIVATION OF NAME From the Greek *corymbos* (corymb) and *orchis* (orchid), referring to the inflorescence of the type species.

TAXONOMY This genus was established by the French botanist Aubert du Petit Thouars in 1822 in his *Orchidées des Iles Australes d'Afrique* (t. 37, 38). *Corymborkis* is a primitive genus most closely allied to *Tropidia* but differing in its unbranched stems, lateral branched inflorescences, elongated flowers, free lateral sepals, spathulate lip and elongate column. The genus was revised by F. Rasmussen (1977) in *Botanisk Tidsskrift* (p. 161). It is very rarely seen in cultivation.

TYPE SPECIES *C. corymbis* Thou.

SYNONYMS include *Hysteria* Reinw.; *Rynchanthera* Bl.; *Chloidia* Lindl.

CULTURE Temp. Winter min. 15°C. Grow as for *Cephalantheropsis* in deep shade. On transfer the roots should not be allowed to dry out.

Corymborkis veratrifolia (Reinw.) Bl.

A tall terrestrial plant 40–310 cm tall. **Leaves** plicate, lanceolate to ovate-elliptic, acuminate, 15–50 cm long, 3–14 cm wide, the margins sometimes undulate. **Inflorescences** erect to drooping, 2- to 9-branched, up to 15 cm long, few- to 70-flowered; peduncle often flattened, up to 14 cm long, hidden in leaf sheaths; bracts ovate to lanceolate, acuminate or apiculate, 3–11 mm long. **Flowers** very variable in size, white or pale green, fragrant, tubular or campanulate; pedicel and ovary 6–13 mm long. **Sepals** spathulate, acute or obtuse, 1.6–5.3 cm long, 0.25–0.6 cm wide. **Petals** curved outwards, obliquely linear-spathulate, acute, up to 5 cm long, 0.2–0.8 cm wide. **Lip** clawed, spathulate, acute, obtuse or mucronate at the apex, 1.6–4.8 cm long, 0.5–1.4 cm wide; callus of 2 fleshy divergent ridges onto the base of the apical lamina. **Column** 1.4–4.5 cm long.

DISTRIBUTION Tropical Asia from India across to the Pacific Islands (Solomon Islands to Samoa); lowland to montane tropical forest on limestone etc. in deep shade; sea level to 2000 m.

HISTORY The Dutch botanist Reinwardt originally described this species as *Hysteria veratrifolia* in 1825 in his *Nova Plantarum Indicarum Genera* (vol. 2: 5). Carl Blume transferred it to *Corymborkis* in 1859 in his *Collection des Orchidées les plus remarquables de l'archipel Indien et du Japon* (p. 125).

SYNONYMS include *Hysteria veratrifolia* Reinw.; *Corymbis veratrifolia* (Reinw.) Rchb.f.; *Rynchanthera paniculata* Bl.; *Corymbis disticha* (Breda) Lindl.; *Corymborchis assamica* Bl.; *C. rhytidocarpa* Hook.f.

Cranichis Sw.
Subfamily Orchidoideae
Tribe Cranichideae
Subtribe Cranichidinae

Terrestrial or epiphytic erect herbs, often with a short creeping rhizome; roots usually fasciculate. **Leaves** in a basal rosette or along the stem, membraneous, sessile or petiolate. **Inflorescences** erect, spicate, laxly to densely few- to many-flowered; peduncle slender. **Flowers** small, non-resupinate. **Sepals** free, subsimilar, the laterals oblique, **petals** smaller, slender, free. **Lip** uppermost in flower, more or less concave, somewhat saccate at the base, sessile or clawed, entire. **Column** short or very short, with a large rostellum; pollinia 2 but deeply divided, pyriform, pulverulent, with a globose viscidium.

DISTRIBUTION A genus of some 30 species in tropical Central and S. America.

DERIVATION OF NAME From the Greek *kranos* (helmet), an allusion to the concave helmet-like lip that projects above the column.

TAXONOMY Olof Swartz established this genus in his *Prodromus* (p. 120) in 1788. It is most closely allied to *Pterichis* but differs in that the inflorescence is terminal, the leaves are present at flowering and the thin-textured flower has a cochleate lip and cyathiform clinandrium.

TYPE SPECIES *C. muscosa* Sw. (lectotype).

CULTURE Temp. Winter min. 10–12°C Cultivation generally as for the terrestrial bromheadias and the other woodland plants.

Cranichis muscosa Sw.

A variable species in size, up to 50 cm tall. **Leaves** up to 7 in a basal rosette, elliptic to ovate-elliptic, acute to subobtuse, 5–10 cm long, 2.5–5 cm wide, with an elongate conduplicate petiole, up to 10 cm long. **Inflorescences** erect, laxly to densely few- to many-flowered; peduncle slender to stout, with 3–4 remote sheaths along length; spike 3–15 cm long; bracts lanceolate to ovate, acuminate, shorter than the ovaries. **Flowers** white or sometimes flushed with pink, with green or dark purple spots on the lip; ovary up to 8 mm long. **Dorsal sepal** elliptic-lanceolate, cucullate, acute, 3–4 mm long, 1.5 mm wide; **lateral sepals** obliquely ovate-lanceolate, acute, 3–4 mm long, 2 mm wide. **Petals** linear, acute to obtuse, 2–3 mm long, 0.5 mm wide. **Lip** sessile, cucullate, obovate to broadly ovate, obtuse to acute, 3.5–4 mm long, 2 mm wide. **Column** 1.5–2 mm long.

DISTRIBUTION Florida, the W. Indies, Central and S. America, south to Peru and Brazil; in forest and scrub, up to 1700 m.

Cranichis muscosa
1 – Habit (× $\frac{4}{5}$)
2 – Flower (× $5\frac{1}{2}$)

HISTORY Olof Swartz discovered this orchid in Jamaica and described it in 1788 in his *Nova Genera et Species Plantarum Prodromus* (p. 120).
SYNONYM *C. bradei* Schltr.

Cremastra Lindl.

Subfamily Epidendroideae
Tribe Calypsoeae
Subtribe Corallorhizinae

Terrestrial plants with clustered, ovoid, 1- or rarely 2-leaved pseudobulbs. **Leaves** plicate, erect or suberect, subtended by a tubular sheath. **Inflorescence** lateral, erect, unbranched, laxly to densely few- to many-flowered. **Flowers** pendent, narrowly tubular. **Sepals** and **petals** linear-spathulate, free, not spreading. **Lip** free, slender, 3-lobed, slightly saccate at the base, callose. **Column** elongate, slender-clavate; pollinia 4, appressed in 2 pairs, attached directly to a semicircular viscidium.
DISTRIBUTION A small genus of one or two species only, widely distributed in the mountains of S.E. Asia and at lower altitudes in temperate E. Asia.
DERIVATION OF NAME From the Greek *kremastra* (flower stalk), descriptive of the conspicuous pedicellate ovary.
TAXONOMY *Cremastra* was established by John Lindley in 1833 in his *Genera and Species of Orchidaceous Plants* (p. 172). It is most closely related to genera such as *Govenia* and *Oreorchis* but is readily distinguished by its flower that does not open widely and has long slender segments.
TYPE SPECIES *C. wallichiana* Lindl.
CULTURE Temp. Winter min. 12–15°C. Cultivation as for calanthes and terrestrial bromheadias.

Cremastra appendiculata (D. Don) Makino
[Colour Plate]
A terrestrial with ovoid uni- or bifoliate pseudobulbs, 1.5–2 cm tall, 2 cm in diameter. **Leaves** erect, narrowly elliptic, lanceolate to oblanceolate, acuminate, 15–40 cm long, 4–12.5 cm wide, shortly petiolate. **Inflorescences** 1–2, secund, 8- to 20-flowered, 20–40 cm long; peduncle purple; bracts linear-lanceolate, acuminate, 7–10 mm long, longer than the ovary. **Flowers** pendent, strongly fragrant; sepals and petals pinkish, purplish or buff; lip white, marked with purple on surface. **Sepals** linear-spathulate, acute, 3–3.5 cm long, 4.5–5 mm wide. **Petals** similar. **Lip** 3-lobed on apical part, 3–3.5 cm long; side lobes erect, falcate, acute, 9 mm long; mid-lobe oblong-ovate, acute; callus smooth, extending to the basal part of the mid-lobe, obscurely 3-lobed in front. **Column** 2.5–3 cm long, slightly clavate, 3-lobed at the apex.
DISTRIBUTION Widespread in E. and S.E. Asia from Nepal and N. India to Japan and Taiwan; 1000–2600 m.
HISTORY Originally described as *Cymbidium appendiculatum* by David Don in 1826 in his *Prodromus Florae Nepalensis* (p. 36) based on material collected in Nepal by Nathaniel Wallich. It was transferred to the present genus by Makino in 1904 in the *Botanical Magazine of Tokyo* (p. 24).
SYNONYMS *Cymbidium appendiculatum* D. Don; *Cremastra wallichiana* Lindl.; *C. triloba* Makino

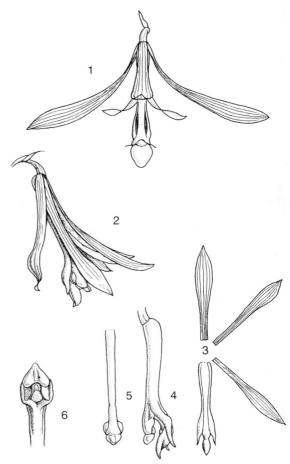

Cremastra appendiculata
1 – Flower, from above (× 1)
1 – Flower, side view (× 1)
3 – Dorsal sepal, petal, lateral sepal and lip (× $\frac{3}{4}$)
4 – Column and lip, side view (× 1)
5 – Column (× 1)
6 – Column apex, ventral view (× 2)

Cryptarrhena R. Br.

Subfamily Epidendroideae
Tribe Cryptarrheneae

Small epiphytes with short leafy stems or with small bilaterally compressed pseudobulbs. **Leaves** distichous, imbricate, coriaceous. **Inflorescences** axillary or basal, unbranched, several-flowered. **Flowers** small. **Sepals** similar, free, spreading, more or less concave. **Petals** similar but smaller than the sepals. **Lip** with a distinct fleshy claw; apical lamina 4-lobed with linear or triangular ovate lobes. **Column** short, dilated above, lacking wings or a foot; pollinia 4 in pairs, waxy.
DISTRIBUTION A small genus of some

four species in tropical Central and S. America and the W. Indies.

DERIVATION OF NAME   From the Greek *kryptos* (hidden) and *arrhen* (stamen), in allusion to the apex of the column which hides the anther.

TAXONOMY   John Lindley described *Cryptarrhena* in 1816 in the *Botanical Register* (t. 153). A key to the accepted species is given by Dressler in 1980 in the journal *Orquidea* (*Mex.*) (p. 288).

TYPE SPECIES   *C. lunata* R. Br.

SYNONYMS   *Clynhymenia* A. Rich. & Gal.; *Orchidofunckia* A. Rich. & Gal.

CULTURE   Temp. Winter min. 12°C. Requires shady humid conditions with even moisture through the year. May be grown mounted or in pots for larger specimens.

Cryptarrhena lunata R. Br. [Colour Plate]

A small epiphyte with a short creeping rhizome and clustered leafy short stems. **Leaves** distichous, erect to spreading, linear to linear-oblanceolate or narrowly elliptic, acute to acuminate, 5–22 cm long, 0.8–2.2 cm wide, articulated to a conduplicate base. **Inflorescences** axillary, laxly many-flowered, 10–30 cm long; peduncle slender, bearing inflated scarious sheaths at the nodes; bracts reflexed, narrowly triangular-lanceolate, 3–7 mm long. **Flowers** small, fleshy, with green sepals and petals and a yellow lip; pedicel and ovary slender, 3–8 mm long. **Sepals** elliptic to elliptic-lanceolate, shortly acuminate or apiculate, 4–5.5 mm long, 1.5–2 mm wide. **Petals** obliquely obovate, rounded to acute, 3.5–4 mm long, 2 mm wide. **Lip** 4-lobed with a prominent fleshy claw, 5 mm long, 6 mm wide; claw 1.5–2.5 m long, with a broad erect flap-like callus on upper side; lamina with 2 short subquadrate basal lobes and 2 longer linear recurved 3–3.5 mm long apical ones. **Column** c. 3 mm long.

DISTRIBUTION   Widespread from Mexico to northern S. America and also in Trinidad and Jamaica, in lowland and lower montane rain forest up to 650 m.

HISTORY   Originally described by Robert Brown in the *Botanical Register* (t. 153) in 1816 based on a specimen from Jamaica cultivated by Messrs Lee and Kennedy of Hammersmith.

SYNONYMS   *Clynhymenia pallidiflora* A. Rich. & Gal.; *Cryptarrhena kegelii* Rchb.f.; *C. unguiculata* Schltr.; *C. brasiliensis* Brade

Cryptochilus Wall.

Subfamily Epidendroideae
Tribe Epidendreae
Subfamily Eriinae

Epiphytic or lithophytic herbs with short creeping rhizomes. **Pseudobulbs** clustered, ovoid to ellipsoid-cylindrical, subtended by imbricate sheaths when young, 2-leaved at the apex. **Leaves** suberect, conduplicate, lanceolate or oblanceolate, acuminate or acute. **Inflorescence** terminal, erect, simple, densely few- to many-flowered; bracts elongate, setose. **Flowers** campanulate, yellow or red, suberect, borne distichously in 2 rows; ovary pubescent. **Sepals** united in the basal two-thirds or three-quarters, with free acute tips, pubescent on the outside. **Petals** hidden within sepals, free. **Lip** articulated to the free apex of the column-foot, simple. **Column** short, apically erose or with elongate stelidia; foot short, free; pollinia 8, attached to a small viscidium.

DISTRIBUTION   A small genus of two species in the Himalayas.

DERIVATION OF NAME   From the Greek *kryptos* (hidden) and *cheilos* (lip), a reference to the campanulate flowers in which the lip is hidden.

TAXONOMY   Nathaniel Wallich established this distinctive genus in 1826 in his *Tentamen Florae Napalensis Illustratae* (p. 36). It is allied to *Eria* but is readily distinguished by its distichously arranged, campanulate, brightly coloured flowers.

TYPE SPECIES   *C. sanguineus* Wall.

CULTURE   Temp. Winter min. 10–12°C. May be mounted or, preferably, grown in pots. As a relative of *Eria*, the roots are fine and should not be allowed to dry out at any time. General conditions should be kept humid and shady especially during growth. Flower stems appear from the young growths.

Cryptochilus sanguineus Wall. [Colour Plate]

An epiphyte or lithophyte with a short creeping rhizome and ovoid to ellipsoid pseudobulbs, 1.5–6 cm long, 0.7–1.8 cm in diameter. **Leaves** narrowly elliptic to oblanceolate, acuminate, 10–26 cm long, 1.8–4.2 cm wide, petiolate; petiole slender, up to 5 cm long. **Inflorescence** produced as the new leaves develop, densely 8- to 28-flowered, 14–28 cm long; bracts erect, linear-lanceolate, acuminate, 7–23 mm long. **Flowers** suberect, produced in 2 rows pointing the same way, red with a darker apical margin, pubescent on the outside, the lip yellow; pedicel and ovary 3–5 mm long, densely shortly pubescent. **Sepals** united almost to the tips to form a tubular elongate perianth with 3 free acute tips,

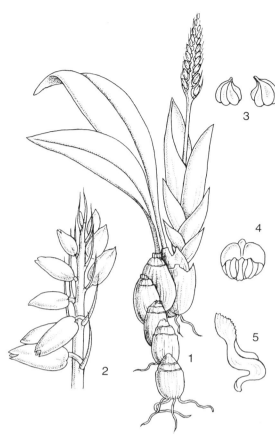

Cryptochilus sanguineus
1 – Habit ($\times \frac{3}{10}$)
2 – Inflorescence ($\times$ 1)
3 – Pollinia ($\times$ 10)
4 – Anther ($\times$ 10)
5 – Lip, side view ($\times$ 5)

12–22 mm long, 5 mm in diameter, slightly gibbous at the base of the lateral sepals. **Petals** oblanceolate, apiculate, 8 mm long, 3 mm wide. **Lip** oblong, obtuse, slightly recurved, with erect sides, 7–8 mm long, 3–4 mm wide. **Column** 10 mm long; foot 3 mm long, incurved.

DISTRIBUTION   N.E. India, Sikkim, Bhutan and Burma; 1300–2300 m.

HISTORY   First collected by Nathaniel Wallich on Mt Chandaghiry in Nepal and described by him in 1826 in his *Tentamen Florae Napalensis Illustratae* (t. 26).

CLOSELY RELATED SPECIES   *C. luteus* Lindl., from the same region, is similar but has shorter yellow flowers.

Cryptopus Lindl.
Subfamily Epidendroideae
Tribe Vandeae
Subtribe Angraecinae

Epiphytic plants with elongate monopodial branched or unbranched leafy stems. **Leaves** coriaceous, distichous, articulated to persistent coriaceous sheathing leaf bases. **Inflorescences** lateral, emerging through the leaf sheaths opposite the leaves, racemose or paniculate, few- to many-flowered, longer than the leaves. **Flowers** showy, white marked sometimes with yellow or red on the lip; column green or yellow. **Sepals** free, subsimilar, lanceolate. **Petals** free, lobed, somewhat resembling the lip in shape. **Lip** 3- or 4-lobed. **Column** short, fleshy; rostellum trilobed, the mid-lobe slightly longer than the side lobes; pollinia 2, each attached by an elastic caudicle to a viscidium.
DISTRIBUTION   A small genus of three species only in Madagascar and the Mascarene Islands.
DERIVATION OF NAME   From the Greek *kryptos* (hidden) and *pous* (foot), given because the author thought that the stipe and viscidia were hidden in a pouch.
TAXONOMY   John   Lindley   established *Cryptopus* in 1824 in the *Botanical Register* (sub t. 817). It is allied to *Angraecum* but readily distinguished by its remarkable lobed petals and similarly lobed lip and its trilobed rostellum.
TYPE SPECIES   *C. elatus* (Thou.) Lindl.
CULTURE   Temp. Winter min. 15°C. Young plants may be grown in pots but as the stem elongates a vertical mount is useful. The plants require moderate humidity and shade with careful watering throughout the year.

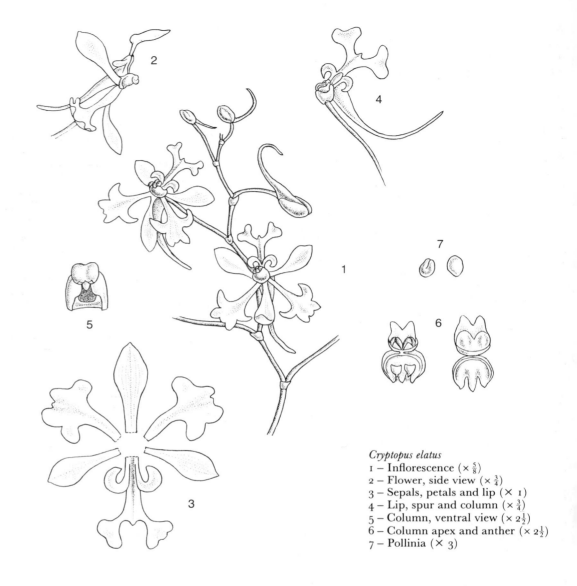

Cryptopus elatus
1 – Inflorescence ($\times \frac{5}{8}$)
2 – Flower, side view ($\times \frac{3}{4}$)
3 – Sepals, petals and lip ($\times$ 1)
4 – Lip, spur and column ($\times \frac{3}{4}$)
5 – Column, ventral view ($\times 2\frac{1}{2}$)
6 – Column apex and anther ($\times 2\frac{1}{2}$)
7 – Pollinia ($\times$ 3)

Cryptopus elatus (Thou.) Lindl.
[Colour Plate]

An erect climbing epiphyte with a long stem up to 50 cm or more long, 4–5 mm in diameter; roots emitted along the stem, emerging through the leaf bases. **Leaves** oblong or elliptic, unequally obtusely bilobed at the apex, 2.5–7 cm long, 1.2–1.6 cm wide. **Inflorescences** erect, 30–60 cm long, 7- to 13-flowered, unbranched or with 1–3 short branches; peduncle elongate, terete; bracts amplexicaul, obtuse, 2–3 mm long. **Flowers** white or creamy-white, sometimes with red markings on the base of the lip; pedicel and ovary 2–3 cm long. **Sepals** spathulate, obtuse or subacute, 1.5–2 mm long. **Petals** 2–2.5 cm long, 1.5 cm wide across apex, longly clawed, unequally 4-lobed at the apex, the 2 outer lobules recurved, the 2 middle ones obliquely ovate. **Lip** 3-lobed, 1.4–1.6 cm long, 2.2–2.5 cm wide across the apical lobules; side

lobes basal, strongly recurved, oblong, ovate, acute, 5–6 mm long; mid-lobe narrowly longly clawed, the apical lamina transversely oblong, shortly apiculate, bilobed, each lobe bilobulate. **Column** short, 5 mm long, green.
DISTRIBUTION   Mascarene Islands only: Mauritius and Réunion; in open situations on the trunks of trees and shrubs throughout the islands.
HISTORY   This strange orchid was first collected by the French botanist Aubert du Petit Thouars on Mauritius and was described by him as *Angraecum elatum* in his *Orchidées des Iles Australes de l'Afrique* (t. 79, 80). Lindley's new genus *Cryptopus* which was established in 1824 in the *Botanical Register* (sub t. 817) was based on this species.
SYNONYMS   *Angraecum elatum* Thou.; *Beclardia elata* (Thou.) A. Rich.

Cryptostylis R. Br.
Subfamily Spiranthoideae
Tribe Cranichideae
Subtribe Cryptostylidinae

Terrestrial plants with short rhizomes and thick spreading roots, rarely saprophytic. **Leaves** solitary, emerging directly from the rhizome, erect, stalked, ovate. **Inflorescences** erect, emerging from the rhizome, unbranched; laxly few- to many-flowered; peduncle terete, elongate. **Flowers** non-resupinate, more or less flat. **Sepals** and **petals** free, subsimilar, linear-lanceolate, acuminate, spreading. **Lip** much larger than the other segments, erect, entire, concave at base, often convex above; lacking a spur and callus. **Column** very short; pollinia 4, mealy, attached to a terminal viscidium; stigma prominent, entire, fleshy.

DISTRIBUTION   A genus of some 15 species in tropical Asia from India across to the Pacific Islands and Australia.

DERIVATION OF NAME   From the Greek *kryptos* (hidden) and *stylis* (style), in allusion to the column which is enclosed by the base of the lip.

TAXONOMY   Robert Brown established *Cryptostylis* in 1810 in his *Prodromus Florae Novae Hollandiae* (p. 317). It is a distinctive genus with spidery non-resupinate flowers and apparently has no close allies.

The five Australian species and their cultivation are discussed by Jones (1988) in his *Native Orchids of Australia* and also by Elliot and Jones (1984) in the *Encyclopedia of Australian Plants* (p. 128).

TYPE SPECIES   Not designated.

CULTURE   Temp. Winter min. 12°C. Compost as for *Acianthus*. Flowers in spring and early summer and should not be kept completely dry when the leaves fade, because the plants have fleshy roots rather than tubers.

Cryptostylis arachnites (Bl.) Hassk.

[Colour Plate]

A creeping terrestrial, 20–60 cm tall, with a subterranean rhizome. **Leaves** erect, ovate, acute, 12–17 cm long, 4–7.5 cm wide, green with darker venation; petiole slender, 5–15 cm long, spotted with purple. **Inflorescence** erect, laxly 3- to 12-flowered; rhachis up to 30 cm long; bracts lanceolate, acuminate, 1–1.2 cm long. **Flowers** non-resupinate, the sepals and petals green or flushed with red, the lip velvety red with darker spots; pedicel and ovary 12–15 mm long. **Sepals** linear, acute, 1.4–1.6 cm long, 2–2.5 mm wide, with the margins recurved. **Petals** linear, acute, 0.8–1 cm long, 1.5–2 mm wide. **Lip** erect, somewhat sigmoid in side view, ovate, acute, 1.5–2 cm long, 5–7 mm wide, papillate-hairy. **Column** 2 mm long.

DISTRIBUTION   Widespread from peninsular Malaya through the Malay Archipelago to the S.W. Pacific islands; in deep shade in lower montane and montane mossy forest; up to 1500 m.

HISTORY   Originally described as *Zosterostylis arachnites*, based on a Javanese plant, by Carl Blume in 1825 in his *Bijdragen* (p. 419). It was transferred to *Cryptostylis* by Hasskarl in his *Catalogus Bogoriensis* (p. 8) in 1844.

SYNONYMS   *Zosterostylis arachnites* Bl.; *Cryptostylis stenochila* Schltr.

Cryptostylis subulata (Labill.) Rchb.f.

A terrestrial plant, often forming colonies, with fleshy roots. **Leaves** leathery, stiffly erect, ovate-lanceolate, acute, 5–15 cm long, 1–3 cm wide, yellow-green; petioles up to 8 cm long. **Inflorescence** erect, 20–80 cm tall, laxly 2- to 20-flowered; bracts 6–16 mm long. **Flowers** 2.5–3.5 cm long, reddish-brown, the lip with 2 longitudinal purple ridges ending in a projecting bilobed callus; pedicel and ovary 15–17 mm long. **Dorsal sepal** reflexed against ovary, linear, acuminate, 2.5–2.8 cm long, 1.5–2.5 mm wide; **lateral sepals** spreading, linear, acuminate 2.2–2.5 cm long, 1–2 mm wide. **Petals** erect, recurved in apical half, linear, acuminate, 1.5–1.6 cm long, 1 mm wide. **Lip** convex, oblong-lanceolate, obtuse, 2.5–3.2 cm long, 9–11 mm wide, the margins recurved, the inner surface glandular hairy. **Column** 3 mm long.

DISTRIBUTION   Australia; from S. Queensland to Victoria, S. Australia and Tasmania; common in marshes and swamps and in moist sandy soil amongst rocks in open woodland.

HISTORY   Originally described by the French botanist Labillardière in *Novae Hollandiae Plantarum* (2: 62) as *Malaxis subulata* and subsequently transferred to *Cryptostylis* by H.G. Reichenbach in *Beitrage zur systematische Pflanzenkunde* (p. 15) in 1871.

This is the easiest of the Australian species to grow and flower. It prefers an open mix of loam, sand and leaf litter.

SYNONYMS   *Malaxis subulata* Labill.; *Cryptostylis longifolia* R. Br.

Cuitlauzina La Llave & Lex.

Subfamily Epidendroideae
Tribe Oncidieae

Epiphytic plants with ovoid, compressed anciptious pseudobulbs, 2-leaved at the apex. **Leaves** ligulate, subcoriaceous, subtended by a few imbricate sheaths. **Inflorescences** basal, pendent, simple, few- to many-flowered. **Flowers** showy, fragrant, more or less flat. **Sepals** free, spreading, subsimilar. **Petals** free, spreading, similar to but broader than the petals. **Lip** deflexed, at an obtuse angle to the column, narrowly clawed, the apical lamina flat, transversely oblong-reniform, bilobed, with a prominent callus on the claw. **Column** short, erect, with 2 lateral wings and hooded above; pollinia 2, attached by a stipe to a viscidium.

DISTRIBUTION   A monotypic genus endemic to Mexico.

DERIVATION OF NAME   Named in honour of Cuitlauhuatzin, the Governor of Itzapalapa in Mexico.

HISTORY   This monotypic genus was established by La Llave and Lexarza in 1824 in their *Novarum Vegetabilium Descriptiones Orchidianum Opusculum* (p. 33) based on *C. pendula*. It was, however, subsequently overlooked as the species was redescribed by European botanists as a species of *Odontoglossum*, *Oncidium* and *Lichterveldia*.

Halbinger resurrected *Cuitlauzina* in 1975 in the journal *Orquidea* (*Mex.*) (p. 3) and it has subsequently been widely adopted despite its tongue-twisting pronunciation. He distinguished it from allied genera such as *Ticoglossum* and *Osmoglossum* because of its pendulous inflorescence, short 3-winged lip, and clawed lip lacking basal side lobes.

In orchid hybrid registration it is still referred to the genus *Odontoglossum*.

TYPE SPECIES   *C. pendula* La Llave & Lex.

SYNONYMS   *Lichterveldia* Lemaire

CULTURE   Temp. Winter min. 10°C. Grows well in a standard epiphyte mix, but should be hung up or grown in a basket as the long inflorescences are pendent and arise at the base of the new growths in the spring. Water well during growth, then give a cool dry rest.

Cuitlauzina pendula La Llave & Lex.

[Colour Plate]

An epiphyte with ovoid, compressed, ancipitous pseudobulbs, 10–15 cm long, 5–7.5 cm wide, 2-leaved at the apex. **Leaves** coriaceous, broadly ligulate, acute, 12–30 cm long, 3 cm wide. **Inflorescences** basal, pendent, simple, up to 1 m long, laxly 2- to 22-flowered; bracts elliptic, cucullate, acute, 3–5 mm long. **Flowers** showy, very fragrant, flat, 6–7.5 cm across, the sepals and petals white, sometimes tinged pink at the base, the lip white to rose-pink, the callus yellow with red spotting; pedicel and ovary 1–1.5 cm long. **Sepals** obovate to ovate-elliptic, rounded or retuse at the apex, 2.3–2.6 cm long, up to 1.5 cm wide. **Petals** elliptic to subcircular, rounded to emarginate at the apex, 2–2.8 cm long, 1–2.5 cm wide, undulate on margins. **Lip** with a narrow claw, the apical lamina transversely reniform, emarginate, 2.2–2.3 cm long, 2.8–4 cm wide; callus fleshy, auriculate at base, concave, bilobed at apex. **Column** short, erect, 7–8 mm long, with 2 lateral obovate, erose wings near the apex.

DISTRIBUTION   Mexico.

HISTORY   This beautiful orchid, which has long been a favourite in collections, was discovered at Jesus del Monte, near Valladolid, Mexico by La Llave and Lexarza who described it in their *Novarum Vegetabilium Descriptiones Orchidianum Opusculum* (p. 33). James Bateman transferred it to *Odontoglossum* in his *Monograph of Odontoglossum* (t. 6) in 1874. For many years this orchid was best known under the Lindley name *Odontoglossum citrosmum* but that name is now recognised as a later synonym.

SYNONYMS   *Odontoglossum citrosmum* Lindl.; *O. pendulum* (La Llave & Lex.) Batem.; *Lichterveldia lindleyi* Lem.; *Oncidium citrosmum* (Lindl.) Beer; *O. galeottianum* Drap.

Cyclopogon Presl

Subfamily Spiranthoideae
Tribe Cranichideae
Subtribe Spiranthinae

Small to medium-sized terrestrial herbs with short fleshy roots. **Leaves** basal, lanceolate, petiolate, lacking prominent venation. **Inflorescence** erect below but limp above, spicate, laxly to densely many-flowered, often secund; peduncle and rhachis pubescent; bracts lanceolate, acuminate. **Flowers** small, mostly green or green and white, pubescent on outer surface, segments not spreading. **Dorsal sepal** porrect, adnate to the hyaline petals over the column; **lateral sepals** similar to dorsal sepal, forming at the base an obscure ventricose mentum. **Lip** pandurate to narrowly oblong, often dilated towards apex and ± 3-lobed at the ± deflexed apex, with a fleshy auricle in the form of a hook on each side at the base. **Column** porrect, ± pubescent on ventral surface; rostellum acute, bifid; pollinia clavate, 4 in 2 closely appressed pairs.
DISTRIBUTION   About 70 species in Florida, Central and S. America and the W. Indies but principally in Brazil.
DERIVATION OF NAME   From the Greek *kyklos* (circle) and *pogon* (beard), apparently an allusion to the pubescent sepals which resemble a circle of beards around the flower when viewed from in front.
TAXONOMY   *Cyclopogon* was described by K.B. Presl in 1827 in *Reliquiae Haenkeanae* (p. 93). Many authors have subsequently included it in the genus *Spiranthes* but R. Schlechter, who revised the Spiranthinae in 1920 in *Beihefte zum Botanischen Zentralblatt* and accepted *Cyclopogon* as a distinct genus, is followed here.
    Cyclopogon is allied to *Pelexia*, *Sarcoglottis*, etc. but is distinguished by its short column-base and obscure mentum, its rather limp rhachis and the pale thin lip of the flower.
TYPE SPECIES   *C. ovalifolium* Presl.
CULTURE   Compost A. Temp. Winter min. 12–15°C. *Cyclopogon* species require humid and well-shaded conditions, and should be carefully watered throughout the year. After flowering, the leaves may die down, in which case less water should be given until the new growths are well started.

Cyclopogon elatus (Sw.) Schltr.

A very variable terrestrial or rarely epiphytic herb with fascicled, stout, tuberous roots. **Leaves** basal, rosulate, 2 or more, petiolate, broadly ovate to oblong-lanceolate, acute or acuminate, up to 20 cm long, 5.8 cm broad. **Inflorescence** erect, racemose, laxly to densely few- to many-flowered, up to 23 cm long; peduncle glabrous below, pubescent above.

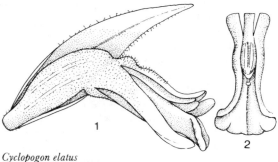

Cyclopogon elatus
1 – Flower, side view (× 4⅓)
2 – Lip from above (× 4⅓)

Flowers small, pubescent, white, greenish, brownish or reddish, rarely striped with violet. **Dorsal sepal** lanceolate, acute or obtuse, 0.4–0.7 cm long; **lateral sepals** linear-lanceolate, oblique, acute or obtuse. **Petals** strongly adnate to the dorsal sepal, linear-oblanceolate, obtuse or rounded at the apex. **Lip** shortly clawed, oblong-pandurate. 0.4–0.9 cm long, trilobulate or entire at the apex, with a pair of flap-like or fleshy retrorse calli at the base. **Column** small, ± pubescent on ventral surface; rostellum ovate, ligulate or lanceolate.
DISTRIBUTION   Florida, the W. Indies, Central and S. America to Argentina and Uruguay.
HISTORY   Discovered in the W. Indies in both Jamaica and Hispaniola and described by O. Swartz as *Satyrium elatum* in 1788 in his *Nova Genera et Species Plantarum* (p. 119). L.C. Richard transferred it to the genus *Spiranthes* in 1818 in *Mémoires du Muséum d'Histoire Naturelle, Paris*. Many botanists still treat this species in the genus *Spiranthes* but R. Schlechter transferred it to *Cyclopogon* in 1919 in *Fedde, Repertorium Specierum Notarum, Beihefte* (p. 53). Schlechter's narrower concept of the genera allied to *Spiranthes* outlined in *Beihefte zum Botanischen Zentralblatt* (1920) is followed here.
SYNONYMS   include *Satyrium elatum* Sw.; *Cyclopogon ovalifolium* Presl; *Spiranthes preslii* Lindl.; *Spiranthes variegata* Kraenzl.; *Gyrostachys ovalifolia* (Presl) O. Ktze.; *Neottia minor* Jacq.; *Sarcoglottis elata* (Sw.) P.N. Don; *Spiranthes elata* (Sw.) L.C. Rich.

Cycnoches Lindl.

Subfamily Epidendroideae
Tribe Gongoreae
Subtribe Catasetinae

Large epiphytic or terrestrial plants. **Pseudobulbs** elongated, fusiform-cylindrical, leafy. **Leaves** plicate, membranaceous. **Inflorescence** lateral, erect to arcuate-pendent, few- to many-flowered, racemose. **Flowers** small to large, unisexual, dimorphic. **Sepals** and **petals** subsimilar, free, spreading or reflexed. **Lip** thin-textured to fleshy, subsessile to distinctly clawed; lamina lanceolate to orbicular, entire to lobed, crested or fringed, mostly bearing calli. **Column** elongated, slender to stout, fleshy, ± arcuate, clavate, lacking a foot; pollinia 2, waxy, ovoid, sulcate.
DISTRIBUTION   A small genus of about 12 species in the American tropics.
DERIVATION OF NAME   From the Greek *kyknos* (swan) and *anchen* (neck), referring to the slender, arcuate column of the male flowers.
TAXONOMY   *Cycnoches* was first described by John Lindley in 1832 in his *Genera and Species of Orchidaceous Plants* (p. 154). It is yet another of the genera in which the presence of dimorphic flowers has made their classification difficult. It has often proved extremely difficult to match male and female specimens, especially when only inadequate herbarium materal is available.
    R. Schlechter revised *Cycnoches* in *Orchis* (1916), dividing the genus into two sections as follows:
1. sect. *(Eu) Cynoches* in which the male and female flowers resemble each other closely, as in *C. loddigesii* Lindl., *C. ventricosum* Batem. and *C. chlorochilum* Klotzsch.
2. sect. *Heteranthae* where the male and female flowers are distinct in lip form as in *C. pentadactylon* Lindl., *C. maculatum* Lindl. and *C. egertonianum* Batem.

    Cycnoches are called "swan" orchids because of the white lip and slender, arched column, downturned in both sexes. There are two conditions in *Cycnoches* which are useful taxonomically; either, in some species, the male and female flowers are morphologically similar or, in other species, the male and female flowers are morphologically distinct. The pollination mechanism in each type is described by L. van der Pijl and C. Dodson in *Orchid Flowers* (1966). In the first group the mechanism depends upon the perfect placement of the bee on the lip in relation to the column. The bee is forced to land in an inverted position on the non-resupinate lip of a male flower. In *C. lehmanii* the pollinators are male bees of *Eulaema cingulata*, which land on the lip, gradually swinging into an inverted position with two pairs of legs grasping the lip margins. In attempting to reach the source of the odour, which is located at the apex of the callus, the bee releases hold of the lip with its back legs so that its abdomen swings downwards to touch the trigger mechanism of the column. This releases the tension-held viscidium, which whips round to strike the apex of the abdomen where it sticks with its rapidly drying cement. During the next

40 minutes or so the stipe joining the viscidium to the pollinia straightens out and the anther-cap eventually dries up and falls off.

The bee eventually visits a female flower. Here, the position of the column and stigma in relation to the lip callus is somewhat different. The bee is attracted again to the lip where it can easily hang and scratch the column-apex. When satiated it drops off the lip before flying away and, in dropping, passes close to the lip so that the pollinia are caught by the finger-like processes of the column.

In the heteromorphic species of the genus, such as *C. egertonianum*, the male flower is adapted to visits by the males of the pollinating bee *Euglossa hemichlora*. Here, the bee lands on the lip, which has a thin, flexible claw and swings down under the bee's weight. This action causes the tip of the bee's abdomen to touch and tip the anther-cap, discharging the pollinia which become fixed to the bee much as in *C. lehmanii*. Pollination of the female flowers then proceeds much as in that species.

TYPE SPECIES   *C. loddigesii* Lindl.

CULTURE   Compost A or B. Temp. Winter min. 15°C. warmer when growing. *Cycnoches*, along with *Catasetum* and *Mormodes*, seem to grow well in a variety of well-drained composts. When the new growths appear, the plants should be moved to a warm, humid atmosphere with only moderate shade. Water must be very carefully given, and only when the new shoots have well-developed roots. After flowering, when the leaves fall, the plants should be kept almost dry in a cooler, drier, place, with good light.

Cycnoches egertonianum Batem.
[Colour Plate]
A large epiphytic plant. **Pseudobulbs** clustered, erect, subfusiform, up to 12 cm long, 2 cm in diameter, 2- to 7-leaved. **Leaves** lanceolate, acuminate, 7–21 cm long, up to 3 cm broad, articulated below to broad leaf-sheaths. **Inflorescence** and **flowers** sexually dimorphic.

Male raceme arcuate-pendulous, up to 85 cm long, up to 20-flowered; bracts lanceolate, acute, 0.7–2 cm long. **Flowers** erect; sepals and petals deep purple to pale green with purple spotting; lip white, lightly marked with rose-purple. **Sepals** and **petals** linear-lanceolate to lanceolate, acute, margins ± reflexed, 1.5–3 cm long, 0.4–0.7 cm broad. **Lip** obovate, uppermost in flowers, narrowly clawed, acute, 1–1.5 cm long, 0.6 cm broad; callus on the mid-lobe of 4 clavate processes on each side with another at the base of the apical part and at the base a pair of green, fleshy, truncate, nearly cylindric outgrowths united along their inner margins. **Column** arcuate, slender, clavate, 2.5–3 cm long.

Female raceme short, erect; bracts ovate-oblong, imbricate below. **Flowers** fleshy, 1 to several, greenish-white with a yellow lip. **Sepals** and **petals** lanceolate, acuminate, 3–4 cm long, 0.8–1.4 cm broad. **Lip** shortly clawed, ovate-lanceolate, acute, very fleshy, somewhat convex, 2.5–3.5 cm long, 1.2–1.5 cm broad. **Column** short, stout, 1–1.2 cm long.

DISTRIBUTION   Belize and Guatemala, south to Costa Rica and Nicaragua; at low altitudes.

HISTORY   This species has been the source of great confusion. According to R.A. Rolfe, the plate accompanying James Bateman's description of it in the *Orchidaceae of Mexico and Guatemala* (t. 40) consists of the large male flowers of *C. ventricosum* as well as the smaller male flowers of *C. egertonianum*. This arose from the composite nature of the illustration. *C. egertonianum*, like *C. ventricosum*, was discovered in Guatemala by George Ure Skinner.

Cycnoches loddigesii Lindl. [Colour Plate]
A large epiphytic plant. **Pseudobulbs** fusiform-cylindric, tapering above, compressed slightly, clothed with white leaf-bases, up to 25 cm long. **Leaves** 5–7, plicate, oblong-oblanceolate, acute to obtuse, up to 40 cm long, 7 cm broad. **Inflorescence** from upper part of pseudobulb, pendent, racemose, up to 10-flowered. **Flowers** male and female superficially similar, large, showy; sepals and petals light olive-green, veined with maroon and with reddish-maroon transverse barring; lip white, ± marked with chocolate-brown spots and with greeny-maroon veining towards the apex; column shiny maroon with a green apex, spotted maroon. **Dorsal sepal** linear-narrowly elliptic, acuminate, 10 cm long, 1.3 cm broad; **lateral sepals** falcate, narrowly elliptic, acute, margins recurved, 7.5 cm long, 2 cm broad. **Petals** falcate, lanceolate, acuminate, 6.5 cm long, 2 cm broad. **Lip** uppermost in flower, clawed, fleshy in basal half, lanceolate, convex, acute or acuminate, 7 cm long, 2 cm broad. **Column** slender, arcuate, winged at the apex, up to 8 cm long.

DISTRIBUTION   Venezuela, Colombia, Brazil, Guyana and Surinam.

HISTORY   Discovered by John Henry Lance in Surinam and sent by him to Messrs Loddiges of Hackney, England. It was named by John Lindley in their honour in 1832 in his *Genera and Species of Orchidaceous Plants* (p. 154).

SYNONYM   *Cycnoches cucullata* Lindl.

Cycnoches pentadactylon Lindl. [Colour Plate]
A large epiphytic plant. **Pseudobulbs** narrowly oblong-fusiform or subconical, many-noded, covered at first with membranaceous sheaths, 10–15 cm long, 2–2.5 cm thick. **Leaves** ligulate-lanceolate, longly acuminate, membranaceous, 15–30 cm long, 2–5 cm broad. **Inflorescences** and **flowers** sexually dimorphic.

Male inflorescence commonly subterminal, pendent, 5–25 cm long, densely many-flowered above. **Male flowers** large, nodding or pendent; sepals and petals yellowish-green or whitish, spotted and transversely banded with chestnut-brown; lip green at the base, white in the middle and yellowish at the apex, purple-spotted; column purple below with a yellowish-white, purple-spotted apex. **Sepals** ligulate-lanceolate, long-acuminate, reflexed, 3.5–5 cm long, 0.9–1.1 cm broad. **Petals** membranaceous, oblong, acute, reflexed, 3.5–4 cm long, 1.5–1.6 cm broad. **Lip** uppermost, fleshy, rigid, longly clawed; hypochile with an erect incurved horn; mesochile 4-lobed; epichile linguiform. **Column** elongate, slender, arcuate, 4–4.5 cm long.

Female inflorescence erect, short, 1- to 3-flowered. **Female flowers** nodding, fleshy; sepals and petals yellowish-white spotted with reddish-maroon in the lower half; lip white, with a yellow claw; column yellow with purple spotting above. **Sepals** and **petals** similar to those of male flowers but slightly smaller. **Lip** uppermost, fleshy, with an entire, ovate-oblong, shortly acuminate lamina, bicallose at the base. **Column** thick, terete, clavate, slightly incurved, 2.5 cm long.

DISTRIBUTION   Brazil.

HISTORY   Discovered in 1841 by William Lobb in Rio de Janeiro province for the firm of Messrs Veitch of Exeter, England, and described in 1843 in the *Botanical Register* (misc. 18) by John Lindley.

Cycnoches ventricosum Batem. [Colour Plate]
A large epiphytic plant. **Pseudobulbs** cylindric-fusiform, somewhat compressed, up to 30 cm long, 3 cm in diameter, leafy. **Leaves** 5–6, elliptic or linear-lanceolate, acute to acuminate, membranaceous, the uppermost the longest, up to 35 cm long, 8 cm broad, articulated to leaf-sheaths. **Inflorescences** and **flowers** sexually dimorphic. **Male** and **female racemes** subsimilar, axillary from the uppermost leaves, up to 30 cm long, several-flowered; bracts broadly ovate, acute, up to 2.5 cm long.

Male flowers greenish with a white lip, callus black, opening simultaneously. **Dorsal sepal** narrowly elliptic, acute to subacuminate, 4–6.2 cm long, 1–1.5 cm broad; **lateral sepals** obliquely lanceolate, acute or acuminate. **Petals** broadly elliptic to elliptic-lanceolate, subacute to acuminate, oblique, 4–6 cm long, 1.8–2.7 cm broad. **Lip** shortly clawed, ovate or ovate-lanceolate, convex, acute, much swollen on the upper side, 4–5 cm long, 2 cm broad; callus basal. **Column** slender-clavate, arcuate, 2.5–

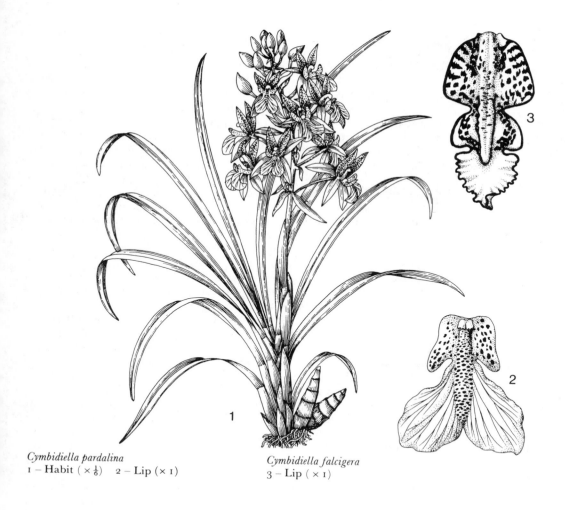

Cymbidiella pardalina
1 – Habit (× 1/6)   2 – Lip (× 1)

Cymbidiella falcigera
3 – Lip (× 1)

3.5 cm long. **Female flowers** similar but smaller and with a shorter, stouter column.
DISTRIBUTION Mexico to Panama; uncommon at altitudes up to 1000 m.
HISTORY First collected by George Ure Skinner at Istapa in Guatemala and described by James Bateman in his monumental work *Orchidaceae of Mexico and Guatemala* (t. 5) in 1837.

Cymbidiella Rolfe
Subfamily Epidendroideae
Tribe Cymbidieae
Subtribe Cymbidiinae

Large, terrestrial or epiphytic plants with elongated pseudobulbs on short to elongate rhizomes. **Leaves** 8–40, arranged in a fan, distichous, persistent, membranaceous, plicate-venose, articulated at the apex of the sheath. **Inflorescence** from the base of the pseudobulb, racemose or paniculate, many-flowered; bracts narrow. **Flowers** large, showy. **Sepals** and **petals** free or sometimes with the lateral

sepals and petals shortly joined to the column-foot. **Lip** 3- to 4-lobed, lacking a spur, with a basal callus or lamellae. **Column** with a short foot; pollinia 2, attached at the base to a retractile stipe; viscidium rectangular or trapezoidal.
DISTRIBUTION Three species, all confined to Madagascar, often epiphytic on palm trees in wet forest.
DERIVATION OF NAME Diminutive of *Cymbidium* to which the species bear a superficial resemblance and were once referred.
TAXONOMY *Cymbidiella* was established by R.A. Rolfe in 1918 in the *Orchid Review* (p. 58).
It is allied to *Eulophiella*, *Eulophia* and *Cymbidium* but is distinguished from *Eulophiella* by its narrow bracts and many leaves which are distichous and borne in a fan; from *Eulophia* by its column-foot and lack of a spur; and from *Cymbidium*, to which the species were originally referred, by (according to Rolfe) 'its epiphytic habit, and its general aspect and floral structure [which] are quite different, the lip being strongly three-lobed with rounded erect side lobes, and an ample, recurved, obcordate or

obovate front lobe, giving quite a different appearance to the flower.'
The nomenclature of the three species of *Cymbidiella* has recently been reviewed in the *Orchid Digest* by L. Garay (1976).
TYPE SPECIES *C. flabellata* (Thou.) Rolfe
CULTURE Compost A. Temp. Winter min. 15°C. These may be grown in well-drained pots or baskets under conditions of moderate shade and good humidity. The plants resent disturbance, so should be left to grow into specimens. *C. pardalina* has been found to grow best in association with *Platycerium madagascariense* and the two should be grown together in a basket if possible.

Cymbidiella falcigera (Rchb.f.) Garay
A large, robust epiphytic plant with stout creeping rhizomes. **Pseudobulbs** 3–4, cylindric, up to 30 cm long, covered by 7–40 leaves. **Leaves** distichous, arranged in a fan, loriform-lanceolate, acuminate, 25–60 cm long, 1–3 cm broad. **Inflorescence** paniculate, 80–150 cm long, many-flowered; bracts lanceolate, acuminate, not reflexed, 2 cm long. **Flowers** large, showy, 8 cm across; sepals and petals pale green; lip pale green, marked especially on side lobes with black or purplish-black. **Sepals** narrowly lanceolate, acute, 4–5 cm long, 1 cm broad; laterals somewhat falcate, recurved, keeled near apex. **Petals** forming a hood with the dorsal sepal, ovate-lanceolate, acute, 3.5–4 cm long, 1.2–1.5 cm broad. **Lip** 3-lobed, up to 4 cm long, 3 cm broad; side lobes erect, ovate, obtuse; mid-lobe reflexed, obovate to elliptic, acuminate, margins undulate-crisped; callus bilamellate at base, prolonged into 3 verrucose keels in front. **Column** 1 cm long; foot 0.4 cm long, channelled; anther-cap dull purple.
DISTRIBUTION E. Madagascar; sea level to 400 m, often epiphytic on *Raphia* palms.
HISTORY Discovered by Charles Curtis in 1878, and at about the same time by L. Humblot, in Madagascar and described by H.G. Reichenbach in 1885 in *Flora* (p. 541) as *Grammangis falcigera*. L. Garay transferred it to *Cymbidiella* in 1976 in the *Orchid Digest* (p. 541). This species is better known under the synonym *Cymbidiella humblotii* (Rolfe) Rolfe.
SYNONYMS *Grammangis falcigera* Rchb.f.; *Cymbidium humblotii* Rolfe; *Cymbidiella humblotii* (Rolfe) Rolfe

Cymbidiella pardalina (Rchb.f.) Garay
[Colour Plate]
A large epiphytic plant. **Pseudobulbs** tufted, oblong-conical, 7.5–12 cm long, 5- to 10-leaved. **Leaves** distichous, linear-loriform, acute, 65–100 cm long, 1.5–2 cm broad, dull green. **Inflorescence** up to 1 m long from the base of the pseudobulb, racemose, up to 20- (or

more) flowered; bracts reflexed, lanceolate, minute. **Flowers** large, 10 cm across, showy; sepals yellowish-green; petals yellowish-green, spotted with black all over; lip red with a yellow base and spotted with black especially in the basal half. **Sepals** subsimilar, lanceolate, acute, 3.7–4.5 cm long, 1.2–1.4 cm broad. **Petals** ovate-elliptic, acute, 3.5–4 cm long, 1.7–1.9 cm broad. **Lip** 3-lobed, 4 cm long, 3 cm broad; side lobes basal, suberect, ovate, acute to obtuse; mid-lobe flabellate-obovate, emarginate, margins often undulate, much larger than the side lobes; callus a raised plate at base of lip terminating in verrucose lines. **Column** suberect, stout, 1 cm long, with a short foot 0.4–0.5 cm long.

DISTRIBUTION E. Madagascar only; in forests from 600 to 800 m, often an epiphyte on *Platycerium* species.

HISTORY Discovered by L. Humblot in Madagascar and described in 1885 by H.G. Reichenbach in *Flora* (p. 541) as *Grammangis pardalina*. Recently, L. Garay has shown that this is conspecific with *Cymbidiella rhodochila* described in 1918 by R.A. Rolfe in the *Orchid Review* (p. 58) and has thus transferred Reichenbach's name to *Cymbidiella* as the earlier, and thus correct, name.

SYNONYMS *Grammangis pardalina* Rchb.f.; *Cymbidiella rhodochila* (Rolfe) Rolfe; *Cymbidium rhodochilum* Rolfe, etc.

Cymbidium Sw.

Subfamily Epidendroideae
Tribe Cymbidieae
Subtribe Cymbidiinae

Epiphytic, lithophytic or terrestrial herbs with short or rarely elongate pseudobulbous stems. **Roots** tufted. **Leaves** long, narrow or rarely lanceolate, plicate or conduplicate and leathery, rarely absent. **Inflorescence** erect, suberect or pendent, racemose, 1- to many-flowered; peduncle loosely covered with sheaths. **Flowers** often large and showy. **Sepals** and **petals** free, spreading or erect. **Lip** 3-lobed, sessile, borne on a short column-foot; side lobes erect around column; mid-lobe recurved; disc with usually 1–3 glabrous or pubescent median ridges. **Column** long; pollinia 2, with deep grooves, or 4, subglobose or pyramidal, almost sessile, on a broad viscid disc or strap.

DISTRIBUTION About 50 species, India, east throughout S.E. Asia, China, Japan, Indonesia to Australia.

DERIVATION OF NAME From the Greek *kymbes* (boat-shaped) in allusion to the shape of lip.

TAXONOMY The genus *Cymbidium* was ori-

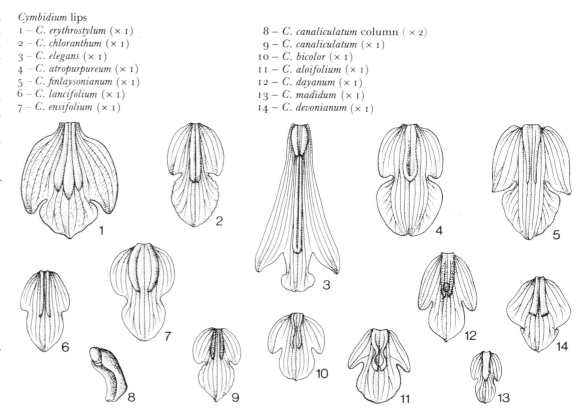

Cymbidium lips
1 – *C. erythrostylum* (× 1)
2 – *C. chloranthum* (× 1)
3 – *C. elegans* (× 1)
4 – *C. atropurpureum* (× 1)
5 – *C. finlaysonianum* (× 1)
6 – *C. lancifolium* (× 1)
7 – *C. ensifolium* (× 1)
8 – *C. canaliculatum* column (× 2)
9 – *C. canaliculatum* (× 1)
10 – *C. bicolor* (× 1)
11 – *C. aloifolium* (× 1)
12 – *C. dayanum* (× 1)
13 – *C. madidum* (× 1)
14 – *C. devonianum* (× 1)

ginally described by Olof Swartz in 1799 in *Nova Acta Regiae Societatis Scientiarum Upsaliensis* (p. 70) and included three of the currently recognised Asiatic species of the genus. Unfortunately he also included several species from the W. Indies and from S. Africa in the genus. The confusion over the exact delimitation of the genus was eventually sorted out by John Lindley, H.G. Reichenbach and George Bentham who, in turn, removed the anomalous species into other genera. Nowadays, the genus *Cymbidium* contains only species from Asia through to Australia.

Some species of *Cymbidium* such as *C. mastersii* and *C. elegans* were separated by Bentham under the genus *Cyperorchis*. These species can be easily recognised as their flowers do not open widely. Although there are other differences, the line of separation between *Cymbidium* and *Cyperorchis* is by no means as clear-cut as some suggest and, in this work, the species segregated as *Cyperorchis* are treated under *Cymbidium*. The genus has been most recently revised by D. Du Puy and P. Cribb (1988) in *The Genus Cymbidium*.

TYPE SPECIES *Epidendrum aloifolium* L. [= *Cymbidium aloifolium* (L.) Sw.].

CULTURE Compost A. Temp. Winter temp. 10 or 15°C, depending on species. *Cymbidium* species may be divided roughly into two groups: those from high altitudes or temperate climates which require cool nights, and those from more tropical regions, requiring generally warmer conditions. All species require good light and humidity while growing, with evenly moist compost. They produce large numbers of roots, so should be grown in relatively large, well-drained containers. Some shading is needed in summer, but only enough to prevent leaf-scorch. When growth is complete, less water should be given, although the plants should never become dry, except for *C. tigrinum* which can be kept drier. The larger-growing cool species, such as *C. lowianum* or *C. tracyanum*, grow well in free-draining beds.

Cymbidium aloifolium (L.) Sw. [Colour Plate]

An epiphytic plant, up to 30 cm high. **Pseudobulbs** very small, hidden by leaf-bases. **Leaves** coriaceous, suberect, linear-ligulate, up to 30 cm or more long, 2 cm broad, obliquely, obscurely 2-lobed at apex. **Inflorescences** pendulous, up to 40 cm or more long, laxly many-flowered. **Flowers** up to 4.3 across; sepals and petals cream, buff or pale greenish with a central purple stripe; lip with all lobes purple-striped, mid-lobe margins white, yellow in centre; column purple with a bright yellow anther-cap. **Sepals** narrowly lanceolate, 2 cm long, 0.5 cm broad, subacute. **Petals** elliptic-lanceolate, 1.8

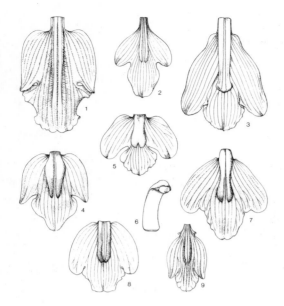

Cymbidium lips (All × 3/5)
1 – *C. tracyanum*
2 – *C. tigrinum*
3 – *C. eburneum*
4 – *C. lowianum*
5 – *C. insigne*
6 – *C. insigne* column
7 – *C. parishii*
8 – *C. lowianum* var. *concolor*
9 – *C. iridioides*

cm long, 0.6 cm broad, obtuse. **Lip** 3-lobed, 1.4 cm long, 1 cm broad; side lobes erect, narrowly acute; mid-lobe ovate, reflexed; disc with 2 ridges, broken in middle, from base of lip to base of mid-lobe. **Column** 1.3 cm long.

DISTRIBUTION India, Sri Lanka, Burma and S. China to Java and Sumatra.

HISTORY This species was described in 1753 by Carl von Linné as *Epidendrum aloifolium* in his *Species Plantarum* (p. 953) based on Rheede's 'Kansyrammaravara' in *Horti Malabarici* (1703), but was transferred to *Cymbidium* by O. Swartz in 1799 in *Nova Acta Regiae Societatis Scientiarum Upsaliensis* (p. 73) when he established the genus.

The name *C. aloifolium*, has produced a great deal of confusion and has been applied by various authors to, for example, *C. finlaysonianum* Lindl., *C. pendulum* Sw. and *C. bicolor* Lindl. Similarly, the name *C. pendulum*, originally described by Swartz, has also been applied to several taxa, e.g. *C. finlaysonianum* Lindl. and *C. simulans* Rolfe. Obviously there is still great confusion surrounding the delimitation of the species of this group of coriaceous-leaved species with pendulous inflorescences and pale yellow flowers variously spotted and striped with crimson-purple.

SYNONYMS *Cymbidium crassifolium* Wall.; *C. erectum* Wight; *C. mannii* Rchb.f.; *Epidendrum aloifolium* L.

CLOSELY RELATED SPECIES *Cymbidium*

bicolor Lindl. is similar to *C. aloifolium* but has a shorter inflorescence, and flowers with a spotted lip, the side lobes of which are shorter than the column.

Cymbidium canaliculatum R. Br.

An epiphytic plant, up to 50 cm high. **Stems** clustered, pseudobulbous, 3–10 cm long, 1.5–4 cm in diameter, greyish-green, base covered by a few large sheaths, 2- to 6-leaved. **Leaves** linear, smaller towards base, erect, rigid, thick but grooved above, 15–50 cm long, 1.5–4 cm broad, acute, dull grey-green. **Inflorescences** erect to pendulous, 1 or 2 per pseudobulb, up to 40 cm long, 12- to many-flowered. **Flowers** up to 5 cm across, with green, brown, purple or dull red sepals and petals and a creamy-white lip marked red or purple. **Sepals** spreading, oblong to oblong-elliptic, 1.2–2.5 cm long, 0.5–1 cm broad, acute. **Petals** elliptic-lanceolate, up to 1.8 cm long, 0.4–0.7 cm broad, acute. **Lip** 3-lobed, up to 2 cm long, 1.5 cm broad; side lobes erect, ovate, subacute; mid-lobe deflexed, ovate, acute; disc bearing 2 parallel pubescent ridges to base of mid-lobe. **Column** short, stout, slightly arcuate, 1 cm long; column-foot very short.

DISTRIBUTION Australia (from central New South Wales to Cape York in Queensland, Northern Territory and northern W. Australia); generally in inland localities often in full sunlight in the drier areas. The plant is most often found growing in hollows in the branches or trunks of trees with the roots penetrating deeply within the tree.

HISTORY Living specimens of this interesting species were first collected by J.C. Bidwill near the Hunter's River in New South Wales but it had earlier been described by Robert Brown in 1810 in his *Prodromus Florae Novae Hollandiae* (p. 331). It received its name for its thick, rigid, grooved leaves. John Gould Veitch first introduced plants into cultivation in Europe, which he had collected in Cape York. Specimens from N. Queensland have flowers much more heavily suffused with deep red-purple (var. *sparkesii*)

SYNONYMS *Cymbidium hillii* F. Muell.; *C. sparkesii* Rendle.

CLOSELY RELATED SPECIES Distinguished from the other Australian species *C. madidum* and *C. suave* by its pseudobulbous stem bearing thick, rigid, grey-green leaves and by the lip callus.

Cymbidium devonianum Lindl. & Paxt.
[Colour Plate]

An epiphytic or lithophytic plant, up to 30 cm high. **Stem** very stout at base, obscurely pseudobulbous, ovoid, 4 cm long, 1.5 cm broad, bearing 2 or more fully developed leaves

at its apex. **Leaves** thick, leathery, petiolate, oblong to oblanceolate, 15–35 cm long, 4 cm broad; petiole stout, grooved, 7.5–12 cm long. **Inflorescence** up to 45 cm long, pendulous, many-flowered; peduncle stout, 20–25 cm long, covered with overlapping membranous sheaths at base. **Flowers** up to 3.5 cm across, somewhat variable in colour; sepals and petals olive-green, speckled red to pale brown streaked dull purple; lip purple with a darker blotch on each side-lobe; column greenish-yellow with some apical red spots. **Sepals** oblong-lanceolate, 2.3 cm long, 0.6 cm broad, subacute. **Petals** slightly shorter but similar to the sepals, acute. **Lip** short, obscurely 3-lobed, broadly ovate, 1.9 cm long, 1 cm broad; side lobes rounded; mid-lobe small, triangular-ovate, reflexed, obtuse; disc bearing 2 short ridges at base. **Column** arcuate, 1.4 cm long, with 2 small wings towards apex.

DISTRIBUTION India (Sikkim Himalayas and Khasia Hills) and Thailand; up to about 1600 m altitude, often in exposed situations as an epiphyte or on mossy rocks.

HISTORY Described in Paxton's *Magazine of Botany* (p. 97) in 1843 and named after the Duke of Devonshire, a well-known orchid enthusiast. The plant was first collected by the Duke's collector John Gibson in the Khasia Hills in India in 1837.

SYNONYM *Cymbidium sikkimense* Hooker f.

Cymbidium eburneum Lindl. [Colour Plate]

Stems obscurely pseudobulbous, clustered, covered at base with imbricating leaf-bases, 9- to 15-leaved. **Leaves** linear-ligulate, rather thin-textured, 30–60 cm long, 2 cm broad, acute or acutely bifid, often drooping in apical half. **Inflorescence** erect to suberect, 1- to 3-flowered, up to 35 cm long; peduncle stout, 20–30 cm long, base covered in 3 alternate lanceolate sheaths. **Flowers** very showy, waxy, 7–10 cm across, creamy-white; lip ± purple-spotted with 3–5 pubescent golden ridges, mid-lobe with a dark yellow blotch; column white with a purple stain in front. **Sepals** lanceolate to oblong, 7 cm long, 1.7 cm broad, acuminate or apiculate. **Petals** subfalcate-lanceolate, 6.5 cm long, 1.8 cm broad, acuminate. **Lip** broadly oblong-ovate, 3-lobed, 5 cm long, 3 cm broad; side lobes narrow, obtuse; mid-lobe short, small, recurved, margins undulately-crenate; disc bearing several pubescent broad ridges onto the base of the mid-lobe, ridges dilated towards apex. **Column** clavate, 4.2 cm long.

DISTRIBUTION India (Sikkim Himalayas) Burma, S. China, at altitudes of 300–1600 m.

HISTORY Described by John Lindley in the *Botanical Register* (t. 67) in 1847. Although it was first collected by William Griffith in 1835 in the Khasia Hills, it was not flowered in

Europe until 1847 when it was flowered by Messrs Loddiges at Hackney, London.

C. eburneum var. *parishii* (considered by some to be a distinct species, *Cymbidium parishii* Rchb.f.) was one of Rev. Charles Parish's earliest discoveries. He sent two plants to Messrs Low of Clapton, London in 1867, but neither flowered until many years later. It may be distinguished by the large purple spots on the lip which has no pubescent lines on the callus and by the finely acute angles of the viscidium.

SYNONYM *Cymbidium syringodorum* Griff.

CLOSELY RELATED SPECIES *Cymbidium mastersii* Griff. ex Lindl. [Colour Plate] has white flowers superficially similar to *C. eburneum* but not opening widely, in an arcuate or pendent inflorescence, and with narrow segments, smaller flowers and distinctive lip structure. *C. mastersii* is also vegetatively similar to *Cymbidium elegans* Blume but is distinguished by its short raceme decurved at the apex, its larger more open flowers which are white or pale rose-coloured often with a little red on the lip and smell of almonds, the broader lip which is quite glabrous and lacks any basal calli, and by the stouter column.

Cymbidium finlaysonianum Lindl.
[Colour Plate]

A robust epiphytic or lithophytic plant, up to 70 cm high, often growing in large clumps. **Pseudobulbs** shortly conical-ovoid, 6 cm long, 3 cm broad, about 5-leaved, covered in leaf-bases. **Leaves** thick, fleshy, narrowly lanceolate, 30–100 cm long, 2–4 cm broad, rounded and unequally 2-lobed at apex, articulated to a leaf-base, 14 cm long. **Inflorescence** 60–150 cm long, slender, pendulous, laxly many-flowered; basal-sheaths inflated, short. **Flowers** up to 6 cm across; sepals and petals dull yellow; lip purplish or white, side lobes streaked red, mid-lobe white, with a red-purple arcuate band towards apex, yellow at base; column yellowish-green, purplish at base. **Sepals** linear-lanceolate, 3 cm long, 0.8 cm broad, acute or obtuse. **Petals** linear-lanceolate, a little smaller than the sepals. **Lip** 3-lobed, 2.1 cm long, 1.4 cm broad; side lobes narrow, acute; mid-lobe oblong, apiculate, curved down at apex; disc with 2 red ridges running onto base of mid-lobe. **Column** 1.8 cm long; foot very short.

DISTRIBUTION S.E. Asia, Malaya and Sumatra to the Philippines; a lowland species often found in exposed places near the sea.

HISTORY Originally collected by Dr N. Wallich. John Lindley described the species in *Genera and Species of Orchidaceous Plants* (p. 164) in 1833, naming it after Finlayson who had discovered it in Cochin China (Vietnam).

SYNONYMS *Cymbidium aloifolium* auct.; *C. pendulum* auct.

CLOSELY RELATED SPECIES Vegetatively very close to *Cymbidium aloifolium* (L.) Sw. but *C. finlaysonianum* has larger flowers with straight ridges on the lip. *Cymbidium atropurpureum* (Hooker) Rolfe is also closely related but its leaves are much narrower, up to 1.5 cm broad, the sepals and petals wine red and the side lobes of the lip are much shorter than the column.

Cymbidium floribundum Lindl. [Colour Plate]

A terrestrial plant. **Pseudobulbs** small, ovoid, clustered, 1–2.5 cm long, 3- to 5-leaved, hidden by leaf-bases. **Leaves** coriaceous, suberect, linear, rounded, 15–40 cm long, 1 cm broad, rounded or acute at apex. **Inflorescences** erect or suberect, many-flowered, up to 30 cm or more long, covered at base by several lanceolate sheaths. **Flowers** 3 cm across, variable in colour; sepals and petals reddish-brown in centre with yellowish margins; lip white, lobes spotted purple, disc bright yellow. **Sepals** obovate, spreading, 1.8–2.1 cm long, 0.5 cm broad, obtuse. **Petals** obovate to elliptic-oblong, incurved, 1.6–2 cm long, 0.5 cm broad, obtuse. **Lip** suberect, 3-lobed, 1.2–1.8 cm long, 0.9–1.4 cm broad; side lobes erect, oblong, obtuse; mid-lobe oblong, recurved, obtuse; disc bearing 2 somewhat obscure longitudinal lamellae. **Column** 1.3 cm long.

DISTRIBUTION S. China and S.E. Tibet.

HISTORY One of the parent species used in the production of the currently popular 'miniature' *Cymbidium* hybrids. *C. floribundum* was described by John Lindley in 1833 in *Genera and Species of Orchidaceous Plants* (p. 162). It is still usually grown under the later synonym *C. pumilum*.

SYNONYM *Cymbidium pumilum* Rolfe

Cymbidium hookerianum Rchb.f.
[Colour Plate]

A large epiphytic or lithophytic orchid. **Pseudobulbs** conical, 3–7 cm long, 1.5–3.5 cm broad, covered in leaf-bases. **Leaves** fairly thin-textured, linear-lanceolate, up to 60 cm long, 1.4–2.5 cm broad, acute to acuminate. **Inflorescence** 7- to 20-flowered, drooping, up to 90 cm long; peduncle very robust, covered below by long-acuminate bracts. **Flowers** 10–12.5 cm across, fragrant; sepals and petals apple-green to yellow-green; lip creamy-white to pale yellow, spotted crimson or purple on side lobes and on margins of mid-lobe; column yellow with a few dorsal purple spots. **Sepals** narrowly elliptic, up to 5.5–6 cm long, 1.8 cm broad, acute. **Petals** similar to sepals. **Lip** 3-lobed, 4 cm long, 2.4 cm broad, pubescent; side lobes narrowly-ovate, acute, with ciliate margins; mid-lobe ovate-rotund, margins undulate, ciliate, curled up; disc bearing 2 pubescent ridges. **Column** 3.5–4 cm long.

DISTRIBUTION Nepal, India (Sikkim), Bhutan, Tibet and S.W. China; 1600–2600 m altitude.

HISTORY The species was introduced into Europe by Thomas Lobb who sent plants to Messrs Veitch & Sons of Chelsea, London, where they flowered for the first time in 1866. The species was described by H.G. Reichenbach in the *Gardeners' Chronicle* (p. 7) in 1866 and was named after Sir Joseph Hooker whose exploration of the Sikkim Himalayas so greatly increased our knowledge of the Himalayan flora.

SYNONYM *Cymbidium grandiflorum* Griff.

CLOSELY RELATED SPECIES See *C. iridioides*.

Cymbidium iridioides D. Don [Colour Plate]

An epiphytic or lithophytic plant, up to 50 cm high. **Stem** short, pseudobulbous, compressed, up to 15 cm long, 3 cm broad, covered by distichous, persistent leaf-bases and sheaths, 4- to 7-leaved. **Leaves** narrowly lanceolate to linear-lanceolate, 25–90 cm long, 2–4.2 cm broad, acuminate, keeled on under side, articulated 6–11 cm above sheathing base. **Inflorescence** suberect or pendulous, 7- to 20-flowered, up to 80 cm long; peduncle very robust, covered at base by several lanceolate imbricating sheaths. **Flowers** 7.5–10 cm across; sepals and petals yellowish-green streaked red or purple; lip cream or yellow, heavily purple-spotted or streaked; column pale greenish-yellow with a dark maroon apex. **Sepals** oblong-lanceolate, 4–5 cm long, 1.2–2 cm broad, acute; **lateral sepals** slightly falcate. **Petals** oblong-lanceolate, 3.5–5 cm long, up to 1.2 cm broad, acute. **Lip** 3-lobed, 3.8–4.7 cm long, 2.5 cm broad, pubescent all over; side lobes erect, narrowly acute; mid-lobe orbicular-ovate, undulate, acute, margins ciliate; 2 ridges on disc diverging at base but converging in apical half, pubescent. **Column** 2.5–3.2 cm long, arcuate.

DISTRIBUTION The tropical Himalayas, the Khasia Hills, Burma and S.W. China; 1200–2200 m altitude.

HISTORY Discovered by Dr N. Wallich in 1821 and subsequently introduced into cultivation by him. *C. iridioides* was described by David Don in 1824 in his *Prodromus Florae Nepalensis* (p. 36) based on Wallich's collection. It is better known as *C. giganteum* (no. 7355 in Wallich's Catalogue of his collections) which was described by John Lindley in *Genera and Species of Orchidaceous Plants* in 1833 (p. 163) but that is a later synonym.

C. wilsonii Rolfe, a slightly smaller-flowered species, was collected by E.H. Wilson at Meng-

tze in Yunnan Province, south western China for the firm of Veitch & Sons of Chelsea, London. Veitch showed a plant at the Royal Horticultural Society show in February 1904 and it received an Award of Merit. This original plant has recently been rediscovered, still living, at the Royal Botanic Garden, Edinburgh. Its history has been fully documented by Peter Taylor and Patrick Woods in the *Botanical Magazine* (1976).
SYNONYM *Iridorchis gigantea* (Lindl.) Blume
CLOSELY RELATED SPECIES Similar to *C. hookerianum* but *C. iridioides* has smaller and distinctively coloured flowers.

C. hookerianum, *C. lowianum* and *C. tracyanum* are undoubtedly closely related to *C. iridioides* and have been considered by some to be varieties or subspecies of a single variable species. However, for horticultural purposes it is more convenient to treat them as separate species and this treatment is followed here.

Cymbidium lancifolium Hooker
[Colour Plate]
A terrestrial plant, up to 30 cm high. **Stems** fusiform, fleshy, 5–15 cm long, 1.2 cm in diameter, bearing 3–6 leaves towards apex, basal part covered with thin sheaths. **Leaves** plicate, thin-textured, elliptic, 15–25 cm long, 4.5 cm broad, acute, with a long, slender petiole, 6 cm long. **Inflorescence** erect, 4- to 8-flowered, 25 cm long; bracts narrow, 1 cm or more long. **Flowers** 3.7–5 cm across; sepals white, yellowish or pale greenish; petals white with a pink or purple mid-rib; lip white, spotted red-purple; column greenish with purple markings. **Sepals** narrowly lanceolate, 1.5–3 cm long, 0.3–0.8 cm broad, shortly pointed. **Petals** ligulate, shorter but similar to sepals, acute. **Lip** 3-lobed, 1.4–2 cm long, 0.8–1.5 cm broad; side lobes narrow, rounded; mid-lobe ovate, obtuse, recurved at apex; disc bearing 2 short fleshy keels, which run onto base of mid-lobe. **Column** 1–1.4 cm long.
DISTRIBUTION Widely distributed in N. India, Burma, Malaya, Indonesia, New Guinea, Taiwan, China and Japan; up to 2300 m altitude.
HISTORY Described in 1823 by Sir William Hooker in *Exotic Flora* (t. 51) based on a Wallich collection from Nepal.
SYNONYMS *Cymbidium gibsonii* Paxt.; *C. javanicum* Bl.; *C. papuanum* Schltr.; *C. aspidistrifolium* Fuk.

Cymbidium lowianum Rchb.f. [Colour Plate]
Stems pseudobulbous, compressed, 10–15 cm long, 3 cm broad, covered in distichous leaf-bases. **Leaves** narrowly linear-lanceolate, 50–90 cm long, up to 3.5 cm broad, acuminate. **Inflorescences** up to 150 cm long, 18- to 25-flowered. **Flowers** 7.5–10 cm across; sepals and petals yellowish-green, with longitudinal brown streaks; lip side lobes dull-yellow, mid-lobe white at base, with a V-shaped red-purple mark with a buff margin in front; column yellow, spotted with red. **Sepals** narrowly lanceolate, up to 4.8–6.2 cm long, 1.4–1.8 cm broad, acute or acuminate, obscurely keeled on reverse. **Petals** falcate, narrowly lanceolate, up to 5.4 cm long, 0.8–1.1 cm broad, acute or acuminate. **Lip** 3-lobed, curvate, 3.5 cm long, 2.8 cm broad, very pubescent; side lobes erect, crescent-shaped, apex rounded; mid-lobe narrowly ovate-lanceolate, decurved, apex rounded or subacute; disc 2-ridged. **Column** triangular in cross-section, arcuate.
DISTRIBUTION Burma, S.W. China and Thailand.
HISTORY Described in the *Gardeners' Chronicle* (n.s. 11: pp. 332, 404, t. 56) of 1879 by H.G. Reichenbach who named it after Stuart Low of the famous horticultural firm. Low's collector, William Boxall, discovered it in Burma in 1877.

R.A. Rolfe described var. *concolor* in the *Gardeners' Chronicle* in 1891. It has pure yellow flowers and was first grown and flowered by Sir Trevor Lawrence of Dorking in Surrey, England.
SYNONYM *Cymbidium giganteum* Lindl. var. *lowianum* Rchb.f.
CLOSELY RELATED SPECIES Sometimes considered a variety of *C. iridioides* from which it can be distinguished by its longer leaves and its lip which has pale yellow-green side lobes and a dark purple mid-lobe edged with yellow. Intermediate in size between *C. iridioides* and *C. hookerianum*.

Cymbidium macrorhizon Lindl.
A saprophytic terrestrial herb, up to 23 cm high. **Rhizome** thick, creeping, branched, bracts membranous. **Leaves** scale-like. **Inflorescence** slender, racemose, erect, 2- to 8-flowered, 15–32 cm long; scape short. **Flowers** 3–4 cm across; sepals and petals pale buff or yellow striated pink; lip white, spotted crimson; column streaked crimson below. **Sepals** linear-lanceolate, 2.5 cm long, 0.5 cm broad, acute or acuminate. **Petals** oblong-lanceolate, 2 cm long, 0.6 cm broad, acute. **Lip** 3-lobed, 2 cm long, 2 cm broad; side lobes narrow, rounded; mid-lobe narrowly ovate, obtuse; disc with 2 keels converging onto base of mid-lobe. **Column** elongate, curved, 1.2 cm long.
DISTRIBUTION N.W. India, east to China, Taiwan and Japan, and south to Thailand and Indochina; growing in deep leaf litter in montane forest, 600–2600 m altitude.
HISTORY *C. macrorhizon* was described by John Lindley in 1833 in *Genera and Species of Orchidaceous Plants* (p. 162). The species re-mained uncollected between 1878 and 1972 when it was re-collected near Kalimpong by Ganesh M. Pradhan.

It is a very distinctive species with flowers similar to those of *C. lancifolium* but easily recognised by its lack of chlorophyll and its scale leaves.

Cymbidium madidum Lindl. [Colour Plate]
Stems pseudobulbous, conical-ovoid, 6–30 cm long, 2–6 cm in diameter, up to 10-leaved. **Leaves** linear, up to 90 cm long, 2–4 cm broad, acute, coriaceous, decurved when long, basal leaves much smaller than the rest. **Inflorescence** pendulous, up to 60 cm long, laxly 12- to 70-flowered. **Flowers** 2–3 cm across, fleshy; sepals and petals pale to dark brown or green on outer surface, olive-green within; lip with a dark brown or black band between the lateral lobes and mid-lobe. **Sepals** obovate, fleshy, 0.9–1.5 cm long, 0.4–0.7 cm broad, obtuse. **Petals** fleshy, porrect, obliquely ovate, 0.7–1.2 cm long, 0.4–0.7 cm broad, obtuse. **Lip** 3-lobed, 0.9–1.5 cm long, 0.4–0.6 cm broad; side lobes ovate, acute; mid-lobe rotund, apical margins upcurved; disc with a low, broad, glandular, viscid keel. **Column** 1.3 cm long, slightly arcuate, dilated towards apex.
DISTRIBUTION Australia (from N.E. New South Wales to the Cape York Peninsula in Queensland); in dense shade or more exposed positions in or near rain forest, from sea level to 1200 m altitude, growing in the hollows of branches and trunks of trees, but rarely on the bark of trees.
HISTORY Described by John Lindley in the *Botanical Register* (misc. 9) of 1840 when it was first introduced into cultivation by the firm of Messrs Rollisson.
SYNONYMS *Cymbidium iridifolium* A. Cunn.; *C. albuciflorum* F. Muell.; *C. leai* Rendle; *C. queenianum* Klinge
CLOSELY RELATED SPECIES See *C. canaliculatum*.

Cymbidium mastersii Griff. ex Lindl.
[Colour Plate]
See under *Cymbidium eburneum*.

Cymbidium suave R. Br. [Colour Plate]
An epiphytic plant, 50 cm or more high. **Stems** not pseudobulbous, 5–35 cm long, thin, woody, covered with remains of leaf-bases which give the stem a compressed appearance. **Leaves** thin-textured, linear, 15–45 cm long, 1–2 cm broad, ± drooping in apical half. **Inflorescence** few- to many-flowered, pendulous. **Flowers** 2–3 cm across; sepals and petals bright green, yellowish-green or brownish-green ± blotched red; lip pale brown or green with a dark red-brown disc. **Sepals** oblong-obovate, 1–1.5 cm

long, 0.5–0.8 cm broad, obtuse, **Petals** obovate, somewhat oblique, 0.8–1.2 cm long, 0.5–0.7 cm broad, mucronate. **Lip** 3-lobed, up to 1.5 cm long, 0.7 cm broad; side lobes oblong, truncate, erect; mid-lobe broadly elliptic, slightly decurved at apex; disc not keeled. **Column** up to 1.2 cm long, slightly arcuate, dilated a little in apical half.

DISTRIBUTION Australia (from S.E. New South Wales to the south end of the Cape York Peninsula); growing from sea level to 1350 m altitude, in the hollows of branches and trunks of hardwood trees in open woodland.

HISTORY First collected and described by Robert Brown in *Prodromus Florae Novae Hollandiae* (p. 331) in 1810.

SYNONYM *C. gomphocarpum* Fitzg.

CLOSELY RELATED SPECIES See *C. canaliculatum*.

Cymbidium tigrinum Parish ex Hooker
[Colour Plate]

A lithophytic plant, up to 20 cm high. **Pseudobulbs** ovoid to ovoid-conical, 2.5–4 cm long, 3 cm broad, covered at base with several sheaths, 3- to 5-leaved. **Leaves** coriaceous, recurved, narrowly elliptic to oblong-lanceolate, 7.5–17.5 cm long, 2–3.3 cm broad; petiole short, 2.5 cm long. **Inflorescence** 3- to 6-flowered, suberect, 15–20 cm long; bracts lanceolate, shorter than the ovary. **Flowers** 5–8.5 cm across; sepals and petals dull yellowish-green; lip white, spotted with red on mid-lobe and striped with red on yellow side lobes; column pale olive-green, spotted red below stigma. **Sepals** linear-oblong, 4–5 cm long, 0.8–1.3 cm broad, subacute or acute. **Petals** linear, somewhat falcate, 3.4–4.5 cm long, 0.6–1 cm broad, acuminate. **Lip** 3-lobed, oblong, 3.8 cm long, 2–3 cm broad; side lobes erect, rounded; mid-lobe oblong, rounded, apiculate; disc with 2 glabrous white ridges. **Column** 2.5–2.8 cm long, arcuate, clavate.

DISTRIBUTION S. Burma and N.E. India; at 1500–2700 m altitude.

HISTORY Described by Sir William Hooker in 1864 in the *Botanical Magazine* (t. 5457). The species was first collected by the Rev. Charles Parish in 1863 in the mountains of Tenasserim. Parish sent living material to Messrs Low of Clapton, London, in the same year.

Cymbidium tracyanum L. Castle
[Colour Plate]

Stem pseudobulbous, compressed, 10–15 cm long, 3 cm broad, covered with distichous leaf-bases. **Leaves** linear-ligulate, 60–95 cm long, 2–4 cm broad, acute, distinctly keeled beneath. **Inflorescences** 100–130 cm long, 15- to 20-flowered, pendulous to suberect. **Flowers** 10–12.5 cm across; sepals and petals greenish-yellow, striped brown or reddish; lip mid-lobe

yellow with purple spots, side lobes purple-veined; column greenish spotted with red. **Sepals** oblong-narrowly obovate, up to 5.5–8 cm long, 1.4–2 cm broad, acute. **Petals** narrowly oblong, 5.6–7.2 cm long, 0.8–1.4 cm broad, acute. **Lip** 3-lobed, 4 cm long, 2.5–3.2 cm broad; side lobes roundish-oblong, erect, with ciliate margins; mid-lobe broadly oblong, reflexed, with crisped-undulate pubescent margins; disc bearing 2–3 dentate ridges. **Column** 3.5 cm long.

DISTRIBUTION Burma, S.W. China and Thailand; 1200–1900 m.

HISTORY Described in the *Journal of Horticulture* (p. 513) in 1890 by L. Castle. The name derives from the original plant which was acquired by Mr Tracy of Twickenham in Middlesex, England in a batch of *C. lowianum*. This single plant eventually was acquired by Baron Schroeder of Egham for his then unrivalled collection.

CLOSELY RELATED SPECIES Somewhat intermediate in character between *C. hookerianum* and *C. iridioides*.

Cynorkis Thou.
Subfamily Orchidoideae
Tribe Orchideae
Subtribe Orchidinae

Terrestrial herbs with elongated fleshy or tuberous roots. **Stems** often glandular-pubescent. **Leaves** almost all radical, few or solitary, the cauline ones small or sheath-like. **Flowers** few or numerous in a lax or dense terminal raceme, usually resupinate but rarely not so, usually pink or mauve, less frequently orange or white. **Sepals** free or slightly adnate to the lip; lateral sepals spreading; dorsal sepal often forming a helmet with the 2 petals. **Lip** free, entire or 3- to 5-lobed, usually larger than the sepals, ecallose, spurred at the base. **Column** short and broad; anther-loculi parallel; canals short or long and slender; caudicles slender; pollinia 2; viscidia 2 or rarely 1; stigmatic processes oblong, papillose; rostellum prominent, several-lobed.

DISTRIBUTION About 125 species mostly natives of Madagascar and the Mascarene Islands but with 17 species in Africa.

DERIVATION OF NAME From the Greek *kynos* (dog) and *orchis* (testicle), in allusion to their small testiculate tubers.

TAXONOMY Described by A. du Petit Thouars in 1809 in the *Bulletin des Sciences par la Société Philomatique de Paris* (p. 317). *Cynorkis* has often erroneously been spelt *Cynosorchis* or *Cynorchis* by later authorities. *Cynorkis* is allied to *Habenaria* but differs in flower colour and in that the stigmatic processes of the column are

united to the column side lobes. In *Habenaria* the latter situation is only found in those species where the lip side lobes are fimbriate.

The genus has not been revised as a whole since F. Kraenzlin's account of it in 1901 in *Orchidacearum genera et species* when he treated 42 species in three sections: (*Eu*) *Cynorkis*, with a 3- to 5-lobed lip; *Auriculatae* in which the side lobes are auriculate; an *Holochilae* with an entire lip. This account is now quite inadequate and although no recent revision of the whole genus exists there are several accounts of the genus from parts of the distribution.

V.S. Summerhayes has revised the W. and E. tropical African species in the *Flora of West Tropical Africa* (2nd ed., 1968) and the *Flora of Tropical East Africa* (1968) respectively. The Madagascan species have been covered by H. Perrier de la Bâthie in the *Flore de Madagascar* (1939) and several new species have recently been described by J. Bosser in *Adansonia* (1969, 1970). Perrier's account is also now out of date and in need of considerable revision.

TYPE SPECIES *C. fastigiata* Thou.

CULTURE Compost C. Temp. Winter min. 15°C, warmer when growing. *Cynorkis* species require conditions similar to those for tropical *Habenaria* species, i.e. very shady and moist when growing and a long dry rest at a cooler temperature. The large leaves remain near the ground, although the inflorescence may be quite tall. *C. fastigiata* frequently appears as a weed amongst collections of tropical orchids, and its seeds germinate readily in pots.

Cynorkis lowiana Rchb.f. [Colour Plate]

A small epiphytic or lithophytic herb, 10–16 cm high. **Tubers** 2, elongate, pubescent. **Stem** very short, 1-leafed, subtended by 2 sheaths; sheaths tubular, brown scarious, 1.2–3 cm long. **Leaf** narrowly linear-lanceolate, longly attenuate-acute above, 4.5–13 cm long, 0.6–1.6 cm broad. **Inflorescence** slender, 7–12 cm long, 1- (rarely 2-)flowered; bract lanceolate, acute, 1.1 cm long, 0.7 cm broad. **Flowers** large; sepals, petals and spur green, flushed rose; lip carmine-red with central darker spot. **Sepals** elliptic-ovate, 0.8–1 cm long. **Petals** elliptic, obtuse, 0.8–1 cm long. **Lip** 3-lobed, 2.2 cm long, 2.7 cm broad; side lobes oblong, ± equal to the mid-lobe; mid-lobe clawed, bilobulate, deeply emarginate; spur slender, 2.5–4.5 cm long. **Column** short; anther 0.3 cm long; caudicles 0.8 cm long; rostellum 0.8 cm long.

DISTRIBUTION E. Madagascar.

HISTORY Originally introduced by S. Low into cultivation when he sent plants from E. Madagascar to Kew. H.G. Reichenbach described the species from these plants in 1888 in *Flora* (p. 150).

SYNONYM *Cynorkis purpurascens* Hooker f.

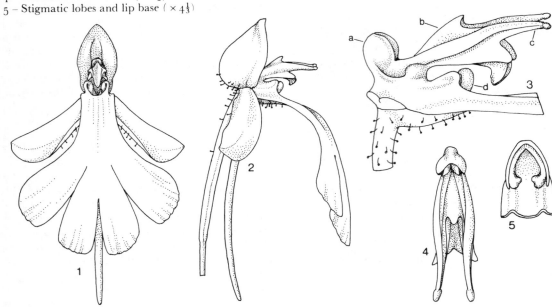

Cynorkis lowiana

1 – Flower (× 2)
2 – Flower, side view (× 2)
3 – Column, rostellum and lip base, side view (× 6½) a Anther, b Rostellum, c Rostellar arms, d Stigma
4 – Rostellum from above (× 6½)
5 – Stigmatic lobes and lip base (× 4⅓)

Cypripedium L.
Subfamily Cypripedioideae

Terrestrial herbs, mostly less than 1 m tall. **Stems** very short to long, produced from a stout creeping rhizome, 1- to several-leaved. **Leaves** plicate, deciduous, reniform or ovate to lanceolate, ± pubescent. **Flowers** 1–several, mostly showy. **Dorsal sepal** erect or somewhat porrect over lip; **lateral sepals** united to apex forming a synsepalum. **Petals** spreading, linear to lanceolate, ± twisted. **Lip** deeply saccate, margins inrolled. **Staminode** peltate-ovate or trullate; anthers 2, behind staminode and beneath the short column.

DISTRIBUTION About 45 species widely distributed in north temperate Asia, Europe, Japan and N. America south to Mexico.
DERIVATION OF NAME From the Greek *Cypros (Cyprus)*, the island sacred to Venus, and *pedilon* (slipper), corrupted to *pedium*, meaning Venus' slipper orchid.
TAXONOMY Carl von Linné (Linnaeus) described the genus in 1753 in his *Species Plantarum* (p. 951). For a discussion of the taxonomy of *Cypripedium* see under *Paphiopedilum*. In horticultural circles many people still refer to the tropical Asiatic lady's slipper orchids, which have fleshy, non-deciduous leaves, as *Cypripedium* species and hybrids. However, these species were transferred over 90 years ago to the genus *Paphiopedilum* and should correctly be referred to as such.

The genus was revised by R.A. Rolfe in 1896 in his *Orchid Review* and again by F. Kraenzlin in A. Engler's *Das Pflanzenreich* (1901). No attempt to account for the whole genus has been made recently but the N. American species (11 in all) have recently been included by C. Luer in his excellent *Native Orchids of the United States and Canada* (1975). A key to the Chinese species is given by S.C. Chen in the *Proceedings of the 12th World Orchid Conference* (1988).
TYPE SPECIES *C. calceolus* L.
CULTURE Compost various, depending on plant origin. Mixtures of sand, peat and leafmould with a little loam and sphagnum are usually suitable. Temp. Hardy outdoors but protect from severe frost. While growing, the plants require very shady and evenly moist conditions, but when the leaves have fallen, less water is needed.

Cypripedium acaule Aiton
[Colour Plate]
An erect, pubescent, terrestrial plant up to 40 cm tall. **Stems** short, mostly 2-leaved, arising from a short rhizome with fibrous roots. **Leaves** plicate, opposite, basal, elliptic, obtuse, 10–28 cm long, 5–15 cm broad. **Inflorescence** erect, 1-flowered, up to 40 cm long. **Flower** showy; sepals and petals yellow-green veined purple or purple-brown; lip purplish-pink (rarely white); staminode greenish to purple. **Dorsal sepal** lanceolate, acute, porrect, with slightly reflexed margins, 4–5 cm long, 0.5–1.9 cm broad; **lateral sepals** united to apex, 3–4 cm long, 1–2 broad. **Petals** spreading-deflexed, linear-lanceolate, twisted slightly, acute, 4–6 cm long, 1–1.5 cm broad. **Lip** elongated, somewhat geniculate towards base, obovoid, pouched, longitudinally sulcate in front, veins prominent, margins, infolded, 4–6 cm long, 2.5–3.5 cm broad. **Staminode** ovate, 1.8 cm long, 1.4 cm broad.
DISTRIBUTION Eastern USA and Canada.
HISTORY Perhaps the best known of the lady's slipper orchids after *C. calceolus* and *C. reginae*, this species is known as the 'moccasin flower'. It is a fairly common species in many N. American woods particularly those in the higher and drier areas.

C. acaule was described in 1789 by William Aiton in his *Hortus Kewensis* (p. 303), the specific epithet referring to the apparently stemless habit.
CLOSELY RELATED SPECIES *C. acaule* is similar to *C. reginae* in lip coloration but the latter differs in having a long leafy stem, much broader white petals and sepals, and a short more globular lip.

Cypripedium calceolus L. [Colour Plate]
An erect terrestrial herb, up to 80 cm tall, ± densely pubescent. **Stem** short, developing from a creeping rhizome, wth fibrous roots. **Leaves** 3–5, plicate, petiolate, elliptic to ovate or ovate-lanceolate, acute, 5–20 cm long, 3–10 cm broad, somewhat 2-ranked, sheathing at the base. **Inflorescence** erect, 1- or 2-flowered. **Flowers** large, showy; sepals and petals yellow-green to deep maroon-purple; lip glossy rich yellow; staminode yellow, ± spotted with red. **Dorsal sepal** ovate-lanceolate, acute, margins ± undulate, twisted, 2.5–8 cm long, 1.5–3.5 cm broad; **lateral sepals** united to apex, similar to dorsal sepal. **Petals** linear to linear-lanceolate, acute, ± twisted into a corkscrew, 4–9 cm long, 0.5–1 cm broad. **Lip** calceolate, an obovoid pouch, margins incurved, somewhat sulcate along veins, 2.2–6.5 cm long, 2–4 cm across. **Staminode** bluntly trullate, 1.1 cm long, 0.4–0.6 cm broad.
DISTRIBUTION Temperate Asia, Europe and N. America; often growing in shaded woodland on limestone except in N. America where it grows extensively in woodlands and also (as var. *parviflorum*) in marshy areas.
HISTORY The lady's slipper is probably the most famous of all orchids, long-prized as a garden plant for its beauty. Unfortunately this has led to its widespread removal from native habitats in both Europe and N. America, so

much so that it is now a great rarity throughout much of its range. Indeed, in the British Isles this formerly fairly widespread species has been reduced to a few plants in a single locality in N. England.

Carl von Linné described and based the genus on this species some 200 years ago. American forms now considered as varieties of *C. calceolus* have until recently been treated as distinct species.

Var. *pubescens* (Willd.) Corr. is widely distributed in N. America and is distinguished from the typical form by its downier appearance and distinctly coloured greenish sepals and petals. Var. *parviflorum* (Salisb.) Fern. is, as its name suggests, distinguished by its smaller flowers and slender, less pubescent vegetative parts. This variety and var. *planipetalum* (Fern.) Victorin & Rousseau, in which the petals are not twisted at all, are confined to the N.E. of N. America.

SYNONYMS *Cypripedium pubescens* Willd.; *C. flavescens* De Cand.; *C. parviflorum* Salisb.; *C. luteum* Aiton; *C. furcatum* Raf.; *C. assurgens* Raf.; *C. aureum* Raf.; *C. parviflorum* Sims & Salisb. etc.
CLOSELY RELATED SPECIES *Cypripedium montanum* Lindl. from N.W. North America may be distinguished from *C. calceolus* by its white lip. *Cypripedium candidum* Muhl. from the Great Lakes area in N. America likewise has a white lip but its flowers are much smaller than those of *C. calceolus* and the plants are shorter and stouter.

Cypripedium reginae Walter [Colour Plate]
A robust terrestrial plant, up to 90 cm tall. **Stems** arising from a stout rhizome, 3- to 7-leaved. **Leaves** ovate-lanceolate, suberect-spreading, subacute, margins undulate, 10–25 cm long, 6–16 cm broad, sheathing the stem at the base. **Inflorescence** erect, 1- to 3- (or rarely 4-)flowered. **Flowers** showy; sepals and petals snow-white; lip rose-purple streaked with white (rarely white); staminode white, lower margins yellow, spotted red. **Dorsal sepal** ovate-orbicular, obtuse or rounded, 3–4.5 cm long, 2.5–4.2 cm broad; **lateral sepals** united, 3–4.2 cm long, 2–3.7 cm broad. **Petals** spreading, oblong or oblong-elliptic, subacute to obtuse, 2.5–4.7 cm long, 1–1.7 cm broad. **Lip** subglobose, saccate, margins infolded, 2.5–5 cm long, 1.5–3.5 cm broad. **Staminode** ovate, 1.4 cm long, 1.7 cm broad.
DISTRIBUTION N.E. and N. Central N. America; commonly growing on the margins of wet bogs.
HISTORY With *C. calceolus* probably the most sought-after slipper orchid. *C. reginae* was described by Carl von Linné in 1753 as a variety of *C. calceolus* but Walter in 1788 in *Flora Carolinensis* (p. 222) raised it to specific rank.

This species is commonly known as the showy or queen lady's slipper orchid.
SYNONYMS *Cypripedium humile* Salisb.; *Fissipes hirsuta* Farwell; *Cypripedium hirsutum* (Farwell) Miller
CLOSELY RELATED SPECIES See *C. acaule*.

Cyrtochilum H.B.K.
Subfamily Epidendroideae
Tribe Oncidieae

Medium-sized to large epiphytic or lithophytic herbs with creeping rhizomes and clustered to remote pseudobulbs. **Pseudobulbs** relatively large, leafy at the apex. **Inflorescences** basal, axillary, simple to branched, elongate, erect to arcuate, sometimes very long and scrambling through the surrounding vegetation, laxly many-flowered. **Flowers** small to large and usually showy, often somewhat stellate; segments more or less spreading, free, often clawed. **Sepals** spreading, subsimilar, the laterals often slightly larger than the dorsal. **Petals** free, spreading, usually slightly smaller than the sepals. **Lip** rather fleshy, dependent, smaller than the sepals and petals, entire to obscurely 3-lobed, with a more or less complex basal ridged callus. **Column** short, erect, with lateral wings near the apex; pollinia 2, obovoid, sulcate, attached by a short to elongate stipe to a small viscidium.
DISTRIBUTION A large genus of perhaps 150 species in tropical Central and S. America, particularly in the Andes.
DERIVATION OF NAME from the Greek *kyrtos* (convex) and *chilum* (lip), in reference to the rather fleshy lip.
TAXONOMY *Cyrtochilum* was established by Humboldt, Bonpland and Kunth in 1815 in their *Nova Genera et Species* (p. 349). It has never been widely accepted and most of the species have usually been included in *Oncidium*, the remainder in *Odontoglossum*. Garay and Stacy in their revision of the infrageneric categories in *Oncidium* considered *Cyrtochilum* a section of *Oncidium*. The species are still usually found in cultivation as oncidiums. Recently, however, the generic delimitation of *Oncidium*, *Odontoglossum* and their allies have been the subject of detailed studies leading most authors to separate off certain taxa in segregate genera. This has been a general trend in the treatment of the larger genera of orchids. *Cyrtochilum* holds together well both as a section of *Oncidium* and as a distinct genus and we have adopted the latter approach which is currently in favour among European workers. *Cyrtochilum* differs from *Oncidium* in having a lip that is smaller than the other segments and is somewhat

triangular to sagittate in outline and either entire or obscurely 3-lobed.

The genus has not been revised since Fritz Kraenzlin's treatment in 1922 in Engler's *Das Pflanzenreich Orchidaceae–Monandrae* pt. 2 (pp. 25–86).
TYPE SPECIES *C. undulatum* H.B.K.
CULTURE Temp Winter min. 12°C. Grow in pots of epiphyte compost under conditions of moderate shade and humidity. Water throughout the year but less when the pseudobulbs are fully swollen. The long inflorescences need to be trained up supports for the best effect.

Cyrtochilum falcipetalum (Lindl.) Kraenzl.
[Colour Plate]
A large epiphytic or occasionally terrestrial plant with a climbing habit. **Pseudobulbs** borne at intervals of 20–25 cm along a creeping ascending rhizome, ovoid or subcylindrical, up to 15 cm long, up to 5 cm in diameter, 1- or rarely 2-leaved at the apex. **Leaves** oblanceolate to narrowly elliptic, acute or shortly acuminate, up to 60 cm long and 5.5 cm wide. **Inflorescence** paniculate, up to 6 m long; peduncle terete; branches short, 3- to 6-flowered; rhachis zigzag. **Flowers** usually 6–7 cm across, variable in size, the sepals rich dark brown with a yellow apex and apical margins, the petals yellower than the sepals, the lip mostly greenish-brown, shiny orange-brown on the sides and yellowish towards the base, the callus bright yellow, the column yellow-brown spotted with red near the base. **Sepals** shortly narrowly clawed, trullate above, acute, 2.6–3.2 cm long, 1.6–2.6 cm wide, with undulate margins, the claw winged at the base. **Petals** similar to the sepals but smaller and with the margins more undulate-crisped, curved forwards in the apical half. **Lip** recurved, obscurely 3-lobed, shortly clawed, narrowly triangular-ovate, acute, 1.1–1.4 cm long, 0.5–0.8 cm wide; callus complex, 3-ridged at the base and 5-ridged at the apex, each ridge with additional projections. **Column** erect, bearing a small porrect digitate projection on each side near the apex.
DISTRIBUTION Venezuela, Colombia, Ecuador and Peru; up to 2700 m elevation in montane forest.
HISTORY Described by John Lindley as *Oncidium falcipetalum* in 1846 in *Orchidaceae Lindenianae* (p. 14) based on collections made by J. Linden and H. Funck near Merida in Venezuela. It was transferred to *Cyrtochilum* in 1922 by F. Kraenzlin in Engler's *Das Pflanzenreich Orchidaceae–Monandrae* (p. 37). It was first introduced into cultivation in 1886 when it was flowered by Messrs. Veitch of Chelsea.
SYNONYM *Oncidium falcipetalum* Lindl.

Cyrtochilum loxense (Lindl.) Kraenzl.

A large epiphyte. **Pseudobulbs** ovoid to pyriform, 7.5–12.5 cm long, 2.5–4 cm in diameter, compressed, arranged in 2 irregular rows on the rhizome, unifoliate. **Leaf** linear to narrowly lanceolate, subacute to acuminate, 22–38 cm long, 3–5 cm wide. **Inflorescence** straggling, 1–3 m long, branching, the branches 1- to 3-flowered; bracts minute, 3 mm long. **Flowers** large, showy, well-spaced, the sepals cinnamon-brown barred with yellow, the petals olive-brown with scattered yellow transverse markings, the lip bright orange-yellow, paler on the disc and crimson-spotted on the callus; pedicel and ovary up to 6 cm long. **Sepals** narrowly clawed, elliptic-oblong to ovate, subacute, 2.2–2.7 cm long, 1.1–1.3 cm wide, keeled on the back. **Petals** similar but less prominently keeled, 2–2.7 cm long, 1–1.4 cm wide. **Lip** fleshy, spathulate, auriculate at the base, 2.1–2.3 cm long, 2.3–2.5 cm wide; callus fleshy, with 4 shallow plates in front and numerous bristles on each side. **Column** erect, with an obscure wing on each side of the stigma.

DISTRIBUTION   Ecuador.

HISTORY   A beautiful species discovered by Th. Hartweg in 1842 near the town of Loxa (now Loja) in Ecuador and described as *Oncidium loxense* by John Lindley in 1852 in his and Paxton's *Flower Garden* (p. 128). It was transferred to *Cyrtochilum* by F. Kraenzlin in Engler's *Das Pflanzenreich Orchidaceae Monandrae–Oncidiinae* (p. 59). It was probably introduced into cultivation in 1883 by E. Klaboch who sent plants to Messrs Sander and Sons of St Albans, England.

SYNONYM   *Oncidium loxense* Lindl.

Cyrtochilum macranthum (Lindl.) Kraenzl.
[Colour Plate]

A large epiphytic plant. **Pseudobulbs** ovoid to conical, more or less compressed, 7–15 cm long, subtended by 3–4 imbricate sheaths, 2-leaved at the apex. **Leaves** linear-oblong to oblanceolate, acute, 25–55 cm long, 2.5–5 cm wide. **Inflorescences** paniculate, 60–300 cm long; branches remote, up to 30 cm long, each 3- to 5-flowered. **Flowers** large, showy, 7–10 cm across, the sepals honey-brown to dull yellow-brown, the petals golden-yellow, the lip white at the base, yellow at the tip and with purple sides; pedicel and ovary 4.5 cm long. **Sepals** clawed, suborbicular-spathulate, rounded at the apex, 3.5–5 cm long, 2.4–3.1 cm wide. **Petals** shortly clawed, suborbicular-ovate, rounded to obtuse, 3–4.5 cm long, 2.5–3 cm wide, with slightly crisped margins. **Lip** shortly clawed, obscurely 3-lobed, flat, triangular, 2.5–3 cm long, 1.9–2.8 cm wide; callus of 3 basally confluent lamellae and 3 smaller teeth in front. **Column** stout, 1 cm long, with small,

fleshy, flabellate wings, irregularly bilobed above.

DISTRIBUTION   Colombia, Ecuador and Peru; in montane forest up to 3000 m elevation.

HISTORY   First collected by H. Ruiz and J. Pavon near Guayaquil in Ecuador and described by John Lindley as *Oncidium macranthum* in his *Genera and Species of Orchidaceous Plants* (p. 205) in 1832. It was subsequently rediscovered near Tunguragua in Ecuador by A. Matthews and later by Th. Hartweg, W. Jameson and R. Spruce. It was introduced into cultivation in 1868 by Lord Londesborough at Norbiton in Surrey, England. It was transferred to *Cyrtochilum* by F. Kraenzlin in Engler's *Das Pflanzenreich Orchidaceae–Monandrae Oncidiinae* (p. 55).

SYNONYM   *Oncidium macranthum* Lindl.

Cyrtochilum microchilum (Lindl.) Cribb
[Colour Plate]

A large lithophyte. **Pseudobulbs** ovoid or suborbicular, much compressed, 2.3–5 cm long, unifoliate at the apex, concealed at the base by acute, imbricate sheaths. **Leaf** rigid, leathery, oblong to elliptic-oblong, subacute, 17–30 cm long, 6–7.5 cm wide, keeled on the reverse, slightly glaucous. **Inflorescence** 100–140 cm long, branching in upper half, subtended by a keeled sheath; branches short, few-flowered; bracts triangular-ovate, acute, 3–5 mm long. **Flowers** small, 2.4–3.5 cm across, variable in colour, the sepals yellow heavily mottled with dull pale to dark brown, the petals yellow heavily suffused with purple-brown or very dark brown, the lip white or lilac spotted with purple on the lobes, the callus purple and yellow, the column lilac spotted with purple and with white wings; pedicel and ovary 1.3–1.5 cm long. **Sepals** clawed, ovate-spathulate to spathulate, obtuse, 1.2–1.4 cm long, 0.8–1 cm wide. **Petals** curved forwards, clawed, oblanceolate, obtuse, 1–1.2 cm long, 0.4–0.7 cm wide. **Lip** very small, 3-lobed, 0.7 cm long, 1.1 cm wide; side lobes curved forwards, dolabriform; mid-lobe obscure, broadly oblong, bluntly apiculate; callus large, many-lobed, occupying the entire disc. **Column** 0.5–0.6 cm long, obliquely triangularly winged on either side of stigma.

DISTRIBUTION   Mexico and Guatemala; growing on rocks in exposed places, up to 2300 m elevation.

HISTORY   This rare orchid was discovered by George Ure Skinner in 1838 near the summit of Cuesta de Puentezuelas in Guatemala. It was described as *Oncidium microchilum* by John Lindley in the *Botanical Register* (misc. 193) in 1840. It is transferred to *Cyrtochilum* below.

SYNONYM   *Oncidium micranthum* Lindl. [*Cyrtochilum microchilum* (Lindl.) Cribb *comb. nov.* Basionym: *Oncidium microchilum* Lindl. in Ed-

wards' Botanical Register 26: misc. 193 (1840)].

Cyrtochilum retusum (Lindl.) Kraenzl.
[Colour Plate]

A large epiphyte or lithophyte. **Pseudobulbs** clustered, ovoid to narrowly ellipsoidal, slightly compressed, 2.5–5 cm long, unifoliate at the apex, subtended by 3–4 pairs of distichous imbricate sheaths. **Leaves** elliptic-linear to linear-oblanceolate, acute to obtuse, up to 29 cm long, 2 cm wide. **Inflorescence** erect, paniculate, up to 60 cm long; peduncle slender; branches slightly fractiflex; bracts ovate-lanceolate, acute, 5–8 mm long. **Flowers** small, red or orange-red, with a red to yellow lip; pedicel and ovary 1.5–1.8 cm long. **Dorsal sepal** concave, broadly lanceolate to oblanceolate, acute, 1.3–1.6 cm long, 0.3–0.5 cm wide; **lateral sepals** longly clawed, similar to the dorsal sepal but longer and narrower. **Petals** narrowly oblong-obovate, slightly oblique, acute, 1–1.3 cm long, 0.4–0.5 cm wide. **Lip** recurved, oblong-quadrate to ovate-cordate, 1–1.2 cm long, 0.75–1 cm wide; callus with 2 close ridges reaching the middle of the lip. **Column** stout, 0.3 cm long, winged on each side.

DISTRIBUTION   Colombia, Ecuador and Peru.

HISTORY   Originally described as *Odontoglossum retusum* in 1844 by John Lindley in Bentham's *Plantae Hartwegianae* (p. 152), based on a collection by Th. Hartweg from Mt Saraguri near Loxa (now Loja) in Ecuador. It was transferred to *Cyrtochilum* by F. Kraenzlin in Engler's *Das Pflanzenreich Orchidaceae–Monandrae Oncidiinae* (p. 86).

SYNONYM   *Odontoglossum retusum* Lindl.; *Oncidium retusum* (Lindl.) Beer

Cyrtochilum superbiens (Rchb.f.) Kraenzl.
[Colour Plate]

Pseudobulbs conical, compressed, 10 cm long, 3.5 cm broad, 1- to 2-leaved at apex, subtended by several leaf-bearing sheaths. **Leaves** oblong-ligulate, broadly linear or oblanceolate, 30–45 cm long, 3.5–4 cm broad, acute. **Inflorescence** flexuose, branched irregularly, laxly 20- to 30-flowered, up to 2 cm long; branches up to 15 cm long, few-flowered; bracts cucullate, 2 cm long, subacute. **Flowers** 6.5–8 cm across; sepals chocolate-brown with a yellow apex and dorsal keel; petals yellow, transversely barred with chocolate-brown; lip maroon-brown, callus yellow; column yellow and brown. **Sepals** spathulate, narrowly clawed, 3–3.5 cm long, 1.5–2.3 cm broad, rounded at apex, margins somewhat undulate. **Petals** shortly clawed, ovate, 2.0 cm long, 1.6 cm broad, apex acute and reflexed, margins undulate-crisped. **Lip** recurved, somewhat hastate, auriculate at base, shortly clawed, 2.3 cm long, 1.5 cm broad, acute; callus fleshy with a central ridge with several smaller tubercles on either side. **Column** with a small wing on either side of stigma.

DISTRIBUTION   Colombia and Venezuela.

HISTORY   First collected by Purdie in 1846 in the Sierra de Santa Marta and by H.C. Funck and L. Schlim between Pamplona and Ocaña in 1847. H.G. Reichenbach described this handsome species in 1848 in *Linnaea* (p. 843) *O. superbiens* is placed by L. Garay and J. Stacy in sect. *Cyrtochilum* with the large-flowered *O. macranthum*. Veitch & Sons first introduced *O. superbiens* into cultivation in 1871. We have followed Kraenzl in (1922) who transferred it to *Cyrtochilum* in Engler's *Pflanzenreich Orchidaceae–Monandreae Cyrtochilum* (p. 49).

SYNONYM   *Oncidium superbiens* Rchb.f.

CLOSELY RELATED SPECIES   See *O. loxense.*

Cyrtopodium R. Br.
Subfamily Epidendroideae
Tribe Cymbidieae
Subtribe Cyrtopodiinae

Medium-sized to large terrestrial, lithophytic or epiphytic plants. **Pseudobulbs** long-fusiform, several-leaved towards apex. **Leaves** deciduous, plicate, membranaceous, sheathing at the base. **Inflorescence** basal, racemose or paniculate, many-flowered; branches spreading; bracts often large. **Flowers** fairly large but often rather dull-coloured, usually whitish or yellow with brown spots. **Sepals** and **petals** free, spreading. **Lip** 3-lobed; side lobes incurved over the column; mid-lobe margins verrucose; disc callose. **Column** semiterete, dilated above, with a short foot; pollinia 2 or 4, waxy, attached by a stipe to a circular viscidium.

DISTRIBUTION   About 15 species confined to the American tropics and subtropics, from Florida and Mexico, south to Argentina.

DERIVATION OF NAME   From the Greek *kyrtos* (curved swelling) and *podion* (little foot), in reference to the shape of the column-foot, which curves upwards.

TAXONOMY   Described by Robert Brown in 1813 in the 2nd edition of William Aiton's *Hortus Kewensis* (p. 216).

Cyrtopodium is allied to *Eulophia* and *Govenia* but lacks the spurred or saccate lip of the former and has a prominently 3-lobed lip in contrast to the simple lip of the latter.

No revision of the genus has been made since that of F. Kraenzlin in 1917 in *Notizblatt des Botanischen Gartens, Berlin.*

TYPE SPECIES   *C. andersonii* (Andrews) R. Br.

CULTURE   Compost A or B. Temp. Winter min. 12–15°C. Although some species grow epiphytically, all grow well in a terrestrial compost. The plants require quite large containers and should be allowed to remain undisturbed for as long as possible. Until the new growths are well developed, water should be very sparingly given. After the leaves have fallen the plants require a cooler dry resting period.

Cyrtopodium andersonii (Andrews) R. Br.
[Colour Plate]

A large plant, 1.6 m or more tall. **Pseudobulbs** erect, fusiform-cylindric, 60–100 cm long, 3–5 cm broad. **Leaves** coriaceous, narrowly linear-lanceolate, shortly acuminate, 30–60 cm long, 2–5 cm broad. **Inflorescence** paniculate, pyramidal in outline above, 90–160 cm long, many-flowered; bracts membranaceous, ovate, acuminate, 3–5 cm long, yellow-green. **Flowers** fairly showy; sepals yellow-green; petals lemon-yellow; lip rich yellow, callus orange. **Sepals** broadly ovate-elliptic, obtuse to shortly apiculate, scarcely undulate, 1.8–2.2 cm long, 1.3–1.7 cm broad. **Petals** broadly obovate, rounded, 1.8–2.3 cm long, 1.2–1.5 cm broad. **Lip** sessile, 3-lobed, 1.8–2 cm long, 2.5–3 cm broad; side lobes obovate, rounded; mid-lobe shorter, broadly obovate-subquadrate; disc longitudinally grooved. **Column** exauriculate, 0.5–0.6 cm long.

DISTRIBUTION   The W. Indies and tropical S. America.

HISTORY   Discovered by Dr J. Anderson on St Vincent and introduced into cultivation in England by T. Stevens of Stepney. It was described in 1811 by Andrews in the *Botanical Repository* (t. 651) as *Cymbidium andersonii*. Robert Brown transferred it to the genus *Cyrtopodium* in 1813 in the 2nd edition of William Aiton's *Hortus Kewensis* (p. 216).

SYNONYM   *Cymbidium andersonii* Andrews

Cyrtopodium punctatum (L.) Lindl.
[Colour Plate]

A large epiphytic or terrestrial plant, 1.2 m tall or more. **Pseudobulbs** clustered, erect, fusiform-elongate, many-noded, 15–40 cm long, 1.5–3.5 cm across, covered by greyish-white sheaths when young. **Leaves** linear to elliptic-lanceolate, acute or acuminate, distichous, spreading or recurved, 10–65 cm long, 1–5 cm broad. **Inflorescence** paniculate, many-flowered; bracts showy, undulate, greenish-yellow, spotted with red-brown. **Flowers** showy; sepals greenish-yellow, spotted with red-brown; petals bright yellow, spotted with red-brown; lip red-brown with a yellow base, mid-lobe purplish with a yellow centre. **Sepals** ovate to oblong-lanceolate, acute, margins undulate, 1.7–2.6 cm long, 0.7–1.1 cm broad.

Petals broadly oblong-ovate to obovate-oblong, clawed, subtruncate, margins undulate-crisped, 1.3–2.1 cm long, 0.8–1.2 cm broad. **Lip** 3-lobed, 1.1–1.6 cm long, 1.7–2.2 cm broad; side lobes erect, obovate or rounded; mid-lobe rigid, deflexed, broadly oblong, margin erose-tuberculate; disc with a sulcate callus. **Column** club-shaped, subapiculate, 0.7 cm long, with a short foot.

DISTRIBUTION   Mexico and Florida, south to Brazil and Paraguay.

HISTORY   One of the earliest of the tropical American orchids to be described, *C. punctatum* was described by Carl von Linné in 1759 as *Epidendrum punctatum* in his *Systema Naturae* (p. 1246). John Lindley transferred it to *Cyrtopodium* in 1833 in his *Genera and Species of Orchidaceous Plants* (p. 188).

SYNONYM   *Epidendrum punctatum* L.

Cyrtorchis Schltr.
Subfamily Epidendroideae
Tribe Vandeae
Subtribe Aerangidinae

Epiphytic or rarely lithophytic herbs. **Stems** elongated, ± branching, covered with leaf-sheaths and emitting aerial roots at intervals. **Leaves** distichous, often imbricate, spreading or recurved, oblong to linear, mostly coriaceous or rarely fleshy, V-shaped in cross-section. **Inflorescences** axillary, spreading or ± recurved, simple, racemose, few- to many-flowered; bracts mostly large and conspicuous, dark brownish. **Flowers** alternate, rather large, white to cream-coloured, turning orange or yellow with age, usually fragrant. **Sepals** and **petals** free, lanceolate, acute, ± strongly recurved. **Lip** similar to petals but broader at base, recurved, with a long tapering spur at the base. **Column** short, stout, footless; anther drawn out into a long beak in front; pollinia 2, globose or elliptic, each attached to a spathulate stipe; viscidium 1, linear or oblong; rostellum long, beak-like, bifid.

DISTRIBUTION   About 15 species widespread in tropical Africa south to S. Africa.

DERIVATION OF NAME   From the Greek *kyrtos (a swelling or curve)* and *orchis* (orchid), probably alluding to the curved sepals, petals and lip or possibly to the fleshy leaves and roots of some species.

TAXONOMY   Rudolf Schlechter described *Cyrtorchis* in 1914 in *Die Orchideen* (p. 595). It is allied to *Angraecum* and many of the species were first described in that genus, but it is distinguished by its characteristic rostellum, the stellate flower with slender lanceolate segments and the large dark brown bracts.

V.S. Summerhayes revised this genus in 1960 in the *Kew Bulletin* dividing the species into two sections:

1. sect. *Cyrtorchis* with a viscidium consisting of an upper indurated saddle-shaped part and a lower thin hyaline part and with the stipites often much widened in the apical half. *C. arcuata* is the type species of this section.
2. sect. *Homocollecticon* with a viscidium of uniform hyaline texture and stipites which are usually only moderately broadened above. Species in the latter section are *C. monteiroae* (Rchb.f.) Schltr.; *C. ringens* (Rchb.f.) Summerh. and *C. praetermissa* Summerh.

TYPE SPECIES *C. arcuata* (Lindl.) Schltr.
CULTURE Compost A. Temp. Winter min. 12–15°C. As they produce numerous, long aerial roots, *Cyrtorchis* species are best grown in baskets, or mounted on large pieces of fern-fibre or cork. They require humid conditions, under moderate shade and should be well watered when in active growth.

Cyrtorchis arcuata (Lindl.) Schltr.
[Colour Plate]
A straggling epiphytic or occasionally lithophytic plant. **Stems** stout, over 70 m long, 1 cm in diameter, pendulous, covered by distichous dark brown persistent leaf-sheaths. **Roots** robust, many, aerial and pendent. **Leaves** 6–12, oblong, obliquely 2-lobed at apex, fleshy-coriaceous, up to 20 cm long, 5.2 cm broad. **Inflorescence** racemose, suberect, commonly 8- to 10-flowered; rhachis zigzag, stout; bracts brown-black, sheathing, very broad, obtuse. **Flowers** star-shaped, translucent, white fading to orange; spur white, tinged pale yellow or green. **Sepals** linear-lanceolate, acuminate, recurved-spreading in apical two-thirds, 2.5–4 cm long, 0.4–0.9 cm broad. **Petals** similar to sepals, 2.2–3.3 cm long, 0.4–0.6 cm broad. **Lip** tapering to an acuminate apex, similar to other segments, 2–3 cm long, 0.5 cm broad; spur tapering to a point, somewhat S-shaped, up to 7 cm long. **Column** short, broad, 0.3 cm long; rostellum long, pendent inside spur.
DISTRIBUTION Common and widespread in tropical and S. Africa.
HISTORY Discovered by J.F. Drége at Albany in S. Africa, this species was described by John Lindley in Hooker's *Companion to the Botanical Magazine* (p. 204) in 1836 as *Angraecum arcuatum* and was transferred to *Cyrtorchis* by Rudolf Schlechter in 1914 in *Die Orchideen* (p. 596).

Five subspecies of *C. arcuata* are known. These are more or less geographically isolated and are distinguished on flower-size and leaf-size.

SYNONYMS include *Listrostachys whitei* Rolfe; *Angraecum arcuatum* Lindl.; *Listrostachys sedenii* (Rchb.f.) Schltr.

Cyrtorchis chailluana (Hooker f.) Schltr.
A medium-sized to large epiphytic plant. **Leaves** distichous, oblong or oblong-oblanceolate, tapering distinctly at both ends, not very rigid or stiff, unequally 2-lobed at apex, 8–26 cm long, 1.7–3.5 cm broad. **Inflorescences** racemose, many-flowered, up to 24 cm long; bracts broad, sheathing, 1–2.5 cm long. **Flowers** scented, pure white or cream-coloured, flushed greenish on the spur. **Sepals** and **petals** subsimilar, recurved, linear-lanceolate, acuminate, 3–5 cm long. **Lip** similar to the other segments, porrect, slightly curvate, 3–5 cm long; spur 9–15 cm long, very slender. **Column** short, stout; viscidium composed of a broad, stiff, hardened upper portion with recurved edges and a linear, hyaline, very thin lower portion.
DISTRIBUTION S. Nigeria, west to Zaïre and Uganda; in tropical rain forest.
HISTORY This, the largest and showiest of all *Cyrtorchis* species, was originally described by Sir Joseph Hooker in 1866 as *Angraecum chailluanum* in the *Botanical Magazine* (t. 5589) based on a plant collected by M. Du Chaillu in the Gabon, which he sent to the Royal Botanic Gardens at Kew, London, where it flowered in May 1866. H.G. Reichenbach transferred it to *Listrostachys* but Rudolf Schlechter transferred it again to *Cyrtorchis* in 1914 in *Die Orchideen* (p. 596).
SYNONYMS *Angraecum chailluanum* Hooker f.; *Listrostachys chailluana* (Hooker f.) Rchb.f.

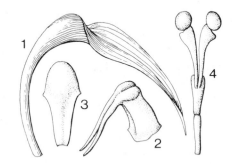

Cyrtorchis chailluana
1 – Lip and base of spur (× 1⅕)
2 – Column and rostellum, side view (× 2)
3 – Anther-cap (× 2)
4 – Pollinia, stipites and viscidium (× 3½)

Dactylorhiza Necker
Subfamily Orchidoideae
Tribe Orchideae
Subtribe Orchidiinae

Terrestrial plants with digitately lobed tuberous roots and leafy erect stems. **Leaves** fleshy, sheathing at base, lanceolate to ovate, green or spotted with black. **Inflorescence** densely many-flowered, pyramidal to cylindrical; bracts prominent, leafy, often overtopping the flowers. **Flowers** usually purple or pink, less commonly yellow or white, often spotted or lined with dark purple on the lip; ovary sessile. **Sepals** and **petals** free, subsimilar; dorsal sepal and petals often connivent to form a hood over the column; lateral sepals spreading to reflexed or erect. **Lip** entire to 3-lobed, ecallose, spurred at the base. **Column** erect, with 2 parallel anther loculi; pollinia 2, mealy, with caudicle and small viscidia.
DISTRIBUTION A genus of about 40 species, widespread in Europe and the Mediterranean region across temperate Asia to the Himalayas, China and Japan, and with single species each in N. America and Madeira.
DERIVATION OF NAME From the Greek *dactylos* (finger), and *rhiza* (root), in allusion to the digitate tuberoids of the genus.
TAXONOMY *Dactylorhiza* was first suggested by Necker, in 1790 in his *Elementa Botanica* (p. 129), as a segregate of the genus *Orchis*. However, it was not formally established until 1937 when Nevski took up the name in the journal *Trudy Batanischeskogo Instituta Akademii Nauk SSSR* (p. 332). *Dactylorhiza* is distinguished from *Orchis* by its digitate tuberoids, and prominent leafy bracts that usually overtop the flowers.

It is a problematic genus taxonomically with many of the species difficult to distinguish morphologically. This may be because the species still appear to be evolving and hybridisation is also frequent in the wild. The most recent accounts of the genus are to be found in the fifth volume of *Flora Europea* and the ninth of the *Flora of Turkey*. The popular accounts of European orchids published in recent years from Germany have in the authors' view tended to oversplit in this genus (and in others) to the extent that they are difficult to use satisfactorily to name plants.
TYPE SPECIES *O. umbrosa* Karelin & Kir.
SYNONYMS *Dactylorchis* Verm.
CULTURE Temp. Winter min. 5°C. Culture as for *Anacamptis* with a little winter moisture. In temperate areas many of the species will grow quite happily out-of-doors in the garden in neutral or slightly acid soils to which peat and leaf mould have been added.

Dactylorhiza foliosa (Solander ex Lowe) Soó
[Colour Plate]

A large terrestrial plant 30–70 cm tall with digitate 2- to 5-lobed tubers. **Leaves** 8–12, distichous, lanceolate to ovate, acute, 10–20 cm long, 2–4.5 cm wide, glossy green. **Inflorescence** densely many-flowered, pyramidal to cylindrical, 5–15 cm long; bracts lanceolate, acuminate, 3–5.5 cm long. **Flowers** pale to rich purple, usually spotted darker purple on the lip; ovary 14–16 mm long. **Dorsal sepal** narrowly elliptic to lanceolate, acute, 10–11 mm long, 5 mm wide; **lateral sepals** reflexed, erect, obliquely lanceolate, acute, 14–16 mm long, 4–5 mm wide. **Petals** porrect, obliquely lanceolate, acute, 9–11 mm long, 3–3.5 mm wide. **Lip** 3-lobed in the apical part, 8–15 mm long, 10–18 mm wide; lobes triangular, more or less equal in length; spur cylindrical-tapering, dorsoventrally flattened, 9–11 mm long. **Column** 3.5–4.5 mm long.

DISTRIBUTION Endemic to the island of Madeira, 400–1000 m, often growing by running water in meadows.

HISTORY Originally described as *Orchis foliosa* in 1831 by Lowe in the *Transactions of the Cambridge Philosophical Society* (p. 13). It was transferred to the present genus by the Hungarian botanist R. Soó in 1962 in his *Nomina nova generis Dactylorhiza* (p. 7). It is nowadays widely grown as a perennial garden plant in the British Isles where it is quite hardy.

SYNONYMS *Orchis foliosa* Solander ex Lowe; *O. maderensis* Summerh.

CLOSELY ALLIED SPECIES The closely allied and equally spectacular *D. elata* (Poiret) Soó from S.W. Europe and N.W. Africa, can be even taller than *D. foliosa* but it differs in having smaller, usually deeper purple flowers with a lip which is narrower than long and with the sides prominently reflexed.

Dactylostalix Rchb.f.
Subfamily Epidendroideae
Tribe Calypsoeae
Subtribe Corallorhizinae

Small terrestrial herbs with creeping underground rhizomes emitting a few roots along the length. **Stems** slender, erect, sheathing at the base, unifoliate at the apex. **Leaf** spreading or suberect, plicate, petiolate. **Inflorescence** erect, terminal, 1-flowered. **Flower** quite large for the plant size, slightly nodding. **Sepals** and **petals** free, spreading, the sepals longer than the petals. **Lip** clawed, broadly ovate, trilobed, with a crested callus but lacking a spur. **Column** slender, elongate; pollinia 4, in 2 pairs, with a distinct viscidium.

DISTRIBUTION A monotypic genus from Japan.

DERIVATION OF NAME From the Greek *dactylos* (finger) and *stalix* (stake), in allusion to the finger-like crests on the lip.

TAXONOMY This genus was established by H.G. Reichenbach in the *Botanische Zeitung* (p. 74) in 1878. It is similar in habit to *Calypso* but lacks the saccate twin-spurred lip of that genus. The placing of *Dactylostalix* in the Corallorhizinae is suspect and it may well be better placed with *Calypso* in the tribe Calypsoinae.

TYPE SPECIES *D. ringens* Rchb.f.

SYNONYM *Pergamena* Rchb.f.

CULTURE Temp. Winter min. 5°C. Culture as for *Calypso*.

Dactylostalix ringens Rchb.f. [Colour Plate]

A small terrestrial with a stout creeping rhizome up to several cm long, 2–4 mm in diameter. **Stems** erect, very short, 1–2 cm long. **Leaf** spreading to suberect, elliptic to ovate-elliptic, obtuse or subacute, 3.5–6 cm long, 2.5–3.5 cm wide, the margins sometimes undulate-crisped, bright green; petiole 1.2–2.4 cm long. **Inflorescence** erect, 10–17 cm tall, 1-flowered; peduncle slender, with 2 distant sheaths along length; bract ovate-elliptic, 2–3 mm long. **Flower** large for plant, with pale green sepals and petals spotted with purple on the basal parts of the dorsal sepal and petals, the lip white with purple blotches on the side lobes, disc and base of the mid-lobe; pedicel and ovary erect, 6–14 mm long. **Dorsal sepal** linear-lanceolate, acute 1.8–2.3 cm long, 2.5–3 mm wide; **lateral sepals** oblanceolate, acute, 1.7–2 cm long, 2–3 mm wide, slightly incurved-deflexed. **Petals** porrect, lanceolate, acute, 1.5–1.7 cm long, 4 mm wide. **Lip** 3-lobed in the basal half, 1.3–1.5 cm long, 8–9 mm wide; side lobes erect, rounded; mid-lobe much larger, subcircular, rounded at the apex, rather undulate; callus of low crests on the disc of the lip. **Column** 9–10 mm long.

DISTRIBUTION Japan from the Kuriles to Kiusiu; growing in subalpine coniferous woodland, up to 1500 m.

HISTORY This pretty delicate orchid was described by H.G. Reichenbach in 1878 in the *Botanische Zeitung* (p. 74) based on a collection from Japan.

SYNONYMS *Pergamena uniflora* Finet; *Calypso japonica* Maxim.

Dendrobium Sw.
Subfamily Epidendroideae
Tribe Dendrobieae
Subtribe Dendrobiinae

Mainly epiphytic but occasionally lithophytic or terrestrial plants of very variable form. **Stems** (a) rhizomatous, (b) erect and many-noded, (c) erect and 1-noded or several-noded from a many-noded rhizome, or (d) with no rhizome and new stems of many nodes starting at base of old ones; 1 or 2 cm to about 5 m long, woody or fleshy, swollen at base or along length, often pseudobulbous, ± covered with sheathing leaf-bases and cataphylls. **Leaves** 1 to many, borne at apex or distichously along stem, linear, lanceolate, oblong or ovate, papery or coriaceous, ± 2-lobed or emarginate at apex. **Inflorescences** racemose, 1- to many-flowered, erect, horizontal or pendent, borne laterally or apparently terminally. **Flowers** often showy, small to large, rather more constant morphologically than the vegetative characteristics. **Sepals** short and broad to long and filiform; lateral sepals form with the elongated column-foot a mentum (or hood) which is often spur-like at the base, 0.1–3 cm long. **Petals** either narrower or occasionally broader than sepals. **Lip** entire to 3-lobed, base joined to column-foot, often forming a closed spur with the lateral sepals to which it may be joined laterally for a short distance; disc bearing 1–7 keels; calli are only occasionally present. **Column** mostly short, terete or subterete, with a pronounced column-foot which is adnate to the base of the lateral sepals; erect teeth (stelidia) present on either side of column at apex; pollinia 4 in 2 appressed pairs, without caudicles or stipe, ± with a viscidium.

DISTRIBUTION About 900 species in India, China, S.E. Asia, Japan, Malaya, the Philippines, New Guinea, Australia and the Pacific Islands including New Zealand.

DERIVATION OF NAME From the Greek *dendros* (tree) and *bios* (life), in allusion to the aerial epiphytic existence of most species.

TAXONOMY *Dendrobium* was established by O. Swartz in 1799 in *Nova Acta Societatis Scientiarum Upsaliensis* (p. 82) and has been conserved as a generic name at the expense of the earlier *Ceraia* Lour. (1790) and *Callista* Lour. (1790).

This genus has caused more problems for the taxonomist than almost any other genus of orchids on two accounts. Firstly, the sheer number of species involved has meant that few botanists have achieved even an adequate knowledge of the genus and thus many species have been described more than once, leading to a superfluity of names. Secondly, the extreme morphological diversity within the genus has defied the efforts of botanists who have attempted to group like-species within the genus into a workable system of sections.

The last comprehensive review of the genus was undertaken by Fritz Kraenzlin in 1910 but this has been the subject of much criticism. Rudolf Schlechter (1912), in his account of the Orchids of German New Guinea, rearranged Kraenzlin's sections and proposed that *Dendrobium* be split into four subgenera with a total of 41 sections in them. Four of these, *Diplocaulobium*, *Goniobulbon*, *Sarcopodium*, *Desmotrichum* have since been elevated to the rank of genus and it is possible that further study may lead to more genera being recognised. It is not possible in a work of this nature to give keys and a description of each section. However, given below is a brief description of each of those sections which contain commonly cultivated species of *Dendrobium* and thus are of some interest to orchid growers. Most of the species described in the text belong to one of the sections outlined below:

1. sect. *Latouria*. Each branch of the sympodium consisting of several internodes, with several swollen nodes, new shoots arising at the base of the old branches. Flowers white, yellow or greenish with a lip which is glabrous within and is borne close to column and bears high keels on disc. Plants of the New Guinea region. This section has recently been revised by Cribb (1983) in the *Kew Bulletin*.

2. sect. *Callista*. Description as for *Latouria* but flowers not green and lip hairy within. Distribution centred in Burma.

3. sect. *Dendrobium* (syn. *Eugenanthe*). Leaves with sheaths; pseudobulbs or stems fleshy; inflorescences borne on leafless stem; mentum short; lip more or less hairy within and not 3-lobed.

4. sect. *Formosae* (syn. *Nigrohirsutae*) As section *Dendrobium* but leaf-sheaths covered with brown or black hairs; mentum moderate to very long; lip not hairy, entire or 3-lobed; flowers borne close to stem apex, large, mostly white.

5. sect. *Phalaenanthe*. Leaf-sheaths glabrous; inflorescence slender, many-flowered, borne near apex of leafy stems or sometimes on leafless stems; petals broad, not twisted; lip papillate within; mentum moderate to long, of two parts at right-angles.

6. sect. *Spatulata* (syn. *Ceratobium*). As sect. *Phalaenanthe* but petals longer than sepals, narrow and often twisted; lip non-papillate, keeled, margins entire; mentum simple forming with the lip a

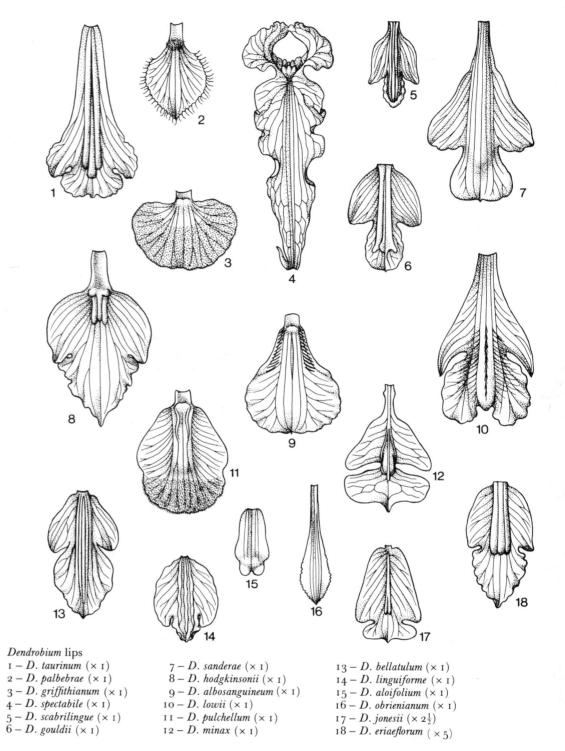

Dendrobium lips
1 – *D. taurinum* (× 1)
2 – *D. palbebrae* (× 1)
3 – *D. griffithianum* (× 1)
4 – *D. spectabile* (× 1)
5 – *D. scabrilingue* (× 1)
6 – *D. gouldii* (× 1)
7 – *D. sanderae* (× 1)
8 – *D. hodgkinsonii* (× 1)
9 – *D. albosanguineum* (× 1)
10 – *D. lowii* (× 1)
11 – *D. pulchellum* (× 1)
12 – *D. minax* (× 1)
13 – *D. bellatulum* (× 1)
14 – *D. linguiforme* (× 1)
15 – *D. aloifolium* (× 1)
16 – *D. obrienianum* (× 1)
17 – *D. jonesii* (× 2½)
18 – *D. eriaeflorum* (× 5)

closed spur. A revision of this sect. has recently been published by Cribb (1986) in the *Kew Bulletin*.

7. sect. *Stachyobium*. As for sect. *Spatulata* but lip margins toothed or fringed.

8. sect. *Pedilonum*. Inflorescences mostly few-flowered, from leafless stems; flowers usually more than 2, fairly large; leaves on young stems, well spaced.

9. sect. *Oxyglossum*. Small plants with clustered pseudobulbs and narrow leaves; flowers narrowly conical, erect, with a tapering mentum. A section centred on New Guinea and recently revised by Woods and Reeve (1990) in *Notes of the Royal Botanical Garden, Edinburgh*.

10. sect. *Dendrocoryne*. Plants with stems tufted, each stem several-noded, swollen

at least partly, 2- to several-leaved near apex; lip not held close to column, keels on disc not very high. Predominantly Australian

Seidenfaden's account in *Opera Botanica* (1985) covering the species from Thailand and adjacent areas is highly recommended and includes many of the horticulturally desirable species. The Australian species are covered by Elliot and Jones (1984) in volume 3 of their *Encyclopaedia of Australian Plants*. A good general account of the most popular species in cultivation is provided by Schelpe and Stewart (1990) in their book *Dendrobiums. An introduction to the species in cultivation.*
TYPE SPECIES *D. moniliforme* (L.) Sw.
CULTURE Compost A. Temp. Winter min. 10–16°C, depending on species. *Dendrobium* species need to be grown according to their natural habits. Upright plants are best grown in relatively small pots, while pendent species need either baskets, or mounting on slabs of fern-fibre or cork. This latter method also suits many of the very small species. All plants require plenty of water and good light while growing, but the treatment when growth is complete must vary. Deciduous species must have a cooler dry period in order to flower and many other Indian plants such as *D. moschatum*, while retaining their leaves, should be given little water at this time. Tropical species like *D. bigibbum* should not become very dry and need a min. temp. of 15°C. Plants from high altitudes should be kept moist throughout the year and will need more shade in summer than other species. In all cases, pseudobulbs should not be allowed to shrivel very much.

Dendrobium aduncum Lindl. [Colour Plate]
Stems pendulous, terete, branching, ± fractiflex, up to 60 cm long, clothed in sheaths which are dilated at apex, flowering on old stems. **Leaves** linear-lanceolate, acuminate, 7–9 cm long, 1.3 cm broad. **Inflorescences** 2- to 5-flowered, racemose, 7 cm long, borne from upper nodes of stem; bracts minute, obtuse, sheathing below, lanceolate, acuminate. **Flowers** 2.5–3.5 cm across, fragrant, semitransparent, white or pink tipped darker pink, green and pink in bud. **Sepals** broadly ovate, acute, spreading, 1.6–2.0 cm long, 0.8–1.2 cm broad; lateral sepals forming a short saccate obtuse mentum, 0.3 cm long. **Petals** shortly oblong, acute, spreading, 1.6–1.8 cm long, 0.7–1.2 cm broad. **Lip** clawed, broadly ovate, concave, acute and deflexed at the apex, 1.2–1.8 cm long, 1.0–1.2 cm broad, puberulous except for the central area, margins ciliate; callus a quadrate flap just below the centre. **Column** puberulous in front; stelidia ovate-lanceolate.

DISTRIBUTION N.E. India, Bhutan, Burma, Thailand, S. China and Indo-China.
HISTORY This delicately-flowered species was first collected in Nepal by Dr N. Wallich of the Calcutta Botanic Garden. He sent living plants to Messrs Loddiges in England where it flowered for the first time in July 1842. John Lindley mentioned it in the same year in the *Botanical Register* (misc. 62) where it was later illustrated for the first time in 1846 (t. 15).
CLOSELY RELATED SPECIES See *D. hercoglossum.*

Dendrobium aemulum R. Br.
Stems clustered in small clumps, about 6-noded, smooth, cylindrical, 15–30 cm long, green when young, covered with sheaths, 2- to 4-leaved at apex. **Leaves** ovate, glossy, 5 cm long, 2.5 cm broad, dark green. **Inflorescence** erect, 2- to 12-flowered, 5–10 cm long, borne at the apex of the stems between the leaves. **Flowers** sweet-scented, 3–4 cm diameter, predominantly white ± suffused with rose; lip white, with purple-marked side lobes and a yellow mid-lobe. **Dorsal sepal** and **petals** linear-lanceolate, acuminate, 1.5–2.5 cm long, 0.1–0.25 cm broad; **lateral sepals** as other segments but broader towards the base, up to 2.7 cm long; mentum small, rotund. **Petals** linear-tapering, 1.5–2.5 cm long. **Lip** 3-lobed, somewhat rhombic, 0.5–0.8 cm long, 0.3 cm broad; side lobes small, triangular, acute; mid-lobe triangular, acute, reflexed; disc 3-keeled below, the central keel longer and flexuose in front. **Column** very short, 0.2 cm long, rounded.
DISTRIBUTION Australia (Queensland and New South Wales); in rain forests and open woodland.
HISTORY Described in 1810 by Robert Brown in his *Prodromus Florae Novae Hollandiae* (p. 333). A. Cunningham sent the first living plants to Europe from New South Wales in 1823 and they flowered at Kew the following year.

A very variable species with several recognisable ecotypic forms.
SYNONYM *Callista aemula* (R. Br.) O. Ktze.
CLOSELY RELATED SPECIES May be distinguished from *D. gracilicaule* by the creamy flowers with slender sepals which are at least 4 times as long as broad and the sinuate keel on the lip.

Dendrobium albosanguineum Lindl.
Stems pseudobulbous, very stout, subclavate or cylindric, clustered, with strongly developed nodes, 12.5–28 cm long, covered in white sheathing bracts. **Leaves** linear-lanceolate, 10–15 cm long, 2.5–3 cm broad, light green, rather translucent, deciduous. **Inflorescences** rather short, 5–7.5 cm long, given off from upper nodes of stem, 2- to 4-flowered; bracts minute, triangular. **Flowers** 9 cm in diameter, rather fleshy, fragrant, predominantly creamy-white or pale yellow; lip marked with a purple or crimson spot at each side of base; column deep purple, stigma green. **Sepals** oblong-lanceolate, acuminate, 3.5–4 cm long, 1–1.3 cm broad; lateral sepals 5 cm long, 1–1.3 cm broad; mentum obtuse. **Petals** elliptic, 4–5 cm long, 2.5 cm broad. **Lip** broadly obovate, convolute below, margin undulate, retuse or emarginate at apex, with 2 elevated lines at base, 5 cm long, 3.5 cm broad. **Column** very short; stelidia obtuse.
DISTRIBUTION Burma and N. Thailand.
HISTORY This species was first collected by T. Lobb from the Attram River, near Moulmein in Burma and was introduced into cultivation by Messrs Veitch of Exeter and Chelsea. John Lindley described it in Paxton's *Flower Garden*, vol. I (t. 5) in 1851.

Dendrobium aloefolium (Blume) Rchb.f.
Stems clustered, thin, rather flattened, 45–90 cm long, densely leafy. **Leaves** alternate, shortly ovate, fleshy, bilaterally flattened, 2.5–3 cm long, 1.2 cm broad, smaller towards apex and base, overlapping at the base, apex obliquely acute. **Inflorescences** borne apparently apically on stems, axis covered in pale-brown sheathing bracts, up to 18 cm long. **Flowers** very small, 0.4 cm across, 0.3–0.5 cm long, white or pale rose, spotted within; lip with purple margin. **Dorsal sepal** ovate, recurved, 0.2 cm long, 0.1 cm broad; **lateral sepals** oblong, recurved, 0.2 cm long, 0.1 cm broad; mentum obtuse, shortly inflated. **Petals** oblong-lanceolate, acute, 0.17 cm long, 0.05 cm broad, recurved. **Lip** almost entire, navicular, cuneate, 0.35 cm long, 0.2 cm broad, apex bilobulate, crisped; disc slightly convex; callus quadrate, fleshy, in middle of lip. **Column** very short.
DISTRIBUTION Borneo, Sumatra, Java, the Philippines, Burma, Thailand and Malaya; in the lowlands.
HISTORY C.L. Blume described this orchid in 1825 as *Macrostomium aloefolium* in his *Bijdragen* (p. 335) based on his own collection from G. Salak in Java. H.G. Reichenbach (1861) transferred it to *Dendrobium* in *Walpers, Annales Botanices* (p. 279). It belongs in sect. *Aporum* of the genus.
SYNONYMS *Macrostomium aloefolium* Bl.; *Aporum serra* Lindl.; *A. micranthum* Griff.; *Dendrobium micranthum* (Griff.) Lindl.
CLOSELY RELATED SPECIES *Dendrobium rhodostele* Ridley which has purple-flushed flowers and erect sepals and petals.

Dendrobium anosmum Lindl. [Colour Plate]

Stems terete, arching to pendulous, many-noded, 60–120 cm long, 0.8 cm broad, each node covered with a loose fitting sheath. **Leaves** oblong-elliptic, 12–18 cm long, 2.5–3 cm broad, acute, deciduous. **Flowers** 9–10 cm across, very showy, 1 or 2 per node, pink to purple with a deep purple throat to the lip, fragrant; column white, apex pink, anther-cap purple. **Sepals** lanceolate, acuminate, 4–5 cm long, 1 cm broad. **Petals** oblong, acute, 4.5–6 cm long, 2 cm broad. **Lip** broadly ovate, acute, margin minutely denticulate, convolute, 3.2–3.5 cm broad; disc pubescent. **Column** very short.

DISTRIBUTION Widespread from Sri Lanka and India to the Malay Peninsula and Archipelago, Laos, Vietnam, the Philippines and New Guinea.

HISTORY First described by John Lindley as *D. macrophyllum* in 1838 in the *Botanical Register* (misc. 36) but that name had already been used for another species by A. Richard. Lindley, therefore, renamed it as *D. anosmum* in 1845 in the *Botanical Register* (misc. 41) based on a Philippines plant sent to him by Messrs Loddiges. H.G. Reichenbach later described the same species as *D. superbum* in *Walpers, Annales Botanices* (p. 282) and this later name is still in current use. Unfortunately, the correct name *D. anosmum* is most inapt as the flowers of this species are sweetly fragrant.

Several varieties are recognised which vary slightly in flower colour and size from that described above.

SYNONYMS *Dendrobium macrophyllum* Lindl. non A.Rich.; *D. superbum* Rchb.f.; *D. leucorhodum* Scholz; *D. scortechinii* Hooker f.; *D. macranthum* Hooker non A.Rich.

Dendrobium aphyllum (Roxb.) C.E. Fisch. [Colour Plate]

Stems slender, pendulous, leafy, 60–90 cm long, 6–10 cm thick. **Leaves** linear-lanceolate or narrowly ovate, acuminate, 5–12 cm long, 2–3 cm broad, deciduous. **Inflorescences** abbreviated, 1- to 3-flowered at each node, borne on old stems; bracts oblong, acute. **Flowers** 5 cm in diameter, fragrant, fragile in texture; sepals and petals white or rosy-mauve; lip tubular at base, cream or pale yellow, purple-veined or marked at base; column white. **Sepals** oblong-lanceolate, acute, 2.5–3 cm long, 0.6–0.8 cm broad. **Petals** broadly oblong-elliptic, obtuse, 2.5 cm long, 1.5 cm broad. **Lip** shortly clawed, suborbicular, convolute, obscurely 3-lobed, pubescent above, 2.5 cm long, 2.5 cm broad, margins erose, almost ciliate; callus at base of lip, 3-ridged. **Column** short, 0.9 cm long.

DISTRIBUTION N.E. India and China, south to Malaya; around 300 m altitude in tropical valleys.

HISTORY First collected in S. India growing on dry rocky slopes, by William Roxburgh and described by him in *Plants of the Coast of Coromandel* (p. 34, t. 41) in 1795 as *Limodorum aphyllum*. C.E. Fischer transferred it to *Dendrobium* in 1928 in J.S. Gamble's *Flora of the Presidency of Madras* (p. 1416).

This species is still commonly grown as *D. pierardii* and *D. amoenum*, both of which are later synonyms.

SYNONYMS include *Dendrobium amoenum* Wall. ex Lindl.; *D. pierardii* (Roxb.) C.E. Fisch.

CLOSELY RELATED SPECIES *D. aphyllum* is closely related to *D. primulinum* which is a smaller plant altogether. *D. aphyllum* also has petals wider than the sepals and the lip with a rounded apex. See also *D. crepidatum*.

Dendrobium arachnites Rchb.f.

Pseudobulbs spindle-shaped, 4- to 5-noded, yellow-coloured. **Leaves** 2–4 per pseudobulb, linear-lanceolate, acute, 4–6.5 cm long, 0.6 cm broad. **Inflorescences** given off near the apex of the old pseudobulb, 2- or 3-flowered. **Flowers** 6 cm across, showy; sepals orange to flame-coloured; lip purple-striped or reticulate; column white with an orange apex. **Sepals** and **petals** linear-lanceolate, 2.2–3.5 cm long, 0.3–0.7 cm broad, acute; lateral sepals forming with the column-foot a short, conical mentum, 0.5–0.7 cm long. **Lip** pandurate-oblong, subacute, as long or longer than the sepals, 1.4 cm broad, with 2 elevated keels at the base. **Column** very short, tridentate.

DISTRIBUTION Burma and India (Manipur).

HISTORY *D. arachnites* was first discovered in 1874 by W. Boxall who sent it to W. Bull in England. Messrs Low & Co. also flowered it in the same year and sent a plant to H.G. Reichenbach who described it in the *Gardeners' Chronicle* (pt. 2: p. 354) in 1874.

CLOSELY RELATED SPECIES *D. unicum* Seidenf. [Colour Plate], from Thailand and Laos, is very closely related to, and often confused with, *D. arachnites*. It differs, however, in having a shorter, broader lip with a callus of 3 obscure central keels running from the base almost to the apex.

Dendrobium atroviolaceum Rolfe [Colour Plate]

Stems clavately-fusiform, deeply sulcate, 20–30 cm long, 1.5 cm thick, greenish when young, yellow-brown when older, 2- to 4-leaved at the apex. **Leaves** ovate-oblong, thick, coriaceous, 7.5–12.5 cm long, 5–6 cm broad, obtusely bidentate at apex, dark green above, paler below. **Inflorescences** subterminal, 8- to many-flowered, scarcely longer than the leaves; bracts small, pellucid, oblong, acute. **Flowers** nodding, glabrous, 7.5 cm across, fragrant, long-lasting; sepals and petals primrose-yellow or greenish-white, purple-spotted in centre; lip green outside with purple at apex and dark purple-striped inside. **Dorsal sepal** ovate, obtuse, 2.8–3 cm long, 1.3 cm broad; **lateral sepals** broadly ovate-triangular, acute, falcate, keeled on reverse, 3 cm long, 1.3 cm broad; mentum broad, incurved, obtuse. **Petals** broadly obovate, acute, margins undulate towards the base, 2.8–3 cm long, up to 1.7 cm broad. **Lip** 3-lobed, 2 cm long, 2 cm broad; side lobes semiobovate, erect, slightly crenulate in front; mid-lobe subrhombic, reflexed; callus bisulcate at base running into a single groove above. **Column** short; stelidia hamate.

DISTRIBUTION New Guinea.

HISTORY This spectacular plant was described by R.A. Rolfe in 1890 in the *Gardeners' Chronicle* (pt. 1: p. 512) and it was illustrated in the *Botanical Magazine* (t. 7271). Rolfe received his plant from the firm of Messrs Veitch & Sons of Chelsea, London, who exhibited it at the Royal Horticultural Society in April 1890.

Dendrobium bellatulum Rolfe [Colour Plate]

Pseudobulbs tufted, very short, ovoid to fusiform, 2–10 cm long, 1.5–1.8 cm in diameter, longitudinally rugose-costate. **Leaves** 2–4, ligulate to narrowly elliptic, leathery, 3–5 cm long, 0.6–1.5 cm broad, covered in black hairs. **Inflorescences** axillary, 1- to 3-flowered, borne on leafy stems. **Flowers** 3.5 cm across, fragrant; sepals and petals light creamy-white; lip mid-lobe yellow, side lobes vermilion, disc with 5 carmine keels; column carmine. **Dorsal sepal** oblong, acute, 2 cm long, 1 cm broad; **lateral sepals** triangular, 3–3.2 cm long, 1 cm broad; mentum short, obtuse. **Petals** obovate-oblong, acute, 2–2.5 cm long, 0.8–1 cm broad. **Lip** pandurate, 3-lobed, 2.5–3 cm long; side lobes rounded; mid-lobe obcordate, bilobulate, with a narrow sinus between the lobules; disc 5-keeled. **Column** dilated above; stelidia minutely rounded.

DISTRIBUTION N.E. India, Burma (Southern Shan States), China (Yunnan), Vietnam (Annam) and Thailand; 900–1600 m altitude.

HISTORY This plant was first discovered in 1898 by A. Henry at Mengtze in Yunnan growing epiphytically at an altitude of about 1600 m. In 1900 Messrs Veitch sent living plants which had been collected by E.H. Wilson to Kew, and further collections were made in 1910 in Burma by W. Micholitz, who was the most zealous of Sander's collectors. It was described in 1903 by R.A. Rolfe in the *Journal of the Linnean Society* (p. 10).

CLOSELY RELATED SPECIES *D. bellatulum* may be distinguished from *D. christyanum* by its narrow lip with a reflexed mid-lobe which is obscurely 2-lobed. In vegetative and floral character it is close to *D. williamsonii* but it is a smaller plant altogether.

Dendrobium bigibbum Lindl. [Colour Plate]

A slender epiphytic or lithophytic plant, growing in small clumps. **Stems** cylindrical, narrow, tapering slightly towards both ends, 15–120 cm long, 1–1.5 cm broad, green or reddish-purple, 3- to 12-leaved in apical half. **Leaves** ovate to lanceolate, 5–15 cm long, 1–3.5 cm broad, acute, often red-striped or suffused. **Inflorescences** 1–4 per stem, horizontal to slightly pendent, 10–40 cm long, bearing up to 20 flowers. **Flowers** showy, about 5 cm in diameter , widely open, white, lilac or purple with a darker lip. **Sepals** oblong, acute 1.5–3 cm long; mentum bilobed, 1–2 cm long. **Petals** spathulate-obovate or suborbicular, shortly acute, up to 3 cm long, 2 cm broad. **Lip** 3-lobed, semiobovate, 1.5–2.5 cm long, 2.5 cm broad; side lobes rounded, erect over column; mid-lobe oblong, notched at apex, much longer than side lobes; disc 5-keeled, whitish, pubescent in middle. **Column** 0.4–0.6 cm long, pubescent ventrally.

DISTRIBUTION S. New Guinea and Australia (Cape York Peninsula and islands in the Torres Strait).

HISTORY J. Lindley described the species in Paxton's *Flower Garden* (p. 25) in 1852. R. Holttum mentions that the first living plants had been received at Kew as early as 1824.

D. bigibbum is a very variable species which is highly prized in cultivation. Three varieties (*bigibbum*, *compactum* and *phalaenopsis*) are recognised by some authorities and have been in cultivation for many years. Var. *phalaenopsis* [Colour Plate] has larger and more variable flowers than the typical variety, flowers in some forms reach 8.5 cm across and vary in colour from pure white to rich purple. The lip is also rather distinct having a pointed mid-lobe and an unthickened disc which is only minutely papillose. Var. *compactum* is, as its name suggests, a dwarf plant with short swollen stems. It is a lithophyte from Cape York.

D. × superbiens Rchb.f. is considered to be a natural hybrid of *D. bigibbum* with *D. discolor* Lindl. It grows on exposed rocks on the Cape York Peninsula and on islands in the Torres Strait.

SYNONYM   *D. phalaenopsis* Fitzg.

Dendrobium bracteosum Rchb.f.

[Colour Plate]
Stems tufted, erect or pendulous, terete, slender at the base, fleshy and thicker above, about 9-noded, yellowish, 20–40 cm long, covered in papery sheaths, up to 6-leaved. **Leaves** ligulate or oblong, tapering to both ends, coriaceous, 4–8 cm long, 1–2 cm broad, rich green. **Inflorescences** short, almost capitate, densely 3- to 8(or more)-flowered; bracts ovate, acuminate, nearly as long as flowers. **Flowers** 2 cm long, 2.5 cm across, fragrant, waxy, white, pink or purple with an orange-red lip; column green. **Dorsal sepal** lanceolate, acuminate, 1–2 cm long; **lateral sepals** narrowly triangular, acuminate; mentum 0.8 cm long. **Petals** obovate-lanceolate, acute, 1–1.2 cm long; mentum 0.7 cm long. **Lip** oblong-elliptic to spathulate, concave, acute; callus shiny, fleshy.
Column 0.4 cm long.

DISTRIBUTION Papua New Guinea and New Ireland; growing as an epiphyte at altitudes of 500 m upwards as far as the montane forest zone.

HISTORY   Discovered by W. Micholitz in the Cloudy Mts, Milne Bay, in New Guinea, *D. bracteosum* was described by H.G. Reichenbach in the *Gardeners' Chronicle* (n.s. 26: p. 809) of 1886. The name was given for its long bracts which nearly equal the flowers in length.

Dendrobium brymerianum Rchb.f.

[Colour Plate]
Stems bulbous in the lower part, terete or fusiform above, sulcate , thickened in middle, 30–50 cm long, 1–1.5 cm thick, yellow. **Leaves** borne near apex, distichous, up to 6, cuneate-oblong or lanceolate, papery, 10–15 cm long, 1.2–2.5 cm broad, acuminate. **Inflorescences** about 11 cm long, lateral but near apex, 1- to few-flowered. **Flowers** large, yellow, 5–6 cm across, short lived; lip side lobes deep orange. **Dorsal sepal** and **petals** ligulate, obtuse, 3 cm long, 1–1.2 cm broad; **lateral sepals** ovate, obtuse, 3 cm long, 1.2 cm broad; mentum obscure. **Lip** shortly clawed, cordate below, ovate above, narrow, acute, 5 cm long, 3.5 cm broad with ± long branched fimbriae on both side and apical margins; fimbriae 1.2 cm long but often shorter; side lobes broad. **Column** short; stelidia obtuse.

DISTRIBUTION Burma, Laos and Thailand; in montane forest, up to 1700 m.

HISTORY   H.G. Reichenbach described this species in 1875 in the *Gardeners' Chronicle* (n.s. 4: p. 323) in honour of W.E. Brymer, Member of Parliament for Dorchester, England, who first flowered it from a plant received from Messrs H. Low & Co.

CLOSELY RELATED SPECIES *Dendrobium harveyanum* Rchb.f. [Colour Plate] from Thailand, Burma and Vietnam is a similar yellow-flowered species but it generally has fewer-flowered inflorescences, its petals are distinctively fimbriate and the lip is paler, the same colour as the sepals and petals.

Dendrobium bullenianum Rchb.f.

[Colour Plate]
Epiphytic herb. **Stems** slender, slightly fractiflex, attenuate below, many-noded, sulcate, 25–60 cm long, 0.5 cm in diameter, covered with sheaths. **Leaves** submembranous, ovate-oblong, obtuse and unequally 2-lobed at apex, 7–14 cm long, 1.5–2.8 cm broad. **Inflorescences** subglobose, up to 6.5 cm long, densely flowered, capitate, on leafless stems at nodes; bracts papery, pellucid, acute. **Flowers** 1.7–2 cm long, orange to yellow with red and purple striations. **Dorsal sepal** oblong, acute, 0.6 cm long, 0.35 cm broad; **lateral sepals** oblong, acute, 1.8–2 cm long, 0.4 cm broad; mentum obtuse, 1.4–1.5 cm long. **Petals** narrowly oblanceolate, acute, 0.6 cm long, 0.3 cm broad. **Lip** rhombic to spathulate, retuse, 1.7 cm long, 0.5 cm broad with a basal semilunate callus on the claw. **Column** short; stelidia triangular, acute; anther-cap tridentate.

DISTRIBUTION The Philippines.

HISTORY   The first importation of this species was made by Messrs Low & Co. and on flowering they sent plants to H.G. Reichenbach. He described it in the *Botanische Zeitung* (p. 214) of 1862, naming it in honour of Bullen, the orchid grower at the Low establishment. *D. bullenianum* is frequently grown now under the name *D. topaziacum* Ames which is a much later synonym.

SYNONYM   *Dendrobium topaziacum* Ames

Dendrobium canaliculatum R. Br.

[Colour Plate]
A very variable species growing in small to medium-sized clumps. **Stems** fusiform, clothed in sheathing bracts, sulcate when old, 3–12 cm long, 1.5–3 cm in diameter, 2- to 6-leaved towards apex. **Leaves** linear, subcylindrical, very fleshy, grooved on upper surface, 5–20 cm long, 0.6–1.2 cm broad, acute. **Inflorescences** erect, 10–40 cm long, many-flowered. **Flowers** 1.8–2.5 cm across, fragrant, predominantly pale yellowish-green with purple or mauve markings on the white lip. **Sepals** and **petals** somewhat twisted, linear, about 1.5 cm long; mentum spur-like, conical, 0.5 cm long. **Lip** 3-lobed in apical third, 1.5 cm long, 0.19 cm broad; side lobes erect, rounded; mid-lobe orbicular, acute; disc with 3 keels extending on to mid-lobe where they are sinuate and crested. **Column** 0.3–0.4 cm long.

DISTRIBUTION N. and E. Australia and Papua New Guinea; where it grows exclusively on papery-barked trees (e.g. *Melaleuca* spp.) often in full sunlight.

HISTORY   The species was first described by Robert Brown in 1810 in his *Prodromus Florae Novae Hollandiae* (p. 333) having been collected

on the Endeavour River in N. Australia by Joseph Banks and D.C. Solander. Several varieties of the species are known in Australia.
SYNONYMS *Dendrobium tattonianum* Batem.; *D. foelschei* F. Muell.

Dendrobium capillipes Rchb.f.
[Colour Plate]
Pseudobulbs spindle-shaped, 6-noded, borne in clusters, 4–15 cm long, 1.5–2 cm thick, aphyllous at flowering time, pale green-striped, covered with red-edged sheaths, yellow when old. **Leaves** ligulate or lanceolate, acuminate, 10–15 cm long, 1–1.5 cm broad, rather laxly held. **Inflorescences** borne towards apex of pseudobulb, 1- to 4-flowered, 12–15 cm long; bracts minute. **Flower** 3 cm across, scentless, bright yellow with an orange centre. **Dorsal sepal** oblong; lanceolate, acute, 1.5 cm long, 0.7–0.8 cm broad; **lateral sepals** similar but 2.3 cm long; mentum obtuse. **Petals** oblong-ovate, obtuse, 1.5 cm long and broad. **Lip** broad, shortly clawed, reniform, 2-lobed, ciliate, 2 cm long, 2.5 cm broad, with a few faint crimson lines near the column-base, margin undulate. **Column** small; anther-cap 3-lobed at apex; stelidia rotund.
DISTRIBUTION N.E. India, Burma, China, Thailand and Vietnam; 800–1300 m altitude.
HISTORY *D. capillipes* was first introduced to cultivation by Messrs H. Low & Co. of Clapton, London, and was described by H.G. Reichenbach in the *Gardeners' Chronicle* (p. 997) in 1867. The Rev. Charles Parish sent living plants, which he had collected on the Sittang River in Burma, to Kew in 1872.
SYNONYMS *D. acrobaticum* Rchb.f.; *D. braianense* Gagnep.

Dendrobium christyanum Rchb.f.
[Colour Plate]
An epiphytic species. **Stems** caespitose, subclavate, abbreviated, 5 cm long, 0.7 cm thick, covered with 3–4 pellucid sheaths which bear black hairs. **Leaves** 2–3 towards apex, lanceolate, 4 cm long, 1.2 cm broad, obtuse, covered with black hairs below, apex obliquely 2-lobed. **Inflorescences** 1- to 2-flowered, terminal or lateral. **Flowers** 2–3 cm across, white with yellow and red on lip. **Dorsal sepal** lanceolate, acute, carinate, 2 cm long; **lateral sepals** triangular, acute. **Petals** broadly linear, acute, 2 cm long. **Lip** pandurate, 3-lobed, 2.5 cm long, 1.5 cm broad; side lobes broadly triangular; mid-lobe cordate, emarginate, with undulate margins; disc with 3 granulose lamellae, fleshy. **Column** short, with long filamentous stelidia.
DISTRIBUTION Vietnam (Annam) and Thailand.
HISTORY Described in 1882 by H.G.

Reichenbach in the *Gardeners' Chronicle* (pt. 1: p. 175) based on a specimen from Thailand that flowered for Messrs Veitch.

This species is well-known under the later synonym *D. margaritaceum* Finet.
SYNONYM *Dendrobium margaritaceum* Finet
CLOSELY RELATED SPECIES See *D. bellatulum*.

D. fuerstenbergianum Schltr., endemic to N. Thailand, is very closely allied but has 5 parallel ridges on the lip.

Dendrobium chrysanthum Wall. ex Lindl.
[Colour Plate]
Stems pendulous, 1–2 m long, sulcate, many-noded, flowering while leafy. **Leaves** ovate-lanceolate, acuminate, 10–21 cm long, 1–3.5 cm broad, but often smaller, bright shining green. **Inflorescences** from the leafy stems, abbreviated, 1- to 3-flowered, given off opposite the leaves. **Flowers** up to 4 cm in diameter, very fragrant, lasting about 14 days, golden-yellow; lip with 2 basal round chestnut or blood-red patches, rarely lacking these markings. **Sepals** oblong, obtuse, 1.6–2.1 cm long, 0.8–1.1 cm broad. **Petals** obovate, broader than sepals, obtuse, 1.6–2.0 cm long, 1.5–1.7 cm broad, minutely dentate towards apex. **Lip** concave, orbicular-subreniform, margins denticulate, involute, disc papillose-pubescent, 2.2–2.4 cm long, 1.5–2.4 cm broad. **Column** short; anther obliquely conical.
DISTRIBUTION N.W. Himalayas to Upper Burma, Thailand and Laos.
HISTORY The species was collected by Dr N. Wallich in 1821 in Nepal and named by him in his *Catalogue* in 1828. It was formally described by John Lindley in 1830 in his *Genera and Species of Orchidaceous Plants* (p. 80) and figured in the *Botanical Register* (t. 1299) of the same year.
SYNONYM *Dendrobium paxtonii* Lindl.
CLOSELY RELATED SPECIES *Dendrobium chryseum* Rolfe [syns. *D. denneanum* A.F.G. Kerr and *D. clavatum* Wall.] is allied to *D. chrysanthum* but is distinguished by its shorter stouter erect stems, its elliptic, coriaceous, obtuse leaves and larger flowers in which the sepals lack any cristate keels on the outer surface. *Dendrobium ochreatum* Lindl. is allied to *D. chrysanthum* and is also found from the Himalayas to Thailand. It may be distinguished by its broader sepals and lip which is hairier on its outer side. See also *D. heterocarpum*.

Dendrobium chrysotoxum Lindl.
[Colour Plate]
Stems clustered, clavate or fusiform, many-angled, much thickened apically, 12–30 cm long, covered with whitish membranous sheaths, bearing 2–3 leaves towards apex.

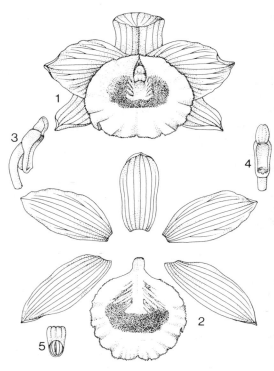

Dendrobium chryseum
1 - Flower (× 1)
2 - Floral dissection (× 1)
3 - Column, side view (× 1)
4 - Column from below (× 1)
5 - Anther (× 3)

Leaves oblong to lanceolate, coriaceous, 10–15 cm long, 2.5 cm broad, acute. **Inflorescence** subapical, lax, arcuate, pendent, up to 15–20 cm long, 12- to 21-flowered; bracts minute. **Flowers** 4–5 cm in diameter, very fragrant, golden and yellow-orange. **Sepals** oblong, obtuse, 2 cm long, 0.7–0.8 cm broad; mentum scarcely prominent, rounded. **Petals** obovate, rotund, 2.2 cm long, 1.5 cm broad. **Lip** thick, fleshy at the base, with a fringed margin, 2 cm long, 2.3 cm broad, densely papillose-hairy; disc with a curved rich orange band. **Column** short, with a broad, blunt tooth on each side of the anther-cap.
DISTRIBUTION India (Assam), Burma, Thailand, China (Yunnan) and Laos.
HISTORY *D. chrysotoxum* was described by John Lindley in the *Botanical Register* (sub t. 19 & t. 36) in 1847. The first importation was made by Messrs Henderson to England from India.
SYNONYM *Dendrobium suavissimum* Rchb.f.
CLOSELY RELATED SPECIES *D. chrysotoxum* may be distinguished from *D. griffithianum* by its densely hairy lip.

Dendrobium crepidatum Lindl. [Colour Plate]
Stems tufted, suberect to pendulous, terete,

15–45 cm or more long, striated, many-noded, internodes covered with papery sheaths. **Leaves** few, about 5–9, oblong to narrowly lanceolate, 5–12 cm long, 1–15 cm broad, acute. **Inflorescences** 1- to 3-flowered, from nodes on leafless stems. **Flowers** up to 2.5–4.5 cm across, long-lived, fragrant; sepals and petals white with pink apices; lip white with a pink or magenta apex and orange-yellow disc. **Sepals** oblong-ovate, obtuse, 2 cm long, 1.2 cm broad; mentum short, very obtuse. **Petals** broadly obovate, obtuse, 2 cm long, 1.2 cm broad. **Lip** shortly clawed, obovate-circular, margins subundulate, rounded at the apex, 2.5 cm long, 1.8–2 cm broad; disc subconcave, pubescent or glabrous. **Column** very short.

DISTRIBUTION N.W. India, Nepal, N.E. India (Assam, Sikkim), Burma, Thailand, S.W. China, Laos and Vietnam.

HISTORY This delightful species first bloomed in cultivation in England in 1850 for Mr Holford. John Lindley described and figured it in Paxton's *Flower Garden* (p. 63) in 1850.

SYNONYMS include *Dendrobium lawanum* Lindl.; *D. roseum* Dalz.

CLOSELY RELATED SPECIES *D. crepidatum* is allied to *D. aphyllum* but has flowers of a firmer texture and with an orange throat to the lip.

Dendrobium cuthbertsonii F. Muell.

[Colour Plate]

Dwarf epiphytic plants. **Stems** clustered, very short, about 1.5 cm long, fusiform. **Leaves** lanceolate, rough-textured, 2 cm long, 0.5 cm broad, dark green, purple-veined below. **Flowers** solitary, large for size of plants, pink, red, magenta, orange or yellow, 3.5 cm long; pedicellate ovary long-hairy. **Sepals** elliptic or ovate-elliptic, obtuse or apiculate, 1–1.2 cm long, 0.6–0.7 cm broad. **Petals** obovate, obtuse, 1–1.3 cm long, 0.7 cm broad. **Lip** cucullate, oblanceolate, rounded or obtuse at the apex, 1.8 cm long, 0.5 cm broad; mentum straight, 1.6 cm long. **Column** short.

DISTRIBUTION New Guinea; 2250–3000 m altitude.

HISTORY *D. cuthbertsonii* was described by Ferdinand von Mueller in the *Transactions of the Royal Society of Victoria* (p. 175) in 1888 based on a collection made by Cuthbertson and Sayer in Papua.

This species is often found in cultivation under the name *D. sophronites* Schltr., a later synonym.

SYNONYM *Dendrobium sophronites* Schltr.

Dendrobium dearei Rchb.f. [Colour Plate]

Stems erect, slightly thickened above, 60–90 cm long, sulcate, leafy throughout; leaf-sheaths covered with black hairs. **Leaves** coriaceous, distichous, oblong-ligulate, 5–23 cm long, 2.5–5 cm broad, obtuse, persisting above. **Inflorescences** several per pseudobulb, 6- to 18-flowered; bracts minute, triangular. **Flowers** long-lasting, 5–6 cm diameter, snow-white with a lime-green or yellow area at base of the lip; ovary winged. **Sepals** ovate, acuminate, keeled, 2.5 cm long, 0.8 cm broad; mentum subulate, tapering. **Petals** broadly ovate, obtuse, 2.5–3 cm long, 2.5 cm broad. **Lip** oblong, 3-lobed, 2.5 cm long; side lobes minute, obtuse; mid-lobe ovate, obtuse, emarginate, crisped; disc with 5 scarcely prominent lines. **Column** much dilated at base.

DISTRIBUTION The Philippines.

HISTORY This species was first collected from a small island near Mindanao in the Philippines and was simultaneously imported by Messrs Low, Veitch and Sander's establishments in 1882. H.G. Reichenbach described it in the same year in the *Gardeners' Chronicle* (pt. 2: p. 361) from two plants received from Low and Col. Deare (after whom he named the species).

CLOSELY RELATED SPECIES See *D. sanderae*.

Dendrobium delacourii Guillaumin

[Colour Plate]

Stems clustered, spindle-shaped, 5- to 6-noded, 14–46 cm long, yellowish, leafy throughout length. **Leaves** stout, papery, narrowly-oblong, acute or unequally 2-lobed above, pale green, 8–12 cm long, 2.5–3 cm broad. **Inflorescence** suberect or nodding, subterminal, laxly 6- to 20-flowered, 12–30 cm diameter, pale greenish, with a yellow leafy stem. **Flowers** 1.6 cm in diameter, pale greenish or off-white, with a yellow-fringed lip streaked with brown or purple, side lobes red-striped. **Dorsal sepal** ligulate, obtuse, 1 cm long; **lateral sepals** triangular, falcate, decurved and slightly recurved; mentum short, obtuse or rounded. **Petals** linear-oblanceolate, obtuse, cuneate below, 1.2 cm long. **Lip** cuneate at base, obscurely 3-lobed above the middle, convolute below, 1.2 cm long, 1 cm broad; side lobes obscure, obliquely triangular, rounded, incurved; mid-lobe broadly triangular, bearing clavate fibrillae; callus excavate at base, 3-ridged above.

DISTRIBUTION Burma, Thailand and Indo-China; 800–1300 m altitude.

HISTORY This species was first collected near the Maymyo Plateau in Burma by the Rev. C. Parish who sent living material back to H. Low & Co. in England. Joseph Hooker published the first description and illustration as *D. ciliatum* in the *Botanical Magazine* (t. 5430) in 1864 keeping the epithet given by Parish to this plant. Unfortunately, this name proved to be a later homonym and thus the first valid name for this species is *D. delacourii* of A. Guillaumin published in 1924 in the *Bulletin du Muséum d'Histoire Naturelle, Paris* (p. 522) based on a plant collected by Delacour at Quangtri in Laos.

SYNONYM *Dendrobium ciliatum* Parish ex Hooker f; *D. rupicola* Rchb.f.

Dendrobium densiflorum Wall. ex Lindl.

[Colour Plate]

Stems erect, borne in tufts, 7- to 12-noded, obscurely 4-angled, fusiform or clavate, thickest at or above the middle, 30–50 cm tall, 2 cm thick, green, each node half covered in a white sheath, 3- to 5-leaved towards apex. **Leaves** elliptic or ovate, persistent, up to 16 cm long, 2–2.5 cm broad, acute. **Inflorescences** pendent, lateral but subapical, very densely many-flowered, cylindrical, up to 26 cm long; bracts lanceolate, acute. **Flowers** 4–5 cm across, pale yellow, delicately fragrant; lip yellow with an orange base; column orange-yellow. **Sepals** ovate-oblong, obtusely acute, 2–2.5 cm long; mentum subglobose, shortly rounded. **Petals** shortly clawed, broadly elliptic to suborbicular, rounded or obtuse, margins 2–2.5 cm long. **Lip** clawed, convolute; lamina orbicular, margin fimbriate-papillate, pubescent-papillate, 2.2 cm long, 2.5–2.8 cm broad. **Column** short.

DISTRIBUTION Nepal, India (Sikkim, Assam), Burma and Thailand; up to 1500 m altitude.

HISTORY The first plants of this species seen in Europe were sent by Dr N. Wallich of the Calcutta Botanic Garden to the Horticultural Society in London. He named it in his *Catalogue* under no. 2000 and John Lindley described it in 1831 in his *Genera and Species of Orchidaceous Plants* (p. 90).

SYNONYM *Dendrobium schroederi* Hort.

CLOSELY RELATED SPECIES *D. thyrsiflorum* Rchb.f. [syn. *D. densiflorum* var. *albo-luteum* Hook.f.] [Colour Plate], which has a slightly wider distribution into S.W. China and Indo-China, differs in having a fewer-flowered inflorescence, white or cream sepals and petals and a lightly grooved rather than 4-angled stem. See also *D. farmeri* and *D. griffithianum*.

Dendrobium denudans D. Don

Plants small. **Stems** cylindrical, up to 20 cm long, but often shorter, 1 cm thick, yellow, covered with loosely fitting, funnel-shaped sheaths. **Leaves** thin-textured, lanceolate or oblong, 9–10 cm long, 1–1.5 cm broad; bracts minute. **Flowers** 2.5 cm long, white, greenish-white or yellowish-green; lip yellowish, red-striped within. **Inflorescences** subapical, laxly many-flowered, pendent. **Dorsal sepal** and **petals** linear-lanceolate, acuminate, 1.5–2.5 cm long, 0.1–0.2 cm broad; **lateral sepals** narrow-

ly obliquely triangular, acuminate; mentum curved, obtuse. **Lip** strongly curved, inflexed, 3-lobed, 0.7–0.8 cm long, 0.4 cm wide; side lobes falcate, obtusely acute, margins serrulate; mid-lobe triangular, acute, margins crispulate, acuminate; disc with 2 longitudinal fleshy lamellae. **Column** slender.
DISTRIBUTION Nepal, N. India and Sikkim; 1200–2000 m.
HISTORY D. Don described *D. denudans* in 1825 in his *Prodromus Florae Nepalensis* (p. 34) based on specimens collected by Dr N. Wallich in Nepal. Living plants of this species were first introduced to Europe by Messrs Veitch & Sons, Exeter, England.
CLOSELY RELATED SPECIES See *D. eriaeflorum*.

Dendrobium discolor Lindl. [Colour Plate]
A very large plant. **Stems** few to numerous, cylindrical with a basal swelling, 30–500 cm long, 1–3 cm broad, tapering a little towards both ends, leafy in apical two-thirds. **Leaves** distichous, ovate or elliptic, leathery, 5–15 cm long, 2–5 cm broad, obtuse. **Inflorescences** 1–6, from the upper nodes, 20–60 cm long, ± horizontal or suberect, few- to many-flowered. **Flowers** 3–8 cm in diameter, waxy, yellow, dull yellow-brown, golden-brown or bronze, turning reddish with age, honey-scented, long-lived. **Sepals** and **petals** twisted and undulate, about 2.5–3.5 cm long; mentum slender, straight or slightly curved, 1–1.2 cm long. **Lip** 3-lobed above middle, 1.5–2.5 cm long, 0.8–1.5 cm broad; side lobes rounded, erect, erose on front margin; mid-lobe triangular, acute, strongly recurved; disc with 5 undulate whitish parallel keels running on to base of mid-lobe. **Column** 0.3–0.6 cm long.
DISTRIBUTION Australia (Cape York Peninsula and islands in the Torres Strait) and South New Guinea; growing on exposed trees and rocks, fairly common near the coast.
HISTORY Described in 1841 by John Lindley in the *Botanical Register* (t. 52) from a plant given to him by Messrs Loddiges. Robert Brown had described it earlier in his *Prodromus Florae Novae Hollandiae* (p. 332) as *D. undulatum* but the name had already been used for another species. Brown based his description on a plant collected by Joseph Banks near the Endeavour River on Captain Cook's voyage of discovery to Australia. At least two varieties are recognised of this very variable but beautiful plant.
SYNONYMS *Dendrobium undulatum* R. Br.; *D. andersonianum* F.M. Bailey

Dendrobium dixanthum Rchb.f.
[Colour Plate]
Stems erect to pendent, terete, scarcely thick-

ened in the centre, 45–100 cm long, about 4-leaved. **Leaves** ligulate or lanceolate, suberect, 7.5–17 cm long, 1 cm broad, acute or acuminate. **Inflorescences** about 5 cm long, borne at nodes after the leaves have fallen, 2- to 5-flowered. **Flowers** up to 4 cm across, yellow but darker yellow and sometimes with red streaks on each side at the base of the lip; column yellow, anther green. **Dorsal sepal** oblong-lanceolate, acute, 2.5–2.8 cm long, 1 cm broad; **lateral sepals** similar; mentum short, obtuse, roundly elongate. **Petals** oblong, obtuse, margins serrulate-papillose, 2.3 cm long, 1.3 cm broad. **Lip** shortly clawed, convolute, suborbicular, bilobulate at the apex, papillose-hairy, margins serrulate-fimbriate, 2.5 cm long, 1.8–2 cm broad; disc puberulous. **Column** short.
DISTRIBUTION Burma, Thailand and Laos; 300–1000 m.
HISTORY Another species discovered by the Rev. C. Parish near Moulmein in Burma. He sent the first living collections to Messrs H. Low & Co. of Clapton, London, in 1864. H.G. Reichenbach described it in the *Gardeners' Chronicle* (p. 674) of 1865 naming it for its flower colour.
SYNONYM *Dendrobium moulmeinense* Parish ex Hooker f.

Dendrobium draconis Rchb.f. [Colour Plate]
Stems tufted, slightly fusiform or clavate, 8- to 9-noded, 30–45 cm long, 1–1.3 cm thick, sheaths covered in short black hairs. **Leaves** rather leathery, ligulate or lanceolate, 6–10 cm long, 1–2 cm broad, dark green, acute or obliquely bilobulate. **Inflorescences** 2- to 5-flowered from upper nodes; bracts minute, triangular-lanceolate, acute. **Flowers** ivory-white, with a crimson- or golden-lined base to the lip and inside of the mentum, fragrant, 6–7 cm across. **Dorsal sepal** lanceolate, acuminate, 4 cm long, 1 cm broad; **lateral sepals** subsimilar; mentum elongate, subulate, 2–3 cm long. **Petals** oblong-lanceolate, acuminate, 4 cm long, 1.5 cm broad. **Lip** cuneate at the base, obscurely 3-lobed, rhombic above, 5.5 cm long, 2 cm broad; side lobes small, rounded, subauriculate; mid-lobe oblong, margins undulate; disc with 3 elevated lines in basal half of lip.
DISTRIBUTION N.E. India, Burma, Thailand and Indo-China; a very common species, 800–2000 m.
HISTORY The species was first collected by the Rev. C. Parish who sent plants to H. Low & Co. of Clapton, London. They sold a plant to John Day and both Low and Day flowered it for the first time in 1862. H.G. Reichenbach described the species from a Parish specimen in the journal *Botanische Zeitung* in 1862 (p. 214).

SYNONYMS *Dendrobium andersonii* J. Scott; *D. eburneum* Rchb.f. ex Batem.
CLOSELY RELATED SPECIES Near *D. longicornu* but stems much shorter and clavate and with broader leaves and a larger mid-lobe to the lip.

Dendrobium eriaeflorum Griff.
Plants dwarf, up to 25 cm high. **Stems** clustered, fleshy at the base, attenuate above, up to 25 cm long, rectangular above, covered with loosely fitting sheaths, yellow. **Leaves** about 9 per stem, deciduous, oblong or lanceolate, obtuse, 7–12 cm long, 1 cm broad. **Inflorescences** given off opposite the leaves, about 8 cm long, 5- to 20-flowered; bracts minute. **Flowers** less than 1 cm long; sepals greenish-white to yellowish; petals white; lip yellow with purple veins, disc bearing 3 undulate green keels. **Dorsal sepal** and **petals** lanceolate, acuminate, 1–1.4 cm long; **lateral sepals** somewhat triangular, acuminate, falcate, incurved, 1.2–1.4 cm long; mentum conical, incurved, obtuse. **Lip** obscurely 3-lobed, obscurely rhombic, 0.6–0.8 cm long; side lobes with serrate-dentate margins; mid-lobe fleshy, triangular, margins crisped; callus 2-ridged, in basal three-quarters of lip. **Column** curved, apex serrulate.
DISTRIBUTION N. India, Nepal, Bhutan and Burma; about 1300 m in tropical valleys.
HISTORY W. Griffith discovered this species in E. Bengal and named it in his *Notulae Botanicae* (p. 316) in 1851.
CLOSELY RELATED SPECIES Very closely allied to *D. denudans* which has larger flowers with narrower longer segments and a 3-lobed lip.

Dendrobium farmeri Paxt. [Colour Plate]
Pseudobulbs clavate or fusiform-thickened and 4-angled above, with a basal hazelnut-like swelling, 2- to 4-leaved, 20–30 cm long, 2–2.5 cm thick. **Leaves** coriaceous, ovate-lanceolate, 8–18 cm long, 3.5–6 cm broad, acute or acuminate. **Inflorescences** pendent, borne on leafless stems 20–30 cm long, densely 14- to 35-flowered; bracts small, oblong. **Flowers** 5 cm in diameter; sepals and petals white or delicate lilac-mauve; lip white with a pink apex and a yellow disc. **Sepals** ovate-oblong, 2–2.5 cm long, 1–1.2 cm broad; mentum very short, rounded. **Petals** shortly clawed, almost orbicular, rounded at the apex, 2–2.5 cm long, 2 cm broad, with erose margins. **Lip** orbicular, shortly clawed, inflexed on both sides, margins erose, 2.2 cm long and broad; disc minutely puberulous; callus small, fleshy, basal, with raised veins on each side. **Column** very short.
DISTRIBUTION Himalayas, Burma, Thailand, Vietnam and Malaya; up to 500 m.
HISTORY The species was first sent by

McClelland of the Calcutta Botanic Gardens to W.F. Farmer of Cheam, Surrey, England. It had been collected in Malaya where it grows on large trees overhanging rivers in primeval forest. J. Paxton described *D. farmeri* in his *Magazine of Botany* (p. 241) in 1849.

SYNONYM *Dendrobium densiflorum* Lindl. var. *farmeri* Regel

CLOSELY RELATED SPECIES *D. farmeri* is closely related to *D. palpebrae* which can be distinguished by the fringe of long hairs near the base of its lip, and to *D. densiflorum* which has yellow flowers, less angular stems and a denser inflorescence.

Dendrobium fimbriatum Hooker
[Colour Plate]

Stem up to 120 cm or more long, erect, arching or pendulous, thickest in middle, light yellow-green when old, many-leaved. Leaves oblong to lanceolate, 8–15 cm long, 2–3 cm broad, acute or acuminate, deciduous. Inflorescences pendulous, bearing 6–15 flowers, up to 18 cm long from apex of leafless stems; bracts minute, triangular. Flowers 4–5.5 cm in diameter, sourly scented; sepals and petals light orange-yellow; lip deep orange-yellow, often with a dark maroon blotch on the disc. Dorsal sepal oblong-elliptic, obtusely acute, 2–3 cm long, 1.2–1.8 cm broad; lateral sepals obliquely ovate, similar in size to dorsal sepal; mentum shortly saccate. Petals subcircular to oblong-elliptic, rounded, shortly clawed, 2–3 cm long and broad. Lip shortly clawed, suborbicular, densely pubescent, 2.5–3 cm long, 3 cm broad, margins fimbriate-barbate. Column short.

DISTRIBUTION Nepal, Burma, Thailand, S. China, Indo-China and Malaya.

HISTORY Described by Sir William Hooker in 1823 in his *Exotic Flora* (t. 71), based on a collection from Nepal by N. Wallich.

Var. *oculatum* Hooker f. [Colour Plate], which has a maroon patch on the lip, was first collected by Dr N. Wallich in Nepal and was first flowered in Europe in 1843 at the Liverpool Botanic Garden. It is commoner than the typical variety in cultivation.

SYNONYM *Dendrobium paxtonii* Paxt.

CLOSELY RELATED SPECIES *D. gibsonii* Lindl. is closely related but lacks the barbate-fimbriate margin to the lip and usually has 2 maroon spots at the base of the lip. Some authors treat it as a variety of *D. fimbriatum*. *D. fimbriatum* is closely related to *D. moschatum* which has a calceolate lip and to *D. pulchellum* which has coppery-orange flowers.

Dendrobium findlayanum Parish & Rchb.f.
[Colour Plate]

Stems compressed bilaterally, much swollen at each node, up to more than 7-noded, 5–50 cm long, 2 cm thick, green turning yellow and wrinkled when older. Leaves deciduous, narrowly elliptic or lanceolate, 9 cm long, 1.5 cm broad, acute, bright green. Inflorescences pendulous, given off near apex of stems, 2-flowered; bracts minute, triangular. Flowers 5–7.5 cm in diameter, fragrant, long-lasting; sepals and petals pale lilac, white towards the base; lip white with a deep yellow disc with a magenta blotch on the claw end, with pale lilac margins; column with 2 deep purple bands. Dorsal sepal oblong-lanceolate, obtuse, 3–3.2 cm long, 0.9 cm broad; lateral sepals oblong, obtuse, 3–3.5 cm long, 0.9 cm broad; mentum very short, obtuse. Petals oblong to ovate, obtuse or acute, 2.6–3.8 cm long, 1.8 cm broad. Lip shortly clawed, circular to broadly ovate, acute, 2–3 cm long, 1.8–2.5 cm broad, sparsely pilose, convolute below. Column short, fleshy.

DISTRIBUTION Mountains of Burma, Thailand and Laos.

HISTORY The Rev. C. Parish and Findlay first collected *D. findlayanum* in Burma in 1869 and it was described by Parish and H.G. Reichenbach in an article in the *Transactions of the Linnean Society* (p. 149) in 1874. *D. findlayanum* was first flowered in cultivation in the same year by Sir Trevor Lawrence of Dorking, England.

CLOSELY RELATED SPECIES *Dendrobium devonianum* Paxton [Colour Plate], from Bhutan, N.E. India, Burma, S.W. China and N. Thailand, is similarly but more brightly coloured than *D. findlayanum*. It also differs in having a slender cylindrical stem, markedly ciliate, acute petals with bright pink tips, and a pubescent, fimbriate and pointed lip with a bright pink tip and 2 yellow blotches at the base.

Dendrobium formosum Roxb. ex Lindl.
[Colour Plate]

A medium-sized epiphytic plant. Pseudobulbs terete, erect, 22–45 cm long, 1.2–1.4 cm in diameter, leafy in apical two-thirds. Leaves spreading, coriaceous, oblong-elliptic, obtuse, up to 12.5 cm long, 3.2 cm broad, articulated to hirsute tubular leaf-sheaths below. Inflorescences terminal or lateral, from nodes near apex, racemose, 1- to 5-flowered; bracts short, ovate, sheathing. Flowers very showy, 7.5–12 cm across, white with a yellow-marked lip. Sepals oblong-lanceolate, subacute, keeled, 4–6 cm long, 1.2–2.5 cm broad. Petals obovate, or suborbicular, cuspidate, up to 6 cm long, 3.6 cm broad, margins undulate. Lip obscurely 3-lobed, obcuneate or broadly obovate, truncate and minutely mucronate at apex, about 5 cm long, 4 cm broad; side lobes small, indistinct, erect; mid-lobe dilated with undulate margins; disc with 2 tuberculate central ridges. Column

rather broad forming a mentum up to 3 cm long.

DISTRIBUTION Nepal to Burma and Thailand; up to 2300 m.

HISTORY Originally described by John Lindley (1830) in Wallich's *Plantae Asiaticae Rariores* (p. 24, t. 29) based on a collection by Dr N. Wallich from Nepal. W. Roxburgh had named this species as early as 1814 in *Hortus Bengalensis* (p. 63) but had not validly described it.

SYNONYM *Dendrobium infundibulum* Rchb.f. non Lindl.

CLOSELY RELATED SPECIES See *D. infundibulum*.

Dendrobium gouldii Rchb.f. [Colour Plate]

An epiphytic or terrestrial plant. Stems clustered or fusiform, up to 200 cm long, many-noded, green. Leaves distichous, rather few, ovate to oblong, coriaceous, up to 15 cm long, 3–8 cm broad, often flushed purple when young, obtuse. Inflorescences up to 70 cm long, many-flowered, erect or arching. Flowers white or pale violet-mauve with mauve lines on lip, to yellow marked with deep chestnut-brown, 6 cm across. Sepals recurved, crisp and slightly undulate. Petals spathulate, obliquely erect, slightly twisted, subacute, up to 4 cm long. Lip 3-lobed, with 3 ridges, raised and flattened at their ends on the mid-lobe; mentum spur-like, 1 cm long, decurved, greenish.

DISTRIBUTION Bougainville and the Solomon Islands; growing down to sea level.

HISTORY *D. gouldii* was described by H.G. Reichenbach in the *Gardeners' Chronicle* (p. 901) of 1867. It is very variable in flower colour, ranging from the white and mauve forms of Bougainville and western Solomon Islands to plants with yellow and brown flowers found on the island of Guadalcanal. *D. gouldii* has been widely used in hybridisation programmes.

SYNONYMS *Dendrobium imthurnii* Rolfe

CLOSELY RELATED SPECIES *D. lineale* Rolfe, from New Guinea, is similar but has spathulate petals rounded at the apex and an oblong mid-lobe to the lip.

Dendrobium gracilicaule F. Muell.
[Colour Plate]

A tall, slender, epiphytic herb, growing in small clumps. Stems erect, swollen at base, cylindrical, 20–60 cm long, 5–6 cm thick, 3- to 6-leaved near apex, greyish. Leaves longly lanceolate to ovate, acuminate, thin-textured, 6–15 cm long, 2–4 cm broad. Inflorescences 5–12 cm long, 5- to 30-flowered; bracts minute. Flowers 1.2 cm across, ± cup-shaped, fragrant, dull yellow with red-brown blotches on the outside of the sepals. Sepals oblong-ovate, obtusely acute, 1–1.3 cm long, 0.3–0.8 cm broad. **Petals** slightly curved, linear, acute, 1 cm long. **Lip** 3-lobed, curved, 0.8 cm long, 0.6 cm broad; side lobes obovate, acute; mid-lobe ovate, acute; disc with 3 parallel keels ending on base of mid-lobe. **Column** 0.3 cm long.

DISTRIBUTION Australia (Central New South Wales to Cape York, Queensland); growing on a variety of rain forest trees.

HISTORY The species was described in 1859 by F. von Mueller in *Fragmenta Phytographiae Australiae* (p. 179) based on a specimen collected by W. Hill at Moreton Bay. The first record of its being grown in Europe is of a plant sent to the Royal Botanic Gardens, Kew in 1883 by J.F. Roberts of Melbourne, Australia.

Two varieties are known in Australia.

SYNONYMS *Dendrobium elongatum* A. Cunn.; *D. brisbanense* Rchb.f.; *D. fellowsii* F. Muell.; *Callista gracilicaulis* (F. Muell.) O. Ktze.

CLOSELY RELATED SPECIES See *D. kingianum* and *D. aemulum*.

Dendrobium gratiosissimum Rchb.f.

Stems swollen at the nodes, usually pendulous, about 10-noded, 30–90 cm long, up to 10-leaved. **Leaves** linear-ligulate, unequally 2-lobed at apex, 7–10 cm long, 1–1.5 cm broad, deciduous, leaf-sheaths reddish. **Inflorescences** 1- to 3-flowered, given off at each node of leafless stems. **Flowers** 6–7 cm in diameter; sepals and petals pink or white with rose-purple tips; lip white with a pink or rose-purple margin; disc yellow, bearing red or purple lines. **Sepals** oblong-lanceolate, acute, 3–3.5 cm long, 1 cm broad; mentum very short, rounded. **Petals** oblong to elliptic, acute, 3–3.5 cm long, 1.8–2 cm broad. **Lip** convolute at base, obovate and subcordate above, obtusely acute, 3 cm long, 2.5 cm broad. **Column** short; stelidia acute.

DISTRIBUTION N.E. India, Burma, Thailand, S.W. China and Laos; 800–1500 m.

HISTORY Described by H.G. Reichenbach in *Botanische Zeitung* (p. 99) of 1865. *D. gratiosissimum* is occasionally still grown under the synonyms *D. bullerianum* Batem. and *D. boxallii* Rchb.f. The type plant was collected by the Rev. C. Parish at Moulmein in Burma and introduced to cultivation by Messrs. Low & Co.

SYNONYMS *Dendrobium boxallii* Rchb.f.; *D. bullerianum* Batem.

Dendrobium griffithianum Lindl.

Stem much thicker towards the apex, clavate-fusiform, deeply sulcate, about 5-noded, 30–45 cm long, 1.5–2.5 cm broad, shiny, yellow, 2- or occasionally 3-leaved at apex. **Leaves** leathery, ovate or oblong, very shortly petiolate, up to 10 cm long, 3–4 cm broad, acute. **Inflorescences** suberect to pendulous, laxly few- to many-

flowered, up to 15 cm long; bracts small. **Flowers** yellow with a darker yellow lip, not scented, short-lived, up to 4 cm across. **Sepals** oblong, obtusely acute, 2–2.4 cm long, 0.7–0.9 cm broad; mentum short, obtuse, nearly half the length of the lateral sepals, 0.5 cm long. **Petals** semiorbicular, obtuse, 1.0–2.2 cm long, 1.6–1.9 cm broad, margins ciliolate. **Lip** shortly clawed, suborbicular, 1.6–1.8 cm long and broad, lower margins involute; disc pilose, margins ciliate. **Column** very short.

DISTRIBUTION N.E. India, Burma and Thailand.

HISTORY The plant was first discovered by W. Griffith who collected it at Limjaik in Burma in 1834. He sent a specimen to John Lindley who described it in the *Botanical Register* (sub t. 1756) in 1836.

CLOSELY RELATED SPECIES *D. griffithianum* may be confused with *D. densiflorum* but the latter has oblong leaves on a longer stem, conspicuous bracts and a denser raceme. See also *D. chrysotoxum*.

Dendrobium hercoglossum Rchb.f.

A medium-sized or small epiphytic plant. **Stems** slender, subclavate, clustered, up to 35 cm long, 0.7 cm broad, almost completely covered by leaf-sheaths. **Leaves** distichous, linear-lanceolate, obtusely and unequally 2-lobed at apex, up to 10 cm long, 0.4–1.1 cm broad. **Inflorescences** from leafy or leafless stems, 2- to 5-flowered; rhachis slightly zigzag, up to 4 cm long; bracts ovate, acute, membranous, 0.4 cm long. **Flowers** fairly showy; sepals and petals rose-purple, paler towards the base; lip white tinged with greenish or cream and with a rose-purple apex; anther-cap magenta. **Sepals** and **petals** spreading, subsimilar, lanceolate, acuminate, 1–2 cm long, 0.5–0.7 cm broad; mentum obscure. **Lip** subsessile, bipartite, 1–1.5 cm long; hypochile orbicular, very concave, sides ± enveloping column, pubescent within, front margin terminating in a transverse fimbriate lamella; epichile triangular-lanceolate, acuminate, glabrous. **Column** up to 0.3 cm long; column-foot broad, 0.2–0.3 cm long.

DISTRIBUTION S.W. China, Thailand, Indo-China and Malaya.

HISTORY Discovered by Foerstermann in Malacca and sent by him to H.G. Reichenbach who described it in 1886 in the *Gardeners' Chronicle* (pt. 1, p. 487).

SYNONYMS *D. vexans* Dammer; *Callista hercoglossa* (Rchb.f.) O. Ktze.; *C. amabilis* Kraenzl. non Lour.

CLOSELY RELATED SPECIES *D. hercoglossum* has in the past been considered conspecific with *D. aduncum*. V.S. Summerhayes in the *Botanical Magazine* (t. 9428) discussed their

affinity in detail and concluded that *D. hercoglossum* may be distinguished by its much less prominent mentum and the separation of the lip into two distinct parts as described above.

D. linguella Rchb.f., which is widespread from Thailand to Borneo, is also closely related but has a very hairy and erect callus at the base of the lip, a subquadrate glabrous central flap and a sparsely hairy apical part to the lip.

Dendrobium heterocarpum Lindl.

[Colour Plate]

A very variable species. **Stems** fusiform or subcylindrical, erect or pendulous, many-noded, in tufts, 40–150 cm long, yellow when older; basal sheaths tubular. **Leaves** deciduous, ligulate or oblong-lanceolate, up to 10–18 cm long, 1.5–2.5 cm broad, acute to obtuse. **Inflorescences** borne on stem after leaves have fallen, borne at nodes, 2- to 3-flowered; bracts scarious. **Flowers** pale creamy-yellow with a yellow disc and maroon or crimson venation on the side lobes and base of the mid-lobe of the lip, fragrant, long-lived, 5–8 cm in diameter. **Sepals** oblong-lanceolate, obtusely acute, up to 4 cm long; mentum very short, obtuse. **Petals** ovate or oblong-elliptic, acuminate 3.5 cm long. **Lip** ovate-lanceolate, cuneate at the base, convolute-cucullate around the column, triangular in front, acute and reflexed at the apex, margins minutely serrulate-fimbriate, 3.5 cm long, 2 cm broad; disc pilose on the veins. Column 0.3–0.4 cm long.

DISTRIBUTION Sri Lanka, India, Burma south to Java and Sulawesi and east to the Philippines; flowering in December and January.

HISTORY *D. heterocarpum* was described in 1830 by John Lindley in *Genera and Species of Orchidaceous Plants* (p. 78). The specific epithet was given in his *Catalogue* by Dr N. Wallich who collected it for the first time in Nepal.

SYNONYMS *Dendrobium atractodes* Ridley; *D. aureum* Lindl.; *D. rhombeum* Lindl.

CLOSELY RELATED SPECIES *Dendrobium ochranthum* Schltr. and *D. chrysanthum* are similar to this species but have yellow flowers.

Dendrobium hodgkinsonii Rolfe

Stems tufted, narrowly clavate or fusiform, deeply sulcate, 12–25 cm tall, 2- to 3-leaved towards apex. **Leaves** elliptic-lanceolate, subcoriaceous, 10–18 cm long, 2.5–4 cm broad, subacute, bright green. **Inflorescences** terminal, about 20 cm long, 5- to 7-flowered, bracts small. **Flowers** nodding, subcampanulate, 4–5 cm across; sepals and petals pale green; lip pale green with broad radiating purple veins; callus white. **Sepals** and **petals** suberect, triangular-lanceolate, acuminate, dorsally keeled, about 3–3.3 cm long, 0.8 cm broad; mentum saccate, obtuse. **Lip** longer, 3 lobed, 3–3.5 cm long; side lobes erect, rounded, crenulate; mid-lobe ovate-cordate, subacute; disc with a large, pronounced, 3-keeled callus. **Column** with erect stelidia.

DISTRIBUTION   New Guinea.

HISTORY   First introduced into cultivation by Messrs Sander & Sons of St Albans, England. A plant of theirs flowered at the Royal Botanic Gardens, Kew in 1899. R. Rolfe described the species in the *Botanical Magazine* (t. 7724) in 1900.

Dendrobium infundibulum Lindl.
[Colour Plate]

Stems erect, cylindrical, up to 10-leaved, 30–100 cm long, 1 cm in diameter, sheaths covered with black hairs. **Leaves** all along new growths, narrowly ovate or linear-lanceolate, dark green, 8.5 cm long, 2 cm broad, obscurely 2-lobed at apex. **Inflorescences** short, few-flowered, borne towards the apex of old growths. **Flowers** 6–8 cm in diameter, ivory-white with scarlet or yellow lines at the base of the lip and inside the mentum. **Sepals** ovate, acute, 3–4.2 cm long, 0.9–1.3 cm broad; mentum 2.5–3 cm long, spur-like, slightly curved. **Petals** almost orbicular or obovate, rounded or shortly apiculate at apex, 3.5–4.8 cm long, 2.9–3.9 cm broad. **Lip** cuneate-obovate, convolute at the base, 3-lobed, 3.2–4.8 cm long, 2.5–3.4 cm broad; side lobes rectangular, almost evolute; mid-lobe cuneate, bilobulate in front, margins serrulate, undulate, papillose within; disc with 5 elevated ridges coalescing at the base. **Column** short; stelidia fleshy, obtuse; anther retuse, hyaline-papillose.

DISTRIBUTION   N.E. India, Burma, Thailand and Laos; 1100–2300 m or higher.

HISTORY   The species was first introduced into England by Messrs H. Low & Co. of Clapton, London, in 1864. They received it from the Rev. C. Parish who had earlier sent a specimen collected at Moulmein to John Lindley who described it in 1859 in the *Journal of the Linnean Society* (p. 16).

SYNONYM   *Dendrobium jamesianum* Rchb.f.

CLOSELY RELATED SPECIES   *D. formosum* is superficially similar but its spur is one-half as long as the dorsal sepal and the sepals are keeled on their outer surface. See also *D. williamsonii*.

Dendrobium johnsoniae F. Muell.
[Colour Plate]

An epiphytic herb sometimes growing in fairly large masses. **Stems** narrowly fusiform, about 9-noded, up to 30 cm long, 1.5 cm in diameter, purple-brown or green, bearing about 4 leaves. **Leaves** suberect, ovate, 5–15 cm long, 1.2–4 cm broad, usually concave on upper side, rather coriaceous, slightly unequally 2-lobed at

apex. **Inflorescences** 1–2, borne towards apex of stem, 7–40 cm long, up to 12-flowered. **Flowers** 6.5–12 cm across, white with some purple markings on the side lobes of the lip and on the column. **Sepals** ovate-lanceolate, acuminate and reflexed at apex, up to 3.8 cm long; mentum 0.7 cm long. **Petals** clawed, rhombic, acute, margins undulate, up to 6 cm long, 3 cm broad. **Lip** 3-lobed in middle, up to 4.5 cm long; side lobes oblong, rounded in front; mid-lobe oblong-ovate, acute to acuminate; callus 2-ridged at the base. **Column** about 0.5 cm long; foot 0.6 cm long.

DISTRIBUTION   New Guinea, Solomon Islands and doubtfully collected once in Australia on Cape York; 650–1300 m altitude often growing in full light on *Casuarina* trees.

HISTORY   The species was first described in 1882 by Baron F. von Mueller in Wing's *South Science Record* (p. 95) who named it after the daughter of the Rev. Johnson of Surrey Hills, New South Wales. Mueller had received the plant from the Rev. J. Chalmers who collected it in 1882 on the E. Peninsula of New Guinea.

SYNONYMS   *Dendrobium macfarlanei* Rchb.f.; *D. monodon* Kraenzl.; *D. niveum* Rolfe; *D. johansoniae* F.M. Bailey; *Callista macfarlanei* (Rchb.f.) O. Ktze.

Dendrobium jonesii Rendle [Colour Plate]

A robust epiphytic or lithophytic plant growing in large clumps. **Stems** swollen at base then fusiform, 15–45 cm long, 1.5–4 cm in diameter, usually sulcate, dark-coloured. **Leaves** 2–7, borne near stem apex, ovate, thin-textured. **Inflorescences** 1–4 per stem, many-flowered, up to 35 cm long. **Flowers** up to 2 cm long, white or cream, yellow with age; lip purple-striped. **Sepals** linear-lanceolate, acute, 1.6–2.2 cm long, 0.3–0.5 cm broad; lateral sepals falcate; mentum 0.3–0.5 cm long. **Petals** linear-lanceolate, acute, 1.6–2.2 cm long, 0.15–0.25 cm broad. **Lip** 3-lobed in apical half, 0.8 cm long, 0.7 cm broad, gently curved; side lobes ± oblong-triangular; mid-lobe only a little longer than side lobes, 0.2 cm long, 0.6 cm broad, truncate, mucronate; disc with a single orange keel. **Column** 0.3–0.4 cm long; foot 0.4–0.5 cm long.

DISTRIBUTION   Australia (Queensland) and New Guinea; growing in rain forest or on the edges of rain forest often on species of *Casuarina* or on rocks. Two varieties of this species are known in Australia.

HISTORY   This attractive orchid was first described by A.B. Rendle in 1901 in the *Journal of Botany* (p. 197), based on a collection made by A. Jones, after whom it is named, on the Johnstone River.

This is a popular species in cultivation and is usually grown under the name *D. ruppianum*

A.D. Hawkes but that has recently been shown to be a later synonym.

SYNONYMS   *Dendrobium speciosum* J.E. Smith var. *fusiforme* F.M. Bailey; *D. fusiform* (F.M. Bailey) F.M. Bailey; *D. ruppianum* A.D. Hawkes

CLOSELY RELATED SPECIES   Distinguished from *D. speciosum* by the broader mid-lobe to the lip and stems which are swollen at the base.

Dendrobium kingianum Bidwill
[Colour Plate]

An extremely variable, lithophytic plant, often growing in large masses. **Stems** cylindrical, erect, slightly broader at base, 8–30 cm long, 1–2 cm broad, up to about 6-leaved. **Leaves** narrowly ovate or obovate, rather thin-textured, 3–10 cm long, 1–2 cm broad, sub-acute. **Inflorescences** apparently terminal, 1–3 per stem, 7–15 cm long, bearing up to 15 flowers. **Flowers** 1.3–2.5 cm across, white, pink or purple with the lip veined or blotched crimson or purple. **Dorsal sepal** oblong, obtusely acute, 1 cm long, 0.5 cm broad; **lateral sepals** ovate-triangular, 1.5 cm long, 0.7–0.8 cm broad; mentum prominent, spur-like, obtuse, slightly incurved, 0.8 cm long. **Petals** linear-lanceolate, acute, 1 cm long, 0.25 cm broad. **Lip** cuneate at the base, 3-lobed, 1.2 cm long, 0.8–0.9 cm broad; side lobes semiobovate or obtriangular, acute; mid-lobe transversely oblong, apiculate; callus fleshy, bisulcate above. **Column** lacking stelidia, margins crenulate.

DISTRIBUTION   Australia (New South Wales and Queensland).

HISTORY   *D. kingianum* was discovered and described in 1844 by J.C. Bidwill in John Lindley's *Botanical Register* (misc. 11). Bidwill sent living plants to Europe in the same year.

At least four varieties of this very variable species are known based mainly on flower colour differences, but var. *pulcherrimum* has shorter stems, shorter inflorescences and larger dark mauve flowers. *D.* × *delicatum* (F.M. Bailey) F.M. Bailey is considered to be a naturally occurring hybrid of *D. kingianum* with *D. speciosum*.

SYNONYM   *Callista kingiana* (Bidwill) O. Ktze.

CLOSELY RELATED SPECIES   *D. gracilicaule* is allied to *D. kingianum* but differs in having pseudobulbs which do not taper to the apex, and in its distinctively coloured flowers with a shorter, broader mentum in side view.

Dendrobium lasianthera J.J. Smith
[Colour Plate]

A very large plant with terete, erect stems reaching 2 m in length, leafy throughout length. **Leaves** elliptic, coriaceous, emarginate, alternate, 3.5–14 cm long. **Inflorescences** erect or spreading, numerous, up to 30 cm long, many-flowered, emerging below the leaves. **Flowers** large, showy, about 8 cm long; sepals pure white at base, yellow-brown to maroon towards apex; petals dark red-brown; lip heavily suffused with purple, mid-lobe brownish-yellow, disc magenta. **Sepals** undulate, 4 cm long; mentum spur-like, up to 2 cm long. **Petals** twisted, ligulate, 4 cm long, acute. **Lip** 3-lobed near apex, 4 cm long, 2.5 cm broad; side lobes short, rounded at apex; mid-lobe obovate, 1 cm long, apiculate; disc with 3 parallel keels.

DISTRIBUTION Northern New Guinea; epiphyte on trees by rivers and lakes at low altitudes.

HISTORY This species was first described in 1932 by J.J. Smith in *Fedde, Repertorium Specierum Novarum* (p. 78) based on a collection made by Stüber in New Guinea. It was later seen on the Sepik River in Papua New Guinea by Captain Blood during the Second World War. Captain Blood returned to the area in 1952 and sent flowers of the species and later living plants to G. Hermon Slade of Manly, New South Wales, Australia. Slade and A.R. Persson flowered it for the first time in cultivation soon afterwards (under the name *D. ostrinoglossum*).

SYNONYM *Dendrobium ostrinoglossum* Rupp
CLOSELY RELATED SPECIES Near *Dendrobium ionoglossum* Schltr. which has much shorter racemes, smaller flowers and only 2 keels on the lip.

Dendrobium lawesii F. Muell. [Colour Plate]
An epiphytic plant with pendulous or subpendulous stems. **Stems** slightly fractiflex, terete, sulcate, up to 45 cm long, covered with maroon leaf-sheaths which turn chaffy with age. **Leaves** ovate-elliptic, distichous, membranous, 6.5 cm long, 2 cm broad, acute or acuminate, grass-green. **Inflorescences** capitate, borne on leafless stems, 1- to 6-flowered. **Flowers** pendulous, white, red, crimson or mauve, about 3 cm long. **Dorsal sepal** broadly ovate-oblong, shortly acute, 0.7–1 cm long; **lateral sepals** broadly oblong, obtusely acute, 2 cm long, 0.7 cm broad; mentum curved, elongate, obtuse, nearly 2 cm long. **Petals** oblong, acute, 0.7–1 cm long. **Lip** spathulate, minutely denticulate on incurved apical margin, lower margins inflexed, up to 1.5 cm long, 0.8–0.9 cm broad. **Column** short; stelidia short, obtuse.

DISTRIBUTION New Guinea and the Solomon Islands (Bougainville to Guadalcanal); up to 2000 m altitude.

HISTORY Discovered in New Guinea by the Rev. W.G. Lawes of the London Missionary Society. He sent it to Baron F. von Mueller at

Melbourne, Australia, who named it after the discoverer. The description of this new species was published in 1884 by Mueller in the *Melbourne Chemist* (June).

Dendrobium leonis (Lindl.) Rchb.f.
Stem thin, flattened, 15–25 cm long. **Leaves** broadly ovate, acute or obtuse, bilaterally flattened, distichous, 2.5 cm long, 1 cm broad, thick and fleshy, overlapping at the base. **Inflorescences** 1- to 2-flowered, borne at the ends of branches. **Flowers** very fragrant, smelling of vanilla, small, 2 cm long, dirty golden-yellow, streaked dull purple at base. **Dorsal sepal** oblong, acute, 0.7–0.8 cm long, 0.6 cm broad; **lateral sepals** obliquely oblong-ovate, rounded below, acute, 1.2 cm long, 0.8–0.9 cm broad; mentum broad. **Petals** oblong-lanceolate to elliptic, with a hairy margin, obtuse or acute, 0.7–0.8 cm long, 0.4–0.5 cm broad. **Lip** ligulate, obtuse to emarginate, entire, margins involute, with a swollen papillose callus at apex, 1.5 cm long, 0.5–0.6 cm broad. **Column** short.

DISTRIBUTION Indo-China, Malaya, Thailand, Sumatra and Borneo; common low-land epiphyte.

HISTORY The species was first described in 1840 by John Lindley as *Aporum leonis* in the *Botanical Register* (misc. 50), the epithet derived somewhat fancifully from the lion's mouth appearance of the flower. Lindley had received the plant from Dr N. Wallich of the Calcutta Botanic Garden who, in turn, had received it from a Mr Prince. Hugh Cuming sent living material from Singapore to Messrs Loddiges in England, who can be credited with introducing it into cultivation. In 1861 H.G. Reichenbach transferred it to *Dendrobium* in *Walpers, Annales Botanices* (p. 280).

SYNONYM *Aporum leonis* Lindl.

Dendrobium lichenastrum (F. Muell.) Kraenzl.
A dwarf creeping epiphytic or lithophytic herb. **Rhizomes** branching, 0.1 cm in diameter, clothed in sheathing bracts, leaves borne at 0.2 cm intervals alternately. **Leaves** prostrate, thick, fleshy, ovate-oblong, obovate or circular, 0.4–1 cm long, 0.3–0.8 cm broad. **Flowers** borne singly, 0.4–0.7 cm in diameter, the sepals and petals hyaline, white, cream or pink with a varying number of red stripes; lip yellow or orange. **Dorsal sepal** broadly ovate-orbicular, 0.3–0.5 cm long; **lateral sepals** obliquely triangular, acute to obtuse, 0.3–0.5 cm long, 0.15–0.4 cm broad; mentum rounded, 0.3 cm long. **Petals** linear-lanceolate, obtuse or acute, 0.2–0.5 cm long. **Lip** clawed, grooved at base, oblong-subpandurate, rugulose above, 0.4–0.5 cm long. **Column** very short, 0.1 cm long.

DISTRIBUTION Tropical E. Australia (NE

Queensland only); epiphyte on rain forest trees or growing on rocks in open forests; commonest above 500 m.

HISTORY A plant of this species was received from Earl Fitzwilliam of Wentworth by the Botanic Gardens in Edinburgh as early as 1836, where it flowered in May of the following year. F. von Mueller originally described this species in his *Fragmenta phytographiae Australiae* (p. 60) as *Bulbophyllum lichenastrum*. F. Kraenzlin transferred it to *Dendrobium* in 1910, in *Das Pflanzenreich. Orchidaceae–Monandrae–Dendrobiinae* (p. 289).

D. lichenastrum is a very variable species and at least two varieties have been recognised, e.g. var. *prenticei* [Colour Plate].

SYNONYM *Bulbophyllum lichenastrum* F. Muell.
CLOSELY RELATED SPECIES In habit *D. lichenastrum* is similar to *D. linguiforme* but it has much smaller leaves and solitary flowers.

Dendrobium lindleyi Steud. [Colour Plate]
Stems ± erect, clustered, thickened upwards from a slender base, almost spindle-shaped, angled, 3–8 cm long. **Leaf** solitary, oblong, 5–16 cm long, 1.5–2.8 cm broad, leathery, obtuse. **Inflorescence** given off from near the apex of the stem, 10–30 cm long, 5- to 15-flowered, often pendent; bracts minute, triangular, 0.2 cm long. **Flower** fragile, 3 cm across, fragrant, pale golden-yellow; lip with orange lines in the throat. **Sepals** small, ligulate, acute, 1.5 cm long, 0.5 cm broad; lateral sepals forming a short obtuse mentum. **Petals** obovate, shortly clawed, acute, 1.7 cm long, 0.8–1 cm broad. **Lip** clawed, transversely oblong or orbicular above, margins undulate and ciliolate, retuse at apex, concave, 2.2 cm long, 2.2 cm broad; disc puberulent. **Column** very short.

DISTRIBUTION India (Assam) and Burma, east to S. China and south to Malaya and Indo-China; in montane forest, 350–1500 m.

HISTORY The earliest record of the cultivation of this species in Europe is of a plant grown at the Edinburgh Botanic Garden in 1836. It had been received from Earl Fitzwilliam of Wentworth and it flowered in May 1837. W. Roxburgh described it in 1832 in *Flora Indica* (p. 477) as *D. aggregatum* but unfortunately that name had already been used by Kunth for a different S. American species. The next valid name for the species is *D. lindleyi* published by Steudel (1840) in his *Nomenclator Botanicus* (p. 490).

Plants are still seen in cultivation under the name *D. aggregatum*.

SYNONYMS *D. aggregatum* Roxb.; *Callista aggregata* (Roxb.) O. Kuntze
CLOSELY RELATED SPECIES *Dendrobium jenkinsii* Wall. ex Lindl. [Colour Plate] from the eastern Himalayas across to Indo-China, i

closely allied to *D. lindleyi* but differs in having shorter pseudobulbs 3–5 cm long, 1- or 2-flowered inflorescences and a lip that is pubescent all over the upper surface.

Dendrobium linguiforme Sw.

An epiphytic or lithophytic herb forming extensive spreading patches. **Stems** terete, consisting of a creeping, branching rhizome, which can form a mat, each branch 1–4 cm long, 0.3–0.4 cm in diameter, clothed with sheaths. **Leaves** sessile, usually alternate, ovate, oblong or obovate 2–4 cm long, 0.8–2 cm broad, very thick, smooth, longitudinally furrowed above. **Inflorescences** erect, 5–15 cm long, up to 20-flowered; bracts minute, triangular. **Flowers** with lip uppermost, about 2 cm across, white or cream with faint purple markings on the apices. **Sepals** linear-lanceolate, 2–2.2 cm long, 0.2–0.25 cm broad; mentum very short, rounded, incurved, 0.2 cm long. **Petals** linear-lanceolate, 1.8–2 cm long, 0.2 cm broad. **Lip** very short, 3-lobed in apical third, 0.4–0.6 cm long, 0.2–0.4 cm broad; side lobes broadly triangular; mid-lobe oblong, obtusely acute and recurved at the apex; disc with 3 lamellae from the base to apex, undulate towards the apex. **Column** very short, 0.2 cm long; stelidia obtuse.

DISTRIBUTION Australia (S.E. New South Wales to Cape York, Queensland); in rain forest and on rocks in open forest, sea level–1000 m.

HISTORY *D. linguiforme* described by O. Swartz as early as 1800 in *Kungliga Svenska Vetenskapsakademiens Avhandlingar*, Stockholm (p. 247).

Two varieties are known: var. *nugentii* F.M. Bailey from N.E. Queensland to Cape York, has larger broader longitudinally-furrowed leaves and often a second inflorescence, whilst var. *huntianum* Rupp has narrow-elongate leaves more pointed than in var. *linguiforme* and flowers similar to var. *nugentii*.

SYNONYM *Callista linguiformis* (Sw.) O. Ktze.

CLOSELY RELATED SPECIES See *D. lichenastrum*.

Dendrobium lituiflorum Lindl. [Colour Plate]

Stems clustered, slender, reed-like, pendulous, 11- to 15-noded, 45 to over 60 cm long, 0.5 cm thick, covered in sheaths, base swollen. **Leaves** deciduous, fleshy, linear-lanceolate, 7.5–12.5 cm long, 1.8–3.5 cm broad, acutish. **Inflorescences** 1- to 5-flowered, given off at each node. **Flowers** 7.5–10 cm across, fragrant, white, pale lilac to dark purple; lip dark violet-purple with a maroon to purple base surrounded by a white or yellow area and with purple recurved margins. **Sepals** oblong or oblong-lanceolate, acute, 2.5–5 cm long, 0.8–1 cm broad; mentum

very short, rounded. **Petals** broadly oblong or elliptic, 2.5–5 cm long, 1.5 cm broad. **Lip** trumpet-shaped, curvate, rounded in front, 2.5 cm long and broad; disc puberulous.

DISTRIBUTION N.E. India, Burma and Thailand.

HISTORY John Lindley described this species in 1856 in the *Gardeners' Chronicle* (p. 372) from plants received from R. Hanbury and John Edwards.

SYNONYM *Dendrobium hanburyanum* Rchb.f.

CLOSELY RELATED SPECIES *D. parishii* is similar but has 2 purple or maroon blotches at the base of the lip.

Dendrobium loddigesii Rolfe [Colour Plate]

Plants small, epiphytic. **Stems** tufted, ± pendent, subterete, striated, 10–17 cm long, 5–7 cm thick, several-noded, white-sheathed. **Leaves** alternate, fleshy, oblong, 4–6 cm long, 1.2–1.8 cm broad, acute. **Flowers** solitary at the nodes, 5 cm across, ± after the leaves have fallen; sepals pale rose-purple; petals lilac-purple; lip purple-edged, disc orange, with a white marginal zone. **Sepals** ovate-oblong, obtuse, 2–2.5 cm long, 0.8–0.9 cm broad; mentum very short, obtuse. **Petals** elliptic, rounded at the apex, 2 cm long, 1.2 cm broad. **Lip** shortly clawed, concave, suborbicular, 1.8 cm long, 1.5 cm broad, margins fimbriate; disc densely pilose. **Column** very short; anther retuse.

DISTRIBUTION Laos and China (Yunnan and Hainan). The distribution of this species is somewhat uncertain but it is probably a native of S. China.

HISTORY The species first figure in George Loddiges' *Botanical Cabinet* (t. 1935) in 1833 as *D. pulchellum*. However, R.A. Rolfe in 1887 in the *Gardeners' Chronicle* (ser. 3, 2: p.155) demonstrated that it most certainly was not *D. pulchellum* of W. Roxburgh and thus renamed it *D. loddigesii*.

SYNONYMS *Dendrobium pulchellum* Lodd. non Roxb.; *D. seidelianum* Rchb.f.

Dendrobium longicornu Wall. ex Lindl. [Colour Plate]

Stems tufted, minutely sulcate, 15–30 cm long, 0.4–0.5 cm thick, somewhat zigzag, several-noded, covered in black hairs, 5- to 11-leaved towards apex. **Leaves** soon deciduous, linear-lanceolate, 7 cm long, 0.5–1.8 cm broad, obliquely acute. **Inflorescences** borne on leafy stems, 1- to 3-flowered, very short, subapical; bracts ovate, acute, hirsute, 1 cm long. **Flowers** fragrant, waxy, long-lived, 5 cm long, white; lip streaked orange-red and edged red and yellow. **Dorsal sepal** ovate, acute, 1.5–2.1 cm long, 0.6–0.7 cm broad; **lateral sepals** ovate-triangular, 4–5 cm long, 0.6–0.7 cm broad; mentum long, attenuate, keeled above,

2–3.2 cm long. **Petals** lanceolate or ovate-lanceolate, acute, 1.5–1.8 cm long, 0.6–0.7 cm broad. **Lip** 3-lobed, rhombic or almost obtriangular; side lobes semiovate, rounded, denticulate on front margins; mid-lobe shortly rounded, fimbriate in front; callus basal, fleshy, divided into 3–4 arms in front. **Column** short; anther retuse in front.

DISTRIBUTION China, Nepal, India (Sikkim) and Burma; 1300–2600 m altitude.

HISTORY Dr N. Wallich first used the name *D. longicornu* in his *Catalogue* (no. 1997) and John Lindley described it in 1830 in *Genera and Species of Orchidaceous Plants* (p. 80).

SYNONYMS *Dendrobium flexuosum* Griff.; *D. fredianum* Hort.; *D. hirsutum* Griff.

CLOSELY RELATED SPECIES See *D. draconis*.

Dendrobium lowii Lindl.

Stem erect, about 9-noded, 25–40 cm long, fairly thick, upper leaf-sheaths covered with brown or black hairs. **Leaves** narrowly ovate, apex obliquely 2-lobed, about 6 borne towards the stem apex, 5–8 cm long, 1.5–2.2 cm broad, covered with black hairs below. **Inflorescences** subapical, rather short, densely 2- to 7-flowered; bracts short, black-hairy, acute. **Flowers** rich yellow, 5 cm across, fragrant; lip-keels orange-red. **Dorsal sepal** broadly oblong, obtuse, apiculate, 2.5 cm long, 1 cm broad; **lateral sepals** ovate-triangular, obtuse, 2 cm long, 1 cm broad; mentum attenuate, subulate, 3 cm long. **Petals** broadly oblong, margins undulate, rounded at the apex, 2.8 cm long, 1.5 cm broad. **Lip** deeply 3-lobed, 3 cm long, 1.2 cm broad; side lobes basal, ligulate or oblong, acute, 1.5 cm long; mid-lobe linear-spathulate, decurved in front, rounded, bilobulate, margin crisped; disc 3- to 7-keeled, longly hairy. **Column** with large, obtuse stelidia.

DISTRIBUTION Sarawak, N. Borneo; 1000 m, epiphytic on trees in exposed places in mountains.

HISTORY The species was first discovered by Hugh Low in N. Borneo in 1861 after whom J. Lindley described it in the *Gardeners' Chronicle* (p. 1046) of the same year.

Dendrobium moniliforme (L.) Sw. [Colour Plate]

An epiphytic or lithophytic plant. **Stem** erect or pendent, tufted, terete, slightly wider in the middle, many-noded, 10–40 cm long, purplish-green, covered in greyish sheaths, yellow when old. **Leaves** narrowly lanceolate, deciduous, 5.5 cm long, 0.8 cm broad, obtuse. **Inflorescences** on leafless stems, 2-flowered at each node. **Flowers** 2–4.5 cm across, very fragrant, white ± with a pinkish flush; base of lip and column-foot greenish-yellow and spotted brown; column white. **Sepals** and **petals** lanceolate to narrowly ovate, up to 3 cm long, 0.8–1.2 cm broad. **Lip** obscurely 3-lobed, elongate-rhombic, 1.4–2.8 cm long, 1.4 cm broad; side lobes rounded, erect; mid-lobe ovate, reflexed; disc with narrow transverse band of red spots. **Column** short, 0.2 cm long, foot 0.8–1.0 cm long.

DISTRIBUTION   Japan,   Korea   and Taiwan.

HISTORY   *D. monile* (Thunb.) Kraenzl. and *D. japonicum* Lindl. are both later synonyms of this species which was known early enough to be described by Carl von Linné in *Species Plantarum* (p. 954) in 1753 as *Epidendrum moniliforme*. O. Swartz transferred it to the genus *Dendrobium* in 1799 in *Nova Acta Regia Societatis Scientiarum Upsaliensis* (p. 85).

SYNONYMS   include   *Dendrobium   monile* (Thunb.) Kraenzl.; *D. japonicum* Lindl.; *D. catenatum* Lindl.

Dendrobium moschatum (Buch. Ham.) Sw. [Colour Plate]

Stems erect, arching or pendulous, terete, up to 150 cm long or more, dark brownish when old, bearing leaves in the apical half. **Leaves** narrowly elliptic to oblong-ovate, leathery, 15 cm long, 3.5 cm broad, acute. **Inflorescences** pendent, up to 20 cm long, 6- to 10-flowered, borne from the upper part of old stems. **Flowers** 6–8 cm across, lasting 7 days, very pale yellow or apricot with lilac veins; lip with 2 large maroon blotches inside. **Sepals** oblong or elliptic, obtuse, 4 cm long, 1.5 cm broad; mentum obscure, rotund. **Petals** broadly elliptic, obtuse, 4 cm long, 2 cm broad. **Lip** shortly clawed, slipper-shaped, densely pilose, 2.5 cm long and broad, margins inflexed. **Column** 0.3–0.4 cm long.

DISTRIBUTION   India,   Sikkim,   Burma, Laos and Thailand; growing in full sun.

HISTORY   Collected very early on, this spectacular orchid was described in 1800 as *Epidendrum moschatum* by Buchanan-Hamilton in Symes's *Embassy to the Kingdom of Ava* (p. 478). It was later transferred by O. Swartz in 1806 in *Schrader, Neues Journal* (p. 94) to the genus *Dendrobium*.

Var. *cupreum* lacks the purple veins on its flowers and is altogether a smaller plant.

SYNONYMS   *Epidendrum moschatum* Buch.-Ham.; *Dendrobium calceolaria* Carey; *D. cupreum* Herbert; *Cymbidium moschatum* (Buch.-Ham.) Willd.

CLOSELY   RELATED   SPECIES   See   *D. fimbriatum*.

Dendrobium nobile Lindl. [Colour Plate]

Stems erect, clustered, 30–50 cm tall, compressed, grooved with age, yellowish. **Leaves** distichous, strap-shaped or oblong, coriaceous, 7–11 cm long, 1–3 cm broad, persistent for 2 years. **Inflorescences** short, given off at each node from leafy or leafless stems, 2- to 4-flowered. **Flowers** very variable, 6–8 cm across, waxy, fragrant, long-lived; sepals and petals white at the base grading to rose or mauve above; lip rich maroon at the base then yellow or white with a mauve or purple margin. **Sepals** oblong-lanceolate, acute, up to 4 cm long, 1.5 cm broad; mentum short, obtuse. **Petals** ovate-oblong, margins slightly undulate, 4 cm long, 2.5 cm broad. **Lip** convolute at the base, obovate-oblong, pubescent above and below, 4.5 cm long, 3 cm broad. **Column** 0.7 cm long, with acute stelidia; anther serrulate in front.

DISTRIBUTION   N.E. India to S. China and south to Laos and Thailand; grows in full sun at altitudes up to 1500 m.

HISTORY   The type specimen of *D. nobile* was collected by Reeves in China and John Lindley described it in 1830 in *Genera and Species of Orchidaceous Plants* (p. 34).

Many varieties and hybrids of this species have been described and it is probably the most commonly cultivated of all *Dendrobium* species.

SYNONYMS   *Dendrobium lindleyanum* Griff.; *D. coerulescens* Lindl.

CLOSELY RELATED SPECIES   *D. pendulum* is closely related but it lacks the maroon-purple area at the base of the lip. See also *D. parishii*.

Dendrobium obrienianum Kraenzl.

Stems clustered, 45 to more than 80 cm long, 1 cm in diameter, pendulous, reddish. **Leaves** oblong-lanceolate, acuminate, papery, 10–12 cm long, 2.5 cm broad, soon deciduous. **Inflorescences** pendulous, up to 20 cm long, about 20-flowered; bracts minute, triangular, acute. **Flowers** yellow-green, ± 2 cm long. **Dorsal sepal** ovate-oblong, obtuse, 1–1.2 cm long, 0.6 cm broad; **lateral sepals** much longer, 2.5–2.8 cm long; mentum cylindric, bent in the middle, slightly clavate at the apex. **Petals** oblong, obtusely acute, 1–1.2 cm long. **Lip** longly clawed; claw linear and grooved; lamina oblong or oblong-lanceolate, margins slightly crenulate denticulate, 1.5–1.8 cm long, 0.9 cm broad; disc with 3 elevated keels.

DISTRIBUTION   The Philippines.

HISTORY   The species was first collected on Luzon by W. Micholitz who sent plants to the firm of Sander & Co. of St Albans, England. When they flowered in 1891, F. Sander sent a specimen to F. Kraenzlin who described it in the *Gardeners' Chronicle* (ser. 3, 11: p. 266) of 1892.

Dendrobium palpebrae Lindl.

Stems 15–50 cm long, 1–1.5 cm in diameter, clustered, rather slender to subclavate, sulcate, covered with membranous sheaths, 2- to 5-leaved towards apex. **Leaves** lanceolate to oblong, 7.5–15 cm long, 1–3 cm broad, acute. **Inflorescences** suberect, 7.5–10 cm long, laxly many-flowered; bracts 0.6–0.8 cm long. **Flowers** lasting only a few days, showy, fragrant, 3.5–6 cm in diameter, white or rose with a yellow or orange disc on the lip. **Sepals** elliptic-oblong, shortly acute, 1–1.4 cm long; mentum very short, rounded. **Petals** ovate-elliptic to subcircular, shortly apiculate or obtuse, 1–1.3 cm long and broad, margins serrulate. **Lip** shortly clawed, ovate-orbicular, slightly concave, pubescent especially in apical half, somewhat acute, margin ciliate; callus small, 3-lobed at the base.

DISTRIBUTION   Burma, N.E. India, Sikkim, Thailand, Laos, Vietnam and China.

HISTORY   The species was originally received by Messrs J. Veitch & Sons from T. Lobb who collected it at Moulmein, Burma in 1847. However, these plants did not survive and the plant was lost until H. Low & Co. reimported it to England in 1868. *D. palpebrae* was described by John Lindley in the *Journal of the Horticultural Society* (p. 33) in 1850 and was figured in Curtis's *Botanical Magazine* (t. 8683). The specific epithet he gave relates to the eyebrow-like appearance of the lip.

CLOSELY RELATED SPECIES   Similar to *D. farmeri* in habit but with laxer inflorescences, shorter broader bracts and smaller flowers which are white with an orange-yellow disc and last only a few days.

Dendrobium parishii Rchb.f. [Colour Plate]

Stems erect or bent downwards, thick throughout, up to about 50 cm long, 1–2 cm thick, yellowish, covered with white membranous sheaths which fall after the first year. **Leaves** narrowly ovate to elliptic, obtuse, stiff, leathery, 5–10 cm long, blunt, notched at apex, deciduous. **Inflorescences** 2- (occasionally 3)-flowered, given off at nodes of leafless stems. **Flowers** 5–6 cm across; sepals and petals light rose-purple, white at base; lip with a rich purple blotch on either side of throat. **Sepals** oblong-lanceolate, acute or obtuse, 3–3.5 cm long, 1.2 cm broad; mentum very short, rounded, 0.5 cm long. **Petals** oblong, acute, 2.5–3 cm long, 1.5–2 cm broad, ciliolate. **Lip** shortly clawed, obscurely 3-lobed, broadly ovate when flattened, convolute below, reniform or subrhombic above, margins slightly fimbriate, 2–2.5 cm long, 2–2.3 cm broad, pubescent all over; disc with 3 elevated calli. **Column** 0.5 cm long; stelidia acute.

DISTRIBUTION   N.E. India, Burma, Thailand, Laos, Kampuchea, Vietnam and S China.

HISTORY   Another species collected by the Rev. C. Parish at Moulmein and introduced to cultivation by H. Low & Co. of Clapton, London. It was described by H.G. Reichenbach in the *Botanische Zeitung* (p. 237) in 1863.

CLOSELY RELATED SPECIES *D. parishii* is not unlike *D. nobile*, but the latter does not have the thick lumpy stems which are arcuately bent. See also *D. lituiflorum*.

Dendrobium pendulum Roxb. [Colour Plate]

Stems forming tufted masses, ± decurved or pendulous, 7- to 16-noded, much swollen at each node, 30–60 cm long, 2.6 cm in diameter at the nodes, sulcate, dull olive-green. **Leaves** deciduous, lanceolate, semiamplexicaul, 10–12 cm long, 1.5–2.5 cm broad, acute. **Inflorescences** given off from nodes of old stems 1- to 3-flowered; bracts boat-shaped, papery. **Flowers** fragrant, long-lived, 4–7 cm in diameter; sepals and petals white with purple apices; lip white, yellow at base and with a purple margin. **Sepals** oblong, obtuse and reflexed at the apex, 2–3.5 cm long, 0.8–1.2 cm broad. **Petals** broadly oblong, obtuse or rounded at apex, 1.0–3.2 cm long, 1.2–1.6 cm broad. **Lip** shortly clawed, orbicular and shell-like, margins ciliolate, pubescent above and below, 2–2.5 cm long, 2–2.6 cm broad. **Column** 0.3–0.4 cm long.

DISTRIBUTION N.E. India, Burma, Thailand, Laos and S. China.

HISTORY *D. pendulum* was described in 1832 by W. Roxburgh in his *Flora Indica* (p. 484). It is perhaps better known today under the later synonym *D. crassinode* Bens. & Rchb.f. The latter was described in 1869 in the *Gardeners' Chronicle* (p. 164) from a plant collected by Col. Benson at Arracau in Burma.

SYNONYMS *Dendrobium crassinode* Bens. & Rchb.f.; *D. wardianum* Warner; *D. melanophthalmum* Rchb.f.

CLOSELY RELATED SPECIES See *D. nobile*.

Dendrobium primulinum Lindl. [Colour Plate]

Stems clustered, ascending, prostrate or pendulous, terete, slightly thickened upwards, 30–45 cm long, 1–1.5 cm in diameter, sulcate, clothed in white sheaths. **Leaves** oblong or lanceolate, coriaceous, 8–10 cm long, 3 cm broad, obliquely emarginate, obtuse. **Inflorescences** 1- or 2-flowered (at nodes); bracts minute. **Flowers** 4.5–7 cm across, very fragrant; sepals and petals white with pink apical half; lip pale yellow or off-white, with red veins, dark red at base inside tube. **Sepals** oblong, obtuse, 2.8–3.5 cm long, 0.8–1.0 cm broad; mentum very short, rounded. **Petals** ovate, obtuse, similar in size to the sepals. **Lip** convolute below, orbicular or transversely elliptic above, margins minutely erose, 3–3.5 cm long, 5 cm broad; disc minutely pubescent; callus obscure, of 3

glabrous ridges coalescent at base. **Column** short.

DISTRIBUTION Himalayas of Nepal and India (Sikkim), S. China, Burma, Thailand, Vietnam and Laos; up to 1600 m.

HISTORY Described by John Lindley in the *Gardeners' Chronicle* (p. 223) of 1858 based largely on specimens collected in the Sikkim foothills by J.D. Hooker.

SYNONYM *Dendrobium nobile* var. *pallidiflora* Hooker

CLOSELY RELATED SPECIES Near to *D. aphyllum* but stem shorter and stouter, sepals and petals narrower and subequal.

Dendrobium pugioniforme A. Cunn. [Colour Plate]

Plant epiphytic or lithophytic, hanging in large masses. **Stems** sympodial, up to 2 m long but often shorter. **Leaves** thick, ovate, shortly petiolate, fleshy, 7 cm long, 0.5–2 cm broad, acuminate, pungent. **Inflorescences** 1- to 3-flowered, borne towards apex of sympodial stems. **Flowers** non-resupinate, 2–2.5 cm in diameter, white to light green with a pale lip bearing some bright purple or red markings on the lateral lobes and at the base of the mid-lobe. **Dorsal sepal** and **petals** lanceolate, acuminate, 1 cm long, 0.25–0.3 cm broad; **lateral sepals** lanceolate, 1.5 cm long. **Lip** rhombic, 3-lobed, ± cuneate, acute, 1.3–1.8 cm long, 0.6–0.9 cm broad; side lobes rounded, obscure; mid-lobe broadly triangular, margins undulate, reflexed; disc 3-keeled, slightly undulate.

DISTRIBUTION Australia (New South Wales, north to the Bunyah Mts in S.E. Queensland); growing in rain forest up to 1150 m altitude but in S. New South Wales it can be found in lowlands.

HISTORY Described by Alan Cunningham in 1839 in Lindley's *Botanical Register* (misc. 34). He discovered it in the Illawarra district of New South Wales. It is colloquially known in Australia as the 'dagger' orchid because of its sharp pointed leaves.

SYNONYM *Dendrobium pungentifolium* F. Muell.

Dendrobium pulchellum Roxb. ex Lindl. [Colour Plate]

Stems erect, rather slender, terete, 100–220 cm long, leaf-sheaths purple-striped, old stem purplish. **Leaves** persistent, linear-oblong, 10–15 cm long, up to 3 cm broad, cordate at base, obtuse or acute. **Inflorescences** pendulous, 5- to 12-flowered, borne on leafy or leafless stems; bracts minute. **Flowers** 7–8 cm across, musk-scented, tawny rose-yellow to creamy yellow; lip white, yellowish towards base with a large maroon patch on each side of disc. **Dorsal sepal** ovate-oblong, acute, 4–4.5 cm long, 2.5 cm

broad; **lateral sepals** similar to dorsal sepal but ovate; mentum scarcely prominent. **Petals** ovate-elliptic, acute, 4–4.5 cm long, 2.5 cm broad. **Lip** broadly obovate to circular, excavated, shell-like, rounded and somewhat emarginate, 2.8 cm long, 2.5 cm broad, with villi in apical half; callus of 3 glabrous ridges, coalescent at the base.

DISTRIBUTION India (Assam), Burma, Thailand, Malaya and Indo-China; a common epiphytic species.

HISTORY First described in 1830 by John Lindley in *Genera and Species of Orchidaceous Plants* (p. 82), based on an unpublished description by W. Roxburgh.

Var. *luteum* O'Brien lacks the maroon markings on the lip.

SYNONYM *Dendrobium dalhousieanum* Wall.

CLOSELY RELATED SPECIES See *D. albosanguineum*.

Dendrobium rigidum R. Br. [Colour Plate]

An epiphytic or lithophytic herb, up to 40 cm long growing in clumps. **Stems** much branching, erect, drooping or pendulous, 1- to 3-noded, 1–4 cm long, 1-leafed at apex. **Leaf** fleshy, ovate or obovate, 2–6 cm long, 1–1.5 cm broad, apiculate, acute or obtuse. **Inflorescences** 2–5 cm long, 2- to 7-flowered, flowers bunched at apex of inflorescence. **Flowers** 1–1.5 cm across, cream with varying amounts of rose-red and with a yellow lip marked with rose-red on the sides. **Sepals** oblong, obtuse or shortly acuminate, 0.6–1 cm long, 0.5 cm broad; mentum very obtuse, bisaccate, 0.4–0.7 cm long. **Petals** oblong or rhombic, acute, 0.6–0.8 cm long, 0.1–0.2 cm broad. **Lip** 3-lobed in apical half, 0.6–1.0 cm long, 0.4–0.7 cm broad; side lobes erect, porrect, ovate, acute; mid-lobe reflexed, obovate-suborbicular, shortly apiculate or obtuse. **Column** 0.3 cm long; stelidia porrect, acute.

DISTRIBUTION Australia (N. Queensland) and New Guinea; a common epiphyte on mangroves and in paperbark swamps and tolerant of high light intensities.

HISTORY Another species described by Robert Brown in his *Prodromus Florae Novae Hollandiae* (p. 333) in 1810, based on a plant collected by D.C. Solander in N. Australia.

SYNONYM *Callista rigida* (R. Br.) O. Ktze.

Dendrobium sanderae Rolfe

Stems erect, somewhat thickened below the middle, up to 80 cm long, longitudinally striate, about 40-leaved, leaf-sheaths covered with blackish hairs. **Leaves** ovate to narrowly ovate, 5 cm long, 1.7 cm broad, 2-lobed at apex. **Inflorescences** racemose, up to about 6 cm long, lateral, 3- to 4-flowered. **Flowers** white with red or purple streaks at the base of the lip and on side lobes, up to 7 cm across. **Sepals** lanceolate, acuminate, 3.5–4.0 cm long. **Petals** elliptic-obovate, 3.5–3.8 cm long, 2–3 cm broad. **Lip** 3-lobed, tubular at base, 4.2 cm long, 3.2 cm broad; mid-lobe truncate, 2.5 cm in diameter; mentum spur-like, 2.2–2.5 cm long.

DISTRIBUTION   The Philippines.

HISTORY   Plants were sent to Messrs Sander & Sons of St Albans, England, by their collectors in the Philippines, and R. Rolfe named it for F. Sander in the *Gardeners' Chronicle* (ser. 3, vol. 45: p. 374) of 1909.

CLOSELY RELATED SPECIES   *D. dearei* and *D. schuetzei* are closely related species.

Dendrobium scabrilingue Lindl.
[Colour Plate]

Stems tufted, fusiform or swollen towards apex, c. 10-noded, up to 30 cm long, 1–1.5 cm in diameter, 4- to 6-leaved sheaths covered with blackish hairs. **Leaves** persistent, ligulate or oblong-linear, up to 10.5 cm long, 1.5–2 cm broad, obscurely 2-lobed at apex. **Inflorescences** very short, 2-flowered from nodes; bracts minute, scarious. **Flowers** very fragrant, 3.5 cm across, ivory-white, with red or green veins on side lobes of lip which has a yellow mid-lobe; mentum green. **Sepals** triangular-lanceolate, acute, 1.9–2.2 cm long, 0.7–0.8 cm broad; mentum conical, obtuse. **Petals** lanceolate to oblong-elliptic, acute, slightly reflexed, 1.3–1.8 cm long, 0.7–0.8 cm broad. **Lip** erect, 3-lobed, 1.8 cm long, 0.8–0.9 cm broad; mid-lobe fleshy, elliptic obtuse, verrucose; side lobes triangular; disc 5- to 7-keeled.

DISTRIBUTION   Burma, Thailand and Laos; in lower montane forest.

HISTORY   J. Lindley described the species in the *Journal of the Linnean Society* (1859). Both Messrs Veitch & Sons and H. Low & Co. had received plants at around that time from T. Lobb and Rev. C. Parish, respectively.

SYNONYMS   *Dendrobium hedyosmum* Batem.; *D. alboviride* Parish; *D. galactanthum* Schltr.

Dendrobium schoeninum Lindl. [Colour Plate]

An erect or semi-erect epiphytic or lithophytic herb, becoming pendulous with age, up to 90 cm long; roots clustered at the base. **Stems** superposed or branching, many-noded, 2–12 cm long, up to 0.3 cm in diameter, unifoliate, yellowish. **Leaves** upright or spreading, terete or obtusely 4-angled, acute, deeply sulcate, 2–16 cm long, 0.2–1.2 cm in diameter. **Inflorescences** up to 3 cm long, 1- to 4-flowered; bracts very small. **Flowers** non-resupinate, 2.5–3.5 cm across, white, cream or pink with dark purple stripes on the proximal half of the segments, the margins of the mid-lobe of the lip purple.

Sepals linear-lanceolate, acute, 1.5–2.4 cm long, 0.35 cm wide; mentum erect, 0.6–0.9 cm long. **Petals** linear-oblanceolate, acute, 1.4–2.4 cm long, 0.2–0.25 cm wide. **Lip** subrhombic, 3-lobed in the apical half, 2–3 cm long, 0.6–1 cm wide; side lobes triangular; mid-lobe reflexed, lanceolate, acuminate, longer than the side lobes, with undulate margins; callus of 3 undulate parallel ridges ending on the mid-lobe. **Column** 0.4–0.5 cm long, with rounded stelidia; foot 0.9 cm long.

DISTRIBUTION   Australia (New South Wales and Queensland); found on rocks and trees, such as *Casuarina*, on rain forest edges, river banks and in swamps growing in shade or bright sunlight in the coastal lowlands and foothills up to 500 m elevation.

HISTORY   This pretty 'pencil' orchid is best known under the name *Dendrobium beckleri* F. Muell., but that is a later synonym. In fact, it was first described nearly 20 years earlier by John Lindley in the *Gardeners' Chronicle* (p. 7) in 1846 as *D. schoeninum*, based on a plant flowered by Messrs Loddiges of Hackney, London.

SYNONYMS   *Dendrobium beckleri* Muell.; *D. striolatum* sensu F.M. Bailey; *Callista beckleri* (Muell.) O. Kuntze

Dendrobium schuetzei Rolfe [Colour Plate]

Epiphytic plant. **Stems** up to 15–40 cm long, erect, thickened above the middle and at the base, about 12-noded, many-leaved. **Leaves** narrowly ovate, suberect, coriaceous, 8.5 cm long, 2.5 cm broad, obscurely 2-lobed. **Inflorescences** shortly 3- to 4-flowered. **Flowers** 8–9.5 cm across, fragrant, showy, white with a small emerald-green disc which is tinged purple at the base of the lip. **Sepals** oblong-lanceolate, 3–5 cm long, acuminate; mentum obtuse, 1.2 cm long. **Petals** broadly ovate-orbicular, up to 5.5 cm long, 4 cm broad. **Lip** 3-lobed, tubular at base, 4–4.5 cm long; side lobes incurved, broadly rotund; mid-lobe recurved, broadly obovate, truncate, apiculate, 3.5–4 cm broad. **Column** 0.6 cm long.

DISTRIBUTION   The Philippines.

HISTORY   The species was first introduced into cultivation by the firm of Sander & Sons of St Albans, England and it was rewarded with a First Class Certificate by the Royal Horticultural Society in 1912. R. Rolfe described it in 1911 in the *Orchid Review* (p. 224).

CLOSELY RELATED SPECIES   *D. sanderae* resembles *D. schuetzei* somewhat but it has smaller less showy flowers.

Dendrobium secundum (Blume) Lindl.
[Colour Plate]

Stems erect or semipendulous, rather stout, tapering to both ends, sulcate, 25 to more than

100 cm long, 1.8 cm in diameter. **Leaves** oblong to oblong-lanceolate, persistent, 6–10 cm long, 3–6 cm broad, unequally 2-lobed and acute at apex, many per stem. **Inflorescences** borne from upper nodes only, tapering, densely many-flowered, up to 12 cm long. **Flowers** waxy, glossy, secund, 1.8 cm long, 0.6 cm broad, light pink to purple or rarely white; lip orange or yellow in front. **Dorsal sepal** and **petals** slightly concave, ovate, acute, 0.7 cm long, 0.4 cm broad; **lateral sepals** 1.5 cm long, 0.4 cm broad; mentum slightly curved, rounded at the apex, 1 cm long. **Lip** spathulate, linear and grooved at the base, acute, 1.4–1.6 cm long, with a transverse lamella in the middle. **Column** with broad stelidia.

DISTRIBUTION   Burma, Thailand, Indo-China through Malaya, Sumatra, the Philippines and some Pacific Islands; very common as an epiphyte in dry forest.

HISTORY   John Lindley transferred C.L. Blume's species *Pedilonum secundum* to the genus *Dendrobium* in the *Botanical Register* (t. 1291) 1829. Blume's original collection was made in Java and he described it in 1825 in *Bijdragen* (p. 322).

SYNONYMS   *Pedilonum secundum* Blume; *Dendrobium bursigerum* Lindl.; *D. heterostigma* Rchb.f.

Dendrobium smillieae F. Muell. [Colour Plate]

A robust plant growing in large clumps. **Stems** slender, fusiform, 15–100 cm long, 1–2 cm in diameter, leafy throughout, sulcate when old and clothed in thin, scarious sheaths. **Leaves** oblong or lanceolate, very thin, often twisted or curved, 5–20 cm long, 2–4 cm broad, acute. **Inflorescences** borne towards apex of leafless stems, densely many-flowered, 4–15 cm long. **Flowers** 1.5–2 cm long, white, cream or pale green with a pink mentum and apical parts of all segments green. **Sepals** oblong, shortly acute or obtuse, 1 cm long; mentum slightly inflated, 0.6–0.9 cm long, obtuse. **Petals** 1 cm long, spathulate, shortly acute. **Lip** uppermost in flower, semicylindrical, forming with the lateral sepals a nectary, apex bright shining green, 1.1–1.6 cm long, 0.4 cm broad. **Column** dilated above, 0.3–0.6 cm long; foot 0.6–0.9 cm long.

DISTRIBUTION   New Guinea and N.E. tropical Australia; growing in open forests at low or moderate altitudes.

HISTORY   Described in 1867 by F. von Mueller in *Fragmenta Phytographiae Australiae* (p. 94). Known as the 'bottle brush' orchid in Australia.

SYNONYMS   *Coelandria smillieae* (F. Muell.) Fitzg.; *Callista smillieae* (F. Muell.) O. Ktze.; *Dendrobium hollrungii* Kraenzl. var. *australiense* Rendle

Dendrobium speciosum J.E. Smith
[Colour Plate]

A small to large epiphytic or lithophytic herb often growing in large masses. **Stems** 8–100 cm long, 1–6 cm broad, swollen throughout or clavate, several-noded, shallowly sulcate, ± clothed with sheathing bracts, 2- to 5-leaved at apex. **Leaves** ovate or oblong, rather thick, coriaceous, 4–25 cm long, 2–8 cm broad, obtuse. **Inflorescences** apparently terminal, suberect or pendent, 10–60 cm long, often densely many-flowered. **Flowers** very fragrant, variable, 2–4 cm long, white, pale cream or yellow with purple or red markings on the lip; column white, spotted red or purple. **Dorsal sepal** linear, acute, 2–4 cm long, 0.5–1 cm broad; **lateral sepals** falcate, tapering, obtuse, 1.5–3.5 cm long, 0.4–1 cm broad. **Petals** linear, acute, 1.5–3.5 cm long, 0.2–0.5 cm broad. **Lip** 3-lobed, up to 3 cm long, 2–4 cm broad, side lobes erect; mentum thick, broad, about 0.5 cm long. **Column** 0.4–0.8 cm long.

DISTRIBUTION   E. Australia.

HISTORY   *D. speciosum*, the 'King' or 'Rock' orchid, was described in 1804 by J.E. Smith in *Exotic Botany* (t. 10).

This is a very variable species with at least five recognised varieties. *D. speciosum* var. *hillii* (often grown as *D. hillii* Hooker f.) has relatively slender stems, up to 1 m long; leaves coriaceous and about 30 cm long; inflorescences 45–60 cm long with many densely packed white flowers rather smaller than in typical *D. speciosum*. It is known from N.E. New South Wales and also from the extreme S.E. of the Cape York Peninsula.

SYNONYM   *Dendrobium hillii* Hooker f.

CLOSELY RELATED SPECIES   *D. jonesii*, *D. gracillimum* (Rupp) Rupp and *D.* × *delicatum* (F.M. Bailey) F.M. Bailey have all at one time been considered varieties of *D. speciosum* but are now considered to be distinct species. *D. jonesii* has a lip whose mid-lobe is 3 times wider than long; the stems of *D.* × *delicatum* taper evenly from base to apex and *D. gracillimum* has stems under 2 cm thick, swollen at the base and tapering for a short distance above with the apical part cylindrical.

Dendrobium spectabile (Blume) Miq.
[Colour Plate]

Stems about 8-noded, semiglobose at base, clavate above, up to 60 cm long, about 5-leaved towards apex. **Leaves** lanceolate to ovate, coriaceous, up to 20 cm long, obtuse. **Inflorescences** laxly several-flowered, up to 30 cm long, arising from stem below leaves; bracts minute, oblong. **Flowers** 7–8 cm long; sepals and petals cream to pale greenish at margins, mottled dull purple and veins same colour; lip almost white at base, yellowish above, strongly purple-veined. **Sepals** and **petals** narrowly ovate-triangular, acuminate, margins irregularly undulate, reflexed at the apex, 3.5 cm long, 0.5–0.9 cm broad; lateral sepals connate at the base. **Lip** similar to other segments but 3-lobed, shortly connate at base with column-foot, 5 cm long, 1.3 cm broad; side lobes oblong, obtuse, minutely dentate on front margins; mid-lobe subpandurate, lanceolate in front, acuminate, undulate; callus at the base of 3 elevated ridges. **Column** stout, very short.

DISTRIBUTION   New Guinea and Solomon Islands.

HISTORY   Originally described by C.L. Blume as *Latouria spectabilis* in 1850 in *Rumphia* (p. 195). He had received his specimen from Leschenault de la Tour (hence Latouria), who was the naturalist on Baudin's voyage to the Pacific, and who had collected the plant in New Guinea. When the true diversity of the genus *Dendrobium* was recognised, Blume's species was transferred to it, where it and several allied species still merit distinction at the sectional level.

SYNONYMS   *Latouria spectabilis* Blume; *Dendrobium tigrinum* Hemsley

Dendrobium stratiotes Rchb.f. [Colour Plate]

Stems clustered, terete to long-fusiform, up to 2 m long, 2 cm in diameter, 5- to many-leaved. **Leaves** rigidly leathery, persistent, narrowly ovate, obtuse, coriaceous, 8 cm long, 2 cm broad, borne near stem apex. **Inflorescences** 8–30 cm long, lateral, erect or suberect; about 3- to 15-flowered. **Flowers** large, 8–10 cm long, creamy-white with greenish petals and a violet-striped white lip. **Dorsal sepal** ovate-triangular to ligulate, undulate, 3.5 cm long, 1 cm broad; **lateral sepals** similar but 4.5 cm long; mentum 1.5 cm long, spur-like. **Petals** linear, erect, acuminate, twisted, 6 cm long, 0.25 cm broad. **Lip** large, 3-lobed, 4 cm long, 2 cm broad; side lobes erect, rhombic; mid-lobe elliptic, acute; disc 3- to 5-keeled.

DISTRIBUTION   The Moluccas and W. New Guinea.

HISTORY   Discovered by August Linden in the Sunda Islands and described by H.G. Reichenbach in the *Gardeners' Chronicle* (n.s. 25: p. 266) of 1886. He named it *D. stratiotes* as the mass of erect stems and petals reminded him of soldiers and their bayonets.

CLOSELY RELATED SPECIES   *Dendrobium antennatum* Lindl. which has smaller flowers.

Dendrobium stricklandianum Rchb.f.
[Colour Plate]

Stems long, clustered, terete, erect or pendent, up to 40 cm long, 0.3–0.4 cm thick, pale green, about 12-leaved. **Leaves** ligulate-lanceolate, 5–7.5 cm long, 1.5–2.5 cm broad, acute, deciduous. **Inflorescences** 2–6 cm long, about 4- to 5- flowered, borne on leafless stems. **Flowers** up to 3 cm across, green or yellow-green with a cream lip, marked with purple stripes, disc with 3 or more dark purple lines; column green, anther purple. **Sepals** and **petals** narrowly ovate, about 1.8 cm long, acute or acuminate; mentum obtuse, 1 cm long. **Lip** oblong-ligulate, entire, 1.7 cm long, 1.1 cm broad, obtuse; disc hirsute. **Column** 0.3 cm long; anther ovate.

DISTRIBUTION   Japan, Ryukyu Islands, Taiwan and China.

HISTORY   Introduced into cultivation in 1875 by W. Strickland of Malton, England. This plant was subsequently described in the *Gardeners' Chronicle* (n.s. 7: p. 749) of 1877 by H.G. Reichenbach who named it *D. stricklandianum*. In recent floras of Taiwan and Japan the name *D. tosaense* is used but as this was described by Makino in the *Illustrated Flora of Japan* in 1891 it must be a later synonym.

SYNONYM   *Dendrobium tosaense* Makino

Dendrobium striolatum Rchb.f.

Small lithophytic plants growing in dense masses. **Stems** sympodial, 5–50 cm long, mostly pendulous, 1-leafed at apex. **Leaf** terete, dorsally grooved, 4–11 cm long, 0.2–0.3 cm broad. **Inflorescences** axillary, 1- to 2-flowered, ± equal to leaf in length. **Flowers** non-resupinate, the sepals and petals whitish-cream or yellow, striped with purple or brown on the base; lip white with a yellow base; ovary purple. **Dorsal sepal** narrowly oblong-ovate, subacute, 1.3–1.5 cm long, 0.2 cm broad; **lateral sepals** oblique, narrowly oblong-lanceolate, subacute, 1.5–2.0 cm long, 0.3–0.5 cm broad, forming with the column-foot a prominent conical mentum up to 0.5 cm high. **Petals** linear-lanceolate to oblanceolate, subacute, 1.2–1.4 cm long, 0.1–0.2 cm broad. **Lip** recurved in apical half, obscurely 3-lobed, 0.7–1.0 cm long, 0.5–0.7 cm broad; side lobes crescentic, acute; mid-lobe ovate to subquadrate, apiculate, margins strongly undulate; callus of 3 parallel keels, sinuate in front. **Column** 0.3–0.4 cm long, slightly papillose.

DISTRIBUTION   Australia (New South Wales, Victoria and Tasmania); sea level to 1000 m, in exposed situations.

HISTORY   H.G. Reichenbach described this pretty orchid in 1857 in the *Hamburger Gartenzeitung* (p. 313) based on a specimen grown by F. Stange in the greenhouses of Consul Schiller.

SYNONYMS   *Dendrobium teretifolium* Lindl. non R. Br.; *D. schoeninum* Lindl.; *D. milliganii* F. Muell.; *Callista striolata* (Rchb.f). O. Ktze.

Dendrobium taurinum Lindl. [Colour Plate]

Stems erect, cylindrical to spindle-shaped, up

to 125 cm long, 1.5–2.5 cm in diameter, nearly cylindrical but slightly compressed, covered in white sheaths. **Leaves** ± persistent, oblong or elliptic, coriaceous, slightly emarginate, 8–15 cm long, 5–6 cm broad, dark shining green, amplexicaul, 3–4 cm apart in the middle of the stem. **Inflorescences** given off from near apex but not terminal, erect, slightly fractiflex, 10–45 cm long, up to 20-flowered; bracts minute, triangular. **Flowers** long-lasting, waxy, about 6.5 cm long; sepals and mentum yellowish-green; petals purple, white at base, once twisted; lip white to purple, margins purple, disc with 3 purple keels; column white with a purple apex. **Dorsal sepal** ovate-triangular, acuminate, 3 cm long, 0.9 cm broad; **lateral sepals** triangular, acuminate, 4 cm long, 1.7 cm broad; mentum spur-like, conical, 1–2 cm long. **Petals** spathulate, obtuse, twisted. **Lip** somewhat elliptic, subentire, 3-lobed in front, 3.5 cm long, 2.5 cm broad; side lobes reduced to a dentate tooth; mid-lobe transversely elliptic, apiculate, crispate, 3-keeled on disc.

DISTRIBUTION The Philippines (Mindanao, Luzon and Ilo-Ilo Islands).

HISTORY Discovered by Hugh Cuming, this species was sent by him to Messrs Loddiges in England. John Lindley described it in 1843 in the *Botanical Register* (t. 28), the flowers reminding him of a bull's head with the petals representing horns.

Dendrobium tetragonum Lindl.

Stems clustered, semipendulous, 4-angled, broadest above the middle, spindle-shaped near apex, about 7- to 10-noded, 6–45 cm long, 1 cm in diameter, 2- to 3-leaved. **Leaves** ovate or oblong, acute, thin-papery but coriaceous, 3–10 cm long, 1.5–3 cm broad, dark green. **Inflorescences** almost apical, very short, 1- to 5-flowered; bracts minute. **Flowers** very variable, 4–9 cm long; sepals yellow, edged brown; petals pale yellow-green; lip dull yellow, ± striped purple on side lobes and spotted purple on mid-lobe. **Sepals** triangular, long-acuminate, 2–5 cm long, 0.3–0.5 cm broad; lateral sepals 4.5 cm long; mentum obtuse, rounded. **Petals** very narrow, linear-lanceolate, long-acuminate, 3.5 cm long, 0.1–0.2 cm broad. **Lip** revolute, 3-lobed, 1–1.4 cm long, 0.8–1.3 cm broad; side lobes semiobovate or triangular, rounded in front; mid-lobe reflexed, suborbicular or broadly cordate, shortly acute, 1–1.5 cm long, 1.2 cm broad; callus bisulcate, decurrent in front. **Column** 0.4–0.5 cm long.

DISTRIBUTION Australia (Queensland and New South Wales); growing on rain forest trees and occasionally on papery-barked species of *Melaleuca*.

HISTORY Originally introduced to England by W. Bull, a plant being received also by the

Royal Botanic Gardens, Kew from Messrs Rollisson & Sons of Tooting, London in 1871. When it flowered in 1872 it was figured in Curtis's *Botanical Magazine*. The plant had, however, been described much earlier in 1839 by John Lindley in the *Botanical Register* (misc. 33).

Three varieties are known of this species, one of which (var. *giganteum* [Colour Plate]) has flowers with sepals 5–8 cm long.

Dendrobium transparens Lindl.
[Colour Plate]

Stems slender, terete, swollen at base, erect to pendulous, 30–60 cm tall, 0.4–0.5 cm in diameter, dark grey marked with faint yellow on the internodes, 5- to 7-leaved. **Leaves** eventually deciduous, linear-lanceolate, recurved, 8–11 cm long, 1.5–2 cm broad, acute. **Inflorescences** borne on old stems, 2- to 3-flowered at the nodes, emerging from large hyaline bracts. **Flowers** 3–5 cm across, delicately scented, short-lived; pedicel pink; sepals and petals transparently white, apices pink; lip white with a pink apex and central purple streaks radiating from the mid-vein, column white, stigma purple. **Dorsal sepal** elliptic, obtuse, 2.2 cm long, 0.6 cm broad; **lateral sepals** triangular, acuminate, 2.5–3.1 cm long, 0.5–0.9 cm broad; mentum short, conical, obtuse. **Petals** oblong or subrhombic, obtuse, 1–1.2 cm long, 0.5 cm broad. **Lip** cuneate and convolute at the base, broadly oblong, rounded at the apex and minutely emarginate, 2.5–2.6 cm long, 1.3–1.6 cm broad, margin fimbriate; disc pilose with a central fleshy sulcate line. **Column** short.

DISTRIBUTION N.E. India (Khasia Hills), Burma (Chin Hills) and Nepal; at an altitude of about 1300 m.

HISTORY *D. transparens* was first discovered in Nepal by Dr N. Wallich and was named by him in his *Catalogue* (no. 2008). John Lindley described in 1830 in his *Genera and Species of Orchidaceous Plants*.

SYNONYM *Dendrobium henshallii* Rchb.f.

Dendrobium trigonopus Rchb.f.
[Colour Plate]

Stems clustered in tufts, fusiform, sulcate, shiny purplish-brown, with 4 well-developed internodes and some shorter ones, 15–20 cm tall, 1 cm in diameter. **Leaves** 1–4, subterminal, ligulate or oblong, thick, papery, 7.5–10 cm long, acute, dull green, long-hispid beneath and on leaf-sheaths. **Inflorescences** 1- or 2-flowered; bracts minute. **Flowers** 5 cm across, golden-yellow with a row of transverse red lines on each side of the lip which is green in the centre; ovary 3-angled in cross-section, 2.5–2.8 cm long, 0.8 cm broad; mentum very short, obtuse. **Petals** oblong, acute, 2.3 cm long, 1 cm

broad. **Lip** broad and longly clawed, 3-lobed, 1.3 cm long and broad; side lobes small, rhombic, angled, front margin denticulate; mid-lobe much larger, broadly oblong, obtuse, margin and disc roughly papillate. **Column** with subquadrate stelidia.

DISTRIBUTION Burma, China (Yunnan), Laos and Thailand; up to 1200 m.

HISTORY The species was first introduced into cultivation by H. Low & Co. of Clapton, London, to whom it was sent from Burma. Low sent plants to John Day who flowered it in 1887 and sent specimens to H.G. Reichenbach who described it in the *Gardeners' Chronicle* (s. 3, 3: p. 682) of the same year.

SYNONYM *Dendrobium velutinum* Rolfe

Dendrobium unicum Seidenf. [Colour Plate]
See under *D. arachnites*.

Dendrobium victoriae-reginae Loher
[Colour Plate]

Stems pendulous, branching near base, 25–60 cm long, about 12-leaved, swollen at the nodes, orange-yellow, covered with persistent sheaths. **Leaves** oblong or lanceolate, papery, 3–8 cm long, 1–2 cm broad, acute to acuminate. **Inflorescences** borne on old stems, 3- to 12-flowered on a very short stalk; bracts paleaceous, oblong, acute. **Flowers** 3 cm across; sepals and petals white at base with a blue blotch above; lip white in throat with 5 violet lines, otherwise blue-violet. **Sepals** oblong, obtusely acute, 1.5–1.8 cm long, 0.6 cm broad; mentum short, straight, obtuse. **Petals** obovate-oblong, 1.5 cm long, 0.6 cm broad, margins minutely erose. **Lip** obovate from a short linear base, slightly concave, shortly acute, denticulate and reflexed on basal margins with 3 elevated lines at the base, 2–3.5 cm long, 0.8–1.1 cm broad; disc minutely sparsely pilose. **Column** with recurved acute stelidia.

DISTRIBUTION The Philippines (Luzon); growing in wet, mossy forests at 1800–2400 m altitude.

HISTORY A. Loher, who discovered this distinctive species, dedicated it to Queen Victoria whose Golden Jubilee was celebrated around the time of its discovery. He described it in the *Gardeners' Chronicle* (pt. 1: p. 399) in 1897.

SYNONYM *Dendrobium coeleste* Loher

Dendrobium wardianum Warner
[Colour Plate]

Stems erect or pendulous, terete, thickened at the nodes, up to 120 cm long, 1–1.8 cm thick. **Leaves** deciduous, oblong-lanceolate, 8–15 cm long, 1.5–2.5 cm broad, acute. **Inflorescences** 1- to 3-flowered, at the nodes of leafless stems; peduncle short. **Flowers** fragrant, long-lived, up to 10 cm across; sepals and petals white with purple tips; lip ochreous-yellow with 2 deep maroon blotches at the base and purple at apex. **Sepals** oblong, obtuse, 4–5 cm long, 2 cm broad; mentum very short, obtuse. **Petals** ovate-elliptic, rounded or obtuse, 4.5–5 cm long, 2.5–3 cm broad. **Lip** convolute, broadly ovate or suborbicular, excavate, minutely puberulent above and below, 4 cm long, 3 cm broad. **Column** 3 mm long; anther deeply sulcate, papillate.

DISTRIBUTION India (Assam); Bhutan, Burma, S. China and Thailand; 1200–2000 m.

HISTORY The species was described by R. Warner in his *Select Orchidaceous Plants* (t. 19) in 1862, based on a plant from N.E. India.

Several named varieties, differing mainly in flower size and colour, are known, e.g. var. *candidum* Veitch which has white flowers with 2 brown spots on the lip.

CLOSELY RELATED SPECIES Very close to *Dendrobium falconeri* Hooker but it has a stouter less nodose stem and broader blunter sepals and petals. Sir Joseph Hooker in the *Flora of British India* (1890) states that he considers the two may be merely forms of a single species.

Dendrobium williamsonii Day & Rchb.f.
[Colour Plate]

Stems upright, elongate-fusiform, velvety, 20–30 cm long, 1 cm thick, many-leaved towards apex. **Leaves** oblong or lanceolate, velvety, 5–10 cm long, 1.5–2 cm broad, obscurely 2-lobed at apex; sheaths densely covered with black hairs. **Inflorescences** 1- to 2-flowered from upper nodes. **Flowers** 6.5–7.5 cm across, waxy, long-lived, fragrant, ivory-white to yellowish; lip with a blood-red or red-brown central spot; column white with orange-red spot below stigma. **Dorsal sepal** ovate, acute, 3 cm long, 0.6–0.7 cm broad; **lateral sepals** falcate, triangular, apex acuminate and deflexed, keeled on reverse, 4.5 cm long, 1.5 cm broad; mentum straight, obtuse. **Petals** ovate, acuminate, 3 cm long, 0.6–0.7 cm broad. **Lip** cuneate at the base, flabellate, 3-lobed in front, 4.5 cm long, 2.5 cm broad; side lobes obtuse, rounded, margins denticulate or ciliate; mid-lobe orbicular, crisped, margin ciliate-denticulate; veins and side lobes long pilose, rest of disc shortly pilose. **Column** with a pilose anther.

DISTRIBUTION India (Assam), Burma, Thailand, Laos, Vietnam and S. China.

HISTORY This species was described in 1869 in the *Gardeners' Chronicle* (p. 78) by John Day of Tottenham near London, a famous grower of orchids, and H.G. Reichenbach. They named if after Day's nephew, W.J. Wil-

liamson, who collected the species in Assam in 1868 and sent it to his uncle.

SYNONYM *Dendrobium cariniferum* Rchb.f.
CLOSELY RELATED SPECIES Similar to *D. infundibulum* in habit but more robust. See also *D. bellatulum*.

Dendrochilum Blume
Subfamily Epidendroideae
Tribe Coelogyneae
Subtribe Coelogyninae

Small or medium-sized epiphytic plants with creeping scaly rhizomes. **Pseudobulbs** tufted or spaced on rhizome, narrow, fusiform or ovoid, 1-leafed. **Leaf** flat, narrow, coriaceous. **Inflorescence** lateral, slender, suberect to pendulous, spicate or racemose, densely many-flowered; bracts often prominent. **Flowers** small, thin-textured. **Sepals** subequal, spreading; lateral sepals adnate to the column-base. **Petals** smaller than the sepals. **Lip** jointed at the foot of the column, subsessile, erect-spreading, oblong, fleshy at the base. **Column** short, winged at apex and laterally or terminally dentate; anther 2-celled; pollinia 4, ovoid, waxy, cohering to a small viscidium.

DISTRIBUTION Over 120 species in S.E. Asia, Indonesia, the Philippines and New Guinea.

DERIVATION OF NAME From the Greek *dendron* (tree) and either *cheilos* (lip) or *chilos* (green food), in allusion either to their prominent lip, or to the epiphytic habit.

TAXONOMY C. Blume described *Dendrochilum* in 1825 in *Bijdragen* (p. 398). It is one of the larger genera with its greatest concentration of species in the mountains of the Philippines, Sumatra and Borneo. Many species are local and many of these are poorly known.

Dendrochilum is allied to *Pholidota* and to *Coelogyne* being distinguished by its smaller flowers in which the column has a winged apex around the anther and also separate lateral arms or wings below.

The most recent revision of the genus is that of E. Pfitzer and F. Kraenzlin in Engler's *Das Pflanzenreich* (1907) where 72 species are recognised in five subgenera. Two of these subgenera, *Platyclinis* and *Acoridium*, have been treated as distinct at the generic level by some authors.

The Philippines species of *Dendrochilum* were revised by Oakes Ames (1908) in *Orchidaceae*, vol. 2. R. Holttum has described the Malayan species in his *Orchids of Malaya* (1964) and J.J. Smith listed the Sumatran species in *Fedde, Repertorium* (1933).

TYPE SPECIES *D. aurantiacum* Blume
SYNONYM *Platyclinis* Benth.

CULTURE Compost A. Temp. Winter min. 12–15°C. *Dendrochilum* species are best grown in pans where they can grow to form large clumps. After flowering, as the new growths develop, water should be freely given, and moderate shade applied. When the psuedobulbs are fully grown, much less water is required.

Dendrochilum cobbianum Rchb.f.
[Colour Plate]

Pseudobulbs clustered, narrowly conical, yellowish, 6–8 cm long, 1–1.5 cm in diameter, yellowish, somewhat glossy when dry, 1-leafed at apex. **Leaf** oblong-lanceolate, acute, petiolate, 6–35 cm long, 2.5–5.5 cm broad, mid-rib prominent. **Inflorescence** drooping above, longer than the leaf, elongated, up to 50 cm long; peduncle erect, up to 30 cm long; bracts glumaceous, ovate, subacute, 0.4–0.7 cm long. **Flowers** 0.7 cm apart; sepals and petals dull white; lip orange. **Sepals** and **petals** oblong-elliptic, obtuse, 0.7–1 cm long, 0.2–0.3 cm broad. **Lip** cuneate-flabellate, retuse in front, apiculate, 0.6–0.7 cm long, 0.3 cm broad, with a depressed semioblong callus at the base. **Column** denticulate at the apex, with linear, acute, porrect side arms.

DISTRIBUTION The Philippines (Luzon).

HISTORY Discovered by W. Boxall in the Philippines whilst collecting there for Stuart Low. It first flowered in cultivation in the collection of Walter Cobb of Silberdale Lodge, Sydenham, England, to whom H.G. Reichenbach dedicated it when he described it in 1880 in the *Gardeners' Chronicle* (n.s. 14: p. 748).

SYNONYMS *Platyclinis cobbiana* (Rchb.f.) Hemsley; *Acoridium cobbianum* (Rchb.f) Rolfe
CLOSELY RELATED SPECIES *D. filiforme* differs from *D. cobbianum* in having smaller yellow-green flowers with an obscure V-shaped basal callus on the lip. It is also generally a smaller plant with less acute leaves.

Dendrochilum filiforme Lindl.
[Colour Plate]

Pseudobulbs conical or ellipsoid-fusiform, 2.5 cm long, 1 cm in diameter, 2-leaved at apex, covered below by papery sheaths. **Leaves** erect, petiolate, narrowly linear-ligulate, subobtuse, about 18 cm long, 1.2 cm broad. **Inflorescence** distichously many-flowered, 35–45 cm or more long; peduncle filiform, up to 25 cm long; rhachis subflexuous, ± pendulous-arcuate, angled; bracts papery, convolute, equal to ovary in length. **Flowers** usually short-lived, fragrant, yellowish-white or yellow; lip often golden yellow. **Dorsal sepal** elliptic-oblong, acute, 0.25–0.3 cm long, 0.1 cm broad; **lateral sepals** lanceolate, 0.25–0.3 cm long, 0.1 cm broad. **Petals** obovate-cuneate, obtuse, 0.25 cm long, 0.12 cm broad. **Lip** obscurely 3-lobed, 0.2 cm long, 0.18 cm broad; side lobes minute, entire; mid-lobe suborbicular-obcordate; disc bearing 2 linear calli. **Column** minute with 2 lateral porrect acute arms.

DISTRIBUTION   The Philippines.

HISTORY   This was the first living species of the genus to be seen in Europe, having been sent from Manila in the Philippines by Hugh Cuming to James Bateman. It was described in 1840 by John Lindley in the *Botanical Register* (misc. 52).

SYNONYMS *Platyclinis filiformis* (Lindl.) Hemsley; *Acoridium filiforme* (Lindl.) Rolfe

CLOSELY RELATED SPECIES   See *D. cobbianum* and *D. glumaceum*.

Dendrochilum glumaceum Lindl.
[Colour Plate]

Pseudobulbs conical to ovoid, clustered, 1.5–4 cm long, 1–1.8 cm in diameter, 1-leafed at apex. **Leaf** grass-like, erect to narrowly elliptic or oblanceolate, acute or acuminate, longly petiolate, 12–45 cm long, 1.8–4 cm broad. **Inflorescences** drooping above, racemose, many-flowered, 18–50 cm long; peduncle erect, up to 30 cm long; bracts spreading, imbricate, distichous, 0.6–0.8 cm long, glumaceous. **Flowers** fragrant, white. **Sepals** lanceolate, acute or acuminate, 0.7–1 cm long, 0.1–0.15 cm broad. **Petals** narrowly oblong-lanceolate, acute or acuminate, 0.4–0.7 cm long, 0.1 cm broad. **Lip** 3-lobed, recurved, 0.3–0.4 cm long, 0.2 cm broad; side lobes erect, short, falcate, acute; mid-lobe ovate-orbicular, apiculate; disc bilamellate. **Column** erect, trifid at the apex, with 2 lateral, acute terminal arms.

DISTRIBUTION   The Philippines (Luzon and Mindanao); on trees and rocks, 700–2000 m altitude.

HISTORY   Described by John Lindley in 1841 in the *Botanical Register* (misc. 23) having been discovered by Hugh Cuming in the Philippines. Messrs Loddiges were the first to flower it in cultivation.

CLOSELY RELATED SPECIES Distinguished from *Dendrochilum latifolium* Lindl. by its roundish mid-lobe, the entire side lobes of the lip and by the arms of the column arising from the apex. *D. filiforme* is vegetatively not unlike *D. glumaceum* (except for the reddish basal sheaths of that species) but is quite distinct otherwise in having smaller bracts, distichous yellow flowers and much broader petals and sepals.

Dendrochilum longifolium Rchb.f.
[Colour Plate]

Pseudobulbs approximate, narrowly conical, up to 8 cm long, 2 cm in diameter, pale green, smooth. **Leaf** narrowly elliptic-lanceolate, acu-

minate, up to 40 cm long, 6.5 cm broad; petiole up to 7 cm long. **Inflorescence** arcuate, proteranthous, up to 40 cm long, densely many-flowered; bracts broad, as long as the pedicel and ovary, distichous. **Flowers** borne in 2 ranks, pale greenish-brown with a sepia lip. **Sepals** narrowly oblong, acute or acuminate, 0.7–0.8 cm long, 0.3–0.4 cm broad. **Petals** narrowly elliptic-oblong, acute or acuminate, 0.7–0.8 cm long, 0.2–0.3 cm broad. **Lip** recurved, 3-lobed, 0.5 cm long, 0.3 cm broad; side lobes small, falcate-triangular, acute; mid-lobe obovate-cuneate; disc with 2 small ridges between side lobes. **Column** erect, with upcurved, acute auricles.

DISTRIBUTION   Malaya and Sumatra to New Guinea; common on old mangroves and on trees by rivers.

HISTORY   This species was first cultivated by F. Stange and was sent by Consul Schiller to H.G. Reichenbach who described it in 1856 in *Bonplandia* (p. 392).

SYNONYM *Platyclinis longifolia* (Rchb.f.) Hemsley

Dendrophylax Rchb.f.
Subfamily Epidendroideae
Tribe Vandeae
Subtribe Angraecinae

Small, leafless epiphytic herbs with densely clustered roots, a very short stem and no pseudobulbs. **Inflorescences** branching or simple, 1- to few-flowered; peduncle slender; bracts small, distant. **Flowers** small to medium-sized or large. **Sepals** subequal, free, spreading. **Petals** similar to sepals. **Lip** sessile at base of column, produced at the base into a long spur much dilated at the mouth, continuous with the column, erect, entire or 2-lobed. **Column** very short, broad, lacking a foot; pollinia 2, somewhat globose, waxy, each with a stipe which is simple or flat and bipartite.

DISTRIBUTION   About five species in the W. Indies.

DERIVATION OF NAME   From the Greek *dendron* (tree), and *phylax* (guard), probably in allusion to the roots which tightly clasp the branches of trees.

TAXONOMY   *Dendrophylax* was established in 1864 by H.G. Reichenbach in *Walpers, Annales Botanices* (p. 903). It is allied to other leafless genera such as *Campylocentrum* and *Polyrrhiza* but is distinguished by its densely papillose stipes.

TYPE SPECIES   *D. hymenanthus* Rchb.f.

CULTURE   Compost: should be mounted. Temp. Winter min. 15°C. These plants, being leafless, are difficult to establish, but may be

grown by mounting them on pieces of fern-fibre or cork. They require moist conditions in moderate shade while growing, but when the roots become inactive, very little water should be given.

Dendrophylax varius (Gmelin) Urban
[Colour Plate]

A small, leafless epiphytic plant with many broad sinuous roots. **Stem** short. **Inflorescences** erect or ascending, arising from the lower part of the stem, 14–30 cm long, simple or branching, bearing flowers towards the apex of short branches; bracts ochre-coloured. **Flowers** white. **Sepals** oblong, acute, 0.3–0.4 cm long. **Petals** oblong, much narrower than the sepals, 0.2–0.3 cm long. **Lip**, erect, large, deeply emarginate at the apex, 1–1.2 cm long; spur 0.6 cm long, with a broad mouth. **Column** very short.

DISTRIBUTION   W. Indies (Cuba, Haiti and Dominican Republic).

HISTORY   Originally described in 1791 by J.F. Gmelin in the 13th edition of Linnaeus's *Systema Naturae* (p. 53) as *Orchis varia*. Ignatz Urban transferred it to *Dendrophylax* in 1918 in *Fedde, Repertorium Specierum Novarum* (p. 306).

Diaphananthe Schltr.
Subfamily Epidendroideae
Tribe Vandeae
Subtribe Aerangidinae

Small to medium-sized epiphytic herbs with short or long stems covered by persistent leaf-bases. **Leaves** mostly linear or ligulate, coriaceous, unequally 2-lobed at apex. **Inflorescences** racemose, many-flowered. **Flowers** translucent or hyaline, white, pale green, pale yellow, ochre or yellow. **Sepals** and **petals** free, spreading, subequal. **Lip** deflexed, mostly broader than long, spurred at the base, ± with a tooth-like callus in the mouth of the spur. **Column** short, porrect; rostellum elongate, pendent; pollinia 2, waxy; stipites 2, linear; viscidia 1 or 2.

DISTRIBUTION   About 45 species, widespread in tropical Africa, south to Natal.

DERIVATION OF NAME   The membranaceous and often translucent perianth of many species suggested the name of this genus which derives from the Greek *diaphanes* (transparent) and *anthos* (flower).

TAXONOMY   *Diaphananthe* was described in 1914 in *Die Orchideen* (p. 593) by Rudolf Schlechter, but the specific limits are still the subject of some debate. It is allied to *Angraecum* but differs in having an elongated rostellum, pollinia with separate stipites and a common viscidium or each with its own stipe and viscidium and often, at the base of the lip, a tooth-like callus obstructing the mouth of the spur.

V.S. Summerhayes revised the genus in the *Botanical Museum Leaflets of Harvard University* (1943) and again in the *Kew Bulletin* (1960). In the latter account he discussed the generic limits of *Diaphananthe* and *Rhipidoglossum* Schltr. and concluded that the latter was not sufficiently distinct to be treated as a distinct genus, particularly as *D. dorotheae* (Rendle) Summerh. is intermediate between the two.

Summerhayes thus divided *Diaphananthe* into 2 sections as follows:

1. sect. *Diaphananthe* characterised by 2 stipites, a common viscidium and a rostrate deflexed rostellum. This section includes *D. pellucida*, *D. plehniana* (Schltr.) Schltr., *D. bidens* (Sw.) Schltr. and *D. fragrantissima* (Rchb.f.) Schltr, amongst others. Most species in section *Diaphananthe* have a distinct tooth-like callus in the mouth of the spur.

2. sect. *Rhipidoglossum* characterised by 2 stipites each being attached to a distinct viscidium and the rostellum being porrect with a spathulate mid-lobe. Species in this section include *D. kamerunensis* (Schltr.) Schltr., *D. pulchella* Summerh., *D. laxiflora* (Summerh.) Summerh., *D. stolzii* Schltr., *D. xanthopollinia* (Rchb.f.) Summerh. and *D. rutila* (Rchb.f.) Summerh.

Recently L. Garay in the *Botanical Museum Leaflets of Harvard University* (1972) has revived *Rhipidoglossum* but as he has given no reason for doing so, Summerhayes' treatment of the genus is followed here.

F. Rasmussen has included *Sarcorhynchus*, a small African genus, in *Diaphananthe* in the *Norwegian Journal of Botany* (1974).

TYPE SPECIES   *D. pellucida* (Lindl.) Schltr.

SYNONYMS   *Rhipidoglossum* Schltr.; *Sarcorhynchus* Schltr.

CULTURE   Compost A or mounted. Temp. Winter min. 15°C for most species. The upright-growing species may be grown in pots, although once the stems have produced lateral roots, the plants are better grown against a support, such as fern-fibre or cork. Pendulous species tend to hang outwards with the flower stems below, so are best tied to pieces of fern-fibre or cork and suspended. *Diaphananthe* species need good shade and plenty of water and humidity when growing. Most species benefit from short dry periods when growth is completed.

Diaphananthe bidens (Sw. ex Pers.) Schltr.
[Colour Plate]
A large, pendulous epiphytic plant. **Stems** elongated, leafy throughout, 1 m or more long. **Roots** adventitious, stout. **Leaves** oblong-lanceolate to narrowly ovate, distinctly and acutely 2-lobed at apex, 5–14 cm long, 1.5–4.5 cm broad. **Inflorescences** pendulous, racemose, many-flowered, 5–18 cm long. **Flowers** salmon-pink, yellowish-pink or white. **Dorsal sepal** oblong or oblong-lanceolate, subacute or acute, 0.3–0.5 cm long, 0.2 cm broad. **Petals** lanceolate, acute, 0.4 cm long, 0.1 cm broad. **Lip** quadrate, deflexed, mucronate, margins erose, 0.35–0.5 cm long, 0.4 cm broad; spur 0.7 cm long, incurved, somewhat inflated in middle. **Column** short; rostellum pointed; stipites joined to a single viscidium.

DISTRIBUTION   Sierra Leone, east to Uganda and south to Angola.

HISTORY   Collected originally by A. Afzelius in Sierra Leone and named as *Limodorum bidens* by O. Swartz in 1800 in *Veteskaps Academiens Nya Handlingar, Stockholm* (p. 243). However, Swartz failed to provide a description to accompany the name and this was provided by C.H. Persoon in 1807 in *Synopsis Plantarum* (p. 521). Schlechter transferred it in 1914 to *Diaphananthe* in *Die Orchideen* (p. 593).

SYNONYMS   include *Limodorum bidens* Sw. ex Pers.; *Angraecum ashantense* Lindl.; *Listrostachys mystacioides* Kraenzl; *Angraecum subfalcifolium* De Wild.

Diaphananthe pellucida (Lindl.) Schltr.
[Colour Plate]
A medium-sized epiphytic plant with a short stem up to 9 cm long, leafy towards apex. **Leaves** oblanceolate, curved, unequally 2-lobed or almost entire at apex, 15–70 cm long, 2.5–7 cm broad. **Inflorescences** pendulous, laxly many-flowered, 15–55 cm long. **Flowers** pellucid, white, pale yellow or pinkish. **Sepals** narrowly oblong, acute, 0.9–1.2 cm long, 0.3–0.5 cm broad. **Petals** narrowly oblong-lanceolate, acute, 0.8–1.1 cm long, 0.3–0.4 cm broad, margins erose. **Lip** subquadrate, margins shortly fimbriate or irregularly dentate, emarginate at the apex, ± apiculate, 0.8–1.1 cm long; spur dependent, inflated in middle, pointed at apex, 0.8–1.1 cm long. **Column** short, fleshy; stipites 2; viscidium 1.

DISTRIBUTION   W. Africa to Zaïre and Uganda.

HISTORY   Originally described in 1862 as *Angraecum pellucidum* by John Lindley in the *Journal of the Linnean Society* (p. 134) based on a specimen imported to England from Sierra Leone by Messrs Loddiges for whom it flowered in November 1842. R. Schlechter transferred it to *Diaphananthe* in *Die Orchideen* (p. 593) in 1914.

SYNONYMS   *Angraecum pellucidum* Lindl.; *Listrostachys pellucida* (Lindl.) Rchb.f.

CLOSELY RELATED SPECIES   *Diaphananthe xanthopollinia* (Rchb.f.) Summerh, widespread in E. Africa, falls into section *Rhipidoglossum* of the genus and is readily distinguished from *D. pellucida* by its mostly longer stem, the shape of its sepals and petals, its broader lip with an obscure tooth in the mouth of the spur and by its 2 pollinia which are joined by their separate stipites to distinct viscidia. *D. xanthopollinia* is widespread in E. and S. Central Africa reaching the northern parts of S. Africa in Natal and N.E. Cape Province.

Dilochia Lindl.
Subfamily Epidendroideae
Tribe Arethuseae
Subtribe Bletiinae

Large or medium-sized epiphytic or terrestrial herbs with cane-like leafy stems. **Leaves** stiff, plicate, distichously arranged along the stem, articulated to a sheathing base. **Inflorescence**

Diaphananthe bidens
1 – Lip and spur (× 5)
2 – Column, side view (× 8)
3 – Pollinia, stipites and viscidium (× 13)

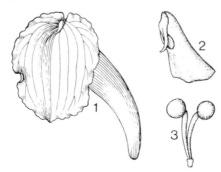

Diaphananthe xanthopollinia
1 – Lip and spur (× 6)
2 – Column, side view (× 13)
3 – Pollinia, stipites and viscidium (× 20)

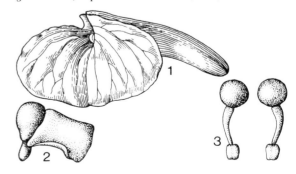

terminal, unbranched, simple or branched, laxly to densely many-flowered; bracts conspicuous, distichous, deciduous. **Flowers** medium-sized, smaller than those of *Arundina*. **Sepals** subsimilar, free, spreading. **Petals** narrower but similar. **Lip** 3-lobed, lacking a spur, with a callus of 3 to 5 longitudinal ridges. **Column** semiterete; pollinia 8, waxy, laterally flattened.

DISTRIBUTION   A genus of about seven species in tropical and subtropical Asia south to the Malay Archipelago.

DERIVATION OF NAME   From the Greek *di* (two) and *lochos* (rows or ranks), a reference to the distichous leaves and bracts.

TAXONOMY   John Lindley established this genus in 1830 in his *Genera and Species of Orchidaceous Plants* (p. 38). It is closely allied to *Arundina* but differs in broader stiffer leaves, large deciduous bracts, smaller flowers, and globose fruits.

TYPE SPECIES   *D. wallichii* Lindl.

CULTURE   Temp. Winter min. 15°C. Culture as for *Arundina*.

Dilochia wallichii Lindl.

A large lithophytic or epiphytic plant with cane-like stems up to 150 cm long. **Leaves** suberect, stiff, elliptic-ovate, acuminate, 10–15 cm long, 4–6 cm wide. **Inflorescence** usually unbranched or with a few branches only, laxly many-flowered; bracts spreading, distichous, cucullate, lanceolate, acute, 2–2.5 cm long. **Flowers** not opening widely, with dull yellow sepals and petals, flushed with purple on the outside, and a greenish-yellow lip marked with purplish-red; pedicel and ovary 1.2–1.5 cm long. **Dorsal sepal** elliptic-lanceolate, acute, 2.2–2.5 cm long, 5–6 mm wide; **lateral sepals** similar but oblique. **Petals** lanceolate, acute, 2.1–2.4 cm long, 3–4.5 mm wide. **Lip** 3-lobed in the apical half, 1.7–1.9 cm long, 0.8–1 cm wide; side lobes erect, narrow, rounded in front; mid-lobe oblong, truncate, with an undulate margin; callus of 3 longitudinal ridges from the base almost to the apex of the lip. **Column** 6 mm long.

DISTRIBUTION   Thailand, Malaya, Java, Sumatra, Borneo and New Guinea; in lowland and lower montane forest.

HISTORY   The type of this large orchid was collected by Nathaniel Wallich in Singapore and was described by John Lindley in 1830 in his *Genera and Species of Orchidaceous Plants* (p. 38).

SYNONYMS   *Dilochia pentandra* Rchb.f.; *Arundina wallichii* (Lindl.) Rchb.f.; *A. pentandra* (Rchb.f.) Rchb.f.

CLOSELY RELATED SPECIES   *D. cantleyi* (Hook.f.) Ridl., from Malaya, Sumatra and Borneo, differs in having decurved, many-branched inflorescences with smaller tracts.

Dimerandra Schltr.

Subfamily Epidendroideae
Tribe Epidendreae
Subtribe Laeliinae

Epiphytes with cane-like stems and smooth flexuous roots. **Stems** clustered, erect, fleshy, leafy along length, covered by thin imbricate leaf sheaths. **Leaves** subcoriaceous, flat, oblonglinear to ligulate, sessile, articulated to the leaf sheaths. **Inflorescences** 1–3, sessile, 1- or 2-flowered, apical. **Flowers** showy, pink. **Sepals** similar, spreading. **Petals** spreading, rhombic to elliptic. **Lip** free or basally adnate to the column, cuneate-flabellate; callus of 3 rows of lamellae below column. **Column** short, somewhat arcuate; pollinia 4, compressed, hard, without a stipe.

DISTRIBUTION   Possibly up to eight closely related species in lowland tropical Central and S. America and the W. Indies.

DERIVATION OF NAME   From the Greek *di* (two), *meros* (part) and *andra* (stamens), in allusion to the 2 large lobes of the clinandrium.

TAXONOMY   *Dimerandra* is a segregate genus of *Epidendrum* that was established by Rudolf Schlechter in 1922 in *Fedde, Repertorium Specierum Novarum, Beihefte* (p. 43). The two most recent accounts of the genus, those of Dressler (1978) in the journal *Orquidea (Mex.)* (p. 99) and Sigerist in 1986 in the *Botanical Museum Leaflets of Harvard University* (p. 199), take diametrically opposite views. Dressler considers the genus to be probably monotypic with one rather variable species whereas Sigerist has identified eight species. We would suggest that many of these are so closely related as to warrant no more than varietal status within *D. emarginata*.

TYPE SPECIES   *Epidendrum rimbachii* Schltr.

CULTURE   Temp. Winter min. 12°C. May be grown mounted or in pots of epiphyte mix under conditions of moderate shade and humidity. Any prolonged dry spells should be avoided.

Dimerandra emarginata (Meyer) Hoehne
[Colour Plate]

An epiphyte with elongate fleshy stems 20–40 cm tall, bulbous at the base. **Leaves** alternate, linear-oblong, obliquely retuse at the apex, 8–11 cm long, 8–10 mm wide. **Inflorescences** fasciculate, produced in succession, 1- or rarely 2-flowered; bracts ovate-cucullate, acute, up to 5 mm long. **Flowers** showy, pink to purple with a white and yellow base to the lip; pedicel and ovary up to 4 cm long; segments spreading. **Dorsal sepal** lanceolate-elliptic, acute, 14–18 mm long, 4–6 mm wide. **Petals** obovate, acute,

14–18 mm long, 7–10 mm wide. **Lip** basally adnate to the column, obovate-flabellate, shortly apiculate, 15–20 mm long, 12–15 mm wide; callus of 3 short rows of tubercles at base of lip. **Column** 5–6 mm long, with 2 subquadrate wings at the apex.

DISTRIBUTION   Mexico to Venezuela, Colombia and Ecuador, and also in Trinidad.

HISTORY   This species was first described as *Oncidium emarginatum*, by G.F.W. Meyer in 1818 in *Primitiae Florae Essequeboensis* (p. 259). It was, however, afterwards considered to belong in *Epidendrum* but because the name *Epidendrum emarginatum* had already been used by Ruiz and Pavon, it became well-known under the name *Epidendrum stenopetalum*. This had been coined by Sir William Hooker in 1835 in Curtis's *Botanical Magazine* (t. 3410). Meyer's name was transferred to the present genus by Hoehne in 1933 in the *Boletim da Agricultura, São Paulo* (p. 618). It should be mentioned that Sigerist considers *D. emarginata* and *D. stenopetala* to be distinct based on lip shape.

SYNONYMS   *Oncidium emarginatum* Meyer; *Epidendrum stenopetalum* Hook.; *E. lamellatum* Westc. ex Lindl.; *Dimerandra stenopetala* (Hook.) Schltr.

Dimorphorchis (Lindl.) Rolfe

Subfamily Epidendroideae
Tribe Vandeae
Subtribe Sarcanthinae

Large epiphytic plants with hanging, often branching stems, rooting near the base. **Leaves** distichous, coriaceous, linear-ligulate, sheathing at the base. **Inflorescences** pendent, unbranched, laxly many-flowered, with a limp tomentose axis. **Flowers** large, fleshy, fragrant, of two sorts; the basal 1–3 very fragrant; the rest less fragrant, distinctively coloured. **Sepals** and **petals** subsimilar, spreading. **Lip** fleshy, versatile, 3-lobed, saccate; mid-lobe with a raised median keel interrupted near the base with a transverse groove, attenuated at the apex. **Column** short, fleshy; pollinia 4, in 2 pairs, subequal; stipe short, broad; viscidium broadly elliptic.

DISTRIBUTION   Two or three closely allied species endemic to Borneo.

DERIVATION OF NAME   From the Greek *di* (two), *morphe* (shape), and *orchis* (orchid), in allusion to the two types of flower produced in the inflorescence.

TAXONOMY   The genus *Dimorphorchis* was established by Robert Rolfe in 1919 in the *Orchid Review* (p. 149) when he raised Lindley's *Vanda* sect. *Dimorphorchis* to generic status. The genus is clearly distinguished from *Vanda*, *Arachnis* and other allied genera by the limp and pendent inflorescence, by its remarkable dimorphic flowers and by its strictly epiphytic habit.

TYPE SPECIES *D. lowii* (Lindl.) Rolfe
CULTURE Temp. Winter min. 18°C. These plants require high humidity and moderate shade. Small plants may be grown in pans or baskets of free-draining epiphyte mix, but larger specimens need the addition of posts to support the long stems.

Dimorphorchis lowii (Lindl.) Rolfe

Stems long, pendent, stout, up to 75 cm long, 1–2 cm in diameter. **Leaves** ligulate, unequally bilobed at the apex, up to 70 cm long, 5 cm wide, articulated to a sheathing leaf base. **Inflorescences** pendent, laxly many-flowered, up to 300 cm long; bracts lanceolate, up to 2 cm long, 7 mm wide. **Flowers** of two sorts; pedicel and ovary furfuraceous, c. 1 cm long. **Basal flowers** yellow spotted with purple, strongly fragrant, 4.5 cm high, 6 cm across, stellately hairy on outer surface, with sepals and petals overlapping. **Apical flowers** yellow with large maroon blotches, 6 cm high, 6.5 cm across, with sepals and petals not overlapping and with undulate margins, stellately hairy on outer surface. **Sepals** spreading-recurved, ovate-lanceolate, acute. 3–3.5 cm long, 1.5 cm wide. **Petals** spreading-recurved, narrowly elliptic, acute, 2.8–3.5 cm long, 1.2–1.5 cm wide, with undulate margins. **Lip** saccate, 1.2 cm long, 3-lobed; side lobes 6 mm long, roundly triangular, with incurved margins; mid-lobe fleshy, at an obtuse angle to the basal part of the lip, laterally compressed, extending into an up-curved attenuated tip; callus oblong, strongly elevated. **Column** terete, 7 mm long, pubescent.

DISTRIBUTION Borneo; on tall trees by rivers and in gulleys; up to 1200 m.
HISTORY This spectacular orchid is named after Sir Hugh Low who discovered it on his expedition to North Borneo. It was described as *Vanda lowii* by John Lindley in 1847 in the *Gardeners' Chronicle* (p. 239) and was transferred to the present genus by Rolfe in the *Orchid Review* (p. 149) in 1919.
SYNONYMS *Vanda lowii* Lindl; *Renanthera lowii* (Lindl.) Rchb.f.; *Arachnanthe lowii* (Lindl.) Bentham; *Arachnis lowii* (Lindl.) Rchb.f.; *Vandopsis lowii* (Lindl.) Schltr.
CLOSELY RELATED SPECIES *D. rossii* Fowlie, from Sabah, differs in being a smaller plant with a shorter fewered-flowered inflorescence, less heavily spotted sepals and petals and a different lip.

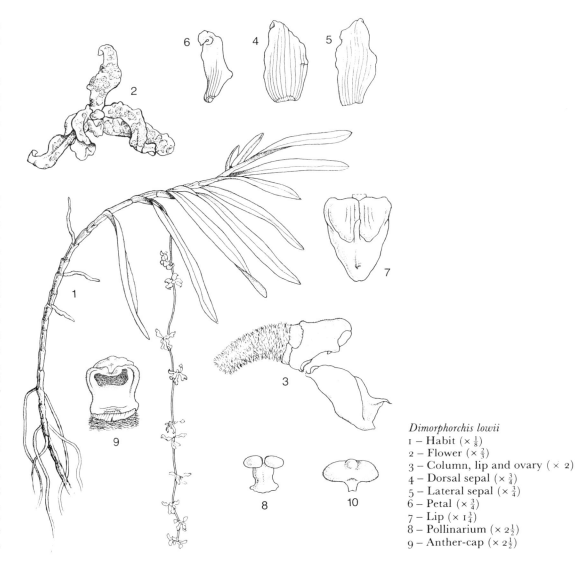

Dimorphorchis lowii
1 – Habit ($\times \frac{1}{8}$)
2 – Flower ($\times \frac{2}{3}$)
3 – Column, lip and ovary ($\times 2$)
4 – Dorsal sepal ($\times \frac{3}{4}$)
5 – Lateral sepal ($\times \frac{3}{4}$)
6 – Petal ($\times \frac{3}{4}$)
7 – Lip ($\times 1\frac{3}{4}$)
8 – Pollinarium ($\times 2\frac{1}{2}$)
9 – Anther-cap ($\times 2\frac{1}{2}$)

Diothonea Lindl.

Subfamily Epidendroideae
Tribe Epidendreae
Subtribe Laeliinae

Medium-sized epiphytic plants with cylindric, branching, leafy stems. **Leaves** distichous, narrow, linear, oblong or oblong-lanceolate, abruptly subobtuse or 2-lobed. **Inflorescence** a terminal raceme, ± pendent, laxly or densely several- to many-flowered. **Flowers** small to rather large; pedicel and ovary long. **Sepals** subequal, suborbicular-ovate to lanceolate, concave; lateral sepals oblique. **Petals** similar to sepals but narrower. **Lip** ± adnate to the sides of the column, ± 3-lobed, auriculate and concave at the base. **Column** short, stout, winged.
DISTRIBUTION A small genus of tropical S. American distribution.

DERIVATION OF NAME From the Greek *di* (two) and *othone* (sail), in allusion 'to the two membranes stretched from the column to the lip like jibs from the foremast to the bowsprit of a ship'.
TAXONOMY A little-known genus closely allied to *Epidendrum* consisting of several closely related and seldom collected species. John Lindley described the genus in 1834 in Hooker's *Journal of Botany* (p. 12).
TYPE SPECIES *D. lloensis* Lindl.
CULTURE Compost A. Temp. Winter min. 12–15°C. Summer max. 25°C. In common with most plants found at high altitudes, these should not remain dry at any time during the year. They grow well in relatively small pots under moderate shade, and with moderate to high humidity. Pendent species may be better grown mounted on fern-fibre or cork, and hung up.

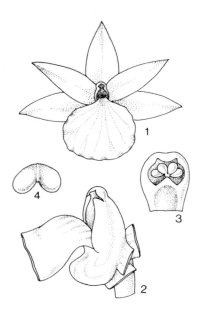

Diothonea lloensis
1 – Flower (× 1½)
2 – Column, base of lip and spur, side view
(× 1½)
3 – Column from below (× 1½)
4 – Anther-cap (× 1½)

Diothonea lloensis Lindl.

A variable epiphytic or terrestrial herb, 20–50 cm tall. **Stems** stout, much branched, leafy, covered by striate leaf-sheaths. **Leaves** linear-oblong or linear-lanceolate, 2-lobed at apex, up to 11 cm long, 1.2 cm broad. **Inflorescences** terminal, short, ± pendulous, several- to many-flowered, 2–11 cm long. **Flowers** membranaceous, pinkish-red, brown or yellowish. **Dorsal sepal** oblong-ovate, acute, concave, 0.8–1 cm long; **lateral sepals** obliquely oblong-ovate, acute or acuminate, ± keeled. **Petals** shorter but broader than the dorsal sepal, elliptic-lanceolate to subrhombic, obtuse to shortly acuminate. **Lip** longer than other segments, adnate to the winged column-base, free part spreading or reflexed, suborbicular, subentire or distinctly 3-lobed above the middle, 0.9–1.4 cm long, margins irregularly, minutely denticulate; disc with several short basal lamellae. **Column** short, stout, arcuate, broadly winged, with a wide, compressed cup formed by the dilated cuneate margins of the column.
DISTRIBUTION Colombia, Ecuador and Peru.
HISTORY Discovered in Ecuador in the Lloa Valley by Col. Hall and described by John Lindley in Hooker's *Journal of Botany* (p. 12) in 1834.
SYNONYM *Diothonea gratissima* Rchb.f.

Diplocaulobium (Rchb.f.) Kraenzl.
Subfamily Epidendroideae
Tribe Dendrobieae
Subtribe Dendrobiinae

Small to medium-sized epiphytic or rarely lithophytic plants usually with a very short rhizome and fibrous roots. **Pseudobulbs** usually clustered, usually swollen at the base and cylindrical above, rarely ovoid-cylindrical and angular in cross-section, unifoliate. **Leaf** erect or suberect, subcoriaceous, linear to oblong-elliptic, blunt. **Inflorescence** axillary, 1-flowered, sessile. **Flower** small to medium-sized, rather drab to showy, ephemeral, lasting less than a day. **Dorsal sepal** and **petals** subsimilar, free, the petals slightly shorter and narrower; lateral sepals oblique at the base but otherwise similar to the dorsal sepal, connate to the column-foot to form a more or less obliquely conical mentum. **Lip** entire to 3-lobed, with a fleshy linear or ridged callus, lacking a spur. **Column** short, fleshy; foot short to long, slightly incurved; pollinia 4, hard, in closely appressed pairs.
DISTRIBUTION A genus of 100 or more species from the Malay Archipelago, New Guinea, the Pacific Islands and N.E. Australia.
DERIVATION OF NAME From the Greek *diplous* (folded), *caulos* (stem) and *bios* (life), referring to the creeping stems with swollen pseudobulbs.
TAXONOMY This genus was originally described as a section of *Dendrobium* by H.G. Reichenbach in the *Journal of the Linnean Society* (p. 112) in 1876. It was raised to generic rank by Fritz Kraenzlin in 1910 in Engler's *Pflanzenreich Orchidaceae-Monandrae-Dendrobiinae* (p. 331).

It differs from *Dendrobium* in having distinctive unifoliate pseudobulbs and axillary solitary ephemeral flowers. The species are not often seen in cultivation because their flowers are so short-lived but they do form good specimen plants and the flowers of some species are delightful even if the pleasure they give is quickly passed.
TYPE SPECIES *Dendrobium nitidissimum* Rchb.f.
SYNONYMS *Dendrobium* sect. *Mekynosepalum* Schltr.; *D.* sect. *Goniobulbum* Schltr.
CULTURE Temp. Winter min. 12–15°C. Compact plants which grow well either mounted or in pots of epiphyte mix under moderate shade and humidity. Water well when growing and less when growth is completed.

Diplocaulobium regale Schltr. [Colour Plate]
A medium-sized to large epiphyte often forming a dense clump. **Stems** cylindrical and slender above, swollen and ovoid at the base, 15–60 cm long, up to 2 cm in diameter below, covered with imbricate sheaths when young, drying bright yellow. **Leaf** erect, oblong-elliptic, subacute to obtuse, 13–22 cm long, 1.9–4 cm wide. **Inflorescence** 1-flowered, up to 7.5 cm long. subtended by a large compressed sheath 2–3 cm long. **Flower** showy, flat, red, pink or white; pedicel and ovary up to 6 cm long. **Sepals** oblong-elliptic, obtuse, 3.5–4 cm long, 1–1.4 cm wide; **lateral sepals** forming a 7 mm-long mentum with the column-foot. **Petals** elliptic, obtuse, 3.5–4 cm long, 1.5–2 cm wide. **Lip** small, recurved, obscurely 3-lobed to rhombic, 1–1.3 cm long, 1.2–1.4 cm wide; side lobes upcurved; mid-lobe triangular-ovate; callus of 2 ridges onto base of mid-lobe. **Column** 0.3–0.4 cm long.
DISTRIBUTION New Guinea only; on mossy trees in tall forest, 700–2100 m.
HISTORY Rudolf Schlechter collected this species in the Finisterre and Dischore Ranges in N.E. New Guinea in 1909. He described it as *Dendrobium regale* in 1912 in *Fedde, Repertorium Beihefte* (p. 476). It was transferred to the present genus in 1957 by A.D. Hawkes in *Lloydia* (p. 127).
SYNONYM *Dendrobium regale* Schltr.

Diploprora Hooker f.
Subfamily Epidendroideae
Tribe Vandeae
Subtribe Sarcanthinae

Small epiphytic herbs with a short slender stem. **Leaves** ± falcate, linear, narrowly elliptic or lanceolate, acuminate to bifid at apex. **Inflorescences** racemose, fairly short, few-flowered. **Flowers** small. **Sepals** and **petals** subsimilar, free, spreading; sepals often keeled. **Lip** as long as, or longer than petals, margins adnate to sides of column, cymbiform to elongate-subpandurate, ± bifid at apex; disc keeled. **Column** very short, lacking a foot; pollinia 2 or 4, globose; stipe short, linear, margins recurved; viscidium small.
DISTRIBUTION India and Sri Lanka, east to China and Taiwan, four species only.
DERIVATION OF NAME From the Greek *diplous* (double), and *prora* (prow), in allusion to the conspicuous bifurcate apex of the lip in the type species.
TAXONOMY *Diploprora* was established by Sir Joseph Hooker in 1890 in the *Flora of British India* (p. 26). It is allied to *Luisia* but is readily distinguished by its flat rather than terete leaves and the rather sigmoid lip which is generally bifid at the apex (rarely truncate).
TYPE SPECIES *D. championii* Hooker f.
CULTURE Compost A in a pot or mounted.

Temp. Winter min. 15°C. These plants may be grown in baskets filled with normal epiphytic compost, but probably grow better when tied to tree-fern-fibre or cork, and hung in a humid atmosphere. Moderate shade should be given in sunny weather. As with other vandaceous plants, when the roots are active, water may be freely given.

Diploprora uraiensis Hayata
[Colour Plate]

A semipendulous epiphytic plant. **Stems** leafy, up to 18 cm long. **Leaves** falcate, oblong-lanceolate, minutely bidentate at apex, 7.5–11 cm long, 2–2.5 cm broad. **Inflorescence** pendulous, racemose, 7–12.5 cm long, 4- to 5 (or more)-flowered; bracts lanceolate. **Flowers** 1.5 cm across, buff-yellow, whiter towards the centre; lip white, spotted yellow. **Sepals** narrowly elliptic, obtuse, 0.8 cm long, 0.15–0.35 cm broad. **Petals** spreading falcate, linear-elliptic, acute, 0.8 cm long, 0.3 cm broad. **Lip** broadly navicular with a linear-caudate apex divided into 2 setae, 0.8 cm long, 0.4 cm broad; callus fleshy, oblong-obtriangular. **Column** 0.25 cm long.

DISTRIBUTION   Taiwan.
HISTORY   Described by Hayata in 1914 in *Icones Plantarum Formosanarum* (p. 87), based on his own collection from Uraisha earlier that year.

Dipodium R. Br.
Subfamily Epidendroideae
Tribe Cymbidieae
Subtribe Cyrtopodiinae

Terrestrial or climbing plants of diverse form. The terrestrials leafy or leafless with stems of limited growth; the climbers with leafy stems that continue to grow indefinitely; roots basal in terrestrials or along stems in climbers. **Leaves** if present distichous, imbricate at base or spaced along stem. **Inflorescences** lateral or terminal, laxly few- to many-flowered. **Flowers** often showy. **Sepals** and **petals** spreading, sub-similar. **Lip** very fleshy, sessile and adnate to column below, 3-lobed, hairy on mid-lobe and callus, lacking a spur. **Column** porrect, sub-clavate; pollinia 2, cleft, often deeply, each attached by a separate stipe to single viscidium.
DISTRIBUTION   A genus of about 20 species from S.E. Asia to Australia and the Pacific Islands.
DERIVATION OF NAME   From the Greek *di* (two) and *podion* (foot), in allusion to 2 stipes attached to the single viscidium.
TAXONOMY   This genus was established by Robert Brown in 1810 in his *Prodromus Florae Novae Hollandiae* (p. 330). It is allied to *Cymbidium* but readily distinguished by its characteristically hairy lip and deeply cleft pollinia borne on separate slender stipes attached to the same viscidium.
TYPE SPECIES   *D. punctatum* (J.E. Sm.) R. Br.
CULTURE   Temp. Winter min. 15°C. Since roots are produced along the stems of the leaf-bearing species, an upright support is required, as well as a container of epiphyte mix at the base. Give good humidity and moderate shade with careful watering throughout the year.

Dipodium pictum (Lindl.) Reichb.f.
[Colour Plate]

A climbing terrestrial with elongate spiralling leafy stems up to 12 m long, 2–3 cm in diameter. **Leaves** distichous, conduplicate, lanceolate, acuminate, 20–50 cm long, 2–4.7 cm wide, sheathing at the base. **Inflorescences** axillary, erect or suberect, laxly 5- to 25-flowered, up to 25 cm long; bracts 4–5 mm long. **Flowers** 3–4 cm across; sepals and petals creamy-white with red spots on outer side; lip creamy-white with 4 to 6 longitudinal red stripes on mid-lobe; pedicel and ovary 2.5–4 cm long. **Dorsal sepal** oblanceolate, obtuse or rounded at the apex, 1.5–2.5 cm long, 5–9 mm wide; **lateral sepals** similar but somewhat falcate. **Petals** oblanceolate, subacute, 1.5–2.5 cm long, 4–6 mm wide. **Lip** obscurely 3-lobed at the base, 1.7–2 cm long, 6–8 mm wide; side lobes oblong-falcate, 1.5–3 mm long; mid-lobe elliptic to obovate, acute, densely covered with white hairs above, with the hairs extending in lines to the base of the lip. **Column** 8–10 mm long.
DISTRIBUTION   Peninsular Malaya to the Solomon Islands and N.E. Australia, in lowland and lower montane forest.
HISTORY   John Lindley originally described this unusual climbing orchid as *Wailesia picta* in 1849 in the *Journal of the Horticultural Society* (p. 262). Reichenbach transferred it to the present genus in 1862 in the second volume of his *Xenia Orchidacea* (pp. 15, 20).
SYNONYMS   *Wailesia picta* Lindl.; *Dipodium pandanum* F.M. Bailey

---

Disa Berg.
Subfamily Orchidoideae
Tribe Diseae
Subtribe Disinae

Terrestrial herbs with tuberous roots. **Stems** unbranched, leafy. **Leaves** scattered along the flowering stem or on separate sterile shoots. **Inflorescence** terminal, 1- to many-flowered. **Flowers** resupinate, variously coloured, often showy. **Sepals** free; dorsal sepal erect, hooded or helmet-shaped, usually spurred; lateral sepals ± spreading. **Petals** at the base ± adnate to the column, often included in the dorsal sepal, variable in shape. **Lip** usually small and narrow, not spurred. **Column** short; anther erect, horizontal or reflexed, the loculi parallel; pollinia 2, sectile, each with a caudicle and naked viscidium; stigmas united into a cushion below the rostellum; rostellum small, ± 3-lobed; side lobes adnate to the petals; mid-lobe small.
DISTRIBUTION   About 130 species, widespread in tropical Africa (particularly E. and S. Central) and in S. Africa with four species in Madagascar and the Mascarene islands.
DERIVATION OF NAME   Meaning obscure but H. Bolus suggested that it derived from the Latin *dis* (*dives*) (rich), in allusion to the beauty of the flowers.
TAXONOMY   The genus *Disa* was described by Petrus Jonas Bergius in 1767 in *Descriptiones Plantarum ex Capite Bonae Spei* (p. 348).

Some of the showiest of the African terrestrial orchids are found in this genus including the famous scarlet and orange *D. uniflora* and *D. tripetaloides*, both from the Cape. These and their showy hybrids are now widely cultivated and have been successfully grown from seed.

The genus was revised by F. Kraenzlin in 1901 in his *Orchidaceae Genera et Species*, where he treated over 90 species in 11 sections. R. Schlechter also monographed *Disa* in the same year in A. Engler's *Botanische Jahrbücher* describing some 100 species in 12 sections. The most recent revision is that of Linder (1981) in a series of papers, the *Journal of South African Botany*, *Bothalia* and the *Bulletin du Jardin Botanique National de Belgique*. Accounts by V.S. Summerhayes of the W. Africa species and of the E. African species have appeared respectively in the *Flora of West Tropical Africa* (2nd ed., 1968) and in the *Flora of Tropical East Africa* (1968).

S. Africa, which has the majority of species, has been covered by H. Bolus in *Orchids of South Africa* (1893–1913), by R.A. Rolfe in *Flora Capensis* (1913), and most recently by J. Stewart et al. (1982) in *Wild Orchids of Southern Africa*. In S. Africa the tendency has been for authors to follow Kraenzlin in keeping the genera *Herschelianthe* (*Herschelia*), *Penthea* and *Monadenia* distinct from *Disa* (see E.A. Schelpe, *An Introduction to the South African Orchids*, 1966). Schlechter (1901) considered these to be congeneric and Summerhayes followed him by treating *Herschelia* as a synonym of *Disa* in the *Flora of Tropical East Africa*. We have followed J. Stewart et al. (1982) in treating these as distinct genera.
TYPE SPECIES   *D. uniflora* Berg.
CULTURE   Compost C with live *Sphagnum* added. Temp. Min. 15°C for warm species.

Min. 10°C for cool species. Low altitude species may be grown as the tropical *Habenaria* species, with a dry rest after the stems have died down. The cool-growing species, including the popular *D. uniflora*, require cool, moist and shady conditions throughout the year, and when growing must remain moist at the root. If offsets are produced, these may be potted up separately to grow into new plants. After flowering, many of these species should be kept somewhat drier.

Disa stolzii Schltr. [Colour Plate]

An erect terrestrial herb, up to 60 cm tall. **Tubers** ovoid or ellipsoid, sparsely hairy and shortly 2-lobed at apex. **Sterile stem** very short, 1- to 3-leaved at apex, with spotted sheaths below; leaves linear or narrowly lanceolate, acute, 9–24 cm long, 0.5–1.5 cm broad. **Flowering stems** erect, almost entirely covered by sheathing leaves, 6- to 11-leaved; leaves lanceolate, acute, 2.5–5.5 cm long, 1–1.5 cm broad, spotted with red below. **Inflorescence** laxly 1- to 5-flowered; bracts lanceolate, acute, 2–4.5 cm long. **Flowers** suberect, showy, orange or scarlet with darker spots. **Dorsal sepal** erect, clawed, with an ovate or elliptic blade, spurred in the middle, 3–5 cm long, 1.5 cm broad; spur cylindric, 1–1.5 cm; **lateral sepals** spreading, oblique, oblong, 2.5–4 cm long, 1 cm broad. **Petals** erect, ovate below, linear or subspathulate above, 2.5–4.5 cm long, 0.5–1 cm broad. **Lip** narrowly linear, pendent, 1.5–2 cm long, 0.1–0.2 cm broad. **Anther** erect, shortly stalked, up to 0.9 cm high.

DISTRIBUTION Tanzania, Malawi and Zambia; in seasonally flooded grasslands, 1000–2800 m altitude.

HISTORY This beautiful orchid so characteristic of the wet grasslands of S. Central Africa was first collected by Adolph Stolz on Mt Rungwe in S.W. Tanzania. Rudolph Schlechter described it in 1915 in A. Engler's *Botanische Jahrbücher* (p. 537).

CLOSELY RELATED SPECIES *Disa erubescens* Rendle is closely allied to this species and is far more widespread in tropical E. Africa but it may be distinguished by its smaller flowers in which the dorsal sepal is less than 3 cm long and by its 9- to 15-leaved flowering stems.

Disa uniflora Berg. [Colour Plate]

A terrestrial plant, 25–70 cm high. **Stem** stout, leafy. **Leaves** lanceolate to elongate-lanceolate, acute, usually somewhat spreading, gradually passing upwards into acuminate sheaths, 7.5–20 cm long. **Inflorescences** 1- or 2 (rarely 5)-flowered; bracts lanceolate, acuminate, 3–5 cm long. **Flowers** large, showy, brilliant scarlet (rarely yellow) with darker veins on the dorsal

sepals and some orange or yellow on the petals. **Dorsal sepal** galeate, broadly ovate, acute or apiculate, 3.5–6 cm long; spur narrowly conical, 1.2 cm long; **lateral sepals** broadly ovate, abruptly acuminate, 3.5–6 cm long. **Petals** obovate or obovate-oblong, subobtuse, 2–2.5 cm long. **Lip** linear-lanceolate, acuminate, 1.2–2 cm long, recurved at the apex. **Column** 2–2.5 cm long; anther reclinate, narrow, acute; rostellum erect, elongate, with short divaricate side lobes.

DISTRIBUTION S. Africa (Cape Province).

HISTORY Described in 1767 by Petrus Jonas Bergius in his *Descriptiones Plantarum ex Capite Bonei Spei* (p. 348).

SYNONYMS *Satyrium grandiflorum* (L.f.) Thunb.; *Disa barelli* Pnydt; *D. grandiflora* L.f.

Disperis Sw.

Subfamily Orchidoideae
Tribe Diseae
Subtribe Coryciinae

Small terrestrial herbs arising from small tubers. **Stems** slender, with scale leaves at the base and 1 to several leaves above. **Leaves** alternate or opposite, rarely almost obsolete. **Inflorescences** racemose, 1- to several-flowered, erect. **Flowers** small, white, pink magenta, yellow or green; bracts leaf-like. **Dorsal sepal** united to petals to form a flat to spurred structure; **lateral sepals** spreading, spurred near the inner margin. **Lip** often much modified and smaller than the sepals, the claw joined to the face of the column and ascending above it, often dilate and papillate and lobed above. **Column** erect; rostellum large, 2-lobed; anther horizontal, with parallel loculi; pollinia 2, granular, each attached to a separate gland.

DISTRIBUTION A genus of about 80 species mostly in S. and tropical Africa and the Mascarene islands, but a few species in tropical Asia across to New Guinea.

DERIVATION OF NAME From the Greek *dis* (two) and *pera* (wallet), in allusion to the pouch-like lateral sepals of some species.

TAXONOMY *Disperis* was established by Olof Swartz in 1800 in *Veteskaps Academiens Nya Handlingar, Stockholm* (p. 218). Despite their small size *Disperis* have flowers of wonderful complexity with highly modified lip and column features. The majority of species are either South African or tropical African and only a few of the former are ever found in cultivation. The most recent account of the South African species is that given by Stewart, Linder, Schelpe and Hall (1982) in *Wild Orchids of Southern Africa* (p. 195). The tropical African species are best covered by Verdcourt (1968) in

the first part of the *Flora of Tropical East Africa, Orchidaceae* (p. 216) and by Summerhayes (1968) in the 2nd ed., of *Flora of Tropical West Africa, Orchidaceae* (p. 203).

TYPE SPECIES *D. secunda* (Thunb.) Sw.

CULTURE As for *Acianthus*.

Disperis capensis (L.f.) Sw.

A small terrestrial plant growing in colonies from a subterranean tuber (root-stem tuberoid). **Stem** erect, bifoliate, pilose towards the base, glabrous above. **Leaves** remote, erect to spreading, lanceolate or linear-lanceolate, acuminate, 4–6 cm long, 0.6–1 cm wide, loosely sheathing at the base. **Inflorescence** apical, 1- or rarely 2-flowered, 12–30 cm or more long; bracts lanceolate, acuminate, 1.5–2.8 cm long. **Flowers** showy, the sepals brown-green to yellowish, the petals purple or rarely white; pedicel and ovary up to 2 cm long. **Dorsal sepal** hooded, bluntly saccate behind, with a filiform, tubular, ascending apical appendage, 1.8–2.2 cm long, 0.8–1 cm wide; **lateral sepals**, spreading, lanceolate, acuminate, bluntly saccate in the basal part, 2–2.5 cm long, 0.5–0.8 cm wide. **Petals** adnate to the dorsal sepal, subrhombic, rounded at the apex, 1.2–1.4 cm long, 0.7–0.9 cm wide. **Lip** hidden within the dorsal sepal hood, spathulate, with a subapical appendage, papillose at the apex, 0.7–0.9 cm long. **Column** reflexed, 0.6–0.7 cm long.

DISTRIBUTION S. Africa: Cape Province only; from sea level to 1000 m.

HISTORY This pretty orchid was described by the younger Linnaeus in 1781 in the Supplement to *Species Plantarum* (p. 405) as *Arethusa capensis* based on a collection from the Cape by Thunberg. It was transferred to *Disperis* by Olof Swartz in 1800 in *Vetenskaps Academiens Nya Handlingar* (p. 218).

SYNONYMS *Arethusa capensis* L.f.; *Dipera capensis* (L.f.) Spreng.; *D. tenera* Spreng.

Disperis fanniniae Harv. [Colour Plate]

A terrestrial herb 15–45 cm tall. **Leaves** 3, cauline, lanceolate or ovate, cordate at the base, acuminate, 2–8 cm long, 1–3 cm wide. **Inflorescences** 1- to 8-flowered, 2.5–10 cm long; bracts leafy, lanceolate, acuminate, 1.3–2.5 cm long. **Flowers** white, flushed with pink or green; pedicel and ovary 1.3–1.8 cm long. **Dorsal sepal** strongly hooded, 12–20 mm long; **lateral sepals** deflexed-spreading, lanceolate, acuminate, 12–14 mm long, undulate, with a short oblong spur in the middle. **Petals** adnate to the dorsal sepal, clawed, apiculate, lobed on free surface. **Lip** linear, 1.5 cm long, dilated in the middle, papillose at the apex, with an ovate green appendage shorter than the limb.

DISTRIBUTION S. Africa: E. Cape Province to the Transvaal, and also in Swaziland, on forest and plantations floors in deep shade, 1200–2000 m.

HISTORY First described in 1863 by Harvey in his *Thesaurus Capensis* (p. 46) based on a collection from Natal by Mrs G. Fannin and from the Draakensberg by T. Cooper.

Diuris J.E. Sm.
Subfamily Orchidoideae
Tribe Diurideae
Subtribe Diuridinae

Terrestrial colony-forming herbs with underground root stem tuberoids. **Leaves** 1–3, slender, erect or suberect, grass-like, occasionally spirally twisted. **Inflorescence** erect, racemose, few-flowered. **Flowers** attractive, white, yellow, pink or purple, often spotted or blotched. **Dorsal sepal** hooded over the column; **lateral sepals** linear, deflexed behind and longer than the lip. **Petals** suberect or erect, spathulate, clawed at base. **Lip** 3-lobed near the base; side lobes spreading or erect, usually smaller than the convex porrect mid-lobe; callus ridged. **Column** short, semiterete, winged; pollinia 4.

DISTRIBUTION A genus of about 40 species, mostly from Australia but with a single species in Timor, Indonesia.

DERIVATION OF NAME The name is derived from the Greek *dis* (two) and *oura* (tail), in allusion to the twin tail-like lateral sepals which project from the base of the flower.

TAXONOMY The genus was established by J.E. Smith in 1798 in the *Transactions of the Linnean Society* (p. 222). The flowers are distinctive with erect spathulate petals that give the species the common name of 'donkey orchids'. Detailed accounts of the Australian species of this genus are given by D. Jones (1988) in his *Native Orchids of Australia* and by M. Clements (1989) in *A Checklist of Australian Orchidaceae*.

The species of *Diuris* have become increasingly popular in cultivation in recent years particularly as methods have been developed for their successful propagation and multiplication in cultivation. Good accounts of culture methods are given by both Jones (1988) and Richards, Datodi and Wooton (1988) in *The Cultivation of Australian Native Orchids*.

TYPE SPECIES *D. maculata* J.E. Smith

CULTURE As for *Acianthus*, but more robust, therefore a weak feed may be beneficial.

Diuris maculata J.E. Smith [Colour Plate]
A medium-sized plant up to 30 cm tall. **Leaves** 2–3, channelled, linear, 10–20 cm long, 3–4 mm broad. **Inflorescence** 2- to 8-flowered; bracts linear, acute, up to 2 cm long. **Flowers** about 3 cm across, yellow with reddish-purple spotting on the sepal and lip margins and the claw of each petal. **Dorsal sepal** ovate, obtuse, 9–10 mm long; **lateral sepals** linear, up to 2 cm long, parallel or crossed. **Petals** suberect, spathulate, obtuse, 1.6–2 cm long, 1 cm wide. **Lip** 3-lobed, 1 cm long, 1.2–1.5 cm wide; side lobes semi-elliptic, rounded, 6–8 mm long; mid-lobe flabellate, truncate, 8 mm long; callus of 2 ridges in basal half of the lip.

DISTRIBUTION Australia, from S.E. Queensland to S. Australia and Tasmania; in open forest and woodland.

HISTORY This species was described in 1804 by J.E. Smith in his *Exotic Botany* (p. 57) based on plants collected at Port Jackson (now Sydney) by Dr White.

SYNONYMS *D. curvifolia* Lindl.; *D. purdina* Lindl.; *D. brevissima* Nicholls

Diuris punctata J.E. Smith [Colour Plate]
A terrestrial plant up to 60 cm tall. **Leaves** 2, erect or lax, channelled, linear, grass-like, 15–25 cm long, 4 mm wide. **Inflorescence** 2- to 10-flowered. **Flowers** attractive, white blotched on all segments with purple, 5–6 cm across. **Dorsal sepal** broadly ovate, obtuse, 1.5–2 cm long; **lateral sepals** linear, deflexed, 4–6 cm long, parallel or crossed, greenish-purple. **Petals** suberect to erect, spathulate, obtuse, 2–2.3 cm long, 1–1.5 cm wide. **Lip** 3-lobed, 1.2–1.5 cm long, 1–1.2 cm wide; side lobes oblong, truncate or rounded, 6 mm long; mid-lobe flabellate to clawed-ovate, 1 cm long; callus of 2 raised ridges onto base of the mid-lobe.

DISTRIBUTION Australia, S.E. Queensland to S.E. of S. Australia, open forest and wet grassland.

HISTORY *D. punctata* was one of the earliest of the Australian orchids to be described in 1804 by J.E. Smith in his *Exotic Botany* (p. 13, t. 8) based on a collection made by Dr White at Port Jackson (now Sydney).

It is a variable species with a number of named forms and varieties.

CLOSELY RELATED SPECIES *D. striata* can be distinguished from *D. punctata* by its slender habit and smaller paler flowers. The latter also has larger darker flowers than *D. cuneata* and *D. alba*, two other closely related species.

Domingoa Schltr.
Subfamily Epidendroideae
Tribe Epidendreae
Subtribe Laeliinae

Small epiphytic herbs with a creeping rhizome. **Stems** clustered, elongate, pseudobulbous, subcylindrical to ellipsoidal, unifoliate, covered by cylindrical papery sheaths. **Leaf** suberect or erect, fleshy-coriaceous, linear-ligulate. **Inflorescence** terminal, erect, elongate, few-flowered, unbranched; peduncle slender, covered by sheaths; rhachis short. **Flowers** borne in succession, not opening widely. **Sepals** and **petals** free, subsimilar, lanceolate, acute or acuminate. **Lip** free, simple, more or less retuse at the apex, disc bearing 2 large calli. **Column** elongate, slightly arcuate and dilated into a foot at the base; clinandrium 3-lobed; pollinia 4, waxy, ovoid, each with a linear caudicle.

DISTRIBUTION A small genus of perhaps four species from Cuba and Hispaniola and Mexico.

DERIVATION OF NAME Named after Santo Domingo, now the Dominican Republic, on the island of Hispaniola.

TAXONOMY Rudolf Schlechter established this small genus in 1913 in Urban's *Symbolae Antillanae* (p. 496). It is allied to *Epidendrum* of which it is a segregate but differs in having a free and entire lip.

TYPE SPECIES *Domingoa hymenodes* (Rchb.f.) Schltr.

CULTURE Temp. Winter min. 15°C. Grow in small pots of free-draining epiphyte compost under moderate shade and humidity. Water carefully throughout the year.

Domingoa hymenodes (Rchb.f.) Schltr. [Colour Plate]
A small to medium-sized epiphyte with clustered, cylindrical, angulate, unifoliate stems, covered by papery sheaths and 2–9 cm long. **Leaf** erect or suberect, linear-ligulate, acute, 4–10 cm long, 0.6–0.9 cm wide. **Inflorescence** erect, 7–30 cm long, covered by papery, acute sheaths; bracts ovate, acute or acuminate, 2–5 mm long. **Flowers** not opening widely, borne successively, the sepals and petals translucent yellow-green, the lip dull purple; pedicel and ovary 8–9 mm long. **Sepals** and **petals** not spreading widely, lanceolate, acute to acuminate, 14–17 mm long, 2.5–4 mm wide. **Lip** slightly deflexed, obovate, retuse, 12–14 mm long, 7–8 mm wide, with 2 calli on the disc. **Column** arcuate, 8–9 mm long, 2-winged at the apex.

DISTRIBUTION Cuba and Hispaniola only; in lowland and lower montane forest, up to 800 m.

HISTORY H.G. Reichenbach originally described this species as *Epidendrum hymenodes* in 1865 in *Flora* (p. 277) based on a collection made by C. Wright in Cuba. It was made the type of Rudolf Schlechter's new genus *Domingoa* in Urban's *Symbolae Antillanae* (p. 497) in 1913.

SYNONYMS *Epidendrum hymenodes* Rchb.f.; *E. haematochilum* Rchb.f.; *E. broughtonioides* Griseb.

Doritis Lindl.

Subfamily Epidendroideae
Tribe Vandeae
Subtribe Sarcanthinae

Small or medium-sized epiphytic plants with a short, leafy stem lacking a pseudobulb. **Leaves** distichous, coriaceous. **Inflorescence** lateral, laxly racemose or paniculate. **Flowers** showy, medium-sized. **Sepals** widely spreading; lateral sepals forming a conical spur-like mentum with the column-foot. **Petals** narrower or broader. **Lip** clawed or sessile, 3-lobed, adnate to the base or foot of the column; side lobes erect; mid-lobe various; disc with a forked plate or callus. **Column** suberect, narrowly winged; foot long; anther 2-celled; pollinia 2, sulcate or bipartite: stipe linear or spathulate; viscidium large or small.

DISTRIBUTION   Two or three species in Sri Lanka, India, Nepal, Burma, Thailand, Indo-China, Malaya and Sumatra.
DERIVATION OF NAME   Either from the Greek *dory* (spear), alluding to the lip shape, or from Doritis, one of the names of the goddess Aphrodite.
TAXONOMY   John Lindley described *Doritis* in 1833 in his *Genera and Species of Orchidaceous Plants* (p. 178). It is allied to *Phalaenopsis* which it vegetatively closely resembles, but it may be distinguished by its conical spur-like mentum.
TYPE SPECIES   *D. pulcherrima* Lindl.
CULTURE   Compost A. Temp. Winter min. 15°C. Upright-growing plants, grow well in pots or baskets. They often shoot from the base, forming clumps. High humidity and good shade are important, with plenty of water when the roots are active – these frequently ramble over the outside of the container. Although they should never become completely dry, the plants need less water when not in active growth.

Doritis pulcherrima Lindl. [Colour Plate]

A very variable terrestrial plant with a short leafy stem about 4–5 cm long. **Leaves** oblanceolate to narrowly elliptic, obtuse to subacute, 6–15 cm long, 1.5–3 cm broad. **Inflorescence** erect, 20–60 cm or more long, simple, laxly many-flowered. **Flowers** showy; sepals and petals deep mauve-purple; lip with reddish side lobes, deep purple mid-lobe and white lines on disc of lip. **Dorsal sepal** narrowly elliptic, obtuse, 1.2–2 cm long, up to 0.7 cm broad; **lateral sepals** oblong, obtuse, 1.2–1.7 cm long, 0.8 cm broad, connate at the base to the column-foot forming a 0.9 cm-long spur-like mentum. **Petals** obovate, rounded at the apex, 1.2–1.7 cm long, up to 0.7 cm broad. **Lip** clawed, 3-lobed above, geniculate in the middle, parallel in basal part with the column-foot,

1.4 cm long, 1.7 cm broad, with a narrow erect-falcate lobe on either side of claw; side lobes oblong, erect; mid-lobe oblong-ovate, apiculate; disc with a callus between the narrow lobes on the claw. **Column** 0.5 cm long; rostellum and anther long-beaked.

DISTRIBUTION   S. China, Burma and Kampuchea, south to Malaya and N. Sumatra.
HISTORY   Originally collected by Finlayson near the River Turon in Cochin China (Vietnam) and named by Dr N. Wallich in his *Catalogue* (no. 7348). John Lindley described it in 1833 in his *Genera and Species of Orchidaceous Plants* (p. 178). R. Holttum in the 3rd edition of *Orchids of Malaya* (1964) states that he does not consider the lip structural differences sufficient to treat *Doritis* as distinct from *Phalaenopsis* and follows J.J. Smith in calling this species *Phalaenopsis pulcherrima*.
SYNONYMS   *Phalaenopsis pulcherrima* (Lindl.) J.J. Smith; *P. esmeralda* Rchb.f.; *P. antennifera* Rchb.f.

Dracula Luer

Subfamily Epidendroideae
Tribe Epidendreae
Subtribe Pleurothallidinae

Small to medium-sized epiphytic herbs with short creeping rhizome producing short, erect, 1-leafed shoots (ramicauls). **Leaf** erect, obovate to oblanceolate, somewhat thin-textured, slightly plicate, with a prominent central mid-rib. **Inflorescences** basal, 1-flowered, erect or more commonly pendent. **Flowers** usually medium-sized, often pendent, flat to bell-shaped; bract sheathing, shorter than the ovary. **Sepals** large, showy, subsimilar, connate for basal third or more, shortly hairy on inner surface, each with a long apical caudate tail. **Petals** very much smaller than the sepals, entire, papillate at thickened apex, parallel to and as long as the column, bearing 2 short keels at the apex. **Lip** bipartite, hinged to the column-foot at the base, the basal part (hypochile) a fleshy oblong cleft claw, the apical part (epichile) transversely elliptic or oblong, cochleate, adorned with radiating grooves from the base. **Column** short, semiterete, porrect, with a short fleshy foot; pollinia 2.
DISTRIBUTION   A genus of some 80 species mainly from Andean S. America and adjacent highland Central America.
DERIVATION OF NAME   From the Latin *dracula* (little dragon) and the eponymous hero of Bram Stoker's novel, in allusion to the fancied resemblance of the somewhat grotesque flowers of most species in the genus.
TAXONOMY   *Dracula* was established as

recently as 1978 by Carlyle Luer in the journal *Selbyana* (p. 190), as a segregate genus from *Masdevallia* in which most of the species were originally described. Luer published at the same time a synopsis of the known species. More recently the first three parts of *Thesaurus Dracularum* (1988–), a finely illustrated account of the genus by Luer and Dalström have appeared, published by the Missouri Botanical Garden.

The fanciful generic name, and specific names such as *D. chimaera* and *D. vampira*, have undoubtedly inspired considerable horticultural interest in the genus over the past decade. Many species are now in cultivation, mostly in small quantities.
TYPE SPECIES   *Masdevallia chimaera* Rchb.f. (= *Dracula chimaera* (Rchb.f.) Luer).
SYNONYM   *Masdevallia* sect. *Chimeroideae* Kraenzl.
CULTURE   Compost A. Temp. Winter min. 11–15°C. depending on the species. The few species which produce erect inflorescences may be grown in pots of free-draining epiphyte compost, while the remainder require baskets of some kind to allow the flowers to burrow and hang. Give high humidity and moderate shade with even water throughout the year.

Dracula bella (Rchb.f.) Luer [Colour Plate]

A caespitose epiphyte with coarse roots and erect stems, 2.5–3 cm long, subtended by 2–3 loose sheaths. **Leaves** erect, thinly coriaceous, elliptic-oblanceolate, acute to obtuse, 15–25 cm long, 2.5–4 cm wide; petiole 3–5 cm long. **Inflorescences** pendent, 1-flowered; peduncle 15–18 long, purple; bracts tubular, 15–18 mm long. **Flowers** pendent, with spreading sepals; sepals pale yellow spotted with maroon; petals yellow, spotted red; lip white with a yellow base; pedicel 15–17 mm long; ovary 8 mm long, with 6 fringed crests. **Sepals** each with a slender apical maroon tail 10–13 cm long; **dorsal sepal** ovate-triangular, 4–4.4 cm long, 2.2–2.4 cm wide, connate to lateral sepals for basal 9–10 mm; **lateral sepals** obliquely triangular-ovate, 4–4.4 cm long, 2.6–2.8 cm wide, connate for basal 3 cm to form a shallow mentum. **Petals** obovate, bilobed at the apex, 5 mm long, 3.5–4 mm wide, papillate in apical half. **Lip** 15–19 mm long, 22–25 mm wide; hypochile oblong, 7 mm long, 5 mm wide; epichile deeply concave, transversely reniform, with tall radiating lamellae within. **Column** 5 mm long; foot stout, 4 mm long.
DISTRIBUTION   Colombia, the western Cordillera.
HISTORY   This species was first described as *Masdevallia bella* by H.G. Reichenbach in 1878 in the *Gardeners' Chronicle* (pt. 1: p. 725) based on a collection made by William Boxall in Col-

ombia and it was flowered in cultivation for the first time by Herr Wendland at the Hamburg Botanic Garden. It was transferred by Luer to the present genus in *Selbyana* (p. 194) in 1978.
SYNONYM *Masdevallia bella* Rchb.f.

Dracula chimaera (Rchb.f.) Luer

A lithophyte or epiphyte with clustered stems 3–6 cm long, subtended by 2–3 loose sheaths. **Leaves** erect, narrowly oblanceolate, 15–30 cm long, 2.5–5 cm wide. **Inflorescences** erect or spreading, 3- to 5-flowered, 15–60 cm long; bracts tubular, 10–12 mm long. **Flowers** produced in succession, pale yellow heavily spotted cinnamon-red, maroon or blackish; lip white to pale yellow; pedicel 12–14 mm long; ovary 9–11 mm long, subverrucose. **Sepals** broadly ovate to triangular, pubescent within, 3–5.5 cm long, 2.5–3 cm broad, connate for basal 1.5–1.8 cm; tails 6–12 cm long. **Petals** spathulate or obovate, bilobed at apex, 3–5 mm long, 1.5–2 mm wide, verrucose in apical part. **Lip** saccate, ellipsoidal, 16–20 mm long, 10–12 mm wide; hypochile large, 4–5 mm long; epichile 12–16 mm long, with dentate margins. **Column** 3–4 mm long; foot 1.5–2 mm long.
DISTRIBUTION Colombia, in cloud forest, 1400–2450 m.
HISTORY This spectacular orchid was discovered in the western Cordillera of Colombia by Benedict Roezl in 1870 and later introduced into cultivation by Gustav Wallis, one of Linden's collectors. Reichenbach described it as *Masdevallia chimaera* in 1872 in the *Gardeners' Chronicle* (pp. 270, 473). Luer transferred it to the present genus in 1978 in *Selbyana* (p. 190).
SYNONYMS *Masdevallia chimaera* Rchb.f.; *M. backhouseana* Rchb.f.; *M. wallisii* Rchb.f. var. *stupenda* Rchb.f.

Dracula erythrochaete (Rchb.f.) Luer
[Colour Plate]
A rather variable epiphyte with short creeping rhizomes and short erect stems. **Leaves** coriaceous, erect, oblanceolate or linear-lanceolate, tridenticulate at the obtuse apex, 15–20 cm long, 1 cm wide, bright green. **Inflorescences** pendent to descending, with 2–3 flowers opening in succession at apex; peduncle slender, terete, up to 12.5 cm long; bracts ovate, sheathing below, apiculate, 1.2 cm long, pale green. **Flowers** with widely spreading segments, the sepals creamy-white tinged with yellow, spotted with crimson-purple and with purple tails, the petals white, the lip white to flesh pink, and the column pale yellow; perianth tube very broad and short; pedicel and ovary 2–2.3 cm long. **Dorsal sepal** broadly ovate at the base, 1.2–1.3 cm long and wide, abruptly narrowing into a slender erect tail,

2.5–5.6 cm long; **lateral sepals** triangular-ovate, 1.3–1.4 cm long and wide, with slender 2.5–5.6 cm long tails; all sepals pubescent within. **Petals** very small, oblong, papillose and 2-lobed at the apex, 4 mm long. **Lip** saccate, clawed, spathulate, 1.3 cm long, 0.5 cm wide, with 3 central lamellae and 5–6 smaller bifurcating ones radiating towards the denticulate margins. **Column** slender, 3–4 mm long, denticulate at the apex.
DISTRIBUTION Costa Rica.
HISTORY Introduced from Central America by Messrs Sander and Sons of St Albans, England in 1882 when H.G. Reichenbach described it as *Masdevallia erythrochaete* in the *Gardeners' Chronicle* (n.s. 18: 392). Carlyle Luer transferred it to the present genus in 1978 in *Selbyana* (p. 195).
SYNONYM *Masdevallia erythrochaete* Rchb.f.
CLOSELY RELATED SPECIES *D. astuta* (Rchb.f.) Luer is very closely allied and may well be conspecific; while *D. gaskelliana* (Rchb.f.) Luer is also similar in its floral morphology but has an erect or suberect inflorescence and differently coloured tails to the sepals.

Dracula robledorum (P. Ortiz) Luer & Escobar [Colour Plate]
A large epiphyte with clustered erect stems 2–3 cm long. **Leaves** erect, oblanceolate, obtuse, 18–24 cm long, 3–5.5 cm wide, with a distinct conduplicate petiole. **Inflorescence** erect, few-flowered with the flowers produced in succession; peduncle slender, erect, 15–18 cm long, dull purple; bracts tubular-obconical, 1–1.2 cm long. **Flower** nutant, cream with dark maroon irregular blotches on the sepals and a white and shell-pink lip; pedicel and ovary 2.2–2.8 cm long. **Sepals** ovate, 3.2–3.3 cm long, 2.6–2.8 cm wide, united for basal 1–1.1 cm, and with long slender filamentous red-brown tails, c. 3.5 cm long. **Petals** oblong, rounded at apex, 6 mm long, 2–2.5 mm wide. **Lip** clawed, calceolate, 1.7–1.9 cm long, 1.2–1.3 cm wide, the apical lamina with a strongly incurved margin and radiating raised lamellae within. **Column** white, 6 mm long with a short, stout, 4 mm-long foot.
DISTRIBUTION Colombia, restricted to a small area in Antioquia Department of the Western Cordillera of Colombia; 2000–2200 m.
HISTORY Pedro Ortiz Valdieva discovered this striking species in June 1975 at Urrao near the headwaters of the Rio Pabon in Colombia. He described it as a variety of *Masdevallia* (now *Dracula*) *chimaera* in the journal *Orquideologia* (p. 222) in the same year. Luer and Escobar raised it to specific rank and transferred it to *Dracula* in 1978 in *Selbyana* (p. 197).
SYNONYM *Masdevallia chimaera* var. *robledorum* P. Ortiz V.

Dracula sodiroi (Schltr.) Luer

An epiphytic or terrestrial plant with densely clustered stout 3–6 cm-long stems subtended by 2–3 sheaths. **Leaves** erect, thinly coriaceous, oblanceolate-narrowly elliptic, acute, 15–25 cm long, 1.2–1.6 cm wide. **Inflorescence** erect, 2- to 3-flowered, campanulate, orange-red with darker central veins to the sepals; pedicel 10–20 mm long; ovary 6–10 mm long; subverrucose, purple. **Sepals** obovate-obtriangular, truncate, 15–20 mm long, connate for basal 15–16 mm, with tails 15–20 mm long. **Petals** obovate-spathulate, obtuse, 7 mm long, 3 mm wide, erose on margin. **Lip** oblong, obtuse, 8 mm long, 2 mm wide, with 2 parallel lamellae on upper side. **Column** semiterete, 7 mm long, yellow; foot 2 mm long.
DISTRIBUTION West-central Ecuador, in cloud forest, 2000–2400 m.
HISTORY The type collection of this unusual species was made by Padre Sodiro on the western slopes of Pichincha in Ecuador and it was described as *Masdevallia sodiroi* in 1915 by Rudolf Schlechter in *Fedde, Repertorum Specierum Novarum* (p. 120). Luer transferred it to *Dracula* in 1978 in *Selbyana* (p. 197).
SYNONYM *Masdevallia sodiroi* Schltr.

Dracula vampira (Luer) Luer

An epiphyte with clustered 4–6 cm-long erect stems enclosed by 2–3 sheaths. **Leaves** erect, elliptic-obovate, acute, 15–28 cm long, 4–5.5 cm wide; petiole 5–8 cm long. **Inflorescences** pendent, laxly several-flowered; peduncle 20–40 cm long; rhachis up to 17 cm long; bracts obliquely tubular, 12–25 mm long. **Flowers** showy, pendent, successive, very pale greenish almost totally obscured by longitudinal blackish-purple veins and intensely suffused blackish-purple above, glabrous; pedicel 18–25 mm long; ovary 10 mm long, subverrucose. **Sepals** spreading, broadly ovate, 3.5–6 cm long, 3–4 mm wide, connate for basal 1.5 cm, with tails 5–11 cm long. **Petals** cartilagenous, oblong, bivalvate at apex, 6 mm long, 2 mm wide, verrucose in apical part. **Lip** 15–24 cm long, 11–17 mm wide; hypochile fleshy, channelled, 7 mm long, 5 mm wide; epichile circular to elliptic-oblong, cochleate, with radiating lamellae within. **Column** 7 mm long, yellow; foot 5–6 mm long.
DISTRIBUTION West-central Ecuador, in cloud forest, 1800–2200 m.
HISTORY For long considered a dark form of *Masdevallia chimaera*, this striking orchid was recognised as distinct by Carlyle Luer in 1978 in *Phytologia* (p. 231). The type collection was collected by Benigno Malo in 1977 on the western slopes of Mt Pichincha. The following year, Luer transferred it to *Dracula* in *Selbyana* (p. 198).

SYNONYMS *Masdevallia vampira* Luer; *Dracula ubanquia* Luer & Andreeta

Dresslerella Luer

Subfamily Epidendroideae
Tribe Epidendreae
Subtribe Pleurothallidinae

Dwarf epiphytic herbs with clustered, unifoliate, erect stems (ramicauls) on a short rhizome. **Stems** erect, spreading or pendent, short or as long as the leaf, bearing 3–4 pubescent or ciliate sheaths. **Leaves** erect, thickly coriaceous or fleshy, minutely to coarsely pubescent, sessile. **Inflorescences** 1-flowered or with several flowers borne one at a time in succession at the apex of a short peduncle, axillary, shorter than the leaf; bract tubular, thin, sometimes pubescent. **Sepals** fleshy, usually dark purple or marked with purple, covered with simple or stellate hairs on outside; **dorsal sepal** more or less triangular, free or connate in the basal part to the lateral sepals; **lateral sepals** often inflated, connate almost to the apex. **Petals** membranous, entire, sometimes clavate. **Lip** more or less clawed, 3-lobed, sagittate or subpandurate; callus more or less bicarinate with a further protuberance on the claw. **Column** slender, more or less winged above, with a short foot at the base; pollinia 4 of 2 sizes.

DISTRIBUTION A genus of perhaps eight species in the tropical Americas from Nicaragua south to Peru.

DERIVATION OF NAME Named in honour of Dr Robert Dressler, a leading orchid taxonomist formerly working at the Smithsonian Institute in Panama.

TAXONOMY Carl Luer established *Dresslerella* as a segregate of *Pleurothallis* in 1970 in the journal *Selbyana* (p. 1). It differs from *Pleurothallis* in its characteristically pubescent leaves and stem sheaths, and the 4 pollinia comprising 2 large and 2 small ones.

TYPE SPECIES *Pleurothallis pertusa* Dressler
CULTURE Temp. Winter min. 12°C. Grow in small pots or pans in a fine epiphyte mix under shady, humid conditions. Water carefully throughout the year.

Dresslerella pertusa (Dressler) Luer

A small plant with clustered 2–4 cm-long, horizontal to pendent stems covered in 3–4 papery imbricate sheaths. **Leaf** prostrate to pendent, thickly coriaceous, elliptic to oblong, obtuse, 4–10 cm long, 2–3.5 cm wide, dark green suffused with purple. **Inflorescence** a succession of single flowers lying on the upper surface of the leaf along the mid-vein; peduncle 3–5 mm long; bract 3–5 mm long, pubescent. **Flower** tubular, yellow below spotted with purple, blackish-purple above, pubescent on outer surface; pedicel and ovary 3 mm long, pubescent. **Sepals** united almost to the apex, 10–14 mm long, the lateral sepals scrotiform-inflated in apical half, with depressed mid-veins. **Petals** linear-oblanceolate, acute, 6–7 mm long, 0.5–1 mm wide. **Lip** clawed, sagittate, 5–7 mm long, 3–4 mm wide, minutely retrorsely auriculate at the base; callus on the claw dentate and retrorse, bilamellate on apical lamina. **Column** slender, bidentate at apex, 5 mm long.

DISTRIBUTION Endemic to Panama; in mist forest at c. 1000 m.
HISTORY Discovered in November 1967 on Cerro Jefe in Panama by Robert Dressler and named by him as *Pleurothallis pertusa* in the journal *Orquideologia* (p. 76). Luer transferred it to *Dresslerella* in *Selbyana* (p. 1) in 1976.
SYNONYM *Pleurothallis pertusa* Dressler

Dressleria Dodson

Subfamily Epidendroideae
Tribe Gongoreae
Subtribe Catasetinae

Vegetatively similar to *Catasetum*. **Flowers** always bisexual, pollinarium and stigma always functional. **Pollinia** release by touching the anther-cap. **Lip** adnate to the base and sides of the short column.

DISTRIBUTION Probably only three or four species from Nicaragua, Costa Rica, Panama, Colombia, Ecuador and Venezuela.
DERIVATION OF NAME Named in honour of Dr Robert Dressler, an orchid taxonomist formerly at the Smithsonian Institute in Panama.

TAXONOMY In 1975 C. Dodson placed three species formerly regarded as species of the genus *Catasetum* into a new genus *Dressleria* in *Selbyana* (p. 131). These species differ from *Catasetum* species in always having bisexual flowers in which the lip is adnate to the column-base and sides and in having pollinia which are discharged by lifting the apex of the anther-cap. L. Garay and G.C.K. Dunsterville (1976) in *Venezuelan Orchids Illustrated* consider these three species to be conspecific.
TYPE SPECIES *Catasetum dilectum* Rchb.f. [= *Dressleria dilecta* (Rchb.f.) Dodson].
CULTURE Compost A or B. Temp. As for *Catasetum*.

Dressleria dilecta (Rchb.f.) Dodson
[Colour Plate]
A lithophytic or epiphytic plant. **Psedobulbs** tufted, fusiform, many-noded, up to 20 cm long, 4 cm in diameter, clothed with distichous leaf-bearing sheaths. **Leaves** oblanceolate, sub-erect, up to 50 cm long, 8 cm broad. **Inflorescence** erect to suberect, 6- to 10-flowered, up to 35 cm long; bracts pale cream, ovate, 2 cm long, 1.2 cm broad. **Flowers** nonresupinate, hermaphrodite, variable in shape and colour, pale brownish-cream to creamy-white. **Sepals** linear, rounded or obtuse, reflexed, 1.8 cm long, 0.4 cm broad. **Petals** ovate, obtuse, reflexed, 1.8 cm long, 0.8 cm broad. **Lip** very fleshy, adnate to base and sides of column, ovate, saccate at base, nectary accessible through a narrow basal slit, 1.5–2 cm long, 1–1.5 cm broad. **Column** very short, stout, lacking antennae.
DISTRIBUTION Costa Rica, Nicaragua, Panama, Venezuela, Colombia and Ecuador.
HISTORY Originally this species was described by H.G. Reichenbach as *Catasetum dilectum* in 1866 in his *Beiträge zu einer Orchideenkunde Zentral-America's* (p. 73). Recently, Calaway Dodson (1975) in *Selbyana* (p. 132) has transferred it to a new genus *Dressleria* named after the American orchidologist Dr Robert Dressler.
SYNONYMS *Catasetum eburneum* Rolfe; *C. suave* Ames & C. Schweinf.; *Dressleria eburnea* (Rolfe) Dodson; *D. suavis* (Ames & C. Schweinf.) Dodson

Dresslerella pertusa
1 – Habit ($\times \frac{3}{4}$)
2 – Sepals and petals ($\times$ 2)
3 – Column and ovary ($\times 2\frac{1}{2}$)
4 – Lip ($\times$ 2)
5 – Pollinarium ($\times$ 6)

Dryadella Luer

Subfamily Epidendroideae
Tribe Epidendreae
Subtribe Pleurothallidinae

Dwarf clump-forming epiphytic plants with short creeping rhizomes and short erect unifoliate stems (ramicauls). **Leaf** suberect, fleshy, obovate to elliptic. **Inflorescences** usually shorter than the leaves, 1-flowered, axillary. **Flowers** small, fleshy, white, cream, yellow, brown or greenish, spotted with maroon or purple; bract small, sheathing. **Sepals** subsimilar, laterals united and shallowly cucullate at the base, caudate at the apex. **Petals** very much smaller than the sepals, short, broad, multiangled. **Lip** with a slender claw and a shovel-shaped apical lamina, bicallose, auriculate at the base of the apical lamina. **Column** semiterete, winged; pollinia 2, hard.
DISTRIBUTION A genus of about 40 species widely distributed from Guatemala to S. Brazil.
DERIVATION OF NAME The diminutive of 'dryad', a tree nymph in classical mythology.
TAXONOMY For many years the species of *Dryadella* were considered to belong to the genus *Masdevallia* until Carlyle Luer convincingly established the segregate genus in 1978 in the journal *Selbyana* (p. 207).
TYPE SPECIES *Masdevallia simula* Rchb.f (= *D. simula* (Rchb.f.) Luer).
SYNONYM *Trigonanthe* (Schltr.) Brieger
CULTURE Temp. Winter min. 11°C. May be grown in pots of epiphyte mix or mounted. They require shade, humidity and moisture throughout the year.

Dryadella lilliputana (Cogn.) Luer
[Colour Plate]
A dwarf densely caespitose epiphyte with very short rhizomes and erect stems. **Leaves** erect or erect-spreading, rigid, subterete, canaliculate, fleshy, slightly arcuate, linear-fusiform, acute, 1.2–1.6 cm long, 2 mm wide. **Inflorescences** many, very short, 1-flowered; peduncle 1–2 mm long; bract membranaceous, subpellucid, 3–4 mm long, white. **Flower** small, erect, glabrous, the sepals cream-coloured spotted with crimson and with yellow tails, the petals white, the lip yellow spotted with crimson; perianth tube campanulate. **Sepals** free part spreading, triangular-ovate, 3 mm long, 2.5 mm wide; tails 4 mm long. **Petals** pellucid, linear, narrow, 1.5 mm long. **Lip** very small, obovate, 1.5 mm long.
DISTRIBUTION Brazil only.
HISTORY Discovered in São Paulo State at the Campos de Bocaina by Edwall and described by Alfred Cogniaux as *Masdevallia lilli-*

putana in 1906 in Martius's *Flora Brasiliensis* (p. 555). Carlyle Luer transferred it to the present genus in 1978 in *Selbyana* (p. 208).
SYNONYM *Masdevallia lilliputana* Cogn.

Dryadella simula (Rchb.f.) Luer
[Colour Plate]
A small epiphyte forming dense tufts; erect stems very short, 1–2 cm long, unifoliate at the apex. **Leaves** erect, arcuate above, linear or oblanceolate, obtuse, 5–8 cm long, 2–6 mm wide. **Inflorescence** 1-flowered, very much shorter than the leaves; bract elliptic, mucronate, 1–2 mm long. **Flowers** small, fleshy; sepals off-white to yellow heavily but finely spotted with purple; petals and lip yellow, heavily flushed with purple; pedicel 5–10 mm long; ovary 2 mm long. **Sepals** spreading, with fleshy tails 2–3 mm long; **dorsal sepal** ovate, caudate, 3.5–8 mm long, 2–5 mm wide; **lateral sepals** ovate, caudate, 3.5–7 mm long, 3–5 mm wide, forming at the base a shallow mentum with the column foot. **Petals** oblong, obtuse, 1.4–2 mm long, 0.7–2 mm wide, with an acute tooth on the lower margin. **Lip** narrowly clawed, with a spade-shaped apical lamina; lamina 1.5–4 mm long, 1–3 mm wide, obtuse and recurved at apex, with 2 back-pointing acute auricles at the base; callus of 2 parallel ridges in the centre of the lip. **Column** slender, 1–2 mm long, winged and denticulate at the apex.
DISTRIBUTION Central America: Guatemala to Panama, and Colombia; montane forest.
HISTORY The type collection was made by Chesterton, one of Messrs Veitch's collectors in Colombia and was described by H.G. Reichenbach in 1875 as *Masdevallia simula* in the *Gardeners' Chronicle* (n.s. 3: p. 8). Reichenbach called it a 'troglodyte among *Masdevallia*' an apt description of the way its flowers are hidden away between the leaves.

Luer transferred it to the present genus in 1978 in *Selbyana* (p. 209).
SYNONYMS *Masdevallia simula* Reichb.f.; *M. guatemalensis* Schltr.; *M. linearifolia* Ames

Dyakia E.A. Christensen

Subfamily Epidendroideae
Tribe Vandeae
Subfamily Sarcanthinae

Small monopodial epiphytic plants with unbranched short to elongate stems. **Leaves** distichous, flat, obtusely bilobed, articulated to a sheathing base. **Inflorescences** erect, lateral, axillary, longer than the flowers, densely many-flowered in a cylindrical raceme. **Flowers** showy, purple with a white lip and spur, open-

ing widely or subringent. **Sepals** and **petals** subsimilar, the dorsal sepal and petals free, spreading; the lateral sepals connate at the base to the base of the lip. **Lip** very short, obscurely 3-lobed, with very small side lobes, spurred at the base; spur elongate, cylindric, pendent, bilaterally flattened, with a prominent callus on the back wall. **Column** short, fleshy; rostellum elongate, tapering, pendent; pollinia 2, ovoid; stipe single, very slender, elongate, with apical appendages; viscidium elliptic.
DISTRIBUTION A monotypic genus in Borneo.
DERIVATION OF NAME From the Malay name 'Dyak', referring to the indigenous people of Borneo.
TAXONOMY This small genus was recently established in 1986 in the *Orchid Digest* (p. 63) by Eric Christensen to accommodate *Saccolabium hendersonianum* which is aberrant in that genus. *Dyakia* is allied to *Ascocentrum* which it superficially closely resembles. It differs, however, in having flat leaves, an abbreviated lip with very small side lobes, a bilaterally compressed spur, the prominent callus on the back wall of the spur, the attenuate rostellum, and the appendaged stipe.
TYPE SPECIES *Saccolabium hendersonianum* Rchb.f.
CULTURE Temp. Winter min. 15°C. Culture as for *Ascocentrum*.

Dyakia hendersoniana (Rchb.f.) E.A. Christensen [Colour Plate]
A small epiphyte with a 5–10 cm-long stem. **Leaves** ligulate to oblanceolate, unequally obtusely bilobed at the apex, 7–15 cm long, 1.2–3 cm wide. **Inflorescences** erect or ascending, 5.5–24 cm long, densely up to c. 40-flowered; peduncle up to 3 mm in diameter; bracts broadly ovate, obtuse, very short, 1–1.5 mm long. **Flowers** showy, rose-purple, with a dark purple spot at the base of each lateral sepal, and with a white lip and spur; pedicel and ovary 1–1.1 cm long. **Dorsal sepal** elliptic, obtuse, 6–7 mm long, 3–4 mm wide; **lateral sepals** cuneate-oblong, obtuse, 7–8 mm long, 5–6 mm wide. **Petals** obovate, obtuse, 5–7 mm long, 2.5–3.5 mm wide. **Lip** obscurely 3-lobed, concave, ovate, acute, 1–1.5 mm long, 3 mm wide; spur pendent, cylindric-clavate, 9–10 mm long. **Column** 1.5 mm long.
DISTRIBUTION Endemic to Borneo; riverine and seasonally swampy forest up to 800 m.
HISTORY H.G. Reichenbach described this pretty orchid in 1875 in the *Gardeners' Chronicle* (n.s. 4: p. 356). The type had been flowered by Messrs Henderson & Sons of the Wellington Nursery, St John's Wood, London, and it was named in their honour as *Saccolabium hendersonianum*. It is best known in cultivation as

Ascocentrum hendersonianum but Christensen transferred it to the present genus in 1986 in the *Orchid Digest* (p. 63).

SYNONYMS *Saccolabium hendersonianum* Rchb.f.; *Ascocentrum hendersonianum* (Rchb.f.) Schltr.

Earina Lindl.

Subfamily Epidendroideae
Tribe Epidendreae
Tribe Glomerinae

Medium-sized epiphytic or terrestrial plants. **Stems** cane-like or pseudobulbous. **Leaves** coriaceous, distichous, conduplicate, articulate to sheathing bases. **Inflorescence** terminal, densely many-flowered, often branched, the branches usually short, distichous. **Flowers** small, yellow, greenish, white or whitish, not opening widely. **Sepals** and **petals** free, subsimilar. **Lip** 3-lobed, constricted in the middle. **Column** short, fleshy; pollinia 4, laterally flattened, with small caudicles.

DISTRIBUTION   A small genus of about four or five species in the islands of the S.W. Pacific from Vanuatu, Samoa and Fiji to New Zealand. Probably centred on New Caledonia.

DERIVATION OF NAME   from the Greek *earinos* (spring time), referring to the flowering season of the New Zealand species.

TAXONOMY   This small genus was established by John Lindley in 1842 in Hooker's *Icones Plantarum* (t. 431). It is one of the few orchid genera endemic to the S.W. Pacific region. It is allied to the genera *Glomera* and *Glossorhyncha*, which are centred on New Guinea, but is readily distinguished by its habit and elongated inflorescences.

TYPE SPECIES   *E. mucronata* Lindl.

CULTURE   Temp. Winter min. 10–12°C. The two New Zealand species are best grown mounted under shady, humid conditions, the more tropical ones in pots. Do not allow the plants to remain dry for more than a day or two. The New Zealand species will tolerate the cooler end of the scale.

Earina mucronata Lindl.

A slender pendent epiphyte often growing in large tufts. **Stems** slender, cylindrical, leafy, up to 1 m in length but usually shorter, covered by black-spotted, flattened leaf bases. **Leaves** distichous, linear-tapering, acuminate, 10–15 cm long, 0.5 cm wide, twisted at base to lie in one plane, deciduous. **Inflorescences** terminal, pendulous, simple or branched, laxly many-flowered; bracts ovate, appressed, papery, 1.5–2.5 mm long. **Flowers** 8–10 mm across, pendent, lightly scented, the sepals pale yellow-green, the petals greenish-white, the lip yellow-orange. **Sepals** spreading, oblong-ovate, obtuse, 4–5 mm long, 1–2 mm wide. **Petals** porrect, obovate, obtuse, 4–5 mm long, 1–2 mm wide. **Lip** 3-lobed, recurved strongly in the middle, 3.5–4.5 mm long, 2–3 mm wide; side lobes erect, obliquely elliptic, rounded in front; mid-lobe transversely bilobed; callus of 2 small fleshy projections between the side lobes. **Column** 2 mm long.

DISTRIBUTION   New Zealand and Chatham Island only; commoner in wetter areas, usually low down on trees and tree ferns, from the coast to upland sites.

HISTORY   Described by John Lindley in 1834 in the *Botanical Register* (sub t. 1699) based on a collection made by Alan Cunningham from the Bay of Islands.

CLOSELY RELATED SPECIES   *Earina autumnalis* (Forst.f.) Hook.f. [Colour Plate], also from New Zealand, differs in having a coarser habit with shorter, broader, less pointed leaves, unspotted leaf sheaths and white flowers with a yellow spot on the lip.

Earina valida Rchb.f.

A medium-sized epiphyte with clustered ovoid pseudobulbs, 4–8 cm long, 2–4 cm in diameter, covered by imbricate persistent leaf sheaths when young. **Leaves** distichous, arranged in a fan, linear-lanceolate, acute or obtuse, 25–40 cm long, 8–22 mm wide, unequally bilobed at the apex; the leaf bases thickened and imbricate. **Inflorescence** terminal, 30–50 cm long, densely many-flowered, many-branched; each branch 4–10 mm long, 2- to 4-flowered; bracts ovate, 2–3 mm long. **Flowers** white; pedicel and ovary 2–4 mm long. **Dorsal sepal** oblong-ovate, obtuse, 3–4 mm long, 1.5 mm wide; **lateral sepals** ovate, shortly apiculate, 4–5 mm long, 2–2.5 mm wide. **Petals** elliptic-oblong, obtuse, 4–4.5 mm long, 2 mm wide. **Lip** saccate at the base, 3-lobed above, constricted in the middle, 5 mm long, 3 mm wide; side lobes erect, rounded; mid-lobe ovate, deflexed at the apex. **Column** 3–4 mm long.

DISTRIBUTION   New Caledonia, Vanuatu, Fiji and Samoa; epiphytic in lower montane and montane forest; 300–1100 m.

HISTORY   H.G. Reichenbach described this species in 1877 in the journal *Linnaea* (p. 96) based on a collection by Vieillard from New Caledonia.

SYNONYMS   *E. samoensium* Muell. & Kraenzl.; *Agrostophyllum drakeanum* Kraenzl.; *Earina brousmichei* Kraenzl.

Elleanthus Presl

Subfamily Epidendroideae
Tribe Arethuseae
Subtribe Sobraliinae

Epiphytic or terrestrial herbs with matted fleshy roots. **Stems** erect, cane-like, simple or branching, leafy. **Leaves** distichous, plicate, sessile, sheathed below, strongly nerved. **Inflorescence** terminal, capitate or racemose; bracts conspicuous. **Flowers** small but often brightly coloured. **Sepals** and **petals** free, subsimilar. **Lip** enclosing column, concave-saccate below; calli 2, basal, in saccate cavity. **Column** erect, footless, winged; anther 2-celled; pollinia 8, waxy.

DISTRIBUTION   About 50 species widespread in the tropical Americas, particularly in the Andes.

DERIVATION OF NAME   Named in honour of the Ancient Greek Helle or Helena, daughter of Athamar and Nephrele. The Hellespont was named after the same mythological character.

TAXONOMY   Described by K.B. Presl in 1827 in *Reliquiae Haenkeanae* (p. 97), *Elleanthus* species closely resemble those of *Sobralia* in the flowerless condition but mostly have much smaller flowers and a lip with a gibbous or subsaccate base ornamented with 2 prominent calli.

TYPE SPECIES   *E. lancifolius* Presl

SYNONYM   *Evelyna* Poepp. & Endl.

CULTURE   Compost B. Temp. Winter min. 12–15°C. As for *Sobralia*, except that *Elleanthus* are generally smaller plants. They should be allowed to form large clumps, and often grow better in beds. During growth they need moderate shade and plenty of water, but after flowering, may be kept much drier, until the new shoots appear.

Elleanthus capitatus (Poepp. & Endl). Rchb.f.

An erect terrestrial plant, 1 m tall. **Stem** slender, terete, erect, up to 1.1 m tall, 0.5 cm in diameter, covered by leaf-sheaths. **Leaves** subcoriaceous, lanceolate, 5–25 cm long, 2–8 cm broad, acuminate, becoming smaller higher up the stem. **Inflorescence** capitate (hence the name), many-flowered, 3–8 cm broad; bracts-imbricate, ovate to lanceolate. **Flowers** rose-purple, embedded in mucilage. **Sepals** lanceolate to elliptic, 0.8–1.2 cm long, up to 0.35 cm broad. **Petals** linear, 1.2 cm long, 0.2 cm broad, subacute. **Lip** triangular-obovate, 1–1.4 cm long and broad, basally saccate, bearing 2 calli, front margin finely toothed. **Column** 0.5–0.6 cm long.

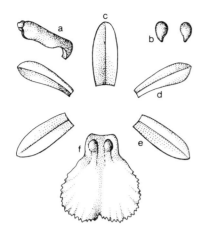

Elleanthus capitatus
Floral dissection
a – Column, side view (× 2)
b – Pollinia (× 9)
c – Dorsal sepal (× 2)
d – Stigma (× 2)
e – Petal (× 2)
f – Lip (× 2)

DISTRIBUTION Mexico south to northern S. America and the W. Indies.

HISTORY This species is widespread and has been described under several different names and in several genera since Robert Brown first described it in the 2nd edition of Aiton's *Hortus Kewensis* (p. 206) as *Bletia capitata* in 1813. H.G. Reichenbach transferred the species to *Elleanthus* in *Walpers, Annales Botanices* (p. 482) in 1861. Unfortunately, he transferred a later synonym, *Evelyna capitata* of E.F. Poeppig and S.L. Endlicher, as he was unaware of Robert Brown's earlier description. As this species is so well known under the name *Elleanthus capitatus* we have left it as this, choosing to ignore the problems which arise if Robert Brown's early name is taken into consideration.

SYNONYMS *Bletia capitata* R.Br.; *Evelyna capitata* Poepp. & Endl.; *Elleanthus cephalotus* Garay & Sweet

Elleanthus furfuraceus (Lindl.) Rchb.f.
[Colour Plate]

A slender plant with a simple or sometimes branching leafy stem. **Leaves** lanceolate or elliptic-lanceolate, acuminate, up to 14 cm long, 2.5 cm broad. **Inflorescence** terminal, densely 4- to 16-flowered; lower bracts lanceolate, acuminate, longer than the flowers. **Flowers** purple, rose-coloured or scarlet. **Dorsal sepal** ovate-oblong, subacute or acuminate, 0.6–0.8 cm long; **lateral sepals** obliquely ovate-lanceolate or ovate-oblong, acute, acuminate or apiculate. **Petals** oblong-oblanceolate, subacute, 0.7 cm long, 0.3 cm broad. **Lip** roundly obovate, concave at the base, denticulate or erose and retuse on anterior margins; disc with a pair of semiellipsoid calli at the base and in front of these a trans-

verse raised ridge. **Column** stout, subclavate, tridenticulate at the apex.

DISTRIBUTION Guyana, Venezuela, Colombia, Ecuador and Peru.

HISTORY First collected at Mérida in Venezuela by Jean Linden and later also at Agua de Obispo. John Lindley described it as *Evelyna furfuracea* in 1846 in *Orchidaceae Lindenianae* (p. 12). H.G. Reichenbach transferred it to *Elleanthus* in 1862 in *Walpers, Annales Botanices* (p. 480).

SYNONYM *Evelyna furfuracea* Lindl.

Elleanthus longibracteatus (Lindl. ex Griseb.) Fawc. [Colour Plate]

A large terrestrial leafy plant, up to 60 cm tall. **Stems** slender, erect, terete, covered by long, tubular leaf-bases. **Leaves** ovate-lanceolate to narrowly lanceolate, acuminate, up to 21 cm long, 4–5 cm broad. **Inflorescence** terminal, spicate, laxly several-flowered; bracts spreading, ovate-lanceolate, acuminate, longer than the flowers. **Flowers** yellow; ovary pubescent. **Dorsal sepal** oblong-ovate, acute, concave, up to 0.8 cm long; **lateral sepals** similar to dorsal sepal but oblique and gibbose at the base. **Petals** narrowly oblong, acute, 0.7 cm long. **Lip** concave, cuneate-flabellate, saccate at base, apical margin erose-denticulate, up to 0.8 cm long, 0.7 cm broad; calli 2, ovoid, basal. **Column** cylindrical, angulate, up to 0.6 cm long.

DISTRIBUTION Central America, Colombia to Bolivia and the W. Indies.

HISTORY Discovered in Ecuador near San Antonio by Prof. William Jameson and described in 1864 by A.H.R. Griesbach in the *Flora of the British West Indies* (p. 623) as *Evelyna longibracteata*, a name suggested by John Lindley. W. Fawcett transferred it to the genus *Elleanthus* in 1893 in his *Flowering Plants of Jamaica* (p. 38).

SYNONYM *Evelyna longibracteata* Lindl. ex Griseb.

Embreea Dodson

Subfamily Epidendroideae
Tribe Gongoreae
Subtribe Stanhopeinae

Epiphytes with clustered, 4-angled, unifoliate pseudobulbs. **Leaf** plicate, heavily veined on the underside, suberect. **Inflorescences** basal, pendent, 1-flowered. **Flowers** fleshy, pendent, short-lived. **Dorsal sepal** and **petals** free; **lateral sepals** oblique, united only at the base. **Lip** 3-partite; the hypochile narrow, channelled; the mesochile with T-shaped lateral erect horns; and the epichile slender, lanceolate. **Column** clavate, narrowly winged; pollinia 2,

hard, obovoid, attached to an elongate stipe to a round viscidium; rostellum bifid.

DISTRIBUTION A monotypic genus from W. Colombia and S.E. Ecuador.

DERIVATION OF NAME Named in honour of Alvin Embree who supported Dodson's studies of *Stanhopea* and its allies.

TAXONOMY *Embreea* is a segregate genus of *Stanhopea*, based on *S. rodigasiana*, which was established by Calaway Dodson in the journal *Phytologia* (p. 389) in 1980.

TYPE SPECIES *Stanhopea rodigasiana* Claes ex Cogn.

CULTURE As for *Stanhopea* in a basket to allow the pendent inflorescences to emerge.

Embreea rodigasiana (Claes ex Cogn.) Dodson

A large epiphyte with ovoid, 4- angled pseudobulbs, 4–6 cm long, 3–4 cm wide, pale green. **Leaf** erect, oblanceolate to elliptic-oblong, acute, 20–50 cm long, 5–10.5 cm wide, pale green. **Inflorescences** 1 to several, pendent, 1-flowered; peduncle 8–25 cm long, slender, bearing several sheaths along length; bract obovate, sheathing at base, acuminate above, 2.5–3.5 cm long. **Flower** large, fleshy, short-lived, 8–10 cm long; pedicel and ovary 7–9 cm long. **Dorsal sepal** concave, lanceolate, acute, 7–8 cm long, 2–2.6 cm wide; **lateral sepals** oblique, ovate, acute, 6.8–7.5 cm long, 2–2.7 cm wide; **Petals** reflexed, lanceolate, acute, 6.5–7.3 cm long, 1–1.5 cm wide. **Lip** tripartite, very fleshy, 5.5–8 cm long, 3–3.5 cm wide; hypochile narrowly oblong, channelled, 3.5–4.5

Embreea rodigasiana
1 – Flower (× ½)
2 – Flower, side view (× ¼)
3 – Column and lip (× ¼)

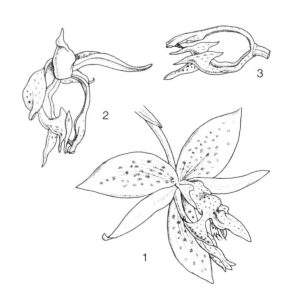

cm long; mesochile with 2 T-shaped erect projections; epichile concave, lanceolate, acute, 2–3 cm long. **Column** arcuate, erosely winged above, 6.5–7 cm long.

DISTRIBUTION W. Colombia and S. Ecuador, on both sides of the Andes, lower montane forest.

HISTORY Originally described as *Stanhopea rodigasiana* by Alfred Cogniaux in 1898 in the *Chronique Orchidienne* (p. 134), based on a collection made by Claes at Antioquia in Colombia. Calaway Dodson made it the type of *Embreea* in 1980 in the journal *Phytologia* (p. 389).

SYNONYM *Stanhopea rodigasiana* Claes ex Cogn.

Encyclia Hooker f.

Subfamily Epidendroideae
Tribe Epidendreae
Subtribe Laeliinae

Stems forming more or less pyriform pseudobulbs, only very rarely slender. **Leaves** fleshy or coriaceous, ligulate to oblong, borne towards apex of pseudobulbs. **Flowers** often showy, borne in racemes or panicles. **Sepals** and **petals** free, subsimilar, ± spreading. **Lip** free from column or partially adnate but never completely adnate. **Column** fleshy; rostellum more or less tongue-like, rarely forming a viscidium, never deeply slit; capsule ± fusiform or strongly 3-winged; pollinia 4.

DISTRIBUTION About 150 species. Predominantly Mexican and W. Indian but with several species in tropical S. America. About 150 species.

DERIVATION OF NAME From the Greek *enkyklein* (to encircle), referring to the manner in which the lip side lobes encircle the column.

TAXONOMY *Encyclia* was established by W.J. Hooker (1828) in the *Botanical Magazine* (t. 2831). It has been treated by some authors as a section of the genus *Epidendrum*, but the tendency now is to accept the well-reasoned views of R. Dressler as stated in *Britonnia* (1961), that *Encyclia* should be removed from *Epidendrum*. The genus may be distinguished from *Epidendrum* by the features given in the description above, in particular, the presence of pseudobulbs and column characteristics (i.e. only partially adnate to the lip).

Dressler further suggested the splitting of *Encyclia* into two sections:

1. sect. *Encyclia* with a capsule circular in cross-section; median-tooth at apex of column small, obtuse or triangular, incurved, separated from the lateral teeth by broad shallow sinuses.
2. sect. *Osmophytum*, with a 3-angled or winged capsule; median-tooth at column-apex erect, large, subquadrate, fleshy and ± fimbriate separated from side teeth by narrow deep sinuses.

As defined above, the genus *Encyclia* cannot really be separated from *Cattleya* from a botanical point of view. However, as both genera are important in horticulture it is convenient to treat them as distinct, with *Encyclia* species having smaller flowers and those of *Cattleya* having larger often showier flowers, 4–20 cm in diameter.

TYPE SPECIES *E. viridiflora* Hooker
CULTURE Compost A. Temp. Winter min. 10–15°C, depending on species. *Encyclia* plants may be grown in pots or shallow pans. While in active growth, the plants need water, with good humidity and moderate shades. Those species with hard pseudobulbs grow well with *Cattleya* plants. All plants benefit from a dry period when the new growth is complete, but care must be taken with the softer-stemmed species.

Encyclia adenocaula (La Llave & Lex.) Schltr. [Colour Plate]

Pseudobulbs clustered, ovoid to subconical, 5–8 cm long, 2–6 cm broad, 2- or 3-leaved. **Leaves** strap-shaped, 11–35 cm long, up to 2.8 cm broad, acute or obtuse. **Inflorescence** paniculate, many-flowered, 100 cm long; peduncle, ovary and rhachis warty. **Flowers**

rose to pale purple; lip with 1 to several purple stripes on mid-lobe. **Sepals** linear-elliptic to narrowly lanceolate, up to 5 cm long, 0.7 cm broad, acute. **Petals** narrowly elliptic or oblanceolate, up to 4.6 cm long, 0.8 cm broad, acute. **Lip** adnate to basal quarter of column, 3-lobed, up to 4.5 cm long; side lobes obliquely oblong-lanceolate, up to 1.2 cm long, acute; mid-lobe suborbicular or ovate-orbicular, up to 3.0 cm long, 2.8 cm broad; callus sulcate, elliptic. **Column** 1.5 cm long, clavate, winged; wings oblong.

DISTRIBUTION Mexico; at 1000–2000 m altitude in rather dry oak and pine/oak forests.

HISTORY Described originally by P. La Llave and J. Lexarza as *Epidendrum adenocaulon* in 1825 in *Novorum Vegetabilium Descriptiones* (p. 22) based on a collection of La Llave from Michoacan in Mexico. R. Schlechter transferred it in 1918 to *Encyclia* in *Beihefte zum Botanischen Zentralblatt* (p. 470).

SYNONYMS *Epidendrum adenocaulon* La Llave & Lex.; *E. nemorale* Lindl.; *Encyclia nemoralis* (Lindl.) Schltr.; *Epidendrum verrucosum* Lindl.

CLOSELY RELATED SPECIES Easily recognised by the pale rose or pink flowers and narrow sepals and petals. The closely related species *Encyclia kennedyi* (Fowlie & Withner) Hagsater has redder flowers, a prominent midvein on the lip and narrower side lobes.

Encyclia baculus (Rchb.f.) Dressler & Pollard [Colour Plate]

An erect epiphyte, up to 45 cm tall. **Pseudobulbs** borne 1.5–2.5 cm apart on the rhizome, ± fusiform, somewhat flattened, up to 35 cm long, 1–2 cm broad, 2- to 3-leaved at apex. **Leaves** lanceolate to ligulate-elliptic, 16–30 cm long, 1.4–3.3 cm broad, obtuse. **Inflorescence** short, 2-(rarely 3)-flowered; peduncle up to 5.5 cm long; basal sheath up to 4.5 cm long. **Flowers** borne 'back to back', non-resupinate, white to cream with lip marked with radiating purple veins, up to 9 cm across, very strongly sweetly scented. **Sepals** elliptic-lanceolate, 4–5.5 cm long, 0.6–0.9 cm broad, acute. **Petals** elliptic, 3.4–4.2 cm long, 0.7–1.4 cm broad, acute or acuminate. **Lip** adnate to the column for half the column length; lamina ovate, concave, up to 2.5 cm long, 1.6 cm broad, acute; base cordate; callus rectangular-oblong, sulcate. **Column** stout, up to 1 cm long; mid-tooth triangular at apex.

DISTRIBUTION Mexico, south to Colombia and possibly Brazil.

HISTORY Well known under the name *Epidendrum pentotis* Rchb.f. Unfortunately, the earlier name *E. baculus* of the same author has priority. H.G. Reichenbach originally described this species in *Bonplandia* (p. 214) in 1856 based on a J. Pavon specimen probably collected by

Encyclia, lips and columns
a Lips, b Columns from above
1 – *E. citrina* (× ⅔)
2 – *E. mariae* (× ⅔)
3 – *E. radiata* (× 2⅔)
4 – *E. calamaria* (× 2⅔)
5 – *E. livida* (× 2⅔)

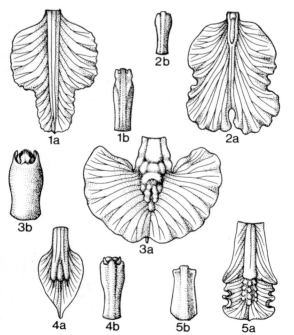

M. Sesse and J.M. Mocino in Mexico. It was transferred to *Encyclia* by R. Dressler and G. Pollard in 1971 in the journal *Phytologia* (p. 436).
SYNONYMS *Epidendrum baculus* Rchb.f.; *E. pentotis* Rchb.f.; *E. fragrans* var. *megalanthum* Lindl.; *E. acuminatum* Sesse & Mocino; *E. beyrodtianum* Schltr.
CLOSELY RELATED SPECIES May be distinguished from *E. fragrans* by its tall, slender, 2- or 3-leaved pseudobulbs which bear 2 flowers placed back to back and by the prominent 'ears' at the base of the lip.

Encyclia belizensis (Rchb.f.) Schltr.
[Colour Plate]
Pseudobulbs clustered, conical-ovoid, 3–4.5 cm long, 1.2–2 cm long, 1.2–2 cm broad, 2-leaved. **Leaves** narrowly elliptic-lanceolate to ligulate, 9–50 cm long, 0.8–2 cm broad, acute or obtuse. **Inflorescence** racemose or paniculate, few- to many-flowered, up to 90 cm long. **Flowers** pale yellow to olive-green, ± streaked brown towards apex; lip cream to pale yellow lined red-brown. **Sepals** oblanceolate, 1.7–2.3 cm long, 0.4–0.7 cm broad, obtuse or subacute. **Petals** narrowly or broadly oblanceolate, 1.6–2.1 cm long, 0.3–0.7 cm broad, acute or obtuse. **Lip** adnate to column-base, 3-lobed, up to 1.7 cm long; side lobes clasping column-apex, oblong, slightly falcate, up to 1.2 cm long, obtuse; mid-lobe suborbicular, 0.9 cm long, 1.1 cm broad, obtuse veins warty, margins undulate; callus elliptic-obovate, sulcate. **Column** clavate, up to 1 cm long, winged; apical teeth triangular.
DISTRIBUTION Belize, Honduras and Mexico; from sea level to 100 m altitude in tropical deciduous forests.
HISTORY Described in 1876 by H.G. Reichenbach in *Linnaea* (p. 78) as *Epidendrum belizense* and transferred by Rudolf Schlechter to *Encyclia* in 1918 in *Beihefte zum Botanischen Zentralblatt* (p. 471). Two subspecies are recognised by R. Dressler and G. Pollard in *The Genus Encyclia in Mexico* (1974). The subspecies *parviflora* is confined to Mexico and it is distinguished from the typical subspecies by its darker flowers, wider sepals and petals and lemony fragrance. This species may be recognised by the winged column, minutely warty lips and oblong side lobes of the lip.
SYNONYMS *Epidendrum belizense* Rchb.f.; *E. virens* Lindl. & Paxt.
CLOSELY RELATED SPECIES *Encyclia megalantha* (Barb. Rodr.) Porto & Brade [Colour Plate] from Brazil is allied to *E. hanburyi*, *E. belizensis* etc. from Central America but is easily distinguished by its larger size and larger flowers with obovate-elliptic to oblong-elliptic concave sepals and petals which are yellow,

heavily suffused with brown, and by its white lip, heavily veined with crimson.

Encyclia brassavolae (Rchb.f.) Dressler
[Colour Plate]
An epiphytic or occasionally lithophytic plant. **Pseudobulbs** widely spaced, about 4.5 cm apart on a creeping rhizome, ovoid to fusiform or pyriform, somewhat flattened, 9–18 cm long, 3–5 cm broad, 2- to 3-leaved at apex. **Leaves** elliptic-oblong, 14–28.5 cm long, 3.5–5 cm broad, obtuse. **Inflorescence** 3- to 15-flowered, 13–40 cm long. **Flowers** pale green, greenish-yellow or olive-tan; lip violet-purple with a creamy base. **Sepals** linear-lanceolate, up to 5.5 cm long, 0.6 cm broad, acuminate. **Petals** linear-lanceolate, 3.3–4.7 cm long, 0.2–0.4 cm broad, acuminate. **Lip** adnate to basal third of column, 3–4.3 cm long, lanceolate-ovate, up to 1.6 cm broad, acuminate, margins fleshy, up-curved at base; callus fleshy, running the length of the lamina. **Column** 1.2–1.5 cm long; mid-tooth at apex flabellate-obovate, laciniate, longer than side teeth.
DISTRIBUTION Central America, Mexico to W. Panama; 1200–2500 m altitude growing in rather wet pine/oak and evergreen forests.
HISTORY Described in 1852 as *Epidendrum brassavolae* by H.G. Reichenbach in *Botanische Zeitung* (p. 729) based on a J. Warscewicz specimen collected in Panama. In 1961 R. Dressler transferred it to the genus *Encyclia* in *Brittonia* (p. 264).
SYNONYM *Epidendrum brassavolae* Rchb.f.
CLOSELY RELATED SPECIES Closely related to *Epidendrum prismatocarpum* Rchb.f. from Central America.

Encyclia bulbosa (Vell.) Pabst [Colour Plate]
An erect epiphytic herb, up to 30 cm tall. **Pseudobulb** fusiform, up to 9 cm long, 1.5 cm broad, shiny green, 2-leaved at apex. **Leaves** strap-shaped, suberect, coriaceous, up to 21 cm long, 2.5 cm broad, obtuse. **Inflorescence** 4- to 5-flowered, erect, racemose, up to 12 cm long, subtended by a large 5 cm-long sheath. **Flowers** non-resupinate, up to 5 cm across, creamy-white with a purple-lined lip. **Sepals** narrowly lanceolate, 2.8 cm long, 0.3 cm broad, acute to acuminate. **Petals** similar to sepals but shorter. **Lip** uppermost, adnate to column at base, free part clawed, lanceolate, acuminate, 1.2 cm long, 0.6 cm broad; callus of 3 truncate ridges at apex of column. **Column** fleshy, triangular in cross-section, dilated towards apex, 0.8 cm long.
DISTRIBUTION Brazil and Paraguay.
HISTORY Originally described by J.M. Velloso in *Flora Fluminensis* (t. 11) in 1827 as *Epidendrum bulbosum* and transferred in 1972 to the genus *Encyclia* by G. Pabst in *Orquidea* (p. 276).

SYNONYMS *Epidendrum inversum* Lindl.; *E. latro* Rchb.f.; *E. bulbosum* Vell.
CLOSELY RELATED SPECIES *Encyclia glumacea* (Lindl.) Pabst [Colour Plate] from Brazil is closely allied to *E. bulbosa*, being distinguished by slightly larger flowers and broader, less acuminate lip. See also *E. calamaria*.

Encyclia calamaria (Lindl.) Pabst
A small epiphytic plant, up to 18 cm tall. **Pseudobulbs** fusiform, glossy green, 2–5 cm long, 0.7–1 cm broad, 2- or 3-leaved at apex. **Leaves** ligulate to narrowly oblanceolate, obtuse or subacute, 4–11 cm long, 0.6–0.8 cm broad. **Inflorescence** up to 6 cm long, 4- to 7-flowered. **Flowers** non-resupinate, small, up to 3 cm across, creamy-white to pale yellowish-green with a few purple stripes on the lip and a yellow anther. **Sepals** linear, acute, up to 1.4 cm long, 0.3 cm broad; lateral sepals slightly dilated towards apex. **Petals** oblanceolate or narrowly spathulate, acuminate, 1.2–1.4 cm long, 0.3 cm broad. **Lip** uppermost, adnate to column at the base, free part cordate or ovate, acute, 0.5–0.8 cm long, 0.4–0.6 cm broad; callus small, 2-ridged below column apex. **Column** short, fleshy, to 0.6 cm long, dilated above.
DISTRIBUTION Brazil.
HISTORY Originally described as *Epidendrum calamarium* by John Lindley in the *Botanical Register* (misc. 88) in 1838 based on a plant imported from Brazil by Messrs Loddiges. G. Pabst transferred it in 1972 to *Encyclia* in *Orquidea* (p. 276).
SYNONYM *Epidendrum calamarium* Lindl.
CLOSELY RELATED SPECIES Closely related to *E. bulbosa* but a much smaller plant with smaller flowers with a broader and shorter lip.

Encyclia chacaoensis (Rchb.f.) Dressler & Pollard [Colour Plate]
An epiphytic or lithophytic plant. **Pseudobulbs** loosely clustered, ovoid to ellipsoid, somewhat flattened, 4–10 cm long, 2–5 cm broad, smooth, pale greyish-green, 2- to 3-leaved at apex. **Leaves** narrowly elliptic or elliptic, 15–20 cm long, 1.7–5 cm broad, obtuse. **Inflorescence** 2- to 7-flowered, up to 10 cm long, subtended by a basal sheath 3 cm long. **Flowers** non-resupinate, creamy-white with lip marked with purple veins, up to 4 cm across. **Sepals** elliptic or ovate-lanceolate, 1.4–2.2 cm long, 0.5–1 cm broad, acute. **Petals** broadly elliptic, up to 2 cm long, 0.6–1 cm broad; acute. **Lip** adnate to column at base; lamina broadly ovate, concave, 1–2 cm long, 1.2–2.5 cm broad, obtuse or acute; callus pubescent. **Column** stout, 1–1.2 cm long, mid-

tooth at apex square or rounded, fleshy; ligule oblong, rounded.

DISTRIBUTION Venezuela, Colombia and Central America, north to Mexico; at an altitude of 750–1100 m growing commonly in oak forests.

HISTORY Described by H.G. Reichenbach in 1854 in *Bonplandia* (p. 20) as *Epidendrum chacaoense* based on a plant collected in Venezuela. It was transferred to *Encyclia* by R. Dressler and G. Pollard in 1971 in *Phytologia* (p. 436).

This very variable species is often self-pollinating, in which form the flowers are rather small. Such a form was described by R. Schlechter as *Epidendrum pachycarpum* but plants with intermediate-sized flowers occur which link this form with the more typical one.

E. chacaoensis is easily distinguished from all allied species by its pale grey-green leaves and smooth pseudobulbs.

SYNONYMS *Epidendrum chacaoense* Rchb.f.; *E. ionophlebium* Rchb.f.; *E. pachycarpum* Schltr.; *E. madrense* Schltr.; *E. hoffmanii* Schltr.

Encyclia citrina (La Llave & Lex.) Dressler [Colour Plate]

An epiphytic plant, up to 32 cm long, often growing in hanging tufts. **Pseudobulbs** in clusters, ovoid, conical or fusiform, 4–6 cm long, 2–3 cm broad, 2- to 4-leaved. **Leaves** elliptic, 18–26 cm long, 3–3.8 cm broad, obtuse or acute. **Inflorescence** pendent, 1- or 2-flowered, 6–10 cm long. **Flowers** sweetly scented, golden yellow; lip mid-lobe orange. **Sepals** fleshy, elliptic-oblong or oblong, 5–6.5 cm long, 1.5–2 cm broad, obtuse or acute. **Petals** oblong to elliptic-obovate, 4.5–6.5 cm long, obtuse. **Lip** adnate to column at base, oblong-obovate, 5.5–6.5 cm long, 3.5–4.8 cm broad, obscurely 3-lobed at apex; mid-lobe quadrate, obtuse or retuse, margins fleshy and crisped; callus fleshy, sulcate running onto base of mid-lobe. **Column** 2.5–3.5 cm long.

DISTRIBUTION Mexico; in dry oak and oak/pine forests, 1300–2200 m altitude.

HISTORY Originally described by P. La Llave and J. Lexarza as *Sobralia citrina* in *Novorum Vegetabilium Descriptiones* (p. 21) in 1825, this species is better known in cultivation as *Cattleya citrina*. However, its closest relative is *Encyclia mariae* and R. Dressler transferred it in 1961 to the same genus in *Brittonia* (p. 264). It is a variable species particularly in lip shape.

SYNONYMS include *Cattleya citrina* (La Llave & Lex.) Lindl.; *Epidendrum citrinum* (La Llave & Lex.) Rchb.f.

CLOSELY RELATED SPECIES See *E. mariae*.

Encyclia cochleata (L.) Lemée [Colour Plate]

A medium-sized epiphytic herb. **Pseudobulbs** loosely clustered, ellipsoid to pear-shaped, somewhat flattened, sometimes shortly stalked, 5.5–26 cm long 2–5 cm broad, 2- to 3-leaved above. **Leaves** elliptic to elliptic-lanceolate, 20–33 cm long, 3–5 cm broad. **Inflorescence** up to 50 cm or more long, many-flowered with flowers opening in succession over a long period; basal sheath 2.5–13 cm long. **Flowers** with lip uppermost; sepals and petals pale green; lip white below with deep purple veins, deep purple above flushed with yellow-green, column green with purple spots. **Sepals** and **petals** subsimilar, reflexed, twisted, narrowly lanceolate, acute, 3–7.5 cm long. 0.3–0.7 cm broad. **Lip** basally adnate to column, deeply concave, broadly triangular-ovate, deeply cordate, obtuse to subacute, 1–2.1 cm long, 1.3–2.6 cm broad; callus rectangular-oblong with a median groove. **Column** stout, broadest in the middle, 0.7–0.9 cm long; apical mid-tooth shorter than side teeth and blunt.

DISTRIBUTION Florida, the W. Indies, Mexico south to Colombia and Venezuela; 100–2000 m in a variety of forest types.

HISTORY Originally described in 1763 as *Epidendrum cochleatum* by Carl von Linné in the 2nd edition of *Species Plantarum* (p. 1351) based on C. Plumier's *Helleborine cochleato flore* (1703) a pre-Linnaean name. A. Lemée transferred it to *Encyclia* in 1955 in *Flore de la Guyane Française* (p. 418).

SYNONYM *Epidendrum cochleatum* L.

CLOSELY RELATED SPECIES A rather distinctive species allied to *Encyclia lancifolia* (Lindl.) Dressler & Pollard but distinguished by its longer sepals and petals and much darker lip. See also *E. fragrans*.

Encyclia cordigera (H.B.K.) Dressler [Colour Plate]

An epiphytic herb, up to 70 cm tall. **Pseudobulbs** erect, clustered, conical-ovoid, 3–11 cm long, 2–8 cm broad. **Leaves** strap-shaped, 12.5–45 cm long, 1.7–4.3 cm broad, obtuse or subacute. **Inflorescence** racemose or paniculate, 3- to 15-flowered, 15–75 cm long. **Flowers** large, fragrant, brown or purplish-brown; lip cream with 3 magenta streaks in centre or pink. **Sepals** and **petals** spathulate-oblanceolate, undulate, 2.6–3.3 cm long, obtuse or mucronate. **Lip** adnate to base of column, 3-lobed, 3.3–4 cm long; side lobes oblong, clasping column, 1.2–1.5 cm long, 0.6 cm broad; mid-lobe suborbicular to ovate, 2.3–3.2 cm long, 2.1–3.4 cm broad, emarginate; callus elliptic, sulcate, passing into 3 fleshy veins on mid-lobe. **Column** 1.5–1.7 cm long, dilated in middle; mid-tooth oblong.

DISTRIBUTION Mexico, Central America, Colombia and Venezuela; sea level to 900 m altitude in rather dry forests.

HISTORY Described by F.H.A. von Humboldt, A. Bonpland and C.S. Kunth in *Nova Genera et Species Plantarum* (p. 341) in 1815 as *Cymbidium cordigerum* but later transferred firstly to *Epidendrum* and later in 1964 to *Encyclia* by R. Dressler in *Taxon* (p. 247). This species is the *Epidendrum atropurpureum* of most authors and it is most frequently cultivated under that name. However, H.G. Reichenbach misapplied the name to this species and unfortunately most authors followed him in this usage.

It is a handsome species, easily recognised by the large mid-lobe to the lip, the narrow lateral lobes, low callus and wide fleshy sepals. Many varieties of this species are grown; most varying in flower colour.

SYNONYMS include *Epidendrum atropurpureum* auct.; *E. macrochilum* Hooker; *Encyclia doeringii* Hoehne

Encyclia fragrans (Sw.) Lemée [Colour Plate]

An erect, stout plant with a creeping rhizome, up to 40 cm tall. **Pseudobulbs** narrowly ellipsoid or fusiform, 5–11 cm long, up to 3 cm in diameter, 1-leafed at apex, subtended by membranous sheaths. **Leaf** coriaceous, ligulate-oblong to elliptic-lanceolate, 10–30 cm long, up to 4.5 cm broad, obtuse, longer than inflorescences. **Inflorescence** few- to several-flowered, racemose, up to 17 cm long with several keeled sheaths at base. **Flowers** non-resupinate, strongly scented, cream to pale greenish-white; lip white, with purple longitudinal stripes along veins. **Sepals** elliptic-lanceolate, spreading, 1.5–3.5 cm long, 0.5 cm broad, acuminate. **Petals** clawed, ovate-lanceolate, 2–3 cm long, acute or acuminate. **Lip** fleshy, erect, ovate, cupped, shortly adnate at column-base, acuminate, 1.5–2.4 cm long, 0.9–1.7 cm broad; disc nervose with 2 small parallel calli at base, **Column** clavate, winged on both sides, dorsally keeled, apically tridentate, up to 0.6–0.8 cm long.

DISTRIBUTION Common in Mexico, Central America, northern S. America and the W. Indies; up to 1500 m.

HISTORY A very variable species, first described by O. Swartz in his *Prodromus* (p. 123) of West Indian Plants (1788) as *Epidendrum fragrans*. Subsequently it has been transferred to the genus *Encyclia* by A. Lemée in the *Flore de la Guyane Française* (1955). *E. fragrans* was one of the first epiphytic orchids to be successfully grown and flowered in cultivation in the late eigthteenth century (1787 at Kew).

CLOSELY RELATED SPECIES *Encyclia spondiada* (Rchb.f.) Dressler [Colour Plate] is allied to *E. fragrans*, *E. vespa*, *E. cochleata* and related species in sect. *Osmophytum*. It is readily distinguished by its long, many-flowered inflorescence, its maroon-spotted segments and its rhombic lip. *E. fragrans* may be distinguished from *E. baculus*, *E. radiata* and *E. cochleata* by unifoliate pseudobulb and rather lax, several-flowered inflorescence.

Encyclia glumacea (Lindl.) Pabst
[Colour Plate]
See under *Encyclia bulbosa*.

Encyclia guatemalensis (Klotzsch) Dressler & Pollard
Pseudobulbs clustered, conical to ovoid, 2.5–5 cm long, 1.8–3.5 cm broad, 2- or 3-leaved. **Leaves** linear-ligulate, 9–32 cm long, 1–2.3 cm broad, acute. **Inflorescence** racemose or paniculate, several- to many-flowered, 17–60 cm long; pedicel and ovary slightly warty. **Flowers** with sepals and petals green, suffused red-brown or chocolate above; lip white with a yellow margin or yellow, purple-veined on mid-lobe. **Sepals** elliptic to obovate-oblanceolate, concave, 1.2–1.7 cm long, up to 0.7 cm broad, acute or obtuse. **Petals** obliquely obovate or spathulate, up to 1.6 m long, acute or obtuse. **Lip** adnate to column at base, 3-lobed, up to 1.5 cm long; side lobes clasping column, oblong or ovate-oblong, up to 0.75 cm long, 0.3–0.5 cm broad; mid-lobe suborbicular, undulate, 0.8 cm long and broad, acute or truncate; callus 2-ridged; veins on lip mid-lobe prominent. **Column** clavate, 0.5–0.8 cm long, winged; mid-tooth obtuse, short.
DISTRIBUTION Guatemala, Honduras, El Salvador, Nicaragua and Mexico; 100–1300 m altitude in a variety of forest types.
HISTORY Originally described in 1852 by O. Klotzsch as *Epidendrum guatemalensis* in F. Otto and A. Dietrich's *Allgemeine Gartenzeitung* (p. 250) based on a plant from Guatemala which flowered in the collection of Herr Kunst. R. Dressler and G. Pollard transferred it in 1971 to *Encyclia* in *Phytologia* (p. 437).

E. guatemalensis is one of a large group of similar small-flowered species such as *E. belizensis*, *E. selligera* and *E. hanburyi* but it may be readily distinguished by its yellow lip lined with purple on the mid-lobe, by its broad dark sepals and petals and by its broad, bowed column which has large squarish wings at the apex.
SYNONYMS *Epidendrum guatemalensis* Klotzsch; *E. dickinsonianum* Withner

Encyclia hanburyi (Lindl.) Schltr.
Pseudobulbs clustered, conical-ovoid, 2.5–8 cm long, 2–4 cm broad, 1- to 2-leaved. **Leaves** elliptic-lanceolate or elliptic-oblong, 8–23 cm long, 1–3 cm broad, obtuse. **Inflorescence** racemose or paniculate, 10- to 35-flowered, up to 100 cm long. **Flowers** showy, brownish-purple; lip white or pink, veined purple. **Sepals**

oblanceolate to spathulate, 1.7–2.4 cm long, 0.5–0.9 cm broad, acute. **Petals** broadly spathulate to obovate, 1.6–2.3 cm long, 0.5–1.1 cm broad, obtuse to mucronate. **Lip** adnate to column at base, 3-lobed, 1.7–2.2 cm long; side lobes pandurate-oblong, spreading, clasping column at base, 0.8–1.2 cm long; mid-lobe suborbicular or subreniform, up to 1.3 cm long, 1.7 cm broad, obtuse or retuse, margins undulate; callus obovate to ovate, sulcate, puberulent, passing into a keel on mid-lobe. **Column** 1 cm long, arcuate; mid-tooth short, triangular.
DISTRIBUTION Mexico; 1200–1800 m altitude in dry oak or scrub oak forests.
HISTORY First cultivated in Europe by Robert Hanbury of Stamford Hill, England. He sent a specimen to John Lindley who described it in 1844 in the *Botanical Register* (misc. 46) as *Epidendrum hanburyi*. Rudolf Schlechter transferred it to *Encyclia* in *Die Orchideen* in 1914.

This is an attractive species distinguished by the long lateral lobes of the lip which are widened near their apices; the large, smooth mid-lobe; and the short high callus.
SYNONYM *Epidendrum hanburyi* Lindl.

Encyclia livida (Lindl.) Dressler
An epiphytic plant, up to 30 cm tall. **Pseudobulbs** 3–3.5 cm apart on rhizome, stalked, fusiform, somewhat flattened, 3.5–8.5 cm long, 0.6–2.6 cm broad, 2-leaved at apex. **Leaves** elliptic or ligulate-elliptic, 11–22 cm long, 0.8–1.8 cm broad, acute or obtuse. **Inflorescence** 3- to 7-flowered, 10–15 cm long. **Flowers** non-resupinate, about 1.5 cm across, pale green, ± heavily suffused orange-brown with a yellow lip lined with red-brown on side lobes. **Sepals** oblong or obovate-oblong, up to 1.1 cm long, 0.5 cm broad, acute or mucronate. **Petals** obovate to oblanceolate, slightly falcate, 1 cm long, 0.4 cm broad, obtuse. **Lip** obscurely 3-lobed, adnate at base to column, up to 1.1 cm long, 0.6 cm broad; side lobes obtuse, 0.2 cm broad and long; mid-lobe orbicular, 0.6 cm in diameter, margin crisped; callus on mid-lobe consisting of 3 verrucose ridges, pubescent. **Column** stout, 0.5 cm long; mid-tooth truncate, longer than side teeth.
DISTRIBUTION Columbia, Venezuela, Central America, north to Mexico; sea level to 1000 m in a variety of forest types.
HISTORY Described in 1838 by John Lindley in the *Botanical Register* (misc. 51) as *Epidendrum lividum* and transferred in 1961 by Robert Dressler to *Encyclia* in *Brittonia* (p. 264). This species is still grown under the synonyms *Encyclia tessellata* and *E. deamii*.

E. livida is the only species of sect. *Osmophytum* with a warty lip and it is quite distinct vegetatively from the other warty-lipped *Encyclia* species.

SYNONYMS *Epidendrum lividum* Lindl.; *E. tessellatum* Batem. ex Lindl.; *E. articulatum* Klotzsch; *E. condylochilum* Lehm. & Kraenzl.; *E. henricii* Schltr.; *E. deamii* Schltr.; *E. dasytaenia* Schltr.; *Encyclia deamii* (Schltr.) Hoehne

Encyclia maculosa (A.H.S.) Hoehne
Pseudobulbs loosely clustered, about 2 cm apart on rhizome, conical-ovoid to fusiform-ovoid, 4–12 cm long, 1–2.7 cm broad, 2- or 3-leaved at apex. **Leaves** elliptic to oblong-ligulate, 6–28 cm long, 0.9–2 cm broad, obtuse or acute. **Inflorescence** 3- to 20-flowered, 6–20 cm long. **Flowers** non-resupinate, orange or orange-brown, ± spotted red-brown; lip white with purple spots. **Sepals** obovate to oblanceolate, 0.5–0.7 cm long, 0.3 cm broad, acute to subobtuse, ± warty on outside. **Petals** cuneate-oblanceolate or spathulate, arched, 0.5–0.7 cm long, 0.3 cm broad, mucronate. **Lip** adnate to basal quarter of column, 3-lobed, up to 0.65 cm long; side lobes clasping column, oblong, 0.3 cm long; mid-lobe oblong-ovate to triangular-ovate, up to 3 cm long, 1.2 cm broad, obtuse; callus thick, obovate, tridentate at front. **Column** up to 0.5 cm long; teeth digitate, subequal.
DISTRIBUTION Mexico; 1400–2400 m altitude in pine/oak or mixed forests.
HISTORY Described originally as *Epidendrum maculosum* by Oakes Ames, Hubbard and C. Schweinfurth in 1935 in the *Botanical Museum Leaflets of Harvard University* (p. 72) based on an H. Galeotti specimen collected in Oaxaca, Mexico. In 1952 F.C. Hoehne transferred it to *Encyclia* in *Arquivos Botanicos do Estado de São Paulo* (p. 151).
SYNONYMS *Epidendrum maculosum* A.H.S.; *E. guttatum* A. Rich. & Galeotti non L.; *Encyclia guttata* (A. Rich. & Galeotti) Schltr.
CLOSELY RELATED SPECIES *E. ochracea* is closely related but has smaller flowers which are never warty on the outside and a smaller lip with an oblong mid-lobe.

Encyclia mariae (Ames) Hoehne
[Colour Plate]
A medium-sized pendent epiphytic species. **Pseudobulbs** ovoid, clustered, 2–4 cm long, 1.5–2.8 cm in diameter, 2- to 3-leaved at apex. **Leaves** oblong or elliptic-oblong, acute, 9–18 cm long, 1.5–2.8 cm broad. **Inflorescence** sub-erect to arching, 2- to 4-flowered, 5–27 cm long. **Flowers** large, showy; sepals and petals yellow to olive-green; lip white with green veins in the throat. **Sepals** elliptic to oblanceolate, obtuse or acute, fleshy, 3.3–4.4 cm long, 0.7–1.1 cm broad. **Petals** oblanceolate or elliptic-oblanceolate, acute, 3.3–4.3 cm long, 0.5–0.8 cm broad. **Lip** basally adnate to the column, subpandurate to oblong-elliptic, 4.7–7.5 cm

long, 3–4.8 cm broad, enfolding the column at the base, deeply retuse at the apex, somewhat undulate-crisped; callus bilamellate, 1.8–3 cm long. **Column** 1.7–1.9 cm long; apical teeth fleshy, truncate, subequal.

DISTRIBUTION Mexico only; 1000–1200 m altitude in dry oak forest.

HISTORY Only discovered in 1937 by E. Oestlund in N. Mexico near the Texas border and described by Oakes Ames in the same year in the *Botanical Museum Leaflets of Harvard University* (p. 36). F.C. Hoehne transferred it to *Encyclia* in 1952 in the *Arquivos Botanicos do Estado de São Paulo* (p. 152).

CLOSELY RELATED SPECIES Allied to *E. citrina* but easily distinguished by its differently coloured flowers.

Encyclia megalantha (Barb. Rodr.) Porto & Brade [Colour Plate]
See under *Encyclia belizensis*.

Encyclia ochracea (Lindl.) Dressler
A medium-sized epiphytic plant. **Pseudobulbs** loosely clustered on rhizome, narrowly ovoid to fusiform-ovoid, 3.5–8 cm long, 0.5–2 cm in diameter, 2- or 3-leaved at apex. **Leaves** narrowly ligulate-elliptic or ligulate-lanceolate, acute or narrowly obtuse, 6–23 cm long, 0.4–1.2 cm broad. **Inflorescence** simple, 6- to 12-flowered, 4–15 cm long; basal sheath 1–2.5 cm long. **Flowers** small, non-resupinate; sepals and petals yellow-brown or brown; lip white with a few red spots, yellowing with age. **Sepals** oblong to oblong-obovate, obtuse or acute, 0.38–0.6 cm long, 0.15–0.25 cm broad. **Petals** cuneate-oblanceolate to obovate, obtuse, 0.36–0.55 cm long, 0.12–0.2 cm broad. **Lip** adnate to basal quarter of column, 3-lobed, 0.32–0.45 cm long; side lobes clasping column, ± subquadrate; mid-lobe triangular-oblong to subquadrate, obtuse or retuse; callus quadrate-oblong, distantly tridentate, mid-vein of mid-lobe crenate. **Column** 0.3–0.4 cm long; apical teeth lacerate.

DISTRIBUTION Costa Rica to Mexico; 800–3000 m altitude in a variety of habitats, although it is commonly a weed in coffee plantations.

HISTORY First collected by George Ure Skinner in Guatemala and described by John Lindley in 1838 in the *Botanical Register* (t. 26, misc. 14) as *Epidendrum ochraceum*. In 1961 R. Dressler transferred it to *Encyclia* in *Brittonia* (p. 264).

SYNONYMS *Epidendrum ochraceum* Lindl.; *E. triste* A. Rich. & Galeotti; *E. parviflorum* Sesse & Mociño

CLOSELY RELATED SPECIES Plants in cultivation as *E. ochracea* are often referable to *E. maculosa* which is easily distinguished by its

flowers which are echinate-warty on the outer surface.

Encyclia polybulbon (Sw.) Dressler
[Colour Plate]
A dwarf creeping epiphyte with an elongate rhizome. **Pseudobulbs** 0.5–3.5 cm apart on the rhizome, ovoid or narrowly ovoid, 1.1–1.2 cm long, 0.3–0.7 cm in diameter. 1- to 3-leaved at the apex. **Leaves** elliptic-lanceolate to elliptic-ovate, retuse, 1–1.5 cm long, 0.4–0.9 cm wide. **Inflorescence** 1-flowered, 1.5–3 cm long; peduncle short, subtended by a slender spathe 1.5–2 cm long. **Flower** large for plant, the sepals and petals pale yellow heavily suffused with brown, the lip white; pedicel and ovary 1–1.5 cm long. **Sepals** spreading, linear-oblanceolate, acute, 0.9–1.7 cm long, 0.15–0.3 cm wide. **Petals** linear-spathulate, acute, 0.8–1.4 cm long, 0.1–0.2 cm wide. **Lip** adnate to the column for the basal 1 mm, clawed, suborbicular above, 1.1–1.4 cm long, 1 cm wide; callus on claw, with 2 low fleshy ridges beneath the column. **Column** fleshy, 7 mm long, with 2 porrect apical toothed obliquely lanceolate wings.

DISTRIBUTION Widespread in Central America from Mexico to Honduras, also in Cuba and Jamaica; in fairly humid mixed forest, 600–2000 m.

HISTORY This pretty little orchid was originally described as *Epidendrum polybulbon* by Olof Swartz in 1788 in his *Nova genera et species seu prodromus . . . . Indiam occidentalem* (p. 124) based on a collection from Jamaica. John Lindley (1831) placed it in its own genus *Dinema* in his *Genera and Species of Orchidaceous Plants* (p. 111) on account of its unusual column morphology, particularly the elongate apical wings. We have, however, followed Dressler (1961) who transferred it to *Encyclia* in *Brittonia* (p. 265) because of its intermediate position between sects. *Osmophytum* and *Encyclia*.

SYNONYMS *Epidendrum polybulbon* Sw.; *Dinema polybulbon* (Sw.) Lindl.; *Bulbophyllum occidentale* Spreng.

Encyclia pygmaea (Hooker) Dressler
A creeping, rhizomatous epiphytic herb, up to 6 cm high. **Rhizome** branching. **Pseudobulbs** about 3 cm apart on rhizome, ovoid or ellipsoid, 2-leaved at apex, each pseudobulb subtended by 2 scarious sheaths. **Leaves** narrowly ovate to elliptic, up to 3.5 cm long, 1.3 cm broad, acute. **Inflorescence** 1-flowered, terminal. **Flowers** minute, up to 0.5 cm long, fleshy, pale green, flushed maroon. **Sepals** lanceolate, 0.5 cm long, 0.2 cm broad, acuminate; lateral sepals adnate in basal quarter. **Petals** ligulate-lanceolate, up to 0.5 cm long, acute. **Lip** adnate to base of column, free part clawed, 3-lobed, 0.3–0.5 cm long, 0.5 cm broad; side

erect around column, rotund; mid-lobe much smaller, triangular. **Column** short, fleshy, 0.2 cm long.

DISTRIBUTION Common throughout tropical America including Florida.

HISTORY Described by Sir William Hooker in the *Journal of Botany* (p. 49, t. 118) in 1833 as *Epidendrum pygmaeum* based on a Brazilian specimen cultivated by Harrison and subsequently transferred in 1961 by R. Dressler to the genus *Encyclia* in *Brittonia* (p. 265).

SYNONYMS include *Epidendrum pygmaeum* Hooker; *E. caespitosum* Poepp. & Endl.; *E. uniflorum* Lindl.; *Hormidium pygmaeum* (Hooker) Benth. & Hooker f.; *H. uniflorum* (Lindl.) Heynh.; *Microstylis humilis* Cogn.

Encyclia radiata (Lindl.) Dressler
Pseudobulb ellipsoid to elliptic-ovoid, somewhat flattened, grooved, 2–2.5 cm apart on rhizome, 7–11 cm long, 1.2–3 cm in diameter, 2- to 4-leaved. **Leaves** lanceolate-elliptic, 14–35 cm long, 1.4–3 cm broad, obtuse or broadly acute. **Inflorescence** 4- to 12-flowered, 7–20 cm long. **Flowers** non-resupinate, creamy or greenish-white with a violet-lined lip. **Sepals** elliptic, up to 2 cm long, 0.7 cm broad, acute. **Petals** elliptic-obovate, or broadly elliptic, up to 2 cm long, 1.1 cm broad, acute. **Lip** adnate to column for half length of column; lamina triangular-reniform, concave, 1.0–1.3 cm long, 1.3–2 cm broad, apex notched, base truncate; callus quadrate-oblong, smooth. **Column** stout 0.8–1 cm long; mid-tooth merging into a broad fan-shaped erose ligule.

DISTRIBUTION Guatemala, Honduras and Mexico; 150–2000 m altitude in various forest types from tropical evergreen to mixed pine/oak forest.

HISTORY Commonly grown, but often misidentified in orchid collections. *E. radiata* was described originally by John Lindley as *Epidendrum radiatum* in the *Botanical Register* (misc. 58) of 1841. In 1961 R. Dressler transferred it to the genus *Encyclia* in *Brittonia* (p. 264).

It is easily recognised by its broad, notched lip and the broad ligule at the apex of the column.

SYNONYM *Epidendrum radiatum* Lindl.

Encyclia selligera (Lindl.) Schltr.
[Colour Plate]
Pseudobulbs clustered, conical-ovoid, 4.5–5.8 cm long, 2–2.5 cm broad, 2-leaved. **Leaves** ligulate or elliptic-ligulate, 15–24.5 cm long, 1.7–4 cm broad, obtuse. **Inflorescence** paniculate, many-flowered, up to 80 cm long. **Flowers** pale green, streaked or suffused reddish-brown; lip cream or pink, ± with basal darker streaks. **Sepals** spathulate-oblanceolate, 1.8–2.4 cm long, 0.5–0.9 cm broad, acute or obtuse. **Petals**

spathulate, 1.8–2.1 cm long, 0.7–0.9 cm broad, obtuse or mucronate. **Lip** adnate to column-base, 3-lobed, 1.7–2.2 cm long; side lobes obliquely ovate-oblong, clasping column at base, up to 1 cm long; mid-lobe suborbicular to ovate, 0.8–1.1 cm long, obtuse; callus 2-keeled at base passing into 3 veins on mid-lobe. **Column** arcuate, dilated near apex, 1.1–1.3 cm long; mid-tooth short, triangular-oblong.

DISTRIBUTION Guatemala and Mexico; 1300–2200 m altitude in oak and oak/pine forests.

HISTORY Described as *Epidendrum selligerum* by John Lindley in 1838 in the *Botanical Register* (misc. 40) based on a specimen collected by George Ure Skinner in Guatemala. James Bateman suggested the specific epithet. In 1914 R. Schlechter transferred it to *Encyclia* in *Die Orchideen* (p. 210).

E. *selligera* may be recognised by its large, branched inflorescences, broad petals which curve upwards, and the white or pink lip with a smooth mid-lobe and recurved side lobes.

SYNONYM *Epidendrum selligerum* Lindl.

Encyclia spondiada (Rchb.f.) Dressler
[Colour Plate]
See under *Encyclia fragrans*.

Encyclia vagans (Ames) Dressler & Pollard.
[Colour Plate]
Pseudobulbs widely spaced on rhizome, up to 7 cm apart, fusiform or ovoid-fusiform, 4.5–5.5 cm long, 1.2–1.5 cm broad, 2- to 4-leaved at apex. **Leaves** ligulate to elliptic-ligulate, up to 12 cm long, 2.5 cm broad, obliquely retuse. **Inflorescence** 2- to 4-flowered, up to 8 cm long. **Flowers** non-resupinate, white or cream, purple-streaked at base of tepals and on lip. **Sepals** elliptic-lanceolate, 1.9–2.4 cm long, 0.5 cm broad, acuminate. **Petals** elliptic or ovate-elliptic, 1.8 cm long, 0.5 cm broad, acute to acuminate. **Lip** adnate to column for half the length of column; lamina ovate, cordate at base, 1.5 cm long, 0.7–1 cm broad, acute to acuminate; callus oblong, pubescent. **Column** up to 0.6 cm long; mid-tooth rounded, shorter than side teeth; ligule sublinear, tridenticulate.
DISTRIBUTION Guatemala to Costa Rica and Mexico; at 1400 m altitude in rather wet oak/pine forests.
HISTORY Described in 1923 by Oakes Ames in *Schedulae Orchidianae* (p. 76) as *Epidendrum vagans* from a plant collected by Charles Lankester in Costa Rica. Over many years Lankester systematically collected the orchids of Costa Rica and in doing so discovered many new and little-known species. R. Dressler and G. Pollard transferred it in 1971 to *Encyclia* in *Phytologia* (p. 438).
SYNONYM *Epidendrum vagans* Ames

CLOSELY RELATED SPECIES Differs from *E. fragrans* in its many-leaved pseudobulbs, long creeping rhizome and pubescent callus.

Encyclia vespa (Vell.) Dressler
[Colour Plate]
A very variable epiphytic species, up to 45 cm tall. **Pseudobulbs** erect, orbicular to fusiform, compressed, 6–20 cm long, 1.5–5 cm broad, 2-leaved, smooth shiny green. **Leaves** oblong-ligulate, up to 25 cm long, 2 cm broad, acute. **Inflorescence** racemose, erect, terminal, few- to many-flowered, up to 30 cm long; bracts small. **Flowers** non-resupinate, creamy-green or yellowish-green, heavily spotted maroon; lip white with pink markings; column pale green. **Sepals** ovate to obovate, obtuse, up to 1.3 cm long, 0.6 cm broad. **Petals** obovate-ligulate, 1.1 cm long, 0.4 cm broad, obtuse. **Lip** adnate to column for half length of column, free part fleshy, entire or very obscurely 3-lobed, transversely elliptic to cordate, apiculate, 0.8 cm long, 0.9 cm broad; callus oblong, retuse, anteriorly pubescent. **Column** rather thick, 0.5 cm long; mid-tooth rounded.
DISTRIBUTION Common epiphyte throughout tropical America.
HISTORY First described by J.M. Velloso in *Flora Fluminense* (t. 27) in 1827 as *Epidendrum vespa*, this very variable species has since been redescribed many times. Recently, R. Dressler has transferred it to the genus *Encyclia* in 1971 in *Phytologia* (p. 441), on account of its partially adnate lip and pseudobulbous stem.
SYNONYMS include *Epidendrum variegatum* Hooker; *E. tigrinum* Linden ex Lindl.; *E. coriaceum* Hooker; *E. leopardinum* Rchb.f.; *E. rhabdobulbon* Schltr.; *E. crassilabium* Poepp. & Endl.; *E. vespa* Vell.
CLOSELY RELATED SPECIES See *E. fragrans*.

Encyclia vitellina (Lindl.) Dressler
[Colour Plate]
A medium-sized epiphytic plant. **Pseudobulbs** clustered, ovoid-conical, slightly flattened, 2.5–5 cm long, 1.5–3 cm in diameter, 1- to 3-leaved at apex. **Leaves** lanceolate-elliptic to elliptic, obtuse or subacute, 7–22 cm long, 0.8–3.6 cm broad. **Inflorescence** simple or few-branched, 4- to 12-flowered, 12–30 cm long; basal spathe up to 1.5 cm long. **Flowers** showy, flat; sepals and petals vermilion; lip and column yellow or orange with lip apex orange-red. **Sepals** lanceolate-elliptic or ovate-elliptic, acute, 1.5–2 cm long, 0.3–0.8 cm broad. **Petals** elliptic, acute, 1.7–2.3 cm long, 0.6–1.1 cm broad. **Lip** basally adnate to the column, 1.1–1.6 cm long, 0.3–0.5 cm broad, elliptic or oblong-elliptic, acute; callus oblong.

Column 0.6–0.7 cm long; apical mid-tooth subquadrate, shorter than side teeth.
DISTRIBUTION Mexico and Guatemala; 1500–2000 m in oak, oak/pine or cloud forests or in scrub on lava flow.
HISTORY Originally described as *Epidendrum vitellinum* by John Lindley in 1831 in his *Genera and Species of Orchidaceous Plants* (p. 97) based on a specimen supposedly collected by J. Pavon in Mexico. R. Dressler transferred it to *Encyclia* in 1961 in *Brittonia* (p. 264).

E. *vitellina* is the only species of Central America *Encyclia* with scarlet flowers.
SYNONYM *Epidendrum vitellinum* Lindl.

Epidanthus L.O. Williams
Subfamily Epidendroideae
Tribe Epidendreae
Subtribe Laeliinae

Dwarf epiphytes with slender elongate leafy branched or unbranched stems and lacking pseudobulbs. **Leaves** linear, distichous, coriaceous. **Inflorescences** terminal, unbranched, fractiflex, few-flowered. **Flowers** small, fleshy, green. **Sepals** and **petals** free, subsimilar, spreading to reflexed; the petals with a callus at the base. **Lip** entire or 3-lobed, concave. **Column** united to the lip for its entire length; pollinia 2, waxy, attached to a distinct viscidium of rostellar origin.
DISTRIBUTION Three species distributed from Mexico to Panama.
DERIVATION OF NAME The name derives from the resemblance of the flowers to those of *Epidendrum*, of which *Epidanthus* is a segregate genus, the first part of the name, *epi*, being taken from *Epidendrum* while the last part comes from the Greek *anthos* (flower).
TAXONOMY The American Botanist L.O. Williams established this genus in 1940 in the *Botanical Museum Leaflets of Harvard University* (p. 148). It is a segregate genus of *Epidendrum* distinguished by the presence of a viscidium derived from the rostellum. A key to the recognised species is given by Dressler in 1983 in *Orquidea* (*Mex.*) (p. 20).
TYPE SPECIES *Epidendrum paranthicum* Reichb.f.
CULTURE Temp. Winter min. 12°C. Requires shady humid conditions without a marked dry season. Probably best mounted, but small plants might adapt to pot culture.

Epidanthus paranthicus (Reichb.f.) L.O. Williams
A dwarf much branched epiphyte often growing in dense masses with slender stems up to 25 cm long and covered by sheathing leaf bases.

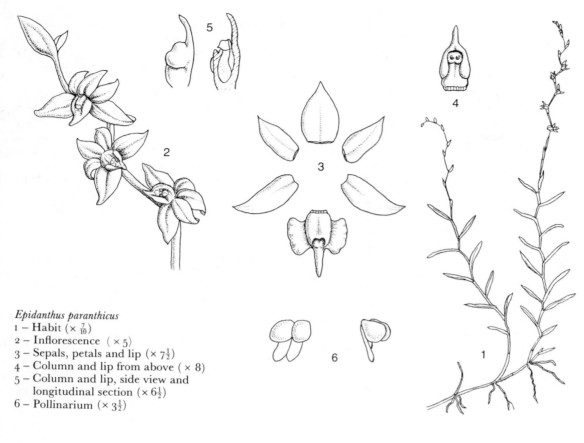

Epidanthus paranthicus
1 – Habit (× $\frac{7}{10}$)
2 – Inflorescence (× 5)
3 – Sepals, petals and lip (× $7\frac{1}{2}$)
4 – Column and lip from above (× 8)
5 – Column and lip, side view and
   longitudinal section (× $6\frac{1}{2}$)
6 – Pollinarium (× $3\frac{1}{2}$)

Leaves erect-spreading or recurved, distichous, fleshy, narrowly linear, 1–2.5 cm long, 1–1.5 mm wide, articulated to sheathing bases. **Inflorescence** terminal, laxly few-flowered, fractiflex; bracts ovate, acuminate, keeled on back, 2–3 mm long. **Flowers** small, yellow, yellowish-green or white, marked with purple; pedicel and ovary 2–3 mm long. **Sepals** oblong-lanceolate, acute or acuminate, 3–4 mm long, 1–1.5 mm wide. **Petals** obliquely linear-oblong, acute, 2–2.5 mm long, 0.7–1.2 mm wide. **Lip** with a short broad claw adnate to the column, deeply 3-lobed above, somewhat reniform when spread, 2–3 mm long, 2.5–3 mm wide; side lobes obliquely oblong, rounded in front; mid-lobe linear, acuminate; callus fleshy on the disc of the lip. **Column** c. 1 mm long, fleshy.
DISTRIBUTION Mexico to Panama. in humid forests up to 1800 m.
HISTORY First described in 1852 as *Epidendrum paranthicum* by H.G. Reichenbach in the journal *Botanische Zeitung* (p. 732). The American botanist L.O. Williams transferred it to his new genus *Epidanthus* in the *Botanical Museum Leaflets of Harvard University* (p. 150) in 1940.
SYNONYM *Epidendrum paranthicum* Reichb.f.

Epidendrum L.
Subfamily Epidendroideae
Tribe Epidendreae
Subtribe Laeliinae

Epiphytic, terrestrial or lithophytic plants, very small to large, erect or creeping, with or without a conspicuous rhizome. **Stems** caulescent, rarely pseudobulbous, ± branching, 1- to many-leaved. **Leaves** terete or flattened, linear to ovate, rounded to long-acuminate. **Inflorescences** terminal or rarely lateral, racemose, subumbellate to paniculate, erect or arcuate. **Flowers** very small to large and showy. **Segments** ± spreading. **Lip** adnate to column-apex; lamina entire or 3-lobed, smooth or callose. **Column** short to elongate, wingless to prominently winged; anther terminal; pollinia 4, equal, waxy, more or less compressed.
DISTRIBUTION One of the largest genera with several hundred species, widely distributed throughout the tropical Americas from N. Carolina, south to Argentina.
DERIVATION OF NAME From the Greek *epi* (upon) and *dendron* (tree), referring to the epiphytic habit of most species in the genus.
TAXONOMY *Epidendrum* was first described

by Carl von Linné (Linnaeus) in *Species Plantarum* in 1753. However, the use of the generic name in the 2nd edition of *Species Plantarum* (p. 1347) in 1763 has been conserved along with the type accepted for that description. *Epidendrum* was the first genus of New World orchids to be described and nearly all of those American epiphytic species collected before 1800 were placed in the genus. With better understanding of the great diversity of New World orchids the delimitation of the genus *Epidendrum* has become better defined and many species have been removed to distinct genera. Even so, *Epidendrum* is probably the largest genus of New World orchids. With such a large genus it is inevitable that attempts continue to try and separate groups previously referred to *Epidendrum*, as distinct genera. One of the most inportant has been the removal of those species with distinct pseudobulbs and a lip adnate only at the column-base as *Encyclia*. Other genera now considered as distinct from *Epidendrum* by most authorities include *Jacquiniella*, *Barkeria*, *Oerstedella* and *Amblostoma*.
TYPE SPECIES *E. nocturnum* Jacq.
CULTURE Compost A. Temp. Winter min. 12–15°C, depending on plant origin. The small creeping species grow well in shallow pans or mounted on cork or fern-fibre. Pseudobulbous species do best in pots or pans and require a drier rest when the pseudobulbs are fully grown. Many of the so-called reed-stemmed species grow equally well in pots, or as terrestrials in beds. In all cases, moderate shade is

Epidendrum lips and columns
1 – *E. coronatum* (× $1\frac{1}{5}$)
2 – *E. cristatum* (× $1\frac{1}{5}$)
3 – *E. secundum* (× $2\frac{2}{5}$)
4 – *E. difforme* (× $1\frac{1}{5}$)

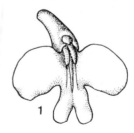
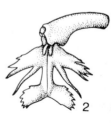
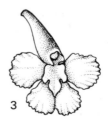
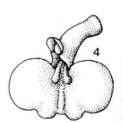

required during the summer, and plenty of water during active growth.

Epidendrum anceps Jacq. [Colour Plate]

An epiphytic or occasionally lithophytic plant, up to 70 cm tall. **Stems** erect, clustered, leafy. **Leaves** about 4 per stem, oblong-elliptic, up to 15 cm long, 4 cm broad, obtuse, green, ± fleck-ed with purple. **Inflorescence** terminal on stem, subumbellate; peduncle long, compressed and covered with scarious sheaths; rhachis ter-ete, brownish-purple. **Flowers** yellowish-brown to greenish-brown, shiny, up to 1.5 cm across; lip pale green, flushed pink; column green, flushed with purple. **Sepals** fleshy, oblong, up to 0.7 cm long, 0.3 cm broad, obtuse. **Petals** narrower than petals, linear, up to 0.6 cm long. **Lip** adnate to column, free part 3-lobed, 0.5 cm long; side lobes elliptic, short; mid-lobe extend-ing beyond side lobes, bifid, with a short, rounded tooth between the lobules. **Column** 0.5 cm long.
DISTRIBUTION Common throughout the American tropics.
HISTORY Described by N.J. Jacquin in *Selectarum Stirpium Americanarum* (p. 224, t. 138) in 1763. Since that time it has been redescribed many times from various parts of its wide range. Recently, in the *Flora of the Lesser Antilles*, L. Garay and H. Sweet have used the name *Epidendrum secundum* for this species as they con-sider that Jacquin's name has been misapplied in the past. Whatever the merits of this conclu-sion, the traditional use of the names *E. anceps* and *E. secundum* is retained here to avoid confu-sion.
SYNONYMS include *Epidendrum musciferum* Lindl.; *E. viridipurpureum* Hooker; *E. galeottianum* A. Rich & Galeotti; *E. cearense* Barb. Rodr.

Epidendrum ciliare L. [Colour Plate]

A coarse, epiphytic or lithophytic plant, up to 50 cm tall, caespitose. **Stems** given off from a creeping rhizome, cylindrical to fusiform, 8–20 cm long, 2 cm in diameter. **Leaves** 1 or 2 (rarely 3), rather fleshy, coriaceous, oblong-lanceolate, glossy, 10–28 cm long, 2.5–8 cm across, obtuse. **Inflorescence** few- to many-flowered, racemose, up to 30 cm long, with large basal sheaths which are imbricating, keeled and purple-spotted. **Flowers** fragrant, 10 cm long, large, yellow-green with a white lip. **Sepals** membranaceous, linear-lanceolate, up to 9 cm long, 0.5 cm broad, acute or acu-minate. **Petals** similar to sepals, slightly smal-ler, obscurely falcate. **Lip** adnate to the basal half of the column, deeply 3-lobed; side lobes narrowly semiovate, deeply and irregularly long-fringed on outer margins, up to 3.5 cm long, 0.4 cm broad; mid-lobe linear, rigid, up to 6 cm long; disc 3-keeled, the middle one ex-tending the length of the lip. **Column** clavate, arcuate, up to 1.8 cm long.
DISTRIBUTION A common and wide-spread species from the W. Indies to Central America and northern S. America.
HISTORY One of the few tropical orchids described by Carl von Linné in 1759 in his *Systema Naturae* (p. 1246).
CLOSELY RELATED SPECIES Easily distinguished from other large white-flowered *Epidendrum* species such as *E. nocturnum* and *E. latifolium* by its fringed side lobes on the lip.

Epidendrum coronatum Ruiz & Pavon
[Colour Plate]

An epiphytic, pendent plant with stems grow-ing in tufts. **Stems** subterete, many-leaved above, up to 90 cm long, 1 cm in diameter. **Leaves** distichous, lanceolate or elliptic, sub-coriaceous, 9–17 cm long, 1.5–4 cm broad, acute. **Inflorescence** arcuate or pendent, race-mose, laxly many-flowered, up to 40 cm long. **Flowers** 3–4 cm across, yellow-green becoming creamy, occasionally with a violet or brownish flush at base of sepals and petals. **Sepals** lanceolate-subspathulate, spreading, up to 2.3 cm long, acute or obtuse. **Petals** ligulate-spathulate, up to 2 cm long, obtuse or sub-acute. **Lip** adnate to column, deeply 3-lobed, 1.5–2.2 cm long, 1.7–2.8 cm broad, margins obscurely undulate-crenulate; side lobes sub-orbicular, much larger than midlobe; mid-lobe 2-lobed, divaricate, rounded. **Column** thickened, clavate, up to 1.4 cm long.
DISTRIBUTION Central America, northern S. America and Trinidad.
HISTORY Discovered by H. Ruiz and J. Pavon at Pozuzo in Peru and described by them in their *Systema Vegetabilium Florae Peru-vianae et Chilensis* (p. 242) in 1798. This species is still grown under the later synonym *E. moyobambae* which F. Kraenzlin described in 1905 in *Fedde, Repertorium Specierum Novarum* based on a specimen collected by Weberbauer at Moyobamba, in Peru.
SYNONYMS *Epidendrum moyobambae* Kraenzl.; *E. compositum* Vell.; *E. subpatens* Schltr.; *E. ama-zonicum* Schltr.

Epidendrum cristatum Ruiz & Pavon

A very variable, erect, epiphytic plant growing in clumps. **Stems** numerous, 0.5–2 m long, leafy, with numerous subcoriaceous sheaths. **Leaves** distichous, erect-spreading, coriaceous, elliptic-lanceolate to ligulate-oblong, 10–24 cm long, 1.5–5 cm broad, subacute to obtuse. **In-florescences** terminal, 1 to several, racemose, laxly many-flowered, pendulous, up to 60 cm long; bracts ovate, 0.4–0.9 cm long. **Flowers** fleshy, whitish, yellowish or pale green, ± purple spotted or banded, segments spreading-

reflexed. **Sepals** oblong-elliptic or elliptic, 1.8–2.8 cm long, 0.3–0.7 cm broad, obtuse. **Petals** linear-subspathulate or elongate-oblanceolate, 1.5–2.5 cm long, up to 0.5 cm broad, obtuse, minutely apiculate. **Lip** adnate to column-apex, irregularly 3-lobed, 1–1.5 cm long, slight-ly broader than long; side lobes dentate to lacerate; mid-lobe 2-lobed, each lobe spreading; disc with a 2-lobed callus and a central ridge. **Column** clavate, up to 1.5 cm long.
DISTRIBUTION Mexico, Belize, Guatema-la, northern S. America and Trinidad.
HISTORY First collected by the pioneer Spanish botanists H. Ruiz and J. Pavon at Pozuzo in Peru and described by them in their *Systema Vegetabilium Florae Peruvianae et Chilensis* (p. 243) in 1798. They did more than anyone to open up the vast plant riches of Peru, and to a lesser extent Mexico, to the view of a curious public in Europe.
SYNONYM *Epidendrum raniferum* Lindl.

Epidendrum difforme Jacq.

An erect or pendent plant, up to 50 cm long. **Stems** numerous, leafy, flexuous, covered with persistent sheaths. **Leaves** leathery to fleshy, oblong to elliptic-lanceolate, 2.5–11 cm long, up to 3.5 cm broad, obtuse. **Inflorescence** ter-minal, subumbellate to umbellate, 1- to many-flowered; bracts hyaline, lanceolate, up to 1.5 cm long. **Flowers** white, yellowish or greenish. **Sepals** membranceous. **Dorsal sepal** lan-ceolate to oblong-obovate, 1.2–3 cm long, 0.8 cm broad, acute to obtuse; **lateral sepals** obli-quely elongate-oblong to obovate, 1.2–3 cm long, 0.4–0.9 cm broad, obtuse or shortly acu-minate. **Petals** filiform to ligulate, up to 3 cm long, 0.1–0.7 cm broad, acute. **Lip** adnate to column-apex, transversely reniform, entire to 3-lobed, 0.7–2 cm long, 1–3 cm broad; mid-lobe entire or shortly 2-lobed, truncate; disc with 2 small calli at base.
DISTRIBUTION A wide-ranging species from Florida, Mexico and Central America, the W. Indies and northern S. America.
HISTORY Another species discovered and described in 1760 by N.J. Jacquin in his *Enumeratio Systematica Plantarum* (p. 29). *E. dif-forme* is a very variable species and was later described several times under different names.
SYNONYMS include *Epidendrum umbellatum* Sw.; *E. latilabre* Lindl.

Epidendrum ibaguense H.B.K. [Colour Plate]

A very variable, erect, terrestrial herb, up to or over 100 cm high. **Stems** terete, covered with grey or brown sheaths. **Leaves** elliptic, dis-tichous, up to 10 cm long, 3.5 cm broad, acute or obtuse. **Inflorescence** in a subcapitate raceme, many-flowered. **Flowers** very variable in size and colour, magenta, scarlet, orange or white; callus yellow or white; column ± yellow at apex. **Sepals** narrowly elliptic-lanceolate, 0.8–1.6 cm long, 0.4 cm broad, acute; **lateral sepals** somewhat falcate. **Petals** obliquely lanceolate, acute, 0.7–1.6 cm long, 0.4 cm broad. **Lip** mostly lowermost in flower, adnate to column for length of column, free part 3-lobed; side lobes oblong, decurved, erose to fimbriate; mid-lobe clawed, longer than side lobes, ± bilobulate, erose or fimbriate; callus 3-keeled at apex of column. **Column** ± slender, 1.5 cm long.

DISTRIBUTION Common throughout tropical America; growing in soil or on rocks.

HISTORY Originally described by F.H.A. von Humboldt, A. Bonpland and C.S. Kunth in *Nova Genera et Species Plantarum* (p. 352) in 1815. The great variability of this species has led to it being redescribed many times and several of these names are still to be found on cultivated material.

Var. *schomburgkii* (Lindl.) Schweinf. is commonly found in cultivation. This handsome plant has brick-red flowers which are rather larger than those of the typical variety with the sepals and petals reaching 3 cm in length.

SYNONYMS include *Epidendrum radicans* auct. non Pavon ex Lindl.; *E. calanthum* Rchb.f. & Warsc.; *E. decipiens* Lindl.; *E. fulgens* Brongn.

CLOSELY RELATED SPECIES May be distinguished from *E. secundum* which it closely resembles vegetatively, by the simpler 3-lobed callus and dependent lip. See also *E. imatophyllum*.

Epidendrum imatophyllum Lindl.
[Colour Plate]

An erect terrestrial herb, up to 1 m high. **Stem** somewhat compressed, leafy in apical two-thirds. **Leaves** oblong-ligulate, fleshy, up to 13 cm long, 2.7 cm broad, obtuse to subacute, margins incurved slightly, light green, **Inflorescence** subcorymbose to shortly racemose, erect, up to 25 cm long; peduncle short; bracts lanceolate, acute, short. **Flowers** non-resupinate, rose-pink grading to white at base; lip darker than sepals and petals, callus white; column pale green at base, pink above. **Sepals** oblanceolate, up to 1.6 cm long, 0.4 cm broad, acute; lateral sepals somewhat oblique. **Petals** narrowly rhombic, 1.7 cm long, 0.7 cm broad, acute. **Lip** erect, adnate to column for whole length of column, free part oblong, 0.8 cm long, 0.6 cm broad, very obscurely 3-lobed; side lobes very shallow, fimbriate or erose; mid-lobe transversely oblong to ovate; callus 3-keeled with side keels truncate and mid-keel running on to base of mid-lobe. **Column** sinuate, dilated towards apex, 1 cm long.

DISTRIBUTION Widespread from Mexico south to Peru and Brazil, also in Trinidad.

HISTORY John Lindley described this species in *Genera and Species of Orchidaceous Plants* (p. 106) in 1831.

SYNONYMS *Epidendrum imetrophyllum* Paxt.; *E. palpigenum* Rchb.f.; *E. lorifolium* Schltr.

CLOSELY RELATED SPECIES Not dissimilar to both *E. ibaguense* and *secundum* which, however, have noticeably 3-lobed lips.

Epidendrum latifolium (Lindl.) Garay & Sweet [Colour Plate]

An epiphytic or lithophytic plant, reaching 55 cm tall. **Stems** erect, terete at base but gradually broadening, compressed above, bearing up to 4 distichously arranged leaves. **Leaves** leathery, broadly elliptic to suborbicular, enveloping the stem at the base, up to 14 cm long, 7 cm broad, obtuse or rounded at apex. **Inflorescence** terminal, 1-flowered, similar to that of *E. nocturnum*. **Flowers** yellowish-green to yellowish-brown with a white lip; pedicel and ovary up to 15 cm long. **Sepals** linear-lanceolate, up to 6 cm long, acuminate. **Petals** oblong-ligulate, up to 6 cm long, acuminate. **Lip** adnate to column, up to 5.5 cm long, free part 3-lobed; side lobes narrowly ovate, acute; mid-lobe twice as long as side lobes, linear-filiform, acute.

DISTRIBUTION Central America, the W. Indies and Venezuela.

HISTORY This species was first described by John Lindley as *Epidendrum nocturnum* var. *latifolium* in the *Botanical Register* (t. 1961) in 1837. Until recently it has been treated as a variety of *E. nocturnum* Jacq. However, in 1972 L. Garay and H. Sweet in the *Journal of the Arnold Arboretum* (p. 392) pointed out that there are no intermediate forms between the two and they thus raised var. *latifolium* to specific rank.

SYNONYM *Epidendrum nocturnum* var. *latifolium* Lindl.

CLOSELY RELATED SPECIES *E. latifolium* may be distinguished from *E. nocturnum* by its broader, ancipitous stem, broadly elliptic to suborbicular leaves, much longer pedicellate-ovary and larger flowers. See also *E. ciliare*.

Epidendrum medusae (Rchb.f.) Sieb.
[Colour Plate]

A small epiphyte with clustered leafy stems, up to 25 cm long. **Leaves** coriaceous, narrowly oblong-ovate, unequally bilobed at the apex, up to 8.5 cm long, 3 cm wide, slightly twisted at the base. **Inflorescences** 1 or more, terminal, 1-flowered, very short. **Flowers** large, showy, the sepals, petals and column green or yellowish-green flushed with purple, the lip dark rich maroon with a pale green throat. **Sepals** and **petals** subsimilar, oblong or oblong-lanceolate, acute to obtuse, 2.5–4.2 cm long, 0.8–1.5 cm wide. **Lip** transversely oblong

to subcircular, emarginate, 3.5–4.5 cm long, 4–5.5 cm wide, with deeply lacerate margins, the basal margins upcurved either side of the column-apex. **Column** stout, fleshy, 1.2–1.3 cm long.

DISTRIBUTION Ecuador.

HISTORY This unusual, even striking and aptly-named orchid was introduced into cultivation by Messrs Backhouse of York and was first flowered in England by John Day of Tottenham. It was described in 1867 by H.G. Reichenbach as *Nanodes medusae* in the *Gardeners' Chronicle* (p. 432) and was figured in the *Botanical Magazine* (t. 5723) in the following year. Unfortunately *Nanodes* can doubtfully be maintained as distinct from *Epidendrum* because of the many species with intermediate features. We have, therefore, included it in *Epidendrum* following Siebert who transferred it there in 1900 in the journal *Gartenflora* (p. 516).

SYNONYM *Nanodes medusae* Rchb.f.

Epidendrum nocturnum Jacq. [Colour Plate]

A stout, tufted, epiphytic plant, up to 60 cm tall but often shorter. **Stem** leafy, compressed, erect. **Leaves** leathery, linear-oblong to oblong-ligulate, sessile, up to 14 cm long, 3 cm broad, acute. **Inflorescence** 1- to 2-flowered, terminal; axis up to 2 cm long. **Flowers** showy, large, yellow-green suffused with brownish-purple with a white lip, up to 6 cm across; pedicel with ovary up to 6 cm long. **Dorsal sepal** linear-lanceolate, up to 3 cm long, long-acuminate; **lateral sepals** similar to dorsal sepal. **Petals** linear, up to 3 cm long, acuminate. **Lip** adnate to column, free part deeply 3-lobed; side lobes obliquely ovate, obtuse, entire, up to 1.5 cm long; mid-lobe twice as long as side lobes, linear, long-acuminate; disc with 2 parallel keels.

DISTRIBUTION Very common in tropical Americas.

HISTORY This widely cultivated species was first described by N.J. Jacquin in his *Enumeratio Systematica Plantarum* (p. 29) in 1760 from a plant he collected on the Caribbean island of Martinique.

SYNONYM *Epidendrum nocturnum* var. *angustifolium* Stehlé

CLOSELY RELATED SPECIES See *E. latifolium*, *E. ciliare* and *E. oerstedii*.

Epidendrum oerstedii Rchb.f. [Colour Plate]

A large epiphytic plant with a creeping terete rhizome, 1 cm in diameter. **Stems** erect, 7–15 cm long, the upper 2 internodes swollen and flattened to form a fusiform pseudobulb 5–9 cm long, 1.5–3.5 cm across, shallowly grooved with age. **Leaves** divergent, somewhat recurved, elliptic or oblong-elliptic, rounded or slightly retuse at the apex, 7–16 cm long, 3–5.5 cm broad, deep green. **Inflorescence** arising from the apex of a fertile stem, 2- or 3-flowered; peduncle compressed, grooved, subtended by a pointed green sheath; bracts oblong-lanceolate, subacute, half length of pedicel and ovary. **Flowers** large; sepals and petals lime-green; lip and column white with a yellow callus and greenish apex to the lip; pedicel and ovary up to 9 cm long. **Sepals** and **petals** linear-lanceolate, acuminate, 5–7 cm long. **Lip** 3-lobed above, united to column below, 4.5–6.5 cm long, 2.8–4 cm broad; side lobes divergent, oblique, semiovate, obtuse or acute, outer margins wavy or irregularly toothed; mid-lobe oblanceolate from a narrow base, acuminate, 2.5–3.5 cm long, 0.7 cm broad; callus at apex of column 2-lobed. **Column** 1.5–2.5 cm long, slightly dilated above, apical margins toothed.

DISTRIBUTION Costa Rica and Panama.

HISTORY Collected for the first time in Costa Rica by the Danish botanist A.S. Oersted and described by H.G. Reichenbach in 1852 in the *Botanische Zeitung* (p. 937).

SYNONYMS *Epidendrum costaricense* Rchb.f.; *E. umlauftii* Zahlbr.; *E. ciliare* var. *oerstedii* (Rchb.f.) L.O. Williams

CLOSELY RELATED SPECIES *E. oerstedii* is closely related to *E. ciliare*, *E. nocturnum* and *E. parkinsonianum* Hooker, all of which have large white flowers. From the first it may be distinguished by its lack of ciliate side lobes to the lip; indeed L.O. Williams considered them close enough to reduce *E. oerstedii* to varietal status in *E. ciliare*; *E. nocturnum* may be distinguished by its longer slender stem and thinner textured leaves; while *E. parkinsonianum* is distinguished by its very short pseudobulbs and very long and fleshy leaves.

Epidendrum paniculatum Ruiz & Pavon [Colour Plate]

A very variable, erect or suberect epiphytic or terrestrial herb, up to 2.5 m tall. **Stems** clustered, terete, clothed in greyish to brown leaf-sheaths. **Roots** in massive knotted masses. **Leaves** lanceolate, thin in texture, up to 20 cm long, 6 cm broad, acute, ± purple-tinged. **Inflorescence** paniculate, up to 250-flowered, apical on stems; rhachis green to purple-brown. **Flowers** pale green with a creamy-white lip. **Sepals** fleshy, oblong, 1 cm long, 0.35 cm broad, acute or apiculate, warty on outer surface. **Petals** linear, dilated towards apex, 1 cm long, acute. **Lip** adnate to column for length of column, free part 0.6 cm long, 0.8 cm broad, 3-lobed; side lobes rounded, margins erose; mid-lobe bifid, short, each lobule curved outwards, erose; callus 2-lobed at base, with 3 fleshy ridges running to apex of lip. **Column** terete, dilated at apex, 0.7 cm long, warty near base.

DISTRIBUTION Common throughout the American tropics.

HISTORY Discovered by H. Ruiz and J. Pavon at Muña in Peru and described by them in 1798 in *Systema Vegetabilium Florae Peruvianae et Chilensis* (p. 243). Since then it has been redescribed many times, as have many widespread species of orchid.

SYNONYMS include *Epidendrum floribundum* H.B.K.; *E. densiflorum* Hooker; *E. laeve* Lindl.; *E. piliferum* Rchb.f.

Epidendrum porpax Rchb.f. [Colour Plate]

A dwarf epiphyte with clustered leafy stems up to 10 cm long. **Leaves** coriaceous-fleshy, distichous, oblong, obtuse or emarginate, up to 2 cm long, 0.9 cm wide. **Inflorescence** terminal, 1-flowered, emerging between the apical leaves, 3–4.5 cm long; bract sheathing, oblanceolate, 1–1.7 cm long, purple. **Flower** fleshy, the sepals and petals purplish-green, the lip purple with a yellowish margin; pedicel and ovary 1.5–3.5 cm long, purplish. **Dorsal sepal** narrowly elliptic, acute, 1.2–1.5 cm long, 0.4–0.5 cm wide; **lateral sepals** obliquely oblong-lanceolate, acute, 1.2–1.5 cm long, 0.5 cm wide. **Petals** spreading, linear, obtuse, 1–1.5 cm long, c. 1 mm wide. **Lip** deflexed-recurved, transversely oblong or transversely elliptic, slightly emarginate, 1–1.4 cm long, 1.2–1.8 cm wide, shiny; callus of 3 small raised fleshy ridges at the apex of the column; spur united to the ovary, cylindrical. **Column** fleshy, dilated at apex, 0.7 cm long.

DISTRIBUTION Widespread in the American tropics from Mexico to Peru and Venezuela; in lower montane forest up to 1500 m.

HISTORY Oersted collected the type of this species on Mt Pantasmi in Nicaragua and it was described by H.G. Reichenbach in 1855 in *Bonplandia* (p. 220) as *Epidendrum porpax*. Garay and Dunsterville transferred it to *Neolehmannia* in 1976 in the sixth volume of *Venezuelan Orchids Illustrated* (p. 37) but we consider that this genus cannot be upheld because of the many species with intermediate features.

SYNONYMS *Epidendrum porpax* Rchb.f.; *E. gnomus* Schltr.; *E. porphyrophyllum* Schltr.; *E. matthewsii* Rchb.f.; *Nanodes matthewsii* (Rchb.f.) Rolfe; *Neolehmannia porpax* (Rchb.f.) Garay & Dunsterville

CLOSELY RELATED SPECIES *Epidendrum peperomia* Rchb.f. (syn. *Neolehmannia peperomia* (Rchb.f.) Garay & Dunsterville) is closely related but differs in having leaves with an acute apex and serrulate apical margin and in the flowers having an obtuse lip and lateral sepals that are fused at the base.

Epidendrum pseudepidendrum (Rchb.f.) Rchb.f. [Colour Plate]

A tall epiphytic plant with tufted stems. **Stems** slender, unbranched, leafy above, naked below, up to 1 m tall. **Leaves** oblanceolate, acute, coriaceous, 6–20 cm long, 1.5–4.5 cm broad. **Inflorescences** 1 or more, 1- to 3-flowered, terminal, racemose; peduncle ± elongate, covered at base by several imbricate bracts. **Flowers** fairly fleshy, glossy, medium-sized, showy; sepals and petals green; lip orange, ± with purple at base; column green at base, rose-purple at apex. **Sepals** oblanceolate, acute to obtuse, 2.2–3.2 cm long, 0.3–0.7 cm broad. **Petals** linear-oblanceolate, obtuse, 2.2–3 cm long, 0.2–0.3 cm broad. **Lip** clawed; claw adnate to the column; lamina transversely oblong to subquadrate or suborbicular, convex, retuse, crenulate, dentate or suborbicular, convex, retuse, crenulate, dentate or lacerate, 1.3–1.7 cm long, 1.5–2.2 cm broad; disc with 2 short lamellate calli at apex of column and a longitudinal 1- to 5-ridged thickening along the mid-line from base to apex.

DISTRIBUTION Costa Rica and Panama.

HISTORY Originally described as *Pseudepidendrum spectabile* (p. 733) by H.G. Reichenbach in the *Botanische Zeitung* (1852). He later transferred it to *Epidendrum*, where the specific epithet *spectabile* had already been used, and thus renamed it in 1856 as *E. pseudepidendrum* in his *Xenia Orchidacea*, vol. 1 (p. 160, t. 53).

SYNONYM *Pseudepidendrum spectabile* Rchb.f.

Epidendrum purum Lindl. [Colour Plate]

An erect epiphytic herb, up to 60 cm high. **Stem** terete, given off from the base of the previous year's growth. **Leaves** linear, thin, once twisted, erect or suberect, light green, up to 20 cm long, 1 cm broad, acute. **Inflorescence** paniculate, branches spreading, many-flowered. **Flowers** white or pale yellow-green; anther-cap pink. **Sepals** narrowly lanceolate, up to 1 cm long, 0.25 cm broad, acute; lateral sepals similar to dorsal but slightly falcate. **Petals** linear, 0.8 cm long, 0.1 cm broad, acute. **Lip** united to column for length of column, free part deeply 3-lobed, 0.7 cm long, 0.55 cm broad; side lobes triangular, acute, directed forwards; mid-lobe longer, slightly spathulate, edges upcurved, acute; callus 3-ridged, at apex of column. **Column** dilated in apical half, 0.5 cm long.

DISTRIBUTION Venezuela, south to Bolivia.

HISTORY John Lindley described this species in 1844 in the *Botanical Register* (misc. 75) based on a plant sent from Caracas to Jean Linden by Rucker.

Epidendrum schlechterianum Ames
[Colour Plate]

A dwarf epiphyte or lithophyte with clustered leafy stems, up to 10 cm long, completely covered by imbricate leaf bases. **Leaves** distichous, fleshy-coriaceous, ovate-lanceolate, acute, up to 2 cm long, 1 cm wide. **Inflorescence** 1- to 3-flowered, inconspicuous, emerging between apical leaves. **Flowers** small pale greeny-brown with a lip marked with purple-brown and with a pale brown column with a purple tip. **Dorsal sepal** narrowly oblong, acute, 0.9–1.1 cm long, 0.4 cm wide, with serrate margins; **lateral sepals** obliquely narrowly oblong, acute, 0.8–1 cm long. **Petals** narrowly elliptic, acute, up to 0.9 cm long, 0.3 cm wide, with serrate margins. **Lip** shortly clawed, reniform above, 0.6–0.7 cm long and wide, shortly apiculate with serrate margins. **Column** 0.6 cm long; anther clavate, incised at the tip.

DISTRIBUTION Mexico to Panama, Venezuela and Colombia south to Brazil and Peru, also in Trinidad; up to 1100 m.

HISTORY John Lindley described this rather insignificant orchid as *Nanodes discolor* in 1832 in his *Genera and Species of Orchidaceous Plants* (p. 139) and in the *Botanical Register* (t. 1541). Many authors have included it in *Epidendrum* as *E. schlechterianum* Ames because the epithet *discolor* has already been used for another species. Ames renamed it in his *Schedulae Orchidinae* (no. 7: p. 9).

The genus *Nanodes* does not stand up to critical examination as distinct from *Epidendrum* because of the number of species with intermediate features.

SYNONYMS *Nanodes discolor* Lindl.; *Epidendrum discolor* (Lindl.). Bentham; *E. brevicaule* Schltr.; *E. congestoides* Ames & C. Schweinf.

Epidendrum secundum Jacq. [Colour Plate]

Stems erect, terete, laxly many-leaved, up to 60 cm long, 1 cm in diameter. **Leaves** ovate-lanceolate, leathery, 8–14 cm long, 1.5–4 cm broad, acute. **Inflorescence** simple, 25–60 cm long, several- to many-flowered in a subcapitate dense head; bracts acuminate. **Flowers** rose-pink with yellow-white marks on lip. **Sepals** lanceolate-spathulate, up to 1 cm long, 0.35 cm broad, acute. **Petals** obovate-oblong, up to 1 cm long, subacute. **Lip** deeply 3-lobed, rotund-subreniform, 0.6 cm long, 0.8 cm broad; side lobes rounded, denticulate; mid-lobe twice as large as the laterals, cuneate, deeply notched; callus concave, acuminate, crenate. **Column** 0.5–0.6 cm long.

DISTRIBUTION The W. Indies and tropical S. America.

HISTORY Described in 1760 by N.J. Jacquin in his *Enumeratio Systematica Plantarum* (p. 29). Recently, L. Garay and H. Sweet in *The Flora of the Lesser Antilles* (1974) have suggested that the Jacquin plant has been misinterpreted by later authors. They suggest that this species should be called *Epidendrum elongatum* with the name *Epidendrum secundum* applying to another species. We have followed the traditional use of *E. secundum* as referring to the plant described above.

CLOSELY RELATED SPECIES See *E. ibaguense* and *E. imatophyllum*.

Epidendrum stamfordianum Batem.
[Colour Plate]

An erect epiphytic herb, 30 cm or more high. **Pseudobulbs** fusiform, 2-leaved, up to 20 cm long, 1.5 cm in diameter, covered with 3 deciduous, scarious sheaths. **Leaves** oblong-elliptic, coriaceous, up to 16 cm long, 3 cm broad, obtuse. **Inflorescence** paniculate or racemose, many-flowered, terminal or basal; scape terete, green, spotted purple. **Flowers** showy, pale greeny-yellow, spotted red-brown; lip white with deep purple on apex of callus; mid-lobe yellow, spotted with purple or crimson. **Sepals** ovate-lanceolate to elliptic, 1.2 cm long, 0.4 cm broad, acute; lateral sepals somewhat oblique. **Petals** elliptic-ligulate, 1.2 cm long, 0.2 cm broad, acute. **Lip** adnate to column, 3-lobed in free part, 1 cm long, 2 cm broad; side lobes spreading oblong, rounded and a little dilated at apex; mid-lobe bilobulate, each lobule erose; callus 3-ridged, mid-ridge longer than blunt side ridges. **Column** sinuate, terete, broadest at apex, 0.5 cm long.

DISTRIBUTION Mexico to Panama, Colombia and Venezuela.

HISTORY Described by James Bateman in *Orchidaceae of Mexico and Guatemala* (t. 11) in 1838 based on a plant collected near Izabal in Guatemala by George Ure Skinner the previous year. Bateman named this species in honour of the Earl of Stamford and Warrington who had at that time a magnificent collection of tropical orchids at Enville Hall, England.

Epigeneium Gagn.
Subfamily Epidendroideae
Tribe Dendrobieae
Subtribe Dendrobiinae

Medium-sized or small epiphytic herbs with elongated rhizomes. **Pseudobulbs** ± ovoid, often enclosed by sheaths, 1- or 2-leaved at apex. **Leaves** oblong or obovate, coriaceous. **Inflorescence** at the apex of the pseudobulb, subtended by a spathaceous bract, racemose, 1- to several-flowered. **Flowers** medium-sized to large, quite often showy. **Dorsal sepal** enclosing the column; **lateral sepals** larger, oblique, forming with the column-foot a mentum. **Petals** triangular, longly decurrent on the mentum. **Lip** pandurate-oblong to 3-lobed; callus lobulate or ridged on basal part. **Column** short; stelidia short or absent, with a long column-foot; pollinia 4 in 2 groups.

DISTRIBUTION About 35 species from India, China, S.E. Asia and Indonesia across to the Philippines.

DERIVATION OF NAME The position of the petals and lateral sepals in relation to the column-foot gives the name from the Greek *epi* (upon) and *geneion* (chin).

TAXONOMY F. Gagnepain described *Epigeneium* in 1932 in *Bulletin du Muséum d'Histoire Naturelle, Paris* (p. 593). The history of this genus which is allied to *Dendrobium* has been summarised by V.S. Summerhayes in the *Kew Bulletin* (1957). John Lindley originally proposed the name *Sarcopodium* for a group of orchids in his and J. Paxton's *Flower Garden* (1850–1). Some of these species are now regarded as being in the genus *Bulbophyllum* whilst others have been included by some authors in *Dendrobium* but as a distinct section. Both R.A. Rolfe and F. Kraenzlin considered these latter species distinct enough to form a genus separate from *Dendrobium* and this treatment is now widely followed.

A.D. Hawkes in *Lloydia* (1956) pointed out that the name *Sarcopodium* Lindl. was a later homonym of *Sarcopodium* Schlectend. (a genus of Fungi). He thus proposed a new name *Katherinea* for the genus. However, he overlooked the work of Tang and Wang who had earlier transferred Gagnepain's genus *Epigeneium* to *Sarcopodium* Lindl. Thus the correct name for the genus is *Epigeneium* on the grounds of priority.

TYPE SPECIES *E. fargesii* (Finet) Gagn.

SYNONYMS *Katherinea* A.D. Hawkes; *Sarcopodium* Lindl.

CULTURE Compost A. Temp. Winter min 12–15°C. Because of their creeping habit, these plants should be grown in shallow baskets or pans, or perhaps be mounted on slabs. They require moderately shady, humid conditions and should be carefully watered throughout the year.

Epigeneium acuminatum (Rolfe) Summerh.

Pseudobulbs ovoid or conical, ± tetragonal roundly angled, ± covered in brown sheath below, shiny yellow, 4–4.5 cm long, 2 cm in diameter, distant on a stout rhizome, 2-leaved. **Leaves** ± very shortly petiolate, oblong or elliptic, obtuse, 2-lobed at apex, 10–15 cm long, 2–4 cm broad, fleshy-coriaceous. **Inflorescence** pendent, laxly 6- to 20-flowered; bracts linear-ligulate, acute, pale green, 1.5–1.8 cm long. **Flowers** with whitish-yellow sepals and petals; lip often purple-suffused at the base, white above. **Sepals** triangular, long acuminate, 3.5–3.8 cm long, 0.8–1 cm broad. **Petals** lanceolate, acuminate, 3.5–3.8 cm long, 0.5–0.6 cm broad. **Lip** 3-lobed, 1.8 cm long, 1.2 cm broad; side lobes obovate, rounded and retuse at apex; mid-lobe broadly ovate-triangular, acute and reflexed at the apex; callus basal, sulcate, produced into a fleshy, 3-angled apex.

DISTRIBUTION   The Philippines.

HISTORY   Originally described by Robert A. Rolfe as *Dendrobium acuminatum* in 1905 in Oakes Ames' *Orchidaceae* (p. 86) based on a collection made by Thomas Borden on the Bamao River, in Bataan Province of Luzon. It has been transferred to *Epigeneium* by V.S. Summerhayes in 1957 in the *Kew Bulletin* (p. 260).

E. acuminatum is quite distinctive with its long arcuate racemes of cream flowers with a yellow lip.

SYNONYM   *Sarcopodium acuminatum* Rolfe
CLOSELY RELATED SPECIES   *Epigeneium lyonii* (Ames) Summerh. [Colour Plate] (sometimes considered as var. *lyonii* (Rolfe) Kraenzl. of *E. acuminatum*), also from the Philippines, has larger red-purple flowers and grows at higher altitudes than *E. acuminatum*.

Epigeneium coelogyne (Rchb.f.) Summerh. [Colour Plate]

A small creeping, epiphytic plant with a stout rhizome bearing pseudobulbs at 5 cm intervals. **Pseudobulbs** very stout, obliquely ellipsoidal, sulcate, 3.8–5 cm long, 1.3 cm broad. **Leaves** 2, broadly elliptic-oblong, obtuse and notched at apex, sessile or shortly petiolate, 10–15 cm long, 4.5 cm broad. **Inflorescence** terminal, 1-flowered; bracts large, sheathing. **Flower** large, cream-coloured or yellowish, mottled with purple-red; lip dull deep purple or chocolate-brown. **Sepals** lanceolate, acute, or acuminate, 4–6.3 cm long; lateral sepals falcate, saccate at base. **Petals** linear-lanceolate, acute, up to 5 cm long, 0.3 cm broad. **Lip** 3-lobed, porrect, 4.5 cm long, 2 cm broad; side lobes narrow, 4.5 cm long, 2 cm broad; side lobes narrow, erect; mid-lobe trapezoid-ovate. **Column** slightly curved, 2 cm long.

DISTRIBUTION   Burma and Thailand.

HISTORY   First collected at Moulmein in Burma by the Rev. Charles Parish who sent it to H.G. Reichenbach who described it in the *Gardeners' Chronicle* (p. 136) in 1871 as *Dendrobium coelogyne*. In 1957 V.S. Summerhayes transferred it to *Epigeneium* in the *Kew Bulletin* (p. 261).

SYNONYMS   *Dendrobium coelogyne* Rchb.f.; *Sarcopodium coelogyne* (Rchb.f.) Rolfe; *Katherinea coelogyne* (Rchb.f.) A.D. Hawkes

Epigeneium cymbidioides (Blume) Summerh. [Colour Plate]

A small epiphytic plant with a fleshy rhizome densely covered with rudimentary cataphylls and bearing well-spaced pseudobulbs. **Pseudobulbs** oviod, fleshy, 3–4 cm high, 2-leaved. **Leaves** oblong, fleshy, 2-lobed and obtuse at apex, up to 15 cm long, 2 cm broad or more. **Inflorescence** erect or arcuate, up to 10-flowered; bracts very small, hyaline, triangular, acute. **Flowers** pale yellow or straw-coloured; lip yellow, suffused with rose or purple with 2 ± confluent golden spots at the base of the mid-lobe. **Sepals** and **petals** oblong-ligulate or ligulate, acute, 2.3–2.5 cm long, 0.6–0.7 cm broad, but petals narrower; mentum short, rounded. **Lip** 3-lobed, 1.5–1.8 cm long, 1.3 cm broad; side lobes broadly semiobovate or obtriangular, rounded in front; mid-lobe shortly ovate-cordate, obtuse, broader than long; calli 3, basal. **Column** short, lacking stelidia.

DISTRIBUTION   Java and the Philippines (Luzon).

HISTORY   Discovered by C.L. Blume on Mt Salak in Java and described by him in 1825 in his *Bijdragen* (p. 332, t. 35) as *Desmotrichum cymbidioides*. John Lindley transferred it to *Dendrobium* in 1830 in his *Genera and Species of Orchidaceous Plants*, but more recently V.S. Summerhayes placed it in *Epigeneium* in the *Kew Bulletin* (p. 260) in 1957.

SYNONYMS   *Desmotrichum cymbidioides* Blume; *Dendrobium cymbidioides* (Blume) Lindl.; *D. marginatum* Teijsm. & Binnend.; *Desmotrichum triflorum* Blume

---

Epipactis Zinn
Subfamily Orchidoideae
Tribe Neottieae
Subtribe Limodorinae

Terrestrial plants with a horizontal rhizome and numerous fleshy roots. **Stems** erect, leafy. **Leaves** spirally arranged, plicate. **Inflorescence** terminal, more or less secund, laxly to densely few- to many-flowered. **Flowers** pedicellate, spreading or pendent. **Sepals** and **petals** free, subsimilar, spreading or connivent. **Lip** bipartite, fleshy; hypochile concave; epichile flat to slightly convex, porrect, with raised swellings at the base. **Column** short; rostellum large and globose but sometimes absent; pollinia 2, mealy.

DISTRIBUTION   A genus of some 15 species widespread in Europe, temperate Asia to Japan, and in N. America.

DERIVATION OF NAME   From the Greek *epipaktis*, a word used by the ancient Greeks for a plant that curdled milk, possibly *Epipactis helleborine*.

TAXONOMY   The genus was established by Johann Zinn in 1757 in the *Catalogus plantarum horti academici et agri Gottingensis* (p. 85). This name has been conserved over earlier usages.

Epipactis is a taxonomically difficult genus in Europe with about five distinct species and a number of self-pollinating taxa that have been given specific rank by some authors. The two species described below, one European and the other N. American are, however, readily recognised.

TYPE SPECIES   *E. helleborine* (L.) Crantz
CULTURE   Temp. Winter min. 5°C. As for *Anacamptis*. The species adapt readily to cultivation in the garden in temperate climates and should be grown in a mixture of a nearly neutral to slightly alkaline soil, leaf mould and peat.

Epipactis gigantea Douglas ex Hooker [Colour Plate]

A terrestrial with short rhizomes. **Stems** up to 100 cm tall. **Leaves** 4–12, ovate-lanceolate, acute, 5–20 cm long, 2–7 cm wide. **Inflorescence** 5- to 15-flowered in lax raceme; bracts leafy, lanceolate, up to 15 cm long. **Flowers** subnutant to spreading; sepals dull yellow or yellow-green heavily flushed with purple and with purple veins; petals pale purple with darker veins; lip yellow with bold purple veins on the side lobes of the hypochile, and with an orange epichile with a pink or white margin. **Sepals** lanceolate, acute, 15–24 mm long, 6–9 mm wide. **Petals** obliquely ovate, acute, 13–15 mm long. 6–8 mm wide. **Lip** bipartite, 13–16 mm long; hypochile deeply concave, with minute warts in the centre and prominent erect side lobes; epichile fleshy, triangular, acute, with 2 raised fleshy calli. **Column** short, 5 mm long, with a pair of spur-like auricles below the anther.

DISTRIBUTION   Western N. America from the Canadian border south to central Mexico; seepage banks and around springs and by rivers and streams.

HISTORY   Originally described in 1839 By Sir William Hooker in the second volume of his *Flora Boreali-Americana* (p. 202) based on a specimen collected in the Rockies by David Douglas. This orchid forms large colonies in cultivation in Europe grown either as a rock or bog garden plant.

SYNONYMS   *E. americana* Lindl.; *Limodorum giganteum* (Hook.) O. Kuntze; *Peramium giganteum* (Hook.) Coulter; *Serapias gigantea* (Hook.) A.A. Eaton; *Helleborine gigantea* (Hook.) Druce; *Amesia gigantea* (Hook.) Nelson & McBride
CLOSELY RELATED SPECIES   The Himalayan *Epipactis royleana* Lindl. is similar but taller and has brightly coloured purple flowers.

Epipactis palustris (L.) Crantz [Colour Plate]
A terrestrial with a long creeping rhizome. **Stems** 15–70 cm tall, pubescent, purplish, with sheathing leaves. **Leaves** 4–8, oblong to oblong-lanceolate, subacute to acuminate, 5–15 cm long, 2–4 cm wide. **Inflorescences** laxly 7- to 14-flowered, 6–20 cm long; bracts lanceolate, equalling or shorter than the flowers. **Flowers** spreading; sepals greenish or brownish with faint violet stripes; petals white with pinkish bases; lip with a pinkish white hypochile with purplish veins and an orange-yellow indumentum, and a white epichile with red veins and a yellow basal callus. **Sepals** lanceolate to ovate-lanceolate, 10–12 mm long. **Petals** similar, 8–10 mm long. **Lip** 10–12 mm long; epichile ovate, obtuse, undulate on margins; callus at base of epichile 2-ridged, fleshy. **Column** 3–4 mm long.

DISTRIBUTION Throughout Europe and temperate Asia to Siberia, in marshes, dune slacks and moorland; sea level to 1600 m.

HISTORY Originally described by Philip Miller as *Serapias palustris* in 1768 in the 8th edition of his *Gardener's Dictionary* (no. 3), based on Linnaeus's *Serapias helleborine palustris* of the 1st edition of *Species Plantarum* (1753). Heinrich Crantz transferred it to the present genus in 1769 in the 2nd edition of his *Stirpium Austriacarum* (p. 462). The Marsh Helleborine is an excellent plant for a bog garden or wet meadow.

SYNONYMS *Serapias palustris* Miller; *Helleborine palustris* (Miller) Schranck

---

Eria Lindl.

Subfamily Epidendroideae
Tribe Epidendreae
Subtribe Eriinae

Epiphytic or rarely terrestrial herbs of very variable habit. **Stems** pseudobulbous, 2- to many-leaved or rarely 1-leafed. **Inflorescence** terminal or axillary, racemose or rarely 1-flowered. **Flowers** mostly small to medium-sized and relatively inconspicuous, rarely showy. **Sepals** free, rarely connate, glabrous or hirsute; lateral sepals adnate to the elongate foot of the column, forming with it a short to long and spur-like or saccate mentum. **Lip** sessile on the foot of the column and incumbent, very rarely mobile. **Column** with an imperfectly quadrilocular anther; pollinia normally 8, waxy, pyriform or broadly obovid, attached in fours by narrow bases to a viscidium.

DISTRIBUTION Over 500 species widespread in tropical Asia, Malaysia to New Guinea, Australia, Polynesia and the adjacent islands.

DERIVATION OF NAME From the Greek *erion* (wool), which refers to the woolly indumentum of the perianth.

TAXONOMY John Lindley described *Eria* in 1825 in the *Botanical Register* (t. 904). It is one of the most polymorphic of all orchid genera. It is allied to *Dendrobium* but is easily distinguished by the number and shape of its pollinia.

In the *Flora of British India* (1890), Sir Joseph Hooker recognised 13 groups within the genus and additionally treated *E. coronaria* in a separate genus as *Trichosma suavis* Lindl. The last attempt to cover the whole genus was made by F. Kraenzlin in A. Engler's *Das Pflanzenreich* but this account is now out of date.

R. Holttum in *Orchids of Malaya* (1964) treats the 60 or so Malayan species in 12 easily distinguishable sections based on the scheme adopted by J.J. Smith. Some of the sections with species most likely to be found in cultivation are:

1. sect. *Trichotosia*. Stems long or short, leafy throughout except at the base, hairy throughout (mostly covered with stiff, red-brown hairs); inflorescences lateral, piercing through the leaf-sheath; bracts hairy, at right-angles to the rhachis; flowers not opening widely, red-hairy on outside; lip entire to obscurely 3-lobed. A large section including *E. teysmannii* J.J. Smith; *E. vestita* Lindl. and *E. ferox* (Blume) Blume. This section is now considered by most botanists as a distinct genus, *Trichotosia*, as we do here.

2. sect. *Callostylis*. Rhizome slender, creeping, with well-spaced, short, erect pseudobulbs, each 2- to 3-leaved; inflorescence short, erect, bearing many flowers in succession; flowers lacking a mentum; column relatively long; lip almost round. This section has been treated as a distinct genus, *Tylostylis*, by some authors and includes *Eria pulchella* Lindl.

3. sect. *Goniorhabdos*. Leaves convolute in bud; inflorescence tall; flowers large in genus; pseudobulbs 1, jointed; leaf-sheaths fused to pseudobulb. This section includes *E. javanica* (Sw.) Blume.

R. Schlechter treated the New Guinea species of *Eria* in three subgenera and eight sections. However, as A. Dockrill points out in *Australian Indigenous Orchids* (1969), species with characteristics between the subgenera are known and the only subgeneric grouping considered by most botanists recently has been the section.

The most recent and most useful treatment of the genus for horticulturists is that of Seidenfaden (1982) in which he revises the species from Thailand and adjacent regions. He considers 67 species in 17 sections but excludes *Trichotosia* which he considers to merit recognition as a distinct genus. Some of the more significant sections containing species common in cultivation are;

1. sect. *Eria*. A monotypic section for *E. javanica*, distinguished by its convolute leaves and stellate flowers.

2. sect. *Xiphosium* Lindl. Distinguished by the conical unifoliate pseudobulbs, proteranthous inflorescences subtended by stiff sheaths, prominent floral bracts and a triquetrous ovary. Species include *E. carinata* and *E. rosea*.

3. sect. *Trichosma* Lindl. Distinguished by its cylindrical or pseudobulbous bifoliate stems, terminal synanthous or hysteranthous inflorescences and lip with a 5- to 9-keeled callus on the mid-lobe. This section includes the popular *E. coronaria*.

4. sect. *Dendrolirium* Lindl. Several-noded pseudobulbous 3- to several-leaved stems produced from a creeping rhizome; heteranthous inflorescence with a woolly rhachis and several large flowers. Species include *E. ornata* and *E. pubescens*.

5. sect. *Pinalia* Lindl. Pseudobulbs several-noded and clustered; inflorescences cylindrical or globose, of many small flowers in which the base of the column-foot is excavate. Includes *E. spicata*.

The Malay Archipelago species are described and keyed out in the third volumne of Backer's *Flora of Java* (1960).

TYPE SPECIES *E. stellata* Lindl. [= *E. javanica* (Sw.) Blume].

CULTURE Compost A. Temp. Winter min. 10–15°C. *Eria* species may be grown either in pans or mounted on slabs of fern-fibre or cork when the natural habit is a spreading one. Humid, shady conditions suit the majority of species, with ample watering being given during growth, and less when the pseudobulbs are fully grown.

Eria bambusifolia Lindl.

A large epiphytic species. **Stem** cylindric, 60–90 cm long, up to 1.4 cm broad, leafy. **Leaves** large, linear-oblong or oblong-lanceolate, acuminate, reflexed, up to 18 cm long, 2.5–5 cm broad. **Inflorescences** as long as or longer than the leaves, simple or branched, slender, laxly many-flowered; bracts small, orbicular, apiculate. **Flowers** densely covered in red-brown hairs, pale brown with darker lines; ridges on lip pale green; column yellow behind and pink in front. **Dorsal sepal** elliptic, obtuse, 1.1–1.3 cm long, 0.4 cm broad; **lateral sepals** ovate-lanceolate, falcate, obtuse, 1.2 cm long, 0.5 cm broad; mentum short, incurved. **Petals** elliptic-oblong or oblanceolate, acuminate, falcate, shorter than the sepals. **Lip** clawed,

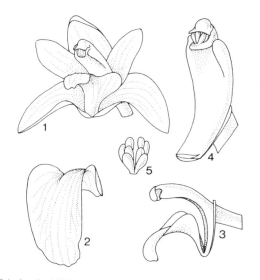

Eria bambusifolia
1 – Flower (× 2)
2 – Lip (× 3)
3 – Lip, column and column-foot, side view (× 3)
4 – Column and column-foot (× 3)
5 – Pollinia (× 6)

ovate-oblong, strongly nerved, deflexed below middle, obtuse, 1 cm long; side lobes very small; mid-lobe small, orbicular, obtuse; disc with 3 pubescent ridges in basal half of lip and 2 smaller ones near the apex. **Column** long, curved; foot straight.

DISTRIBUTION India (tropical Sikkim Himalayas, Peninsular India and the Khasia Hills), Burma, S. China and Thailand; 600–1400 m altitude.

HISTORY Collected on the Khasia Hills at an altitude of 600 m by Simonds and also by William Griffith and described by John Lindley in the *Journal of the Linnean Society* (p. 61) in 1859.

Eria carinata Gibs.

Pseudobulbs on a stout or slender rhizome, ovoid-oblong, sulcate, 5–10 cm long, 3 cm in diameter, 1-leafed at apex. **Leaf** elliptic-oblong, acute, thickly coriaceous, stoutly petiolate, 15–45 cm long, 3.2–8.5 cm broad. **Inflorescence** 15–30 cm long, subtended up to the base of the raceme by a sword-shaped upper sheath; bracts linear-lanceolate, equitant, 3–4 cm long. **Flowers** with greenish-yellow or green and white sepals with red nerves; petals yellow or greenish-yellow; lip pale yellow marked with red-brown to pale faded purple. **Sepals** ovate or ovate-lanceolate, strongly keeled, 2.5 cm long, 0.6 cm broad; mentum rounded, 0.5 cm high. **Petals** oblong-rhombic, acute, 2.2 cm

long, 0.7 cm broad. **Lip** obscurely 3-lobed, obovate-oblong, decurved in the middle, 2 cm long; side lobes narrow; mid-lobe oblong or ovate, apiculate, much recurved, the upper surface with a central ridge and 2 shorter lines between the side lobes. **Column** short, much curved; foot shorter but broader.

DISTRIBUTION India (Sikkim Himalayas and the Khasia Hills) and Thailand; up to 2300 m.

HISTORY Discovered by William Griffith in the Khasia Hills at Churra Punjee in E. Bengal in 1837 and described by him as *Xiphosium acuminatum* in the *Calcutta Journal of Natural History* (p. 365, t. 25) in 1845. In a footnote he mentions that John Gibson had called it *Eria carinata* in the Calcutta Botanic Gardens. This species is now regarded as being in the genus *Eria* and as both Gibson and Griffith's names appear in the same article, the Gibson name has prevailed.

SYNONYMS include *Eria rosea* auct. non Lindl.; *E. fordii* Rolfe; *Xiphosium acuminatum* Griff.

Eria coronaria (Lindl.) Rchb.f. [Colour Plate]

A medium-sized terrestrial plant. **Pseudobulbs** tufted, from an underground soft rhizome, fleshy, naked, 7.5–15 cm long, 0.5 cm broad, 2-leaved at apex; basal sheaths lax, few, pubescent. **Leaves** ovate-lanceolate, acuminate, coriaceous, 12.5–15 cm long, 3–4 cm broad. **Inflorescence** terminal, 2.5–5 cm long, 2–6 flowered; bracts large, narrowly lanceolate. **Flowers** 2.5 cm across, fragrant, white, yellowish or purplish; lip streaked with purple; disc yellow. **Dorsal sepal** elliptic-oblong, subacute, 1.5–2 cm long, 0.8 cm broad; **lateral sepals** ovate-lanceolate, acute, 1.4–2.2 cm long; mentum short, 0.5 cm long. **Petals** oblong, subacute, smaller than the dorsal sepal, 1.8 cm long, 1 cm broad. **Lip** subsessile, ovate-oblong, 3-lobed, 1.8 cm long, 1.2 cm broad; side lobes large, rounded; mid-lobe small, suborbicular, revolute; disc with 2 thick crenate ridges at the base, with 6 or 7 crenate ridges on the mid-lobe. **Column** short, stout, longer than the tapering column-foot.

DISTRIBUTION India (Sikkim Himalayas and the Khasia Hills).

HISTORY Discovered by John Gibson when collecting for the Duke of Devonshire in the Khasia Hills and described as *Coelogyne coronaria* by John Lindley in 1841 in the *Botanical Register* (misc. p. 83). H.G. Reichenbach transferred it to *Eria* in *Walpers, Annales Botanices* (p. 272) in 1864.

SYNONYMS *Coelogyne coronaria* Lindl.; *Trichosma suavis* Lindl.; *Eria cylindropoda* Griff.; *E. suavis* (Lindl.) Lindl.

Eria javanica (Sw.) Blume [Colour Plate]

Pseudobulbs ovoid, sheathed, 5–7.5 cm long, 1.5 cm in diameter, 1- or 2-leaved. **Leaves** lanceolate, acuminate, 20–30 cm long, 3.3–4.5 cm broad. **Inflorescences** suberect to drooping, pubescent, longer than the leaves; bracts lanceolate. **Flowers** sweetly scented, white or creamy with red spots on side lobes to the lip, pubescent on outer surface and ovary. **Dorsal sepal** lanceolate, acuminate, pubescent on outer surface, 2–2.3 cm long; **lateral sepals** similar to dorsal sepal, 1.8 cm long; mentum rounded, incurved. **Petals** lanceolate, acuminate, falcate, smaller than the sepals, glabrous. **Lip** 3-lobed, narrowly oblong, deflexed in middle, 1.2 cm long; side lobes auriculate, subfalcate, rounded; mid-lobe lanceolate, acute or acuminate; disc with 5 crenulate ridges almost to the apex. **Column** very short, broad, shorter than the curved foot.

DISTRIBUTION Himalayas, Burma and Thailand, south to Indonesia and across to New Guinea and the Philippines.

HISTORY Originally described as *Dendrobium javanicum* by O. Swartz in *Acta Holmiae* (p. 247) in 1800. Carl Blume transferred it in 1836 to *Eria* in *Rumphia* (p. 23).

SYNONYMS *Dendrobium javanicum* Sw.; *Eria*

Eria javanica
1 – Flower, front view (× 2)
2 – Flower, side view (× 2)
3 – Lip (× 3)
4 – Column and ovary (× 4)
5 – Anther (× 11)

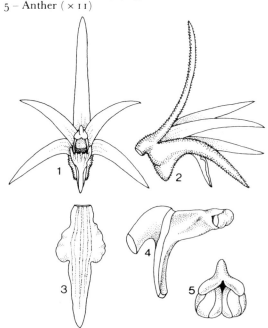

fragrans Rchb.f.; *E. stellata* Lindl.; *E. rugosa* Lindl.; *E. vaginata* Benth. ex D. Jackson; *E. pseudostellata* Schltr.

Eria monostachya Lindl.
Stems clustered, pendulous, subancipitous, few-noded, leafy, 10–15 cm long. **Leaves** spreading, linear, acuminate, sulcate, shiny, up to 30 cm long, 1.5 cm broad. **Inflorescences** 1 or 2, many-flowered, up to 40 cm long, sparsely woolly; bracts reflexed, pilose, 2 cm long. **Flowers** 0.8 cm across, pale greenish-yellow; lip white, spotted with violet. **Dorsal sepal** ovate, 0.5 cm long, 0.2 cm broad; **lateral sepals** broadly triangular, forming with the column-foot a long, obtuse mentum. **Petals** oblong, pellucid, obtuse, 0.3 cm long, 0.15 cm broad. **Lip** 3-lobed, more or less obtriangular, 0.45 cm long, 0.3 cm broad; side lobes triangular, horizontal; mid-lobe bilobulate, with diverging lobules deflexed, triangular and obtuse; mid-line of disc farinaceous, fleshy, clavate in front.
DISTRIBUTION Java and Sumatra.
HISTORY Described by John Lindley in 1859 in the *Journal of the Linnean Society* (p. 55) based on a specimen collected by Zollinger on Mt Gembolo in E. Java.

Eria pubescens (Hook.) Steud. [Colour Plate]
A medium-sized epiphytic plant with a stout creeping rhizome. **Pseudobulbs** large, furrowed, compressed, 7.5–10 cm long, 3 cm across, sheathed at the base, 3- to 5-leaved. **Leaves** petiolate, ± narrowly oblong, tapering to the base, acuminate, subcoriaceous, 15–25 cm long, 2–3 cm broad. **Inflorescence** stout, erect, 15–25 cm long, white-tomentose, bearing several sessile flowers; bracts lanceolate, as long as flowers. **Flowers** white-tomentose without, yellow or green lined with purple on sepals and petals and with purplish markings on the disc of the lip. **Dorsal sepal** lanceolate, acute, 1.4 cm long, 0.5 cm broad; **lateral sepals** triangular or ovate-lanceolate, obtuse, 1.8 cm long, 0.7 cm broad; mentum subcylindric. **Petals** ovate-oblong, obtuse, lying parallel over the column, 1.2 cm long. **Lip** 3-lobed, clawed, oblong, 1.6 cm long, 0.8 cm broad; side lobes short, broad, rounded at the apex; mid-lobe subquadrately rounded or oblong, emarginate, deflexed; callus thick, trifid in front. **Column** erect, at right-angles to the foot.
DISTRIBUTION Tropical Himalayas and Burma.
HISTORY Originally described as *Dendrobium pubescens* by William Hooker in his *Exotic Flora* (t. 124) in 1825 based on a Wallich collection. Steudel (1840) transferred it to *Eria* in his *Nomenclator Botanicus* (p. 566).

This species is still perhaps best known under the later synonym *Eria flava* Lindl.
Var. *lanata* (Griff). Hooker, which has smaller flowers and a narrower lip with a purplish mid-lobe and thickened nerves on the disc, is recorded from Sikkim and Tenasserim.
SYNONYMS *Eria flava* Lindl.; *E. laniceps* Rchb.f.; *Dendrobium pubescens* (Lindl.) Hooker; *Octomeria pubescens* (Lindl.) Sprengel

Eria rosea Lindl. [Colour Plate]
Pseudobulbs large, ovoid or conical, rugose, 5 cm long, 3 cm broad, 1-leafed, covered when young by several green imbricate sheaths. **Leaf** petiolate, coriaceous, linear-lanceolate or oblong, obtuse, up to 22 cm long, almost 3 cm broad; petiole 5 cm long. **Inflorescence** nodding, 3- to 4-flowered, ± equalling the leaf in length; bracts long, linear, acute, up to 4.5 cm long. **Flowers** showy, rose-coloured or white, tinged with rose. **Dorsal sepal** oblong-lanceolate, obtuse, 1.3 cm long; **lateral sepals** ovate-triangular, 1.3 cm long, 0.6 cm broad, forming with the column-foot a rectangular mentum. **Petals** narrowly obovate, obtuse, margins crenulate, 1 cm long. **Lip** 3-lobed, 1.2 cm long; side lobes semiobovate, rotund; mid-lobe oblong, acute, margin undulate, crenulate; disc with 2 undulate lamellae, pilose. **Column** 0.7 cm long.
DISTRIBUTION China and Hong Kong.
HISTORY Described in the *Botanical Register* (t. 978) in 1826 by John Lindley based on a plant brought from China in 1824 by J.D. Parks for the Horticultural Society for whom it flowered at Chiswick, London, in October 1825.

Eria spicata (D.Don) Hand.-Mazz. [Colour Plate]
A small to medium-sized epiphytic plant. **Stems** after flowering very stout, 5–20 cm long, 2.5 cm in diameter, about 4-leaved at apex. **Leaves** elliptic-lanceolate, acuminate, arcuate, plicate, 10–18 cm long, 2.5–5 cm broad, loosely sheathed. **Inflorescence** arcuate or nodding, spicate, densely many-flowered in an ovoid spike; peduncle stout. **Flowers** subglobose, small, glabrous or sparsely pilose, white to straw-coloured. **Sepals** elliptic, very broad, obtuse, 0.5–0.6 cm long, 0.4–0.5 cm broad; lateral sepals forming an obtuse mentum. **Petals** elliptic-obovate, obtuse, 0.5 cm long, 0.35 cm broad. **Lip** cuneate, obscurely 3-lobed, 0.3 cm long and broad, truncate or with a broadly triangular verrucose apex. **Column** short, semiterete; foot slightly arcuate.
DISTRIBUTION Nepal, N. India, Burma, S. China and Thailand; up to 2100 m altitude.
HISTORY This species was first described in 1825 by D. Don in his *Prodromus Florae*

Nepalensis (p. 31) as *Octomeria spicata* based on plants collected by F. Buchanan-Hamilton and N. Wallich at Narainhetty in Nepal. H. Handel-Mazzetti transferred it to *Eria* in 1936 in his *Symbolae Sinicae* (p. 1353). The species is probably better known and is still cultivated as *E. convallarioides* Lindl.
SYNONYMS *Octomeria spicata* D. Don; *Eria convallarioides* Lindl.

Eriopsis Lindl.
Subfamily Epidendroideae
Tribe Cymbidieae
Subtribe Cyrtopodiinae

Medium-sized epiphytic plants. **Pseudobulb** conical or cylindric, concealed at first by imbricating sheaths which are leaf-bearing in the upper part, 2- or 3-leaved. **Leaves** oblong-elliptic or oblong, plicate-veined. **Inflorescences** lateral, basal, distantly few-sheathed below, racemose, laxly or subdensely several to many-flowered above, mostly longer than the leaves. **Flowers** medium-sized, relatively showy, with spreading segments, slender pedicelled. **Sepals** subequal; lateral sepals slightly oblique. **Petals** similar to sepals but slightly smaller and narrower. **Lip** distinctly 3-lobed, shorter but much broader than other segments; side lobes large, incurved or erect; mid-lobe commonly small, entire or 2-lobed; disc longitudinally lamellate with toothed or entire crests or with a pair of flattened horn-like calli. **Column** arcuate, subclavate above, with a short foot; pollinia 2 and bipartite or 4.
DISTRIBUTION From Costa Rica and northern S. America to Peru and Brazil; about half a dozen species.
DERIVATION OF NAME From the *Eria*-like appearance of some species of the genus; *Eria* (a genus of orchids) and *opsis* (appearance).
TAXONOMY John Lindley described *Eriopsis* in 1847 in the *Botanical Register* (sub t. 9 and t. 18). It is allied to *Warrea*, *Bollea* and *Bifrenaria* but is easily distinguished by the peculiar lamellae of the lip and the almost quadrangular viscidium.
TYPE SPECIES *E. biloba* Lindl.
CULTURE Compost A. Temp. Winter min. 10–13°C. These plants should be grown in pots, and given moderate shade and humidity. While growing, they require ample water, but when the pseudobulbs are fully formed, less water should be given.

Eriopsis biloba Lindl. [Colour Plate]
An epiphytic or terrestrial herb. **Pseudobulbs** arising along a rhizome, very variable, subterete to ovoid, 14–45 cm long, 3–8 cm in

diameter, dark purple-brown or greenish-brown, 2- to 4-leaved. **Leaves** rigid or membranous, narrowly lanceolate to narrowly ovate, 30–50 cm long, 2–8 cm broad, shiny green above. **Inflorescence** from base of pseudobulb, erect, up to 110 cm high, up to 35-flowered. **Flowers** ± open simultaneously; sepals and petals brownish-yellow suffused with maroon; lip white, marked with brown on side lobes and dark maroon spotted on mid-lobe; column yellow-green. **Sepals** and **petals** oblong-elliptic to elliptic, rounded at the apex, 2–2.5 cm long, 0.7–1 cm broad. **Lip** variously 3-lobed, broadly ovate, up to 2.3 cm long, 2.1 cm broad; side lobes elliptic, spreading, with somewhat erose margins; mid-lobe small, bilobulate, with spreading lobules; callus a pair of broad undulate or serrate lamellae with 2 ± separate teeth in front. **Column** up to 1 cm long, slender, terete, arcuate.

DISTRIBUTION Costa Rica to Brazil and Peru; mostly above 1000 m.

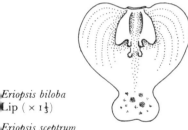

Eriopsis biloba
Lip (× 1⅓)

Eriopsis sceptrum
1 – Habit (× ¼)
2 – Flower (× ⅔)
3 – Lip (× 1½)
4 – Column, side view (× 1⅘)

HISTORY Described by John Lindley in the *Botanical Register* (sub t. 9, t. 18) in 1847 based on a plant sent him by J.J. Blandy of Reading, England, which had originally been in George Barker's collection at Springfield, England.
SYNONYMS *Eriopsis rutidobulbon* Hooker; *Pseuderiopsis schomburgkii* Rchb.f.; *Eriopsis schomburgkii* (Rchb.f.) Rchb.f.; *E. fuerstenbergii* Kraenzl.
CLOSELY RELATED SPECIES *Eriopsis sceptrum* Rchb.f. & Warsc. from Peru differs in having a lip on which the calli consist of a pair of divaricate, flattened, triangular or horn-like lamellae.

Erycina Lindl.
Subfamily Epidendroideae
Tribe Oncidieae

Small to medium-sized epiphytic herbs. **Pseudobulbs** 1-leafed at apex, subtended by several distichous imbricate ± leaf-bearing sheaths. **Inflorescence** axillary, from the base of the pseudobulb, racemose or paniculate, several-flowered; bracts short, rigid. **Flowers** showy, mainly yellow. **Dorsal sepal** convex below, acuminate and reflexed above; **lateral sepals** similar, slightly connate below, spreading. **Petals** reflexed, similar to sepals. **Lip** very much longer than other segments, 3-lobed; lobes subsimilar; calli on disc 2, ligulate, parallel, erect. **Column** with two ligulate arms on either side of the stigma; anther elongated; rostellum elongated; stipe elongate, geniculate just above the ovate gland; pollinia 2, ovoid.
DISTRIBUTION Two species in Mexico.
DERIVATION OF NAME *Erycina* was the Aphrodite of Mt Eryx in Sicily.
TAXONOMY John Lindley described *Erycina* in *Folia Orchidacea* (*Erycina*) in 1853 based on *Oncidium echinatum* H.B.K. Lindley separated it from *Oncidium* which it superficially resembles in its flowers on account of its dwarf column, long sigmoid rostellum and the very large, fleshy column-arms. From *Zygostates* it differs in the column-arms not being free, in its peculiar lip and minute petals; from *Leochilus* it differs in rostellum and lip structure; and from *Ornithocephalus* in the column-arms and its possession of 2 rather than 4 pollinia.
TYPE SPECIES *E. echinata* (H.B.K.) Lindl.
CULTURE Compost A or mounted. Temp. Winter min. 12–15°C. These small plants are probably best grown on slabs of fern-fibre or cork. While growing, they need to be well-watered, and shaded, but when growth is completed, a drier period is required, with more light.

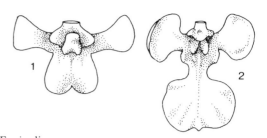

Erycina lips
1 – *E. diaphana* (× ⅘)
2 – *E. echinata* (× ⅘)

Erycina echinata (H.B.K.) Lindl. [Colour Plate]
A small epiphytic herb with a short leafy stem terminated by a solitary 2-leaved pseudobulb. **Stems** tufted, 5–15 cm long. **Leaves** distichous, ovate-oblong, acuminate, 5–10 cm long, bright green, articulated below to imbricating leaf-sheaths. **Inflorescence** axillary, arcuate, racemose, laxly many-flowered; peduncle slender, long, with several lanceolate, amplexicaul, rigid, sterile bracts along its length. **Flowers** 2 cm across, bright yellow with brown or green sepals and a red anther-cap; column white. **Dorsal sepal** galeate, acuminate, 0.4–0.5 cm long; **lateral sepals** connate at the base, linear-oblong, acuminate. **Petals** ovate, acuminate, reflexed, 0.4 cm long. **Lip** very large, deeply 3-lobed, 1 cm long, 0.8 cm broad; side lobes subequal, clawed side, reniform or flabelliform; mid-lobe apiculate; callus with 2 spreading oblong basal lobes and 2 erect, porrect, oblong lobes in front on either side of a low, fleshy, central ridge. **Column** very short, curved, lacking any wings; rostellum long, subulate.
DISTRIBUTION Mexico.
HISTORY Discovered by F.H.A. von Humboldt near Acapulco in Mexico and later by H. Galeotti at the Laguna de Tutupeque in Oaxaca Province. Humboldt, A. Bonpland and C. S. Kunth described it in 1815 as *Oncidium echinatum* in their *Nova Genera et Species Plantarum* (p. 345, t. 79). John Lindley transferred it to his new genus *Erycina* in *Folia Orchidacea* (*Erycina*) in 1853.
SYNONYMS *Oncidium echinatum* H.B.K.; *Erycina major* Schltr.
CLOSELY RELATED SPECIES *Erycina diaphana* (Rchb.f.) Schltr. is similar to *E. echinata* but differs in having a smaller lip with narrow side lobes and a subquadrate, emarginate mid-lobe and a distinct callus.

Esmeralda Rchb.f.
Subfamily Epidendroideae
Tribe Vandeae
Subtribe Sarcanthinae

Large, erect, lithophytic or terrestrial herbs with stout, terete, scandent stems. **Leaves** coriaceous, distichous, twisted at base to lie in one plane, unequally 2-lobed at apex, sheathing and articulated below; aerial roots piercing the leaf-sheaths along the stem. **Inflorescences** longer than the leaves, erect, few-flowered; bracts persistent, scarious, sheathing. **Flowers** pale yellow, transversely marked with red-brown stripes, showy. **Petals** and **sepals** subsimilar, spreading, overlapping, ligulate to ovate. **Lip** free, pendulous, 3-lobed; side lobes small; mid-lobe clawed, reniform with a crenate upturned border, bicallose. **Column** short, stout; anther terminal; pollinia 4 in 2 pairs, dorsally compressed.

DISTRIBUTION Two species in Himalayas, S. China, Burma and Thailand.

DERIVATION OF NAME From the Greek *smaragdus* (emerald green), probably an allusion to the jewel-like beauty of the flower or alternatively in reference to the deep green colour of the foliage.

TAXONOMY *Esmeralda* was established by H.G. Reichenbach in 1874 in vol. 2 of *Xenia Orchidacea* (p. 38). *Esmeralda* was distinguished by Reichenbach from *Vanda* by its mobile, rather than articulate, lip. G. Bentham and J. Hooker considered *Esmeralda* synonymous with *Arachnanthe* Blume which itself is a later synonym of *Arachnis* Blume. Recently, Kiat Tan in *Selbyana* (1975) has discussed the taxonomy of *Esmeralda* and its related genera *Arachnis*, *Armodorum*, *Vandopsis* and *Dimorphorchis*, in detail and distinguishes the first on its well-developed spur or nectary which is concealed in the lip.

TYPE SPECIES *E. cathcartii* (Lindl.) Rchb.f.

CULTURE As for larger *Arachnis* species.

Esmeralda clarkei Rchb.f. [Colour Plate]
Stems terete, stout, scandent, up to 1 m long. **Leaves** coriaceous, ligulate, unequally 2-lobed at apex, margins undulate, 15–23 cm long, 2.2–3.5 cm broad, articulated to a sheath below. **Inflorescences** erect, 3- to 4-flowered, up to 35 cm long. **Flowers** 5.5–7.5 cm across, slightly fragrant, yellow, transversely streaked with chestnut-brown; lip mid-lobe brown with 7–9 radiating white keels; column yellow, spotted with brown. **Dorsal sepal** erect, ligulate, 3.5 cm long, 1 cm broad; **lateral sepals** falcate, ligulate, cuneate, 3.2 cm long, 1.2 cm broad. **Petals** falcate, ligulate, 3.5 cm long, 0.8 cm broad. **Lip** free, pendulous, 3-lobed, up to 1.7 cm long; side lobes auriculate; mid-lobe clawed, reniform, with a crenate margin, with 7–9 radiating keels and 2 raised calli in centre of lip. **Column** 1 cm long, stout.

DISTRIBUTION E. Himalayas, Burma, China and Thailand.

HISTORY Discovered in 1875 at an altitude of about 1700 m at Yoksun in the Sikkim Himalayas by C.B. Clark and described by H.G. Reichenbach as *Esmeralda clarkei* in his honour in 1886 in the *Gardeners' Chronicle* (n.s. 26: p. 552). Messrs Low & Co. introduced it into cultivation in 1885 or 1886 and it was flowered in cultivation for the first time in 1886 by John Day of Tottenham, London.

SYNONYMS *Arachnanthe clarkei* (Rchb.f.) Rolfe; *Arachnis clarkei* (Rchb.f.) J.J. Smith; *Esmeralda bella* Rchb.f.; *Arachnis bella* (Rchb.f.) J.J. Smith

Euanthe Schltr.
Subfamily Epidendroideae
Tribe Vandeae
Subtribe Sarcanthinae

Large monopodial epiphytic plants. **Stems** elongate, covered by imbricating sheathing bases. **Leaves** distichous, coriaceous, articulated below to persistent leaf-sheaths. **Inflorescence** erect, axillary, few- to several-flowered. **Flowers** large, flat, very showy, pink and pale orange, lined and suffused with deep wine red. **Sepals** and **petals** free, subsimilar but petals smaller. **Lip** very much smaller than the other segments, bipartite; hypochile saccate, sides erect on either side of column; epichile deflexed, spreading, broader than hypochile, with 3 longitudinal central ridges to apex. **Column** very short; pollinia 2, sulcate, waxy; stipe linear, slightly dilated in apical half; viscidium ovate-elliptic.

DISTRIBUTION A single species from the Philippines.

DERIVATION OF NAME From the Greek *euanthes* (blooming), referring to the showy inflorescence.

TAXONOMY Described by R. Schlechter in 1914 in *Die Orchideen* (p. 567) based on *Vanda sanderiana* which he removed from that genus on account of the peculiar structure of the lip which is bipartite rather than being 3-lobed as in other *Vanda* species.

TYPE SPECIES *E. sanderiana* (Rchb.f.) Schltr.

CULTURE Compost A. Temp. Winter min. 15°C. These plants should be given light and humid conditions, with shade applied during the middle of the day in summer. At all times they should be well watered, although less will be needed in the winter.

Euanthe sanderiana (Rchb.f.) Schltr.
[Colour Plate]
A large, spectacular, epiphytic plant. **Leaves** ligulate, unequally 2-lobed or truncate at apex, curved, coriaceous, 30–40 cm long. **Inflorescence** suberect, mostly shorter than the leaves, 6- to 10-flowered. **Flowers** flat, very showy, 8–11.5 cm across; dorsal sepal delicate rose-coloured suffused with white; lateral sepals tawny-yellow with carmine-red anastomosing venation; petals similar in colour to the dorsal sepal but with a tawny blotch spotted with red on the lower basal part; lip variable in colour at the base, mostly dull tawny-yellow streaked with red within, reddish-brown at the apex; column buff-yellow. **Sepals** elliptic-suborbicular to broadly obovate, obtuse or rounded, 5–6 cm long, 4 cm broad. **Petals** ovate-rhombic, obtuse, 4 cm long, 3.5 cm broad. **Lip** 3-lobed, concave at the base, up to 3 cm long, 2 cm broad; side lobes rounded, erect; mid-lobe fleshy, shortly clawed, spreading, oblong-rotund, strongly recurved at the apex, 1.5 cm long, prominently 3-ridged on the disc. **Column** very short, stout, 0.6 cm long.

DISTRIBUTION The Philippines (Mindanao); on trees close by the sea.

HISTORY Discovered by M. Roebelin for Messrs Sander & Co. in 1882 in the S.E. of Mindanao and a few months later also by David Burke for Messrs Veitch & Sons in the same area. It flowered for the first time in Britain in 1883 in the collection of Mr Lee of Downside, Leatherhead. H.G. Reichenbach described it in 1882 in the *Gardeners' Chronicle* (n.s. 17: p. 588) as *Vanda sanderiana* but R. Schlechter transferred it in 1914 to *Euanthe* in *Die Orchideen* (p. 567).

SYNONYMS *Esmeralda sanderiana* (Rchb.f.) Rchb.f.; *Vanda sanderiana* Rchb.f.

Eulophia R. Br. ex Lindl.
Subfamily Epidendroideae
Tribe Cymbidieae
Subtribe Cyrtopodiinae

Small to large terrestrial or rarely lithophytic plants arising from stout rhizomes, pseudobulbs or underground tuber-like corms. **Leaves** several or rarely absent, clustered, sheathing the lower part of the scape. **Inflorescence** erect, lateral, racemose or rarely paniculate, few- to many-flowered. **Flowers** small to large, ± showy. **Sepals** and **petals** free, subsimilar. **Lip** saccate or spurred at base, entire to 3-lobed; side lobes erect; mid-lobe spreading, ± recurved; disc ± bearing calli, papillae, hairs or lamellae. **Column** short to long, ± winged; column-foot short; pollinia 2, often deeply cleft waxy.

DISTRIBUTION Over 200 species throughout the tropics but particularly numerous in tropical Africa and S. Africa.

DERIVATION OF NAME From the Greek *eu* (well, true) and *lophos* (plume), in reference to the crests on the lip.

TAXONOMY *Eulophia* was described by John Lindley in 1823 in the *Botanical Register* (t. 686) but it has had to be conserved against *Eulophia* C.A. Agardh (1822) in the Algae.

The genus is still rather poorly known, especially in tropical Africa. V.S. Summerhayes revised some species such as *E. paivaeana* and *E. shupangae* in the *Kew Bulletin* but did not extend either study to S. Africa where the former undoubtedly occurs and is known as *E. streptopetala*. More recently the S. African species have been studied by A.V. Hall (*Journal of South African Botany*, 1965) and the E. African species by P.J. Cribb (1990) in the *Flora of Tropical East Africa Orchidaceae* (pt. 3). Undoubtedly the critical area for study is in S. Central Africa where recent collections have greatly elucidated our understanding of the distribution and variability of many of the more widespread species.

Formerly, the genus *Lissochilus* was considered distinct from *Eulophia* (e.g. R.A. Rolfe in *Flora of Tropical Africa*, 1897) but, as more collections were received from Central Africa, many species with intermediate features were discovered and these genera are now considered synonymous.

One interesting feature of *Eulophia* is that the genus contains saprophytic species such as *E. galeoloides* Kraenzl. and species such as *E. subsaprophytica* and *E. florulenta*, in which the leaves are poorly developed. These latter are sometimes referred to as being subsaprophytic.

TYPE SPECIES *E. guineensis* Lindl.

SYNONYM *Lissochilus* R. Br.; *Cyrtopera* Lindl.

CULTURE Compost B. Temp. Winter min. 15°C. when resting; more when growing. While in active growth, all *Eulophia* species require careful watering but when the current pseudobulbs are completed, all should have a dry rest, except for those species found growing by streams, e.g. *E. horsfallii*. Shade requirements vary according to natural habit; forest species needing more than those, such as *E. petersii*, found in hot dry areas. All plants should be repotted when new growth commences.

Eulophia cucullata (Sw. ex Pers.) Steud.
[Colour Plate]
A large, showy, rather variable, terrestrial species, 1 m or more tall. **Pseudobulbs** rounded, several-leaved. **Leaves** tufted, narrowly lanceolate (grass-like), acute, 25–30 cm long, up to 1.5 cm broad. **Inflorescence** appearing before the leaves, 50–75 cm or more tall, 5- to 10-flowered. **Flowers** showy, 2.5–5 cm across; sepals olive-green to brown; petals and lip vivid royal-purple, magenta or rose-pink, throat of lip paler and spotted with purple; callus yellow. **Sepals** triangular, reflexed, acute, 2 cm long. **Petals** broadly elliptic, rounded, 2 cm long and broad. **Lip** cucullate, truncate in front, obscurely 3-lobed, 2.5 cm long, 3–3.5 cm broad; disc with 2 quadrate erect calli in centre of lip; spur broadly conical, short.

DISTRIBUTION Very widely distributed in tropical Africa; growing in grassland and on poor pasture.

HISTORY Originally named as *Limodorum cucullatum* by O. Swartz based on an A. Afzelius specimen but not described until 1807 by C.H. Persoon in his *Synopsis Plantarum* (p. 521). Ernst Steudel transferred it to *Eulophia* in 1840 in the 2nd edition of *Nomenclator Botanicus* (p. 205).

SYNONYMS *Limodorum cucullatum* Sw. ex Pers.; *Lissochilus arenarius* Lindl.

Eulophia guineensis Lindl. [Colour Plate]
A large, handsome terrestrial plant. **Pseudobulbs** clustered on a stout rhizome, ovoid-conical, 2- to 3-noded, 3–5 cm long, 3–4 cm in diameter, 2- to 4-leaved. **Leaves** elliptic to broadly lanceolate, veins depressed, acute, up to 25 cm long, 5–8 cm broad. **Inflorescence** arising when the leaves are present, up to 35 cm long, 6- to 15-flowered; peduncle purple-brown, clothed with several greyish sheaths. **Flowers** showy, about 5 cm across; sepals and petals purplish-green or brownish; lip rose-purple, light mauve or white with darker veins, pale towards the base. **Sepals** and **petals** sub-similar, narrowly lanceolate, 2–3 cm long, 0.3–0.4 cm broad. **Lip** cordate or obscurely 3-lobed, apiculate, flat, with undulate margins, 2.4–3 cm long, 1.6–2.6 cm broad; side lobes rounded; spur slender, tubular, 2–2.5 cm long. **Column** short, stout.

DISTRIBUTION Widespread in tropical Africa, south to Angola.

HISTORY Introduced into cultivation by the Horticultural Society of London who were sent plants by their collector, George Don, from Sierra Leone. John Lindley described it in 1823 in the *Botanical Register* (t. 686).

CLOSELY RELATED SPECIES Very similar and possibly conspecific with *Eulophia quartiniana* A. Rich. but that species flowers before the leaves have developed, has an orbicular obtuse lip and reflexed sepals and petals.

Eulophia petersii (Rchb.f.) Rchb.f.
A large terrestrial plant 1–3.5 m tall. **Pseudobulbs** conical to fusiform, 4- to to 6-noded, 6–23 cm long, 1.4–4 cm in diameter, 2- to 3-leaved in the apical part, orange to yellow when dry. **Leaves** very thick, fleshy-coriaceous, lanceolate, acute, 14–80 cm long, 1.4–6 cm wide, with serrulate margins. **Inflorescence** erect, paniculate; peduncle stout, up to 90 cm long; branches up to 7, up to 35 cm long; bracts lanceolate, 5–16 mm long. **Flowers** with brown or greenish-brown sepals, whitish petals and a white lip veined with purple; pedicel and ovary 2–2.6 cm long. **Sepals** linear-oblanceolate, apiculate, recurved in the apical half, 1.7–2.3 cm long, 0.4–0.5 cm wide. **Petals** oblong, shortly apiculate, 1.6–1.8 cm long, 0.5–0.7 cm wide. **Lip** 3-lobed, 1.4–2 cm long, 0.8–1.5 cm wide; side lobes erect, elliptic; mid-lobe circular to subquadrate, obtuse; callus of 3 fleshy ridges, raised and erose on mid-lobe; spur incurved, shortly cylindrical, 0.4–0.6 cm long. **Column** 0.8–0.9 cm long; foot 0.1–0.2 cm long.

DISTRIBUTION Widespread in the drier parts of E. and S.E. Africa, also in S.W. of the Arabian peninsula; in rocky places and sandy soils in woodland, thickets and bushland, sea level to 1800 m.

HISTORY Originally described by H.G. Reichenbach as *Galeandra petersii* in 1847 in *Linnaea* (p. 679) based on a collection made by Peters in Mozambique. Reichenbach transferred it to *Eulophia* in 1865 in the journal *Flora* (p. 186). This species is commonly grown under the later synonym *Eulophia schimperiana*.

SYNONYMS include *Galeandra petersii* Rchb.f.; *Eulophia schimperiana* A. Rich.; *E. caffra* Rchb.f.

CLOSELY RELATED SPECIES *Eulophia taitensis* Cribb & Pfenning, from coastal Kenya and Tanzania, differs in having 6- to 14-leaved pseudobulbs almost covered by the leaf bases, a racemose inflorescence of 5–15 flowers, and larger flowers with broader yellow-green sepals and petals and a broader very obscurely lobed lip.

Eulophia speciosa (R. Br. ex Lindl.) Bolus
[Colour Plate]
A large terrestrial herb, 1 m or more tall. **Pseudobulbs** ovoid, 5 cm or more long, 3- to 5-leaved. **Leaves** elongate-linear, acute, slightly fleshy, conduplicate below, 15–30 cm long, 1.8–2.5 or more cm broad. **Inflorescences** erect, up to 1 m or more long, racemose, laxly many-flowered; bracts ovate-oblong to ovate-lanceolate, acuminate, 1.8–2.5 cm long. **Flowers** quite showy; sepals green; petals bright yellow; lip yellow, whitish on side lobes and flecked and lined with red in centre. **Sepals** ovate or oblong-ovate, acute, reflexed, 0.8 cm long, 0.35 cm broad. **Petals** spreading, ovate or suborbicular, subobtuse, up to 1.8 cm long, 1.6 cm broad. **Lip** 3-lobed, nearly as long as the petals; side lobes suberect, transversely oblong; mid-lobe broadly elliptic, reflexed at the sides; disc converse, with 3 obtuse keels; spur very

short, broadly conical, obtuse. **Column** oblong, 0.6 cm long.

DISTRIBUTION Tropical E. Africa, south to S. Africa (Cape Province); sea level to 1000 m, in sandy soil in bush or grassland.

HISTORY Originally described by John Lindley in 1821 in his *Collectanea Botanica* (t. 31) as *Lissochilus speciosus* a name suggested by Robert Brown.

H. Bolus transferred it to *Eulophia* in 1889 in the *Journal of the Linnean Society* (p. 184).

SYNONYMS *Lissochilus speciosus* R. Br. ex Lindl.; *Satyrium giganteum* L.; *Limodorum giganteum* (L.) Thunb.; *Cymbidium giganteum* (L.) Sw.; *Cyrtopera* (?) *gigantea* (L.) Lindl.

Eulophia streptopetala Lindl. [Colour Plate]

A large, erect, terrestrial plant. **Pseudobulbs** ovoid or ovoid-oblong, 3.5–7.5 cm long, 4- to 7-leaved. **Leaves** elongate-linear to lanceolate, acute or acuminate, arching, plicate, 15–45 cm long, 1.2–6.5 cm broad. **Inflorescence** erect, 45–100 cm long, racemose, laxly many-flowered; bracts oblong or oblong-lanceolate, acute, 0.8–1.3 cm long. **Flowers** medium-sized; sepals green, marked with brown or purple-brown; petals bright yellow; lip yellow, striped with reddish-brown on side lobes and in centre of lip. **Sepals** elliptic-oblong, apiculate or subobtuse, 1.2–1.7 cm long, reflexed. **Petals** ovate-orbicular, broadly clawed, obtuse, 1.2–1.7 cm long, spreading, twisted somewhat. **Lip** 3-lobed, up to 1.5 cm long; side lobes erect, broadly oblong or subquadrate, obtuse; mid-lobe ovate-orbicular to broadly ovate, obtuse, sides reflexed; disc thickened at the base with 3 or 4 obtuse keels running to middle of mid-lobe; spur broadly conical, obtuse, 0.6 cm long. **Column** oblong, 0.6 cm long.

DISTRIBUTION S. and tropical E. Africa; on the margins of forests and woodland.

HISTORY Described originally by John Lindley in 1826 in the *Botanical Register* (t. 1002) from a plant said to have come from Brazil but, as suggested by Lindley, most probably from tropical Africa.

SYNONYMS include *Lissochilus streptopetalus* (Lindl.) Lindl.; *Eulophia krebsii* (Rchb.f.) Bolus; *Lissochilus krebsii* Rchb.f.; *E. paivaeana* (Rchb.f.) Summerh.

Eulophiella Rolfe

Subfamily Epidendroideae
Tribe Cymbidieae
Subtribe Cyrtopodiinae

Medium to large epiphytic plants with large pseudobulbs, borne on a stout creeping rhizome. **Leaves** 3–6, membranaceous, plicate-venose, persistent, articulated at the apex of the sheath. **Inflorescence** basal, racemose, erect, many-flowered; bracts broad, not caducous. **Flowers** often showy, 2–9 cm in diameter. **Sepals** and **petals** free, subsimilar; lateral sepals adnate to column-foot forming a short mentum. **Lip** suborbicular, 3-lobed, lacking a spur, inserted at the apex of the column-foot; disc bearing several crests or lamellae. **Column** fleshy, arcuate, with a foot; rostellum 3-lobed; pollinia 2, sessile on a common viscidium.

DISTRIBUTION Two or three species only in Madagascar.

DERIVATION OF NAME Diminutive of *Eulophia*, given for the superficial resemblance of the species to those of the latter genus.

TAXONOMY *Eulophiella* was described by R. A. Rolfe in 1891 in *Lindenia* (p. 77). It is allied to *Eulophia* and *Cymbidiella* being distinguished from the former by its column which has a prominent foot and the lip which lacks a spur and from the latter by its very broad bracts and non-distichous leaves which are not disposed in a fan. R. Schlechter wrote an account of the genus in *Orchis* in 1920, and the genus has recently been revised by J. Bosser and P. Morat in *Adansonia* (1969) who accept only two species in the genus.

TYPE SPECIES *E. elisabethae* Linden & Rolfe

CULTURE Compost A. Temp. Winter min. 15°C. *Eulophiella* species require considerable growing room, so are probably best cultivated in large shallow baskets. They require humid conditions at all times, with moderate shade during the summer months. While growing, water should be freely given, with less needed after the pseudobulbs are fully grown.

Eulophiella elisabethae Linden & Rolfe

A medium-sized epiphytic herb with a long, creeping rhizome. **Pseudobulbs** green, compressed, ovoid to narrowly ovoid, up to 15 cm long, 2- to 4-leaved. **Leaves** narrowly lanceolate, acuminate, tapering to the base, 60–120 cm long, 3–5 cm broad. **Inflorescence** 60–90 cm long, from the base of the pseudobulb, spreading horizontally or arcuate-drooping, up to 40-flowered; bracts ovate, acute, up to 1.4 cm long. **Flowers** showy, 4 cm across, almost hemispherical in shape; sepals and petals pale pinkish-white within, rose-purple without; lip white with a yellow callus and central area and red spotting around the callus. **Sepals** elliptic, obtuse to slightly retuse, 2.3–2.5 cm long, 1.5 cm broad. **Petals** obovate, obtuse, 2.2–2.4 cm long, 1.4 cm broad. **Lip** articulated to column-foot, smaller than tepals, 1.3 cm long, 3-lobed; side lobes oblong; mid-lobe orbicular, emarginate, margins obscurely crenulate, setose at the base; disc with a hippocrepiform callus at the base terminating in a

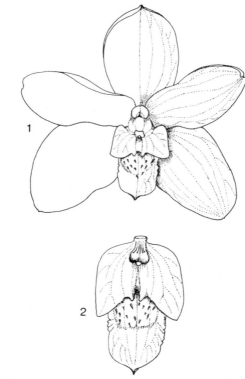

Eulophiella elisabethae
1 – Flower (× 1½)
2 – Lip (× 2)

double tooth. **Column** about 0.9 cm long; foot 0.3 cm long.

DISTRIBUTION Madagascar; in wet rain forests epiphytic on the palm *Vonitra fibrosa*.

HISTORY Discovered by M. Hamelin and described by J. Linden and Robert Rolfe in *Lindenia* (t. 325) in 1891. They named it for Queen Elisabeth of Romania.

CLOSELY RELATED SPECIES *Eulophiella perrieri* Schltr. is probably conspecific with *E. elisabethae*.

E. roempleriana (Rchb.f.) Schltr. is a much larger plant with a stout creeping rhizome and larger pink flowers or an inflorescence up to 1 m or more long.

Eurychone Schltr.

Subfamily Epidendroideae
Tribe Vandeae
Subtribe Aerangidinae

Small to medium-sized epiphytic herbs with very short leafy stems covered by persistent leaf sheaths. **Leaves** elliptic-ligulate, unequally bilobed at the apex, coriaceous, articulated at the base to a persistent leaf base. **Inflorescences** axillary, scarcely exceeding the leaves in length, laxly 10-flowered; bracts small. **Flowers** large, showy, white with a green mark on the lip or pink. **Sepals** and **petals** spreading, free, subsimilar. **Lip** obscurely 3-lobed, obconical-funnel-shaped, ecallose, with an elongate basal spur. **Column** short, fleshy, semiterete; rostellum pendent, elongate, entire or slightly bifid at the apex; pollinia 2, broadly ellipsoidal, attached by a single linear stipe to an oblong or oval viscidium.

DISTRIBUTION   A small genus of two species from tropical Africa.

DERIVATION OF NAME   From the Greek *eurys* (broad) and *stylis* (style), a reference to the short broad column of the species.

TAXONOMY   *Eurychone* was established as a segregate genus from *Angraecum* by Rudolf Schlechter (1918) in *Beihefte zum Botanisches Centralblatt* (p. 134). It differs from *Angraecum* in having a lip lacking a callus, a column with an elongate entire rostellum, and pollinia attached by a single linear stipe to a small viscidium.

TYPE SPECIES   *E. galeandrae* (Rchb.f.) Schltr. & *E. rothschildianum* (O'Brien) Schltr.

CULTURE   Temp. Winter min. 15°C. Grow much as *Phalaenopsis* in pots or mounted, with good shade and even watering throughout the year.

Eurychone rothschildiana (O'Brien) Schltr.
[Colour Plate]

An epiphyte with a short stem, 1–10 cm long, 4–8 mm in diameter. **Leaves** obliquely obovate, unequally obtusely or subacutely bilobed at the apex, 5.5–21 cm long, 3–6 cm wide. **Inflorescences** densely 1- to 7-flowered, up to 9 cm long; rhachis zigzag; bracts ovate-triangular, obtuse, 3–5 mm long. **Flowers** large for size of plant, white with a dark green mark on the lip, sweetly scented; pedicel and ovary 10–12 mm long. **Dorsal sepal** oblong-narrowly elliptic, obtuse, 2–2.5 cm long, 0.5–0.6 cm wide; **lateral sepals** lanceolate, acute, 2.2–3 cm long, 0.6 cm wide. **Petals** oblong-lanceolate, acute, 1.8–2.5 cm long, 0.6–0.7 cm wide. **Lip** almost circular, funnel-shaped, obtuse, 2–3 cm long and wide; spur pointing backwards, with a broad mouth, constricted and geniculate in the middle and clavate at apex, 2–2.5 cm long. **Column** short, broad, 4–6 mm long.

DISTRIBUTION   Tropical Central and W. Africa: Sierra Leone and Guinea to Uganda and Zaïre; in lowland and riverine forests; up to 1300 m.

HISTORY   James O'Brien described this attractive orchid as *Angraecum rothschildianum* in 1903 in the *Gardeners' Chronicle* (s. 3, 34: p. 131) based on a plant from Uganda flowered by the Hon. Walter Rothschild. It was transferred to

Eurychone by Rudolf Schlechter in 1918 in *Beihefte zum Botanisches Centralblatt* (p. 135).

SYNONYM   *Angraecum rothschildianum* O'Brien

CLOSELY ALLIED SPECIES   *E. galeandrae* (Rchb.f.) Schltr., from Cameroon, Gabon and the Central African Republic, is readily distinguished by its narrower leaves, longer laxer inflorescences, and pink flowers with a straighter 2–2.5 cm long spur.

Flickingeria A.D. Hawkes
Subfamily Epidendroideae
Tribe Epidendreae
Subtribe Dendrobiinae

Epiphytic or lithophytic plants with a creeping rooting rhizome producing erect branching stems. **Stems** several-noded with the apical node usually swollen and pseudobulbous, unifoliate but covered by sheaths below when young, usually branching from the upper nodes to form elongate superposed erect or hanging clumps. **Leaf** coriaceous, erect. **Inflorescences** several, axillary, terminal or subterminal on each stem, 1-flowered. **Flowers** ephemeral, lasting usually less than a day, thinly membranous. **Sepals** subsimilar, the laterals oblique and forming a chin-like mentum with the column-foot. **Petals** narrower than the sepals but similarly coloured. **Lip** complex, tripartite; the hypochile short concave, with 2 erect side lobes; the mesochile oblong, usually narrow and claw-like; the epichile bilobed, transversely oblong or reniform, often pleated, sometimes with each lobe deeply lacerate; callus of 2–3 longitudinal raised lamellae. **Column** short, fleshy, with a distinct elongate foot; pollinia 4, in 2 appressed pairs.

DISTRIBUTION   A genus of some 60 species in S.E. Asia, the Malay Archipelago, the Pacific Islands and N.E. Australia. The centre of diversity lies in the large islands of Indonesia.

DERIVATION OF NAMED   Named after Edward A. Flickinger, a friend of A.D. Hawkes.

HISTORY   *Flickingeria* is a segregate genus of *Dendrobium* which was first recognised as distinct at generic rank by Carl Blume in his *Bijdragen* (p. 329) in 1825 under the name *Desmotrichum*. For more than century afterwards, however, most authorities reincorporated it as a section into *Dendrobium*. Upon its reinstatement it was realised that the name *Desmotrichum* had already been used by Kuetzing for another genus. Almost simultaneously in 1961 it was renamed by A.D. Hawkes as *Flickingeria* in the *Orchid Weekly* (p. 451) and by P.F. Hunt and Victor Summerhayes as *Ephemerantha* in the journal *Taxon* (p. 102). The former is now

generally accepted as having priority by a matter of a few days.

Flickingeria is distinguished from *Dendrobium* and other allies by its strange vegetative habit, the characteristic ephemeral 1-flowered inflorescences, and the tripartite lip. The mainland Asiatic species have recently been revised by Gunnar Seidenfaden (1980) in *Dansk Botanik Archiv*.

TYPE SPECIES   *Desmotrichum angulatum* Bl.

CULTURE   Temp. Winter min. 15°C. Generally they are untidy growers that can form large masses on a suitable slab of branch. Small plants will establish in pots. They require moderate shade and humidity with plenty of water when actively growing.

Flickingeria comata (Bl.) A.D. Hawkes
[Colour Plate]

A large, erect or pendent, clump-forming epiphyte 40–100 cm long. **Stems** 7- to 8-noded, clavate, branching from the upper two nodes, 5–25 cm long, 1–1.5 cm in diameter, unifoliate, drying yellow or orange. **Leaf** very coriaceous, elliptic, obtuse, 5–16 cm long, 2.5–8 cm wide. **Inflorescences** 1-flowered, axillary; bracts chartaceous, ovate, acute, 4–10 mm long. **Flowers** ephemeral, the sepals and petals pale yellow spotted with purple, the lip cream with a yellow base, the anther-cap purple; pedicel and ovary 13–18 mm long. **Dorsal sepal** linear-lanceolate, acute, 10–12 mm long, 2–3 mm wide; **lateral sepals** obliquely ovate, acute, 12 mm long, 6–7 mm wide, forming a broadly conical mentum 5–6 mm long. **Petals** linear, acute, 10–12 mm long, 1 mm wide. **Lip** 12–14 mm long, 8–10 mm wide; hypochile short, with 2 erect rounded side lobes; mesochile narrow-tapering; epichile bilobed, with each lobe deeply lacerate; callus of 2 undulating ridges from the base of the lip onto the epichile. **Column** 4 mm long; foot 5–6 mm long.

DISTRIBUTION   Java and Sulawesi to N.E. Australia, New Guinea and the Pacific Islands; sea level – 850 m; in littoral, riverine or lowland forest, often on trees overhanging water.

HISTORY   Originally collected in Java by Carl Blume and described by him as *Desmotrichum comatum* in his *Bijdragen* (p. 230) in 1825. It was transferred to the present genus in 1961 by A.D. Hawkes in the *Orchid Weekly* (p. 453). The wide range of this attractive species is responsible for its large synonymy.

SYNONYMS   include *Desmotrichum comatum* Bl.; *Dendrobium comatum* (Bl.) Lindl.; *D. thysanochilum* Schltr.; *Ephemerantha comata* (Bl.) Hunt & Summerh.

Galeandra Lindl.

Subfamily Epidendroideae
Tribe Cymbidieae
Subtribe Cyrtopodiinae

Medium-sized to large terrestrial or epiphytic herbs. **Pseudobulbs** fusiform, short to elongated, concealed by leaf-sheaths. **Leaves** distichous, plicate, narrow, articulated to sheaths. **Inflorescence** terminal, racemose or paniculate. **Flowers** showy, **Sepals** and **petals** free, spreading. **Lip** tubular below, spreading-porrect and lobed above, with a prominent tapering basal spur; disc crested or lamellate. **Column** short to elongate, with a short foot, dorsally rostrate; pollinia 4, often in pairs, ovoid, ceraceous.

DISTRIBUTION   About 20 species in the American tropics.

DERIVATION OF NAME   From the Latin *galea* (helmet-shaped), referring to the anther-cap of the type species.

TAXONOMY   *Galeandra* was named by John Lindley in 1830 in his and F. Bauer's *Illustrations of Orchidaceous Plants* (t. 8). It is a distinct genus which is allied to *Polystachya* but may be distinguished easily by its much larger flowers and spurred lip. It is also allied to *Cyrtopodium* and *Eulophia* differing in its convolute lip which encloses the column.

TYPE SPECIES   *G. baueri* Lindl.

CULTURE   Compost B or C. Temp. Winter min. 12–15°C. *Galeandra* species grow well as terrestrials in well-drained pots. While the new shoots are growing, water may be freely given and the plants should be well shaded, but as the stems mature, less water and shade are required. After flowering, the plants benefit from a cooler, dry rest period, taking care not to allow the stems to shrivel.

Galeandra baueri Lindl.

An epiphytic plant often growing in clumps, up to 45 cm tall. **Stems** ancipitous, fusiform, slightly zigzag, up to 27 cm long, concealed by red-spotted, scarious leaf-sheaths. **Leaves** erect-spreading, linear to linear-lanceolate, acute or acuminate, up to 23 cm long, 2 cm broad. **Inflorescence** racemose or branched, few-flowered; peduncle erect, bearing slender, spotted sheaths; bracts lanceolate, acuminate, up to 0.5 cm long. **Flowers** showy; sepals and petals yellowish-brown; lip purple with a white or brownish base. **Sepals** narrowly oblanceolate, acute, 2 cm long, 0.5 cm broad. **Petals** similar to sepals, 1.8 cm long, 0.5 cm broad. **Lip** involute below, spreading above, rhombic-ovate, margins crenulate, 5 cm long up to 3.5 cm broad; callus of 2 small parallel ridges near base; spur tapering, curved, about 2 cm long.

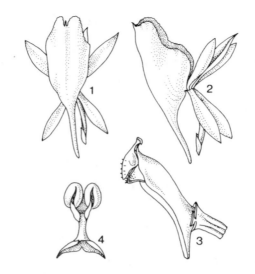

Galeandra baueri
1 – Flower from below (× ¾)
2 – Flower, side view (× ¾)
3 – Column (× 2)
4 – Pollinia, stipe and viscidium (× 6½)

Column arcuate, with a pair of ciliate side lobes at the apex; rostellum dorsal, recurved, 1 cm long.

DISTRIBUTION   Mexico to Panama and Surinam; up to 800 m altitude.

HISTORY   Named by John Lindley after Francis Bauer, the brilliant botanist and artist, and described in Lindley and Bauer's *Illustrations of Orchidaceous Plants* (t. 8) in 1832.

CLOSELY RELATED SPECIES   *Galeandra batemanii* Rolfe, often considered a synonym of *G. baueri*, differs from that species in its flower colour and lip and sepal shape.

Galeandra batemanii
Flower (× 1)
a – spur

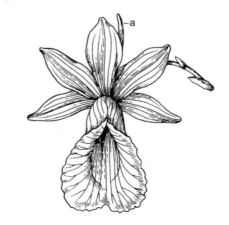

Galeandra devoniana Lindl. [Colour Plate]

A large epiphytic plant, up to 90 cm high. **Pseudobulbs** erect, fusiform, ± swollen at the base, up to 75 cm long, several-leaved, concealed by grey sheaths below, often bright red-brown above. **Leaves** linear, bright green, up to 20 cm long, 1 cm broad. **Inflorescence** terminal, racemose, several-flowered. **Flowers** showy; sepals and petals pale greenish-brown flushed or veined with maroon; lip white with maroon or pink veining near the apex and maroon or pale green veining on the spur; column cream. **Sepals** and **petals** erect, subsimilar, narrowly elliptic-lanceolate, acute, 4–4.2 long, 0.7–1 cm broad; lateral sepals and petals falcate. **Lip** tubular, subquadrate-obcordate when spread out, obscurely 3-lobed towards the apex, up to 5 cm long, 4.5 cm broad; side lobes oblong, incurved over column; mid-lobe broadly oblong, margins undulate; callus of 2 longitudinal ridges in the basal half; spur incurved, 1.5 cm long. **Column** arcuate-clavate, 1.3 cm long.

DISTRIBUTION   Guyana, Venezuela and Brazil.

HISTORY   Sent by Sir Robert Schomburgk to Messrs Loddiges of Hackney, London, from Guyana where he had collected it near Barcellos (Marina) on the banks of the Rio Negro. It was described for the first time by John Lindley in 1838 in *Sertum Orchidacearum* (t. 37).

Galeandra lacustris Barb. Rodr.

[Colour Plate]

A large epiphytic plant. **Pseudobulbs** fusiform, lightly compressed, up to 13 cm long, several-leaved towards apex, clothed below with grey sheaths and leaf-bases. **Leaves** ligulate, attenuate, spreading, mid-vein sulcate, up to 14 cm long, 0.7 cm broad. **Inflorescence** apical, 1- to 3-flowered. **Flowers** showy; sepals and petals green, flushed with maroon, bronze in appearance; lip white with pinkish margins and pink marks at the base; callus white; spur light greenish-yellow; column white with purple marks on ventral surface. **Sepals** and **petals** subsimilar, narrowly oblong-oblanceolate, acute, 2.1–2.2 cm long, 0.5–0.6 cm broad. **Lip** tubular-involute below; lamina broadly flabellate-obcordate when spread-out, obscurely 3-lobed towards the apex, 3 cm long, 4 cm broad; side lobes oblong-rounded, incurved over column; mid-lobe broadly oblong, margins undulate; callus of 4 ridges in basal half of lip; spur tapering, slightly upcurved, somewhat pubescent within, 2 cm long. **Column** terete, pointed at the apex, 2 cm long.

DISTRIBUTION   Brazil and Venezuela; in forest near rivers at low altitude.

HISTORY   Discovered on the Rio Negro in the Amazonas province of Brazil by J. Barbosa

Rodrigues and described by him in 1877 in his *Genera et Species Orchidearum Novarum* (p. 86).

Gastrochilus D. Don

Subfamily Epidendroideae
Tribe Vandeae
Subtribe Sarcanthinae

Epiphytic herbs with short to long, monopodial stems. **Leaves** coriaceous, distichous. **Inflorescence** axillary, short, few-flowered; peduncle and rhachis short. **Flowers** fleshy, conspicuous. **Sepals** and **petals** ± similar, spreading. **Lip** adnate to base of column, consisting of a ± round or globose saccate base, the sides of which are adnate to the wings of the column; mid-lobe pointing forward, broad and rounded, nearly flat, sometime hairy or fringed. **Column** very short, stout; pollinia 2, somewhat sulcate, on a long narrow stipe.

DISTRIBUTION   About 20 species in India, E. Asia, Malaysia and the adjacent islands.

DERIVATION OF NAME   From the Greek *gaster* (belly) and *cheilos* (lip), referring to the lip shape.

TAXONOMY   David Don described *Gastrochilus* in 1825 in his *Prodromus Florae Nepalensis* (p. 32). Rudolf Schlechter reviewed the genus in 1913 in *Fedde, Repertorium Specierum Novarum* accepting 16 species in it. *Gastrochilus* has been included by some authors in *Saccolabium* but is kept distinct by R. Holttum in the *Orchids of Malaya* (1964), by L. Garay in *Botanical Museum Leaflets of Harvard University* (1972), and by G. Seidenfaden (1988) in *Opera Botanica* (p. 285). The last account covers 12 species from Thailand and adjacent area. *Saccolabium* has been conserved against *Gastrochilus* but this only applied if the two are considered congeneric.

Gastrochilus is characterised by the very short, stout column lacking a foot; the subglobose lip with sides firmly adnate to the column, the 2 porate or slightly notched pollinia on a linear stipe and the short bifid rostellum.

TYPE SPECIES   *Aerides calceolare* J.E. Smith [= *G. calceolaris* (J.E. Smith) D. Don].

CULTURE   Compost A. Temp. Winter min. 15°C. As with many small vandaceous plants, these can be grown well in small pots or baskets, hanging near the glass. The smallest species also grow well mounted on a piece of cork or fern-fibre. High humidity is important while the plants are growing and water should be freely given, so long as drainage is perfect. Moderate shade is required during the summer.

Gastrochilus acutifolius (Lindl.) O. Ktze.

Stems elongate, slender, clothed by leaf-bases, 10–30 cm long, 0.5 cm in diameter. **Leaves** distichous, linear-oblong, acute or acuminate, 10–15 cm long, 1.7–4 cm broad. **Inflorescences** densely many-flowered, corymbose, much shorter than the leaves. **Flowers** fleshy, yellowish-red or more often yellowish-green and spotted or mottled brown; lip white with a yellow centre and ± speckled red; column stained with pale purple. **Sepals** obovate-oblong, obtuse, 0.4–0.7 cm long, 0.2 cm broad. **Petals** similar but slightly narrower than the sepals. **Lip** subglobose or almost hemispherical with a small triangular blade fringed with glandular hairs, 0.4–0.6 cm long; disc naked or very sparingly tuberculate. **Column** very short.

DISTRIBUTION   India (Sikkim Himalayas and the Khasia Hills).

HISTORY   Introduced into cultivation by the Rev. J. Clowes of Broughton Hall, near Manchester in 1837, having been collected somewhat earlier by Dr N. Wallich in N.E. India. John Lindley described it as *Saccolabium acutifolium* in 1833 in his *Genera and Species of Orchidaceous Plants* (p. 223). Otto Kuntze transferred it to *Gastrochilus* in 1891 in his *Revisio Genera Plantarum* (p. 661).

SYNONYMS   *Saccolabium denticulatum* Paxt.; *Aerides umbellatum* Wall.; *Saccolabium acutifolium* Lindl.

Gastrochilus bellinus (Rchb.f.) O. Ktze.

Stem short to long. **Leaves** falcate, narrowly oblanceolate, deeply unequally subacutely bifid at apex, 15–30 cm long, up to 2.5 cm broad. **Inflorescence** very short; bracts large, suborbicular, apiculate or obtuse, 1 cm long. **Flowers** medium-sized; sepals and petals greenish or pale yellow, spotted with chocolate-brown or purple; lip white, spotted with purple, yellow on disc and in saccate base. **Sepals** and **petals** subsimilar, slightly incurved, obovate, obtuse or rounded at the apex, 0.9–1.4 cm long, 0.4–0.5 cm broad. **Lip** saccate below, epichile spreading, broadly elliptic, margin erose, verrucose and with long white hairs on upper surface on each side, 1.3 cm long, 1.1–

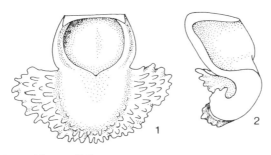

Gastrochilus acutifolius
1 – Lip, front view (× $3\frac{1}{2}$)
2 – Lip, longitudinal section (× $3\frac{1}{2}$)

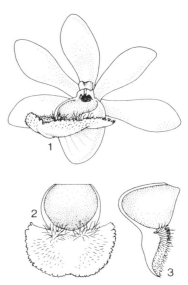

Gastrochilus bellinus
1 – Flower (× $1\frac{1}{2}$)
2 – Lip from above (× $1\frac{1}{2}$)
3 – Lip, longitudinal section (× $1\frac{1}{2}$)

1.5 cm broad. **Column** short, stout, 0.3 cm long.

DISTRIBUTION   Burma, Thailand, S.W. China and Laos; 600–1600 m.

HISTORY   Originally described in 1884 in the *Gardeners' Chronicle* (n.s. 21, p. 174) by H.G. Reichenbach as *Saccolabium bellinum* based on a plant collected by W. Boxall in Burma. O. Kuntze transferred it to *Gastrochilus* in 1891 in his *Revisio Genera Plantarum* (p. 661).

SYNONYM   *Saccolabium bellinum* Rchb.f.

Gastrochilus calceolaris (J.E. Smith) D. Don
[Colour Plate]

An epiphytic plant, up to 15 cm high. **Stem** very short, 0.6 cm in diameter. **Leaves** strongly falcate, linear-lanceolate, acutely unequally 2-lobed at apex, 15–30 cm long, 0.8–2 cm broad. **Inflorescence** short, corymbose, pendent, up to 5.5 cm long; bracts small, acute. **Flowers** 1.2–1.8 cm across; sepals and petals yellow or greenish, speckled, barred or blotched with red-brown; lip white or yellow, speckled with red. **Sepals** narrowly elliptic, subacute or rounded, 0.6–0.8 cm long, 0.35 cm broad. **Petals** subspathulate, obtuse, similar to sepals but shorter. **Lip** sessile, 0.7 cm long, 0.5–0.6 cm broad; front lobe reniform, margin denticulate; disc echinate; base saccate-globose, 0.4 cm deep. **Column** short, fleshy.

DISTRIBUTION   Tropical Himalayas, India (Assam and the Khasia Hills), Bangladesh (Sylhet), Burma, Malaya and Java.

HISTORY   This species was described in 1818 as *Aerides calceolaris* by J.E. Smith in A.

Rees's *Cyclopaedia* (p. 39) based on plants collected at Narainhetty in Nepal by F. Buchanan-Hamilton and also by Dr N. Wallich. It was transferred to *Gastrochilus* by David Don in his *Prodromus Florae Nepalensis* (p. 32) in 1825 as the type species in his new genus *Gastrochilus*.

SYNONYMS *Gastrochilus calceolaris* D. Don; *Sarcochilus nepalensis* Sprengel; *Aerides calceolaris* J.E. Smith; *Saccolabium calceolare* (D. Don) Lindl.

Gastrochilus dasypogon (J.E. Smith) O. Ktze.
Stem very short, 1–3 cm long; roots densely clustered below. **Leaves** ovate-oblong, acute, obliquely bidentate, 10–15 cm long, 1.8–2.5 cm broad. **Inflorescence** corymbose or subumbellate, up to 2.5 cm long; bracts ovate, cucullate, 0.5 cm long. **Flowers** with creamy-yellow or greenish sepals and petals, ± spotted violet; lip white or yellow, spotted with blood-red or purple. **Sepals** and **petals** obovate, obtuse, up to 0.8 cm long, 0.2 cm broad. **Lip** deeply saccate below, broadly spreading-reniform above, front margin erose, 0.6–0.7 cm long, 0.5 cm deep.

DISTRIBUTION Himalayas.
HISTORY Originally described as *Aerides dasypogon* by J.E. Smith in 1818 in the Supplement to A. Rees's *Cyclopaedia*, (p. 39) based on a collection from Nepal by F. Buchanan-Hamilton. It was transferred by John Lindley to *Saccolabium* in 1833 in his *Genera and Species of Orchidaceous Plants* (p. 222). Otto Kuntze transferred it to *Gastrochilus* in 1891 in his *Revisio Genera Plantarum* (p. 661).

Sir Joseph Hooker in the *Flora of British India* treated this species under the 'doubtful and imperfectly known species' section of *Saccolabium* and notes that it is probably *S. calceolare* (D. Don) Lindl. [= *G. calceolaris* D. Don]. G. Seidenfaden and T. Smitinand included *G. dasypogon* in their account of the *Orchids of Thailand* (1963) but Seidenfaden (1988) in *Opera Botanica* (p. 298) now considers this to be *G. obliquus*.

Gastrochilus dasypogon
1 – Lip from above (× 3⅘)
2 – Lip, longitudinal section (× 3⅘)

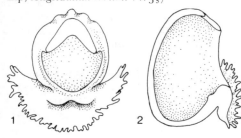

SYNONYM *Saccolabium dasypogon* Lindl.
CLOSELY RELATED SPECIES *G. obliquus* (Lindl.) O. Ktze., widely distributed from Sikkim to Indo-China, is often confused with *G. dasypogon*, but it differs in having a shorter inflorescence and flowers with yellow-green sepals and petals and a lip with a narrower epichile bearing a smaller almost obscure fleshy callus.

Genyorchis Schltr.
Subfamily Epidendroideae
Tribe Cymbidieae
Subtribe Genyorchidinae

Small epiphytic herbs with an elongate creeping rhizome bearing well-spaced small, ovoid or cylindrical, 1- or 2-leaved pseudobulbs. **Leaves** elliptic to linear, subcoriaceous to somewhat fleshy. **Inflorescence** basal, lateral, erect, racemose, laxly few-flowered. **Flowers** non-resupinate, small, not opening widely. **Dorsal sepal** free; **lateral sepals** obliquely triangular, forming a distinct conical mentum with the column-foot. **Petals** free, present or almost absent. **Lip** uppermost in the flower, 3-lobed, small. **Column** short, sometimes winged or with minute stelidia, with a long foot; pollinia 2 on a short but distinct stipe.

DISTRIBUTION A small genus of six species in tropical Africa.
DERIVATION OF NAME From the Greek *genys* (jaw) and *orchis* (orchid) a reference to the side view of the flower, which resembles an open jaw.
TAXONOMY Rudolf Schlechter established this genus of small *Bulbophyllum*-like orchids in 1901 in the *Westafrika Kautschuk-Expedition* (p. 280) and in greater detail in 1905 in Engler's *Botanische Jahrbucher* (p. 11). The genus has flowers that closely resemble those of some species of *Polystachya* and some of the smaller *Dendrobium* species. It is, however, not closely allied to them and Dressler (1981) in his *The Orchids. Natural History and Classification* places it in its own subtribe close to the Cyrtopodiinae.
TYPE SPECIES *G. pumila* (Sw.) Schltr.
CULTURE Temp Winter min. 15°C. As for some of the small *Bulbophyllum* species. These small creeping epiphytes are best grown mounted, but may be grown in pans. Give humid conditions and water throughout the year.

Genyorchis pumila (Sw.) Schltr.
A small creeping epiphyte with an elongate slender rhizome. **Pseudobulbs** ovoid-oblong, 4-angled, 6–15 mm long, 4–5 mm in diameter, 2-leaved at the apex. **Leaves** spreading, elliptic-oblong, obtuse, 0.7–2.5 cm. long, 0.4–

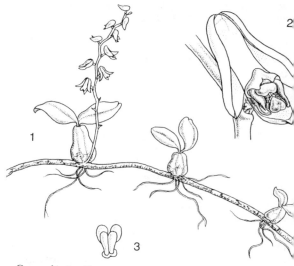

Genyorchis pumila
1 – Habit (× ¾)
2 – Flower (× 4½)
3 – Pollinarium (× 5)

0.7 cm wide. **Inflorescence** erect, 6–10 cm long or rarely longer, laxly 4- to 6- to 12-flowered; peduncle wiry; bracts triangular, 1–1.5 mm long. **Flowers** distichous, white with a yellow patch at the base and apex of the lip and purple apex to the column; ovary up to 1 mm long, glabrous. **Dorsal sepal** elliptic-lanceolate, acute, 2.5–3 mm long, 1–1.7 mm wide; **lateral sepals** obliquely triangular, acute, 4–4.5 mm long, 2–2.5 mm wide; mentum obliquely conical, 2–2.5 mm long. **Petals** very small, semicircular, obtuse. **Lip** obscurely 3-lobed, fleshy, 2.5–3.5 mm long, recurved and papillose near apex. **Column** 1.5 mm long; foot 2–2.5 mm long, incurved.
DISTRIBUTION Tropical Africa from Sierra Leone across to Zaïre and Uganda; in forest, up to 1400 m altitude.
HISTORY Olof Swartz described this tiny species as *Dendrobium pumilum* in 1805 in Scrader, *Neues Journal* (p. 97), based on a collection made by Afzelius in Sierra Leone. It was transferred to the present genus as the type species by Rudolf Schlechter in 1901 in the *Westafrika Kautschuk-Expedition* (p. 280).
SYNONYMS *Dendrobium pumilum* Sw.; *Bulbophyllum pumilum* (Sw.) Lindl.; *Polystachya bulbophylloides* Rolfe

Geodorum G. Jacks.
Subfamily Epidendroideae
Tribe Cymbidieae
Subtribe Cyrtopodiinae

Terrestrial herbs with ovoid fleshy pseudobulbs, produced at the soil surface, covered when young by leaf sheaths. **Leaves** 2 to 4, plicate, erect or suberect, broad, petiolate. **Inflorescence** erect, but the rhachis curling through 180° as the flowers open, simple, racemose. **Flowers** off-white, yellow or pink, campanulate, sometimes self-pollinating. **Sepals** and **petals** subsimilar, free. **Lip** lowermost in flower, entire, obscurely 3-lobed, concave, with a saccate base, usually with an obscure ridged callus. **Column** elongate, with a distinct foot; pollinia 2, attached by a stipe to a viscidium.

DISTRIBUTION A genus of about 10 species, widespread from India throughout S.E. Asia across to Australia and the islands of the S.W. Pacific.

DERIVATION OF NAME From the Greek *geo* (ground) and *doron* (gift) referring to the distinctive recurved apex of the inflorescence, whose apex points towards the ground.

TAXONOMY *Geodorum* was established by Jackson in Andrews' *Botanical Repository* (t. 626) in 1810. It is a taxonomically difficult genus in which the specific limits are unclear. It can either be considered to comprise a few species, of which one or two are widespread and variable, or of many closely related but similar species. A discussion of the problems is given by Seidenfaden (1983) in *Opera Botanica* (p. 47).

TYPE SPECIES *G. citrinum* G. Jacks.

CULTURE Temp. Winter min. 15°C. Grown in a similar manner to *Eulophia* species. After flowering, the leaves gradually die down and the plants then need a much drier resting period until new growth begins again.

Geodorum purpureum R. Br. [Colour Plate]

A medium-sized terrestrial plant with ovoid **pseudobulbs**, 1.5–2.5 cm long, 1–2 cm in diameter. **Leaves** ovate-lanceolate, acute or acuminate, 15–35 cm long, 4.5–8 cm wide. **Inflorescence** up to 45 cm tall, rather densely 8- to 20-flowered; rhachis up to 5 cm long, recurved; bracts linear-lanceolate, 0.6–4 cm long. **Flowers** campanulate, often self-pollinating, pale purple with a yellow blotch and purple spotting on the lip; pedicel and ovary 6–7 mm long. **Sepals** oblong, acute or subacute, 0.9–1.4 cm long, 3–5 mm wide. **Petals** similar but broader. **Lip** saccate at the base, ovate, 3-lobed, 8–10 mm long, 7–8 mm wide. **Column** 5 mm long; foot 3 mm long.

DISTRIBUTION S.E. Asia, from Burma and Thailand south to the Malay archipelago and Australia and the islands of the S.W. Pacific; in grassy places and scrub sea level to 500 m.

HISTORY Robert Brown described this species in the second edition of Aiton's *Hortus Kewensis* (p. 207).

It is a widespread and variable species and may be conspecific with *G. densiflorum* (Lam.) Schltr.

SYNONYMS include *G. pictum* R. Br.; *G. pacificum* Rolfe; *G. neocaledonicum* Kraenzl.

Gomesa R. Br.
Subfamily Epidendroideae
Tribe Oncidieae

Small epiphytic herbs. **Stems** short, pseudobulbous, 1- or 2-leaved at apex. **Leaves** oblong or elongate, petiolate below. **Inflorescence** from the base of the pseudobulb, axillary, simple, racemose; bracts narrow often longer than the pedicel. **Flowers** small, rather insignificant. **Dorsal sepal** and **petals** subsimilar, free, spreading; **lateral sepals** free or ± connate. **Lip** fixed to the column-base, incurved-erect or erect at the base then reflexed above, spurless, entire to 3-lobed; side lobes erect, obsolete to prominent and enclosing the column; mid-lobe spreading or reflexed; disc with two longitudinal calli. **Column** erect, footless, semiterete, straight, narrow or clavate or 2-winged above; pollinia 2, waxy, ovoid or subglobose, sulcate, with a narrow stipe and an ovate viscidium.

DISTRIBUTION About 20 species in Brazil.

DERIVATION OF NAME Dr Bernardino Antonio Gomes was a Portuguese naval physician and botanist who wrote a book on the medicinal plants of Brazil.

TAXONOMY *Gomesa* was described by R. Brown in 1815 in the *Botanical Magazine* (t. 1748). He distinguished it by its spurless, entire, bicristate, sessile lip which is continuous with the base of the wingless column, by the connate lateral sepals and by the 2 pollinia which are sulcate and obliquely 2-lobed and are attached to a single disc.

G. Pabst and F. Dungs in *Orchidaceae Brasilienses* (1977) have separated the Brazilian species of *Gomesa* into 3 groups as follows:

1. *G. crispa* alliance – rhizome short; pseudobulbs approximate; lateral sepals free (or rarely partially connate in abnormal flowers).

2. *G. recurva* alliance – rhizome short; pseudobulbs approximate: lateral sepals always more or less connate.

3. *G. glaziovii* alliance – rhizome long; pseudobulbs always distantly placed.

TYPE SPECIES *G. recurva* R. Br.

CULTURE Compost A. Temp. Winter min. 15°C. *Gomesa* species grow well in pots under shady, humid conditions. When growth is complete, the plants should be given more light, and carefully watered, so that the pseudobulbs remain firm. The inflorescences appear from the side of the pseudobulbs as in *Odontoglossum* and *Oncidium*.

Gomesa crispa (Lindl.) Klotzsch ex Rchb.f.
[Colour Plate]

A medium-sized epiphytic herb. **Pseudobulbs** narrowly oblong-conical, strongly compressed, ancipitous, 5–10 cm long, 1–2.5 broad, 2-leaved at apex. **Leaves** erect-spreading, membranaceous, narrowly ligulate-lanceolate, acute or shortly acuminate, long-attenuate below, 15–28 cm long, 2–3.5 cm broad. **Inflorescence** pendent, densely many-flowered above, 15–22 cm long. **Flowers** fragrant, green with yellow margins or yellow. **Sepal** oblong-ligulate, more or less free to the base, subabruptly acute, 0.9–1 cm long, 0.2–0.25 cm broad. **Petals** oblong-subspathulate, abruptly subacute, 0.8–1 cm long, 0.3 cm broad. **Lip** subconvex, strongly recurved, broadly oblong, obtuse, 0.7–0.8 cm long, 0.3–0.4 cm broad; disc broadly bicristate, margins of each undulate-denticulate in front. **Column** slender, subclavate, 0.5 cm long.

DISTRIBUTION Brazil

HISTORY Originally described without citing any specimens by John Lindley in 1839 in the *Botanical Register* (misc. 86) as *Rodriguezia crispa*. H.G. Reichenbach transferred it to *Gomesa* in 1852 in the *Botanische Zeitung* (p. 772).

SYNONYMS *Rodriguezia crispa* Lindl.; *Odontoglossum crispulum* Rchb.f.

Gomesa recurva R.Br. [Colour Plate]

A medium-sized epiphytic plant. **Pseudobulbs** narrowly ovoid, ancipitous, compressed, 5–7 cm long, 2.5–3.5 cm broad, 2- or 3-leaved at apex. **Leaves** coriaceous, linear-oblanceolate, acute, long-attenuate below, 20–30 cm long, 2–3 cm broad. **Inflorescence** arcuate, nodding, densely many-flowered, 20–35 cm long. **Flowers** rather small, long-pedicellate, yellowish-green, with a yellow basal streak on the lip, fragrant. **Sepals** spreading, narrowly oblong-spathulate, abruptly acute, 1–1.2 cm, long, 0.4 cm broad; lateral sepals connate almost to the apex. **Petals** flat or slightly undulate, oblong-spathulate, rounded or apiculate at the apex, 1.1 cm long, 0.4 cm broad. Lip strongly recurved, ovate, acute, 0.9–1 cm long, 0.5–0.6 broad; disc broadly bilamellate, terminating in 2 lower rounded calli. **Column** fleshy, clavate, truncate at the apex, 0.4–0.5 cm long.

DISTRIBUTION Brazil

HISTORY Cultivated for the first time by William Anderson, curator of the Chelsea Botanic Garden, London, this pretty Brazilian species was described by Robert Brown in 1815 in Curtis's *Botanical Magazine* (t. 1748).

SYNONYMS *Rodriguezia recurva* (R. Br.) Lindl.; *Odontoglossum recurvum* (R. Br.) Rchb.f.

CLOSELY RELATED SPECIES *Gomesa planifolia* (Lindl.) Klotszch & Rchb.f. is allied to *G. recurva*, being distinguished by its ovate-elliptic lip, the calli which extend to beyond the middle of the lip, and the shorter, more incurved sepals and petals.

Gongora Ruiz & Pavon

Subfamily Epidendroideae
Tribe Gongoreae
Subtribe Stanhopeinae

Epiphytic plants with fleshy 2-leaved pseudobulbs. **Leaves** large, plicate, contracted at the base. **Inflorescence** from the base of the pseudobulb, racemose, flexuose, pendulous, laxly many-flowered. **Flowers** medium-sized, often rather dully coloured and somewhat grotesque. **Dorsal sepal** erect, spreading; **lateral sepals** broader, spreading and reflexed, oblique. **Petals** adnate to the side of the column, spreading and erect above. **Lip** complex, continuous with the column-foot, spreading to ascending, narrow, fleshy; side lobes thick, erect, aristate or horned; mid-lobe compressed or saccate, 2-lobed, acute or acuminate at the apex. **Column** slender, arcuate, ± winged above; pollinia 2, ovoid to narrowly oblong.
DISTRIBUTION Some 25 species in the American tropics from Mexico and the W. Indies south to Peru and Brazil.
DERIVATION OF NAME Named in honour of Don Antonio Caballero y Gongora, one time Viceroy of New Granada (Colombia and Ecuador) and later Bishop of Córdoba. He was an enthusiastic patron of Don Celestino Mutis, after whom Ruiz and Pavon named the genus *Mutisia* (Compositae).
TAXONOMY Described by H. Ruiz and J. Pavon in 1794 in their *Prodromus Florae Peruvianae et Chilensis* (p. 227). Several species in the genus have extremely variably coloured flowers and in the past many cultivated forms have been described as species which are now considered merely as colour variants. Although the variability of these species is now well recognised, cultivated plants are often difficult to name because of the great variability and still poorly defined specific limits in some species.

Undoubtedly the problem is exacerbated by the extreme complexity of the fleshy lip in *Gongora* which often defies description. Additionally many of the original descriptions have only a superficial description of the lip and also lack an accompanying illustration. P. Allen in *Flora of Panama* (1949) states 'Of the many published names, perhaps about a dozen fairly well marked entities can be segregated, but even these often are subject to a considerable amount of variation.' For example, Pabst and Dungs in *Orchidaceae Brasilienses*, vol. 2 (1977) have resurrected several names for Brazilian species which have previously been relegated to synonymy within *G. quinquenervis*. A series of articles by R. Jenny in the journal *Die Orchideen* from 1982 onwards has clarified some of the complex taxonomy of this genus.
TYPE SPECIES *G. quinquenervis* Ruiz & Pavon
CULTURE Compost A. Temp. Winter min. 15°C. Except for their 2-leaved pseudobulbs, *Gongora* species resemble *Stanhopea*, and may be grown in the same way. Although the inflorescences do not grow so quickly, the plants are best grown in hanging baskets or pots. During active growth, they need high humidity, moderate shade and plenty of water at the roots, but when the new pseudobulbs are fully grown, much less water should be given.

Gongora galeata (Lindl.) Rchb.f.
[Colour Plate]
A large epiphytic plant. **Pseudobulbs** ovoid, sulcate to pyriform, clustered, covered with 2 or 3 membranous sheaths up to 4.5 cm long, 2.5 cm broad, 1- or 2-leaved at apex. **Leaves** broadly lanceolate, plicate, acute, 16–32 cm long, 4–4.5 cm or more broad. **Inflorescence** basal, arcuate-pendulous, up to 28 cm long, mostly 10- to 15-flowered arranged in 3 rows: bracts very small, purple; peduncle and rhachis purple. **Flowers** buff to creamy-green faintly mottled orange below; pedicel and ovary curved and purple; lip yellow-brown; column yellow-green, spotted with purple. **Sepals** oblong-ovate, obtuse, margins reflexed, 2–2.5 cm long, 1.2 cm broad. **Petals** very short, oblong-falcate, truncate and with 2 spreading teeth at sides at apex, 0.4–0.5 cm. **Lip** articulated to column-base, 3-lobed, 1.2 cm long, 0.9 cm broad; side lobes large, inflexed; mid-lobe saccate. **Column** somewhat winged on margins, 1 cm long.
DISTRIBUTION Mexico.
HISTORY Introduced from Xalapa, Mexico by George Loddiges, having been originally collected there by F. Deppe in 1828. John Lindley described it as *Maxillaria galeata* in 1830 in Loddiges' *Botanical Cabinet* (t. 1645). H.G. Reichenbach transferred it in 1854 to *Gongora* in *Xenia Orchidacea* (p. 51).
SYNONYMS *Maxillaria galeata* Lindl.; *Acropera loddigesii* Lindl.

Gongora quinquenervis Ruiz & Pavon
[Colour Plate]
Pseudobulbs ovoid-oblong to conical, 4.5–8 cm long, 2.5–3.5 cm in diameter, deeply grooved and ridged, 2-leaved at apex. **Leaves** lanceolate, ligulate or elliptic-obovate, 25–40 cm long, 5–14 cm broad, acute, suberect, plicate, margins undulate, shortly petiolate. **Inflorescence** pendulous, laxly many-flowered, up to 80 cm long; bracts ovate-lanceolate, up to 0.5 cm long. **Flowers** fragrant, lip uppermost, reddish or brownish-red with yellow or white spots and bands, or yellow with maroon spotting. **Sepals** membranaceous, acuminate; dorsal sepal lanceolate, margins curved back, up to 2.3 cm long, 0.6 cm broad; lateral sepals reflexed, obliquely ovate-lanceolate, 2–3 cm long, 1.5 cm broad, margins curved back. **Petals** joined to sides of column in basal half, linear-lanceolate, up to 1 cm long, 0.2 cm broad. **Lip** very fleshy, up to 2.5 cm long, 3-lobed; side lobes triangular, acuminate, erect, each bearing a basal erect protuberance; mid-lobe hastate, very fleshy. **Column** suberect, arcuate, up to 2.5 cm long, dilated towards apex.
DISTRIBUTION Mexico, Central America, northern S. America and Trindad.
HISTORY This very variable species was first collected by H. Ruiz and J. Pavon at Pozuzo in Peru. They described it in 1798 in their *Systema Vegetabilium Florae Peruvianae et Chilensis* (p. 227). It is still cultivated under other later names such as *G. maculata* which was described by John Lindley in the *Botanical Register* (t. 1616). The type of *G. maculata* was collected by Thomas Moss in Demerara (Georgetown) in Guyana and he sent living plants to Richard Harrison of Liverpool in 1832.
SYNONYMS include *Gongora maculata* Lindl.; *G. atropurpurea* Hooker; *G. nigrita* Lindl.; *G. retrorsa* Rchb.f.

Goodyera R. Br.

Subfamily Spiranthoideae
Tribe Cranichideae
Subtribe Goodyerinae

Small to medium-sized terrestrial herbs with a creeping rhizome, rooting at the nodes sending up erect secondary stems at intervals. **Leaves** basal or clustered in lower part of stem, fleshy, several, petiolate from somewhat inflated sheaths, sometimes with reticulately coloured leaves. **Inflorescences** erect, few- to many-flowered, racemose; peduncle and rhachis pubescent or glandular-hairy. **Flowers** relatively small and insignificant, often secund, often pubescent or glandular on outer surface. **Sepals** parallel to the floral axis or with lateral sepals spreading; dorsal sepal forming a hood with the petals. **Lip** hollow or saccate, with bristly hairs within, narrowed to an acute apex which is sometimes reflexed but not lobed. **Column** short, lacking appendages at the base; rostellum long, deeply cleft; stigma not divided, large, on front of column; pollinia 2, often deeply cleft, granulose, pyriform to narrowly clavate; viscidium elongate.
DISTRIBUTION A genus of about 40

species, widely distributed in the N. temperate zone south to Mexico in the New World, S.E. Asia, the Pacific Islands, New Guinea and Australia. Also in Madagascar.

DERIVATION OF NAME Named in honour of John Goodyer (1592–1664), an early English botanist.

TAXONOMY *Goodyera* was established in 1813 by Robert Brown in the 2nd edition of W. Aiton's *Hortus Kewensis* (p. 197). It is allied to *Hetaeria* and *Zeuxine* amongst other genera but is easily distinguished by its unlobed lip which is hairy within and the large, undivided stigma at the front of the column. Rudolf Schlechter in *Die Orchidaceen von Deutsch-Neu-Guinea* recognised two sections: *Otosepalum*, in which the lateral sepals are spreading or deflexed and diverge well away from each other; and (*Eu*)*Goodyera* where the lateral sepals are ± porrect and parallel to each other.

TYPE SPECIES *Satyrium repens* L. lectotype [= *G. repens* (L.) R. Br.].

CULTURE Compost C. Temp. Winter min. 12–15°C for tropical species, lower for temperate ones. *Goodyera* species are generally creeping plants, so should be grown in shallow pans. They soon cover quite a large area and may readily be propagated from side shoots. The compost needs to be kept evenly moist throughout the year, and good shade is required.

Goodyera hispida **Lindl.** [Colour Plate]

A small terrestrial plant, up to 15 cm tall. Leaves 6–8, basal, subsessile, ovate-lanceolate, acuminate, 2.5–5 cm long, 1.5–2 cm broad, **Inflorescences** erect, spicate, hispidly glandular, twisted above; bracts shorter than the flowers. **Flowers** small, white. **Sepals** ovate-oblong, obtuse and recurved at apex, 0.6 cm long, 0.2 cm broad. **Petals** oblong-lanceolate, nearly straight, 0.5 cm long, 0.15 cm broad, subacute. **Lip** saccate, shortly obtusely beaked, shortly setose within, 0.6 cm long, 0.3 cm broad, apex recurved. **Column** with subulate arms; anther lanceloate.

DISTRIBUTION India (Khasia Hills, Sikkim and near Darjeeling) and Bhutan; above 1000 m.

HISTORY Described by John Lindley in the *Journal of the Linnean Society* (p. 183) in 1857, based on a plant collected by J.D. Hooker and T. Thompson in the Khasia Hills.

CLOSELY RELATED SPECIES Allied to *Goodyera repens* R. Br. but distinguished by its larger leaves and the lip which has a setose saccate base. Also allied to *Goodyera secundiflora* Griff. which is distinguished by its secund inflorescence.

Goodyera maximowicziana **Makino**
[Colour Plate]

A small fleshy plant with a long creeping rhizome and short leafy erect stems, 6–10 cm tall. **Leaves** ovate, acute, 2.5–5 cm long, 1–2 cm wide, green, with undulate margins. **Inflorescence** densely 3- to 9-flowered, 1.5–4 cm long; bracts lanceolate, acuminate, up to 22 mm long. **Flowers** white, more or less flushed with pink, glabrous; pedicel and ovary 10–13 mm long. **Dorsal sepal** concave, lanceolate, rounded at the apex, 9–14 mm long, 4–4.5 cm wide; **lateral sepals** falcate, lanceolate, acuminate, 10–14 mm long, 4–5 mm wide. **Petals** oblanceolate, acute, 10–13 mm long, 3.5–4 mm wide, adnate to the dorsal sepal to form a hood over the column. **Lip** saccate at the base, ovate, 9–10 mm long, 4–5 mm wide, with many papillae within the saccate part. **Column** 3 mm long; rostellum bifid, 4 mm long.

DISTRIBUTION Japan and Taiwan; in leaf litter on the floor of forests.

HISTORY Described by T. Makino in the *Botanical Magazine, Tokyo* (p. 137) in 1909, based on his own collection from Japan. *Goodyera henryi* Rolfe, from China, may be conspecific and is an earlier name.

CLOSELY RELATED SPECIES Very close to *Goodyera foliosa* (Lindl.) Bentham, also from the Far East, which differs mainly in having glandular pubescent flowers.

Govenia **Lindl. ex Lodd.**

Subfamily Epidendroideae
Tribe Calypsoeae
Subtribe Corallorhizinae

Terrestrial plants with corm-like pseudobulbs surrounded by leaf-sheaths. **Leaves** 2, sub-opposite, or rarely 1, plicate, strongly veined, petiolate. **Inflorescence** lateral, erect, few- to many-flowered. Flowers fleshy, medium-sized. **Sepals** and **petals** free but dorsal sepal and petals connivent to form a hood over the column. **Lip** entire, thin-textured. **Column** incurved, winged at the apex, with a short foot; pollinia 4, hard, superimposed, attached by an oblong or broad stipe to the small or dilated viscidium.

DISTRIBUTION Some 25 or so species distributed from Mexico south to Bolivia.

DERIVATION OF NAME This genus commemorates the English gardener and naturalist, J.R. Gowen, who collected plants in Assam in the early nineteenth century.

TAXONOMY The genus was established in 1831 in Loddiges' *Botanical Cabinet* (t. 1709).

Govenia is taxonomically a difficult genus with several species that are readily separated in the field but whose differences disappear in herbarium material. The synonymy of some of the species is therefore possibly inflated, and

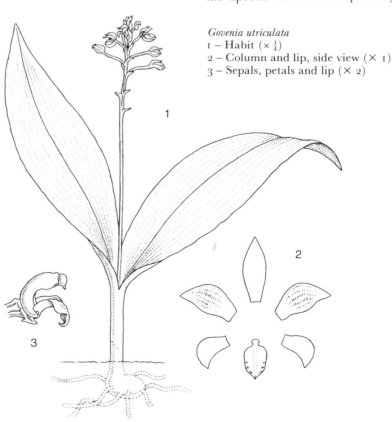

Govenia utriculata
1 – Habit (× $\frac{1}{4}$)
2 – Column and lip, side view (× 1)
3 – Sepals, petals and lip (× 2)

the distributions given in Floras may reflect the range of a number of closely related taxa rather than that of the species being described.

TYPE SPECIES   *Maxillaria superba* La Llave & Lex.

SYNONYM   *Eucnemis* Lindl.

CULTURE   As for *Eulophia*, but rather cooler growing. The soft leaves are liable to rot, so that water needs to be carefully applied. When the leaves die down, very little water is required until the new growth begins.

Govenia utriculata (Sw.) Lindl.

A medium-sized terrestrial plant up to 90 cm tall. **Pseudobulbs** 2-leaved, enclosed when young by several inflated sheaths up to 22 cm long. **Leaves** narrowly elliptic to oblanceolate, acute to obtuse, 30–60 cm long, 8–15 cm wide. **Inflorescence** laxly 5- to 15-flowered; bracts linear-lanceolate to elliptic-lanceolate, acute to acuminate, 1–1.5 cm long. **Flowers** white to pale yellow, flushed with purple on the outer surface and marked inside with dark purple spots and lines; pedicel and ovary 1.5–2 cm long. **Dorsal sepal** elliptic-oblanceolate to elliptic-oblong, subacute to obtuse, 1.3–2.5 cm long, 0.3–0.7 cm wide; **lateral sepals** elliptic-oblong to elliptic, falcate, obtuse, 1–1.5 cm long, 0.3–0.6 cm wide. **Petals** elliptic to oblanceolate, obtuse, 1–2.2 cm long, 0.5–0.9 cm wide. **Lip** entire, shortly clawed, ovate to ovate-elliptic, obtuse to rounded at the apex, 0.6–1.2 cm long, 0.4–0.8 cm wide. **Column** stout, 5–9 mm long.

DISTRIBUTION   Widespread in tropical Americas from Mexico to Argentina, and also in the West Indies; up to 2000 m in wet montane forest.

HISTORY   This species was originally described as *Limodorum utriculatum* by Olof Swartz in 1788 and was transferred to *Govenia* by John Lindley in the *Botanical Register* (misc. 47) of 1839. It is closely allied to *G. superba* (Llave & Lex.) Lindl., another widespread species from Mexico to Venezuela, but differs principally in having whitish rather than yellow flowers.

SYNONYMS   *Limodorum utriculatum* Sw.; *Govenia gardneri* Hook.; *G. boliviensis* Rolfe; *G. ernestii* Schltr.; *G. sodiroi* Schltr.

Grammangis Rchb.f.
Subfamily Epidendroideae
Tribe Cymbidieae
Subtribe Cymbidiinae

Large epiphytic plants. **Pseudobulbs** large, 3- to 5-leaved at apex. **Leaves** flat, fleshy, coriaceous, articulated. **Inflorescences** from the base of the pseudobulb, racemose. **Flowers** large, showy, fleshy. **Dorsal sepal** free; **lateral**

sepals and **petals** free, dissimilar, decurrent at the base. **Lip** 3-lobed, spurless, inserted at the apex of the column-foot; disc several-ridged. **Column** fleshy, with a short thick foot and a deep nectary; pollinia 2, sessile on an elliptic viscidium.

DISTRIBUTION   Two species in Madagascar.

DERIVATION OF NAME   From the Greek *gramma* (letter or mark) and *angos* (vessel) possibly referring to the conspicuous red-purple lines of the lip.

TAXONOMY   Described by H.G. Reichenbach in 1860 in the *Hamburger Gartenzeitung* (p. 520). *Grammangis* is allied to *Cymbidium* and was originally referred to the Malaysian genus *Grammatophyllum* by John Lindley. H.G. Reichenbach separated it from that genus on account of the very different form of the perianth.

Grammangis has most recently been revised by J. Bosser and P. Morat in *Adansonia* (1969) where they accept two species in the genus. Two other species, *G. falcigera* Rchb.f. and *G. pardalina* Rchb.f., treated in this genus by Henri Perrier de la Bâthie in *Flore de Madagascar* (1941) are now considered to be species of *Cymbidiella* (see L. Garay (1976) in the *Orchid Digest*).

TYPE SPECIES   *G. ellisii* (Lindl.) Rchb.f.

CULTURE   Compost A. Temp. Winter min. 15°C. These plants resent disturbance and so should be potted in a container of sufficient size to accommodate at least 2 year's growth. While growing they need high humidity, plenty of water and moderate shade. When growth is complete, less water should be given, and shading may be reduced. The inflorescences arise at the same time as the new shoots.

Grammangis ellisii (Lindl.) Rchb.f.
[Colour Plate]

A large epiphytic plant, 50–60 cm high. **Pseudobulbs** ovoid-tetragonal, 8–10 cm long, covered by numerous sheaths when young, 3- to 5-leaved. **Leaves** oblong, plicate, obliquely rounded at apex, 16–40 cm long, 1.3–4 cm broad. **Inflorescence** basal, arcuate, up to 65 cm long, 15- to 40-flowered; peduncle 25–35 cm long; bracts lanceolate, 5 cm long, 1.2 cm broad. **Flowers** large, segments waxy; sepals glossy-brown, spotted yellow and with a yellow margin; petals cream, pinkish-yellow above; lip white, pale pinkish-orange above, callus white; column white. **Dorsal sepal** spreading, obovate, attenuate into an apical point, 4 cm long, 2 cm broad; **lateral sepals** spreading, obovate, acuminate, 4 cm long, 2.5 cm broad, margins of sepals undulate. **Petals** porrect, similar to sepals but smaller. **Lip** erect, obovate, 3-lobed above the middle, 1.8 cm long and broad; side

lobes falcate; mid-lobe longer and narrower than side lobes; disc with a large bifurcate callus. **Column** 1 cm long, with triangular-obtuse wings.

DISTRIBUTION   E. Madagascar.

HISTORY   Discovered in the forests of E. Madagascar by the Rev. W. Ellis and named after him by John Lindley as *Grammatophyllum ellisii* in 1860 in the *Botanical Magazine* (t. 5179). Later the same year H.G. Reichenbach transferred it to the genus *Grammangis* in the *Hamburger Gartenzeitung* (p. 520).

SYNONYM   *Grammatophyllum ellisii* Lindl.

Grammatophyllum Blume
Subfamily Epidendroideae
Tribe Cymbidieae
Subtribe Cymbidiinae

Medium-sized to very large epiphytic plants. **Pseudobulbs** clustered, short or long, few- to many-leaved. **Roots** stiff, white, growing upwards or outwards, many-branched. **Leaves** 2-ranked relatively long and narrow, flexible. **Inflorescences** erect or drooping, many-flowered, racemose. **Flowers** large or medium-sized, often showy. **Sepals** and **petals** large, showy, sub-similar. **Lip** smaller than other segments, with 3 low keels. **Column** short; pollinia 2, cleft, each joined by a caudicle to a separate outgrowth from the laterally extended ± crescent-shaped viscidium.

DISTRIBUTION   Possibly up to 12 species in S.E. Asia and Indonesia to New Guinea, the Philippines and S.W. Pacific.

DERIVATION OF NAME   From the Greek *gramma* (letter) and *phyllon* (leaf), in reference to the dark and conspicuous markings of the sepals and petals.

TAXONOMY   *Grammatophyllum* was established by C.L. Blume in 1825 in *Bijdragen* (p. 377, t. 20). This genus comprised about 12 rather confused species which was revised by R. Schlechter in *Orchis* (1915). In particular, there has been confusion over the name *G. scriptum* which was given to two distinct species by G.E. Rumphius.

There are two distinct growth-forms in the genus. Sect. *Grammatophyllum* has very long pseudobulbs which are really fleshy stems bearing many leaves, this corresponding to Schlechter's sect. *Gabertia;* the other has rather short thick pseudobulbs which are not covered by leaf-bases and bear a few leaves towards the apex and corresponds to Schlechter's sect. *Pattonia*. The flowers are essentially similar in both, and both have erect branching white roots.

Grammatophyllum is closely allied to *Cymbidium* and the plants of the second section closely approach that genus in habit. The two genera are most notably distinct in their pollinia which are directly attached to the viscidium in *Cymbidium* but attached by separate straps to the viscidium in *Grammatophyllum*.

Schlechter (1915) placed one species *G. stapeliaeflorum* (Teijsm. & Binnend.) J.J. Smith in its own section, *Stictorchis*, of *Grammangis* but R. Holttum in the *Orchids of Malaya* (1964) agrees with J.J. Smith that this species is better placed in *Grammatophyllum*.

TYPE SPECIES *G. speciosum* Blume

CULTURE Compost A. Temp. Winter min. 15°C. Species such as *G. scriptum* may be grown in large pots or baskets, under humid and only moderately shady conditions. Plenty of water is required during growth, with a drier period when the pseudobulbs are fully grown. *G. speciosum*, because of its potential size, requires a suitable large container and should not be disturbed too often. Good light and plenty of water throughout the year are other requirements.

Grammatopyllum speciosum Blume

[Colour Plate]

A very large epiphytic plant. **Pseudobulbs** erect to spreading or drooping, cylindric, up to 3 m or more long, 5 cm in diameter, yellowish with age, many-ridged and many-noded.

Leaves thin-textured, distichous, linear or ovate, obtuse or acute, decurved in apical half, usually 50–60 cm long, 3 cm broad. **Inflorescences** erect, basal, up to 2 m or more long, racemose, many-flowered, lower flowers distant and abnormal, upper flowers perfect and clustered. **Flowers** (perfect) about 10 cm across; sepals and petals pale greenish-yellow to yellow or ivory-white with large dull orange-brown or maroon spots; lip side lobes yellow striped with brown, mid-lobe lined with red; column pale greenish above, white and spotted with purple below. **Sepals** and **petals** spreading, subsimilar, oblong-elliptic, obtuse, up to 5.5 cm long, 2.5–3 cm broad. **Lip** much smaller, 3-lobed, 3 cm long, 2.5 cm broad; side lobes narrowly oblong, bluntly pointed, erect; mid-lobe ovate, obtuse, 1 cm across; disc with 3 keels terminating on the mid-lobe. **Column** clavate, slightly arcuate above, 2.2 cm long, with 2 outgrowths at the base forming a cup-shaped hollow at the base of the lip.

DISTRIBUTION Malaya and Sumatra across to the Philippines and the Solomon Islands; in lowland forests often near streams.

HISTORY *G. speciosum* often forms enormous plants and is reputedly the largest of all orchids with a specimen shown at the Crystal Palace in London in 1851 weighing nearly 2 tons. C. Blume described it in his *Bijdragen*

(p. 378) in 1825 based on a plant he collected in the forest near Buitenzorg (Bogor), Java.

G. speciosum may be distinguished from other species in the genus by its very long leafy stems and by its lip in which the side lobes are bluntly pointed and a little incurved.

CLOSELY RELATED SPECIES *Grammatophyllum rumphianum* Miq. from the Moluccas and Borneo may be distinguished from *G. speciosum* by its short, thick, smooth pseudobulbs bearing only a few leaves and by the flowers with many, almost round, rather large brown spots on them and its 4 cm-long sepals.

G. scriptum Bl., common throughout the Malay Archipelago to the Philippines and Solomon Islands, is closely allied to *G. rumphianum* but has green, rather than yellow, ridged pseudobulbs, and smaller flowers with yellow sepals and petals heavily suffused or blotched with maroon-brown.

Graphorkis Thou.

Subfamily Epidendroideae
Tribe Cymbidieae
Subtribe Cyrtopodiinae

Medium-sized epiphytic herbs. **Pseudobulbs** clustered, several-noded, ovoid to cylindric-fusiform, leafy. **Roots** clustered around base

Grammatophyllum speciosum

1 – Flower (× $\frac{2}{3}$)
2 – Lip (× 1)
3 – Column (× 1 $\frac{1}{3}$)

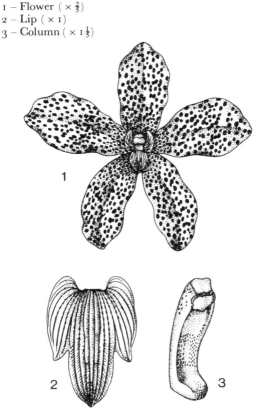

Grammatophyllum rumphianum

1 – Habit (× $\frac{1}{10}$)   3 – Lip (× 1)
2 – Flower (× $\frac{2}{3}$)   4 – Column (× 2)

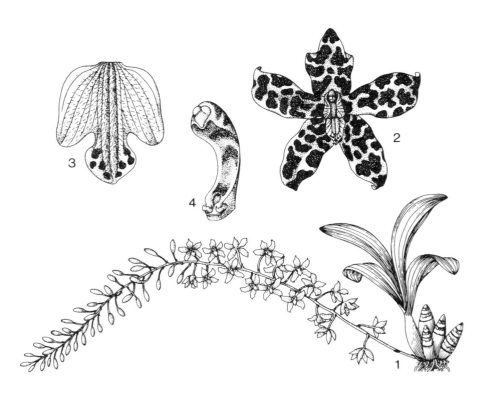

of pseudobulbs, with erect aerial branches. **Leaves** lanceolate, plicate, petiolate. **Inflorescence** erect, paniculate, many-flowered. **Flowers** small to medium-sized, yellow and marked with brown or maroon. **Sepals** and **petals** sub-similar, free, spreading. **Lip** 3-lobed, spurred at the base, 2-keeled on disc. **Column** with a hairy mound on each side at the base; rostellum long, beak-like; pollinia 2, waxy.

DISTRIBUTION Five species in Madagascar, the Mascarene Islands and tropical Africa.

DERIVATION OF NAME From the Greek *graphe* (writing) and *orchis* (orchid). The significance of this name is obscure as there are no such markings on the flowers of the type species.

TAXONOMY *Graphorkis* (often misspelt *Graphorchis*) was described by Aubert du Petit Thouars in 1809 in *Nouvelle Bulletin des Sciences par la Société Philomatique de Paris* (p. 318).

Vegetatively the species are very like smaller forms of *Ansellia* but the flowers are quite distinct in being spurred at the base.

V.S. Summerhayes has revised the genus in *Kew Bulletin* (1953).

TYPE SPECIES *G. scripta* (Thou.) O. Ktze

SYNONYM *Eulophiopsis* Pfitz.

CULTURE Compost A. Temp. Winter min. 15°C. During growth, the plants need plenty of water and only minimal shade from direct sunlight. After the leaves have fallen, cooler conditions are beneficial, and very little or no water should be given until the flower stems appear. At the commencement of new leaf growth, the plants may be returned to a warmer house.

Graphorkis lurida (Sw.) O. Ktze
[Colour Plate]

A medium-sized epiphytic plant, ± with many erect spikey roots at base of pseudobulbs. **Pseudobulbs** cylindric-fusiform or conical ovoid, 3–9 cm long, 1–3 cm in diameter, 4- to 6-leaved. **Leaves** lanceolate, acute, plicate, up to 40 cm long, 3.5 broad. **Inflorescence** appearing before the leaves, 15–50 cm long, erect, paniculate, with spreading branches, many-flowered. **Flowers** small, yellow and brown. **Sepals** spathulate-oblong, subacute, 0.5–0.6 cm long, 0.15 cm broad. **Petals** elliptic, slightly shorter than the sepals. **Lip** 3-lobed, 0.6 cm long, 0.3 cm broad; side lobes oblong and erect; mid-lobe more or less retuse or bifid; disc of lip with 2 keels at the base; spur bent sharply forwards, nearly as long as the lip. **Column** with a hairy auricle on each side of the base.

DISTRIBUTION W. Africa across to Uganda, Burundi and Tanzania.

HISTORY Originally described in 1805 by O. Swartz in *Schrader, Neues Journal* (p. 87) as *Limodorum luridum* based on a plant collected by

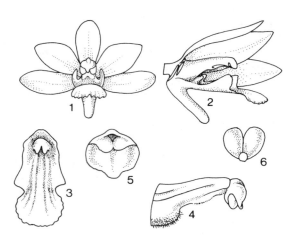

Graphorkis lurida
1 – Flower, front view (× 3)
2 – Flower, side view with petal and lateral sepal removed (× 3)
3 – Lip (× 4)
4 – Column, side view (× 4)
5 – Anther-cap (× 6)
6 – Pollinia and viscidium (× 6)

A. Afzelius in Sierra Leone. O. Kuntze transferred it to *Graphorkis* in 1891 in *Revisio Genera Plantarum* (p. 662).

SYNONYMS *Limodorum luridum* Sw.; *Eulophia lurida* (Sw.) Lindl.; *Eulophiopsis lurida* (Sw.) Schltr.

Grobya Lindl.

Subfamily Epidendroideae
Tribe Cymbidieae
Subtribe Cyrtopodiinae

Small epiphytic herbs with short, many-leaved stems, forming fleshy pseudobulbs at the base. **Leaves** long, narrow, plicate. **Inflorescence** from the base of the pseudobulb, simple, recurved or deflexed, many-sheathed at the base. **Flowers** medium to large, shortly pedicellate. **Dorsal sepal** free, erect; **lateral sepals** spreading or deflexed, connate to the middle, flexuose at the apex. **Petals** erect-spreading, broader than the dorsal sepal. **Lip** articulated with the column-foot, with a very shortly incumbent claw, erect, broad, 3-lobed; side lobes erect; mid-lobe spreading; disc callose or cristate. **Column** erect, semiterete, biauriculate near the base, with a short fleshy foot; pollinia 2, waxy, deeply sulcate or bipartite; stipe long; viscidium ovate.

DISTRIBUTION Three species in Brazil.

DERIVATION OF NAME Named in honour of Lord Grey of Groby, England, a keen

orchid grower and also a patron of horticulture in that country.

TAXONOMY *Grobya* was described by John Lindley in 1835 in the *Botanical Register* (t. 1740) where he states that it is most nearly allied to *Cymbidium*, *Cyrtopodium* and *Eriopsis*, but is distinguished by the lateral sepals being united at the base; by the large size of the petals; by the lip having no parallel elevated lines, and by the pollen masses being united to the gland (viscidium) by two distinct caudiculae attached to a single stipe.

R. Dressler in his recent article on the classification of the Orchid family has placed *Grobya* together with *Cyrtopodium* and *Eriopsis* in the subtribe *Cyrtopodiinae*.

TYPE SPECIES *G. amherstiae* Lindl.

CULTURE Compost A. Temp. Winter min. 15°C. As with many plants having hard pseudobulbs, *Grobya* species need moderate shade and humidity during growth, with plenty of water at the roots, followed by a cooler dry period when the pseudobulbs have fully formed. At this stage, very little water is required.

Grobya amherstiae Lindl. [Colour Plate]

A small epiphytic herb with short branched rhizomes and fleshy roots. **Pseudobulbs** densely tufted, erect, ovoid to almost spherical, up to 3.5 cm long, covered when young with persistent, whitish, fibrous leaf-bases, about 6-leaved towards apex. **Leaves** firm-textured, erect and arching, linear-lanceolate, subacute, slightly grooved, up to 40 cm long, 1–1.6 cm broad. **Inflorescence** erect or arcuate, from the bases of the older pseudobulbs, up to 10-flowered, densely racemose, up to 15 cm long; bracts narrowly lanceolate, 1–1.3 cm long, becoming brown with age. **Flowers** fairly showy; sepals pale green or pale yellow faintly tinged or spotted purple; petals almost transparent covered with longitudinal lines of small vinous blotches; lip pale yellow with a dull purple callus. **Dor-**

Grobya amherstiae
Flower (× 1)

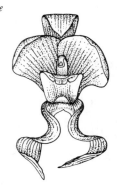

sal sepal narrowly obovate-spathulate, acute, 2 cm long, 0.6–0.7 cm broad; **lateral sepals** oblong-lanceolate, connate at the base, curved and twisted with margin strongly incurved in the middle, 2 cm long, 0.7 cm broad. **Petals** erect, obliquely elliptic, obtuse, 2 cm long, 1 cm broad. **Lip** 3-lobed, about 0.7 cm long, 0.8 cm broad; side lobes curved upwards, rounded above; mid-lobe transversely, narrowly elliptic, about 1.5 cm long, 0.4 cm broad, with 7 parallel longitudinal ridges on upper surface; callus at base of mid-lobe of 2 lateral narrow lamellae with a central short mucro. **Column** erect, arching forwards at apex.

DISTRIBUTION   E. Brazil; 600–900 m.

HISTORY   First collected by Hayne in Brazil who sent a plant to Countess Amherst. When it flowered, John Lindley named it in her honour in the *Botanical Register* (t. 1740) in 1855.

Gymnadenia R. Brown

Subfamily Orchidoideae
Tribe Orchideae
Subtribe Orchidinae

Medium-sized or small terrestrial herbs growing from subterranean palmately lobed tapering tubers (root-stem tuberoids). **Leaves** along the stem, fleshy, sheathing at the base. **Inflorescence** terminal, densely many-flowered in a cylindrical-tapering spike. **Flowers** small, pink, purple or rarely white, fragrant. **Sepals** and **petals** subsimilar, free; **dorsal sepal** forming a hood over the column with the petals; **lateral sepals** spreading. **Lip** 3-lobed, deflexed or recurved, with a long slender spur at the base, lacking a callus. **Column** short, erect; pollinia 2, clavate, mealy, sectile, each attached by a caudicle to a naked viscidium.

DISTRIBUTION   A genus of some six species in Europe and temperate Asia across to Japan.

DERIVATION OF NAME   From the Greek *gymnos* (naked) and *aden* (gland), in reference to the naked viscidium characteristic of the genus.

TAXONOMY   Robert Brown established the genus in 1813 in the 2nd edition of Aiton's *Hortus Kewensis* (p. 191). It is similar in floral features to *Anacamptis* but differs in having palmately lobed tubers, a cylindrical rather than a pyramidal inflorescence and in the lack of basal calli on the lip.

TYPE SPECIES   *G. conopsea* (L.) R. Br.

CULTURE   Temp. Winter min. 5°C. Culture as for *Anacamptis*.

Gymnadenia conopsea (L.) R. Br.
[Colour Plate]

A terrestrial plant, 20–80 cm tall. **Leaves** 3–7 linear or linear-lanceolate, acuminate, 10–25 cm long, 0.5–3.5 cm wide, green, unspotted. **Inflorescence** cylindrical, densely many-flowered; spike 6–25 cm long; bracts erect, lanceolate, acuminate, 0.8–1.4 cm long, green flushed with purple. **Flowers** rose-purple, pink or rarely white, sweetly scented; ovary arcuate, 0.8–1 cm long. **Dorsal sepal** elliptic, obtuse, 4–7 mm long, 2–3 mm wide; **lateral sepals** spreading, oblong-elliptic, obtuse, 4–7 mm long, 2–3 mm wide. **Petals** obliquely ovate, obtuse, 4–6 mm long, 2.5–3 mm wide. **Lip** flabellate, 3-lobed in apical half, 5–7 mm long and wide, the lobes subequal; spur slender, cylindrical, slightly incurved, 12–20 mm long. **Column** short, erect, 2–3 mm long.

DISTRIBUTION   Widespread throughout Europe and Asia across to Japan; growing in grassland on calcareous soils, up to 2800 m.

HISTORY   Originally described by Linnaeus as *Orchis conopsea* in 1753 in his *Species Plantarum* (p. 942). It was transferred to *Gymnadenia* by Robert Brown in 1813 in the 2nd edition of Aiton's *Hortus Kewensis* (p. 196).

The clove-scented var. *densiflora* is a fine plant usually growing to a greater size than the typical variety and with darker flowers. It characteristically grows in marshes and wet meadows.

SYNONYMS   include *Orchis conopsea* L.; *Gymnadenia ornithis* L.C. Rich.; *G. transsilvanica* Schur; *G. gracillima* Schur; *G. pseudoconopsea* Gren.

Habenaria Willd.

Subfamily Orchidoideae
Tribe Orchideae
Subtribe Orchidinae

Small to large, leafy, terrestrial herbs with simple or lobed tubers and fleshy roots. **Leaves** smooth, sheathing at the base. **Flowers** in a terminal spike or raceme, small to large, mostly green or white, less commonly yellow, orange, pink or red. **Sepals** subequal, the dorsal shorter than the laterals which may be ascending, spreading, reflexed or deflexed. **Petals** simple, cleft or bifid, often adnate to dorsal sepal. **Lip** continuous with the base of the column, entire or 3-lobed, spurred at the base. **Column** complex, very short; anther with cells parallel or divergent below; bases ± produced into long or short tubes; pollinia clavate or pyriform; viscidia exposed; staminodes ± present on either side of the anther; stigmatic processes distinct, often stalked and clavate; rostellum small, erect between the anther cells, with divergent lateral lobes.

DISTRIBUTION   Over 500 species, widespread in the temperate and tropical grassland areas but particularly numerous in tropical S. America, Africa and Asia.

DERIVATION OF NAME   From the Latin *habena* (reins), in reference to the long strap-like divisions of the petals and lip.

TAXONOMY   Described by C.L. Willdenow in the 4th edition of *Species Plantarum* (p. 44) in 1805. *Habenaria* forms one of the largest genera of terrestrial orchids and was most recently revised by F. Kraenzlin in A. Engler's *Das Pflanzenreich* where he described over 460 species in 32 sections. Some of these sections, such as *Bonatea* and *Platycoryne*, are now treated as distinct genera albeit closely allied to *Habenaria*.

Most species are rather sombrely coloured with green or white flowers but some species are extremely beautiful with scarlet, orange or yellow flowers and are quite worthy of cultivation. Even some of the green-flowered species such as *H. praestans* and *H. splendens* would repay cultivation.

The most thorough recent study of *Habenaria* species has been that by V.S. Summerhayes on the African species published in the *Flora of West Tropical Africa* (2nd ed., 1968) and in the *Flora of Tropical East Africa* (1968). In the latter he deals with 113 species in 14 sections. Many of the American species have been treated by Oakes Ames in his *Orchidaceae* – Fascicle 4 (1910); by C. Luer in *The Native Orchids of The United States and Canada* (1975); by O. Ames and D.S. Correll in *Orchids of Guatemala* (1953); by F.C. Hoehne in *Flora Brasilica* – *Orchidaceae* (1940) and by G. Pabst and F. Dungs in *Orchidaceae Brasilienses*, vol. 1 (1976).

Elsewhere the only recent accounts have been by R. Holttum in *Orchids of Malaya* (1964); G. Seidenfaden and T. Smitinand (1959–65) in *Orchids of Thailand;* and by Seidenfaden (1977) in *Dansk Botanisk Arkiv* (p. 65). The last covers 55 species from Thailand and adjacent areas.

TYPE SPECIES   *Orchis habenaria* L. [= *Habenaria macroceratitis* Willd.].

CULTURE   Compost C. Temp. Tropical spp. resting 15°C, growing 18°C min.; other spp. somewhat cooler. After flowering, the plants die down, leaving the fleshy tubers underground. At this stage, they should remain almost completely dry, but there is always the risk that they will become too desiccated. When the new green shoots appear the tubers should be repotted and grown under moderate to heavy shade. Water may be carefully given at first, but in full growth, the plants should not dry out at any time. The inflorescence appears at the top of the mature shoot.

Habenaria medusae Kraenzl.

A terrestrial herb up to 20 cm tall. **Leaves** 4–5 along stem, lanceolate, acute or acuminate, 10–15 cm long, 2–2.5 cm wide, sheathing at the base. **Inflorescence** laxly 6- to 10-flowered, up to 18 cm long; bracts erect, lanceolate, acuminate-setose, 1.5–2.7 cm long. **Flowers** showy, white with green sepals; pedicel and ovary 2–3 cm long. **Dorsal sepal** hooded over column, ovate, acute, 7–8 mm long, 3.5 mm wide; **lateral sepals** spreading, oblong-ovate, acute, 8–9 mm long, 4 mm wide. **Petals** adnate to dorsal sepal, linear, obtuse, erose, 6–7 mm long, 1 mm wide. **Lip** deflexed, spreading, 3-lobed, 2–2.2 cm long, 3.5–4 cm wide; side lobes deeply lacerate, 1.7–1.9 cm long, ciliate on outer margins; mid-lobe linear, 5 mm long, ciliate; spur dependent, filiform, slightly inflated towards apex, 3–3.7 cm long. **Column** 6 mm long.

DISTRIBUTION   Java only; in light forest in drier areas up to 1000 m.

HISTORY   F. Kraenzlin described this attractive species in 1896 in the third volume of *Xenia Orchidacea* (p. 149, t. 286). The provenance of the type was unknown to him.

CLOSELY ALLIED SPECIES   Similar to *H. radiata* but with more and larger flowers.

Habenaria radiata Thunb.

An erect terrestrial herb, up to 45 cm high. **Tubers** small, ovoid or ellipsoid, mostly less than 1 cm long. **Stem** erect, 3- to 7-leaved, slender, terete. **Leaves** linear-lanceolate, acuminate, suberect, sheathing at base, longest in the middle of the stem, 2–10 cm long, 0.3–0.7 cm broad. **Inflorescence** terminal, 1- to 3-flowered; bracts lanceolate, acuminate, 1 cm long. **Flowers** showy; sepals and spur green; petals, lip and column pure white. **Sepals** ovate-lanceolate, acuminate, 1 cm long, 0.5 cm broad. **Petals** suberect, ovate, subacute, 1.2 cm long, 0.6 cm broad, margins erosely denticulate. **Lip** clawed, deeply 3-lobed, up to 2 cm long, 3 cm broad; side lobes spreading, obovate, lacerate on back and side margins, entire on front margin; mid-lobe linear-ligulate, acute, much smaller than the side lobes; spur dependent, cylindric, slightly dilated towards apex, 3.5–5 cm long. **Column** erect.

DISTRIBUTION   Japan and Korea.

HISTORY   Discovered by C.P. Thunberg in Japan and illustrated by him as *Habenaria radiata* in his *Icones Plantarum Japonicarum* (1794–1805).

SYNONYMS   *Pecteilis radiata* (Thunb) Raf.; *Plantanthera radiata* (Thunb.) Lindl.; *Orchis susannae* Thunb. non L.; *Hemihabenaria radiata* (Thunb.) Finet

Habenaria rhodocheila Hance [Colour Plate]

A showy terrestrial plant with bulbous or cylindric fleshy roots. **Stem** 10–30 cm long. **Leaves** 1 or 2 below, sessile, 3–4 above, linear-lanceolate, attenuate into a petiole below, acuminate or mucronate at apex, 6–12 cm long, 0.8–3 cm broad, those above bract-like. **In-**florescence densely 2- to 15-flowered; bracts ovate, acuminate, 1–2 cm long. **Flowers** showy, the sepals and petals greenish; the lip scarlet or brick-red, rarely orange or yellow. **Dorsal sepal** deeply concave, elliptic, acuminate, 0.5–0.6 cm long, 0.4–0.5 cm broad; **lateral sepals** spreading, elliptic-lanceolate, oblique, 0.7–1 cm long, 0.5 cm broad. **Petals** adnate to dorsal sepal, linear-lanceolate, 0.4–0.7 cm long, 0.25 cm broad. **Lip** 4-lobed, 1.8–3 cm long, 1.8–2.2 cm broad, narrow clawed at the base; side lobes oblique, oblong, 0.7–1.5 cm long, 0.4–1.2 cm broad; mid-lobes similar; spur slender, 4–5 cm long. **Column** oblique, 1 cm high; rostellum lying well in front of the anther.

DISTRIBUTION   Thailand, Indo-China and Malaya, north to S. China, also in the Philippines (Mindanao).

HISTORY   Described in 1856 by Hance in *Annales des Sciences Naturelles* (p. 243) based on a plant collected by Sampson in Canton.

SYNONYMS   *Habenaria militaris* Rchb.f.; *H. xanthocheila* Ridley; *H. pusilla* Rchb.f.

Habenaria splendens Rendle [Colour Plate]

An erect terrestrial herb, up to 75 cm tall with ellipsoid tubers up to 3 cm long. **Stem** erect, stout, leafy. **Leaves** 6–8, ovate-lanceolate or lanceolate, acute, up to 20 cm long, 2.5–8 cm broad. **Inflorescence** 8–20 cm long, laxly 4- to 17-flowered; bracts lanceolate, acuminate. **Flowers** suberect, often fragrant; sepals pale green; petals and lip white. **Dorsal sepal** erect, lanceolate-elliptic, apiculate, 2–3 cm long, 0.9–1.5 cm broad; **lateral sepals** very oblique, lanceolate, acuminate, up to 2.8 cm long, 1.3 cm broad. **Petals** erect, adherent to dorsal sepal, very curved, ligulate, up to 3 cm long, 0.5–0.9 cm broad. **Lip** with a long narrow claw, 0.7–1.3 cm long, deeply 3-lobed above, densely pubescent below; side lobes diverging, with 6–12 fimbriae on outer margin, up to 3.5 cm long; mid-lobe linear, deflexed, 2–3 cm long, 0.2–0.3 cm broad; spur incurved, somewhat S-shaped, 3–4 cm long. **Anther-connective** horseshoe-shaped, 1.1–1.8 cm broad, loculae at each end; stigmas united to rostellum side lobes below, 0.5–0.7 cm long.

DISTRIBUTION   E. Africa, Ethiopia, south to Malawi and Zambia; in open grassland and on woodland margins, 1000–2400 m.

HISTORY   *H. splendens* is one of the largest of the African species of the genus and was discovered on Mt Kilimanjaro in Tanzania by H.H. Johnston. A.B. Rendle described it in 1895 in the *Journal of the Linnean Society* (p. 395).

CLOSELY RELATED SPECIES   *H. splendens* is closely allied to *Habenaria praestans* Rendle which has a shorter spur, up to 2.5 cm long, and to *Habenaria macrantha* A. Rich. which has a glabrous base to the lip.

Hagsatera R. Gonzales T.

Subfamily Epidendroideae
Tribe Epidendreae
Subtribe Laeliinae

Small epiphytic or lithophytic plants with creeping rhizomes. **Pseudobulbs** distant, fusiform, unifoliate at the apex. **Leaf** erect or suberect, coriaceous, linear-lanceolate. **Inflorescence** shorter than the leaf, axillary, few-flowered. **Flowers** nodding or subnutatant; **sepals** and **petals** free, spreading; sepals slightly larger than the petals. **Lip** fleshy, obscurely 3-lobed, pendent; side lobes obscure, much smaller than the mid-lobe; callus obscure, of fleshily thickened veins. **Column** free almost to the base, short, fleshy, lacking a foot; pollinia 8, compressed, each attached by a caudicle to the viscidium; rostellum laminar, very short.

DISTRIBUTION   Two species only in Mexico.

DERIVATION OF NAME   Named in honour of Eric Hagsater, editor of the journal *Orquidea (Mexico)* and an authority on Mexican orchids and the genus *Epidendrum*.

TAXONOMY   This genus was established in 1974 by Roberto Gonzales Tamayo in the journal *Orquidea (Mexico)* (p. 345) as a segregate of the large genus *Epidendrum*.

Hagsatera is most closely allied to *Encyclia* and the type species was indeed placed in that genus by Robert Dressler in 1961 in the journal *Brittonia*. It is distinguished, however, by its short free column, 8 pollinia attached by elastic caudicles to the viscidium and the fruit which is triangular in cross section.

TYPE   SPECIES   *Epidendrum brachycolumna* L.O. Williams

CULTURE   Temp. Winter min 12°C. As for *Epidendrum* and *Encyclia* species with a creeping rhizome. Small plants can be grown in a pot with an epiphyte mix while larger specimens can be mounted on a cork slab.

Hagsatera brachycolumna (L.O. Williams) R. Gonzales T.

A creeping medium-sized epiphyte with an ascending rhizome 3–3.5 mm in diameter. **Pseudobulbs** borne 1–6.5 cm apart on rhizome, narrowly conical-fusiform, somewhat compressed, 1.5–4.5 cm long, 4–9 mm wide. **Leaf** suberect-arcuate, linear, obtuse, 7.5–15 cm long, 0.9–1.3 cm wide. **Inflorescence** axillary, 3–4 cm long, unbranched, 4- to 6-flowered; peduncle 2–2.2 cm long; bracts triangular, acute, 1–2 mm long. **Flower** subcampanulate, nutant; sepals brownish-yellow; petals yellow or pale brown; lip rich purple on callus and in apical half, yellow on disc; pedicel slender, 8–10 mm long; ovary curved, 6 mm long. **Dorsal sepal** lanceolate, obtuse, 1.6–1.7 cm long, 0.5 cm wide; **lateral sepals** slightly falcate, linear-lanceolate, obtuse, 1.8–2 cm long, 0.6–0.7 cm wide. **Petals** porrect, oblanceolate, obtuse, 1.4 cm long, 0.3–0.4 cm wide. **Lip** ovate, very obscurely 3-lobed in basal half, 1.8 cm long, 0.8–0.9 cm wide; side lobes narrowly oblong, spreading; mid-lobe ovate, obtuse, with undulate margins; callus of 7 parallel raised veins, the central one longest and almost reaching the apex of the lip. **Column** 2 m long.

DISTRIBUTION   Mexico only.

HISTORY   L.O. Williams described this species in the *American Orchid Society Bulletin* (p. 309) of 1942 as *Epidendrum brachycolumna*. It was transferred to the new genus *Hagsatera* by R. Gonzales Tamayo in *Orquidea (Mexico)* (p. 345) in 1974. At the same time he described a second species *H. rosilloi* from Jalisco State in Mexico where it grows as a lithophyte at 1500–1600 m. It differs from *H. brachycolumna* in having yellow sepals and petals, and an obovate lip concave at the base and with much shorter side lobes and an obscure callus.

SYNONYMS   *Epidendrum brachycolumna* L.O. Williams; *Encyclia brachycolumna* (L.O. Williams) Dressler

Hagsatera brachycolumna
1 – Habit (× 1½)
2 – Flower (× 1)
3 – Pollinia (× 2)

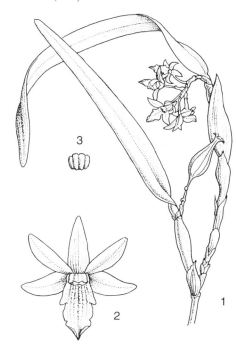

Haraella Kudo
Subfamily Epidendroideae
Tribe Vandeae
Subtribe Sarcanthinae

Small epiphytic herbs with very short stems. **Leaves** distichous, spreading, fleshy, sheathing the stem at the base. **Inflorescences** lateral, flexuous, simple, few-flowered. **Flowers** medium-sized, fairly showy. **Sepals** and **petals** subsimilar, free, spreading, ± obovate. **Lip** sessile on the base of the column, lacking a spur or basal sack, somewhat elongate-elliptic, constricted in the middle; front lobe orbicular with a minutely and irregularly pectinate-fimbriate margin; callus 2-ridged. **Column** short, broad, wingless; pollinia 2, globose, deeply sulcate; stipe linear; viscidium relatively large; rostellum bifid in front, somewhat porrect.

DISTRIBUTION   Taiwan; two species only.

DERIVATION OF NAME   In honour of Yoshi Hara of the Taihoken Imperial University of Formosa (Taiwan) who discovered the type material of the genus.

TAXONOMY   *Haraella* was described by Y. Kudo in 1930 in the *Journal of the Society of Tropical Agriculture, Formosa* (p. 26). There he compares it with *Gastrochilus* but states that it differs in lacking a spur on the lip.

TYPE SPECIES   *H. odorata* Kudo and *H. retrocalla* (Hayata) Kudo

CULTURE   Mounted on bark or tree fern. Temp. Winter min. 12–15°C. In common with other vandaceous orchids, these plants appreciate high humidity and moderate shade at all times, and grow best when hung up. When the roots are growing, plenty of water can be given, but at other times misting over is sufficient.

Haraella odorata Kudo
A small epiphytic plant, up to 5 cm or so tall. **Stem** short, 1.5 cm long, leafy. **Leaves** distichous, fleshy, falcate, oblong to oblanceolate, acute, 3–8 cm long, 0.9–1.1 cm broad. **Inflorescences** axillary, shorter than the leaves, few-flowered; bracts deltoid, acute, pale green, 0.1–0.15 cm long. **Flowers** up to 2 cm across; sepals and petals greenish-yellow; lip greenish-yellow with a central maroon area and a few marginal maroon spots. **Sepals** free, oblanceolate-elliptic, obtuse or mucronate, 0.9 cm long, 0.35 cm broad. **Petals** obovate-oblong, obtuse, 0.8 cm long, 0.25 cm broad. **Lip** sessile, elongate-elliptic, densely puberulent above, 1.3 cm long and broad, margins denticulate or erose. **Column** short, broad, wingless.

DISTRIBUTION   Taiwan only.

HISTORY   Described in 1930 by Yushun

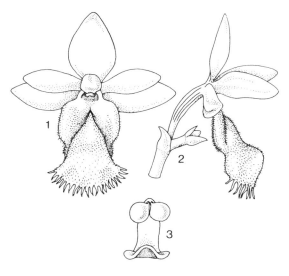

Haraella odorata
1 – Flower (× 2)
2 – Flower, side view (× 2)
3 – Pollinia, stipe and viscidium (× 6)

Kudo in the *Journal of the Society of Tropical Agriculture, Formosa* (p. 26) based on a plant cultivated by Yoshi Hara.

Helcia Lindl.
Subfamily Epidendroideae
Tribe Oncidieae

Medium-sized epiphytic plants with oblong-ovoid pseudobulbs. **Leaves** linear-oblong, shortly petiolate below. **Inflorescences** ascending, 1- or rarely 2-flowered. **Flowers** medium-sized, showy. **Sepals** and **petals** subsimilar. **Lip** oblong, 2-lobed at the apex; lobes slightly divergent, crisped and denticulate at the margin, with 2 basal auricles adnate to the column, between which there are 2 short protuberances. **Column** terete, terminating in a fibriate hood.

DISTRIBUTION   A single species in Ecuador and Colombia.

DERIVATION OF NAME   From the Latin *helcium* (horse-collar or yoke), referring to the hollow hairy pit at the base of the lip which, when seen from in front, looks, with the anther and column, like an old-fashioned Elizabethan head-dress or horse-collar decorated with ribbons.

TAXONOMY   *Helcia* was first described by John Lindley in 1845 in the *Botanical Register* (misc. p. 17). It is allied to *Trichopilia*, differing in having the column standing erect and clear of the lip. The anther is 2-celled and has 2 lateral processes on its bed (androclinium) and is surrounded by a deep fringed border. Finally, the lip is contracted in the middle and below is furnished with a pair of thick fleshy lobes, hollowed out in the middle and standing erect on each side of the column. The space between the lobes and the column-base is a hollow hairy pit.

This genus is also allied to *Aspasia* from which it differs in having the column free from the lip and by its fringed androclinium.

TYPE SPECIES   *H. sanguineolenta* Lindl.

CULTURE   Compost A. Temp. Winter min. 12–15°C. *Helcia sanguineolenta* appreciates small pots and while growing require ample water and high humidity. After the pseudobulbs are fully grown, much less water should be given. During the summer months, the plants must be well-shaded from strong sunlight.

Helcia sanguineolenta Lindl. [Colour Plate]

A medium-sized epiphytic plant. **Pseudobulbs** ovate, elongate, subterete, up to 8 cm long, 1 cm broad, 1-leafed at apex. **Leaf** erect, undulate, petiolate, narrowly canaliculate, oblong to elliptic, 11–20 cm long, 3.5–4.5 cm broad. **Inflorescence** longer than the pseudobulbs, 1-flowered, up to 19 cm long, bibracteate. **Flowers** showy; sepals and petals yellow or olivaceous, spotted heavily with chocolate-brown; lip white with broken crimson venation; callus yellow, flecked with crimson. **Sepals** narrowly oblong, acute, margins reflexed, 3–3.2 cm long, 0.6–1.1 cm broad. **Petals** similar to sepals but slightly smaller. **Lip** spreading, obovate, emarginate, margins undulate in front, pubescent at the base, 3 cm long, 1.2 cm broad; callus bilobulate on each side of the column, hollowed out in the middle. **Column** free, terete, fimbriate at the apex.

DISTRIBUTION   Ecuador and Colombia.

HISTORY   Theodore Hartweg first collected this species at Paccha in the Andes above Guayaquil and it was described by John Lindley in 1845 in the *Botanical Register* (misc. p. 17).

Hexadesmia Brongn.

Subfamily Epidendroideae
Tribe Epidendreae
Subtribe Laeliinae

Small epiphytic plants with caespitose or superposed stems. **Stems** pseudobulbous, often stipitate, 1- or 2-leaved at apex. **Inflorescence** terminal, fasciculate or racemose, 1- to several-flowered. **Flowers** small, rarely showy. **Sepals** and **petals** spreading, free; lateral sepals adnate to the column-foot forming a mentum. **Lip** articulate with the column-foot, ± recurved. **Column** erect or arcuate, clavate, with a foot; anther terminal; pollinia 6, waxy, unequal in size, held together by a small viscidium.

DISTRIBUTION   About 15 species distributed in the American tropics.

DERIVATION OF NAME   From the Greek *hex* (six) and *desmos* (chain or bond), referring to the 6 pollinia joined in 2 groups.

TAXONOMY   Described in 1842 by A. Brongniart in *Annales des Sciences Naturelles* (p. 44). It is allied to *Scaphyglottis*, in which it is included by some authors, but is distinguished by its 6 pollinia.

TYPE SPECIES   *H. fasciculata* Brongn.

CULTURE   Compost A. Temp. Winter min. 12–15°C. As for *Hexisea* and *Scaphyglottis*. The plants are often untidy in their growth habit and species such as *H. dunstervillei* require support for the long stems.

Hexadesmia fusiformis Griseb.

A small epiphytic herb, up to 20 cm or so tall. **Stems** caespitose at base but superposed above (i.e. each new growth arises from the apex of the old growth), slender at base, swollen above, up to 6 cm long, 0.8 cm in diameter, 1-leafed at apex. **Leaf** erect, flexuous, linear, minutely 2-lobed at the apex, up to 10 cm long, 0.5 cm broad. **Inflorescences** terminal, 1-or 2-flowered, emerging from a short sheath. **Flowers** small; sepals and petals pale creamy-green, semitranslucent with pinkish nerves; lip white; column yellow-green. **Sepals** similar, lanceolate, acuminate, 0.8–1 cm long, 0.2–0.3 cm broad. **Petals** oblong-elliptic, acute, 0.8 cm long, 0.3 cm broad. **Lip** obovate-pandurate, truncate, 0.8 cm long, 0.5 cm broad, with a basal, slightly fleshy, central thickening. **Column** slender, subterete, slightly clavate, 0.5 cm long.

DISTRIBUTION   Costa Rica, Venezuela and Trinidad.

HISTORY   Originally described by A.H.R. Grisebach in 1864 in the *Flora of the British West Indies* (p. 623).

SYNONYM   *Scaphyglottis fusiformis* (Griseb.) R.E. Schultes

Hexadesmia jiminezii Schltr.

An erect epiphytic plant, 8–14 cm tall, with an abbreviated rhizome. **Stems** slender below, fusiform-fleshy above, up to 10 cm long, 0.4 cm broad. **Leaves** erect-spreading, lanceolate-oblong, acute, sessile, coriaceous, up to 5 cm long, 1.4 cm broad. **Inflorescence** short, solit-

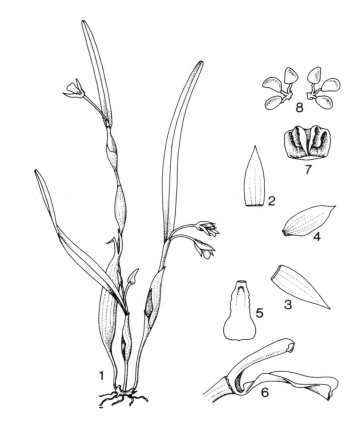

Hexadesmia fusiformis
1 – Habit ($\times \frac{1}{2}$)
2 – Dorsal sepal ($\times 2$)
3 – Lateral sepal ($\times 2$)
4 – Petal ($\times 2$)
5 – Lip ($\times 2$)
6 – Column and lip, side view ($\times 3$)
7 – Anther-cap ($\times 12$)
8 – Pollinia ($\times 12$)

ary, 2- to 3-flowered; bracts scarious. **Flowers** large for genus. **Sepals** ovate-lanceolate, subacute, 1 cm long; lateral sepals oblique. **Petals** obliquely ovate-lanceolate, obtuse, 1 cm long. **Lip** cuneate-obovate, with undulate margins in front, 1.3 cm long, 0.8 cm broad. **Column** dilated towards apex, 0.5 cm long; foot short.
DISTRIBUTION Costa Rica.
HISTORY Discovered near Sangabe in Costa Rica by O. Jiminez and sent by A. Tonduz to Rudolf Schlechter who described it in 1923 in *Fedde, Repertorium Specierum Novarum, Beihefte* (p. 293).

Hexisea **Lindl.**
Subfamily Epidendroideae
Tribe Epidendreae
Subtribe Laeliinae

Small epiphytic herbs. **Stems** simple or branched, segmented, with thickened and constricted segments alternating. **Sheaths** numerous, scarious, arising from constricted sections. **Leaves** 1 or 2, rigid. **Inflorescences** terminal, racemose, abbreviated, few-flowered; peduncles hidden by leathery imbricating sheaths. **Flowers** small, often brightly coloured, orange-red or yellow. **Sepals** erect, spreading; lateral sepals basally connate forming a small saccate mentum. **Petals** similar to the sepals. **Lip** simple or lobulate, erect, connate at the base to the column forming a pouch-like nectary. **Column** short, apically broad, 3-lobed; pollinia 4, collateral, waxy.
DISTRIBUTION Possibly five or six species from Central America, northern S. America and the W. Indies.
DERIVATION OF NAME From the Greek *hex* (six) and *isos* (equal), referring to the 6 more or less equal perianth segments
TAXONOMY John Lindley described *Hexisea* in 1834 in Hooker's *Journal of Botany* (p. 7). It is characterised by its lip which is geniculate below the column and may be sigmoid; the lip base is not jointed as is usual in the closely allied *Scaphyglottis*, and the margins of the lip are united with the column to form a deep nectary which does not extend back beyond the base of the sepals.
    The affinities of the genus have been fully discussed by R. Dressler in *Orquidea* (*Mex.*) in 1974 where he accepts four species in the genus and provides a key to them.
TYPE SPECIES *H. bidentata* Lindl.
CULTURE Compost A. Temp. Winter min. 12–15°C. These plants may be grown in pots, or mounted on slabs of fern-fibre or cork. They should be given humid conditions, under moderate shade, with plenty of water while grow-

ing, and less when growth is complete. Flowers may appear more than once each year.

Hexisea bidentata **Lindl.** [Colour Plate]
A tufted epiphytic plant, up to 45 cm tall. **Stem** composed of superposed pseudobulbs. **Pseudobulbs** sulcate, of 1 or more internodes, up to 9 cm long, 0.8 cm in diameter, bases of pseudobulbs covered by scarious imbricate sheaths, each 2-leaved at the apex. **Leaves** linear to linear-lanceolate, obliquely tridentate at the apex, coriaceous, up to 11 cm long, 1.2 cm broad. **Inflorescence** terminal, abbreviated, several-flowered, up to 3 cm long, covered by imbricate scarious sheaths. **Flowers** scarlet or vermilion. **Sepals** elliptic-lanceolate, acute to obtuse, 1.2–1.9 cm long, 0.3–0.5 cm broad; lateral sepals dorsally keeled. **Petals** obliquely oblanceolate, obtuse or acute, 0.9–1.3 cm long, 0.3–0.35 cm broad. **Lip** saccate at base, arcuate, oblong-elliptic, acute or obtuse, 0.7–1.2 cm long, 0.3–0.4 cm broad; callus fleshy, transverse in basal part of lip. **Column** short, fleshy, tridentate at apex, 0.3–0.4 cm long.
DISTRIBUTION Mexico, south to Panama and northern S. America.
HISTORY Discovered in both Panama and W. Colombia by H. Cuming and described by John Lindley in 1834 in Hooker's *Journal of Botany* (p. 8).

Himantoglossum **Koch**
Subfamily Orchidoideae
Tribe Orchideae
Subtribe Orchidinae

Large and robust terrestrial herbs growing from subterranean ovoid or ellipsoidal tubers (root-stem tuberoids). **Leaves** several, fleshy, along lower part of stem, oblong-ovate sheathing at the base. **Inflorescence** terminal, laxly to densely many-flowered in a cylindrical spike; bracts leafy, prominent. **Flowers** elongate, foul-smelling. **Sepals** and **petals** subsimilar, free but adnate, curved forwards over the column to form a hood. **Lip** porrect to pendent, 3-lobed at the base, elongate, with a short spur at the base; mid-lobe very long, linear, bifid at the apex. **Column** erect; pollinia 2, sectile, mealy, attached by stalks to the viscidium.
DISTRIBUTION A small genus of about four or five species in Europe and the Middle East; usually growing on calcareous soils.
DERIVATION OF NAME from the Greek *himas* (strap) and *glossa* (tongue), in allusion to the strange lip of the genus.
TAXONOMY The genus was established by W.D. Koch in 1837 in the *Synopsis Florae Germanicae et Helveticae* (p. 689). This usage of the

name has been conserved over that of Sprengel (1826) and over *Loroglossum* L.C. Rich. It is allied to *Aceras* and *Barlia* but the species are much more robust and are readily distinguished by their elongate linear mid-lobe of the lip.
TYPE SPECIES *H. hircinum* (L.) Sprengel
SYNONYM *Loroglossum* L.C. Rich.

Himantoglossum hircinum **(L.) Sprengel**
A large terrestrial plant 30–90 cm tall. **Leaves** 6–12, ovate to broadly lanceolate, acute, 11–15 cm long, 3–5 cm wide, green, unspotted. **Inflorescence** cylindrical, densely 15- to 120-flowered; spike 18–30 cm long; bracts lanceolate, acuminate, 10–15 mm long. **Flowers** elongate, smelling of goats, the sepals green or greyish-green striped and spotted with red, the lip white at the base with reddish tufts and with green, brown, greyish or brownish-purple lobes; ovary 10–13 mm long. **Sepals** elliptic, obtuse, incurved, 10–13 mm long, 5–6 mm wide. **Petals** smaller. **Lip** clawed, 3-lobed above the claw, 5–6 cm long; claw with undulate margins; side lobes short, incurved, linear-tapering, 1–2 cm long; mid-lobe linear, bifid at apex, up to 5 cm long; spur incurved-conical, 4–5 mm long. **Column** erect, 4.5 mm long.
DISTRIBUTION Europe across to N. Turkey and in N.W. Africa; in calcareous soils up to 1800 m.
HISTORY Popularly known as the Lizard Orchid in the British Isles where it is a rarity, this striking species was originally described by Linnaeus as *Satyrium hircinum* in his *Species Plantarum* (p. 944) in 1753. It was transferred to the present genus by Sprengel in his *Systema Vegetabilium* (p. 694) in 1826.
    Three subspecies are known of the Lizard Orchid: the typical subspecies is widespread in W. Europe and N. Africa; subsp. *caprinum* with fewer larger flowers is found in the Balkans and Turkey; and subsp. *calcaratum* with the largest flowers of a pretty rose-pink is found in Yugoslavia and Albania.
SYNONYMS *Satyrium hircinum* L.; *Orchis hircinum* (L.) Crantz; *Aceras hircina* (L.) Lindl.

Hispaniella **Braem**
Subfamily Epidendroideae
Tribe Oncidieae

Small epiphytic herbs with elongate creeping or ascending rhizomes and well-spaced, erect, short-stemmed, leafy shoots. **Leaves** fleshy, bilaterally compressed (equitant), grooved on upper surface, lanceolate-falcate in side view,

denticulate. **Inflorescences** few-flowered, elongate. **Flowers** appearing in succession, bee-like. **Sepals** and **petals** free, subsimilar, reflexed. **Lip** much larger than the other segment, convex, entire or obscurely 3-lobed, emarginate, pubescent; callus of a subquadrate fleshy pubescent basal area and tapering hairy protuberances in front. **Column** short, erect, with short linear wings; pollinia 2, attached by a linear-oblanceolate stipe to a small viscidium.
DISTRIBUTION A monotypic genus from Hispaniola.
DERIVATION OF NAME Named after the W. Indian island of Hispaniola.
TAXONOMY For many years *Hispaniella* has been included in *Oncidium* but was established as a distinct genus by G. Braem in 1980 in the journal *Die Orchidee* (p. 144). It had previously been included in with the 'equitant' oncidiums (now *Tolumnia*), such as *O. variegatum*. Vegetatively, it does indeed resemble *O. variegatum* but the flower, with its hairy bee-like lip, is rather distinctive.
TYPE SPECIES *O. henekenii* Schomb. ex Lindl.
CULTURE Temp. Winter min. 15°C. Must be mounted on a bare twig or small branch and hung under minimal shade, enough to prevent scorching. Mist lightly daily, because of its intolerance of excessive moisture.

Hispaniella henekenii (Schomb. ex Lindl.) Braem

A small epiphyte with a slender creeping rhizome. **Stems** very short, leafy. **Leaves** distichous, bilaterally compressed, falcate, elliptic-lanceolate, acute, 1.5–5 cm long, 0.5–1 cm wide, erose-denticulate on the margins. **Inflorescences** erect-arcuate, unbranched, laxly few-flowered, to 30 cm or more long; peduncle slender, up to 25 cm long; rhachis zigzag; bracts triangular-lanceolate, acute, 2–3 mm long. **Flowers** produced in succession, bee-like,

Hispaniella henekenii
Flower (× 2)

the sepals and petals off-yellow flushed at the base with purple, the lip dark maroon with a yellow apical margin, the callus orange; pedicel and ovary 8–9 mm long. **Sepals** and **petals** oblong-obovate, obtuse, 4–5 mm long, 1.5–2 mm wide. **Lip** convex, obscurely 3-lobed to entire, emarginate, 11–13 mm long, 8–10 mm wide, pubescent; callus at base subquadrate, fleshy, pubescent, with 3 elongate, tapering, hairy protuberances on each side in front. **Column** 2.5–3 mm long.
DISTRIBUTION Known only from the island of Hispaniola; in dry areas growing on cacti and other spiny shrubs.
HISTORY This strange orchid was described by John Lindley in his *Folia Orchidacea Oncidium* (p. 11) as *Oncidium henekenii* in 1855, based on a collection made by Schomburgk in Santo Domingo in 1852. It was transferred to *Hispaniella* in 1980 by G. Braem in *Die Orchidee* (p. 144). D. Dod (1976), in the *American Orchid Society Bulletin* (p. 792), has elucidated its pollination by pseudocopulation.
SYNONYM *Oncidium henekenii* Schomb. ex Lindl.

Holcoglossum Schltr.

Subfamily Epidendroideae
Tribe Vandeae
Subtribe Sarcanthinae

Medium-sized monopodial epiphytic plants with short to elongate unbranched stems covered by sheathing leaf bases; roots from the lower part of the stems, thick, bootlace-like. **Leaves** coriaceous, terete to triquetrous, articulated at base. **Inflorescences** lateral, racemose, few- to many-flowered. **Flowers** often showy, with spreading sepals and petals. **Sepals** and **petals** free, subsimilar but with lateral sepals usually larger than the dorsal sepal. **Lip** sessile, bipartite, usually with a slender arcuate elongate spur with a ridged callus on the epichile. **Column** short, lacking a foot, with prominent wings; clinandrium deeply cleft in front; rostellum short, bifid; pollinia 2, porate, on a linear tapering stipe attached to a small circular or elliptic viscidium.
DISTRIBUTION A small genus of perhaps eight species in tropical S.E. Asia from Burma across to Taiwan.
DERIVATION OF NAME from the Greek *holkos* (strap) and *glossa* (tongue), in allusion to the strap-shaped lip of the type species.
TAXONOMY *Holcoglossum* was established by Rudolf Schlechter in 1919 in *Fedde, Repertorium Specierum Novarum, Beihefte* (p. 285). It has been revised by Tsi (1982), who recognised four species in the genus, in *Acta Phytotaxonomica Sinica* (p. 439) and by Christensen (1987), who

recognised eight species, in *Notes of the Royal Botanical Garden, Edinburgh* (p. 249).
Holcoglossum is allied to *Vanda* but is readily distinguished by its longer spur, different lip shape and porate pollinia
TYPE SPECIES *Saccolabium quasipinifolium* Hayata
CULTURE Temp. Winter min. 12–15°C. Best grown as a hanging mounted plant in conditions of moderate shade and good humidity. A drier period with cooler nights is appropriate in winter.

Holcoglossum amesianum (Rchb.f.) Christensen

A pendent epiphyte with 1–8 cm-long leafy stems; roots basal, stout, 3–5 mm in diameter. **Leaves** rigid-coriaceous, arcuate or straight, channelled, linear-tapering, acuminate or acute, 10–30 cm long, 0.5–1.6 cm wide, dark green. **Inflorescences** 1–8, 14–80 cm long, simple or branched, (4) 15- to 50-flowered; bracts ovate-elliptic, obtuse, 2–3 mm long. **Flowers** 5–6.8 cm across, with spreading segments, thin-textured, creamy-white with a rich rosy hue on the lip, fading to yellow with age; pedicel and ovary 2.5–3.1 cm long. **Dorsal sepal** ovate-elliptic, obtuse, 1.6–2.1 cm long, 0.9–1 cm wide; **lateral sepals** obliquely elliptic, obtuse, 1.7–1.9 cm long, 0.9–1 cm wide. **Petals** obovate to elliptic, obtuse, 1.7–2 cm long, 0.9–1.1 cm wide. **Lip** erect, bipartite, 1.2–1.9 cm long, 1.2–1.8 cm wide; hypochile saccate, with erect oblong side lobes; epichile shortly broadly clawed, reniform, emarginate, with a callus of 3 ridges in centre; spur conical-cylindrical, 5–6 mm long. **Column** short, fleshy, 3–4 mm long.

Holcoglossum amesianum
1 – Flower (× 1)
2 – Lip (× 1)
3 – Column (× 3)
4 – Pollinarium (× 6)

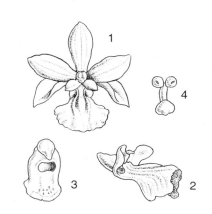

DISTRIBUTION Burma, N. Thailand, S. China, Laos and Vietnam; at high elevations.
HISTORY This attractive species was originally described by H.G. Reichenbach in 1887 as *Vanda amesiana* in the *Gardeners' Chronicle* (s. 3, 1: p. 764) based on a plant introduced from Burma by Messrs H. Low & Co. of Clapton. It was named for Mr F.A. Ames of Boston, Massachusetts.

Eric Christensen transferred it to the present genus in 1987 in the *Notes of the Royal Botanical Garden, Edinburgh* (p. 255).
SYNONYM *Vanda amesiana* Rchb.f.

Holcoglossum kimballianum (Rchb.f.) Garay
A pendent epiphyte with stems 1–25 cm long, 3–4 mm in diameter; roots 2–2.5 cm in diameter. **Leaves** terete, acuminate, 18–40 cm long, 2–3.5 cm in diameter, articulated to tapering leaf bases, 1.5–2.3 cm long. **Inflorescences** 17–26 cm long, laxly 7- to 10-flowered; peduncle terete, 1.5–2 mm in diameter; rhachis zigzag; bracts elliptic, obtuse, 3–4 mm long. **Flowers** white to pale pink with a purple lip,

Holcoglossum kimballianum
1 – Habit ($\times \frac{1}{2}$)
2 – Inflorescence ($\times \frac{1}{2}$)

with a brown hypochile, and a white column; pedicel and ovary 2–3.5 cm long. **Dorsal sepals** elliptic, obtuse, clawed at the base, 2–3 cm long, 0.6–1.1 cm wide; **lateral sepals** obliquely ovate, obtuse or subacute, 2.2–3.5 cm long, 0.9–1.6 cm wide. **Petals** obliquely spathulate or elliptic-obovate, obtuse, clawed at the base, 1.5–3 cm long, 0.5–1.1 cm wide. **Lip** bipartite; hypochile saccate, with erect triangular side lobes, incurved at the apex; epichile broadly flat, deflexed, ovate, emarginate, 1.2–2 cm long, 0.8–1.9 cm wide, erose, bearing 3 keels in the basal part. **Column** terete, 5–6 mm long.
DISTRIBUTION Thailand, Burma and S. China; 5–6 mm long.
HISTORY Originally described as *Vanda kimballiana* by H.G. Reichenbach in the *Gardeners' Chronicle* (s. 3, 5: p. 232) in 1889 based on a plant collected in the southern Shan States of Burma. It was transferred to the present genus by Leslie Garay in 1972 in the *Botanical Museum Leaflets of Harvard University* (p. 182).
SYNONYM *Vanda kimballiana* Rchb.f.

Holcoglossum quasipinifolium (Hay.) Schltr.
[Colour Plate]
A medium-sized epiphyte with a spreading stem up to 10 cm long and covered by sheathing leaf-bases; roots clustered in basal part of the stem. **Leaves** V-shaped in cross-section, linear, acute, 9–11 cm long, 2.5–3.5 mm wide, articulated to a broad short imbricate basal sheath. **Inflorescences** laxly 1- to 5-flowered, about as long as the leaves; bracts ovate, acute, 3 mm long. **Flowers** showy, 4 cm long, white with pink central veins to the sepals and with tawny spots on the side lobes of the lip; pedicel and ovary 2.5 cm long. **Dorsal sepal** erect, oblong-elliptic, obtuse, 1.6 cm long, 0.5–0.6 cm wide, twisted somewhat; **lateral sepals** similar but slightly broader, 1.6–1.7 cm long, 0.7–0.85 cm wide. **Petals** spreading or reflexed, spathulate, acute, 1.5–1.6 cm long, 0.7–0.8 cm wide. **Lip** 3-lobed, 1.5–1.7 cm long; side lobes erect, somewhat deltoid, 0.7 cm wide; mid-lobe porrect-deflexed, oblong, obtuse, 1.6 cm long, 1.3 cm wide, with erose undulate margins; callus of 7 parallel ridges on basal part of the lip, spur pendent, cylindrical-tapering from a broad mouth, 1.7–1.9 cm long. **Column** porrect, cylindrical, 0.7 cm long.
DISTRIBUTION Taiwan only; in montane forest up to 2200 m.
HISTORY Originally described by the Japanese botanist Hayata as *Saccolabium quasipinifolium* in 1912 in his *Icones Plantarum Formosanarum* (p. 144) based on his and Sasaki's collection from Taiwan. It was transferred to the present genus by Rudolf Schlechter in 1919 in his *Orchidologiae Sino-Japonicae Prodromus* (p. 285).
SYNONYM *Saccolabium quasipinifolium* Hay.

Houlletia Brongn.
Subfamily Epidendroideae
Tribe Gongoreae
Subtribe Stanhopeinae

Large, stout, eipiphytic or terrestrial herbs. **Pseudobulbs** ovoid to narrowly ovoid, 1-leafed. **Leaf** elliptic or lanceolate, petiolate, plicate. **Inflorescence** erect to pendent, racemose, laxly 1- to 12-flowered. **Flowers** large. **Sepals** subsimilar, spreading, free or with lateral sepals somewhat connate. **Petals** similar to the sepals but narrower. **Lip** 3-lobed; side lobes basal, narrowly lanceolate-falcate or broad; mid-lobe jointed, often separated from basal part by a mesochile, ovate to ligulate, often with a truncate, auriculate base. **Column** arcuate, clavate, ± with a short foot; pollinia 2, oblong-cylindric.
DISTRIBUTION A small genus of about seven species distributed from Guatemala and Costa Rica to Colombia, Brazil, Peru and Bolivia.
DERIVATION OF NAME Named in honour of M. Houllet who collected the type species in Brazil He later became the head gardener of the Jardin des Plantes in Paris.
TAXONOMY A. Brongniart described the genus in 1841 in the *Annales des Sciences Naturelles* (p. 37).

Houlletia is allied to *Paphinia* but may be distinguished by its 1- rather than 2- or more-leaved pseudobulbs. R. Schlechter revised the genus in *Orchis* in 1915.
TYPE SPECIES *H. stapeliaeflora* Brongn.
CULTURE Compost A or C. Temp. Winter min. 12–15°C. Species such as *H. brocklehurstiana* which have erect inflorescences generally grow terrestrially, and require moderate shade and plenty of water during active growth. Epiphytic species such as *H. tigrina*, with downward-growing inflorescences should be grown as *Stanhopea*, in hanging baskets. All species should be given much less water when growth is complete.

Houlletia odoratissima Linden ex Lindl. & Paxt.
A large terrestrial plant. **Pseudobulbs** pyriform, clustered, grooved, up to 6 cm long, 3 cm in diameter, almost concealed by grey nervose sheaths, 1-leafed at apex. **Leaf** erect, long-petiolate, narrowly elliptic, subobtuse, plicate, up to 32 cm long, 11 cm broad; petiole slender, up to 22 cm long. **Inflorescence** basal, erect, racemose, up to 40 cm long, laxly several-flowered above. **Flowers** nodding, very fragrant; sepals and petals fleshy, dark maroon with light brown near the base and margins;

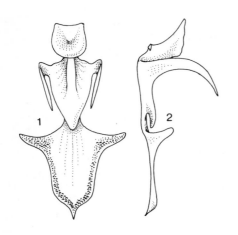

Houlletia odoratissima
1 – Lip, front view (× 7)
2 – Lip, side view (× 7)

lip white, lined and spotted below with pinkish-red; column pale brown wth a pale yellow-green apex marked with red-maroon, foot bright red. **Sepals** elliptic or elliptic-ovate, obtuse, 3.5 cm long, 1.1–1.9 cm broad; lateral sepals forming a short mentum with the column-foot. **Petals** oblanceolate, subobtuse, 3 cm long, 1 cm broad. **Lip** complex, 3-lobed, fleshy in basal half, 2 cm long, 2.4 cm broad; side lobes erect, linear-lanceolate, falcate, curved forwards in apical half; mid-lobe (epichile) separated from basal part of lip by a narrow isthmus, trilobulate, side lobules suberect, linear, acute, mid-lobule subquadrate, apiculate. **Column** slender, slightly arcuate, 2.3 cm long.

DISTRIBUTION   Venezuela, Colombia, Peru Bolivia and Brazil.

HISTORY   Originally discovered by L. Schlim in 1849 on the east side of the R. Magdalena in Soto province and again near Ocaña, Colombia, two years later. It was introduced from the latter locality into cultivation through J. Linden's nursery in Brussels and it flowered for the first time in Europe in 1852 in the greenhouse of M. Pescatore of St-Cloud near Paris. John Lindley described it the following year in his and Paxton's *Flower Garden* (p. 172).

SYNONYMS   *Houlletia picta* Linden & Rchb.f.; *H. juruenensis* Hoehne; *H. antioquiensis* Hort.; *H. buchtienii* Kraenzl.; *H. boliviana* Schltr.

Huntleya Lindl.
Subfamily Epidendroideae
Tribe Maxillarieae
Subtribe Zygopetalinae

Tufted epiphytic herbs lacking pseudobulbs. **Leaves** many, distichous, arranged in a fan-shape, plicate, membranaceous to thinly coriaceous, elongate-lanceolate, acute. **Inflorescences** axillary, 1-flowered, shorter than the leaves. **Flowers** large, fleshy, showy, often with a glossy sheen. **Sepals** and **petals** subsimilar, spreading; lateral sepals and petals inserted on the column-foot. **Lip** articulated at the apex of the column-foot, contracted basally, dilated above, clawed; basal callus transverse, long-fimbriate. **Column** arcuate, apically dilated and subcrenulate, biauriculate above; pollinia 4, flattened, superimposed, attached by a short stipe to a flattened viscidium.

DISTRIBUTION   Possibly up to ten species from Central and S. America and Trinidad.

DERIVATION OF NAME   Named in honour of an Englishman, the Rev. J.T. Huntley, a keen orchid grower of the early nineteenth century.

TAXONOMY   *Huntleya* was described by John Lindley in 1837 in the *Botanical Register* (sub t. 1991). Lindley states that *Huntleya* differs from *Maxillaria* in its distichously-arranged leaves; its flat spreading lip which is unguiculate (clawed) with a free base of the column and is furnished with a fine fringed appendage at its base; and the column which is broadly winged towards the apex.

From *Zygopetalum*, where the species of *Huntleya* have sometimes been placed, it differs in having leaves conduplicate in venation, whilst its applanate flowers and its pectinately fringed lip callus distinguishes it from *Chondrorhyncha* and *Pescatorea*.

R.A. Rolfe revised the genus *Huntleya* in the *Orchid Review* (1900) where he recognised six species and one variety, albeit noting that many of these are similar both vegetatively and florally, differing mainly in characters such as flower size and coloration.

J. Fowlie in the *Orchid Digest* (1967 and 1974) has also revised *Huntleya* and considers that the genus now consists of 10 species; considerably more than is accepted by most other botanists who have tended to consider many of these taxa conspecific with *H. meleagris*. From the illustrations in Fowlie's work it seems that several taxa may be distinguished based on floral differences which are often difficult to quantify. Whether these differences are sufficient to recognise the taxa at specific rank or lower would seem to be a matter of opinion.

TYPE SPECIES   *H. meleagris* Lindl.

CULTURE   Compost A. Temp. Winter min. 12–15°C. *Huntleya* species should be grown in well-drained pots or may succeed mounted on fern-fibre or cork slabs. They require shady and very humid conditions and should be carefully watered throughout the year so that the roots never become very dry.

Huntleya heteroclita (Poepp. & Endl.) Garay
[Colour Plate]
A large epiphytic plant with very short, tufted, leafy stems. **Leaves** distichous, spreading, oblanceolate, acute or shortly acuminate, plicate, up to 44 cm long, 6.5 cm broad, articulated below to elongate, conduplicate sheaths. **Inflorescence** basal, axillary, erect, 1-flowered, 7–15 cm long; bract tubular below, acute. **Flowers** large; segments spreading; sepals and petals dull yellow, heavily suffused with purple-brown; lip violet with a white callus; column maroon. **Sepals** lanceolate, acuminate, 2.7–3.9 cm long, 0.8–0.9 cm broad; lateral sepals oblique. **Petals** oblong-lanceolate, acuminate, slightly shorter than the sepals. **Lip** obscurely 3-lobed, 2.2–2.4 cm long, 1.3–1.5 cm broad; side lobes auriculate, erect; mid-lobe large, spreading, rhombic-ovate, acuminate, apex recurved; callus fleshy, basal, semiorbicular, plurilamellate. **Column** erect, short, stout, with a pair of basal suborbicular wings, densely tomentose in front, up to 1.3 cm long; foot short, 0.7 cm long.

DISTRIBUTION   Ecuador and Peru.

HISTORY   Originally described by E.F. Poeppig and S.L. Endlicher as *Maxillaria heteroclita* in 1827 in their *Nova Genera et Species Plantarum* (p. 37, t. 63) based on a specimen collected by the former in Peru. In 1969 L. Garay transferred it to *Huntleya* in *Orquideologia* (p. 146).

SYNONYM   *Zygopetalum rhombilabium* Schweinf.

Huntleya meleagris Lindl. [Colour Plate]
A medium-sized epiphytic plant. **Leaves** linear-lanceolate or elliptic-lanceolate, acute, thinly coriaceous, 20–40 cm long, 3–5 cm broad. **Inflorescence** erect, 1-flowered; bract triangular, acute, 1–2 cm long. **Flower** showy; sepals glossy red-brown, flecked with yellow with yellowish-white and white in the basal third; petals and lip similar but streaked with purple below. **Sepals** elliptic-ovate to elliptic-lanceolate, acute or acuminate, 4.5–6 cm long, 1.8–2.5 cm broad. **Petals** narrowly ovate, acuminate, margins undulate, 3.5 cm long, 1.6–2.5 cm broad. **Lip** shortly clawed, ovate, trilobulate, long-recurved, acuminate above, 2.5–3.5 cm long, 1.7–2.5 cm broad; callus with a fimbriate crest. **Column** attenuate below, di-

lated above, dorsally keeled, up to 2 cm long; wings broadly round-triangular.

DISTRIBUTION Brazil, Venezuela, Ecu-Colombia and Guyana; in wet cloud forest, up to 1200 m.

HISTORY Discovered by M.E. Descourtilz in Brazil and described by John Lindley in 1837 in the *Botanical Register* (sub t. 1991).

SYNONYMS *Batemannia burtii* Endres & Rchb.f.; *B. meleagris* (Lindl.) Rchb.f; *Huntleya albo-fulva* Lemaire; *Zygopetalum meleagris* (Lindl.) Benth.; *Z. burtii* (Endres & Rchb.f.) Benth. & Hooker ex Hemsley; *Huntleya burtii* (Endres & Rchb.f.) Rolfe

---

Hygrochilus Pfitzer
Subfamily Epidendroideae
Tribe Vandeae
Subtribe Sarcanthinae

Large monopodial epiphytic plants with stout erect, rather short stems covered by sheathing leaf bases; roots stout, emerging along stem opposite the leaves. **Leaves** distichous, coriaceous, ligulate to obovate-oblanceolate, twisted at the base somewhat, articulated to persistent sheathing bases. **Inflorescences** erect or spreading, unbranched, laxly few- to several-flowered; bracts large, persistent. **Flowers** large, fleshy, flat, showy. **Sepals** subsimilar, free, spreading. **Petals** similar but broader. **Lip** mobilely attached to the column-foot, L-shaped in side view, bipartite or obscurely 3-lobed; hypochile with a narrow nectar-filled channel and a fleshy raised basal callus between the small side lobes; epichile with a central raised ridge. **Column** fleshy, elongate, incurved, with a short foot; anther long-beaked; pollinia 4, ovoid, of two sizes; stipe spathulate; viscidium semicircular to broadly ovate.

DISTRIBUTION A monotypic genus from N. India and S. China across to Laos and Vietnam.

DERIVATION OF NAME From the Greek *hygros* (wet or moist) and *chilos* (lip), in reference to the nectar-producing channel of the hypochile of the lip of the type species.

TAXONOMY *Hygrochilus* is a segregate genus of *Vandopsis* distinguished by its distinct elongate, arcuate column, the mobile lip, and the distinctively shaped pollinia. It is probably most closely allied to *Esmeralda* but differs in habit and pollinarium structure. It is still often found in cultivation as a *Vandopsis*.

The genus was established by Pfitzer in 1897 in Engler's *Die Naturlichen Pflanzenfamilien* (II, 6 Nachtr. 3: 112). For many years Pfitzer's name was ignored but it was resurrected by Garay in 1974 in the *Botanical Museum Leaflets of Harvard*

University (p. 374) and has been generally accepted since then.

TYPE SPECIES *Vanda parishii* Veitch & Rchb.f.

CULTURE Temp. Winter min. 15°C. Best grown in a hanging basket or mounted. Moderate shade, high humidity and plenty of water when in growth, but requiring a cooler drier period when growth ceases.

Hygrochilus parishii (Veitch & Rchb.f.) Pfitzer [Colour Plate]

A large epiphyte with a short stout stem, up to 20 cm long. **Leaves** elliptic-oblong, unequally obtusely bilobed or deeply emarginate at the apex, 11–23 cm long, 2.4–7.5 cm wide, bright green. **Inflorescences** very robust, longer than the leaves, 20–40 cm long, 1- to 6-flowered; bracts ovate-elliptic, acute or subacute, cucullate, 1–1.5 cm long. **Flowers** 3.5–5 cm across, very fleshy, the sepals and petals white at the base, yellow or yellow-green above, densely spotted with red-brown, (in var. *marrottianus* Rchb.f. the tepals are purple in the middle and dark brown above), the lip purple with a paler base and margins, and the column white; pedicel and ovary 2–3 cm long. **Dorsal sepal** elliptic, obtuse or shortly apiculate, 1.6–2.5 cm long, 1–1.4 cm wide; **lateral sepals** oblong-spathulate, shortly apiculate, keeled on reverse, 1.6–2.2 cm long, 0.9–1.3 cm wide. **Petals** elliptic or broadly elliptic, obtuse, 1.5–2 cm long, 1.2–2 cm wide. **Lip** bipartite, 1–1.6 cm long, 0.9–1.2 cm wide; hypochile narrowly channelled and nectariferous, with erect small triangular side lobes; epichile obovate or broadly clawed with a transversely elliptic to oblong apical lamina, with a central raised keel and a higher raised callus at the base. **Column** 6–7 mm long.

DISTRIBUTION N.E. India, Burma, Thailand, S. China, Laos and Vietnam; in deciduous forest up to 1300 m.

HISTORY Charles Parish discovered this spectacular orchid in 1862 at Moulmein in Burma and sent it to H.G. Reichenbach who described it as *Vanda parishii* in 1867 in the *Gardeners' Chronicle* (p. 180).

Pfitzer transferred it to his new genus *Hygrochilus* in 1897 in Engler's *Die Naturlichen Pflanzenfamilen* (II, 6 Nachtr. I: p. 112).

SYNONYMS *Vanda parishii* Rchb.f.; *Vandopsis parishii* (Rchb.f.) Schltr.; *Stauropsis parishii* (Rchb.f.) Rolfe

Ionopsis H.B.K.
Subfamily Epidendroideae
Tribe Oncidieae

Small epiphytic or rarely terrestrial plants. **Rhizomes** short to long, leafy. **Pseudobulbs** small, leafless or 1-leafed. **Leaf** coriaceous, rigid, distichous; subtending leaves imbricate. **Inflorescences** 1–3, paniculate, laxly many-flowered. **Flowers** showy. **Sepals** and **petals** similar, erect, spreading; lateral sepals united to form a short pouch below the lip. **Lip** clawed, much larger than the other segments, callose. **Column** stout, lacking wings or a foot; pollinia 2, waxy.

DISTRIBUTION About ten species in the tropical and subtropical Americas from Florida and Mexico to Bolivia and Paraguay.

DERIVATION OF NAME From the Greek *ion* (violet) and *opsis* (appearance), referring to the flowers which somewhat resemble violets (*Viola* species).

TAXONOMY Described in F.H.A. von Humboldt, A. Bonpland and C.S. Kunth's *Nova Genera et Species Plantarum* (p. 348, t. 83) in 1815. *Ionopsis* is allied to *Comparettia* but the lip of the former lacks any filiform appendages at its base.

TYPE SPECIES *I. pulchella* H.B.K.

CULTURE Compost A. Temp. Winter min. 12–15°C. These plants are best grown in small pots or mounted on slabs of fern-fibre or cork. They should be given conditions of good humidity and moderate shade, and not allowed to become very dry.

Ionopsis utricularioides (Sw.) Lindl. [Colour Plate]

A glabrous, epiphytic or rarely terrestrial plant, 7–75 cm tall. **Pseudobulbs** smooth, ellipsoid, conical, up to 3 cm long, leafless or 1-leafed at apex, concealed by leaf-bases. **Leaves** arising from the rhizome, 2–3, articulated with leaf-sheaths, linear to oblong-lanceolate, acute to obtuse, coriaceous, 3–17 cm long, 0.6–18 cm broad, ± red-brown below. **Inflorescence** racemose or paniculate, laxly few- to many-flowered, up to 75 cm long; peduncle slender to stout; bracts minute. **Flowers** attractive, whitish to rose-red, tinged lavender, purple or magenta. **Dorsal sepal** oblong to oblanceolate, obtuse or apiculate, up to 0.6 cm long, 0.3 cm broad; **lateral sepals** ovate-lanceolate, acute, up to 0.6 cm long, 0.2 cm broad, united to form a small saccate mentum at the base. **Petals** oblong or ovate-oblong, rounded to acute and recurved at the apex, 0.7 cm long, 0.3 cm broad. **Lip** shortly clawed, flabellate-obcordate, emarginate, margins entire, undulate or crenulate, up to 1.6 cm long, 0.7–0.8 cm broad.

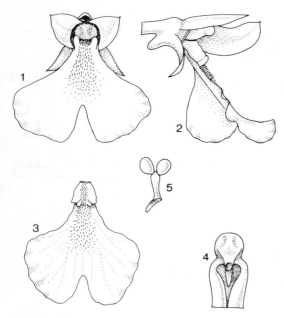

Ionopsis utricularioides
1 – Flower, front view (× 4)
2 – Flower, side view, nearside petal removed (× 4)
3 – Lip (× 3)
4 – Column from below (× 8)
5 – Pollinia, stipe and viscidium (× 17)

Claw auriculate at base; disc bearing 2 thin basal calli. **Column** stout, 0.2 cm long.
DISTRIBUTION Widespread in tropical America as far north as Florida; from sea level to 1050 m altitude.
HISTORY O. Swartz originally described this pretty species as *Epidendrum utricularioides* in his *Prodromus* (p. 122) of W. Indian plants in 1788. John Lindley transferred it to *Ionopsis* in 1821 in his *Collectanea Botanica* (t. 39).
SYNONYMS *Epidendrum utricularioides* Sw.; *Dendrobium utricularioides* (Sw.) Sw.; *I. paniculata* Lindl.

Ipsea Lindl.
Subfamily Epidendroideae
Tribe Arethuseae
Subtribe Bletiinae

Medium-sized terrestrial puberulous herbs with irregular underground pseudobulbs (like tubers); roots fibrous, elongate. **Leaf** solitary or rarely 2, erect, plicate, lanceolate, slenderly petiolate. **Inflorescence** erect, laxly 1- to few-flowered; peduncle slender, terete, puberulous; bracts spathaceous. **Flowers** large, showy. **Dorsal sepals** free, hooded; **lateral sepals**

spreading, attached at the base to base of the column forming with the base of the lip a short broadly conical mentum. **Petals** narrower than the sepals, free. **Lip** sessile, 3-lobed, with a callus, lacking a spur at the base. **Column** slender, elongate, with a short foot; pollinia 8, pyriform, in 2 groups of 4 attached to an obscure viscidium.
DISTRIBUTION A small genus of three species in India and Sri Lanka.
DERIVATION OF NAME Probably from the Latin *ipse* (itself), given by Lindley to this genus which he considered rather isolated from other orchids. Alternatively it may be derived from the Greek *ips* (woodworm), from the appearance of the roots.
TAXONOMY John Lindley established this genus in 1831 in his *Genera and Species of Orchidaceous Plants* (p. 124). It is related to *Calanthe* and *Phaius* but is readily distinguished vegetatively and by the distinct mentum of the flower.
TYPE SPECIES *I. speciosa* Lindl.
CULTURE Temp. Winter min. 12°C. Grow in a well-drained loam-based compost as for other grassland terrestrials. Give moderate shade and careful watering while in leaf, but a cooler and much drier resting period when the leaves fall.

Ipsea speciosa Lindl.
A terrestrial plant with irregularly cylindrical underground tubers, 2–3 cm long, 1.2–2.5 cm in diameter. **Leaves** linear-lanceolate to oblanceolate, acuminate, 15–25 cm long, 0.5–2.2 cm wide; petiole slender, puberulous. **Inflorescence** erect, 1- to several-flowered towards the apex, 15–40 cm tall; bracts ovate, acuminate, 1.5–2 cm long. **Flowers** large, golden-yellow, 5–6.6 cm across; pedicel and ovary decurved, 1–1.5 cm long. **Dorsal sepal** oblong-elliptic, obtuse, 2.7–3 cm long, 1.2–1.7 cm wide; **lateral sepals** obliquely oblong-ovate, acute, 3–3.5 cm long, 0.9–1.4 cm wide. **Petals** oblanceolate, obtuse, 2.8–3.1 cm long, 0.8–1 cm wide. **Lip** 3-lobed, 3–3.2 cm long, 2.7–2.9 cm wide; side lobes erect, suborbicular; mid-lobe orbicular-ovate, recurved, with an undulate margin; callus of 3–5 crenulate ridges ending on the mid-lobe. **Column** 1.9–2 cm long.
DISTRIBUTION Sri Lanka, endemic; common in grassy places in the mountains, 900–1830 m.
HISTORY Macrae collected the type material in Ceylon (now Sri Lanka) and it was described by John Lindley in 1831 in his *Genera and Species of Orchidaceous Plants* (p. 124). It is popularly called the Daffodil Orchid in Sri Lanka and its tubers are collected by local sorcerers for love charms and potions.
SYNONYM *Pachystoma speciosum* (Lindl.) Rchb.f.

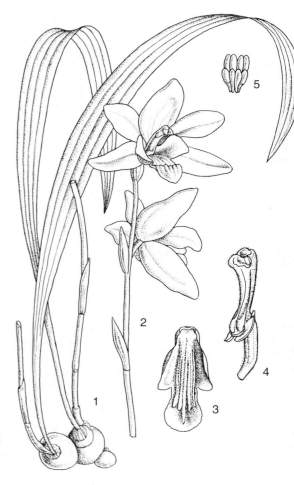

Ipsea speciosa
1 – Habit (× ½)
2 – Inflorescence (× ½)
3 – Lip (× 1)
4 – Column and ovary (× 1½)
5 – Pollinia (× 2½)

Isabelia Barb. Rodr.
Subfamily Epidendroideae
Tribe Epidendreae
Subtribe Laeliinae

Dwarf creeping epiphytic herbs with a short to long slender rhizome. **Pseudobulbs** small, ovoid, clustered or well-spaced on the rhizome, covered when young by fibrous basal sheaths, unifoliate at the apex. **Leaf** erect, terete, very slender-aciculate. **Inflorescence** 1-flowered, short. **Flowers** small, pale pink to purple. **Sepals** and **petals** free, the petals narrower than the sepals. **Lip** entire, saccate at the base and appressed to the column, recurved above, somewhat thickened on the disc. **Column** fleshy, terete; pollinia 8, pyriform, 4 in each locule attached to a filiform caudicle.

DISTRIBUTION A small genus of two species only in E. Brazil.

DERIVATION OF NAME Named in honour of Dona Isabel, Comtessa d'Eu.

TAXONOMY This distinctive dwarf genus was established by the Brazilian botanist João Barbosa Rodrigues in 1877 in his *Nova Genera et Species Orchidearum Novarum* (p. 75). In habit it resembles some of the aciculate-leaved *Maxillaria* species but its floral morphology places it with *Laelia* and allied genera.

TYPE SPECIES *I. virginalis* Barb. Rod .

CULTURE Temp. Winter min. 12–15°C. Best grown mounted under conditions of moderate shade and humidity. Water well while growing, but less when growth is complete.

Isabelia virginalis Barb. Rodr. [Colour Plate]

A small creeping epiphyte with clustered ovoid-globose pseudobulbs, 5–8 mm in diameter, covered by dense fibrous sheaths when young, unifoliate. **Leaf** erect, terete, curved and flexuous, blunt, 4.5–15 cm long, 1–2 mm in diameter. **Inflorescence** 1-flowered; peduncle short, slender, 3–5 mm long; bract spathaceous, obtuse, 1 mm long. **Flowers** small, spreading, off-white flushed with rose or pale purple, and purple on the column and anther-cap; pedicel and ovary 2–3 mm long. **Dorsal sepal** suberect, ovate-oblong, obtuse, somewhat concave, 4–5 mm long, 2 mm wide; **lateral sepals** somewhat spreading, ovate-oblong, obtuse, 5 mm long, 2 mm wide. **Petals** oblanceolate, obtuse, 4–5 mm long, 1 mm wide. **Lip** recurved in the middle, obovate, truncate or rounded, saccate at the base, 3–4.5 mm long, 3 mm wide, fleshily swollen in the basal part. **Column** 2.5–3 mm long.

DISTRIBUTION E. Brazil only: Rio de Janeiro, São Paulo, Parana and Minas Geraes states.

HISTORY George Gardner first collected this pretty little orchid in March 1837 in the Organ Mountains but thought it was a *Maxillaria*. It was not described until 1877 when João Barbosa Rodrigues named it in his *Nova Genera et Species Orchidearum Novarum* (p. 75) based on his own collection from Caldas in the state of Minas Geraes. It was introduced into cultivation in 1904 by K. Grossman who sent living plants from Brazil to the Berlin Botanical Garden in Dahlem.

CLOSELY RELATED SPECIES *I. pulchella* (Kraenzl.) Senghas & Teuscher differs in having well-spaced pseudobulbs on an elongate slender rhizome and darker purple flowers.

Isochilus R. Br.

Subfamily Epidendroideae
Tribe Arethuseae
Subtribe Sobraliinae

Small, tufted or creeping, epiphytic, terrestrial or lithophytic herbs. **Stem** slender, bearing numerous distichous leaves. **Leaves** articulate to the leaf-sheaths, linear, lanceolate or oblong, subcoriaceous to rigid membranaceous. **Inflorescences** terminal, racemose, 1- to many-flowered. **Flowers** secund or distichous, small, white to dark purple. **Sepals** subequal, free to united to apex, ± dorsally keeled. **Petals** slender, clawed, oblique. **Lip** shortly clawed, linear or linear-oblanceolate, acute to obtuse, sigmoid below or above middle. **Column** erect, wingless, dentate at apex; ± with an obscure foot; pollinia 4, waxy, ovoid-oblong, elongate, laterally compressed.

DISTRIBUTION A small genus of a few species and four varieties from Central America and northern S. America and the W. Indies.

DERIVATION OF NAME From the Greek *iso* (equal) and *cheilos* (lip), as the lip more or less equals the other floral segments in length.

TAXONOMY *Isochilus* was first described by Robert Brown in 1813 in the 2nd edition of W. Aiton's *Hortus Kewensis* (p. 209) and has most recently been revised by D.S. Correll in the *Botanical Museum Leaflets of Harvard University* (1941). The taxa included in *Isochilus* are difficult to distinguish on floral morphology but are identifiable more readily by their vegetative morphology. Variation in flower shape and size seems to be more or less continuous from one taxon to the next.

Isochilus may be distinguished from *Ponera* by its lip which is S-shaped at the base and in its inflorescence which is always terminal. It is most closely allied to *Elleanthus* being distinguished by its distinct lip and 4 pollinia.

According to Steyermark the plants of *Isochilus* are used medicinally in Guatemala to treat various intestinal orders.

TYPE SPECIES *I. linearis* (Jacq.) R. Br.

CULTURE Compost A. Temp. Winter min. 12–15°C. *Isochilus* species grow well in pots or pans. They need moderate humidity and shade, and careful watering throughout the year.

Isochilus linearis (Jacq.) R. Br.

[Colour Plate]

A terrestrial, lithophytic or epiphytic plant, up to 60 cm tall. **Stems** subcaespitose, slender, leafy, up to 0.2 cm in diameter, covered by verrucose leaf-sheaths. **Leaves** linear, retuse and obtuse at apex, suberect or spreading, up to 6.5 cm long, 0.25 cm broad. **Inflorescence** racemose, 1- to several-flowered; bracts paleaceous, suborbicular to oblong. **Flowers** small, ± distichous, white, orange-yellow, red or purple. **Sepals** concave, ± coherent, ± keeled dorsally, obtuse to subacuminate, up to 0.8 cm long; lateral sepals forming a short mentum at the base. **Petals** clawed, oblong-lanceolate to obovate, up to 0.6 cm long. **Lip** shortly clawed, linear or linear-oblanceolate, acute or obtuse, S-shaped, 0.8 cm long, 0.2 cm broad. **Column** erect, wingless, toothed at the apex, with a short foot.

DISTRIBUTION Widespread in the tropical Americas; from sea level to 3900 m altitude.

HISTORY Described by N.J. Jacquin in 1763, based on a C. Plumier species collected in Martinique, as *Epidendrum lineare* in his *Selectarum Stirpium Americanarum Historia* (p. 221, t. 131). Robert Brown transferred it to *Isochilus* in 1813 in the 2nd edition of W. Aiton's *Hortus Kewensis* (p. 209).

SYNONYM *Epidendrum lineare* Jacq.

CLOSELY RELATED SPECIES *Isochilus major* Cham. & Schltr. [Colour Plate], may be distinguished from *I. linearis* by its numerous dense compact unilateral scorpioid inflorescences and characteristically smooth and green-spotted leaf-sheaths. It is widespread in Central America from S. Mexico to Panama and also in Jamaica growing either terrestrially or epiphytically between 600 and 2000 m in open or cloud forest.

Isochilus major Cham. & Schltr.

[Colour Plate]
See under *Isochilus linearis*.

Jumellea Schltr.

Subfamily Epidendroideae
Tribe Vandeae
Subtribe Angraecinae

Small to medium-sized epiphytic or lithophytic plants with very short to elongated stems which are rarely branched. **Leaves** often distichous and loriform, ± 2-lobed at the apex. **Inflorescences** always 1-flowered; peduncle mostly shorter than the ovary and pedicel. **Flowers** white. **Sepals** and **petals** subsimilar; lateral sepals ± united at the base around the base of the spur. **Lip** entire, contracted at the base with 1 or 2 dilations above, with a central linear or tapering callus; spur short to very long, filamentous or slender. **Column** short, fleshy; rostellum bifid; pollinia 2, each on a separate stipe or directly attached to a viscidium.

DISTRIBUTION About 40 species mostly in Madagascar, the Comoros and Mascarene Islands but with two species in continental Africa.

DERIVATION OF NAME Named in honour of Dr Henri Jumelle, a celebrated French botanist who collected and studied plants of Madagascar.

TAXONOMY Described by Rudolf Schlechter in 1914 in *Die Orchideen* (p. 609), *Jumellea* is another genus which has been split off from *Angraecum* as the orchids of Africa and Madagascar have become better understood.

Jumellea is a remarkably uniform genus particularly in the form of the flowers which, because of the narrow segments and reflexed sepals and petals, appear very narrow in front view. The characteristic flower form and lanceolate lip which never envelops the column, serve to distinguish it easily from *Angraecum* and allied genera.

The delimitation of the species within the genus is not easy and as many species have very similar flowers, the vegetative organs are important in identification as well as the inflorescence.

The most recent account of the genus is that by H. Perrier de la Bâthie in *Flore de Madagascar* (1941) where 37 species are treated. This account is now out of date as several more species have been described and many further specimens have been collected which indicate the interspecific variability may be much greater than Perrier supposed.

TYPE SPECIES *Jumellea recurva* (Thou.) Schltr.

CULTURE Compost A. Temp. Winter min. 15°C. *Jumellea* species enjoy high humidity and moderate shade throughout the year, with plenty of water while growing. They are often very untidy plants, so should be grown in baskets or pans so that the roots are free to ramble. Some species have an upright habit, while others prefer to hang. All tend to branch, forming clumps, and flowers may appear at any time of the year.

Jumellea sagittata H. Perr. [Colour Plate]

A large epiphytic plant, up to 50 cm high or more. **Stems** very short, 5- or 6-leaved. **Leaves** ligulate, obtuse at apex, conduplicate toward base, 25–30 cm long, 3–3.5 cm broad. **Inflorescence** spreading, 1-flowered; peduncle 7–9 cm long; bract green, 1 cm long. **Flowers** white, a little furfuraceous on outer surface. **Dorsal sepal** lanceolate, acuminate, 2.5–3 cm long, 0.4–0.8 cm broad; **lateral sepals** a little longer and narrower, 3–4 cm long, 0.6 cm broad. **Petals** similar to dorsal sepal. **Lip** lanceolate, acuminate, basal margins incurved to form a tube, 3.6–4 cm long, 1.8–2 cm broad; spur cylindrical, 5–6 cm long. **Column** thick, 0.4 cm long, 0.3 cm broad.

DISTRIBUTION Madagascar; in mossy forests up to 1400 m altitude.

HISTORY Discovered by H. Perrier de la

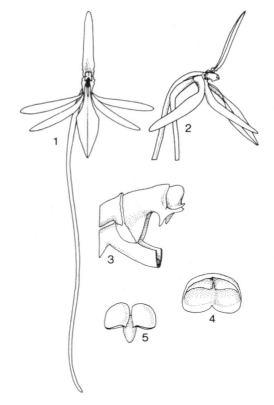

Jumellea comorensis
1 – Flower, front view ($\times \frac{3}{4}$)
2 – Flower, side view ($\times \frac{3}{4}$)
3 – Column, side view ($\times 4$)
4 – Anther-cap ($\times 6$)
5 – Pollinia and viscidium ($\times 6$)

Bâthie at Ankeramadinika in Central Madagascar and described by him in *Notulae Systematiae* (p. 52) in 1938.

CLOSELY RELATED SPECIES *Jumellea comorensis* Schltr. has a quite different habit from *J. sagittata* in that its stems are much more slender and elongate and its leaves are much shorter. It also differs in having a delicate flower with a more slender lip and longer filiform spur.

Kefersteinia Rchb.f.

Subfamily Epidendroideae
Tribe Maxillarieae
Subtribe Zygopetalinae

Small to medium-sized epiphytic plants lacking pseudobulbs. **Stems** very short, tufted, 2- to 3-leaved. **Leaves** oblanceolate or lanceolate, thinly coriaceous. **Inflorescence** pendulous, few-flowered. **Flowers** medium-sized, hyaline, whitish to pale straw-coloured, ± well-spotted with red, purple or maroon. **Sepals** and petals spreading, free, subsimilar. **Lip** articulate to column-foot, entire, often saccate at base, geniculate in the middle, margins erose or fringed; callus basal, plate-like. **Column** semi-terete, with a distinct vertical keel in front, ± with a weakly developed foot forming an inconspicuous mentum; rostellum tripartite, median tooth linear-lanceolate, porrect; pollinia 4, superposed, with a prominent viscidium and stipe.

DISTRIBUTION About 20 species mostly poorly known, Costa Rica and Nicaragua, south to Brazil and Peru.

DERIVATION OF NAME Named after Herr Keferstein of Krollwitz who was a contemporary of H.G. Reichenbach and a keen orchid grower who assembled an outstanding collection during his lifetime.

TAXONOMY *Kefersteinia* was described by Reichenbach in 1852 in the *Botanische Zeitung* (p. 633). The genus is most closely allied to *Chondrorhyncha* and *Cochleanthes*, differing in that the column has a distinct vertical keel in front and the lip which is geniculate or reduplicate with a free basal plate-like callus. It has often been considered congeneric with *Chondrorhyncha* but the recent tendency has been to keep them separate (L. Garay in *Orquideologia*, 1969).

Several species have been illustrated in colour by J.A. Fowlie in the *Orchid Digest* (1970). These complement his previous article on the Central American species of *Kefersteinia* in the *Orchid Digest* (1966).

TYPE SPECIES *K. graminea* (Lindl.) Rchb.f.

CULTURE Compost A. Temp. Winter min. 12–15°C. As for *Chondrorhyncha*. The plants may be grown in pots or baskets under conditions of good humidity and shade. The roots should never become very dry but water must always be applied carefully.

Kefersteinia graminea (Lindl.) Rchb.f.

A medium-sized epiphytic plant. **Leaves** suberect-spreading, linear-oblanceolate, acute or acuminate, 35 cm long, 2.5 cm broad, articulate below to a conduplicate leaf-sheath, keeled behind. **Inflorescences** several, erect, 1- to 3-flowered. **Flowers** thin-textured; sepals and petals pale green with maroon spotting; lip very pale green spotted with reddish maroon; callus dark maroon; column white. **Sepals** narrowly ovate-elliptic, acute, spreading, 2–2.3 cm long, 0.9–1 cm broad. **Petals** narrowly elliptic, acute, 2 cm long, 0.9 cm broad. **Lip** broadly ovate, emarginate; side margins upturned; apical half deflexed, 2.1 cm long, 2.4 cm broad; apical margins erose-undulate; callus fleshy, porrect, bifid in front, velvety to glandular pubescent in the centre. **Column** erect, obscurely biauriculate.

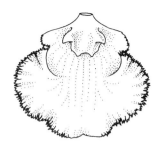

Kefersteinia graminea
Lip (× 2)

DISTRIBUTION Venezuela, Colombia and Ecuador.
HISTORY Originally described by John Lindley in 1844 in the *Botanical Register* (misc. 10) as *Zygopetalum gramineum* based on a plant collected in Ecuador.

H.G. Reichenbach transferred it to *Kefersteinia* in 1852 in the *Botanische Zeitung* (p. 634).
SYNONYM *Zygopetalum gramineum* Lindl.

Kefersteinia lojae Schltr. [Colour Plate]

A small epiphytic plant, up to 25 cm tall. **Stems** abbreviated, clustered, covered with 4 or 5 distichous, imbricating leaf-sheaths. **Leaves** articulated to conduplicate leaf-bases, oblanceolate to linear, subacute, up to 20 cm long, 0.8–2 cm broad. **Inflorescences** 2 or 3, basal, very short, 1-flowered, spreading or ascending. **Flowers** similar to *K. graminea* but smaller, small to medium-sized with membranous segments, white except for densely red-dotted central part. **Dorsal sepal** oblong, acute, 1.4 cm long, 0.6 cm broad; **lateral sepals** obliquely oblong-lanceolate, subacute, concave at the base. **Petals** shorter but broader than the dorsal sepal, slightly crenulate. **Lip** shortly clawed, rhombic-ovate, retuse or 2-lobed at the apex, cuneate at the base, margins erose-denticulate, 1.3 cm long, 1.2 cm broad; callus basal, suborbicular-rhombic, 2-lobed. **Column** short, stout, with a short foot, subauriculate above.
DISTRIBUTION Ecuador and Peru.
HISTORY Originally described by Rudolf Schlechter in 1921 in *Fedde, Repertorium Specierum Novarum, Beihefte* (p. 93) as *Kefersteinia lojae* from a specimen collected by F.C. Lehmann at Las Juntas near Loja in Ecuador. C. Schweinfurth transferred it to the genus *Chondrorhyncha* in 1944 in the *Botanical Museum Leaflets of Harvard University* (p. 216), but changed his mind and resurrected the genus *Kefersteinia* in the *First Supplement* to the *Orchids of Peru* in 1970.
SYNONYM *Chondrorhyncha lojae* (Schltr.) Schweinf.

Kegeliella Mansfeld
Subfamily Epidendroideae
Tribe Gongoreae
Subtribe Stanhopeinae

Medium-sized or small epiphytic herbs resembling a small *Gongora* plant. **Pseudobulbs** ovoid, somewhat compressed, angled, 2- to 3-leaved at the apex. **Leaves** plicate, suberect, elliptic to elliptic-lanceolate, acute. **Inflorescences** pendent, racemose, laxly few-flowered; rhachis covered in dense hairs. **Flowers** medium-sized. **Sepals** subequal, free, spreading, covered on outer surface with glandular hairs. **Petals** similar to sepals but narrower. **Lip** membranous to fleshy, 3-lobed; the side lobes large, spreading or erect; mid-lobe small, subcordate to triangular; callus erect, fleshy, laterally compressed or carinate, dorsally sulcate, bilobed or acute. **Column** elongate, more or less arcuate, broadly winged above, lacking a foot; rostellum elongate; pollinia 2, elongate, waxy, attached by a linear or oblanceolate stipe to a deltoid viscidium.
DISTRIBUTION A small genus of two species in Central America, the W. Indies and Surinam.
DERIVATION OF NAME Named in honour of Herr Kegel, the gardener of the Halle University in Germany. He collected orchids in Surinam in the mid-nineteenth century.
TAXONOMY This genus was originally described by H.G. Reichenbach who named it *Kegelia* in 1852 in the *Botanische Zeitung* (p. 670). Unfortunately, that name had previously been used for another genus and R. Mansfeld, therefore, renamed it *Kegeliella* in 1934 in *Fedde, Repertorium Specierum Novarum* (p. 60).

Kegeliella is allied to *Polycycnis* and *Gongora*.
TYPE SPECIES *Kegelia houtteana* Rchb.f.
CULTURE Temp. Winter min. 12°C. Grow as for *Gongora* but give a less pronounced dry period when growth is complete.

Kegeliella kupperi Mansf.

Small epiphyte with ovoid somewhat compressed angulate pseudobulbs 2–3 cm long, 1–2 cm wide. **Leaves** elliptic-lanceolate, acute, 4–8 cm long, 1.5–6 cm wide. **Inflorescences** pendent, up to 4- to 8-flowered, up to 30 cm long; peduncle and rhachis coarsely glandular-pubescent; bracts lanceolate, acute, 4–6 mm long. **Flowers** with white sepals and petals marked with red-brown bars all over and with a green lip; ovary recurved, c. 1.5 cm long. **Sepals** concave, lanceolate, acute, 1.6–2 cm long, 0.5–0.7 cm wide, minutely pubescent on outside. **Petals** lanceolate, acute, 1–1.4 cm long, 0.3–0.4 cm wide. **Lip** fleshy, 3-lobed, 1–1.3 cm long and wide; side lobes large, round-

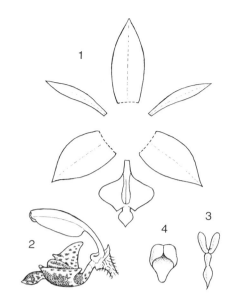

Kegeliella kupperi
1 – Sepals, petals and lip (× 1½)
2 – Column and lip, side view (× 2½)
3 – Pollinarium (× 4)
4 – Anther-cap (× 5)

ed, acute in front; mid-lobe small, subcordate, acute; callus erect, fleshy, carinate, acute, linguiform. **Column** 1–1.2 cm long, broadly winged above.
DISTRIBUTION Costa Rica and Panama; at low altitudes.
HISTORY R. Mansfeld described this rare species in 1934 in *Fedde, Repertorium Specierum Novarum* (p. 60) based on a plant flowered in the Munich Botanical Garden by Walter Kupper.

Kingidium P.F. Hunt
Subfamily Epidendroideae
Tribe Vandeae
Subtribe Sarcanthinae

Small epiphytic herbs with very short stems. **Leaves** rather thin-textured. **Inflorescence** racemose or paniculate, many-flowered. **Flowers** showy but rather small. **Dorsal sepal** and **petals** free, subsimilar; **lateral sepals** united with base of lip, forming a spur-like mentum. **Lip** saccate at base, markedly 3-lobed; side lobes erect; mid-lobe widening from a narrow base, callus flattened, bifid. **Column** short, fleshy; pollinia 4, borne on a linear-oblanceolate stipe attached to a cordate viscidium.
DISTRIBUTION Five species in China,

India, Sri Lanka, Burma, Thailand, Malaya, Indonesia and the Philippines.
DERIVATION OF NAME Named in honour of Sir George King who was joint author with R. Pantling of *Orchids of the Sikkim-Himalaya*.
TAXONOMY P.F. Hunt established the genus *Kingidium* in 1970 in the *Kew Bulletin* (p. 97). This genus has previously been known as *Kingiella* Rolfe but that name had been predated by the orthographic variant *Kingella* van Tiegh. and was thus a later homonym and invalid under the *International Code of Botanical Nomenclature*.

Kingidium is closely allied to *Phalaenopsis* and is occasionally considered congeneric by some authors. It is distinguished, however, by its saccate mentum on which the lip lobes are borne directly and without a claw bearing linear appendages. K. Senghas (1990) in the 3rd edition of Schlechter's *Die Orchideen* (p. 140) provides a key to the five recognised species.
TYPE SPECIES *K. decumbens* (Griff.) P.F. Hunt and *K. taenialis* (Lindl.) P.F. Hunt
SYNONYM *Kingiella* Rolfe
CULTURE Compost A. Temp. Winter min. 15°C. As for *Phalaenopsis* and *Doritis*. The relatively thin leaves need to be well shaded from direct sunlight and humidity should be high at all times. Although the plants need water at all times, less is required when the roots have completed active growth.

Kingidium decumbens (Griff.) P.F. Hunt
A very variable epiphytic plant. Stem short, 0.3–1 cm long, 0.3–0.8 cm broad, forming large tortuous tufts. **Leaves** few, obovate-oblong, obtuse or subacute, narrowed to a sessile base, soft when dry, 7.5–15.5 cm long, about 3.5 cm broad. **Inflorescences** 1 to several, single or branched, 6–12 cm long; bracts small, triangular. **Flowers** small with white sepals and petals; lateral sepals spotted purple at the base; lip purple. **Dorsal sepal** narrowly elliptic, subobtuse, 0.6–0.9 cm long; **lateral sepals** very broad, oblong-falcate, obtuse. **Petals** broadly clawed, elliptic, rounded, 0.7–0.9 cm long, 0.4 cm broad. **Lip** 3-lobed, spreading, slightly saccate at base, up to 1.3 cm long, 0.8 cm broad; side lobes slightly spreading, broader above, cuneate-obovate; mid-lobe obcordate, 0.6 cm long and broad, apex broad and deeply cleft; callus flattened, divided into 2 spreading teeth. **Column** somewhat elliptic in front view.
DISTRIBUTION Bhutan, India, Burma, Sri Lanka, Malaya, Indonesia and the Philippines.
HISTORY Originally described as *Aerides decumbens* by William Griffith in his *Icones Plantarum Asiaticum* (t. 320) in 1851, based on his own collection from Mogoung in Burma. R.A. Rolfe transferred it to the new genus *Kingiella*, be-

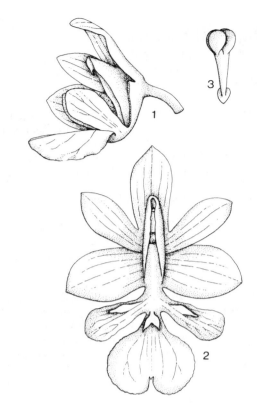

Kingidium decumbens
1 – Flower, side view (× 4)
2 – Flower with segments spread out (× 4)
3 – Pollinia, stipe and viscidium (× 15)

cause of its saccate lip base, in 1917 in the *Orchid Review*. R. Holttum did not consider this sufficient to separate this species from *Phalaenopsis* and thus treated it as *P. decumbens* in his account of the orchids in the 3rd edition of *Flora of Malaya* (1964). More recently P.F. Hunt has transferred it to the new genus *Kingidium* in 1970 in the *Kew Bulletin* (p. 97), the new generic name being necessary because *Kingiella* Rolfe was predated by 2 years by *Kingiella* van Tiegh. in the Loranthaceae.
SYNONYMS *Phalaenopsis wightii* Rchb.f.; *Aerides latifolium* Thwaites; *Doritis wightii* (Rchb.f.) Benth.; *Aerides decumbens* Griff.; *Kingiella decumbens* (Griff.) Rolfe; *Phalaenopsis hebe* Rchb.f.; *P. deliciosa* Rchb.f.; *P. decumbens* (Griff.) Holttum

---

Koellensteinia Rchb.f.
Subfamily Epidendroideae
Tribe Maxillarieae
Subtribe Zygopetalinae

Terrestrial or epiphytic plants with an abbreviated rhizome. **Stems** short, leafy, often thickening with maturity into ± conspicuous pseudobulbs. **Pseudobulbs**, if present, 1- to 3-leaved at apex, sometimes with a long caulescent neck. **Leaves** linear to oblong-elliptic, ± distinctly petiolate, plicate. **Inflorescences** lateral, erect or spreading, distantly few-sheathed below, racemose or somewhat paniculate above. **Flowers** small to medium-sized, with spreading segments. **Sepals** and **petals** subsimilar, free; lateral sepals slightly oblique. **Lip** articulated to column-foot, distinctly 3-lobed; side lobes erect or spreading; mid-lobe larger, broad, entire or somewhat 2-lobed. **Column** very short, often dilated or winged above, with a conspicuous foot; pollinia 2, deeply 2-lobed.
DISTRIBUTION A small genus of about ten species, widespread in S. America from Colombia and Venezuela, south to Bolivia and Brazil.
DERIVATION OF NAME Named in honour of Capt. Kellner von Koellenstein, an Austrian.
TAXONOMY *Koellensteinia* was described in 1854 in *Bonplandia* (p. 17) based on *Koellensteinia kellneriana* which had been collected in Colombia by Wagener. R. Schlechter revised the genus in 1918 in *Orchis*.

Koellensteinia is one of several genera allied to *Zygopetalum* which are discussed by L. Garay in *Orquideologia* (1973). It is most closely allied to *Paradisanthus*, differing in that the lip side lobes are distinct and ascend obliquely and the callus is commonly 2-lobed and more or less retrorse.
TYPE SPECIES *K. kellneriana* Rchb.f.
CULTURE Compost A. Temp. Winter min. 12–15°C. *Koellensteinia* species may be grown in pans or baskets under shady, humid conditions. They require careful watering throughout the year and may flower for several months at a time.

Koellensteinia graminea (Lindl.) Rchb.f.
A small epiphytic plant with very short non-pseudobulbous stems. **Leaves** 1–3, narrowly linear, grass-like, acute, erect to arcuate, 6–26 cm long, 0.4–0.9 cm broad. **Inflorescences** erect, axillary, racemose or loosely paniculate, few-flowered, 6–25 cm long, ± shorter than the leaves; bracts very small, ovate, spreading. **Flowers** rather small, cream-coloured, straw-coloured or white, often greenish-tinged, marked with rose, violet or red-brown on basal part of each segment and yellow around callus. **Sepals** oblong-ovate to elliptic, acute or subacute, concave, 1–1.1 cm long, 0.4–0.6 cm broad. **Lip** 3-lobed at base, articulated to column-foot, 0.6 cm long, 0.9 cm broad; side lobes erect, oblong to ovate; mid-lobe sessile, transversely oblong or reniform, apiculate to retuse at apex; callus between side lobes fleshy,

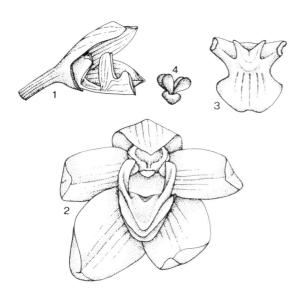

Koellensteinia graminea
1 – Flower, side view with nearside lateral sepal and petal removed (× 2)
2 – Flower, front view (× 4)
3 – Lip (× 4)
4 – Pollinia and viscidium (× 14)

2-lobed, pointing backwards. **Column** short, stout, with 2 short apical wings, extended below into a slightly curved foot.
DISTRIBUTION Venezuela and Colombia, south to Bolivia.
HISTORY This species was first described in 1836 by John Lindley in the *Botanical Register* (sub t. 1802), as *Maxillaria graminea*, based on a plant imported by Messrs Low from Demerara (Georgetown), Guyana, and flowered by Messrs Loddiges in January 1835. H.G. Reichenbach subsequently transferred it in 1856 to *Koellensteinia* in *Bonplandia* (p. 323).
SYNONYM *Maxillaria graminea* Lindl.

Lacaena Lindl.
Subfamily Epidendroideae
Tribe Gongoreae
Subtribe Stanhopeinae

Epiphytic plants with short, thickened, 1-noded, 2- to 4-leaved pseudobulbs. **Leaves** plicate, petiolate. **Inflorescences** basal, pendent, unbranched, distantly many-flowered. **Flowers** fleshy, showy. **Sepals** subsimilar, spreading; laterals joined to form a short mentum with the column-foot at the base. **Petals** free, smaller than the sepals. **Lip** 3-lobed, articulated to the column-foot; side lobes upcurved; mid-lobe spreading, deflexed. **Column** semiterete, slight-

ly incurved, subclavate, narrowly winged above; pollinia 2, waxy, attached by a slender stipe to a small viscidium.
DISTRIBUTION Two species only in Central America.
DERIVATION OF NAME From the Greek *Lakaina*, meaning a woman of Laconia in Greece and an alternative name for Helen of Troy.
TAXONOMY A small genus allied to *Stanhopea* but distinguished by its more numerous, smaller and simpler flowers reflecting a different pollination syndrome.
  Lacaena was established by John Lindley in 1843 in the *Botanical Register* (misc. no. 101).
TYPE SPECIES *L. bicolor* Lindl.
CULTURE Temp. Winter min. 15°C. Grown as for *Acineta* and *Stanhopea* in baskets, to allow the pendent inflorescences to grow naturally.

Lacaena bicolor Lindl. [Colour Plate]
A large epiphyte or lithophyte. **Pseudobulbs** clustered, elongated-conical, slightly bilaterally compressed, 6–10 cm long, 2–7 cm diameter, several ribbed, yellowish-green. **Leaves** 2–4, plicate, elliptic-lanceolate, acute, 30–45 cm long, 8–15 cm wide; petiole 4–9 cm long. **Inflorescences** pendent, up to 60 cm long, 15- to 50-flowered; peduncle fleshy, up to 20 cm long, 5 mm diameter; bracts scarious, cucullate, elliptic-lanceolate, obtuse, 17–30 cm long. **Flowers** fleshy, furfuraceous on outside, cream or off-cream, lightly spotted on the basal halves of the sepals and petals with purple; lip cream heavily spotted and blotched with purple on the disc, side lobes and base of the mid-lobe; column cream with ventral purple-spotting; pedicel and ovary 3–3.2 cm long, scabrid, green. **Dorsal sepal** elliptic, acute or subacute, 2–3 cm long, 1–1.7 cm wide; **lateral sepals** obliquely ovate-elliptic, subacute, 2.5–3 cm long, 1.3–1.7 cm wide. **Petals** ovate-elliptic, obtuse, 1.4–1.6 cm long, 0.8–1 cm wide. **Lip** 3-lobed, 1.8–2.5 cm long, 1.3–2 cm wide; side lobes erect, semicircular, obtuse, 7 mm long, 4 mm wide; mid-lobe reflexed, subquadrate-obovate, obtuse, 13 mm long and wide; callus a raised mound at the base running into 2 ridges in front, puberulent. **Column** clavate, narrowly winged above, 14–17 mm long.
DISTRIBUTION Mexico, Guatemala, Honduras, Nicaragua and Costa Rica; in oak and pine forest and thickets, up to 2200 m.
HISTORY John Lindley described this species in 1843 in the *Botanical Register* (misc. p. 68) based on a collection by Th. Hartweg from Guatemala which flowered at Chiswick in May 1843 in the collection of the Horticultural Society.
SYNONYMS *Peristeria longiscapa* A. Rich. & Gal.; *Acineta longiscapa* (A. Rich. & Gal.)

Rchb.f.; *A. hrubyana* Hort.; *A. wightii* Fraser; *Lueddemannia sanderiana* Kraenzl.

Laelia Lindl.
Subfamily Epidendroideae
Tribe Epidendreae
Subtribe Laeliinae

Epiphytic, lithophytic or terrestrial herbs. **Pseudobulbs** thickened, ± hollow, fusiform, ovoid or cylindrical, 1- or 2(or more)-leaved at apex. **Leaves** coriaceous. **Inflorescence** terminal, 1- to several-flowered, racemose or rarely paniculate. **Flowers** mostly large and showy, white, yellow, orange, pink or purple. **Sepals** and **petals** free, spreading, flat or undulate. **Lip** free or adnate to base of column, entire to 3-lobed, tubular at base around the column, ± spreading above; disc smooth or lamellate. **Column** long, toothed at the apex; anther apiculate; pollinia 8, 4 in each cell of the anther, waxy, ovoid or compressed.
DISTRIBUTION A genus of about 50 species distributed widely from Mexico, south to Peru, the W. Indies and Brazil.
DERIVATION OF NAME Dedicated to Laelia, one of the Vestal Virgins.
TAXONOMY The genus *Laelia* is closely related to *Cattleya* and *Epidendrum* but may be conveniently identified by its 8 rather than 4 pollinia. Undoubtedly, this distinction is somewhat artificial as is evidenced by the ease with which hybrids can be produced between these genera.
  Laelia was described by John Lindley in 1831 in his *Genera and Species of Orchidaceous Plants* (p. 115). This name has been conserved at the expense of *Laelia* Adanson (1763) in the *Cruciferae*.
  Rudolf Schlechter revised the genus in *Orchis* (1917) dividing the genus into seven sections as follows:

1. sect. *Cattleyodes* – Species resembling *Cattleya* but with 8 pollinia; includes *L. crispa* Rchb.f., *L. lobata* Lindl., *L. purpurata* Lindl. and *L. tenebrosa* Rolfe.
2. sect. *Hadrolaelia* – Species with heteroblastic pseudobulbs and a lip with distinctive crests or keels; *L. pumila* Rchb.f. and *L. jongheana* Rchb.f.
3. sect. *(Eu) Laelia* – As above but pseudobulbs homoblastic; *L. speciosa* (H.B.K.) Schltr.
4. sect. *Microlaelia* – Similar to sect. *Laelia* but sepals and petals of equal width; *L. lundii* Rchb.f. only.
5. sect. *Cyrtolaelia* – *L. cinnabarina* Batem. and the other rupicolous species in which the lip is narrow. Many species have yellow

or orange-red flowers. This section has recently been called *Parviflorae* and has most recently been revised by Pabst (1978) in the *Orchid Digest* (pp. 156–165, 196–200).

6. sect. *Podolaelia* – Species in which the stem is articulated and bears sheaths; includes *L. albida* Batem., *L. autumnalis* (La Llave & Lex.) Lindl., *L., anceps* Lindl. and *L. rubescens* Lindl.

7. sect. *Calolaelia* – A single species, *L. superbiens*, now placed in *Schomburgkia* by most authors.

H.G. Jones has recently reviewed the sectional limits of *Laelia* in the *Botanische Jahrbücher* (1976). He retains five of Schlechter's sections for 19 species but excludes *Cyrtolaelia* which, in *Acta Botanica Academiae Scientiarum Hungaricae* (1968), he has elevated to generic status as *Hoffmannseggella* and *L. superbiens* in sect. *Calolaelia* which he considers to be a species of *Schomburgkia*. So far, Jones has only made the necessary combination in *Hoffmannseggella* for *L. cinnabarina* and his treatment of the rupicolus *Laelia* species has not been generally accepted.

Recently, some botanists have placed species of the genus *Schomburgkia* in *Laelia* following the work of L.O. Williams in *Botanical Museum Leaflets of Harvard University* (1941). *Schomburgkia* is regarded as a distinct genus in this work.

The genus has most recently been revised by Carl Withner (1990) in the second volume of his *The Cattleyas and their relatives*.

TYPE SPECIES *L. grandiflora* (La Llave and Lex.) Lindl. [syn. *Bletia grandiflora* (La Llave and Lex.] typ. cons.

CULTURE Compost A. Temp. Mostly 12–15°C min.; Mexican species a little cooler in winter. As for *Cattleya*. *Laelia* species require moderate shade and humidity during growth. Most species grow well in pots, but *L. anceps* and similar species are better in hanging baskets. Plenty of water should be given when the roots are growing, but less is needed when resting. Mexican species such as *L. anceps* should be kept cooler and drier in winter than those species from Brazil etc., especially at night.

Laelia albida Lindl. [Colour Plate]
An epiphytic herb, up to 55 cm high. **Pseudobulbs** clustered, ovoid or pear-shaped, wrinkled when old, 3–4 cm long, 2-leaved at apex. **Leaves** linear-lanceolate, leathery, 10–17 cm long, 1.2 cm broad, acute, dark green. **Inflorescence** laxly 5- to 9-flowered, 35–50 cm long; scape slender, jointed, nearly covered in sheaths borne at each node. **Flowers** 5 cm across, fragrant, white delicately tinged with pink towards apex; lip with 3 parallel yellow ridges, of which the outer may be purple-spotted; column white. **Sepals** oblong-lanceolate, 3 cm long, 0.8 cm broad, acute. **Petals** similar to sepals, broader, 2.5 cm long, 1.2 cm broad, acute, margin undulate. **Lip** 3-lobed, oblong, 2 cm long, 1.6 cm broad; side lobes erect oblong, only partly covering the column; mid-lobe reflexed, ovate, margin undulate. **Column** arched, 1.5 cm long.

DISTRIBUTION Mexico; 1300–2600 m growing on oak trees.

HISTORY John Lindley described *L. albida* in the *Botanical Register* (t. 54, misc. 2) in 1839. The specific epithet refers to the pale pinkish-white flower colour. Count Karwinsky had earlier introduced it into cultivation in 1832 from near Oaxaca in Mexico.

Several colour varieties of *L. albida* are known, e.g. *rosea* with a bright rose-coloured lip and *salmonea* with salmon-pink sepals and petals.

CLOSELY RELATED SPECIES Similar to, but smaller and paler flowered than *L. autumnalis*.

SYNONYM *Bletia albida* (Lindl.) Rchb.f.

Laelia anceps Lindl. [Colour Plate]
An epiphytic or lithophytic herb. **Pseudobulbs** ovate-oblong, compressed, 7 cm long, 2.5 cm broad, edges acute, flattened sides ribbed, 1- or rarely 2-leaved at apex. **Leaves** oblong-lanceolate, leathery, 15–22 cm long, 3.4 cm broad, acute. **Inflorescence** 60–75 cm long, 2- to 5-flowered; scape bears alternate keeled sheaths along length at nodes. **Flowers** up to 10 cm across; sepals pale rose-purple, petals darker; lip side lobes pale rose, rich yellow striped purple, bordered purple, mid-lobe rich crimson-purple, disc bright yellow, bordered white in front. **Sepals** ligulate-lanceolate, 6 cm long, 1.6 cm broad, acute, reflexed at apex. **Petals** oblong-elliptic, 6 cm long, 2.6 cm broad, acute. **Lip** 3-lobed in middle, 4.5 cm long, 3.8 cm broad; side lobes oblong, curved up around column, rounded; mid-lobe oblong, reflexed, undulate, blunt; disc with a thick longitudinal ridge. **Column** semiterete, wingless.

DISTRIBUTION Mexico, widely distributed on the eastern side of the Cordillera; growing on tree trunks and branches or on rocks, often in full sunlight.

HISTORY Messrs Loddiges first introduced this striking species into England from Mexico in 1835 and it was described by John Lindley in the same year in the *Botanical Register* (t. 1751). The specific epithet refers to the ancipitous (compressed) appearance given to the scape by the keeled sheaths.

Several varieties of *L. anceps* are known which differ from the typical form in flower size and/or flower colour. White-flowered varieties are known.

SYNONYM *Bletia anceps* (Lindl.) Rchb.f.

Laelia autumnalis Lindl. [Colour Plate]
An epiphytic or rarely lithophytic herb, up to 1 m high. **Pseudobulbs** ovoid, subconical or pyriform, tapering, curved, up to 15 cm long, 2.3 cm broad, ribbed and furrowed, 2- or 3-leaved at apex. **Leaves** lanceolate, leathery, 12.5–18 cm long, 3.5 cm broad, acute. **Inflorescence** 50–100 cm long, laxly 5- to 15-flowered; scape jointed, fairly stout, purplish, with a scale-like bract at each joint. **Flowers** 7.5–10 cm across; sepals and petals bright rose-purple; lip white on side lobes, mid-lobe whitish at base, rose-purple at apex, disc white with a yellow central line and purple-spotted on edges; column purplish above, white below, anther yellow. **Sepals** lanceolate, 5.5–6.5 cm long, 1.3 cm broad, acuminate. **Petals** ovate, 5–6.5 cm long, 1.8 cm broad, acuminate, undulate. **Lip** 3-lobed, 4 cm long, 2.6 cm broad; side-lobes erect, partly enclosing column, rounded; mid-lobe oblong, apex recurved, acuminate; disc 3-ridged, central ridge extending beyond side-ridges. **Column** clavate, terete, 2.7 cm long.

DISTRIBUTION Mexico; on rocks and small trees in highlands, 1600–2600 m altitude, often in full sunlight.

HISTORY This species was first introduced into cultivation by Tayleur of Liverpool who was sent plants from Mexico in 1836. It had earlier, in 1831, been described by John Lindley in *Genera and Species of Orchidaceous Plants* (p. 115). The specific epithet was given for its flowering time in Europe: October and November.

SYNONYMS *Bletia autumnalis* (Lindl.) Rchb.f.

CLOSELY RELATED SPECIES L.O. Williams in the *Orchidaceae of Mexico* (1951) considers *Laelia gouldiana* Rchb.f. [Colour Plate] to be merely a richer coloured showy form of *L. autumnalis* while G. Kennedy in the *Orchid Digest* (1975) suggests that *L. gouldiana* may be a natural hybrid of *L. autumnalis* and *L. anceps*. Nowadays, it is usually treated as a distinct species. See *L. albida*.

Laelia cinnabarina Lindl. [Colour Plate]
A lithophytic herb. **Stems** cylindrical, swollen at base, 12.5–25 cm long, clothed with white striated sheaths, 1- or rarely 2-leaved. **Leaves** linear-oblong, erect or spreading, 12.5–25 cm long, 3.2 cm broad, ± tinged purple. **Inflorescence** 10- to 15-flowered; scape slender, 38–50 cm long, subtended by a narrow compressed sheath, blooms over an extended period. **Flowers** about 6 cm across, bright cinnabar-red; pedicels red, 5 cm long. **Sepals** linear-lanceolate, 3.2–5 cm long, 0.5–0.8 cm broad, acuminate or acute. **Petals** linear-lanceolate, 3–5 cm long, 0.6–0.8 cm broad, acuminate,

In the following colour plate section the species under which plants were previously known are shown in brackets.

Acacallis cyanea

Acampe papillosa

Acianthus caudatus

Acineta chrysantha

Acineta superba

Acoridium saccolabium

Ada aurantiaca

Ada glumacea

Ada keiliana

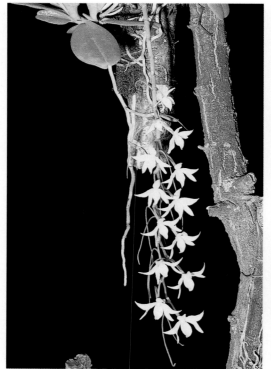

Aerangis articulata

Aerangis brachycarpa

Aerangis confusa

Aerangis fastuosa

Aerangis kirkii

Aerangis kotschyana

Aerangis luteoalba var. *rhodosticta*
(*A. rhodosticta*)

Aerangis ugandensis

Aeranthes grandiflora

Aeranthes henricii

Aerides jarckiana (*A. jarckianum*)

Aerides maculosa (*A. maculosum*)

Aerides multiflora (*A. multiflorum*)

Aerides odorata (*A. odoratum*)

Aerides odorata var. *lawrenciae*

Aerides rosea (A. fieldingii)

Alamania punicea

Amblostoma tridactylum

Amesiella philippinensis

Anacamptis pyramidalis

Ancistrochilus rothschildianus

Ancistrorhynchus cephalotes

Angraecum calceolus

Angraecum dasycarpum

Angraecum distichum

Angraecum eburneum

Angraecum eichlerianum

Angraecum gabonense

Angraecum infundibulare

Angraecum leonis

Angraecum magdalenae

Angraecum reygaertii

Angraecum scottianum

Angraecum sesquipedale

Anguloa cliftonii

Anguloa clowesii

Anguloa uniflora

Anneliesia candida (Miltonia candida)

Ansellia africana

Ansellia gigantea var. *gigantea*

Arachnis flosaëris

Armodorum sulingii

Arpophyllum giganteum

Arundina graminifolia

Ascocentrum ampullaceum

Ascocentrum curvifolium

Ascocentrum miniatum

Ascoglossum calopterum

Aspasia epidendroides

Baptistonia echinata

Barbosella cucullata

Barkeria cyclotella

Barkeria lindleyana

Barkeria skinneri

Barkeria spectabilis

Barlia robertiana

Bartholina burmanniana

Bifrenaria atropurpurea

Bifrenaria harrisoniae

Bletia catenulata

Bletilla striata

Bollea voilacea

Bolusiella maudiae (B. imbricata)

Bothriochilus bellus

Brachycorythis henryi

Brassavola cucullata

Brassavola flagellaris

Brassavola nodosa

Brassavola tuberculata

Brassia arcuigera (*B. longissima*)

Brassia caudata

Brassia gireoudiana

Brassia lawrenceana

Brassia verrucosa

Bromheadia finlaysoniana

Broughtonia sanguinea

Bulbophyllum barbigerum

Bulbophyllum careyanum

Bulbophyllum cocoinum

Bulbophyllum dearei

Bulbophyllum distans

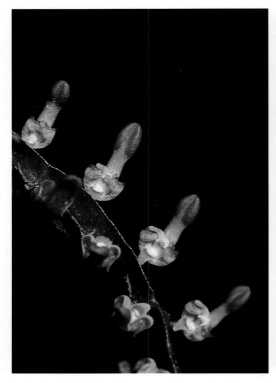

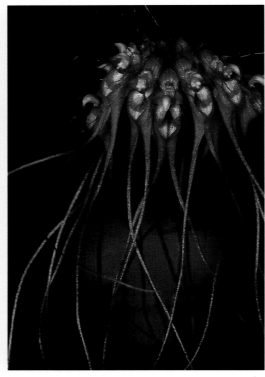

Bulbophyllum falcatum

Bulbophyllum gracillimum
(*Cirrhopetalum gracillimum*)

Bulbophyllum lasiochilum

Bulbophyllum leopardinum

Bulbophyllum lobbii

Bulbophyllum longissimum
(*Cirrhopetalum longissimum*)

Bulbophyllum masterianum

Bulbophyllum medusae

Bulbophyllum ornatissimum
(Cirrhopetalum ornatissimum)

Bulbophyllum patens

Bulbophyllum rothschildianum
(Cirrhopetalum rothschildianum)

Bulbophyllum roxburghii
(Cirrhopetalum roxburghii)

Caladenia menziesii

Calanthe discolor

Calanthe rubens

Calanthe striata (*C. discolor* var. *flava*)

Calanthe sylvatica

Calanthe triplicata

Calanthe vestita var. *regnieri*

Calopogon tuberosus

Calypso bulbosa

Calyptrochilum christyanum

Campylocentrum micranthum

Capanemia superflua

Catasetum barbatum

Catasetum discolor var. *roseo-album*

Catasetum fimbriatum

Catasetum gnomus

Catasetum integerrimum

Catasetum macrocarpum

Catasetum maculatum

Catasetum microglossum

Catasetum pileatum

Catasetum platyglossum

Catasetum saccatum var.
christyanum

Cattleya aclandiae

Cattleya amethystoglossa

Cattleya aurantiaca

Cattleya bicolor

Cattleya bowringiana

Cattleya dormaniana

Cattleya dowiana

Cattleya eldorado

Cattleya forbesii

Cattleya gaskelliana

Cattleya granulosa

Cattleya guttata

Cattleya intermedia

Cattleya iricolor

Cattleya labiata

Cattleya lawrenceana

Cattleya leopoldii

Cattleya loddigesii

Cattleya luteola

Cattleya maxima

Cattleya mendelii

Cattleya mossiae

Cattleya percivaliana

Cattleya rex

Cattleya schilleriana

Cattleya schroederae

Cattleya skinneri

Cattleya trianaei (C. trianae)

Cattleya velutina

Cattleya violacea

Cattleya walkeriana

Cattleya warneri

Cattleya warscewiczii

Caularthron bicornutum

Ceratostylis retisquama

Chelonistele sulphurea

Chiloglottis gunnii

Chiloschista parishii (C. lunifera)

Chrysocycnis schlimii

Chysis aurea

Chysis bractescens

Chysis tricostata

Cirrhaea dependens

Cleisostoma filiforme

Cleisostoma scortechinii

Cleistes rosea

Cochleanthes discolor

Cochlioda rosea

Coelia triptera

Coeliopsis hyacinthosma

Coelogyne asperata

Coelogyne corymbosa

Coelogyne cristata

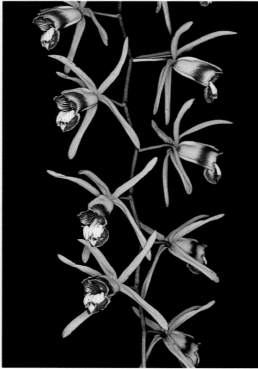

Coelogyne dayana

Coelogyne flaccida

Coelogyne fuliginosa

Coelogyne lawrenceana

Coelogyne lentiginosa

Coelogyne massangeana

Coelogyne mooreana

Coelogyne nitida

Coelogyne ovalis

Coelogyne pandurata

Coelogyne parishii

Coelogyne rochussenii

Coelogyne speciosa

Comparettia coccinea

Comparettia falcata

Comparettia macroplectron

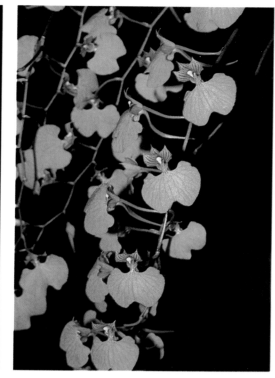

Comparettia speciosa

Corybas diemenicus

Cremastra appendiculata

Cryptarrhena lunata

Cryptochilus sanguineus

Cryptopus elatus

Cryptostylis arachnites

Cuitlauzina pendula (*Odontoglossum pendulum*)

Cycnoches egertonianum

Cycnoches egertonianum

Cycnoches loddigesii

Cycnoches pentadactylon

Cycnoches ventricosum

Cymbidiella pardalina

Cymbidium aloifolium

Cymbidium devonianum

Cymbidium eburneum

Cymbidium finlaysonianum

Cymbidium floribundum

Cymbidium hookerianum

Cymbidium iridioides (C. giganteum)

Cymbidium lancifolium

Cymbidium lowianum

Cymbidium madidum

Cymbidium mastersii

Cymbidium suave

Cymbidium tigrinum

Cymbidium tracyanum

Cynorkis lowiana

Cypripedium acaule

Cypripedium calceolus

Cypripedium reginae

Cyrtochilum falcipetalum
(Oncidium falcipetalum)

Cyrtochilum macranthum
(Oncidium macranthum)

Cyrtochilum microchilum
(*Oncidium microchilum*)

Cyrtochilum retusum
(*Odontoglossum retusum*)

Cyrtochilum superbiens
(*Oncidium superbiens*)

Cyrtopodium andersonii

Cyrtopodium punctatum

Cyrtorchis arcuata

Dactylorhiza foliosa

Dactylostalix ringens

Dendrobium aduncum (D. hercoglossum)

Dendrobium anosmum

Dendrobium aphyllum

Dendrobium atroviolaceum

Dendrobium bellatulum

Dendrobium bigibbum

Dendrobium biggibum var. *phalaenopsis*
(*D. phalaenopsis*)

Dendrobium bracteosum

Dendrobium brymerianum

Dendrobium bullenianum

Dendrobium canaliculatum

Dendrobium capillipes

Dendrobium christyanum (D. margaritaceum)

Dendrobium chrysanthum

Dendrobium chrysotoxum

Dendrobium crepidatum

Dendrobium cuthbertsonii (D. sophronites)

Dendrobium dearei

Dendrobium delacourii

Dendrobium densiflorum

Dendrobium devonianum

Dendrobium discolor

Dendrobium dixanthum

Dendrobium draconis

Dendrobium farmeri

Dendrobium fimbriatum

Dendrobium fimbriatum var. *oculatum*

Dendrobium findlayanum

268

Dendrobium formosum

Dendrobium gouldii

Dendrobium gracilicaule

Dendrobium gratiosissimum

Dendrobium harveyanum

Dendrobium heterocarpum

Dendrobium infundibulum

Dendrobium jenkinsii (D. aggregatum)

Dendrobium johnsoniae

Dendrobium jonesii

Dendrobium kingianum

Dendrobium lasianthera

Dendrobium lawesii

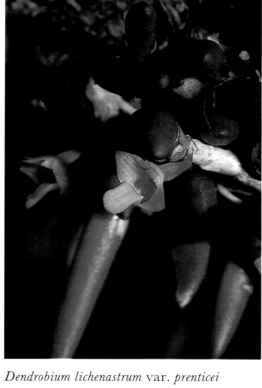

Dendrobium lichenastrum var. *prenticei*

Dendrobium lindleyi

Dendrobium lituiflorum

Dendrobium loddigesii

Dendrobium longicornu

271

Dendrobium moniliforme

Dendrobium moschatum

Dendrobium nobile

Dendrobium parishii

Dendrobium pendulum

Dendrobium primulinum

Dendrobium pugioniforme

Dendrobium pulchellum

Dendrobium rigidum

Dendrobium scabrilingue

Dendrobium schoeninum (D. beckleri)

Dendrobium schuetzei

273

Dendrobium secundum

Dendrobium smillieae

Dendrobium speciosum

Dendrobium spectabile

Dendrobium stratiotes

Dendrobium stricklandianum

Dendrobium taurinum

Dendrobium tetragonum var. *giganteum*
(*D. tetragonum*)

Dendrobium thyrsiflorum
(*D. densiflorum* var. *alboluteum*)

Dendrobium transparens

Dendrobium trigonopus

Dendrobium unicum

Dendrobium victoria-reginae

Dendrobium wardianum

Dendrobium williamsonii

Dendrochilum cobbianum

Dendrochilum filiforme

Dendrochilum glumaceum

Dendrochilum longifolium

Dendrophylax varius

Diaphananthe bidens

Diaphananthe pellucida

Dilochia cantleyi

Dimerandra emarginata

Dimorphorchis rossii

Diplocaulobium regale

Diploprora uraiensis

Dipodium pictum

Disa stolzii

Disa uniflora

Disperis fanniniae

Diuris maculata

Diuris punctata

Domingoa hymenodes

Doritis pulcherrima

Dracula bella

Dracula erythrochaete
(Masdevallia erythrochaete)

Dracula robledorum

Dressleria dilecta

Dryadella lilliputana (Masdevallia lilliputana)

Dryadella simula

Dyakia hendersoniana

Earina autumnalis

Elleanthus furfuraceus

Elleanthus longibracteatus

Encyclia adenocaula

Encyclia baculus

Encyclia belizensis

Encyclia brassavolae

Encyclia bulbosa

Encyclia chacaoensis

Encyclia citrina

Encyclia cochleata

Encyclia cordigera

Encyclia fragrans

Encyclia glumacea

Encyclia guatemalensis

Encyclia mariae

Encyclia megalantha

Encyclia polybulbon

Encyclia selligera

Encyclia spondiada

Encyclia vagans

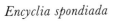

Encyclia vespa

Encyclia vitellina

Epidendrum anceps

Epidendrum ciliare

Epidendrum coronatum

Epidendrum ibaguense

Epidendrum imatophyllum

Epidendrum latifolium

Epidendrum medusae

Epidendrum nocturnum

Epidendrum oerstedii

Epidendrum paniculatum

Epidendrum porpax

Epidendrum pseudepidendrum

Epidendrum purum

Epidendrum schlechterianum

Epidendrum secundum

Epidendrum stamfordianum

Epigeneium coelogyne

Epigeneium cymbidioides

Epigeneium lyonii

Epipactis gigantea

Epipactis palustris

Eria coronaria

Eria javanica

Eria pubescens (E. flava)

Eria rosea

Eria spicata

Eriopsis biloba

Erycina echinata

Esmeralda clarkei

Euanthe sanderiana

Eulophia cucullata

Eulophia guineensis

Eulophia speciosa

Eulophia streptopetala

Eurychone rothschildiana

Flickingeria comata

Galeandra devoniana

Galeandra lacustris

Gastrochilus calceolaris

Geodorum purpureum

Gomesa crispa

Gomesa recurva

Gongora galeata

Gongora quinquenervis

Goodyera hispida

Goodyera maximowicziana

Grammangis ellisii

Grammatophyllum speciosum

Graphorkis lurida

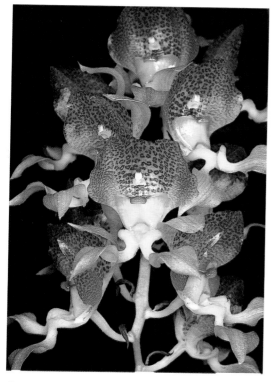

Grobya amherstiae

Gymnadenia conopsea

Habenaria rhodocheila

Habenaria splendens

Helcia sanguineolenta

Hexisea bidentata

Holcoglossum quasipinifolium

Huntleya heteroclita

Huntleya meleagris

Hygrochilus parishii (Vandopsis parishii)

Ionopsis utricularioides

Isabelia virginalis

Isochilus linearis

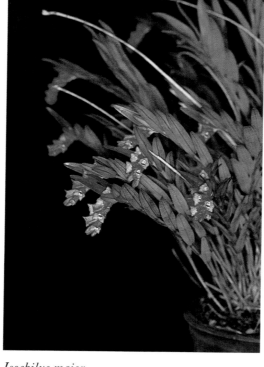

Isochilus major

Jumellea sagittata

Kefersteinia lojae

Lacaena bicolor

Laelia albida

Laelia anceps

Laelia autumnalis

Laelia cinnabarina

Laelia crispa

Laelia dayana

Laelia flava

Laelia gouldiana

Laelia grandis

Laelia harpophylla

Laelia jongheana

Laelia longipes var. *alba*

Laelia lundii

Laelia perrinii

Laelia pumila

Laelia purpurata

Laelia tenebrosa

Laelia xanthina

Lanium avicula

Lemboglossum bictoniense
(*Odontoglossum bictoniense*)

Lemboglossum cervantesii
(*Odontoglossum cervantesii*)

Lemboglossum cordatum
(*Odontoglossum cordatum*)

Lemboglossum maculatum
(*Odontoglossum maculatum*)

Lemboglossum majale
(*Odontoglossum majale*)

Lemboglossum rossii

Lemboglossum uroskinneri
(*Odontoglossum uroskinneri*)

Leochilus scriptus

Lepanthes calodictyon

Lepanthopsis floripecten

Leptotes bicolor

Leptotes tenuis

Leucohyle subulata

Liparis bowkeri (L. neglecta)

Liparis viridiflora

Listrostachys pertusa

Lockhartia oerstedii

Ludisia discolor

Luisia volucris

Lycaste aromatica

Lycaste brevispatha

Lycaste cruenta

Lycaste deppei

Lycaste lasioglossa

Lycaste leucantha

Lycaste longipetala

Lycaste skinneri

Lycaste xytriophora

Macodes petola

Macodes petola

Macradenia brassavolae

Masdevallia barlaeana

Masdevallia caloptera

Masdevallia caudata

Masdevallia coccinea

Masdevallia coccinea

Masdevallia coriacea

Masdevallia infracta

Masdevallia laucheana

Masdevallia macrura

Masdevallia maculata

Masdevallia mejiana

Masdevallia mendozae

Masdevallia militaris

Masdevallia racemosa

Masdevallia reichenbachiana

Masdevallia schlimii

Masdevallia schroederiana

Masdevallia tovarensis

Masdevallia triangularis

Masdevallia tubulosa

Masdevallia veitchiana

Masdevallia ventricularia

Masdevallia wageneriana

Maxillaria arachnites

Maxillaria densa

Maxillaria desvauxiana

Maxillaria lepidota

Maxillaria luteoalba

Maxillaria meleagris

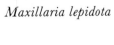

Maxillaria nigrescens

Maxillaria parkeri

Maxillaria picta

Maxillaria rufescens

Maxillaria sanderiana

Maxillaria tarumaensis

Maxillaria tenuifolia

Maxillaria valenzuelana

Maxillaria variabilis

Mediocalcar decoratum

Meiracyllium trinasutum

Mendoncella grandiflora

Mexicoa ghiesbrechtiana
(Oncidium ghiesbrechtianum)

Microcoelia globulosa (*M. guyoniana*)

Miltonia clowesii

Miltonia cuneata

Miltonia flavescens

Miltonia regnellii

Miltonia spectabilis

Miltonia spectabilis var. *moreliana*

Miltonioides confusa (*Miltonia schroederiana*)

Miltonioides laevis (*Odontoglossum laeve*)

Miltonioides reichenheimii
(*Odontoglossum reichenheimii*)

Miltonioides warscewiczii
(*Miltonia warscewiczii*)

Miltoniopsis phalaenopsis

Miltoniopsis roezlii

Miltoniopsis vexillaria

Miltoniopsis warscewiczii

Mischobulbum cordifolium

Mormodes colossus

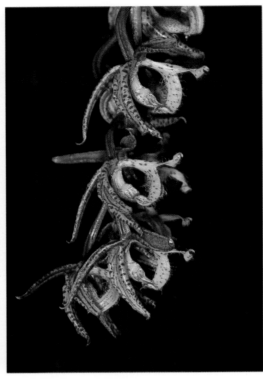

Mormodes maculata var. *unicolor*

Mormodes warscewiczii

Mormolyca ringens

Myrmecophila brysiana

Myrmecophila tibicinis

Nageliella purpurea

Neobathiea filicornu

Neobathiea perrieri

Neogardneria murrayana

Neomoorea wallisii (*N. irrorata*)

Nidema boothii

Notylia barkeri

Octomeria grandiflora

Odontoglossum blandum

Odontoglossum cirrhosum

Odontoglossum constrictum

Odontoglossum crispum

Odontoglossum cruentum

Odontoglossum hallii

Odontoglossum harryanum

Odontoglossum lindenii

Odontoglossum luteopurpureum

Odontoglossum odoratum

Odontoglossum ramosissimum

Odontoglossum spectatissimum (O. triumphans) *Odontoglossum weirii* *Oeceoclades angustifolia*

Oeceoclades saundersiana *Oeonia volucris* *Oeoniella polystachys*

Oerstedella endresii (*Epidendrum oerstedii*)

Oerstedella wallisii (*Epidendrum wallisii*)

Oncidium ampliatum

Oncidium ansiferum

Oncidium barbatum

Oncidium baueri

Oncidium bicallosum

Oncidium bifolium

Oncidium blanchetii

Oncidium bracteatum

Oncidium cariniferum
(*Odontoglossum cariniferum*)

Oncidium carthagenense

Oncidium cavendishianum

Oncidium cebolleta

Oncidium cheirophorum

Oncidium concolor

Oncidium crispum

Oncidium cucullatum

Oncidium dayanum

Oncidium divaricatum

Oncidium excavatum

Oncidium flexuosum

Oncidium forbesii

Oncidium gardneri

Oncidium harrisonianum

Oncidium hastatum

Oncidium hastilabium

Oncidium hookeri

Oncidium incurvum

Oncidium jonesianum

Oncidium lanceanum

Oncidium leucochilum

Oncidium longipes

Oncidium luridum

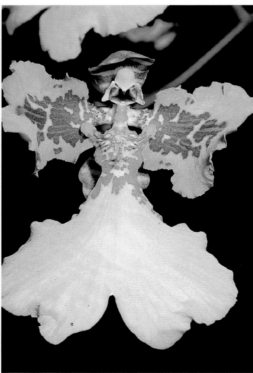

Oncidium marshallianum

Oncidium micropogon

Oncidium nanum

Oncidium nubigenum

Oncidium obryzatum

Oncidium ornithorhynchum

Oncidium phymatochilum

Oncidium pubes

Oncidium pumilum

Oncidium raniferum

Oncidium sarcodes

Oncidium sphacelatum

Oncidium spilopterum

Oncidium splendidum

Oncidium stramineum

Oncidium waluewa

Oncidium wentworthianum

Ophrys lutea var. *galilea*

Ophrys vernixia (*Ophrys speculum*)

Orchis militaris

Orchis papilionacea

Ornithocephalus kruegeri

Ornithocephalus myrticola

Osmoglossum pulchellum
(Odontoglossum pulchellum)

Otochilus porrectus

Otoglossum brevifolium

Pabstia jugosa

Palumbina candida

Panisea uniflora

Paphinia cristata

Paphiopedilum acmodontum

Paphiopedilum appletonianum

Paphiopedilum argus

Paphiopedilum armeniacum

Paphiopedilum barbatum

Paphiopedilum bellatulum

Paphiopedilum bullenianum

Paphiopedilum callosum

Paphiopedilum charlesworthii

Paphiopedilum ciliolare

Paphiopedilum concolor

Paphiopedilum delenatii

Paphiopedilum druryi

Paphiopedilum emersonii

Paphiopedilum exul

Paphiopedilum fairrieanum

Paphiopedilum glaucophyllum

Paphiopedilum haynaldianum

Paphiopedilum hirsutissimum

Paphiopedilum insigne

Paphiopedilum insigne var. *sanderae*

Paphiopedilum javanicum

Paphiopedilum kolopakingii

Paphiopedilum lawrenceanum

Paphiopedilum lowii

Paphiopedilum malipoense

Paphiopedilum mastersianum

Paphiopedilum micranthum

Paphiopedilum niveum

Paphiopedilum parishii

Paphiopedilum philippinense

Paphiopedilum primulinum

Paphiopedilum purpuratum

Paphiopedilum randsii

Paphiopedilum rothschildianum

Paphiopedilum spicerianum

Paphiopedilum stonei

Paphiopedilum sukhakulii

Paphiopedilum supardii

Paphiopedilum superbiens

Paphiopedilum superbiens var. *sanderae*

Paphiopedilum tonsum

Paphiopedilum venustum

Paphiopedilum victoriaregina
(*P. chamberlainianum*)

Paphiopedilum villosum

Paphiopedilum violascens

Papilionanthe teres (*Vanda teres*)

Papilionanthe vandarum (*Aerides vandarum*)

Paraphalaenopsis denevei

Paraphalaenopsis labukensis

Paraphalaenopsis laycockii

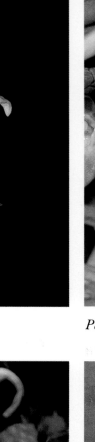

Pecteilis sagarikii

Pelatantheria insectifera

Pescatorea cerina

Pescatorea dayana var. *rhodacra*

Phaius mishmensis

Phaius tankervilleae

Phaius tuberculosus

Phalaenopsis amabilis

Phalaenopsis cornucervi

Phalaenopsis equestris

Phalaenopsis fasciata

Phalaenopsis fimbriata

Phalaenopsis gigantea

Phalaenopsis hieroglyphica

Phalaenopsis × *intermedia*

Phalaenopsis lindenii

Phalaenopsis lueddemanniana

Phalaenopsis mannii

Phalaenopsis mariae

Phalaenopsis pallens

Phalaenopsis pulchra

Phalaenopsis schilleriana

Phalaenopsis stuartiana

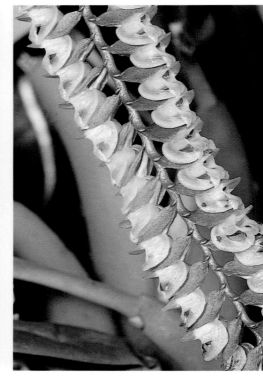

Phalaenopsis sumatrana

Phalaenopsis violacea

Pholidota imbricata (*P. pallida*)

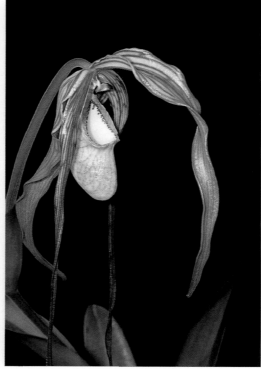

Phragmipedium besseae

Phragmipedium caudatum

Phragmipedium klotzschianum

Phragmipedium lindenii

Phragmipedium longifolium (Phragmipedium hartwegii)

Phragmipedium pearcei

Phragmipedium schlimii

Phymatidium tillansioides

Physosiphon tubatus

Platanthera psycodes

Platystele stenostachya

Pleione aurita

Pleione bulbocodioides var. *limprichtii*

Pleione formosana (Pleione bulbocodioides)

Pleione forrestii

Pleione hookeriana

Pleione maculata

Pleione praecox

Pleurothallis bivalvis

Pleurothallis endotrachys

Pleurothallis glandulosa

Pleurothallis grobyi

Pleurothallis loranthophylla

Pleurothallis octomerioides

Pleurothallis phalangifera

Pleurothallis quadrifida

Pleurothallis tuerkheimii

Plocoglottis acuminata

Podangis dactyloceras

Polycycnis barbata

Polycycnis muscifera

Polystachya affinis

Polystachya bifida

Polystachya concreta

Polystachya cultriformis

Polystachya fallax

Polystachya odorata

Polystachya paniculata

Polystachya pubescens

Polystachya virginea

Polystachya vulcanica

Ponerorchis graminifolia

Ponthieva maculata

Porroglossum muscosum (P. echidna)

Prescottia plantaginea

Promenaea xanthina

Psychopsiella limminghei
(*Oncidium limminghei*)

Psychopsis krameriana
(*Oncidium kramerianum*)

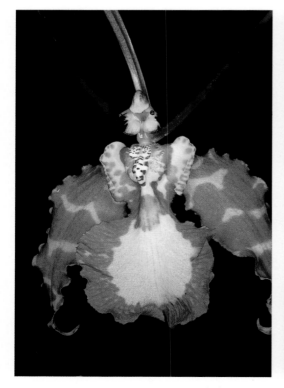

Psychopsis papilio (*Oncidium papilio*)

Psygmorchis pumilio (*Oncidium pumilio*)

Pterostylis baptistii

Pterostylis curta

Rangaeris muscicola

Renanthera imschootiana

Renanthera matutina

Renanthera monachica

Renanthera storiei

Renantherella histrionica var. *auyongii*

Restrepia elegans

Restrepia maculata

Rhyncholaelia digbyana (*Brassavola digbyana*)

Rhyncholaelia glauca (*Brassavola glauca*)

Rhynchostylis gigantea

Rhynchostylis retusa

Robiquetia spathulata

Rodriguezia candida

Rodriguezia decora

Rodriguezia lanceolata

Rodrigueziella gomezoides

Rossioglossum grande

Rossioglossum insleayi

Rossioglossum schlieperianum

Rossioglossum williamsianum

Rudolfiella aurantiaca

Sarcochilus fitzgeraldii

Sarcochilus hartmannii

Sarcoglottis sceptrodes

Satyrium nepalense

Scaphosepalum verrucosum

Scaphyglottis amethystina

Schlimmia trifida

Schoenorchis gemmata

Schomburgkia crispa

Schomburgkia superbiens

Schomburgkia undulata

Scuticaria hadwenii

Scuticana steelii

Sedirea japonica

Seidenfadenia mitrata

Serapias neglecta

Sievekingia peruviana

Sigmatostalix bicallosa

Sobennikoffia robusta

Sobralia dichotoma

Sobralia leucoxantha

Sobralia macrantha

Solenidium racemosum

Sophronitella violacea

Sophronitis cernua

Sophronitis coccinea

Spathoglottis petri

Spathoglottis plicata

Sphyrarhynchus schliebenii

Spiranthes cernua var. *odorata*

Stanhopea ecornuta

359

Stanhopea graveolens

Stanhopea hernandezii

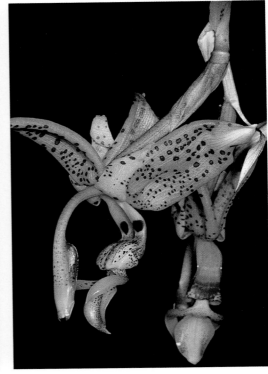

Stanhopea oculata

Stanhopea platyceras

Stanhopea tigrina

Staurochilus fasciatus (Trichoglottis fasciatus)

Stelis argentata

Stenia guttata

Stenoglottis longifolia

Stenorrhynchus lanceolatus

Stolzia repens

Sunipia cirrhata

Symphyglossum sanguineum

Tainia hookeriana

Teuscheria wageneri

Thecopus maingayi

Thecostele alata

Thelymitra antennifera

Thelymitra variegata

Thrixspermum centipeda

Thunia marshalliana

Ticoglossum krameri (Odontoglossum krameri)

Ticoglossum oerstedii (Odontoglossum oerstedii)

Trichocentrum tigrinum

Trichoceros antennifer

Trichoglottis philippinensis

Trichopilia fragrans

Trichopilia laxa

Trichopilia marginata

Trichopilia suavis

Trichopilia tortilis

Trichotosia ferox

Tridactyle bicaudata

Tridactyle gentilii

Trigonidium egertonianum

Trudelia alpina (Vanda alpina)

Trudelia cristata (Vanda cristata)

Vanda coerulea

Vanda coerulescens

Vanda stangeana

Vanda tricolor

Vandopsis lissochiloides

Vanilla phalaenopsis

Vanilla planifolia

Warmingia eugenii

Warrea warreana

Xylobium leontoglossum

Xylobium variegatum

Zeuxine strateumatica

Zootrophion atropurpureum
(*Cryptophoranthus atropurpureus*)

Zygopetalum crinitum

Zygopetalum intermedium

Zygosepalum labiosum

Zygosepalum lindeniae

slightly undulate. **Lip** 3-lobed, 2.2–3.5 cm long, 1–1.5 cm broad; side lobes triangular, acute, curved over column to form a tube, streaked red within; mid-lobe narrowly ovate, crisped, reflexed acute. **Column** clavate, 3-angled in cross-section.

DISTRIBUTION Brazil (states of Rio de Janeiro, Minas Gerais and São Paulo) 800–1500 m.

HISTORY Mr Young of Epsom, Surrey, England introduced this delightful *Laelia* in 1836 and John Lindley, naming it for its rich flower colour, described it in *Sertum Orchidacearum* (t. 28) in 1838.

SYNONYM *Bletia cinnabarina* (Lindl.) Rchb.f.

CLOSELY RELATED SPECIES Closely related to *Laelia milleri* Blumensch. and *L. harpophylla* Rchb.f. The former has blunt obtuse rather than acute side lobes to the lip, whilst the latter is an epiphytic species with a shorter inflorescence equal to or shorter than the leaf.

Laelia crispa (Lindl.) Rchb.f. [Colour Plate]

An epiphytic or occasionally lithophytic plant. **Stems** club-shaped, 18–30 cm long, compressed, with 2 or 3 grooves on each flattened side, 1-leafed at apex. **Leaf** suberect, oblong-lanceolate, 15–30 cm long, 5 cm broad, obtuse or notched at apex. **Inflorescence** 4- to 7(or more)-flowered, up to 30 cm long, subtended by a compressed sheath. **Flowers** 10–12.4 cm across, very showy; sepals and petals white, ± tinted purple at base; lip yellow at base, streaked purple in centre, rich purple in apical half, veined and reticulated darker purple; column white, purple below. **Sepals** obovate-lanceolate, 6–7.5 cm long, 1.5 cm broad, acute, undulate. **Petals** ovate-lanceolate, 7.5 cm long, 2.5 cm broad, acute, margin crisped-undulate. **Lip** 3-lobed, 5 cm long, 4.5 cm broad; side lobes erect over column, rounded, margins crisped; mid-lobe oblong, reflexed, crisped. **Column** club-shaped.

DISTRIBUTION Brazil (states of Espirito Santo, Rio de Janiero, Minas Gerais and in S. Brazil); at altitudes of 800–1150 m.

HISTORY One of the earliest *Laelia* species to be introduced into cultivation by Sir Henry Chamberlain in 1826. It flowered at the Horticultural Society of London's Chiswick garden in the following year and John Lindley described it in 1828 in the *Botanical Register* (t. 1172) as *Cattleya crispa*. H.G. Reichenbach transferred it to the genus *Laelia* in 1853 in *Flore des Serres* (p. 102) on account of its 8 rather than 4 pollinia.

SYNONYMS *Cattleya crispa* Lindl.; *Bletia crispa* (Lindl.) Rchb.f.

Laelia crispata (Thunb.) Garay

A lithophytic herb, up to 35 cm high. **Pseudo-bulb** terete, cylindrical, 4–10 cm long, 1 cm broad, covered in a stout sheath, 1-leafed at apex. **Leaf** erect, very leathery, narrowly oblong, up to 16 cm long, 3.2 cm broad, obtuse. **Inflorescence** much longer than the leaf, up to 26 cm long, 2- to 10-flowered, subtended at base by a sheath. **Flowers** up to 4.5 cm across; sepals and petals rose-pink; lip with a white or creamy throat, a rich purple mid-lobe and pink side lobes. **Dorsal sepal** oblong, 2 cm long, 0.8 cm broad, obtuse; **lateral sepals** slightly oblique. **Petals** oblong-elliptic, 2.2 cm long, 0.8 cm broad, obtuse, margin slightly undulate. **Lip** cucullate, 3-lobed, 1.6 cm long, 1.2 cm broad; side lobes erect, oblong; mid-lobe ovate, acute, margin very crisped; disc 2-ridged.

DISTRIBUTION Brazil (Minas Gerais State); growing on iron-ore hills, 400–500 m altitude.

HISTORY This species was originally described in 1818 as *Cymbidium crispatum* by C.P. Thunberg in *Plantarum Brasiliensium* (p. 18) based on a collection from near Rica in Brazil. In 1973 L. Garay transferred it to *Laelia* in *Bradea* (p. 302). The species is better known under the later synonym *L. rupestris*.

SYNONYMS *Cymbidium crispatum* Thunb.; *Laelia rupestris* Lindl.; *L. tereticaulis* Hoehne

CLOSELY RELATED SPECIES *Laelia crispata* is one of the rupicolous or lithophytic species in which the inflorescence overtops the leaves as in *L. longipes*. However, it is readily distinguished by its stout peduncle, its rose-purple flowers with a broader purple lip, white throat and yellowish calli.

Other species allied to *L. crispata* and with similarly coloured flowers are as follows:

(a) *Laelia mantequeira* Pabst – Flowers smaller than *L. crispata*, margins of lip with a narrow purple band rather than a broad band. According to G. Pabst, this species is often incorrectly named, being grown as *L. crispilabia*.

(b) *Laelia ghillanyi* Pabst – Flower segments paler, lip with a narrow pink margin and a central purple spot at the apex of the yellow throat.

(c) *Laelia longipes* Rchb.f. – The yellow area in the throat extends onto the mid-lobe which is white. Flower segments very pale pink.

(d) *Laelia reginae* Pabst – Lip orange-yellow. Inflorescence only slightly overtops leaf.

Laelia dayana Rchb.f. [Colour Plate]

See under *Laelia pumila*.

Laelia flava Lindl. [Colour Plate]

A lithophytic herb, up to 50 cm high. **Stems** stout, cylindrical, 4–20 cm long, pseudobulbous at base, ± tinged purple, 1-leafed. **Leaf** lanceolate or linear-lanceolate, 10–15 cm long, 2.7 cm broad, obtuse, very leathery, dark green above, purple below. **Inflorescence** 5- to 9-flowered; scape 30–45 cm long, much longer than the leaf, subtended by a basal compressed sheath. **Flowers** 3.2 cm across, light orange-yellow or canary-yellow; column greenish-yellow at base. **Sepals** ligulate or oblong-ligulate, 2–3.5 cm long, 0.6–0.9 cm broad; lateral sepals somewhat falcate. **Petals** ligulate, 2.2–3.3 cm long, 0.6–1.1 cm broad, subacute. **Lip** narrowly 3-lobed, 2.4–3 cm long, 1.8 cm broad; side-lobes erect, semiovate, curved over column; mid-lobe oblong, crisped with 4 thickened nerves running to base of lip, blunt. **Column** short, 0.9 cm long.

DISTRIBUTION Brazil (Minas Gerais State); growing on iron-ore outcrops, 800–1250 m altitude.

HISTORY The first of several small yellow-flowered *Laelia* species to be described. John Lindley named it, for its colour, as *L. flava* in the *Botanical Register* (misc. 88) in 1839, plants having been introduced in the same year into the collection of Sir Charles Lemon of Carclew, Cornwall, England.

SYNONYMS *Laelia fulva* Lindl.; *Cattleya lutea* Beer

CLOSELY RELATED SPECIES Several miniature yellow-flowered *Laelia* species have been described, some of them quite recently. Undoubtedly these are all closely related and some, no doubt, will eventually be reduced to the status of subspecies or even varieties. They may be distinguished from *Laelia flava* as follows:

(a) *Laelia briegeri* Blumensch. ex Pabst – Broader segments to its flowers and an emarginate mid-lobe to the lip.

(b) *Laelia mixta* Hoehne – Orangey-yellow flowers; the basal part to the lip forming a long narrow tube and mid-lobe undulate but not crisped.

(c) *Laelia bradei* Pabst – Lip has an obscure erose mid-lobe and the inflorescence is scarcely longer than the leaf.

(d) *Laelia kautskyi* Pabst – Also has a shorter inflorescence and is epiphytic rather than lithophytic.

(e) *Laelia esalqueana* Blumensch. ex Pabst – A diminutive species with an inflorescence scarcely longer than the leaves. Flowers canary yellow.

(f) *Laelia itambana* Pabst – Very close to *L. esalqueana*, but the side lobes of the lip overlap the mid-lobe considerably when the lip is spread.

(g) *Laelia macrobulbosa* Pabst – Narrower segments to the flower than either of the two previous species and shorter oblong side lobes and a less frilled mid-lobe to the lip than *L. flava*.

See also *L. xanthina*.

Laelia gouldiana Rchb.f. [Colour Plate]
See under *Laelia autumnalis*.

Laelia grandis Lindl. [Colour Plate]
An epiphytic herb, up to 45 cm high. **Stem** clavate-fusiform, compressed, narrowed below, 22 cm long, 3.5 cm broad, 1-leafed at apex. **Leaf** oblong-lanceolate, rigid, 20–35 cm long, up to 4.5 cm broad, obtuse. **Inflorescence** 3- to 5-flowered, up to 25 cm long, subtended by a basal compressed sheath. **Flowers** 10–12.5 cm across; petals and sepals rich greeny-yellow; lip white outside, white veined rose-purple within; column greenish. **Sepals** elliptic-lanceolate, wavy, twisted, 6–7 cm long, 1.4 cm broad, undulate. **Petals** rhombic-ovate, broader than sepals, up to 5 cm long, 1.8 cm broad, margins undulate, **Lip** 3-lobed, 6 cm long, 3.5 cm broad; side lobes curved over column to form a tube; mid-lobe oblong, crisped-undulate along margins. **Column** short, 2 cm long.
DISTRIBUTION   Brazil (Bahia State).
HISTORY   A fine species which first appeared in cultivation in the establishment of G.M. Morel of Paris where it flowered early in 1850 for the first time. John Lindley described it in 1850 in his and J. Paxton's *Flower Garden* (p. 60) from a flower sent to him by Morel. The species disappeared from cultivation until 1864 when Messrs H. Low & Co. of Clapton, London, imported more plants from Bahia. The plant figured here is an albino.
CLOSELY RELATED SPECIES   *L. tenebrosa*.

Laelia harpophylla Rchb.f. [Colour Plate]
An epiphytic plant. **Stems** clustered, very thin, terete, up to 30 cm long, 0.3 cm in diameter, 1-leafed. **Leaf** ligulate-lanceolate, coriaceous, up to 25 cm long, 1.1 cm broad, acuminate. **Inflorescence** equal to or shorter than leaf, about 7-flowered, up to 17 cm long, subtended at base by a short sheath. **Flowers** up to 6.5 cm across, bright orange-red. **Sepals** linear-ligulate, 3.3–4 cm long, 0.5 cm broad, acute or obtuse. **Petals** narrowly lanceolate, 3.2–4 cm long, 0.6 cm broad, acute, margins undulate. **Lip** 3-lobed, 2.9 cm long, 1.4–1.7 cm broad; side lobes erect over column, acute; mid-lobe lanceolate, reflexed, margins crisped-undulate, acute. **Column** arched, 0.9 cm long.
DISTRIBUTION   Brazil (Minas Gerais and Espirito Santo States).
HISTORY   Described by H.G. Reichenbach in the *Gardeners' Chronicle* (p. 542) of 1873 from flowers and a sketch sent to him by John Day of Tottenham and also from specimens sent to him by Messrs Veitch & Sons.

CLOSELY RELATED SPECIES   The flowers of *L. harpophylla* are similar to those of *L. cinnabarina* but the latter is a rupicolous species with an inflorescence much longer than its leaf and a much broader stem.

Laelia jongheana Rchb.f. [Colour Plate]
An epiphytic herb, up to 21 cm high. **Pseudobulb** ovoid to ellipsoid, up to 5.5 cm long, 1.5 cm broad, dark green, covered in a white appressed sheath, 1-leafed at apex. **Leaf** very leathery, oblong-elliptic, 12 cm long, 4 cm broad, obtuse or emarginate. **Inflorescence** 1- to 2-flowered, up to 14 cm long. **Flowers** 12.5 cm across; sepals and petals pale lilac; lip white with a rich yolk-coloured throat and pink margins and side lobes. **Dorsal sepal** oblong-oblanceolate, 6 cm long, 1.4 cm broad, obtuse; **lateral sepals** deflexed-falcate, acute. **Petals** obovate, 6–7 cm long, 2.8 cm broad, obtuse, margin irregular-undulate near apex. **Lip** 3-lobed, 5.5 cm long, 3 cm broad; side lobes oblong, round, curved around column; mid-lobe deflexed, oblong, margin crisped-undulate; disc with 7 lamellae onto base of mid-lobe. **Column** clavate, 2.8 cm long.
DISTRIBUTION   Brazil (Minas Gerais State).
HISTORY   Collected sometime before 1856 by J. Libon who collected plants in Brazil for J. de Jonghe of Brussels. It remained unnamed until 1872 when M. Lueddeman sent a plant to H.G. Reichenbach from the collection of M.M. Thibaut and Keteleer of Paris. Reichenbach named it in 1872 after de Jonghe in *Flora* (p. 158).

This is probably the most striking of the *Laelia* species and one which Reichenbach considered

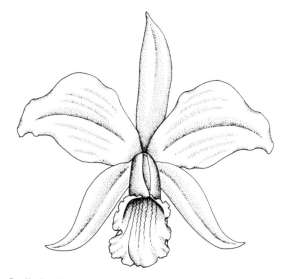

Laelia jongheana
Flower ($\times \frac{1}{2}$)

a rival to the showiest *Cattleya* species. An albino form is known.

Laelia longipes Rchb.f.
A lithophytic plant, up to 30 cm high. **Pseudobulbs** conical, 2–8 cm long, 2 cm broad, 1-leafed at apex. **Leaf** erect, fleshy, rigid, elliptic-oblong, 3–14 cm long, 2.5 cm broad, subacute, dark green. **Inflorescence** much longer than leaf, 2- to 4-flowered or more. **Flowers** 3–4 cm across; sepals and petals very pale pink or off-white; lip yellow or white with a yellow throat extending onto apex of side lobes and base of mid-lobe, disc stained brown towards base; column streaked with purple. **Sepals** oblong-ligulate, 1.6–2.3 cm long, 0.5–0.9 cm broad, acute. **Petals** narrowly elliptic, 1.5–2.3 cm long, 0.5–0.9 cm broad, acute, slightly undulate. **Lip** 3-lobed, 1.2–1.5 cm long, 1–1.2 cm broad; side lobes oblong, curved over column; mid-lobe oblong, with very crisped-undulate margins. **Column** short.
DISTRIBUTION   Brazil (Minas Gerais State).
HISTORY   Described by H.G. Reichenbach in *Xenia Orchidacea* (p. 59) in 1873 based on a collection made by F. Sellow in Brazil.

There is white-flowered variety, *L. longipes* var. *alba* [Colour Plate].
SYNONYM   *Bletia longipes* (Rchb.f.) Rchb.f.
CLOSELY RELATED SPECIES   *Laelia lucasiana* Rolfe is considered by some botanists to be synonymous with *L. longipes*, but it has a shorter inflorescence and smaller flowers with rather narrow segments. See also *L. crispata*.

Laelia lundii Rchb.f. & Warming [Colour Plate]
A small epiphytic plant. **Pseudobulbs** short, robust, oblong-fusiform, slightly compressed, 3.5–4 cm long, 1.2–1.3 cm in diameter, 2-leaved at apex. **Leaves** small, erect-spreading, fleshy, semicylindric, linear, very acute, slightly arcuate, deeply channelled above, 3–9 cm long, 0.4–0.5 cm broad. **Inflorescence** ascending, ± arcuate, 1–3-flowered at the apex, much shorter than the leaves; bracts minute. **Flowers** erect-spreading, white, with rose-purple venation on lip. **Sepals** fleshy, subequal, ligulate-oblong, acute, 2–2.2 cm long, 0.4–0.5 cm broad; lateral sepals falcate. **Petals** linear-lanceolate, acute, margins scarcely undulate, 2–2.2 cm long, 0.35–0.4 cm broad. **Lip** fleshy, narrowly elliptic-ovate or subquadrate, deeply 3-lobed, 2–2.3 cm long, 1.1–1.2 cm broad; side lobes erect, semiovate, acute; mid-lobe semirotund, reflexed, margin crisped and lobulate; disc slightly puberulous and fleshily 4-ridged. **Column** short, broad, 0.7–0.8 cm.
DISTRIBUTION   E. Brazil only.
HISTORY   Discovered at Lagao Santa in

Minas Gerais by Eugenius Warming and described by him and H.G. Reichenbach in 1881 in *Otia Botanica Hamburgiensis* (p. 92).
SYNONYMS *Bletia lundii* (Rchb.f. & Warming) Rchb.f. & Warming; *Laelia regnellii* Barb. Rodr.; *L. reichenbachiana* Wendl. & Kraenzl.
CLOSELY RELATED SPECIES Similar to *Laelia cattleyoides* Barb. Rodr. in its habit.

Laelia perrinii Lindl. [Colour Plate]
Stem ovoid-ellipsoid to clavate, 7–16 cm long, 1.5–3 cm broad, covered in scarious sheaths, 1-leafed at apex. **Leaf** ligulate, leathery, 26 cm long, 3–4.5 cm broad, rounded at apex. **Inflorescence** 2- to 3-flowered, up to 25 cm long, subtended by a broad compressed sheath. **Flowers** 11 cm across; sepals and petals delicate pink; lip white, anterior margin and apical area of mid-lobe rich purple; column pink or white. **Dorsal sepal** lanceolate, 6.5 cm long, 1.5 cm broad, obtuse to subacute; **lateral sepals** oblong, slightly deflexed-falcate, 5.1 cm long, 1.3 cm broad, subacute. **Petals** narrowly ovate, 6.5 cm long, 2 cm broad, obtuse. **Lip** 3-lobed, 5 cm long, 3.4 cm broad; side lobes oblong, curved up around column but not completely concealing it; mid-lobe rotund, margin erose, undulate. **Column** 3.6 cm long, very slender.
DISTRIBUTION Brazil (Espirito Santo, Rio de Janeiro and Minas Gerais States); 700–900 m.
HISTORY Originally described by John Lindley in 1838 as *Cattleya perrinii* in the *Botanical Register* (t. 2) and transferred by him to *Laelia* in the same journal (sub t. 62) in 1842. It was named it after Mr Perrin the gardener of R. Harrison who was a keen grower of South American epiphytic species at that time.

A white-flowered variety known as var. *alba* is known. It was originally collected by one of Messrs Sander's collectors in Brazil.
SYNONYM *Cattleya intermedia* Graham var. *angustifolia* Hort.

Laelia pumila (Hooker) Rchb.f.
[Colour Plate]
A dwarf epiphytic species, up to 15 cm tall. **Pseudobulbs** small, ovoid, 2–3 cm long, 1 cm broad, 1-leafed at apex. **Leaf** narrowly oblong-ligulate, leathery, 10–12.5 cm long, 2.5 cm broad. **Inflorescence** 1- or rarely 2-flowered, 9 cm tall, subtended by a membranous sheath. **Flowers** 8–11 cm across; sepals and petals rich rose-purple; lip similar but with a white throat and darker purple area on mid-lobe and front margins of side lobes. **Sepals** spreading, oblong, 4–5.5 cm long, 1.3 cm broad, acute; dorsal sepal reflexed. **Petals** elliptic, 3.5–5.5 cm long, 3 cm broad, subacute, margins waved. **Lip** very obscurely 3-lobed or undivided, 4.5

cm long, 3.5 cm broad; sides curved over column to give the lip a trumpet shape; mid-lobe transversely oblong, truncate or emarginate, margin crisped; disc with 3–5 parallel ridges. **Column** clavate, arcuate, 2.3 cm long.
DISTRIBUTION Brazil (E. Minas Gerais State); 600–900 m altitude growing epiphytically in tall trees.
HISTORY Originally described by William Hooker in 1839 in the *Botanical Magazine* (t. 3656) as *Cattleya pumila* and transferred to the genus *Laelia* by H.G. Reichenbach in 1853 in *Flore des Serres* (p. 62). The original importations from Brazil were made by John Allcard who collected it on the Essequibo River in 1838 and by M. Pinel the following year.

A great number of varieties of this species have been introduced into cultivation since its first introduction. These vary from the typical *L. pumila*, with a flower colour all shades of pink, to pure white varieties.
SYNONYMS *Cattleya pumila* Hooker; *C. marginata* Hort.; *C. pinelii* Lindl.; *Bletia pumila* (Hooker) Rchb.f.
CLOSELY RELATED SPECIES *L. pumila* may be distinguished from the closely related *Laelia dayana* Rchb.f. [Colour Plate] by its lack of purple striping in the throat of the lip and from *Laelia praestans* Rchb.f. by the callosities on the lip and by its longer clavate column.

Laelia purpurata Lindl. [Colour Plate]
An epiphytic herb, up to 50 cm high. **Stem** clavate, 15 cm long, 2–3 cm broad, 1-leafed at apex. **Leaf** oblong-ligulate, leathery, erect, 22–30 cm long, 4.8 cm broad, rounded at apex. **Inflorescence** 2- to 5-flowered, 20–32 cm long, subtended by a long compressed sheath. **Flowers** about 15 cm across, very showy; sepals and petals white to delicate pink; lip pink outside and at apex, throat yellow, veined purple, side lobes and base of mid-lobe rich deep purple. **Sepals** oblanceolate-ligulate, 7–10 cm long, 1.8 cm broad, obtuse. **Petals** elliptic-ovate, 8–10 cm long, 4–6 cm broad, rounded at apex, margins undulate. **Lip** trumpet-shaped, obscurely 3-lobed, 7–9 cm long, 6–7.5 cm broad; side lobes rounded, curved up around column; mid-lobe round, spreading, with margin undulate. **Column** 2.5 cm long.
DISTRIBUTION S. Brazil (São Paulo, Santa Catarina and Rio Grande do Sul States) in coastal areas.
HISTORY Described in 1852 by John Lindley in Lindley and Paxton's *Flower Garden* (p. 111) from a specimen grown by Messrs Backhouse of York, England, and sent to them from Santa Catarina in Brazil.
SYNONYMS *Cattleya brysiana* Lemaire; *C. casperiana* Rchb.f.

Laelia rubescens Lindl.
An epiphytic or lithophytic plant, up to 40 cm high. **Pseudobulb** ovoid, compressed, furrowed, 3–5 cm long, 2.5 cm broad, dark green, clothed in papery sheaths when young, 1-leafed at apex. **Leaf** oblong-ovate, spreading or suberect, leathery, ± V-shaped in cross-section, up to 14 cm long, 3.5 cm broad, obtuse. **Inflorescence** 2- to 8-flowered, very much longer than leaf, jointed from apex of new growth; scape almost covered in sheaths borne at each joint; bracts papery, lanceolate, up to 1.2 cm long. **Flowers** up to 6 cm across, borne in a cluster at apex of scape; sepals and petals white, flushed pink or pale purple; lip white, throat deep purple with pale yellow on base of mid-lobe. **Sepals** lanceolate, up to 3.3 cm long, 0.5 cm broad, acute. **Petals** ovate-lanceolate, 2.7 cm long, 0.9 cm broad, acute, margins undulate. **Lip** 3-lobed, 2.5 cm long, 1.3 cm broad; side lobes oblong, curved up around column, reflexed at apex; mid-lobe spreading, oblong, reflexed, acute, undulate, especially at margins; disc 3-ridged, ridges pubescent towards apex. **Column** 0.8 cm long.
DISTRIBUTION Mexico, Costa Rica, Nicaragua, and Guatemala; sea level to 800 m altitude. altitude.
HISTORY Described by John Lindley in the *Botanical Register* (t. 41, misc. pp. 17, 20) in 1840.
SYNONYMS *Laelia acuminata* Lindl.; *L. peduncularis* Lindl.

Laelia tenebrosa Rolfe [Colour Plate]
Stem clavate, up to 18 cm long, 3 cm broad, 1-leafed at apex. **Leaf** erect, oblong-ovate to ligulate, leathery, up to 28 cm long, 6 cm broad, rounded at apex. **Inflorescence** 2–4-flowered, 30 cm long. **Flowers** 14 cm across; sepals and petals bronzy-green; lip rose-purple, pale greenish at base and with 2 very rich purple marks in centre; column green. **Sepals** lanceolate-ligulate, 8 cm long, 1.6 cm broad, acute; lateral sepals slightly falcate-deflexed. **Petals** obliquely elliptic-oblong, 7 cm long, 2.5 cm broad, obtuse. **Lip** 3-lobed, 6.5 cm long, 4 cm broad; side lobes curved up around column; mid-lobe spreading, rotund, crisped-undulate. **Column** 2–3 cm long.
DISTRIBUTION Brazil (Bahia and Espirito Santo States).
HISTORY Described by R.A. Rolfe in the *Orchid Review* (p. 146) in 1893 based on W.H. Gower's *Laelia grandis* var. *tenebrosa* described in *The Garden* (p. 36). The type collection was made in Brazil by E. Shuttleworth.
CLOSELY RELATED SPECIES *L. grandis*.

Laelia xanthina Lindl. [Colour Plate]
An epiphytic herb, up to 50 cm high. **Stem**

clavate, up to 22 cm long, 2–3 cm broad, 1-leafed at apex. **Leaf** oblong-ligulate, obtuse or rounded, rigid, erect, 28 cm long, 3–8 cm broad, rounded. **Inflorescence** 4- to 5-flowered, up to 24 cm long, subtended by a large sheath. **Flowers** up to 7.5 cm across; sepals and petals rich canary-yellow; lip white, with a rich yolk-coloured throat, striped purple or crimson; column pale creamy-white. **Sepals** oblanceolate, 4 cm long, 1–2 cm broad, acute or subacute. **Petals** oblong, 4 cm long, 1–3 cm broad, obtuse, margins recurved. **Lip** obscurely 3-lobed, flabellate, 3.2 cm long, 2.8 cm broad; side lobes oblong, curved up around column; mid-lobe short, rounded. **Column** clavate, 2.2 cm long.

DISTRIBUTION   Brazil (Bahia and Espirito Santo States).

HISTORY   Introduced into cultivation in Europe by Messrs Backhouse & Sons of York, England, who imported it from Brazil. A specimen sent to John Lindley was described in the *Botanical Magazine* (t. 5144) in 1859.

SYNONYM   *Laelia wetmorei* Ruschi

CLOSELY RELATED SPECIES   Much larger flowered than *L. flava* which is similar coloured. The lip also lacks the raised veins found in that species.

Laeliopsis Lindl.

Subfamily Epidendroideae
Tribe Epidendreae
Subtribe Laeliinae

Medium-sized or small epiphytic or lithophytic plants. **Pseudobulbs** ovoid to fusiform-cylindrical, prominently 2- to 3-noded, 2- to 3-leaved at the apex. **Leaves** fleshy-rigid, linear-ligulate, erose on the margins. **Inflorescences** erect to arcuate, terminal from between apical leaves, simple or with a few branches, laxly few- to several-flowered; bracts small. **Flowers** small to medium-sized, showy. **Sepals** and **petals** not spreading widely, free, subsimilar. **Lip** entire, lacking a spur, ecallose but with pubescent central veins. **Column** slender, clavate, elongate, lacking basal appendages; pollinia 4, equal.

DISTRIBUTION   A monotypic genus from Hispaniola and Mona Island in the Caribbean.

DERIVATION OF NAME   From the resemblance of the flowers to those of *Laelia*.

TAXONOMY   *Laeliopsis* was described by John Lindley in his and Paxton's *Flower Garden* (p. 155) in 1853. This monotypic genus is closely allied to *Broughtonia* and to *Cattleyopsis* with both of which it is often confused. However, it is readily distinguished from the former by its fleshy-rigid erose leaves, elongate column lacking the short thick wings of *Broughtonia* and the

lack of a prominent swollen nectary. From *Cattleyopsis*, it differs in having 4 equal, rather than 8 unequal, pollinia and a column that lacks basal appendages.

An account of these three genera, in which keys to the genera and species are given, has recently been provided by Sauleda and Adams (1989) in the *Orchid Digest* (p. 39).

TYPE SPECIES   *Cattleya domingensis* Lindl.

CULTURE   Temp. Winter min. 15°C. Grow as for *Broughtonia*.

Laeliopsis domingensis (Lindl.) Lindl.

An epiphyte or lithophyte with ovoid to fusiform-cylindrical pseudobulbs, 3–5.5 cm long, 1.5–2.1 cm in diameter, 2- to 3-leaved at the apex. **Leaves** linear to ligulate, unequally roundly or obtusely bilobed at the apex, 7–11 cm long, 1.2–2 cm wide, with serrulate margins. **Inflorescence** erect to arcuate, laxly 5- to several-flowered, up to 60 cm long, the branches short, 5- to 7-flowered; bracts triangular-ovate, acute to subacute, 2–2.5 mm long. **Flowers** not opening widely, rose to lilac with a white base to the lip and a yellow central stripe; pedicel and ovary 1.5–3.1 cm long. **Sepals** and **petals** lanceolate, acute, 2.2–3.7 cm long, 0.4–0.8 cm wide. **Lip** obovate, emarginate, 2.8–4 cm long, 2–3 cm wide, with the veins pubescent in the basal two-thirds. **Column** 1–1.1 cm long, clavate, arcuate, narrowly winged above.

DISTRIBUTION   Hispaniola: Haiti   and

Laeliopsis domingensis
1 – Flower ($\times \frac{3}{4}$)
2 – Dorsal sepal ($\times$ 1)
3 – Lateral sepal ($\times$ 1)
4 – Petal ($\times$ 1)
5 – Lip ($\times$ 1)
6 – Column ($\times \frac{3}{4}$)

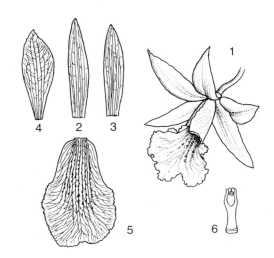

Dominican Republic, and Mona Island only; in xeric conditions, sea level to 200 m.

HISTORY   This attractive orchid was discovered by Mackenzie in Santo Domingo and shortly afterwards by Jaeger in the woods near Miragoane. Lindley described it as *Cattleya domingensis* in 1831 in his *Genera and Species of Orchidaceous Plants* (p. 118), but transferred it to his new genus *Laeliopsis* in 1853 in Paxton's *Flower Garden* (t. 105). The plant first flowered in cultivation in the collections of Rucker, Messrs Henderson of Pineapple Place Nursery, and W.F.G. Farmer of Nonsuch Park, the last's plant being illustrated in Paxton's *Flower Garden*.

SYNONYMS   *Cattleya domingensis* Lindl.; *Broughtonia domingensis* (Lindl.) Rolfe

---

Lanium Lindl.

Subfamily Epidendroideae
Tribe Epidendreae
Subtribe Laeliinae

Small epiphytic herbs with an abbreviated or long, creeping, sheathed, ± branched rhizome. **Stems** ± distant, short, 2-leaved at apex if pseudobulbous or distichously 2- to 8-leaved. **Leaves** subterete, oblong or broadly elliptic ovate. **Inflorescence** ± longer than the leaves, racemose or paniculate, laxly several- to many-flowered. **Flowers** small, with spreading segments; outside of sepals, pedicel and ovary woolly-pubescent. **Sepals** ovate-lanceolate to linear-lanceolate, subacute to acuminate; lateral sepals oblique, adnate to the column at the base. **Petals** linear. **Lip** adnate to the column up to the apex; lamina simple, ovate or rhombic, concave, acute or acuminate. **Column** prominent, dilated avove, auriculate or dentate at the apex; pollinia 4 in 2 superimposed pairs.

DISTRIBUTION   A small genus from northern S. America.

DERIVATION OF NAME   From the Latin *lana* (wool), probably referring to the 'downy flowers'.

TAXONOMY   John Lindley described this genus in Sir William Hooker's *Journal of Botany* (p. 85) in 1841. It is closely allied to *Epidendrum*, but readily distinguished by its tomentose inflorescence and flowers.

TYPE SPECIES   *L. avicula* Benth.

CULTURE   Compost A or mounted. Temp. Winter min. 12–15°C. As in the case of *Encyclia polybulbon*, *Lanium* species are small creeping plants, so should be grown either mounted on fern-fibre or cork, or potted in shallow pans or baskets. While growing, they need moist shady conditions but, after flowering, more light and less water are beneficial.

Lanium avicula (Lindl.) Benth. [Colour Plate]

A small, creeping, epiphytic plant, with a stout rhizome covered by loose, scarious sheaths. **Stems** ± remote, abbreviated, somewhat pseudobulbous with age, 1–3 cm long, obliquely 2-leaved at the apex. **Leaves** sessile, spreading, boradly elliptic to circular, acute or rounded at the apex, 1.5–3.5 cmlong, up to 1.5 cm broad. **Inflorescences** terminal, racemose or paniculate, laxly serveral- to many-flowered, longer than their bases; axis, ovary and sepals all densely white-tomentose. **Flowers** small, segments spreading, yellowish-brown, pale greenish-red or yellowish-green, ± spotted red. **Sepals** ovate-lanceolate or lanceolate, 0.6–0.7 cm long. **Petals** linear, acute or acuminate, 0.5 cm long. **Lip** adnate to the column almost to apex; lamina ovate-subrhombic, acuminate to apiculate, 0.45 cm long, 0.4 cm broad, with somewhat irregular margins. **Column** stout, dilated above, bidentate at the apex, 0.5 cm long.
DISTRIBUTION Brazil and Peru.
HISTORY Discovered by George Gardner in the Organ Mts of Brazil and described by John Lindley as *Epidendrum avicula* in Hooker's *Journal of Botany* (p. 85) in 1841. George Bentham transferred it to the genus *Lanium* in Hooker's *Icones Plantarum* (t. 1335) in 1881.
SYNONYM *Epidendrum avicula* Lindl.
CLOSELY RELATED SPECIES Allied to *Lanium microphyllum* (Lindl.) Benth. which lacks any pseudobulbs and has distichous, 2- to 8-leaved stems.

Lemboglossum Halbinger
Subfamily Epidendroideae
Tribe Oncidieae

Epiphytic, lithophytic or rarely terrestrial plants. **Pseudobulbs** rounded, ovoid to elongate, enclosed by sheaths that may be leaf-bearing, 1- to 3-leaved at the apex. **Leaves** thinly coriaceous, linear to lanceolate or elliptic. **Inflorescences** lateral, axillary from basal sheaths, simple or few-branched, with few to many flowers. **Flowers** showy, large. **Sepals** and **petals** subequal, free, spreading. **Lip** shortly clawed, with claw partly united to the column at the base, ovate to cordate, with a basal callus on the claw. **Column** long, slender, auriculate or winged; pollinia 2, with a laminar stipe; viscidium almost always bent to form a hook at the base of the stipe.
DISTRIBUTION A genus of about 14 species in Central America from Mexico south to Costa Rica.
DERIVATION OF NAME From the Greek *lembos* (boat) and *glossa* (tongue), in allusion to the shape of the callus on the lip.

TAXONOMY The genus was recognised as distinct from *Odontoglossum* by Federico Halbinger in 1983 in the journal *Orquidea (Mex.)* (p. 8) under the name *Cymbiglossum*. Unfortunately, that name is a later homonym and Halbinger replaced it with the name *Lemboglossum* in the following year in the same journal (p. 348).
For orchid hybrid registration purposes, these species of this genus are still treated as odontoglossums.
TYPE SPECIES *Odontoglossum rossii* Lindl.
SYNONYMS *Odontoglossum* sect. *Leucoglossum* Lindl.; *Cymbiglossum* Halbinger
CULTURE Temp Winter min. 10–12°C. Grow well in pots of epiphyte mix, but small species may be mounted. Shady and humid conditions are appreciated while in growth but cooler and drier conditions when growth is complete.

Lemboglossum bictoniense (Batem. ex Lindl.) Halbinger [Colour Plate]
Plant terrestrial or lithophytic. **Pseudobulbs** ovoid to ellipsoid, compressed, 4–6 cm tall, 3 cm wide, 1- to 3-leaved at apex, enclosed below by several leafy or non-leafy bracts. **Leaves** linear to elliptic-lanceolate, acute, 11–45 cm long, 1.5–5.5 cm wide, conduplicate at the base. **Inflorescence** erect, basal, 40–80 cm tall, simple or few-branched, many-flowered; bracts narrowly elliptic-lanceolate, acute to acuminate, 0.7–2 cm long. **Flowers** showy, the sepals and petals pale or yellowish-green transversely marked with brown or red-brown, the lip white, lilac or rose-purple; pedicel and ovary 2.5–5 cm long. **Dorsal sepal** elliptic-lanceolate, acute, slightly recurved, 1.8–2.3 cm long, 0.6–0.9 cm wide; **lateral sepals** oblique, elliptic-lanceolate, acute to acuminate, 2.1–2.7 cm long, 0.5–0.6 cm wide, dorsally keeled. **Petals** obliquely oblanceolate to elliptic-lanceolate, acute to obtuse, 1.8–2.3 cm long, 0.4–0.8 cm wide. **Lip** with a short 2–3 mm long claw, entire, heart-shaped, acute to rounded, 1.5–3 cm long, 1.6–2.4 cm wide, with an undulate-crenulate margin; callus fleshy, with upcurved sides and bilobed in front. **Column** slender, 1.2–1.5 cm long, with subquadrate apical wings.
DISTRIBUTION Mexico, Guatemala and El Salvador; in humid mixed forests, 1800–2800 m.
HISTORY George Ure Skinner discovered this attractive orchid in 1835 in Guatemala and sent living plants of it to James Bateman. Other specimens were also received by Sir Charles Lemon and Lord Rolle, the former flowering it for the first time in cultivation in his collection at Bicton. Bateman described it as *Cyrtochilum bictoniense* in 1838 in his celebrated *Orchidaceae of Mexico and Guatemala* (t. 6).

Halbinger recently transferred it to the present genus in 1984 in *Orquidea (Mexico)* (p. 352).
This orchid is best known in cultivation under the name *Odontoglossum bictoniense* (Batem.) Lindl. and it graces many collections. It has been an important parent in hybridising, producing many colourful progeny.
SYNONYMS *Cyrtochilum bictoniense* Batem.; *Odontoglossum bictoniense* (Batem.) Lindl.; *Zygopetalum africanum* Hook.

Lemboglossum cervantesii (La Llave & Lex.) Halbinger [Colour Plate]
An epiphyte with ovoid slightly compressed, ancipitous pseudobulbs, 2.5–7 cm tall, 1.5–4 cm wide, brown or spotted with brown, unifoliate at the apex, subtended by 2–3 sheaths. **Leaf** oblong, acute, 6.5–21 cm long, 1.9–3 cm wide, with a conduplicate petiole. **Inflorescence** 2- to 6-flowered, arcuate to pendent, 15–30 cm long; bracts linear, acuminate, 3–6 cm long. **Flowers** 3.5–6 cm across, white or pink marked with bands or spots of reddish-brown in basal parts of the sepals and petals, the callus yellow marked with red; pedicel and ovary 3–3.5 cm long. **Dorsal sepal** obovate, acute, 1.8–3.5 cm long, 1–1.8 cm wide; **lateral sepals** oblong-lanceolate, acute, 1.9–3.5 cm long, 0.8–1.4 cm wide. **Petals** oblong-lanceolate to ovate, obtuse, 1.9–3.5 cm long, 1–2.2 cm wide. **Lip** shortly clawed, cordate, acute or obtuse, 1.3–3 cm long, 1.5–3 cm wide, with undulate and erose margins; callus fleshy, on claw of lip, with 2 upcurved rounded sides, a central raised knob and 3-lobed in front. **Column** slender, clavate, 1–1.7 cm long.
DISTRIBUTION Endemic to Mexico; in mixed pine/oak forests, 1400–3000 m.
HISTORY The Mexican botanists La Llave and Lexarza discovered this pretty orchid near Irapeo in Michoacan State and described it as *Odontoglossum cervantesii* in 1825 in their *Novarum Vegetabilium Descriptiones Orchidianum Opusculum* (p. 34). They dedicated it to Vincentio Cervantes, a Mexican professor of botany. It was transferred to *Lemboglossum* by Halbinger in 1984 in the journal *Orquidea (Mex.)* (p. 352).
SYNONYMS *Odontoglossum cervantesii* La Llave & Lex.; *Oncidium cervantesii* (La Llave & Lex.) Beer; *Odontoglossum membranaceum* Lindl.
CLOSELY RELATED SPECIES *L. apterum* (La Llave & Lex.) Halbinger differs in having a much smaller ovate lip and narrower sepals and petals.

Lemboglossum cordatum (Lindl.) Halbinger [Colour Plate]
An epiphyte with ellipsoid-ovoid, compressed pseudobulbs, 4.5–9 cm tall, 2–4 cm wide, unifoliate at the apex but subtended by several imbricate sheaths, 2–4 of which are foliaceous,

the pseudobulbs borne on an ascending rhizome. **Leaves** elliptic-lanceolate, apiculate, 9–30 cm long, 2.5–4.5 cm wide, conduplicate at the base. **Inflorescence** basal, erect, unbranched, 30–50 cm long, laxly 5- to 12-flowered; peduncle slightly flattened; bracts lanceolate, acuminate, 2.5–3 cm long. **Flowers** showy, 4–7 cm across, the sepals and petals yellow-green spotted with pale or reddish-brown, the lip whitish with pale or red-brown spots; pedicel and ovary 3–4.5 cm long. **Sepals** elliptic-lanceolate to narrowly lanceolate, acuminate, 3.5–5 cm long, 0.4–1 cm wide, dorsally keeled. **Petals** ovate-lanceolate, long-acuminate, 2.5–4 cm long, 0.7–1.1 cm wide. **Lip** shortly clawed, cordate-deltoid, abruptly acuminate, 1.8–2.5 cm long, 1.5–1.9 cm wide, with entire margins; callus united to the claw, fleshy, with upcurved sides and bidentate at the apex, 7–8 mm long. **Column** slender, incurved, 1.2–1.5 cm long, shortly hairy, yellow-green, the wings shallow, rounded.

DISTRIBUTION   Mexico to Costa Rica, and also in Venezuela; in humid mixed forest in the mist zone, 1900–2500 m.

HISTORY   John Lindley described this species as *Odontoglossum cordatum* in 1838 in the *Botanical Register* (misc. p. 50) based on a specimen introduced into cultivation from Mexico by George Barker of Birmingham. Halbinger transferred it to *Lemboglossum* in 1984 in the journal *Orquidea* (*Mex.*) (p. 352).

SYNONYMS   *Odontoglossum cordatum* Lindl.; *O. hookeri* Lem.; *O. lueddemannii* Regel

Lemboglossum maculatum (La Llave & Lex.) Halbinger [Colour Plate]

An epiphyte with oblong compressed pseudobulbs, 6–12 cm tall, 2.5–6 cm wide, subtended by 1–2 foliaceous sheaths at the base, unifoliate at the apex. **Leaf** lanceolate, apiculate, 15–30 cm long, 3–6 cm wide. **Inflorescence** erect, basal, 2- to 7-flowered, 20–35 cm long; bracts lanceolate, acuminate, 3–5 cm long. **Flowers** 4–7 cm across, the sepals and petals yellow with blotches of pale to dark brown, the lip yellow with brown or red-brown blotches, the callus yellow with red streaks; pedicel and ovary 3.5–7.5 cm long. **Dorsal sepal** linear-lanceolate to elliptic-lanceolate, acute, 2.5–4 cm long, 0.6–1.1 cm wide; **lateral sepals** similar but 3–4.5 cm long, 0.6–0.8 cm wide. **Petals** oblong, elliptic or elliptic-obovate, acuminate, 2.5–3 cm long, 1.5–3 cm wide. **Lip** shortly clawed, triangular-cordate, acuminate, 1.5–2.5 cm long, 2–2.5 cm wide, erose-denticulate on the margins; callus on the claw of the lip, fleshy, boat-shaped, bilobed at the apex. **Column** slender, clavate, 1–1.5 cm long.

DISTRIBUTION   Mexico, Guatemala and Costa Rica; in mixed mist forest, 2000–2700 m.

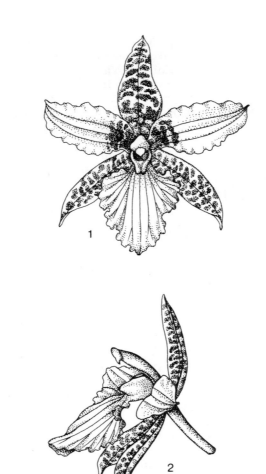

Lemboglossum rossii
1 – Flower, front view (× 1)
2 – Flower, side view (× 1)

HISTORY   Discovered by La Llave and Lexarza near Irapeo in Michoacan State of Mexico, and described by them as *Odontoglossum maculatum* in 1825 in their *Novarum Vegetabilium Descriptiones Orchianum Opusculum* (p. 35). Halbinger transferred it to the present genus in 1984 in the journal *Orquidea* (*Mex.*) (p. 353).

SYNONYMS   *Odontoglossum maculatum* La Llave & Lex.; *Brassia oestlundiana* L.O. Williams.

CLOSELY RELATED SPECIES   Allied to *L. cordatum* but distinguished by its lack of an ascending rhizome, the broader leaves, fewer-flowered inflorescences, broad petals spotted only in the basal part, and acute rather than caudate sepals, petals and lip.

Lemboglossum rossii (Lindl.) Halbinger [Colour Plate]

An epiphyte with ovoid to subspherical pseudobulbs, up to 5 cm long, 3.5 cm wide, enclosed

at the base by 2 sheaths, unifoliate at the apex. **Leaf** elliptic to elliptic-lanceolate, acute, 5–20 cm long, 1.5–4 cm wide. **Inflorescence** arcuate to pendent, basal, laxly 1- to 4-flowered, 6–20 cm long; peduncle terete; bracts lanceolate, acuminate, 1.5–3 cm long. **Flowers** 5–7.5 cm across, white or pale pink with spots or blotches of brown or reddish-brown on sepals and base of petals, the callus yellow, streaked or spotted red; pedicel and ovary 3–5 cm long. **Sepals** oblong-lanceolate to oblong-elliptic, acuminate, 2.5–4.5 cm long, 0.5–1.1 cm wide. **Petals** broadly elliptic, subacute, 2.5–3.8 cm long, 0.8–2 cm wide. **Lip** shortly clawed, suborbicular-subcordate above, rounded to obtuse, 2.5–3.2 cm long, 1.8–3.2 cm wide, with undulate margins; callus fleshy, with upcurved sides and a central ridge bifid at the apex. **Column** slender, slightly incurved above, 1.7–2 cm long, pubescent.

DISTRIBUTION   Mexico, Guatemala, Honduras and Nicaragua; in mixed cloud forest, 2000–2400 m.

HISTORY   Discovered by John Ross in 1837 in the Oaxaca District of Mexico. John Lindley described this attractive orchid as *Odontoglossum rossii* the following year in his *Sertum Orchidacearum* (sub t. 25) based on a Ross specimen flowered by Mr George Barker of Birmingham.

It was transferred to the present genus by Halbinger in 1984 in *Orquidea* (*Mex.*) (p. 353).

SYNONYMS   *Odontoglossum rossii* Lindl.; *O. caulescens* A. Rich. & Gal.; *O. rubescens* Lindl.; *O. warnerianum* Rchb.f.; *O. humeanum* Rchb.f.; *O. asperum* Rchb.f.; *O. youngii* Gower

Lemboglossum uroskinneri (Lindl.) Halbinger [Colour Plate]

A terrestrial or more commonly a lithophyte with ovoid, compressed, ancipitous pseudobulbs up to 9 cm long, 3.5 cm wide, subtended by 3–4 foliose sheaths, 1- to 3-leaved at the apex. **Leaves** flexuose, lanceolate, acute, 10–20 cm long, 2–4 cm wide. **Inflorescence** erect, basal, simple or branched, 7- to 25-flowered, up to 1 m or more long; bracts lanceolate, acuminate, up to 3.5 cm long. **Flowers** showy, long-lasting, c. 5 cm across, the sepals and petals yellow-green spotted and banded with reddish-brown or brown, the lip white more or less marked with spots, lines and blotches of rose-lilac or pink; pedicel and ovary 5–6 cm long. **Dorsal sepal** ovate, acuminate, 2.5–2.7 cm long, 1.1–1.3 cm wide, dorsally keeled; **lateral sepals** falcate, oblanceolate, acuminate, 2.5–3 cm long, 0.8–1.3 cm wide, dorsally keeled. **Petals** ovate, acuminate, 2.5–2.7 cm long, 1.1–1.3 cm wide. **Lip** shortly clawed, triangular-cordate to suborbicular, obtuse to rounded, 2.5–2.8 cm long, 2.8–3.5 cm wide, denticulate, undulate on margins; callus auriculate at base, fleshy, with upcurved sides, bidentate at apex, pubescent. **Column** slender, slightly incurved, 1.6–1.8 cm long, with 2 subquadrate wings at apex.

DISTRIBUTION   Guatemala and S. Mexico; now very rare usually on rocks in humid mixed forest, 1800–2200 m.

HISTORY   It is fitting that George Ure Skinner, who collected so many orchids in Guatemala for James Bateman and others, should be commemorated by this fine species. He discovered it near the town of Santa Catarina Ixtahuacan and sent living plants to Messrs Veitch in 1854. They flowered it in 1859 and it was described as *Odontoglossum uroskinneri*, by John Lindley in the same year in the *Gardeners' Chronicle* (p. 708).

Halbinger transferred it to the present genus in 1984 in *Orquidea* (*Mex.*) (p. 353).

SYNONYM   *Odontoglossum uroskinneri* Lindl.

CLOSELY RELATED SPECIES   Allied to *L. majale* (Rchb.f.) Halbinger [Colour Plate] which differs in its much shorter inflorescence, narrower unspotted sepals and petals, and broad blunt lip. Also close to *L. bictoniense* which differs in having smaller flowers and differently shaped sepals and petals.

Leochilus **Knowles & Westcott**
Subfamily Epidendroideae
Tribe Oncidieae

Small, tufted, epiphytic herbs with pseudobulbous stems. **Pseudobulbs** covered at the base by 1 to several leaf-sheaths, 1- or 2-leaved above. **Leaves** coriaceous, ligulate or lanceolate. **Inflorescences** 1 or 2, racemose or paniculate, laxly few-flowered. **Flowers** small, mostly inconspicuous. **Sepals** and **petals** spreading, free or variously connate. **Lip** adnate to the base of the column, entire or 3-lobed, mostly longer than the petals; disc bearing a fleshy callus. **Column** lacking a foot, bearing stelidia on each side near the middle, truncate at the apex; rostellum elongate.

DISTRIBUTION   A genus of about 15 species distributed from Mexico to Argentina and in the W. Indies.

DERIVATION OF NAME   From the Greek *leios* (smooth) and *cheilos* (lip), referring to the smooth surface of the lip.

TAXONOMY   *Leochilus* was described in the *Floral Cabinet* (p. 143) of 1838 by G. Knowles and F. Wescott. It is a genus closely allied to *Oncidium*, differing in that the anther is produced in front into a membranaceous appendage equalling or mostly longer than the locule.

The genus has not been revised since F. Kraenzlin (1922) included the genus in his account of the Orchidaceae in A. Engler's *Das Pflanzenreich*.

TYPE SPECIES   *L. oncidioides* Knowles & Westcott

SYNONYMS   *Leochilus* Benth.; *Rhynchostelis* Rchb.f.

CULTURE   Compost A or mounted. Temp. Winter min. 12–15°C. *Leochilus* species grow well either in pots or when tied to slabs of fern-fibre or cork. Moderate shade and humidity are required during the growing season with a drier rest period when the pseudobulbs are fully formed. Being small plants they should never be allowed to become too dry.

Leochilus scriptus (Scheidw.) **Rchb.f.**
[Colour Plate]

A small epiphytic plant, growing in dense clumps, 4–24 cm tall. **Pseudobulbs** ovoid, compressed, sulcate, 1–5 cm long, 1–2.5 cm broad, 1-leafed at apex, subtended by 2 leaf-bearing sheaths below. **Leaves** elliptic-ligulate to ellipticlanceolate, oblique, tridentate at the obtuse apex, coriaceous, 3–14.5 cm long, 1–3 cm broad. **Inflorescence** basal, axillary, erect-ascending, 4–23 cm long, racemose or paniculate, few- to several-flowered; bracts triangular-lanceolate, acuminate, 0.4–1.8 cm long. **Flowers** pale greenish-yellow, spotted or striped brownish-purple. **Dorsal sepal** hooded over column, elliptic or suboblanceolate, acute or obtuse, 0.8–1.2 cm long, 0.3–0.6 cm broad; **lateral sepals** spreading-decurved, elliptic or elliptic-lanceolate, apiculate to acuminate, margins somewhat reflexed, 0.9–1.3 cm long, 0.4–0.5 broad. **Petals** ovate-elliptic to elliptic-lanceolate, obtuse, porrect and uncurved, 0.8–1.1 cm long, 0.4 cm broad. **Lip** arcuate below, spreading above, obovate-cuneate to obcordate, retuse or 2-lobed at the apex, 1–1.3 cm long, 0.6–0.9 cm broad; callus cup-like, silky-pubescent inside, with a fleshy, subquadrate, sulcate, puberulent callus in front. **Column** short, thick, up to 0.4 cm long, with a slender projection on each side in the middle.

DISTRIBUTION   Brazil, Mexico, Guatemala to Panama and possibly in Cuba as well; from sea level to 900 m in wet montane or open pine forests.

HISTORY   Originally described in 1843 by M.J. Scheidweiler as *Cryptosaccus scriptus* from a plant of supposedly Brazilian origin in F. Otto and A. Deitrich's *Allgemeine Gartenzeitung* (p. 101). It was transferred to the genus *Leochilus* by H.G. Reichenbach in 1854 in his *Xenia Orchidacea* (p. 15, t. 6).

SYNONYMS   *Cryptosaccus scriptus* Scheidw.; *Leochilus major* Schltr.

CLOSELY RELATED SPECIES   Often confused with *Leochilus oncidioides* Knowles & Westcott, but distinguished from that species by its rigidly erect, stout, straw-coloured peduncle. *L.*

oncidioides has a weak, filiform, often fractiflex, pendent, purplish-tinged peduncle.

Lepanthes **Sw.**
Subfamily Epidendroideae
Tribe Epidendreae
Subtribe Pleurothallidinae

Dwarf or small, epiphytic or lithophytic herbs with a short rhizome. **Secondary stems** erect, slender, concealed by tubular sheaths which are dilated and mostly ciliate at the apex. **Leaves** ± sessile, suberect, coriaceous, linear to orbicular, tridentate at the apex. **Inflorescences** axillary, solitary or fasciculate. **Flowers** small, 1 to many, 2-ranked. **Sepals** the most prominent segments of the flower, spreading, subequal; lateral sepals ± connate. **Petals** minute, mostly broader than long. **Lip** minute, 2- to 3-lobed. **Column** short, fleshy; pollinia 2, waxy, pyriform; rostellum linear, well developed, erect.

DISTRIBUTION   100 or more species, mostly confined to the higher altitudes of mountainous Central and S. America and the W. Indies.

DERIVATION OF NAME   From the Greek *lepis* (scale), *anthos* (flower), referring to the very small flowers of many species in this genus.

TAXONOMY   *Lepanthes* was described in 1799 by O. Swartz in *Nova Acta Regiae Societatis Scientiarum Upsaliensis* (p. 85). A taxonomically complex group with many species which are little known and poorly defined or not yet described.

Lepanthes is allied to *Pleurothallis* being distinguished by its mostly strongly 2-lobed transverse petals from a very oblique base. In many species of *Lepanthes* the flower opens widely so as to be almost flat.

TYPE SPECIES   *L. concinna* Sw. nom. illeg.

CULTURE   Compost A. Temp. Winter min. 10–12°C. Most species are found in forests at fairly high altitudes and, in cultivation, should be given shady humid conditions at all times although no shade will be needed in winter. *Lepanthes* grow well in small pots or they may be mounted on fern-fibre or cork. In either case they must never remain dry for long. In hot weather, moving air and frequent mistings overhead will help the plants – this applies equally to other genera such as *Stelis* and *Pleurothallis* from similar habitats.

Lepanthes calodictyon **Hook.** [Colour Plate]

A dwarf epiphyte with clustered erect stems, 3.5–5 cm long, covered with obconical, acute, ciliate sheaths. **Leaves** pendent, broadly ovate to subcircular, obtuse or shortly apiculate, 1–2.5 cm long, 0.8–2 cm wide, green with broad brown reticulate venation on upper surface, the margins hyaline and undulate. **Inflorescences** fasciculate, several, shorter than the leaves, 1- to several-flowered, the flowers produced in succession. **Flowers** very small, with greenish sepals and orange-yellow to red petals and a red or purple lip. **Sepals** spreading to reflexed, elliptic-ovate, acute, 2–2.5 mm long 1.5 mm wide. **Petals** complex, bilobed, 2–2.5 mm long, 1 mm wide, each ovate lobe bearing a filiform apical extension longer than the lobe. **Lip** spathulate, the apical lamina fleshy and transversely elliptic-reniform, 1–1.5 mm long. **Column** as long as the lip.

DISTRIBUTION   Ecuador only; 900–1200 m in mist forest.

HISTORY   Richard Spruce, the Amazon explorer and botanist, discovered this distinctive species in August 1860 on the lower slopes of Mt Chimborazo. Sir William Hooker described it the following year in Curtis's *Botanical Magazine* (t. 5259), the illustration based on a plant flowered by Mr Osborne of the Clapham Nursery. In February 1980 the cultivar 'Eichenfels', shown by Mr and Mrs H. Phillips Jesup of Bristol, Connecticut, received an award of the Certificate of Horticultural Merit from the American Orchid Society, which was an amazing distinction for a plant with such tiny flowers.

Lepanthes lindleyana Oersted & Rchb.f.

A small, tufted, epiphytic plant, up to 15 cm high. **Stems** slender, erect, covered by tubular sheaths with expanded ciliate, inrolled margins, up to 9 cm long. **Leaves** ovate-lanceolate, acuminate, coriaceous, up to 4.5 cm long, 1.4 cm broad. **Inflorescences** 1 to several, axillary, shorter than the leaves. **Flowers** minute, borne in succession from a lengthening rhachis; sepals yellow or yellow-brown, flushed red-brown on nerves; petals red and yellow; lip maroon or red; column pink. **Sepals** connate below, ovate, shortly acuminate, 0.25 cm long, 0.1 cm broad, margins ciliate; lateral sepals connate for basal two-thirds. **Petals** transversely narrowly elliptic or reniform, covered with glandular hairs, 0.05 cm long, 0.2 cm broad. **Lip** broader than long, fleshy, complex, glandular-hairy or papillate, transversely oblong-bilobulate, 0.1 cm long, 0.15 cm broad; lobes densely pubescent or papillose. **Column** slender, 0.1 cm long, lying in groove between lobes of lip.

DISTRIBUTION   Costa Rica, Nicaragua, Panama, Colombia and Venezuela.

HISTORY   Discovered at Cartagena in Costa Rica by A.S. Oersted and described by him and H.G. Reichenbach in 1856 in *Xenia Orchidacea* (p. 149, t. 50).

SYNONYM   *L. micrantha* Ames

Lepanthopsis (Cogn.) Ames

Subfamily Epidendroideae
Tribe Epidendreae
Subtribe Pleurothallidinae

Dwarf epiphytes with short rhizomes and clustered erect stems, each bearing several obconical ciliate sheaths and a terminal leaf. **Leaf** erect or suberect, elliptic or ovate, coriaceous. **Inflorescences** axillary, terminal, 1 to several, densely many-flowered. **Flowers** small, flat, 2-ranked. **Sepals** flat, most prominent segments of flower; **lateral sepals** united in basal part, more or less parallel. **Petals** small, free, spreading. **Lip** small, entire, often auriculate at base, with a depression at the base below the column. **Column** very short, broad, often enclosed by basal auricles of the lip; stigma bilobed; pollinia 2, ovoid.

DISTRIBUTION   About 25 species widespread from Florida, Mexico and the W. Indes south to Peru and Brazil.

DERIVATION OF NAME   From the resemblance of the species to the allied genus *Lepanthes*.

TAXONOMY   For many years *Lepanthopsis* was recognised as a section of *Pleurothallis*. However, Oakes Ames raised it to specific rank in 1933 in the *Botanical Museum Leaflets of Harvard University* (1(9); p. 3). It is distinguished by the lepanthiform sheaths on the erect stems, the small flowers with a short column bearing an apical anther, 2 pollinia and a bilobed stigma.

SYNONYM   *Pleurothallis* sect. *Lepanthopsis* Cogn.

TYPE SPECIES   *Pleurothallis floripecten* Rchb.f.

CULTURE   Temp. Winter min. 10–12°C. As for *Lepanthes*, requiring shady and humid conditions, never being allowed to dry out. Probably easier to grow mounted than in pots.

Lepanthopsis floripecten (Rchb.f.) Ames
[Colour Plate]

A dwarf epiphyte with clustered erect stems, up to 3 cm long, covered by obconical ciliate sheaths. **Leaves** elliptic, obtuse, 2–3.5 cm long, 1–1.5 cm wide. **Inflorescences** 1 to several, erect, racemose, up to 20-flowered, 4–6 cm long; peduncle 2–3 cm long, wiry; bracts c. 1 mm long. **Flowers** 2-ranked and closely spaced along rhachis, flat, tiny, c. 5 mm long, purplish to brownish with a yellow lip; pedicel and ovary 1 mm long. **Dorsal sepal** ovate, acute, 2–2.5 mm long, 1 mm wide; **lateral sepals** united for basal two-thirds, oblong, obtuse, 2.5 mm long. **Petals** circular, 0.5 mm in diameter. **Lip** deflexed, obovate, rounded in front, 0.7 mm long. **Column** very short, 0.2 mm long.

DISTRIBUTION   Central America: Mexico

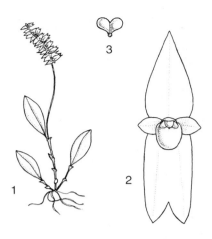

Lepanthopsis floripecten
1 – Habit (× 1)
2 – Flower (× 8)
3 – Pollinarium (× 13)

to Panama, and S. America: Colombia to Peru and Brazil.

HISTORY   H.G. Reichenbach originally described this tiny but unusual orchid as *Pleurothallis floripecten* in 1854 in *Bonplandia* (p. 25). Oakes Ames transferred it to his new genus *Lepanthopsis* in 1933 in the *Botanical Museum Leaflets of Harvard University* (1(9): p. 11).

SYNONYMS   *Pleurothallis floripecten* Rchb.f.; *Lepanthes secunda* Barb. Rodr.; *Pleurothallis unilateralis* Cogn.; *Lepanthopsis secunda* (Barb. Rodr.) Hoehne

Leptotes Lindl.

Subfamily Epidendroideae
Tribe Epidendreae
Subtribe Laeliinae

Small epiphytic herbs, seldom more than 10 cm high, with creeping rhizomes. **Stems** very short, 1-leafed. **Leaf** subterete, erect, fleshy, acute. **Inflorescences** terminal, laxly racemose, 1- to few-flowered; peduncle short, slender, rigid; bracts small. **Flowers** medium-sized. **Sepals** and **petals** subsimilar, free, ± spreading. **Lip** free, fixed to the column at the base, 3-lobed; side lobes with a short distinct claw, small and auriculate, enveloping the column; mid-lobe longer, entire, margins reflexed; disc naked or costate. **Column** erect, short, fleshy, obscurely biauriculate above; pollinia 6, waxy, 4 large and 2 small.

DISTRIBUTION   Three species in Brazil, Paraguay and Argentina.

DERIVATION OF NAME   From the Greek

leptotes (delicateness), referring to the delicate leaves of most species in the genus.

TAXONOMY   Described in the *Botanical Register* (t. 1625) in 1833. It is allied to *Epidendrum* and *Sophronitis* but differs in having 6 pollinia and terete leaves, and less showy flowers than the latter; from *Loefgrenianthus* Hoehne which is also closely allied, it differs in having terete rather than flat and fleshy leaves.

TYPE SPECIES   *L. bicolor* Lindl.

CULTURE   Compost A or mounted. Temp. Winter min. 15°C. *Leptotes* species may be grown either mounted on blocks or in shallow pans. Being small plants, they must be carefully watered especially while growing. After flowering, less water is required but shrivelling must be avoided. Moderate shade and humidity are needed.

Leptotes bicolor **Lindl.** [Colour Plate]

A small epiphytic plant with a stout, elongate, creeping rhizome. **Stems** short, fleshy, cylindric or subfusiform, erect or ascending, 1–3 cm long, 0.4–0.8 cm thick, covered with several membranous sheaths. **Leaf** erect or spreading, subcylindric, acute, deeply grooved dorsally, 5–10 cm long, 0.5–0.8 cm broad, shiny, dark green. **Inflorescence** erect to arcuate, shorter than the leaves, often 3-flowered. **Flowers** long-pedicellate; sepals and petals white; lip with white or greenish side lobes and a deep purple mid-lobe and disc with a white apical margin; column green or purple. **Sepals** linear-lanceolate, acute, 1.6–2.2 cm long, 0.4–0.5 cm broad. **Petals** linear-ligulate, very acute, membranaceous, 1.6–2.2 cm long, 0.3 cm broad. **Lip** fleshy, erect, ± convex, 3-lobed, 1.4–2 cm long, 0.6–0.7 cm broad; side lobes small, rotund or subquadrate; mid-lobe sessile, narrowly ovate, abruptly acute; disc fleshy, 1-ridged. **Column** fleshy, obscurely 3-angled, 0.5 cm long.

DISTRIBUTION   E. Brazil.

HISTORY   Discovered by W. Harrison in the

Leptotes bicolor
Lip (× 2)

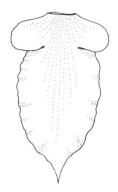

Organ Mts near Rio de Janeiro and described by John Lindley in 1833 in the *Botanical Register* (t. 1625). Several named varieties of *L. bicolor* have been collected which vary from the typical variety described above in either flower or leaf colour.

SYNONYM   *Tetramicra bicolor* (Lindl.) Benth.

Leptotes tenuis **Rchb.f.** [Colour Plate]
See under *Leptotes unicolor*.

Leptotes unicolor **Barb. Rodr.**

A very small, pendulous, epiphytic plant with a short, 1-leafed stem. **Leaf** straight or slightly arcuate, fleshy, subcylindric, acute, deeply sulcate above, 2–5.5 cm long, 0.3–0.8 cm broad. **Inflorescence** pendent, 2-flowered. **Flowers** hanging, pale rose-lilac coloured or white; column greenish-white. **Sepals** linear-ligulate, acute, 2–2.5 cm long, 0.3 cm broad. **Petals** membranaceous, linear-subspathulate, acute, 2–2.5 cm long, 0.2–0.25 cm broad. **Lip** 3-lobed, fleshy, straight or slightly recurved, 2–2.5 cm long, 0.8–1 cm broad; mid-lobe lanceolate, acuminate; side lobes very small, subtriangular. **Column** short, stout, 0.5 cm long.

DISTRIBUTION   Brazil.

HISTORY   Discovered by the banks of the River Dourado between Antas and Sapucahy and near the town of Alfenas by J. Barbosa Rodrigues and described by him in 1877 in his *Genera et Species Orchidearum Novarum* (p. 74).

CLOSELY RELATED SPECIES *Leptotes tenuis* Rchb.f. [Colour Plate] is similar to *L. unicolor* but its lip is distinctly coloured with a transversely oblong or elliptic, obtuse or emarginate mid-lobe.

Leucohyle **Klotzsch**
Subfamily Epidendroideae
Tribe Oncidieae

Medium-sized epiphytic herbs with a short creeping rhizome. **Stems** erect, very short, somewhat pseudobulbous, 1-leafed at apex. **Leaf** linear or linear-lanceolate, subcoriaceous, terete, arcuate, acuminate. **Inflorescence** basal, from the axils of the sheaths covering the pseudobulbs, racemose, several-flowered; bracts scarious. **Flowers** white, spotted with crimson or purple. **Sepals** and **petals** lanceolate, free, spreading, subsimilar. **Lip** porrect, parallel to column, entire or obscurely 3-lobed, erect around base of column below; callus basal, obscure to very shortly 2-ridged. **Column** erect, somewhat dilated around stigma; apex with an oblong hood over anther; pollinia 2, pyriform, attached by a linear-oblong stipe to a small viscidium.

DISTRIBUTION   About four species in Venezuela, Panama, Colombia, Ecuador, Guyana, Surinam, French Guiana, Trinidad and Brazil.

DERIVATION OF NAME   From the Greek *leukos* (white) and *hyle* (wool or stuff), referring to the white woolly indumentum on the stiff floral axis.

TAXONOMY   Described by O. Klotzsch in 1854 in *Index Seminum in Horto Botanico Berolinense* (App. 1). Klotzsch removed this species from *Trichopilia* to which it is undoubtedly closely related, on account of its lip shape which is concave and broader at the base and never convolute and almost concealing the column at its cuneate base as in *Trichopilia*.

TYPE SPECIES   *L. warscewiczii* Klotzsch

CULTURE   Compost A. Temp. Winter min. 12–15°C. As for *Trichopilia*. During growth, the plants require moderate shade and plenty of water. When growth is complete much less water should be given.

Leucohyle subulata **(Sw.) Schltr.** [Colour Plate]

A tufted epiphytic plant. **Pseudobulbs** subcylindric-conical, up to 3 cm long, 0.4 cm in diameter, 1-leafed at apex. **Leaf** fleshy, linear, acute, with a sulcate mid-vein on upper surface, up to 25 cm long, 1 cm broad. **Inflorescence** basal, pendent, racemose, laxly 5- to 6-flowered. **Flowers** showy, almost translucent, white; lip spotted pinky-mauve in basal half; column white. **Sepals** and **petals** lanceolate, acute, twisted once, 1.9 cm long, 0.3–0.4 cm broad. **Lip** subcircular, apiculate, adnate at base to the column, 1.5 cm long and broad, margins curved up around column at the base and erose; callus almost basal, 1 obscure fleshy transverse notched ridge. **Column** suberect, hooded over anther at apex, apical margin erose.

DISTRIBUTION   Trinidad, Panama, Venezuela, Colombia and Peru.

HISTORY   Originally described in 1788 by O. Swartz in his *Prodromus* (p. 123) of W. Indian plants as *Epidendrum subulatum*. H.G. Reichenbach transferred it to the genus *Trichopilia* in 1865 in *Flora* and, to this day, the plant is grown under the name *T. subulata*. However, R. Schlechter transferred it to the genus *Leucohyle* in 1914 in *Die Orchideen* (p. 469) and L. Garay and G.C.K. Dunsterville have followed the treatment in *Venezuelan Orchids Illustrated* (vol. 6: 40).

SYNONYM   *Trichopilia subulata* (Sw.) Rchb.f.

Liparis L.C. Rich.

Subfamily Epidendroideae
Tribe Malaxideae

Small terrestrial, lithophytic or less commonly epiphytic herbs arising from pseudobulbs or corms. **Leaves** 1 to several, plicate, sheathing at the base. **Inflorescence** erect, racemose, laxly few- to many-flowered. **Flowers** small, green, purple, yellow-green or dull orange. **Sepals** free, spreading. **Petals** filiform to linear. **Lip** usually recurved, entire to 3-lobed, acute, obtuse or emarginate ± callose. **Column** mostly elongate, incurved, narrowly winged above; pollinia 4, ovoid, waxy.

DISTRIBUTION   A large genus of about 250 species widespread in the tropics of the world and less common but still widespread in temperate regions.

DERIVATION OF NAME   From the Greek *liparos* (shiny or greasy), referring to the smooth glossy sheen of the leaves of many species.

TAXONOMY   L.C. Richard described *Liparis* in 1818 in *Mémoires du Muséum d'Histoire Naturelle, Paris* (pp. 43, 52). Species of this large genus are seldom found in cultivation for the flowers are generally rather small and drab.

Liparis is closely allied to *Malaxis* but may generally be distinguished by its resupinate flowers in which the lip lacks the auricles on either side at the base which encircle the column in *Malaxis*. The column in *Liparis* species is also mostly rather long and the anther incumbent, in contrast to the short, almost obsolete column and erect anther found in *Malaxis*.

H.N. Ridley (1886) originally monographed the genus in the *Journal of the Linnean Society* dividing it into two sections: *Mollifoliae* with three subsections and *Coriifoliae* with three or four subsections. Since then no complete revision has been attempted but R. Schlechter (1911) in *Die Orchidaceen von Deutsch-Neu Guinea* proposed a new system, establishing four subgenera and a total of 12 sections. J.J. Smith subsequently introduced some further sections, at the same time accepting some of Schlechter's sections. A. Dockrill in *Australian Indigenous Orchids* (1969) more or less follows Schlechter's treatment of the genus for the Australian species.

The most recent work on the genus has been that of G. Seidenfaden (1976) who considered the Thai species in *Dansk Botanisk Arkiv*. Here he reviews the previous work and bases his treatment of the genus on that adopted by J.D. Hooker in the *Flora of British India* (1890). In all he treats some 87 species in three sections as follows:

1. sect. *Liparis* – Plants with non-jointed leaves, usually of a membranaceous thin texture, most often terrestrial. This is the same as Ridley's sect. *Mollifoliae*.

2. sect. *Coriifoliae* – Plants with jointed leaves, often coriaceous, usually epiphytic, inflorescence lax, lacking prominent imbricate bracts.

3. sect. *Distichae* – Plants with jointed leaves, often coriaceous, usually epiphytic. Inflorescence with close, distichous, imbricate bracts.

TYPE SPECIES   *Ophrys loeselii* L. [= *Liparis loeselii* (L.) L.C. Rich.].

CULTURE   Compost A or C. Temp. Winter min. 12–15°C. Tropical and subtropical species may be grown in pans, using the appropriate compost, as plants may naturally grow terrestrially or as epiphytes. They all require moist, shady conditions while growing and should be kept rather drier when growth is complete.

Liparis bowkeri Harv. [Colour Plate]

A small terrestrial or rarely lithophytic plant, up to 20 cm tall. **Pseudobulbs** clustered, conical, 1.5–2 cm long, 0.5 cm in diameter, 2- or 3-leaved. **Leaves** plicate, rather thin-textured, broadly elliptic, petiolate, acute or shortly acuminate, up to 8 cm long, 3.5 cm broad. **Inflorescence** erect, racemose, 9–10 cm long, up to 5-flowered. **Flowers** pale green fading to ochre or orange. **Dorsal sepal** linear-lanceolate, acute, 0.9–1.4 cm long, 0.1 cm broad; **lateral sepals** falcate-elliptic, subacute, 0.8–1 cm long. **Petals** linear, decurved, 0.9 cm long or more. **Lip** geniculate, subreniform or suborbicular, shortly auriculate at the base, 0.7 cm long, 0.8 cm broad, margins slightly irregular; callus basal, transverse, fleshy. **Column** dilated at the base, incurved above, 0.35 cm long.

DISTRIBUTION   Uganda, Kenya and Tanzania, south to the Transvaal, Natal and Cape Province of S. Africa; in woodlands and forests, 100–1500 m.

HISTORY   Discovered by H. Bowker at Fort Bowker, Kaffraria in the Cape Province of S. Africa and described by Harvey in 1863 in his *Thesaurus Capensis* (p. 6, t. 109).

SYNONYM   *Liparis neglecta* Schltr.

Liparis viridiflora (Blume) Lindl.
[Colour Plate]

A very variable terrestrial or epiphytic herb. **Pseudobulbs** short and ovoid to long and cylindric, up to 15 cm long. **Leaves** 2, obovate-oblong or oblanceolate, obtuse, acute or acuminate, 10–30 cm long, 3.8–5 cm broad. **Inflorescence** cylindric, 15–25 cm long, slender, densely many-flowered, with a few bracts below the raceme; bracts small, lanceolate, acuminate, scarious. **Flowers** very small, white, with a yellow lip. **Sepals** revolute, linear-ligulate, free, obtuse, 0.25 cm long, 0.08 cm broad. **Petals** linear, subacute, spreading-reflexed, 0.2 cm long, 0.04 cm broad. **Lip** recurved, broadly ovate, subacute, rather fleshy, lacking calli, 0.25 cm long, 0.2 cm broad. **Column** incurved, wings rounded, 0.15 cm long.

DISTRIBUTION   Tropical Himalayas eastwards to the Khasia Hills and Manipur, and southwards to Malaya and Sri Lanka, also in the Pacific Islands and China; 400–1500 m altitude.

HISTORY   Originally described in 1825 by C.L. Blume in *Bijdragen* (p. 392) as *Malaxis viridiflora* based on his own collection at Tjanjor in Java. John Lindley transferred it in 1830 to *Liparis* in his *Genera and Species of Orchidaceous Plants* (p. 31). This plant is perhaps better known as *L. longipes* Lindl. but J.J. Smith and G. Seidenfaden both consider this to be a later synonym of this very variable species.

SYNONYMS   include *Liparis pendula* Lindl.; *L. spathulata* Lindl.; *L. longipes* Lindl.; *L. boothii* Regel; *L. triloba* Ridley; *L. pleistantha* Schltr.

Listrostachys Rchb.f.

Subfamily Epidendroideae
Tribe Vandeae
Subtribe Aerangidinae

Small epiphytic plants with stems up to 20 cm long. **Leaves** narrowly oblong or linear, equally or slightly unequally 2-lobed at the apex, lobes obtuse. **Inflorescences** axillary, long, many-flowered. **Flowers** distichous, small, white, ± spotted or flushed red. **Sepals** and **petals** subsimilar, free. **Lip** entire, ± apiculate, spurred; spur swollen at apex, short, mouth of spur some distance from base of lip and column. **Column** short; rostellum short; stipites 2; viscidium 1, as broad as long.

DISTRIBUTION   A small genus of two or three species in W. and Central Africa.

DERIVATION OF NAME   From the Greek *listron* (spade) and *stachys* (ear), in allusion to the compactly many-flowered and distichous inflorescence of the type species.

TAXONOMY   *Listrostachys* was established by H.G. Reichenbach in 1852 in the *Botanische Zeitung* (p. 930). Many species originally described in this genus have subsequently been transferred to others such as *Bolusiella* and *Cyrtorchis* as the genus limits of African angraecoid orchids have become better understood.

TYPE SPECIES   *L. jenischiana* Rchb.f. [= *L. pertusa* (Lindl.) Rchb.f.].

CULTURE   Compost A. Temp. Winter min. 15°C. These plants may be grown in baskets or mounted on slabs of fern-fibre or cork. They require humid, shady conditions and should be carefully watered throughout the year.

Listrostachys pertusa (Lindl.) Rchb.f.

[Colour Plate]

A small epiphytic plant with a short stem, 6–15 cm long. **Leaves** ligulate, conduplicate, coriaceous, almost equally or slightly unequally obtusely 2-lobed at the apex, 8–35 cm long, 1–2 cm broad. **Inflorescences** 10–25 cm long, laxly many-flowered, suberect-flexuous; peduncle 2–5 cm long. **Flowers** white, ± minutely spotted red towards the base and with a red spur. **Sepals** ovate, 0.23–0.26 cm long, 0.17–0.2 cm broad. **Petals** a little shorter and narrower. **Lip** obovate or almost quadrate, shortly and broadly apiculate, 0.45–0.5 cm long, 0.26–0.28 cm broad; spur clavate at the apex, 0.35–0.5 cm long. **Column** short, stout; stipites 2; viscidium elliptic.

DISTRIBUTION Sierra Leone to Cameroun, Gabon and Zaïre, also on Príncipe.

HISTORY Described by John Lindley in 1836 in Hooker's *Companion to the Botanical Magazine* (p. 205) based on a plant imported to England from Sierra Leone by Messrs Loddiges which flowered for them on 9 October 1835. It was transferred to *Listrostachys* by H.G. Reichenbach in the *Botanische Zeitung* (p. 930) in 1852.

SYNONYMS *Angraecum pertusum* Lindl.; *Listrostachys jenischiana* Rchb.f.

Lockhartia Hooker

Subfamily Epidendroideae
Tribe Pachyphylleae
Subtribe Lockhartiinae

Small or medium-sized, epiphytic, tufted herbs lacking any pseudobulbs. **Stems** erect or pendulous, simple, leafy throughout. **Leaves** distichous, equitant, spreading to suberect. **Inflorescences** from the axils of the upper leaves, racemose or paniculate, laxly few- to many-flowered; bracts amplexicaul, conspicuous. **Flowers** small to medium-sized, white or yellow, ± marked with red-brown. **Sepals** and **petals** subsimilar, free, spreading or reflexed. **Lip** longer than sepals, entire to 3-lobed; side lobes linear, incurved or recurved; mid-lobe obovate or oblong, 2- to 4-lobulate; callus papillose or tuberculate. **Column** very short, 2-winged above, lacking a foot.

DISTRIBUTION About 30 species distributed from Mexico, south to northern S. America, also in Trinidad.

DERIVATION OF NAME Named in honour of the first Superintendent of the Trinidad Botanic Gardens, David Lockhart (1818–46) who collected the type species and sent herbarium material of it to Kew.

TAXONOMY Sir William Hooker described *Lockhartia* in 1827 in the *Botanical Magazine* (t. 2715).

The flowers of many species of *Lockhartia* closely resemble those of *Oncidium*, being yellow or cream with red or red-brown markings. However, the two genera are only remotely allied and *Lockhartia* species may be easily distinguished by their non-articulated, equitant, approximate leaves borne on elongate stems. Lip and callus shape may be extremely complex in the genus and is of prime importance in classifying the species. No attempt has been made to monograph this genus since that of F. Kraenzlin in A. Engler's *Das Pflanzenreich* (1923).

TYPE SPECIES *L. elegans* Hooker
SYNONYM *Fernandezia* Lindl.
CULTURE Compost A. Temp. Winter min. 12–15°C. Small pots suit *Lockhartia* species well. The plants require fairly shady and humid conditions especially when growing. They should never become very dry but need careful watering when not in active growth.

Lockhartia acuta (Lindl.) Rchb.f.

A medium-sized epiphytic plant, 20–50 cm tall. **Leaves** coriaceous, ovate-triangular, subacute, 1.5–3 cm long, 0.4–1 cm broad, ventrally somewhat carinate. **Inflorescences** several, often many-flowered, a terminal or lateral panicle, 8–9 cm long; bracts small, hyaline. **Flowers** small, 0.8–1 cm across, yellowish or white with a yellow lip. **Sepals** spreading, ovate, obtuse, 0.4 cm long, 0.25 cm broad. **Petals** elliptic-oblong, obtuse, 0.5 cm long, 0.2 cm broad. **Lip** 3-lobed, oblong in outline, 0.6 cm long, 0.4 cm broad; side lobes linear, rounded; mid-lobe obtusely subquadrate, deeply emarginate; callus 2-ridged to middle of lip, velvety, with a basal tubercle. **Column** wings triangular, marginally undulate.

DISTRIBUTION Panama, Colombia, Venezuela and Trinidad.

HISTORY Introduced into cultivation from Trinidad by J. Knight who flowered it in June 1835. It was described by John Lindley in 1836 in the *Botanical Register* (t. 1806) as *Fernandezia*

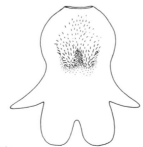

Lockhartia acuta
Lip (× 7)

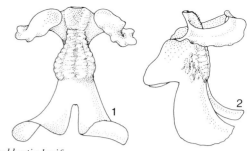

Lockhartia lunifera
1 – Lip, front view (× 3)
2 – Lip, side view (× 3)

acuta. H.G. Reichenbach transferred it to the genus *Lockhartia* in 1852 in *Botanische Zeitung* (p. 767).

SYNONYMS *Fernandezia acuta* Lindl.; *Lockhartia pallida* Rchb.f.

Lockhartia lunifera (Lindl.) Rchb.f.

A small epiphytic plant lacking pseudobulbs. **Stems** slender, erect or suberect, leafy throughout, 10–35 cm long. **Leaves** rigid, small, densely imbricate, subcoriaceous, bilaterally compressed, narrowly triangular-ligulate, rounded or subtruncate at the apex, 1.6–2 cm long, 0.5–0.7 cm broad. **Inflorescence** straight or slightly arcuate, subterminal, 1- to few-flowered; bracts small, hyaline, broadly ovate-orbicular, acute or minutely apiculate. **Flowers** long-pedicellate, golden-yellow, minutely purple-spotted on the lip; column purple-spotted. **Sepals** broadly obovate to ovate or oblong, reflexed, acute to rounded and minutely apiculate, 0.5–0.6 cm long, 0.3–0.5 cm broad. **Petals** broadly oblong, obtuse or retuse at the apex, 0.4–0.5 cm long, 0.3 cm broad. **Lip** spreading-reflexed, sessile, deeply 3-lobed, 0.8 cm long, 0.4 cm broad; side lobes erect, elongate, linear, acute, divaricate, 0.4 cm long; mid-lobe obovate-quadrate, almost 4-lobulate, deeply emarginate; disc verrucose. **Column** short, erect, broadly biauriculate, 0.2 cm long; wings with denticulate margins.

DISTRIBUTION Brazil.

HISTORY Discovered by M.E. Descourtilz near Bananal in Brazil and described by John Lindley as *Fernandezia lunifera* in the *Botanical Register* (misc. 147) of 1839. H.G. Reichenbach transferred it to *Lockhartia* in 1852 in *Botanische Zeitung* (p. 767).

SYNONYMS *Fernandezia lunifera* Lindl.; *F. robusta* Klotzsch non Batem.

Lockhartia micrantha Rchb.f.

A small, caespitose, epiphytic plant. **Stems** erect or pendulous, flattened, 5–40 cm long, 1–2 cm broad, leafy throughout. **Leaves** equitant, imbricate, distichous, narrowly

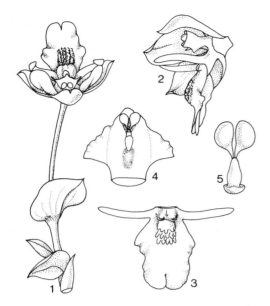

Lockhartia micrantha
1 – Flower and bract (× 4)
2 – Flower, side view with nearside lateral sepal and petal removed (× 4)
3 – Lip (× 6)
4 – Column, from below (× 11)
5 – Pollinia, stipe and viscidium (× 18)

triangular, obtuse or truncate at the apex, 0.8–2 cm long, 0.35–1 cm broad. **Inflorescences** shortly racemose or paniculate, 1- to few-flowered, produced from the central or terminal leaf-axils; bracts ovate-cordate, membranaceous. **Flowers** small, yellow. **Sepals** subsimilar, free, concave, ovate to elliptic-oblong, acute or apiculate, 0.2–0.4 cm long, 0.2–0.3 cm broad. **Petals** broadly ovate to elliptic-ovate, obtuse, 0.25–0.4 cm long, 0.15–0.2 cm broad. **Lip** complex, 3-lobed, 0.25–0.5 cm long and broad; side lobes linear-ligulate, obtuse, spreading or reflexed; mid-lobe obovate, deeply retuse at the apex; callus low, somewhat concave, ± bifid. **Column** very short, with spreading lateral wings.

DISTRIBUTION   Nicaragua to Surinam and Brazil.

HISTORY   First collected by R.B. Hinds near Veraguas, this species was described by H.G. Reichenbach in 1852 in the *Botanische Zeitung* (p. 767).

SYNONYMS   *Lockhartia chiriquensis* Schltr.; *L. lankesteri* Ames

Lockhartia oerstedii Rchb.f. [Colour Plate]

A caespitose epiphytic plant. **Stems** erect, leafy throughout, 10–45 cm long. **Leaves** distichous, equitant, imbricate, semitriangular in outline, obtuse or acute, 2–4 cm long. **Inflorescences** axillary from the uppermost leaves, pendulous,

longer than the leaves, up to 3.5 cm long, 1- to several-flowered; bracts cordate-semiorbicular, apiculate, amplexicaul, glaucous, 0.4–0.8 cm long, 0.6 cm broad. **Flowers** small, bright yellow, spotted and barred dark red on column and the lower part of the lip. **Sepals** reflexed, suborbicular-ovate, rounded, minutely apiculate, concave, 0.6–0.8 cm long, 0.4–0.5 cm broad. **Petals** deflexed, elliptic-quadrate, truncate, side margins reflexed, 0.6–0.9 cm long, 0.5 cm broad. **Lip** complexly 5-lobed, 1–1.4 cm long; basal lobes elliptic or linear-elliptic, slightly denticulate at the rounded apex, antrorsely falcate; central lobes ovate-triangular, obtuse, erect; mid-lobe bilobulate, undulate; disc with a fleshy quadrate, puberulent callus at the base, with several papillose ridges in the centre. **Column** short, fleshy, 0.4 cm long; wings subquadrate, denticulate.

DISTRIBUTION   Mexico to Panama; rather common in dense tropical forests up to 2650 m altitude.

HISTORY   First collected on the Barba Volcano in Costa Rica by Dr A.S. Oersted and described by H.G. Reichenbach in 1852 in the *Botanische Zeitung* (p. 767).

SYNONYMS   *Fernandezia robusta* Batem.; *Lockhartia verrucosa* Rchb.f.; *L. robusta* (Batem.) Schltr.

Ludisia A. Rich.

Subfamily Spiranthoideae
Tribe Cranichideae
Subtribe Goodyerinae

Terrestrial herbs with a creeping rhizome. **Leaves** cauline, petiolate, attractively marked, often ± purplish-black with red or gold venation. **Inflorescences** erect, terminal, racemose, several-flowered; peduncle and rhachis pubescent. **Flowers** relatively small and inconspicuous. **Dorsal sepal** and **petals** forming a hood; **lateral sepals** broad, spreading widely. **Lip** adnate to the base and sides of the column, twisted and saccate at base, grooved below with 2 large calli at base, apex of lip transversely oblong. **Column** large, clavate, twisted in a clockwise direction; anther large, subhorizontal; pollinia 2, slender, elongate, granular, attached by a fleshy viscidium to a forked rostellum.

DISTRIBUTION   One very variable species in China and S.E. Asia.

DERIVATION OF NAME   The origin and meaning of *Ludisia* are unknown but may refer to a personal name.

TAXONOMY   *Ludisia* was established by A. Richard in 1825 in *Dictionnaire Classique d'Histoire Naturelle* (p. 437) but for some unknown reason this name was ignored and John Lind-

ley's name, *Haemaria*, published later in the same year in *Collectanea Botanica* had been incorrectly used until P.F. Hunt resurrected *Ludisia* in the *Kew Bulletin* (1970).

Ludisia is allied to *Macodes* and both have a similarly twisted lip and column, but the lip in *Ludisia* is in the usual position at the bottom of the flower. *Ludisia* is also allied to *Goodyera* and *Zeuxine* but it is distinguished by the twisted lip with a slender claw, its slender twisted column and its single stigma placed in front of the column.

TYPE SPECIES   *L. discolor* (Ker-Gawl.) A. Rich.

SYNONYM   *Haemaria* Lindl.

CULTURE   Compost C. Temp. Winter min. 15°C. Whilst these plants have a reputation for being difficult to keep growing, under the right conditions they grow strongly. A very humid and shady place is required and water should be given throughout the year. Because of their creeping growth-habit, the plants should be grown in shallow pans.

Ludisia discolor (Ker-Gawl.) A. Rich.
[Colour Plate]

A terrestrial herb with a creeping rhizome. **Stems** 20–25 cm long, shortly softly hairy, leafy towards the base. **Leaves** elliptic-lanceolate, shortly attenuate at the base, attenuate-acute at the apex. 4–7 cm long, 2.5–3 cm broad, purplish with red or gold venation; petiole 1.5–3 cm long, clasping at the base. **Inflorescence** cylindric, 3–8 cm long, densely hairy; bracts lanceolate, acuminate, nearly glabrous but with ciliate margins, 1 cm long. **Flowers** distichous, glabrous, 2.3 cm long, white with a yellow lip. **Dorsal sepal** forming with the petals a hood which is narrowly elliptic, obtuse, obtusely tridentate at the apex, 0.7–0.8 cm long, 0.5 cm broad; **lateral sepals** elliptic-lanceolate, obtuse, 0.9 cm long, 0.5 cm broad. **Lip** 0.5–0.6 cm long, 0.35 cm broad below, connate at the base to the column, saccate below, 2-lobed above, 0.6–0.7 cm broad; lobes oblong, obtuse. **Column** 0.55 cm long; rostellum triangular.

DISTRIBUTION   India, Burma, S. China, Indo-China to Malaya and the Malay Archipelago; on rocks by streams and on forest floor, up to 1800 m.

HISTORY   Originally described in 1818 by John Ker-Gawler in the *Botanical Register* (t. 271) as *Goodyera discolor* in 1818 based on a plant mistakenly thought to come from Brazil. A. Richard transferred it to the genus *Ludisia* in 1825 in *Dictionnaire Classique d'Histoire Naturelle* (p. 437). Unfortunately, John Lindley was either unaware of or ignored Richard's generic name when he transferred this species (which he correctly considered to be Asiatic) to *Haemaria* in 1840 in his *Genera and Species of*

Orchidaceous Plants (p. 490). Recently, P.F. Hunt has discussed the nomenclature of this species in the *Kew Bulletin* (1970) and concluded that the name *Ludisia discolor* is the correct one for this species.

SYNONYMS include *Haemaria discolor* (Ker-Gawl.) Lindl.; *Ludisia furetii* Blume; *L. odorata* Blume; *Goodyera discolor* Ker-Gawl.; *Myoda rufescens* Lindl.

Lueddemannia Linden & Rchb.f.

Subfamily Epidendroideae
Tribe Gongoreae
Subtribe Stanhopeinae

Large, epiphytic plants with large, clustered, ovoid, slightly ribbed, 1-noded pseudobulbs, 2- to 3-leaved at the apex. **Leaves** plicate, large. **Inflorescences** pendent, elongate, basal. **Flowers** fleshy, large. **Sepals** and **petals** free. **Lip** 3-lobed, the claw bearing a tooth-like laterally flattened callus with an entire apical lobe. **Column** slender, winged on each side of the stigma; pollinia 2, deeply lobed, hard, attached by a small, oblong stipe to the small, reniform viscidium.

DISTRIBUTION Two or three species only from Venezuela to Ecuador.

DERIVATION OF NAME Named in honour of Herr Lueddemann, an orchid grower and friend of Reichenbach and Jean Linden.

TAXONOMY A small genus allied to *Stanhopea* and distinguished by different flowers which reflect its distinctive pollination syndrome.

Lueddemannia was established by Jean Linden and Reichenbach in 1854 in the journal *Bonplandia* (p. 281).

TYPE SPECIES *Cycnoches pescatorei* Lindl.

CULTURE Temp. Winter min. 12–15°C. Grow in baskets as for *Lacaena* and *Stanhopea*. Give moderate shade and humidity with plenty of water while in growth, but less water when growth slows.

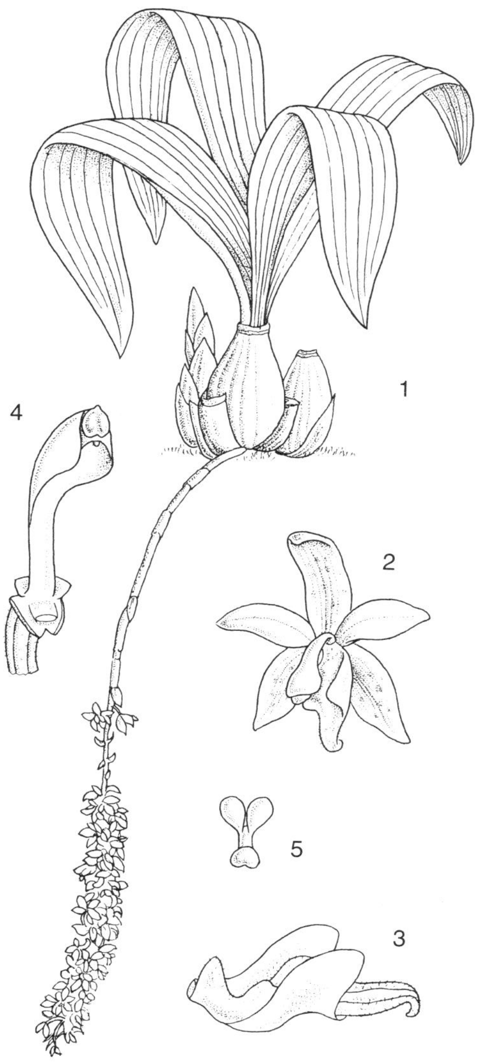

Lueddemannia pescatorei (Lindl.) Linden & Rchb.f.

A large epiphyte with ovoid, slightly compressed, grooved pseudobulbs, 7–13 cm long, 2.5–9 cm in diameter, yellow-green. **Leaves** 2–4, narrowly elliptic-lanceolate, acute, 30–75 cm long, 5–8.5 cm wide, articulated at the apex of the pseudobulb. **Inflorescence** pendulous, 50–100 cm long, densely 20- to 50-flowered; peduncle stout, 10–30 cm long, 3–5 mm in diameter, red-green; bracts narrowly elliptic, acute, 1–1.5 cm long, brown. **Flowers** sweetly scented; sepals red-brown with red veins; petals and lip orange with base of lip speckled with red; callus yellow or red; column pale creamy green;

Lueddemannia pescatorei
1 – Habit ($\times \frac{1}{4}$)
2 – Flower ($\times \frac{1}{2}$)
3 – Lip, side view ($\times 1$)
4 – Column ($\times 1$)
5 – Pollinarium ($\times 4$)

pedicel and ovary 2 cm long, scurfy, green. **Sepals** oblong-elliptic, acute, 2.1–2.8 cm long, 0.9–1.4 cm wide; **lateral sepals** slightly oblique. **Petals** obovate or oblong-obovate, subacute, 1.8–2.3 cm long, 0.9–1.2 cm wide. **Lip** waxy-fleshy, 3-lobed in the apical half, clawed at base, 2.3–2.4 cm long, 2 cm wide; side lobes erect, oblong-elliptic, rounded in front; midlobe triangular, 9 mm long, 5 mm wide; callus of an erect bilaterally flattened conical pubescent dark puce tooth on the claw and with a fleshy slightly raised pubescent area in front between the side lobes. **Column** 1.5–1.7 cm long, winged at the apex, slightly incurved-clavate.

DISTRIBUTION Colombia and Venezuela to Peru, in montane rain forest, 1300–1600 m.

HISTORY Originally described in 1851 in the short-lived journal Paxton's *Flower Garden* (p. 123) by John Lindley as *Cycnoches pescatorei* based on a specimen cultivated by the well-known Belgian orchid grower M Pescatore. It was subsequently transferred to the genus *Lueddemannia* by Jean Linden and H.G. Reichenbach in the journal *Bonplandia* (p. 281) in 1854.

SYNONYMS *Acineta glauca* Rchb.f.; *Cycnoches pescatorei* Lindl.; *C. lindleyi* Hort. ex Rchb.f.

Luisia Gaud.

Subfamily Epidendroideae
Tribe Vandeae
Subtribe Sarcanthinae

Epiphytic herbs with simple or occasionally branched, monopodial, leafy stems. **Leaves** alternate, fleshy, terete. **Inflorescences** axillary, short, racemose, few- to several-flowered. **Flowers** fleshy. **Sepals** and **petals** subsimilar, ± spreading. **Lip** deflexed, sessile, adnate to the column-base, mostly longer than the sepals and petals, entire or lobed. **Column** very short, fleshy, lacking a foot; anther terminal; pollinia 2, on an ovate stipe with a replicate viscidium (gland).

DISTRIBUTION About 40 species in tropical Asia, Malaysia, Australia and Polynesia north to Japan.

DERIVATION OF NAME Named in honour of Don Luis de Torres; a Portuguese botanist of the nineteenth century.

TAXONOMY Described by Charles Gaudichaud in Louis de Freycinet's *Voyage sur l'Uranie et la Physicienne* (p. 426, t. 37) in 1826 based on *L. teretifolia* from Guam.

Luisia seems to be a well-defined genus quite distinct from allied genera, but specific limits within the genus have caused botanists many problems. The present state of our knowledge of the genus is summed up by G. Seidenfaden in *Dansk Botanisk Arkiv* (1971) where he recognises 36 species. He emphasises the problems encountered in studying the genus, particularly the failure to find type material or where found this often proved to be incomplete. The latter is largely due to the difficulty experienced in pressing fleshy leaves and flowers and is a common problem experienced by orchid taxonomists in a wide range of genera.

TYPE SPECIES *L. teretifolia* Gaud.

CULTURE Compost A. Temp. Winter min. 15°C. Most species have an upright growth habit so may be grown either in pots or

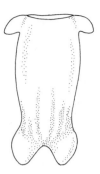

Luisia birchea
Lip (× 3)

mounted on slabs of fern-fibre or cork. They require conditions of high humidity and moderate shade and plenty of water when the roots are actively growing. Less water should be given at other times.

Luisia birchea (A. Rich.) Blume

Stem long, slender, straight or curved-ascending, 0.4 cm in diameter. **Leaves** very variable in thickness, sometimes long and slender, 10–18 cm long, 0.2–0.4 cm in diameter. **Inflorescence** short, several-flowered. **Flowers** large; sepals yellowish-green, stained and streaked red; petals greenish; lip white or greenish with deep purple at the base and on lobes, or purple and streaked with paler lines. **Sepals** ovate, concave, subacute, 0.8–1 cm long, 0.3 cm broad; lateral sepals dorsally apiculate. **Petals** narrow, lanceolate, acute, up to 1.5 cm long, 0.25 cm broad. **Lip** narrowly panduriform, fleshy, auriculate and convex at the base, with 2 divergent apical lobes, up to 1.2 cm long, 0.4 cm broad; disc with 3 large rounded calli at the base.

DISTRIBUTION India and Sri Lanka.
HISTORY Originally dscribed as *Birchea teretifolia* by A. Richard in 1841 in *Annales des Sciences Naturelles* (p. 67). C.L. Blume considered it correctly placed in *Luisia* in *Rumphia* (p. 50) in 1848. The name *L. tenuifolia* (L.) Blume has been incorrectly applied to this species (see Seidenfaden (1971) in *Dansk Botanisk Arkiv* (p. 35).
SYNONYMS *Luisia birchea* Blume; *L. zeylandica* Thwaites; *Birchea teretifolia* A. Rich.

Luisia teretifolia Gaud.

Stem stout, terete, rigid, 15–30 cm long, 0.4 cm thick, nodes 1.2–1.8 cm apart, **Leaves** variable in thickness, terete, obtuse, 4–20 cm long, about 0.3 cm thick. **Inflorescence** axillary, few-flowered; rhachis 0.4–0.8 cm long. **Flowers** small, pale pink, green or yellow; lip yellow or greenish and purple below. **Dorsal sepal** ellip-

tic, obtuse or subacute, 0.55 cm long, 0.3 cm broad; **lateral sepals** lanceolate, keeled on reverse, with a fleshy apical point, 0.75 cm long, 0.25 cm broad. **Petals** linear-oblong, obtuse, 0.3–0.7 cm long, 0.4 cm broad. **Lip** subquadrate below, broadly cordate above, up to 0.75 cm long, gibbous at the base, 3-lobed; side lobes elliptic, falcate, undulate at the apex; mid-lobe cordate, undulate on the margins. **Column** 0.2 cm long.

DISTRIBUTION India, Sri Lanka, S.E. Asia, Indonesia to New Caledonia and Guam.
HISTORY Discovered on the island of Guam in the Pacific Ocean during the voyage round the world of the *Uranie* and the *Physicienne* led by Louis de Freycinet. Charles Gaudichaud described it in the account of the botany of that voyage (p. 426) published in 1826. *L. teretifolia* is the type species of the genus.
SYNONYMS include *Luisia burmanica* Lindl.; *L. platyglossa* Rchb.f.; *L. zeylandica* Lindl.; *Cymbidium triste* Roxb.; *C. tenuifolium* Wight

Luisia volucris Lindl. [Colour Plate]

Stem stout, 15–30 cm long, 0.5 cm in diameter, nodes 1.3 cm apart. **Leaves** terete, obtuse, rigid, 7.5–12.5 cm long, 0.3 cm broad. **Inflorescences** with a short stout rhachis, 1.2 cm long. **Flowers** 6 cm across, with pale yellow-green segments and a purple lip with a green base. **Dorsal sepal** erect, linear, cucullate, 1.2–1.9 cm long, 0.3 cm broad; **lateral sepals** cymbiform, winged on outer surface, similar to dorsal sepal in length. **Petals** linear-subspathulate, dilated at the rounded apex, 2.5–3.8 cm long, 0.4 cm broad. **Lip** auriculate at base, with an oblong hypochile and a much broader convex, ovate-cordate, fleshy, obtuse epichile, 1.2 cm long, 0.8 cm broad.

DISTRIBUTION India (Sikkim Himalayas and the Khasia Hills) and Bangladesh (Sylhet).
HISTORY Described in 1853 by John Lindley in *Folia Orchidacea* (*Luisia;* p. 1) from a plant collected by Thomas Lobb in the Khasia Hills.

Lycaste Lindl.

Subfamily Epidendroideae
Tribe Maxillarieae
Subtribe Zygopetalinae

Epiphytic, terrestrial or lithophytic herbs with short, thick pseudobulbs. **Leaves** plicate, several at apex of each pseudobulb, large, deciduous. **Inflorescence** lateral, several borne from the base of a pseudobulb, erect or erect-spreading, 1-flowered in most species. **Flowers** large, showy, often fragrant. **Sepals** subequal, spreading; lateral sepals forming with the column-foot a distinct saccate mentum. **Petals**

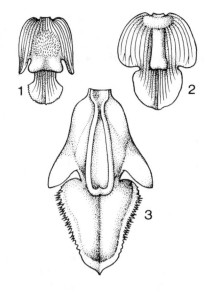

Lycaste lips (All × 1)
1 – *L. aromatica*
2 – *L. cruenta*
3 – *L. longipetala*

similar to sepals but often distinctly coloured. **Lip** 3-lobed, ± pubescent; disc ± pubescent, with a variously shaped callus. **Column** long, wingless to narrowly 2-winged above, produced into a foot at base; pollinia 4 or 2 and sulcate, with 2 very short or elongate stipites.
DISTRIBUTION About 25 species, widely distributed from Mexico south to Peru and Bolivia and in the W. Indies.
DERIVATION OF NAME Lycaste was the beautiful daughter of King Priam of Troy.
TAXONOMY John Lindley described *Lycaste* in 1843 in the *Botanical Register* (misc. p. 14).

Most of the species of *Lycaste* have been placed in *Maxillaria* at one time or another but they are readily distinguished from that genus by their plicate leaves. *Lycaste* is also allied to *Xylobium* but the species of that genus have few- to many-flowered inflorescences. The genus has recently been monographed by J.A. Fowlie in *The Genus Lycaste* (1970). The genus may be conveniently divided into those species such as *L. barringtoniae* (J.E. Smith) Lindl. in which the mid-lobe of the lip is fimbriate and the callus is bifid; and the species such as *L. cruenta* Lindl., *L. deppei* Lindl. and *L. skinneri* (Lindl.) Lindl. where the lip mid-lobe is not fimbriate and the callus is entire and finger-like.
TYPE SPECIES *L. plana* Lindl.
CULTURE Compost A. Temp. Winter min. 12°C. While the hard pseudobulbs are leafless, *Lycaste* species require a cool, dry rest with only a little water given from time to time. When the new shoots appear, the plants should be given

conditions of moderate shade and humidity but very little water until the roots are seen to be growing. When in full growth, water may be freely given until the new pseudobulbs are fully formed.

Lycaste aromatica (Hooker) Lindl.
[Colour Plate]
An epiphytic or lithophytic plant, up to 60 cm high. **Pseudobulbs** ovate, compressed, 7–10 cm long, up to 4.5 cm across, subtended by fibrous sheaths. **Leaves** lanceolate, plicate, up to 55 cm long, 10 cm broad, acuminate. **Inflorescences** lateral, several (up to 18) borne at a time, each 1-flowered, up to 15 cm long; peduncle bearing several inflated brown sheaths. **Flowers** showy, fragrant, yellow, spotted slightly with orange on lip; column deep yellow. **Sepals** ovate-lanceolate to elliptic-oblong, pubescent on inner surface at base, 3–4 cm long, 1.3–1.8 cm broad, acute; lateral sepals oblique, forming a blunt mentum with the column-foot. **Petals** ovate-elliptic or elliptic, 2.8–3.5 cm long, 1.5–2 cm broad, acute to obtuse. **Lip** concave below, 3-lobed above, 2.8–3.2 cm long, 1.5–2 cm broad; side lobes elliptic to lanceolate, porrect, obtuse, crenulate on front margin; mid-lobe elliptic-orbicular, recurved, undulate on margins; disc thickened in centre, pubescent; callus flap-like and truncate. **Column** pubescent on anterior surface, 2.5 cm long.

DISTRIBUTION Mexico, Belize, Honduras and Guatemala; in rain forests up to 1200 m altitude.

HISTORY First collected in Mexico by Lord Napier who sent plants to the Edinburgh Botanic Garden where they flowered in May 1826. It was originally described as *Maxillaria aromatica* by Sir William Hooker (who was sent a specimen and drawing by Dr Graham) in 1826 in *Exotic Flora* (t. 219) but was transferred by John Lindley to the genus *Lycaste* in 1843 in the *Botanical Register* (misc. p. 16).

SYNONYMS *Maxillaria aromatica* Hooker; *Colax aromaticus* (Hooker) Sprengel; *Lycaste suaveolens* Summerh.

CLOSELY RELATED SPECIES Allied to *Lyaste cochleata* Lindl. but distinguished by the lack of red markings on the lip which lacks a saccate base.

Lycaste brevispatha (Klotzsch) Lindl.
[Colour Plate]
Pseudobulbs ovate-conical, compressed, 3.5–6.5 cm long, 4 cm in diameter. **Leaves** deciduous, oblanceolate-acuminate, 22–50 cm long, up to 10 cm broad. **Inflorescence** up to 10 cm long, 1-flowered, borne after leaves fall. **Flowers** about 5 cm across; sepals pale green, ± spotted pale rose; petals whitish, ± tinted

rose; lip white with a few rose-purple spots, callus yellowish; column white, spotted with rose. **Sepals** ovate-oblong, reflexed and acute at apex, 2.5–3 cm long, 1.5 cm broad. **Petals** subequal to the sepals, ovate-elliptic, obtuse, up to 2.6 cm long, 1.5 cm broad. **Lip** oblong-obovate, obscurely 3-lobed, 2.8 cm long, 1.8 cm broad; side lobes obscurely oblong, upcurved in basal half, spreading above; mid-lobe orbicular, deflexed; disc with a thin oblong plate, emarginate at apex. **Column** slender, terete, pubescent below the stigma, 2 cm long.

DISTRIBUTION Costa Rica, Nicaragua and Panama; 600–1600 m altitude.

HISTORY Discovered by J. Warscewicz in 1849–50 in Central America and introduced to Europe by him shortly afterwards. O. Klotzsch described it as *Maxillaria brevispatha* in *Allgemeine Gartenzeitung* (p. 217) in 1851 and it was transferred to the genus *Lycaste* by John Lindley in 1852 in J. Paxton's *Flower Garden* (p. 44).

SYNONYMS *Lycaste candida* Lindl.; *L. lawrenceana* Hort.; *Maxillaria brevispatha* Klotzsch

Lycaste cruenta Lindl. [Colour Plate]
An epiphytic plant, up to 50 cm high. **Pseudobulbs** large, ovoid-oblong, compressed, up to 10 cm long, 5 cm across, several-leaved, subtended by several imbricate, scarious bracts. **Leaves** elliptic-lanceolate to broadly elliptic, plicate, up to 45 cm long, 15 cm broad, acute or acuminate. **Inflorescences** lateral, 1-flowered, 7–17 cm long; peduncle covered by several tubular sheaths each 2 cm long. **Flowers** showy; sepals yellow-green; petals yellow to orange-yellow; lip yellow, spotted maroon with a crimson spot at the base. **Sepals** ovate to oblong-elliptic, recurved in apical half, 3–5 cm long, 1.8–2.5 cm broad, acute, ± pubescent at base. **Petals** elliptic, 3–4 cm long, 2–2.3 cm broad, obtuse or retuse at apex. **Lip** saccate, 3-lobed, 2.5 cm long, with long white hairs in saccate part; side lobes erect, rounded; mid-lobe ovate to orbicular, emarginate, decurved, pubescent, margins crisped; disc with a subquadrate, truncate callus. **Column** stout, arcuate, pubescent below, 2 cm long.

DISTRIBUTION Mexico, Guatemala and El Salvador; up to 2200 m altitude.

HISTORY Discovered in Guatemala by George Ure Skinner and described as *Maxillaria cruenta* by John Lindley in 1842 in the *Botanical Register* (t. 13). The following year in the same journal (misc. 16) he transferred it to the genus *Lycaste*.

SYNONYMS *Maxillaria cruenta* Lindl.; *Lycaste balsamea* A.Rich. ex Lindl.

Lycaste deppei (Lodd.) Lindl. [Colour Plate]
An epiphytic or lithophytic plant, up to 60 cm tall. **Pseudobulbs** ovoid, compressed, 6–10 cm

long, 5 cm across, subtended by scarious sheaths, several-leaved at apex. **Leaves** elliptic-lanceolate, plicate, 20–50 cm long, 8–10 cm broad, acuminate, deciduous but leaving several short spines at apex of pseudobulb. **Inflorescences** erect, 1-flowered, 12–15 cm long; peduncle dotted with inflated red-brown scarious sheaths. **Flowers** showy; sepals pale green, marked with red flecks; petals white, flecked red towards base; lip bright yellow with red lines and spots on basal half; column white, flecked red. **Sepals** elliptic or ovate-elliptic, 5–6 cm long, 2–2.4 cm broad, subacute or obtuse. **Petals** elliptic-obovate, recurved above, 4–4.5 cm long, 2 cm broad, obtuse. **Lip** arcuate, 3-lobed, granular-ciliate, 3.5 cm long, nerves prominent; side lobes erect, rounded, forming a tube around column; mid-lobe ovate-oblong, obtuse, decurved, margins undulate; disc thickened in middle, with a short rounded callus at base. **Column** arcuate, 2.5 cm long, pubescent on lower surfaces.

DISTRIBUTION Mexico and Guatemala: up to 1200 m altitude.

HISTORY Discovered by F. Deppe near Jalapa in Mexico and introduced into cultivation by Messrs Loddiges who described it in the *Botanical Cabinet* (t. 1612) in 1830 as *Maxillaria deppei*. John Lindley transferred it to the genus *Lycaste* in 1843 in the *Botanical Register* (misc p. 15).

SYNONYM *Maxillaria deppei* Lodd.

Lycaste lasioglossa Rchb.f. [Colour Plate]
A terrestrial plant, up to 60 cm tall. **Pseudobulbs** ovoid, compressed, 5–10 cm long, 4 cm across, 2-leaved. **Leaves** elliptic-lanceolate, plicate, shortly petiolate, up to 55 cm long, 12 cm broad, acute or acuminate. **Inflorescence** 1-flowered, up to 25 cm long; peduncle bearing several conduplicate scarious sheaths, each up to 3 cm long. **Flowers** showy; sepals red-brown; petals yellow; lip yellow, striped and flecked with red-purple. **Sepals** elliptic-lanceolate, 5–7 cm long, 1.5–2 cm broad, acute to acuminate; lateral sepals forming a sharp mentum with the column-foot. **Petals** elliptic, arched over the column, 3.5–4 cm long, 1.5–2 cm broad, recurved at the rounded or mucronate apex. **Lip** 3-lobed, obovate, tubular below, 3.5–4 cm long, 2 cm broad; side lobes narrowly oblong, truncate; mid-lobe oblong, densely softly pubescent, obtuse, decurved; callus ovate-triangular, notched at apex. **Column** arcuate, densely pubescent in middle below, 2.5–3 cm long including the foot.

DISTRIBUTION Guatemala only.

HISTORY This species was discovered in Guatemala in 1871 from where it was introduced into Europe by Messrs Veitch. It was described in 1872 by H.G. Reichenbach in the

Gardeners' Chronicle (p. 215). The specific epithet refers to the rough or hairy tongue-like lip of this species.

Lycaste leucantha (Klotzsch) Lindl.
[Colour Plate]

Pseudobulbs ovoid, slightly compressed, 5–7.5 cm long, 3.5 cm in diameter, 2- or 3-leaved at the apex. **Leaves** narrowly oblong or oblanceolate, acute, 40–65 cm long, 3.5–6 cm broad, deciduous. **Inflorescence** up to 20 cm long, borne after the leaves have fallen. **Flowers** large, 7.5–10 cm across; sepals brownish-green to apple-green; petals yellowish-white; lip light yellow on side lobes, mid-lobe creamy-white; column yellowish-white. **Sepals** oblong, spreading, obtuse, 4–4.5 cm long, 1.8 cm broad. **Petals** elliptic. recurved in apical third, rounded, 3.8 cm long, 1.8 cm broad. **Lip** 3-lobed, 2.8 cm long, 2 cm broad; side lobes elliptic-oblong, erect; mid-lobe oblong-ovate, obtuse, pubescent, margin denticulate, reflexed slightly; disc bearing a narrow sulcate plate. **Column** semiterete, curved.

DISTRIBUTION Costa Rica and Panama: 1200-1800 m altitude, in montane evergreen forest.

HISTORY Discovered in 1849 in Costa Rica by J. Warscewicz and described by O. Klotzsch in the following year in the *Allgemeine Gartenzeitung* (p. 402) as *Maxillaria leucantha*. John Lindley transferred it to *Lycaste* in 1851 in J. Paxton's *Flower Garden* (p. 37).

SYNONYMS *Maxillaria leucantha* Klotzsch; *Lycaste leuco-flavescens* Hort.; *L. candida* auct. non Lindl.

CLOSELY RELATED SPECIES Distinguished from *Lycaste macrophylla* (Poepp. & Endl.) Lindl. by its smaller habit and lack of any red markings on the flower segments.

Lycaste longipetala (Ruiz & Pavon) Garay
[Colour Plate]

A variable, large and showy terrestrial plant. **Pseudobulb** large, broadly cylindrical or oblong-ovoid, compressed, sulcate or rugose with age, 7–15 cm long, 2- or 3-leaved at apex. **Leaves** long-petiolate, oblong-elliptic or oblong-lanceolate, up to 80 cm long, 9.5 cm broad, acute or acuminate; petiole stout, up to 25 cm long. **Inflorescence** robust, basal, 1-flowered, up to 60 cm long; peduncle bearing several large, loose, tubular sheaths. **Flowers** fleshy, large; sepals and petals yellowish or yellow-green, more or less tinged pink or brown; lip red, purple or brown. **Dorsal sepal** narrowly oblong-elliptic or oblong-lanceolate, up to 10 cm long, 2.5 cm broad, acute or obtuse; **lateral sepals** falcately-decurved, 8.5 cm long, 3 cm broad, forming with the column-foot a narrowly conical mentum, 1.6 cm long.

Petals obliquely elliptic-oblong, up to 8 cm long. **Lip** elliptic-obovate, 5.5 cm long, 3-lobed in the middle; side lobes small, semiobovate, subacute or obtuse; mid-lobe oblong-ovate, margins irregularly dentate or fimbriate, apex abruptly recurved; disc with a pair of fleshy ridges merging into a broad, retuse plate above. **Column** stout, arcuate, up to 2.5 cm long, hairy below.

DISTRIBUTION Peru, Ecuador, Colombia and Venezuela.

HISTORY H. Ruiz and J. Pavon first collected this species in Peru and described it in 1798 in *Systema Vegetabilium Florae Peruvianae et Chilensis* (p. 220) as *Maxillaria longipetala*. This name has been overlooked until recently and the plant has become well known under the John Lindley name *Lycaste gigantea*. However, Leslie Garay, in 1962 in *Caldasia* (p. 524), transferred the Ruiz and Pavon species to the genus *Lycaste* and this name must be used on grounds of priority.

SYNONYMS *Lycaste gigantea* Lindl.; *Maxillaria longipetala* Ruiz & Pavon; *Maxillaria gigantea* (Lindl.) Beer

CLOSELY RELATED SPECIES Allied to *Lycaste fulvescens* Hooker but differs in having more widely spreading floral segments.

Lycaste skinneri (Batem. ex Lindl.) Lindl.
[Colour Plate]

An epiphytic plant, 75 cm tall or more. **Pseudobulbs** ovoid, compressed, 5–10 cm long, 3.5 cm across, several-leaved at apex when young. **Leaves** elliptic-lanceolate, up to 75 cm long, 15 cm broad, acuminate. **Inflorescence** lateral, 1-flowered, up to 30 cm long; peduncle concealed by inflated sheaths, each 3–6 cm long. **Flowers** very showy; sepals white to rose-coloured; petals reddish-violet; lip white, lined and flecked with red-violet; column white with crimson spots above, crimson below. **Sepals** elliptic-oblong or elliptic-ovate, keeled on reverse, 5.5–8 cm long, 3–3.5 cm broad, subacute to obtuse at apex; lateral sepals forming a short blunt mentum. **Petals** broadly elliptic, reflexed above, 4.5–7.5 cm long, 2.5–4 cm broad, apiculate. **Lip** 3-lobed, 4.5–5 cm long; side lobes erect, forming a tube, pubescent, truncate; mid-lobe suborbicular, obtuse, strongly decurved; callus fleshy, ligulate; disc pilose in centre. **Column** arcuate, pubescent below, 3–3.5 cm long.

DISTRIBUTION Mexico, Guatemala and Honduras.

HISTORY Considerable confusion has existed over the correct name for this spectacular plant. It was described by John Lindley in 1840 in the *Botanical Register* (misc. p. 48) as *Maxillaria skinneri* in honour of George Ure Skinner who discovered it, and subsequently also described by M.J. Scheidweiler as *Maxillaria virginalis* in the *Bulletin of the Royal Academy of Sciences of Brussels* (p. 25) in 1842. The former name was transferred to the genus *Lycaste* by Lindley in 1843 in the *Botanical Register* (misc. p. 15) and has been widely used for this species. For many years the name *Lycaste virginalis* had been accepted as the correct name but J.A. Fowlie (1970) has detailed the evidence to show that on grounds of priority the name *Lycaste skinneri* (Batem. ex Lindl.) Lindl. should now be used.

This is the national flower of Guatemala, where it is known as 'Monja Blanca'.

SYNONYMS *Maxillaria virginalis* Scheidw.; *M. skinneri* Batem. ex Lindl.; *Lycaste virginalis* (Scheidw.) Linden

Lycaste xytriophora Rchb.f. [Colour Plate]

Pseudobulbs ovoid, compressed, 7.5–10 cm long, 5–6 cm across, 1- to 3-leaved at apex. **Leaves** deciduous, lanceolate, acuminate, 30–50 cm long, 11–12 cm broad, leaving long spines at the apex of the pseudobulbs when they fall. **Inflorescence** 10–12.5 cm long, borne when new growth is half-grown; bracts large, 3–4 cm long. **Flowers** 7.5–10 cm across; sepals light greenish-brown; petals yellowish-green below, white above; lip white, stained rose-pink above, callus reddish grading to deep yellow above, spotted red in apical half. **Sepals** oblong, acuminate, 3–4 cm long, 1.5–1.8 cm broad. **Petals** oblong to narrowly elliptic, reflexed and obtuse at apex. 2.8–3.2 cm long, 1.5–1.8 cm broad. **Lip** oblong-ligulate, 3-lobed, 2.6–3 cm long, 1.5 cm broad; side lobes incurved; mid-lobe thickened in middle, margins undulate; disc with a narrow sulcate plate. **Column** 3-angled in cross-section, pubescent below the stigma, 2.5–2.8 cm long.

DISTRIBUTION Panama and Ecuador; 600–1500 m altitude.

HISTORY Probably first collected near Loxa (Loja) in Ecuador by G. Wallis for J. Linden in 1867 and described by H.G. Reichenbach in 1872 in Saunders' *Refugium Botanicum* (t. 131).

CLOSELY RELATED SPECIES Distinguished from *Lycaste dowiana* Endres & Rchb.f. by the armed apices of the mature pseudobulbs and the lack of red or crimson coloration of the petals.

Lycomormium Rchb.f.

Subfamily Epidendroideae
Tribe Gongoreae
Subtribe Stanhopeinae

Large epiphytic or terrestrial plants with clustered large, ovoid, slightly ribbed pseudobulbs, 2- to 3-leaved at the apex, enclosed when young by several foliaceous sheaths. **Leaves** large, sub-erect, plicate with prominent veins. **Inflorescences** basal, pendulous. **Flowers** fleshy, medium-sized. **Dorsal sepal** and **petals** free, hooded over the column; **lateral sepals** united at the base to the column-foot. **Lip** bipartite with a rigid epichile and lobed hypochile. **Column** thick, lacking wings, with a long foot; pollinia 4, hard, superimposed in 2 pairs and attached by a very short stipe to a reniform viscidium.

DISTRIBUTION Some eight species distributed in the Andes from Colombia to Peru.

DERIVATION OF NAME The name derives from the Greek *lykos* (wolf) and *mormo* (hobgoblin), in allusion to the rather grotesque look of the flowers.

TAXONOMY *Lycomormium* was described by H.G. Reichenbach in 1852 in the journal *Botanische Zeitung* (p. 833). It has simple gullet-shaped flowers of a rather primitive structure when compared to allied genera such as *Stanhopea* and *Coryanthes*. Its closest allies are probably *Peristeria* and *Coeliopsis* but it differs in its lip which is divided into a distinct hypochile and movable epichile and its pollinia which are sulcate and rather slender and are attached almost directly to the viscidium.

TYPE SPECIES *L. squalidum* (Poepp. & Endl.) Rchb.f.

CULTURE Temp. Winter min. 12–15°C. Grow in baskets as for *Lacaena* and *Stanhopea*. Give moderate shade and humidity with plenty of water while in growth, but less water when growth is complete.

Lycomormium squalidum (Poepp. & Endl.) **Rchb.f.**

A large epiphyte or terrestrial plant with a short rhizome and large 3- to 5-leaved pseudobulbs, up to 7 cm long. **Leaves** thin-textured, oblanceolate to elliptic-oblong, acute, longly petiolate, up to 120 cm long, 6 cm broad. **Inflorescence** suberect or deflexed, up to 30 cm long, densely up to 13-flowered. **Flowers** fleshy, campanulate, white to straw-yellow with red-brown spots; pedicel and ovary 1–2 cm long. **Sepals** more or less connate at the base; **dorsal sepal** elliptic-oblong, obtuse, up to 2.5 cm long, 1.4 cm wide; **lateral sepals** obliquely broadly ovate, obtuse, slightly shorter and broader than the dorsal sepal. **Petals** obovate or elliptic-obovate, obtuse, slightly shorter and much narrower that the sepals. **Lip** rigidly attached to the column-foot, 3-lobed in apical part, shorter than the lateral sepals; side lobes erect, semicircular, obtuse; mid-lobe recurved, obovate, trilobed at apex. **Column** 0.8–1 cm long, with a long curved foot.

DISTRIBUTION Peru and E. Ecuador; on

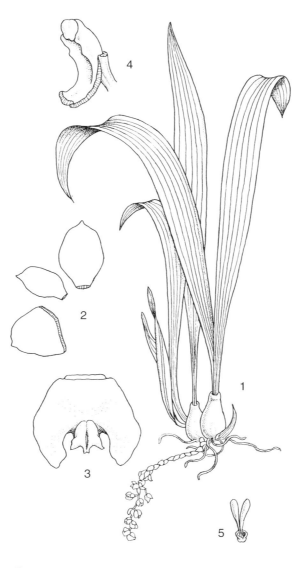

Lycomormium squalidum
1 – Habit ($\times \frac{1}{10}$)
2 – Dorsal sepal, petal and lateral sepal ($\times \frac{1}{2}$)
3 – Lip, flattened ($\times 1$)
4 – Column ($\times \frac{3}{4}$)
5 – Pollinarium ($\times 1\frac{1}{2}$)

steep embankments in wet montane forest, 900–1500 m.

HISTORY Originally collected by Poeppig near Cuchero and Pampayaco in Peru and described as *Anguloa squalida* by Poeppig and Endlicher in 1836 in their *Genera ac Species Plantarum* (p. 43), and transferred to *Lycomormium* as the type species by H.G. Reichenbach in the journal *Botanische Zeitung* (p. 833) in 1852.

SYNONYMS *Anguloa squalida* Poepp. & Endl.; *Peristeria fuscata* Lindl.; *Lycomormium elatum* C. Schweinf.

Macodes Lindl.

Subfamily Spiranthoideae
Tribe Cranichideae
Subtribe Goodyerinae

Stems erect, rather fleshy, arising from a short rhizome. **Leaves** several, rather fleshy, often beautifully marked with white or coloured veins. **Inflorescence** erect, terminal, glandular, pubescent, racemose, few- to many-flowered; bracts small, often coloured pink or brown. **Flowers** rather small, with lip uppermost (non-resupinate), pubescent, not strikingly coloured, asymmetric due to twisting of column and lip. **Lateral sepals** enclosing base of lip. **Petals** much narrower than sepals. **Lip** 3-lobed, with saccate base containing two small glands; side lobes short, rounded; mid-lobe narrow at base, spreading above. **Column** short, twisted, with 2 thin parallel wings in front, the wings descending into base of lip; rostellum bifid; stigma large, entire; anther acute; pollinia 2, sectile, attached by long caudicles to a large viscidium.

DISTRIBUTION A small genus of about nine species distributed from Malaya, Java and Sulawesi across to New Guinea, the Solomon Islands and Vanuatu.

DERIVATION OF NAME From the Greek *mak(r)os* (long), in allusion to the elongated mid-lobe of the lip.

TAXONOMY This genus was established by John Lindley in 1840 in his *Genera and Species of Orchidaceous Plants* (p. 496) based on *Neottia petola* Blume. It is allied to *Ludisia* and *Goodyera* with small flowers similar to the former in having the lip and column twisted, but in *Macodes* the lip is uppermost in the flower.

TYPE SPECIES *Neottia petola* Blume [= *Macodes petola* (Blume) Lindl.]

CULTIVATION As for *Goodyera* and *Spiranthes*.

Macodes petola (Blume) **Lindl.** [Colour Plate]

A showy terrestrial herb. **Leaves** few, mostly basal and close together, ovate, shortly pointed, up to 6.5 cm long, 4.2 cm broad, very dark green with 5 longitudinal golden veins and groups of small golden cross veins; petiole narrow, 1–25 cm long. **Inflorescence** erect, up to 25 cm long, up to 15-flowered; peduncle pubescent, bearing 2 sterile bracts; fertile bracts shorter than the ovary, up to 0.8 cm long. **Flowers** reddish-brown with a white lip. **Dorsal sepal** ovate, subacute about 5–6 cm long; **lateral sepals** spreading, ovate-orbicular, obtuse, 0.6 cm long, 0.4 cm broad. **Petals** narrowly lanceolate, acuminate, 0.3 cm long. **Lip** uppermost, asymmetric, 3-lobed, saccate at base, 0.5 cm long, 0.3 cm broad, with 2 glands in the saccate base; mid-lobe shortly narrowly clawed, transversely oblong above. **Column** short, twisted, with 2 thin parallel wings in front, descending downwards into the spur; rostellum cleft.

DISTRIBUTION Sumatra and Malaya, east to the Philippines.

HISTORY Originally described as *Neottia petola* by C.L. Blume in 1825 in his *Bijdragen* (p. 407, t. 2) based on a Rumphius name 'Folium petolatum' published in the pre-Linnaean *Herbarium Amboinensis* (1750). John Lindley transferred it in 1840 to *Macodes* in his *Genera and Species of Orchidaceous Plants* (p. 496).

SYNONYM *Neottia petola* Blume

Macradenia R. Br.
Subfamily Epidendroideae
Tribe Oncidieae

Small epiphytic plants with small, cylindrical, 1-leafed pseudobulbs. **Leaf** thickly fleshy or coriaceous. **Inflorescence** basal, erect or pendulous, racemose, laxly many-flowered. **Flowers** small to medium-sized. **Sepals** and **petals** free, ± spreading, subsimilar. **Lip** deeply 3-lobed; side lobes erect, embracing the column; mid-lobe short, spreading. **Column** wingless, lacking a foot, sulcate on lower surface; anther produced into a long, membranaceous appendage embracing the rostellum.

DISTRIBUTION Florida, the W. Indies and Mexico, south to northern S. America, about a dozen species.

DERIVATION OF NAME From the Greek *makros* (long) and *aden* (gland), alluding to the long anther appendage.

TAXONOMY Robert Brown described this genus in 1822 in the *Botanical Register* (t. 612).

Macradenia is allied to *Cryptarrhena* R. Br. but differs in having a 3-lobed rather than a 4-lobed lip which has suborbicular-ovate to semiorbicular side lobes.

TYPE SPECIES *M. lutescens* R. Br.

CULTURE Compost A. Temp. Winter min. 12–15°C. *Macradenia* species may be grown in small pots or mounted on fern-fibre or cork slabs. They should be given moderately shaded and humid conditions. Water must be carefully given throughout the year, more being required when the plants are actively growing.

Macradenia brassavolae Rchb.f.
[Colour Plate]

A medium-sized epiphytic plant. **Pseudobulbs** clustered, pyriform-cylindric, slightly compressed, sulcate, up to 5 cm long, 3 cm broad, 1-leafed at apex. **Leaf** narrowly oblong-oblanceolate, subacute, coriaceous, 18-22 cm long, 3.5–4.5 cm broad. **Inflorescence** pendu-

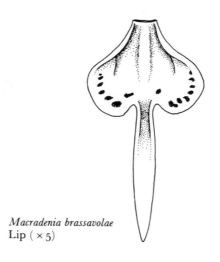

Macradenia brassavolae
Lip (× 5)

lous, racemose, densely many-flowered; axis maroon. **Flowers** showy; sepals and petals red, maroon-red with a yellow margin; lip white, marked with maroon spots; column white, yellow at apex. **Sepals** and **petals** subsimilar, lanceolate, acute or acuminate, spreading, 1.4–1.7 cm long, 0.3–0.5 cm broad. **Lip** fleshy and 3-lobed in basal half, 1.2 cm long, 0.6 cm broad; side lobes rounded, erect; mid-lobe recurved, ligulate, acute; disc with a central thickened ridge. **Column** clavate, 2-winged at the apex, apical margins erose, 0.6 cm long; wings spreading, obtriangular-subquadrate; rostellum long, porrect.

DISTRIBUTION Mexico, south to Colombia and Venezuela.

HISTORY Originally described by H.G. Reichenbach in 1852 in *Botanische Zeitung* (p. 734) from a plant collected in Guatemala.

SYNONYMS *Serrastylis modesta* Rolfe; *Macradenia modesta* (Rolfe) Rolfe

CLOSELY RELATED SPECIES *Macradenia multiflora* (Kraenzl.) Cogn. from Brazil is very closely allied to the more widespread *M. brassavolae*, differing mainly in its lip which has longer acute side lobes and a shorter mid-lobe.

Malaxis Sw.
Subfamily Epidendroideae
Tribe Malaxideae

Small, terrestrial or less commonly epiphytic herbs, caespitose or with a distinct rhizome. **Secondary stem** fleshy, basally extended into a jointed, small pseudobulb. **Leaves** 1 to several, membranaceous to fleshy, plicate, or conduplicate, ± petiolate and articulate to a tubular leaf-sheath. **Inflorescence** terminal, pedunculate, racemose to subumbellate, laxly to densely many-flowered. **Flowers** small to minute, non-

resupinate. **Sepals** free, subequal, spreading; lateral sepals often connate at the base. **Petals** mostly filiform. **Lip** free from column, sessile, entire or lobed, basally cordate or auriculate and enveloping the column-base. **Column** short, lacking a foot; pollinia 4, waxy, lacking a caudicle or viscidium; stigmas transverse, confluent under the rostellum.

DISTRIBUTION About 300 species, found almost throughout the world but most frequent in S.E. Asia and the adjacent islands.

DERIVATION OF NAME From the Greek *malaxis* (softening), referring to the soft texture of the leaves.

TAXONOMY The genus *Malaxis* was described in 1788 by O. Swartz in his *Nova General et Species Plantarum* (p. 119), and has most recently been revised as long ago as 1889 in the *Journal of the Linnean Society, Botany*. The New Guinea species have been divided into nine sections by Schlechter (1911) in *Fedde, Repertorium Specierum Novarum, Beihefte* (p. 111). Seidenfaden (1978) revised the 24 species from Thailand in *Dansk Botanisk Arkiv* (p. 42), recognising six sections.

Although allied to *Liparis*, *Malaxis* species are easily distinguished by their non-resupinate flowers in which the lip is uppermost. The lip is also auriculate at the base with the auricles almost encircling the short column. Most *Malaxis* species are small plants with rather dull flowers but some species warrant cultivation for their vegetative coloration such as *M. metallica* which has shiny deep purple leaves and stems.

TYPE SPECIES *M. spicata* Sw. is the lectotype chosen by Britton and Brown in 1913 in the *Illustrated Flora of the Northern United States and Canada*.

SYNONYM *Microstylis* Blume

CULTURE Compost C. Temp. Winter min. 15°C. While growing, *Malaxis* species require humid, shady conditions and should be well watered. When growth is complete, after flowering, pseudobulbous species lose their leaves and should be kept much drier. Other species should not become very dry.

Malaxis calophylla (Rchb.f.) O. Ktze
Pseudobulbs stout, short, erect, about 3- to 4-leaved. **Leaves** shortly petiolate, oblong-lanceolate, acute, 7-13 cm long, 3-4.8 cm broad, bronze with crisped-undulate green-spotted margins; petiole 2 cm long, sheathing below. **Inflorescence** 15-25 cm long, densely many-flowered; bracts narrow, linear-setaceous, 0.5 cm long. **Flowers** small, pale pink or pink and cream. **Dorsal sepal** oblong, obtuse, about 0.35 cm long; **lateral sepals** oblong, curved, obtuse, 0.25 cm long, 0.1 cm broad. **Petals** narrowly linear, obtusely acute, 0.35 cm long. **Lip** uppermost in flower, auricu-

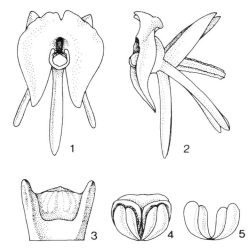

Malaxis calophylla
1 – Flower, front view ($\times 4\frac{1}{3}$)
2 – Flower, side view ($\times 4\frac{1}{3}$)
3 – Column—apex, from below ($\times 9$)
4 – Anther ($\times 18$)
5 – Pollinia ($\times 18$)

late, saggitate or subhastate, 0.3–0.7 cm long and broad, apex bidentate; auricles lanceolate, acute, pointing downwards.
DISTRIBUTION   Sikkim, Burma, S. Thailand, Cambodia, Malaya and Borneo.
HISTORY   Introduced into cultivation from Dutch India (probably Malaya), it first flowered in cultivation for Messrs Groenewegen who showed it at Amsterdam in 1877. Later, Messrs Veitch sent a plant to H.G. Reichenbach who described it in 1879 in the *Gardeners' Chronicle* (n.s. 12: p. 718) as *Microstylis calophylla*. O. Kuntze transferred it to the genus *Malaxis* in 1891 in *Revisio Genera Plantarum* (p. 673).
SYNONYM   *Microstylis calophylla* Rchb. f.; *M. scottii* Hook.f.

Masdevallia Ruiz & Pavon

Subfamily Epidendroideae
Tribe Epidendreae
Subtribe Pleurothallidinae

Small to medium-sized epiphytic or lithophytic herbs with creeping rhizomes. **Stem** erect, short, covered by scarious sheaths, 1-leafed at apex.   **Leaf** erect or suberect, fleshy, coriaceous, narrowly oblong, oblanceolate or linear. **Inflorescence** erect to spreading, 1- to several-flowered, racemose. **Flowers** ± showy, variously coloured. **Sepals** most obvious segments of flower, more or less connate to form a tube at the base; free parts spreading, terminating in short to long tails. **Petals** small, mostly linear-oblong, with a callus on lower part. **Lip** small, oblong to obovate, entire or 3-lobed, straight or recurved, sessile or shortly clawed. **Column** erect or arcuate, ± toothed at apex; foot short, forming with the base of the lateral sepals a short mentum; pollinia, 2, waxy.
DISTRIBUTION   A large genus of about 340 species widely distributed from Mexico south through tropical S. America but diversifying particularly in the Andes from Peru to Venezuela.
DERIVATION OF NAME   Dr Jose Masdevall was an eighteenth-century Spanish physician and botanist.
TAXONOMY   Named by H. Ruiz and J. Pavon in 1794 in their *Prodromus Florae Peruvianae et Chilensis* (p. 112). *Masdevallia* is allied to *Pleurothallis*, differing mainly in having larger, showier flowers and in having the sepals united at the base into a more or less narrow campanulate tube. Some of the smaller flowered species of *Masdevallia* such as *M. allenii* L.O. Williams are very close to *Pleurothallis* and could possibly be considered in that genus.

Some of the species of *Masdevallia* are extremely variable in sepal size, shape and colour. Much of this may be due to the continued growth of the sepals and sepal tails after anthesis.

The early monographs of the genus by Miss Florence Woolward in 1898 and F. Kraenzlin in *Fedde, Repertorium Specierum Novarum, Beihefte* in 1925 are now out-of-date. The former is a beautiful work the original of which is virtually unobtainable.

Recently, a great deal of taxonomic work has been published on this genus by H. Sweet (*Botanical Museum Leaflets of Harvard University*), C. Luer (*Selbyana* etc.) and L. Braas (*Orchid Review* and *Die Orchidee*). The major contribution of their combined researches has been to define more strictly the generic limits of *Masdevallia* and to describe several new genera such as *Dracula*, *Dryadella*, *Andreetaea* and *Trisetella* for aberrant species previously placed in that genus. Luer's work on the genus is now approaching completion. In the second part of *Icones Pleurothallidinarum* in 1986 he has revised the infrageneric treatment of the genus, recognising five subgenera, two of which are further subdivided into 17 sections. Nearly half of the species have so far been monographed by Luer in his and Koeniger's admirable *Thesaurus Masdevalliarum* (1983 onwards), the 15th part of which has recently been published.
TYPE SPECIES   *M. uniflora* Ruiz & Pavon
CULTURE   Compost A. Temp. Winter min. 10–12°C. As for   *Pleurothallis* and related genera. Most *Masdevallia* species grow well in pots. All species require moist shady conditions, with water carefully supplied throughout the year.

Masdevallia barlaeana Rchb.f. [Colour Plate]

A dwarf, caespitose plant with a very short stem. **Leaves** elliptic-lanceolate, petiolate, up to 12 cm long, 2.5 cm broad, obtuse or acute. **Inflorescence** slender, erect, 1-flowered, up to 20 cm long, **Flowers** with a narrow, 1.6 cm long perianth-tube, slightly bent and keeled, coral-red; dorsal sepal orange-red with marginal and median red lines; lateral sepals carmine shaded with scarlet and with 3 sunken crimson lines; lip white with a purple apical spot. **Dorsal sepal** free part small, subquadrate to ovate-triangular, with a red filiform apex, 2.5–3.8 cm long; **lateral sepals** elliptic-oblong, connate in basal two-thirds; apices long, filiform, crossing over, 1.4 cm long. **Petals**   minute, oblong-linear, tridentate at apex, keeled, 0.6 cm long. **Lip** minute, oblong, 0.6 cm long, longitudinally bicarinate in middle, apex subacute, recurved.
DISTRIBUTION   Peru;   on   rocks   2200–2500 m.
HISTORY   Discovered by Walter Davis, one of Veitch's collectors, near Cuzco in the Peruvian Andes in 1875. H.G. Reichenbach named it after Señor J.B. Barla, the Brazilian consul at Nice and an orchid enthusiast, in 1876 in the *Gardeners' Chronicle* (n.s. 5: p. 170).
CLOSELY RELATED SPECIES   Allied to *Masdevallia amabilis* Rchb.f. & Warsc. but differs in having more divergent lateral sepals with a broader, shorter sinus between them and by the crossing tails of the lateral sepals.

Masdevallia caloptera Rchb.f. [Colour Plate]

A dwarf epiphytic plant. **Leaves** suberect, oblong-ovate, petiole, keeled on reverse, 7.5 cm long, 1.8 cm broad, minutely tridenticulate at apex. **Inflorescence** erect, 3- to several-flowered; peduncle slender, terete, pale green, 10–12.5 cm long; bracts minute, apiculate. **Flowers** small; sepals white, streaked with crimson, tails orange-yellow; petals white with prominent anterior crimson ridge; lip yellow-spotted and streaked with crimson; column pale green with crimson on apex side margins and foot; perianth-tube narrow, 0.8 cm long, with a pouch on low side of base. **Dorsal sepal** ovate-triangular, cucullate, keeled on reverse; tail erect, slender, 1.3 cm long; **lateral sepals** oblong, margins recurved; tails decurved, spreading, 1.3 cm long. **Petals** oblong-obovate, 0.6 cm long, apical margins denticulate. **Lip** obscurely 3-lobed; side lobes oblong; mid-lobe obovate-orbicular, apiculate.
DISTRIBUTION   N. Peru and S. Ecuador; 1800–2000 m altitude in dense, moist woods.
HISTORY   Discovered in N. Peru by B. Roezl and described by H.G. Reichenbach in 1874 in the *Gardeners' Chronicle* (n.s. 1: p. 338 & n.s. 2: p. 322).
SYNONYM   *Masdevallia biflora* Regel

CLOSELY RELATED SPECIES A very variable species allied to *Masdevallia polysticta* Rchb.f. and *M. melanopus* Rchb.f. with which it often grows in the wild.

Masdevallia calura Rchb.f.

An epiphytic plant. **Leaves** oblanceolate, coriaceous, petiolate, 7.5 cm long. **Inflorescence** 7.5 cm long, 1-flowered. **Flowers** deep chocolate-red with a blackish hue; sepal apices orange-yellow; petals rich crimson with a white apex; lip deep crimson; column white; perianth-tube cylindric, bent, 1.5 cm long. **Dorsal sepal** triangular; apex filiform, 3.5–5 cm long; **lateral sepals** connate for basal 2 cm, ovate-oblong, reflexed, minutely papillose on inner surface; sinus between tails triangular; apices filiform, parallel. **Petals** ovate, triangular to apex with a small angle below, 0.8 cm long. **Lip** pandurate, fleshy, 2-lobed at base, bicarinate, apex rounded and deflexed.

DISTRIBUTION Costa Rica.

HISTORY Discovered by Consul Lehmann in 1882 on the western slopes of the volcano Irazu in Costa Rica. He sent plants to Messrs Sander & Co. and it was described by H.G. Reichenbach in 1883 in the *Gardeners' Chronicle* (n.s. 20: p. 230). The specific epithet refers to the 'beautiful tail' of each sepal.

CLOSELY RELATED SPECIES *M. calura* is similar to *M. reichenbachiana* but is distinguished by its flower colour.

Masdevallia caudata Lindl. [Colour Plate]

A tufted epiphytic plant. **Leaves** oblanceolate, suberect, coriaceous, petiolate, rounded at apex, up to 12 cm long, 3 cm broad. **Inflorescence** spreading-suberect or horizontal, as long as or shorter than the leaves, 1-flowered; peduncle terete, 4–10 cm long. **Flowers** campanulate, variable in colour; dorsal sepal white, yellow or yellow-green with darker nerves and purple spotting in apical half; lateral sepals rose-coloured or white, tails light green; petals white; lip white, spotted purple; column white, spotted purple on margins; perianth-tube broad with a saccate pouch on lower side. **Dorsal sepal** concave, lamina ovate-elliptic, 2.3 cm long, 2 cm broad, abruptly narrowing into tail; tail slender, up to 6.5 cm long; **lateral sepals** rounded-ovate with a basal saccate projection, 1.7 cm long, 1.5 cm broad, abruptly contracted at apex into long slender tails; tails deflexed, slender, 5–6.5 cm long. **Petals** oblong, with a flap-like extension on basal part, obliquely toothed at apex, 0.5 cm long. **Lip** oblong, recurved in apical half, 0.6 cm long, 0.4 cm broad, with 2 fleshy thickenings at base extending as ridges on to centre of lip and a small raised mound near the apex. **Column** 0.7 cm long; foot arcuate, as long as column.

DISTRIBUTION Venezuela, Colombia, Ecuador and Peru; in cloud forest at high altitude, 2000–2500 m.

HISTORY First collected by Justin Goudot near San Fortunato in Colombia in 1833 and described by John Lindley in his *Genera and Species of Orchidaceous Plants* (p. 193) in the same year.

SYNONYMS *Masdevallia shuttleworthii* Rchb.f.; *M. klabochorum* Rchb.f.

CLOSELY RELATED SPECIES See *M. estradae*.

Masdevallia civilis Rchb.f. & Warsc.

A tufted epiphytic, lithophytic or terrestrial plant. **Stem** short. **Leaves** oblanceolate, very shortly petiolate, suberect, coriaceous, 10–23 cm long, 1–1.8 cm broad, rounded at apex. **Inflorescence** 1-flowered; peduncle green, up to 7.6 cm long. **Flower** at right-angles to peduncle; sepals pale yellow-brown or green-brown, spotted heavily with maroon; petals white with a central purple stripe; lip maroon, ± with a central creamy stripe along groove; column yellow-brown, with purple line along margin; perianth-tube broad, short. **Sepals** ovate-lanceolate, acuminate, 2.4 cm long; tails short, tapering, spreading only slightly; lateral sepals united for basal 0.7 cm. **Petals** narrowly elliptic-oblanceolate, acute, with a fleshy ridge on one side, 0.8 cm long, 0.25 cm broad. **Lip** fleshy, narrowly oblong-elliptic, sulcate almost to apex which is papillose, 1.1–1.5 cm long, 0.5 cm broad. **Column** 0.6 cm long.

DISTRIBUTION Colombia, Peru, Ecuador and Venezuela; in high altitude cloud forests up to 2500 m.

HISTORY Originally discovered by J. Warscewicz on the eastern slopes of the Peruvian Andes and described by Warscewicz and H.G. Reichenbach in *Bonplandia* (p. 115) in 1854.

It is distinctive in possessing a large lip for the genus.

SYNONYMS *Masdevallia leontoglossa* Rchb.f.; *M. aequiloba* Regel; *M. ellipes* Rchb.f.; *M. macroglossa* Rchb.f.; *M. porcellipes* Rchb.f.; *M. haematosticta* Rchb.f.; *M. fragrans* Woolward; *M. sulphurea* Kraenzl.

Masdevallia coccinea Linden ex Lindl. [Colour Plate]

A plant forming large tufts. **Stem** short, up to 6 cm long, concealed by sheaths. **Leaves** oblong-lanceolate to spathulate, petiolate, 15–23 cm long, 2–3.4 cm broad, rounded and minutely tridentate at apex. **Inflorescence** slender, up to 40 cm long, 1-flowered at apex, 3- to 4-noded, with a spotted bract at each node. **Flowers** large, showy, variable in size and colour, scarlet, magenta or magenta-purple to yellow or white; perianth-tube cylindric-campanulate, curved, 1–1.8 cm long. **Dorsal**

sepal narrowly triangular-lanceolate or linear, 3–6 cm long, including the slender recurved tail; **lateral sepals** connate in basal third, free parts deflexed, incurved, obliquely oblong-ovate, 4.5–6 cm long, 2.2–2.6 cm broad, with short tails at apices. **Petals** very small, linear-oblong, retuse or 2-lobed at apex, keeled close to anterior margin and auricled at base. **Lip** oblong or linguiform, bicarinate, cordate at base, rounded at the apex, 0.6–1 cm long.

DISTRIBUTION Colombia and Peru; 2400–2800 m altitude.

HISTORY Jean Linden discovered this beautiful plant on the southern slopes of the Andes near Pamplona in Colombia in 1842 and it was described from dried material by John Lindley in *Orchidaceae Lindenianae* (p. 5, no. 26) in 1846. Subsequently, it was rediscovered and introduced into cultivation by Gustav Wallis who sent living plants to Linden's nursery in Ghent, Belgium.

Of more value in cultivation than the typical form, is var. *harryana* which was introduced in 1871 by J. Chesterton from near Sugamosa in the Cordillera Oriental of the Andes. This variety exhibits a broader range of colour (from purple to yellow and white) than the typical form, and can be further distinguished by its lateral sepals which have broadly ovate-falcate blades terminating in acuminate tips which turn towards each other.

Two of the various flower colours of *M. coccinea* are shown in the colour plates.

SYNONYMS *Masdevallia lindenii* André; *M. harryana* Rchb.f.

CLOSELY RELATED SPECIES For many years in the nineteenth century *M. coccinea* was confused with both *M. militaris* and *M. ignea* Rchb.f., the former error arising from a misidentification by Lindley.

Masdevallia coriacea Lindl. [Colour Plate]

A small tufted, epiphytic or lithophytic plant. **Leaves** linear-oblanceolate, erect, coriaceous, keeled beneath, 12.5–18 cm long. **Inflorescence** up to 18 cm long, 1-flowered at apex; peduncle pale green, spotted dull purple. **Flowers** medium-sized with a pale-yellow perianth-tube and dorsal sepal, spotted purple along the veins; lateral sepals yellowish; petals white with a purple mid-lobe; lip greenish-yellow with a purple mid-line and marginal spots; perianth-tube broadly cylindrical; 1.3 cm long. **Dorsal sepal** triangular, keeled above, 1–3 cm long, with a short broad tail, 1.2–2.5 cm long; **lateral sepals** oblong, with acuminate apices, 1.2–2.5 cm long. **Petals** oblong, 1.2 cm long. **Lip** 1.2 cm long, linguiform, reflexed, pubescent above.

DISTRIBUTION Colombia; 2200–2800 m altitude.

HISTORY Th. Hartweg discovered this plant in 1842 in the Cordillera Oriental of Colombia near Bogotá and his herbarium specimens were described by John Lindley in 1845 in the *Annals and Magazine of Natural History* (p. 257). The specific epithet refers to the leathery leaves.

SYNONYM *Masdevallia bruchmuelleri* Hort.

Masdevallia estradae Rchb.f.

A small epiphytic plant. **Leaves** obovate, suberect, coriaceous, shortly petiolate, obtuse and minutely tridenticulate at the apex, 5–7.5 cm long, 3 cm broad. **Inflorescence** erect, 1-flowered; peduncle terete, slender, 7.5–10 cm long; bract oblong-ovate, acuminate, 1.2 cm long. **Flowers** with widely spreading segments; dorsal sepal rich magenta with yellow-orange margins and tail; lateral sepals magenta on basal half, white above, tails orange-yellow; perianth-tube short, shallow, 0.8 cm long; column white, margins purple-spotted, apex and foot purple. **Dorsal sepal** free part obovate, cucullate, 1.4 cm long; **lateral sepals** oblong, spreading, 1.4 cm long. **Petals** narrowly oblong, apiculate, 0.8 cm long, keeled on anterior margin, keel terminates below in a curved auricle. **Lip** oblong, apiculate, fleshy and sulcate at base, 0.8 cm long. **Column** 0.8 cm long, apex dentate.

DISTRIBUTION Colombia; in mist forest 2000–2500 m altitude.

HISTORY First introduced into cultivation by Gustav Wallis in Colombia who sent dried specimens of plants found in the garden of Señora Estrada to H.G. Reichenbach. It was first discovered as a wild plant in Antioquia by the Belgian collector, C. Patin, in 1873. Plants were purchased from him by B.S. Williams of Holloway, London, who flowered it the following year when Reichenbach also described it in the *Gardeners' Chronicle* (n.s. 2: p. 435).

SYNONYM *Masdevallia ludibunda* Rchb.f.

CLOSELY RELATED SPECIES See *M. xanthina*. It is also allied to *M. caudata* but has quite distinctively coloured flowers and a deeply concave, rather than oblong-elliptic dorsal sepal.

Masdevallia floribunda Lindl.

A small, tufted plant, often very floriferous. **Leaves** oblong-lanceolate, petiolate, 7.5–10 cm long. **Inflorescences** decumbent, numerous, 1-flowered, longer than the leaves. **Flowers** pale yellow or buff-yellow, spotted brown-purple, tails reddish; petals white; lip with a red-brown blotch at apex; perianth-tube cylindrical. **Dorsal sepal** free part very short, triangular, 0.6–1.1 cm long, 0.4 cm broad; tail long, slender and recurved, 1.2 cm long; **lateral sepals** free part oblong, 1–1.6 cm long, 1–1.2 cm broad;

tails long, slender and recurved, 0.6 cm long. **Petals** linear-oblong, dentate at apex, 0.4–0.5 cm long, 0.1–0.2 cm broad. **Lip** cordate at base, constricted below centre, 0.5 cm long, 0.2 cm broad.

DISTRIBUTION Mexico; 900–1300 m altitude.

HISTORY The first Mexican *Masdevallia* known to science. Henri Galeotti, the French botanist, discovered it near Veracruz in 1840 and he sent living plants to Europe which survived for a few years. One of these cultivated by Mr Rodgers of Sevenoaks in Kent, England, was sent to John Lindley who described it in 1843 in the *Botanical Register* (misc. 72).

SYNONYMS *Masdevallia galeottiana* A. Rich. & Galleotti; *M. myriostigma* C. Morr.

Masdevallia infracta Lindl. [Colour Plate]

A medium-sized, tufted, epiphytic plant, up to 21 cm high. **Stem** short. **Leaves** erect, oblanceolate-oblong to oblong-obovate, petiolate, coriaceous, 8–12.7 cm long, up to 2 cm broad, subobtuse and minutely tridentate at apex, glossy green. **Inflorescence** erect, up to 25 cm long, 1- to 5-flowered; peduncle 2- or 3-winged. **Flowers** medium-sized, nodding, campanulate, variable in colour; purplish-pink to dull red with a yellow flush outside, purple to wine-red within; tails pale yellow; petals white; lip apex spotted red-brown; perianth-tube broadly campanulate, bent, yellow-white. **Dorsal sepal** free part rotund-triangular, concave; tail filiform, 2–3.7 cm long; **lateral sepals** oblong-rotund, connate for lower half, keeled; tails spreading, 3.8–5 cm long. **Petals** linear-oblong, dentate or oblique at apex, 0.8 cm long. **Lip** oblong or slightly pandurate, reflexed at apex, bicarinate, 0.6–0.9 cm long, apiculate.

DISTRIBUTION Brazil and Peru; montane forest up to 2000 m.

HISTORY Another of the many orchid species discovered by the Frenchman M.E. Descourtilz near Rio de Janeiro and later collected by George Gardner in 1837 in the Organ Mts. John Lindley described it in 1831 in his *Genera and Species of Orchidaceous Plants* (p. 193).

SYNONYMS *Masdevallia longicaudata* Lemaire; *M. albida* Pinel

Masdevallia laucheana Bohnhof
[Colour Plate]

A small epiphytic plant. **Leaves** oblanceolate-obovate, suberect, shortly petiolate, 10–12.5 cm long, 2.5 cm broad, bright green. **Inflorescence** erect, 1-flowered, shorter than the leaves; peduncle slender, terete, 5 cm long, pale green; bract sheathing, pale green. **Flowers** small, segments spreading in apical two-thirds; sepals white with a central purple nerve, tails

orange; petals white with green apices; lip pale yellow below, orange on margins above, with apical crimson spot; column white with purple margins; perianth-tube slightly gibbous, 0.9 cm long. **Dorsal sepal** ovate, with a slender erect, somewhat recurved tail 2.5 cm long; **lateral sepals** spreading, obliquely ovate-triangular; tails slightly incurved or outcurved towards apex, slender. **Petals** oblanceolate, 0.6 cm long, with 2 thickened ridges on surface, acuminate. **Lip** linear-oblong, 2-lobed at base, apex papillose, 2-ridged above, 1 cm long. **Column** apex denticulate.

DISTRIBUTION Costa Rica; 800–1000 m altitude.

HISTORY Described from a plant of unknown provenance by Bohnhof in 1892 in *Gartenflora* (p. 184). The specific epithet was given in honour of Herr Lauche of Eisgrub in Austria.

Masdevallia macrura Rchb.f. [Colour Plate]

A robust, lithophytic plant. **Stem** up to 15 cm long. **Leaves** oblong-elliptic, coriaceous, 25–30 cm long, 6–7.5 cm broad. **Inflorescence** up to 30 cm long, 1-flowered; bract, membranous, keeled, white, **Flowers** large, whitish at base, deep rich or dull tawny-yellow above, with blackish-purple warts within; sepals orange-yellow; lip tawny-yellow, spotted purple below; column yellow, spotted crimson on foot; perianth-tube 1.3 cm long, cylindrical, short, broad, ribbed. **Dorsal sepal** free part lanceolate, acuminate, tapering, 10–15 cm long; tail erect; **lateral sepals** up to 12.5 cm long, connate for basal 2.5 cm or so, tapering into long, dependent tails. **Petals** oblong-curved, anterior margin much thickened, 1 cm long. **Lip** oblong, fleshy, papillose, bicarinate, reflexed at apex, 0.8 cm long. **Column** 0.8 cm long.

DISTRIBUTION Colombia; 2300–2600 m altitude.

HISTORY B. Roezl discovered this large-flowered species in 1871 near Sonsón in Colombia and H.G. Reichenbach described it in 1874 in the *Gardeners' Chronicle* (n.s. 1: p. 240). He named it for the long tails to its sepals.

CLOSELY RELATED SPECIES *M. peristeria*.

Masdevallia maculata Klotzsch & Karst.
[Colour Plate]

A large tufted plant. **Stem** very short. **Leaves** oblanceolate to narrowly spathulate, coriaceous, petiolate, 10–18 cm long, up to 2.9 cm broad, acute or subacute and minutely tridentate at apex. **Inflorescence** up to 25 cm long, several-flowered; peduncle sharply 2- to 4-angled. **Flowers** large, showy; segments spreading, yellow or yellow-green, shaded and spotted red; tails yellow or orange; petals white; lip dull purple or pale pink with dark red spotting; perianth-tube short with a prominent rib above, orange-yellow or yellow. **Dorsal sepal** ovate-triangular, with a longer slender tail, altogether 6.5–8 cm long; **lateral sepals** connate to above the middle, forming a broadly ovate lamina, with 2 parallel, slender, filiform tails. **Petals** very small, oblong-ligulate, oblique and apiculate at apex. **Lip** oblong, papillose and denticulate at acute apex, 0.9 cm long. **Column** 0.5 cm long.

DISTRIBUTION Peru, Venezuela and Colombia; montane forest up to 2000 m.

HISTORY Introduced into cultivation by H. Wagener who discovered it near Caracas in Venezuela and sent it to the Berlin Botanic Garden where it first flowered in 1847. O. Klotzsch and Karsten described it in the same year in F. Otto and A. Dietrich's *Allgemeine Gartenzeitung* (p. 330).

CLOSELY RELATED SPECIES *Masdevallia bicolor* Poepp. & Endl. is very closely related to *M. maculata* but it is a smaller plant altogether, barely reaching 10 cm in height.

Masdevallia mejiana Garay [Colour Plate]

A tufted epiphytic plant, up to 12 cm high. **Leaves** suberect, fleshy-coriaceous, oblong-lanceolate, up to 12 cm long, 1.5 cm broad, obtuse. **Inflorescence** erect or ascending, up to 10 cm long, 1- or 2-flowered; peduncle terete; bracts up to 7 cm long. **Flowers** white, spotted with minute pink dots, tails yellow or orange; petals white; perianth-tube campanulate, 2.4 cm long. **Dorsal sepal** triangular-ovate; tail long, suberect, 3–3.8 cm long; **lateral sepals** broadly ovate, connate for basal 1.5 cm, spreading above; tails deflexed, 3–3.5 cm long, spreading. **Petals** narrowly oblong, tridenticulate at apex, keeled on outer surface, 0.7 cm long, 0.2 cm broad. **Lip** fleshy, shortly clawed, oblong-quadrate, rounded at base, truncate at apex, 0.6 cm long, 0.3 cm broad; disc glabrous. DISTRIBUTION Colombia; 800 m altitude, on western slope of the central Cordillera. HISTORY Originally collected by Don Alvaro Mejia in the department of Antioquia in Colombia and named after him by Dr Leslie Garay in 1970 in the Colombian orchid journal *Orquideologia* (p. 17).

Masdevallia mendozae Luer [Colour Plate]

A small epiphyte with clustered erect stems, 1–2 cm long. **Leaf** erect to spreading, oblanceolate, obtuse, 3–8 cm long, 1–1.5 cm wide; petiole 1–2 cm long. **Inflorescence** as long as the leaf or slightly longer, 1-flowered, suberect to arcuate-spreading; peduncle slender, 3–6 cm long; bract papery, tubular, acute, 5–6 mm long. **Flower** showy, tubular, bright orange; pedicel and ovary 5–11 mm long. **Sepals** united to form a slender somewhat arching tube 2.7–3.1 cm long, the free parts broadly ovate, 5–7 mm long, with short spreading 2–5 mm long tails. **Petals** obliquely oblong, truncate and obscurely tridentate at the apex, slightly dilated below on lower margin, 5–6 mm long, 1.5–1.8 mm wide. **Lip** fleshy, oblong, obscurely shortly apiculate at the truncate apex, 7–8 mm long, 3 mm wide; callus of 2 obscure linear ridges. **Column** slender, 5–6 mm long with a short foot.

DISTRIBUTION A rare species in S. Ecuador; in cloud forest 2000–2300 m altitude.

HISTORY Despite its colourful flowers this pretty orchid was only discovered in 1979 when Hartman Mendoza, after whom it is named, found it in a remote region at Loma de Aguila. It has subsequently been collected in some quantity and is found in many collections nowadays. It was described in 1983 by Carlyle Luer in the journal *Phytologia* (p. 382).

Masdevallia militaris Rchb.f. [Colour Plate]

A large, tufted, lithophytic plant. **Leaves** oblong-lanceolate, coriaceous, suberect, keeled beneath, 20–23 cm long, 3.5 cm broad, minutely tridentate at apex. **Inflorescence** longer than the leaves, 1-flowered; peduncle 30–38 cm long, terete, green, streaked with crimson; bract ovate, apiculate, yellow-green. **Flowers** showy, almost nodding; sepals varying shades of orange and scarlet, veins and margins cinnabar-red; column white, sides lined with purple; perianth-tube curved, cylindric, 2 cm long. **Dorsal sepal** free part triangular, 1 cm long, tapering into a deflexed slender tail; tail 3–4 cm long; **lateral sepals** united for 2.5 cm, elliptic-ovate, margin reflexed, ending in short blunt tails. **Petals** linear-oblong, 0.8 cm long, keeled near anterior margin, prolonged below into a backcurved tooth, acute at apex. **Lip** oblong, fleshy, sulcate, bicarinate, margins crenate, 0.8 cm long, apex recurved, apiculate. **Column** 0.8–1 cm long, apex denticulate.

DISTRIBUTION Colombia; at high altitudes as a lithophyte in the mist zone.

HISTORY Discovered by J. Warscewicz in 1849 near Ocaña in the mountains of Santander in Colombia and H.G. Reichenbach described it from a plant of Warscewicz's importation in 1854 in *Bonplandia* (pp. 115 & 283). It is a very variable species, particularly in flower colour.

CLOSELY RELATED SPECIES See *M. coccinea*.

Masdevallia nidifica Rchb.f.

A dwarf epiphytic species. **Leaves** ovate-oblong or spathulate, petiolate, suberect, coriaceous, 3.7–5 cm long, 1 cm broad. **Inflorescence** as long as the leaves, 1-flowered; peduncle slender, terete, 3–7 cm long, dull greenish-crimson; bract membranous, sheathing, apiculate, 0.6 cm long. **Flowers** small, variable in size and colour; sepals whitish or pale yellow, somewhat transparent, spotted and striped with crimson, minutely pubescent within; dorsal sepal tail crimson, lateral sepal tails yellow; petals creamy with a central purple streak; lip yellow with 3 central longitudinal purple stripes; column pink, marked with crimson; perianth-tube gibbous below, 0.9 cm long. **Dorsal sepal** rotundate, cucullate, minutely pubescent within; tail suberect, slender, 1.8 cm long. **Petals** oblong, keeled on anterior margin, 0.3 cm long. **Lip** pandurate-oblong, curved, 0.4 cm long. **Column** 0.4 cm long.

DISTRIBUTION Costa Rica, Colombia, Ecuador and Peru; 500–2000 m altitude.

HISTORY Discovered by Consul Lehmann in 1877 in the Andes near Quito in Ecuador and described from dried specimens of his collection by H.G. Reichenbach in 1878 in *Otia Botanica Hamburgensia* (p. 18).

Masdevallia peristeria Rchb.f.

An epiphytic plant. **Leaves** linear-lanceolate, suberect, thick, fleshy, obscurely petiolate, 12.5 cm long, 2 cm broad. **Inflorescence** short, 1-flowered; peduncle arising from joint at base of petiole, terete, 6 cm long, pale green spotted with crimson. **Flowers** variable in colour, apex of segments spreading; sepals rich yellow or greenish-yellow, heavily spotted with crimson, greenish-yellow on reverse; petals pale greenish at apex; lip greenish-white, heavily mottled maroon-crimson; column pale green with white apex and margins; perianth-tube broad, with a distinct basal pouch on lower side, up to 2 cm long. **Sepals** ovate-triangular, tapering into fleshy tails; tails 3.3 cm long, triquetrous towards the apex. **Petals** oblanceolate, curved, fleshy, 1.2 cm long, minutely bidenticulate. **Lip** oblong-pandurate, 1.3 cm long, base fleshy and sulcate, bilamellate above, apex reflexed crenate and papillate. **Column** 1.2 cm long, apex denticulate.

DISTRIBUTION Colombia; 1600–2200 m altitude in open park-like woodland or by rivers, growing low down on the trunks of trees.

HISTORY First collected by Gustav Wallis in 1873 in Colombia. He sent plants to Messrs Veitch who supplied H.G. Reichenbach with material from which he described it in 1874 in the *Gardeners' Chronicle* (n.s. 1: p. 500).

CLOSELY RELATED SPECIES *M. peristeria* is allied to *Masdevallia leontoglossa* Rchb.f. but is distinctive in its erect inflorescences and yellower flowers with longer tails which are markedly deflexed.

It is also allied to *M. macrura* but has smaller leaves, shorter peduncles and yellower flowers with more spreading and shorter tails to the lateral sepals.

Masdevallia racemosa Lindl. [Colour Plate]

A terrestrial or rarely epiphytic plant with a long creeping rhizome. **Stems** ascending, given off from the rhizome at 0.5–3 cm intervals. **Leaves** oblong-ovate, petiolate, suberect, coriaceous, tridentate at apex, 10–12.5 cm long, 2 cm broad, dull greyish-green. **Inflorescence** erect or arcuate, with 2 to several flowers developing in succession; peduncle slender, terete, dull red-green. **Flowers** showy, orange-scarlet, with vermilion nerves and margins; petals pale yellow; lip ivory-white; column pale yellow above, pink below; perianth-tube narrow, straight, 1.3 cm long. **Dorsal sepal** free part ovate-triangular; tail short, suberect, 0.6 cm long; **lateral sepals** united for basal 2.5 cm, broadly cordate, apiculate. **Petals** ovate, shortly clawed, acute, 0.8 cm long. **Lip** narrowly oblong, bicarinate, 1 cm long, rounded at apex. **Column** 1 cm long.
DISTRIBUTION Colombia; 2900–4200 m altitude.
HISTORY *M. racemosa* was discovered by Th. Hartweg near Popayan in Colombia in 1845 and he sent dried specimens to John Lindley who named it in the *Annals and Magazine of Natural History* (p. 256) in the same year. The first living specimens reached Europe in 1887 when E. Shuttleworth and J. Carder succeeded in importing a small number into England.

Masdevallia reichenbachiana Endres

[Colour Plate]

An epiphytic plant, up to 20 cm high. **Leaves** suberect, oblanceolate, coriaceous, keeled below, 10–12.5 cm long, 2–2.5 cm broad, minutely tridentate at apex. **Inflorescence** erect, 1- to 3-flowered; peduncle terete, bright green, 15–18 cm long; bract ovate, apiculate, 1.2 cm long. **Flowers** spreading; sepals pale yellow or pale pink, lined with red within on dorsal sepal, rich dark red on outer surface, tails greenish-yellow or green; column white; perianth-tube slightly curved, broad, 2.5 cm long. **Dorsal sepal** free part triangular, 1.2 cm long, 3-nerved; tail slender recurved, 5 cm long; **lateral sepals** united for basal 3 cm, triangular-ovate, keeled behind; tails 3.5 cm long, pointing backwards. **Petals** small, oblong-ovate, truncate at apex, thickened on anterior margin, 0.8 cm long, apex denticulate. **Lip** oblong-pandurate, 0.6 cm long, with 2 short longitudinal keels, apex narrow and recurved. **Column** 0.8 cm long, apex denticulate.
DISTRIBUTION Costa Rica; growing in dense, damp forests at 1600–2200 m altitude in the central Cordillera between the Vulcan de Barba and the Pico Blanco.
HISTORY Discovered in 1873 in the mountains of Costa Rica by A.R. Endres and named by him in honour of H.G. Reichenbach in the *Gardeners' Chronicle* (n.s. 4: p. 257) in 1875.
SYNONYM *Masdevallia normanii* Hort.
CLOSELY RELATED SPECIES See *M. calura* and *M. rolfeana*.

Masdevallia rolfeana Kraenzl.

A small epiphytic plant. **Leaves** suberect, obovate-oblanceolate, thick, fleshy, keeled on reverse, 12.5 cm long, 2 cm broad, obtuse and tridenticulate at apex. **Inflorescence** shorter than the leaves, 1-flowered; penduncle erect, terete, slender, 7.5 cm long, bright green; bract ovate, apiculate, brownish, 1.2 cm long. **Flowers** somewhat campanulate; sepals rich purplish-crimson, apex crimson; column white; perianth-tube slender at base, broader above, 1.2 cm long. **Dorsal sepal** ovate, cucullate; tail slender, slightly deflexed in basal half, and reflexed above, 3.7 cm long; **lateral sepals** oblong-oval; tails up to 3.3 cm long. **Petals** oblong-oval, apiculate, 0.8 cm long. **Lip** oblong, apiculate, fleshy at base, 2-ridged above, 1 cm long, apex recurved. **Column** apex denticulate.
DISTRIBUTION Costa Rica; in the central Cordillera.
HISTORY Introduced into cultivation by F. Sander in 1891 and described the same year in the *Gardeners' Chronicle* (s. 3, 9: p. 488) by F. Kraenzlin who named it in honour of Robert Allen Rolfe of the Royal Botanic Garden, Kew, the founder of the *Orchid Review*.
CLOSELY RELATED SPECIES *M. rolfeana* is allied to *M. reichenbachiana* but differs in having an inflorescence which is shorter than the leaves, smaller darker flowers with only a small area of yellow in the throat and a shorter perianth-tube.

Masdevallia schlimii Linden ex Lindl.

[Colour Plate]

An epiphytic plant. **Leaves** suberect, fleshy, petiolate, obovate, or oblanceolate, obtuse or rounded apex, up to 17 cm long, 4.5 cm broad. **Inflorescence** erect, longer than the leaves, up to 6-flowered; peduncle terete, light green, up to 25 cm long; bracts grey or white, tubular. **Flowers** light greeny-yellow, heavily spotted maroon-red on lamina of sepals; tails light greeny-yellow; petals white; lip white, marked with short maroon transverse bars; column white with purple margins; perianth-tube broad, 0.5 cm long. **Sepals** ovate, with a long slender tail, ± at right-angles to lamina, filiform, 5–5.8 cm long, 0.8–0.9 cm broad; lateral sepals united for basal 1.5 cm. **Petals** falcate-oblong, acute, with a small fleshy knob at base, 0.6 cm long, 1.7 cm broad. **Lip** oblong, 0.6 cm long, 0.2 cm broad, subacute at apex, with 2 converging ridges towards apex. **Column** 0.5 cm long.
DISTRIBUTION Colombia and Venezuela; 1800–2500 m altitude.
HISTORY Discovered in 1843 by Louis Schlim as an epiphyte at Valle near Mérida in Venezuela and described by John Lindley in 1846 in his *Orchidaceae Lindenianae* (p. 5). The specific name was suggested by Jean Linden in honour of the plant's discoverer who was also his fellow traveller and half-brother. Living plants were first imported into Europe by Messrs Sander of St Albans, England, in 1883.

Masdevallia schroederiana Hort.

[Colour Plate]

A medium-sized, densely-tufted plant. **Leaves** oblanceolate, petiolate, minutely tridentate at apex, up to 15 cm long, 2.5 cm broad. **Inflorescence** erect, slightly longer than the leaf, 1-flowered; peduncle up to 21 cm long. **Flowers** large for plant; dorsal sepal rich orange-yellow with 2 dark spots; lateral sepals violet on outer sides, white on inner side; tails of all sepals orange-yellow; petals and lip pale pink, spotted with rose-purple; perianth-tube campanulate, 2 cm long, white, lined with violet. **Dorsal sepal** broadly ovate-triangular; tail erect, arching backwards, 5–7.5 cm long; **lateral sepals** much longer than dorsal sepal, united almost to apices of the laminae, 3 cm long, 1.5 cm broad; tails deflexed, 5 cm long or more. **Petals** oblong, fleshy, margins waved, 0.8 cm long. **Lip** oblong, fleshy at base, bicarinate in entre, apex recurved, 0.9 cm long. **Column** denticulate at apex.
DISTRIBUTION Peru.
HISTORY This species was named by F. Sander and was described in 1890 in the *Gardeners' Chronicle* (ser. 3, 8: p. 51). The origins of this plant are unknown other than that it was first introduced from Peru. It was first exhibited in 1890 by Baron Schroeder of Egham, Surrey, England, when it was awarded a First Class Certificate by the Royal Horticultural Society.
CLOSELY RELATED SPECIES Very closely related to *Masdevallia fulvescens* Rolfe if not conspecific. *M. fulvescens* was also imported in 1890 but from Colombia.

Masdevallia tovarensis Rchb.f.

[Colour Plate]

An epiphytic caespitose plant, up to 18 cm high. **Stem** very short. **Leaves** suberect, oblanceolate or oblong-elliptic, petiolate, coriaceous, obtuse, up to 14 cm long, 2 cm broad, minutely tridentate at apex. **Inflorescence** erect or suberect, 1- to 4-flowered at apex, up to 18 cm long; peduncle glabrous, triangular cross-section; bracts green, ovate, cucullate, apiculate, up to 1.5 cm long. **Flowers** showy, white; column purple, apex and base white; ovary green; perianth-tube short, subtriangular in cross-section, 0.6 cm long. **Dorsal sepal** free part lanceolate, long-acuminate, 4 cm long, 0.6 cm broad; tail erect; **lateral sepals** connate for over half their length, ovate, acuminate, 3.7 cm long, 1 cm broad; tails converging or crossing over. **Petals** small, narrowly oblong, acute, 0.6 cm long, 0.15 cm broad. **Lip** pandurate-oblong, 0.6 cm long 0.2 cm broad, apex recurved, papillose, acute, with 2 ± parallel ridges in middle. **Column** 0.4 cm long, subterete.

DISTRIBUTION   Venezuela.

HISTORY   Jean Linden discovered this beautiful species in 1842 near Tovar in Venezuela. H.G. Reichenbach described it in 1849 in *Linnaea* (p. 818) from specimens collected in the same locality in 1846 by J.W. Moritz. The first living plants seen in Europe were sent to Germany by H. Wagener from near Caracas several years later.

SYNONYM   *Masdevallia candida* Klotzsch & Karst.

Masdevallia triangularis Lindl.
[Colour Plate]

A tufted epiphytic plant. **Leaves** suberect, obovate or oblanceolate, long-petiolate, coriaceous, margins strongly recurved, up to 15 cm long, 3 cm broad, obtuse; petiole dark purple towards base. **Inflorescence** erect, 1-flowered; peduncle slender, up to 13 cm long. **Flowers** with spreading segments; sepals yellow-green, heavily spotted dark brown within, tails dark purple; petals and column white; lip white, flecked purple; perianth-tube broad. **Sepals** free part ovate, 2 cm long; tails slender, up to 4 cm long. **Petals** oblong, drawn out into a retrorse spur at base, apex tridentate, 0.6 cm long. **Lip** fleshy, narrowly flabellate, 3-lobed near apex, 0.6 cm long, 0.3 cm broad; side lobes obscure, truncate in front; mid-lobe reflexed, orbicular, with many purple glandular attachments at apex. **Column** 0.5 cm long.

DISTRIBUTION   Colombia and Venezuela; in mist forest, 1400–2300 m altitude.

HISTORY   Discovered in 1842 by Jean Linden near Bailadores in the province of Mérida in Venezuela and described by John Lindley in 1846 in *Orchidaceae Lindenianae* (p. 5). The first living plants were imported by Messrs Sander of St Albans, England in 1881.

It is easily recognised by its very characteristic lip.

Masdevallia trochilus Linden & André
Leaves narrowly elliptic-lanceolate, petiolate, 12.5–18 cm long. **Inflorescence** erect, 30 cm long, 1- or 2-flowered; scape stout, triangular in cross-section; bracts compressed. **Flowers** large, chestnut-brown or tawny with a yellowish perianth-tube which is short and cylindrical. **Dorsal sepal** 7.5–10 cm long, suborbicular, keeled outside with long diverging flexuose tails. **Petals** linear-oblong, acute or 3-toothed towards apex. **Lip** oblong, clawed, auriculate at base, apiculate, toothed towards apex.

DISTRIBUTION   Colombia and Ecuador.

HISTORY   Discovered by G. Wallis in 1873 near Antioquia in Colombia and later near Medellin by B. Roezl and C. Patin. J. Linden & E. André described it in the *Gardeners' Chronicle* (p. 711) in 1873 based on a plant sold by Stevens salesroom in London. They called it the 'hummingbird' *Masdevallia* and '*King of the Masdevallias*'.

Masdevallia trochilus is readily distinguished by its very large flowers in which the lateral sepals form a cucullate lamina very much larger than the dorsal sepal and in which the tails to the lateral sepals diverge markedly from the base.

SYNONYMS   *Masdevallia acrochordonia* Rchb.f.; *M. ephippium* Rchb.f.

Masdevallia tubulosa Lindl. [Colour Plate]
A tufted epiphytic plant. **Leaves** oblanceolate, petiolate, erect or suberect, coriaceous, up to 11 cm long, 1.3 cm broad, obtuse. **Inflorescence** erect, 1-flowered; peduncle terete, slender, pale green, 6–10 cm long. **Flowers** variable in size of segments; sepals pale cream or white, tails yellow-green; petals, lip and column white; perianth-tube long, slender, 1.2–2 cm long. **Sepals** linear-tapering, long-acuminate, 3–7 cm long; tails 2.5–6 cm long, tapering ± at right-angles to the lamina. **Petals** clawed, lamina oblong, 0.4–0.5 cm long, 0.2 cm broad. **Lip** narrowly oblong, thickened at base, obtuse at apex, 0.5 cm long 0.15 cm broad. **Column** straight, 0.4 cm long; foot obscure.

DISTRIBUTION   Colombia and Venezuela.

HISTORY   Another of Jean Linden's discoveries and described by John Lindley in his *Orchidaceae Lindenianae* (p. 4) in 1846.

Masdevallia veitchiana Rchb.f. [Colour Plate]
A larger, showy, tufted, lithophytic plant. **Leaves** linear-oblanceolate or linear-oblong, up to 25 cm long, 2.5 cm broad, minutely 3-toothed at apex. **Inflorescence** longer than the leaves, 1-flowered. **Flowers** variable in size, large and showy, 5–7.5 cm across; sepals orange-scarlet within, covered on free part with numerous crimson-purple papillae; perianth-tube campanulate-cylindric, 3.2 cm long. **Dorsal sepal** triangular-ovate, lamina 2.5 cm long; tail 2.5–6 cm long; **lateral sepals** larger than

dorsal sepal, oblong, obliquely acute at apex, keeled, 1.3 cm long. **Lip** oblong or ovate-oblong, bicarinate on upper surface, papillosely thickened on reflexed apex, 1.3 cm long.

DISTRIBUTION   Peru; 2200–4000 m altitude. This species is frequently seen in flower amongst the ancient Inca ruins of Macchu-Picchu near Cuzco.

HISTORY   This most spectacular orchid was discovered near Cuzco by Pearce, one of Messrs Veitch & Sons' collectors, in 1867. They introduced it into cultivation in the same year and it was named in their honour by H.G. Reichenbach in the following year in the *Gardeners' Chronicle* (p. 814).

M. veitchiana hybridises in the wild with *M. barlaeana* and this cross has also been reconstructed in cultivation.

Masdevallia ventricularia Rchb.f.
[Colour Plate]

An epiphytic plant. **Leaves** oblong-lanceolate, petiolate, suberect-spreading, coriaceous, 12.5–15 cm long, 2.5 cm broad. **Inflorescence** shorter or equal to leaves in length, 1-flowered; peduncle erect or erect-spreading, terete, slender, 5–7.5 cm long; bract membranous, sheathing, apiculate, 1.2 cm long. **Flowers** narrowly cylindrical-campanulate, suberect; sepals rich maroon or brownish-crimson with darker longitudinal streaks, tails yellow; petals white with a few crimson spots; lip dull purple; column white; perianth-tube narrow, inflated slightly in middle, curvate, up to 6.2 cm long. **Dorsal sepal** free part ovate, 1.2 cm long; tail erect, slender, 2.5–7.8 cm long; **lateral sepals** ovate-triangular; tails dependent, spreading slightly, 2.5–7.5 cm long. **Petals** small, oblong, acute or apiculate. **Lip** ligulate to oblong-ovate, 2-ridged above. **Column** erect, slender, apex denticulate.

DISTRIBUTION   Ecuador; 1800–2200 m altitude, growing low down on the trunks of forest trees.

HISTORY   First collected by Dr Jameson in Ecuador and later in 1877 by Consul Lehmann near Quito. H.G. Reichenbach described this species from the Lehmann collection in 1878 in *Otia Botanica Hamburgensia* (p. 14).

Masdevallia wageneriana Lindl.
[Colour Plate]

A small, tufted, epiphytic plant. **Leaves** elliptic, petiolate, suberect, coriaceous, 3–5 cm long, 1–1.5 cm broad, minutely tridentate at apex, glossy dark green above, minutely purple-spotted on blade. **Inflorescence** suberect-spreading, 1-flowered; peduncle about 5 cm long. **Flowers** large for size of plant; sepals yellowish-green, orange-yellow towards base, spotted and streaked violet, tails pale green and yellow; petals pale yellow; lip pale greenish-yellow, spotted purple; column pale violet, spotted violet. **Sepals** free part, ovate-triangular to oblong, 1 cm long, 1 cm broad; tails slender, borne at right-angles to lamina, up to 4.5 cm long. **Petals** fleshy, narrowly oblong, truncate or tridentate, 0.4 cm long, 0.13 cm broad. **Lip** hastate, clawed, 0.4 cm long, 0.2–0.3 cm broad, acute or rounded at apex. **Column** 0.4–0.5 cm long.

DISTRIBUTION Venezuela.

HISTORY Discovered by J.W. Moritz in 1849 near Tovar in Venezuela and the following year by H. Wagener at an altitude of 1800 m near Carabobo, also in Venezuela. This pretty species was described by John Lindley in J. Paxton's *Flower Garden* (p. 74) in 1852 from plants sent by Wagener to Jean Linden in Brussels.

CLOSELY RELATED SPECIES See *M. xanthina*.

Masdevallia xanthina Rchb.f.

A small epiphytic plant. **Leaves** oblong-obovate, suberect, shortly petiolate, tridenticulate at apex, 6.5–7.5 cm long, 2 cm broad. **Inflorescence** erect, 1-flowered; peduncle slender, terete, pale green, 7.8 cm long; bracts sheathing below, apiculate, 1.1 cm long, brown to blackish-green. **Flowers** with spreading segments; sepals brilliant yellow, rarely cream, with darker nerved lateral sepals with a basal purple spot, tails orange-yellow; petals white; lip pale yellow, minutely spotted crimson; column white with purple margins, apex and foot; perianth-tube obscure. **Dorsal sepal** cucullate, obovate-oblong, margins recurved at base; tail erect, 3.3–3.7 cm long; **lateral sepals** spreading, lanceolate; tails slender, dependent, 2.5–3.3 cm long. **Petals** oblong, keeled on anterior margin, 0.4 cm long. **Lip** oblong, fleshy and grooved at base, 0.4 cm long. **Column** tridentate at apex.

DISTRIBUTION Colombia and Ecuador; in damp woods, 1800–2500 m altitude.

HISTORY *M. xanthina* was described by Professor Reichenbach in 1880 in the *Gardeners' Chronicle* (n.s. 13: p. 631) from specimens of unknown provenance given him by Messrs Veitch & Sons. Later its distribution was established by Consul Lehmann who collected orchids and drew them over a number of years in Colombia.

CLOSELY RELATED SPECIES A very variable species closely allied to *M. estradae*, but differing in its flower colour.

Also allied to *M. wageneriana* but differs in having an entire-margined lip, a narrower obovate-oblong dorsal sepal and narrower lanceolate lateral sepals.

Maxillaria Ruiz & Pavon

Subfamily Epidendroideae
Tribe Maxillarieae
Subtribe Maxillariinae

Epiphytic or lithophytic, caespitose or rhizomatous plants. **Rhizome** very short to elongate, creeping, ascending or suberect, clothed with evanescent, papery sheaths. **Pseudobulbs** (secondary stems) clustered or remote, 1- or 2-leaved (rarely more). **Inflorescence** 1-flowered, fasciculate, glomerate or solitary. **Flowers** small to large, sometimes showy. **Sepals** free, subsimilar, ringent, rarely connivent and urceolate; lateral sepals somewhat oblique, adnate to or decurrent on column-foot, and forming with it a ± distinct mentum. **Petals** similar to dorsal sepal, free. **Lip** adnate to or articulate with column-foot, entire or 3-lobed, commonly sessile; disc usually with a distinct callus. **Column** erect or arcuate, stout, lacking wings, extended at base into a ± distinct foot; pollinia 4, waxy, usually compressed, sessile on a semilunate viscidium.

DISTRIBUTION About 300 species widely distributed in the American tropics and subtropics.

DERIVATION OF NAME From the Latin *maxilla* (jaw-bone), alluding to the column and lip inside the ringent flowers of some species which somewhat resemble the jaws of an insect.

TAXONOMY Described by H. Ruiz and J. Pavon in 1794 in their *Prodromus Florae Peru-*

Maxillaria lips
1 – *M. crassipes* (× 2)
2 – *M. echinochila* (× 2)
3 – *M. plebeja* (× 4)
4 – *M. gracilis* (× 3)
5 – *M. ringens* (× 3)
6 – *M. fletcheriana* (× 1)
7 – *M. juergensii* (× 2)
8 – *M. mosenii* (× 3)
9 – *M. ferdinandiana* (× 4)
10 – *M. uncata* (× 2)
11 – *M. grandiflora* (× 1½)

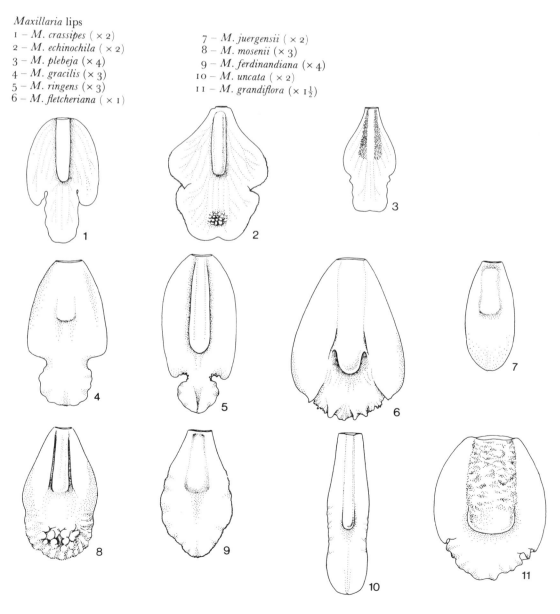

vianae et Chilensis (p. 116, t. 25), *Maxillaria* is one of the largest genera of New World orchids. The genus is easily distinguished by coriaceous non-plicate leaves, its prominent mentum formed by the uniting of the bases of the lateral sepals to the column-foot and by its distinctive rounded or semilunate viscidium.

No recent revision of the genus has been made but many species originally described in the genus have subsequently been removed to allied genera such as *Lycaste* and *Xylobium*. *Maxillaria* may conveniently be divided into those species with a tufted (caespitose) habit and those in which the pseudobulbs are borne on a more or less elongate rhizome. These latter were once considered to form a distinct genus *Camaridium* but many species intermediate between that and *Maxillaria* exist and it is more realistic to consider the two as congeneric.

TYPE SPECIES *M. ramosa* Ruiz & Pavon. This species was selected as lectotype of the genus by L. Garay and H. Sweet in 1972 in the *Journal of the Arnold Arboretum*.

SYNONYMS *Camaridium* Lindl.; *Psittacoglossum* La Llave & Lex.; *Heterotaxis* Lindl.; *Dicrypta* Lindl.; *Menadenia* Raf.; *Onkeripus* Raf.; *Pentulops* Raf.; *Ornithidium* Salisb.

CULTURE Compost A. Temp. Winter min. 12–15°C. The majority of *Maxillaria* species may be grown in pots but species such as *M. sanderiana* and *M. valenzuelana* are better grown in baskets. All plants require good humidity and moderate shade with plenty of water while growing. Pseudobulbous species should be given less water when fully grown but other species must never remain dry for long.

Maxillaria arachnites Rchb.f. [Colour Plate]
An epiphytic plant with a short ascending rhizome. **Pseudobulbs** small, compressed, ancipitous, 2.5 cm long, 1.8 cm broad, 1-leafed at apex, subtended by several ± leaf-bearing imbricating sheaths. **Leaf** oblanceolate, erect or suberect-spreading, up to 25 cm long, 3 cm broad, subacute. **Inflorescence** erect, 1-flowered; peduncle up to 20 cm long, almost covered by several tubular acute sheaths; bract lanceolate, acute, longer than ovary, green, spotted with purple. **Flowers** large; sepals pale yellow-green, suffused maroon towards base; petals white, pale purple at base; lip golden-yellow, flushed maroon-red towards apex but apex golden-yellow, callus yellow. **Sepals** linear-lanceolate, very acute, up to 6 cm long, 0.9 cm broad at base; lateral sepals forming with the column-foot a short, curved, conical mentum. **Petals** similar to sepals but shorter. **Lip** 3-lobed towards apex, 1.7 cm long, 1 cm broad, minutely pubescent above; side lobes truncate, erose on front margin; mid-lobe sub-

quadrate; callus pubescent. **Column** 1 cm long, erose at apex.

DISTRIBUTION Colombia, Venezuela and Ecuador.

HISTORY Introduced into cultivation from Colombia by Messrs Backhouse of York, England, and described in the *Gardeners' Chronicle* (n.s. 13: p. 394) in 1880 by H.G. Reichenbach.

Maxillaria consanguinea Klotzsch
A pendulous epiphytic plant. **Pseudobulbs** clustered, ovoid-pyriform, compressed, shiny, deeply grooved with age, 4–7 cm long, 2.5–4 cm broad, 1- or more commonly, 2-leaved at apex. **Leaves** fleshy-coriaceous, narrowly ligulate, acute, attenuate or distinctly petiolate below, 20–35 cm long, 2–5 cm broad. **Inflorescences** many, 1-flowered, basal, up to 16 cm long; bracts ovate lanceolate, acute, sheathing, 2–3 cm long. **Flowers** erect-spreading; sepals and petals yellowish-brown; lip white sparsely spotted with crimson. **Sepals** fleshy-coriaceous, oblong ligulate, acute, about 2–5 cm long, 0.6 cm broad; lateral sepals fusing with the column-foot to form a short, broadly rounded mentum. **Petals** ligulate, acute, 2.0–2.2 cm long, 0.5 cm broad. **Lip** erect-spreading, rigid, fleshy, slightly furfuraceous-puberulent above, broadly oblong, deeply 3-lobed above the middle, 2.4–2.5 cm long, 1 cm broad; side lobes small, erect, semioblong; mid-lobe oblong-ligulate, obtuse, margins undulate-denticulate; callus linear-ligulate, fleshy, furfuraceous. **Column** fleshy, subclavate.

DISTRIBUTION Brazil.

HISTORY Originally described by O. Klotzsch in 1852 in the *Index Seminum in Horto Botanico Berolinensi* (p. 1). In Martius's *Flora Brasiliensis*, A. Cogniaux treated this species as a variety of *M. picta* Hooker but it differs from that species in its smaller, distinctly coloured flowers.

Maxillaria consanguinea
Floral dissection (× 1)

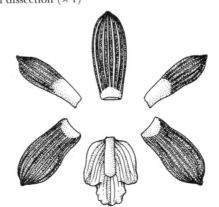

SYNONYMS *Maxillaria picta* var. *brunnea* Rchb.f.; *M. serolina* Hoehne

Maxillaria crassipes Kraenzl.
A repent epiphytic plant. **Rhizome** creeping, fleshy, bearing pseudobulbs at intervals of 1–1.5 cm. **Pseudobulbs** conical, 4-angled, up to 2.5 cm long, 1 cm across, 2-leaved at apex. **Leaves** fleshy-coriaceous, lanceolate, petiolate, acute, up to 9 cm long, 1.2–1.5 cm broad. **Inflorescences** erect, about 2 per pseudobulb, up to 12 cm long. **Flowers** yellow, paler on outer surface, margins red; lip purple at apex; column flushed lilac. **Sepals** ovate-lanceolate, long-acuminate, fleshy, 2.5 cm long, 0.5 cm broad; lateral sepals forming a short, rounded mentum. **Petals** ligulate-lanceolate, acute, 1.8 cm long, 0.3 cm broad. **Lip** 3-lobed above the middle, 0.5 cm long, 0.7–0.8 cm broad; side lobes erect, rounded in front; mid-lobe oblong-ligulate, margins undulate; callus ligulate, fleshy, rounded in front, minutely pilose. **Column** clavate, curved. 0.8 cm long.

DISTRIBUTION Brazil.

HISTORY Discovered near Santos in Brazil by C.W. Mosen and described in *Kungliga Svenska Vetenskapsakademiens Avhandlingar, Stockholm* (46(10): p. 72) in 1911 by Dr F. Kraenzlin.

Maxillaria cucullata Lindl.
A very variable, terrestrial, lithophytic or epiphytic herb growing in large clumps. **Pseudobulbs** clustered, ovoid-oblong, compressed, 2.5–9.5 cm long, 1–3 cm across, 1-leafed at apex, subtended by several distichous sheaths. **Leaf** linear to oblong-elliptic, coriaceous, 11–40 cm long, 1–5 cm broad, obtuse or rounded at the apex. **Inflorescences** several, borne in the axils of the sheaths subtending the pseudobulb, each 1-flowered, 4–20 cm long; bracts almost covering the peduncle, scarious-fibrous, 2–3 cm long. **Flowers** yellowish to almost black, striped or spotted deep maroon; segments fleshy. **Sepals** linear to elliptic-lanceolate, 2.3–4.5 cm long, 0.4–1.1 cm broad, acute to acuminate, keeled on reverse; lateral sepals forming a short mentum with the column-foot. **Petals** narrowly lanceolate to broadly elliptic, forming a hood over the column, 1.5–2.9 cm long, 0.5–0.9 cm broad, subacute to acuminate. **Lip** erect-arcuate, ± 3-lobed in the middle, 1.5–3 cm long, 0.7–1 cm broad; side lobes short, bluntly triangular, clasping the column; mid-lobe obovate or oblong-subquadrate, subobtuse or acute at apex, verrucose; callus between side lobes broadening towards apex, sulcate. **Column** stout. 1.3–1.5 cm long.

DISTRIBUTION Mexico, Belize, Guatemala, Honduras and Costa Rica; rather common in open or dense rain or mist forests, up to 3300 m altitude.

HISTORY Discovered by J. Henchman in Central America and described by John Lindley in 1840 in the *Botanical Register* (t. 12) from plants sent him by the Duke of Devonshire from Chatsworth, England.

SYNONYMS *Maxillaria rhombea* Lindl.; *M. atrata* Rchb.f.; *M. obscura* Linden & Rchb.f.; *M. praestans* Rchb.f.

CLOSELY RELATED SPECIES See *M. tenuifolia*.

Maxillaria curtipes Hooker

A medium-sized epiphytic plant with a straggly, ascending or pendulous habit. **Rhizome** stout, with pseudobulbs borne at intervals. **Pseudobulbs** ellipsoid-oblong, compressed, 4–6.5 cm long, up to 2 cm across, 1-leafed at apex. **Leaf** linear, coriaceous, obtuse and obliquely retuse at apex, 10–30 cm long, 1.5–2.5 cm broad. **Inflorescence** axillary; peduncle 2–4 cm long, concealed by imbricating sheaths. **Flowers** fleshy, showy; sepals and petals yellowish on outer surface, deep red within, margins orange; lip deep yellow, spotted and striped red-brown; column yellowish, spotted red-brown. **Sepals** elliptic to ovate-lanceolate or lanceolate, acute to acuminate, spreading, 2–2.8 cm long, 0.4–0.6 cm broad; lateral sepals forming with the column foot a short blunt mentum. **Petals** linear or linear-oblong, subobtuse to subacuminate, incurved, forming a hood over column, 2 cm long, 0.5 cm broad. **Lip** arcuate, oblong to broadly elliptic; subobtuse or rounded at apex, 1.7–2 cm long, 0.8–1.1 cm broad; disc papillose-puberulent; callus fleshy, papillose, broad. **Column** semiterete. arcuate, 1.5 cm long.

DISTRIBUTION Mexico, Guatemala and Costa Rica; up to 3000 m altitude. An uncommon species.

HISTORY *M. curtipes* was discovered by J. Parkinson in Mexico and it was described by Sir William Hooker in 1841 in *Icones Plantarum* (t. 384). This species is still occasionally grown under the later synonym *M. houtteana* Rchb.f.

SYNONYM *Maxillaria houtteana* Rchb.f.

CLOSELY RELATED SPECIES *Maxillaria elatior* Rchb.f. and *M. tenuifolia*.

Maxillaria densa Lindl. [Colour Plate]

A medium-sized epiphytic or terrestrial plant with thick, elongated, ± branching rhizomes. **Pseudobulbs** clustered or spaced on rhizome, elliptic-oblong or ovate-oblong, compressed-ancipitous, 1.5–7 cm long, 1–2.5 cm in diameter, yellow-green, 1-leafed at apex. **Leaf** linear or linear-oblong to oblanceolate, retuse at the obtuse apex, conduplicate below, up to 30 cm long, 1–4 cm broad. **Inflorescences** of dense fascicles of 1-flowered peduncles in the axils of the basal cataphylls of new growths. **Flowers** variable in colour, greenish-white and yellowish-white with a purple tinge to deep maroon or reddish-brown. **Sepals** linear-lanceolate to elliptic-lanceolate, acute to acuminate, apex fleshily keeled, 0.6–0.9 cm long, 0.2–0.3 cm broad; lateral sepals oblique, forming an inconspicuous mentum with the column-foot. **Petals** elliptic-lanceolate, acute, oblique, 0.5–0.75 cm long, 0.15–0.25 cm broad. **Lip** continuous with column-foot, fleshy, 3-lobed, 0.4 cm long, 0.3 cm broad; side lobes auriculate, rounded; mid-lobe suborbicular to ovate, rounded to obtuse; disc with a plate-like, concave callus between side lobes. **Column** short, stout, clavate; foot 0.3 cm long.

DISTRIBUTION Mexico south to Honduras; rather common in damp woods at low elevations, in cloud forests or as a terrestrial in pine forests, up to 2500 m.

HISTORY Described by John Lindley in the *Botanical Register* (t. 1804) in 1835 based on a plant imported from Mexico by Messrs Loddiges. This plant is still treated by some authors in the genus *Ornithidium* to which H.G. Reichenbach transferred it in 1855 in *Bonplandia* (p. 217).

SYNONYM *Ornithidium densum* (Lindl.) Rchb.f.

Maxillaria desvauxiana Rchb.f.

[Colour Plate]

A medium-sized epiphytic or lithophytic plant. **Pseudobulbs** clustered on a stout repent rhizome, ovoid, slightly compressed, up to 4.5 cm long, 2.5 cm in diameter, 1-leafed at apex. **Leaf** erect, petiolate, narrowly elliptic, acute, up to 45 cm long, 4.5 cm broad, coriaceous. **Inflorescence** 1-flowered, from base of pseudobulb, spreading-erect, very short, up to 5 cm long. **Flower** fleshy; sepals dull yellowish-pink flushed with maroon at apex, and base; petals maroon with paler margins; lip shiny vinous-maroon with a pale margin to mid-lobe; column pinkish-maroon. **Sepals** spreading, ovate-lanceolate apiculate, margins reflexed, 2.6–3 cm long, 1.1–1.3 cm broad. **Petals** parallel to column, oblong-obovate, rounded and slightly recurved at apex, up to 2.3 cm long, 1.4 cm broad. **Lip** parallel to column, reflexed at apex, 3-lobed in apical half, to 2.1 cm long, 1.5 cm broad; side lobes erect, narrowly oblong, rounded in front; mid-lobe rounded with several glossy longitudinal verrucose ridges to apex; disc with an oblong fleshy callus. **Column** semiterete, 1.3 cm long.

DISTRIBUTION Tropical S. and Central America; from sea level to 1500 m.

HISTORY Described in 1855 by H.G. Reichenbach in *Bonplandia* (p. 67) based on a

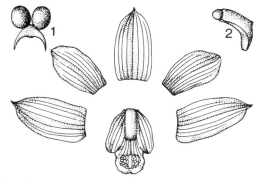

Maxillaria desvauxiana
Floral dissection (× 1)
1 – Pollinia and viscidium (× 4)
2 – Column, side view (× 1)

collection made by H. Wagener at Pericos, Mexico which flowered in the collection of M. Desvaux in Paris.

SYNONYMS *Maxillaria coriacea* Barb. Rodr.; *M. petiolaris* Rchb.f.

CLOSELY RELATED SPECIES Allied to *M. parkeri* which has larger, distinctly coloured flowers and lacks the verrucose callus on the mid-lobe of the lip. See also *M. echinochila*.

Maxillaria echinochila Kraenzl.

A tufted epiphytic plant. **Pseudobulbs** clustered, elongate-ovoid, 3–3.5 cm long, 1 cm across, 2-leaved at apex. **Leaves** linear, curvate, acute, up to 10 cm long, 4–5 mm broad. **Inflorescence** erect. **Flowers** brown. **Dorsal sepal** oblong, cucullate, acute, 2 cm long, 0.5–0.6 cm broad; **lateral sepals** slightly falcate, otherwise as dorsal sepal. **Petals** obovate-oblong, apex obtusely acute and reflexed, 2 cm long, 0.4 cm broad. **Lip** simple obovate, almost clawed, margins crenulate 1.5 cm long, 0.8 cm broad; callus linear. **Column** slender.

DISTRIBUTION Brazil.

HISTORY Discovered in the state of Paraná in Brazil by Dusen and described by F. Kraenzlin in 1921 in the Swedish journal *Arkiv för Botanik* (p. 22).

CLOSELY RELATED SPECIES Allied to *M. desvauxiana*.

Maxillaria elegantula Rolfe

A rather large plant with a stout creeping rhizome. **Pseudobulbs** narrowly ellipsoid, compressed, up to 5.7 cm long, 1-leafed at apex, subtended by several large distichous sheaths. **Leaf** petiolate, oblong-elliptic, chartaceous, up to 30 cm long, 5.6 cm broad, acute; petiole compressed, up to 20 cm long. **Inflorescence** erect or suberect, lateral, basal, 1-flowered, up to 25 cm long. **Flowers** showy, large, white, more or less suffused with purplish-brown or dark bluish. **Dorsal sepal** elliptic-oblong, concave, 2.5–4.1 cm long, up to 1.6 cm broad, subacute, margins revolute; **lateral sepals** similar to dorsal sepal but oblique, forming a prominent mentum with the column-foot. **Petals** obliquely lanceolate, up to 3.5 cm long, 1.4 cm broad, acute, **Lip** short, arcuate, ovate, lobulate-denticulate in front, 1.7 cm long, 1.2 cm broad, obtuse at apex; disc thickened below in centre. **Column** very short, stout, arcuate, up to 1 cm long, with a 1.2–1.7 cm long foot.

DISTRIBUTION Ecuador and Peru; 750–2400 m altitude.

HISTORY First introduced into cultivation from Ecuador by Messrs Sander & Co. of St Albans, England, and described by Robert Rolfe in the *Kew Bulletin* (p. 196) in 1898. *M. dichroma* was described by Rolfe at the same time but further research has shown it to be conspecific with *M. elegantula*.

M. elegantula is a distinctive rhizomatous species readily recognised by its large flowers which are distinctively coloured.

SYNONYM *Maxillaria dichroma* Rolfe

Maxillaria ferdinandiana Barb. Rodr.

A creeping epiphytic plant. **Stems** long, robust, branching, 10–25 cm long, bearing pseudobulbs at spaced intervals. **Pseudobulbs** erect or erect-spreading, narrowly ovate-subrhomboid, compressed, 1-leafed at apex. **Leaf** subcoriaceous, shortly petiolate, linear-lanceolate, very acute, 6–9 cm long, 0.6–0.8 cm broad. **Inflorescence** erect, solitary, shorter than the pseudobulb, 0.5–1.5 cm long; peduncle slender; bract ovate-lanceolate, scarious, long-acuminate, 1–1.5 cm long. **Flowers** erect or erect-spreading; sepals and petals greenish-white, spotted purple below; lip greenish on outside, white within with purple spots; column white. **Sepals** oblong or ovate-oblong, acute, 1–1.1 cm long, 2.5–4 cm broad; lateral sepals forming an obtuse mentum with the column-foot. **Petals** oblong, abruptly acute, 0.9–1 cm long, 0.25–0.3 cm broad. **Lip** rigid, erect, fleshy, shortly clawed, broadly ovate, obscurely 3-lobed above, 1 cm long, 0.8 cm broad; side lobes erect, rounded; mid-lobe semirotund, very obtuse; callus fleshy, ligulate, rounded in front. **Column** short, slender, clavate, 0.6 cm long.

DISTRIBUTION Eastern states of Brazil.

HISTORY Discovered by J. Barbosa Rodrigues at Juiz de Fora in Minas Gerais State and described by him in his *Genera et Species Orchideanum Novarum* (p. 204) in 1882.

Maxillaria fletcheriana Rolfe

A large robust plant with a stout rhizome. **Pseudobulbs** oblong-ovoid, slightly compressed, 3–5 cm long, 1-leafed at apex, subtended by 2 distichous leaf-bearing sheaths. **Leaf** vari-

able, ± petiolate, elliptic-oblong or oblong, 15–24 cm long, up to 5.5 cm broad, acute or obtuse; petiole stout, channelled, 5–13 cm long. **Inflorescence** erect, 1-flowered, 25–35 cm long; peduncle more or less covered by loose conduplicate, tubular sheaths. **Flowers** showy; sepals and petals white or yellow, lined purple; lip rich yellow lined with purple below and on side lobes. **Dorsal sepal** recurved, spreading, ovate, up to 4.5 cm long, 2.5 cm broad, acute or subacute; **lateral sepals** similar to dorsal sepal but oblique, forming a conical mentum 3 cm or more long. **Petals** obliquely elliptic-ovate, up to 4 cm long, 2 cm broad, shortly acuminate. **Lip** erect, parallel to column, strongly recurved, elliptic-obovate or oblong-obovate, obscurely 3-lobed, up to 5 cm long, 3 cm broad; side lobes erect, semiobovate, front margins crisped-undulate; mid-lobe suborbicular, obtuse, undulate; disc with an obovate-oblong, fleshy callus above the middle. **Column** short, stout, arcuate, about 1.5 cm long, with a prominent foot 3–4 cm long.

DISTRIBUTION Peru.

HISTORY First collected by Forget in S. Peru for the firm of Messrs Sander of St Albans, England, and described by Robert Rolfe in the *Gardeners' Chronicle* (ser. 3, 53: p. 258) in 1913.

Maxillaria gracilis Lodd.

A small tufted epiphytic plant. **Pseudobulbs** clustered, ovoid-pyriform, compressed, 2–2.5 cm long, 1–1.3 cm across, 2-leaved at apex. **Leaves** subcoriaceous, linear-ligulate, petiolate and conduplicate below, acute at apex, 10–20 cm long, 0.8–1.5 cm broad. **Inflorescence** ascending, 1-flowered, up to 10 cm long; peduncle slender, pale green or reddish; bract pale, 1.2–1.5 cm long. **Flowers** erect-spreading, fragrant; sepals and petals yellow, flushed with purple on the outer margins; lip yellow, lined or spotted with purple. **Sepals** fleshy, erect-spreading, narrowly triangular-lanceolate, acute, 1.7–2.2 cm long, 0.5–0.7 cm broad. **Petals** fleshy, narrowly linear-lanceolate, very acute, 1.2–2 cm long, 0.2–0.3 cm broad. **Lip** rigid, erect, fleshy, deeply 3-lobed above the middle, furfuraceous at base, 1.2–1.5 cm long, 0.7–1 cm broad; side lobes erect, semiovate, rounded at apex; mid-lobe broadly oblong-linguiform, apex shortly sulcate, margins undulate-denticulate; disc with a callus reaching the middle; callus fleshy, ligulate.

DISTRIBUTION E. Brazil.

HISTORY *M. gracilis* was introduced into cultivation from near Rio de Janeiro by Messrs Loddiges who named it in 1832 in their *Botanical Cabinet* (t. 1837). The plant described by Loddiges as *M. punctata* was reduced to varietal

rank by A. Cogniaux in Martius's *Flora Brasiliensis*. It differs from the typical variety in having slightly larger flowers with a slightly 3-lobed lip.

SYNONYMS *Maxillaria queirogana* Barb. Rodr.; *M. punctata* Lodd.

Maxillaria grandiflora (H.B.K.) Lindl.

A large, tufted, epiphytic plant. **Pseudobulbs** ovoid, compressed, wrinkled, 5 cm long, 3 cm broad, 1-leafed at apex, subtended by several imbricate leaf-bearing sheaths. **Leaf** narrowly oblong-ligulate, conduplicate at base, thin-textured, keeled below, up to 45 cm long, 7 cm broad. **Inflorescence** 1-flowered; peduncle terete, up to 25 cm long, covered by several overlapping compressed sheaths. **Flowers** nodding with an arcuate ovary, large, showy; sepals and petals pure white; lip white, creamy-yellow at base, with a maroon-red spot visible from below on either side of mid-lobe; column white to yellow with some red flecks on inner side. **Dorsal sepal** ovate-elliptic, acute, 3.5–5.5 cm long, 2.2 cm broad; **lateral sepals** falcate, lanceolate, acute, up to 6 cm long, 2.4 cm broad, forming a short, broad mentum with the column-foot. **Petals** projecting forwards on either side of the column, lanceolate, oblique, acute, up to 4.7 cm long, 1.7 cm broad. **Lip** fleshy, oblong or oblong-elliptic, subacute, 2.5–3 cm long, 1.3–1.6 cm broad, densely farinaceous above; callus flat, undercut at apex, densely farinaceous. **Column** short, arcuate, 3 cm long including the foot.

DISTRIBUTION Colombia, Ecuador, Venezuela, Guyana, Peru and Bolivia; at high altitudes in cloud forest.

HISTORY Collected by F.H.A. von Humboldt and A. Bonpland and described by them and C.S. Kunth in *Nova Genera et Species Plantarum* (p. 359, t. 88) in 1816 as *Dendrobium grandiflorum*. Subsequently, it had been transferred to the genera *Broughtonia* and *Lycaste* but finally to *Maxillaria* by John Lindley in 1832 in his *Genera and Species of Orchidaceous Plants* (p. 147).

SYNONYMS *Dendrobium grandiflorum* H.B.K.; *Broughtonia grandiflora* (H.B.K.) Sprengel; *Lycaste grandiflora* (H.B.K.) Beer; *Maxillaria eburnea* Lindl.; *M. lehmannii* Rchb.f.

Maxillaria juergensii Schltr.

A small epiphytic plant. **Rhizome** short, ascending, with closely-spaced pseudobulbs, 0.25–0.3 cm apart. **Pseudobulbs** ovoid to fusiform-cylindric, 1–1.5 cm long, 0.3–0.4 cm across. 2-leaved at apex. **Leaves** suberect, more or less circular or triangular in cross-section, mucronate, 1.5–4 cm long, 0.8–1.5 cm in diameter. **Inflorescence** erect; peduncle 1–1.5 cm long. **Flowers** showy, more or less fleshy; sepals and petals maroon with a whitish base; lip white at base, spotted maroon, rich maroon above; column white, striped purple with a green base; anther-cap rich purple. **Dorsal sepal** oblong, obtuse or rounded at the apex, 1–1.2 cm long, 0.4–0.5 cm broad; **lateral sepals** oblong-ovate, obtuse, 1.2–1.5 cm long, 0.6–0.7 cm broad. **Petals** oblong-ligulate, obtuse, 1 cm long, 0.4–0.5 cm broad. **Lip** oblong-obovate, sessile, 1.2–1.3 cm long, 0.7 cm broad; callus claviform, rounded at apex. **Column** erect, slender.

DISTRIBUTION   Brazil.

HISTORY   *M. juergensii* was discovered by C. Jürgens in 1922 at São João in Brazil at an altitude of 350 m and was described by Rudolf Schlechter in 1925 in *Fedde, Repertorium Specierum Novarum, Beihefte* (p. 88).

Maxillaria lepidota Lindl. [Colour Plate]

A large epiphytic or lithophytic herb. **Pseudobulbs** clustered, ovoid to cylindric, up to 5 cm long, 1.5 cm in diameter, 1-leafed at apex, covered when young by acute, nervose, leaf-bearing sheaths. **Leaf** linear-ligulate to linear-oblanceolate, acute, suberect, up to 35 cm long, 2 cm broad, conduplicate below, carinate. **Inflorescence** basal, 1-flowered; peduncle slender, up to 12 cm long, covered by slightly inflated sheaths. **Flower** large; sepals and petals yellow with a splash of red at the base; lip creamy-yellow with maroon markings along the dorsal axis, the ventral surface being covered by a yellow-green farina. **Sepals** linear-lanceolate, long-acuminate, up to 6 cm long, 0.7 cm broad, margins slightly recurved; lateral sepals slightly falcate, forming a short obtuse mentum at the base. **Petals** falcate, linear-attenuate, long-acuminate, up to 4.5 cm long, 0.4 cm broad. **Lip** 3-lobed in the apical half, fleshy, up to 2 cm long, 1.2 cm broad; side lobes erect, narrowly oblong, rounded in front; mid-lobe ovate, apiculate, with undulate margins; callus oblong, rounded in front, pubescent. **Column** short, slightly arcuate, 1.2 cm long; foot short, 0.6 cm long.

DISTRIBUTION   Venezuela, Colombia and Ecuador.

HISTORY   Described by John Lindley in 1845 in the *Annals and Magazine of Natural History* (p. 383) based on a collection made near Popayan in Colombia by Th. Hartweg.

SYNONYMS   *Maxillaria pertusa* Lindl. ex Rchb.f.; *M. saxicola* Schltr.

Maxillaria luteoalba Lindl. [Colour Plate]

A large epiphytic plant. **Pseudobulbs** clustered, ovoid-oblong, slightly compressed, dark brown, 5 cm long, 2 cm broad, 1-leafed at apex. **Leaf** narrowly oblong-elliptic, petiolate, rigid, suberect, up to 50 cm long, 5 cm broad, obtuse. **Inflorescence** suberect or erect, 1-flowered;

peduncle up to 12 cm long, covered by sheaths which are green and spotted with brown. **Flowers** large; sepals and petals yellow, white towards base; lip white marked with yellow in centre and in centre of mid-lobe, side lobes lined purple on nerves; column white, marked purple below. **Sepals** linear, acute, 5–6 cm long. 0.7–0.9 cm broad; lateral sepals slightly oblique, mentum very short. **Petals** falcate. linear-lanceolate, acute, 4.5–5 cm long, 0.8 cm broad. **Lip** 3-lobed in apical half, 2.2–2.5 cm long, 1.2–1.4 cm broad, pubescent in centre; side lobes very narrowly oblong, ± truncate at front; mid-lobe ovate-orbicular, deflexed, obtuse; callus in basal half, a longitudinal ridge rounded in front.

DISTRIBUTION   Costa Rica, Panama, Colombia, Ecuador and Venezuela.

HISTORY   Discovered by Jean Linden in the forests of Mérida in Venezuela between 1600 and 1850 m and described by John Lindley in 1846 in *Orchidaceae Lindenianae* (p. 20).

SYNONYM   *Maxillaria luteograndiflora* Hort.

Maxillaria meleagris Lindl. [Colour Plate]

An epiphytic plant, with a short stout rhizome. **Pseudobulbs** clustered, ellipsoid-ovoid to ovoid, compressed, 2–5.5 cm long, 1–2.2 cm in diameter, 1-leafed at apex, subtended by several distichous, imbricating sheaths. **Leaf** linear to linear-ligulate, coriaceous, 15–40 cm long, 0.6–2.2 cm broad, obtuse. **Inflorescence** from base of new growth, 1-flowered, 3–8 cm long; peduncle covered by tubular sheaths; bracts scarious, acute or acuminate, 1.3–2 cm long. **Flowers** variable in texture and size; sepals and petals tawny, olive-buff or flesh-coloured, spotted or mottled dark red; lip dark red. **Sepals** elliptic-lanceolate to linear-elliptic, dorsally keeled, 1.2–2.9 cm long, 0.4–0.7 cm broad, acuminate to obtuse; lateral sepals similar to dorsal but oblique, forming with the column-foot a short mentum. **Petals** connate to dorsal sepal, elliptic to elliptic-lanceolate, 1–2.2 cm long, 0.3–0.65 cm broad, obtuse to subacuminate. **Lip** arcuate, 3-lobed at the base, 0.7–1.6 cm long, 0.4–0.8 cm broad; side lobes small, rounded, erect; mid-lobe much larger, fleshy, ovate-orbicular to broadly elliptic, rounded at apex; disc thickened between side lobes, with a transverse ridge between side lobes at front, with small lamellae superimposed on the thickened portion between the side lobes. **Column** stout, 5–10 mm long including the foot.

DISTRIBUTION   Mexico, Guatemala and Panama; rare in humid forests, up to 1800 m altitude.

HISTORY   Described in 1844 by John Lindley in the *Botanical Register* (misc. p. 3) from a plant imported from Mexico by Messrs Loddiges.

SYNONYMS   *Maxillaria lindeniana* A. Rich. & Galeotti; *M. punctostriata* Rchb.f.

Maxillaria mosenii Kraenzl.

An erect or pendent epiphytic plant with an ascending rhizome bearing closely-spaced pseudobulbs. **Pseudobulbs** fusiform, plurisulcate, 2–4.5 cm long, 0.4–1 cm across, 2-leaved at apex. **Leaves** linear-oblanceolate, acute to long-acuminate, 10–15 cm long, 0.6–0.7 cm broad. **Inflorescence** a little longer than the pseudobulb; peduncle covered by ovate, acuminate sheaths. **Flowers** yellow, spotted with red-purple; lip yellow, heavily spotted and marked purple in the middle. **Dorsal sepal** oblong-elliptic, acute, 1.7–1.8 cm long, 0.6–0.8 cm broad; **lateral sepals** oblong-lanceolate, oblique, acute, 1.7–1.9 cm long, 0.8 cm broad. **Petals** spathulate to oblanceolate, obtuse, 1.6–1.7 cm long, 0.6–0.8 cm broad. **Lip** shortly clawed, oblong, 1.6–1.8 cm long, 0.7–0.9 cm broad; callus in basal half bisulcate. **Column** slender, curved, 1 cm long.

DISTRIBUTION   Brazil.

HISTORY   Discovered by the River Buturoca near Santos in Brazil by C.W. Mosen, *M. mosenii* was described by F. Kraenzlin in 1911 in the Swedish journal *Kungliga Svenska Vetenskapsakademiens Avhandlingar, Stockholm* (46(10), p. 73).

Var. *hatschbachii* (Schltr.) Hoehne and var. *echinochila* (Kraenzl.) Hoehne are similar florally to the typical variety (with the latter having somewhat buff-coloured flowers with a broader lip) but both can be readily distinguished vegetatively. Var. *hatschbachii* has slender grass-like leaves whilst var. *echinochila* has shorter acuminate leaves and is altogether a smaller plant.

SYNONYM   *Maxillaria hatschbachii* Schltr.

Maxillaria nigrescens Lindl. [Colour Plate]

A large epiphytic plant. **Pseudobulbs** narrowly ovoid, compressed, ancipitous, up to 9 cm long, 3.5 cm broad, 1-leafed at apex, subtended by several imbricate, grey sheaths. **Leaf** ligulate, rigid, suberect, up to 35 cm long, 3.5 cm broad, acute or minutely unequally 2-lobed at apex. **Inflorescence** suberect or erect, much shorter than the leaves, 1-flowered; peduncle up to 14 cm long, ± concealed by green sheaths which are flecked with brown. **Flowers** large, 5 cm across; sepals and petals maroon-red, base of sepals yellow; lip and column dark maroon-purple, shiny; anther yellow on either side. **Sepals** linear, acute, 4–6 cm long, 0.7–1 cm broad; lateral sepals slightly falcate, forming a short mentum with the column-foot. **Petals** falcate, acute, 4–5.5 cm long, 0.6 cm broad. **Lip** oblong, margins upcurved, obtuse and decurved at apex, 1.7 cm long, 1.2 cm broad; callus half length of lip. **Column** 1.3 cm long.

DISTRIBUTION   Colombia and Venezuela;

in high altitude rain forests up to 2500 m altitude.

HISTORY Another species discovered by Jean Linden near Mérida at between 1600 and 2500 m altitude and described by John Lindley in his *Orchidaceae Lindenianae* (p. 20) in 1846.

SYNONYM *Maxillaria rubrofusca* Klotzsch

Maxillaria parkeri Hooker [Colour Plate]

A medium-sized epiphytic plant. **Pseudobulbs** ovoid or elongate-ovoid, compressed, 4 cm long, 2–3 cm across, 1-leafed at apex, smooth, dark green, subtended by large grey-brown spotted sheaths. **Leaf** lanceolate-ligulate, coriaceous, obscurely striate, up to 45 cm long, 4 cm broad, subacute, smooth, mid-green. **Inflorescence** erect, basal, 1-flowered, up to 10 cm long; peduncle covered by about 5 overlapping sheaths; sheaths and bract green, lined and flushed purple. **Flowers** faily large, erect-spreading; sepals yellow-buff coloured; petals white, lined with purple; lip off-white, side lobes lined with crimson, callus yellow; column yellow at base, purple above. **Sepals** nearly similar, erect-spreading, elliptic, obtuse or rounded, 3.3 cm long, 1.8–2 cm broad; mentum obscure. **Petals** linear-lanceolate, suberect, 2.8 cm long, 1 cm broad. **Lip** 3-lobed, 2.3 cm long, 1.6 cm broad; side lobes erect, rounded in front; mid-lobe ovate-orbicular, margins undulate; callus a longitudinal, pubescent, fleshy ridge to the centre of the lip.

DISTRIBUTION Guyana, Venezuela, Surinam, Brazil and Peru.

HISTORY Discovered by Charles Parker in Demerara (Georgetown) and sent by him to the Liverpool Botanical Gardens, England. Sir William Hooker described it in 1827 in the *Botanical Magazine* (t. 2729).

SYNONYMS *Menadenia parkeri* Raf.; *Maxillaria hirtilabia* Lindl.; *M. lorifolia* Rchb.f.; *M. kegelii* Rchb.f.; *M. loretoensis* Schweinf.

CLOSELY RELATED SPECIES *M. parkeri* belongs to a group of species, including *M. rufescens*, which have no basal leaves subtending the 1-leafed pseudobulbs. It differs from *M. rufescens* in having a petiolate leaf and paler flowers with a purple-lined lip. See also *M. desvauxiana*.

Maxillaria picta Hooker [Colour Plate]

An epiphytic or occasionally lithophytic plant with clustered pseudobulbs. **Pseudobulbs** ovoid-pyriform, somewhat compressed, many-grooved when old, 4–7 cm long, 2.5–4 cm across, 2- (or rarely 1)-leaved at apex. **Leaves** erect or erect-spreading, fleshy-coriaceous, narrowly ligulate, acute, shortly but distinctly petiolate at base, 20–35 cm long, 2–5 cm broad. **Inflorescences** many on each plant, erect or ascending, 8–16 cm long; peduncle

terete, slender, pale green, 0.2–0.3 cm in diameter; bract appressed, pale green, 2–3 cm long. **Flowers** erect-spreading, fragrant; sepals and petals yellow with purple-spotting, paler on outer surface; lip yellowish-white, spotted and striped purple above; column purple. **Sepals** fleshy, oblong-ligulate, acute, 3 cm long, 0.6 cm broad. **Petals** fleshy, oblique, ligulate, acute, 2.6–2.8 cm long, 0.3 cm broad. **Lip** erect-spreading, slightly recurved above, overall broadly oblong, deeply 3-lobed a little above the middle, 2.4–2.5 cm long, 1 cm broad; side lobes erect, semioblong, obtuse; mid-lobe oblong-linguiform, obtuse, margins slightly undulate-subdenticulate; disc with a furfuraceous, fleshy callus to middle. **Column** erect, slightly incurved, 1–1.2 cm long.

DISTRIBUTION Eastern states of Brazil.

HISTORY Collected by the brother of Mrs A. Harrison in the Organ Mts of Brazil and described in the *Botanical Magazine* (t. 3154) in 1832 by Sir William Hooker from a plant grown by Mrs Harrison. Several varieties of *M. picta* have been described. The plant sometimes cultivated as *M. consanguinea* Klotzsch was earlier described as *M. picta* var. *brunnea* by H.G. Reichenbach. It differs from *M. picta* in having brown sepals.

SYNONYMS *Maxillaria leucocheila* Hoffmannsegg; *M. kreysigii* Rchb.f.; *M. fuscata* Klotzsch; *M. rupestris* Barb. Rodr.

Maxillaria plebeja Rchb.f.

An epiphytic plant with a branching rhizome bearing pseudobulbs at closely spaced intervals. **Pseudobulbs** oblong-cylindrical, 2 cm long, 0.4 cm broad, 1-leafed at apex. **Leaf** oblanceolate, erect, 2.5–3.5 cm long, 0.4–0.6 cm broad. **Inflorescence** very short, about 2–2.5 cm long. **Flowers** large for plant; sepals and petals ochre-yellow to chestnut-brown with a purple base and spotted red; lip purple with a chestnut-brown apex; column chestnut-brown above, purple below. **Dorsal sepal** oblong-elliptic, obtuse, 0.9 cm long, 0.4 cm broad; **lateral sepals** obliquely oblong-ovate, obtuse, 1 cm long, 0.5 cm broad. **Petals** narrowly oblong-elliptic, obtuse, 0.7 cm long, 0.15 cm broad. **Lip** pandurate, emarginate or truncate, margins ciliate, ecallose, 0.8–0.9 cm long, 0.5–0.6 cm broad. **Column** elongate, slightly arcuate, 0.8 cm long.

DISTRIBUTION Brazil.

HISTORY Introduced into cultivation by Consul Schiller who received it from Brazil, *M. plebeja* was described by H.G. Reichenbach in 1859 in the *Hamburger Gartenzeitung* (p. 57).

Maxillaria ringens Rchb.f.

A large, variable, epiphytic plant with a short, stout rhizome. **Pseudobulbs** clustered, cylin-

drical or ovoid, compressed, up to 6.5 cm long, 1-leafed at apex, subtended by several distichous, imbricating sheaths. **Leaf** petiolate, elliptic-oblong, up to 54 cm long, 5 cm broad, subacute or rounded at apex; petiole conduplicate, up to 15 cm long. **Inflorescence** lateral, basal, 1-flowered, erect, lax or flexuous, up to 18 cm long; peduncle concealed more or less by imbricating tubular sheaths. **Flowers** very variable in size, yellow-green to creamy-yellow, with a more or less purple-spotted lip. **Dorsal sepal** oblong or linear-oblong, concave, 1.8–3.9 cm long, 0.6–0.8 cm broad, acute or subacute; **lateral sepals** similar but oblique, forming a short prominent mentum. **Petals** linear-lanceolate or oblong-lanceolate, oblique, smaller than the sepals, acute. **Lip** erect, parallel to column, elliptic, deeply 3-lobed near apex, 1.3–1.7 cm long, 0.6 cm broad; side lobes erect, narrowly semiobovate, with irregular free margins; mid-lobe ovate, fleshy, with irregular margins; disc with a central longitudinal ridge with an acute apex. **Column** small, 0.6–0.7 cm long, slightly arcuate, with a prominent foot.

DISTRIBUTION Common in Mexico, Central America, Venezuela, Guatemala and Peru; in dense humid forests, up to 1700 m altitude.

HISTORY This species was discovered by J. Warscewicz in Guatemala and was described by H.G. Reichenbach in *Walpers, Annales Botanices* (p. 523) in 1864.

SYNONYMS *Maxillaria amparoana* Schltr.; *M. tuerckheimii* Schltr.; *M. yzabalana* S. Wats.; *M. lactea* Schltr.; *M. rousseauae* Schltr.; *M. pubilabia* Schltr.

Maxillaria rufescens Lindl. [Colour Plate]

A very variable epiphytic plant with a long creeping rhizome. **Pseudobulbs** more or less proximate, 2–3 cm apart, cylindrical to ellipsoidal, compressed, more or less 4-angled in cross-section, 1.5–6 cm long, 1-leafed at apex, subtended by several distichous, membranous sheaths. **Leaf** sessile or shortly petiolate, narrowly elliptic, elliptic-oblong or lanceolate, coriaceous, 2–4.5 cm long, up to 2.5 cm broad, acute. **Inflorescence** basal, 1-flowered, 1.5–7 cm long; peduncle erect or arcuate, with several ventricose, remote sheaths. **Flowers** small to medium-sized, yellow or orange and spotted purple or red, rarely white or greenish and striped red or purple. **Dorsal sepal** oblong to elliptic-oblong, concave, 0.9–2.4 cm long, 0.3–0.9 cm broad, acute; **lateral sepals** broader and oblique. **Petals** obliquely oblong-lanceolate or oblong-elliptic, up to 2 cm long, 0.9 cm broad, subacute. **Lip** erect, parallel to column, ovate or elliptic, sharply 3-lobed in middle, 0.8–2.1 cm long, 0.6–1.2 cm broad; side lobes erect, obliquely triangular; mid-lobe oblong to subquadrate, truncate; disc with a linear-oblong central ridge to the middle of the lip. **Column** arcuate, clavate, 0.7–1.6 cm long, with a short foot.

DISTRIBUTION Colombia, Venezuela, Guyana, Brazil, Peru, Mexico, Central America and the W. Indies; common in rain forests up to 1700 m altitude.

HISTORY Imported to England from Trinidad by Messrs Low & Co. One of their plants, sold to the Duke of Devonshire, flowered in December 1834 at Chatsworth, Derbyshire, and was described by John Lindley in the *Botanical Register* (sub t. 1802 & t. 1848) of 1836.

M. rufescens is easily distinguished by its sharp falcate side lobes to the lip.

SYNONYMS *Maxillaria acutifolia* Lindl.; *M. rugosa* Scheidw.; *M. articulata* Klotzsch; *M. vanillodora* Rchb.f.; *M. abelei* Schltr.

CLOSELY RELATED SPECIES See *M. parkeri*.

Maxillaria sanderiana Rchb.f. [Colour Plate]

A large, robust epiphytic or terrestrial plant with a short or more or less elongate rhizome. **Pseudobulbs** clustered, subglobose to ovoid, compressed, up to 5 cm long, 1-leafed at apex, subtended by 2 or more evanescent sheaths. **Leaves** petiolate, oblong-elliptic or narrowly oblong, up to 40 cm long, 5.7 cm broad, acute or cuspidate at the apex. **Inflorescence** basal, lateral, 1-flowered, ascending or arcuate, up to 25 cm long; peduncle more or less concealed by several imbricating tubular sheaths. **Flowers** large, showy, fleshy; sepals and petals white, with deep purple blotches at the base; lip mid-lobe margins bright yellow within. **Dorsal sepal** oblong or oblong-lanceolate, concave, up to 7.5 cm long, 2 cm broad, acute; **lateral sepals** oblique but similar to dorsal sepal, forming with the column-foot a prominent conical mentum. **Petals** obliquely lanceolate, up to 6.5 cm long, 1.8 cm broad, acute. **Lip** erect, parallel to column, recurved, ovate, 3-lobed above the middle, up to 3.5 cm long; side lobes obscure; mid-lobe rounded, margins crisped-undulate; disc with central flattened clavate ridge in the basal half. **Column** short, stout, clavate, up to 1.5 cm long.

DISTRIBUTION Ecuador and Peru.

HISTORY Discovered by Edward Klaboch in Peru at an altitude of 1200 m. He sent plants to Messrs Sander & Sons of St Albans, England. H.G. Reichenbach named it in honour of Frederick Sander in 1888 in Sander's monumental work on orchids *Reichenbachiana* (p. 57, t. 25).

CLOSELY RELATED SPECIES See *M. striata*.

Maxillaria sophronitis (Rchb.f.) Garay

A dwarf, creeping epiphytic plant with a long, slender rhizome completely covered with brown sheaths. **Pseudobulbs** ovoid, compressed, 2.5–3.5 cm apart on the rhizome, dull brown, 1.2 cm long, 0.8 cm broad, 1-leafed at apex, subtended by 1 or 2 leaf-bearing sheaths. **Leaf** oblong-elliptic, minutely apiculate, coriaceous, suberect-spreading, 2 cm long, 0.9 cm broad. **Flowers** large for plant, showy; sepals and petals bright orange-red; lip bright orange-yellow with creamy-yellow side lobes and margins; column pale green. **Sepals** elliptic, acute or apiculate, 1.1–1.3 cm long, 0.7 cm broad; mentum obscure. **Petals** obovate-elliptic, apiculate, 0.8 cm long, 0.6 cm broad. **Lip** 3-lobed in basal half, clawed, 0.7 cm long and broad when spread out; side lobes erect, rounded, front margins erose and inrolled; mid-lobe fleshy, oblong-elliptic, papillose, margins erose; callus raised behind, flat and smooth above. **Column** 0.5 cm long.

DISTRIBUTION Venezuela.

HISTORY Collected by both J.W. Moritz at Tovar and by H. Wagener at Guareima in July 1844 at an altitude of 1200 m, this species was originally described by H.G. Reichenbach in 1854 in *Bonplandia* (p. 18) as *Ornithidium sophronitis* as the flowers are similarly coloured to those in the genus *Sophronitis*. L. Garay transferred it to the genus *Maxillaria* in 1958 in the *Botanical Museum Leaflets of Harvard University* (p. 208).

M. sophronitis is a most distinctive miniature species readily recognised by its small 1-leafed pseudobulbs borne at intervals on a creeping rhizome and by its relatively large scarlet flowers with an orange-yellow lip.

SYNONYM *Ornithidium sophronitis* Rchb.f.

Maxillaria striata Rolfe

A large, stout, showy plant. **Pseudobulbs** clustered, ovoid to oblong-cylindrical, compressed, 4.7–8 cm long, 1-leafed at apex, subtended and partly concealed by several distichous, imbricating sheaths. **Leaves** petiolate, oblong or oblong-elliptic, coriaceous, up to 24 cm long, 4–6 cm broad, acute or obtuse. **Inflorescence** lateral, basal, suberect or arcuate, 1-flowered, up to 30 cm long; peduncle concealed by several tubular sheaths. **Flowers** large, showy; sepals greenish-yellow, closely striped reddish-purple; lip white with reddish-purple stripes on side lobes. **Dorsal sepal** oblong-lanceolate, concave, 4.6–7 cm long, up to 1.2 cm broad, subacute; **lateral sepals** very obliquely triangular-lanceolate, up to 7 cm long, 3 cm broad or more, acute, forming with the column-foot a conspicuous mentum, 2.5 cm long. **Petals** obliquely lanceolate, up to 5 cm long, 1 cm broad, apex recurved. **Lip** erect, parallel to column, recurved, obscurely 3-lobed towards apex, rhombic, 3.5–4 cm long; side lobes erect, semiobovate, free part rounded; mid-lobe ovate-lanceolate, subobtuse; margins crenulate-undulate; disc linear-oblong, many-grooved, rounded at apex. **Column** short, stout, clavate, 1.1 cm long; foot up to 2.2. cm long.

DISTRIBUTION Peru; 1500 m altitude on eastern edge of the Andes.

HISTORY Introduced into cultivation from Peru by Messrs Linden of Brussels and described by Robert Rolfe in 1893 in the *Orchid Review* (p. 265).

CLOSELY RELATED SPECIES *M. striata* is a large-flowered species not unlike *M. sanderiana* in habit. It is, however, readily distinguished by its slightly smaller distinctively coloured flowers in which the lip mid-lobe has crenulate margins.

Maxillaria tarumaensis Hoehne

[Colour Plate]

An epiphytic plant. **Pseudobulbs** small, slightly compressed, up to 3 cm long, greeny-brown, concealed by several imbricating leaf-bearing sheaths. **Leaves** ligulate, conduplicate at base, coriaceous, up to 50 cm long, 2.5 cm broad, unequally acutely 2-lobed at apex, one margin recurved, the other incurved. **Inflorescence** 1-flowered, very short in comparison with leaves; peduncle pale green, up to 5 cm long. **Flowers** relatively small; sepals and petals pale browny-yellow; lip red-purple with a ventral longitudinal green stripe; column cream with dark purple base. **Sepals** oblong-elliptic, subacute or obtuse, 1.4 cm long, 0.6 cm broad; mentum obscure. **Petals** narrowly linear-elliptic, acute, 1.4 cm long, 0.4 cm broad. **Lip** obscurely 3-lobed, subelliptic, rounded at apex, 1.3 cm long, 0.65 cm broad; callus raised, sticky.

DISTRIBUTION Brazil and Venezuela.

HISTORY Originally described in 1877 as *Dicrypta longifolia* by J. Barbosa Rodrigues in *Genera et Species Orchidearum Novarum* (p. 125). A. Cogniaux in Martius's *Flora Brasiliensis* transferred it to the genus *Maxillaria* as *M. longifolia*. Unfortunately, this name had already been used by John Lindley in 1832 for a different species and so F.C. Hoehne renamed the plant *M. tarumaensis* in 1947 in the *Arquivos de Botanica do Estado de São Paulo* (p. 73).

SYNONYMS *Maxillaria longifolia* (Barb. Rodr.) Cogn.; *Dicrypta longifolia* Barb. Rodr.

Maxillaria tenuifolia Lindl. [Colour Plate]

A straggling, pendent or ascending plant up to 60 cm or more long, with a rhizome concealed by appressed sheaths. **Pseudobulbs** 4 cm or more apart on the rhizome, ovoid to ellipsoid, somewhat compressed, rugose, 2–6 cm long, 1–2 cm broad, 1-leafed at apex, subtended by imbricating sheaths. **Leaf** linear, thin-textured but subcoriaceous, grass-green, 12–50 cm long,

0.2–0.7 cm broad, acuminate. **Inflorescence** 1-flowered, up to 6 cm long; bracts scarious, thin, imbricating. **Flowers** showy; sepals and petals dark red marked with yellow or red; lip dark red and yellow or whitish, marked with purple spots, callus dark purple. **Sepals** elliptic-lanceolate to linear-lanceolate, recurved in apical half, 1.7–2.8 cm long, 0.3–1 cm broad, subobtuse to acute; lateral sepals oblique, forming with the column-foot a short mentum. **Petals** appressed to column, lanceolate, oblique, 1.5–2.5 cm long, 0.3–0.7 cm broad, acute or obtuse. **Lip** arcuate-decurved, oblong-elliptic to oblong-subpandurate, acute or retuse at apex, 1.5–2.2 cm long, 0.5–1.1 cm broad; side lobes erect; disc papillose, with a narrow, puberulent callus on the lower third. **Column** clavate, arcuate, 1–1.5 cm long including the foot.

DISTRIBUTION Mexico south to Costa Rica; in rain forests at low altitudes up to 1500 m altitude.

HISTORY Discovered near Veracruz in Mexico by Th. Hartweg and described by John Lindley in 1837 in the *Botanical Register* (sub t. 1986).

SYNONYM *Maxillaria gracilifolia* Kraenzl.

CLOSELY RELATED SPECIES Flowers similar to those of *M. curtipes* and *M. cucullata* which, however, differ markedly in their vegetative habitat.

Maxillaria uncata Lindl.

A small epiphytic plant, up to 35 cm long, growing in clumps or with straggling pendent stems. **Rhizome** short or long. **Pesudobulbs** fusiform-cylindrical, 0.8–1.5 cm long, 0.2–0.3 cm across, 1-leafed at apex, dark green. **Leaf** linear, semiterete, fleshy, erect-recurved, sulcate above, 2–7 cm long, 0.2–0.6 cm broad, pale green. **Inflorescence** axillary; peduncle less than 1 cm long. **Flowers** variable in colour, white, pink or pale green, tinged or veined with purple or red-brown; column lavender or red-brown. **Dorsal sepal** oblong-elliptic or elliptic-lanceolate, acute to obtuse, 0.8–1.1 cm long, 0.3–0.4 cm broad; **lateral sepals** obliquely triangular-lanceolate, acute to obtuse, 1.3–1.7 cm long, 0.6–0.9 cm broad, forming with the column-foot a prominent mentum. **Petals** linear or linear-lanceolate, acute to obtuse, 1 cm long, 0.2–0.35 cm broad. **Lip** linear, elliptic-lanceolate or linear-spathulate, narrowed and sulcate below the middle, minutely carinate and decurved at the obtuse apex. 1.3–1.6 cm long. 0.3–0.4 cm broad, margins cellular-ciliate; callus flat, linear rounded in front. **Column** slender, erect, 1.1–1.6 cm long including the foot.

DISTRIBUTION Belize, Guatemala, Honduras, Costa Rica, Panama and S. America;

rather common from sea level to 1200 m altitude.

HISTORY Introduced into cultivation by Messrs Loddiges of Hackney, London, and described by John Lindley in 1837 in the *Botanical Register* (sub t. 1986).

SYNONYMS *Maxillaria maclaei* Lindl.; *M. striatella* Kraenzl.

Maxillaria valenzuelana (A. Rich.) Nash [Colour Plate]

A pendent or suberect epiphytic plant. **Stem** very short. **Leaves** iris-like, radiating fan-like from the short stem, bilaterally compressed, falcate, coriaceous, acute, up to 18 cm long, 1.6 cm across, light blue-green. **Inflorescence** 1-flowered; peduncles often curved, about 5 cm long. **Flowers** with light green or yellow-green sepals and petals; lip pale brown, spotted purple. **Sepals** ovate-elliptic, acute, 1.1–1.4 cm long, 0.6 cm broad; lateral sepals slightly oblique. **Petals** oblong, acute, 0.9 cm long, 0.3 cm broad. **Lip** very obscurely 3-lobed, acute at apex, 1 cm long, 0.5 cm broad; side lobes suberect; callus in 3 parts along mid-line, glandular-pubescent. **Column** short, stout, 0.3 cm long.

DISTRIBUTION Central and tropical S. America and the W. Indies.

HISTORY Originally collected in Cuba by J.M. Valenzuela, this species was described in *Flora Cubana* (p. 234) by A. Richard in 1850 as *Pleurothallis valenzuelana* but was transferred by G. Nash to the genus *Maxillaria* in 1907 in the *Bulletin of the Torrey Botanical Club* (p. 121).

SYNONYMS *Pleurothallis valenzuelana* A. Rich.; *Dicrypta iridifolia* Batem.; *Maxillaria iridifolia* (Batem.) Rchb.f.; *Marsupiaria iridifolia* (Batem.) Hoehne; *M. valenzuelana* (A. Rich.) Garay

Maxillaria variabilis Lindl. [Colour Plate]

A terrestrial, lithophytic or epiphytic plant with slender, simple or branched rhizomes. **Pseudobulbs** subclustered, ovoid to ellipsoid, 3 cm apart on the rhizome, 1.5–5 cm long, 0.7–1.5 cm broad, 1-leafed at apex, subtended by several sheaths. **Leaf** linear or linear-elliptic, subcoriaceous, grass-green, 5–25 cm long, 0.5–2.3 cm broad, acute to obtuse. **Inflorescence** up to 5 cm long, 1-flowered, subtended by several thin, scarious sheaths; bracts thin, scarious, translucent, lanceolate, acuminate. **Flowers** rather inconspicuous, variable in colour, white to dark red, often deep orange or greenish-yellow, marked column wine-red, blotched red and white at base. **Sepals** oblong-elliptic or lanceolate, concave, recurved in apical half, 1–1.7 cm long, 0.35–0.6 cm broad, rounded or acute; lateral sepals somewhat oblique, forming with the column-foot a short mentum. **Petals**

appressed to column, elliptic-oblanceolate, margins papillose, 0.9–1.4 cm long, 0.3–0.4 cm broad, subobtuse to acute. **Lip** erect, fleshy, obscurely 3-lobed in middle, oblong-elliptic to oblong-subquadrate, rounded or truncate at apex, 1–1.3 cm long, 0.5–0.6 cm broad; disc with a triangular-subquadrate glossy callus. **Column** semiterete, arcuate, 1 cm long including the foot.

DISTRIBUTION Common from Mexico to Panama; in rain forests, up to 1900 m altitude.

HISTORY Discovered by several collectors in Mexico at about the same time and described by John Lindley in 1837 in the *Botanical Register* (sub t. 1986). The specific epithet was given by James Bateman in reference to the very variable flowers found in this species.

SYNONYM *Maxillaria angustifolia* Hooker

Mediocalcar J.J. Smith
Subfamily Epidendroideae
Tribe Epidendreae
Subtribe Eariinae

Small epiphytic plants with creeping rhizomes, often forming dense clumps. **Stems** pseudobulbous, conical to obliquely conical, close together or well-spaced, enveloped when young by several sheaths, 1- to 5-leaved at the apex. **Inflorescences** 1 to several, apical, 1-flowered, produced from the new growths. **Flowers** campanulate, red or orange with white, yellow or green tips to the sepals. **Dorsal sepal** united in the basal part to the lateral sepals, porrect; **lateral sepals** united at the base to the column-foot to form a chin-like mentum. **Petals** hidden within the sepals, free, linear-lanceolate. **Lip** bipartite, the hypochile a short claw, the epichile saccate, ovate, separated from the hypochile by a fleshy transverse callus. **Column** short, fleshy; pollinia 8, waxy.

DISTRIBUTION A genus of some 40–50 species centred on the island of New Guinea with a few species in the Moluccas and extending into the Pacific Islands to Fiji.

DERIVATION OF NAME From the Latin *medius* (middle) and *calcar* (spur), in reference to the saccate middle part of the lip.

TAXONOMY The Dutch botanist J.J. Smith described this genus in 1900 in the *Bulletin de l'Institut Botanique de Buitenzorg* (7: p. 3). It is closely allied to *Eria* but is easily distinguished by its small 1-flowered inflorescences of red or orange campanulate flowers. These are similar to those of *Epiblastus*, another close relative but whose habit is quite different and whose flowers are borne in clusters.

TYPE SPECIES *M. bicolor* J.J. Sm.

CULTURE Temp. Winter min. 12°C. These

orchids are best mounted and grown under shaded, humid conditions. Water all year.

Mediocalcar alpinum J.J. Sm.

A creeping ascending epiphyte with elongate rhizomes, often forming mats. **Pseudobulbs** obliquely ovoid, 0.5–1.5 cm long, 0.5–1 cm in diameter, green, 1- to 2-leaved at the apex. **Leaves** oblanceolate, obtuse or acute, 6–9 cm long, 0.6–1.2 cm wide. **Inflorescences** 1 or 2, 1-flowered, axillary, terminal, very short; bract hidden in sheath. **Flowers** campanulate, orange or red with yellow or greenish tips; pedicel and ovary 1–2 cm long. **Sepals** united in basal half, 7–9 mm long. **Petals** hidden inside sepals, lanceolate, acute, 7–8 mm long, 1 mm wide. **Lip** with a broad claw, saccate in the middle, ovate, subacute, 7 mm long. **Column** 3 mm long.
DISTRIBUTION   New Guinea, the Solomon Islands and Vanuatu; in montane forest up to 1800 m.
HISTORY   J.J Smith, the Dutch botanist, described this orchid in 1914 in the *Bulletin du Jardin Botanique de Buitenzorg* (p. 62) based on collections by de Kock in W. New Guinea.
SYNONYM   *M. bifolium* var. *validum* J.J. Sm.

Mediocalcar decoratum Schuiteman

[Colour Plate]
A dwarf mat-forming epiphytic plant with a creeping rhizome bearing pseudobulbs 1–5 mm apart. **Pseudobulbs** cylindrical to slightly clavate, 0.5–2 cm long, 0.3–0.6 cm in diameter, 3- to 4-leaved at the apex. **Leaves** fleshy, spreading in one plane, linear-narrowly elliptic, subacute to obtuse, 1–2.3 cm long, 0.2–0.4 cm wide, shortly petiolate. **Inflorescences** heteranthous or rarely synanthous, 1-flowered; peduncle 0.3–0.7 cm long; bract sheathing. **Flower** campanulate, not opening widely, orange-red with yellow tips to the sepals and petals; pedicel and ovary 0.5–0.7 cm long. **Sepals** fused in the basal two-thirds to form a saccate cup, 6.5–8.5 mm long, the free parts recurved, triangular, subacute, 2.5–3.5 mm long. **Petals** linear, acute, 5.5–7 mm long, 1 mm wide. **Lip** saccate at base, obscurely 3-lobed, 5–7 mm long, 3 mm wide; side lobes rounded, erect; mid-lobe oblong, acute. **Column** much dilated apically, 3 mm long, with a very short foot.
DISTRIBUTION   New Guinea; montane forest at 900–2000 m. Usually in shaded positions.
HISTORY   Although frequently seen in collections over the past 20 years this delightful miniature was described for the first time by A. Schuiteman in 1989 in the journal *Blumea* (p. 169) based on a collection made in February 1978 at Efogi in Central Province of Papua New Guinea by Alasdair Morrison.

Meiracyllium Rchb.f.

Subfamily Epidendroideae
Tribe Epidendreae
Subtribe Meiracylliinae

Small epiphytic plants with creeping rhizomes that are concealed by scarious sheaths. **Secondary stems** short or obsolete, 1-leafed, somewhat thickened. **Leaf** short, broad, sessile, fleshy-coriaceous. **Inflorescence** terminal, several-flowered. **Flowers** not large for size of plant, delicate. **Sepals** similar, erect-spreading; lateral sepals oblique, forming an inconspicuous mentum at the base. **Petals** narrower than the sepals. **Lip** simple, adnate to the base of the column, conspicuously saccate or gibbous. **Column** short, with a slender or triangular-thickened base, lacking wings; rostellum prominent, apical; pollinia 8, in 2 groups, oblong or clavate, waxy.
DISTRIBUTION   Two species, both uncommon, in Mexico and Guatemala.
DERIVATION OF NAME   From the Greek *meirakyllion* (stripling or little fellow), probably in reference to the low, creeping habit.
TAXONOMY   *Meiracyllium* was described by H.G. Reichenbach in 1854 in *Xenia Orchidacea* (p. 12). It is distantly allied to *Laelia* but its anther is not operculate and the 8 pollinia are not borne in 4 pairs but in 2 fascicles. Because of these rather distinctive features, R. Dressler (1972) has placed it in a subtribe of its own in the Epidendreae.

The relationship of *Meiracyllium* to the other orchid genera has been discussed in full by Dressler in *Brittonia* (1960).
TYPE SPECIES   *M. trinasutum* Rchb.f.
CULTURE   Compost A. Temp. Winter min. 12–15°C. *Meiracyllium* species are best grown in shallow pans or baskets or on slabs of fern-fibre or cork. While growing they require plenty of moisture with moderate shade. Less water should be given when growth is complete after flowering.

Meiracyllium trinasutum Rchb.f.

[Colour Plate]
A small creeping epiphytic or lithophytic plant with a terete rhizome concealed by tubular scarious sheaths when young. **Stems** obscure, 1-leafed. **Leaf** sessile, orbicular to broadly elliptic, obtuse or rounded, fleshy-coriaceous, 2.8–5 cm long, 1.5–3.5 cm broad. **Inflorescences** shorter than the leaves, several-flowered; bracts short, triangular, acute, 0.2 cm long. **Flowers** reddish-purple. **Sepals** oblong-elliptic, acute or shortly acuminate, margins reflexed; 0.8–1.1 cm long, 0.35–0.5 cm broad. **Petals** oblique, elliptic, acute, 0.7–1 cm long, 0.3 cm broad.

Lip sessile, fleshy, saccate-cucullate, acuminate, ± cordate-ovate, auriculate on basal margins, 0.7–0.9 cm long, 0.4–0.5 cm broad. **Column** short, stout, broad at base, with a long pointed apex, 0.4–0.6 cm long.
DISTRIBUTION   Mexico and Guatemala; in forests or on rocks up to 1300 m.
HISTORY   Originally described in 1854 by H.G. Reichenbach in *Xenia Orchidacea* (vol. 1 t. 6) based on a plant of unknown origin in the Pavon herbarium owned by Mr Boissier.
CLOSELY RELATED SPECIES   Very closely allied to *M. wendlandii* but distinguished by its elliptic petals, the strongly saccate lip and by its column which has a broad base.

Meiracyllium wendlandii Rchb.f.

A small, creeping, prostrate, epiphytic plant with a stout rhizome. **Stems** curved, ascending, up to 1 cm long. **Leaves** sessile, obovate or oblong, rounded or obtuse, fleshy-coriaceous, up to 5 cm long, 2.3 cm broad. **Inflorescence** 1-flowered; peduncle short, up to 3.5 cm long; bracts triangular-ovate, acute, 0.1–0.3 cm long. **Flowers** purple, yellowish at the base. **Dorsal sepal** oblong-elliptic, acute, concave, 1–1.7 cm long, 0.4 cm broad; **lateral sepals** obliquely oblong-lanceolate to oblanceolate, dorsally keeled, acute to acuminate, 1–1.7 cm long, 0.3–0.4 cm broad. **Petals** linear-oblanceolate, margins denticulate, 0.8–1.5 cm long, 0.1–0.25 cm broad. **Lip** fleshy, concave, obovate or flabellate when spread, margins upturned, apex decurved and acuminate, 1–1.3 cm long, 0.7 cm broad. **Column** slender. 0.8 cm long, with a long apical point.
DISTRIBUTION   Mexico and Guatemala.
HISTORY   Discovered by H. Wendland in 1857 by the Rio Sucio in Guatemala and named after him by H.G. Reichenbach in 1866 in *Beiträge zu einer Orchideenkunde Zentral-Amerika's.* (p. 73).
SYNONYM   *Meiracyllium gemma* Rchb.f.
CLOSELY RELATED SPECIES   Similar to *M. trinasutum* Rchb.f. but distinguished by its more oblong leaves and better developed stems, linear-oblanceolate petals and slenderer column.

Mendoncella A.D. Hawkes

Subfamily Epidendroideae
Tribe Maxillarieae
Subtribe Zygopetalinae

Medium-sized epiphytes with clustered, 2-leaved pseudobulbs. **Leaves** plicate. **Inflorescences** basal, few-flowered, erect or spreading. **Flowers** fleshy, medium-sized to large, often showy. **Sepals** and **petals** free; lateral sepals borne on column-foot; petals decurrent on column-foot. **Lip** 3-lobed, with a fimbriate margin; side lobes small; callus fan-shaped, grooved. **Column** incurved, semiterete, fimbriately or entirely winged at apex, with a prominent foot; pollinia 4, hard, attached by a quadrate stipe to the viscidium.

DISTRIBUTION Eleven species, widespread in the American tropics from Mexico to Peru and Brazil.

DERIVATION OF NAME Named in honour of Dr Luys de Mendonça e Silva, the editor of the Brazilian orchid journal *Orquidea*.

TAXONOMY Originally described in 1845 as *Galeottia* by A Richard and Galeotti in *Annales des Sciences Naturelles* (p. 25) based on their *Galeottia grandiflora*. Unfortunately, that name is a later homonym and A.D. Hawkes replaced it with *Mendoncella* in 1963 in the journal *Orquidea* (p. 7). *Mendoncella* is allied to *Zygopetalum*.

TYPE SPECIES *Galeottia grandiflora* A. Rich.
SYNONYM *Galeottia* A. Rich. & Gal.
CULTURE Temp. Winter min. 12–15°C. May be grown in pots of epiphyte mix under moderate shade and humidity. Inflorescences appear at the side of new growths as in *Zygopetalum*. Give less water when growth is complete.

Mendoncella fimbriata (Linden & Rchb.f.) Garay

A medium-sized epiphyte or rarely a lithophyte with clustered, ovoid, 2-leaved pseudobulbs, 5–6 cm long, 1–2.5 cm wide, subtended by imbricate distichous acute sheaths. **Leaves** oblanceolate, acute to acuminate, 30–40 cm long, 4.5–8 cm wide, petiolate. **Inflorescences** erect, 2- to 3-flowered, 13–22 cm tall; peduncle 0.5–0.6 cm in diameter; bracts rigid, lanceolate, acuminate, 2.5–5 cm long. **Flowers** fleshy; sepals and petals light brown to pale yellow, boldly veined with purple-brown; lip creamy-white with broad dark purple veins; column pale cream with brown at the base; pedicel and ovary 3.5–4.5 cm long. **Dorsal sepal** lanceolate, acuminate, 4.3–4.6 cm long, 1.5–1.8 cm wide; **lateral sepals** falcate, lanceolate, acuminate, saccate at the base, 4.8–5 cm long, 2–2.5 cm wide. **Petals** falcate, lanceolate-ovate, acuminate, 4–4.5 cm long, 1.5–1.8 cm wide. **Lip** 3-lobed at base, 3–3.3 cm long, 2–2.5 cm wide, pubescent on margins of the mid-lobe; side lobes falcate, lanceolate, acuminate, erose on front margin; mid-lobe ovate to broadly ovate, acuminate, fimbriate; callus several-ridged, fleshy, broad across base of mid-lobe. **Column** 1.2–1.4 cm long, with erose apical wings; foot 1 cm long.

DISTRIBUTION Colombia and Venezuela; in shade on tree trunks in rain forest, 200–1600 m.

HISTORY Originally described by Jean Linden and Reichenbach as *Batemannia fimbriata* in 1854 in *Bonplandia* (p. 280) based on a collection made by L. Schlim, Linden's nephew, at Ocaña in Colombia. Leslie Garay transferred it to the present genus in 1969 in the journal *Orquideologia* (p. 80).

SYNONYM *Batemannia fimbriata* Linden & Rchb.f.

Mendoncella grandiflora (A. Rich.) A.D. Hawkes [Colour Plate]

A large epiphyte with clustered ovoid narrow pseudobulbs 4–8 cm long, 2–3 cm wide, 2-leaved at the apex, subtended by scarious sheaths. **Leaves** lanceolate to elliptic-oblanceolate, acuminate, 25–40 cm long, 5–7 cm wide. **Inflorescences** 1 to several, lateral from base of pseudobulb, 2- to 4-flowered, 10–20 cm long; bracts semicircular-ovate to ovate-lanceolate, acute, 3–4.5 cm long, 2–3 cm wide. **Flowers** large, showy; sepals and petals yellow-green, striped with 5–7 reddish-brown stripes; lip white with longitudinal streaks of red; column whitish streaked with red. **Sepals** lanceolate, acuminate, recurved at apex, 4.5–5 cm long, 1.1–1.5 cm wide; **lateral sepals** with undulate margins and forming a prominent mentum with the column-foot. **Petals** obliquely falcate-lanceolate, acuminate, 4–4.5 cm long, 1.3–1.5 cm wide. **Lip** hinged to the column-foot, 3-lobed, 2.7–3 cm long, 2 cm wide, concave at the base, with erose margins; side lobes small, obliquely ovate; mid-lobe arcuate, rhombic, ovate, acuminate; callus basal, fleshy, several ridged and toothed in front. **Column** arcuate, 2.5–3 cm long, with a pair of subquadrate wings at the apex.

DISTRIBUTION Mexico to Costa Rica, in open woodland to about 1100 m.

HISTORY Originally described in 1845 as *Galeottia grandiflora* by the French botanist Achille Richard in the *Annales des Sciences Naturelles* (p. 25), based on a Mexican collection made by Galeotti. It was for many years considered to be a species of *Zygopetalum* but was transferred to the segregate genus *Mendoncella* by A.D. Hawkes in 1964 in the journal *Orquidea* (p. 7).

SYNONYMS *Galeottia grandiflora* A. Rich.; *Zygopetalum grandiflorum* (A. Rich.) Benth. & Hook.f.; *Batemannia grandiflora* (A. Rich.) Rchb.f.

Mesoglossum Halbinger
Subfamily Epidendroideae
Tribe Oncidieae

Lithophytic or terrestrial plants with elongate rhizomes and ovoid pseudobulbs; roots thick, white, unbranched. **Leaves** 2 to 3, thin-textured, deciduous. **Inflorescences** basal, erect, elongate, simple or few-branched, many-flowered in upper third; peduncle elongate, bearing several sheaths along length. **Flowers** showy, long-lasting, yellow and marked with red-brown. **Sepals** free, subsimilar. **Petals** spreading, free, larger than the sepals. **Lip** dependent, solidly attached to the base of the column, 3-lobed, with a fleshy basal callus; side lobes small, auriculate; mid-lobe clawed, large, spreading. **Column** slender, arcuate, lacking wings; pollinia 2, obovate, sulcate; stipes laminar, linear; viscidium small, elliptic.

DISTRIBUTION A monotypic genus endemic to Mexico.

DERIVATION OF NAME From the Greek *mesos* (middle) and *glossum* (tongue), alluding to the intermediate position of this genus in the *Odontoglossum/Oncidium* alliance.

TAXONOMY A segregate genus of *Odontoglossum* distinguished by its deciduous habit with elongate rhizomes, flowers that resemble a typical *Oncidium* in tepal shape and colour, a wingless column, a complex callus bordered by 2 thin erect plates, and the transverse apical lamina of the lip.

The genus was established by Federico Halbinger in the journal *Orquidea* (Mex.) (p. 194) in 1984.

TYPE SPECIES *Odontoglossum londesboroughianum* Rchb.f.

CULTURE Temp. Winter min. 12°C. This is a difficult orchid to grow requiring a distinct resting season when it drops its leaves. In the growing season plants should be well watered and misted daily and should be grown in a well-ventilated position in full sun.

Mesoglossum londesboroughianum (Rchb.f.) Halbinger

A lithophyte or terrestrial plant, often 1 m or more long, with an ascending rhizome and ovoid bilaterally compressed pseudobulbs, up to 7.5 cm long, 4.5 cm wide, olive-green, 2- to 3-leaved at the apex, subtended by two pairs of foliaceous sheaths at the base. **Leaves** linear-lanceolate, acute, up to 45 cm long, 4.5 cm wide, deciduous after flowering. **Inflorescence** erect, 70–100 cm long, 15- to 30-flowered, with flowers arranged alternately along the rhachis. **Flowers** golden-yellow, heavily marked with red-brown on the sepals and petals and on the base of the lip and callus, 3–3.5 cm across; pedicel and ovary 2.9–4 cm long. **Dorsal sepal** ovate, acute or shortly acuminate, 1.3 cm long, 0.8 cm wide; **lateral sepals** similar but oblique, 1.5 cm long, 0.8 cm wide. **Petals** ovate, rounded at apex, truncate at base, 1.3 cm long, 1.2 cm wide. **Lip** deflexed, 3-lobed, 2.5–2.8 cm long, 2.8–3 cm wide; side lobes

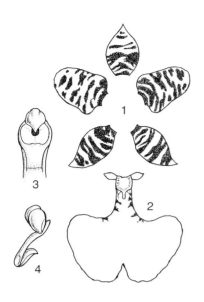

Mesoglossum londesboroughianum
1 – Sepals and petals (× 1)
2 – Lip (× 1)
3 – Column, ventral view (× 1½)
4 – Pollinarium (× 5)

basal, tiny, auriculate, spreading; mid-lobe narrowly clawed, apical lamina reniform, deeply emarginate; callus concave with a raised rim at the base and with 5 teeth at the apex. **Column** slender, arcuate, 1.4 cm long.

DISTRIBUTION Mexico: Guerrero State only; in mixed vegetation on rocks and ground in full sun, 1000–1200 m.

HISTORY H.G. Reichenbach described this orchid in 1876 in the *Gardeners' Chronicle* (n.s. 6: 772) as *Odontoglossum londesboroughianum* based on a specimen that flowered in the collection of Lord Londesborough. It had been introduced into cultivation by Messrs Backhouse of York.

This species has always been regarded as a misfit in that genus somewhat intermediate in its characteristics between *Oncidium*, *Odontoglossum*, *Lemboglossum* and *Rossioglossum*. Since it does not fit comfortably in any of these, Halbinger (1984) placed it in its own genus in the journal *Orquidea* (*Mex.*) (p. 194).
SYNONYM *Odontoglossum londesboroughianum* Rchb.f.

Mexicoa **Garay**

Subfamily Epidendroideae
Tribe Oncidieae

Small epiphytic herbs with short rhizomes, often forming large clumps. **Pseudobulbs,** ovoid to conical, 1- to 2-leaved at the apex,

subtended by 1 leaf-bearing sheath. **Leaves** thinly coriaceous, linear. **Inflorescence** laxly few-flowered, simple, emerging with the new growth; peduncle slender. **Flowers** showy, more or less flat. **Sepals** and **petals** free, subsimilar, the sepals spreading, the petals porrect-ascending, more or less parallel to the column. **Lip** articulated to the column-foot, dependent, 3-lobed, with a basal ridged callus. **Column** elongate, arcuate, lacking wings, with a short foot; rostellum prominent, decurved, truncate; pollinia 2, globose, sulcate, attached by a linear-triangular stipe to an ovate viscidium.

DISTRIBUTION A monotypic genus endemic to Mexico.
DERIVATION OF NAME Named after the country Mexico.
TAXONOMY *Mexicoa* is a segregate genus of *Oncidium* that was established by Leslie Garay in 1974 in the journal *Bradea* (p. 424). It differs from *Oncidium* in having a slender arcuate column, lacking wings but with a short obliquely descending column-foot, and in the lip being articulate to the column-foot.
TYPE SPECIES *Oncidium ghiesbrechtianum* A. Rich. & Gal.

Mexicoa ghiesbrechtiana **(A. Rich. & Gal.) Garay** [Colour Plate]

A small epiphyte often forming a clump. **Pseudobulbs** ovoid, conical or pyriform, 2–5 cm long, up to 2 cm in diameter, grooved, usually bifoliate at the apex. **Leaves** linear or linear-lanceolate, acute, 8–14 cm long, 0.7–1.2 cm wide. **Inflorescence** erect to arcuate, laxly 3- to 6-flowered, up to 20 cm long; bracts sheathing, 2 mm long. **Flowers** c. 1.5 cm across, the sepals and petals off-white or dull yellow longitudinally striped with purple, the lip yellow with an orange-yellow callus; pedicel and ovary up to 1.5 cm long. **Sepals** oblong to oblong-lanceolate, acute, 1.5–1.6 cm long, 0.5–0.6 cm wide. **Petals** porrect-ascending, oblong-obovate, subacute, 1.2–1.5 cm long, 0.4 cm wide. **Lip** deflexed, 3-lobed, 1.7–2 cm long and wide; side lobes spreading, obliquely elliptic, rounded in front; mid-lobe flabellate, bilobulate in front, each lobule subquadrate; callus hairpin-shaped with a basal cup-shaped depression. **Column** slender, arcuate, 0.5 cm long.

DISTRIBUTION Mexico: States of Oaxaca, Michoacan and Guerrero; in montane oak forest at about 2000 m altitude.
HISTORY This pretty and distinctive little orchid, referred to as a 'charming little maverick' by Rebecca Northern in 1980 in the *American Orchid Society Bulletin* (p. 745), was originally described as *Oncidium ghiesbrechtianum* by A. Richard and H. Galeotti in 1845 in the *Annales*

des Sciences Naturelles (p. 27) based on a collection from Mexico by Ghiesbrecht. It was transferred to the present genus by Leslie Garay in 1974 in the Brazilian journal *Bradea* (p. 424).
SYNONYMS *Oncidium ghiesbrechtianum* A. Rich. & Gal.; *Odontoglossum warneri* Lindl.; *Oncidium warneri* (Lindl.) Lindl.

Microcoelia **Lindl.**

Subfamily Epidendroideae
Tribe Vandeae
Subtribe Aerangidinae

Small, leafless, epiphytic plant with a very short or short stem. **Roots** elongate, ± branching, often dorsoventrally flattened, silvery when dry, photosynthetic and green when wet. **Inflorescences** several-flowered, racemose but often very short; bracts very small. **Flowers** small to minute, often translucent, white, ± with green on the lip, ± flushed salmon or brown on sepals and spur. **Sepals** and **petals** free, subsimilar. **Lip** entire, spurred at the base; spur globose to filiform, short to elongate, rarely dilated towards the apex. **Column** short, stout; pollinia 2, ovoid; stipe tapering to a slender base, ± forked at apex; viscidium elliptic.

DISTRIBUTION About 27 species in tropical Africa to S. Africa and Madagascar.
DERIVATION OF NAME From the Greek *mikros* (small) and *koilia* (abdomen), in allusion to the minute globose spur of the type species.
TAXONOMY John Lindley established *Microcoelia* in 1830 in his *Genera and Species of Orchidaceous Plants* (p. 60).

Microcoelia is characterised by its short, leafless stems, simple racemose inflorescences, almost entire lip, the short column in which the androclinium slopes markedly upwards towards the back, the common stipe and viscidium and the deeply cleft rostellum. The genus was revised by V.S. Summerhayes in the *Botanical Leaflets of Harvard University* (1943). Summerhayes recognised three sections in the genus and a total of 25 species. Six other leafless species previously considered in the genus were removed by him and placed in the genera *Solenangis*, *Encheiridion*, *Chauliodon*, *Taeniorrhiza* and *Ankylocheilos*, the last four being newly described by him. The genus has most recently been revised by L. Jonsson (1981) in *Symbolae Botanicae Upsalienses*. He considers *Encheiridion* congeneric with *Microcoelia*.
TYPE SPECIES *M. exilis* Lindl.
SYNONYM *Encheiridion* Summerh.
CULTURE Best mounted. Temp. Winter min. 12–16°C. As for *Chiloschista*.

Microcoelia globulosa (Hochst.) L. Jonsson
[Colour Plate]

A small epiphytic plant often growing in masses on branches and twigs of trees and shrubs. **Stem** very short, leafless. **Roots** grey when dry, greenish when moist, 16–30 cm long. **Inflorescences** numerous, slender, racemose, 5–10 cm long, 20- to 50-flowered; bracts amplexicaul, obtuse. **Flowers** white, secund. **Sepals** ovate, obtuse, 0.2–0.35 cm long, 0.1–0.18 cm broad. **Petals** similar to sepals but slightly smaller. **Lip** oblong-obovate, obtuse or apiculate, 0.2–0.35 cm long, 0.13–0.18 cm broad; spur conical, pendent or incurved, 0.2–0.35 cm long. **Column** stout, minute.

DISTRIBUTION Tropical Africa from Nigeria and Ethiopia south to Zimbabwe; in savanna woodlands and in montane forests.

HISTORY Discovered in 1840 by Schimper near Dscheladscharem in Ethiopia, it was originally described by Hochstetter in 1844 on the printed herbarium label (no. 1565) as *Angraecum globulosum*. L. Jonsson transferred it to *Microcoelia* in 1981 in *Symbolae Botanicae Upsaliensis* (p. 78).

H.G. Reichenbach named it in 1849, based on the same Schimper collection, as *Angraecum guyonianum* in *Linnaea* (p. 865). Summerhayes (1943) transferred it to *Microcoelia* in the *Botanical Museum Leaflets of Harvard University* (p. 144), and the species is well known under that name.

SYNONYMS *Angraecum guyonianum* Rchb.f.; *A. globulosum* Hochst.; *Microcoelia guyoniana* (Rchb.f.) Summerh.; *Gussonia globulosa* (Hochst.) Ridl.

CLOSELY RELATED SPECIES Similar to *Microcoelia obovata* Summerh. which has larger flowers with a longer lip; and to *M. stolzi* (Schltr.) Summerh. which is easily distinguished by its amplexicaul bracts.

Miltonia Lindl.
Subfamily Epidendroideae
Tribe Oncidieae

Epiphytic herbs with short, usually rather inconspicuous, compressed pseudobulbs bearing 2 leaves at apex, the base enveloped in few to many distichous, imbricate, foliaceous sheaths. **Leaves** elliptic-lanceolate to narrowly linear, coriaceous to subcoriaceous, contracted at the base into short or elongate conduplicate petioles. **Inflorescences** axillary from the base of the pseudobulb, often short, erect or arching, 1- to few-flowered scapes or sometimes elongate, many-flowered racemes. **Flowers** medium-sized to large, showy, on long slender pedicels, segments all in one plane so that the flower is flat. **Sepals** subequal, spreading, free,

or with laterals very shortly connate. **Petals** subequal to sepals or slightly broader. **Lip** entire, broadly spreading, apex often bifid; base sessile or very shortly to broadly clawed and affixed to the base of the column at a right-angle; disc inconspicuous or sometimes prominently lamellate. **Column** short, rarely membranaceous and dilated, lacking a foot, apex biauriculate or bialate, truncate or 2-lobed; pollinia 2, waxy.

DISTRIBUTION About 10 species found mostly in Brazil.

DERIVATION OF NAME Dedicated to Earl Fitzwilliam, Viscount Milton (1786–1857) of Wentworth House, Yorkshire, England, an eminent patron of horticulture at the time and a keen orchid grower.

TAXONOMY *Miltonia* was established in 1837 by John Lindley in the *Botanical Register* (sub t. 1976). The short column separates this genus from *Oncidium* and *Odontoglossum* and its auricles separate it from *Brassia* according to Lindley in *Folia Orchidacea* (1854).

Some species previously referred to *Miltonia* have recently been removed to the segregate genera *Miltoniopsis* and *Miltonioides*. L. Garay and G.C.K. Dunsterville in *Venezuelan Orchids Illustrated* (1976) have revived the genus *Miltoniopsis* Godefroy-Lebeuf for the Costa Rican and Andean species of *Miltonia*. The distinctions they emphasise are that the Brazilian *Miltonia* species are characterised by having a scandent rhizome, 2-leaved pseudobulbs, an auriculate column, excavate in front and with the sides united with the nectariferous lip-base. Conversely, the genus *Miltoniopsis* has clustered, 1-leafed pseudobulbs, an exauriculate column which is united with the lip through a central raised ridge. G. Pabst and F. Dungs in *Orchidaceae Brasilienses* (1977) have divided the Brazilian species into 2 groups; namely:

1. *M. spectabilis* alliance of *M. anceps*, *M. flavescens* and *M. spectabilis* which are distinguished by their compressed ancipitous peduncle and bracts which are as long as the ovary.
2. *M. clowesii* alliance of 6 species with a terete peduncle and bracts much shorter than the ovary.

TYPE SPECIES *M. spectabilis* Lindl.
CULTURE Compost A. Temp. Winter min. 12–15°C. Those species such as *M. candida* with clustered pseudobulbs may be grown in pots, whilst those such as *M. spectabilis* with creeping rhizomes are better grown in shallow pans or baskets. All species require plenty of water and moderate shade while growing, and less water when the pseudobulbs are fully grown.

Miltonia clowesii Lindl. [Colour Plate]
An epiphytic plant. **Pseudobulbs** narrowly

oblong-ovate, compressed, 7.5–10 cm long, 2-leaved at apex. **Leaves** linear-ligulate, 30–45 cm long, 1.8–2.4 cm broad, subacute, yellow-green. **Inflorescence** racemose, up to 45 cm long, 7- to 10-flowered. **Flowers** 5–7.5 cm across; sepals and petals chestnut-brown transversely barred with yellow; lip white with a violet-purple basal half, callus white or yellow. **Sepals** lanceolate, 3.6–3.9 cm long, 0.9 cm broad, acuminate, margins revolute. **Petals** similar to sepals, 3.4 cm long, 1 cm broad, acuminate. **Lip** subpanduriform, acuminate or apiculate at the apex, 3.2 cm long, 2 cm broad; callus of 5–7 raised ridges of unequal length. **Column** with narrow entire wings.

DISTRIBUTION Brazil.

HISTORY Discovered in the Organ Mts near Rio de Janeiro by George Gardner and sent by him to the Rev. John Clowes of Manchester, England, who flowered it for the first time in 1839. John Lindley named it in honour of its cultivator in 1839 in *Sertum Orchidacearum* (t. 34).

CLOSELY RELATED SPECIES *Anneliesia candida* (Lindl.) Brieger & Lueckel from Brazil is similar to *M. clowesii* but is readily distinguished by its more oblong-obtuse sepals and petals and the lip which enfolds the column at the base and is shorter than the other segments. *Miltonia cuneata* Lindl. [Colour Plate] is also allied to *M. clowesii* but has distinctly coloured flowers which are blotched rather than spotted brown on the sepals and petals and an obovate lip which is white and has a 2-ridged callus in the basal part.

Miltonia cuneata Lindl. [Colour Plate]
See under *Miltonia clowesii*.

Miltonia flavescens Lindl. [Colour Plate]
An epiphytic plant. **Pseudobulbs** ovate-oblong in outline, compressed, 5–12.5 cm long, 2-leaved at apex. **Leaves** linear-ligulate, 30–35 cm long, 1.3 cm broad, subacute or acute. **Inflorescence** racemose, 7- to 10-flowered; peduncle bearing distichous, alternate, pale brown membranous sheaths; bracts distichous, linear, acuminate, longer than the pedicels, up to 6.5 cm long. **Flowers** fragrant; sepals and petals straw-yellow; lip white or yellow, striped red-purple in basal half. **Sepals** linear-oblong, 3.5–5 cm long, 0.4 cm broad, acute. **Petals** similar to sepals. **Lip** ovate-oblong, acute, margins undulate, 2.5 cm long, base pubescent. **Column** wings obscure.

DISTRIBUTION Brazil.

HISTORY Discovered by M.E. Descourtilz near Bananal in Minas Gerais State in Brazil, *M. flavescens* was later introduced into cultivation by William Harrison who sent plants to his brother Richard in Liverpool, England. John

Lindley described it in 1839 in *Sertum Orchidacearum* (sub t. 48).

SYNONYMS *Cyrtochilum stellatum* Lindl.; *Oncidium flavescens* (Lindl.) Rchb.f.

Miltonia regnellii Rchb.f. [Colour Plate]
Pseudobulbs ovate-oblong, compressed, 5–10 cm long, 1.2 cm across, pale yellow-green, 2-leaved at apex. **Leaves** linear-ligulate, 19–30 cm long, 1.3–1.5 cm broad, acute. **Inflorescence** up to 40 cm long, racemose, 3- to 5-flowered. **Flowers** 5–7.5 cm across; sepals and petals white, ± tinged pale rose towards the base; lip pale rose, streaked with rose-purple, margins white, callus pale yellow. **Sepals** oblong-lanceolate, 3 cm long, 0.9 cm broad, apiculate. **Petals** broader than sepals, elliptic-oblong, 2.7 cm long, 1.1 cm broad, acute. **Lip** broadly obcordate, obscurely 3-lobed, 3–3.5 cm long, 2.1–3.4 cm broad, emarginate; callus of 7–9 radiating lines. **Column** wings narrow, prolonged above.
DISTRIBUTION Brazil (eastern states).
HISTORY This beautiful species was discovered in 1846 by Dr Regnell in Minas Gerais State of Brazil. H.G. Reichenbach described it two years later in *Linnaea* (p. 851). However, it was not introduced into cultivation until 1855 when a plant introduced from Santa Catarina was shown in Hamburg.
SYNONYM *Oncidium regnellii* (Rchb.f.) Rchb.f.

Miltonia spectabilis Lindl. [Colour Plate]
An epiphytic plant with a stout, creeping, scaly rhizome. **Pseudobulbs** spaced, ovate-oblong, compressed, 7.5–10 cm long, 2 cm in diameter, 2-leaved at apex, ochreous-yellow. **Leaves** linear-ligulate, 10–15 cm long, 1.3 cm broad, rounded at apex, ochreous-yellow. **Inflorescence** erect, up to 25 cm long, 1-flowered; peduncle covered by imbricating ancipitous sheaths; bracts covering the ovary completely, up to 7 cm long. **Flowers** flat, 7.5 cm across; sepals and petals white or cream-coloured, tinged rose towards the base; lip vinous-purple with 6–8 darker radiating lines, margins white or pale-rose, callus yellow; column rose-purple. **Sepals** oblong-lanceolate, 3.5–4 cm long, 1.6 cm broad, subacute or acute. **Petals** similar to sepals but broader. **Lip** large, spreading, obovate-orbicular, 4.5–5 cm long, 4–4.6 cm broad; callus trilamellate, with lamellate ending in small, erect plates. **Column** wings subtriangular.
DISTRIBUTION Brazil.
HISTORY *M. spectabilis* is the type species of the genus *Miltonia*. John Lindley described it in the *Botanical Register* (sub t. 1976) of 1837 basing his description on a plant collected by Weddell supposedly in the Sierra de Estrada in Brazil. Plants were also sent to the Birmingham Botanical and Horticultural Society in 1835 by Mr Fry from Brazil and it was flowered by Messrs Loddiges and George Barker of Birmingham in 1837.

The remarkable var. *moreliana* Henfrey [Colour Plate] has larger flowers with plum coloured sepals and petals and a bright rose lip with deeper veins and reticulations. It was sent to G.M. Morel of St-Mandé near Paris from Brazil in 1846 by M. Porte.
SYNONYM *Macrochilus fryanus* Knowles & Westcott

Miltonioides Brieger & Lueckel
Subfamily Epidendroideae
Tribe Oncidieae

Large epiphytic or, less commonly, lithophytic herbs with ovid compressed one-noded pseudobulbs, subtended at the base by leaf-bearing sheaths and 1- 2-leaved at the apex. **Leaves** coriaceous, linear or ligulate. **Inflorescences** axillary from the basal leaf sheaths, laxly few-flowered, simply racemose. **Flowers** showy, flat. **Sepals** and **petals** subsimilar, spreading, free, lanceolate-oblong to spathulate-oblong, rarely undulate. **Lip** pandurate or somewhat oblong, sessile, usually bicoloured, with margins usually recurved, more or less parallel to the column at the base but deflexed in basal part sharply at right angles to the column; the callus obscure of low raised veins in the basal part of the lip. **Column** erect, with or without erose lateral wings and an erose apex; pollinia 2, deeply cleft, attached by on obovate stipe to a small ovate viscidium.
DISTRIBUTION A genus of possibly five or six species in tropical Central and S. America.
DERIVATION OF NAME From its resemblance to the genus *Miltonia*.
TAXONOMY *Miltonioides* was established in 1983 by F.G. Brieger and Emil Lueckel in the journal *Die Orchidee* (p. 131). They give a key to the species and a discussion of their motives.

The species included by Brieger and Lueckel in *Miltonioides* were previously assigned to *Miltonia* or *Odontoglossum* by most recent authorities. The generic delimitation of these genera and their allies, which includes *Miltonioides*, has caused problems for generations of taxonomists. However, the recent work of Garay, Kennedy, Halbinger, Bockemuehl and others has better defined the generic limits of *Miltonia* and *Odontoglossum* sensu stricto. They have also established some well-defined segregate genera such as *Rossioglossum*, *Lemboglossum* and *Miltoniopsis*. Because of the anomalous presence of these species in *Odontoglossum* and *Miltonia*, we have decided to follow here the recognition of *Miltonioides* by Brieger and Lueckel. However, we are sure that further detailed work on this subtribe, particularly on its chemistry, will lead to further rearrangements of some of the species in different genera. It is worth noting that several other species, such as *Oncidium cariniferum*, *O. hastilabium* and *Miltonia clowesii*, may also belong here but the formal transfers have yet to be made.
TYPE SPECIES *M. karwinskii* (Rchb.f.) Brieger & Lueckel
CULTURE Winter min. 12°C. Grow as for *Odontoglossum* and *Miltonia*.

Miltonioides confusa (Garay) Brieger & Lueckel [Colour Plate]
A large epiphyte. **Pseudobulbs** ovoid-cylindrical, 3.5–5 cm long, bifoliate at the apex. **Leaves** linear-oblong, acute, 12.5–20 cm long. **Inflorescence** erect, racemose, laxly 7- to 9-flowered; bracts lanceolate, acute, 1 cm long. **Flowers** 6–6.5 cm tall, fleshy, fragrant, the sepals and petals chestnut-brown, marked and tipped with yellow, the lip milk-white above, rose-purple below, the column white, yellow in front. **Sepals** spreading, linear-lanceolate, acute, 2.5–3.2 cm long, 0.5–0.6 cm wide. Petals falcate, erect, lanceolate, acute, 2.5–2.8 cm long, 0.5–0.6 cm wide. **Lip** deflexed, convex, subpandurate-obovate, shortly apiculate, 2.3–2.5 cm long, 1.5–1.7 cm wide; callus obscurely 2-ridged in basal part of lip. **Column** suberect, 0.1 cm long, with two narrowly oblong lateral wings.
DISTRIBUTION Costa Rica.
HISTORY Introduced into cultivation by Messrs Sander of St. Albans in England before 1885 and described as *Odontoglossum schroederianum* by H.G. Reichenbach in 1887 in the *Gardeners' Chronicle* (pt. 2: p. 364). Unfortunately that name had already been used for a different species by Reichenbach (1882). Therefore Leslie Garay renamed it as *Odontoglossum confusum* in the *American Orchid Society Bulletin* (p. 950) in 1964. Brieger and Lueckel placed it in *Miltonioides in Die Orchidee* (p. 131) in 1983.
SYNONYMS *Odontoglossum schroederianum* Rchb.f. (1887 non 1882); *Miltonia schroederiana* (Rchb.f.) O'Brien; *Odontoglossum confusum* Garay

Miltonioides laevis (Lindl.) Brieger & Lueckel [Colour Plate]
A large epiphyte or lithophyte, up to 1 m or more tall. **Pseudobulbs** ovoid to ovoid-ellipsoidal, compressed bilaterally, 5–12 cm long. 2.5–6.5 cm in diameter, 2- to 3-leaved at the apex. **Leaves** coriaceous-flexible, linear-ligulate to oblong-ligulate, rounded or subacute at the apex, 15–45 cm long, 2.5–5.5 cm wide. **Inflorescence** erect, paniculate, up to 1 m or more long, subtended by a large sheath; bracts scarious, ovate-cucullate, acute, up to 1.5 cm

long. **Flowers** fleshy, showy, the sepals and petals yellow, blotched and banded red-brown, the white in apical part, purple below. **Sepals** spreading, narrowly elliptic to oblanceolate, acute, 2.5–3.5 cm long, 0.6–0.9 cm wide; lateral sepals keeled on the reverse, the margins reflexed. **Petals** erect, falcate, obliquely oblong-elliptic, acute, 2.5–3 cm long, 0.7–0.8 cm wide. Lip deflexed, convex, oblong-pandurate, shortly apiculate, 2–3 cm long, 1–1.3 cm wide, sulcate in the lower part; callus obscurely 2-ridged in the basal part. Column erect, clavate, 1 cm long, with spreading obliquely ovate wings.

DISTRIBUTION Mexico and Guatemala; rare in rain forest up to 1600 m elevation.

HISTORY Discovered in Guatemala by George Ure Skinner and later by Theodore Hartweg and described by John Lindley in 1844 in the *Botanical Register* (t. 39). Lindley named it *Odontoglossum laeve* and it is still frequently met with under that name in collections.

Brieger and Lueckel transferred it to *Miltonioides* in 1983 in *Die Orchidee* (p. 131).

SYNONYMS *Odontoglossum laeve* Lindl.; *Miltonia laevis* (Lindl.) Rolfe; *Odontoglossum leucomelas* Rchb.f.; *Miltonia leucomelas* (Rchb.f.) Rolfe

CLOSELY RELATED SPECIES The Mexican species *Miltonioides reichenheimii* (Linden & Rchb.f.) Brieger & Lueckel (syn. *Odontoglossum reichenheimii* Linden & Rchb.f.) [Colour Plate] is similar to *M. laeve* but differs in lacking column wings and in having a 3-ridged callus in the basal part of the lip.

Miltonioides stenoglossa (Schltr.) Brieger & Lueckel, sometimes considered a variety of *M. laeve* and found from Mexico to Costa Rica, differs in having a narrower almost linear lip.

Miltonioides reichenheimii (J. Linden & Rchb.f.) Brieger & Lueckel
See under *M. laevis*.

Miltonioides warscewiczii (Rchb.f.) Brieger & Lueckel [Colour Plate]
A large epiphyte. **Pseudobulbs** oblong-cylindrical, compressed, 8–12.5 cm long, 2.5 cm wide, unifoliate at apex, subtended by 1–2 leaf-bearing sheaths. **Leaf** linear-lanceolate to oblong, acute or rounded, 12.5–33 cm long, 2–3.5 cm wide. **Inflorescence** longer than the leaves, racemose or more commonly paniculate, many-flowered; bracts lanceolate, acuminate, 2 cm long. **Flowers** clustered, 5 cm across, the sepals and petals brownish-red, yellow or white at the apex, the lip rose-purple with a red-brown disc edged with white and with a yellow callus, the column red-purple. Sepals spreading, oblong-spathulate, obtuse to retuse and mucronate, 1.7–2.3 cm long, 0.5–0.75 cm wide,

undulate. **Petals** similar to dorsal sepal but broader below. **Lip** convex, ovate-orbicular or orbicular-obovate, deeply bilobed at the rounded or truncate apex, up to 2.8 cm long, 2.5 cm wide; callus bilobed and very obscure at the base of the lip. **Column** very short and stout, 0.4–0.5 cm long, with a pair of rounded inconspicuous wings.

DISTRIBUTION Costa Rica, Colombia, Ecuador and Peru.

HISTORY Discovered by the German botanist E.F. Poeppig in 1830 near Cuchero in the Peruvian Andes. However, it was not described until 1856 when H.G. Reichenbach named it as *Miltonia warscewiczii* in his *Xenia Orchidacea* (p. 129).

The placing of this species in *Miltonioides* is perhaps contentious but it equally seems out of place in other allied genera. We have, for the time being, followed Brieger and Lueckel who transferred it to *Miltonioides* in *Die Orchidee* (p.132) in 1983.

SYNONYMS *Miltonia warscwewiczii* Rchb.f.; *Oncidium fuscatum* Rchb.f.; *O. weltonii* Hort.; *Odontoglossum weltonii* Hort.

Miltoniopsis Godefroy-Lebeuf
Subfamily Epidendroideae
Tribe Oncidieae

Epiphytic or lithophytic plants with clustered bilaterally flattened pseudobulbs, 1-leafed at apex and subtended by several distichous leaf-bearing sheaths. **Inflorescence** lateral, basal, erect to arcuate, 1- to few-flowered. **Flowers** large, attractive, rather flat. **Sepals** and **petals** spreading; petals ± reflexed in the middle. **Lip** large, flat, auriculate at base, firmly united at the base to the column by a keel-like ridge. **Column** rather short, lacking wings, keeled in front, footless; stigma large, subquadrate; rostellum broadly triangular, bifid; pollinia 2; stipe 1, linear; viscidium small.

DISTRIBUTION A small genus of five species in Costa Rica, Panama, Venezuela, Ecuador and Colombia.

DERIVATION OF NAME The name refers to the resemblance of the flowers to those of the genus *Miltonia*.

TAXONOMY The genus *Miltoniopsis* was established by Godefroy-Lebeuf in 1889 in *Orchidophile* (9: p. 63). However, subsequent authors failed to take up this name and referred four of the five species to the genus *Miltonia*. In 1976 L. Garay and G.C.K. Dunsterville in *Venezuelan Orchids Illustrated*, vol. 6 (p. 276) in describing a new species, *Miltoniopsis santanaei*, have resurrected the genus for the four other Central American and Andean species previously referred to *Miltonia*. This treatment

seems eminently reasonable, confining the use of *Miltonia* to the Brazilian species and is gaining acceptance. Garay and Dunsterville distinguish *Miltoniopsis* from *Miltonia* by its 1- rather than 2-leaved pseudobulbs which are aggregated rather than being spread on a scandent rhizome and by its exauriculate column which is united to the lip through a keel and is not excavate at the base. The species of this genus are treated as *Miltonia* for hybrid registration purposes.

TYPE SPECIES *Miltoniopsis vexillaria* (Rchb.f.) Godefroy-Lebeuf

CULTURE Compost A. Temp. Winter min. 12–15°C. *Miltoniopsis* should be grown in relatively small pots in conditions of good shade and humidity. They should be well watered while growing and given less water when growth is complete.

Miltoniopsis phalaenopsis (Linden & Rchb.f.) Garay & Dunsterville [Colour Plate]
An epiphytic plant. **Pseudobulbs** ovoid, compressed, 2.5–3.8 cm long, pale green, 1-leafed at apex. **Leaves** linear, pale green, 12.5–22 cm long, 0.6 cm broad, acuminate. **Inflorescence** racemose, shorter than the leaves, 3- to 5-flowered. **Flowers** flat, 5–6.5 cm across; sepals and petals white; lip white with some light purple streaks on side lobes and white, blotched with purple on mid-lobe. **Sepals** ovate-oblong, 2 cm long, 0.8 cm broad, acute. **Petals** broadly ovate-oblong, 2 cm long, 1.2 cm broad, obtuse. **Lip** 3-lobed, 2.6 cm long, 2.8 cm broad; side lobes rounded; mid-lobe flabellate, emarginate; callus of 3 small blunt teeth. **Column** wings very short.

DISTRIBUTION Colombia; in shade in humid situations, 1200–1500 m altitude.

HISTORY Discovered in Colombia on the western slopes of the Cordillera Oriental by L. Schlim in 1850 and sent by him to Messrs Linden of Brussels. H.G. Reichenbach described it in *Bonplandia* (p. 278) in 1854 as *Odontoglossum phalaenopsis*.

Many still accept it in the genus *Miltonia* to which G. Nicholson transferred it in 1886 in the *Illustrated Dictionary of Gardening*. In 1976, L. Garay and G.C.K. Dunsterville have transferred it to *Miltoniopsis* in *Venezuelan Orchids Illustrated*, vol. 6 (p. 278).

SYNONYMS *Odontoglossum phalaenopsis* Linden & Rchb.f.; *Miltonia phalaenopsis* (Linden & Rchb.f.) Nicholson

CLOSELY RELATED SPECIES *M. warscewiczii*.

Miltoniopsis roezlii (Rchb.f.) Godefroy-Lebeuf [Colour Plate]
Pseudobulbs ovate-oblong, compressed, 5–6.5

cm long, pale green, 1-leafed at apex. **Leaf** linear to linear-ligulate, 22–30 cm long, 1.5 cm broad, pale green. **Inflorescence** racemose, up to 30 cm long, 2- to 5-flowered; bracts lanceolate, acute, 0.9 cm long, **Flowers** flat, 8–10 cm across, white with a purple blotch at the base of each segment; disc orange-yellow. **Sepals** obovate-oblong, up to 5 cm long, 2.1 cm broad, acute. **Petals** similar to sepals but broader, up to 2.5 cm broad, acute. **Lip** broadly obcordate, emarginate, with an apicule in the sinus, 3–5.1 cm long, 3.5–5.5 cm broad, with a small horn-like auricle on each side at base; callus of 3 raised ridges at base with 2 small teeth in front. **Column** wings obsolete.

DISTRIBUTION   Colombia (Antioquia Province); 300–700 m altitude.

HISTORY   This spectacular species was discovered in the Cordillera Occidental of Colombia in 1873 by Benedict Roezl. The plant he discovered was eventually flowered by William Bull of Chelsea, London. H.G. Reichenbach described it in 1873 as *Odontoglossum roezlii* in *Xenia Orchidacea* (p. 191, t. 182) but for many years this species has been known as *Miltonia roezlii*. G. Nicholson having transferred it there in the *Illustrated Dictionary of Gardening* (1886). Godefroy-Lebeuf transferred it in 1889 to *Miltoniopsis* in *Orchidophile* (p. 145) a name that has now been resurrected.

SYNONYMS   *Odontoglossum roezlii* Rchb.f.; *Miltonia roezlii* (Rchb.f.) Nicholson

CLOSELY RELATED SPECIES   *M. warscewiczii*

Miltoniopsis vexillaria (Rchb.f.) Godefroy-Lebeuf [Colour Plate]

An erect or suberect epiphytic plant, up to 30 cm high. **Pseudobulbs** strongly compressed, ovoid-conical, 4 cm long, 1.8 cm broad, 1-leafed at apex, but pseudobulb subtended by 3–6 leaves of which the outer ones are very reduced. **Leaves** ligulate, articulated to leaf-base, up to 20 cm long, 2 cm broad, obliquely acute, pale green, V-shaped in cross-section. **Inflorescence** lateral from base of pseudobulb, about 4-flowered, up to 30 cm long; bracts small, lanceolate, keeled on reverse, 1 cm long. **Flowers** large, showy, white, pink or white flushed and striped pink; lip with yellow marking at base, striped maroon and surrounded by a maroon area. **Sepals** obovate, 3 cm long, 1.6 cm broad, minutely apiculate. **Petals** oblong-obovate, recurved at apex, 3 cm long, 1.8 cm broad, apiculate. **Lip** broadly flabellate or reniform, auriculate, with a deep apical sinus, lobes broadly rounded; callus small, 3-ridged. **Column** short, erect.

DISTRIBUTION   Colombia and N. Ecuador; 1300–2150 m altitude on the margins of montane forests.

HISTORY   Originally discovered by Bowman, one of Veitch's collectors, whilst collecting in Colombia in 1866 or 1867. Unfortunately, he died before he could send plants to Europe. It was rediscovered by Gustav Wallis for Jean Linden and again by B. Roezl for the same firm. Eventually J. Chesterton succeeded in collecting it in 1872 for Messrs Veitch who flowered it for the first time the following year. H.G. Reichenbach had originally described this species as *Odontoglossum vexillarium* in 1867 in the *Gardeners' Chronicle* (p. 901) but in 1886 G. Nicholson transferred it to *Miltonia* under which generic name it is still often grown. Godefroy-Lebeuf transferred it to his new genus *Miltoniopsis* as the type species in 1889 in *Orchidophile* (p. 148).

SYNONYMS   *Odontoglossum vexillarium* Rchb.f.; *Miltonia vexillaria* (Rchb.f.) Nicholson

Miltoniopsis warscewiczii (Rchb.f.) Garay & Dunsterville [Colour Plate]

Pseudobulbs ovate-oblong, compressed, 3.8–5 cm long, 1-leafed at apex. **Leaf** linear-lanceolate, 22–30 cm long, acute, pale green. **Inflorescence** racemose, up to 30 cm long, 3- to 5-flowered; bracts small, acute, appressed. **Flowers** flat, 6.5 cm across; white with a pale reddish-purple blotch at the base of each segment; callus yellow; column-wings light rose. **Sepals** ovate-oblong, acute, 2.6–2.7 cm long, 1.4–1.5 cm broad. **Petals** similar to sepals. **Lip** broadly panduriform, 3.5 cm long, 3.3 cm broad; basal lobes small, rounded; mid-lobe emarginate; callus semilunar with 3 short ridges in front, pubescent. **Column** with narrow wings.

DISTRIBUTION   Costa Rica; 1400–2000 m.

HISTORY   Discovered in 1849 by J. Warscewicz in the Cordillera de Veragua growing on leguminous trees. H.G. Reichenbach described it in 1852 in the *Botanische Zeitung* (p. 692) as *Odontoglossum warscewiczii*. This was transferred recently to *Miltoniopsis* by L. Garay and G.C.K. Dunsterville in 1976 in *Venezuelan Orchids Illustrated*, (vol. 6 p. 278). If placed in the genus *Miltonia*, the correct name for this species would be *Miltonia endresii* as *Miltonia warscewiczii* has been used for a distinct species. It was first imported by Messrs Veitch & Sons in 1873 when their collector A.R. Endres found it in Central America. G. Nicholson named it in honour of Endres in 1886 in the *Illustrated Dictionary of Gardening* (p. 368).

SYNONYMS   *Odontoglossum warscewiczii* Rchb.f.; *O. warscewiczianum* Rchb.f. ex Hemsley; *Miltonia endresii* Nicholson; *M. superba* Schltr.

CLOSELY RELATED SPECIES   *M. phalaenopsis* and *M. roezlii*.

Mischobulbum Schltr.
Subfamily Epidendroideae
Tribe Arethuseae
Subtribe Bletiinae

Small to medium-sized terrestrial herbs with a fleshy short stout creeping rhizome. **Pseudobulbs** cylindrical, unifoliate. **Leaf** fleshy, ovate-triangular to cordate, sometimes mottled above, shortly petiolate, articulated near the base of the lamina. **Inflorescence** erect, lateral from the base of the pseudobulb, laxly to densely few-flowered; peduncle covered by sheaths. **Flowers** somewhat showy, non-resupinate to erect. **Sepals** and **petals** subsimilar, free but the lateral sepals decumbent on the column-foot. **Lip** obscurely 3-lobed or entire, lacking a spur, with a linear ridged callus. **Column** subterete, quite long, with a more or less prominent foot; pollinia 8.

DISTRIBUTION   A small genus of about six species in S.E. Asia and the Malay Archipelago across to New Guinea.

DERIVATION OF NAME   From the Greek *mischos* (stalk) and *bulbos* (bulb), descriptive of the pseudobulbs.

HISTORY   Rudolf Schlechter established this genus in 1911 in *Fedde, Repertorium Specierum Novarum* (p. 98) to accommodate a few species that seemed intermediate between *Tainia* and *Nephelaphyllum*. They differ from the former in their *Nephelaphyllum*-like habit and from the latter in having a column-foot and no spur.

TYPE SPECIES   Not selected.

CULTURE   Temp. Winter min. 12–15°C. Grow as for *Nephelaphyllum*.

Mischobulbum cordifolium (Hook.f.) Schltr. [Colour Plate]

Medium-sized terrestrial plants with a short creeping rhizome. **Pseudobulbs** cylindrical, up to 7 cm long, 0.5 cm in diameter, covered by loose sheaths when young, 1-leaved at the apex. **Leaf** spreading, ovate, obtuse to subacute, 8–10 cm long, 6–7 cm wide, green blotched with dark green on the upper side. **Inflorescence** erect, laxly 4- to 8-flowered, up to 25 cm long; bracts lanceolate, acuminate, 7–8 mm long. **Flowers** showy, the sepals and petals brown with darker veins, the lip white with red spots on the side lobes and a yellow-brown mid-lobe. **Dorsal sepal** and **petals** not spreading widely, lanceolate, acuminate, 2–2.4 cm long, 0.4–0.8 cm wide; **lateral sepals** obliquely lanceolate, acuminate, 2.2–2.3 cm long, 0.6–0.8 cm wide; mentum 0.7–0.8 cm long. **Lip** obscurely 3-lobed, recurved, 2.3–2.5 cm long, 1.9–2.1 cm wide; side lobes spreading, rounded; mid-lobe triangular, acute; callus of 3 ridges from the

base almost to the apex of the lip. **Column** 1 cm long; foot 1.2–1.3 cm long, incurved.
DISTRIBUTION S.E. China, Hong Kong and Taiwan; in forest, 500–1000 m altitude.
HISTORY Sir Joseph Hooker first described this attractive orchid as *Tainia cordifolia* in 1889 in Hooker's *Icones Plantarum* (t. 1861). It was transferred to *Mischobulbum* by Rudolf Schlechter in 1911 in *Fedde, Repertorium Specierum Novarum* (p. 98).
SYNONYM *Tainia cordifolia* Hook.f.

Mormodes Lindl.
Subfamily Epidendroideae
Tribe Gongoreae
Subtribe Catasetinae

Epiphytic or terrestrial herbs. **Pseudobulbs** oblong to fusiform, fleshy, several-leaved. **Leaves** elongate, distichous, plicate. **Inflorescences** lateral, 1 to several, arising from the nodes of the pseudobulbs, racemose, often pendulous. **Flowers** ± showy, monomorphic or polymorphic. **Sepals** and **petals** free, spreading or reflexed, rarely connivent. **Lip** entire, 3-lobed or dentate below, glabrous to pubescent, incurved-ascending, reduplicate or rarely concave; side lobes contorted or reflexed; mid-lobe apiculate. **Column** thick, erect, twisted to one side in male flowers, without a foot; pollinia 4, waxy, oblong.
DISTRIBUTION About 20 species in Central and S. America.
DERIVATION OF NAME From the Greek *mormo* (phantom) and *eides* (looking like) referring to the grotesque appearance of the flowers.
TAXONOMY John Lindley described *Mormodes* in 1836 in *An Introduction to the Natural System of Botany*, 2nd edition (p. 446). Taxonomically it is a difficult group which is particularly interesting for the polymorphic flowers found in some species and for the exotic pollination mechanisms. Charles Darwin was the first person to elucidate how *Mormodes* flowers were pollinated when he studied *M. ignea* (in *The Various Contrivances by which British and Foreign Orchids are Fertilised*, 1862). C. Dodson and L. van der Pijl in *Orchid Flowers* (1966) have summarised our knowledge on the pollination mechanisms of 12 species studied in the wild. All species studied so far have been pollinated by bees of the genus *Euglossa*. *Mormodes* species may have separate male and female flowers or, alternatively, in some species, the flowers are protandrous. In male flowers the column is twisted to one side so that the apex of the column lies in a hollow in the lip surface (the lip being uppermost) and the anther thus faces outwards. A male bee attracted by the flower's

odour will land on the lip disturbing the column-apex at which stimulus the viscidium is released. The apex of the anther-cap acts as a hinge so that the viscidium and attached stipe and pollinia are swung in and arc upwards above the lip striking the back of the bee. The cement of the viscidium dries quickly, leaving the pollinarium attached to the insect but tightly curled. In 30 minutes or so the stipe uncurls and the pollinia are held erect from the bee's thorax so that when it enters a female flower the pollinia are in the correct position to be placed in the stigma.

Mormodes is allied to other genera which exhibit dimorphism, such as *Catasetum* and *Cycnoches*, being distinguished by the twisted column so vital in the mechanism of pollination.

The Brazilian species of *Mormodes* has been covered by F.C. Hoehne in *Flora Brasilica* (1942) and by G. Pabst and F. Dungs in *Orchidaceae Brasilienses* (1975) and the 17 Colombian species by Pabst in *Orquideologia* (1968, 1969). The Central American species are fewer in number and are covered by the relevant orchid floras of Panama, Guatemala and Mexico.
TYPE SPECIES *M. atropurpurea* Lindl.
CULTURE Compost A or B. Temp. Winter min. 12–15°C, more while growing. As for *Catasetum*. The plants require good light, warmth and plenty of water with a dry cooler rest after the leaves are shed. The flowers appear from various points on the mature pseudobulbs.

Mormodes colossus Rchb.f. [Colour Plate]
A large epiphytic plant. **Pseudobulbs** almost cylindric, up to 30 cm long, 4.5 cm in diameter, tapering. **Leaves** plicate, deciduous, with persistent imbricating bases. **Inflorescences** produced near the bases of the pseudobulbs up to 60 cm or more long, arching, racemose. **Flowers** variable in size and colour, fragrant; sepals and petals olive-green, yellowish-brown or cream; lip brown, tan or yellow. **Sepals** subequal, spreading, linear-lanceolate, acuminate, 3.5–5 cm long, 0.6–0.8 cm broad. **Petals** similar to sepals, lanceolate, 3.2–4.5 cm long, 0.7–1 cm broad. **Lip** shortly clawed, elliptic-ovate, to rhombic-ovate, acute or acuminate, 3.2–5 cm long, 1.6–2.5 cm broad, side margins strongly recurved. **Column** twisted to one side, 1.5–1.7 cm long.
DISTRIBUTION Costa Rica and Panama.
HISTORY Described in 1852 by H.G. Reichenbach in the *Botanische Zeitung* (p. 636) from a plant collected by J. Warscewicz in 1850 in the mountains of Central America at between 1800 and 2100 m.
SYNONYMS *Mormodes macranthum* Lindl. & Paxt.; *M. wendlandii* Rchb.f.; *M. powellii* Schltr.

Mormodes maculata (Klotzsch) L.O. Williams
A medium-sized epiphytic plant. **Pseudobulbs** more or less fusiform, 12.5–15 cm long, several-leaved. **Leaves** linear-lanceolate, long-acuminate, 30–38 cm long, 3 cm broad, articulated to persistent bases. **Inflorescence** up to 40 cm long, arching, densely many-flowered, racemose; bracts small, ovate, acuminate. **Flowers** subsecund, pleasantly fragrant, light tawny-yellow densely spotted with chocolate-red, rarely lacking any spots. **Sepals** and **petals** similar, ovate, acuminate, incurved, 2.8–3.5 cm long, 0.8 cm broad. **Lip** smaller than other segments, 3-lobed. all lobes acuminate, 2.4 cm long, 1.6 cm broad. **Column** twisted, 1.8 cm long.
DISTRIBUTION Mexico.
HISTORY Discovered by Count Karwinsky in 1836 in the Mexican province of Oaxaca and sent by him to J. Bateman of Knypersley, England where it flowered in July 1838. Bateman described it in his *Orchidaceae of Mexico and Guatemala* where it was also illustrated for the first time (t. 14) as *Mormodes pardina*. However, L.O. Williams noted in *Ceiba* (1950) that O. Klotzsch has described this species in the *Allgemeine Gartenzeitung* (p. 306), just before Bateman in 1838, as *Cyclosia maculata*, thus the correct name for this species is *Mormodes maculatum*.

Var. *unicolor* (Hooker) L.O. Williams [Colour Plate] with bright lemon-yellow flowers was collected in Mexico by John Ross for G. Barker.
SYNONYM *Mormodes pardina* Batem.

Mormodes warscewiczii Klotzsch [Colour Plate]
An epiphytic plant, up to 50 cm or more tall. **Pseudobulbs** fusiform-cylindric, many-noded, slightly compressed, up to 16 cm long, 5 cm broad, covered by white scarious sheaths. **Leaves** linear-lanceolate to elliptic-lanceolate, acuminate, articulated to leaf-sheaths, 15–23 cm long, 1–4.5 cm broad. **Inflorescences** several, arising from the nodes of the pseudobulbs, up to 50 cm long, racemose, several-flowered; peduncle slender; bracts ovate-cucullate, acute, up to 0.7 cm long. **Flowers** variable in size and colour; sepals and petals fleshy, green, yellowish or maroon, heavily marked with brownish-purple; lip reddish-brown, greenish-white or yellow, spotted red or purple. **Sepals** oblong-lanceolate to lanceolate, acute or acuminate, 1.7–13.5 cm long, 0.5–11.2 cm broad. **Petals** elliptic-lanceolate, acute to shortly acuminate and recurved at apex, 1.7–3.2 cm long, 0.6–1.3 broad, margins undulate-crisped. **Lip** deeply 3-lobed towards base,

pilose or pubescent, 1.7–3 cm long; side lobes linear-oblanceolate, twisted, 0.8–1.5 cm long; mid-lobe tapering or linear, truncate or rounded at apex, 1.2–2 cm long, up to 1.2 cm broad. **Column** somewhat twisted, arcuate, sulcate, 1.3–2.7 cm long.

DISTRIBUTION   Mexico and Peru.

HISTORY   This polymorphic species was first collected by J. Warscewicz in Peru and it was described the following year by O. Klotzsch in F. Otto and A. Dietrich's *Allgemeine Gartenzeitung* (p. 65) in 1854.

SYNONYM   *Mormodes histrio* Linden & Rchb.f.

Mormolyca Fenzl

Subfamily Epidendroideae
Tribe Maxillarieae
Subtribe Maxillariinae

Small epiphytic plants. **Pseudobulbs** emitted from a short rhizome, fleshy, 1-leafed above. **Leaf** coriaceous, erect, ligulate. **Inflorescences** basal, erect, 1-flowered; peduncles slender. **Sepals** and **petals** similar, free; lateral sepals not forming a mentum. **Lip** suberect, 3-lobed; side lobes minute, erect; mid-lobe large, decurved; disc callose. **Column** arcuate, lacking wings; pollinia 4, waxy; viscidium lunate.

DISTRIBUTION   Six species only in Central America and northern S. America.

DERIVATION OF NAME   From the Greek *mormolyca* (hobgoblin), in allusion to the rather grotesque appearance of the flower in side view and its coloration.

TAXONOMY   E. Fenzl described *Mormolyca* in 1850 in *Denkschriften Akademie Wien der Mathematisch Naturwissenschaftlichen* (p. 253). It is allied to *Maxillaria* but distinguished by its lunate viscidium and the inflorescence which is as long as the leaves. From *Trigonidium* which is also closely allied, *Mormolyca* can be readily separated by its lack of a short sepaline tube at the base of the flower. L. Garay and M. Wirth (1959) revised the genus in the *Canadian Journal of Botany* giving a key to the species and giving reasons for considering *Cyrtoglottis* Schltr. congeneric with *Mormolyca*.

TYPE SPECIES   *M. lineolata* Fenzl [= *M. ringens* (Lindl.) Schltr.].

SYNONYM   *Cyrtoglottis* Schltr.

CULTURE   Compost A. Temp. Winter min. 12–15°C. As for *Maxillaria*. The plants may be grown in pots or pans as each pseudobulb tends to produce two new shoots. While growing, the plants need moderate shade with plenty of water and a somewhat drier period when the pseudobulbs are fully grown.

Mormolyca peruviana C. Schweinf.

A medium-sized epiphytic plant, up to 16 cm tall. **Pseudobulbs** clustered, ellipsoid, compressed, up to 2 cm long, 1-leafed at apex. **Leaf** ligulate, subacute above, coriaceous, about 14 cm long, 1.2 cm broad. **Inflorescences** many, basal, erect, 1-flowered, 8–12 cm long. **Flower** large in genus, ringent, 3 cm across, yellow. **Sepals** oblong-lanceolate, mucronate, 2 cm long, 0.5 cm broad, margins reflexed. **Petals** linear-oblong, acute or apiculate, 1.9 cm long, 0.4 cm broad. **Lip** erect and parallel to the column, 3-lobed in the middle, 1.5 cm long, 0.7 cm broad; side lobes porrect, erect, obliquely lanceolate-acuminate; mid-lobe oblong, rounded or truncate in front; callus central, ovate, porrect, trilobulate in front. **Column** arcuate, lacking a foot, concave in front, 1.3 cm long.

DISTRIBUTION   Peru; 1800 m altitude.

HISTORY   Discovered by Schunke in the Chanchamayo Valley in Peru and described and illustrated by Charles Schweinfurth in 1944 in the *American Orchid Society Bulletin* (p. 196).

CLOSELY RELATED SPECIES   *M. peruviana* differs from the more frequently cultivated *M. ringens* in having larger flowers with elongate side lobes to the lip.

Mormolyca ringens (Lindl.) Schltr.
[Colour Plate]

A small epiphytic plant, growing in dense clumps. **Pseudobulbs** arising from a slender wiry rhizome, subrotund to ellipsoid, compressed, 2–4 cm long, 2–3 cm broad, 1-leafed at apex, subtended by distichous sheaths. **Leaf** coriaceous, linear-ligulate to narrowly lanceolate, acute to obtuse, 9–35 cm long, 1.5–3.5 cm broad. **Inflorescences** erect, 1-flowered, ± equal in length to the leaf, 6–33 cm long; bracts brownish, scarious, acute, up to 1.5 cm long. **Flower** fleshy, yellow to lavender; sepals lined with purple; lip lavender or maroon. **Sepal** oblong-elliptic, rounded or obtuse, 1.6–1.9 cm long, up to 0.8 cm broad. **Petals** linear-elliptic, obtuse or rounded, convex, 1.3–1.5 cm long, 0.4–0.6 cm broad. **Lip** suberect, 3-lobed in middle, obovate-elliptic to elliptic-oblong, downy-pubescent, ciliolate, 1 cm long, 0.3–0.5 cm broad; side lobes minute, erect, obtuse to acute; mid-lobe broadly orbicular, fleshy, decurved; disc fleshy with a tridentate callus in the middle. **Column** downy-pubescent, arcuate, 1 cm long.

DISTRIBUTION   Mexico to Costa Rica; common in forests from sea level to 1000 m altitude.

HISTORY   John Lindley originally described this species as *Trigonidium ringens* in 1840 in the *Botanical Register* (misc. 57) based on a Th.

Hartweg collection from Mexico. R. Schlechter transferred it to the monotypic genus *Mormolyca* in 1914 in *Die Orchideen* (p. 436).

SYNONYMS   *Mormolyca lineolata* Fenzl; *Trigonidium ringens* Lindl.

CLOSELY RELATED SPECIES   See *M. peruviana*.

Myoxanthus Poepp. & Endl.

Subfamily Epidendroideae
Tribe Epidendreae
Subtribe Pleurothallidinae

Small epiphytes with creeping rhizomes and many erect unifoliate stems (ramicauls) covered by loose easily shed, often hispid sheaths. **Leaves** erect, coriaceous. **Inflorescences** axillary. **Flowers** small, fleshy; pedicel separated from the ovary by a thickened node. **Sepals** free. **Petals** with fleshily thickened knob-like tips. **Lip** small. **Column** well-developed, winged or toothed; pollinia 2, hard.

DISTRIBUTION   About 40 species in Central and S. America.

DERIVATION OF NAME   From the Greek *myoxos* (dormouse) and *anthos* (flower), in some obscure allusion to the flower of the type species.

TAXONOMY   Poeppig and Endlicher established this genus in 1835 in the first volume of their *Nova Genera ac Species* (p. 50). The genus was for many years considered synonymous with *Pleurothallis* but the critical work of Luer (see *Icones Pleurothallidinarum* 1: p. 35) has led to its recent resurrection. The genus is distinguished from *Pleurothallis* by the hispid sheaths that cover the erect stems, the single flowers produced successively or simultaneously in the leaf axil and the variously thickened and extended tips to the petals.

TYPE SPECIES   *M. monophyllos* Poepp. & Endl.

SYNONYMS   *Reymondia* Karst. & Kuntze; *Duboisia* Karst.; *Chaetocephala* Barb. Rodr.

CULTURE   Temp. Winter min. 12°C. May be grown in pots but more readily mounted, when they will form large masses. Water throughout the year and give conditions of moderate shade and humidity.

Myoxanthus reymondii (Rchb.f.) Luer

An erect caespitose epiphyte with a very short rhizome. **Stems** erect, terete, 15–30 cm long, covered by roughly hispid sheaths along length, unifoliate at the apex. **Leaf** erect, coriaceous, convex, lanceolate, acute, 8–17 cm long, 1–1.5 cm wide, dorsally carinate. **Inflorescences** 1 to many, axillary, fasciculate, 1-flowered, 1.5–2 cm long; bracts scarious, ovate, acute, 4–6 mm long. **Flowers** spreading, fleshy, the sepals greeny-brown to honey-brown, the petals yellow-brown spotted with purple and with purple tips, the lip dark brown and yellow; pedicel 1.5–3 mm long; ovary 1.5–3 mm long, hispid. **Dorsal sepal** oblong, obtuse, 6–7 mm long, 3–4 mm wide; **lateral sepals** obliquely ovate-elliptic, obtuse, 7 mm long, 4–4.5 mm wide, united in basal half; all sepals hispid on outer surface. **Petals** porrect, ovate below with a prominent fleshy stalked clavate shiny apex, 4.5–5 mm long, 2.5 mm wide at base. **Lip** recurved strongly in middle, clawed, ligulate, rounded at apex, 2–2.5 mm long, 1–1.5 mm wide, with 2 lateral erect teeth. **Column** slight-

ly arcuate, with 2 lateral rounded auricles towards the apex, 2 mm long.
DISTRIBUTION Venezuela and Colombia.
HISTORY Originally described in 1847 by Hermann Karsten as *Duboisia reymondii* in *Allgemeine Gartenzeitung* (p. 394) based on a collection from Petaquire in Venezuela and named for Dr Du Bois Reymond. It was transferred to *Pleurothallis* by Reichenbach in *Bonplandia* (p. 26) in 1854 and is still often met with under that name in cultivation. Luer transferred it to the present genus in *Selbyana* (p. 49) in 1982.
SYNONYMS *Duboisia reymondii* Karst.; *Pleurothallis reymondii* (Karst.) Rchb.f.; *Duboisreymondia pulpiguera* Karst.

Myrmecophila Rolfe
Subfamily Epidendroideae
Tribe Epidendreae
Subtribe Laeliinae

Large or medium-sized epiphytes with conical, tapering, hollow pseudobulbs, 2- to 4-leaved at the apex. **Leaves** short, very coriaceous. **Inflorescences** apical, elongate, erect, multi-flowered, paniculate; peduncle terete, often very long. **Flowers** often showy, medium-sized to large. **Sepals** and **petals** spreading, similar. **Lip** 3-lobed porrect, attached to the short column-foot, with a longitudinal callus of ridges. **Column** elongate, arcuate; pollinia 8.
DISTRIBUTION A genus of some eight species in tropical Central and S. America and the W. Indies.
DERIVATION OF NAME From the Greek *myrmex* (an ant), and *philos* (a friend), referring to the ant associations of the plant.
TAXONOMY Established in 1917 by Robert Rolfe in the *Orchid Review* (p. 50) as a segregate genus of *Schomburgkia*. It differs from the latter in having conical hollow pseudobulbs that taper upwards, usually 3–4 short leaves at the apex, branched paniculate inflorescences, short bracts, broad side lobes to the lip and a smaller mid-lobe usually lacking any keels. The hollow pseudobulbs are the home of ant colonies which reportedly protect the delicate root tips and other parts of the plant from damage by other insects.
    A illustrated account of the genus is given by George Kennedy in the *Orchid Digest* (p. 205) in 1979.
TYPE SPECIES *Schomburgkia tibicinis* Bateman
CULTURE Temp. Winter min. 15°C. Light-loving plants which grow and flower well when hung in baskets under conditions suitable for *Cattleya*. Water well while growing and then much less when the large pseudobulbs are completed.

Myrmecophila brysiana (Lem.) Kennedy
[Colour Plate]
An epiphyte up to 70 cm tall. **Pseudobulbs** fusiform-conical, up to 21 cm long, 2.5 cm in diameter. **Leaves** 2, very coriaceous, ovate-elliptic, retuse at the rounded apex, up to 12 cm long, 5 cm wide. **Inflorescence** erect, up to 50 cm long; peduncle up to 40 cm long, partly covered by 1.5–2 cm long, sterile sheathing bracts; fertile bracts triangular, acute, 5 cm long. **Flowers** showy, deep yellow flushed on the sepals and petals with orange-brown and marked with purple-violet on the mid-lobe of the lip; pedicel and ovary 3 cm long. **Sepals** oblanceolate, obtuse or apiculate, 3.3–3.5 cm long, 1–1.2 cm wide, with undulate margins. **Petals** oblanceolate-obovate, acute to obtuse, 3–3.5 cm long, 1.3–1.5 cm wide, with strongly undulate margins. **Lip** 3-lobed, 4 cm long, 4–4.5 cm wide; side lobes upcurved, obliquely elliptic, rounded in front; mid-lobe broadly clawed, bilobulate in front; callus of 3 longitudinal low ridges from base onto claw of mid-lobe. **Column** arcuate, 2 cm long.
DISTRIBUTION Guatemala, Honduras, Belize and Nicaragua; also in the W. Indies; sea level to 200 m.
HISTORY Originally described as *Schomburgkia brysiana* by Lemaire in 1851 in *Le Jardin Fleuriste* (p. 34) based on a specimen flowered by M. Arnould Brys of Bornhem near Antwerp in Belgium. It was transferred to the present genus by George Kennedy in 1979 in the *Orchid Digest* (p. 210).
SYNONYM *Schomburgkia brysiana* Lem.
CLOSELY RELATED SPECIES This species is very closely allied to *S. tibicinis* with which it sometimes hybridises in the wild. It differs in being a smaller plant and in having smaller differently coloured flowers with a shortly clawed mid-lobe to the lip and 3 raised callus ridges on the lip.
    M. wendlandii (Rchb.f.) Kennedy is similar in habit but has much smaller flowers with narrower segments and is distinctively coloured with greenish-brown sepals and petals and a greenish-cream lip.

Myrmecophila tibicinis (Batem.) Rolfe
[Colour Plate]
A large erect epiphyte or lithophyte up to 2 m tall with fusiform-conical pseudobulbs up to 40 cm long, 3- to 4-leaved at the apex. **Leaves** coriaceous, rigid, ovate-elliptic, obtuse or retuse, 10–30 cm long, 3.5–7 cm wide. **Inflorescence** a multi-flowered panicle; peduncle purple almost covered with c. 15 sheaths; bracts triangular, 1.5 cm long. **Flowers** showy, with reddish-purple sepals and petals and a lip with a yellow disc, red-purple veins on the whitish side lobes and a magenta apex to the mid-lobe;

Myoxanthus reymondii
1 – Habit (× ⅔)
2 – Dorsal sepal (× 2)
3 – Petal (× 4)
4 – Lateral sepals (× 2)
5 – Column and ovary (× 7)

pedicel and ovary 5 cm long. **Sepals** oblong, obtuse, 4–4.5 cm long, 1–1.3 cm wide, somewhat undulate on margins, the laterals oblique. **Petals** oblanceolate, acute, 4.5–4.7 cm long, 1 cm wide, with undulate margins. **Lip** 3-lobed, 4.5–5 cm long, 4.5–4.7 cm wide; side lobes upcurved, obliquely elliptic, rounded in front; mid-lobe flabellate, deeply emarginate; callus of 3 elevated ridges from base to halfway along the mid-lobe. **Column** arcuate, 3 cm long, with a short foot.

DISTRIBUTION Mexico south to Costa Rica; at low altitude usually near to water.

HISTORY Originally described as *Epidendrum tibicinis* in 1838 in the *Botanical Register* (p. 8). James Bateman figured a plant, collected by George Ure Skinner from Guatemala, in his *Orchidaceae of Mexico and Guatemala* (t. 30) in 1837. Rolfe transferred it to *Myrmecophila* in 1917 in the *Orchid Review* (p. 51).

SYNONYMS *Epidendrum tibicinis* Batem. ex Lindl.; *Schomburgkia tibicinis* (Batem. ex Lindl.) Batem.; *Laelia tibicinis* (Batem. ex Lindl.) L.O. Williams

Mystacidium Lindl.
Subfamily Epidendroideae
Tribe Vandeae
Subtribe Aerangidinae

Dwarf or small epiphytic or rarely lithophytic herbs with short stems covered by imbricate leaf bases. **Leaves** distichous, fleshy or coriaceous, twisted at the base to lie in one plane, linear to oblanceolate, unequally bilobed at the apex, articulated to a sheathing leaf base. **Inflorescences** 1 to several, spreading to pendent, few- to several-flowered, simply racemose, axillary. **Flowers** usually stellate, small to medium-sized, white or pale green or pale yellow. **Sepals** and **petals** subsimilar, free, the petals usually narrower than the sepals. **Lip** entire or obscurely 3-lobed, ecallose, usually similar to the other segments but with an elongate slender spur tapering from a broader mouth at the base. **Column** short, fleshy; rostellum 3-lobed, pendent, papillate or barbate; pollinia 2, sulcate, each attached by a slender elongate stipe to a separate narrow viscidium.

DISTRIBUTION A genus of 13 species in S. and E. Africa.

DERIVATION OF NAME From the Greek *mystax* (moustache) probably an allusion to the barbate rostellar lobes.

HISTORY John Lindley established the genus *Mystacidium* in 1836 in W.D. Hooker's *Companion to the Botanical Magazine* (p. 205). It is most closely allied to *Angraecopsis* and *Aerangis*, the flowers resembling closely some of the smal-

ler flowered *Aerangis* species. It differs, however, in the characteristic barbate or papillate 3-lobed rostellum and the pollinarium structure.

The majority of the species are S. African and these have recently been described in *The Wild Orchids of Southern Africa* by Joyce Stewart et al. (1983).

TYPE SPECIES *M. filicorne* Lindl.

CULTURE Temp. Winter min. 12°C. Probably best grown as mounted epiphytes under shady humid conditions. Water throughout the year, but less when not growing actively.

Mystacidium capense (L.f.) Schltr.
A small epiphyte often forming sizeable clumps. **Stems** 1–2 cm long, covered by sheathing leaf bases and numerous greyish 1.5–2 mm diameter roots flecked with white streaks, 3- to 5-leaved. **Leaves** spreading, obovate to oblanceolate, unequally roundly or obtusely bilobed at the apex, 4–13 cm long, 0.8–1.4 cm wide, articulated to a sheathing leaf base and twisted at the base to lie in one plane. **Inflorescences** 1 to several, 7–20 cm long, 6- to 12-flowered; peduncle and ovary terete, slender; bracts ovate to obovate, acute or apiculate,

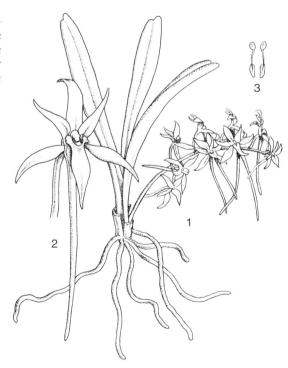

Mystacidium capense
1 – Habit (× ½)
2 – Flower (× ½)
3 – Pollinaria (× 4)

3–4 mm long. **Flowers** stellate, white to creamy-white, 1.5–2 cm across; pedicel and ovary 7–15 mm long. **Sepals** lanceolate, acuminate, 8–16 mm long, 1.5–2.5 mm wide. **Petals** lanceolate, acuminate, 8–13 mm long, 1.5–2 mm wide. **Lip** lanceolate, acuminate, 6–9 mm long, 1–1.5 mm wide; spur filiform from a conical base, pendent, 4–6 cm long. **Column** 2–3 mm long.

DISTRIBUTION S. Africa, from the E. Cape to the Transvaal, and Swaziland; in deep shade in dryish forest and bush; sea level to 500 m.

HISTORY This was one of the first epiphytic orchids described from S. Africa. It was described in 1781 as *Epidendrum capense* by the younger Linnaeus in his *Supplement* (p. 407) to his father's *Species Plantarum*. But it was not transferred to *Mystacidium* until 1914 by Rudolf Schlechter in his *Die Orchideen* (p. 597).

SYNONYMS *Epidendrum capense* L.f.; *Limodorum longicorne* Sw.; *Angraecum capense* (L.f.) Lindl.; *Mystacidium filicorne* Lindl.

Nageliella L.O. Williams
Subfamily Epidendroideae
Tribe Epidendreae
Subtribe Laeliinae

Small epiphytic, or rarely terrestrial herbs with creeping rhizomes. **Stems** short, pseudobulbous, 1-leafed above. **Leaf** fleshy-coriaceous. **Inflorescence** terminal, subumbellate, racemose or paniculate; branches short, congested. **Flowers** small, few to many. **Sepals** connivent; lateral sepals forming with the column-foot a ± prominent mentum. **Petals** linear to elliptic-lanceolate. **Lip** ± adnate to column, constricted above or below the middle, entire or 3-lobed. **Column** slender, auriculate towards the apex, arcuate; pollinia 4, waxy, compressed.

DISTRIBUTION Two species only in Central America.

DERIVATION OF NAME Named in honour of Otto Nagel who collected plants extensively in Mexico.

TAXONOMY *Nageliella* was described by L.O. Williams in 1940 in the *Botanical Museum Leaflets of Harvard University* (p. 144). It is allied to *Hexisea* and *Epidendrum* but differs in having a gibbous or saccate base to the lip and flowers with a definite mentum.

The genus was originally described by John Lindley as *Hartwegia* in honour of Th. Hartweg but unfortunately this name was a later homonym of *Hartwegia* Nees and as such was invalid.

TYPE SPECIES *N. purpurea* (Lindl.) L.O. Williams

SYNONYM *Hartwegia* Lindl.
CULTURE Compost A. Temp. Winter min. 12–15°C. The plants form compact clumps and are thus better left undivided. During active growth they should be watered freely but when the new leaves are fully grown, very little water is needed. The inflorescences appear on top of the new growths in the spring and slowly elongate for several months, before flowering in summer. The plants need only moderate shade from strong sunlight and good humidity while growing.

Nageliella purpurea (Lindl.) L.O. Williams
[Colour Plate]
A tufted epiphytic plant, 10–55 cm tall. **Stems** slender, erect, pseudobulbous, clavate-thickened, 1.5–8 cm long. **Leaves** clasping at the base, lanceolate or ovate-lanceolate, acute or subacute, coriaceous, 3–12 cm long, 0.7–3 cm broad, ± spotted bronze-purple. **Inflorescence** erect, a subumbellate raceme or panicle, up to 48 cm long; bracts small, ovate, scarious. **Flowers** purplish-red. **Dorsal sepal** elliptic, concave, acute, 0.7–0.9 cm long, 0.2–0.4 cm broad; **lateral sepals** obliquely oblong-lanceolate, obtuse to acute, keeled dorsally, 0.7–1 cm long, 0.2 cm broad. **Petals** elliptic-lanceolate, acute to obtuse, 0.6–0.8 cm long, 0.12–0.2 cm broad, margins minutely ciliate. **Lip** 0.7–1.1 cm long, less then 0.5 cm wide, saccate at base, basal part geniculate and constricted, adnate to the column; apical part deflexed, cordate-ovate, obtuse to acute. **Column** slender, arcuate above the middle, 0.6–0.7 cm long.
DISTRIBUTION Mexico, Guatemala and Honduras; up to 1500 m altitude.
HISTORY Discovered near Veracruz in Mexico by Theodore Hartweg, collecting for the Horticultural Society in London. It was described in 1837 in his honour by John Lindley as *Hartwegia purpurea* in the *Botanical Register* (sub t. 1970). L.O. Williams transferred it to the genus *Nageliella* in 1940 in the *Botanical Museum Leaflets of Harvard University* (p. 144) as *Hartwegia* had unfortunately already been used for a genus in the Liliaceae.
SYNONYM *Hartwegia purpurea* Lindl.

Neobathiea Schltr.
Subfamily Epidendroideae
Tribe Vandeae
Subtribe Angraecinae

Small to medium-sized epiphytic herbs with very short to short stems. **Leaves** coriaceous, often obovate or oblanceolate, obscurely unequally 2-lobed at apex. **Inflorescences** longer than the leaves, 1- to several-flowered, racemose. **Flowers** large or medium-sized, mostly white or white and green but rarely yellow. **Sepals** and **petals** subsimilar, spreading or reflexed. **Lip** much larger than the other segments, entire or 3-lobed, spurred at the base; spur with a broad mouth, filamentous below, often very long. **Column** short, fleshy, auriculate at the apex; rostellum short, with a prominent mid-lobe, thick, fleshy; pollinia 2, globose; viscidia 2.
DISTRIBUTION Seven species in Madagascar and the Comoros.
DERIVATION OF NAME Named in honour of Henri Perrier de la Bâthie, author of the Orchidaceae in the *Flore de Madagascar*.
TAXONOMY Described by Rudolf Schlechter in 1925 in *Fedde, Repertorium Specierum Novarum, Beihefte* (p. 369), *Neobathiea* is allied to *Aeranthes* but lacks the saccate column-foot of that species, and to *Jumellea* which never has a 3-lobed lip and in which the mouth of the spur is narrow and never inflated. It is further characterised by its short column with a cleft apex, the short rostellum, and two pollinia each attended directly to a viscidium. The genus has recently been revised by J. Bosser in *Adansonia* (1969).
TYPE SPECIES *Aeranthes perrieri* Schltr. [= *N. perrieri* (Schltr.) Schltr.].
CULTURE Compost A. Temp. Winter min. 15°C. *Neobathiea* species should best be grown in small pots, under conditions of good humidity and moderate shade. They should receive plenty of water while growing and less at other times, without becoming very dry.

Neobathiea filicornu Schltr. [Colour Plate]
A small epiphytic herb. **Stem** short, up to 6 cm long, 4- to 5-leaved. **Leaves** ligulate to elliptic, unequally obtusely 2-lobed above, 4–4.8 cm long, 0.8–1.2 cm broad. **Inflorescence** 1-flowered, a little shorter than the leaves; peduncle 2–2.3 cm long; bract ovate-deltoid. **Flowers** large for size of plant, pure white or pale green ± turning yellow with age. **Sepals** oblong-ligulate to oblanceolate, acute, reflexed, 1.3 cm long, 0.4 cm broad. **Petals** similar to sepals, 1.1 cm long. **Lip** ovate-lanceolate or cordate, acuminate, 2 cm long, 1 cm broad; spur with a broad mouth, filiform and pendent, 14 cm long. **Column** short, fleshy, 0.3 cm long.
DISTRIBUTION Central Madagascar and the Comoros.
HISTORY Discovered in 1923 by H. Perrier de la Bâthie at Manakazo, to the N.E. of Ankazobe in Madagascar at an altitude of 1500 m, *Neobathiea filicornu* was described by R. Schlechter in 1925 in *Fedde, Repertorium Specierum Novarum, Beihefte* (p. 369).

Neobathiea perrieri (Schltr.) Schltr.
[Colour Plate]
A small almost stemless epiphytic species. **Leaves** 4–6, oblong-spathulate, margins undulate, unequally and obscurely roundly 2-lobed at apex, 3.5–7 cm long, 1–1.9 cm broad. **Inflorescence** 6–12 cm long, 1- or 2-flowered; peduncle erect or suberect, slender; bracts ovate, acute, 0.4 cm long. **Flowers** white. **Sepals** reflexed lanceolate-spathulate, narrow at the base, acuminate, 2.2 cm long, 0.3 cm broad. **Petals** reflexed, similar to sepals. **Lip** 3-lobed in middle, cordate at the base, 2 cm long and broad; side lobes triangular, subacute or truncate; mid-lobe ovate, acuminate, longer than the side lobes; spur with a broad mouth, filiform-attenuate, 7–10 cm long. **Column** very short.
DISTRIBUTION W. Madagascar.
HISTORY Discovered by H. Perrier de la Bâthie on the edges of the River Besafotra in W. Madagascar and named after him by R. Schlechter in 1913 as *Aeranthes perrieri* in *Annales du Musée Colonial de Marseille* (p. 198). Schlechter later based his new genus *Neobathiea* on this species in *Fedde, Repertorium Specierum Novarum, Beihefte* (p. 371) in 1925.
SYNONYMS *Aeranthes perrieri* Schltr.; *Bathiea perrieri* (Schltr.) Schltr.

Neocogniauxia Schltr.
Subfamily Epidendroideae
Tribe Epidendreae
Subtribe Laeliinae

Small epiphytic plants with slender, short, terete, erect stems, 1-leafed at apex, covered by 1–3 tubular sheaths. **Leaf** suberect, linear-lanceolate to linear-oblong, coriaceous. **Inflorescence** longer than the leaf, slender, erect or arching, 1-flowered at the apex. **Flower** showy, scarlet or orange. **Sepals** and **petals** free, spreading, subsimilar. **Lip** much smaller than other segments, ± entire, ± papillose above, lying parallel to the column. **Column** semiterete, arcuate above, denticulate at the apical margin; pollinia 8.
DISTRIBUTION Two, or possibly three, species in Jamaica, Cuba, Haiti and Dominican Republic.
DERIVATION OF NAME Named in honour of Alfred Cogniaux (1841–1916), a Belgian botanist who wrote the Orchidaceae in Martius's *Flora Brasiliensis*.
TAXONOMY R. Schlechter established the genus *Neocogniauxia* in 1913 in I. Urban's *Symbolae Antillanae* (p. 495). The genus is distinguished from *Laelia* by its habit, its lip which is very short in relation to the other segments and by the toothed apex to its column.

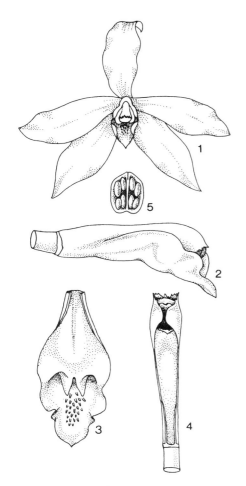

flowered; bract sheath-like, purple-spotted. **Flower** very attractive, rich scarlet to orange-scarlet with an orange column and purple anther. **Sepals** spreading, oblong-elliptic, obtuse, 1.7–2.2 cm long, 0.6–0.8 cm broad. **Petals** spreading, obovate-elliptic, obtuse, 1.4–1.7 cm long, 0.6–0.9 cm broad. **Lip** obovate, appressed to the column, 3-lobed near apex, somewhat apiculate, 0.7–0.9 cm long; disc papillate with a sac-like outgrowth on the midline. **Column** 0.6–0.9 cm long, auriculate, apical margin erosely denticulate.

DISTRIBUTION Jamaica; in woods at about 1000 m and above.

HISTORY Originally described in 1864 as *Trigonidium monophyllum* by A.H.R. Grisebach in the *Flora of the British West Indies* (p. 269) based on a specimen collected by Bancroft. It was later transferred to both *Octadesmia* and *Laelia* finally ending up in *Neocogniauxia* to which R. Schlechter transferred it in 1913 in I. Urban's *Symbolae Antillanae* (p. 495).

SYNONYMS *Trigonidium monophyllum* Griseb.; *Octadesmia monophylla* (Griseb.) Benth.; *Laelia monophylla* (Griseb.) Hooker f.

Neocogniauxia monophylla
1 – Flower (× 2)
2 – Column and lip, side view (× 4½)
3 – Lip (× 4½)
4 – Column, from below (× 4½)
5 – Anther (× 6½)

TYPE SPECIES *Trigonidium monophyllum* Griseb. [= *Neocogniauxia monophylla* (Griseb.) Schltr.].

CULTURE Compost A. Temp. Winter min. 10°C. These small plants may be grown in pots or mounted on slabs. They should never become dry and require moderate shade and good humidity.

Neocogniauxia monophylla (Griseb.) Schltr.

A small epiphytic plant, 10–30 cm high. **Stems** arising from a creeping rhizome, slender, erect, 2–9 cm long, 1-leafed at apex, covered by 2–3 speckled sheaths. **Leaf** erect to arcuate, linear-elliptic or linear-oblong, obtuse, 12–25 cm long, 0.7–1 cm broad. **Inflorescence** erect or arcuate, arising from the base of the stem, 5–30 cm long, mostly longer than the leaf, 1-

Neoescobaria Garay
Subfamily Epidendroideae
Tribe Oncidieae

Epiphytes with clustered conical-elongate unifoliate pseudobulbs. **Leaves** fleshy-coriaceous, shortly petiolate. **Inflorescences** lateral 1- to 3-flowered; peduncle with 3–5 sheaths along length. **Flowers** conspicuous, fleshy. **Sepals** and **petals** similar, free, spreading. **Lip** enfolding column, sessile, scarcely connate with the column at the base. **Column** short, cylindrical, lacking a foot, erose-denticulate at the apex; pollinia 2, with a broad stipe attached to a small viscidium.

DISTRIBUTION Two species only, in Andean S. America.

DERIVATION OF NAME Named in honour of Don Gilberto Escobar R., an eminent orchid grower in Colombia.

TAXONOMY Leslie Garay established this small genus in 1972 in the Colombian orchid journal *Orquideologia* (p. 194) as a segregate genus from *Trichopilia*. It differs in having the lip which is bell-shaped and only loosely encircles the column and which is scarcely fused to the base of the column.

A key to the species is also provided by Garay.

TYPE SPECIES *Trichopilia callichroma* Rchb.f.

Neoescobaria brevis (Rolfe) Garay

A medium-sized epiphyte with elongate, cylindric-ovoid unifoliate pseudobulbs, 8–12

Neoescobaria brevis
1 – Habit (× 1/6)
2 – Flower (× 1/2)

cm long. **Leaf** coriaceous, elliptic-lanceolate, acute, 10–16 cm long, 4–5 cm wide. **Inflorescences** 2- to 3-flowered, shorter than the leaves, spreading-suberect; bracts oblong, subobtuse, c. 2 cm long. **Flowers** showy; sepals and petals yellowish-green with large ochre-brown markings; lip white with a yellow mark in the throat. **Sepals** and **petals** broadly lanceolate, acute, subrevolute, 3.5–4 cm long, 1.2–1.5 cm wide. **Lip** conical at base, obscurely 3-lobed, 3–3.5 cm long, 4.5–5 cm wide, with crisped-undulate margins; mid-lobe broadly rotund, retuse, up to 2.5 cm wide; callus 3-keeled, without divergent horns. **Column** short, subclavate, 1.2–1.3 cm long, with entire wings, serrulate at apex.

DISTRIBUTION Colombia to Peru.

HISTORY Originally described as *Trichopilia brevis* by Robert Rolfe in 1892 in *Lindenia* (p. 91, t. 332), based on a plant flowered in Belgium by L'Horticole Internationale in August 1891 and said to have originated in Peru. Garay transferred it to the present genus in 1972 in the journal *Orquideologia* (p. 194).

SYNONYM *Trichopilia brevis* Rolfe

Neofinetia H.H. Hu
Subfamily Epidendroideae
Tribe Vandeae
Subtribe Sarcanthinae

Epiphytic plants with short, leafy, monopodial stems. **Leaves** distichous, fleshy, conduplicate, channelled above. **Inflorescence** racemose, axillary, laxly several-flowered. **Flowers** conspicuous, white. **Sepals** and **petals** similar, free, spreading. **Lip** erect, obscurely 3-lobed, with a long, filiform, arcuate spur at the base. **Column** rather short, winged, fleshy, lacking a foot; pollinia 2, cartilaginous; stipe ± broadly triangular; stigma large.

DISTRIBUTION A monotypic genus widespread in China, Korea, Japan and the Ryukyu Islands.

DERIVATION OF NAME Named in honour of Achille Finet (1862–1913) a French botanist who worked on the orchids of China and Japan.

TAXONOMY *Neofinetia* was described by H.H. Hu in 1925 in *Rhodora* (p. 107). This monotypic genus was recently transferred by L. Garay and H. Sweet in the *Botanical Museum Leaflets of Harvard University* (1972) to *Holcoglossum*. However, in their more recent *Orchids of the Southern Ryukyu Islands* (1974) the genus *Neofinetia* is resurrected.

Neofinetia is characterised by its short, prominently winged column without a foot, by its deeply cleft clinandrium with a short bifid rostellum, its 2-notched pollinia borne on a tapering stipe and by its slender lip.

TYPE SPECIES *Orchis falcata* Thunb. [= *Neofinetia falcata* (Thunb.) H.H. Hu].

CULTURE Compost A. Temp. Winter min. 10–12°C. *Neofinetia* may be grown in a small pot or basket under humid conditions and moderate shade. While the roots are active, plenty of water is required but, on completion of growth, less should be given.

Neofinetia falcata (Thunb.) **H.H. Hu**

A small epiphytic plant, up to 15 cm tall. **Stem** short, complanate, covered by conduplicate leaf-bases. **Leaves** coriaceous, distichous, fleshy, conduplicate, linear-falcate, up to 10 cm long. **Inflorescence** axillary, erect, racemose

Neofinetia falcata
Habit (× ½)

above, laxly several-flowered. **Flowers** conspicuous, white, with a long pedicellate-ovary. **Sepals** and **petals** subsimilar, linear-oblong to linear-lanceolate, acute, up to 1 cm long. **Lip** recurved, 3-lobed, up to 0.9 cm long; side lobes erect, obtuse, semiovate with long decurrent margins; mid-lobe ligulate; spur filiform, arcuate up to 4 cm long.

DISTRIBUTION Japan, Korea and the Ryukyu Islands.

HISTORY Discovered in Japan by Carl Thunberg and described by him as *Orchis falcata* in 1784 in his *Flora Japonica* (p. 26). H.H. Hu transferred it to his new genus *Neofinetia* in 1925 in *Rhodora* (p. 107).

SYNONYMS include *Orchis falcata* Thunb.; *Oeceoclades falcata* (Thunb.) Lindl.; *Angraecum falcatum* (Thunb.) Lindl.; *Aerides thunbergii* Miq.; *Angraecopsis falcata* (Thunb.) Schltr.; *Finetia falcata* (Thunb.) Schltr.; *Nipponorchis falcata* (Thunb.) Masamune; *Holcoglossum falcatum* (Thunb.) Garay

---

Neogardneria **Schltr.**
Subfamily Epidendroideae
Tribe Maxillarieae
Subtribe Zygopetalinae

Medium-sized or rather small epiphytic herbs with ovoid, bifoliate pseudobulbs subtended by 2 or more acute, often leaf-bearing sheaths. **Leaves** deciduous, plicate, suberect, narrowly elliptic to oblanceolate. **Inflorescences** produced with the new growth, suberect to spreading, laxly 2- to 5-flowered; peduncle and rhachis slender; bracts large. **Flowers** with green sepals and petals and a white lip spotted with red at the base. **Sepals** and **petals** subsimilar, spreading, free. **Lip** subsessile, clawed at the base, 3-lobed above, bearing a flabelliform cristate callus; side lobes erect; mid-lobe narrow, more or less geniculately deflexed. **Column** fleshy, narrowly winged above, with a short foot below; rostellum tridentate, with a lanceolate mid-tooth; pollinia 4 of unequal size, paired, each pair attached to a small triangular viscidium.

DISTRIBUTION A monotypic genus from Brazil.

DERIVATION OF NAME Named in honour of George Gardner who collected orchids in E. Brazil between 1836 and 1841.

TAXONOMY Rudolf Schlechter established this genus in 1921 in *Notizblatt des Botanischen Garten, Berlin* (p. 471) as a segregate of *Zygopetalum* from which it is readily distinguished by its distinctly clawed lip bearing a flabellate or horse-shoe shaped callus.

TYPE SPECIES *Zygopetalum murrayanum* Hook.

CULTURE Temp. Winter min. 12–15°C. Grow in pots of epiphyte mix under moderate shade and humidity. Water well when growing and give less when growth is complete.

Neogardneria murrayana (Hook.) **Schltr.**
[Colour Plate]

An epiphyte with clustered ovoid pseudobulbs, 2.5–3.5 cm long, 1.5–1.8 cm in diameter, borne on a very short rhizome. **Leaves** narrowly elliptic to oblanceolate, acute, 12–20 cm long, 2–3 cm wide. **Inflorescences** arcuate or suberect, 2- to 5-flowered, 9–25 cm long; bracts elliptic-lanceolate, acute, cucullate, 1–1.8 cm long. **Flowers** with green sepals and petals and a white lip spotted with red; pedicel and ovary 1.8–2.7 cm long. **Sepals** oblong-lanceolate, acute or apiculate, 1.6–2.1 cm long, 0.6–0.8 cm wide. **Petals** narrowly elliptic-lanceolate, acute or apiculate, 1.8–2.3 cm long, 0.5–0.6 cm wide. **Lip** clawed at the base, 3-lobed above, 1.2–1.4 cm long, 1 cm wide; side lobes erect, small, rounded; mid-lobe narrowly elliptic, obtuse, deflexed-recurved; callus flabellate, cristate. **Column** 0.6–0.7 cm long.

DISTRIBUTION E. Brazil; montane mist-forest at 1000–1400 m.

HISTORY Sir W.J. Hooker described this species as *Zygopetalum murrayanum* in 1838 in the *Botanical Magazine* (t. 3674) based on a collection made by Gardner in the Organ Mts of Brazil. Gardner suggested the specific name in honour of his friend Mr Murray. Rudolf Schlechter transferred it to *Neogardneria* in *Notizblatt des Botanischen Garten, Berlin* (p. 471) 1921.

SYNONYMS *Zygopetalum murrayanum* (Hook.) Rolfe; *Z. binotii* De Wild.; *Eulophia murrayana* (Hook.) Steud.; *Neogardneria binotii* (De Wild.) Hoehne

---

Neomoorea **Rolfe**
Subfamily Epidendroideae
Tribe Maxillarieae
Subtribe Zygopetalinae

Epiphytic herbs with stout ovoid pseudobulbs, 2-leaved at apex. **Leaves** plicate, elliptic-lanceolate, acute or shortly acuminate. **Inflorescences** erect or arcuate, racemose, from the base of the pseudobulbs. **Flowers** relatively large, conspicuous. **Sepals** subequal, free, spreading. **Petals** similar to sepals but narrower at the base. **Lip** deeply 3-lobed, articulated to the column-foot; side lobes large, spreading, subreniform; mid-lobe concave, lanceolate, acuminate, basal crest shortly pedicellate, with 2 lateral, erect or spreading wings. **Column** subclavate, semiterete, somewhat arcuate, lacking wings, produced at the base into a short broad foot; pollinia 4 in 2 unequal pairs, waxy.

DISTRIBUTION A rare monotypic genus from Colombia and Panama.

DERIVATION OF NAME Named in honour of F.W. Moore, one-time curator of the famous Glasnevin Botanic Garden in Dublin.

TAXONOMY R.A. Rolfe described *Neomoorea* in 1904 in the *Orchid Review* (p. 30). He had earlier described the genus as *Moorea*, only subsequently discovering that the name had already been used for a distinct genus. *Neomoorea* is allied to *Stanhopea* differing in that its lip hypochile is not saccate-concave and the lip is distinctly 3-lobed. From *Acineta* and *Peristeria* it may be distinguished by the narrowly lanceolate and acuminate mid-lobe of its lip.

TYPE SPECIES *N. irrorata* (Rolfe) Rolfe

SYNONYM *Moorea* Rolfe

CULTURE Compost B or C. Temp. Winter min. 15°C. These plants should be grown under conditions of moderate shade, with good humidity while growing. Water must be carefully given when the new shoots first appear but the plants should be well watered when in full growth. When the pseudobulbs are fully grown, very little water should be given until growth again begins.

Neomoorea wallisii (Rchb.f.) Schltr.
[Colour Plate]

An erect epiphytic plant with white, spiny erect roots forming a dense mat at the base of the plant. **Pseudobulbs** stout, ovoid, compressed, sulcate, 4–11 cm long, 2.5–6 cm in diameter, 2-leaved at apex. **Leaves** plicate, elliptic-lanceolate, acute or shortly acuminate, strongly veined, subcoriaceous, 45–75 cm long, 10–13 cm broad. **Inflorescences** erect or arcuate, racemose, 15–34 cm long, few- to 12-flowered. **Flowers** large, showy; sepals and petals chestnut- or reddish-brown, white at the base; lip pale yellow, marked and banded with brown-purple, mid-lobe yellow, spotted red. **Sepals** subequal, spreading, concave, elliptic-lanceolate or elliptic-ovate, acute, 2–2.8 cm long, 1–1.8 cm broad. **Petals** elliptic-obovate, acute, 2.2–2.5 cm long, 1.2–1.4 cm broad. **Lip** deeply 3-lobed, articulated to the base of the short column-foot, 1.4–1.6 cm long; 1.5–1.7 cm broad; side lobes large, spreading, subreniform; mid-lobe concave, lanceolate, acuminate; callus conspicuous, cristate, erect. **Column** subclavate, arcuate, 1.2–1.4 cm long, with a short broad foot.

DISTRIBUTION Colombia and Panama.

HISTORY Originally described by H.G. Reichenbach in 1877 as *Lueddemannia wallisii* in *Linnaea* (p. 109) based on a collection from Colombia by Gustav Wallis. Rudolf Schlechter transferred it to the present genus in 1924 in the *Orchid Review* (p. 355).

This species is perhaps better known in cultivation as *Neomoorea irrorata* (Rolfe) Rolfe, but that name is a later synonym.

SYNONYMS *Lueddemannia wallisii* Rchb.f.; *Moorea irrorata* Rolfe; *Neomoorea irrorata* (Rolfe) Rolfe

Nephelaphyllum Bl.
Subfamily Epidendroideae
Tribe Arethuseae
Subtribe Bletiinae

Small terrestrial herbs with creeping fleshy rhizomes covered with thin sheaths and erect slender cylindrical unifoliate pseudobulbs. **Leaves** fleshy, erect or suberect, ovate to cordate, shortly petiolate, mottled dark and lighter green above, often purple beneath. **Inflorescence** lateral, erect, densely or laxly few-flowered, shorter than or slightly longer than the leaf. **Flowers** non-resupinate, medium-sized. **Sepals** and **petals** often recurved or spreading, subsimilar, free, slender, acute. **Lip** large, uppermost in the flower, entire or 3-lobed, with a callus and with a short basal spur. **Column** short, slightly winged; pollinia 8.

DISTRIBUTION A small genus of about 16 species in N. India, S.E. Asia and the Malay Archipelago.

DERIVATION OF NAME From the Greek *nephela* (cloud) and *phyllon* (leaf), in reference to the cloud-like mottling of the upper surface of the leaf.

TAXONOMY Carl Blume established this genus in 1825 in his *Bijdragen* (p. 372, t. 22). It is allied to *Mischobulbum* and *Tainia*, being distinguished by its vegetative anatomy and non-resupinate flowers.

TYPE SPECIES *N. pulchrum* Bl.

CULTURE Temp. Winter min. 15°C. Grow as for *Macodes* or *Ludisia* with a drier period after growth is complete.

Nephelaphyllum pulchrum Bl.

A small terrestrial herb with a creeping fleshy rhizome and closely spaced unifoliate cylindrical fleshy pseudobulbs 1–2 cm long, 0.2–0.4 cm in diameter. **Leaf** erect, ovate-triangular to cordate, acute or obtuse, 4–10 cm long, 2.5–6 cm wide, mottled dark and light green above, flushed with purple. **Inflorescence** 3–5 cm long at flowering but elongating afterwards to 10 cm long, densely 2- to 3-flowered; bracts lanceolate, acuminate, 0.6–1 cm long. **Flowers** erect, non-resupinate, with pinkish sepals and petals and a white or pale yellow lip, pinkish at the base and with a yellow callus; ovary 0.5–

0.8 cm long. **Sepals** and **petals** subsimilar, recurved, lanceolate or oblanceolate, acute, 1.2–1.4 cm long, 0.3–0.4 cm wide. **Lip** fleshy, entire, oblong-elliptic, emarginate, 1.5–1.7 cm long, 1–1.2 cm wide; callus of 3 papillose ridges; spur clavate-orbicular, bilobed, 0.3–0.4 cm long, **Column** 0.5 cm long.

DISTRIBUTION Sikkim, Bhutan, N.E. India, Burma, Thailand, Indo-China, Malaya, Java, Borneo and the Philippines; in lowland and lower montane forest.

HISTORY The type was collected by C.L. Blume on Mt Salak in Java and was described by him in his *Bijdragen* (p. 373) in 1825.

Nephelaphyllum latilabre Ridl., from Borneo and Malaya, is closely allied but differs in having a broader lip well marked with purple veins.

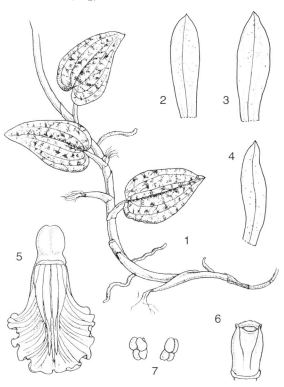

Nephelaphyllum latilabre
1 – Habit (× 1/3)
2 – Dorsal sepal (× 2)
3 – Lateral sepal (× 2)
4 – Petal (× 2)
5 – Lip (× 2)
6 – Column, ventral view (× 3½)
7 – Pollinia (× 3)

Nervilia Gaud.

Subfamily Epidendroideae
Tribe Gastrodieae
Subtribe Nerviliinae

Small terrestrial herbs arising from underground ovoid to ellipsoid tubers. **Leaf** solitary, petiolate, plicate, ovate to cordate, erect or parallel to the substrate, rarely appressed to the ground, glabrous or pubescent, appearing after the inflorescence has withered. **Inflorescence** erect, hysteranthous, 1- to several-flowered, racemose; peduncle brittle. **Flowers** not opening widely, sometimes self-pollinating, subnutant, spreading or erect. **Sepals** and **petals** free, subsimilar, lanceolate, acute. **Lip** entire to 3-lobed or rarely pandurate, with or without a longitudinal callus, papillate or pubescent. **Column** clavate, elongate; pollinia 2, granular-mealy.

DISTRIBUTION A genus of about 80 species in tropical Africa, Madagascar, tropical Asia, the Malay Archipelago, the Pacific Islands and N. Australia.

DERIVATION OF NAME From the Latin *nervus* (veined), descriptive of the leaves.

TAXONOMY Originally described by the French botanist Gaudichaud-Beaupré in 1826 in Freycinet's *Voyage Botanique* (p. 421, t. 35). *Nervilia* is taxonomically rather difficult because the inflorescence disappears before the leaves develop. In some species the leaves and flowers have proved difficult to match as several species can grow in the same area.

The African species are described by V. Summerhayes (1968) in the *Flora of West Tropical Africa Orchidaceae* and by P. Cribb (1984) in the *Flora of Tropical East Africa Orchidaceae*. These have recently been somewhat superseded by the account of the African and Arabian species by B. Pettersson (1991) in the 5th volume of *Orchid Monographs*. The species from Thailand and adjacent areas are covered by G. Seidenfaden (1978) in *Dansk Botanisk Arkiv*.

TYPE SPECIES *N. aragoana* Gaud.

CULTURE Temp. Winter min. 12–15°C. Grow in a terrestrial mix such as that used for *Acianthus*, then repot when dormant. Give shady, humid conditions and plenty of water when growing, but keep almost dry when dormant.

Nervilia plicata (Hance) Schltr.

A small terrestrial herb with a round tuber. **Leaf** prostrate, cordate, acute or apiculate at the apex, 4–8 cm long, 5–9 cm wide, pubescent, dark green above, purple beneath; petiole short, 1–2 cm long. **Inflorescence** erect, usually 2-flowered; peduncle up to 25 cm long;

bracts ovate to lanceolate, acute to acuminate, 2–12 mm long. **Flowers** subnutant, with green or brown sepals and petals and a white lip usually with purple veins and a purple marginal band; pedicel and ovary 7–12 mm long. **Sepals** and **petals** spreading, lanceolate, acuminate, 17–40 mm long, 3–5 mm wide. **Lip** porrect, more or less obscurely 3-lobed, 14.5–25 mm long, ecallose; side lobes erect, narrowly elliptic; mid-lobe ovate to transversely oblong, emarginate. **Column** 10–15 mm long.

DISTRIBUTION India, Bhutan, Burma, Thailand, S. China, Laos, Vietnam, Malaya, the Malay Archipelago across to New Guinea and the Philippines.

HISTORY Originally described in Andrew's *Botanical Repository* (t. 321) as *Arethusa plicata* based on a specimen flowered in cultivation by Lambert. It was transferred to *Nervilia* by Rudolf Schlechter in 1911 in Engler's *Botanische Jahrbücher* (p. 403). It is a widespread and variable species.

SYNONYMS include *Arethusa plicata* Andrews; *Cordyla discolor* Bl.; *Pogonia discolor* (Bl.) Bl.; *Nervilia velutina* (Par. & Rchb.f.) Schltr.; *N. discolor* (Bl.) Schltr.

Nervilia plicata
Plant ($\times \frac{1}{2}$)

Nidema Britton & Millspaugh

Subfamily Epidendroideae
Tribe Epidendreae
Subtribe Laeliinae

Small epiphytic plants with caespitose pseudobulbous stems on an elongate rhizome. **Pseudobulbs** fusiform or clavate, 1- to 2-leaved at the apex. **Leaves** suberect or erect, coriaceous, linear, obtuse. **Inflorescence** produced from the new growth as the leaf develops, erect, laxly few-flowered; bracts conspicuous, chartaceous, brown. **Flowers** small, spreading. **Sepals** and **petals** subsimilar but the petals slightly smaller, free. **Lip** entire, lacking a spur, with an obscure linear sulcate callus, attached to the base of the column. **Column** slender, slightly incurved; pollinia 4, of two different sizes, waxy, attached to prominent caudicles.

DISTRIBUTION A genus of two species widespread from Mexico to Panama, Cuba and Surinam.

DERIVATION OF NAME An anagram of the generic name *Dinema*.

TAXONOMY Established by the American taxonomists Britton and Millspaugh in 1920 in their *Flora of the Bahamas* (p. 94). It is a segregate genus of *Epidendrum* distinguished by its lip which is completely free from the column to the base. In some ways the flowers resemble those of certain *Maxillaria* species.

TYPE SPECIES *N. ottonis* (Rchb.f.) Britton & Millsp.

CULTURE Temp. Winter min. 12°C. May be grown in a pan but, because of its spreading habit, is better suited to being mounted. Grow under conditions of moderate shade and humidity with a drier period when growth is complete.

Nidema boothii (Lindl.) Schltr. [Colour Plate]

A small glabrous epiphyte up to 30 cm tall, with a creeping rhizome. **Pseudobulbs** 2–3 cm apart on the rhizome, clavate or fusiform, somewhat compressed, 2.5–6 cm long, 1- or 2-leaved at the apex. **Leaves** linear, obtuse, 6–25 cm long, 0.8–1.5 cm wide, shiny dark green. **Inflorescence** laxly few-flowered, 5–15 cm long; peduncle covered by brown sterile bracts; bracts lanceolate, acuminate, up to 3 cm long, scarious, brown. **Flowers** creamy-white or greenish-white; pedicel and ovary 1.5–2.5 cm long, covered by a scurfy indumentum. **Sepals** lanceolate, acuminate, recurved, 12–22 mm long, 2.5–5 mm wide, dorsally keeled. **Petals** elliptic-lanceolate, acuminate, 11–15 mm long, 2.5–4.5 mm wide. **Lip** obovate-subpandurate, obtuse, arcuate above the middle, 9–11 mm long, 3–4 mm wide, with an erose apical margin; callus a sulcate depression in the basal half of the lip. **Column** 7–8 mm long.

DISTRIBUTION Widespread in Central America from Mexico to Panama, also in Cuba and Surinam; in tropical forests up to 1500 m.

HISTORY John Lindley described this species in 1838 as *Maxillaria boothii* in the *Botanical Register* (misc. 52). It was transferred to *Nidema* by Rudolf Schlechter in 1922 in *Fedde, Repertorium Specierum Novarum, Beihefte* (p. 43). It is still perhaps best known in cultivation as *Epidendrum boothii* (Lindl.) L.O. Williams

SYNONYMS *Maxillaria boothii* Lindl.; *Dinema paleacea* Lindl.; *Epidendrum auritum* Lindl.; *E. paleaceum* (Lindl.) Rchb.f.; *E. boothii* (Lindl.) L.O. Williams

---

Notylia Lindl.

Subfamily Epidendroideae
Tribe Oncidieae

Small epiphytic herbs with or without pseudobulbs. **Stems** abbreviated, several-leaved. **Pseudobulbs,** when present, small, fleshy, 1-leafed at apex. **Leaves** often distichous, imbricate or equitant. **Inflorescence** either from the base of a pseudobulb or from the axil of a leaf, arcuate or pendent, racemose to paniculate, few- to many-flowered. **Flower** small. **Sepals** and **petals** erect or spreading, free or with lateral sepals variously connate. **Lip** clawed, simple; callus ± present. **Column** erect, apically recurved, terete or sulcate, lacking wings or a foot, with a long erect rostellum.

DISTRIBUTION About 40 or so species in tropical Central and S. America.

DERIVATION OF NAME From the Greek *noton* (back) and *tylon* (a hump) referring to the recurved apical part of the column.

TAXONOMY John Lindley described *Notylia* in 1825 in the *Botanical Register* (sub t. 930). This genus is allied to *Macradenia* and *Cryptarrhena* R. Br., but differs from both in having a simple unlobed lip.

A. Cogniaux divided the species into two well-marked subgenera; firstly *Eunotylia* in which the plants have small but distinct, 1-leafed pseudobulbs with flat leaves; and secondly *Macroclinium* in which the leaves are equitant and distichously imbricate with the leaf-bases sometimes enclosing a small complanate pseudobulb.

G. Pabst and F. Dungs in *Orchidaceae Brasilienses* (1977) have conveniently treated the 27 Brazilian species in these two sections with four groups in the first section as follows:

A. sect. *Notylia* – leaves normal, flat.

1. *N. aromatica* alliance – lip lacking keels on the claw.
2. *N. micromera* alliance – lip with keels on the claw; apex acute and shorter than the column.
3. *N. pubescens* alliance – as group 2 but lip longer than the column and long-acuminate.
4. *N. punctata* alliance – lip carinate with a blunt or rounded apex.

B. sect. *Macroclinium* – leaves complanate and connate, equitant.

Undoubtedly some extra-Brazilian species would fit into the above divisions to some extent.

TYPE SPECIES *N. punctata* (Ker) Lindl. and *N. multiflora* Lindl. are both cited by Lindley.

SYNONYMS *Tridachne* Liebm. ex. Lindl.; *Macroclinium* Barb. Rodr.

CULTURE Compost A. Temp. Winter min. 12–15°C. *Notylia* species may be grown in small pots or mounted on slabs of fern-fibre or cork. They require humid, shady conditions with plenty of water while growing and somewhat less when growth is complete.

Notylia barkeri Lindl. [Colour Plate]

A medium-sized epiphytic plant, up to 33 cm tall. **Pseudobulbs** clustered, ellipsoid, compressed, 1–3.5 cm long, 0.6–1.6 cm across, 1-leafed at apex, subtended by leafy and non-leafy scarious sheaths. **Leaf** coriaceous, erect or spreading, oblong-ligulate to broadly elliptic, obliquely tridentate at the rounded or subacute apex, 3.5–20 cm long, 1.5–4.5 cm broad, pale green. **Inflorescence** axillary, pendulous, racemose or rarely paniculate, 5–32 cm long, laxly many-flowered; bracts small, scarious, triangular-lanceolate, acuminate, 0.2 cm long. **Flowers** small, variable, greenish-white ± dotted yellow on petals, slightly fragrant, **Sepals** oblong-ligulate to elliptic-lanceolate, apex revolute, obtuse to acute, 0.3–0.7 cm long, 0.2–0.3 cm broad; lateral sepals ± united to middle. **Petals** elliptic-lanceolate, obtuse, 0.3–0.6 cm long, 0.1–0.2 cm broad. **Lip** white, shortly clawed, lamina ovate to subhastate-lanceolate, subobtuse to acuminate, ecallose, 0.3–0.6 cm long, 0.1–0.2 cm broad. **Column** terete, 0.3 cm long.

DISTRIBUTION Mexico south to Panama; in forests, swamps and in coffee plantations, up to 1600 m altitude.

HISTORY Described by John Lindley in 1838 in the *Botanical Register* (misc. p. 90) based on a Mexican specimen sent to Lindley by George Barker in 1837.

SYNONYMS *Notylia trisepala* Lindl. & Paxt.; *N. bipartita* Rchb.f.; *N. albida* Klotzsch; *N. guatemalensis* S. Wats.; *N. guatemalensis* Schltr.; *N. bernoullii* Schltr.

Notylia carnosiflora C. Schweinf.

A small epiphytic plant with an abbreviated rhizome. **Pseudobulb** short, cylindric-compressed, 1 cm long, 1-leafed at apex, subtended by several distichous, imbricating, ± leaf-bearing sheaths. **Leaf** elliptic-oblong, rounded above, cuneate below, 4.5–6.5 cm long, 1.3–1.9 cm broad. **Inflorescence** basal, arcuate-recurved, ± equal to the leaves or shorter, racemose, subdensely several-flowered; bracts small, reflexed. **Flower** small, fleshy, reflexed, segments spreading. **Dorsal sepal** concave, oblong, subacute, 0.7 cm long, 0.3 cm broad: **lateral sepals** connate forming an oblong lamina, obscurely bifid-truncate at the apex. **Petals** 0.5 cm long, 0.1 cm broad, falcate, oblong-oblanceolate, acute. **Lip** clawed, triangular-ovate above, 0.4 cm long, 0.2 cm broad; claw fleshy; disc minutely pubescent. **Column** short, stout, dilated below, 0.3 cm long, minutely pubescent.

DISTRIBUTION Peru; 1800 m altitude.

HISTORY Discovered in the Chanchamayo Valley in Peru by Schunke and described by Charles Schweinfurth in 1946 in the *Botanical Museum Leaflets of Harvard University* (p. 199, t. 28).

Oberonia Lindl.

Subfamily Epidendroideae
Tribe Malaxideae

Small to medium-sized erect to pendent epiphytic herbs with short to elongate, usually clustered, leafy stems; roots basal, fibrous. **Leaves** fleshy, distichous, arranged in a fan or along the stem, bilaterally compressed to terete, often articulated to a persistent compressed leaf base. **Inflorescence** terminal, densely many-flowered, cylindrical, spicate. **Flowers** non-resupinate, flat, minute to small, purple, yellow, green or off-white, arranged in a spiral or verticillately. **Sepals** and **petals** spreading, free, subsimilar but with the petals smaller and narrower. **Lip** sessile, deflexed, entire or variously lobed, auriculate at the base, ecallose, often erose. **Column** very short, fleshy, usually enclosed by the basal auricles of the lip; pollinia 4, pyriform, waxy.

DISTRIBUTION A genus of over 100 species centred on tropical Asia but extending to the Pacific Islands, Australia and with a single species in Madagascar and tropical Africa.

DERIVATION OF NAME Named after Oberon, the mythical King of the Fairies.

TAXONOMY John Lindley described this genus in 1830 in his *Genera and Species of Orchidaceous Plants* (p. 15). It is allied to *Malaxis* but is readily distinguished by its characteristic habit and tiny flowers in a dense cylindrical spike.

The 77 mainland Asiatic species have been revised by G. Seidenfaden (1968) in *Dansk Botanisk Arkiv* (pp. 1–125).

TYPE SPECIES *O. iridifolia* (Roxb.) Lindl.
CULTURE Temp. Winter min. 12–15°C. May be grown either in small pots or mounted under conditions of moderate shade and humidity. These fine-rooted species need to be watered carefully throughout the year.

Oberonia iridifolia (Roxb.) Lindl.

A small epiphyte with clustered short leafy stems less than 1 cm long. **Leaves** 3–4, arranged in a fan, iridiform, acute, 5–25 cm long, 0.5–1.2 cm wide, articulate at the base to imbricate compressed leaf bases. **Inflorescence** apical, elongate-cylindrical, densely many-flowered with the flowers borne in whorls, 12–35 cm long; peduncle terete, 4–9 cm long; bracts elliptic, 0.5–1.5 mm long, erose. **Flowers** tiny, yellow, 1–1.5 mm across; ovary 0.5 mm long. **Dorsal sepal** reflexed, ovate-elliptic, obtuse, 1 mm long, 0.7 mm wide; **lateral sepals** reflexed, elliptic, obtuse, 1 mm long, 0.7 mm wide. **Petals** elliptic, obtuse, 1–1.4 mm long, 0.8–1 mm wide, erose. **Lip** spreading, 3-lobed, deeply emarginate, 1–1.5 mm long

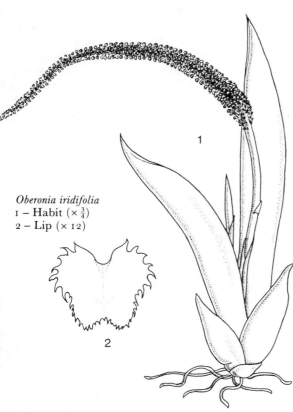

Oberonia iridifolia
1 – Habit (× ¾)
2 – Lip (× 12)

and wide, with lacerate margins to the lobes. **Column** very short 0.3–0.4 mm long.
DISTRIBUTION India, Nepal, Burma, S. China, Thailand, Malaya, the Malay Archipelago across to Australia; widespread in lowland and lower montane forests.
HISTORY William Roxburgh described this widespread species in 1814 in his *Hortus Bengalensis* (p. 63) as *Cymbidium iridifolium*. John Lindley transferred it to the present genus in his *Genera and Species of Orchidaceous Plants* (p. 15) in 1830.
SYNONYMS *Cymbidium iridifolium* Roxb.; *Malaxis iridifolia* (Roxb.) Hook.f.

Octomeria R. Br.
Subfamily Epidendroideae
Tribe Epidendreae
Subtribe Pleurothallidinae

Small epiphytic plants with creeping rhizomes (primary stems) and erect secondary stems which are 1-leafed at apex and covered with 1 to several sheaths below. **Leaf** sessile to shortly petiolate, coriaceous to fleshy, flattened to terete. **Inflorescences** axillary, 1- to many-flowered, often fasciculate. **Flowers** small, often dully coloured. **Sepals** and **petals** spreading, free or basally connate. **Lip** very short, articulated to the base of the column, entire or 3-lobed, apically spreading or reflexed; callus bilamellate. **Column** very short, slightly incurved, wingless; pollinia 8, oblong-clavate.
DISTRIBUTION About 50 or so species widely distributed in Central and S. America and the W. Indies.
DERIVATION OF NAME From the Greek *octo* (eight) and *meros* (part) referring to the 8 pollinia characteristic of species in the genus.
TAXONOMY *Octomeria* was described by Robert Brown in 1813 in the 2nd edition of W. Aiton's *Hortus Kewensis* (p. 211).

Superficially many species resemble those of *Pleurothallis* but all *Octomeria* species have 8 pollinia whereas in *Pleurothallis* 4 or 2 pollinia is normal. Taxonomically, *Octomeria* is still poorly known, due mainly, no doubt, to their rather insignificant appearance.
TYPE SPECIES *O. graminifolia* (Willd.) R. Br.
CULTURE Compost A. Temp. Winter min. 10–12°C. As for *Pleurothallis* and *Masdevallia*. The species mostly have an upright growth habit, so should be grown in small pots.

Octomeria diaphana Lindl.
A small epiphytic plant. **Stems** slender, terete, erect, 3- to 4-noded, 6–8 cm long. **Leaf** erect or slightly spreading, rigid, fleshy, sessile, oblong-

lanceolate, acute, 4–6 cm long, 1.2–1.3 cm broad, ± purplish-tinged. **Inflorescence** 1-flowered. 0.3–0.5 cm long. **Flowers** white; lip yellow marked with maroon, diaphanaceous, not scented. **Sepals** concave, membranaceous, elliptic-lanceolate, acuminate, about 1 cm long. **Petals** linear-lanceolate, acuminate, 1 cm long. **Lip** membranaceous, glabrous. ovate-oblong, cuneate at the base, obscurely 3-lobed, apex subtruncate and distinctly tridentate, margins subcrisped, 0.6–0.7 cm long; disc shortly bicristate.
DISTRIBUTION E. Brazil.
HISTORY Introduced into cultivation from the Organ Mts near Theresopolis in Brazil by Messrs Loddiges of Hackney, London, and described by John Lindley in 1839 in the *Botanical Register* (misc. 91).

Octomeria grandiflora Lindl. [Colour Plate]
A medium-sized epiphytic plant. **Stems** terete below, laterally compressed above, tufted, up to 20 cm long, 1-leafed at apex. **Leaf** linear-lanceolate to narrowly linear-rhombic, acute, erect or arcuate, coriaceous-rigid, up to 20 cm long, 1.5 cm broad. **Inflorescence** fasciculate, axillary, several-flowered. **Flowers** large in genus; sepals and petals straw-yellow to yellow; lip yellow marked with purple on callus and on side lobes. **Sepals** narrowly elliptic-lanceolate, acute, up to 1.3 cm long, 0.3 cm broad. **Petals** similar. **Lip** 3-lobed just below the middle, shortly clawed, 0.8 cm long, 0.6 cm broad; side lobes rounded in front, erect; mid-lobe obovate to cuneate-flabellate, emarginate or shortly bifid at apex; with a short fleshy ridge on each side at base of mid-lobe. **Column** short, stout.
DISTRIBUTION Brazil, Surinam, Trinidad, Bolivia and Paraguay.
HISTORY Imported to England by Messrs Loddiges from Brazil and described by John Lindley in 1842 in the *Botanical Register* (misc. 64). *O. grandiflora* is one of the largest species, both vegetatively and florally, in the genus.
SYNONYMS *Octomeria arcuata* Rolfe; *O. surinamensis* Focke; *O. ruthiana* Hoehne; *O. robusta* Barb. Rodr.

Octomeria saundersiana Rchb.f.
A small epiphytic plant with short stems, up to 2.5 cm long. **Leaf** terete, subulate, canaliculate, 5–6 cm long. **Inflorescence** fasciculate. **Flowers** membranaceous, ochre-yellow, ± purple-striped. **Sepals** and **petals** subsimilar, triangular, acute. **Lip** 3-lobed; side lobes triangular, obtuse; mid-lobe oblong, acute, slightly undulate; disc keeled between the side lobes. **Column** clavate, incurved.
DISTRIBUTION Brazil.
HISTORY Described from a Brazilian plant lacking exact locality data by H.G. Reichen-

Octomeria oxycheila Barb. Rodr.

A small epiphytic herb with a slender creeping rhizome. **Stems** 1-leafed, terete, 5-noded, erect or slightly flexuous, 7–11 cm long, up to 2 cm thick. **Leaf** erect or slightly spreading, fleshy, sessile, oblong-lanceolate, acute, 6–8 cm long, 1.5 cm broad, **Flowers** densely fasciculate, spreading or nodding, small, whitish-yellow, slightly fragrant. **Sepals** fleshy, oblong-lanceolate, acute, 0.5 cm long, 0.15 cm broad. **Petals** broadly rhombic, acute, 0.45 cm long, 0.2 cm broad. **Lip** fleshy, shortly and narrowly clawed, 3-lobed, 0.4 cm long, 0.25 cm broad; side lobes small, erect, subrotund; mid-lobe rectangular, broad, truncate and tridenticulate at apex; disc glabrous, with 2 median calli and a fleshy keel to the apex. **Column** short, fleshy.

DISTRIBUTION Brazil.

HISTORY Discovered near Rodeio in Rio de Janeiro Province by J. Barbosa Rodrigues and decribed by him in 1882 in his *Genera et Species Orchidearum Novarum* (p. 99).

O. oxycheila is recognised by its relatively large size lanceolate leaves and thin, rather than compressed as in *O. grandiflora*, stems. Its oblong-ovate lip is 3-lobed at the apex.

Odontoglossum H.B.K.
Subfamily Epidendroideae
Tribe Oncidieae

Medium-sized to large epiphytic or lithophytic plants with short rhizomes. **Pseudobulbs** ± compressed, covered by distichous ± leaf-bearing sheaths, 1–3 leaved at apex. **Leaves** coriaceous or fleshy, rigid or flexible. **Inflorescence** basal, erect or arcuate, 1- to many-flowered, racemose or paniculate. **Flowers** large and showy to small and inconspicuous. **Sepals** and **petals** subsimilar, spreading; lateral sepals ± adnate. **Lip** entire to 3-lobed, base of lip parallel to the column or somewhat adnate to it; side lobes erect or revolute; mid-lobe deflexed, spreading; disc lamellate, cristate or callose. **Column** long, slender; pollinia 2, waxy, entire or sulcate; stipe strap-like; viscidium small, ± elliptic.

DISTRIBUTION About 60 species mainly confined to the mountainous regions of tropical and subtropical Central and S. America.

DERIVATION OF NAME From the Greek *odonto* (tooth) and *glossa* (tongue) referring to the tooth-like projections of the lip callus.

TAXONOMY *Odontoglossum* was first described in 1815 by A. von Humboldt, A. Bonpland and C.S. Kunth in *Nova Genera et Species*

(p. 350, t. 85). The genus *Odontoglossum* is closely allied to *Oncidium* differing mainly in the lip which is parallel to the column in its basal part and not at right-angles to it as in *Oncidium* and the lack of spreading column-wings. Other minor features which separate these genera are column length and callus type. Nevertheless, with several species it is difficult to assess to which genus they should belong and sometimes these have been arbitrarily placed in one genus or the other.

It is interesting to note the comments of L.O. Williams in the *Annals of the Missouri Botanical Garden* (1946) in a footnote to the generic key, that the concepts of *Odontoglossum, Miltonia, Mesospinidium, Aspasia, Brassia, Leochilus* and *Osmoglossum* are technically inseparable from that of the earlier *Oncidium* and might be logically treated as subgeneric sections of that genus. However, the species in each category are generally sufficiently distinctive to be readily recognisable with only the border-line species presenting any difficulty. Practical ends seem to be better served by the maintenance of these entities as distinct.

Recently, L. Garay and G. Kennedy, in the *Orchid Digest* (1976), have removed *Odontoglossum grande* and its allies to the genus *Rossioglossum* and this treatment has been followed in this account. Halbinger (1983 onwards) in a series of articles in the journal *Orquidea* (Mexico) removed the Mexican and C. American species to a series of segregate genera – *Lemboglossum, Ticoglossum, Mesoglossum, Osmoglossum*, etc. This treatment is followed here.

John Lindley first revised the genus in his *Folia Orchidacea* in 1852 and this was followed by James Bateman's *Monograph* of the genus (1854–74). The genus was revised by F. Kraenzlin in 1922 in A. Engler's *Das Pflanzenreich*. This account although still useful is out of date and should be used with caution. The most recent revision of the genus is that by Leonore Bockemuehl (1989) in her book entitled *Odontoglossum. Monographie und Ikonographie*. Her concept of the genus is the narrowest to date and she recognises only 57 species in the genus which is predominantly Andean in distribution.

TYPE SPECIES *O. epidendroides* H.B.K.

CULTURE Compost A. Temp. Winter min. 12–15°C. The majority of species come from high altitudes and so, in cultivation, require constantly humid conditions with ample shade in hot weather. The roots should never dry out but water must be given very carefully when the new growths first appear. Fresh moving air is important especially in warm weather. Species from low altitudes may be grown as *Oncidium* with a drier period after the pseudobulbs have completed.

Odontoglossum blandum Rchb.f.
[Colour Plate]

A medium-sized epiphytic plant. **Pseudobulbs** ellipsoid, compressed, 3 cm long, 2 cm broad, 2-leaved at apex. **Leaves** linear-lanceolate, 15–25 cm long, 1.2–2.4 cm broad, acute to subacute at apex. **Inflorescence** racemose, arcuate, 12–25 cm long with up to 8 flowers clustered towards the apex; bracts ovate, acute, 0.5–0.8 cm long. **Flowers** showy, scented, up to 4.5 cm across; sepals and petals white, spotted purple-red; lip white, spotted purple; callus yellow. **Sepals** lanceolate, 2.2–2.7 cm long, 0.3 cm broad, long-acuminate. **Petals** similar to sepals but slightly shorter and narrower. **Lip** clawed, obovate, apiculate, margins erose-dentate and undulate, 2.3 cm long, 1.1 cm broad; callus of 2 parallel ridges terminated by 2 slender upturned teeth, pubescent. **Column** with 3–4 tapering cirri on each side at apex.

DISTRIBUTION Colombia, Ecuador and Peru; in the Cordillera Oriental of the Andes; 1700–2700 m.

HISTORY Discovered in the forests of Ocaña in Colombia by H. Blunt whilst collecting for the firm of Messrs Low & Co. during the period 1863–65. Unfortunately Blunt's collection failed to survive and it was not successfully cultivated until 1871 when it was flowered by the Royal Horticultural Society at Chiswick, London. H.G. Reichenbach described it in 1870 in the *Gardeners' Chronicle* (p. 1342).

Odontoglossum cirrhosum Lindl.
[Colour Plate]

A large epiphytic plant. **Pseudobulbs** oblong-ovoid, compressed, 3–8 cm long, 1-leafed at apex, subtended by 3 pairs of distichous, imbricating leaf-bearing sheaths. **Leaves** linear-oblong to elliptic-oblong, 10–30 cm long, 2.5–3 cm broad, acute. **Inflorescence** lateral, basal, longer than the leaves, up to 60 cm long, racemose or paniculate, laxly many-flowered. **Flowers** large, up to 10 cm across, milk-white with brown blotches on the sepals, petals and lip mid-lobe, basal part of lip yellow, lined with red. **Dorsal sepal** narrowly lanceolate, 4–5 cm long, 0.7 cm broad, long-acuminate, with undulate margins; lateral sepals similar, somewhat oblique. **Petals** rhombic-lanceolate, 3.8–5 cm long, 1.4–1.8 cm broad, long-acuminate, with undulate margins. **Lip** 3-lobed near base, basal part clasping the column, 3 cm long; side lobes broadly rounded, erect-spreading, denticulate; mid-lobe recurved, elongate, narrowly lanceolate, long-acuminate; disc with 2 S-shaped ascending horns between the side lobes. **Column** straight, 1 cm long, with 2 ascending tendrils at the apex.

DISTRIBUTION S. Colombia, Ecuador and

Peru; growing in the Cordillera Occidental of the Andes; 1700–2600 m.

HISTORY Discovered in the Mindo valley in the Andes of Ecuador by Colonel Hall and subsequently by Prof. W. Jameson and described by John Lindley in *Genera and Species of Orchidaceous Plants* (p. 211) in 1833. The specific epithet refers to the tendril-like extensions to the column. The first living introductions were made in 1875 by the Klaboch brothers. Var. *hrubyanum* Rchb.f. is an albino.

SYNONYMS *Oncidium cirrhosum* (Lindl.) Beer; *Odontoglossum hrubyanum* Hort.

Odontoglossum constrictum Lindl.
[Colour Plate]
An epiphytic plant. **Pseudobulbs** ovoid, ancipitous, 5–7.5 cm long, light green when young, 2-leaved at apex. **Leaves** linear-lanceolate, 16–43 cm long, 1.5–2 cm broad, subacute or acute. **Inflorescence** slender, arcuate, racemose or laxly paniculate, up to 65 cm long, many-flowered; bracts ovate-triangular, acute, 0.4 cm long. **Flowers** 3.5–5 cm across, fragrant; sepals and petals yellow or greenish-yellow, blotched with red-brown; lip white with a rose blotch in front of the callus; column white. **Sepals** linear-lanceolate, spreading, 1.8–2.4 cm long, 0.45–0.6 cm broad, acute to acuminate. **Petals** similar to sepals. **Lip** obscurely 3-lobed in basal half, subpandurate, apiculate, 2.3–2.5 cm long, 1 cm broad; mid-lobe deflexed, with erose-undulate margins; callus bidentate with erose margins. **Column** bicirrate at the apex.

DISTRIBUTION Venezuela, Colombia and Ecuador.

HISTORY Introduced in 1843 from La Guayra and Caracas by J. Linden and flowered in England by Rucker of Westhill and the Rev. Clowes of Broughton Hall. They sent it to John Lindley who described it in 1843 in the *Botanical Register* (misc. p. 17).

SYNONYMS *O. sanderianum* Rchb.f.; *O. boddaertianum* Rchb.f.

Odontoglossum crispum Lindl. [Colour Plate]
An epiphytic plant. **Pseudobulbs** broadly ovoid or oblong-ovoid, ancipitous, up to 7.5 cm long, 2-leaved at apex. **Leaves** suberect, linear-lanceolate, 30–42 cm long, 1.8–3.2 cm broad, acute. **Inflorescence** arching or pendulous, racemose or paniculate, many-flowered, up to 50 cm or more long; bracts small, lanceolate, cucullate, up to 1.2 cm long. **Flowers** variable, 6–10 cm across, very showy, mostly white or white tinged rose, rarely pale yellow, ± spotted or blotched red or purple; disc of lip bright yellow. **Sepals** ovate-lanceolate, undulate, 3.1–5 cm long, 1.2–2.2 cm broad, obtuse to acuminate with undulate-crenulate margins keeled on reverse. Petals ovate-elliptic to oblong-

elliptic, margins erose or dentate, 3–4.5 cm long, 1.7–3.8 cm broad, acute to acuminate, with undulate-crenulate margins. **Lip** oblong or subpandurate, margins dentate and undulate, rounded, emarginate or apiculate at apex, 2–3 cm long, 1.2–1.5 cm broad; callus fleshy, with 2 diverging lobes at apex. **Column** arching slightly, 1.6–1.9 cm long, with 2 broad lacerate apical wings.

DISTRIBUTION Colombia, western spurs and slopes of the Cordillera Oriental of the Andes; 2250–3000 m altitude.

HISTORY If for nothing else, Theodore Hartweg will be remembered as the discoverer of this, the most famous of all the *Odontoglossum* species. He collected it in 1841 in the Colombian Andes whilst collecting for the Horticultural Society of London. John Lindley described Hartweg's specimen in 1852 in the *Annals and Magazine of Natural History* (p. 256). Surprisingly *O. crispum* was not introduced into cultivation until 1863 when J. Weir, H. Blunt and L. Schlim collected it for, respectively, the Horticultural Society of London, Messrs Low and Jean Linden of Brussels. Of the collections, the one made by Blunt was sold to John Day of Tottenham, London, who became the first person to successfully flower it in cultivation.

Many varieties and colour forms of this popular orchid are in cultivation.

SYNONYMS *Odontoglossum alexandrae* Batem.; *O. bluntii* Rchb.f.

Odontoglossum cruentum Rchb.f.
[Colour Plate]
An epiphytic plant. **Pseudobulbs** ovoid-pyriform, compressed, 2.5–7 cm long, 1.5–3.5 cm across, 2-leaved at apex, subtended by 2–3 leaf-bearing sheaths. **Leaves** linear-ligulate, sub-erect, up to 22 cm long, 1.9–2.2 cm broad, acute. **Inflorescence** erect, arching slightly, racemose or weakly branching, up to 45 cm long, loosely many-flowered; bracts lanceolate, acute, up to 1 cm long. **Flowers** 5 cm across; sepals and petals greenish-yellow with a few large maroon blotches on inner surface; lip yellow with a central maroon blotch; callus white; column white, wings red. **Sepals** linear-oblanceolate, 2.5–3.2 cm long, 0.5–0.6 cm broad, acuminate; lateral sepals twisted slightly. **Petals** narrowly elliptic-lanceolate, margins undulate, 2–2.8 cm long, 0.5 cm broad, acute or acuminate. **Lip** oblong-elliptic, apiculate, sharply deflexed after basal third, 1.8–2 cm long, 0.6 cm broad, margins reflexed; callus on claw fleshy, bifurcate above, with teeth on each side at base. **Column** arcuate, clavate, 1–1.2 cm long; wings narrowly oblong.

DISTRIBUTION Ecuador and N. Peru; 2000–2500 m altitude in mist forests.

HISTORY Discovered by G. Wallis in

February 1866 at Chuquiribamba in Ecuador and described by H.G. Reichenbach in 1874 in *Xenia Orchidacea* vol. 2 (t. 174).

Odontoglossum hallii Lindl. [Colour Plate]
A large, variable, epiphytic plant with a short rhizome. **Pseudobulbs** oblong-ovoid or ovoid, strongly compressed, 5–10 cm long, 1- or 2-leaved at apex, subtended by distichous leaf-bearing sheaths. **Leaves** oblong-lanceolate to ligulate, 13–30 cm long, 2–4.5 cm broad, acute. **Inflorescence** lateral, in the axil of a sheath, 30–90 cm long or more, racemose or rarely paniculate, laxly 4- to 20-flowered; rhachis somewhat fractiflex. **Flowers** large, up to 10 cm across; sepals and petals yellow, spotted and blotched, purplish-brown; lip white with a few dark purple spots and a yellow callus. **Dorsal sepal** lanceolate to elliptic-lanceolate, 3.6–5.5 cm long, up to 1.2 cm broad, long-acuminate; with undulate margins; **lateral sepals** similar but somewhat oblique. **Petals** obliquely ovate-lanceolate, up to 5 cm long, 1.5 cm broad, acute. **Lip** shortly clawed and adnate for 5 mm to column; lamina strongly deflexed, pandurate-oblong, lacerate-dentate on front margins, up to 2.5 cm long, 2.3 cm wide; disc with a callus of several multifimbriate ridges. **Column** strongly arcuate, 1.6–1.9 cm long; wings divided into narrow teeth or tendrils.

DISTRIBUTION Ecuador; up to an altitude of 3000 m.

HISTORY One of the fine *Odontoglossum* species discovered in the Loxa (now Loja) valley in the Ecuadorian Andes by Col. Hall in 1837 and described by John Lindley in the same year in the *Botanical Register* (sub t. 1992). It was first introduced into cultivation in 1864 and 1865 by the establishments of Messrs Low, Linden, Backhouse and Veitch.

SYNONYMS *O. chaetostroma* Rchb.f.; *O. victor* Rchb.f.

Odontoglossum harryanum Rchb.f.
[Colour Plate]
A large plant. **Pseudobulbs** clustered, oblong-ovoid to shortly conical, 6–8 cm long, 2-leaved at apex, subtended by several leaf-bearing sheaths. **Leaves** oblong-elliptic to narrowly oblong, distinctly petiolate, up to 44 cm long, 2.5–4 cm broad, acute to obtuse. **Inflorescence** racemose, up to 1 m long, suberect, 6- to 8-flowered. **Flowers** large, up to 9 cm across, showy, the sepals and petals yellow marked with pale to chestnut-brown; petals purple-lined at base; lip white, purple-lined at base; callus yellow. **Dorsal sepal** elliptic-oblong to subelliptic, up to 4.5 cm long, 1.3–2.5 cm broad, subacute; **lateral sepals** similar but oblique. **Petals** elliptic-oblong to narrowly elliptic, 4–4.2 cm long, 1.6–2.3 cm broad,

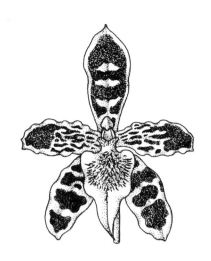

Odontoglossum harryanum
Flower (× $\frac{3}{5}$)

acute. **Lip** shortly clawed, auriculate on claw; lamina ovate-pandurate or obscurely 3-lobed, 4.5 cm long, up to 3.3 cm wide; sides incurved; anterior part subcordate, apiculate; disc with a prominent lacerate or fimbriate callus. **Column** small, 1.2–1.7 cm long, with dentate wings above.
DISTRIBUTION Colombia; on margins of lower montane forest; 1800–2300 m.
HISTORY Introduced into cultivation by Messrs Horsman & Co. of Colchester, England, for whom it was purchased by Messrs Veitch. It was described by H.G. Reichenbach in 1886 in the *Gardeners' Chronicle* (pt. 2: p. 486). Reichenbach named this species in honour of Harry Veitch of the famous nursery firm.
CLOSELY RELATED SPECIES Often confused with *O. wyattianum* Wilson, from Ecuador and Peru, which is distinguished by its more evenly coloured yellow-brown sepals, more spreading petals and lip lacking a mucronate apex.

Odontoglossum lindenii **Lindl.** [Colour Plate]
A tufted, terrestrial plant. **Pseudobulbs** ovoid, 6 cm long, 2–5 cm broad, 2-leaved at apex. **Leaves** erect, linear, thin-textured, margins inrolled, 10–45 cm long, 2–5 cm broad, subacute. **Inflorescence** erect, much longer than the leaves, paniculate, pyramidal, 40–100 cm long, with up to 50 flowers; branches short, often twisted somewhat; bracts membranous, cucullate, oblong, apiculate up to 2.6 cm long. **Flowers** bright yellow; about 4 cm across. **Sepals** oblanceolate or spathulate, shortly clawed 1.5–2 cm long, 0.3 cm broad, obtuse, margins very undulate. **Petals** elliptic-spathulate, 1.7 cm

long, 0.7–0.8 cm broad, subacute to obtuse, margins very undulate. **Lip** deflexed, ovate, apiculate, occasionally obscurely 3-lobed, 1.6–1.8 cm long, 1 cm broad; callus bilamellate at base with several long projections in front. **Column** terete, 0.8 cm long.
DISTRIBUTION Venezuela, Colombia and Ecuador; terrestrial in areas bordering the paramo; 2700–3000 m.
HISTORY Discovered by Jean Linden in Colombia at an altitude of 2800 m and named after him in *Folia Orchidacea Odontoglossum* (no. 46) in 1852 by John Lindley.

Odontoglossum lindleyanum **Rchb.f.**
Pseudobulbs broadly ovoid, compressed, ancipitous, up to 7.5 cm long, 1.6–3.2 cm broad, 2-leaved at apex. **Leaves** suberect, acute, linear-lanceolate, 12–30 cm long, 1.2–2.5 cm broad, racemose or paniculate, up to 10-flowered; bracts small, ovate, acute, 0.5–0.8 cm long. **Flowers** stellate, 5–7.5 cm across; sepals and petals yellow with a central red-brown blotch and spotted red-brown towards base; lip red-brown with a yellowish apex, white at base and spotted purple. **Sepals** linear-lanceolate, up to 2.9 cm long, up to 0.6 cm broad, acute or acuminate. **Petals** similar to sepals, 2.7 cm long, 0.7 cm broad, acute or acuminate. **Lip** obscurely 3-lobed; geniculate in middle, 2.5–3 cm long, 1 cm broad; side lobes small; mid-lobe lanceolate, reflexed, acute; calli 2, horn-like. **Column** 1.8 cm long, straight, wings narrow, acuminate, suberect.
DISTRIBUTION Venezuela, Colombia (Cordilleras Central and Oriental) and Ecuador; on margins and in clearings in montane forest; 1800–2400 m.
HISTORY Discovered in Colombia in 1842 or 1843 by Jean Linden who sent specimens to Lindley who mistakenly thought it was *O. epidendroides* H.B.K. Subsequently, H.G. Reichenbach concluded that Linden's plant was a new species which he named *O. lindleyanum* in honour of that most eminent of all orchid taxonomists. Reichenbach described it in 1854 in *Bonplandia* (p. 99).
CLOSELY RELATED SPECIES *O. lindleyanum* is allied to *O. odoratum* but differs in its flower colour and markings, in its lip which has a prominent keel which is bifid and spreading in front, and by its column which lacks elongated arms at the apex.

Odontoglossum luteopurpureum **Lindl.**
[Colour Plate]
An epiphytic plant. **Pseudobulbs** ovoid, compressed, up to 10 cm long, 3–4.5 cm broad, 2-leaved at apex, subtended by a few leaf-bearing sheaths. **Leaves** linear or narrowly linear-lanceolate, suberect, 23–60 cm long, 1.6–

4 cm broad, acute. **Inflorescence** erect, up to 100 cm long, racemose, up to 12-flowered. **Flowers** showy, 6–10 cm across; sepals and petals bright chestnut-brown, margins and apices yellow; lip yellowish-white or white, spotted red-brown, callus deep yellow. **Sepals** lanceolate, undulate, 4–5 cm long, up to 1.4 cm broad, acute or acuminate. **Petals** lanceolate, margins erose and crisped-undulate, up to 4.2 cm long, 1.2 cm broad, acuminate. **Lip** deflexed, obscurely 3-lobed, up to 3 cm long, 2.5 cm broad; side lobes small; mid-lobe clawed, obovate to pandurate, emarginate, margins lacerate; callus of many subulate cirri. **Column** 1.8–2 cm long, wings lacerate-dentate.
DISTRIBUTION Colombia; 2300–2900 m altitude.
HISTORY A very variable species first collected by Jean Linden in the forests of Quindio at 2500 m altitude and described in *Orchidaceae Lindenianae* (p. 16) in 1846 by John Lindley.
  Many named varieties of this species of orchid have been introduced into cultivation in the past.
SYNONYM *Odontoglossum hystrix* Batem.

Odontoglossum odoratum **Lindl.**
[Colour Plate]
Pseudobulbs broadly ovoid, compressed, ancipitous, 4–9 cm long. **Leaves** suberect, linear-lanceolate, 15–30 cm long, 3–4 cm broad, acute, keeled on reverse. **Inflorescence** racemose or paniculate, laxly many-flowered, 50–75 cm long; branches fractiflex. **Flowers** fragrant, 3.8–6 cm across, pale to deep yellow, spotted dark maroon or red-brown; lip callus white. **Sepals** narrowly lanceolate, 1.9–3.5 cm long, 0.4–0.7 cm broad, long-acuminate and reflexed at apex. **Petals** lanceolate, up to 3.0 cm long, 0.6–0.7 cm broad, long-acuminate, margins undulate. **Lip** deflexed, 3-lobed, shortly clawed, geniculate in basal third, 2.4–2.9 cm long, 1 cm broad; side lobes rounded, erect; mid-lobe lanceolate to oblong-elliptic, recurved in apical half, glandular pubescent in basal half, acuminate; callus bidentate, covered with glandular hairs. **Column** 0.9 cm long, with 2 cirri at apex.
DISTRIBUTION Venezuela and Colombia; lower montane forests, 1500–2500 m.
HISTORY First collected in W. Venezuela by Jean Linden in 1842 or 1843 and later by L. Schlim in the Cordillera Oriental of Colombia. John Lindley described it in 1846 in *Orchidaceae Lindenianae* (p. 16) naming it for its pleasant hawthornlike fragrance.
SYNONYM *Odontoglossum gloriosum* Linden & Rchb.f.
CLOSELY RELATED SPECIES See *O. lindleyanum*.

Odontoglossum ramosissimum Lindl.
[Colour Plate]

An epiphytic plant. **Pseudobulbs** oblong-ovoid, ancipitous, up to 12 cm long, 5 cm broad, 1-leafed at apex, subtended by several distichous leaf-bearing sheaths. **Leaves** linear-lanceolate, 30–60 cm long, up to 5 cm broad, acute. **Inflorescence** erect, paniculate, 100 cm or more long, densely many-flowered towards apex; apex of inflorescence often pyramidal in outline; bracts 0.8 cm long. **Flowers** 5 cm across, white (yellow in var. *xanthinum* Rchb.f.), spotted violet; callus white; column white, stained with purple. **Sepals** narrowly lanceolate, 2.4–2.6 cm long, 0.8 cm broad, acuminate, margins undulate and reflexed. **Petals** narrowly lanceolate, 2.3 cm long, 0.8 cm broad, acuminate, margins undulate and reflexed. **Lip** elongate, deltoid, reflexed, acuminate, 1.8 cm long, 0.7–1 cm broad; callus bilamellate, many-toothed in front. **Column** 0.8 cm long, obscurely winged.

DISTRIBUTION Colombia, Venezuela and Ecuador; in montane forest, 2200–3300 m.

HISTORY First collected near Mérida in Venezuela in 1843 by Jean Linden and described in 1852 by John Lindley in *Folia Orchidacea Odontoglossum* (p. 16), who named it for its many-branched inflorescence. Gustav Wallis sent the first living plants to Linden's nursery in 1871.

SYNONYMS *O. liliiflorum* Hort.; *Oncidium ramosissimum* (Lindl.) Beer

Odontoglossum spectatissimum Lindl.
[Colour Plate]

Pseudobulbs ovoid, compressed, 7.5–10 cm long, 2-leaved at apex. **Leaves** petiolate, linear or ligulate, 8–45 cm long, 2–3 cm broad, acute. **Inflorescence** arching, racemose or rarely paniculate, up to 15-flowered, 60–90 cm long; bracts small, ovate-cucullate, acute, up to 0.4 cm long. **Flowers** 7.5 cm across, scented; sepals and petals golden-yellow, heavily spotted with cinnamon-brown; lip white or pale yellow with a large red-brown blotch in the apical half, callus white or yellow; column white. **Sepals** oblong-lanceolate or narrowly elliptic, 3.8–5.3 cm long, 0.9–1.6 cm broad, acute or acuminate. **Petals** elliptic-subrhombic to lanceolate, 3–4.4 cm long, 1.1–1.6 cm broad, acute, margin undulate. **Lip** clawed, oblong-ovate and deflexed, apiculate, margin denticulate, 3–3.6 cm long, 1.6–2 cm broad; callus a raised plate terminating in 2 diverging teeth. **Column** arcuate, 1.7–2.2 cm long, with 2 erose, truncate wings.

DISTRIBUTION W. Venezuela and Colombia; in dense forest from 1500–3200 m altitude.

HISTORY Discovered near Pamplona in the Cordillera Oriental of Colombia by Jean Linden in 1842 and by J. Warscewicz in the same area around 1848. J. Lindley described it in *Folia Orchidacea Odontoglossum* (p. 19) in 1852. This species is well-known as *O. triumphans* which H.G. Reichenbach described in 1854 in *Bonplandia*. However, it was not introduced into cultivation in Europe until 1867 when Messrs Low of Clapton, London, were sent some living plants.

SYNONYM *Odontoglossum triumphans* Rchb.f.

Odontoglossum weirii Rchb.f. [Colour Plate]

An epiphytic plant. **Pseudobulbs** clustered, ovoid, compressed, 5–6 cm tall, 4 cm across, 1- to 2-leaved at apex. **Leaves** oblanceolate-ligulate, acute, 10–25 cm long, 2.5–3.5 cm broad. **Inflorescence** paniculate; branches spreading, laxly arranged, about 6-flowered; bracts ovate-cucullate, 1 cm long, acute. **Flowers** about 4.5–5 cm across; sepals and petals pale yellow, blotched and barred pale red-brown in basal half; lip red, apex yellow. **Sepals** narrowly clawed, lamina lanceolate, acuminate, 2.3–3.4 cm long, 0.5 cm broad. **Petals** falcate-lanceolate, 2.5 cm long, 0.6 cm broad, acuminate, margins undulate. **Lip** shortly clawed, ovate-subhastate; lamina deflexed, undulate, 1.5–2.1 cm long, 0.7–1.1 cm broad, acuminate; callus on base of lamina, fleshy, verrucose-velvety, papillate. **Column** long, clavate, 1–1.2 cm long, lacking apical wings.

DISTRIBUTION Colombia; montane forest, 2700–3300 m.

HISTORY Discovered in 1868 in Colombia by J. Weir who sent living plants to James Bateman in England. Bateman, in turn, sent flowering material to H.G. Reichenbach who described it in 1875 in the *Gardeners' Chronicle* (ser. 2,3: p. 461).

CLOSELY RELATED SPECIES Somewhat similar to *Odontoglossum tetraplasium* Rchb.f. but distinguished by its longer column, widely diffuse panicle and larger flowers with an almost solid red lip.

Oeceoclades Lindl.

Subfamily Epidendroideae
Tribe Cymbidieae
Subtribe Cyrtopodiinae

Small to large terrestrial or rarely epiphytic plants. **Pseudobulbs** more or less proximate, apparently 1-noded, 1- to 3-leaved at apex. **Leaves** coriaceous, conduplicate, ± petiolate. **Inflorescence** lateral, racemose or paniculate. **Flowers** small, thin-textured, resupinate. **Sepals** and **petals** free, spreading. **Lip** sessile, 3-lobed, spurred at base; calli quadrate or triangular, at entrance to spur. **Column** erect, short, oblique at base; rostellum short; anther cucullate to cristate; pollinia 2 on a short, rudimentary stipe; viscidium large.

DISTRIBUTION 31 species in tropical S. America, the W. Indies, Florida, tropical Africa, Madagascar, the Mascarene Islands and the Seychelles.

DERIVATION OF NAME From the Greek *oikeios* (private) and *klados* (branch) possibly referring to Lindley's separation of certain species from *Angraecum* to form a distinct tribe or 'private' branch.

TAXONOMY Described by John Lindley in 1832 in the *Botanical Register* (sub t. 1522). Until recently, species of *Oeceoclades* were referred to the genus *Eulophidium* of E. Pfitzer (a name which reflects this genus's affinity with *Eulophia*). However, L. Garay and P. Taylor in 1976 in *Botanical Museum Leaflets of Harvard University* have revised the genus and shown that Pfitzer was wrong to describe the genus *Eulophidium* when Lindley had already described the genus *Oeceoclades* some fifty years before based on the same type species, namely *Oeceoclades (Angraecum) maculata* Lindl.

Unfortunately both botanists and horticulturalists followed Pfitzer in placing *O. maculata* and its allies in the genus *Eulophidium*. Garay and Taylor have now made the necessary combinations in the genus *Oeceoclades* for all species previously referred to *Eulophidium* and they also provide a key to identify the species.

TYPE SPECIES *O. maculata* Lindl.

SYNONYM *Eulophidium* Pfitz.

CULTURE Compost B. Temp. Winter min. 15–18°C. Conveniently divided into 2 groups: (1) Forest species from tropical Africa and S. America. These plants need quite heavy shade and require only a short dry rest. When growing, they should be carefully watered as they produce relatively few thick roots. Most species have beautifully-marked leaves. (2) Species from Madagascar. These plants are much tougher than those in group (1) and require much less shade. They must also be carefully watered when growing but must remain nearly dry when growth is complete.

Oeceoclades angustifolia (Senghas) Garay & Taylor [Colour Plate]

A terrestrial herb. **Pseudobulbs** ovoid-pyriform, clustered, 2 cm long and in diameter, 1-leafed at apex (rarely 2-leaved). **Leaves** linear, erect or suberect, acute, coriaceous, up to 10 cm long, 0.7 cm broad, dull green, mottled with purple. **Inflorescence** erect, racemose or rarely poorly branched, up to 30 cm long, 5- to 15-flowered; bracts appressed, narrowly triangular, acuminate, 0.15 cm long. **Flowers** small; sepals greenish-white below, brownish above; petals white, striped with green; lip white, margin of mid-lobe ochre-yellow, side lobes and disc red-spotted, spur green. **Sepals** elliptic to oblanceolate, acute, 0.8 cm long, 0.3 cm broad. **Petals** concave, elliptic, acute, 0.6 cm long, 0.45 cm broad. **Lip** 3-lobed, 1–1.2 cm long, 1.4–1.6 cm broad; side lobes erect subquadrate-orbicular; mid-lobe bilobulate, spreading, obovate; callus bilobulate; spur subsphaerical, slightly incurved, 0.3 cm long. **Column** semiglobose, 0.3 cm long, 0.35 cm broad.

DISTRIBUTION N. Madagascar; in moss-filled cracks between calcareous boulders.

HISTORY Discovered by W. Rauh and Buchloch near Diego Suarez in 1961 in N. Madagascar and described by K. Senghas as *Eulophidium angustifolium* in *Adansonia* (p. 558) in 1966. L. Garay and P. Taylor transferred it to the genus *Oeceoclades* in 1976 in *Botanical Museum Leaflets of Harvard University* (p. 259).

SYNONYM *Eulophidium angustifolium* Senghas

CLOSELY RELATED SPECIES Related to *Oeceoclades decaryana* (H. Perr.) Garay & Taylor but distinguished by its petiolate leaves and differently proportioned lip.

Oeceoclades cordylinophylla (Rchb.f.) Garay & Taylor

A terrestrial or lithophytic herb, 60–80 cm tall. **Pseudobulbs** conical, narrowing towards the apex, 1-leafed at apex. **Leaf** persistent, coriaceous, longly petiolate, broadly elliptic, narrowly acute, 13–19 cm long, 6–8 cm broad; petiole 16–30 cm long, articulated 5–9 cm above the base. **Inflorescence** developing before the pseudobulb, paniculate; peduncle 40–50 cm long; bracts acute, reddish, 0.3 cm long. **Flowers** small, yellow-green, spotted purple with a purple mark in front of the column. **Sepals** spathulate, obtuse, 0.7 cm long, 0.35 cm broad. **Petals** broadly obovate, 0.6 cm long, 0.5 cm broad. **Lip** 3-lobed, pubescent towards base, with 2 basal calli; side-lobes erect, 0.2 cm high, 0.3 cm broad; mid-lobe lobules divergent, subrectangular, 0.6 cm long, 0.4 cm broad; spur conical, 0.6 cm long, pilose at the mouth. **Column** margins ciliolate-hirsute, 0.45 cm long.

DISTRIBUTION Comoros and Madagascar; growing in the deep shade on rocks.

HISTORY Discovered by L. Humblot in the Comoros and described by H.G. Reichenbach in 1885 as *Eulophia cordylinophylla* in *Flora* (p. 541). V.S. Summerhayes later transferred it to *Eulophidium* but it was transferred again to *Oeceoclades* when *Eulophidium* was recognised as a later synonym by L. Garay and P. Taylor in the *Botanical Museum Leaflets* (p. 261).

SYNONYMS *Eulophia cordylinophylla* Rchb.f.; *Lissochilus cordylinophyllus* (Rchb.f.) H. Perr.; *Eulophia lokobensis* H. Perr.; *Lissochilus lokobensis* (H. Perr.) H. Perr.; *Eulophidium lokobense* (H. Perr.) Summerh.

Oeceoclades maculata (Lindl.) Lindl.

An erect terrestrial herb. **Stems** ovoid, up to 2.5 cm long, dark greenish-brown, lightly sulcate, 1-leafed at apex. **Leaf** suberect-spreading, coriaceous, oblong-elliptic, up to 22 cm long, 6 cm broad, green, mottled with darker green. **Inflorescence** up to 40 cm long, erect, laxly 12- or more-flowered. **Flowers** small; sepals and petals pinkish-green; lip white, lined dark red on side lobes, pink on isthmus, spur brownish-green. **Sepals** linear, obtuse, 0.8–1 cm long, 0.2 cm broad; lateral sepals slightly falcate. **Petals** narrowly oblong, obtuse, 1 cm long, 0.35 cm broad. **Lip** 3-lobed, 0.8 cm long and broad; side lobes erect, rounded, shorter than mid-lobe; mid-lobe broadly oblong, shortly clawed, emarginate; spur pendent, cylindrical with a bulbous apex, 0.4 cm long. **Column** with a short foot, 0.5 cm long.

DISTRIBUTION Florida, the W. Indies, tropical S. America and tropical Africa from Senegal to Angola and Zimbabwe, and Tanzania (Zanzibar and Pemba).

HISTORY The type species of the genus. Originally introduced into cultivation from Brazil by Messrs Loddiges and described by John Lindley in 1821 as *Angraecum maculatum* in his *Collectanea Botanica* (t. 15). Lindley transferred it to the new genus *Oeceoclades* in 1833 in *Genera and Species of Orchidaceous Plants* (p. 237). Unfortunately, E. Pfitzer chose to ignore Lindley's genus even though he knew of its existence and placed this species in a new genus *Eulophidium* in 1837. The name *Eulophidium maculatum* has been the accepted name for this plant until L. Garay and P. Taylor's recent revision of the genus (1976) showed otherwise.

SYNONYMS *Angraecum maculatum* Lindl.; *Limodorum maculatum* Lodd.; *Aerobion maculatum* (Lindl.) Sprengel; *Eulophia maculata* (Lindl.) Rchb.; *Eulophidium maculatum* (Lindl.) Pfitz.; *Graphorkis maculata* (Lindl.) O. Ktze.; *Geodorum pictum* Link & Otto; *Eulophia ledienii* (Stein ex N.E. Br.) De Wild.; *Eulophidium warneckianum* Kraenzl.; *Eulophidium nyassanum* Schltr. Undoubtedly the wide geographical distribution of this species has led to the proliferation of names.

Oeceoclades roseovariegata (Senghas) Garay & Taylor

A terrestrial plant. **Pseudobulbs** clustered, ovoid, brownish-violet, 2.5 cm long, 2.5 cm in diameter, 2-leaved at apex. **Leaves** prostrate, ovate or elliptic ovate, acuminate, margins undulate, up to 4 cm long, 3.5 cm broad, dark purplish-black, mottled pale rose. **Inflorescence** erect, racemose or sparingly branched, laxly many-flowered, up to 55 cm long; bracts triangular, acuminate, 0.2–0.8 cm long. **Flowers** small; sepals and petals dull green, flushed purple on outer surface; lip white, densely spotted with red; column yellowish-green, anther ivory-white. **Sepals** oblanceolate, obtuse, 0.5–0.6 cm long, 0.2 cm broad; lateral sepals somewhat falcate. **Petals** oblong-lanceolate, obtuse, 0.4–0.5 cm long, 0.3 cm broad. **Lip** 3-lobed, 0.35–0.4 cm long, 0.7–0.8 cm broad; side lobes erect, oblong, truncate; mid-lobe strongly recurved, subquadrate, emarginate; callus quadrate, sulcate; spur cylindrical, pendent, 0.5 cm long.

DISTRIBUTION N. Madagascar; amongst mossy cracks in calcareous rocky terrain.

HISTORY The type of *O. roseovariegata* was collected by W. Rauh and Buchloch near Diego Suarez in N. Madagascar and was described by K. Senghas in 1966 in *Adansonia* (p. 501) as *Eulophidium roseovariegatum*. L. Garay and P. Taylor transferred it to *Oeceoclades* in their recent revision of the genus (p. 270). H. Perrier de la Bâthie first collected *O. roseovariegata* many years before Rauh and Buchloch in the same locality.

SYNONYM *Eulophidium roseovariegatum* Senghas

Oeceoclades saundersiana (Rchb.f.) Garay & Taylor [Colour Plate]

An erect terrestrial herb. **Pseudobulbs** tufted, up to 15 cm long, 2.5 cm thick, dark glossy green, narrowly conical-fusiform, 2- to 3-leaved at apex. **Leaves** petiolate, suberect, coriaceous, elliptic or elliptic-lanceolate, acuminate, glossy dark green, 10–27 cm long, 3–8.5 cm broad; petiole slender, up to 20 cm long. **Inflorescence** up to 90 cm long, laxly many-flowered. **Flowers** large in genus; sepals and petals brownish-green with darker venation; lip dull yellow, lined with crimson. **Sepals** linear-oblanceolate, obtuse, 1.2 cm long, 0.5 cm broad. **Petals** elliptic, slightly oblique, obtuse, 1.2 cm long, 0.3 cm broad. **Lip** 3-lobed, 1.5 cm long, 1.2 cm broad; side lobes erect, rounded; mid-lobe with a narrow claw, deeply bifid in front, flabellate-obcordate, dependent; spur tapering, 0.4 cm long; callus 2-lobed at mouth of spur.

DISTRIBUTION Widespread in tropical Africa from Sierra Leone east to Kenya and Tanzania and south to Zambia.

HISTORY First collected in W. Africa by G. Mann and described by H.G. Reichenbach in 1866 as *Eulophia saundersiana* in the *Botanische Zeitung* (p. 378). L. Garay and P. Taylor trans-

Oeceoclades saundersiana
1 – Habit (× ⅕)
2 – Flower (× 1½)
3 – Column, side view (× 3)

ferred it in 1976 to the genus *Oeceoclades* in their recent revision of the genus (p. 270).

O. saundersiana is easily recognised by its 2- to 3-leaved pseudobulbs and long-petiolate leaves.
SYNONYMS *Eulophia saundersiana* Rchb.f.; *Eulophidium saundersianum* (Rchb.f.) Summerh.; *Graphorkis saundersiana* (Rchb.f.) O. Ktze.; *Lissochilus barombensis* Kraenzl.; *Eulophia bierleri* De Wild.; *Eulophia mildbraedii* Kraenzl.

Oeonia Lindl.
Subfamily Epidendroideae
Tribe Vandeae
Subtribe Angraecinae

Small to medium-sized epiphytic herbs. **Stems** slender, flexuose, climbing or branching, or very short and almost obsolete. **Leaves** several, short to long, distichous, coriaceous. **Inflorescence** erect, longer than the leaves, racemose, several-flowered. **Flowers** white, often spotted rose or red on the lip. **Sepals** and **petals** free, spreading, subsimilar. **Lip** 3- to 6-lobed, with the base enfolding the column. **Column** short; mid-lobe of rostellum as long as the auricles; pollinia 2, each sessile on a separate viscidium.
DISTRIBUTION Five species in Madagascar and the Mascarene Islands.
DERIVATION OF NAME From the Greek *oionos* (bird of prey), possibly in allusion to the flower which fancifully resembles a bird in flight.
TAXONOMY John Lindley described this genus in 1824 in the *Botanical Register* (sub t. 817) but misspelt it as *Aeonia*. Lindley corrected the spelling himself in the following year in *Collectanea Botanica*. *Oeonia* is closely allied to *Cryptopus* Lindl. but has entire petals and a 3- to 6-lobed lip, the claw of which embraces the column. The genus has most recently been revised by J. Bosser (1989) in *Adansonia* (pp. 157–65).
TYPE SPECIES *O. aubertii* Lindl. nom illeg. [= *O. volucris* (Thou.) Dur. & Schinz].
CULTURE Compost A. Temp. Winter min. 15°C. *Oeonia* species are probably best grown in shallow pans or baskets. They require good humidity and shade with ample water while growing. Less water should be given when growth is completed.

Oeonia volucris (Thou.) Dur. & Schinz
[Colour Plate]
A slender epiphytic plant. **Stems** pendent or climbing, branching somewhat, many-leaved. **Leaves** spaced, ovate-oblong or elliptic, attenuate below, unequally acutely 2-lobed above, 2.5 cm long, 0.8 cm broad. **Inflorescence** very long, erect, several-flowered, 30–35 cm long. **Flowers** white, spotted red on the lip. **Dorsal sepal** oblong-obovate, subacute, 1.2 cm long; **lateral sepals** longer, acute. **Petals** oblong-obovate, subacute, 1.2 cm long. **Lip** 3-lobed, 1.8 cm long, 1.2 cm broad; side lobes basal, inrolled somewhat; mid-lobe clawed, bilobulate-flabellate; disc papillate; spur short, gradually attenuate, 0.6 cm long. **Column** very short.
DISTRIBUTION Madagascar and the Mascarene Islands; sea level to 1200 m altitude.
HISTORY Originally collected by A. du Petit Thouars in Mauritius and figured by him as *Epidendrum volucre* in his *Orchidées des Iles Australes de l'Afrique* (t. 81) in 1822. Th. Durand and Schinz transferred it to *Oeonia* in their *Conspectus Florae Africae* (p. 51) in 1895.
SYNONYMS *Epidendrum volucre* Thou.; *Oeonia aubertii* Lindl. nom illeg.; *Aeranthus volucris* (Thou.) Rchb.f.; *Epidorchis volucris* (Thou.) O. Ktze.; *Oeonia humblotii* Kraenzl.

Oeoniella Schltr.
Subfamily Epidendroideae
Tribe Vandeae
Subtribe Angraecinae

Epiphytic herbs with long stems. **Leaves** distichous, spreading, coriaceous, linear. **Inflorescence** lateral, axillary, racemose, simple, few- to many-flowered. **Flowers** subsecund, white, non-resupinate. **Sepals** and **petals** free, linear-lanceolate, acuminate. **Lip** much larger, trumpet-shaped, 3-lobed at the apex, with a short spur at the base; side lobes rounded; mid-lobe subulate, longer than side lobes. **Column** short, stout; pollinia 2, ovoid, sulcate; stipites 2, linear; viscidium 1, subquadrate-cordate.
DISTRIBUTION Two or possibly three species confined to Madagascar, the Mascarene Islands and the Seychelles.
DERIVATION OF NAME The diminutive of *Oeonia*, another Madagascan orchid genus, which it superficially resembles.
TAXONOMY This genus was established by R. Schlechter in *Beihefte zum Botanischen Zentralblatt* (p. 439) in 1915. Vegetatively it is quite typical of many of the monopodial Vandoid orchid genera but its pretty fragrant white flowers are quite distinct with the trumpet-shaped lip having a short conical basal spur and a long subulate apical lobe.
TYPE SPECIES *O. polystachys* (Thou.) Schltr.; *O. aphrodite* (J.B. Balf. & S. Moore) Schltr.
CULTURE Compost A. Temp. Winter min. 15°C. As for *Vanda*. Although their stems are narrower than those of *Vanda* species, they have the same habit of growth with numerous aerial roots. The plants may be grown in pots or baskets under conditions of high humidity and moderate shade.

Oeoniella polystachys (Thou.) Schltr.
[Colour Plate]
A common epiphytic species. **Stems** erect, rigid, leafy, 7–50 cm long. **Roots** grey, stout, adventitious. **Leaves** oblong, fleshy, 2.5–5 cm long, 1.2 cm broad. **Inflorescence** more or less horizontal or suberect, 7- to 12-flowered; bracts short and rounded. **Flowers** 3–6 cm across, white; sepals and petals off-white, greenish towards the base. **Sepals** linear-lanceolate, acuminate, 1.2–1.6 cm long. **Petals** linear, acuminate, 1.2–1.6 cm long. **Lip** obcordate, trumpet-shaped, 3-lobed at the apex, 1.6 cm long; side lobes erect, crenulate; mid-lobe narrowly linear-filiform; spur attenuate towards apex, 0.6 cm long. **Column** short.

DISTRIBUTION Madagascar, Mascarene Islands, the Comoros and the Seychelles.

HISTORY Discovered in E. Madagascar by A. du Petit Thouars and described by him in 1822 as *Epidendrum polystachys* in his *Orchidées des Iles Australes de l' Afrique* (t. 82). R. Schlechter transferred it to his new genus *Oeoniella* in *Beihefte zum Botanischen Zentralblatt* (p. 439) in 1915.

SYNONYMS *Epidendrum polystachys* Thou.; *Angraecum polystachyum* (Thou.) Rchb.f.; *Oeonia polystachya* (Thou.) Benth.; *Monixus polystachys* (Thou.) Finet

---

Oerstedella Rchb.f.

Subfamily Epidendroideae
Tribe Epidendreae
Subfamily Laeliinae

Epiphytic or terrestrial plants with cane-like leafy stems and lacking pseudobulbs. **Leaves** distichous, coriaceous, flat, with rugulose or verrucose sheathing bases. **Inflorescences** terminal or lateral at the nodes, emerging through the leaf sheaths opposite the leaves. **Flowers** with free, spreading sepals and petals. **Lip** united at base to the column forming a nectary, deflexed, 3-lobed. **Column** semiterete; rostellum projecting downwards at 90° to the column; pollinia 4, hard, with caudicles but lacking a semi-liquid viscidium.

DISTRIBUTION A genus of about 40 species widespread from Mexico south to Bolivia.

DERIVATION OF NAME Named in honour of Anders Sandoe Oersted, the collector of the type material and a prolific plant collector in Mexico.

TAXONOMY The genus was established by Reichenbach in 1852 in the journal *Botanische Zeitung* (p. 932). Some authors have included the genus in the synonymy of *Epidendrum* but recent workers have tended to keep it as a distinct entity (see Hagsater in *Orquidea* (*Mex.*) 8(1): 19). It is allied to *Epidendrum* but is easily distinguished by the tubercular sheaths on the stems and by the rostellum and pollinarium structure.

TYPE SPECIES *Epidendrum centropetalum* Rchb.f.

CULTURE Temp. Winter min. 12°C. Pot in epiphyte mix and grow under shady, humid conditions. Water throughout the year, but less when not actively growing.

Oerstedella centropetala (Rchb.f.) Rchb.f.

A large terrestrial with loosely clustered erect stems, up to 75 cm long, sometimes branching, covered by sheathing leaf bases. **Leaves** distichous, spreading, linear-lanceolate to lanceolate, acute or obtuse, 2.5–8 cm long, 0.3–1.7 cm wide, articulated to 2–3 cm long, verrucose leaf bases. **Inflorescences** lateral, simple, few- to many-flowered, up to 10 cm long; bracts lanceolate, acuminate, up to 5 mm long. **Flowers** small, greenish-brown to purplish-brown or rose-purple; pedicel and ovary c. 5 mm long. **Dorsal sepal** elliptic to oblanceolate, acute to obtuse, 7–9 mm long, 2–3 mm wide; **lateral sepals** oblong to oblanceolate, acute, arcuate, 7–10 mm long, 2–3.5 mm wide. **Petals** linear-oblanceolate, obtuse, 6–9 mm long, 1–2.3 mm wide. **Lip** adnate to column in lower part of claw, the free part 3-lobed, up to 10 mm long, 8 mm wide; side lobes oblong, falcate, upcurved; mid-lobe deeply bilobulate with a mucro in the sinus; callus bilobed, yellow. **Column** abruptly recurved in the middle, 7–8 mm long, crenate at the apex.

DISTRIBUTION Guatemala to Costa Rica and Panama; montane forest up to 2400 m.

HISTORY H.G. Reichenbach originally described this orchid as *Epidendrum centropetalum* in 1852 in the *Botanische Zeitung* (p. 752) based on a collection made in December 1875 by Bernoulli and Cario in Guatemala. Reichenbach transferred it to his new genus *Oerstedella* in the same journal and in the same year (*Botanische Zeitung* p. 952).

SYNONYMS *Epidendrum centropetalum* Rchb.f.; *E. aberrans* Schltr.; *E. leprosum* Schltr.

Oerstedella endresii (Rchb.f.) Hagsater
[Colour Plate]

A small epiphyte with clustered terete stems, 8–20 cm long. **Leaves** convex, ovate to elliptic-ovate, obtuse or retuse, 1.2–4 cm long, 0.5–1.3 cm wide, glossy dark green above, articulated to green, sheathing, purple pustular leaf-bases, 0.8–1.1 cm long. **Inflorescence** erect, terminal. 3- to 10-flowered, 4–6 cm long; bracts lanceolate, acuminate, 5–8 mm long. **Flowers** flat, scented, white with bright purple markings at the base of the mid-lobe of the lip and the apex of the column, the lip lobes flushed with lilac in their basal parts; pedicel and ovary 1.2–1.7 cm long. **Sepals** oblong to ovate-oblong, acute to obtuse, 0.8–1 cm long, 0.3–0.4 cm wide. **Petals** obliquely obovate-spathulate, round to obtuse, 0.8 cm long, 0.3–0.5 cm wide. **Lip** deflexed, flat, 3-lobed at base, 1.1–1.3 cm long, 0.8 cm wide; side lobes short, spreading, emarginate; mid-lobe clawed, the apical lobules oblong, emarginate, divergent, separated by a broad obtuse sinus. **Column** clavate, 4 mm long, with truncate apical wings, united to lip for half its length.

DISTRIBUTION Endemic to Costa Rica; 1800–1900 m in montane forest.

HISTORY This pretty species was discovered by Endres in Costa Rica and was described as *Epidendrum endresii* by H.G. Reichenbach in 1883 in the *Gardeners' Chronicle* (pt. 1: p. 432). Eric Hagsater transferred it to the present genus in 1981 in *Orquidea* (*Mex.*) (p. 21).

SYNONYMS *Epidendrum endresii* Rchb.f.; *E. adolphii* Schltr.

Oerstedella wallisii (Rchb. f.) Hagsater
[Colour Plate]

A large terrestrial plant with erect stems up to 1 m or more tall. **Leaves** distichous, spreading-arcuate, lanceolate or ligulate-lanceolate, acute, 5.5–11 cm long, 1.4–2.8 cm wide, articulated at the base to purplish pustular-verrucose sheathing leaf-bases, up to 4 cm long. **Inflorescences** lateral and terminal, simple or little branched, 2- to 4-flowered, 4–5 cm long; rhachis zigzag; bracts ovate, acuminate, cucullate, 5–8 mm long. **Flowers** fleshy, honey-scented, the sepals and petals yellow usually finely spotted with purple, the lip white with radiating pink or purple streaks; pedicel and ovary 3–3.5 cm long. **Sepals** elliptic-obovate or elliptic-ovate, acute to obtuse, 2–2.2 cm long, 0.6–0.7 cm wide. **Petals** elliptic-obovate, subacute to obtuse, 1.8–2 cm long, 0.6 cm wide. **Lip** deflexed, flabellate in outline, 3-lobed, 2.3–2.5 cm long, 2–2.6 cm wide; side lobes obliquely oblong, truncate and erose at the apex; mid-lobe flabellate, deeply bilobulate, erose at apex of each lobule, the sinus triangular. **Column** 6–7 mm long, orange at the apex.

DISTRIBUTION Colombia; montane forest, 1500–1800 m.

HISTORY Discovered in Colombia by Gustav Wallis, one of Veitch's collectors, and described as *Epidendrum wallisii* by H.G. Reichenbach in 1875 in the *Gardeners' Chronicle* (n.s. 4: p. 66). Eric Hagsater transferred it to the present genus in 1981 in *Orquidea* (*Mex.*) (p. 24).

SYNONYM *Epidendrum wallisii* Rchb.f.

Oncidium Sw.

Subfamily Epidendroideae
Tribe Oncidieae

Small to very large epiphytic, lithophytic or terrestrial plants with short to long rhizomes. **Pseudobulbs** very small to large, 1- or 2-leaved at apex, subtended by distichous, ± leaf-bearing sheaths. **Leaves** flat or terete, membranaceous to fleshy-coriaceous. **Inflorescence** basal, racemose to paniculate, few- to many-flowered. **Flowers** variously coloured, inconspicuous to very showy. **Sepals** subsimilar, often free or with lateral sepals more or less united. **Petals** similar to dorsal sepal but often larger. **Lip** borne at a right-angle to the column, entire to 3-lobed; side lobes auriculate to large, spreading or reflexed; mid-lobe spreading, ± emarginate; callus basal, fleshy, ± tuberculate, papillose or pubescent. **Column** short, stout, erect, mostly auriculate above; pollinia 2, waxy, deeply sulcate.

DISTRIBUTION   A very large genus of over 400 species native to the American tropics and subtropics.

DERIVATION OF NAME   The diminutive form of the Greek word *onkos* (pad or mass), referring to the fleshy warty callus on the lip of many species in the genus.

TAXONOMY   Described by O. Swartz in 1800 in *Kungliga Svenska Vetenskapsakademiens Avhandlingar, Stockholm* (p. 239).

Oncidium is not only one of the largest and most widely cultivated genera but is also one that has provided taxonomists with many problems. These have recently led to great controversy over the delimitation of sectional limits in the genus and also over the boundary between *Oncidium*, *Odontoglossum* and *Miltonia* where there are intermediate species which have often arbitrarily been placed in one or more of these genera by different botanists. R. Dressler has recently written an interesting article on the species linking *Oncidium* and *Odontoglossum* in *Orquidea (Mexico)* in 1975. The most recent treatment of the whole genus at sectional level and including a more or less complete synonymy is that of L. Garay and J. Stacy in *Bradea* (1974). Although this work aroused some controversy, none of the other protagonists has attempted to state fully their treatment of the genus so far.

The most recent revision of the genus as a whole is that of F. Kraenzlin in A. Engler's *Das Pflanzenreich* (1922). It is still useful but must be used with caution as much additional information has since been accumulated. Kraenzlin's account can still be usefully referred to if used in conjunction with the corrections listed by L. Garay in *Taxon* (1970).

In the past decade several of Garay's sections have been raised to generic rank notably *Cyrtochilum*, *Hispaniella*, *Psychopsis*, *Psychopsiella* and *Tolumnia*. These are discussed here under the respective genera.

TYPE SPECIES   *O. altissimum* (Jacq.) Sw.
CULTURE   Compost A. Temp. Winter min. 12–15°C. During growth, *Oncidium* species require humid conditions under moderate shade and plenty of water at the roots. When growth is complete, all species should be given less water but especially those with large tough leaves, i.e. *O. luridum* etc. Very small species may be mounted on cork or tree-fern slabs.

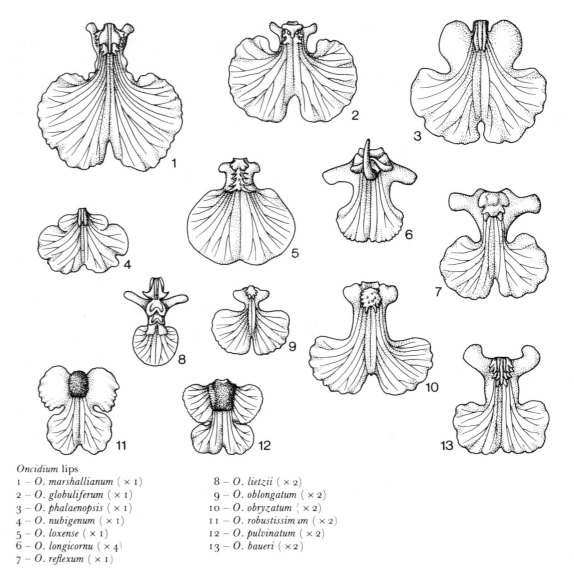

Oncidium lips
1 – *O. marshallianum* (×1)
2 – *O. globuliferum* (×1)
3 – *O. phalaenopsis* (×1)
4 – *O. nubigenum* (×1)
5 – *O. loxense* (×1)
6 – *O. longicornu* (×4)
7 – *O. reflexum* (×1)
8 – *O. lietzii* (×2)
9 – *O. oblongatum* (×2)
10 – *O. obryzatum* (×2)
11 – *O. robustissimum* (×2)
12 – *O. pulvinatum* (×2)
13 – *O. baueri* (×2)

Oncidium altissimum (Jacq.) Sw.

An epiphytic plant up to 30 cm high. **Pseudobulbs** clustered, ovoid to suborbicular, compressed, up to 10 cm long, 7 cm broad, 1-(rarely 2-)leaved at apex. **Leaves** oblong-ligulate, up to 20 cm long, 3 cm broad, acute. **Inflorescence** arcuate to pendent, paniculate, up to 3 m long; branches short, 2- to 3-flowered. **Flowers** small, up to 3.5 cm across; petals and sepals yellowish-green, marked with maroon blotches; lip deep yellow with a maroon blotch on base of mid-lobe. **Sepals** fleshy, elliptic-lanceolate, dorsally keeled, 1.8 cm long, 0.5 cm broad, acute or subacuminate. **Petals** similar to sepals, 1.5 cm long, 0.5 cm broad. **Lip** sessile, minutely auriculate at base, 1.2 cm long, 1 cm broad; mid-lobe bilobulate, each lobule suborbicular; callus many-toothed. **Column** slightly arcuate, 0.5 cm long, wings auriculate.

DISTRIBUTION   Lesser Antilles (islands of Martinique and St Vincent).

HISTORY   Described as *Epidendrum altissimum* by N.J. Jacquin in 1760 in *Enumeratio* of Caribbean plants (p. 30) based on his own collection and transferred by Olof Swartz to the genus *Oncidium* in 1800. Leslie Garay and John Stacy in 1974 in *Bradea* consider that the name *O. altissimum* should be applied to the species commonly known as *O. luridum* and they use the name *O. jacquineanum* Garay & Stacy for this species. The arguments they use have met with

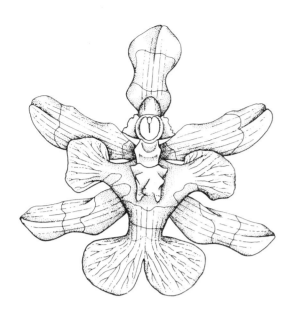

Oncidium altissimum
Flower (× 2)

some disagreement among other botanists and the names in pre-1974 usage will be retained here.

O. altissimum was one of the earliest tropical orchids in cultivation having been introduced into cultivation at the Royal Botanic Gardens, Kew in 1793 by Captain William Bligh who later achieved notoriety in the 'Bounty' mutiny.
CLOSELY RELATED SPECIES See *O. baueri*.

Oncidium ampliatum Lindl. [Colour Plate]
An epiphytic plant, up to 60 cm high. **Pseudobulbs** clustered on a short rhizome, orbicular, strongly bilaterally compressed, up to 10 cm high, 8 cm broad, 1- or 2-leaved at apex, bright shiny green, spotted purple-brown. **Leaves** elliptic-oblanceolate to linear-elliptic, up to 25 cm long, 7 cm broad, obtuse or rounded at apex. **Inflorescence** racemose or paniculate, erect, up to 60 cm long, many-flowered; peduncle terete, green. **Flowers** 2.2 cm across; sepals pale yellow to browny-yellow with dark chocolate-brown markings; petals similar but less heavily spotted; lip bright yellow with a creamy callus. **Sepals** obovate to broadly spathulate, concave, 0.9 cm long, 0.7 cm broad, rounded at apex. **Petals** broadly spathulate, 1 cm long, 0.8 cm broad, rounded at apex. **Lip** obscurely 3-lobed, up to 2.5 cm long, 1–8 cm broad; side lobes very narrow, small; mid-lobe broadly oblong, bilobulate; callus 3-ridged; mid-ridge small, side ridges rather butterfly-shaped. **Column** erect, winged; wings elliptic with a shallowly erose margin.

DISTRIBUTION Guatemala to Panama, Colombia, Ecuador, Peru, Venezuela and Trinidad; an epiphyte on trees in hot lowland areas up to 600 m altitude.
HISTORY Described by John Lindley in *Genera and Species of Orchidaceous Plants* (p. 202) in 1833, *O. ampliatum* was discovered in 1831 by Hugh Cuming in Costa Rica. Later introductions were made by George Ure Skinner, J. Warscewicz and other collectors from elsewhere in Central America.
SYNONYM *Oncidium bernoullianum* Kraenzl.
CLOSELY RELATED SPECIES See *O. isthmii*.

Oncidium ansiferum Rchb.f. [Colour Plate]
A large epiphytic plant, up to 1 m or more tall. **Pseudobulbs** clustered or closely spaced on rhizome, suborbicular or elliptic-oblong, strongly compressed, 6–14 cm long, 3.5–7 cm broad, 1- to 2-leaved at apex. **Leaves** oblong-elliptic to oblanceolate, conduplicate at base, 10–45 cm long, 2–5.5 cm broad, acute or obtuse. **Inflorescence** flexuose, a long open panicle, up to 1 m or more long; peduncle terete, subtended by a leaf; branches short, 3- to 8-flowered. **Flowers** malodorous, numerous; sepals and petals red-brown, apex and margins yellow; lip yellow, marked with yellow-brown on isthmus; callus off-white, spotted with pale brown. **Sepals** reflexed, clawed, oblong-elliptic to narrowly lanceolate, 1.2–1.7 cm long, 0.4–0.6 cm broad, acute or acuminate, margins crisped undulate. **Petals** oblong to broadly elliptic-lanceolate, 1–1.6 cm long, 0.4–0.7 cm broad, obtuse, margins undulate-crisped. **Lip** 3-lobed, pandurate, 1.4–1.8 cm long, 0.9–1.3 cm broad; side lobes auriculate, rounded, up to 0.3 cm broad; mid-lobe with a broadly triangular claw, semiorbicular, bilobulate or broadly obreniform, emarginate; callus fleshy, obovate in outline, 3-toothed in front and 2–4 teeth on each side above the middle. **Column** stout, 0.6 cm long; wings broad, toothed-crenulate.
DISTRIBUTION Costa Rica, Guatemala and Panama; epiphytic on trees up to 2500 m.
HISTORY Described by H.G. Reichenbach in 1852 in the *Botanische Zeitung* (p. 696).
SYNONYMS *Oncidium delumbe* Lindl.; *O. lankesteri* Ames; *O. naranjense* Schltr.
CLOSELY RELATED SPECIES Similar to *O. baueri* and *O. sphacelatum*, but differing in its flower colour, much smaller leaves and suborbicular pseudobulbs. See also *O. incurvum*.

Oncidium barbatum Lindl. [Colour Plate]
A dwarf plant of compact habit. **Pseudobulbs** ovate-oblong, compressed, 3–6.5 cm long, 2–3.5 cm broad, 1-leafed at apex. **Leaf** erect-

spreading, rigid, linear or ovate-oblong, 7.5–10 cm long, 1–2.5 cm broad, acute or emarginate, intensely green above, paler below. **Inflorescence** loosely paniculate, erect to arcuate, 40–60 cm long; peduncle slender, compressed, pale green, spotted red-brown; branches short, slender; bracts concave, appressed; 3–5 cm long. **Flowers** 2.5 cm across; sepals and petals yellow, blotched with chestnut-brown; lip bright yellow, callus dotted with red. **Sepals** clawed, elliptic-oblong, undulate, 1.2–1.4 cm long, 0.5 cm broad, acute; lateral sepals similar to dorsal sepal but narrower, connate in basal third, 1.5–1.8 cm long, 0.5 cm broad, acute. **Petals** clawed, oblong, oblique, 1–1.2 cm long, 0.6–0.7 cm broad, rounded at apex. **Lip** deeply 3-lobed, flat, 1.1–1.2 cm long, 2 cm broad; side lobes obovate obtuse, 0.6–0.7 cm long; mid-lobe obovate, or transversely oblong, similar in size to side lobes, emarginate to apiculate; callus circular, 5-toothed, margin fringed; disc slightly puberulous. **Column** wings roundish to subquadrate.
DISTRIBUTION Brazil.
HISTORY W. Swainson discovered *O. barbatum* in Pernambuco and sent plants to Sir William Hooker at the Glasgow Botanic Garden where it flowered in 1819. John Lindley described it in his *Genera and Species of Orchidaceous Plants* (p. 200) in 1833 naming it for its fringed callus.
SYNONYM *Oncidium microglossum* Klotzsch
CLOSELY RELATED SPECIES See *O. micropogon*.

Oncidium baueri Lindl. [Colour Plate]
A large epiphytic plant with a stout creeping rhizome. **Pseudobulbs** cylindric to ovoid, strongly compressed, 5–15 cm long, 2-leaved at apex, subtended by 2 or more pairs of leaf-bearing sheaths. **Leaves** linear-oblong to ligulate, 20–78 cm long, 2–6 cm broad, obtuse to shortly acuminate. **Inflorescence** straggling, up to 3 m or more high, paniculate, many-flowered. **Flowers** relatively small, up to 3 cm across; sepals and petals greenish-yellow to bright yellow, marked with brown bars; lip yellow with brown markings towards base. **Sepals** elliptic-lanceolate to oblanceolate, 1.2–1.7 cm long, 0.3–0.5 cm broad, acute. **Petals** obliquely elliptic-oblong, up to 1.2 cm long, 0.3 cm broad, acute, apex recurved. **Lip** 3-lobed, up to 1.8 cm long, 1.0–1.2 cm broad; side lobes auriculate; mid-lobe reniform, emarginate, 1.1–1.5 cm broad; callus subquadrate, with many teeth in 3 series, with 3 subequal apical teeth above. **Column** stout, up to 0.6 cm long, with a short, broad, dolabriform wing on each side.
DISTRIBUTION Brazil, Peru, Bolivia and Ecuador; from sea level to 1200 m altitude.

HISTORY Named by John Lindley after Francis Bauer, the brilliant botanical illustrator, in his and Bauer's *Illustrations of Orchidaceous Plants* (t. 7) in 1833. This species was first cultivated by J. Colvill of Chelsea who won a medal with it in 1833 at the Horticultural Society of London.
CLOSELY RELATED SPECIES Occasionally confused with *O. altissimum* from which it is distinguished by its larger, smoother pseudobulbs, longer narrower leaves, and smaller flowers with a distinctly-shaped lip and callus. See also *O. ansiferum*; *O. bracteatum*; *O. incurvum*.

Oncidium bicallosum Lindl. [Colour Plate]
An epiphytic plant. **Pseudobulbs** small, borne on a short thick rhizome, up to 1.5 cm long, covered by several distichous sheaths, 1-leafed at apex. **Leaf** oblong-elliptic, fleshy coriaceous, sulcate, 14–33 cm long, 4–8.5 cm broad, obtuse. **Inflorescence** pendulous, racemose, 20–65 cm long, many-flowered; peduncle with scarious bracts at the nodes. **Flowers** showy, large, 5 cm across; sepals and petals green-yellow to deep yellow, suffused with brown, margins yellow or crimson; lip yellow, callus white, spotted red. **Sepals** obovate-spathulate to suborbicular-obovate, 1.5–2 cm long, 1.2–1.6 cm broad, obtuse. **Petals** suborbicular-obovate, 1.5–2 cm long, 1–1.5 cm broad, rounded, margins undulate-crisped. **Lip** strongly 3-lobed, 2–3 cm long; mid-lobe large, transversely oblong to broadly reniform, separated by a broad claw from the side lobes; callus bituberculate, basal one broad, upper one narrow and trilobulate. **Column** stout, 1.0–1.2 cm long, with a fleshy falcate deflexed wing on either side at apex.
DISTRIBUTION Mexico, El Salvador and Guatemala; up to 1500 m altitude.
HISTORY Th. Hartweg collected the type specimen in Guatemala and it was described by John Lindley in Bentham's *Plantae Hartwegianae* (p. 94) in 1842. George Ure Skinner had earlier discovered it in Guatemala and had sent plants to James Bateman who flowered it for the first time in 1842.
CLOSELY RELATED SPECIES Similar to *O. cavendishianum* which it resembles in habit but it differs in having a racemose inflorescence, larger yellowish brown-yellow unspotted flowers, smaller side lobes to the lip and a bituberculate (not trituberculate) callus.

Oncidium bifolium Sims [Colour Plate]
A small epiphytic herb. **Pseudobulbs** ovoid or oblong-ovoid, 3–4 cm long, 1–2 cm in diameter, deeply sulcate with age, 2- or rarely 1-leaved at apex. **Leaves** somewhat coriaceous, linear-oblong, acute, 6–12 cm long, 0.6–1.4 cm

broad. **Inflorescence** commonly nodding, simple or rarely branched, 20–35 cm long, laxly 7- to 20-flowered; bracts rigid, narrowly triangular, acute, 0.3–0.5 cm long. **Flowers** 2–2.5 cm across; sepals and petals yellow, marked with chestnut-brown; lip yellow, callus marked with chestnut-brown. **Dorsal sepal** elliptic-ovate, rounded or minutely apiculate, 0.6–0.65 cm long, 0.4–0.45 cm broad; **lateral sepals** broadly oblong, acute, 0.9 cm long, 0.3–0.35 cm broad. **Petals** ovate-pandurate, rounded or emarginate at apex, 0.7–0.75 cm long, 0.5–0.6 cm broad. **Lip** deflexed, sessile, 3-lobed, 1.8–2.0 cm long, 2–2.5 cm broad, margins undulate; side lobes small, basal, auriculate; mid-lobe much larger, shortly clawed, transversely oblong-reniform, deeply emarginate; callus fleshy, cristate, tuberculate in front. **Column** short, auriculate on each side of the stigma, margins of wings sinuate-denticulate.
DISTRIBUTION Brazil, Uruguay, Argentina and Bolivia.
HISTORY Originally described in 1812 in the *Botanical Magazine* (t. 1491) by John Sims based on a specimen flowered by Messrs Loddiges which they received from Uruguay. On the journey home from Montevideo it flowered for the whole journey while hung up in a cabin.
SYNONYMS *Oncidium vexillarium* Rchb.f.; *O. celsium* A. Rich.
CLOSELY RELATED SPECIES See *O. flexuosum*.

Oncidium blanchetii Rchb.f. [Colour Plate]
Pseudobulbs clustered, erect, oblong or narrowly ovoid-oblong, compressed, smooth at first, sulcate later, 6–9 cm long, 2.5–3.5 cm in diameter, 3-leaved at apex. **Leaves** erect, rigid, coriaceous, narrowly linear-ligulate, 35–50 cm long, 1.5–3 cm broad, acute. **Inflorescence** erect, robust, much longer than the leaves, branched above, many-flowered, 60–140 cm long; branches spreading or suberect, slender; bracts concave, lanceolate, 0.3–0.5 cm long. **Flowers** yellow, segments fleshy at the base, membranaceous above. **Dorsal sepal** shortly clawed, oblong, 0.6–0.65 cm long, 0.25 cm broad, acute; **lateral sepals** shortly clawed, obliquely lanceolate, 0.7–0.75 cm long, 0.15–0.2 cm broad, connate at the base, hooked at apex. **Petals** oblong to subpanduriform, margins undulate, 0.6–0.65 cm long, 4–5 cm broad. **Lip** subdeflexed, sessile, 3-lobed, 1.2–1.3 cm long, 1.1 cm broad; side lobes retrorse, oblong-subspathulate, much smaller than mid-lobe: mid-lobe narrowly clawed, broadly reniform, emarginate, margins undulate; callus fleshy, subrectangular, warty. **Column** short, fleshy; wings obtuse, quadrangular, margin undulate.
DISTRIBUTION Brazil.

HISTORY Discovered near Jacobina in Bahia State in Brazil by Blanchet and named after him by H.G. Reichenbach who described it in *Linnaea* (p. 845) in 1849.

Oncidium bracteatum Rchb.f. & Warsc. [Colour Plate]
Pseudobulbs oblong-ovoid, much compressed, 7.5 cm long, 3.8 cm broad, 2-leaved at apex. **Leaves** linear-ligulate, flexuose, arching, 20–30 cm long, 2.5 cm broad, acute. **Inflorescence** arcuate, 1–1.3 m long, paniculate; branches short, 2- to 3-flowered; bracts papery, deciduous, pale chestnut-brown, up to 1.2 cm long. **Flowers** 2.5 cm across; sepals and petals yellow-green, heavily spotted with brownish-purple; lip yellow or pale yellow with a red-brown claw. **Dorsal sepal** linear-oblong, undulate, 1.7 cm long, 0.45 cm broad, acute; **lateral sepals** linear, prominently keeled behind, undulate, 1.7 cm long, 0.5 cm broad. **Petals** linear-oblong, undulate, 1.4 cm long, 0.4 cm broad, acute. **Lip** very obscurely 3-lobed, 1.3 cm long, 1.5 cm broad; side lobes auriculate, margins recurved, 0.6 cm long; mid-lobe shortly clawed, transversely oblong, emarginate; callus fleshy, verrucose, 3-toothed in front. **Column** wings narrow.
DISTRIBUTION Costa Rica and Panama.
HISTORY Discovered by J. Warscewicz in 1849 on the slopes of the Chiriqui Volcano, Panama, at an elevation of 6000–7000 m and described by H.G. Reichenbach in the *Botanische Zeitung* (p. 695) in 1852.
CLOSELY RELATED SPECIES Allied to *O. baueri*, *O. sphacelatum* and *O. ansiferum*.

Oncidium cariniferum (Rchb.f.) Beer [Colour Plate]
A large epiphyte with oblong, compressed, smooth pseudobulbs, 7.5–10 cm long, 5 cm broad, 2-leaved at the apex. **Leaves** coriaceous, narrowly oblong-ligulate, subacute to obtuse, 25–43 cm long, 3–4 cm wide. **Inflorescence** paniculate, robust, laxly many-flowered; branches spreading, fractiflex; bracts narrowly ovate-triangular, acute, up to 8 mm long. **Flowers** 5 cm across; sepals and petals yellow or greenish heavily blotched with reddish-brown; lip white fading to yellow-brown with age; callus crimson-mauve; column white stained with purple. **Sepals** lanceolate, acute to acuminate, keeled on the back, 2.5–2.6 cm long, 0.4–0.5 cm wide; the laterals dependent. **Petals** incurved, elliptic-lanceolate, acute, 2.1–2.3 cm long, 0.4–0.5 cm wide. **Lip** long-clawed; apical lamina obreniform, apiculate, 1.5 cm long, 2 cm wide, with erose margins; callus of 2 rhombic dentate lateral plates on the claw of the lip and 3 erect short subcylindrical pro-

tuberances in front. **Column** scarcely winged, sigmoid, swollen near the base.

DISTRIBUTION Costa Rica, in montane forests on the west-facing slopes of the Cordillera.

HISTORY Discovered by J. Warscewicz in 1848 in the Cordillera de Chiriqui and introduced into cultivation by him in Germany. It was described as *Odontoglossum cariniferum* by H.G. Reichenbach in 1852 in the *Botanische Zeitung* (p. 638). Beer transferred it to *Oncidium* in 1854 in his *Praktische Studien an der Familien der Orchideen* (p. 283).

This species occupies an anomalous position in the genus and is possibly allied to *O. laeve*, *O. reichenheimii* and *O. schroederianum* which have recently been placed in the new genus *Miltonioides* by Lueckel and Brieger (1983) in *Die Orchideen* (p. 131).

SYNONYM *Odontoglossum cariniferum* Rchb.f.

Oncidium carthagenense (Jacq.) Sw.
[Colour Plate]

An epiphytic plant, 2 m or more high. **Pseudobulbs** very small, up to 2.5 cm long, concealed by scarious sheaths, 1-leafed at apex. **Leaf** elliptic, oblong or lanceolate, rigid, coriaceous, 9–40 cm long, 3–7 cm broad, acute to subacuminate. **Inflorescence** erect, paniculate, many-flowered, up to 2 m or more long; peduncle subtended by a scarious sheath, with smaller scarious sheaths at nodes. **Flowers** small but showy, 2.5 cm across, pale yellow or white, blotched with red-brown, magenta or lavender. **Sepals** clawed, spathulate, 0.8–1.3 cm long, 0.4–0.8 cm broad, rounded or rarely retuse at apex, margins undulate-crisped. **Petals** shortly, broadly clawed, broadly obovate, 0.7–1.2 cm long, 0.6–0.6 cm broad, rounded, margins undulate-crisped. **Lip** 3-lobed, pandurate, 0.9–1.6 cm long, 0.7–1.4 cm broad; side lobes semi-orbicular, margins recurved; mid-lobe reniform to broadly flabellate, separated from side lobes by a broad claw; callus fleshy, with a pair of porrect projections below and a short trilobulate thickening above. **Column** short, fleshy, with 3 2-lobed wings at apex.

DISTRIBUTION Common and widespread from Florida through Mexico and Central America to Panama, northern S. America and the W. Indies; from sea level to 1500 m altitude.

HISTORY Described by N.J. Jacquin in 1762 in his *Enumeratio* of Caribbean plants (p. 30) as *Epidendrum carthagenense* but later transferred by Olof Swartz to the genus *Oncidium* in 1800. Jacquin discovered it near Cartagena on the Caribbean coast of Colombia and named it after the town.

SYNONYM *Oncidium kymatoides* Kraenzl.

CLOSELY RELATED SPECIES Allied to *O. luridum* which it closely resembles in its vegetative parts, but the flowers of *O. carthagenense* are somewhat smaller, the lip mid-lobe equals the width across the side lobes and the blotches of colour on the flower are lavender instead of reddish-brown.

Oncidium cavendishianum Batem.
[Colour Plate]

A large epiphytic plant, up to 1.5 m or more high. **Pseudobulbs** very small, up to 2 cm long, concealed by several distichous scarious sheaths, 1-leafed at apex. **Leaf** erect, broadly lanceolate or elliptic, fleshy-coriaceous, 15–45 cm long, 5–13 cm broad, acute or subobtuse. **Inflorescence** erect, stout, paniculate, 60–150 cm long, many-flowered. **Flowers** showy, 3.8 cm across, very fragrant; sepals and petals yellow or yellow-green, spotted reddish-brown or chocolate-brown; lip deep yellow, callus white with red-brown flecks; column-wings red-spotted. **Sepals** obovate to suborbicular, concave, 1.2–1.7 cm long, 0.7–1.2 cm broad, obtuse or rounded, margins crisped-undulate. **Petals** shortly clawed, oblong-obovate to elliptic-subquadrate, 1.2–1.6 cm long, 0.8–1.1 cm broad, rounded or emarginate, margins crisped-undulate. **Lip** deeply 3-lobed, 1.4–2.5 cm long; side lobes obliquely obovate-suborbicular, 0.7–1.3 cm long, 0.6–1.2 cm broad, rounded; mid-lobe broadly reniform or transversely oblong, bilobulate, margins undulate-crisped; callus of erect tubercles below, trilobulate-tuberculate above. **Column** short, thick, 0.8–1 cm long; apex with a falcate, deflexed, wing on each side.

DISTRIBUTION Mexico, Honduras and Guatemala; a rare plant at altitudes up to 2800 m.

HISTORY Described by James Bateman in 1837 in his monumental *Orchidaceae of Mexico and Guatemala* (t. 3) based on a collection made by George Ure Skinner near Guatemala City. Bateman dedicated this species to the then Duke of Devonshire under whose patronage Sir Joseph Paxton commenced the modern system of orchid culture at Chatsworth, England.

SYNONYM *Oncidium pachyphyllum* Hooker

CLOSELY RELATED SPECIES Closely allied to *O. bicallosum*.

Oncidium cebolleta (Jacq.) Sw.
[Colour Plate]

A common and somewhat variable epiphytic species. **Pseudobulbs** obscure, conical, up to 1.5 cm long and broad, forming a slight swelling at the base of each leaf, concealed by large white sheaths, 1-leafed at apex. **Leaf** terete, sulcate, erect or suberect, fleshy, 7–40 cm long, 1–2.5 cm broad, tapering to a sharp point, greyish-green, spotted purple. **Inflorescence** a raceme or shortly branched panicle, up to 150 cm long, erect to arcuate, many-flowered. **Flowers** small, 2–3.5 cm across; sepals and petals yellow or greenish-yellow with dark red-brown markings; lip bright yellow with red-brown spotting around callus. **Sepals** spathulate, 0.8–1.4 cm long, 0.4–0.8 cm broad, obtuse. **Petals** oblong, obscurely clawed, 0.9–1.3 cm long, 0.4–0.6 cm broad, truncate. **Lip** 3-lobed, up to 2 cm long, 2.5 cm broad; side lobes somewhat obovate, spreading, fairly large; mid-lobe bilobulate, transversely oblong, lobules overlapping; callus 3-ridged, mid-ridge a high keel, side ridges much shorter. **Column** erect, short; wings oblong, entire.

DISTRIBUTION American tropics; where it grows in relatively hot areas with a fairly long dry period which accounts for its xerophytic character, up to 1700 m altitude. *O. cebolleta* is the most widespread of all *Oncidium* species.

HISTORY Described by N.J. Jacquin as *Dendrobium cebolleta* in his *Enumeratio* of Caribbean plants (p. 30) in 1760 and it was transferred in 1800 by O. Swartz to the genus *Oncidium*. Jacquin discovered it in the forest near Cartagena in Colombia. It first flowered in cultivation in Europe in the nursery of Messrs Low & Co. of Clapham, London, in 1837.

SYNONYM *Dendrobium cebolleta* Jacq.

CLOSELY RELATED SPECIES *O. cebolleta* may be distinguished from *Oncidium ascendens* Lindl. by its blunt column-wings, the broadly obovate side lobes of the lip and the several-toothed (not many-toothed) callus. See also *O. jonesianum*.

Oncidium cheirophorum Rchb.f.
[Colour Plate]

A dwarf plant. **Pseudobulbs** ovoid to oblong-conical, compressed, 2.5 cm long, 1.5 cm broad, 1-leafed at apex. **Leaf** oblanceolate to ligulate, erect, 11 cm long, 1.3 cm broad, subacute. **Inflorescence** erect or arching, up to 20 cm long, paniculate; densely many-flowered; branches suberect, fractiflex; bracts triangular-ovate, 2 cm long. **Flowers** 1.4 cm across; rich golden-yellow, fragrant. **Dorsal sepal** obovate, concave, 0.5 cm long, 0.3 cm broad, rounded; **lateral sepals** hidden behind lip, obovate, 0.4 cm long, 0.3 cm broad, margins recurved. **Petals** rotund, shortly clawed, 0.3 cm long, 0.25 cm broad. **Lip** 3-lobed, 1 cm long, 1.5 cm broad; side lobes erect, spreading, oblong, lower margin recurved; mid-lobe rotund emarginate, margins upcurved; callus fleshy, longitudinal, with 3 free apical teeth. **Column** erect; wings pointing forwards, oblong with an apical point; anther long beaked in front.

DISTRIBUTION Panama and Colombia.

HISTORY Described by H.G. Reichenbach in 1852 in the *Botanische Zeitung* (p. 695). *O.*

cheirophorum was discovered by J. Warscewicz who found it on the Chiriqui Volcano, 2500 m above sea level. The plant was first flowered in Europe by Senator Jenisch and Consul Schiller of Hamburg.

CLOSELY RELATED SPECIES *O. cheirophorum* is allied to *O. ornithorhynchum* in sect. *Rostrata* of the genus but it is easily recognised by its yellow flowers and 3-lobed callus.

Oncidium cimiciferum (Rchb.f.) Lindl.

A large straggling epiphytic plant. **Pseudobulbs** oblong-cylindrical, up to 7.5 cm, subtended by several imbricating leaf-bearing sheaths, 1- or 2-leaved at apex. **Leaves** narrowly lanceolate to ligulate, 20–65 cm long, 3–5 cm broad, acute or acuminate. **Inflorescence** paniculate, up to or more than 3 m long; branches of panicle short and numerous; rhachis fractiflex. **Flowers** fleshy, small, greenish-yellow or brown. **Dorsal sepal** spathulate to oblanceolate, 0.9–1.2 cm long, 0.4 cm broad, acute, reflexed; **lateral sepals** obliquely oblong-oblanceolate, up to 1.4 cm long, 0.35 cm broad, acute. **Petals** obliquely obovate-elliptic, up to 1 cm long, 0.6 cm broad, acute. **Lip** simple, sessile, ovate-triangular, convex, 0.9 cm long, 0.8 cm broad, acute or acuminate; callus multilobulate. **Column** stout, 0.4 cm high, with a broad fleshy thickening on each side at base; 2 obscure, broad wings above.

DISTRIBUTION Peru and Ecuador; in montane forest up to 2300 m altitude or more.
HISTORY Described by H.G. Reichenbach as *Odontoglossum cimiciferum* in *Linnaea* (p. 849) in 1849 but transferred in 1855 by John Lindley to the genus *Oncidium* in *Folia Orchidacea Oncidium* (p. 9).

O. cimiciferum and its allies in sect. *Cimicifera* are readily recognised by their broadly ovate lip. The long branching inflorescence and callus of this species are quite distinctive.
SYNONYMS *Oncidium flexuosum* Lindl.; *Cyrtochilum flexuosum* (Lindl.) H.B.K.

Oncidium concolor Hooker [Colour Plate]

A small, epiphytic plant, up to 15 cm high. **Pseudobulbs** clustered, narrowly oblong or ovoid-oblong, 3–5 cm long, 1–2.5 cm broad, becoming sulcate with age, 2-leaved at apex. **Leaves** rigid, erect-spreading, lanceolate-ligulate, 9–15 cm long, 1.5–2.5 cm broad, acute. **Inflorescence** arcuate, 12–30 cm long, laxly few- to many-flowered; peduncle terete, a little fractiflex above; bracts appressed, concave, pale green, 0.7–1 cm long. **Flowers** rich lemon-yellow. **Dorsal sepal** concave, narrowly obovate-oblong, 1.4–2.1 cm long, 0.5–0.9 cm broad; **lateral sepals** connate almost to middle, longer and narrower than dorsal sepal. **Petals** elliptic-oblong, 1.4–2 cm long, 0.5–0.9

cm broad, apex rounded and minutely apiculate, margins a little undulate. **Lip** undivided, slightly convex, up to 3.5 cm long, 3.2 cm broad; claw narrow, up to 1 cm long; limb 1.8–2.5 cm long, up to 3.2 cm broad, obscurely 4-lobed; callus bilamellate with a minute peg on each side of ridge. **Column** erect, winged near apex; wings oblong.

DISTRIBUTION Brazil (states of Rio de Janeiro and Minas Gerais) and N. Argentina.
HISTORY Described by William Hooker in the *Botanical Magazine* (t. 3752) in 1839 based on a collection of George Gardner from the Organ Mts of Brazil in 1837. Gardner, F. Sellow and Glaziou all sent living plants of *O. concolor* to Europe but it remained rare in cultivation until 1876 when Veitch & Sons imported a large quantity from Rio de Janeiro.
SYNONYMS *Oncidium unguiculatum* Klotzsch; *Cyrtochilum citrinum* Hooker
CLOSELY RELATED SPECIES *Oncidium brachyandrum* Lindl. is allied to *O. concolor* but has greenish sepals heavily marked with brownish-purple and a 3- (rather than 2-) ridged callus.

Oncidium crispum Lodd. [Colour Plate]

A medium-sized to large epiphytic plant. **Pseudobulbs** large, ovoid, strongly compressed, clustered, deeply sulcate with age, 7–10 cm long, 3–5 cm in diameter, 2- or 3-leaved at apex. **Leaves** large, coriaceous, oblong-lanceolate, abruptly acute above, attenuate below, spreading or erect-spreading, 15–20 cm long, 3–5 cm broad, slightly red-spotted at base. **Inflorescence** erect to drooping, longer than the leaves, 70–110 cm long, paniculate, many-flowered; bracts ovate-triangular, acute or shortly acuminate, 0.3–0.6 cm long. **Flowers** large, showy, spreading or subnutant; sepals and petals coppery-red to olive-brown; lip similar in colour but yellow at base and on callus. **Sepals** obovate or oblong-obovate,

Oncidium crispum
1 – Flower, front view (× $\frac{3}{4}$)
2 – Flower, side view (× $\frac{3}{4}$)

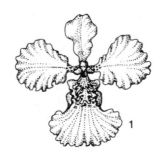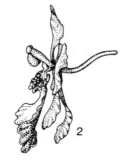

acute, rounded or retuse at apex, 1.5–2.6 cm long, 0.6–1.3 cm broad, margins undulate. **Petals** ovate, rounded at the apex, margins undulate-crisped, 1.8–2.6 cm long and broad. **Lip** deflexed, shortly clawed, suborbicular above, obscurely 3-lobed at base, 2–3 cm long, 2–3 cm broad; side lobes auriculate; mid-lobe suborbicular or transversely oblong-elliptic, obtuse to emarginate, margins undulate; callus trilamellate with mid-lamella extending into a hook in front, side lamellae multidentate. **Column** short, fleshy, winged; wings subquadrate with denticulate margins.

DISTRIBUTION Brazil.
HISTORY Introduced from Brazil by Messrs Loddiges who described it in 1832 in the *Botanical Cabinet* (t. 1854).
CLOSELY RELATED SPECIES *O. forbesii*; *O. marshallianum*.

Oncidium cucullatum Lindl. [Colour Plate]

A medium-sized epiphytic plant. **Pseudobulbs** small, clustered or approximate, ovoid to slightly pyriform, slightly compressed, 2–5 cm long, 0.8–2.5 cm in diameter, enveloped by several imbricate ± leaf-bearing sheaths, 1- or 2-leaved at apex. **Leaves** linear or narrowly lanceolate, subcoriaceous, 15–20 cm long, 1.8–3.6 cm broad. **Inflorescence** emitted from axils of basal sheaths, up to 50 cm or more long, slender, erect to suberect, racemose or branching, few- to many-flowered; bracts small, ovate, acute. **Flowers** to about 3.5 cm across; sepals and petals dark maroon-black with a pale greenish margin; lip white to rose-purple, spotted dark crimson, callus yellow and red. **Dorsal sepal** oblong-elliptic, concave, acute, 1.2 cm long, 0.6 cm broad; lateral sepals connate, deeply concave, bifid at apex, 1.3 cm long, 0.8 cm broad. **Petals** oblong-elliptic, acute, 1.2 cm long, 0.8 cm broad. **Lip** 3-lobed at base, up to 2.5 cm long, 3.5 cm broad; side lobes spreading, subquadrate; mid-lobe clawed, reniform above, margins undulate, apiculate; callus of 3 keel-like parallel ridges, mid-ridge longer than side ridges, pubescent at base. **Column** short, stout.

DISTRIBUTION Ecuador and possibly S. Colombia.
HISTORY Discovered by Prof. William Jameson on the western side of Pichincha in Ecuador and described by John Lindley in 1838 in his *Sertum Orchidacearum* (sub t. 21).
CLOSELY RELATED SPECIES See *O. nubigenum*.

Oncidium dayanum Rchb.f. [Colour Plate]

A medium-sized epiphytic herb. **Pseudobulbs** small, clustered or approximate, ovoid to sub-pyriform, slightly compressed, 2–5 cm long, 0.7–2.5 cm in diameter, enveloped by ± leaf-bearing sheaths below, 1- or 2-leaved at apex. **Leaves** narrowly lanceolate or linear, acute, subcoriaceous, up to 20 cm long, 3.5 cm broad. **Inflorescence** suberect, few-flowered, racemose or branching, up to 30 or more cm long. **Flowers** up to 3 cm across; sepals and petals white, spotted or barred with crimson; lip white, spotted with crimson around callus and on side lobes, callus shiny, yellow. **Dorsal sepal** narrowly elliptic, acute, 1.3 cm long, 0.6 cm broad; **lateral sepals** connate, bifid, 1.6 cm long, 0.7 cm broad. **Petals** subspathulate, elliptic, acute, 1.3 cm long, 0.7 cm broad. **Lip** 3-lobed at base, 2 cm long, 2.4 cm broad; side lobes spreading, rounded; mid-lobe transversely oblong, emarginate, with the margin undulate; callus of 3 keels, acute in front, the mid-keel shorter and raised above the outer keels, pubescent at base. **Column** short, stout.

DISTRIBUTION Ecuador.

HISTORY Originally described in 1871 by H.G. Reichenbach in the *Gardeners' Chronicle* (p. 834) as *O. cucullatum* var. *dayanum* based on a plant flowered by John Day of Tottenham, near London.

In 1975 J. Stacy raised it to specific rank in the *Botanical Museum Leaflets of Harvard University* (p. 150) when he revised sect. *Cucullata* of the genus.

SYNONYMS *Oncidium cucullatum* var. *dayanum* Rchb.f.; *O. phalaenopsis* var. *brandtiae* Hort.

CLOSELY RELATED SPECIES *O. dayanum* is closely allied and often confused with *O. phalaenopsis* but it differs in having a convex callus of 3 parallel ridges of which the outer 2 are obscurely lobulate and the middle 1 originates from the base of the lip between the column-wings.

Oncidium tripterygium Rchb.f. also differs in its callus, which has a median keel longer than the lateral keels. *Oncidium mimeticum* Stacy is also closely allied to *O. dayanum* but differs in its stouter column with a cucullate clinandrium (apex), its callus shape and its flower colour which is closer to that of *O. cucullatum*.

Oncidium divaricatum Lindl. [Colour Plate]

A small, epiphytic plant. **Pseudobulbs** suborbicular, strongly compressed, discoid, 2.5–3.8 cm in diameter, 1-leafed at apex. **Leaf** narrowly oblong to oblong-elliptic, coriaceous, suberect, 14–30 cm long, 4–8 cm broad, obtuse. **Inflorescence** 120–200 cm long, paniculate; peduncle dull purple; branches many-flowered, often branching again; bracts narrowly ovate, very acute, 0.1–0.3 cm long. **Flowers** 2.5 cm across; sepals and petals yellow with a chestnut-brown basal blotch; lip yellow, spotted with chestnut-brown. **Sepals** spathulate, concave, 1.1–1.2 cm long, 0.6 cm broad, rounded at apex. **Petals** oblong, shortly clawed, un-

dulate, 1.2–1.3 cm long, 0.8 cm broad, obtuse. **Lip** 3-lobed, lobes subequal 1.2–1.3 cm long, 1.5 cm broad across base; side lobes spreading rotund, margins erose; mid-lobe transversely oblong, emarginate, 0.6 cm long, 0.9 cm broad, margins undulate; callus of 4 equal cushion-like papillose lobes. **Column** erect, short, glabrous; wings subrotund, rigid.

DISTRIBUTION Brazil.

HISTORY First collected by the French traveller M.E. Descourtilz in the Sierra das Argoas and at Corcovado near Rio de Janeiro in Brazil, *Oncidium divaricatum* was introduced into cultivation by A.J. Heatherly, the British Consul in Brazil. He sent plants to the Horticultural Society of London in 1826 and John Lindley described it in the *Botanical Register* (t. 1050), the specific epithet being given for its divaricate lateral sepals.

CLOSELY RELATED SPECIES *O. divaricatum* is one of several species placed in Lindley's section *Pulvinata* characterised by the papillose cushion-like callus on the lip. *O. divaricatum* may be distinguished from the closely related *O. harrisonianum* and *O. pulvinatum* by its 4-lobed callus and the flat lateral lobes of the lip. See also *O. robustissimum*.

Oncidium excavatum Lindl. [Colour Plate]

A large, robust plant, up to 1 m or more high. **Pseudobulbs** numerous, clustered, ovoid or oblong-ovoid, slightly compressed, 7–18 cm long, clothed at base with a few leaf-bearing sheaths, 1- or 2-leaved at apex. **Leaves** linear to narrowly oblong, 30–50 cm long, 2.5–4 cm broad, with a long-attenuate apex, base subpetiolate. **Inflorescence** paniculate, 60–150 cm long, erect or arcuate, laxly many-flowered. **Flowers** variable in size, up to 3.8 cm broad; sepals and petals yellow, spotted and barred red-brown in lower half; lip similarly coloured. **Dorsal sepal** obovate or oblanceolate, 1.2–1.6 cm long, 0.9 cm broad, abruptly acute at apex; **lateral sepals** oblong-oblanceolate, slightly oblique, up to 1.9 cm long, 0.7 cm broad, acute. **Petals** oblong-obovate or triangular-obovate, up to 1.7 cm long, 1.5 cm broad, apex retuse, margins undulate. **Lip** 3-lobed, 1.2–2.2 cm long, up to 2 cm broad; side lobes small, rotund; mid-lobe with a broad short claw, cordate-reniform, obscurely bilobulate; callus convex, with 4 verrucose lines extending into 2 ridges in front, with several free tubercules on either side. **Column** stout, 0.5 cm long; wings membranous, porrect, dolabriform or quadrangular.

DISTRIBUTION Ecuador and Peru.

HISTORY Described by John Lindley in 1838 in *Sertum Orchidacearum* (sub t. 25) from a specimen collected by A. Mathews in the same year at Chachapoyas in N. Peru. It was first

flowered in cultivation in Europe by Messrs Loddiges of Hackney, London, in 1834. The specific epithet *excavatum* was given by Lindley because of the deep pit at the base of the underside of the lip.

SYNONYM *Oncidium aurosum* Rchb.f.

Oncidium flexuosum Sims [Colour Plate]

A medium-sized epiphytic plant. **Pseudobulbs** narrowly ovoid or ovate-elliptic, strongly compressed, ancipitous, 4–8 cm long, 2–3 cm in diameter, spaced 3–5 cm apart on the rhizome, (1- or) 2-leaved at apex. **Leaves** ± spreading, somewhat coriaceous, narrowly oblong-ligulate, obtuse or abruptly acute, 10–22 cm long, 1.5–3 cm broad. **Inflorescence** erect or ascending, longer than the leaves, up to 1 m long, branched above, many-flowered; bracts very short, narrowly triangular, acute. **Flowers** fairly small; sepals and petals yellow, barred with chestnut-brown; lip rich yellow, marked red-brown around callus, ± spotted finely with orange on lamina; callus yellow. **Dorsal sepal** obovate-oblong, subrotund at apex, concave, 0.35–0.4 cm long, 0.2 cm broad; **lateral sepals** oblong, obtuse, 0.4 cm long, 0.15 broad. **Petals** obovate, subrotund, 0.5 cm long, 0.25 cm broad. **Lip** 3-lobed at base, 1.2–1.3 cm long, 1.2–1.5 cm broad; side lobes auriculate; mid-lobe shortly clawed, broadly reniform above, deeply emarginate; callus fleshy, cristate, with 3 lacerate lobes in front. **Column** short, fleshy, slightly furfuraceous, with a broad subquadrate wing on either side of stigma.

DISTRIBUTION Brazil, Argentina and Paraguay.

HISTORY Described by John Sims in the *Botanical Magazine* (t. 2203) in 1821, based on a plant introduced from Brazil by Messrs Loddiges of Hackney, London.

SYNONYMS *Oncidium haematochrysum* Rchb.f.; *O. haematoxanthum* Rchb.f.; *Epidendrum lineatum* Vell.

CLOSELY RELATED SPECIES *O. flexuosum* is closely allied to *O. bifolium* which differs in its slightly larger flower, longer petals which are less regularly barred with red-brown, the more divided callus and the undulate margins to the lip.

Oncidium forbesii Hooker [Colour Plate]

A epiphytic plant. **Pseudobulbs** oblong, or elliptic ovoid, compressed, 5–7.5 cm long, 2.5–4 cm across, 1- or rarely 2-leaved. **Leaves** lanceolate or oblong-ligulate, coriaceous, 15–25 cm long, 2.5–4 cm broad, acute to mucronate. **Inflorescence** erect or nodding, 45–90 cm long, paniculate or racemose; peduncle mottled dull purple and green, slender; bracts membranous, narrowly triangular, acute, 0.4–0.5 cm long. **Flowers** large, 5–6 cm across; segments slightly membranous; sepals, petals and lip chestnut-brown with a narrow golden-yellow margin; column purplish-violet, red-spotted. **Dorsal sepal** shortly clawed, broadly ovate-elliptic, margins undulate, 2 cm long, 1.2–1.5 cm broad, rounded at apex; **lateral sepals** shortly clawed, narrowly oblong, connate in basal third, hidden by lip, 2.2–2.4 cm long, 0.8–1 cm broad, rounded at apex. **Petals** clawed, suborbicular or obovate, 2.6–2.8 cm long, 2–3.3 cm broad, margin crisped, rounded or retuse at apex. **Lip** obscurely 3-lobed, 3.2–3.4 cm long, 3 cm broad; side lobes auriculate, 0.3 cm long; mid-lobe broadly clawed, flabellate, 2-lobed, margins crisped-undulate; callus warty, 5-lobed. **Column** short; wings subrounded, fleshy.

DISTRIBUTION   Brazil.

HISTORY   Another of the splendid *Oncidium* species from the Organ Mts in E. Brazil. *O. forbesii* was discovered by George Gardner there in 1837 and he sent plants to the Duke of Bedford at Woburn Abbey, England. Sir William Hooker named it after the Duke's gardener, H.O. Forbes in 1839 in the *Botanical Magazine* (t. 3705).

SYNONYMS   *Oncidium crispum* var. *forbesii* Burb.; *O. crispum* var. *marginatum* Hort.

CLOSELY RELATED SPECIES   *O. crispum.*

Oncidium gardneri Lindl. [Colour Plate]

Pseudobulbs narrowly ovoid, much compressed, longitidinally grooved when old, 5–7.5 cm long, 3–4 cm across, 2-leaved at apex. **Leaves** coriaceous, linear to oblong-lanceolate, 15–30 cm long, 2.5–5 cm broad, obtuse, dark green above, ± purplish below. **Inflorescence** erect or ascending, paniculate, 45–90 cm long, many-flowered; branches spreading, densely many-flowered; bracts triangular-lanceolate, very acute, 0.4–0.5 cm long. **Flowers** about 5 cm across; sepals brown, barred with yellow; petals chestnut-brown marked with yellow spots along margins; lip bright yellow, with a broad band of confluent red-brown spots near the margin, callus marked with red-brown spots; column yellow-green, wings yellow, spotted purple. **Sepals** clawed, obovate-oblong, concave, 1.2–1.5 cm long, 0.7–0.9 cm broad, rounded at apex, margins undulate; lateral sepals connate to beyond middle, similar to dorsal sepal, 1.4–1.7 cm long, 0.5–0.6 cm broad. **Petals** shortly clawed, suborbicular, concave, 1.6–1.8 cm long, 1.2–1.4 cm broad, emarginate, margin undulate. **Lip** obscurely 3-lobed, 2–2.5 cm long, 2.2–2.5 cm broad; side lobes auriculate, 0.4–0.5 cm long; mid-lobe spreading, flabellate, margins undulate; callus a fleshy triangular plate, apex verrucose with a verrucose protuberance on each side. **Column**

slightly arcuate, 0.3–0.4 cm long; column-wings rotund, 0.15–0.2 cm broad.

DISTRIBUTION   Brazil.

HISTORY   Another of George Gardner's collections from the Organ Mts of Brazil and named after him by John Lindley in 1843 in Hooker's *London Journal of Botany* (p. 662). Living plants were first introduced into cultivation by Messrs Rollinson in 1856.

SYNONYMS   *Oncidium flabelliferum* Paxt.; *O. praetextum* Morr.; *O. forbesio-dasytele* Rolfe

CLOSELY RELATED SPECIES   *Oncidium curtum* Lindl.; *O. praetextum* Rchb.f.

Oncidium globuliferum H.B.K.

A creeping epiphytic plant, up to 9 cm high, with an intertwining flexuose rhizome. **Pseudobulbs** widely spaced on a creeping rhizome, suborbicular-oblong, compressed, 2.5 cm long, 2 cm broad, 1-leafed at apex, subtended by 1 or 2 leaf-bearing sheaths at base. **Leaves** fleshy, suberect, oblong, up to 6.5 cm long, 2.4 cm broad, obtuse. **Inflorescence** 1-flowered, up to 9 cm high; peduncle up to 5 cm long, dull purple-coloured. **Flowers** up to 3.7 cm across; sepals, petals and lip yellow, marked with red or pale red spots towards the base; column-wings yellow. **Dorsal sepal** obovate, 0.8–1.6 cm long, 0.4–0.7 cm broad, subacute to obtuse, margins undulate; **lateral sepals** falcate, oblong, shortly clawed, 1–1.7 cm long, 0.3–0.7 cm broad, acute, undulate. **Petals** shortly clawed, oblong, 1–1.8 cm long, 0.5–0.8 cm broad, subacute, undulate. **Lip** 3-lobed at base, 1.7–3.1 cm long, 2–3.7 cm broad; side lobes auriculate, margins recurved; mid-lobe shortly clawed, flabellate, deeply bilobulate, margins undulate; callus small with a basal obtriangular plate and several peg-like tubercles in front. **Column** erect, 0.5 cm long, 2-winged on either side of stigma; wings obliquely dolabriform, yellow.

DISTRIBUTION   Peru, Colombia, Venezuela, Costa Rica and Panama; 1000–2000 m.

HISTORY   *O. globuliferum* was described in 1815 by F.H.A. von Humboldt, A. Bonpland and C.S. Kunth in *Nova Genera et Species Plantarum* (p. 347).

SYNONYMS   *Oncidium scansor* Rchb.f.; *O. werklei* Schltr.

Oncidium harrisonianum Lindl. [Colour Plate]

A dwarf epiphytic plant. **Pseudobulbs** small, elliptic-oblong to orbicular, disc-like, compressed, 2.5 cm long, 0.8–1.8 across, 1-leafed at apex. **Leaf** small, suberect or recurved, fleshy, linear-oblong to oblong-lanceolate, 7.5–15 cm long, 3 cm broad, subacuminate, glaucous, spot-

ted with grey. **Inflorescence** erect or arcuate, 30 cm long, paniculate; branches about 6-flowered; bracts very short, triangular-lanceolate, acute. **Flowers** about 1.6 cm across; sepals and petals yellow or orangy-yellow with a few large chocolate-brown spots in centre; lip yellow, side lobes with a few faint longitudinal chocolate-brown stripes; callus brown. **Dorsal sepal** concave, obovate, up to 0.9 cm long, 0.4 cm broad, apex subacute, recurved; **lateral sepals** spreading widely, obliquely spathulate, 0.9 cm long, 0.4–0.5 cm broad, subacute. **Petals** spathulate, 0.8–1 cm long, 0.3–0.4 cm broad, subacute. **Lip** spreading-subdeflexed, 3-lobed, 0.9–1.0 cm long, 0.7–0.3 cm broad; side lobes subquadrate, suberect; mid-lobe clawed, bilobulate, reniform, lobules upcurved; callus 5-lobed. **Column** very short, fleshy; wings deltoid.

DISTRIBUTION   Brazil.

HISTORY   William Harrison discovered this species in the Organ Mts of Brazil and sent living plants to his relative, Mrs Arnold Harrison of Liverpool, England. She flowered it in 1832 and John Lindley described it in the following year in his *Genera and Species of Orchidaceous Plants* (p. 202) and also in the *Botanical Register* (t. 1569).

SYNONYMS   *Oncidium pallidum* Lindl.; *O. pantherinum* Hoffmannsegg; *O. acrobotryum* Klotzsch

CLOSELY RELATED SPECIES   Related to *O. divaricatum*, *O. robustissimum* and *O. pulvinatum* but easily recognised by its 5-lobed callus.

Oncidium hastatum Lindl. [Colour Plate]

An epiphytic or lithophytic plant. **Pseudobulbs** large, ovoid-conical, compressed, 7.5–11 cm long, 5–6 cm broad, 2-leaved at apex, with 4 distichous leaf-bearing sheaths at base. **Leaves** linear to linear-oblanceolate, arcuate, fairly flexible, 15–43 cm long, 1.5–3 cm broad, acute or acuminate. **Inflorescence** paniculate, up to 1 m or more long; branches suberect, 6- or more-flowered; bracts lanceolate, 0.6 cm long. **Flowers** with yellow sepals and petals, heavily spotted with deep maroon; lip off-white, mid-lobe marked with rose-purple blotches, especially towards the base, callus white, lined with rose-purple. **Sepals** narrowly lanceolate, undulate on margins, 2–2.4 cm long, 0.3–0.7 cm broad, acuminate. **Petals** lanceolate, 2 cm long, 0.4–0.7 cm broad, acuminate. **Lip** 3-lobed at base, 1.7–2.1 cm long, 1.5 cm broad at base; side lobes oblong or rotund-subquadrate, spreading; mid-lobe elliptic-ovate, shortly clawed, acuminate; callus fleshy, longitudinal, 4-lobed at front, 2 mid-lobes longer than outer ones. **Column** wings incurved, subquadrate-rounded.

DISTRIBUTION   Mexico; 1000–2000 m altitude.

HISTORY   Discovered at Oaxaca in Mexico by H. Galeotti at an altitude of 1200 m and described by John Lindley in 1850 in Paxton's *Flower Garden* (p. 9, no. 2).

CLOSELY RELATED SPECIES   Similar to *Oncidium karwinskii* (Lindl.) Lindl. and *O. maculatum* (Lindl.) Lindl. which have broader, more obscurely-lobed lips which lack the heavy rose-purple suffusion on the mid-lobe.

Oncidium hastilabium (Lindl.) Garay & Dunsterville [Colour Plate]

A creeping epiphytic plant. **Pseudobulbs** clustered, oblong-ovoid, compressed, ancipitous, up to 6 cm long, 4 cm broad, 1- or 2-leaved at apex, subtended by several leaf-bearing sheaths. **Leaves** oblong-ligulate to oblanceolate, spreading, up to 20 cm long, 4 cm broad, obtuse or mucronate at apex. **Inflorescence** arching or suberect, paniculate, up to 75 cm long or more. **Flowers** opening in succession, 6–7.5 cm across, fragrant; sepals and petals pale yellow-green, transversely striped chocolate-brown in basal two-thirds; lip white with a purple base; column lavender with a yellow base. **Sepals** narrowly lanceolate, 4 cm long, 0.8–1 cm broad, acuminate. **Petals** similar to sepals, 3.4 cm long, 0.9 cm broad. **Lip** 3-lobed, 3.2 cm long, 1.8–2.4 cm broad; side lobes small, falcate, porrect; mid-lobe clawed, cordate above, apiculate or acute; callus of 3 parallel ridges, mid-ridge trilobulate at front. **Column** wings very narrowly oblong.

DISTRIBUTION   Colombia.

HISTORY   Discovered at Tesqua in the province of Pamplona at an altitude of 760 m by Jean Linden and described as *Odontoglossum hastilabium* by John Lindley in 1846 in *Orchidaceae Lindenianae* (p. 16). In 1976 L. Garay and G.C.K. Dunsterville transferred it to the genus *Oncidium* in *Venezuelan Orchids Illustrated* (p. 302) but this species is probably more closely allied to *Miltonioides* species.

SYNONYM   *Odontoglossum hastilabium* Lindl.

Oncidium heteranthum Poepp. & Endl.

An epiphytic plant, up to or more than 70 cm high. **Pseudobulbs** clustered, ovoid-conical, bilaterally compressed, smooth, lightly sulcate, up to 5 cm long, 3 cm broad, 2- (rarely 1-)leaved. **Leaves** oblanceolate, thin-textured, dorsally carinate, up to 15 cm long, 2 cm broad, acute. **Inflorescence** paniculate, erect or drooping, up to 70 cm high; peduncles minutely verrucose; branches have 1–3 fertile flowers towards apex only, lower flowers abortive; bracts minute, narrowly triangular. **Flowers** 1 cm across; sepals and petals pale

greenish-yellow, marked with brown; lip bright yellow, marked brown around callus; callus white, marked brown; column yellow. **Sepals** oblanceolate, 0.7 cm long, 0.2 cm broad, obtuse. **Petals** obovate, 0.7 cm long, 0.4 cm broad, obtuse. **Lip** 3-lobed, up to 1.5 cm long and broad; side lobes triangular, margins recurved; mid-lobe transversely ovate, bilobulate; callus about 5-ridged, mid-ridge ends in an erect recurved hook-like projection. **Column** erect, with oblong wings enclosing anther-cap.

DISTRIBUTION   Costa Rica, Panama, Venezuela, Colombia, Ecuador, Bolivia, and Peru; an epiphyte in mountain forest.

HISTORY   Described in 1836 by E.F. Poeppig and S.L. Endlicher in *Nova Genera ac Species Plantarum* (p. 34, t. 60) and named on account of the presence of both sterile and fertile flowers in the inflorescence. Poeppig discovered this species in the Bolivian Andes.

SYNONYMS   *Oncidium bryolophotum* Rchb.f.; *O. ionops* Cogn. & Rolfe; *O. megalous* Schltr.

Oncidium hookeri Rolfe [Colour Plate]

A small, pendulous, epiphytic plant, up to 45 cm long. **Pseudobulbs** narrowly conical, ridged, 3–6 cm long, 1.5 cm broad, 1- or 2-leaved at apex, subtended by 1 or 2 basal leaf-bearing sheaths. **Leaves** erect or erect-spreading, coriaceous, oblanceolate, rounded or obtuse at apex, 8–20 cm or more long, 0.5–1.5 cm broad. **Inflorescence** paniculate, erect or arcuate, 2.0–4.5 cm broad, many-flowered; branches long, bearing flowers towards apex; bracts membranous, triangular, acuminate, 0.1–0.2 cm long. **Flowers** small, 1 cm across; sepals and petals yellow, flushed flesh-brown; lip yellow, pale brown on and around callus; column yellow-green. **Sepals** reflexed completely, oblong-lanceolate, 0.5 cm long, 0.15 cm broad, acute. **Petals** similar to sepals, slightly concave, 0.45 cm long, 0.2 cm broad. **Lip** more or less convex, 3-lobed, 0.6 cm long, 0.5 cm broad; side lobes oblong-triangular; mid-lobe clawed, narrowly flabellate, bilobulate; callus 5-lobed, lobes flattened, somewhat concave and fleshy. **Column** short, wingless, 0.2 cm long.

DISTRIBUTION   Brazil.

HISTORY   First collected together with *O. forbesii* Hooker from the Organ Mts in Brazil by George Gardner in 1837 and described by R.A. Rolfe in the *Gardeners' Chronicle* (s. 3, 2; p. 520) in 1887.

CLOSELY RELATED SPECIES   Similar to *Oncidium loefgrenii* Cogn. which has a more complexly lobed callus. When first introduced it was misidentified as *O. raniferum*, which led to its being undescribed for 50 years after its introduction. *O. hookeri* is easily distinguished from *O. raniferum* by its larger flowers which

have lateral sepals which are connate for half their length.

Oncidium incurvum Lindl. [Colour Plate]

Pseudobulbs ovoid, compressed, ridged, 7.5–10 cm long, 2–3 cm broad, ribbed on flattened sides, 2- or 3-leaved. **Leaves** linear-ligulate, 30–85 cm long, 2 cm broad or more, acute. **Inflorescence** 1–2 m long, paniculate; branches distichous, alternate, laxly flowered. **Flowers** 2.5 cm across; sepals and petals off-white and spotted pale violet; lip pink with a white blade; callus yellow, marked with brown; column white, wings tinged pink. **Dorsal sepal** linear-oblanceolate, undulate, 1.2 cm long, 0.3 cm broad, acute; **lateral sepals** curved, narrowly oblanceolate, 1.7 cm long, 0.3 cm broad, acute. **Petals** linear-lanceolate, undulate, 1.4 cm long, 0.3 cm broad, subacute. **Lip** 3-lobed, 1.5 cm long, 1.1 cm broad; side lobes small, oblong to rounded, 0.4 cm long; mid-lobe clawed, spreading, subrotund, apiculate; callus 5-toothed, mid-tooth largest. **Column** erect, 0.7 cm long, bidentate.

DISTRIBUTION   Mexico.

HISTORY   Introduced into cultivation by George Barker of Birmingham in 1840. Both John Ross and H. Galeotti collected it in Oaxaca Province at an elevation of between 1200 and 1500 m. John Lindley described it in 1840 in the *Botanical Register* (misc. p. 75) using the epithet given to the species by Barker which refers to the incurved petals of its young flowers.

A pure white-flowered var. *album* is known in cultivation.

CLOSELY RELATED SPECIES   Placed by L. Garay and J. Stacy in sect. *Planifolia* with *O. baueri* and *O. ansiferum* but easily recognised by its white and pale violet flowers.

Oncidium isthmii Schltr.

Pseudobulbs narrowly conical, compressed, 10 cm long, 3 cm broad, 2-leaved at apex, subtended by about 4 leaf-bearing sheaths. **Leaves** narrowly linear-lanceolate, suberect, conduplicate at base, 28–41 cm long, 2.6 cm broad, acute or acuminate. **Inflorescence** long, paniculate, up to 1 m or more long, many-flowered; branches spreading, up to 10-flowered; bracts scarious, concave, ovate, acute, 0.7 cm long. **Flowers** yellow, marked with copper-brown on the base of all the segments. **Dorsal sepal** oblanceolate, undulate on margins, 1 cm long, 0.3 cm broad, obtuse; **lateral sepals** linear-oblanceolate, 1.4 cm long, 0.3 cm broad, acute. **Petals** oblong-oblanceolate, 1.2 cm long, 0.35 cm broad, obtuse. **Lip** spreading-deflexed, 3-lobed at base, 1.3 cm long, 1.6 cm broad; side lobes spreading, auriculate, 0.3 cm long; mid-lobe narrowly clawed, transversely oblong, emarginate; callus fleshy, several-lobed, with 3 spreading lobes in front. **Column** short, erect; wings obliquely dolabriform.

DISTRIBUTION Costa Rica and Panama; at low elevations.

HISTORY *O. isthmii* was described in 1922 by Rudolf Schlechter in *Fedde, Repertorium, Beihefte* (p. 84).

CLOSELY RELATED SPECIES Allied to *O. oblongatum* which has larger flowers. Also allied to *O. ampliatum*, but differs in having longer branches to the inflorescence, a smaller lip and a distinctive callus.

Oncidium jonesianum Rchb.f. [Colour Plate]

An erect or pendulous epiphytic plant. **Pseudobulbs** very small, ovoid, 1 cm long and broad, 1-leafed at apex. **Leaf** fleshy, terete, linear, grooved for entire length, 20–40 cm long, 0.5–1.5 cm in diameter, apex thorn-like. **Inflorescence** arching to pendulous, racemose, 6- to 16-flowered, 30–50 cm long; peduncle slender, compressed; bracts ovate-triangular, shortly acuminate, 0.5–0.8 cm long. **Flowers** showy, nodding, 5.5 cm across; sepals and petals pale green with large maroon spots; lip white, auriculate side lobes of lip yellow-orange; side lobes, callus and base of mid-lobe crimson-spotted; column pale green, spotted crimson. **Sepals** and **petals** oblong-obovate to elliptic, undulate, 2.2–2.7 cm long, 0.8–1.1 cm broad, rounded at apex. **Lip** 3-lobed, sessile, 2.1–2.3 cm long, 1–1.2 cm broad; side lobes auriculate, spreading; mid-lobe broadly oblong, emarginate, margins undulate; callus fleshy, several-lobed, each lobe covered with small tubercles. **Column** erect, 0.6–0.7 cm long, with a wing on each side of stigma; wings pointed above.

DISTRIBUTION Brazil and Paraguay; in riverine forest.

HISTORY Described by H.G. Reichenbach in 1883 in the *Gardeners' Chronicle* (n.s. 19: p. 781).

CLOSELY RELATED SPECIES Vegetatively similar to *O. cebolleta* but easily distinguished when in flower by its larger, pale green, purple-spotted sepals and petals and white lip.

Oncidium lanceanum Lindl. [Colour Plate]

An epiphytic herb, up to 30 cm or more high. **Pseudobulbs** lacking or minute, erect, narrowly ovoid, strongly compressed, up to 2 cm long. **Leaves** coriaceous, ± prostrate, oblong-lanceolate, up to 4.8 cm long, 1.2 cm broad, green, spotted purple. **Inflorescence** up to 30 cm high, 10- to 12-flowered; peduncle erect, stout, dark green with grey-brown sheaths near base. **Flowers** very showy, 6 cm across, fragrant; sepals and petals yellow, heavily spotted

brown-purple; lip rose to violet-purple, darker in basal half, callus rich violet-purple; column greenish-yellow below, dark purple above, anther-cap purple. **Sepals** elliptic, very shortly clawed, 3.5 cm long, 2.2 cm broad, obtuse, margins undulate; lateral sepals slightly concave, longer and narrower than dorsal sepal. **Petals** broadly obovate-spathulate, 3.5 cm long, 2 cm broad, obtuse. **Lip** 3-lobed, 3.8 cm long, 2.4 cm broad; side lobes basal, auriculate to shortly oblong, 0.6 cm long, 0.5 cm broad, mid-lobe long-clawed, spathulate, as broad or broader than base of lip; callus 3-lobed, mid-lobe carinate, longer than side lobes. **Column** short, 0.8 cm long; wings elliptic.

DISTRIBUTION Brazil, Guyana, Surinam, French Guiana, Venezuela and Trinidad.

HISTORY Described by John Lindley in the *Transactions of the Horticultural Society of London* (p. 100, t. 7) in 1836, it was first introduced into cultivation two years later from Surinam by John Henry Lance.

Oncidium leucochilum Lindl. [Colour Plate]

A large epiphytic plant, up to 3 m or more in height. **Pseudobulbs** ovoid to ovoid-ellipsoid, compressed, with 2–3 prominent ribs on flattened sides, 5–13 cm long, 3–6 cm broad, subtended by several scarious sheaths, 1- or 2-leaved at apex. **Leaves** ligulate, coriaceous, conduplicate at base, 10–60 cm long, 1.5–4.5 cm broad, obtuse. **Inflorescence** paniculate, many-flowered, up to about 3 m long; peduncle subtended by a leaf-sheath. **Flowers** with sepals and petals yellow or green to pale green, blotched red-brown; lip white, ± tinged pink or yellow, callus purple-tinged; column-wings purple. **Sepals** oblong-elliptic to elliptic-lanceolate, 1.3–2.3 cm long, 0.5–1.2 cm broad, obtuse to slightly acuminate, keeled on reverse. **Petals** similar to sepals. **Lip** deeply 3-lobed, pandurate, 1.6–2.5 cm long, 1.4–2.3 cm broad; side lobes small, semiovate to oblong, margins reflexed; mid-lobe separated from side lobes by a narrow claw, transversely oblong or reniform, margins undulate-crenulate; callus oblong, with 5–9 slender fleshy teeth, the 3 apical teeth being recurved. **Column** short, fleshy, 0.7 cm long, with a crenulate apical wing on each side.

DISTRIBUTION Mexico, Honduras and Guatemala; a rare species growing in dry to humid forest, up to 2000 m altitude.

HISTORY The type collection of this species was made by George Ure Skinner in Guatemala in 1835 and it was described by John Lindley in the *Botanical Register* (sub t. 1920) in 1837, the same year the species was figured in James Bateman's *Orchidaceae of Mexico and Guatemala* (t. 1). The epithet *leucochilum* refers to the white lip in this species.

SYNONYM *Oncidium digitatum* Lindl.

Oncidium lietzii Regel

Pseudobulbs subfusiform or conical, 5–12 cm long, 1–2 cm broad, 1- or 2-leaved at apex, glossy green. **Leaves** rigid, erect-spreading, oblong-elliptic or ligulate, 11–20 cm long, 3–5 cm broad, acute, apex recurved, deep green above, paler below. **Inflorescence** arching, racemose or paniculate, 40–70 cm long or more; peduncle purple, spotted with white; bracts concave, appressed, pale green 0.9–1.2 cm long. **Flowers** subsecund, 2.2–3.3 cm across; sepals and petals yellow or greeny-yellow, with transverse red-brown lines; lip side lobes yellow with 1 or 2 chocolate-brown spots, mid-lobe chocolate-brown, callus pale orange-brown; column yellow, wings yellow with a central purple-brown marking. **Dorsal sepal** spathulate, concave, up to 1.5 cm long, 0.8 cm broad, obtuse; **lateral sepals** united to apex, 1.2 cm long, 0.8 cm broad, emarginate. **Petals** incurved, spathulate, 1.4–1.6 cm long, 0.9 cm broad, obtuse. **Lip** slightly convex, 3-lobed, 1 cm long, 0.9 cm broad; side lobes incurving, narrowly oblong, margins recurved; callus very large compared to lip, verrucose-tuberculate. **Column** pubescent, 0.4–0.5 cm long; wings incurved, ligulate.

DISTRIBUTION Brazil.

HISTORY First collected by H.W. Lietz in Brazil and named after him by E.A. Regel in 1880 in *Acta Horti Petropolitani* (p. 387).

CLOSELY RELATED SPECIES Allied to *Oncidium amictum* Lindl.

Oncidium longicornu Mutel

Pseudobulbs clustered, oblong-conical, slightly compressed, ridged, 3–7 cm long, 1–2 cm broad, 1- or 2-leaved at apex. **Leaves** erect, rigid, oblong to oblong-ligulate, 8–16 cm long, 1–2 cm broad, subacute, deep green above, paler below. **Inflorescence** paniculate, many-flowered, 25–45 cm long; branches elongate, subdistichous, slender, spreading; bracts membranous, 1–1.5 cm long. **Flowers** relatively small, membranous; sepals yellow-green or suffused reddish-brown; petals reddish-brown with yellow apices; lip pale red below, yellow above; column yellow-green. **Dorsal sepal** oblong-elliptic, concave, 0.5–0.6 cm long, 0.25–0.3 cm broad, acute; **lateral sepals** fused to middle, oblong, up to 0.6 cm long, 0.2 cm broad. **Petals** oblong, undulate, slightly concave, 0.6 cm long, 0.3 cm broad, truncate. **Lip** 3-lobed, slightly convex, 1–1.1 cm long, 0.6–0.8 cm broad; side lobes oblong, margins recurved; mid-lobe clawed, flabellate, emarginate; callus a long recurved horn-like appendage. **Column** incurved slightly, subclavate, 0.4–0.45 cm long, wingless.

DISTRIBUTION Brazil.

HISTORY Described by Mutel in 1838 in *Mémorial de la Scarpe* (p. 10).
SYNONYMS *O. unicorne* Lindl.; *O. monoceras* Hooker

Oncidium longipes Lindl. & Paxt.
[Colour Plate]
A small epiphytic plant, up to 20 cm high. **Pseudobulbs** ovoid, elongate, in clusters of 3 or 4 on a thick ascending rhizome, 2–2.5 cm long, 0.7 cm broad, 1- or 2-leaved at apex. **Leaves** linear-oblong, 10–15 cm long, 1.7 cm broad, mucronate. **Inflorescence** up to 15 cm long, erect, 2- to 5-flowered. **Flowers** 2–3.3 cm across; sepals and petals buffish-yellow or pale reddish-brown, streaked transversely with yellow and with a yellow tip; lip light bright canary yellow, spotted dull red on and around callus, callus with whitish warts. **Sepals** narrowly oblong to spathulate, 1.3 cm long, 0.4 cm broad, acute, apex reflexed; lateral sepals oblanceolate, connate at base, 1.6 cm long, 0.4 cm broad, acute. **Petals** spathulate, 1.1 cm long, 0.6 cm broad, obtuse. **Lip** 3-lobed, 1.2 cm long, 1.1 cm broad; side lobes spreading upwards, oblong-obovate, margins undulate; mid-lobe broadly emarginate, somewhat undulate on margins, claw of mid-lobe more or less fimbriate: callus with many warty projections. **Column** with a broad plate below the stigma; wings very narrow, obscure.
DISTRIBUTION Brazil.
HISTORY Described by John Lindley in Paxton's *Flower Garden* (p. 46) in 1851 based on a collection made the previous year from near Rio de Janeiro, Brazil.
SYNONYM *Oncidium janeirense* Rchb.f.
CLOSELY RELATED SPECIES *Oncidium uniflorum* Lindl. is closely related but differs in having 1-flowered peduncles, in the column-wings being 2-lobed and in having a distinct callus consisting of an oblong cluster of small smooth projections. *Oncidium croesus* Rchb.f. is considered by some botanists to be a superior variety of *O. longipes* but its flowers are quite distinct in their larger size and colouring, having contrasting purple sepals and petals and a golden lip.

Oncidium luridum Lindl. [Colour Plate]
A very large epiphytic plant, up to 2 m or more high. **Pseudobulbs** very small, up to 1.5 cm long, concealed by scarious imbricating sheaths, 1-leafed at apex. **Leaf** oblong-elliptic to elliptic-lanceolate, rigid, coriaceous, 12–85 cm long, 3.5–15 cm broad, acute to obtuse. **Inflorescence** paniculate, many-flowered, up to 1.5 m long; peduncle subtended at base by a scarious sheath. **Flowers** variably coloured, 3.8 cm across; sepals, petals and lip commonly yellow or greenish-yellow, mottled or spotted red-brown to purplish, callus yellow, spotted purple. **Sepals** with a narrow claw, spathulate, obovate or suborbicular, 1.5–2 cm long, 0.7–1.2 cm broad, rounded, margins crisped-undulate. **Petals** with a narrow claw, suborbicular to oblong-spathulate, 1.2–1.8 cm long, 0.7–1.2 cm broad, truncate, margins crisped-undulate. **Lip** 3-lobed, 1.4–2 cm long, 0.7–0.9 cm broad; side lobes auriculate, margins recurved, mid-lobe with a short broad claw, much wider than side lobes, semiorbicular-reniform, margins entire or crenulate; callus of 5 fleshy lobules which are tuberculate. **Column** short, 0.5 cm long, with a bilobulate wing on each side.
DISTRIBUTION A widespread species, common in Florida, Mexico through Central America to Honduras, the W. Indies and northern S. America to Peru; sea level to 1400 m altitude.
HISTORY Described by John Lindley in 1823 in the *Botanical Register* (t. 727). He based his description on a plant cultivated by Mr Griffin of S. Lambeth, London. However, this species was known to Linnaeus who described it as *Epidendrum guttatum*. More recently L. Garay and H. Sweet in the *Flora of the Lesser Antilles* (1974) consider the correct name for this species to be *Oncidium altissimum* (Jacq.) Sw. However, their arguments are at present not accepted by all botanists.
CLOSELY RELATED SPECIES *O. luridum* is allied to *O. carthagenense* from which it may be distinguished by its lip which has a mid-lobe far broader than the side lobes.

Oncidium marshallianum Rchb.f.
[Colour Plate]
An epiphytic plant. **Pseudobulbs** ovoid-oblong, slightly compressed, 5–15 cm long, 2.5–4 cm in diameter, 2-leaved at apex. **Leaves** erect-spreading, rigid, oblong-lanceolate, 21–30 cm long, 2.5–4 cm broad, acute. **Inflorescence** spreading or arcuate, 1–1.8 m long, paniculate, laxly many-flowered; branches spreading or erect-spreading, slender, subdistichous; bracts rigid, narrowly triangular, very acute, 0.2–0.4 cm long. **Flowers** variable in colour and size, up to 5.5 cm across; sepals dull yellow with pale red-brown bars; petals bright canary-yellow, spotted red-brown in centre; lip bright yellow, claw and callus spotted orange-red; column yellow, wings whitish. **Dorsal sepal** oblong-obovate, concave, 1.2–1.5 cm long, 0.9–1.1 cm broad, rounded and apiculate at apex; **lateral sepals** hidden by lip, oblong, connate in basal third, 1.8–2.1 cm long, 0.5–0.7 broad. **Petals** narrowly clawed, broadly obovate-oblong, undulate, 2–2.5 cm long, 1.6–1.9 cm broad, apex emarginate. **Lip** obscurely 3-lobed, 3.5–4 cm long and broad; side lobes auriculate; mid-lobe large, spreading, 2-lobed, broadly oblong; callus with a medium triangular erect plate with 2 basal teeth and 2 smaller ones in front. **Column** 0.6–0.7 cm long; wings short, quadrate.
DISTRIBUTION Brazil.
HISTORY *O. marshallianum* was first collected for Messrs Low & Co. in 1865 by their collector Henry Blunt near Novo Friburgo in the Organ Mts in Rio de Janeiro State, Brazil. H.G. Reichenbach named it in 1866 in the *Gardeners' Chronicle* (p. 682) after William Marshall of Bexley, England, a well-known orchid grower.
CLOSELY RELATED SPECIES *O. crispum*, which was also collected by Blunt in the Organ Mts, is allied to *O. marshallianum* which is distinguished by its bright green pseudobulbs and distinct flowers. *Oncidium pectorale* Lindl. is distinguished from *O. marshallianum* by its predominantly chestnut-coloured flowers; larger, less cucullate dorsal sepal; and a lip callosity which is divided into 2 obovoid, divergent lobes.

Oncidium micropogon Rchb.f. [Colour Plate]
Pseudobulbs broadly ovoid, compressed with acute edges, 2- to 3-ribbed on flattened sides, 5–6.5 cm long, 1- or 2-leaved. **Leaves** suberect, coriaceous, linear-oblong, 10–15 cm long, 3–4 cm broad, rounded. **Inflorescence** erect, flexuous, 30–45 cm long, racemose, 3- to 10-flowered; bracts ovate-triangular, acute, 4 cm long. **Flowers** variable in size, up to 3.8 cm across; sepals yellow, barred with reddish-brown; petals bright canary-yellow, spotted red-brown on claw; lip yellow, callus and basal part of mid-lobe yellow, spotted red-brown at base. **Dorsal sepal** linear-oblong, 2.4 cm long, 0.9 cm broad, acuminate; **lateral sepals** connate at base, oblong-lanceolate, 2.4 cm long, 0.8 cm broad, acute. **Petals** clawed, suborbicular, 2.1 cm long, 2 cm broad, emarginate, apiculate. **Lip** 3-lobed, 1.5 cm long, 2.7 cm broad; side lobes orbicular, equal in size to mid-lobe; mid-lobe broadly obcordate or suborbicular, apiculate; callus fleshy, covered with conical tubercles, margins pectinately toothed. **Column** wings deltoid.
DISTRIBUTION Brazil.
HISTORY *O. micropogon* was first cultivated in 1853 in Europe by Consul Schiller at Ovelgonne, near Hamburg and was described the following year by H.G. Reichenbach in *Bonplandia* (p. 90). The plants of the original importation died out but the species was reintroduced in 1886 by Messrs Sander & Sons.
SYNONYM *Oncidium dentatum* Klotzsch
CLOSELY RELATED SPECIES Closely related to *O. barbatum* but distinguished by its

larger flowers with distinctly shaped segments and callus.

Oncidium nanum Lindl. [Colour Plate]

A small epiphytic plant, up to 25 cm high. **Pseudobulbs** obsolescent, up to 1.5 cm long, 1 cm broad, 1-leafed at apex. **Leaf** oblong-elliptic, fleshy-coriaceous, up to 13 cm long, 4 cm broad, subacute, dull green, flushed and spotted purple, dorsally keeled near base. **Inflorescence** paniculate, pendent, few- to many-flowered, 10–25 cm long. **Flowers** 1.3 cm across; sepals and petals browny-yellow, marked reddish-chocolate; lip yellow marked with chocolate-red on side lobes, callus honey-coloured; column yellow-brown with a maroon flush, anther maroon. **Sepals** spathulate, concave, up to 0.8 cm long, 0.5 cm broad, obtuse. **Petals** spathulate, truncate, 0.8 cm long, 0.5 cm broad. **Lip** very obscurely 2-lobed, 0.8 cm long, 0.9 cm broad; side lobes obscure; mid-lobe transversely oblong, obscurely bilobulate. **Column** erect, with 2 forward-pointing peg-like projections in middle; anther glandular.

DISTRIBUTION Guyana, Venezuela, Peru and Brazil; an epiphytic species in lowland forests below 100 m altitude.

HISTORY Described by John Lindley in the *Botanical Register* (misc. p. 37) in 1842 from a plant grown by Messrs Loddiges in 1842 which Sir Richard Schomburgk had collected on the banks of the Pomeroon River in Guyana.

CLOSELY RELATED SPECIES See *O. pumilum*.

Oncidium nubigenum Lindl. [Colour Plate]

A medium-sized to large plant, one of a large group of closely related species, which have often been confused in the past. **Pseudobulbs** clustered, narrowly ovoid to conical, somewhat compressed, 3–10 cm long, with 2 pairs of imbricating sheaths at base, 1- or 2-leaved. **Leaves** linear-elliptic to oblanceolate, 5–40 cm long, up to 3 cm broad, acute or acuminate. **Inflorescence** up to 25 cm or more long, suberect or arching, racemose or rarely paniculate, 3- to 10-flowered (rarely more). **Flowers** small to medium-sized; sepals and petals rose-purple with white margins; lip pale rose or white, spotted with rose, purple or pale pink at base; callus yellow. **Sepals** oblong to obovate, cucullate, 1.1–1.5 cm long, 0.5–0.8 cm broad, truncate; lateral sepals connate for basal third, free ends apiculate. **Petals** elliptic or obovate, up to 1.4 cm long, 1 cm broad, acute or obtuse. **Lip** obovate-suborbicular, 3-lobed, 1.6–1.8 cm long, 2.2–2.8 cm broad; side lobes auriculate; mid-lobe sessile, transversely reniform to cordate-reniform; callus 3- or 5-lobulate at base, without a basal tuft of hairs. **Column** stout, 0.3 cm long, wingless.

DISTRIBUTION Peru, Ecuador and Colombia; up to 3000 m altitude.

HISTORY Described by John Lindley in his *Genera and Species of Orchidaceous Plants* (p. 197) in 1833 based on a collection of Prof. W. Jameson from the Azuay Mts in Ecuador.

CLOSELY RELATED SPECIES In the past, *O. nubigenum* has often been treated as a synonym of *O. cucullatum* Lindl., but John Stacy in 1975 in a paper in the *Botanical Museum Leaflets of Harvard University* shows them to be distinct species. His elucidation of the specific limits in sect. *Cucullata* of *Oncidium* has enabled him to distinguish 19 species in the section. *O. cucullatum* can easily be separated from *O. nubigenum* by its tuft of hairs present at the base of the callus where it is enclosed by the auriculate base of the column.

Oncidium oblongatum Lindl.

A compact epiphytic plant. **Pseudobulbs** ovoid to ovoid-ellipsoid, compressed, 6–10 cm long, 2.5–3.5 cm broad, 2-leaved at apex. **Leaves** oblong-ligulate to linear-lanceolate, subcoriaceous, suberect, narrowed at base, 15–45 cm long, 1.5–2.5 cm broad, acute to obtuse. **Inflorescence** paniculate, many-flowered, up to 1.4 m long. **Flowers** showy, bright yellow marked with irregular brown or red-brown blotches. **Sepals** elliptic-oblanceolate to obovate-oblanceolate, 1.2–1.5 cm long, 0.3–0.5 cm broad, subobtuse to acute. **Petals** obliquely elliptic-oblanceolate, 1.3–1.5 cm long, 0.5–0.7 cm broad, rounded, margin undulate. **Lip** large, 1.9–2.5 cm long, 1.1–1.3 cm broad; side lobes small, obliquely rounded, reflexed; mid-lobe large, with a short narrow claw, suborbicular, deeply retuse; callus fleshy, obscurely 4-lobulate below, tridentate above. **Column** stout, fleshy, 0.5–0.7 cm long; wings rounded and borne towards apex of column.

DISTRIBUTION Mexico and Guatemala; where it is an uncommon epiphyte in dry forests up to 2100 m altitude.

HISTORY Described by John Lindley in 1844 in the *Botanical Register* (misc. p. 4) based on a plant by Messrs Loddiges.

CLOSELY RELATED SPECIES Similar in habit to *O. sphacelatum* but easily recognised by its differently coloured flowers and by the differently shaped column-wings. See also *O. isthmii*.

Oncidium obryzatum Rchb.f. [Colour Plate]

A compact, epiphytic plant. **Pseudobulbs** erect, conical, compressed, ridged, up to 10 cm high, 4 cm broad, shiny green, 1-leafed at apex. **Leaf** oblong-ligulate, suberect, up to 35 cm long, 4–6 cm broad, obscurely unequally 2-lobed at apex. **Inflorescence** paniculate, suberect to drooping, up to 1 m or more long,

bearing 100 or more flowers. **Flowers** variable in size; sepals, petals and lip yellow marked with chocolate-brown; callus yellow or white with a few chocolate-brown spots. **Sepals** spathulate to oblong, clawed, 1–1.5 cm long, 0.4–0.6 cm broad, truncate. **Petals** obovate to spathulate, 1.1–1.5 cm long, 0.8 cm broad, rounded. **Lip** 3-lobed, 1.8–2.5 cm long, 1.6–2.5 cm broad; side lobes auriculate, much smaller than mid-lobe; mid-lobe bilobulate, clawed, lobules elliptic; callus with a central ridge flanked on either side at base by 2 toothed ridges and towards apex by a protruding ridge on either side. **Column** erect; wings with erose margins.

DISTRIBUTION Venezuela, Colombia, Ecuador, Peru, Costa Rica and Panama.

HISTORY Described in *Bonplandia* (p. 108) in 1854 by H.G. Reichenbach, *O. obryzatum* was first collected by J. Warscewicz in Peru in 1852. The specific epithet is derived from a Greek work meaning 'refined gold', an allusion to the flower colour.

SYNONYMS *Oncidium obryzatoides* Kraenzl.; *O. fulgens* Schltr.; *O. varians* Schltr.; *O. brenesii* Schltr.; *O. graciliforme* C. Schweinf.

Oncidium ornithorhynchum H.B.K. [Colour Plate]

Pseudobullbs ellipsoid-conical, compressed, 6 cm long, 3 cm broad, 2-leaved at apex. **Leaves** somewhat arched, oblong-oblanceolate, up to 24 cm long, 3.5 cm broad, acute. **Inflorescence** pendulous or arcuate, paniculate, up to 30 cm or more long. **Flowers** 2.2–2.5 cm across; sepals, petals and lip purple, pink or white; callus golden-yellow. **Dorsal sepal** oblong-lanceolate, undulate, 0.8 cm long, 0.3 cm broad, acute; **lateral sepals** joined at base, spreading at right-angles to lip, falcate, 0.8 cm long, 0.25 cm broad, subacute. **Petals** oblong-lanceolate, shortly clawed, undulate, 0.7 cm long, 0.25 cm broad, subacute. **Lip** shortly clawed, obscurely 3-lobed to hastate, 1 cm long, 0.8 cm broad; side lobes obscurely recurved on upper and lower margins; mid-lobe bilobulate at apex, upper margins recurved; callus cristate, irregular. **Column** erect; wings spreading, obliquely dolabriform.

DISTRIBUTION Mexico, Guatemala. El Salvador and Costa Rica.

HISTORY *O. ornithorhynchum* was described in 1815 by F.H.A. von Humboldt, A. Bonpland and C.S. Kunth in *Nova Genera et Species Plantarum* (p. 345, t. 80). It had been discovered by Humboldt during his travels in the mountains near Valladolid in Michoacan State, Mexico. The specific epithet derives from the Greek for 'beak of a bird', in allusion to the beak-like rostellum. *O. ornithorhynchum* was first introduced into cultivation simultaneously by James

Bateman who received plants from George Ure Skinner in Guatemala and by Messrs Loddiges who were sent plants from Mexico by Count Karwinsky.

CLOSELY RELATED SPECIES   Related to *O. cheirophorum* which is easily distinguished by its yellow flowers.

Oncidium phalaenopsis Linden & Rchb.f.

Pseudobulbs ovoid to ovoid-conical, 1.5–4.5 cm long, 1–2 cm diameter, sulcate when older, 2-leaved at apex. **Leaves** linear-oblanceolate, suberect-arcuate, 7–18 cm long, 1.5–2 cm broad, subobtuse. **Flowers** showy, 3.5 cm across; sepals and petals white, spotted with dark purple; lip white to pale pink, flushed and spotted purple in middle, callus yellow. **Dorsal sepal** oblong-obovate, concave, 1.8 cm long, 0.9 cm broad, obtuse; **lateral sepals** connate, bifid at apex, 1.8 cm long, 0.7 cm broad. **Petals** elliptic, shortly clawed, spreading, 1.7 cm long, 1 cm broad, acute. **Lip** spreading-deflexed, obscurely 3-lobed at base, 3.3 cm long, 2.2 cm broad at base, 3.2 cm broad across mid-lobe; side lobes subrotund, somewhat obscure; mid-lobe transversely oblong, emarginate, margins undulate; callus obovate, concave, bidentate at the apex, with a shorter central ridge.

DISTRIBUTION   Ecuador.

HISTORY   The type specimen of this showy species was collected in Ecuador by G. Wallis and was described by Jean Linden and H.G. Reichenbach in 1869 in the *Gardeners' Chronicle* (p. 416).

One of the species of sect. *Cucullata* which has recently been revised by John Stacy in the *Botanical Museum Leaflets of Harvard University* (1975). The species of this group are closely allied to *O. phalaenopsis* which is readily distinguished by its obovate, concave callus which is bidentate at apex.

CLOSELY RELATED SPECIES   See *O. dayanum*.

Oncidium phymatochilum Lindl.
[Colour Plate]

A short, erect, epiphytic plant, up to 60 cm or more high. **Pseudobulbs** fusiform, slightly compressed, 5.5–12.5 cm long, 2.5 cm broad, subtended at the base by several large imbricating sheaths, 1-leafed at apex. **Leaf** elliptic to elliptic-oblanceolate, coriaceous, 25–35 cm long, 4.5–7.5 cm broad, acute or obtuse, dark green, speckled red below. **Inflorescence** up to 60 cm long, paniculate, laxly many-flowered; peduncle tinged purple-brown; rhachis zigzag. **Flowers** showy, up to 5 cm across; sepals and petals yellow or pale green, marked with red-brown blotches below the middle; lip white, callus yellow, spotted reddish-orange. **Sepals**

delicate, flaccid, somewhat twisted, 1.8–3.5 cm long, 0.3 cm broad at base, dorsally carinate. **Petals** similar to sepals but shorter, recurved. **Lip** pandurate, 3-lobed, 1.5–1.8 cm long, 1.1 cm broad; side lobes auriculate, rounded, undulate, 0.4 cm broad; mid-lobe broadly ovate-cordate, apiculate, apex recurved; callus fleshy, with a toothed flap on each side at base and trituberculate above. **Column** erect, slender, 0.5 cm long, with a semicordate wing on either side at apex.

DISTRIBUTION   Mexico, Guatemala and Brazil; a rare plant of forests up to 1300 m altitude.

HISTORY   *O. phymatochilum* was first grown in Europe by Rev. J. Clowes of Manchester, England, and by Messrs Loddiges in about 1849. John Lindley described it in 1848 in the *Gardeners' Chronicle* (p. 139). The specific epithet refers to the tumour-like callus on the lip.

It is a very distinct species somewhat resembling species in the genus *Brassia*.

Oncidium pubes Lindl. [Colour Plate]

An epiphytic plant, up to 23 cm high. **Pseudobulbs** oblong-cylindrical, clustered, slightly compressed, 5–7 cm long, 1–1.5 cm broad, green, 1- or 2-leaved at apex. **Leaves** erect or spreading, subcoriaceous, narrowly oblong-lanceolate, 7–12 cm long, 2–3 cm broad, acute, intensely green above. **Inflorescence** 30–60 cm long, arcuate, many-flowered, paniculate. **Flowers** 2 cm across; sepals and petals brownish-purple with transverse yellow or green bands; lip yellow or brownish-purple with a yellow margin; column white. **Dorsal sepal** obovate, truncate, up to 1.2 cm long, 0.8 cm broad; **lateral sepals** united almost to apex, recurved, linear-ligulate, 1 cm long, 0.45–0.5 cm broad, acute or subacute. **Petals** narrowly obovate-spathulate, 1.2 cm long, 0.6 cm broad, rotund-subtruncate at apex. **Lip** deeply 3-lobed, 1.1 cm long, 0.7 cm broad; side lobes 0.3 cm long; mid-lobe broadly reniform, recurved, truncate-subcordate at base, emarginate at apex; callus pubescent, 2-ridged, 2-horned at front. **Column** erect, 0.4 cm long, with villose hairs around the stigma, wings 0.2 cm long.

DISTRIBUTION   Brazil (states of Rio de Janeiro and Minas Gerais) and Paraguay.

HISTORY   Described by John Lindley in 1826 in the *Botanical Register* (t. 1007), based on a specimen sent to the Horticultural Society of London in 1824 from Rio de Janeiro by David Douglas. It had first been discovered somewhat earlier by M.E. Descourtilz in Minas Gerais State. The specific epithet related to the soft villose hairs around the stigma margins.

SYNONYMS   *Oncidium bicornutum* Hooker; *O. pubescens* Duchartre

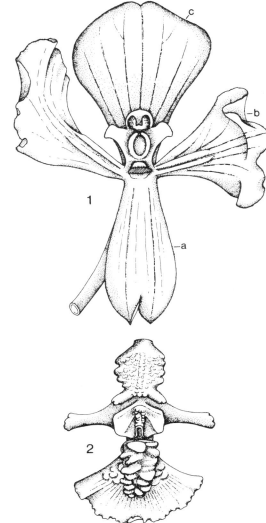

Oncidium pubes
1 – Flower with lip removed (× 4)
  a Lateral sepals, b Petal, c Dorsal sepal
2 – Lip (× 4)

Oncidium pulvinatum Lindl.

A compact, epiphytic plant. **Pseudobulbs** suborbicular-oblong, compressed, 3.5–5 cm in diameter, 1-leafed at apex. **Leaf** rigid, suberect, oblong, 24–30 cm long, 5–8 cm broad, acute. **Inflorescence** flexuose, 1.7–3 m long, loosely paniculate, many-flowered, branches spreading, simple or branching again; bracts linear-triangular, very acute, 0.2–0.4 cm long, **Flowers** 2.5 cm across; sepals and petals orange-red below, yellow above; lip yellow, spotted red or orange-red, callus white, spotted with red; column-wings purple-lined. **Sepals** spathulate, up to 1.3 cm long, 0.6 cm broad, subacute to obtuse. **Petals** similar to sepals but obtuse-truncate, 1.1–1.3 cm long, 0.5–0.6 cm broad. **Lip** 3-lobed, up to 1.4 cm long, 1.1 cm broad;

439

side lobes spreading, semicircular, dentate-undulate on margins; mid-lobe broadly oblong, bilobulate; callus a papillate fleshy cushion. **Column** erect, clavate, 0.4 cm long; wings rounded.

DISTRIBUTION   Brazil.

HISTORY   Another species collected in Brazil by William Harrison of Rio de Janeiro. He sent plants to his brother Richard in Liverpool in 1838 in which year it was described by John Lindley in the *Botanical Register* (misc. p. 61).

CLOSELY RELATED SPECIES   Similar to *O. divaricatum* but easily recognised by its entire, cushion-like callus and distinct lip shape.

Oncidium sphegiferum Lindl. is also allied to *O. pulvinatum* but differs in its larger, more richly coloured flowers in which the callus is oblong and the mid-lobe of the lip has an undulate margin. See also *O. harrisonianum*.

Oncidium pumilum Lindl. [Colour Plate]

A small epiphytic plant. **Stems** clustered, minute, broadly ovoid, compressed, 0.3–0.5 cm long, 0.4–0.6 cm across, 1-leafed at apex. **Leaf** coriaceous, suberect, oblong to ligulate, 5–12 cm long, 1.6–3.5 cm broad, subacute. **Inflorescence** commonly erect, paniculate, densely many-flowered, 8–15 cm long; peduncle slender; bracts coriaceous, ovate, acute, 0.1–0.15 cm long. **Flowers** small, somewhat campanulate, 0.6 cm across; sepals and petals mustard-yellow, spotted with chocolate-brown; lip pale yellow with a brown transverse line on either side of the callus; column green and purple. **Dorsal sepal** concave, obovate, 0.3 cm long, 0.1 cm broad, obtuse; **lateral sepals** oblong, 0.2 cm long, 0.1 cm broad, obtuse. **Petals** curved forwards, 0.25 cm long, 0.1 cm broad, obtuse. **Lip** broadly 3-lobed, 0.5 cm long, 0.35 cm broad; side lobes curved forward, ovate-oblong, 0.3 cm long, 0.2 cm broad; mid-lobe ovate to triangular-ovate, curved forwards, subacute; callus of 4 fleshy, slightly diverging longitudinal ridges, free at apex. **Column** erect; wings on either side of stigma spreading, each a down-pointing peg-like projection joined at upper end to the column.

DISTRIBUTION   Brazil.

HISTORY   Described by John Lindley in the *Botanical Register* (t. 920) in 1825, *O. pumilum* was first cultivated by Dean William Herbert of Spofforth, Yorkshire in the same year. Herbert received it from one of his Brazilian correspondents who found it growing on *Bombax ceiba* between Botofogo and Rio de Janeiro.

SYNONYM   *Epidendrum ligulatum* Vell.

CLOSELY RELATED SPECIES   Similar to *O. nanum* but this species has smaller flowers with a distinct callus and lip.

Oncidium raniferum Lindl. [Colour Plate]

A small to medium-sized epiphytic herb.

Pseudobulbs ovoid to narrowly ovoid, 2.5–6.5 cm long, 0.7–2 cm in diameter, subtended by several scarious bracts and 2 or 3 leaf-bearing sheaths. **Leaves** suberect, thinly coriaceous, linear or linear-oblanceolate, subacute, 6–17 cm long, 0.5–1.5 cm broad. **Inflorescence** erect, greatly-branched, many-flowered, up to 35 cm tall; branches spreading, up to 11 cm long; bracts lanceolate, acute, 0.15 cm long. **Flowers** small but showy; sepals and petals pale yellow, spotted red-brown; lip yellow, red-brown on disc; callus rich red-brown. **Sepals** spreading oblong-elliptic, obtuse, 0.2 cm long, 0.1 cm broad. **Petals** similar but slightly smaller. **Lip** 3-lobed, dependent, 0.4–0.5 cm long, 0.2–0.3 cm broad; side lobes at base of lip, small, spreading; mid-lobe obovate-obcordate, emarginate; callus of 6 glossy bosses between side lobes. **Column** erect, short, very narrow winged on each side of stigmatic cavity.

DISTRIBUTION   E. Brazil (Rio de Janeiro and Pernambuco States only).

HISTORY   John Lindley described this species in 1837 in the *Botanical Register* (sub t. 1920) based on a collection made by George Gardner in the Organ Mts of Brazil. It was illustrated in the same journal (t. 48) the following year.

CLOSELY RELATED SPECIES   See *O. hookeri*.

Oncidium reflexum Lindl.

A medium-sized plant. **Pseudobulbs** ovoid, compressed, 3–8 cm long; 1.5–4 cm across, 1- or 2-leaved at apex. **Leaves** linear-lanceolate, 15–30 cm long, 1.5–4 cm broad, acute. **Inflorescence** straggling, paniculate, 60–75 cm long; peduncle pale green mottled with dull crimson. **Flowers** 3.8 cm across; sepals and petals light yellow-green barred with dull red-brown; lip bright gamboge-yellow, red-spotted on and around callus. **Sepals** linear-oblong, reflexed, undulate, 1.5 cm long, 0.5 cm broad, acute; lateral sepals curved in basal third, similar to dorsal sepal. **Petals** linear-oblong, undulate, reflexed, 1.7 cm long, 0.6 cm broad, acute. **Lip** 3-lobed, 1.5–1.8 cm long, 2.1–2.4 broad; side lobes rounded-oblong, margins revolute; midlobe clawed, transversely oblong with a sinus in front margin; callus of 10 equal-sized tubercles. **Column** wings dolabriform, denticulate; anther beaked.

DISTRIBUTION   Mexico and Guatemala.

HISTORY   First collected by Count Karwinsky in 1832 in S. Mexico and described by John Lindley in 1837 in the *Botanical Register* (sub t. 1920).

SYNONYMS   *Oncidium pelicanum* Lindl.; *O. cruentum* Hort.; *O. suave* Lindl.

Oncidium robustissimum Rchb.f.

Pseudobulbs short, stout, elliptic, compressed, 1-leafed at apex. **Leaf** fleshy, olive-green, oblong, keeled below, 30–40 cm long. **Inflorescence** paniculate, up to 2 m long; rhachis strong, stout; branches numerous, straight, 6–15 cm long, spreading, several-flowered; bracts triangular-lanceolate, 3 cm long, acute. **Flowers** sepals and petals yellow above, brown below; lip yellow marked with cinnamon-brown spots or stripes; column-wings striped light brown. **Sepals** cuneate-oblong, 1.2 cm long, 0.4 cm broad, rounded at apex. **Petals** oblong-oblanceolate, 1.1 cm long, 0.5 cm broad, obtuse or truncate at apex. **Lip** 3-lobed at base, 1.1 cm long, 1 cm broad; side lobes rounded, serrate; mid-lobe flabellate, deeply emarginate at apex; callus with a pilose cushion at the base. **Column** wings transversely oblong.

DISTRIBUTION   Brazil.

HISTORY   First cultivated by Frederick Horsman of Colchester, England. He sent a plant to H.G. Reichenbach who described it in the *Gardeners' Chronicle* (ser. 3, 4: p. 352) in 1888.

CLOSELY RELATED SPECIES   *O. harrisonianum*; *Oncidium sphegiferum* Lindl. and *O. divaricatum*.

Oncidium sarcodes Lindl. [Colour Plate]

Pseudobulbs variable in size, subfusiform, slightly compressed, 10–15 cm long, 1.5–3 cm across, 2- or rarely 3-leaved. **Leaves** suberect or spreading, oblong, 15–25 cm long, 3.5–6 cm broad, acute. **Inflorescence** arcuate, 1–1.8 m long, paniculate; peduncle slender, dull purple, spotted with green; branches short, few-flowered; bracts narrowly triangular, acute, 4–6 cm long. **Flowers** 3.7–5 cm across; sepals and petals chestnut-brown with a yellow margin; lip bright yellow with a few reddish-brown spots around the callus, callus whitish or yellow, spotted red-brown. **Dorsal sepal** obcordate, to obovate, concave, 1.3–1.5 cm long, 1.3 cm broad, rounded at apex; **lateral sepals** obovate-oblong, keeled on reverse, 1.3–1.5 cm long, 0.6–0.8 cm broad, margins of sepals slightly undulate. **Petals** obovate, 1.6–1.7 cm long, 1.1–1.3 cm broad, obtuse, margins undulate. **Lip** 3-lobed, 1.7–2 cm long, 1.7–1.9 cm broad; side lobes spreading, small, oblong, 0.2–0.3 cm long, margin reflexed; mid-lobe transversely oblong, margins undulate; callus an oblong plate, lobed in front, with a tooth on each side near middle. **Column** subclavate, slightly pubescent, 0.4–0.5 cm long; wings short, fleshy, triangular-semirotund.

DISTRIBUTION   Brazil.

HISTORY   *O. sarcodes* was first cultivated by the Horticultural Society of London in 1849 which received it from P.N. Don, probably

from Rio de Janeiro in Brazil. Later collections of this beautiful species were said to have originated from near Novo Friburgo in the Organ Mts of Brazil. The specific epithet *sarcodes* was given by John Lindley in 1849 in the *Journal of the Horticultural Society* (p. 266) and refers to the red-brown ('flesh-like') colour of the flowers.
SYNONYM *Oncidium rigbyanum* Paxt.

Oncidium sphacelatum Lindl. [Colour Plate]
Pseudobulbs almost oblong, compressed, edges acute, 10–15 cm long, 2.5–3.5 cm broad, 2- to 3-leaved. **Leaves** linear-ligulate, suberect, rigid, 37–60 cm long, 2–3.5 cm broad, acute. **Inflorescence** 1–1.8 cm long, paniculate, many-flowered; branches many, suberect, short; bracts triangular, 2.5 cm long. **Flowers** brightly coloured, 3 cm across; sepals and petals with apices recurved in bud, dark chestnut-brown barred with yellow; lip golden-yellow with a red-brown band before the callus, callus white, spotted yellow-orange; column white with crimson spots on margins. **Sepals** narrowly oblong, undulate, 1.3 cm long, 0.5 cm broad, acute and reflexed at apex; lateral sepals reflexed, similar to but larger than dorsal sepal. **Petals** narrowly oblong-ovate, undulate, 1.5 cm long, 0.6 cm broad, subacute or obtuse, reflexed at apex. **Lip** subpanduriform or obscurely 3-lobed, 1.6 cm long, 1.7 cm broad; side lobes obscure, subquadrate; mid-lobe transversely oblong, emarginate or shortly apiculate, margins undulate; callus a fleshy plate, 3-lobed in front, toothed on sides. **Column** wings small, oblong, margins undulate.
DISTRIBUTION Mexico to El Salvador.
HISTORY Collected by Theodore Hartweg in Mexico in 1840 and sent by him to the Horticultural Society of London. Messrs Lodiges also received plants from Honduras in 1841. John Lindley described it in *Sertum Orchidacearum* (sub t. 48) in the same year.
SYNONYM *Oncidium massangei* C. Morr.
CLOSELY RELATED SPECIES *O. wentworthianum*; *O. stenotes* Rchb.f.; *O. ansiferum*; *O. bracteatum*; *O. oblongatum*.

Oncidium spilopterum Lindl. [Colour Plate]
A small to medium-sized epiphytic plant. **Pseudobulbs** clustered, ovoid-conical, slightly compressed, deeply sulcate with age, 3–4 cm long, 2–2.5 cm in diameter, 2-leaved at apex. **Leaves** somewhat coriaceous, erect-spreading, linear-lanceolate, acute, dorsally keeled, 15–20 cm long, 1.5–2.5 cm broad. **Inflorescence** arcuate, erect to nodding, simple, laxly 6- to 10-flowered, 30–40 cm long; bracts rigid, triangular-linear, acuminate, 0.4–0.6 cm long. **Flowers** nodding; sepals and petals brownish-violet, variegated with greenish-yellow; lip sulphur-yellow with a rich purple-violet callus.

Dorsal sepal ovate to ovate-oblong, acute, 0.9–1 cm long, 0.5 cm broad; **lateral sepals** oblong-falcate, acute, shortly connate at base, 1.3–1.4 cm long, 0.35–0.4 cm broad. **Petals** ovate-subquadrate, shortly clawed at base, rounded-submarginate above, 0.9–1 cm long, 0.5–0.6 cm broad. **Lip** 3-lobed at base, deflexed, 2–2.5 cm long, 2–3 cm broad; side lobes oblong-spathulate, auriculate; mid-lobe shortly clawed, reniform, emarginate at apex, margins crisped; callus fleshy, subrotund, densely multituberculate. **Column** short, fleshy; wings porrect, obtusely quadrate.
DISTRIBUTION Brazil and Paraguay.
HISTORY Described by John Lindley in the *Botanical Register* (misc. no. 75) in 1844 based on a plant imported from Brazil by Messrs Loddiges.
SYNONYMS *Oncidium saint-legerianum* Rolfe; *O. ghillanyi* Pabst

Oncidium splendidum Duchartre
[Colour Plate]
A large epiphytic plant, up to 1 m high. **Pseudobulbs** clustered, suborbicular, compressed, 4–5 cm long, 3–4.5 cm broad, subtended by fibrous sheaths at base, 1-leafed at apex. **Leaf** oblong-elliptic, coriaceous, sulcate, V-shaped in cross-section, 14–27 cm long, 3–4.5 cm broad, obtuse. **Inflorescence** erect, up to 1 m or more long, paniculate, many-flowered. **Flowers** large, showy; sepals and petals bright lemon-yellow, spotted and blotched reddish-brown; lip yellow, side lobes marked with lavender, callus white. **Sepals** elliptic-lanceolate, up to 2.5 cm long, 1 cm broad, acute to apiculate, recurved towards apex. **Petals** obliquely elliptic-oblong, 3 cm long, 1 cm broad, obtuse. **Lip** shallowly 3-lobed, 4 cm long, 1.8 cm broad; side lobes obscure, rounded, reflexed; mid-lobe with a short broad claw, transversely oblong, margins undulate; callus tricarinate with short side keels and a broad elongated mid-keel, up to 1 cm long, **Column** stout, 1 cm long with an apical rounded concave wing on each side.
DISTRIBUTION Guatemala and Honduras; very rare.
HISTORY Described by Duchartre in *Journal de la Société Impériale et Centrale d'Horticulture, Paris* (p. 50) in 1862 based on a herbarium collection of M. Herment, made in Guatemala in 1852 and preserved in A. Richard's herbarium.

Oncidium stramineum Lindl. [Colour Plate]
Pseudobulbs obscure, 1-leafed at apex. **Leaf** thick, leathery, rigid, suberect, narrowly oblong-elliptic or oblong-lanceolate, 14–20 cm long, 3.5–4.2 cm broad, obtuse. **Inflorescence** arching, paniculate, many-flowered; branches

short, fairly few-flowered; bracts triangular, acute, up to 0.4 cm long. **Flowers** 2.2 cm across; sepals and petals creamy-white; lip creamy-white, yellow on side lobes and callus, these and base of mid-lobe spotted with purple; column white, wings purple-marked. **Sepals** oblong-subcircular, 0.8 cm long, 0.65 cm broad, emarginate at apex. **Petals** oblong, shortly clawed, 0.8 cm long, 0.5 cm broad, truncate at apex. **Lip** 3-lobed, 0.8 cm long and broad; side lobes oblong, spreading, slightly incurved; mid-lobe clawed, reniform, emarginate; callus with a central fleshy lobe running on to the claw of the mid-lobe and with 2 lobes on either side. **Column** erect; wings on either side of stigma.
DISTRIBUTION Mexico.
HISTORY First collected by Th. Hartweg for the Horticultural Society of London in 1837, probably from Orizaba near Vera Cruz in Mexico and described the following year by John Lindley in the *Botanical Register* (misc. p. 29) The specific epithet refers to the straw-coloured flowers.

Oncidium tigrinum La Llave & Lex.
A large free-flowering epiphytic plant. **Pseudobulbs** subglobose, compressed, obtuse or subacute, 7.5–10 cm long, 1.7–6 cm across, 2- or 3-leaved at apex. **Leaves** linear-oblong or lanceolate, coriaceous, 24–45 cm long, 1.3–2.6 cm broad, acute. **Inflorescence** loosely paniculate, erect, 60–90 cm long. **Flowers** about 7.5 cm high, fragrant; sepals and petals bright yellow, heavily blotched with brown; lip yellow. **Sepals** narrowly oblong, undulate, 2.4–2.7 cm long, 0.6–0.8 cm broad, acute and reflexed at tip; lateral sepals falcate. **Petals** narrowly oblong, undulate, 2.2 cm long, 0.8 cm broad, acute and reflexed at tip. **Lip** narrowly clawed, spreading, large, obscurely 3-lobed, 3.4 cm long, 3–4 cm broad; side lobes auriculate, rounded; mid-lobe narrowly clawed, broadly oblong, emarginate, apiculate; callus of 2 short ridges and a large central one ending in 3 blunt teeth. **Column** wings auriculate.
DISTRIBUTION Mexico; 2000–2500 m altitude, epiphytic on oak trees.
HISTORY Discovered by the pioneering Mexican botanists P. La Llave and J. Lexarza who described it in 1825 in *Novorum Vegetabilium Descriptiones* (p. 36). It was first cultivated in Europe from Mexico by George Barker of Birmingham in 1839 or 1840.
SYNONYM *Oncidium unguiculatum* Lindl.

Oncidium waluewa Rolfe [Colour Plate]
A small epiphytic plant. **Pseudobulbs** narrowly oblong-cylindric, compressed somewhat, 4–6 cm long, 0.8–1.5 cm in diameter, deeply sulcate, 1-leafed at apex. **Leaf** erect or erect-

spreading, somewhat coriaceous, lanceolate, acute, petiolate, 6 cm long, 1.2 cm broad. **Inflorescence** erect or nodding, densely 6- to 20-flowered above, 10 cm long; bracts ovate-triangular, acute, greenish-white, 0.3–0.4 cm long. **Flowers** strongly concave, white to greenish-yellow, transversely barred on petals with pinkish-purple, lined and barred with pinkish-purple on lip and with a purple callus. **Dorsal sepal** incurved over column, oblong-spathulate, obtuse, 0.8–0.9 cm long, 0.35 cm broad; lateral sepals united almost to apex, 0.7–0.8 cm long, 0.4–0.5 cm broad. **Petals** spreading, somewhat deflexed, obovate, obtuse, 0.8 cm long, 0.5 cm broad. **Lip** sessile, shortly connate with column at base, deeply 3-lobed above the middle, cuneate at base, 0.7–0.8 cm long, 0.5–0.6 cm broad; side lobes reflexed, broadly deltoid, rounded; mid-lobe obovate-reniform; callus linear, minutely tuberculate at base, fleshy and tuberculate at apex. **Column** short, with a forward-curving, narrowly linear wing on each side of stigma.

DISTRIBUTION Brazil and Paraguay.
HISTORY Originally described by E.A. Regel in 1890 in *Acta Horti Petropolitani* (p. 309) as *Waluewa pulchella* based on a collection made by H.W. Lietz in Minas Gerais, Brazil, R.A. Rolfe (1904) transferred it to *Oncidium* as *O. waluewa* in the *Kew Handlist of Orchids*, 2nd edition (p. 167), the new epithet being given as the specific epithet *pulchellum* had already been used for a different species in the genus *Oncidium*.
SYNONYMS *Waluewa pulchella* Regel; *Leochilus pulchellus* (Regel) Cogn.

Oncidium wentworthianum Lindl.
[Colour Plate]
A large epiphytic plant, up to 1 m or more high. **Pseudobulbs** ovoid-ellipsoid, compressed, 7.5–10 cm high, up to 4.5 cm broad, subtended by fibrous-scarious sheaths, 2-leaved at apex. **Leaves** linear-ligulate to lanceolate, subcoriaceous, 13–35 cm long, 1.5–2.8 cm broad, acute. **Inflorescence** up to 1 m or more long, paniculate, many-flowered; branches of panicle short, 3- to 10-flowered. **Flowers** showy, large, 3 cm or more across; sepals and petals dark yellow with irregular red-brown blotches; lip yellow with red-brown blotches across base of mid-lobe; callus and column mottled red-brown. **Sepals** elliptic-obovate, reflexed, 1.4–2.2 cm long, 0.5–0.9 cm broad, acute, obtuse or apiculate. **Petals** obliquely ovate-elliptic, 1.2–2.2 cm long, 0.6–1 cm broad, rounded. **Lip** 3-lobed, deflexed, 1.5–2.3 cm long, 1.4–2.3 cm broad; side lobes oblique, suborbicular-obovate, auriculate, margin crenate; mid-lobe with a long broad claw, obcordate to obreni-form, bilobulate, margins undulate; callus fleshy, with 2 teeth on either side and a longer

central tooth in front. **Column** stout, 0.6–0.7 cm long, with a triangular-auriculate wing on either side at apex.
DISTRIBUTION Mexico and Guatemala; where it is a rare plant of forest to 1500 m altitude.
HISTORY Described by John Lindley in 1840 in the *Botanical Register* (misc. p. 82) from a plant collected by George Ure Skinner in the Santa Rosa Mts of Guatemala in 1839 and sent to James Bateman. It was first cultivated in Europe by the Horticultural Society of London from plants sent from Mexico by Th. Hartweg. The specific epithet was given in honour of Earl Fitzwilliam of Wentworth near Rotherham, England.
CLOSELY RELATED SPECIES *O. sphacelatum.*

Ophrys L.
Subfamily Orchidoideae
Tribe Orchideae
Subtribe Orchidinae

Erect terrestrial herbs, mostly under 60 cm high. **Tubers** (root-stem tuberoids) 2, rarely 3, globose or ovoid, entire. **Leaves** mostly basal, 3 to several, ± prostrate. **Inflorescence** erect, 2- to several-flowered. **Flowers** often mimicking insects, ± showy, mostly pollinated by insects by pseudocopulation. **Sepals** spreading, green or pink. **Petals** often smaller than sepals, sometimes antennae-like. **Lip** ± 3-lobed, often very hairy particularly around margins, with a central shiny area (speculum) mostly of blue, grey or steel-blue. **Column** suberect; anther loculi on each side towards apex.
DISTRIBUTION Europe, N. Africa and the Middle East, about 30 species.
DERIVATION OF NAME From the Greek *ophrys* (eyebrow).
TAXONOMY *Ophrys* was described by Carl von Linné in 1753 in *Species Plantarum* (p. 945). One of the most studied of all orchid genera. *Ophrys* species have attracted great interest because of their method of pollination which involves pseudocopulation of males of some solitary bee species. These bees are attracted to *Ophrys* flowers by a combination of flower shape and smell.

Many *Ophrys* species are very variable in flower colour and shape, no doubt due to genetic drift in isolated populations in the Mediterranean regions. However, a great deal of the variation is due to hybridisation arising where previously geographic or ecologically isolated species have been brought together in areas severely disturbed by man.

The treatment of this genus in *Flora Europaea*

is somewhat inadequate. The accounts by Davies et al. (1983) in *Wild Orchids of Britain and Europe* and Buttler (1986) in *Orchideen* are recommended. Baumann and Kuenkele (1982) in *Die wildwachsenden Orchideen Europas* is also useful but in their most recent treatment of *Ophrys* in *A.H.O. Mitteilungsblatt* in 1989 they have inexplicably raised most infraspecific taxa to specific rank making the treatment difficult to use.
TYPE SPECIES *O. insectifera* L.
CULTURE Various combinations of calcareous soil and sand have been used successfully. Good drainage is essential. Temp. In cultivation should be frost-free. Being plants predominantly of the Mediterranean region, *Ophrys* species begin growth very early in the year so that, in colder climates, they need the protection of a frame or cold-house. While growing, they should be carefully watered but after flowering, when the plants have completely withered away, the pots should be kept almost completely dry. Great care must be taken when the tubers are disturbed for repotting.

Ophrys lutea Cav. [Colour Plate]
A small, tuberous-rooted, terrestrial herb, 10–30 cm tall. **Leaves** more or less prostrate on the substrate, elongate-ovate, yellow-green, subacute or acute, up to 8 cm long, 2.5 cm broad. **Inflorescence** erect, laxly 2- to 10-flowered. **Flowers** showy, well-spaced on rhachis; sepals yellow-green; petals yellow or yellow-green; lip yellow with a central dark purple-brown area around a greyish-blue speculum. **Dorsal sepal** oblong, concave, margins reflexed, rounded at apex, 1 cm long, 0.4 cm broad; **lateral sepals** spreading, oblong-elliptic, rounded, 1 cm long. **Petals** short, linear, 0.3–0.5 cm long, 0.15 cm broad. **Lip** 3-lobed in apical quarter, obovate, margins flat, 0.9–1.8 cm long; side lobes narrowly oblong, truncate; mid-lobe emarginate, broadly oblong-flabellate; disc with an entire speculum or one of two longitudinal, narrowly oblong, greyish-blue marks. **Column** 0.5–0.6 cm long, blunt at apex.
DISTRIBUTION Mediterranean coasts of Europe, N. Africa and the Middle East; usually in scrub and grassy places, up to 1800 m.
HISTORY Originally collected in Spain by A. Cavanilles and described by him in 1793 in vol. 2 of his *Icones et Descriptiones Plantarum* (p. 46, t. 160). Three subspecies of *O. lutea* are recognised. The typical subspecies is found from Spain east to the Aegean region; subsp. *galilaea* (Fleischm. & Bornm.) Soó [Colour Plate] is found throughout the range and is recognised by its small lip which has a glabrous narrow marginal zone; subsp. *melena* Renz is

restricted to Greece and Cyprus, it again has a small lip with a narrow marginal zone covered with blackish-purple hairs.

SYNONYMS *Ophrys vespifera* Brot.; *O. sicula* Tineo; *Arachnites lutea* (Cav.) Tod.

Ophrys vernixia Brot. [Colour Plate]

A small, tuberous-rooted, terrestrial herb, 10–30 (rarely to 50) cm tall. **Basal leaves** large, oblong, subobtuse; **cauline leaves** lanceolate, acute. **Inflorescence** erect, 2- to 6-flowered in a tight spike. **Flowers** showy; sepals dull green, ± striped pale brown; petals brown or orange-brown; lip russet with a glossy deep-blue speculum with a yellow or brown margin. **Dorsal sepal** elliptic, rounded, deeply concave, margins recurved, 0.6–0.8 cm long, 0.3 cm broad; **lateral sepals** spreading, slightly concave, subacute, 0.8 cm long, 0.4 cm broad. **Petals** short, oblong, 0.2–0.3 cm long, 0.15 cm broad. **Lip** 3-lobed in basal half, margins densely bearded with russet or brown hairs, 1.3–1.5 cm long; side lobes spreading or decurved, ± oblong or linear; mid-lobe much longer, obovate or rotund; speculum large, occupying most of the mid-lobe. **Column** erect, 0.4 cm long, blunt at apex.

DISTRIBUTION Mediterranean coasts of N. Africa, Europe and the Middle East; in scrub and open places on limestone, up to 800 m.

HISTORY Originally collected in Portugal and described by Felix Brotero in his *Flora Lusitanica* (p. 24) in 1804. This species is, however, better known under the synonym *O. speculum*.

SYNONYM *Ophrys speculum* Link; *O. scolopax* Willd. non Cav.

Orchis L.

Subfamily Orchidoideae
Tribe Orchideae
Subtribe Orchidinae

Erect terrestrial herbs, mostly under 1 m tall. **Tubers** (root-stem tuberoids) 2(3), ovoid or ellipsoid. **Leaves** glabrous, ± forming a basal rosette. **Inflorescence** erect, spicate, laxly to densely many-flowered. **Flowers** showy, white, pink or purple, rarely yellow or yellow-green; segments all free. **Sepals and petals** convergent into a hood or the lateral sepals spreading and deflexed. **Lip** porrect or decurved, entire or 3-lobed, glabrous, smooth or papillose, with a basal spur. **Column** erect; rostellum 3-lobed; anther bilocular; viscidia in a simple bursicle.

DISTRIBUTION About 30 species widely distributed in Europe and Asia east to China.

DERIVATION OF NAME From the Greek *orchis* (testicle), in allusion to the shape of the tubers.

TAXONOMY Carl von Linné described *Orchis* in *Species Plantarum* (p. 939) in 1753. Many species originally described in this genus have now been removed to other genera so that the genus *Orchis* is now fairly homogeneous consisting of terrestrial plants with the characteristics given in the description. The most recent species removed from *Orchis* are those species now placed in the genus *Dactylorhiza* (*Dactylorchis*) which have flowers that are somewhat similar to those of *Orchis* species but here the floral segments rarely form a galea (hood) and the 2 tubers are usually palmately 2- to 5-lobed and more or less elongated at the apex.

Detailed treatments of the European, N. African and Middle Eastern species are to be found by Baumann and Kuenkele (1982) in *Die wildwachsenden Orchideen Europas*; Davies et al. (1983) in *Wild Orchids of Britain and Europe*; and K.P. Buttler (1986) in *Orchideen*. The account in *Flora Europaea* vol. 5 is now somewhat outdated.

TYPE SPECIES *O. militaris* L.

CULTURE Compost. More varied than for *Ophrys* – depending on plant habitat. Some require lime, others a more acid medium, but good drainage is always necessary in pots. Temp. Generally frost-free, but some species are hardy when planted out. Most species may be naturalised in their country of origin, so long as the site is carefully selected. Species from differing climates may adapt to pot culture, as with *Ophrys*, and, in this case, a cold-house or frame is necessary. Water requirements depend on habitat but all species need ample water while growing and less or much less when flowering is over and the plants have died down completely.

Orchis militaris L. [Colour Plate]

An erect, terrestrial herb, 20–60 cm tall. **Tubers** ovoid or ellipsoid. **Leaves** oblong-lanceolate or oblong-ovate, prostrate, 10–18 cm long, 2–5 cm broad. **Inflorescence** erect, many-flowered; spike conical at first, becoming cylindrical; bracts often violet, shorter than ovary. **Flowers** showy; sepals and petals forming a pink hood, spotted and streaked violet; lip white or pink with purple spotting. **Sepals** ovate or ovate-lanceolate, acute, 1–1.5 cm long. **Petals** linear. **Lip** 3-lobed at base, 1.2–1.5 cm long; side lobes linear, obtuse; mid-lobe narrow below, bilobulate towards apex, lobules spreading; spur narrowly cylindrical, pendent, half the length of the ovary.

DISTRIBUTION From S. and E. England and N.W. Russia south to N. Central Spain, Central Italy and Bulgaria; grows in meadows and thickets on marl or calcareous soils; sea level to 1600 m altitude; nowhere common.

HISTORY Described by Carl von Linné in 1753 in *Species Plantarum* (p. 941).

CLOSELY RELATED SPECIES *O. militaris* (Military orchid) is readily distinguished from the closely allied *Orchis simia* Lam. (Monkey orchid) as the flowers in the spike open from the base upwards. In *O. simia* the uppermost flowers open first and the lip has slender lobules.

Orchis papilionacea L. [Colour Plate]

An erect terrestrial herb, 10–40 cm tall. **Tubers** ovoid or globose. **Leaves** in a basal rosette, lanceolate to linear-lanceolate, acute. **Inflorescence** laxly to densely few-flowered; peduncle angular, reddish towards apex. **Flowers** showy, purple, rarely red or brownish; lip purple-spotted on a lighter background; segments convergent into a galea (hood). **Sepals** ovate-oblong, acute, 1–1.8 cm long. **Petals** ovate-oblong, similar to sepals. **Lip** entire, clawed, obcordate or suborbicular, 1.2–2.5 cm long, 1.2–2.5 cm broad; spur deflexed, cylindrical, shorter than the ovary.

DISTRIBUTION Mediterranean shores of Europe and the Middle East and the Mediterranean islands; growing in dry maquis vegetation, in turf or in olive groves in dry stone soil.

HISTORY *O. papilionacea* was described by Carl von Linné in 1759 in *Systema Naturae* (p. 1242).

Var. *grandiflora* from Spain has much larger flowers than the typical form with the lip up to 2.5 cm long, 2.5 cm broad.

Ornithocephalus Hooker

Subfamily Epidendroideae
Tribe Maxillarieae
Subtribe Ornithocephalinae

Epiphytic plants lacking pseudobulbs. **Stems** short, covered completely by distichous imbricating leaf-sheaths. **Leaves** equitant, fleshy, articulate to leaf-sheaths, arranged in a fan-shape. **Inflorescence** axillary, racemose, laxly few- to several-flowered. **Flowers** small. **Sepals** and **petals** subsimilar; ± spreading or reflexed, free. **Lip** entire or lobed; callus basal thickened, inflexed in front. **Column** short, lacking wings or a foot; anther distinctly beaked; pollinia 4, waxy, borne on a slender stipe with a small viscidium.

DISTRIBUTION Some 50 species distributed throughout the American tropics.

DERIVATION OF NAME The name alludes to the curious shape of the column-apex which resembles a bird's head in the type species, hence from the Greek *ornis, ithos* (bird) and *kephale* (head).

TAXONOMY *Ornithocephalus* was established by Sir William Hooker in 1825 in his *Exotic Flora* (t. 127). It is somewhat similar to *Lockhartia* but is easily recognised by its much shorter stem, racemose inflorescence and flowers with 4 rather than 2 pollinia and a distinctive callus and anther. It is most closely allied to *Zygostates* and *Dipteranthus*.

TYPE SPECIES *O. gladiatus* Hooker

CULTURE Compost A. Temp. Winter min. 12–15°C. *Ornithocephalus* species may be grown either in small pots or tied to slabs of fern-fibre or cork. They require humid shady conditions at all times although the roots should dry a little between waterings.

Ornithocephalus bicornis Lindl.

A small, stemless, epiphytic plant, 3.5–10 cm tall. **Leaves** arranged fan-wise, equitant, rigid, lanceolate or oblong-lanceolate, acute, articulated, 1.5–7 cm long, 0.4–1.2 cm broad; sheaths imbricate, 1–3 cm long. **Inflorescence** racemose, axillary, few- to many-flowered, ± equal the leaves; peduncle slender, flexuose; bracts broadly ovate or orbicular, acute, ciliate, 0.2–0.5 cm long. **Flowers** small, greenish-white or greenish-yellow; pedicel and ovary shortly hispid. **Sepals** free, spreading, suborbicular, apiculate, concave, hispid on outer surface, 0.15–0.2 cm long and broad. **Petals** suborbicular, erose, concave, 0.15–0.2 cm long and broad. **Lip** 3-lobed, fleshy at base, 0.4–0.5 cm long; side lobes obscure, linear-spathulate, recurved, 0.1 cm long; mid-lobe narrowly linear, acute, dorsally keeled, curved. **Column** small, slender, less than 0.1 cm long.

DISTRIBUTION Guatemala. Honduras, Costa Rica and Panama: in forests, sea level to 1100 m altitude.

HISTORY Discovered in Panama during the voyage round the world of the H.M.S. *Sulphur* and described in 1846 by John Lindley in George Bentham's *Botany of the Voyage of H.M.S. Sulphur* (p. 172).

Ornithocephalus iridifolius Rchb.f.

A small, stemless, epiphytic plant, 3.5–8 cm long. **Leaves** arranged fan-wise, linear-ensiform, fleshy, acute to acuminate, 2.5–7.5 cm long, 0.3–0.6 cm broad. **Inflorescence** racemose, axillary, laxly many-flowered, 4–8 cm long; rhachis fractiflex, winged; wings serrate; bracts suborbicular-cordate, keeled on reverse, erose-ciliate, 0.5 cm long. **Flowers** small, white. **Sepals** concave, spreading, suborbicular or broadly elliptic, apiculate, ciliate, 0.25 cm long, 0.2 cm broad. **Petals** flabellate, erose-ciliate and rounded at the apex, 0.35 cm long, 0.4 cm broad. **Lip** spreading, deeply 3-lobed, 0.5 cm long, 0.5 cm broad; side lobes fleshy, suborbicular, rounded; mid-lobe thin, ovate-

triangular, obtuse, concave. **Column** short, fleshy, 0.3 cm long.

DISTRIBUTION Mexico and Guatemala; a rare plant in open forests and coffee plantations, up to 900 m altitude.

HISTORY First collected by Liebold at Zacuapan in Mexico and described by H.G. Reichenbach in *Walpers, Annales Botanices* (p. 494) in 1863.

Ornithocephalus kruegeri Rchb.f.
[Colour Plate]

A very small epiphytic plant with a very short stem. **Leaves** distichous, arranged in a fan, oblong-lanceolate, conduplicate, compressed, acute, 2–4 cm long, 0.4–0.9 cm broad, articulated to a conduplicate leaf-base, 1.5 cm long. **Inflorescences** axillary, erect, racemose, many-flowered; axis and bracts and outside of flowers covered with short peg-like hairs. **Flowers** small; sepals and petals creamy-white, sepals with a central green nerve; lip creamy-white with 5 green nerves, callus dark green on each side; column cream, anther bright green. **Sepals** obovate, rounded, 0.24 cm long, 0.2 cm broad. **Petals** obovate-circular, truncate at apex, 0.3 cm long and broad. **Lip** geniculate below callus, oblong, obtuse, 0.4 cm long, 0.25 cm broad; callus basal, fleshy, several-lobed. **Column** short, acute; rostellum long-pointed.

DISTRIBUTION Trinidad, Surinam, Venezuela, Brazil and Peru.

HISTORY First collected at Arima in Trinidad by Krueger and described by H.G. Reichenbach in 1863 in *Walpers, Annales Botanices* (p. 495).

Ornithocephalus myrticola Lindl. [Colour Plate]

A small epiphytic plant with a very short stem. **Leaves** distichous, imbricate, arranged in a fan, narrowly lanceolate-ligulate, falcate, acute or acuminate, margins broadly pellucid, 1.5–2.5 cm long, 0.5–0.7 cm broad, articulated to a rigid sheath below. **Inflorescence** ascending, axillary, ± arcuate, fractiflex above, 4–8 cm long, densely many-flowered; peduncle and outside of flowers longly and densely glandular-hispid. **Flowers** small, shortly pedicellate, white and green, fragrant, smelling of lemon. **Sepals** broadly ovate, rounded, margins denticulate, 0.3–0.4 cm long, 0.2 cm broad. **Petals** pellucid, broadly rounded margins entire or undulate, 0.45 cm long and broad. **Lip** entire, oblong-ligulate, cordate at the base, acute at the apex, reflexed in the middle, 0.5 cm long, 0.25 cm broad; disc fleshy, 5-callose, outer calli densely papillose. **Column** erect, 0.2 cm long.

DISTRIBUTION Brazil and Bolivia.

HISTORY M.E. Descourtilz first collected this plant near Bom Jesus de Bananal in Brazil

where it was growing on Myrtaceous trees. John Lindley described it in 1840 in the *Annals and Magazine of Natural History* (p. 583).

Ornithochilus (Lindl.) Bentham
Subfamily Epidendroideae
Tribe Vandeae
Subtribe Sarcanthinae

Small monopodial epiphytes with short unbranched leafy stems covered by sheathing leaf bases. **Leaves** coriaceous-fleshy, large. **Inflorescences** axillary, branching, many-flowered, as long as or longer than the leaves. **Flowers** small. **Sepals** and **petals** free, the petals smaller and narrower than the sepals, more or less spreading. **Lip** immobile 3-lobed or bipartite, the side lobes erect, smaller than the mid-lobe, with a prominent cylindrical spur; callus of a pilose cushion between the side lobes and sometimes a raised keel in front on the fringed or dentate mid-lobe. **Column** small, fleshy, with a short foot; rostellum elongate, fleshy, obtuse; pollinia 4 in unequal pairs; stipe obovate or oblanceolate; viscidium small, semi-elliptic.

DISTRIBUTION A small genus of three species in S.E. Asia, from N.W. Himalayas to the Malay Archipelago.

DERIVATION OF NAME From the Greek *ornis, ithos* (bird) and *cheilos* (lip), descriptive of the bird-like appearance of the lip.

TAXONOMY *Ornithochilus* was first recognised as a monotypic section of *Aerides* by Lindley in 1833 in his *Genera and Species of Orchidaceous Plants* (p. 242). George Bentham raised it to generic rank in 1833 in *Genera Plantarum* (p. 334) distinguishing it from other vandaceous genera by its spurred lip, fringed or dentate lip mid-lobe, and stipe which is four times as long as the diameter of the pollinia.

TYPE SPECIES *O. fuscus* Lindl. (= *O. difformis* (Wall. ex Lindl.) Schltr.).

CULTURE Temp. Winter min. 15°C. May be grown mounted or in pots with free-draining epiphyte mix. Give good light and humidity while in growth but should not be allowed to dry out completely when dormant.

Ornithochilus difformis (Wall. ex Lindl.) Schltr.

A small epiphyte with a short stem 1–8 cm long; roots 2 mm in diameter. **Leaves** falcate, oblong-elliptic or obovate-elliptic, acuminate to obtuse at very unequally bilobed apex, 7–18 cm long, 2.4–4.2 cm wide. **Inflorescences** spreading to pendent, simple to several-branched, laxly many-flowered, up to 35 cm long; branches spreading, up to 21 cm long; bracts triangular, acute, 1–2.5 mm long. **Flow-**

ers small, up to 1 cm across, rather insect-like, the sepals and petals yellow with several longitudinal red-brown stripes, the lip dark maroon with some yellow marking towards the base; pedicel and ovary 7–12 mm long. **Dorsal sepal** oblong-elliptic, obtuse, incurved, 3–5 mm long, 2 mm wide; **lateral sepals** obliquely oblong-ovate, subacute, widely spreading, 3.5–6 mm long, 2–3 mm wide. **Petals** linear, obtuse, 3–4 mm long, 1 mm wide. **Lip** bipartite, 4–7 mm long, 4 mm wide; the hypochile at a right angle to the column, with 2 narrowly elliptic erect side lobes, spurred above the base; epichile borne at right angles to the hypochile, 3-lobed, lacerately fringed, the side lobes erect, spreading, falcate, with a central longitudinal broadly triangular raised keel; spur cylindrical, decurved, 3–5 mm long. **Column** 4 mm long, papillate ventrally.

DISTRIBUTION N.W. Himalayas, Nepal, Sikkim, Bhutan, Burma and Thailand south to Sumatra and Borneo; montane forest up to 1600 m.

HISTORY Another of Nathaniel Wallich's Nepalese introductions. It was described by Lindley in 1833 in his *Genera and Species of Orchidaceous Plants* (p. 242) as *Aerides difforme*. Rudolf Schlechter transferred it to the present genus in 1919 in *Fedde, Repertorium Specierum Novarum, Beihefte* (p. 277).

SYNONYMS *Aerides difforme* Lindl.; *Ornithochilus eublepharon* Hance; *O. fuscus* Lindl.; *Sarcochilus difformis* (Lindl.) Tang & Wang; *Trichoglottis difformis* (Lindl.) Ban & Huyen

---

Ornithophora Barb. Rodr.
Subfamily Epidendroideae
Tribe Oncidieae

Small epiphytic herbs. **Pseudobulbs** borne at intervals on slender rhizomes, ovoid-pyriform, glossy green, subtended by 1–2 leaf-bearing sheaths, 2-leaved at apex. **Leaves** suberect, slender, linear, acute, channelled. **Inflorescence** basal, simply racemose, erect, laxly several-flowered; bracts minute; pedicel and ovary slender, ± at right-angles to the rhachis, elongate. **Flowers** small, resupinate. **Sepals** and **petals** subsimilar, free, spreading to reflexed. **Lip** with a long slender claw; lamina transversely lunate with an acute back-pointing auricle on each side, spreading; callus of 3 fleshy lobules on claw and of 4 fan-like ridges on base of the lamina. **Column** erect, slender, over half of the lip length, papillose on ventral surface, with a very short column-foot; stigma concave, elliptic-subcircular, rostellum elongate, triangular; pollinia 2, waxy; stipe 1,

oblanceolate, elongate; viscidium 1, very small.

DISTRIBUTION One species only in Brazil.

DERIVATION OF NAME From the Greek *ornis, ithos* (bird) and *phoros* (bearing), an allusion to the column which is bird-like in side view.

TAXONOMY Originally described by J. Barbosa Rodrigues in 1881 in his *Genera et Species Orchidearum Novarum* (p. 225). *Ornithophora* is allied to *Sigmatostalix* with which it is considered congeneric by some authorities. It differs, however, in having 2-leaved pseudobulbs, a short free column-foot and in the column being papillose around the stigma.

TYPE SPECIES *O. quadricolor* (Rchb.f.) Barb. Rodr. [= *O. radicans* (Linden & Rchb.f.) Garay & Pabst].

CULTURE Compost A. Temp. Winter min. 12–15°C. These small, creeping plants are best grown is shallow pans or baskets or may be established on slabs of fern-fibre or cork. While growing, they need humid conditions under moderate shade with a drier period when the pseudobulbs are fully grown. They should not become so dry as to shrivel.

Ornithophora radicans (Linden & Rchb.f.) Garay & Pabst

A small epiphytic herb. **Pseudobulbs** oblong-ligulate, compressed, ancipitous, 2-leaved at apex, subtended by several distichous leaf-bearing sheaths below. **Leaves** cuneate, linear-ligulate, acute, membranaceous, 10–18 cm long, 0.2–0.4 cm broad. **Inflorescence** erect or erect-spreading, elongate, laxly few- to many-flowered, 7–15 cm long. **Flowers** greenish-yellow or whitish-green; lip white with a yellow callus; column violet-purple in front. **Dorsal sepal** narrowly oblong-subspathulate, acute, 0.4 cm long, 0.1 cm broad; **lateral sepals** narrowly ovate-falcate, 0.5 cm long, 0.2 broad. **Petals** oblong-spathulate, rounded-subtruncate at the apex, 0.5 cm long, 0.2 cm broad. **Lip** narrowly clawed, membranaceous 3-lobed, margins slightly undulate, 0.3–0.4 cm long, 0.5–0.6 cm broad; side lobes narrowly longly acuminate, basal; mid-lobe sagittate-semirotund, emarginate; disc 2- to 6-cristate at the base. **Column** slender, triangular-subulate, 0.25 cm long.

DISTRIBUTION Brazil.

HISTORY Described as *Sigmatostalix radicans* by J. Linden and H.G. Reichenbach in *Hamburger Gartenzeitung* (p. 16) in 1860 from specimens collected in province of Rio Grande do Sul at Porto Alegre. Leslie Garay and Guido Pabst transferred it to the present genus in 1951 in *Orquidea* (Brasil) (p. 50).

SYNONYMS *Ornithophora quadricolor* Barb. Rodr.; *Sigmatostalix radicans* Linden & Rchb.f.

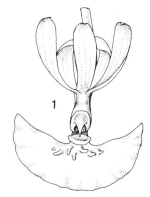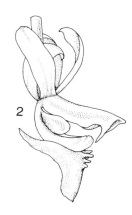

Ornithophora radicans
1 – Flower, front view (×6)
2 – Flower, side view (×6)

Osmoglossum Schltr.
Subfamily Epidendroideae
Tribe Oncidieae

Medium-sized epiphytic herbs often forming large clumps. **Pseudobulbs** ovoid or ellipsoid, clustered on short rhizomes, bifoliate at the apex, subtended by distichous sheaths. **Leaves** erect-spreading, linear-ligulate, conduplicate at the base, coriaceous. **Inflorescences** few- to many-flowered, racemose, axillary from the basal sheaths, erect. **Flowers** non-resupinate, showy, white or pink, fragrant. **Sepals** free, subsimilar, spreading, or with lateral sepals united almost to the apex, **Petals** similar but smaller. **Lip** uppermost in the flower, narrowly clawed, entire, with a complex callus at the base, spurless, borne at 90° or more to the column. **Column** slender, clavate, rather short, fleshy, obscurely winged; pollinia 2, pyriform, waxy; stipe short, oblong; viscidium oblong to ovate.

DISTRIBUTION A small genus of three closely allied species in Central America.

DERIVATION OF NAME From the Greek *osme* (scent or odour) and *glossa* (lip), because of the marked fragrance of the flower of the type species.

TAXONOMY *Osmoglossum*, a segregate genus of *Odontoglossum*, was established by Rudolf Schlechter in 1916 in the journal *Orchis* (p. 164). It is readily distinguished from *Odontoglossum* by its non-resupinate flowers, the fleshy, short, winged column and the lip borne at 90° or more from the column. It is most closely allied to the Central American genus *Ticoglossum*.

A key to the species is given by Senghas

445

and Bockemuehl (1977) in *Die Orchidee* (Orchideenkartei 47, 48).
TYPE SPECIES *O. pulchellum* (Batem. ex Lindl.) Schltr.
CULTURE Temp. Winter min. 12°C. A compact pot plant which may form large clumps. Requires moderate shade and humidity with less water given when growth is complete. A general epiphyte mix is suitable.

Osmoglossum pulchellum (Batem. ex Lindl.) Schltr. [Colour Plate]

An erect epiphyte often growing to form large clumps. **Pseudobulbs** clustered, ovoid to ovoid-ellipsoid, compressed, ancipitous, 6–10 cm long, 3–4 cm wide, 2-leaved at the apex, subtended by several distichous, membranous, imbricate sheaths. **Leaves** coriaceous, erect-spreading, linear-ligulate, acute, 10–35 cm long, 0.8–1.4 cm wide. **Inflorescences** erect, 12–50 cm long, simple, laxly 3- to 10-flowered; bracts triangular-lanceolate, acuminate, 8–13 mm long. **Flowers** non-resupinate, fleshy, white with a yellow callus spotted with red, fragrant; pedicel and ovary 1.2–1.5 cm long, bent in middle. **Dorsal sepal** obovate or elliptic-ovate, shortly acuminate, 1–2 cm long, 0.6–1.3 cm wide; **lateral sepals** united in basal part, ovate to lanceolate, acuminate, 1–2 cm long, 0.5–1 cm wide. **Petals** obovate to suborbicular-obovate, obtuse or apiculate, 1.3–2 cm long, 0.7–1.5 cm wide, with undulate margins. **Lip** strongly recurved, uppermost in flower, panduriform, obtuse, 1–1.8 cm long, 0.8–11 cm wide, with undulate-crisped margins; callus fleshy, 3-ridged in basal half, bilobed at apex. **Column** very fleshy, stout, 4–5 mm long; wings trilobate.
DISTRIBUTION Mexico, Guatemala and El Salvador; common in montane forests up to 2600 m.
HISTORY Introduced into cultivation by James Bateman from Guatemala where it was probably discovered by George Ure Skinner. It was described as *Odontoglossum pulchellum* by John Lindley in 1841 in the *Botanical Register* (t. 48). Rudolf Schlechter transferred it to the present genus in 1916 in the journal *Orchis* (p. 164).
SYNONYM *Odontoglossum pulchellum* Batem. ex Lindl.
CLOSELY RELATED SPECIES *O. egertonii* (Lindl.) Schltr. differs in having a zigzag rhachis, a lip that is as wide in the apical half as in the basal half, and lateral sepals that are united above the middle; *O. convallarioides* Schltr. has a flat rather than a recurved lip and a column with more or less entire wings.

Otochilus Lindl.
Subfamily Epidendroideae
Tribe Coelogyneae
Subtribe Coelogyninae

Epiphytic herbs with a creeping habit. **Pseudobulbs** each arising from the apex or near the apex of the previous pseudobulb, cylindric, fleshy, 2-leaved at apex. **Leaves** plicate, thin-textured, shortly petiolate. **Inflorescence** racemose, arising between the apical leaves in the young shoot, laxly few- to many-flowered, arcuate. **Flowers** similar to *Coelogyne* but smaller. **Sepals** and **petals** subequal, free, narrow, spreading. **Lip** sessile at base of column, saccate at base, 3-lobed, with or without callus ridges; side lobes erect, auriculate; mid-lobe tongue-shaped, elongate. **Column** elongate, erect, semiterete, wingless, clavate above; anther subterminal, operculate; pollinia 4, waxy, ovoid, paired.
DISTRIBUTION About four species in the Himalayas, China, Burma and Thailand.
DERIVATION OF NAME From the Greek *otos* (ear) and *cheilos* (lip).
TAXONOMY *Otochilus* was described by John Lindley in 1830 in his *Genera and Species of Orchidaceous Plants* (p. 35) based on three species collected in Nepal and E. India by Dr N. Wallich. It is most closely allied to *Coelogyne* in its floral structure but is distinguished by its column which lacks a margin, its subterminal dehiscent anther and the different column structure. Vegetatively it closely resembles some species of *Pholidota* but its flowers are quite distinct.
    A key to the species is given by Seidenfaden (1986) in *Opera Botanica* (p. 90).
TYPE SPECIES *O. albus* Lindl.; *O. fuscus* Lindl.; *O. porrectus* Lindl.
SYNONYMS *Broughtonia* Lindl. non R. Br.; *Tetrapeltis* Lindl.
CULTURE Compost A. Temp. Winter min. 12–15°C. As for *Coelogyne*. Although the plants may be grown in pots with some support for the chains of pseudobulbs, they are perhaps better grown up a slab of fern-fibre or cork. They require humid, shady conditions with careful watering throughout the year.

Otochilus porrectus Lindl. [Colour Plate]
Pseudobulbs each arising from the apex of the previous one, subcylindric, elongate-fusiform or clavate, 3–10 cm long, up to 1.3 cm broad. **Leaves** elliptic-lanceolate or oblong-lanceolate, long-petiolate, 12–25 cm long, 3.6–6.5 cm broad; petiole narrow, 2–3.5 cm long. **Inflorescences** decurved; bracts linear, broad, acute, caducous. **Flowers** white or pale flesh-

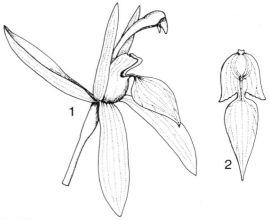

Otochilus porrectus
1 – Flower in side view (× 2)
2 – Lip flattened, from above (× 2)

coloured, ± with pale brown markings. **Sepals** linear-oblong, acute, 0.8–1.8 cm long, 0.2–0.35 cm broad. **Petals** linear, acute, similar in size to sepals. **Lip** 3-lobed. linear-lanceolate, acute, up to 1.5 cm long, 0.3–0.5 cm broad; side lobes erect, falcate, obtuse, much shorter than mid-lobe; mid-lobe lanceolate to elliptic, acute; callus of 3 keels. **Column** slender, dilated above, 1.6 cm long; pollinia globose.
DISTRIBUTION Subtropical Himalayas from Nepal eastwards, India (the Khasia Hills and Manipur), Burma, Thailand and S.W. China (Yunnan); 800–2700 m altitude.
HISTORY Discovered at Pundua in India by Dr N. Wallich and described by John Lindley in 1830 in his *Genera and Species of Orchidaceous Plants* (p. 36).
SYNONYMS *Otochilus latifolius* Griff.; *Coelogyne porrecta* (Lindl.) Rchb.f.; *Tetrapeltis fragrans* Wall. ex Lindl.

Otoglossum (Schltr.) Garay & Dunsterville
Subfamily Epidendroideae
Tribe Oncidieae

Medium-sized to large epiphytic herbs. **Pseudobulbs** well-spaced on creeping rhizome, 1- or 2-leaved. **Leaves** fleshy. **Inflorescence** elongate, erect, racemose, longly pedunculate. **Flowers** commonly clustered, showy. **Sepals** and **petals** subsimilar, spreading. **Lip** deflexed, pandurate, replicate at the base and adnate to the column-foot. **Column** small, cucullate at apex, auriculate, produced at the bases into an obliquely decurved foot, forming an obtuse mentum with the ovary; pollinia 2, attached to a small viscidium by a subquadrate stipe.
DISTRIBUTION Some seven species in Central and S. America; mostly confined to

montane forests from Costa Rica south to Peru.

DERIVATION OF NAME From the Greek *otos* (ear), and *glossa* (tongue or lip), in reference to the auriculate side lobes of the lip of the type species.

TAXONOMY Rudolf Schlechter established *Odontoglossum* sect. *Otoglossum* for *O. hoppii* and related species in *Fedde, Repertorium Specierum Novarum, Beihefte* (p. 107) in 1924 remarking that the species of this section differ from other *Odontoglossum* species in their growth habit, the shape of their flowers and in lip and column structure. In reviewing the generic limits in the Oncidieae, L. Garay and G. Dunsterville in 1976 in *Venezuelan Orchids Illustrated*, vol. 6 (p. 41) have concluded that Schlechter's section warrants recognition at the generic level. *Otoglossum* is characterised by the deflexed lip with its replicate base firmly attached to the obliquely descending column-foot, the cucullate-auriculate clinandrium and the obtuse mentum formed by the ovary and the column-foot.

TYPE SPECIES *Odontoglossum hoppii* Schltr. [= *Otoglossum hoppii* (Schltr.) Garay & Dunsterville].

SYNONYM *Odontoglossum* sect. *Otoglossum* Schltr.

CULTURE As for higher altitude *Odontoglossum* species.

Otoglossum brevifolium (Lindl.) Garay & Dunsterville [Colour Plate]

A large, stout, variable, terrestrial or epiphytic plant with a stout creeping rhizome. **Pseudobulbs** more or less spaced, ovoid to cylindric-ovoid, compressed, 4–11 cm long, 1-leafed at apex, subtended by 2 pairs of imbricating ± leaf-bearing sheaths. **Leaves** oval to elliptic-oblong, coriaceous, 10–30 cm long, up to 9 cm broad, retuse or subacute at apex. **Inflorescence** stout, erect or rarely nodding above, 3- to many-flowered, racemose, up to 60 cm long. **Flowers** large and showy; sepals and petals chestnut-brown, edged with yellow; lip yellow with a brown transverse band in centre. **Dorsal sepal** obovate or oblong-obovate, 1.6–3 cm long, 1–2 cm broad, obtuse or retuse at apex; **lateral sepals** obovate-oblong, slightly oblique, up to 3.2 cm long, 1.8 cm broad. **Petals** obovate or elliptic-oblong, up to 3 cm long, 2 cm broad, obtuse or retuse at apex. **Lip** 3-lobed at base, 1.7–2.5 cm long, basal part parallel to column; side lobes small, erect or spreading, semiovate, rounded at apex; mid-lobe cuneate to spathulate, ± 2-lobed at apex; disc with a small fleshy ridge with a retuse callus in front and a fleshy callus at the base of each side lobe. **Column** short, stout, 0.8 cm high with a rounded wing on each side and a denticulate apex.

DISTRIBUTION Colombia, Peru and Ecuador; up to 3000 m altitude.

HISTORY This species was originally described by John Lindley in 1844 as *Odontoglossum brevifolium* in G. Bentham's *Plantae Hartwegianae* (p. 152) based on a collection of Th. Hartweg from near Loxa (Loja) in Ecuador. Recently, L. Garay and G. Dunsterville have transferred it to *Otoglossum* in *Venezuelan Orchids Illustrated*, vol. 6 (p. 41).

At various times, both *O. coronarium* (Lindl.) Garay & Dunsterville and *O. chiriquense* (Rchb.f.) Garay & Dunsterville have been considered conspecific but, in our opinion, these are certainly distinct having much larger flowers, the latter with with well-spotted sepals and petals.

SYNONYMS *Odontoglossum brevifolium* Lindl.; *O. brachypterum* Rchb.f.

Pabstia Garay

Subfamily Epidendroideae
Tribe Maxillarieae
Subtribe Zygopetalinae

Medium-sized epiphytic herbs. **Pseudobulbs** elongate-ovoid, 2-leaved. **Leaves** broadly lanceolate. **Inflorescences** as long as the leaves, 2- to 3-flowered. **Flowers** large, showy. **Sepals** and **petals** subsimilar, free; petals often distinctly coloured. **Lip** shorter than other segments, entire or 3-lobed, shortly clawed; callus basal, fleshy with several longitudinal grooves. **Column** stoutish, bent towards the apex, hairy in front; pollinia 4, waxy; stipe oblong-obovate, membranaceous with a central raised line, narrowing to a point where the viscidium usually is.

DISTRIBUTION A small genus of about five species in tropical Brazil.

DERIVATION OF NAME Named in honour of Dr Guido Pabst, co-author of Pabst and Dungs's *Orchidaceae Brasilienses* (1975–77) and numerous other articles on Brazilian orchids.

TAXONOMY The name *Colax* was originally given in 1825 by John Lindley in the *Botanical Register* (t. 897) to a genus which proved synonymous with *Bifrenaria*. He later in 1843 in the same journal (misc. p. 50) used the same name for a different group of species. Unfortunately, although Lindley realised what he was doing, the latter name is now treated as an invalid later homonym under the rules of *International Code of Botanical Nomenclature*. This situation was rectified by L. Garay in 1973 in *Bradea* (p. 306) when he renamed the genus *Pabstia*.

John Lindley originally placed three species previously referred to *Maxillaria* in *Colax* on the basis of their peculiar pollinary appendage. The genus is closely allied to *Zygopetalum* as is shown by their various intergeneric hybrids. It differs from that genus in having a distinctly clawed or long-obovate lip, in lacking a flabellate or horseshoe-shaped crest on the lip and in its globose or subglobose pollinia borne on an oblong-obovate stipe.

TYPE SPECIES *Maxillaria viridis* Lindl. (lectotype) [= *Pabstia viridis* (Lindl.) Garay].

CULTURE Compost A. Temp. Winter min. 12–15°C. As for *Zygopetalum*. The plants should have humid, shady conditions while growing with plenty of water. When the pseudobulbs are fully formed, much less water should be given.

Pabstia jugosa (Lindl.) Garay [Colour Plate]

A medium-sized epiphytic or lithophytic plant. **Pseudobulbs** clustered, narrowly ovoid or ovoid-oblong, compressed, ancipitous, slightly sulcate, 5–7 cm long, 2–3 cm broad, 2-leaved at apex. **Leaves** subcoriaceous, elongate-lanceolate, shortly acuminate, long-attenuate below, 15–25 cm long, 3–5 cm broad. **Inflorescence** erect, laxly 2- to 4-flowered, 12–20 cm long; bracts oblong-lanceolate, long-acuminate. **Flowers** large, showy, rather fleshy, subglobose; sepals ivory-white; petals greenish-white covered with deep purple marmorations; lip white, blotched and spotted rose-purple; column white, spotted purple above. **Sepals** spreading, broadly oblong, obtuse, 2.9–3.1 cm long, 1.3–1.7 cm broad; mentum short. **Petals** erect-spreading, narrowly oblong-obovate, obtuse or rounded at the apex, 2.6–2.8 cm long, 1.4–1.6 cm broad. **Lip** narrowly clawed, obovate-oblong in outline, deeply 3-lobed, 2.5 cm long, 1.2–1.3 cm broad; side lobes small, erect; mid-lobe semicircular, rounded at the apex; disc 4-sulcate to the middle, slightly puberulent at the base. **Column** stout, clavate, 1.3 cm long,

DISTRIBUTION Brazil.

HISTORY Introduced into cultivation in 1840 from Rio de Janeiro Province by Messrs Loddiges, it was originally described by John Lindley in 1841 in the *Botanical Register* (misc. p. 51) as *Maxillaria jugosa*, but he transferred it to the genus *Colax* as one of the type species in 1843 in the same journal. Unfortunately, Lindley had already established *Colax* based on another type species in the *Botanical Register* in 1825. *Colax* (1843) is therefore a later homonym, this being recognised by L. Garay in 1973 who proposed the new generic name *Pabstia* for it in *Bradea* (p. 307).

SYNONYMS *Maxillaria jugosa* Lindl.; *Colax jugosus* (Lindl.) Lindl.; *Lycaste jugosa* (Lindl.) Nichols; *Zygopetalum jugosum* (Lindl.) Schltr.

Palumbina Rchb.f.
Subfamily Epidendroideae
Tribe Oncidieae

Small epiphytic plants. **Pseudobulbs** small, 1-leafed. **Leaf** narrow, subcoriaceous-flexuose. **Inflorescences** basal, racemose, few-flowered. **Flowers** small, pretty. **Dorsal sepal** free, erect; **lateral sepals** united to the apex, lamina elliptic. **Petals** spreading, free. **Lip** entire. sessile, deflexed; callus basal, fleshy, bilobulate. **Column** short, winged at the apex; pollinia 4, oblong-pyriform.

DISTRIBUTION   One species only, endemic to Guatemala.

DERIVATION OF NAME   From the Latin *palumbina* (belonging to a dove), probably in reference to the white flowers, white being a colour associated with the dove.

TAXONOMY   H.G. Reichenbach described *Palumbina* in 1863 in *Walpers, Annales Botanices* (p. 699). It is a monotypic genus and some botanists consider that it should be included in *Oncidium* as the only distinguishing character is that the lateral sepals of the former are totally united whereas in *Oncidium* they are free or only partially united.

TYPE SPECIES   *P. candida* (Lindl.) Rchb.f.

CULTURE   Compost A. Temp. Winter min. 12°C. *Palumbina candida* grows well in small pots or pans under conditions of moderate shade and good humidity. While growing, the plants require plenty of water with less being given after the pseudobulbs are fully formed.

Palumbina candida (Lindl.) Rchb.f.
[Colour Plate]

A small epiphytic plant, up to 40 cm or more tall. **Pseudobulbs** oblong-ellipsoidal, compressed, up to 4.5 cm long, 1.5–2 cm across, 1-leafed at apex. **Leaf** linear-lanceolate, acute or acuminate, subcoriaceous, flexuose, 10–30 cm long, 1–1.5 cm broad. **Inflorescence** erect or spreading, racemose, few-flowered; bracts minute, triangular, acute, scarious, up to 0.1 cm long. **Flowers** fleshy; segments spreading, pure white, spotted purple at base of segments; callus yellow, spotted with red. **Dorsal sepal** erect, elliptic or oblong-elliptic, rounded, 1 cm long, 0.5 cm broad; **lateral sepals** united to form an elliptic lamina, bifid at the apex, 0.9–1 cm long, 0.5 cm broad. **Petals** obovate, rounded or emarginate, 1–1.1 cm long, 0.7 cm broad. **Lip** ovate-elliptic, obtuse or rounded, convex, 1.4–1.6 cm long, 0.8 cm broad; callus basal, tuberculate. **Column** short, with subquadrate, erose wings, 0.4 cm long.

DISTRIBUTION   Guatemala.

HISTORY   Originally collected by Theodore Hartweg in Guatemala in 1840 and described

by John Lindley in 1843 as *Oncidium candidum* in the *Botanical Register* (misc. no. 76). H.G. Reichenbach based the monotypic genus *Palumbina* on Lindley's species in 1863 in *Walpers, Annales Botanices* (p. 699).

SYNONYM   *Oncidium candidum* Lindl.

Panisea Lindl.
Subfamily Epidendroideae
Tribe Coelogyneae
Subtribe Coelogyninae

Small sympodial epiphytes or lithophytes with a branching short rhizome. **Pseudobulbs** 1-noded, ovoid or obliquely ovoid, 1- or 2-leaved at the apex. **Leaves** narrowly elliptic to linear, petiolate. **Inflorescences** produced before the developing pseudobulbs (synanthous or proteranthous respectively), after it has developed (hysteranthous) or on a separate shoot (heteranthous), unbranched, 1- to several-flowered. **Flowers** small to medium-sized, white, greenish-white, yellowish-white or apricot-coloured. **Sepals** and **petals** free, subsimilar. **Lip** entire or 3-lobed, with a sigmoid curve at the base; with or without a callus. **Column** slender, incurved, hooded at the apex, with a short foot; pollinia 4, waxy, superposed.

DISTRIBUTION   A small genus of seven species from the Himalayas of Nepal and N.E. India to Indo-China.

DERIVATION OF NAME   From the Greek *pan* (all) and *isos* (equal), in reference to the similarity of the sepals and petals.

TAXONOMY   Lindley (1830) treated *Panisea* as a section of *Coelogyne* in his *Genera and Species of Orchidaceous Plants* (p. 44). Steudel raised it to generic level in 1841 in the second edition of his *Nomenclator botanicus* (p. 265).

Panisea is closely allied to *Coelogyne* but differs in its conduplicate foliar leaves, 1- to few-flowered inflorescences, subsimilar sepals and petals and the lip which is sigmoidly bent at the base and entire or with very small side lobes. The genus has recently been revised by Ingelise Lund (1987) in the *Nordic Journal of Botany* (p. 511).

TYPE SPECIES   *Coelogyne uniflora* Lindl.

CULTURE   Temp. Winter min. 12°C. May be grown in pans of epiphyte mix, or mounted, because of their spreading habit. Give moderate shade and humidity, with less water when growth is complete.

Panisea uniflora (Lindl.) Lindl.
[Colour Plate]

A small epiphyte or lithophyte. **Pseudobulbs** narrowly ovoid or ovoid, 1.7–3.5 cm long, 0.4–1.5 cm in diameter, 2-leaved at the apex.

Leaves linear, acute, 7–15.5 cm long, 0.5–1.2 cm wide. **Inflorescences** proto- or heteranthous, erect, 3–4 cm long, 1- or rarely 2-flowered; bracts ovate or obovate, acuminate, 7–9 mm long. **Flowers** pale apricot with a darker lip; pedicel and ovary 8–16 mm long. **Sepals** lanceolate, acuminate, not spreading widely, 1.4–2.1 cm long, 0.3–0.8 cm wide. **Petals** lanceolate-elliptic, acuminate, 1.2–1.8 cm long, 0.2–0.7 cm wide. **Lip** obscurely 3-lobed in the basal half, narrowly obovate, obtuse, 1.2–2.2 cm long, 0.4–1 cm wide; side lobes short, falcate, 2 mm long, 1 mm wide; callus of 2 obscure thickenings on lateral veins in the middle of the lip. **Column** arcuate, 0.7–1.1 cm long, with blunt shallow triangular wings towards the apex; foot 2 mm long.

DISTRIBUTION   Nepal, India and Burma to Thailand, Laos and Vietnam; in humid forest on trees and limestone rock; 500–1500 m.

HISTORY   Lindley described this species in 1830 in his *Genera and Species of Orchidaceous Plants* (p. 42) as *Coelogyne uniflora* based on a Wallich collection from Nepal. He transferred it to the present genus 10 years later in *Folia Orchidacea* (*Panisea*, p. 2).

SYNONYMS   *Coelogyne uniflora* Lindl.; *C. thuniana* Rchb.f.; *C. biflora* Rchb.f.; *C. falcata* Hook.f.

Paphinia Lindl.
Subfamily Epidendroideae
Tribe Gongoreae
Subtribe Stanhopeinae

Medium-sized epiphytic plants with leafy pseudobulbs. **Pseudobulbs** usually small, ovoid, 2- or more-leaved. **Leaves** membranaceous, plicate. **Inflorescences** pendent or rarely erect, few-flowered, 1 or more produced at base of the pseudobulb. **Flowers** showy. **Sepals** and **petals** subsimilar; petals slightly smaller. **Lip** smaller than other segments, unguiculate, 3-lobed, variously crested with glandular hairs and fleshy calli: side lobes oblong, porrect: mid-lobe obliquely triangular to sagittate. **Column** clavate, semiterete, auriculate at the apex, produced into a foot at the base; anther subterminal; pollina 4, obovate, with a long stipe; viscidium roundish.

DISTRIBUTION   About five species in northern S. America north to Guatemala.

DERIVATION OF NAME   Paphia is the Cypriot name for Aphrodite, for whom the city of Paphos is also named.

TAXONOMY   *Paphinia* was described by John Lindley in 1843 in the *Botanical Register* (misc. p. 14). It is allied to *Houlletia* but may be distinguished by its 2- or more-leaved pseudobulbs. From *Lacaena* it may be distinguished by

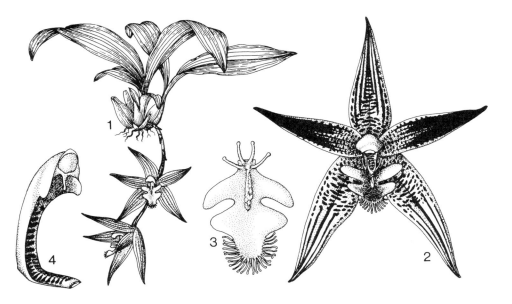

Paphinia cristata
1 – Habit (× ¼)   3 – Lip (× 1⅓)
2 – Flower (× ⅔)   4 – Column and column-foot (× 1⅓)

the slender claw and oblong-falcate, acute side lobes to the lip.

The type species was originally described in *Maxillaria* but was removed because of its very different pollinary apparatus.

TYPE SPECIES   *P. cristata* (Lindl.) Lindl.
CULTURE   Compost A. Temp. Winter min. 15°C. *Paphinia* species are best grown in small pans under humid and shady conditions. During active growth, the compost should be kept moist but when the pseudobulbs are fully grown much less water is required.

Paphinia cristata (Lindl.) Lindl.
[Colour Plate]
A medium-sized epiphytic plant. **Pseudobulbs** tufted, elongate-ovoid, sulcate, somewhat compressed, up to 5 cm long, 1.5–2.5 cm across, 2-leaved at apex. **Leaves** membranaceous, soft-textured, broadly lanceolate to elliptic-lanceolate, acute, plicate, 15–25 cm long, 2.5–4.5 cm broad. **Inflorescence** pendent, slender, 1- to 3-flowered, 5–10 cm long. **Flowers** large and showy, 8 cm or more across; sepals white with red stripes; lip purple with white teeth on the green claw; column greenish with a yellowish apex. **Sepals** and **petals** rather fleshy, broadly lanceolate, acute, 4–5 cm long, 1–1.5 cm broad. **Lip** fleshy, up to 2 cm long, 1.8 cm broad, 3-lobed, sparsely setulose at base; side lobes erect, linear-falcate, acute; mid-lobe ovate to hastate, acute, marginally cristate-fimbriate or coarsely ciliate; callus fleshy, lacinate. **Col-**

umn 2–3 cm long, with 2 apical wings; foot 0.7–0.8 cm long.
DISTRIBUTION   Columbia, Venezuela, Guyana, Surinam, French Guiana and Trinidad.
HISTORY   Originally described by John Lindley in the *Botanical Register* (t. 1811) in 1836 as *Maxillaria cristata* based on a plant from Trinidad cultivated by Mr Knight of the King's Road Nursery, Chelsea. Lindley transferred it later to *Paphinia* in the *Botanical Register* (misc. p. 14) in 1843.
SYNONYMS   *Maxillaria cristata* Lindl.; *Lycaste cristata* (Lindl.) Benth.

Paphiopedilum Pfitz.
Subfamily Cypripedioideae

Terrestrial or occasionally epiphytic sympodial herbs mostly under 50 cm tall with thick, horizontal, spreading roots borne at the base of the plant. **Leaves** conduplicate, ovate, elliptic or ligulate, distichous, 2 to several, coriaceous, green or green mottled with light green above or purple markings beneath, acute to obtuse, often minutely 2-lobed or 3-lobed at apex. **Inflorescence** terminal, terete. **Flowers** 1 to several per inflorescence, waxy in appearance. **Dorsal sepal** erect, large; **lateral sepals** united to form a synsepalum. **Petals** spreading, horizontal or pendent. **Lip** saccate, pouch forming ± half the total length; side lobes incurved, ±

auriculate. **Column** horizontal, short with a fleshy staminode at apex in front of 2 fertile ventral anthers; pollinia 2, glutinous; stigma large, ventral, fleshy, borne on a short stalk, ± hidden by side lobes of lip.
DISTRIBUTION   About 65 species in India, Burma, S.E. Asia, S.W. China, Indonesia, New Guinea, the Solomon Islands (Bougainville and Guadalcanal) and the Philippines.
DERIVATION OF NAME   These orchids are popularly called Lady's or Venus's slipper orchids due to the slipper-shaped lip. The generic name has the same meaning, Paphos being a city on Cyprus with a temple dedicated to Venus and *pedilum* being the Greek for slipper. This derivation is similar to that of the name *Cypripedium* (Cyprus being an island dedicated to Venus and *pedium* being a corruption of *pedilum*). Species of the genus *Paphiopedium* are often erroneously called *Cypripedium* by horticulturists. *Cypripedium* is correctly used only for the deciduous species of slipper orchids from northern temperate zones.
TAXONOMY   E. Pfitzer described *Paphiopedilum* in *Morphologische Studien über die Orchideenblüthe* (p. 11) in 1886. The genus has been divided into three subgenera which form more or less natural groupings by Pfitzer in A. Engler's *Das Pflanzenreich* (1903).

Paphiopedilum is closely related to the three other genera of slipper orchids. *Cypripedium*, *Selenipedium* and *Phragmipedium*. Indeed, they have all been treated in one genus *Cypripedium* in the past.

The following key (after R.A. Rolfe in *Orchid Review*, 1896) may be used to separate the genera:

1. Leaves plicate, alternate; rhizome prominent; leafy shoots with conspicuous internodes.
   (a) Leafy shoots often branching; inflorescences of numerous small flowers having trilocular ovaries; up to 5 m tall; Central and S. America.
                    Selenipedium (3 species)
   (b) Leafy shoots never branching; inflorescence of a few relatively large flowers with unilocular ovaries; up to 1 m tall; temperate and subtropical America, Europe and Asia.
                    Cypripedium (about 40 species)
2. Leaves conduplicate, distichous; rhizome present but condensed; leafy shoots without conspicuous internodes; often with lengthy inflorescence axes.
   (a) Sepals imbricate in bud; unilocular ovaries; S.E. Asia.
                    Paphiopedilum (about 65 species)
   (b) Sepals valvate in bud; trilocular ovaries; Central and S. America.
                    Phragmipedium (about 12 species)

Many species are variable in such characters as colour and size of floral parts and this has led to some species being redescribed many times from minor variants and often from a single plant in a population. Thus, many names still used horticulturally are either synonyms or invalidly used. Many critical species have been discussed and illustrated in colour in recent issues of the *Orchid Digest*, notably by J.A. Fowlie, and in the *Orchid Review* by M.W. Wood. The genus has received considerable interest in recent years particularly as a number of spectacular new species have been introduced into cultivation. The revisions by Karasawa (1982) and by Cribb (1987), both entitled *The Genus Paphiopedilum* are recommended. Lance Birk's (1983) *The Paphiopedilum Grower's Manual* also contains much of interest for growers.

Several naturally occurring hybrids are known to occur in the genus *Paphiopedilum* and quite spectacular plants are often produced by hybridisation. Several natural hybrids have been described as new species before their hybrid nature was discovered. Some of the better known ones are:

P. × siamense	= callosum × appletonianum
P. × kimballianum	= rothschildianum × dayanum
P. × frankeanum	= superbiens [curtisii] × tonsum
P. × littleanum	= dayanum × lawrenceanum
P. × nitens	= villosum × insigne
P. × shipwayae	= hookerae × dayanum

TYPE SPECIES *P. insigne* (Lindl.) Pfitz. typ. cons.

CULTURE Compost A. Temp. Winter min. 10–15°C depending on species. *Paphiopedilum* species fall into two groups: those such as *P. insigne* which require cooler conditions, and those such as *P. callosum* or *P. concolor* which require warmer conditions. All species need constant good humidity and careful shading from direct sunlight. As they have no means of water storage, the plants must never be allowed to become too dry.

Paphiopedilum acmodontum M. Wood
[Colour Plate]

A medium-sized terrestrial plant with a short stem. **Leaves** distichous, elliptic-oblong, acuminate and minutely tridentate at apex, up to 18 cm long, 4 cm broad, upper surfaces tessellated light and dark green, basal margins sparsely ciliate, **Inflorescence** erect, 1-flowered, up to 25 cm long; peduncle sparsely pubescent, green with purple markings; bract ovate, up to 3 cm long, sparsely hirsute, **Flowers** large; dorsal sepal white heavily flushed with pink-purple and lined with purple-green, synsepalum white, lightly flushed purple, lined green and purple; petals greenish-white with a purple apical half, lined dark green, with raised purple spots near margin below; lip pale olive-green; staminode pale green, tinted darker green and purple. **Dorsal sepal** ovate, acuminate, 4 cm long, 3 cm broad; **synsepalum** ovate, acute, 3.2 cm long, 1.5 cm broad. **Petals** oblanceolate, spreading, slightly recurved, rounded and tridentate at apex, up to 4.5 cm long, 1.5 cm broad, inner surface sparsely pubescent, margins sparsely ciliate. **Lip** slipper-shaped, 3-lobed, 4 cm long, 2.3 cm broad, auriculate at base of pouch, apiculate, minutely pubescent. **Staminode** obovate, with proximal margin bifid, distal margin with a short tooth on each side and a longer central tooth, minutely pubescent, 1 cm long, 0.9 cm broad.
DISTRIBUTION Although this species was first referred to by G. Schoser in the *Proceedings of the 6th World Orchid Congress* (1971), it was not validly described until 1976 when Mark Wood described it in the *Orchid Review* (p. 350).

Paphiopedilum appletonianum (Gower) Rolfe
[Colour Plate]

A terrestrial plant, up to 60 cm tall. **Leaves** narrowly elliptic, 21 cm long, 3.5 cm broad, bright green, veined darker and mottled with darker green. **Inflorescence** up to 50 cm long; peduncle brown, pubescent; bract 1.8 cm long, one-third the length of the ovary. **Flower** 8–9 cm tall, 12 cm broad; dorsal sepal green with darker veins, **synsepalum** green; petals bright green at base with small brown spots, apex purple; lip purplish-brown, paler below; staminode green with a paler border. **Dorsal sepal** ovate, 3.5 cm, long, 2.6 cm broad, acute; **synsepalum** ovate-lanceolate, 2.4 cm long, acute. **Petals** ligulate-spathulate, 5 cm long, 1.4 cm broad, widened towards apex, acute, ciliate. **Lip** saccate, 4.5 cm long; side lobes with shiny warts. **Staminode** oblong-obcordate, with a tooth in the ventral sinus.
DISTRIBUTION Hainau, Thailand, Laos and Cambodia; up to 1000 m altitude.
HISTORY This species was first mentioned in 1893 by W.H. Gower in *The Garden* (p. 95) as *Cypripedium appletonianum*, having been introduced earlier that year in a consignment of *P. hookerae*. It flowered in cultivation for the first time for W.M. Appleton of Weston-super-Mare, England. R.A. Rolfe transferred it to the genus *Paphiopedilum* in 1896 in the *Orchid Review* (p. 364). *P. appletonianum* is also grown under the synonym *P. wolterianum* described by F. Kraenzlin in the *Gardeners' Chronicle* (1895) after D. Walter of Magdeburg.
SYNONYMS *Cypripedium appletonianum* Gower; *Paphiopedilum wolterianum* Kraenzl.
CLOSELY RELATED SPECIES *P. appletonianum* is closely related to *P. bullenianum* which has more boldly mottled leaves and a narrower staminode with parallel apical lobes.

Paphiopedilum argus (Rchb.f.) Stein
[Colour Plate]

A terrestrial herb, up to 45 cm tall. **Leaves** elliptic or oblong-elliptic, 16 cm long, 4 cm broad, light green, mottled and veined darker green, ciliate on the margins at the base, apex bifid and minutely serrate. **Inflorescence** up to 40 cm long, 1-flowered; bract up to 4.5 cm long, up to half the length of the ovary. **Flowers** up to 7.5 cm across; dorsal sepal whitish with green stripes, synsepalum paler-veined; petals white with pale green veins, marked with dark purple spots and warts, some ocellated, purple in apical third; lip dull brownish-purple above, pale greenish-brown below, side lobes pale purple, spotted deep purple. **Dorsal sepal** broadly ovate-cordate, 3.5–4.5 cm long, 3.5 cm broad, acuminate, minutely ciliate on margins; **synsepalum** smaller, notched at apex. **Petals** ligulate, deflexed, undulate, 4.5–6.5 cm long, 1–1.5 cm broad, acute, margins ciliate. **Lip** broadly calceiform, 3–4.2 cm long, 2.4 cm broad; side lobes unfolded. **Staminode** nearly horseshoe-shaped with 2 incurved ventral cusps.
DISTRIBUTION The Philippines (Negros and Luzon); on limestone, between 600 and 2000 m altitude.
HISTORY *P. argus* was discovered by Gustav Wallis, one of the collectors for the firm of Veitch & Sons, Exeter, England, on Luzon in 1872. He sent plants to Veitch immediately afterwards and these plants first flowered in April 1873. H.G. Reichenbach described it as *Cyripedium argus* in the same year in the *Gardeners' Chronicle* (p. 608) naming it after Argus, the hundred-eyed beast of Greek mythology, for the eye-like spotting of its petals. B. Stein transferred it to *Paphiopedilum* in 1892 in his *Orchideenbuch* (p. 453).
SYNONYM *Cypripedium argus* Rchb.f.
CLOSELY RELATED SPECIES *P. argus* is related to *P. superbiens* and *P. ciliolare* but has smaller flowers and petals with much bolder spots.

Paphiopedilum armeniacum S.C. Chen & Liu
[Colour Plate]

A terrestrial plant with an elongate rhizome bearing very short leafy stems. **Leaves** distichous, 5–7, oblong, obtuse to acute, 6–15 cm long, 1.8–2.5 cm wide, with serrulate apical margins, checkered dark and paler green above, heavily purple-spotted beneath. **Inflorescence** terminal, erect, 1-flowered; peduncle slender, 20–26 cm tall, green, purple-spotted, hispid; bract lanceolate-ovate, acute, 1–1.5 cm long. **Flower** relatively thin-textured, golden-yellow to pale yellow, red-dotted at base of petals, with red veins on the staminode and purplish spotting inside the lip; pedicel and ovary 3–3.5 cm long, hispid, green. **Dorsal sepal** ovate, subacute, 2.2–4.8 cm long, 1.4–2.5 cm wide; **synsepalum** ovate, obtuse, 2–3.5 cm long, 1.5–2 cm wide. **Petals** elliptic to ovate, obtuse, 2.8–5.5 cm long, 2.5–5.3 cm wide, densely pubescent at base within. **Lip** very inflated, ovoid to sphaerical, 4–5 cm long, 3.5–4.5 cm wide. **Staminode** heart-shaped, convex, 1–2.2 cm long and wide.

DISTRIBUTION Known only from W. Yunnan in China, up to 1800 m.

HISTORY This beautiful orchid caused a sensation when it first appeared in cultivation outside of China in 1984. Its flower colour is unique in the genus. It was first described by the Chinese botanists, S.C. Chen and Liu, in 1982 in the journal *Acta Botanica Yunnanica* (p. 163), based on a specimen collected by Zhang at Bijiang in Yunnan. It is most closely allied to the rare Vietnamese species *P. delenatii*.

Paphiopedilum barbatum (Lindl.) Pfitz.
[Colour Plate]

A terrestrial herb, up to 36 cm tall. **Leaves** narrowly elliptic, thin in texture, 10–20 cm long, 2–3 cm broad, dull green, mottled darker green. **Inflorescence** up to 25 cm tall, 1 (occasionally 2)-flowered; bract 1.5 cm, one-quarter the length of the ovary. **Flowers** up to 8 cm in diameter; dorsal sepal white or pale green marked with 14 longitudinal stripes which are green at base and purple towards apex; petals brownish-green towards base, purple towards apex, upper margin with a few black hairy warts; lip deep brownish-purple, paler below, side lobes purple with small purplish warts and spots; staminode green with purplish markings. **Dorsal sepal** large, suborbicular, up to 4 cm long, margin reflexed towards base; **synsepalum** shorter, 2.1 cm long, narrowly elliptic, obtuse. **Petals** linear-oblong, drooping slightly, almost straight, 4.5 cm long, 1.2 cm broad, widened towards apex, margins ciliate. **Lip** calceiform, about 3.6 cm long, as long as dorsal sepal; side lobes inflexed. **Staminode** horseshoe-shaped with a prominent basal projection at either side.

DISTRIBUTION Malaya and peninsular Thailand; in moist shady valleys in mountains on granite boulders covered with moss, or in mossy places on sandy or peaty ground, 700–1300 m altitude.

HISTORY The species was first discovered by Hugh Cuming on Mt Ophir, Malaya in 1838. Cuming sent living material to Messrs Loddiges who first flowered it in 1841. Thomas Lobb re-collected it in quantity in 1844 and sent a large consignment of living plants to Veitch & Sons of Exeter, England. The Loddiges' plant was described in 1841 by John Lindley in the *Botanical Register* (misc. p. 53) as

Cypripedium barbatum, named for the shiny black warts on the upper margins of the petals which are bearded with black hairs. E. Pfitzer transferred it to *Paphiopedilum* in 1888 in *Pringsheim, Jahrbücher für Wissenschaftliche Botanik* (p. 159).

P. barbatum was one of the parents of the first two artificially produced hybrid paphiopedilums: *P.* Harrisianum which was made by John Dominy in 1869, *P. villosum* being the other parent; and in 1870 *P.* Vexillarium which was a hybrid of *P. barbatum* and *P. fairrieanum*.

SYNONYM *Cypripedium barbatum* Lindl.

CLOSELY RELATED SPECIES *P. barbatum* is closely related to *P. callosum* but it has smaller, darker flowers with scarcely deflexed and straight petals. See also *P. purpuratum*.

Paphiopedilum bellatulum (Rchb.f.) Stein
[Colour Plate]

A small terrestrial herb, up to 10 cm tall (occasionally taller). **Leaves** similar to those of *P. niveum* but rather larger, 17–25 cm long, 7.5–8.5 cm broad, deep green above but sparingly mottled, deep purple-spotted below. **Inflorescence** very short so that the flower touches the leaves; scape deep purple, pubescent, more than half as long as ovary. **Flower** 6–8 cm or more broad, white or pale yellow conspicuously spotted with purple-brown; lip fewer-spotted than other flower parts. **Dorsal sepal** elliptic to orbicular, 2.5 cm long, 4 cm broad, minutely ciliate as are the synsepalum and petals; **synsepalum** broadly ovate, nearly as long as the dorsal sepal but narrower. **Petals** very large, broadly oval-oblong, slightly deflexed, 4.7–6.3 cm long, 3–4.7 cm broad, notched at apex. **Lip** saccate, compressed, 3.5 cm long, 2 cm broad. **Staminode** suborbicular, oblong-elliptic or subcircular, somewhat variable, narrower than in *P. niveum* with small basal teeth.

DISTRIBUTION Burma and Thailand; on wet mossy limestone rocks in shady places, up to 1500 m altitude.

HISTORY *P. bellatulum* was first introduced to Europe by Messrs Low & Co. of Clapton, England in the spring of 1888. H.G. Reichenbach described it the same year in the *Gardeners' Chronicle* (ser. 3, 3: p. 648) as *Cypripedium bellatulum*. Stein transferred it to *Paphiopedilum* in his *Orchideenbuch* (p. 456).

SYNONYM *Cypripedium bellatulum* Rchb.f.

CLOSELY RELATED SPECIES *P. bellatulum* is closely related to *P. godefroyae* and *P. niveum*. Postulated hybrids with intermediate coloration, flower and staminode shapes have often been cultivated and further study may reveal that the three species are merely variants of one widespread species.

Paphiopedilum bullenianum (Rchb.f.) Pfitz.
[Colour Plate]

A terrestrial herb, up to 38 cm tall. **Leaves** elliptic to narrowly elliptic, 15 cm long, 3 cm broad, light bluish-green, faintly mottled darker green. **Inflorescence** up to 30 cm long, 1-flowered; bract 1.5 cm long, one-quarter length of ovary. **Flower** up to 7 cm in diameter; dorsal sepal pale green with a darker central band; petals greenish, 3–4 small black warts on each margin, apex with a central purple flush, apical margin pale yellow; lip purplish-red. **Dorsal sepal** ovate, 2.4–3.5 cm long, 1.4–2.1 cm broad, margins reflexed towards base; **synsepalum** shorter and narrower than dorsal sepal. **Petals** spreading horizontally with widened ends somewhat drooping, 4–5 cm long, 0.9–1.5 cm broad. **Lip** saccate, 3–4 cm long, 1.7 cm broad; inflexed side lobes with large warts. **Staminode** ovate, deeply indented dorsally, bifid at apex, the lobes parallel.

DISTRIBUTION N. Borneo, Sumatra, Malaya, probably other Indonesian islands such as Sulawesi.

HISTORY Hugh Low collected the type specimen in N. Borneo whilst collecting there for the firm of Messrs H. Low & Co. When it flowered, they sent it to H.G. Reichenbach who described it in 1865 in the *Botanische Zeitung* (p. 99) as *Cypripedium bullenianum*. E. Pfitzer transferred it in 1894 to *Paphiopedilum* in A. Engler's *Botanische Jahrbücher* (p. 40).

SYNONYMS *Cypripedium bullenianum* Rchb.f.; *Paphiopedilum amabile* Hall.

CLOSELY RELATED SPECIES *P. bullenianum* closely resembles *P. appletonianum* but it has more heavily mottled leaves and a deeply indented staminode. In *P. appletonianum* the petals are purple at the apex not just centrally.

Paphiopedilum callosum (Rchb.f.) Stein
[Colour Plate]

A terrestrial herb, up to 45 cm tall. **Leaves** elliptic, up to 25 cm long, 5 cm broad, pale green with a few darker mottlings above, equally 2-lobed at apex. **Inflorescence** up to 38 cm long, 1 (occasionally 2)-flowered; peduncle dark purple, pubescent; bracts 2.2 cm long, one-third length of ovary. **Flowers** showy; dorsal sepal white, lined dark green at base, purple-shaded and lined above; petals green, lined darker green with apical third rose-purple, upper margin with black warts; lip dark bronze, side lobes green with large black warts. **Dorsal sepal** ovate to cordate, 4–5.5 cm long, 4–6 cm broad, margins recurved above the centre; **synsepalum** ovate to lanceolate, 2.6–3.5 cm long, acute. **Petals** ligulate, somewhat sigmoid, spreading at 45° below horizontal, 4.6–6.8 cm long, 1–1.8 cm broad, margins long-ciliate. **Lip** helmet-shaped, 3–4.7 cm long,

2.2 cm broad. **Staminode** horseshoe-shaped, deeply cleft on dorsal side; ventral side lobes cusped with a projecting tooth between them.
DISTRIBUTION Thailand and Indo-China; at low altitudes up to 1300 m.
HISTORY *P. callosum* was discovered in Thailand or in Indo-China by Alexandre Regnier of Paris and was introduced by him into cultivation in 1885. H.G. Reichenbach described it as *Cypripedium callosum* in the *Gardeners' Chronicle* (ser. 2, 26: p. 326) in 1886. B. Stein transferred it in 1892 to *Paphiopedilum* in his *Orchideenbuch* (p. 457).
SYNONYM *Cypripedium callosum* Rchb.f.
CLOSELY RELATED SPECIES *P. callosum* may be distinguished from *P. barbatum* by its ovate, acute synsepalum, sigmoid petals and its much larger flower. *P. lawrenceanum* differs in having black warts on both upper and lower margins.

Paphiopedilum charlesworthii (Rolfe) Pfitz.
[Colour Plate]
A terrestrial herb, up to 25 cm tall. **Leaves** linear, up to 25 cm long, 2.5 cm broad, glossy green, purple mottled at base and beneath. **Inflorescence** up to 15 cm long; peduncle pubescent; bract 2.6 cm long, two-thirds the length of the ovary. **Flower** with dorsal sepal white, veined and flushed pink to carmine-purple; petals and lip chestnut-brown; staminode shining white. **Dorsal sepal** broadly ovate, 4.4–5.7 cm long, 4.7–6.6 cm broad; **synsepalum** 3.3–4 cm long. **Petals** narrowly spathulate, 4–5 cm long, 1–1.7 cm broad, margins ciliate. **Lip** rather shallowly cupped, 3.5–4.3 cm long. **Staminode** ovate but slightly concave on dorsal and ventral margins, with a small central wart.
DISTRIBUTION Burma and India (E. Assam); up to at about 1600 m altitude, on isolated peaks.
HISTORY First discovered by R. Moore in 1893 about 25 miles S.W. of Lake Inle, Burma. It was introduced into cultivation the same year. R.A. Rolfe (1893) named this species in the *Orchid Review* (p. 303) as *Cypripedium charlesworthii* after J. Charlesworth of Keaton, Bradford, who was the first to flower it in the British Isles. E. Pfitzer transferred it the following year to the genus *Paphiopedilum* in A. Engler's *Botanische Jahrbücher* (p. 40).
    This distinctive species is easily recognised by its large pink or carmine-purple veined dorsal sepal.
SYNONYM *Cypripedium charlesworthii* Rolfe

Paphiopedilum ciliolare (Rchb.f.) Stein
[Colour Plate]
A terrestrial herb, up to 45 cm tall. **Leaves** narrowly oblong or elliptic-oblong, 20 or more cm long, 4 cm broad, obtuse, tessellated deep and pale green, **Inflorescence** up to 38 cm long, 1-flowered; scape very pubescent; bract ovate, 1.7 cm long, one-quarter length of ovary. **Flower** up to 10 cm long and broad; dorsal sepal purple at base, rest white with alternating long and short green or purplish veins; synsepalum whitish with green veins; petals with basal two-thirds green, densely spotted with black warts, apex pale purple; lip dull purplish-brown, side lobes pale yellow-green, spotted with purple warts; staminode greenish, stained pale rose. **Dorsal sepal** broadly ovate, 4.5–5 cm long, 3.5–4.5 cm broad, acuminate, margin ciliate; **synsepalum** ovate, much smaller, 2.7 cm long, acuminate. **Petals** ligulate, deflexed and recurved, 5.5–7.2 cm long, 1.5–2.5 cm broad, upper margin with large black warts, both margins with long black hairs. **Lip** deeply saccate, 4.5–6 cm long; side lobes infolded. **Staminode** reniform, dorsally notched, ventrally 3-toothed.
DISTRIBUTION The Philippines (Mindanao, Camiguin, Dinagat and Luzon); 300–1830 m.
HISTORY The first introduction of *P. ciliolare* was made by Messrs Low & Co. of Clapton, London in 1881 and H.G. Reichenbach described it in the same year in the *Gardeners' Chronicle* (n.s. 18: p. 488) as *Cypripedium ciliolare*. The following year Messrs Veitch & Sons received a large importation of it from Mindanao. B. Stein transferred it to *Paphiopedilum* in 1892 in his *Orchideenbuch* (p. 462).
SYNONYM *Cypripedium ciliolare* Rchb.f.
CLOSELY RELATED SPECIES *P. ciliolare* is closely related to the Sumatran species *P. superbiens* but it may be distinguished by its shorter, distinctly coloured dorsal sepal; the denser margin hairs on the petals which are more deeply coloured and reflexed; by the smaller and more deeply coloured lip and by its shorter, broader staminode. See also *P. argus*.

Paphiopedilum concolor (Batem.) Pfitz.
[Colour Plate]
A terrestrial plant, up to 20 cm tall. **Leaves** 5, elliptic, 10–15 cm long, 4–5 cm broad, dark green with paler irregular mottlings, ± spotted deep purple beneath, unequally 2-lobed at apex. **Inflorescence** up to 10 cm long, 1- to 2-flowered (occasionally more); scape dark brown, pubescent; bract ovate, 1–2 cm long, much shorter than ovary. **Flowers** 5–7.5 cm tall, pale yellow, spotted finely with purple; staminode yellow with deep yellow blotch in centre, dotted purple. **Dorsal sepal** ovate, 2.7–3.5 cm long, 2.2–3.3 cm broad, trifid at apex; **synsepalum** similar, 1.9 cm long, slightly smaller. **Petals** broadly elliptic-oblong 3–4.3 cm long, 1.7 cm broad, obtuse, both petals and sepal margins minutely hairy. **Lip** narrowly conical-saccate, compressed, 2.4 cm long, 1.4 cm broad. **Staminode** variable, cordate tridentate at apex.
DISTRIBUTION Burma, Thailand, Laos, N. and S. Vietnam and Kampuchea, S. China; in hollows in limestone rocks, up to 1000 m.
HISTORY *P. concolor* was collected first by the Rev. C. Parish in 1859 near Moulmein in Burma and it was described by James Bateman in the *Botanical Magazine* (t. 5513) in 1865 as *Cypripedium concolor*. E. Pfitzer transferred it in 1888 to *Paphiopedilum* in Engler and Prantl's *Natürliche Planzenfamilien* (p. 84).
SYNONYM *Cypripedium concolor* Batem.
CLOSELY RELATED SPECIES *P. concolor* falls into the same group as *P. niveum, P. bellatulum* and *P. godefroyae* from which it has been distinguished by its usually yellow flower. However, the flowers of some forms of the other species occasionally have a yellowish background. *P. niveum* and *bellatulum* form the opposite ends of a range of variation which encompasses the other two species. *P. niveum* may be distinguished from *concolor* by its broader, more rounded petals, smaller synsepalum, more inflated lip and reniform staminode.

Paphiopedilum delenatii Guillaumin
[Colour Plate]
A terrestrial plant, up to 25 cm tall. **Leaves** narrowly elliptic, 13 cm long, 5 cm broad, light green, mottled and veined dark green, purple-spotted beneath, unequally 2-lobed at apex. **Inflorescence** up to 20 cm tall, 1- or 2-flowered; scape reddish. **Flowers** mostly pink, up to 8 cm across; dorsal sepal white, faintly tinged pink; petals white, tinged pink; staminode pink with a yellow centre and base, darker pink around the yellow area. **Dorsal sepal** ovate, 1.7–3.5 cm long, 1.8–2.5 cm broad, acute; **synsepalum** ovate, 1.9–2.7 cm long, 2 cm broad. **Petals** ovate, 3–4 cm long, 2.4–3.5 cm broad, obtuse, **Lip** saccate, narrowly mouthed, 2.5–3.5 cm long, 1.8–3 cm broad, rounded below. **Staminode** convex, ovate.
DISTRIBUTION N. and Central Vietnam, possibly extinct in the wild.
HISTORY *P. delenatii* was first found in 1913 and was introduced into Europe from Tonkin by M. Delenat. The species was described in 1924 by A. Guillaumin in the *Journal de la Société National d'Horticole, France* (p. 127). A second site was discovered in Central Vietnam in 1922.
CLOSELY RELATED SPECIES This very distinctive species is closely related to the *P. armeniacum,* differing in its smaller pink flowers.

Paphiopedilum druryi (Bedd.) Stein
[Colour Plate]
An erect, terrestrial plant, up to or over 25 cm tall. **Stems** short, clustered, 4- or 5-leaved.

Leaves oblong-ligulate, coriaceous, suberect or spreading, rounded at apex, up to 15 cm long, 3.4 cm broad, mid-green. **Inflorescence** erect, 1-flowered; peduncle purple, terete, subtended by a short, compressed, green sheath, densely glandular-pubescent; bract pale green, pubescent, up to 2 cm long. **Flowers** slightly nodding, about 7.5 cm across, shortly pubescent on outer surface; dorsal sepal pale greenish-yellow with a central, longitudinal, broad deep-maroon stripe, synsepalum very pale greenish with 2 longitudinal purple stripes; petals yellow with a central, longitudinal maroon stripe, spotted purple; lip glossy, dull yellow outside, spotted purple within; staminode dull yellow with a central yolk-yellow spot. **Dorsal sepal** broadly ovate, curved forwards, obtuse, 3–3.8 cm long, 2.5–3.3 cm broad; **synsepalum** ovate-elliptic, subacute, 2.7–3.5 cm long, 2–2.3 cm broad. **Petals** curving forwards and downwards, oblanceolate-oblong, margins undulate in basal half, apex tridentate with ciliate margins, 4–4.5 cm long, 1.3–2 cm broad, with a few maroon hairs at the base. **Lip** 3-lobed, saccate, 3.3–4.5 cm long, 1.2–1.9 cm broad; side lobes obscure, incurved under staminode; mid-lobe inverted helmet-shaped, emarginate. **Staminode** obcordate, 3-toothed at apex, 2-lobed above.

DISTRIBUTION S. India but probably extinct in the wild; 1500–1700 m altitude.

HISTORY Discovered in the Travancore Hills in S. India at an altitude of between 1500 and 1700 m by Col. Drury, and named after him in 1874 as *Cypripedium druryi* by R. Beddome in *Icones Plantarum Indiae Orientalis* (p. 23, t. 112).

The exact source of *P. druryi* remained a mystery for many years until Peter Mammen, using allusions to golden flowers he found in Indian literature, traced it to the hill area of Travancore. He reintroduced it into cultivation in 1968 in some numbers but it remains a rarity in collections.

SYNONYM *Cypripedium druryi* Bedd.

Paphiopedilum emersonii **Koopowitz & Cribb** [Colour Plate]
A terrestrial plant forming large clumps with a short rhizome producing clustered growths with very short leafy stems. **Leaves** oblong, acute to obtuse, 12–25 cm long, 2.5–4 cm wide, dark green above, paler below and often purple-flushed at the base. **Inflorescence** 1-flowered; peduncle up to 15 cm long, whitish, pubescent; bract papery, elliptic, acute, 2–3 cm long. **Flower** large, up to 10 cm across, white, flushed pink at the base of the petals, with a creamy to yellow lip, flushed with pink around the rim and spotted with purple within, and a yellow staminode with red markings; pedicel

and ovary 2.5–3.5 cm long, whitish, densely pubescent. **Dorsal sepal** hooded, curving forwards over the lip, elliptic-ovate, obtuse, 4–4.5 cm long, 3–3.5 cm wide; **synsepalum** elliptic-subcircular, obtuse, 3–3.5 cm long and wide; sepals pubescent on both surfaces. **Petals** slightly deflexed from horizontal, broadly elliptic to subcircular, rounded at apex, 4–5 cm long and wide, pubescent on inner surface towards the base. **Lip** deeply saccate, 3.5 cm long, 3 cm wide, flared at the base, with opaque windows on the surface. **Staminode** convex, trullate, truncate, 2 cm long, 1 cm wide, longitudinally deeply sulcate with groove dilating towards the apex.

DISTRIBUTION Known only from Yunnan Province in China, growing in clayey soils in forest.

HISTORY This beautiful orchid appeared quite unexpectedly in cultivation in California in 1986 and its spectacular large flowers created a sensation. It was described for the first time by Harold Koopowitz and Phillip Cribb in the *Orchid Advocate* journal (p. 86) in late 1986.

Paphiopedilum exul **(Ridley) Rolfe**
[Colour Plate]
A terrestrial herb, up to 40 cm high. **Leaves** linear, suberect, up to 20–33 cm long, 2–4 cm broad, glossy green. **Inflorescence** up to 30 cm long, 1-flowered; scape long-pubescent; bract 4 cm long, almost covering ovary. **Flowers** 6–8 cm broad; dorsal sepal yellow-green with several brown spots towards base and a white margin; synsepalum pale green; petals yellow with purple longitudinal streaks in middle; lip shining ochre-yellow; staminode dull yellow. **Dorsal sepal** broadly ovate, 3–5 cm long, 2.5–3 cm broad, obtuse, keeled and pubescent on outer surface, shiny on inner surface; **synsepalum** as large as dorsal sepal, curving forwards. **Petals** narrowly oblong, curving forwards, slightly broadened towards apex, 4.5–5 cm long, 1.2–1.7 cm broad. **Lip** 3–4.5 cm long, 2 cm broad, ± cylindrically pouched, almost at right-angles to dorsal sepal, prominently auricled. **Staminode** almost round to obcordate, with a small wart in centre.

DISTRIBUTION Peninsular Thailand; like *P. niveum* in rock crevices at low elevations.

HISTORY *P. exul* was first reported by H. Ridley in the *Gardeners' Chronicle* (ser. 3, 10: p. 94) of 1891 as *Cypripedium insigne* var. *exul* and it was raised to specific rank as *C. exul* by James O'Brien in the same journal the following year. The species was introduced into cultivation in 1892 by several firms, notably Messrs F. Sander & Co. in England and by Messrs J. Linden on the Continent. R.A. Rolfe transferred it

to *Paphiopedilum* in 1896 in the *Orchid Review* (p. 364).

SYNONYMS *Cypripedium exul* (Ridley) Rolfe; *C. insigne* var. *exul* Ridley

CLOSELY RELATED SPECIES This species is somewhat similar to *P. insigne* and was first described as a variety of that species. However, *P. insigne* has more prostrate leaves and a more heavily spotted dorsal sepal.

Paphiopedilum fairrieanum **(Lindl.) Stein**
[Colour Plate]
A dwarf herb, up to 27 cm tall. **Leaves** narrowly elliptic to ligulate, 10–15 cm long, 2.5 cm broad, dull green, mid-rib prominent on underside. **Inflorescence** 10–20 cm high, 1-flowered; peduncle covered with purplish hairs. **Flower** 6–7.5 cm long, 4 cm broad; dorsal sepal greenish-white, veins purple, synsepalum pale green, striped with purple; petals similar in colour to dorsal sepal, margin purple; lip brownish-green with purple reticulations, side lobes creamy-white. **Dorsal sepal** ovate, 3.5–8 cm long, 2.4–7 cm broad, 2-lobed at apex, margin undulate-ciliate; **synsepalum** smaller, 2.5–3.5 cm long. **Petals** lanceolate, decurved-sigmoid, with a recurved apex, 4–5 cm long, 0.9–1.5 cm broad, margins undulate, ciliolate. **Lip** cup-shaped with a wide mouth, up to 4 cm long; side lobes infolded. **Staminode** elliptic, 2-lobed ventrally, with a long central extension on the ventral side.

DISTRIBUTION India (Assam, Sikkim) and Bhutan; 1300–2200 m altitude.

HISTORY Introduced into cultivation in 1857. Mr Fairrie of Liverpool was among the first to flower this species. The origin of the species remained obscure until it was rediscovered by G.C. Searight in W. Bhutan over 40 years later. John Lindley described it in 1857 in the *Gardeners' Chronicle* (p. 740) as *Cypripedium fairrieanum* and it was later transferred to *Paphiopedilum* by B. Stein (1892) in the *Orchideenbuch* (p. 467). It is worth noting that the correct spelling of the specific epithet is *fairrieanum* and not *fairieanum* as is commonly seen in the literature.

P. fairrieanum is a most distinctive species.
SYNONYM *Cypripedium fairrieanum* Lindl.

Paphiopedilum glanduliferum **(B.R.) Stein**
A terrestrial herb, up to or over 50 cm tall. **Leaves** narrowly oblong, rather fleshy, up to 30 cm long, 3 cm broad, rounded at apex, green, **Inflorescence** up to 50 cm long, up to 5-flowered; scape finely pubescent; bract lanceolate, up to 4.5 cm long, about half to two-thirds the length of the ovary. **Flowers** up to 10 cm long and broad; dorsal sepal light yellow with dark lines; petals yellow-green with a darker central line; lip pale green, veined darker;

staminode yellow; ovary almost glabrous. **Dorsal sepal** ovate, up to 5.5 cm long, 2 cm broad, acute; **synsepalum** lanceolate, 4–5.5 cm long, acute. **Petals** ribbon-like, twisted, pendent-spreading, up to 12 cm long, 0.5–0.8 cm broad, margins undulate and black warted at base, ciliate. **Lip** slipper-shaped, lacking prominent auricles, similar to that of *P. stonei*, 4.5 cm long, 2 cm broad. **Staminode** oblong, fleshy, noduled on sides, with a short ventral point.

DISTRIBUTION Islands N.W. of New Guinea and W. and Central New Guinea; up to 1700 m.

HISTORY This attractive species, which is somewhat intermediate in character between *P. stonei* and *P. rothschildianum*, was introduced into Europe by the firm of J. Linden in December 1886. However, it was described much earlier in 1848 by C.L. Blume in *Rumphia* (p. 56, tt. 195 & 198) as *Cypripedium glanduliferum*. Stein (1892) transferred it to *Paphiopedilum* in *Orchideenbuch* (p. 481). This species is better known in cultivation under the later name *P. praestans*.

SYNONYMS *Cypripedium glanduliferum* Bl.; *C. praestans* Rchb. f.; *C. glanduliferum* Veitch; *Paphiopedilum praestans* (Rchb.f.) Pfitz.

CLOSELY RELATED SPECIES *P. glanduliferum* may be distinguished from *P. philippinense* by its larger dorsal sepal and shorter, more spreading petals and from *P. rothschildianum* by its oblong staminode and twisted petals.

Paphiopedilum glaucophyllum J.J. Smith
[Colour Plate]

A terrestrial herb, up to or over 50 cm tall. **Leaves** narrowly elliptic, up to 25 cm long, 6 cm broad, somewhat glaucous, purple-flushed at base on underside, unequally 2-lobed at apex. **Inflorescence** several-flowered but opening most commonly 1 at a time; scape terete, up to about 30 cm tall, deep purple with white pubescence; bracts ovate, 1.5 cm long, green with white purple veins, pubescent; ovary 3.5 cm long, purple, pubescent. **Flowers** superficially similar to *P. liemianum;* dorsal sepal green with white margins, brown-shaded at base, veins darker coloured; petals white, heavily spotted with purple; lip pink with darker mottling; staminode brown with white dorsal margin. **Dorsal sepal** ovate, 2–3.3 cm long, 2.5–3.2 cm broad; **synsepalum** ovate, 2.6–3.2 cm long, 1.2–1.8 cm broad. **Petals** linear, somewhat deflexed, 4–5 cm long, 0.6–0.9 cm broad, obtuse, margins undulate, ciliate. **Lip** deeply saccate, rounded at apex, 3–4.1 cm long, 1.2–2 cm in diameter. **Column** short; staminode trullate, depressed centrally.

DISTRIBUTION Java, on cliffs, 200–700 m.

HISTORY *P. glaucophyllum* was described in the *Bulletin de l'Institute Botanique de Buitenzorg* (1900) by the Dutch botanist J.J. Smith based on a specimen collected near Turen in Central Java. Var. *moquetteanum*, from E. Java has larger flowers with a yellow dorsal sepal.

CLOSELY RELATED SPECIES *P. glaucophyllum* is closely related to *P. victoriaregina* of which it is considered to be a subspecies by M. Wood in the *Orchid Review* (1976). It differs in having glaucous leaves and rather different floral morphology.

Paphiopedilum godefroyae (Godefroy-Lebeuf) Stein

A terrestrial herb, up to 15 cm tall. **Leaves** linear-oblong, 18 cm long, 4 cm broad, deep green, more or less marbled and spotted paler green, purple-brown spotted below. **Inflorescence** 3–10 cm long, 1- or 2-flowered; scape pale green, spotted purple, tomentose; bracts one-third the length of ovary. **Flowers** 5–7.5 cm in diameter, white or pale yellow, lightly to heavily spotted magenta, obscurely pubescent. **Dorsal sepal** broadly ovate or suborbicular, 2.5–3.3 cm long, 2–3.7 cm broad; **synsepalum** elliptic-oblong, 2–3 cm long, smaller than dorsal sepal. **Petals** elliptic-oblong, broad, deflexed, 3.5–5.5 cm long, 2–3 cm broad. **Lip** ellipsoidal to subcylindrical, 2.5–3.5 cm long, 1.5 cm broad, minutely magenta-spotted. **Staminode** variable, round-oblong, 1- or 3-toothed ventrally, minutely purple-spotted, yellow-stained in centre.

DISTRIBUTION Peninsular Thailand and adjacent islands and possibly S. Burma; on limestone, at low elevations.

HISTORY Found originally by Murton probably in Thailand, this species was introduced to Europe in 1876 by Godefroy-Lebeuf who acquired plants from an Englishman named Alabaster who knew Murton. The species was originally described in *Orchidophile* (p. 830) in 1882 as *Cypripedium godefroyae* and was transferred in 1892 to *Paphiopedilum* by B. Stein in his *Orchideenbuch* (p. 468).

SYNONYMS *Cypripedium godefroyae* Godefroy-Lebeuf; *C. concolor* Batem. var. *godefroyae* Hemsley; *C. godefroyae* var. *leucochilum* Rolfe; *Paphiopedilum leucochilum* (Rolfe) Fowlie

CLOSELY RELATED SPECIES For a discussion of the relationships of *P. godefroyae* see under *P. bellatulum* and *P. niveum* to which it is closely related.

Paphiopedilum haynaldianum (Rchb.f.) Stein
[Colour Plate]

A terrestrial herb, up to or over 1 m tall. **Leaves** 6 per stem, ligulate or narrowly elliptic, up to 35 cm long, 4.5 cm broad, dull deep green. **Inflorescence** 3- to 6-flowered, 50–75 cm long; bracts half the length of the ovary, both bracts and ovary covered with long pubescence; peduncle 1.4 cm long; ovary 4 cm long. **Flowers** 7.5–10 cm broad; dorsal sepal yellowish-green with large brown spots along veins, synsepalum whitish with pale green veins; petals yellow-green with 8–12 large dark brown spots at base, apical half purple; lip pale greenish tinged with purple-brown. **Dorsal sepal** ovate, 3.5–6.2 cm long, 2.5–4 cm broad, acute, margins reflexed in basal two-thirds; **synsepalum** broadly ovate, 2.5–4.5 cm long. **Petals** linear-spathulate, ± horizontal and then drooping at apex, 5.8–10 cm long, 1–1.4 cm broad, slightly twisted. **Lip** saccate, with mouth 3.5–4.9 cm long, 2–2.3 cm broad, infolded side lobes the same colour, auricled. **Staminode** obovate with a dorsal tooth.

DISTRIBUTION The Philippines; widely distributed on limestone hills from sea level to 1400 m.

HISTORY *P. haynaldianum* was first collected by Gustav Wallis in 1873 near Manila in the Philippines. Wallis sent specimens in the same year to Veitch & Sons in England and it was named in 1875 as *Cypripedium haynaldianum* by H.G. Reichenbach in *Xenia Orchidacea* (p. 222) after Dr Haynald, the Archbishop of Kalocsa, Hungary, who was a keen horticulturist. It was transferred to *Paphiopedilum* by Stein (1892) in his *Orchideenbuch* (p. 470).

SYNONYM *Cypripedium haynaldianum* Rchb.f.

CLOSELY RELATED SPECIES Very closely related to *P. lowii* but it has a broader and distinctly coloured dorsal sepal with large basal spotting, larger more leathery leaves and a narrower staminode. Closer study is needed to see whether it merits its separate specific status.

Paphiopedilum hirsutissimum (Lindl. ex Hooker) Stein [Colour Plate]

An epiphytic or terrestrial herb, up to 35 cm tall. **Leaves** linear-oblong, 16–40 cm long, 1.5–3 cm broad, uniform green, acute. **Inflorescence** up to 30 cm long, 1-flowered; scape green, covered with dark purple hairs; bract 2.6 cm long, about a quarter the length of the ovary. **Flower** up to 10–15 cm across, all segments ciliate; bract, ovary and sepal backs covered with purple hairs; dorsal sepal densely spotted with blackish-purple in central and basal areas, broad marginal area deeper or paler green, synsepalum pale green with purplish veins; petals green in basal half, blotched and spotted deep purple, covered with numerous black hairs, distal half bright violet-purple; lip dull green stained with brownish-purple and dotted with minute blackish warts; staminode green with 2 dorsal white spots. **Dorsal sepal** broadly cordate, 4–4.5 cm long, 3–4 cm broad; **synsepalum** ovate, 3.2–3.9 cm long, smaller than dorsal sepal. **Petals** broadly spathulate, spreading horizontally, slightly twisted, 5.5–7.5 cm long, 1.2–2.2 cm broad, margins ciliate, crisped and undulate on upper margin of basal half. **Lip** helmet-shaped, 3.5–5 cm long, 2–3.3 cm broad. **Staminode** nearly square, convex, dorsally hairy.

DISTRIBUTION India (Assam), Thailand and Burma; an epiphyte on tree branches or in thin deposits of soil on rocks, 700–1300 m altitude.

HISTORY *P. hirsutissimum* was first sent to England in about 1857 by Simons but its original locality was unknown. However, in 1868 or 1869, John Day of Tottenham near London received a plant collected in the Khasia Hills by Capt. Williamson. Sir William Hooker described a plant of the original importation in 1857 in the *Botanical Magazine* (t. 4990) as *Cypripedium hirsutissimum*. The specific epithet was given by John Lindley for the very hairy flower-stalk, pedicel, ovary, bract and outer surface of the sepals. Stein transferred it to *Paphiopedilum* in his *Orchideenbuch* (p. 470).

Var. *esquirolei* (Schltr.) Cribb, from Thailand and S. China, is distinguished by its slightly larger flowers and shorter pubescence on the peduncle and ovary.

SYNONYM *Cypripedium hirsutissimum* Lindl.

Paphiopedilum insigne (Lindl.) Pfitz.
[Colour Plate]
A terrestrial plant, up to 30–50 cm tall. **Leaves** strap-shaped, 20–30 cm long, 2.5 cm broad, pale green, minutely 2-lobed at apex. **Inflorescence** up to 30 cm long, 1 (occasionally 2)-flowered; scape dark green-brown with a reddish pubescence; bract ovate, up to 5.2 cm long; ovary 4.5 cm long, pubescent. **Flowers** with a glossy appearance, 10–12.5 cm high; dorsal sepal green, marked with large brown spots, margins white; synsepalum pale green, lightly spotted dark brown in basal half; petals yellowish-green, veined pale brown; lip golden-brown, veined darker brown, side lobes deep yellow-brown with paler margins; staminode golden with a central orange-yellow wart. **Dorsal sepal** broadly ovate, 4–6 cm long, 2.5–4 cm broad; margins minutely pubescent; **synsepalum** ovate-elliptic, 4–5 cm long, 1.8–2.5 cm broad, acute. **Petals** narrowly oblanceolate, 4–6.3 cm long, 1–1.7 cm broad, minutely pubescent, margins undulate. **Lip** saccate, wide-mouthed, 4–5 cm long; side lobes inflexed. **Staminode** subquadrate, with a central raised boss, pubescent.

DISTRIBUTION India (Assam) and Nepal; on limestone fully exposed to the monsoon rains, 1000–2000 m.

HISTORY *P. insigne* was discovered by N. Wallich in the Sylhet district of N.E. India during the second decade of the nineteenth century. It was sent by him in either 1819 or 1820 to England where it first flowered in the autumn of 1820 in the Liverpool Botanic Garden. Subsequently, W. Griffith found *P. insigne* in the Khasia Hills. John Lindley described it in 1821 as *Cypripedium insigne* in his *Collectanea Botanica* (t. 32) and E. Pfitzer transferred it in 1888 to *Paphiopedilum* in Pringsheim, *Jahrbücher für wissenschaftliche Botanik* (p. 165).

P. insigne has been extensively used in the production of artificial hybrids.

Var. *sanderae* [Colour Plate] is an albino form which lacks any of the brown pigmentation of the typical form, the whole being yellowish-green with a white margin to the dorsal sepal.

SYNONYM *Cypripedium insigne* Lindl.

CLOSELY RELATED SPECIES The closely related *P. exul* from lower Thailand has narrow, more erect leaves and a less spotted dorsal sepal. The Chinese *P. barbigerum* Tang & Wang is rather like a dwarf *P. insigne* with an unspotted dorsal sepal. *P. henryanum* Braem, also from China, is similar in size to *P. barbigerum* but has an almost circular dorsal sepal, that has large bold black spots all over, and a pink lip.

Paphiopedilum javanicum (Lindl.) Pfitz.
[Colour Plate]
A terrestrial herb, up to 40 cm tall. **Leaves** narrowly elliptic or elliptic-oblong, up to 20 cm long, 5 cm broad, tessellated pale and dark green, apex minutely 2-lobed. **Inflorescence** up to 25 cm long, 1 (occasionally 2)-flowered; scape mottled pale green and crimson; bract 2 cm long, one-third length of ovary. **Flower** up to 10 cm across, all segments ciliate except lip, dorsal sepal pale green with deeper green veins, whitish towards apex; petals pale green, spotted with minute black warts in basal two-thirds, distal third dull purple; lip brownish-green, paler below, side lobes pale green, spotted purple. **Dorsal sepal** cordate, 3–4.3 cm long, 2.5–2.9 cm broad, acuminate; **synsepalum** ovate-oblong, 2.5–3.1 cm long, smaller than dorsal sepal. **Petals** broadly ligulate, slightly deflexed, 4.2–5 cm long, 1.3–1.5 cm broad, **Lip** almost cylindrical, 3.6–4.5 cm long. **Staminode** broadly reniform, dorsally notched and with a short ventral sinus.

DISTRIBUTION Sumatra, E. Java, Flores, Bali and Borneo; 900–2100 m altitude.

HISTORY This species was first found by the Dutch botanist C.G.E. Reinwardt in the mountains of E. Java in 1823 and it was named by C. Blume in the catalogue of the plants in the Buitenzorg (now Bogor) Botanic Garden, Java. However, it remained undescribed until 1850 when John Lindley described it, in his and Paxton's *Flower Garden* (p. 38), as *Cypripedium javanicum*. E. Pfitzer transferred it to *Paphiopedilum* in 1888 in Pringsheim, *Jahrbücher für*

wissenschaftliche Botanik (p. 165). The first plants of this orchid seen in Europe were introduced in 1840 by Thomas Lobb.

The pretty Bornean var. *virens* (Rchb.f.) Stein (syn. *P. virens* Rchb.f.) differs in having smaller flowers of a deeper brighter green; spreading, more horizontal petals reflexed beyond the middle; and a lip that is deeper brown with a glossier surface.

Paphiopedilum kolopakingii Fowlie
[Colour Plate]
A large terrestrial plant with a fan of 8–10 leaves. **Leaves** strap-shaped, obtuse, 40–90 cm long, 6–10 cm wide, green. Inflorescence 6- to 14-flowered, 40–70 cm long; peduncle stout; bracts elliptic-lanceolate, acuminate, 4–5 cm long, purple-striped. **Flowers** 6–10 cm across, sepals whitish with purple veins; petals greenish; lip pale ochre; staminode yellow. **Sepals** ovate, acute, 3.5–6.5 cm long, 2–3.5 cm wide. **Petals** linear-tapering, acute, 5–7 cm long, 0.5–0.7 cm wide. **Lip** narrow, grooved on back surface, 4–6 cm long, 2.2–2.8 cm wide. **Staminode** convex, subquadrate, obtuse at upcurved apex, 9–15 mm long, 6–10 mm wide.

DISTRIBUTION Borneo; C. Kalimantan only; 600–1000 m.

HISTORY Although the flowers of *P. kolopakingii* are not the showiest in the genus, this extraordinary species produces more flowers open simultaneously in the spike than any other species.

It was discovered by a collector of A. Kolopaking (Liem Khe Wie), the well-known Javanese orchid nurseryman, in a remote part of central Borneo and was described in 1984 in the *Orchid Digest* (p. 41) by Jack Fowlie. It is most closely allied to *P. stonei*.

SYNONYM *P. topperi* Braem & Mohr

Paphiopedilum lawrenceanum (Rchb.f.) Pfitz.
[Colour Plate]
A terrestrial herb, up to 40 cm tall. **Leaves** elliptic, up to 22 cm long, 5 cm broad, strongly tessellated dark green and olive-green, minutely acutely 2-lobed at apex. **Inflorescence** up to 30 cm long, 1 (rarely 2)-flowered; bracts small 1.7 cm long, one-quarter length of ovary. **Flower** up to 10 cm broad; dorsal sepal white, flushed with green at base, with 11 prominent green and purple longitudinal stripes with shorter ones between; petals pale green at base grading to purplish-brown at apex, each margin with 5–10 black warts; lip more or less purple-flushed, tinged with brown above, side lobes with small separate warts. **Dorsal sepal** nearly orbicular, 5–6.2 cm long and broad, shortly acuminate; **synsepalum** narrowly oblong-ovate, 2.5–4 cm long. **Petals** spreading, almost horizontal, straight, narrowly oblong,

5.5–6 cm long, 1 cm broad, each margin ciliolate. **Lip** 4.5–6.5 cm long, nearly as long as dorsal sepal, pouch-like; side lobes inflexed. **Staminode** similar to *P. barbatum* but larger, lunate, with acute incurved ventral cusps and 5 projections in the sinus, deeply cleft dorsally.
DISTRIBUTION N. Borneo; on rocks and on ground in leaf litter, up to 450 m.
HISTORY *P. lawrenceanum* was discovered by F.W. Burbidge who collected plants for Veitch and Sons in Borneo in 1878. H.G. Reichenbach described it as *Cypripedium lawrenceanum* in the *Gardeners' Chronicle* (n.s. 10: p. 748) of the same year and dedicated it to Sir Trevor Lawrence, the President of the Royal Horticultural Society and a keen orchid grower. E. Pfitzer transferred it to *Paphiopedilum* in *Pringsheim, Jahrbücher für wissenschaftliche Botanik* (p. 163) in 1888.
SYNONYM *Cypripedium lawrenceanum* Rchb.f.
CLOSELY RELATED SPECIES This species is allied to *P. barbatum*, from which it may be distinguished by its larger dorsal sepal and smaller synsepalum, the only slightly deflexed petals which are warty on both margins and by the staminode which is similarly shaped but a darker green. The relatively minor nature of these distinctions has led M. Wood in the *Orchid Review* (1976) to reduce *P. lawrenceanum* to subspecific status in *P. barbatum*. Furthermore, he has described from the Philippines a new variety, *hennisianum*, of subsp. *lawrenceanum*. This latter plant has been widely grown for many years as *P. hennisianum*, a name that had not been validly described until recently. It differs from *P. lawrenceanum* in its smaller elliptic dorsal sepal, broader synsepalum and shorter, broader petals.

Paphiopedilum lowii (Lindl.) Stein
[Colour Plate]
An epiphytic herb, up to 100 cm tall. **Leaves** linear to narrowly elliptic, rather tough, fleshy, 30 cm long, 4 cm broad, uniformly dark green. **Inflorescence** 60–100 cm long, 2- to 5 (rarely more)-flowered; bracts 2.2 cm long, one-third the length of the ovary. **Flowers** 10–14 cm broad, pubescent; dorsal sepal yellow-green with purple-brown suffusion and radiating lines in basal few mm; petals basally greenish-yellow with large dark-brown markings, some ocellated, apically purple-flushed; lip greenish with brown markings, side lobes yellowish. **Dorsal sepal** broadly elliptic to ovate, 4–5 cm long, 2.5–3.2 cm broad, shortly acuminate, upper part concave, margins reflexed towards base; **synsepalum** narrower but as long as dorsal sepal, reflexed away from lip. **Petals** spathulate, basal part spreading horizontally, apical part drooping, once twisted, 6–9 cm long, 1.5–2 cm broad. **Lip** saccate, 3.6–4 cm long, nearly as long as dorsal sepal; side lobes inturned.

Staminode obcordate, with a blunt tooth in the ventral sinus, bordered with purple hairs.
DISTRIBUTION Malaya, Sumatra, Borneo, Sulawesi and Java; an epiphyte on large trees, 1000–1600 m altitude.
HISTORY Sir Hugh Low discovered this species which bears his name in Sarawak, N.W. Borneo in 1846. He sent plants to Low & Co. of Clapton, England the same year and John Lindley described it in the *Gardeners' Chronicle* (p. 765) in 1847. It was transferred to *Paphiopedilum* in 1892 by Stein in his *Orchideenbuch* (p. 476).
SYNONYM *Cypripedium lowii* Lindl.
CLOSELY RELATED SPECIES See under *P. haynaldianum*, which bears a striking resemblance to *P. lowii* but has a spotted dorsal sepal.

Paphiopedilum malipoense S.C. Chen & Tsi
[Colour Plate]
A terrestrial plant with a basal fan of 7–8 leaves and long creeping rhizomes. **Leaves** oblong, acute to obtuse, 10–25 cm long, 2.5–4.5 cm wide, mottled and veined above dark and light green, heavily purple-spotted below, ciliate on margins. **Inflorescence** 1-flowered; peduncle slender, up to 40 cm long, green spotted with purple, hirsute; bract ovate-lanceolate, acute, 1–2 cm long, purple-spotted. **Flower** large, smelling of raspberry; sepals and petals apple-green striped and spotted with purple; lip greyish, spotted within with purple; staminode white with a glossy purple apex. **Dorsal sepal** elliptic-lanceolate, acuminate, 4–4.5 cm long, 1.8–2.2 cm wide; **synsepalum** ovate-lanceolate, acutely bidentate at apex, 3.5–4 cm long, 2–2.5 cm wide. **Petals** obovate, subacute, 3.8–4.5 cm long, 3–4 cm wide, villose within. **Lip** very inflated, thin-textured, 4–5 cm long, 3–4 cm wide. **Staminode** broadly ovate-oblong, truncate, 1.3–1.4 cm long, 1–1.3 cm wide.
DISTRIBUTION S.W. China; S.E. Yunnan only; 1300–1600 m.
HISTORY It is remarkable that this attractive orchid remained unknown until 1984. In that year it was described by the Chinese botanists S.C. Chen and Tsi in *Acta Phytotaxonomica Sinica* (p. 119) based on a specimen collected at Ma-li-po in S.E. Yunnan by K.M. Feng. This is the same area that yielded the spectacular *P. micranthum* a few years earlier.
P. malipoense was first seen in cultivation outside of China in 1986 but wild-collected material has appeared in some quantity since then.

Paphiopedilum mastersianum (Rchb.f.) Stein
[Colour Plate]
A medium-sized terrestrial plant. **Stem** short. **Leaves** narrowly oblong, tridentate at the obtuse apex, up to 22 cm long, 4.5 cm broad,

deep green, tessellated with pale green. **Inflorescence** 1-flowered, up to 40 cm high; peduncle deep purple, pubescent; bract very short, ovate, subacute, 2–2.5 cm long. **Flower** 10–12 cm across, about 7.5 cm across vertically; dorsal sepal green, veined darker green, with a white or cream margin; synsepalum pale green; petals copper-coloured to reddish-purple, spotted in upper halves with dark purple, lower halves greenish towards the base; lip pale chestnut-brown, yellowish above, side lobes olive-brown, speckled with purple; staminode greenish-brown with a yellow margin. **Dorsal sepal** broadly ovate, obtuse, ciliate, 3–4 cm long, 3–4.5 cm broad; **synsepalum** ovate, acute, up to 3 cm long. **Petals** spathulate, rounded at the apex, spreading, ciliolate, 4.5–6 cm long, 1.2–2 cm broad. **Lip** slipper-shaped, 4.5–5.5 cm long, 2–2.5 cm broad. **Staminode** obovate; side teeth on ventral side long and incurved; mid-tooth blunt.
DISTRIBUTION The Moluccas (Ambon, Buru); 900–2000 m.
HISTORY Described in 1879 by H.G. Reichenbach in the *Gardeners' Chronicle* (n.s. 12: p. 102) as *Cypripedium mastersianum* in honour of Maxwell Masters. The type specimen was introduced by Messrs Veitch from the Moluccas. B. Stein transferred it in 1892 to *Paphiopedilum* in his *Orchideenbuch* (p. 477).
SYNONYM *Cypripedium mastersianum* Rchb.f.

Paphiopedilum micranthum Tang & Wang
[Colour Plate]
A terrestrial plant with elongate slender rhizomes and very short erect leafy stems. **Leaves** 4–5, oblong-elliptic, obtuse to subacute, 5–18 cm, long, 1.5–2.5 cm wide, chequered dark and paler green on the upper surface, heavily purple-spotted on the under surface. **Inflorescence** erect, 1-flowered; peduncle 9–25 cm long, green, spotted with purple, hirsute; bract lanceolate-narrowly elliptic, acute 1–2 cm long. **Flower** very attractive, large for size of plant; sepals and petals pale yellow heavily veined with purple; lip pale to rose-pink. **Sepals** ovate, obtuse to acute, 1.5–2.4 cm long, 1.1–3 cm wide. **Petals** elliptic-subcircular, obtuse or rounded at apex, 1.9–3.3 cm long, 2.3–3.4 cm wide, white-pubescent on inner surface. **Lip** thin-textured, very inflated, 5–6.5 cm long, 3.4–4.7 cm wide. **Staminode** circular to elliptic, longitudinally conduplicate, 1–1.3 cm long and wide, white with a pink base and yellow apex, spotted with red.
DISTRIBUTION S.W. China; S.E. Yunnan only, c. 1000–1500 m.
HISTORY Although described in *Acta Phytotaxonomica Sinica* (p. 56) in 1951 by the Chinese botanists Tang and Wang, this beautiful orchid was not seen in cultivation outside China until

1984. Since then it has appeared in large numbers in trade and it must now be severely depleted in the wild if not threatened by extinction.

Its inappropriate name deserves some comment and it seems probable that the type collection made by Wang from the hills between Ma-li-po and Shi-chou was in bud when collected.

Paphiopedilum niveum (Rchb.f.) Stein
[Colour Plate]
A small herb, up to 26 cm tall. **Leaves** elliptic, 10–15 cm long, 2.7–3.3 cm broad, dark green with grey-green markings on upper surface and purple-spotted beneath. **Inflorescence** erect, up to 17 cm long, 1- or 2-flowered. **Flowers** 7.5 cm in diameter, white with fine purple spots at base of tepals. **Dorsal sepal** ovate, 2.6–3 cm long, 2–4 cm broad; **synsepalum** much smaller. **Petals** spreading, oblong, 3.5–4 cm long, 2–2.6 cm broad. **Lip** ellipsoidal, up to 3 cm long, mouth small, almost closed by column and staminode. **Column** short; staminode somewhat variable, ± elliptic, keeled centrally.
DISTRIBUTION Langkawi Islands off W. Malaysia, Thailand and possibly the Tambelan Islands between Borneo and Singapore; on limestone often near the sea.
HISTORY *P. niveum* was introduced into cultivation in 1868 by Messrs Veitch & Co. from Moulmein, Burma where the plant was probably introduced by a Burmese collector from further south. H.G. Reichenbach described it in 1869 in the *Gardeners' Chronicle* (p. 1038) as *Cypripedium niveum* but it was later transferred to *Paphiopedilum* by B. Stein in his *Orchideenbuch* (p. 478) in 1892.
SYNONYM *Cypripedium niveum* Rchb.f.
CLOSELY RELATED SPECIES The closely related *P. godefroyae* and *P. bellatulum* may be distinguished by the marked purple spotting of their larger flowers. Intermediate geographic variants do occur and field work may show that the three are merely forms of one widespread species or, alternatively, that hybridisation has occurred in nature. See also *P. concolor*.

Paphiopedilum parishii (Rchb.f.) Stein
[Colour Plate]
An epiphytic plant, up to 70 cm tall. **Leaves** oblong-ligulate, leathery, up to 40 cm long, 6.5 cm broad, bright glossy green, bifid at apex. **Inflorescence** stoutish, suberect, up to 60 cm long, 4- to 8-flowered; scape pale green, downy; bracts ovate, inflated, 4 cm long, covering half to three-quarters of the ovary, acute. **Flowers** up to 7.5 cm across, up to 13 cm long; dorsal sepal pale yellow with green veins; petals green in basal half with a few scattered black spots,

distal half blackish-purple with a pale margin; lip deep green, shaded brown-purple; staminode pale yellow, mottled green; ovary hairy. **Dorsal sepal** elliptic-oblong, upper half bent forwards, lateral margins reflexed at base, 3–5 cm long, 2.5–3 cm broad, acute; synsepalum similar but smaller with 2 dorsal keels. **Petals** linear, twisted, spreading at first and then pendulous, 9–12.5 cm long, 0.6–1.2 cm broad, basal margins undulate. **Lip** calceiform, wide-mouthed, 3–4.5 cm long; side lobes narrow, smooth. **Staminode** oblong-obovate, with a dorsal tooth and an apical sinus.
DISTRIBUTION Burma, Thailand and China (Yunnan); epiphytic on large trees amongst bird's nest ferns etc. and occasionally on the bases of ferns, 1250–2200 m elevation.
HISTORY This spectacular slipper orchid was discovered by the Rev. Charles Parish in the Moulmein district of Burma in 1859. He re-collected it in 1866 when he sent flowers to Kew. Messrs Low & Co. of Clapton, London received the first living plants in 1868 and sent flowers of these to H.G. Reichenbach, who described it in the *Flora* (p. 322) of 1869.
Var. *dianthum* (Tang & Wang) Cribb & Tang, from S. China, can be distinguished by its white dorsal sepal and staminode and glabrous ovary.
SYNONYM *Cypripedium parishii* Rchb.f.
CLOSELY RELATED SPECIES *P. parishii* bears a strong resemblance to *P. philippinense* in habit but it has far larger and quite differently coloured flowers. It also resembles *P. lowii* especially in its staminode but is readily distinguished by its longer, narrower petals.

Paphiopedilum philippinense (Rchb.f.) Stein
[Colour Plate]
Terrestrial herb, up to 50 cm tall. **Leaves** longly elliptic, glossy green, 35 cm long, 4 cm broad. **Inflorescence** 3- to 5-flowered, 20–50 cm tall; peduncle pubescent, greenish streaked with brownish-purple; bract 2.2–2.9 cm long, one-third length of ovary. **Flowers** with dorsal sepal white, striped with brown-purple, synsepalum white, with green veins; petals purple-red with yellow base and pale green apex; lip buff-yellow with pale green-brown venation; ovary pubescent. **Dorsal sepal** ovate, 4–5 cm long, 2–3 cm broad, margin pubescent, apex acute; **synsepalum** ovate 3.7–4 cm long, smaller than dorsal sepal. **Petals** linear, ribbon-like, spreading or pendulous, twisted, 8–16 cm long, tufts of hair on margins in basal half. **Lip** helmet-shaped, 3–4 cm long, 1.7 cm broad. **Staminode** ovate to subcordiform but 2-lobed at apex and base, lobes rounded, side margins pubescent.
DISTRIBUTION The Philippines and islands of N.E. coast of Borneo; growing near the

sea shore on limestone and the roots of *Vanda batemanii* etc.
HISTORY Introduced into cultivation by J.G. Veitch who discovered it on Guimaras Island in 1865. H.G. Reichenbach had earlier described *Cypripedium philippinense* in *Bonplandia* (p. 335) in 1862 from a dried herbarium specimen. It was transferred to *Paphiopedilum* by Stein in 1892 in his *Orchideenbuch* (p. 480).
SYNONYMS *Paphiopedilum roebelinii* (Rchb.f.) Pfitz.; *P. laevigatum* (Batem.) Pfitz.
CLOSELY RELATED SPECIES The pendent twisted petals, pubescent ovary and the lip with its auriculate rather than involute margins distinguish *P. philippinense* from the superficially similar Bornean species *P. rothschildianum* which also possesses a narrower 2-lobed staminode. From the New Guinean species *P. glanduliferum*, it differs in having smaller flowers with a pubescent ovary and longer, less spreading petals. *P. sanderianum*, from Borneo, has much longer petals up to 30 cm long. See also *P. randsii*.

Paphiopedilum primulinum M. Wood & P. Taylor [Colour Plate]
A medium-sized terrestrial stemless herb. **Leaves** 4–8, distichous, oblong-lanceolate, tridenticulate at apex, 14–33 cm long, 2.5–4 cm broad, dark green above, paler green below. **Inflorescence** erect, of 7–10 flowers opening in succession from lowest upwards; peduncle 10–30 cm long, green, pubescent. **Flowers** with greenish-yellow sepals and petals and a primrose-yellow lip (a form with a purplish-flushed lip is known in cultivation). **Dorsal sepal** ovate, obtuse, 2.5–2.7 cm long, 2.3–2.5 cm broad, ciliate, shortly pubescent on outer surface; **synsepalum** similar but smaller, half size of dorsal sepal. **Petals** linear, obtuse, spreading, 2.8–3 cm long, 0.7 cm broad, twisted once near apex, margins undulate and ciliate. **Lip** deeply pouched, 2.7–2.9 cm long, 1.5 cm broad, with 2 prominent lateral auricles, incurved margins in basal part touching each other. **Column** 0.2 cm long; staminode subcircular with a small central projection, 0.7 cm long, 0.6 cm broad.
DISTRIBUTION N. Sumatra only; 400–500 m.
HISTORY One of the recently described species of this popular genus and one of the most controversial. *P. primulinum* was described in 1973 by M. Wood and P. Taylor in the *Orchid Review* (p. 220) based on a plant collected by Liem Khe Wie on Gunung Leuser in N. Sumatra in 1972. It is closely allied to *P. victoria-regina* differing in its narrower leaves, the broader and less acute apical margin of the staminodes and in its flower colour. This has led to its being considered a subspecies or form of that species by some authors. In our opinion

P. primulinum differs as much if not more from *P. victoria-regina* as, for example, *P. callosum* does from *P. barbatum*.

SYNONYMS *Paphiopedilum victoria-regina* (Sander) M. Wood subsp. *primulinum* (M. Wood & P. Taylor) M. Wood; *P. chamberlainianum* (Sander) Stein subsp. *liemianum* forma *primulinum* Fowlie

CLOSELY RELATED SPECIES *P. victoria-regina*; *P. liemianum*; *P. glaucophyllum*.

Paphiopedilum purpuratum (Lindl.) Stein
[Colour Plate]

A terrestrial herb, up to 29 cm tall. **Leaves** oblong-elliptic, 12.5 cm long, 4 cm broad, mottled light and dark green, pale green below, apex unequally 3-lobed. **Inflorescence** up to 18 cm long, 1-flowered; scape purple with white pubescence; bract 2.2 cm long, half the length of the ovary, pale green, pubescent. **Flower** 7.5–8.5 cm long; dorsal sepal white with greenish central stain and 8–10 curved brown-purple stripes, synsepalum greenish; petals purple-crimson with deep purple or green veins, base covered with numerous small black warts; lip brownish-purple with deeper purple veins, side lobes purple with numerous small warts; staminode dull green, stained purple. **Dorsal sepal** suborbicular, 2.5–4.5 cm long, 2.2–4.6 cm broad, acute, ciliate, sides reflexed towards base; **synsepalum** ovate, 2–4.2 cm long, acuminate. **Petals** subspathulate, spreading, wavy, 4–6 cm long, 0.8–1.8 cm broad, ciliate. **Lip** subcylindric, 3.3–4.6 cm long, 2–2.6 cm broad, side lobes infolded. **Staminode** semi-lunate, notched dorsally, ventral side has a small central tooth.

DISTRIBUTION Known only from Hong Kong and adjacent areas of S.E. China.

HISTORY *P. purpuratum* was the third species of the genus introduced into cultivation in Europe when J. Knight of the Royal Exotic Nursery successfully grew it in 1836 or thereabouts. The species was described by John Lindley in the *Botanical Register* (t. 1991) in 1837 as *Cypripedium purpuratum*. Stein (1892) transferred it to *Paphiopedilum* in his *Orchideenbuch* (p. 481).

CLOSELY RELATED SPECIES *P. purpuratum* resembles the S.E. Asian species *P. barbatum* somewhat, but it lacks the black marginal warts on its wider petals and its dorsal sepal is acute at the apex and less heavily lined.

Paphiopedilum randsii Fowlie [Colour Plate]

A medium-sized terrestrial or epiphytic plant with a very short stem. **Leaves** basal, oblong or elliptic-oblong, rounded at apex, 12–35 cm long, 5–6 cm broad, not tessellated or mottled. **Inflorescence** erect, 3- to 5-flowered, 25–40 cm long, densely pilose, bracts lanceolate, acute to acuminate, pilose, 2.5–3 cm long, 1.6–2 cm broad. **Flowers** large; sepals white or pale greenish-white, longitudinally striped with maroon; lip pale yellow-green veined with darker green; staminode pale green. **Dorsal sepal** ovate, acute and slightly cucullate at the apex, concave, 3.8–4.2 cm long, 1.8–2.2 cm broad; **synsepalum** similar to dorsal sepal but subtruncate at apex, 3–3.2 cm long, 1.8–2 cm broad. **Petals** linear, decurved, rounded at the apex, 3.8–4.5 cm long, 0.4–0.6 cm broad, margins shortly ciliate. **Lip** slipper-shaped, 3-lobed, 2.8–3.2 cm long, 1.2–1.5 cm broad; side lobes incurved, obtuse; mid-lobe auriculate at base, broad and grooved at apex. **Staminode** elliptic, truncate below, 0.5 cm long, 0.4 cm broad, pubescent on sides.

DISTRIBUTION The Philippines (Mindanao); about 500 m altitude.

HISTORY Discovered in 1968 by Mrs Patricia K. Manuel at Agusan on Mindanao and imported into the USA by Ray Rands after whom it was named by J.A. Fowlie in 1969 in the *Orchid Digest* (p. 321).

CLOSELY RELATED SPECIES *P. randsii* is allied to *P. philippinense* and *P. stonei*, being easily recognised by its boldly marked sepals and petals and its distinctive lip and staminode shapes.

Paphiopedilum rothschildianum (Rchb.f.) Stein [Colour Plate]

A terrestrial herb, up to about 55 cm tall. **Leaves** very narrowly elliptic or ligulate, suberect, 40–60 cm long, 4.5–7.5 cm broad. **Inflorescence** up to 45 cm long, 3- or more-flowered; scape reddish with a few short hairs; bracts nearly as long as the glabrous ovary, tridentate at apex, pale yellow-green, black-lined. **Flowers** with a yellowish dorsal sepal with numerous longitudinal blackish stripes, white around margins; petals yellow-green with dark longitudinal lines, dark blotches at base; lip cinnamon with an ochre margin around mouth; ovary glabrous. **Dorsal sepal** cuneate-oblong, 4.5–6.6 cm long, 3.5–4.5 cm broad, acute; **synsepalum** 4.2–5.7 cm long, nearly as large as dorsal sepal, slightly shorter. **Petals** linear, not twisted, tapering slightly to apex, undulate at base, 11–14 cm long, 0.7–1 cm broad. **Lip** apex angular from side, 4.5–5.7 cm long, 2.2 cm broad. **Staminode** beak-like, narrowing to bifid apex where it is hairy.

DISTRIBUTION N. Borneo (Mt Kinabalu); up to 1200 m altitude.

HISTORY This beautiful species, arguably the most handsome in the genus, was introduced almost at the same time in 1887 by F. Sander & Co. of St Albans into England and by J. Linden into Belgium. Both flowered it then, but some clones at present cultivated have a name for being poor flowerers. The species was described in 1888 as *Cypripedium rothschildianum* by H.G. Reichenbach in the *Gardeners' Chronicle* (ser. 3, 3: p. 457) who dedicated it to Baron F. de Rothschild of Waddesdon Manor near Aylesbury, an eminent patron of horticulture at that time in England. B. Stein later transferred it in 1892 to *Paphiopedilum* in his *Orchideenbuch* (p. 482).

SYNONYM *Cypripedium rothschildianum* Rchb.f.

CLOSELY RELATED SPECIES *P. rothschildianum* is a most distinctive species, amongst the finest in the genus. It may be distinguished from the somewhat similar *P. glanduliferum* by its untwisted petals and narrowly pointed staminode. See also *P. philippinense*.

Paphiopedilum spicerianum (Rchb.f.) Pfitz. [Colour Plate]

A terrestrial herb, up to 20 cm tall. **Leaves** 5, oblong, up to 22 cm long, 5.5 cm broad but often narrower, dull green, purple-mottled beneath, central vein dull dark purple, apex minutely, acutely bilobed. **Inflorescence** 1 (occasionally 2)-flowered, up to 30 cm long; peduncle arcuate, terete, purple, glabrous, up to 10 cm long; bract ovate, acute, pale green, spotted purple; ovary purple, glabrous. **Flower** up to 9 cm high, 7.5 cm broad, showy; dorsal sepal white with central purple stripe and yellow-green base; synsepalum pale green, faintly striped purple; petals yellow-green, heavily mottled with dark purple and with central purple stripe; lip dull bronzy-green outside with yellow margins, side lobes dull yellow with small purple spots; column white, mottled purple with a central yellow raised area. **Dorsal sepal** cordate, 2.7–4 cm long, 3.5–5.6 cm broad, sides reflexed to give obovate appearance to sepal; **synsepalum** 2.7–3.5 cm long, 1.6–2.5 cm broad. **Petals** narrowly oblong, 3–4 cm long, 0.8–1.3 cm broad, dorsal margin undulate, apex rounded. **Lip** saccate, 3.5–4.1 cm long, 2.5–2.9 cm across at widest. **Column** short; staminode ± ovate, 2-lobed dorsally, lobes recurved, 1 cm diameter.

DISTRIBUTION N.E. India (Assam); in steep river gorges, 1000–2000 m altitude.

HISTORY *P. spicerianum* was first flowered in Europe by Herbert Spicer of Godalming, Surrey, England in 1878. His plant was brought from Messrs Veitch in a consignment of mixed slipper orchids from India. H.G. Reichenbach named the species as *Cypripedium spicerianum*, in honour of its first successful cultivator, in the *Gardeners' Chronicle* (n.s. 12: p. 40) of 1880. Later gatherings by the collectors of Low & Co. and Sander & Sons were made when they rediscovered *P. spicerianum* growing in Assam. E. Pfitzer transferred it to *Paphiopedilum* in 1888 in

Pringsheim, *Jahrbücher für wissenschaftliche Botanik* (p. 164).

Extensively used for the production of commercial hybrids in the past, *P. spicerianum* still figures in the pedigrees of many of today's most popular hybrids.

SYNONYM *Cypripedium spicerianum* Rchb.f.

CLOSELY RELATED SPECIES The closely related *P. insigne* may be distinguished by the spotting on the dorsal sepal, staminode shape and flower colour.

Paphiopedilum stonei (Hooker f.) Stein [Colour Plate]

A lithophytic species over 60 cm tall. **Leaves** strap-shaped, 30–38 cm long, 4 cm broad, leathery, grass-green. **Inflorescence** up to 60 cm long, 3- to 5-flowered; scape dull greenish-purple, sparsely pubescent; bracts lanceolate, one-third to one-half the length of the ovary, acuminate. **Flowers** up to 12 cm across; dorsal sepal white with 2 or 3 purple stripes; petals yellowish with elongated red-brown spots towards base, apical third crimson-brown; lip dull rose or ochre, veined darker, whitish below, side lobes whitish; ovary glabrous. **Dorsal sepal** ovate to cordate, 4.5–6 cm long, 3–4.2 cm broad, acuminate; **synsepalum** as long as dorsal sepal but narrower. **Petals** linear, decurved-pendent, not twisted, 12–15 cm long, 0.5–0.8 cm broad, with a few black hairs towards base. **Lip** calceiform, 4.5–6 cm long, 2.5 cm broad. **Staminode** convex, almost oblong as in *P. philippinense* but longer, margins ciliate.

DISTRIBUTION W. Borneo; on limestone hills, up to 400 m altitude.

HISTORY This beautiful species was first collected by Sir Hugh Low in Sarawak. He sent plants back to Low & Co. of Clapton, London in 1860, and the species first flowered in the collection of John Day of Tottenham, near London in 1861. Day sent flowers to J.D. Hooker who named it in 1862 in the *Botanical Magazine* (t. 5349) as *Cypripedium stonei* after Day's gardener, Mr Stone. B. Stein transferred the species to *Paphiopedilum* in 1892 in his *Orchideenbuch* (p. 487).

The most prized of all *Paphiopedilum* species is probably the spectacular wide-petalled *P. stonei* var. *platytaenium*. This arose from a single plant which flowered in 1867 in Day's collection and he successfully propagated it so that four plants were sold for high prices when he disposed of his collection. Var. *platytaenium* has been shown to be a mutation of the typical species and a preserved flower of the plant at Kew has a flower with one normal petal and one typical *platytaenium*-type petal. The other flowers on the plant were all of the *platytaenium* form.

SYNONYM *Cypripedium stonei* Hooker f.

Paphiopedilum sukhakulii Schoser & Senghas [Colour Plate]

A terrestrial plant, up to 30 cm tall. **Leaves** narrowly elliptic, up to 13 cm long, 5 cm broad, mottled pale and dark green with dark green veins, minutely trifid at apex. **Inflorescence** up to 25 cm long, 1-flowered; bract ovate, 1.5–2.5 cm long, one-third the length of the ovary. **Flower** broader than long; dorsal sepal white or pale green, lined with darker green; synsepalum white, lined with green; petals pale yellow-green, spotted deep purple all over; lip pale green, veined and mottled deep purple, side lobes purple-mottled; staminode pale yellow, mottled green in centre. **Dorsal sepal** cordate to ovate, 3.8–4 cm long, 2.6–3 cm broad, acuminate; **synsepalum** smaller, lanceolate. **Petals** narrowly oblong, slightly broader in apical half, about 6 cm long, 1.5–2 cm broad, acute. **Lip** deeply saccate, narrowing at apex, 4.5–5 cm long, 2.3–3 cm broad. **Staminode** lunate with 3 short teeth in sinus formed by ventral cusps.

DISTRIBUTION N.E. Thailand; at 250–1000 m altitude, in sandy loam rich in leaf mould.

HISTORY *P. sukhakulii* was introduced into Europe in 1964 when Fritzer and Netzer in Germany found a plant growing with recently imported specimens of *P. callosum* from Thailand. They did not recognise the plant immediately, although when it flowered, its similarity to *P. wardii* was recognised. G. Schoser and K. Senghas described the plant in 1965 as *P. sukhakulii* in *Die Orchidee* (pp. 110, 224) and named it after P. Sukhakul of Bangkok whose company collected the original plants.

CLOSELY RELATED SPECIES *P. sukhakulii* is undoubtedly closely allied to *Paphiopedilum wardii* Summerh., from N. Burma, as Schoser and Senghas mention in their article. They state that it is distinct in lacking any purple marking beneath the leaves. In addition the petals are held more nearly horizontally, lack the slight apical twist of *P. wardii* and the staminode ventral teeth are rather more prominent. However, the limited geographical distribution of *P. sukhakulii* and its undoubted resemblance to *P. wardii* may indicate that with further study it should more realistically be treated as a subspecies of the latter.

Paphiopedilum supardii Braem & Loeb [Colour Plate]

A large terrestrial or lithophytic herb. **Leaves** in a fan, linear, obtuse, 25–55 cm long, 3–5.5 cm wide, glossy mid-green above. **Inflorescence** suberect to arcuate, 30–40 cm long, 3- to 6-flowered; peduncle and rhachis red-purple, pubescent; bracts large, deeply cucullate, lanceolate, acute, 3.5–5.2 cm long, yellow-green striped boldly with maroon. **Flowers** appearing somewhat deformed, the sepals yellow striped

with maroon, the petals yellow spotted with maroon, the lip whitish-yellow flushed on the front with red, and the staminode yellow with red hairs on the margins; pedicel and ovary up to 4.5 cm long, purple-red, glabrous. **Dorsal sepal** ovate, acute, 4.5–5.5 cm long, 2.4–2.6 cm wide; **synsepalum** ovate, acute, 4–5 cm long, 2–2.4 cm wide. **Petals** arcuate-pendent, contorted-twisted, linear-tapering, obtuse, 8–9 cm long, 0.7–0.9 cm wide. **Lip** narrow, pipe-shaped, 4.4–4.7 cm long, 1.5–1.8 cm wide. **Column** short; staminode convex, rounded at base, suboblong, 0.8–0.9 cm long and wide, with short hairy base and sides.

DISTRIBUTION Borneo: S.E. Kalimantan only.

HABITAT Growing on limestone rocks in leaf-mould-filled hollows in half shade; 600–960 m altitude.

HISTORY Although this strange slipper orchid was introduced into cultivation in the 1930s by Dutch horticulturalists, it was not recognised as distinct until Eduard de Vogel collected it in S.E. Kalimantan in 1972. It was finally described in 1985 by G. Braem and U. Loeb in the journal *Die Orchidee* (p. 142), based on a specimen collected by Supardi in Kalimantan and flowered in cultivation by Braem.

Paphiopedilum superbiens (Rchb.f.) Stein [Colour Plate]

A terrestrial herb, up to 40 cm tall. **Leaves** elliptic to oblong, up to 20 cm long, 8 cm broad, mottled light and dark green, veins dark green, minutely bifid at apex. **Inflorescence** up to 30 cm tall, 1-flowered; scape dark purple with purple pubescence; bract 2.1 cm long, one-third the length of the ovary. **Flower** segments ciliate; dorsal sepal white, longitudinally lined purple and dark green, central area pale green, synsepalum white with green longitudinal lines; petals pinkish-white with darker purple veining and covered with small black warts, largest warts along upper margin; lip rich deep purple, side lobes pale purple covered with purple warts. **Dorsal sepal** almost cordate, 3.4–5.8 cm long, 3–5.3 cm broad, acuminate; **synsepalum** ovate, 2.6–4 cm long, smaller than dorsal sepal, acuminate. **Petals** ligulate, deflexed slightly, down-curved, 5.2–7.5 cm long, 1.6 cm broad, margins ciliate. **Lip** large, saccate, 4.2–6.5 cm long, 2.6–3.1 cm broad; side lobes infolded. **Staminode** broadly horseshoe-shaped, dorsally notched, ventrally with 3 small teeth between incurved side arms.

DISTRIBUTION Sumatra; in leaf litter in woods, 900–1300 m altitude.

HISTORY This species was described in 1855 as *Cypripedium superbiens* by H.G. Reichenbach in *Bonplandia* (p. 227) based on a plant said to be from Java and grown by Consul

Schiller. *P. superbiens* was originally known from two separate introductions each of a single plant. The first was a plant received by Messrs Rollison and said to be from Java or Assam (undoubtedly from neither place), and the second was sent by T. Lobb to Messrs Veitch & Sons from Mt Ophir, Sumatra. These were successfully propagated and represented the total germ plasm of *P. superbiens* in cultivation until the more recent introductions which have been made from Sumatra. The form known until recently as *P. curtisii* was introduced from Sumatra in 1883 having been collected by Charles Curtis near Padang at between 900 and 1200 m altitude.

Paphiopedilum superbiens var. 'Sanderae' [Colour Plate] is a beautiful albino variant which is rare in cultivation.

SYNONYMS *Cypripedium superbiens* Rchb.f.; *C. curtisii* Rchb.f.; *Paphiopedilum curtisii* (Rchb.f.) Stein

CLOSELY RELATED SPECIES See under *P. ciliolare* and *P. argus*.

Paphiopedilum tonsum (Rchb.f.) Stein
[Colour Plate]
A terrestrial herb, up to 40 cm or so tall. **Leaves** oblong-elliptic, up to 20 cm long, 5 cm broad, pale and dark green-mottled, usually densely purple-spotted beneath. **Inflorescence** up to 38 cm tall, 1-flowered; scape dull green- and purple-marked; bract 2 cm long, one-third length of ovary. **Flower** dorsal sepal pinkish-white, lined green and dark purple; petals pale green with darker green veins, sometimes stained dull purple; lip dull green, tinged brown and crimson; staminode pale green. **Dorsal sepal** broadly cordate, 4–5 cm long, 4 cm broad, acute, margins minutely ciliate; **synsepalum** elliptic-oblong, 3.5–4 cm long, much smaller than dorsal sepal, acute. **Petals** subspathulate, up to 6.5 cm long, 2 cm broad, mid-vein with warts along it, upper margin very finely ciliate towards apex only and with a few small warts. **Lip** helmet-shaped, 5.6 cm long, 2–3.5 cm broad; side lobes warted. **Staminode** reniform, dorsally deeply cleft, ventral side with two incurved cusps between which is a small rounded tooth.

DISTRIBUTION Sumatra, at 1000–1800 m.
HISTORY *P. tonsum* was described as *Cypripedium tonsum* by H.G. Reichenbach in the *Gardeners' Chronicle* (n.s. 20: p. 262) in 1883 based on plants collected in Sumatra by Charles Curtis for the firm of Veitch & Sons. B. Stein transferred it to *Paphiopedilum* in 1892 in his *Orchideenbuch* (p. 488).
SYNONYMS *Cypripedium tonsum* Rchb.f.; *Paphiopedilum braemii* Mohr

Paphiopedilum venustum (Wall.) Pfitz.
[Colour Plate]
A terrestrial herb, up to 40 cm tall. **Leaves** narrowly elliptic, 17–29 cm long, 4.5 cm broad, mottled very dark bluish-green and lighter green, deep purple below, minutely, equally, acutely 2-lobed at apex. **Inflorescence** 17–30 cm tall; scape deep purple, pubescent; bract ovate, 2.2 cm long; ovary 3.5 cm long, pubescent. **Flower** 5–6 cm long, 5.5–8.2 cm broad; dorsal sepal white, lined with green; petals green at base, lined with darker green, purple in apical half, with a few black spots; lip bronze-green, lined darker green, paler within. **Dorsal sepal** ovate, 3–3.8 cm long, 2.5–3 cm broad; **synsepalum** narrowly ovate, 2.4–2.8 cm long. **Petals** recurved, narrowly obovate, 4.3–5.4 cm long, 1.2–1.5 cm broad, acute, margins ciliate. **Lip** up to 4.3 cm long. **Staminode** semilunate, with a dorsal notch and a smooth ventral tooth.

DISTRIBUTION Nepal, Bhutan, Bangladesh (Sylhet) and India (Sikkim and Assam); at between 1000 and 1500 m.
HISTORY *P. venustum* was one of the first *Paphiopedilum* species to be discovered when it was found by N. Wallich in Sylhet (now in Bangladesh). The first plants were introduced into cultivation by Messrs Whitley, Brames and Milne who flowered the species in November 1819. It was described shortly afterwards in the *Botanical Magazine* (t. 2129) as *Cypripedium venustum*. It was transferred to *Paphiopedilum* by E. Pfitzer in 1888 in *Pringsheim, Jahrbücher für wissenschaftliche Botanik* (p. 165).

This species was one of the first used in the production of artificial hybrids. *P. Crossii* produced in 1871 by Mr Cross, the gardener of Lady Ashburton of Melchett Court, Hampshire, England, was a hybrid of *P. venustum* and *P. insigne*. Since that time *P. venustum* has continued to play a small role in the breeding of many of our more important hybrid slipper orchids.
SYNONYM *Cypripedium venustum* Wall.

Paphiopedilum victoriaregina (Sander) M.W. Wood [Colour Plate]
A terrestrial or lithophylic herb, up to or over 50 cm tall. **Leaves** large, oblong, up to 45 cm long, 10 cm broad, dull green, ± faintly mottled lighter green, minutely 2-lobed at apex. **Inflorescence** ± erect, many-flowered (up to 30) but opening 1 at a time, up to ± 60 cm long; peduncle dark brown; fertile bracts ovate, acute, almost envelop younger buds, markedly distichous, up to 3.7 cm long, margins ciliate. **Flower** showy, 7.5 cm tall, 8 cm broad; dorsal sepal greenish- to creamy-white, striped deep brown longitudinally, base purple-spotted; synsepalum greenish-white; petals creamy-white

with purple markings, apex pink; lip pink but heavily spotted with light purple; column brown with white dorsal margin. **Dorsal sepal** ovate, 2.8–3 cm tall, 2.5 cm broad; **synsepalum** ovate, 2.7 cm long, ± as large as lip. **Petals** linear, horizontal, spirally twisted, pubescent along margins, 4 cm long, 0.8 cm broad, apical margins ciliolate. **Lip** deeply saccate, broadly rounded at apex, wide-mouthed, about 4 cm long. **Column** short; staminode rhombic.

DISTRIBUTION Sumatra.
HISTORY This unusual species was introduced into cultivation by F. Sander and was first described by him in 1892 in the *Gardeners' Chronicle* (ser. 3 , 11: p. 194) as *Cypripedium victoria-regina* in honour of Queen Victoria. It was transferred to the present genus in 1976 in the *Orchid Review* (p. 134) by M. Wood who has placed *P. chamberlainianum* (O'Brien) Stein, under which name this species is still commonly grown, *P. liemianum* Fowlie, *P. glaucophyllum* and *P. primulinum* all as subspecies of one widespread species *P. victoriaregina* (Sander) M. Wood. This treatment undoubtedly reflects the close affinities of each of these taxa. However, each differs as much from each other as, for example, does *P. barbatum* from *P. callosum* and thus the long-established and well-known names for these taxa have been retained here.
SYNONYMS *Cypripedium chamberlainianum* O'Brien; *C. victoriaregina* Sander; *Paphiopedilum chamberlainianum* (Sander) Stein *Paphiopedilum victoriaregina* (Sander) M. Wood
CLOSELY RELATED SPECIES *P. glaucophyllum* [Colour Plate] may be distinguished by its glaucous leaves and the flowers which lack the brown striping on the dorsal sepal and have a trullate staminode depressed centrally. The yellow-flowered *P. primulinum* [Colour Plate] is undoubtedly closely related but differs in flower colour and in having a ± 6-sided staminode. *P. primulinum* has a form with purple shading on the lip. *P. liemianum* has oblong to elliptical leaves, dark green or mottled above and purple-spotted below, up to 20 cm long, 6.5 cm broad. The leaf margins are ciliate and the leaf has an unequally 2-lobed, obtuse apex.

Paphiopedilum villosum (Lindl.) Stein
[Colour Plate]
An epiphytic herb, up to 30 cm tall. **Leaves** narrowly lanceolate, suberect, 25–40 cm long, 4 cm broad, dark yellow-green, purple-spotted beneath at base, unequally acutely 2-lobed at apex. **Inflorescence** up to 15 cm tall; peduncle dark green covered with long purple hairs; bract 5 cm long, nearly as long as ovary. **Flower** has a glossy, varnished look; dorsal sepal bright green with deep brown-purple shading over basal two-thirds, margins white; synsepa-

lum pale yellow-green; petals yellow-brown in front with darker purple central line, paler brown behind; lip pale golden-brown with a darker central line in front; staminode tawny-yellow. **Dorsal sepal** broadly ovate, 4.5–6.5 cm long , 3–3.5 cm broad, margins ciliate, reflexed towards base; **synsepalum** ovate, reflexed, 3.8–4.5 cm long, smaller than dorsal sepal. **Petals** spathulate, curved forwards, 4.7–7 cm long, 2.5–3 cm broad, rounded at apex, margins ciliolate. **Lip** pouch rather pointed, calceiform, 4–5.5 cm long, 3 cm broad, wide-mouthed. **Staminode** cordate with a wart just below the centre and a short mucro in the centre of the base.

DISTRIBUTION   India (Assam), Burma and Thailand; an epiphytic species growing in areas of abundant rainfall, up to about 2100 m altitude.

HISTORY   First discovered by T. Lobb in the mountains near Moulmein, Burma in 1853, *P. villosum* was described by John Lindley the following year in the *Gardeners' Chronicle* (p. 135) as *Cypripedium villosum*. The specific epithet refers to the shaggy pubescence covering the peduncle, ovary and bract. B. Stein transferred it to *Paphiopedilum* in his *Orchideenbuch* (p. 490) in 1892.

This species is the progenitor of many modern hybrids. One of the first artificially produced hybrid Paphiopedilums, *P.* Harrisianum, resulted from a cross made in 1869 between *P. barbatum* and *P. villosum*.

Var. *boxallii* (Rchb.f.) Pfitz., from Burma, differs in having a boldly spotted dorsal sepal.

SYNONYM   *Cypripedium villosum* Lindl.

CLOSELY RELATED SPECIES   *P. gratrixianum* (Masters) Guill., from Laos and Vietnam, differs in having a smaller flower with a white-margined and heavily spotted dorsal sepal.

Paphiopedilum violascens Schltr.
[Colour Plate]

A terrestrial plant with a short stem. **Leaves** 4–6, erect or spreading, oblong-lanceolate, minutely tridentate at the apex, 13–21 cm long, 2.5–4 cm broad, tessellated grey-green on a darker green background above. **Inflorescence** erect, up to 30 cm long, 1-flowered; peduncle pubescent, dark brown to black; bract greenish-brown pubescent, 1.5–2 cm long. **Flower** 6–7 cm across vertically; dorsal sepal white or pinkish, longitudinally striped with magenta, green or dark purple; synsepalum paler than dorsal sepal; petals white and purple at the base, veined with purple; lip brown and olive-green, shiny; staminode creamy-yellow veined and mottled green. **Dorsal sepal** ovate, acute, ciliate, 2.7–3.2 cm long, 2.8–3 cm broad; **synsepalum** ovate-lanceolate, acute, 2–2.4 cm long,

1.5 cm broad. **Petals** oblong to linear-ligulate, deflexed-falcate, ciliate, 3.9–4.5 cm long, 1.5–1.7 cm broad. **Lip** slipper-shaped, 3-lobed, 4.4–5 cm long, 2.7 cm broad; side lobes unfolded; pouch with veins outlined. **Staminode** reniform to lunate, slightly cleft above, side teeth below longer than mid-tooth, 1.2 cm long, 1 cm broad.

DISTRIBUTION   New Guinea and adjacent islands

HISTORY   Described by R. Schlechter in 1911 in *Fedde, Repertorium Specierum Novarum, Beihefte* (p. 2) based on a plant he had collected in 1908 in the Finisterre Mts at an altitude of 1200 m.

Papilionanthe Schltr.
Subfamily Epidendroideae
Tribe Vandeae
Subfamily Sarcanthinae

Terrestrial scrambling plants or more usually epiphytes with monopodial erect to pendent terete stems, unbranched or branching near the base, covered by sheathing leaf bases. **Leaves** distichous, terete, fleshy-coriaceous, articulated to sheathing leaf bases. **Inflorescences** axillary, 1- to several-flowered. **Flowers** large, showy, flat. **Sepals** and **petals** subsimilar, free, spreading. **Lip** 3-lobed, continuous with the column-foot. **Column** short, fleshy, with a short foot; rostellum elongate; pollinia 2, sulcate, attached by a broad triangular to subquadrate stipe to the large viscidium.

DISTRIBUTION   A genus of 11 species in S.E. Asia and the Malay Archipelago.

DERIVATION OF NAME   The generic name derives from the Greek *papilio* (butterfly) and *anthe* (flower), in allusion to its beautiful flowers that fancifully resemble butterflies.

HISTORY   *Papilionanthe* is a segregate genus of *Vanda*, indeed many of the species are still grown as vandas. Rudolf Schlechter established the genus in 1915 in the journal *Orchis* (p. 78) but the genus only became widely accepted after 1972 following the treatment of Leslie Garay in the *Botanical Museum Leaflets of Harvard University* (p. 149). This account was usefully reprinted by the *Orchid Digest* (p. 88) in 1979.

SYNONYMS   *Vanda* sect. *Teretifolia* Pfitz.; *Aerides* sect. *Phalaenidium* Pfitz.

TYPE SPECIES   *Aerides vandarum* Rchb.f. (= *Papilionanthe vandarum* (Rchb.f.) Schltr).

CULTURE   Temp. Winter min. 18°C. Tall straggling plants which require high humidity and as much light as possible, short of scorching, under glass. Grow up poles from a pot or bed or coarse epiphyte mix and water well.

Papilionanthe hookerianum (Rchb.f.) Schltr.
A large scrambling terrestrial plant. **Stems** slender, terete, up to 2.2 m long; internodes 4–5 cm long. **Leaves** terete, nearly straight, sulcate, constricted some 2 cm below the apex, mucronate, 7–10 cm long, 0.3 cm in diameter. **Inflorescences** up to 30 cm long, 2- to 12-flowered; bracts broad, 3 mm long. **Flowers** large, showy; dorsal sepal and petals white to pale mauve, tessellated with darker mauve and somewhat spotted; lateral sepals almost white; lip rich purple, deeper coloured near the base of the side lobes, and pale mauve marked with rich purple spots on the mid-lobe; pedicel and ovary 1.8–2.5 cm long. **Dorsal sepal** erect, obovate-oblong, obtuse, 1.8 cm long, 1.3 cm wide, with crisped-undulate margins; **lateral sepals** spreading, less undulate. **Petals** twisted at the base, broadly elliptic, obtuse, 2.2 cm long, 1.5 cm wide, with strongly undulate-crisped margins. **Lip** deflexed, 3-lobed, 2–3.3 cm long, 3.3–5.3 cm wide, when flattened; side lobes erect-spreading, oblong to triangular-falcate, 1.3 cm long, 0.7 cm wide; mid-lobe reniform-flabellate, somewhat trilobulate, 2.8 cm long, 4 cm wide; callus fleshy, 2-ridged, small, basal; spur conical, about 2 mm long. **Column** terete, incurved, about 1 cm long, pubescent around the stigma and at the base.

DISTRIBUTION   Malaya, Borneo and Sumatra; in swampy areas near the coast.

HISTORY   Both Sir William Hooker and H.G. Reichenbach received specimens of this spectacular orchid from Motley who had collected it in Borneo. Reichenbach described it as *Vanda hookeriana* in 1856 in *Bonplandia* (p. 324). The first living plants to reach Europe arrived in 1879 from Labuan in Borneo at the nursery of Messrs Veitch of Chelsea.

Rudolf Schlechter included it in *Papilionanthe* in 1915 in the journal *Orchis* (p. 80).

SYNONYM   *Vanda hookeriana* Rchb.f.

Papilionanthe teres (Roxb.) Schltr.
[Colour Plate]

A large scrambling epiphytic plant. **Stems** branching, terete, very long. **Leaves** straight and suberect or curved, terete, 15–20 cm long, 4 mm in diameter. **Inflorescences** 15–30 cm long, 3- to 6-flowered; bracts short, ovate. **Flowers** large, showy, 5–10 cm across, white to rose-coloured with a darker rose lip and yellowish mouth to the spur; column white; pedicel and ovary 1.8–3.2 cm long. **Dorsal sepal** spreading, ovate to subrhombic, obtuse, up to 3.8 cm long, 3 cm wide, undulate; **lateral sepals** similar. **Petals** twisted at the base, more or less orbicular, rounded at apex, up to 4.5 cm long, 3.8 cm wide, undulate on margins. **Lip** 3-lobed, up to 3.8 cm long, 3.2 cm wide, pubescent; side lobes erect, semicircular; mid-lobe

flabellate-obcordate, deeply cleft; spur funnel-shaped, compressed, up to 2.5 cm long. **Column** 9 mm long, pubescent in front.
DISTRIBUTION Thailand, Laos, Burma and the Himalayan foothills; in the lowlands and in valleys, often in full sun on the branches of large trees.
HISTORY Discovered in Sylhet in N. India by Nathaniel Wallich and introduced into cultivation by him in 1829. John Lindley described it as *Vanda teres* in 1833 in his *Genera and Species of Orchidaceous Plants* (p. 217).

Rudolf Schlechter made it the type species of his new genus *Papilionanthe* in 1915 in the journal *Orchis* (p. 78).
SYNONYMS *Vanda teres* Lindl.; *Dendrobium teres* (Lindl.) Roxb.

Papilonanthe vandarum (Rchb.f.) Schltr.
[Colour Plate]
An epiphyte forming large masses. **Stems** branching, hanging, terete, flexuous, 60 cm or more long; roots long, flat, up to 6 mm in diameter. **Leaves** suberect, terete, acuminate, sulcate, 15–25 cm long, 3 mm in diameter; leaf bases longitudinally grooved. **Inflorescences** 1- to 3-flowered, up to 30 cm long; bracts 2–3 mm long. **Flowers** 3.8–5 cm across, white with a purple-flushed base to the lip and spur; pedicel and ovary 1.5–3.3 cm long, pink. **Sepals** obovate-oblong, obtuse, up to 3.6 cm long, 1.5 cm wide, undulate. **Petals** twisted at the base, subrhombic, obtuse, up to 2.5 cm long, 1.9 cm wide, undulate. **Lip** 3-lobed, up to 2.2 cm long, and broad; side lobes flexuous, erect, narrowly ovate, falcate, dentate on apical margin; mid-lobe clawed, obovate, dilated and bilobulate at the apex, with each lobule orbicular; spur cylindric from a conical base, straight, 1.8–2.5 cm long. **Column** short, fleshy.
DISTRIBUTION India (Sikkim, Manipur and the Khasia Hills), Burma and S. China; 1200–1500 m.
HISTORY Sir William Hooker originally described this species as *Aerides cylindricum* in the *Botanical Magazine* (t. 4982) in 1857. Unfortunately that name had already been used for another species in Wight's *Icones Plantarum Indiae Orientalis*. H.G. Reichenbach therefore renamed it as *Aerides vandarum* in 1867 in the *Gardeners' Chronicle* (p. 997).

Leslie Garay transferred it to the present genus in 1974 in the *Botanical Museum Leaflets of Harvard University* (p. 372).
SYNONYMS *Aerides cylindricum* Hooker non Wight; *A. vandarum* Rchb.f.

Paraphalaenopsis A.D. Hawkes
Subfamily Epidendroideae
Tribe Vandeae
Subtribe Sarcanthinae

Pendent or less commonly erect epiphytes with short leafy stems and stout fleshy roots. **Leaves** few, terete, channelled, often very long. **Inflorescences** short, axillary, few-flowered, subcapitate, with a distinct peduncle and obscure rhachis. **Flowers** showy, fleshy. **Sepals** free, spreading, subsimilar; **lateral sepals** decurrent on the column-foot. **Petals** spreading to reflexed, clawed, inserted on the column-foot. **Lip** rigidly attached to the column-foot, 3-lobed, excavate at the base behind the callus; side lobes erect, parallel to the column; mid-lobe narrow; callus fleshy, plate-like, at the base of the mid-lobe. **Column** cylindrical, with a foot; pollinia 2 on a broad cuneate stipe and a large viscidium.
DISTRIBUTION A genus of four species endemic to the island of Borneo.
DERIVATION OF NAME From the Greek *para* (near) and *Phalaenopsis*, the orchid genus of that name, in allusion to the close affinity of the two genera.
TAXONOMY *Paraphalaenopsis* is a small segregate genus of *Phalaenopsis* distinguished by its cylindrical, terete leaves, from which the commonly used horticultural name 'Rat-tailed phalaenopsis' derives. It also differs in having the clawed petals inserted on the column-foot, the excavate base of the lip and in its breeding behaviour. These features were enough to allow A.D. Hawkes to establish *Paraphalaenopsis* as a distinct genus in 1964 in the Brazilian journal *Orquidea* (p. 212). The most recent account of the genus is that given by Herman Sweet in *The genus Phalaenopsis* in 1980.
TYPE SPECIES *Phalaenopsis denevei* J.J. Smith [Colour Plate]
CULTURE Temp. Winter min. 18°C. Small plants can be grown in pots or mounted, but larger plants should be grown in baskets hung on a slope to accommodate the pendent habit. They require humid, well-shaded conditions, similar to those for *Phalaenopsis*, with water given throughout the year.

Paraphalaenopsis laycockii (M.R. Henderson) A.D. Hawkes
[Colour Plate]
A pendent epiphyte. **Leaves** up to 5, terete, grooved, pointed, up to 1 m long, 1 cm in diameter, dark green. **Inflorescence** subcapitate, densely 2- to 12-flowered; bracts ovate, acute, up to 1 cm long. **Flowers** fleshy, pinkish-mauve to lilac with yellow-brown markings on the lip side lobes and a yellow

callus with transverse brown stripes; pedicel and ovary 4–6 cm long. **Dorsal sepal** narrowly lanceolate-elliptic, acute to subacuminate, 3–4 cm long, 1–1.5 cm wide; **lateral sepals** obliquely ovate-lanceolate, acute, 3.5–4.5 cm long, 1.3–1.7 cm wide. **Petals** subfalcate-lanceolate, acute, 3–4 cm long, 1–1.4 cm wide, fleshily clawed. **Lip** 3-lobed, 1.5–1.8 cm long; side lobes linear-oblong, rounded, up to 1.8 cm long, 0.7 cm wide; mid-lobe porrect, linear-spathulate, acutely bilobed at the apex, up to 1.2 cm wide; callus quadrate, conduplicate. **Column** up to 1 cm long, white.
DISTRIBUTION Central and S. Borneo only, a rare species in the wild.
HISTORY The type specimen of this beautiful orchid was imported from central Borneo (now Kalimantan) by the well-known Singaporean grower John Laycock. It was named in his honour, as *Phalaenopsis laycockii*, on flowering in cultivation by M.R. Henderson in 1935 in the *Orchid Review* (p. 108).

A.D. Hawkes transferred it to the present genus in 1964 in *Orquidea (Brasil)* (p. 212).
SYNONYM *Phalaenopsis laycockii* M.R. Henderson
CLOSELY RELATED SPECIES *P. laycockii* is similar to *P. serpentilingua* (J.J. Smith) A.D. Hawkes, also from Kalimantan, but that has longer inflorescences of white flowers with a distinctly coloured lip with spreading subulate apical lobules to the mid-lobe. The recently described *P. labukensis* Lamb, Chan & Shim [Colour Plate] from Mt Kinabalu in Sabah has very long leaves, up to 1.5 m long, and striking yellow flowers heavily banded with chestnut.

Pecteilis Raf.
Subfamily Orchidoideae
Tribe Orchideae
Subtribe Orchidinae

Small to medium-sized terrestrial herbs with elongate tubers. **Stems** erect, leafy throughout or leaves in basal rosette. **Inflorescence** erect, few-flowered. **Flowers** mostly showy, white or white and yellow. **Sepals** free, subsimilar, spreading. **Petals** much narrower than the sepals. **Lip** 3-lobed; side lobes spreading, ± fimbriate; mid-lobe entire; spur long, slender. **Column** with widely set anther-loculi; rostellum mid-lobe blunt; stigma sessile; pollinia 2, narrow, long-clavate; viscidia small, ovate.
DISTRIBUTION A small genus of about nine species in S.E. Asia north to Japan.
DERIVATION OF NAME From the Greek *pectein* (comb), descriptive of the pectinate side lobes of the lip.
TAXONOMY *Pecteilis* was established by C.

S. Rafinesque in 1836 in his *Flora Telluriana* (p. 37).

Pecteilis is very closely allied to *Habenaria* and *Platanthera*, being included by many botanists in the former. However, it may be distinguished from both by its characteristic sessile, 2-lobed stigma. Seidenfaden (1977) in *Dansk Botanisk Arkiv* (p. 22) discusses the current status of the genus and its affinities.

TYPE SPECIES Three species *(Habenaria gigantea* (J.E. Smith) D. Don; *Orchis susannae* L. and *O. radiata* Pers.) are mentioned by Rafinesque following the generic description.

CULTURE Compost C. Temp. Winter min. 15°C. While dormant the small tubers should be repotted and kept almost dry until green shoots appear on the surface of the compost. The plants then need more water and warm, shady and humid conditions. After flowering when the leaves have died down, the pots should again be kept a little cooler and almost dry.

Pecteilis sagarikii Seidenf. [Colour Plate]

A medium-sized terrestrial herb, up to 25 cm tall. **Tubers** ovoid, about 3 cm in diameter. **Leaves** 2–3, in a basal rosette, prostrate, ovate, rounded or obtuse at apex, 10–12 cm long, 6–9 cm broad, glossy dark green. **Inflorescence** erect, subdensely 2- to several-flowered; scape with 4 or more acute sheaths along length; bracts lanceolate, acute or acuminate, about 3 cm long. **Flowers** showy, slightly fragrant, white or cream with a cream or bright yellow lip. **Dorsal sepal** erect, ovate, acute, 2.4 cm long, 1.4 cm broad; **lateral sepals** suberect-spreading, lanceolate, acute, 2.4 cm long, 0.9 cm broad. **Petals** suberect-spreading, lanceolate, acute, 2 cm long, 0.9 cm broad. **Lip** slightly decurved, convex, obscurely 3-lobed at base, subovate, obtuse or rounded at apex, 2.4 cm long, 2 cm broad; side lobes obscure, rounded, much smaller than mid-lobe; spur pendent, filiform, slightly incurved, 3–5 cm long. **Column** erect; anther loculi 0.5 cm apart.

DISTRIBUTION Thailand.

HISTORY This attractive terrestrial was first collected by R. Sagarik at Pracinburi in Thailand. He sent living plants via Dr T. Smitinand to G. Seidenfaden who flowered it and subsequently described it in 1973 in *Botanisk Tidsskrift* (p. 46).

Pecteilis susannae (L.) Raf.

A large terrestrial herb up to 75 cm tall growing from tubers. Leaves cauline ovate-elliptic, acute, up to 19 cm long, 4–6.5 cm wide. **Inflorescence** few-flowered; bracts leaf-like, up to 8 cm long. **Flowers** large, showy, white, fragrant at night; pedicel and ovary 3.5–5.5 cm long. **Dorsal sepal** spreading,

ovate, obtuse, 2.5–4 cm long, 2.5–4.5 cm wide; **lateral sepals** spreading-suberect, ovate, obtuse, 3–4.5 cm long, 1.5–2.4 cm wide. Petals suberect, linear-elliptic, obtuse, 3–3.5 cm long, 0.2–0.3 cm wide. **Lip** 3-lobed at base, 3–3.6 cm long; side lobes spreading, obtriangular, fimbriate, 3–3.5 cm long; mid-lobe dependent, linear, acute, 2.2–3.7 cm long; spur incurved-pendent, slenderly cylindrical, 9–14 cm long. **Column** broad, shield-like, 1.5 cm long, with two divergent anther loculi.

DISTRIBUTION Widespread in S.E. Asia from India to Hong Kong and south to Indonesia; in grassy places to 2000 m.

HISTORY Originally described by Linnaeus in the first edition of *Species Plantarum* (p. 939) in 1753 as *Orchis susannae* based on a collection from Ambon in the Moluccas. It was named in honour of the wife of Rumphius who lived in Ambon and was the first to collect orchids there. C. Rafinesque transferred it to *Pecteilis* in his *Flora Telluriana* (2: p. 38) in 1836.

SYNONYMS *Orchis susannae* L.; *Habenaria susannae* (L.) R.Br.; *Platanthera susannae* (L.) Lindl.; *Platanthera robusta* Lindl.; *Hemihabenaria susannae* (L.) Finet

---

Pelatantheria Ridley
Subfamily Epidendroideae
Tribe Vandeae
Subtribe Sarcanthinae

Epiphytic herbs with long erect monopodial stems. **Leaves** oblong, obtuse, coriaceous, 2-lobed at the apex. **Inflorescences** lateral, short, racemose. **Flowers** small or medium-sized. **Sepals** lanceolate or ovate-lanceolate; petals subsimilar. **Lip** spurred; side lobes adnate to column; mid-lobe flat, larger; basal callus situated in the spur opening, callus on mid-lobe of lip dentiform. **Column** short, broad; stelidia elongate, erect; anther large, ovate, bilocular; pollinia 2; stipe short, broad, subquadrate; viscidium large, reniform or subquadrate.

DISTRIBUTION A small genus of about five species in S.E. Asia, S. China and Indonesia.

DERIVATION OF NAME From the Greek *pelates* (approaching, neighbour) and *anthera* (anther). The meaning of this name is obscure unless it possibly refers to 'stelidia which enfold the anther-cap and approach each other in doing so'.

TAXONOMY This genus was described by H.N. Ridley in 1896 in the *Journal of the Linnean Society* (p. 371) based on three species from S.E. Asia. He compared the genus with *Sarcanthus* but distinguished it by the totally different

habit, the remarkably broad, thick column, the distinct pollinia, the broad, short, quadrate stipe and large viscidium. Seidenfaden (1988) in *Opera Botanica* (p. 115) discusses the current status of the genus and provides a key to the species.

TYPE SPECIES *P. cristata* (Ridley) Ridley; *P. ctenoglossum* Ridley; *P. insectifera* (Rchb.f.) Ridley

CULTURE Compost A. Temp. Winter min. 15°C. *Pelatantheria* species, having a slender upright growth habit, may be started in a pot but require some support for their numerous aerial roots. They require good humidity and moderate shade with frequent mistings when the roots are active.

Pelatantheria insectifera (Rchb.f.) Ridley
[Colour Plate]

A medium-sized epiphytic plant. **Stems** robust, scandent, up to or over 30 cm long, 0.5 cm broad, leafy. **Leaves** subimbricate, oblong, unequally obtusely 2-lobed at apex, up to 5 cm long, 1.6 cm broad, coriaceous. **Inflorescence** sessile, very short, few-flowered, up to 2 cm long; bracts small, deciduous. **Flowers** 1.3 cm across, thickly coriaceous, greenish-yellow striped with red-brown; lip white and pink or purple, mid-lobe greenish. **Sepals** ovate-oblong, obtuse, 0.5–0.7 cm long, 0.25–0.3 cm broad. **Petals** oblong, acute, 0.6 cm long, 0.2 cm broad. **Lip** 3-lobed, 1.2 cm long, 0.6 cm broad; side lobes rounded; mid-lobe broadly triangular-ovate, acute or acuminate, fleshy; spur short, broadly conical, semiseptate, mouth with a pubescent ridge; dorsal callus large. **Column** very short, stout, apex reclinate with uncinate recurved arms.

DISTRIBUTION India, Nepal, Burma, Thailand and Malaya; up to 1000 m.

HISTORY Originally described in 1857 as *Sarcanthus insectifer* by H.G. Reichenbach in the *Botanische Zeitung* (p. 159) based on a plant introduced from Calcutta by Consul Schiller. N. Ridley transferred it to *Pelatantheria* in 1896 in the *Journal of the Linnean Society* (p. 373).

SYNONYM *Sarcanthus insectifer* Rchb.f.

Pelexia L.C. Rich.
Subfamily Spiranthoideae
Tribe Cranichideae
Subtribe Spiranthinae

Terrestrial plants with numerous, fleshy, fasciculate roots. **Leaves** in basal rosette, petiolate. **Inflorescence** erect, few- to many-flowered, racemose; peduncle often densely pubescent. **Flowers** medium-sized. **Dorsal sepal** erect, forming with the petals a narrow hood; **lateral sepals** linear, decurrent at the base and forming a long, linear, spur-like mentum. **Lip** attached to the base of the column, erect, linear, canaliculate below, spreading above, often produced at the base on either side into the sepaline spur. **Column** short, lacking a foot; rostellum flat, membranaceous, longly subulate-acuminate; pollinia 2, narrowly obovoid, granulose.

DISTRIBUTION About 50 species widely distributed in tropical and temperate S. America south to Argentina and Paraguay but commonest in Brazil.

DERIVATION OF NAME From the Greek *pelex* (helmet), referring to the helmet-shaped structure formed by the adnate dorsal sepal and petals.

TAXONOMY *Pelexia* was established by L.C. Richard in 1818 in *Mémoires du Muséum d'Histoire Naturelle, Paris* (p. 59) and was described by John Lindley in 1840 in his *Genera and Species of Orchidaceous Plants*.

Pelexia is closely allied to *Spiranthes, Cogniauxiocharis* (Schltr.) Hoehne, *Lankesterella* Ames, *Stenorrhynchus* L.C. Rich. and other American spiranthoid genera, but may be distinguished by the dorsal sepal being connate to the petals to form a hood; the lateral sepals which are connate below and prolonged into a free, long, linear, spur-like mentum; and the rostellum which is flat, membranaceous and rounded at the apex.

The genus was revised by R. Schlechter in *Beihefte zum Botanischen Zentralblatt* (1919–20) when he divided the 49 species recognised by him into five sections. F.C. Hoehne raised one of these sections to generic level as *Cogniauxiocharis* (Schltr.) Hoehne in *Arquivos de Botânicos do Estado de São Paulo* (1944).

Hoehne described and illustrated some 43 species in *Flora Brasilica–Orchidaceas* (1945). This account included most of the species in the genus which is predominantly Brazilian. Only one section, *Potosia*, with a single species from Mexico and Guatemala, is unknown in Brazil. The three other sections are all well represented.

The most recent account of the Brazilian species is that of G. Pabst and F. Dungs in *Orchidaceae Brasilienses* (1975) where the flowers of some 40 species are illustrated by line drawings.

TYPE SPECIES *P. spiranthoides* Lindl. nom. illeg. [= *P. adnata* (Sw.) Sprengel].

CULTURE Compost A. Temp. Winter min. 12–15°C. *Pelexia* species require humid and well-shaded conditions and should be carefully watered throughout the year. After flowering, the leaves may die down in which case less water should be given until the new growths are well started.

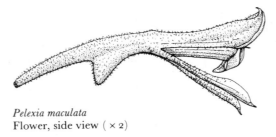

Pelexia maculata
Flower, side view (× 2)

Pelexia maculata Rolfe

A terrestrial plant, up to 75 cm or so tall, with numerous, fascicled, tuberous roots. **Leaves** 3–4, basal, rosulate, long-petiolate, ovate to lanceolate, somewhat oblique, acute or rounded at apex, up to 19 cm long, 8 cm broad, dark green, spotted with lighter green above. **Inflorescence** up to 75 cm high, racemose, densely to laxly many-flowered; peduncle glabrous below, pubescent above. **Flowers** ascending, pubescent on outer surface, green with a white lip. **Dorsal sepal** broadly oblanceolate, acute, concave above, 1–1.2 cm long; **lateral sepals** obliquely linear-oblanceolate, acute, spreading, connate and produced below into a cylindric spur with an ovoid-conical free apex. **Petals** adnate to the dorsal sepal, finely ciliolate on the margins. **Lip** adnate to the sepaline sac, narrowly oblanceolate or cuneate-spathulate, 1.7 cm long, 0.5 cm broad, margins adnate to the column below, with a transversely ovate, acute lobule at apex, retrorsely bicallose at the base. **Column** slender, dilated above; rostellum a subulate process.

DISTRIBUTION Venezuela(?), Peru and Bolivia.

HISTORY Described as *Pelexia maculata* from a plant of unknown provenance by Robert A. Rolfe in 1893 in the *Kew Bulletin* (p. 7). C. Schweinfurth transferred it to the genus *Spiranthes* in 1941 in the *Botanical Museum Leaflets of Harvard University* (p. 30), but R. Schlechter's treatment of the Spiranthinae is followed here.

SYNONYM *Spiranthes maculata* (Rolfe) C. Schweinf.

Peristeria Hooker

Subfamily Epidendroideae
Tribe Gongoreae
Subtribe Stanhopeinae

Large, epiphytic or rarely terrestrial herbs with fleshy pseudobulbs, 1- to several-leaved at apex. **Leaves** plicate, large, often very long, petiolate. **Inflorescences** lateral, basal, racemose, erect or arcuate. **Flowers** showy, subglobose. **Sepals** connivent into a sphere, broad; lateral sepals basally connate. **Petals** similar to sepals but smaller. **Lip** fleshy, 3-lobed, continuous with the column; side lobes erect, surrounding the column; mid-lobe continuous or articulated at base; disc often callose. **Column** very short, stout, footless, ± biauriculate near the apex; pollinia 2, often sulcate or subdivided.

DISTRIBUTION A small genus of about six species confined to the American tropics, from Costa Rica and Panama south to Peru and Brazil.

DERIVATION OF NAME From the Greek *peristerion* (dove), because of the fancied resemblance of the column-apex and anther within the lateral lobes of the lip to a dove.

TAXONOMY Sir William Hooker described *Peristeria* in 1831 in the *Botanical Magazine* (t. 3116). It is a small genus allied to and reminiscent of *Acineta*, but distinguished by the side lobes of the lip which are not joined by a central callus and by the short and inconspicuous hypochile of the lip.

Peristeria elata Hooker is known as the 'Holy Ghost orchid' or 'dove orchid' and is the national flower of Panama.

TYPE SPECIES *P. elata* Hooker

SYNONYM *Eckardia* Rchb.f. ex Endl.

CULTURE Compost A or C, depending on species. Temp. Winter min. 12–15°C. *P. elata* should be grown in well-drained terrestrial compost, while species such as *P. pendula* should be grown as *Acineta* species in baskets. All plants require moderate shade and plenty of water while growing but after the pseudobulbs have fully formed the plants should be kept almost dry.

Peristeria elata Hooker

A large terrestrial or lithophyte. **Pseudobulbs** clustered, large, ovoid or conical, 4–12 cm long, 4–8 cm in diameter, covered below by imbricate papery sheaths when young, the upper two leaf-bearing, 3- to 5-leaved above. **Leaves** plicate, broadly lanceolate to elliptic, acute or acuminate, 30–100 cm long, 6–12 cm wide. **Inflorescence** basal from the new growth, erect, laxly 10- to 15 (or more)-flowered, simple, 80–130 cm long; bracts ovate, acute, 1–1.5 cm long. **Flowers** campanulate-subglobose, waxy-fleshy, white with rose-red spotting on the sides of the lip, opening from the base of the inflorescence upwards. **Sepals** concave, broadly ovate, obtuse, 2.5–3 cm long, 2–3 cm wide; **lateral sepals** somewhat connate at the base. **Petals** obovate, shortly apiculate or obtuse, 2–2.5 cm long, 1.5–1.8 cm wide. **Lip** very fleshy, broadly clawed, 3-lobed; side lobes erect, thickened at the apex into a fleshy lobule; mid-lobe articulated at the base, subquadrate, truncate; callus a ventricose or suborbicular crest. **Column** erect, subconical, 0.9–1.1 cm long.

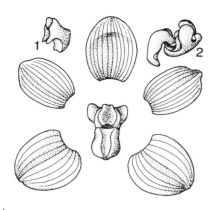

Peristeria pendula
Floral dissection ($\times 1\frac{1}{2}$)
1 – Column, side view ($\times 1\frac{1}{2}$)
2 – Lip, side view ($\times 1\frac{1}{2}$)

DISTRIBUTION Costa Rica, Panama, Venezuela and Colombia; in shaded places on the edge of grassland or on rocky outcrops in forest, at low to medium elevations up to about 700 m.

HISTORY *Peristeria elata* was described in 1831 by William Hooker in the *Botanical Magazine* (t. 3116). The 'Holy Ghost orchid' is the national flower of Panama and is now a rare plant in the wild because of over-collection. It is, consequently, one of the few orchids on Appendix 1 of the CITES Convention.

Peristeria pendula Hooker

A large, epiphytic plant with tomentose roots. **Pseudobulbs** prominent, approximate, ovoid-conical to oblong-subconical, deeply sulcate, 8–15 cm long, 3- to 4-leaved at apex. **Leaves** lanceolate-elliptic or oblong-lanceolate, acute or acuminate, up to 80 cm long, 12 cm broad, with a slender, sulcate petiole. **Inflorescence** pendent, up to 18 cm long, racemose, densely 4- to 8-flowered. **Flowers** subglobose, large, fleshy, greenish-white without, reddish-purple within, spotted purple; lip yellowish, spotted purple. **Dorsal sepal** ovate-subrotund, deeply concave, obtuse, 2.8–3.5 cm long; **lateral sepals** connate at base. **Petals** similar to dorsal sepal but shorter and narrower. **Lip** enclosed by lateral sepals, deeply 3-lobed; side lobes erect, basal, oblong-ovate, separated by a lunate or deeply sulcate callus; mid-lobe ovate-rhombic or ovate-ligulate, obtuse, recurved, transversed by a large V-shaped, sulcate callus. **Column** stout, short, auriculate near the summit.

DISTRIBUTION Guyana, Surinam, Venezuela and Peru.

HISTORY Introduced into cultivation from Demerara (now Georgetown) in Guyana by

John Allcard of Stratford Green, England. It flowered for the first time for him in 1836 and was described by William Hooker and illustrated in the *Botanical Magazine* (t. 3479) in the same year.

Pescatorea Rchb.f.

Subfamily Epidendroideae
Tribe Maxillarieae
Subtribe Zygopetalinae

Erect, tufted, epiphytic herbs, lacking pseudobulbs. **Leaves** plicate, contracted below into conduplicate, imbricating petioles which are distichously arranged in the form of an open fan. **Inflorescence** short, slender, arcuate, 1-flowered, produced from axil of non-foliaceous basal sheaths. **Flowers** relatively large, showy. **Sepals** more or less fleshy, subsimilar, concave; dorsal sepal erect, free; lateral sepals connate at the base, obliquely inserted on the column-foot. **Petals** subsimilar to the sepals. **Lip** rather fleshy, 3-lobed, abruptly contracted below into a conspicuous ligulate claw, continuous and at an obtuse angle with the column-foot, the base apparently with a deep concavity below the column, surrounded by an erect semicircular, plurisulcate callus; mid-lobe ± convex or ventricose, lateral margins often recurved. **Column** stout, semiterete, produced at base into a short foot; pollinia 4, waxy.

DISTRIBUTION A small genus of about 14 species ranging from Costa Rica to Colombia.

DERIVATION OF NAME Dedicated to V. Pescatore of Château Celle-St-Cloud near Paris, who had a fine collection of living orchids.

TAXONOMY H.G. Reichenbach described this genus in 1852 in the *Botanische Zeitung* (p. 667).

P. Allen discussed the situation of *Pescatorea* and allied genera in the *Flora of Panama* (1949) stating: 'In the exceedingly perplexing association of closely allied generic concepts embracing *Bollea*, *Chondrorhyncha*, *Kefersteinia*, *Huntleya*, *Pescatorea*, *Warscewiczella* and *Zygopetalum*, it becomes largely a matter of individual opinion which are to be rejected and which retained. Probably something very nearly approaching a logical treatment of the situation was proposed by Reichenbach filius (in *Walp. Ann.* 6: 650–662, 1863) in his reduction of nearly all of these to sections of *Zygopetalum*. This solution has never been universally accepted, however, the more recent tendency being to recognise some as valid genera and to reduce others to synonymy.'

If *Pescatorea* is treated as a distinct genus (as in this account) then it can be distinguished from *Zygopetalum* by its lack of pseudobulbs;

from *Chondrorhyncha* by its clawed lip and from *Huntleya* by the lack of broad, projecting, lateral wings at the column-apex and by its plurisulcate, but never fimbriate, basal callus. L. Garay has reviewed this group of genera in *Orquideologia* (1969, 1973) where he suggests that the relationship of *Pescatorea* to *Zygopetalum* is remote as the latter has prominent pseudobulbs. Furthermore, he maintains *Pescatorea* as a genus emphasising its distinction from *Bollea* with which it frequently hybridises in nature, the latter having a lip which is fairly adnate and continuous with the column-foot.

A key and annotated check list of the genus have been given by J.A. Fowlie in the *Orchid Digest* (1968) and the article is accompanied by fine colour illustrations of several of the species. Fowlie points out that some species such as *P. ruckeriana* Rchb.f. and *P. backhousiana* Rchb.f. may prove on further study to be natural hybrids of *Pescatorea* and *Bollea*.

TYPE SPECIES *P. cerina* (Lindl.) Rchb.f.

CULTURE Compost A. Temp. winter min. 10–12°C. As for *Chondrorhyncha*. The plants require humid, shady conditions with evenly moist roots throughout the year.

Pescatorea cerina (Lindl.) Rchb.f.
[Colour Plate]

A caespitose epiphytic plant, lacking any pseudobulbs. **Leaves** erect or arcuate, plicate, subcoriaceous, linear-lanceolate to elliptic-lanceolate, acute or acuminate, 15–60 cm long, 3–5 cm broad. **Inflorescence** short, axillary, 1-flowered, erect or arcuate, 3.5–10 cm long. **Flower** large, showy; sepals white, blotched greenish-yellow at the base of the lateral sepals; petals white; lip marked reddish-brown on callus; column white. **Dorsal sepal** linear-elliptic to obovate, obtuse, 2.5–3.2 cm long, 1.6–1.8 cm broad; **lateral sepals** connate at the base, elliptic-lanceolate to oblanceolate, obtuse, 2.5–3.5 cm long, 1.8–2 cm broad. **Petals** spreading, similar to the dorsal sepal. **Lip** rather fleshy, clawed, 3-lobed, 2–3 cm long, 2.5 cm broad, geniculate at base of lamina; side lobes subfalcate, resting against the base of the column; mid-lobe convex, margins often reflexed; callus plurisulcate. **Column** short, stout, 1.3–1.5 cm long, with a short foot.

DISTRIBUTION Costa Rica and Panama; in wet highland forest at about 1000–2600 m altitude.

HISTORY Discovered in Veragua by J. Warscewicz on the Chiriqui Volcano at about 2400 m and sold in Stevens' Sale Rooms in 1851. Rucker was the first to flower it, and it was originally described in 1852 as *Huntleya cerina* by John Lindley in his and J. Paxton's *Flower Garden* (p. 62). H.G. Reichenbach trans-

ferred it to the genus *Pescatorea* in the same year in the *Botanische Zeitung* (p. 667).
SYNONYMS *Huntleya cerina* Lindl.; *Zygopetalum cerinum* (Lindl.) Rchb.f.

Pescatorea dayana Rchb.f. [Colour Plate]
A large epiphytic herb. **Stem** very short, about 7-leaved. **Leaves** suberect, oblong-oblanceolate, acuminate, 20–60 cm long, 2–5 cm broad, petiolate. **Inflorescence** 1-flowered, axillary, up to 11 cm long; peduncle terete, bearing 2 short sheaths; bract lanceolate, acute, 1–1.5 cm long. **Flower** showy, up to 8 cm across; sepals and petals white, ± rose-purple in apical half; lip white or purple with a purple-violet callus; column white with a purple anther. **Sepals** obovate, obtuse, up to 4.5 cm long, 2.5 cm broad. **Petals** similar but slightly smaller. **Lip** shortly clawed, ovate to elliptic, convex, 3 cm long, 2.3 cm broad; callus lunate, longitudinally several-ridged. **Column** fleshy, slightly arcuate.
DISTRIBUTION Colombia; 300–1500 m.
HISTORY This showy species was described in 1874 by H.G. Reichenbach in the *Gardeners' Chronicle* (p. 1618) based on a specimen flowered by John Day of Tottenham, near London. Reichenbach rightly supposed it to grow in Colombia, having just received flowers in spirit sent to him from there by G. Wallis.
P. dayana occurs in several colour varieties, that illustrated being var. *rhodacra* Rchb.f. [Colour Plate].

Phaius Lour.
Subfamily Epidendroideae
Tribe Arethuseae
Subtribe Bletiinae

Large or medium-sized terrestrial herbs. **Stems** ± pseudobulbous or cylindric, few-leaved. **Leaves** large, petiolate, plicate. **Inflorescence** lateral or axillary halfway up the stem, laxly or subdensely racemose. **Flowers** conspicuous, often showy. **Sepals** and **petals** ± fleshy, subsimilar, spreading. **Lip** erect, sessile and shortly adnate to column below, gibbous or spurred at base; lamina entire or ± lobed with sides parallel to the column. **Column** fleshy, free, rather short to long, produced at base into an inflexed foot; anther 2-celled; pollinia 8, waxy, lacking a gland.
DISTRIBUTION About 30 species widely distributed in tropical Asia, Africa, Madagascar, Indonesia, New Guinea, Australia and the Pacific Islands.
DERIVATION OF NAME From the Greek *phaios* (grey or swarthy) referring to the flowers which turn dark with age or if damaged.

TAXONOMY *Phaius* was described in 1790 by Juan Loureiro in *Flora Cochinchinensis* (p. 524). It is allied to *Calanthe* but may be distinguished by its long, free column and short, saccate or non-existent spur. Although a smaller genus in number of species, *Phaius* is almost as widespread as *Calanthe*.
In *Die Orchidaceen von Deutsch-Neu-Guinea* (1914), R. Schlechter reduced the four sections of the genus recognised until then to two. These were *(Eu) Phaius* in which the stems are short and thick and *Pesomeria* where they are elongated and rather thin. Later, in *Fedde, Specierum Novarum, Beihefte* (1924) he raised C.L. Blume's subgenus of *Phaius*, *Gastrorchis*, (with Madagascan species only) to generic rank, distinguishing his new genus from *Phaius* on account of its ecalcarate lip entirely free from the column and furnished with various calli.
However, V.S. Summerhayes in the *Kew Bulletin* (1964) has shown that *Gastrorchis* Schltr. cannot be kept as distinct from *Phaius*, because species with intermediate characters exist. He proposed that *Gastrorchis* therefore be reduced to sectional rank within *Phaius*. This treatment is followed here with the species of sect. *Gastrorchis* being distinguished by their lack of a spurred lip and by their characteristic lip-calli.
J. Bosser has recently reviewed the nine Madagascan species of *Phaius* in *Adansonia* (1971) giving a key to identify them and illustrating several species by line drawings.
TYPE SPECIES *P. grandifolius* Lour. [= *P. tankervilleae* (Banks) Blume].
SYNONYMS *Gastrorchis* (Blume) Schltr.; *Gastorkis* [*Gastrorchis*] Thou.
CULTURE Compost B or C. Temp. Winter min. 15°C. During growth these plants require ample water, good shade and high humidity but it is important that water is not allowed to fall on the leaves. When growth is complete, they should be kept almost dry in slightly cooler conditions.

Phaius mishmensis (Lindl.) Rchb.f.
[Colour Plate]
A large terrestrial plant, up to 140 cm tall but mostly much shorter. **Stems** obscurely pseudobulbous, fleshy, narrowly fusiform-cylindric, sheathed below, 6- to 8-leaved above. **Leaves** plicate, alternate, elliptic-lanceolate to oblong-ovate, acuminate or acute, 15–30 cm long, 8–12.5 cm broad. **Inflorescences** 1–2, axillary, racemose, laxly-flowered, not exceeding the leaves, up to 30 cm long; bracts lanceolate, caducous. **Flowers** erect, 5–6 cm across; sepals and petals pale rose-coloured, dark red or purplish-brown; lip white or pink, speckled with purple, spur ± yellowish. **Sepals** erect-spreading, linear-oblong, subacute, concave, up to 3.5 cm long, 1 cm broad. **Petals** narrowly

linear-oblanceolate, acute, up to 3 cm long, 0.6 cm broad. **Lip** cuneate at base, 3-lobed, joined to base of column, 3 cm long, 2.5 cm broad; side lobes erect, rounded, enfolding the column; mid-lobe entire, reflexed, subquadrate or oblong, emarginate or retuse at apex, with a central raised lamella highest in the apical part; disc with a central pubescent ridge; spur narrowly cylindrical, acute, arcuate, up to 1.5 cm long. **Column** straight, 1.2 cm long; anther-cap pubescent.
DISTRIBUTION India (Sikkim Himalayas, Assam), Bhutan, Burma, Thailand, S. China, Laos, Vietnam, Taiwan and adjacent islands, and the Philippines.
HISTORY Originally described by John Lindley in 1852 in his and J. Paxton's *Flower Garden* (p. 36) as *Limatodes mishmensis*. H.G. Reichenbach transferred it to the genus *Phaius* in 1857 in *Bonplandia* (p. 43).
SYNONYMS *Limatodes mishmensis* Lindl.; *Phaius roseus* Rolfe; *P. gracilis* Hayata; *P. crinita* (Gagnep.) Seid.

Phaius tankervilleae (Banks) Blume
[Colour Plate]
A large, terrestrial plant, 60–200 cm tall. **Pseudobulbs** conical or ovoid, green, 2.5–6 cm long, sheathed by leaf-bases. **Leaves** elliptic-lanceolate, acuminate, thin-textured, 30–100 cm long, up to 20 cm broad; petiole 15–25 cm long. **Inflorescence** very tall, 10- to 20-flowered, 60–200 cm long; peduncle stout; bracts spathaceous, caducous, 5 cm long. **Flowers** 10–12.5 cm across; sepals and petals white, greenish or rosy on outer surface, reddish or yellow-brown with a golden margin or rarely white inside; tube of lip pink to wine-red with a yellow base inside, whitish outside, mid-lobe orange, red or white and pink. **Sepals** and **petals** spreading, lanceolate or oblanceolate, acuminate, 4.5–6.5 cm long, 1.2 cm broad. **Lip** tubular below, 3-lobed when spread, obovate, acute or apiculate or sometimes truncate, front margin crisped-undulate and recurved, about 5 cm long or more, 4.5 cm broad; spur slender, short, ± forked at apex, 0.6–1.5 cm long; callus of 3 low ridges, the central one in front of the lateral ones. **Column** clavate, 2 cm long.
DISTRIBUTION China, N. India (Sikkim, N.W. and N.E. Himalayas, Assam), Bangladesh (Sylhet), Burma, Sri Lanka, Thailand, Indo-China, China, Malaya, Indonesia to New Guinea, Australia and the S.W. Pacific Islands; up to 1300 m altitude, in lowland and lower montane forests.
HISTORY This widespread species was cultivated in Europe as early as 1788 when it was described by Sir Joseph Banks in L'Heritier's *Sertum Anglicum* (p. 28) and shortly afterwards in W. Aiton's *Hortus Kewensis* as

Limodorum tankervilleae. C.L. Blume transferred it to *Phaius* in 1856 in *Museum Botanicum Lugdunum Batavium* (p. 177).

The specific epithet is often misspelt '*tancarvilliae*'.

SYNONYMS include *Phaius bicolor* Lindl.; *P. grandifolius* Lour.; *Limodorum tankervilleae* Banks; *P. wallichii* Hooker f.; *Limodorum incarvilliae* Pers.

Phaius tuberculosus (Thou.) Blume
[Colour Plate]
A large terrestrial plant with a short ascending rhizome, bearing pseudobulbs at intervals. **Pseudobulbs** short, small, hidden by the leaf-sheaths, up to 2.5 cm long, 0.4 cm broad, 5- to 6-leaved. **Leaves** suberect-spreading, longly petiolate, narrowly lanceolate, acute, plicate, 30–60 cm long, 2–3 cm broad; petiole sheathing. **Inflorescence** equalling the leaves or slightly longer, 40–65 cm long, 6- to 8-flowered; bracts caducous, white, narrowly lanceolate. **Flowers** showy; sepals and petals pure white; lip side lobes yellow covered with many red spots, mid-lobe white with lilac- or violet-spotted margins, disc and callus yellow; column white. **Sepals** broadly elliptic-lanceolate, apiculate, 3.2–4.4 cm long, 1.4–1.6 cm broad. **Petals** a little smaller than the sepals, 2.4 cm long, 1 cm broad. **Lip** broadly spread out, obscurely 3-lobed; side lobes glabrous, erect-spreading, semiorbicular, margins undulate; mid-lobe deflexed, spreading, margins very undulate; disc bearing 3 verrucose ridges onto base of mid-lobe, glandular pubescent at the base. **Column** 1.8 cm long.
DISTRIBUTION E. Madagascar.
HISTORY This attractive species was first collected and described in 1822 by Aubert du Petit Thouars who named it *Limodorum tuberculosum* in his *Orchidées des Iles Australes de l'Afrique* (t. 31). C.L. Blume transferred it to the genus *Phaius* in 1856 in *Museum Botanicum Lugdunum Batavium* (p. 181).
SYNONYMS *Gastrorchis tuberculosa* (Thou.) Schltr.; *Limodorum tuberculosum* Thou.; *Bletia tuberculosa* (Thou.) Sprengel; *Phaius warpurii* Weathers
CLOSELY RELATED SPECIES Similar to *Phaius humblotii* Rchb.f. and *P. francoisii* (Schltr.) Summerh. which are distinguished by their pink sepals and petals and distinct lip shape.

Phalaenopsis Blume
Subfamily Epidendroideae
Tribe Vandeae
Subtribe Sarcanthinae

Epiphytic or lithophytic plants. **Roots** adventitious, fleshy, chlorophyll-bearing in leafless species. **Stems** short, leafy, lacking pseudobulbs.

Leaves distichous, usually broadest towards the apex, often twisted to lie in one plane, with a conduplicate base, rarely petiolate, **Inflorescence** lateral, racemose or paniculate, 1- to many-flowered; bracts smaller than the pedicellate ovary. **Flowers** small to large, long-lasting, often showy, variously coloured white, pink, mauve, violet or yellow with red-brown markings. **Sepals** free, spreading. **Petals** similar to sepals or much larger and broader, base clawed or tapered. **Lip** 3-lobed; side lobes erect, parallel with the column, with a fleshy swelling in or near the middle; mid-lobe porrect, fleshy, often with a central ridge, ± pubescent; disc between side lobes bearing a more or less complex fleshy callus. **Column** erect, lacking wings, basally extended into a short column-foot; stigma large; pollinia 2, subglobose, winged.
DISTRIBUTION About 46 species in India, S.E. Asia, Indonesia, the Philippines and N. Australia.
DERIVATION OF NAME From the Greek *phalaina* (moth) and *opsis* (appearance), refer-

Phalaenopsis lips (All × 1)
(After Sweet, 1968–69)

1 – *P. sanderiana*	10 – *P. lueddemanniana*
2 – *P. lowii*	11 – *P. pallens*
3 – *P. equestris*	12 – *P. hieroglyphica*
4 – *P. fimbriata*	13 – *P. schilleriana*
5 – *P. amabilis*	14 – *P. cornucervi*
6 – *P. sumatrana*	15 – *P. intermedia*
7 – *P. gigantea*	16 – *P. mannii*
8 – *P. violacea*	17 – *P. stuartiana*
9 – *P. aphrodite*	

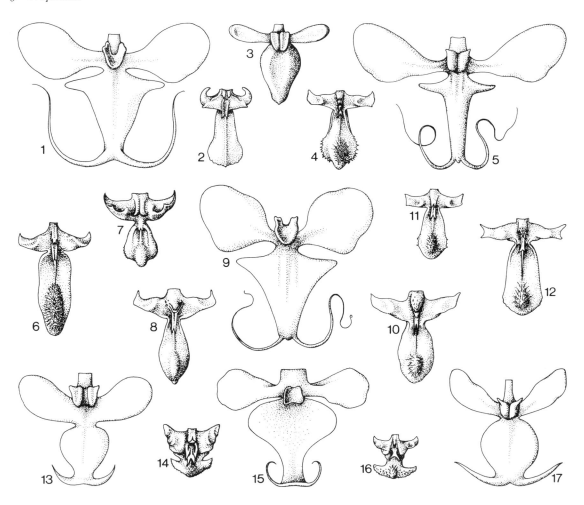

ring to the delicate, moth-like, predominantly white flowers of some species.

TAXONOMY Since the genus *Phalaenopsis* was established in 1825 by C.L. Blume in his *Bijdragen* (p. 294), it has been revised several times, notably by H.G. Reichenbach in *Xenia Orchidacea* in 1862, R.A. Rolfe in 1886 in the *Gardeners' Chronicle* and recently by H. Sweet in the *American Orchid Society Bulletin* (1968–69) and in *The Genus Phalaenopsis* (1980). Reichenbach's account mentioned some 11 species in two groups, but further introductions meant that Rolfe dealt with about 24 species placing them in four sections. Sweet's revision covers 46 species which he places in nine sections. Following the treatment of A.D. Hawkes, Sweet leaves the terete-leaved species in a distinct genus, *Paraphalaenopsis*. Species of *Paraphalaenopsis* also behave rather distinctively in their breeding behaviour. The species described here occur in five of Sweet's sections as follows:

1. sect. *Phalaenopsis* – Species with broad petals; lip with a pair of antennae-like projections at the apex. This section includes *P. amabilis*, *P. schilleriana* and *P. stuartiana*.
2. sect. *Polychilos* (Breda) Rchb.f. – Species with fleshy flowers; sepals and petals similar; lip with a central gibbous cavity; mid-lobe apex ± anchor-shaped; base of lip continuous with column-foot. This section includes *P. cornucervi* and *P. mannii*.
3. sect. *Stauroglottis* (Schauer) Benth. – Sepals and petals narrow, subsimilar; lip 3-lobed, with a peltate callus at the base of the mid-lobe. This section includes *P. equestris* and *P. lindenii*.
4. sect. *Amboinensis* Sweet – Flowers rotund; petals broad, elliptic; lip mid-lobe fleshy, convex; with a thin central ridge. This section includes *P. gigantea*.
5. sect. *Zebrinae* Pfitz. – Flowers stellate; petals oblanceolate to narrowly obovate. This section includes *P. fasciata*, *P. fimbriata*, *P. lueddemanniana*, *P. mariae*, *P. pallens*, *P. sumatrana* and *P. violacea*. The difficult taxonomy of this group has led to the section being referred to as the 'lueddemanniana complex'. However, Sweet's authoritative account has now clarified greatly the specific limits in this section.

TYPE SPECIES *P. amabilis* (L.) Blume

CULTURE Compost A. Temp. Winter min. 15°C. Although they grow well in pots, *Phalaenopsis* species are often better grown in baskets where the roots are more exposed to the air. As with *Paphiopedilum*, the plants require careful shading, especially in the spring when the young leaves are growing. Apart from good humidity, water should be given throughout the year especially when the plants are in active growth.

Phalaenopsis amabilis (L.) Blume
[Colour Plate]

A variable, robust, epiphytic plant. **Stem** pendulous, short, robust, covered by imbricating leaf-bases. **Leaves** 3–5, fleshy or coriaceous, arcuate, pendent, ovate-elliptic, obovate or oblong-oblanceolate, up to 50 cm long, 10 cm broad, obtuse to subacute, shiny green above. **Inflorescence** ± slender, racemose or paniculate, laxly few- to many-flowered, up to 1 m long; bracts small, scarious, triangular, up to 0.5 cm long. **Flowers** variable in size and colour, delicate in texture, showy, fragrant and long-lasting; sepals and petals milky-white with a pinkish suffusion on reverse, especially towards the base; lip white, margins rich yellow, callus golden-yellow, spotted with crimson. **Dorsal sepal** elliptic or ovate-elliptic, ± shortly clawed, up to 4 cm long, 2.5 cm broad, obtuse; **lateral sepals** ovate, ovate-elliptic or ovate-lanceolate, oblique, up to 4 cm long, 2.5 cm broad, acute or rarely shortly acuminate. **Petals** subrotund to subreniform, cuneate at base, up to 4.5 cm long, 5 cm broad, rounded at apex. **Lip** fleshy, clawed, 3-lobed in basal half, up to 2.3 cm broad; side lobes obliquely spathulate, erect; mid-lobe cruciform, side arms short, triangular, acute, with 2 whip-like tendrils at apex; callus subquadrate, fleshy, 2-lobed. **Column** short, cylindrical.

DISTRIBUTION Australia (Queensland), New Guinea, Indonesia to Sumatra in the west and the Philippines (Palawan).

HISTORY Originally described from the island of Amboina by G.E. Rumphius in 1750 as *Angraecum album majus*, a pre-Linnaean trinomial. However, it was re-collected in Java in 1752 by Peter Osbeck while on his way from China to England and an herbarium specimen of his eventually reached Carl von Linné who described it in *Species Plantarum* (p. 953) in 1753 as *Epidendrum amabile*. This species was transferred to the new genus *Phalaenopsis* by C.L. Blume in 1825 in his *Bijdragen* (p. 294) as the type species of that genus.

SYNONYMS include *Epidendrum amabile* L.; *Cymbidium amabile* (L.) Roxb.; *Synadena amabilis* (L.) Raf.; *Phalaenopsis grandiflora* Lindl.; *P. gloriosa* Rchb.f.; *P. rimestadiana* (Linden) Rolfe

CLOSELY RELATED SPECIES Sometimes confused with *Phalaenopsis aphrodite* Rchb.f., from the Philippines, which has a distinct callus which is 4-lobed behind and a much broader rhombic mid-lobe to the lip.

Phalaenopsis cornucervi (Breda) Blume & Rchb.f. [Colour Plate]

A robust, epiphytic plant. **Stem** rhizomatous, short, enclosed in imbricating leaf-bases. **Leaves** fleshy, oblong-ligulate to oblong-oblanceolate, 12–22 cm long, 2–4 cm broad,

obtuse. **Inflorescence** several-flowered, racemose or paniculate, 9–42 cm long; rhachis compressed, flexuose, winged; bracts distichous, ovate-cucullate, keeled dorsally, up to 5 cm long. **Flowers** fleshy, waxy, several opening simultaneously; yellow or greenish-yellow, spotted or blotched with cinnamon or red-brown; lip white, marked with parallel red-brown stripes on side lobes and at base of column. **Dorsal sepal** elliptic to oblanceolate; dorsally keeled, 1.6–2.3 cm long, 0.5–0.8 cm broad, acute, margins recurved; **lateral sepals** similar but somewhat oblique, 1.9–2.3 cm long, 0.7–0.9 cm broad, acute or subacuminate. **Petals** lanceolate or elliptic-lanceolate, 0.7–1.8 cm long, 0.5–0.6 cm broad, acute or obtuse. **Lip** very fleshy, 3-lobed, 1.8 cm long, 1 cm broad; side lobes erect, oblong, truncate, with a basal fleshy thickening; mid-lobe anchor-shaped, side lobules erose; callus complex of 3 appendages in series, reaching onto mid-lobe, 2-pronged in front. **Column** fleshy, arcuate, up to 0.8 cm long.

DISTRIBUTION Indonesia (Sumatra to Borneo), Malaya, Thailand and Burma; in relatively exposed habitats.

HISTORY First discovered by van Hasselt in Bantam Province in Java and described by Breda in Kuhl and Breda's *Genera et Species Orchidacearum* (t. 1) in 1827 as *Polychilos cornu-cervi*. However, C.L. Blume and H.G. Reichenbach transferred it to the genus *Phalaenopsis* in 1860 in the *Hamburger Gartenzeitung* (p. 116).

Var. *picta*. (Hassk.) Sweet differs from the typical form in having its sepals and petals marked with transverse red-brown bars and not with spots.

In the wild, *P. cornucervi* occasionally forms natural hybrids with *P. violacea*.

SYNONYM *Polychilos cornucervi* Breda

Phalaenopsis equestris (Schauer) Rchb.f.
[Colour Plate]

An epiphytic plant. **Stem** short, covered by imbricating leaf-bases, up to 5-leaved. **Leaves** fleshy, recurved, oblong-elliptic to oblong-ovate, up to 20 cm long, 6.5 cm broad, acute or subobtuse. **Inflorescence** suberect, arcuate, racemose or paniculate, many-flowered; rhachis slightly flexuose, purple; bracts small, up to 0.2 cm long. **Flowers** delicate in texture, variable in size and colour; sepals and petals commonly white or pale rose; lip darker rose with yellow on the side lobes. **Dorsal sepal** oblong-elliptic to ovate-elliptic, margins recurved, 1–1.7 cm long, 0.5–0.8 cm broad. **Petals** elliptic to rhombic, margins somewhat recurved, 0.8–1.5 cm long, 0.5–0.8 cm broad, acute or obtuse. **Lip** 3-lobed, 1–1.4 cm long, 1–1.6 cm broad; side lobes oblong-ovate, obtuse or rounded, fleshy on anterior margins; mid-lobe ovate to elliptic, concave in the middle, fleshy and acute at the apex; callus between side lobes fleshy, subquadrate, peltate. **Column** arcuate, up to 0.9 cm long.

DISTRIBUTION   Widespread in the Philippines; from sea level to 300 m altitude.

HISTORY   Collected for the first time on the island of Luzon by Meyen and described by Schauer in *Nova Acta...Naturae Curiosorum* (Suppl. 1: p. 432) in 1843 as *Stauroglottis equestris*. H.G. Reichenbach transferred it to the genus *Phalaenopsis* in *Linnaea* (p. 864) in 1849.

SYNONYMS   *Stauroglottis equestris* Schauer; *Phalaenopsis stauroglottis* Hort.; *P. esmeralda* auct. non Rchb.f.; *P. riteiwanensis* Masamune; *P. rosea* Lindl.

CLOSELY RELATED SPECIES   *P. lindenii* may be distinguished by its marmorated leaves, green rhachis and the orbicular mid-lobe to the lip. *P. x intermedia* Lindl., from Luzon, is a natural hybrid of *P. equestris* and *P. aphrodite*.

Phalaenopsis fasciata Rchb.f. [Colour Plate]

An epiphytic plant. **Stem** short, completely covered by imbricating persistent sheaths. **Roots** numerous, fleshy, glabrous. **Leaves** distichous, elliptic, obovate-elliptic or obovate, dorsally keeled, 14–20 cm long, 6–7.5 cm broad, obtuse or rounded. **Inflorescence** lateral, suberect or arcuate, racemose, longer than the leaves; rhachis fractiflex; bracts triangular, up to 0.4 cm long, acute. **Flowers** fleshy, waxy; sepals and petals pale yellow with numerous cinnamon bars; lip sulphur-yellow, bright purple in front. **Dorsal sepal** elliptic or ovate-elliptic, dorsally carinate, 2–3.1 cm long, 1.2–1.5 cm broad; **lateral sepals** obliquely ovate or ovate-elliptic, dorsally keeled, 2–3.1 cm long, 1.2–1.5 cm broad. **Petals** ovate to ovate-elliptic, 2.2–2.6 cm long, 0.9–1.3 cm broad, acute or obtuse. **Lip** shortly clawed, 3-lobed, 2–2.7 cm long, 1.2–1.8 cm broad; side lobes spreading, narrowly oblong, dilated and truncate at apex, fleshy in the middle; mid-lobe cuneate-flabellate, obscurely erose towards the apex, with a central ridge, merging into a rounded callus at apex; disc with a callus bearing many backpointing teeth, bifid in front. **Column** arcuate, 1.2–1.6 cm long.

DISTRIBUTION   The Philippines.

HISTORY   *P. fasciata* was introduced into cultivation by Messrs Low & Co. of Clapton, England in 1882 from the Philippines. H.G. Reichenbach described it the same year in the *Gardeners' Chronicle* (n.s. 18: p. 134).

CLOSELY RELATED SPECIES   *P. fasciata* is commonly cultivated species which is often confused with *P. lueddemanniana* Rchb.f. var. *ochracea* Rchb.f. However, it can easily be separated from *P. lueddemanniana* and its varieties by its many retrorse callosities.

Phalaenopsis fimbriata J.J. Smith
[Colour Plate]

An epiphytic plant. **Stem** short, covered with imbricating persistent leaf-sheaths. **Leaves** suberect, oblong-elliptic to elliptic-obovate, 14–23 cm long, 3–7 cm broad, acute or obtuse. **Inflorescence** more or less recurved, laxly many-flowered, up to 27 cm long; rhachis angled; bracts ovate-triangular, 0.2–0.4 cm long. **Flowers** fleshy, all opening simultaneously; sepals and petals white, pale green towards the apex; lateral sepals ± faintly striated with magenta-purple; lip side lobes white, purple at apex and base, mid-lobe magenta or purple with white hairs, callus golden-yellow. **Dorsal sepal** elliptic or oblong-elliptic, dorsally slightly keeled, 1.5–2 cm long, 0.6–0.9 cm broad, obtuse; **lateral sepals** obliquely ovate-elliptic or oblong-elliptic, keeled dorsally, 1.3–2 cm long, 0.8–1.2 cm broad, acute to subacute. **Petals** oblong-elliptic, 1.5–1.8 cm long, 0.6–0.8 cm broad, subacute to obtuse. **Lip** 3-lobed, 1.4–1.6 cm long, 1–1.4 cm broad; side lobes erect, obliquely oblong, fleshy in middle; mid-lobe convex, very fleshy, ovate-rhomboid, margins dentate-fimbriate; apical callus fleshy ovoid, densely covered with long hairs; disc with 2 superposed lamellae with a bifid projection in front. **Column** fleshy, erect, 0.6–0.8 cm long.

DISTRIBUTION   Java and Sumatra.

HISTORY   First collected in Java at Blitar by Tollens and cultivated successfully in the Buitenzorg (now Bogor) Botanic Garden. J.J. Smith described it in 1921 in the *Bulletin du Jardin Botanique de Buitenzorg* (p. 300), naming it for the densely fimbriate margins to the mid-lobe of the lip.

Phalaenopsis gigantea J.J. Smith
[Colour Plate]

An epiphytic plant. **Stem** short, completely enclosed by the leaf-bases, 5- to 6-leaved. **Leaves** pendulous, leathery, shiny on both sides, oblong-ovate to elliptic, up to 50 cm long, 20 cm broad, obtuse. **Inflorescence** from the leaf-axils, lateral, pendulous, up to 40 cm long, densely 20- to 30-flowered; bracts triangular, acute, 0.5–0.6 cm long. **Flowers** fleshy, all open simultaneously, about 5 cm across; sepals and petals greenish-yellow to white covered with closely spaced brown or maroon spots; lip white with crimson or carmine spots or blotches. **Dorsal sepal** spreading, elliptic or ovate-elliptic, up to 3.1 cm long, 2.1 cm broad, obtuse; **lateral sepals** obliquely elliptic or ovate-elliptic, adnate at base to column-foot, up to 3.1 cm long, 2.1 cm broad, obtuse. **Petals** elliptic or rhombic-elliptic, up to 2.7 cm long, 2 cm broad, acute or obtuse. **Lip** 3-lobed, small, very fleshy, 1.5 cm long, 1.5 cm broad; side lobes triangular-subfalcate, with a central cal-

lus; mid-lobe ovate, with an ovoid callus at apex, side margins dentate, with a bidentate, plate-like callus at base of mid-lobe; disc with a fleshy subcylindrical callus with a bifurcate apex. **Column** short, fleshy, cylindric, 1.1 cm long.

DISTRIBUTION   Borneo; where it grows as an epiphyte in primaeval forest.

HISTORY   *P. gigantea* was first collected during the Niewenhuis Expedition to Borneo in 1896–97 by Mantri Jaheri. One plant of this original collection survived until just after 1909 when J.J. Smith described it in the *Bulletin du Département de l'Agriculture aux Indes Néerlandaises* (p. 45). No more was heard of *P. gigantea* until 1937 when it was collected in large quantities from a new locality in Borneo. Recent information suggests that *P. gigantea* is probably nearly extinct in all its known wild localities.

Phalaenopsis hieroglyphica (Rchb.f.) Sweet
[Colour Plate]

A pendent or suberect epiphytic plant with coarse, fleshy, rather flexuous roots. **Stem** short, covered by imbricating leaf-bases. **Leaves** few to many, rather coriaceous, oblong-ligulate, acute or obtuse, up to 30 cm long, 9 cm broad. **Inflorescence** suberect to arcuate, simple or branching, up to 32 cm long, many-flowered; bracts ovate-cucullate, 0.5 cm long. **Flowers** long-lasting; sepals and petals ochre-white covered with small cinnamon figures, circles or spots; lip whitish with a pink-purple flush. **Sepals** elliptic to ovate-elliptic, acute, dorsally keeled towards apex, 2.3–4.1 cm long, 1–1.7 cm broad. **Petals** ovate-elliptic, acute to apiculate, 2.2–3.3 cm long, 1.1–1.6 cm broad. **Lip** shortly clawed, 3-lobed, 2–2.5 cm long, 1.4–1.8 cm broad; side lobes obliquely oblong-linear, truncate, with a cushion-like central ridge; mid-lobe cuneate-flabellate, obscurely erose towards apex, fleshy and covered with hairs in centre; callus between side lobes and on base of mid-lobe much divided below and with a pair of long appendages in front. **Column** slightly arcuate, cylindric, up to 1.2 cm long.

DISTRIBUTION   The Philippines (Polillo and Palawan only).

HISTORY   Originally described by H.G. Reichenbach in the *Gardeners' Chronicle* (ser. 3, 2: p. 586) in 1887 as a variety of *P. lueddemanniana* but raised to specific rank in 1969 by H. Sweet in the *American Orchid Society Bulletin* (p. 36).

SYNONYMS   *Phalaenopsis lueddemanniana* var. *hieroglyphica* Rchb.f.; *P. lueddemanniana* var. *palawanensis* Quis.; *P. lueddemanniana* var. *surigadensis* Hort.

CLOSELY RELATED SPECIES   Closely allied to *P. lueddemanniana* from which Sweet separated it because of its multidigitate glabrous callus and the hieroglyphic patterning of the sepals and petals. He further noted that no intermediate forms between these species have been recorded.

Phalaenopsis × intermedia Lindl.
[Colour Plate]
See under *Phalaenopsis equestris*.

Phalaenopsis lindenii Loher [Colour Plate]
A pendent epiphytic plant. **Stem** very short, enclosed completely in imbricating leaf-bases. **Leaves** oblong-lanceolate or oblong-oblanceolate, up to 25 cm long, 4 cm broad, acute or obtuse at unequally 2-lobed apex, green, mottled with silvery-white. **Inflorescence** racemose, rarely branched, slender; rhachis flexuose; bracts small, 0.1–0.2 cm long. **Flowers** delicate, white suffused with pale rose, with a few rose-coloured dots at base of sepals and petals; lip mid-lobe amethyst-rose with several darker lines radiating out from the base, side lobes white, minutely spotted with orange and with 3 purple lines above; column purple. **Dorsal sepal** oblong-elliptic, 1.6 cm long, 0.7 cm broad, obtuse or rounded; **lateral sepals** oblong-ovate, slightly carinate, 1.5 cm long, 0.8 cm broad, acute. **Petals** elliptic-rhombic, acute or subobtuse, 1.4 cm long, 0.8 cm broad. **Lip** shortly clawed, 3-lobed near base, 1.4 cm long, 1.8 cm broad; side lobes oblanceolate to oblong, rounded at apex, fleshy along front margin; mid-lobe orbicular to elliptic, apiculate, slightly concave in centre; callus between side lobes 6- to 8-sided. **Column** cylindric, slightly arcuate, 1 cm long.
DISTRIBUTION The Philippines (Luzon).
HISTORY *P. lindenii* was collected on the island of Luzon by A. Loher and was subsequently described by him in the *Journal des Orchidées* (p. 103) in 1895. Loher named this species in honour of Jean Linden of the famous Belgian orchid nursery firm.
CLOSELY RELATED SPECIES Closely related to *P. equestris* from which it may be distinguished by its mottled leaves and the orbicular mid-lobe of its lip. Some authorities consider that *P. lindenii* may be a natural hybrid of *P. equestris* and *P. schilleriana* Rchb.f.

Phalaenopsis lowii Rchb.f.
A medium-sized epiphytic or lithophytic herb. **Stem** very short, covered entirely by imbricating leaf-bases. Roots few, elongate, fleshy. **Leaves** 1–5, ovate-lanceolate to oblong-lanceolate, acute, up to 9 cm long, 3 cm broad, channelled above, dark green above, speckled with purple below, articulated below to leaf-base. **Inflorescence** arcuate to pendent, simple or rarely branched, laxly many-flowered, up to 30 cm long; bracts triangular, acute, 0.3–0.4

cm long. **Flowers** showy, delicate in texture; sepals and petals pale rose; lip mid-lobe and column-apex deep rose-purple to violet, bases of side lobes yellow. **Dorsal sepal** oblong-elliptic to ovate-elliptic, subacute, 1.5–2 cm long, 0.9–1.2 cm broad; **lateral sepals** oblique, ovate to ovate-elliptic, subacute, 1.5–2 cm long, 0.9–1.2 cm broad. **Petals** flabellate-reniform or suborbicular, broadly rounded above, 1.7–2.2 cm long, 1.8–2.4 cm broad. **Lip** 3-lobed, 1.5 cm long, 1 cm broad when spread; side lobes erect, falcate-hamate, bearing a fleshy diagonal ridge; mid-lobe obovate-oblong, obtuse, with a central, longitudinal, fleshy ridge, front margin irregular; callus between side lobes fleshy, bifid and porrect in front. **Column** arcuate, short, with an elongate, proboscis-like, deflexed rostellum at apex.
DISTRIBUTION Burma (Tenasserim): in limestone areas.
HISTORY *P. lowii* was discovered by Rev. Charles Parish in Tenasserim in Burma. He sent plants to Messrs Low, who sent a flowering specimen to H.G. Reichenbach who, in turn, described it in 1862 in the *Botanische Zeitung* (p. 214).
SYNONYM *Phalaenopsis proboscidioides* Rchb.f.

Phalaenopsis lueddemanniana Rchb.f.
[Colour Plate]
An epiphytic plant, very variable in size. **Stem** erect or ascending, covered by imbricating leaf-bases. **Leaves** elliptic, obovate or oblong-elliptic, fleshy, ± drooping, up to 30 cm long, 9 cm broad, acute or obtuse. **Inflorescence** suberect, arcuate to pendulous, racemose or branching, much larger than the leaves; rhachis somewhat fractiflex; bracts distichous, ovate-triangular, up to 0.5 cm long, acute. **Flowers** up to 6 cm across, waxy and fleshy, variously coloured; sepals and petals with purple to magenta transverse bars on a whitish background on inner side only; lip yellowish at base and on calli of the side lobes, rest of lip carmine; column purple, anther greenish-yellow. **Dorsal sepal** elliptic or oblong-elliptic, dorsally keeled, 2.2–3 cm long, 1–1.4 cm broad, acute or obtuse; **lateral sepals** obliquely ovate-elliptic, dorsally keeled, 2–3 cm long, 1–1.4 cm broad. **Petals** elliptic or ovate-elliptic, up to 2.7 cm long, 1.2 cm broad, acute or obtuse. **Lip** 3-lobed, 1.8–2.2 cm long, 1.5–1.8 cm broad; side lobes narrowly oblong, spreading, with a fleshy thickening in the middle; mid-lobe variable in shape, narrowly oblong, ovate or oblong-ovate, fleshy, convex, with a central ridge ending in a fleshy raised cushion at the apex, cushion covered in coarse hairs in front; callus between side lobes fleshy, papillose in basal half, bifid in front.
DISTRIBUTION The Philippines.

HISTORY The type specimen of *P. lueddemanniana* was introduced into cultivation by Lueddemann of Paris in 1865 and it was described the same year by H.G. Reichenbach in the *Botanishe Zeitung* (p. 146).
Two commonly cultivated varieties of *P. lueddemanniana* are var. *delicata* Rchb.f. which has the apical halves of its sepals and petals marked with cinnamon or ochre bars, and var. *ochracea* Rchb.f. which has flowers marked with ochre bars on a pale yellow background. Both varieties are structurally identical with the typical form.
CLOSELY RELATED SPECIES *P. lueddemanniana* may be distiguished from the closely related *P. violacea* by its coarsely hairy callus on the mid-lobe of its lip and by its distinctly barred sepals and petals. See also *P. hieroglyphica*, *P. pulchra* and *P. fasciata*.

Phalaenopsis mannii Rchb.f. [Colour Plate]
A pendent epiphytic plant. **Stem** short, completely covered by imbricating leaf-bases. **Leaves** 4–5, oblong-oblanceolate to oblong-ligulate, fleshy, up to 37 cm long, 7 cm broad, acute, rarely obtuse. **Inflorescence** slender, pendulous, racemose or rarely branched, as long as the leaves; rhachis laxly many-flowered; bracts ovate-lanceolate, up to 1 cm long. **Flowers** waxy, fleshy, opening in succession; sepals and petals yellow, ± spotted or blotched with cinnamon-brown; lip white and purple; column yellow. **Dorsal sepal** obovate-oblanceolate, margins revolute, dorsally keeled towards apex, 2–2.4 cm long, 0.7–0.8 cm broad, acute; **lateral sepals** obliquely ovate-elliptic, dorsally keeled, margins revolute, 2.2–2.5 cm long, 0.9–1.1 cm broad, acute. **Petals** lanceolate, subfalcate, 1.7–2 cm long, 0.5–0.6 cm broad, acute. **Lip** very fleshy, shortly clawed, 3-lobed, 0.9–1.1 cm long, 1–1.1 cm broad; side lobes narrowly oblong, spreading, obliquely truncate at apex, with a fleshy callus in middle; mid-lobe clawed, bilobulate, lobules papillate, erose-dentate on margins, with an apical fleshy callus, ± hairy; callus between side lobes bicirrhose in front.
DISTRIBUTION India (Sikkim, Assam) and Vietnam.
HISTORY Described by H.G. Reichenbach in 1871 in the *Gardeners' Chronicle* (p. 902). Reichenbach named it in honour of its discoverer G. Mann who collected it in Upper Assam.
SYNONYM *Phalaenopsis boxallii* Rchb.f.

Phalaenopsis mariae Burb. ex Warner & B.S. Williams [Colour Plate]
An epiphytic plant. **Stem** short, covered by imbricating leaf-bases. **Leaves** distichous, oblong-ligulate to obovate-ligulate, fleshy,

deflexed, up to 30 cm long, 7 cm broad, acute or obtuse. **Inflorescence** lateral, pendulous, racemose or branched, few- to many-flowered, shorter than the leaves; bracts distichous, triangular-ovate, up to 0.4 cm long. **Flowers** fleshy, up to 5 cm across; sepals and petals white or cream with large maroon to chestnut-brown spots; lip pale mauve or purple with yellow calli on side lobes; column white with a purple base. **Sepals** oblong-elliptic to narrowly elliptic, 1.6–2.2 cm long, 0.7–1.1 cm broad, obtuse. **Petals** oblong-elliptic, 1.5–1.7 cm long, 0.6–0.9 cm broad, obtuse. **Lip** fleshy, 3-lobed, 1.2–1.5 cm long, 1.2 cm broad; side lobes narrowly oblong, spreading, truncate, each with a central semilunate callus; mid-lobe obovate, subacute, margins erose-dentate, with a central ridge running into an apical fleshy callus covered with short soft hairs; callus between side lobes fleshy, 2-lobed, acicular. **Column** slightly arcuate, up to 0.7 cm long.

DISTRIBUTION The Philippines and Borneo.

HISTORY F.W. Burbidge, one of Veitch's collectors, found the type specimen on Sulu (now Jolo) Island in the Philippines. Although Burbidge suggested the specific epithet for this species in honour of his wife, it was left for R. Warner and B.S. Williams to publish the name validly in 1883 in the *Orchid Album* (t. 80). *P. mariae* was first imported in large numbers by Messrs Low & Co. whose collectors found it plentiful on Mindanao Island.

CLOSELY RELATED SPECIES Somewhat similar in its lip shape to *P. pallens* but *P. mariae* may easily be distinguished by its flower colour pattern, the erose-dentate margins to the side lobes of the lip and the densely hairy callus on the apex of the lip mid-lobe.

Phalaenopsis pallens (Lindl.) Rchb.f.
[Colour Plate]

A dwarf epiphytic plant. **Stem** short, ascending, covered by distichous leaf-bases. **Leaves** distichous, elliptic to obovate, fleshy, drooping, 12–18 cm long, 4.5–6 cm broad, rounded or obtuse and obscurely unequally 2-lobed at apex. **Inflorescence** slender, rarely exceeding the leaves in length, 1- to few-flowered; rhachis fractiflex; bracts ovate-triangular, up to 0.4 cm long, acute. **Flowers** rather delicate in texture, up to 4.8 cm across; sepals and petals white or pale yellow-green, transversely lined with brown; lip white with a yellow callus. **Dorsal sepal** oblong-elliptic, dorsally mucronate, 1.2–2.3 cm long, 0.5–1 cm broad, acute or obtuse; **lateral sepals** similar to dorsal sepal, 1.5–2.2 cm long, 0.8–1 cm broad. **Petals** similar but smaller than lateral sepals, 1.1–2 cm long, 0.5–0.9 cm broad. **Lip** 3-lobed, 1.3–1.7 cm long, 1.2–1.4 cm broad; side lobes narrowly oblong,

truncate, with a central semilunate callus; mid-lobe obovate, rounded or mucronate at apex; margins erose-dentate towards apex, with a central longitudinal ridge and a hairy fleshy cushion towards the apex; callus between side lobes fleshy and consisting of 2 forward-pointing bifid projections 1 in front of the other. **Column** slightly arcuate, 0.8 cm long.

DISTRIBUTION The Philippines.

HISTORY Originally introduced from the Philippines and flowered by the Duke of Devonshire in 1849. John Lindley described it in 1850 in the *Journal of the Horticultural Society* (p. 34) as *Trichoglottis pallens* but H.G. Reichenbach transferred it to the genus *Phalaenopsis* in *Walpers, Annales Botanices* (p. 932) in 1864.

SYNONYMS *Trichoglottis pallens* Lindl.; *Phalaenopsis lueddemanniana* var. *pallens* Burb.; *P. foerstermanii* Rchb.f.; *P. mariae* var. *alba* Ames & Quis.

CLOSELY RELATED SPECIES Often grown incorrectly under the name *P. lueddemanniana* but easily separable from the yellow-flowered forms of that species by the features of its callus. See also *P. mariae*.

Phalaenopsis pulchra (Rchb.f.) Sweet
[Colour Plate]

A medium-sized suberect or ascending epiphytic plant with fleshy, rather flexuous, glabrous roots. **Stem** very short, enclosed by imbricating leaf-bases. **Leaves** suberect, arcuate, oblong-elliptic to narrowly obovate, fleshy, acute or subobtuse, up to 15 cm long, 6 cm broad. **Inflorescence** lateral, simple, suberect or arcuate, shorter than the leaves, laxly few-flowered; bracts triangular, acute, short. **Flowers** fleshy, brilliant deep magenta-purple. **Sepals** elliptic to ovate, acute or subobtuse, 1.9–2.8 cm long, 0.9–1.5 cm broad. **Petals** obliquely elliptic or ovate-elliptic, acute or obtuse, 1.8-2.3 cm long, 0.8–1.1 cm broad. **Lip** 3-lobed, fleshy, 1.7–2.3 cm long, 1.6–2 cm broad; side lobes narrowly oblong, erect, truncate, fleshily thickened in the centre; mid-lobe flabellate or cuneate-flabellate, front margin erose-dentate, keeled in basal half above and fleshy with scattered hairs in centre towards the apex; callus between side lobes plate-like, papillate apically, with 1 or 2 superimposed plate-like calli in front and terminating with a fleshy, bifurcate, acicular projection on base of mid-lobe. **Column** fleshy, erect or slightly arcuate and clavate, 0.8–1.3 cm long.

DISTRIBUTION The Philippines.

HISTORY Originally introduced by Messrs Low from the Philippines and described in 1875 by H.G. Reichenbach in the *Gardeners' Chronicle* (n.s. 4: p. 36) as *P. lueddemanniana* var. *pulchra*. H. Sweet raised it to specific rank in 1968 in the *American Orchid Society Bulletin* (p. 1102).

SYNONYM *Phalaenopsis lueddemanniana* var. *pulchra* Rchb.f.; *P. lueddemanniana* var. *purpurea* Ames & Quis.

CLOSELY RELATED SPECIES Allied to *P. lueddemanniana* of which many consider it a variety but distinguished by its distinct callus and distinctly-coloured flowers which lack any barring on the sepals.

Phalaenopsis schilleriana Rchb.f.
[Colour Plate]

A stout, epiphytic plant. **Stem** short, stout, enclosed completely by leaf-bases and roots. **Leaves** fleshy, elliptic, oblong-elliptic, to oblanceolate, up to 45 cm long, 11 cm broad, obtuse, dark green, mottled with silver-grey on the upper surface. **Inflorescence** pendulous; generally paniculate, laxly few- to more than 250-flowered; bracts small, ovate-cuculate, up to 0.5 cm long. **Flowers** showy, rather delicate in texture, fragrant, 7 cm across, variable in colour; sepals and petals soft rose-pink fading to white on margins; sepals spotted with purple towards base; lip white to deep purple, base of side lobes yellow, spotted carmine. **Dorsal sepal** elliptic to ovate-elliptic, up to 3.5 cm long, 1.6 cm broad, rounded or obtuse at apex; **lateral sepals** similar to dorsal sepal but oblique. **Petals** shortly clawed, rhombic, somewhat undulate, 4 cm long and broad, rounded or obtuse at apex. **Lip** variable, clawed, 3-lobed, up to 2.2 cm long, 3.4 cm broad; side lobes spreading, elliptic or suborbicular; mid-lobe ovate, with 2 divergent, recurved, tapering appendages in front; callus between base of side lobes fleshy, subquadrate, truncate. **Column** short, fleshy.

DISTRIBUTION The Philippines (Luzon and smaller adjacent islands).

HISTORY This beautiful species was named by H.G. Reichenbach in 1860 in the *Hamburger Gartenzeitung* (p. 115) after Consul Schiller who introduced it from Luzon and flowered it for the first time in 1858.

Because of the great variation in flower colour and form, several distinct varieties have been introduced into cultivation. Var. *immaculata* Rchb.f. lacks any of the pink and purple marking of the typical form, whilst var. *splendens* Warner has distinctly marmorated leaves and larger flowers than the typical form.

CLOSELY RELATED SPECIES See *P. stuartiana*.

Phalaenopsis stuartiana Rchb.f.
[Colour Plate]

An epiphytic plant. **Stem** short, covered by imbricating leaf-bases. **Leaves** few, arcuate to pendent, fleshy, elliptic-oblong or oblanceolate, up to 35 cm long, 8 cm broad, obtuse, green, mottled with silvery-grey above. **Inflorescence** arcuate to pendulous, racemose or paniculate, laxly many-flowered, up to 60 cm long; bracts ovate-cucullate, up to 1 cm long. **Flowers** delicate in texture, slightly fragrant; sepals and petals white or light sulphur-yellow, spotted inside with cinnamon in the basal half; lip side lobes white at apex, orange below, mid-lobe pale yellow with white margins and tails, callus orange; all spotted cinnamon. **Dorsal sepal** elliptic or ovate-elliptic, up to 3.5 cm long, 1.5 cm broad, obtuse; **lateral sepals** obliquely oblong-elliptic or ovate-elliptic, up to 3.2 cm long, 1.5 cm broad, obtuse or rounded at apex. **Petals** subrhombic to rhombic-ovate, up to 3.3 cm long, 2.6 cm broad, rounded or obtuse at apex. **Lip** with a short narrow claw, 3-lobed in basal half, up to 2.5 cm long, 3 cm broad; side lobes spreading, obovate, rounded at apex; mid-lobe ovate, with 2 special diverging tapering lobes, emarginate; callus between side lobes bilobulate, fleshy, lobules acutely pointed behind. **Column** cylindrical, fleshy.

DISTRIBUTION The Philippines (Mindanao).

HISTORY This showy species was first collected by W. Boxall on the island of Mindanao for the firm of Low & Co. in 1881. Stuart Low sent it to H.G. Reichenbach who named it after that famous nurseryman in the *Gardeners' Chronicle* (n.s. 16: p. 748) of 1881.

SYNONYMS *Phalaenopsis schilleriana* var. *vestalis* Rchb.f.; *P. schilleriana* var. *stuartiana* (Rchb.f.) Burb.

CLOSELY RELATED SPECIES *P. stuartiana* is closely related to *P. schilleriana* from which it may be separated by its distinct coloration and by the shape of its lip callus. Indeed, *P. stuartiana* has been treated by some authors as a variety of *P. schilleriana*.

Phalaenopsis sumatrana Korth. & Rchb.f. [Colour Plate]

A robust epiphytic plant. **Stem** short, covered by persistent leaf-sheaths. **Leaves** fleshy, oblong-elliptic or obovate, arched or pendent, acute or rounded, 15–30 cm long, 4–11 cm broad. **Inflorescence** erect or slightly arching, laxly several- to many-flowered, racemose or with a few branches, up to 30 cm long; rhachis slightly fractiflex; bracts triangular, up to 0.6 cm long. **Flowers** up to 5 cm across, fleshy, variable, the typical form with sepals and petals off-white to pale yellow, transversely barred with reddish-brown; lip off-white or pale yellow with 2 magenta stripes on each side of the mid-ridge. **Sepals** oblong- to elliptic-lanceolate, dorsally carinate, 2–4 cm long, 1–1.5 cm broad, acute. **Petals** lanceolate, 2.2–2.5 cm long, 0.9–1.2 cm broad, acute. **Lip** 3-lobed, 2.5 cm long, 1.5 cm broad, fleshy; side lobes erect, fleshy, linear-oblong, obliquely truncate; mid-

lobe convex, mid-ridge oblong-elliptic, thickened towards the apex, cushion-like, densely pubescent; disc with a multidigitate callus, fleshily bifurcate at base of mid-lobe. **Column** fleshy, arcuate, up to 1.5 cm long.

DISTRIBUTION Sumatra, Java, Borneo, Malaya and Thailand; on trees by streams.

HISTORY Discovered in 1839 by Korthals in the province of Palembang, Sumatra and it was described by him and H.G. Reichenbach in 1860 in *Hamburger Gartenzeitung* (p. 115). The plant was figured in Curtis's *Botanical Magazine* (t. 5527) from a plant flowered by John Day.

A number of varieties of *P. sumatrana* are cultivated which vary mainly in flower colour and size.

SYNONYMS *Phalaenopsis zebrina* Witte; *P. zebrina* Teijsm. & Binnend.; *P. acutifolia* Linden

CLOSELY RELATED SPECIES Closely related to *Phalaenopsis corningiana* Rchb.f. which, however, has a simpler excavate callus and sepals and petals longitudinally, not transversely, striped with reddish-brown.

Phalaenopsis violacea Witte [Colour Plate]

An epiphytic plant. **Stem** erect, enclosed by imbricating leaf-sheaths. **Roots** stout, flexuose, glabrous. **Leaves** fleshy or leathery, obovate, oblong-elliptic or elliptic, articulated to leaf-sheaths, 20–25 cm long, 7–12 cm broad, shiny dark green. **Inflorescence** suberect or arcuate, few-flowered; rhachis markedly flattened and fractiflex; bracts ovate, concave, up to 0.7 cm long, acute. **Flowers** fleshy, 5–8 cm across, waxy, 1 or 2 at a time in succession; sepals and petals violet with greenish apices; column and mid-lobe of lip magenta-purple; side lobes marked with yellow. **Dorsal sepal** elliptic, ovate or ovate-lanceolate, concave, dorsally carinate, 2–3.5 cm long, 1.1–1.7 cm broad; **lateral sepals** obliquely adnate to the base of the column, ovate-lanceolate, subfalcate above, dorsally keeled, 2.2–3.5 cm long, 1.1–1.7 cm broad. **Petals** elliptic or ovate-elliptic, 2–3 cm long, 0.7–1.7 cm broad, acute to subobtuse. **Lip** 3-lobed, 2–2.8 cm long, 1.6–2.3 cm broad; side lobes spreading, narrowly oblong, truncate; mid-lobe obovate, apiculate, fleshy towards the apex; callus fleshy and irregularly warty, merging into 1–3 superimposed lamellae in front. **Column** fleshy, slightly arcuate, 1.5 cm long.

DISTRIBUTION Sumatra, Borneo, Malaya; in shady places by rivers at low altitudes.

HISTORY *P. violacea* was discovered by Teijsman who sent living material to Witte at the Leiden Botanic Garden in the Netherlands. Witte described it in the *Annales d'Horticulture et de Botanique, Leiden* (p. 129) in 1860.

SYNONYM *Stauritis violacea* (Witte) Rchb.f.

CLOSELY RELATED SPECIES *P. violacea*

has a similarly-shaped lip to *P. lueddemanniana* which, however, has a hairy fleshy thickening at the apex of the mid-lobe.

Pholidota Lindl. ex Hooker

Subfamily Epidendroideae
Tribe Coelogyneae
Subtribe Coelogyninae

Medium-sized epiphytic or lithophytic herbs, with a creeping or pendent rhizome. **Pseudobulbs** closely- or well-spaced, sometimes superposed, 1- or 2-leaved. **Leaves** herbaceous to thickly coriaceous, petiolate. **Inflorescence** slender, racemose; rhachis flexuous, often zigzag; bracts rather large, concave, ± deciduous. **Flowers** borne in 2 ranks, small, globose. **Sepals** usually concave; lateral sepals asymmetric, often keeled dorsally. **Petals** flat, broad or narrow. **Lip** sessile on base of column, erect, saccate at base, subentire or bipartite. **Column** short, with a wide wing around the anther; pollinia 4, subglobose or pyriform, free or cohering in pairs by a viscidium.

DISTRIBUTION About 30 species in India, S. China, Malaya, Indonesia, New Guinea, the Pacific Islands and Australia.

DERIVATION OF NAME From the Greek *pholidotos* (scaly), descriptive either of the large inflorescence bracts or of the large sheaths surrounding the pseudobulbs.

TAXONOMY *Pholidota* was described by John Lindley in 1826 in Sir William Hooker's *Exotic Botany* (t. 138).

Sir Joseph Hooker in the *Flora of British India–Orchideae* (1890) divided the Indian species into two groups dependent on whether the new pseudobulb arises from the base of the old pseudobulb or from its apex.

R. Holttum in *Orchids of Malaya* (1964) extended the generic concept to include *Crinonia* and *Chelonanthera* noting that the three species of *Crinonia* form a distinct group in *Pholidota* but one which does not warrant generic rank.

The genus has been recently revised by E. de Vogel (1988) in the third volume of *Orchid Monographs*. He recognises 29 species providing a key for their identification and a detailed account of each, together with a black and white line drawing.

TYPE SPECIES *P. imbricata* Lindl.

SYNONYMS *Crinonia* Blume; *Chelonanthera* Blume; *Ptilocnema* D. Don; *Acanthoglossum* Blume

CULTURE Compost A. Temp. Winter min. 12–15°C. Those species with hard pseudobulbs such as *P. pallida* require ample water while growing and moderate shade. When the pseudobulbs are fully formed, much less water is required until the new growths appear. Species such as *P. articulata* with a vertical growth habit need support such as a slab of fern-fibre or cork.

Pholidota convallariae (Rchb.f.) Hooker f.

A medium-sized epiphytic plant with a creeping rhizome. **Pseudobulbs** sessile, subcylindric to ovoid-conical, 2.5–7 cm long, 1–1.5 cm in diameter. **Leaves** 1 or 2, linear to oblong-lanceolate, acuminate, coriaceous, 12.5–20 cm long, 0.5–2.5 cm broad; petiole narrow, 1–4 cm long. **Inflorescence** racemose, erect or sub-erect, stout, up to 28-flowered, 5–10 cm long, produced at apex of young shoot; bracts caducous, deciduous, lanceolate or ovate, obtuse, 1.2 cm long, equalling the flowers. **Flowers** whitish, 0.5–0.6 cm across, secund. **Dorsal sepal** oblong or ovate-lanceolate, obtuse, 0.5–0.8 cm long, 0.3 cm broad; **lateral sepals** ovate or lanceolate, acuminate, mid-rib thickened, 0.4–0.8 cm long. **Petals** a little smaller than the sepals, lanceolate to ovate, obtuse. **Lip** cymbiform, nearly orbicular, obscurely bilobed at apex, 3-ridged at base within, emarginate, 0.4–0.6 cm long, 0.2–0.3 cm broad; basal calli minutely elongate. **Column** broadly obovate, apex contracted, obtuse, 0.3 cm long.

DISTRIBUTION India (Assam Khasia Hills, Naga Hills), Burma, China, Thailand, Vietnam, Sumatra and Java; 800–1750 m altitude.
HISTORY Originally described in 1872 in *Flora* (p. 277) as *Coelogyne convallariae* by H.G. Reichenbach based on an illustration made by Oliver in India. Sir Joseph Hooker transferred it to *Pholidota* in 1889 in *Icones Plantarum* (p. 161, t. 1880) noting that it had been collected in the Khasia Hills by himself and Dr T. Thomson, by Dr Prain in the Naga Hills at Kohima, and by C. Parish at Moulmein in Burma.
SYNONYMS *Coelogyne convallariae* Rchb.f.; *Pholidota fragrans* Ridl.

Pholidota pallida Lindl.

Pseudobulbs densely clustered, ovoid to sub-cylindric, 2.5–7.5 cm long, 1-leafed at apex. **Leaf** thinly herbaceous, elliptic-lanceolate to oblanceolate, petiolate, 15–52 cm long, 1.6–9 cm broad; petiole 5 cm long. **Inflorescence** longly pedunculate, elongate, pendulous, 7.5–30 cm long, many-flowered; bracts semicircular, persistent, distichous, concave, 0.8 cm broad. **Flowers** distichous, 0.6–0.7 cm across, pale flesh-coloured or white; anther brown. **Dorsal sepal** circular, obtuse, 0.5 cm long, 0.3 cm broad; **lateral sepals** connate at the base, cymbiform, dorsally keeled, 0.6 cm long, connate at the base. **Petals** linear-oblong, falcate, narrower than the sepals, acute, 0.4 cm long, 0.15 cm broad, forming with the dorsal sepal a hood. **Lip** bipartite, 5–8 mm long, saccate at the base; side lobes erect, broadly rounded;

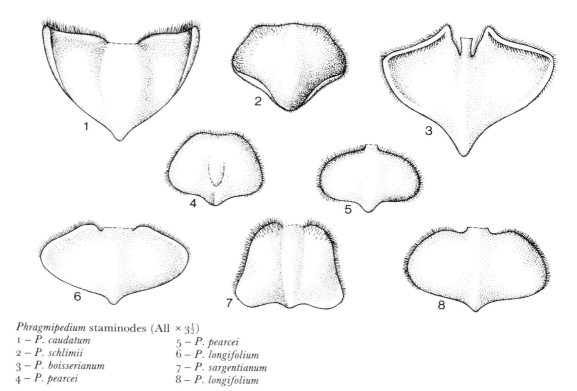

Phragmipedium staminodes (All × 3½)
1 – *P. caudatum*
2 – *P. schlimii*
3 – *P. boissierianum*
4 – *P. pearcei*
5 – *P. pearcei*
6 – *P. longifolium*
7 – *P. sargentianum*
8 – *P. longifolium*

epichile smaller, spreading, deeply bifid. **Column** circular when spread out, broadly winged; rostellum truncate.
DISTRIBUTION The tropical Himalayas from Kumaon eastwards, N. India (the Khasia Hills), Burma, S. China and Indo-China; epiphytic or lithophytic, 1000–2300 m altitude.
HISTORY Originally described by John Lindley in the *Botanical Register* (t. 1777) in 1836 based on a plant introduced from India by Dr N. Wallich in 1828. This species is still commonly known as *P. imbricata* Lindl. but that name had already been used for another species by W. Roxburgh.
SYNONYMS *Pholidota imbricata* sensu Lindl. (1827 non 1824); *C. pallida* (Lindl.) Rchb.f.
CLOSELY RELATED SPECIES *Pholidota imbricata* Lindl. [Colour Plate] and *P. pallida* Lindl. have often been confused. Lindley in 1836 distinguishes between them saying that *P. pallida* has white flowers, smaller leaves and very rounded blunt bracts whilst *P. imbricata* has yellowish flowers with a dash of violet, very long strong leaves and pointed bracts. De Vogel (1988) in *Orchid Monographs* (p. 58) distinguished *P. pallida* by its thin herbaceous leaves, floral bracts with fewer than 25 coarse nerves, and lateral sepals which are connate at the base.

Phragmipedium Rolfe
Subfamily Cypripedioideae

Large terrestrial, lithophytic, or, less commonly, epiphytic herbs with short stems, short to long rhizomes and fibrous roots. **Leaves** coriaceous, ligulate, conduplicate, sulcate. **Inflorescences** erect, racemose, few-flowered. **Flowers** large, showy. **Sepals,** spreading; dorsal sepal free; lateral sepals united for entire length into a synsepalum. **Petals** free, spreading, similar to dorsal sepal or long-caudate. **Lip** sessile, inflated, slipper-shaped. **Column** short, stout, with 2 laterally-placed fertile stamens, each bearing a 2-celled anther, and a dorsally-placed sterile, shield-shaped staminode; pollen granular; stigma stalked, ventral; ovary 3-celled.
DISTRIBUTION About 12 to 20 species in S. America north to Panama and Guatemala.
DERIVATION OF NAME From the Greek *phragma* (fence or division) and *pedion* (slipper), in allusion to the divisions of the trilocular ovary and to the slipper-shaped lip.
TAXONOMY This genus was established by Robert A. Rolfe in 1896 in the *Orchid Review* (p. 330) when he revised all the slipper orchids and placed the tropical American species in two

genera: *Selenipedium* and *Phragmipedium*. The genus was revised by E. Pfitzer in 1903 in A. Engler's *Das Pflanzenreich* where 11 species and many varieties are treated in five sections.

One species of *Phragmipedium*, *P. lindenii*, is of particular interest in that in its commonest form the lip is replaced by a third petal. John Lindley originally described this in a new genus, *Uropedium*, as *U. lindenii*. Until recently, under the *International Code of Botanical Nomenclature*, this name could be ignored as being based upon a monstrosity. When this rule was recently changed it became necessary to take the name *Uropedium* into account as it predates *Phragmipedium*. Consequently R. Dressler and Norris Williams have put forward a proposal (see *Taxon*, 1976) to conserve *Phragmipedium* Rolfe against the earlier *Uropedium* Lindl. on the grounds that the former name is so well established that resurrection of *Uropedium* would cause confusion to all.

L. Garay in *Orchid Digest* (1979) has completely revised the genus. In this article he has adopted a narrow concept of the species recognising 20 in all. L. McCook considers several of these conspecific in her recent account of the genus in the *American Orchid Society Bulletin* (p. 1095) in 1989, where each species is illustrated and a key to the species provided.

TYPE SPECIES *P. caudatum* (Lindl.) Rolfe
SYNONYM *Uropedium* Lindl.
CULTURE Compost A. Temp. Winter min. 12–15°C. Although some species are found at quite high altitudes, they are better kept somewhat warmer in cultivation. Having little means of water storage, the plants should be kept evenly moist throughout the year taking care to avoid stagnation of the compost. Moderate shade and good humidity are required during the summer months. In general, it is better to allow the plants to form large clumps rather than to divide them too often.

Phragmipedium besseae Dodson & Kuhn
[Colour Plate]
A lithophytic or terrestrial plant with a long creeping rhizome producing well-separated short-stemmed leafy growths. **Leaves** 6–10, coriaceous, linear to narrowly elliptic, 5–12 cm long, 1–2.5 cm broad, glossy green. **Inflorescence** terminal, erect, 1- to 4-flowered; peduncle terete, shortly pubescent; bracts elliptic, boat-shaped, acute, up to 2.5 cm long. **Flowers** spectacular, orange-red to scarlet, up to 6 cm across, pubescent on the outer surface of the sepals and petals; pedicel and ovary 5–7 cm long, densely pubescent. **Dorsal sepal** ovate-elliptic, obtuse, slightly concave, 2.4–2.7 cm long, 1.5–1.6 cm broad; **synsepalum** narrowly elliptic, acute, 2–2.7 cm long, 1.5–2 cm broad. **Petals** spreading to somewhat decurved, ellip-

tic or narrowly elliptic, acute, 2.8–3 cm long, 1.4–1.8 cm broad, pubescent within. **Lip** calceolate, ovoid, rather pointed, 2.2–2.4 cm long, 1.5–1.7 cm broad, very shortly pubescent-papillose, with translucent slit-like windows around the front margin. **Column** short; **staminode** transversely elliptic, obtuse or bluntly apiculate.

DISTRIBUTION Ecuador and Peru; on steep cliffs and slopes above rivers on the eastern side of the Andes, 1100–1500 m elevation.
HISTORY The type collection of this sensational orchid was made in northern Peru in 1981 by Mrs Libby Besse, after whom it was described by Calaway Dodson and Janet Kuhn in the same year in the *American Orchid Society Bulletin* (p. 1308). It had first been collected some 60 years earlier in Colombia by Werner Hopp but had not at that time been recognised as distinct from the smaller pink-flowered *P. schlimii*. It seems to be commonest in Ecuador but the several localities it has been found in have been systematically stripped by collectors in recent years.

Phragmipedium caricinum (Lindl.) Rolfe
A terrestrial or lithophytic herb, up to 40 cm high. **Stem** very short, about 5- to 6-leaved. **Leaves** linear, suberect, rigid, up to 43 cm long, 0.6 cm broad, narrowing to apex. **Inflorescence** up to 30 cm long, racemose or paniculate, about 4- to several-flowered; peduncle terete, densely pubescent, with a basal leaf-like cataphyll; bracts lanceolate, distichous, 2–5 cm long, acute. **Flowers** 5–7.5 cm long, lime-green; petals with pale purple margins; lip side lobes spotted dark green and purple. **Dorsal sepal** lanceolate, 2.5–4 cm long, 1.3 cm broad, acute, margins undulate. **Synsepalum** ovate, 2.5–3.5 cm long, 1.5 cm broad, acute. **Petals** linear, ribbon-like, 5–12.7 cm long, 0.4 cm broad, acute, densely pubescent at the tip. **Lip** slipper-shaped, up to 3.5 cm long, with a slightly bulbous pouch; side lobes incurved, spotted. **Staminode** obtriangular, hairy on dorsal margin.

DISTRIBUTION Ecuador, Bolivia and Peru; often on boulders in rivers.
HISTORY Described in 1851 by John Lindley as *Cypripedium caricinum* in his and Paxton's *Flower Garden* (sub t. 9), but subsequently transferred in 1896 by Robert A. Rolfe to the genus *Phragmipedium* in the *Orchid Review* (p. 332). This is a very variable species in both flower size and leaf length and width.
SYNONYM *Cypripedium caricinum* Lindl.; *Phragmipedium ecuadorense* Garay
CLOSELY RELATED SPECIES Vegetatively very similar to *P. klotzscheanum*.

Phragmipedium pearcei (Rchb.f.) Senghas & Rauh [Colour Plate] is similar but differs in

having a sparsely pubescent inflorescence axis, sparsely pubescent petal apices, and a green lip with a white claw spotted with green near base and red-brown above.

Phragmipedium caudatum (Lindl.) Rolfe
[Colour Plate]
An erect, epiphytic or lithophytic plant, up to 70 cm high. **Stem** very short, about 5-leaved. **Leaves** strap-shaped, fairly rigid but drooping in apical half, up to 50 cm long, 5.5 cm broad, erose. **Inflorescence** 3- to 4-flowered, suberect, up to 60 cm tall; peduncle slightly compressed, finely hairy, with a large, leafy, sterile bract near base; bracts lanceolate, boat-shaped, acute, up to or more than 10 cm long. **Flowers** very large, up to 35 cm long or more; sepals and petals pale green with darker nerves; petals pale pink on margins and towards apex; lip white near base, flushed pink towards apex and green-nerved; staminode pale yellow with purple hairy margins. **Dorsal sepal** curved forwards, lanceolate, 10–15 cm long, 1.5–2.5 cm broad, acute margins very undulate; **synsepalum** 8–10 cm long, 2.5–4.5 cm broad, margins undulate. **Petals** pendent, twisted, linear, very long, 30–70 cm long, 0.6–1 cm broad, rounded, margins purple-ciliate towards apex. **Lip** slipper-shaped, 3-lobed, 5–7 cm long, 2–3 cm broad; side lobes incurved, green-spotted; midlobe inflated.
DISTRIBUTION Mexico, Guatemala, Costa Rica, Panama, Colombia, Ecuador, Peru and Venezuela.
HISTORY Originally described by John Lindley as *Cypripedium caudatum* in 1840 in his *Genera and Species of Orchidaceous Plants* (p. 531). R.A. Rolfe transferred it to the genus *Phragmipedium* in the *Orchid Review* (p. 332) of 1896.
SYNONYMS *Cypripedium caudatum* Lindl.; *C. humboldtii* Rchb.f.; *C. warscewiczianum* Rchb.f.; *Paphiopedilum caudatum* (Lindl.) Pfitz.; *Phragmipedium warscewiczianum* (Rchb.f.) Schltr.
CLOSELY RELATED SPECIES A lipless form described by Lindley as *Uropedium lindenii* is considered by many to be a variety of *P. caudatum*. However, occasional forms with a lip are found in predominantly lipless populations and these differ slightly from *P. caudatum*. On this evidence, R. Dressler and N. Williams have recently proposed the name *Phragmipedium lindenii* [Colour Plate] for this species.

Phragmipedium klotzscheanum (Rchb.f.) Rolfe [Colour Plate]
A terrestrial herb, up to 30 cm high. **Stem** very short, about 6-leaved. **Leaves** linear, rigid, suberect, up to 25 cm long, 1 cm broad, acutely 2-lobed at apex, shiny green, paler on lower surface. **Inflorescence** 2- to 3-flowered, erect, up to 30 cm long, flowers opening one at a

time; peduncle red or pale maroon, pubescent; sheathing sterile bracts red; bracts maroon-brown, or pale brown with green and maroon nerves. **Flowers** up to 6 cm long; sepals pink-brown with darker nerves; petals light brown with green and maroon veins; lip light or olive-green with darker nerves, side lobes yellow, spotted brown, mid-lobe white; staminode pale green with dark purple hairs on margins. **Dorsal sepal** lanceolate, 3 cm long, 1 cm broad, subacute; **synsepalum** ovate, 2.8 cm long, 1.7 cm broad, obtuse. **Petals** linear, pendent, twisted in apical half, up to 5 cm long, 0.7 cm broad, rounded, finely pubescent at base and at apex. **Lip** slipper-shaped, 3-lobed, 2.7 cm long, 1.5 cm broad; side lobes incurved, finely hairy; mid-lobe margins inrolled. **Staminode** triangular-undulate.

DISTRIBUTION Venezuela and Guyana; often growing near water and in places which may be seasonally flooded.

HISTORY The type was collected in Guyana by Sir Robert Schomburgk in 1848 and H.G. Reichenbach described it as *Cypripedium klotzscheanum* in *Linnaea* (p. 811) the following year. It was later transferred in 1896 by Robert Rolfe to the genus *Phragmipedium* in the *Orchid Review* (p. 332).

SYNONYMS *Cypripedium schomburgkianum* Klotzsch ex Schomb.; *Paphiopedilum klotzscheanum* (Rchb.f) Pfitz.; *Selenipedium schomburgkianum* (Klotzsch ex Schomb.) Desbois

CLOSELY RELATED SPECIES See *P. longifolium* and *P. caricinum*.

Phragmipedium lindenii (Lindl.) Dressler & N.H. Williams [Colour Plate]
See under *Phragmipedium caudatum*.

Phragmipedium lindleyanum (Schomb. ex Lindl.) Rolfe
A terrestrial herb, up to 1 m high. **Stem** very short, about 5-leaved. **Leaves** linear-lanceolate, suberect, fairly rigid, up to 50 cm long, 6 cm broad, acuminate. **Inflorescence** several-flowered, racemose or a shortly branched panicle, up to 1 m tall; peduncle terete, reddish-green, finely pubescent; bracts lanceolate-ovate, up to 7.5 cm long, acute. **Flowers** up to 8.5 cm across; sepals and petals green or yellow-green; petals purple on veins, margins and towards apex; lip ochre-yellow with darker veins and light purple-spotted side lobes; all segments pubescent on outer surfaces; staminode yellowish. **Dorsal sepal** ovate, concave, 2.8–3.5 cm long, 1.8 cm broad, obtuse; **synsepalum** ovate, 2.7 cm long, 2.5 cm broad, obtuse. **Petals** slightly twisted towards apex, linear-oblong, 4–5.5 cm long, 1 cm broad, obtuse or emarginate, margins undulate. **Lip** slipper-shaped, 3-lobed, 3 cm long, 1.4 cm broad; side lobes incurved;

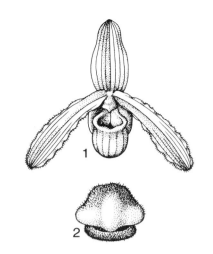

Phragmipedium lindleyanum
1 – Flower (× ⅔)
2 – Staminode (× 2½)

mid-lobe rather bulbous, margins incurved. **Staminode** truncately triangular, margin purple-ciliate.

DISTRIBUTION Guyana and Venezuela; growing in thin soil covering rocks, in open or dappled shady areas.

HISTORY Originally collected by Sir Robert Schomburgk in 1838 and described by John Lindley as *Cypripedium lindleyanum* in *Genera and Species of Orchidaceous Plants* (p. 531) in 1840. Robert Rolfe transferred it in 1896 to the genus *Phragmipedium* in the *Orchid Review* (p. 332). Schomburgk collected the type specimen on Mt Roraima, Guyana.

CLOSELY RELATED SPECIES Closely related to *P. sargentianum* from which it may be distinguished by its narrower, yellower flowers, the more bulbous apex to the lip, the drooping petals and lack of white tubercles on the lip side lobes.

Phragmipedium longifolium (Warsc. & Rchb.f.) Rolfe [Colour Plate]
A terrestrial plant, often growing in large clumps. **Stem** very short, several-leaved. **Leaves** linear-lanceolate, arcuate, up to 80 cm long 1–4 cm broad, acuminate, dark green above, paler below, lowest leaves somewhat shorter than rest. **Inflorescence** about 40 cm long, several-flowered with flowers opening 1 at a time; peduncle stout, terete, purplish, almost covered by 3 sterile, compressed linear bracts; bracts distichous, lanceolate, 4–9 cm long, acute. **Flowers** up to 13 cm or so across, pale yellowish-green, nerves of sepals darker green, dorsal sepal side margins whitish; petals edged purple; lip side lobes spotted light purple; staminode pale green. **Dorsal sepal** lanceolate, curved forward, 3–5 cm long, 1–1.6 cm broad, acute, side margins reflexed; **synsepalum**

ovate, similar to dorsal sepal, 2.5–5 cm long, 1.7–2.5 cm broad. **Petals** linear, very twisted, tapering towards apex, 8–10 cm long, 0.4–0.8 cm broad, rounded. **Lip** slipper-shaped, 3-lobed, 2.5–5 cm long, 1.5–2 cm broad; side lobes incurved; mid-lobe margin incurved. **Column** 0.7 cm long; **staminode** obtriangular, top margin lined with purple hairs, resembling an eyebrow on either side.

DISTRIBUTION Costa Rica, Panama, Ecuador and Colombia.

HISTORY Described by J. Warscewicz and H.G. Reichenbach in 1852 in *Botanische Zeitung* (p. 690) as *Selenipedilum longifolium* from an herbarium specimen collected by Warscewicz, who discovered it in the Cordillera de Chiriqui. Robert Rolfe subsequently transferred it in 1896 to the genus *Phragmipedium* in the *Orchid Review* (p. 332). L. Garay (1979) in the *Orchid Digest* considers *P. hartwegii* (Rolfe) L.O. Williams to be distinct from *P. longifolium* on account of its staminode which is trilobulate in front and muricate-puberulent on the basal margins. However, L. McCook (1989) in the *American Orchid Society Bulletin* considers *P. longifolium* to be a variable species encompassing *P. hartwegii*.

SYNONYM *Selenipedilum longifolium* Warsc. & Rchb.f; *Phragmipedium hartwegii* (Rchb.f.) L.O. Williams; *P. hincksianum* Rchb.f. (Garay); *P. roezlii* Rchb.f. (Garay).

CLOSELY RELATED SPECIES *P. klotzscheanum* differs from *P. longifolium* in its slender-er habit, its lack of auricles on the lip, its densely velutinous ovary and peduncle and in having glabrous petals.

Phragmipedium sargentianum (Rolfe) Rolfe
Stems very short, about 7-leaved. **Leaves** bright green, lanceolate or oblong-lanceolate, 20–50 cm long, 3–6 cm broad, often shorter, acute to acuminate. **Inflorescence** erect, up to 40 cm long, 2- to 4-flowered, opening 1 at a time; scape pubescent, erect, reddish-purple; bracts lanceolate, green, pubescent. **Flowers** up to 10 cm across; sepals, petals and lip green or greenish-yellow, margins of petals and nerves purplish especially towards apex; lip yellow, purple-veined, side lobes heavily purple-spotted; staminode yellowish-green. **Dorsal sepal** ovate-elliptic, 3 cm long, 1.6 cm broad, concave, acute, margins ciliate; **synsepalum** 3 cm long, 2.1 cm broad, acute, margins ciliate. **Petals** ligulate-oblong, ± slightly twisted, ± horizontal, 5.5 cm long, 1.2 cm broad, acute, margins ciliate. **Lip** slipper-shaped; side lobes incurved, bearing a pair of white tubercles. **Staminode** truncately triangular.

DISTRIBUTION Brazil (Pernambuco State).
HISTORY This delightful species was introduced into cultivation by Messrs Sander & Son

of St Albans, England in 1892. Robert Rolfe described it in the *Orchid Review* (p. 239) of 1893 as *Selenipedium sargentianum* but, in 1896 in the same journal (p. 332), he transferred it to the genus *Phragmipedium* [= *Phragmopedilum* = *Phragmipedilum;* both occasionally-used orthographic variants]. Rolfe gave the specific epithet in honour of Professor C.S. Sargent, then the Director of the Arnold Arboretum in the USA. It has been suggested by L. McCook (1989) in the *American Orchid Society Bulletin* that this is conspecific with *P. lindleyanum.*

SYNONYM *Selenipedium sargentianum* Rolfe
CLOSELY RELATED SPECIES See *P. lindleyanum.*

Phragmipedium schlimii (Linden & Rchb.f.) Rolfe [Colour Plate]

A terrestrial plant, up to 50 cm high, but much smaller. **Stem** very short, about 8-leaved. **Leaves** linear-lanceolate, suberect, rigid, up to 35 cm long, 2.3 cm broad, acute to acuminate. **Inflorescence** erect, up to or over 30 cm high, 6- to 10-flowered; scape very hairy; bracts ovate, 3 cm long. **Flowers** small in genus; sepals and petals pure white, mottled rose-pink especially towards base; lip rose-coloured; ovary densely pubescent; staminode yellow with a pink apex. **Dorsal sepal** oblong-ovate, 1.7 cm long, 0.8 cm broad, obtuse, densely hairy on outer surface; **synsepalum** similar to dorsal sepal. **Petals** spreading, elliptic, 2 cm long, 0.9 cm broad. **Column** 0.6 cm long; **staminode** trullate, ciliate especially on upper margins.
DISTRIBUTION Colombia; 1500–1800 m by rivers.
HISTORY Described in 1854 by J. Linden and H.G. Reichenbach in *Bonplandia* (p. 278) as *Cypripedium schlimii,* the specific epithet being suggested by Linden, the eminent Belgian orchid nurseryman. Robert Rolfe subsequently transferred it to the genus *Phragmipedium* in the *Orchid Review* (p. 332) of 1896.

It is a very distinct species easily recognised by its white or pink ± marked with crimson spots, and yellow staminode.
SYNONYMS *Selenipedium schlimii* Rchb.f.; *Cypripedium schlimii* (Rchb.f.) Batem.

Phreatia Lindl.

Subfamily Epidendroideae
Tribe Epidendreae
Subtribe Thelasiinae

Epiphytic plants of very diverse form. **Stems** may be almost vestigial, thin and either short or of moderate length, or pseudobulbous with the pseudobulbs either closely-tufted or spaced on a rhizome. **Leaves** in thin-stemmed species few to many, short to long, thin or thick and

fleshy, distichous, imbricate or even equitant: leaves in pseudobulbous species 1 or 2, long and slender, thin-textured. **Flowers** few to many, small to minute, usually white, segments often not opening widely. **Sepals** and **petals** subsimilar; lateral sepals forming a mentum with the column-foot. **Lip** usually narrow at the base, upcurved just above base to become ± erect or suberect for a distance then curved forwards into an entire or obscurely-lobed lamina. **Column** with a foot; pollinia 8, in 2 equal groups, usually on a long slender stipe.
DISTRIBUTION About 150 species from N. India through S.E. Asia, Indonesia, New Guinea to Australia and the Pacific Islands.
DERIVATION OF NAME From the Greek *phreatia* (well), probably referring to the well-like mentum formed by the lateral sepals and lip.
TAXONOMY John Lindley described this genus in 1830 in his *Genera and Species of Orchidaceous Plants* (p. 63). F. Kraenzlin revised the genus in A. Engler's *Das Pflanzenreich* (1911), describing and keying out 77 species in three sections: Octarrhena, *(Eu) Phreatia,* and *Thelasiformes.* R. Schlechter in *Die Orchidaceen von Deutsch-Neu-Guinea* (1914) raised the first to generic rank and subdivided *Phreatia* into six sections (with a total of 75 species in New Guinea alone).
TYPE SPECIES *P. elegans* Lindl.
CULTURE Compost A. Temp. Winter min. 12–15°C. *Phreatia* species have fine roots so should be grown in relatively small pots or pans. They require humid, shady conditions and should be carefully watered throughout the year.

Phreatia elegans Lindl.

A small, tufted epiphytic herb with a small pseudobulb. **Leaves** coriaceous, linear-lanceolate to oblanceolate, retuse, 6–12.5 cm long; 0.7 cm broad. **Inflorescence** larger than the leaves, densely many-flowered, up to 15 cm long: bracts ovate-lanceolate, longer than the ovary. **Flowers** small, white. **Dorsal sepal** ovate, acute or acuminate, up to 0.2 cm long, 0.1 cm broad; **lateral sepals** triangular, acute, 0.25 cm long, forming a short, rounded mentum. **Petals** broadly ovate-elliptic, acute, up to 0.2 cm long, 0.1 cm broad. **Lip** with a short saccate claw, triangular to broadly ovate above, pilose within, obtuse with an undulate-triangular to almost circular margin. **Column** very short; column-foot 0.1 cm long.
DISTRIBUTION N. India to Sri Lanka and across to Java.
HISTORY John Lindley decribed *P. elegans* in 1830 in his *Genera and Species of Orchidaceous Plants* (p. 63) based on a collection of J. Macrae from Ceylon (now Sri Lanka).

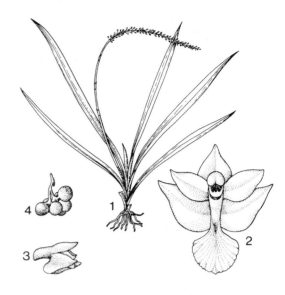

Phreatia elegans
1 – Habit ($\times \frac{1}{4}$)
2 – Flower with lip spread out ($\times 12$)
3 – Flower, side view ($\times 7$)
4 – Pollinia and viscidium ($\times 30$)

SYNONYM *Thelasis elegans* (Lindl.) Blume

Phymatidium Lindl.

Subfamily Epidendroideae
Tribe Oncidieae

Dwarf epiphytes with very short leafy stems. **Leaves** few to many, distichous and arranged in a fan or spirally arranged, linear, very slender, articulated to persistant leaf sheaths at the base. **Inflorescences** usually longer than the leaves, simple, laxly to densely many-flowered; bracts distichous, slender, elongate, falcate. **Flowers** distichous, small, white, semitranslucent. **Sepals** free, spreading. **Petals** similar but narrower. **Lip** broadly clawed, entire, with a fleshy callus, attached to the column base, lacking a spur. **Column** slender, elongate, sometimes sigmoid, sometimes winged at the apex, tumid at the base; pollinia 4, ovoid-pyriform, waxy, attached by an elongate spathulate stipe to a small circular viscidium.
DISTRIBUTION A small genus of about a dozen species in tropical S. America.
DERIVATION OF NAME The name derives from the diminutive of the Greek word *phyma* (growth).
TAXONOMY *Phymatidium* was established by John Lindley in 1833 in his *Genera and Species of Orchidaceous Plants* (p. 209).

The genus is closely allied to *Ornithocephalus*

but is distinguished by much slenderer leaves and a shorter rostellum.

TYPE SPECIES *P. delicatulum* Lindl. & *P. falcifolium* Lindl.

CULTURE Temp. Winter min. 12°C. Grow mounted under shady, humid conditions and water throughout the year.

Phymatidium tillansioides **Barb. Rodr.**

[Colour Plate]

Dwarf epiphytes with a very short leafy stem. **Leaves** spirally arranged, linear-aciculate, acute, recurved, 3–6 cm long, 0.5–1 mm wide, bilaterally flattened. **Inflorescences** erect, laxly 3- to 10-flowered; peduncle slender; bracts linear, 1–6 mm long. **Flowers** white with a green mark at the base of the column; pedicel and ovary 5–6 mm long. **Sepals** oblong-lanceolate, acute, 3–4 mm long, 1 mm wide; the laterals oblique. **Petals** similar. **Lip** ovate-elliptic, truncate, with lacerate margins, 3 mm long, 2 mm wide, the sides recurved; callus large, fleshy, elliptic, occupying most of the lip. **Column** 2.5 mm long, incurved, with a bulbous 3-lobed swelling at the base.

DISTRIBUTION E. Brazil only.

HISTORY Discovered by João Barbosa Rodrigues in the Serra da Prata in Paraná State and described by him in his *Genera et Species Orchidiarum Novarum* (p. 228).

Physosiphon **Lindl.**

Subfamily Epidendroideae
Tribe Epidendreae
Subtribe Pleurothallidinae

Small, epiphytic, caespitose herbs with a solitary leaf at apex. **Secondary stems** erect or ascending, provided with tubular sheaths. **Roots** fibrous from a short creeping stem. **Leaf** fleshy or coriaceous, narrowed at the base. **Inflorescences** elongate, racemose, axillary. **Flowers** small, secund, tubular. **Sepals** connate for more than half their length forming a 3-angled inflated tube which is spreading or ventricose at the base and constricted at the mouth, free above and spreading. **Petals** minute, enclosed at base of sepaline tube. **Lip** minute, articulated to base of column or column-foot, 3-lobed or entire, fleshy, caniculate. **Column** small, erect, arcuate, subterete, 3-lobed; pollinia 2, ovoid, ceraceous.

DISTRIBUTION A small genus of about six species in the American tropics.

DERIVATION OF NAME From the Greek *physa* (bellows) and *siphon* (tube) and referring to the basally-inflated tube formed by the lateral sepals.

TAXONOMY *Physosiphon* was established by John Lindley in 1835 in the *Botanical Register*

(sub t. 1797). It is closely allied to *Masdevallia* and to *Pleurothallis;* differing from the former in having a racemose inflorescence and sepals with relatively short, free lobes, and from the latter in having a sepaline tube. Luer (1986) in *Icones Pleurothallidinarum* treats this as a section of *Pleurothallis*.

TYPE SPECIES *P. loddigesii* Lindl. nom. illeg.

CULTURE Compost A. Temp. Winter min. 10–12°C. As for *Pleurothallis*. The plants grow well in pans and flower well if left undivided. During growth they need plenty of water with less being required when growth is complete.

Physosiphon tubatus **(Lodd.) Rchb.f.**

[Colour Plate]

A small epiphytic plant. **Stems** erect or ascending, clustered, covered by tubular scarious sheaths, 1.5–12 cm long, 1-leafed at apex. **Leaf** suberect to erect, fleshy, elliptic to oblanceolate, obtuse and minutely retuse at the apex, 4–15 cm long, 1.5–3 cm broad, shortly petiolate. **Inflorescence** arcuate, 8–42 cm long, laxly many-flowered; bracts tubular-spathaceous, acute or acuminate, scarious, 0.3–0.7 cm long. **Flowers** cylindric-campanulate, greenish-yellow to brick-red. **Sepals** united for over half their length into a cylindric sepaline tube; free parts spreading elliptic-oblong to elliptic-lanceolate, obtuse to acute, 0.6–2.2 cm long including the tube. **Petals** obovate, obtuse to rarely 3-lobed at apex, 0.15–0.25 cm long, 0.1 cm broad. **Lip** 3-lobed towards apex, somewhat arcuate, canaliculate, dorsally carinate, 0.2–0.35 cm long, 0.1–0.2 cm broad; side lobes suberect, rounded; mid-lobe ovate, obtuse, crenulate on margins. **Column** slender, semiterete, arcuate, 3-lobed at apex, 0.2–0.3 cm long.

DISTRIBUTION Mexico and Guatemala; fairly common in rain and drier forests up to 3500 m.

HISTORY Discovered by F. Deppe at Xalapa in Mexico in 1828 when collecting for Messrs Loddiges, who described it their *Botanical Cabinet* (t. 1601) in 1830 as *Stelis tubatus*. H.G. Reichenbach transferred it to *Physosiphon* in 1864 in *Walpers, Annales Botanices* (p. 188).

SYNONYMS *Stelis tubatus* Lodd.; *Physosiphon guatemalensis* Rolfe; *Pleurothallis tubata* (Lodd.) Steud.

Platanthera **L.C. Rich.**

Subfamily Orchidoideae
Tribe Orchideae
Subtribe Orchidiinae

Small to large terrestrial plants growing from a fascicle of subterranean fleshy, swollen roots.

Leaves basal and cauline, elliptic, lanceolate to oblanceolate, green, conduplicate, convolute. **Inflorescence** erect, terminal, laxly to densely few- to many-flowered, simply racemose. **Flowers** often quiet showy, white, yellow, green, pink or purple. **Dorsal sepal** more or less adnate to the petals to form a hood over the column; **lateral sepals** spreading, free. **Lip** entire and ligulate or 3-lobed and fringed on the lobes, pendent to spreading, with a slender spur at the base. **Column** erect, short, broad; anther fixed, the anther loculi separated or divergent; pollinia 2, clavate, mealy, each attached by a caudicle to a separate viscidium.

DISTRIBUTION A large genus of perhaps 100 species in the north temperate regions of both hemispheres.

DERIVATION OF NAME From the Greek *platys* (broad) and *anthera* (stamen or anther), referring to the broad anther.

TAXONOMY *Platanthera* was established by the French botanist Louis-Claude-Marie Richard in 1818, in the *Mémoires du Muséum d'Histoire Naturelle, Paris* (p. 48), to accommodate those European orchids that fell between *Orchis* and *Habenaria* but were distinguished by their broad column with well separated parallel or divergent anther loculi.

The most distinctive species in this genus are the N. American fringed orchids with showy white, yellow or purple flowers and broad, lobed lips with fringed margins. They have even been separated as a distinct genus, *Blephariglottis*, by some authorities but they are probably best considered as a distinct section of *Platanthera*.

TYPE SPECIES *P. bifolia* (L.) L.C. Rich.

SYNONYMS *Blephariglottis* Raf.; *Tulotis* Raf.

CULTURE Temp. Winter min. 5°C. Mix as for *Anacamptis*.

Platanthera psycodes **(L.) Lindl.**

[Colour Plate]

Large terrestrial plants up to 90 cm tall, with numerous fleshy roots. **Leaves** 2–5, elliptic to lanceolate, acute, 10–20 cm long, 2–5 cm wide, keeled on the back, sheathing at the base, becoming bract-like above, dark green. **Inflorescence** laxly- to densely 20- to 50-flowered; rhachis 8–14 cm long; bracts lanceolate, acuminate, 8–15 mm long, green edged with purple. **Flowers** pale to rose-purple; pedicel and ovary purplish, 12–15 mm long. **Dorsal sepal** concave, elliptic, obtuse, 5–6 mm long, 3–4 mm wide; **lateral sepals** oblique, elliptic-ovate, obtuse, 5–7 mm long, 3–4 mm wide. **Petals** oblong-elliptic, obtuse, 5–7 mm long, 3–6 mm wide, erose-denticulate on the margins. **Lip** deflexed, 3-lobed, 7–12 mm long, 8–15 mm wide; side lobes spreading, cuneate, fringed on apical margin; mid-lobe flabellate, fringed on the apical margins; spur filiform, somewhat sigmoid, 12–18 mm long. **Column** 2 mm long.

DISTRIBUTION Widespread in N.E. of N. America across to the Great Lakes; in damp meadows and pastures, bogs and open wet woods.

HISTORY Linnaeus originally named this pretty orchid as *Orchis psycodes* in 1753 in his *Species Plantarum* (p. 943). It was transferred to *Platanthera* in 1835 by John Lindley in his *Genera and Species of Orchidaceous Plants* (p. 294). SYNONYMS include *Orchis psycodes* l.; *O. cristata* W. Bart.; *Platanthera incisa* (Willd.) Lindl.; *P. cristata* Lindl.; *Blephariglottis psycodes* (L.) Ryd.

CLOSELY RELATED SPECIES *P. grandiflora* (Bigelow) Lindl. is similar in flower colour and shape but its flowers are much larger, the lip up to 18 mm long and 25 mm wide; *P. ciliaris* (L.) Lindl. and *P. cristata* (Mich.) Lindl. have yellow-orange flowers with a deeply lacerate but narrower lip; *P. blephariglottis* (Willd.) Lindl. has similar white flowers.

Platystele Schltr.

Subfamily Epidendroideae
Tribe Epidendreae
Subtribe Pleurothallidinae

Small epiphytic herbs. **Stems** caespitose, very short, 1-leafed. **Inflorescences** terminal, slender, subdensely many-flowered, racemose; bracts hyaline. **Flowers** small. **Sepals** subspreading, subequal, oblong, obtuse or shortly acuminate. **Petals** smaller than sepals. **Lip** minute, broadly ovate or suborbicular, shortly acuminate, with an inconspicuous transverse lamella at the base. **Column** very short, lacking a foot; pollinia 2, obliquely ellipsoidal.

DISTRIBUTION About half a dozen species in Central and S. America.

DERIVATION OF NAME From the Greek *platys* (broad) and *stele* (column), descriptive of the short column which is dilated above.

TAXONOMY Described by Rudolf Schlechter in 1910 in *Fedde, Repertorium Specierum Novarum* (p. 565), *Platystele* closely resembles some species of *Pleurothallis* and *Masdevallia* in habit. Indeed, L.O. Williams in his *Enumeration of the Orchidaceae of Central America* considers it congeneric with *Pleurothallis*. *Platystele* may, however, be distinguished from *Pleurothallis* by its short, stout column, by its lanciform entire lip which lacks a callosity, and by its petals which equal the sepals in length.

TYPE SPECIES *P. bulbinella* Schltr. [= *Platystele compacta* (Ames) Ames].

CULTURE Compost A or mounted. Temp. Winter min. 12–15°C. Most grow well in pots or pans, while creeping species may be better grown on slabs of fern-fibre or cork. During active growth, good shade and humidity are needed, with plenty of water at the roots, but when the new leaves are fully formed, less water should be given, without the plants ever remaining dry.

Platystele stenostachya (Rchb.f.) Garay
[Colour Plate]

A minute, tufted epiphytic plant. **Leaf** obovate, sulcate above, suberect-spreading, up to 3.4 cm long, 0.5 cm broad. **Inflorescence** axillary, shorter than the leaf, racemose, few-flowered; bracts sheathing at the base. **Flowers** minute, appearing in succession on a lengthening rhachis; sepals and petals yellowish-brown; lip dark maroon with a gold or white marginal fringe. **Sepals** elliptic, acute, 0.12–0.17 cm long, 0.1 cm broad; lateral sepals united to middle. **Petals** narrowly elliptic, acute, 0.1–0.15 cm long, 0.03–0.06 cm broad. **Lip** elliptic-ligulate, very fleshy, 0.1–0.13 cm long, 0.05–0.07 cm broad, densely papillose. **Column** very short; pollinia, 2, obpyriform.

DISTRIBUTION Widespread from Mexico to Panama, Venezuela and Colombia; up to 1500 m.

HISTORY Another species described many times under various names and in three different genera. It was first described by H.G. Reichenbach in 1844 in *Linnaea* (p. 399) as *Pleurothallis stenostachya* from a specimen collected by Leibold at Temperirtes in Mexico. In 1962 Garay transferred it to the genus *Platystele* in *Caldasia* (p. 320).

SYNONYMS *Pleurothallis stenostachya* Rchb.f.; *dubia* Rchb.f.; *P. minutiflora* S. Wats.; *Humboldtia dubia* (Rchb.f.) O. Ktze.; *H. stenostachya* (Rchb.f.) O. Ktze.; *Pleurothallis myriantha* Lehm. & Kraenzl.; *P. lankesteri* Rolfe

Platystele stenostachya
1 – Flower (× 17)
2 – Anther-cap (× 36)
3 – Pollinia and viscidium (× 36)

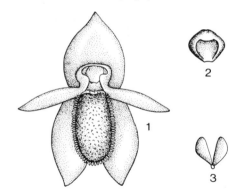

Pleione D. Don

Subfamily Epidendroideae
Tribe Coelogyneae
Subtribe Coelogyninae

Small, epiphytic, terrestrial or lithophytic plants. **Stems** pseudobulbous, clustered, annual, ovoid, conical or cylindrical, ± warty, 1- or 2-leaved at apex. **Leaves** plicate, 7.5–30 cm long, deciduous, ± falling before flowering. **Inflorescences** usually 1- or rarely 2-flowered, 1 or 2 per pseudobulb. **Flowers** short-lived, large, showy; peduncles short. **Sepals** and **petals** free, narrow, subsimilar. **Lip** obscurely 3-lobed, somewhat trumpet-shaped, embracing the column; disc bearing 2–9 longitudinal entire or dissected lamellae. **Column** slender, long, dilated towards apex; pollinia 4.

DISTRIBUTION A genus of some 16 or so species, in Nepal, N. India (Sikkim and Assam), Bhutan, Burma, S. China, Taiwan, Thailand and Laos; 1000–3300 m or more altitude in forest regions with high rainfall where the species lose their leaves in the autumn as the pseudobulbs mature in preparation to survive the severer climate of the winter season.

DERIVATION OF NAME From the Greek name Pleione, the mother of the Pleiads of Greek mythology who were transformed into a cluster of stars by Zeus.

TAXONOMY *Pleione* was established in 1825 by D. Don in his *Prodromus Florae Nepalensis* (p. 36). The genus is closely allied to *Coelogyne* to which genus those species discovered before 1825 were previously ascribed. However, *Pleione* differs in having distinctly shaped pseudobulbs, which are deciduous and have a distinct rest period during the dry season; a generally far fewer-flowered inflorescence and a quite distinctive lip shape.

The genus was first reviewed by R.A. Rolfe in the *Orchid Review* (1903) where he discussed the generic distinction of *Pleione* from *Coelogyne* and briefly described the 11 species in cultivation at that time. F. Kraenzlin revised the genus shortly afterwards in A. Engler's *Das Pflanzenreich* (1907) accepting 13 species which he divided into two sections:

1. sect. *(Eu) Pleione* in which the pseudobulbs are ovate or bottle-shaped, usually unifoliate, and the sheaths are not inflated and have subparallel variation. The species flower in the spring, e.g. *P. humilis*, *P. hookeriana* and *P. bulbocodioides*.

2. sect. *Dictyopleione* where the pseudobulbs are shortly cylindric, usually bifoliate, and the inflated sheaths are prominently reticulately veined. These flower in the autumn, e.g. *P. praecox* and *P. maculata*.

R. Schlechter reviewed the genus in *Orchis*

(1914) but followed Kraenzlin's treatment. The account of the genus by P.F. Hunt and C.G. Vosa in the *Kew Bulletin* (1971) differs from earlier accounts in that only nine species are accepted in the genus and that several names are reduced to synonymy, particularly in *P. bulbocodioides* which assimilated the horticulturally well-known *P. formosana*, *P. pricei* and others.

The most recent account of the genus is that of Cribb and Butterfield (1988) in *The genus Pleione* in which the species and their hybrids are discussed in detail with all of the species being fully illustrated.

TYPE SPECIES   *P. humilis* (J.E. Smith) D. Don and *P. praecox* (J.E. Smith) D. Don

CULTURE   Compost A. Temp. Winter min. 5–7°C. Summer max. below 25°C if possible. Autumn-flowering species such as *P. praecox* should be repotted after flowering and kept cool and dry until the new shoots are growing. The plants then require careful watering and warmer shady conditions. After the leaves are fully grown, the plants should again be cool and, after leaf-fall, completely dry. The other species should be repotted when the new shoots are 1–2 cm tall. Water should be given only when the roots appear and then very carefully. During growth, moderate shade and humidity are required. After leaf-fall, the plants must be kept cool and dry again.

Pleione aurita Cribb & Pfennig
[Colour Plate]
A terrestrial plant. **Pseudobulb** conical, angular in cross-section, 2–4.5 cm long, 1–2 cm in diameter, unifoliate. **Leaf** erect, narrowly elliptic, acute, up to 20 cm long, 2.5–3.5 cm wide. **Inflorescence** 1-flowered, up to 16 cm tall, spring-flowering; peduncle slender, erect, 5–7 cm long; bract elliptic-oblanceolate, acute, 2–2.5 cm long. **Flower** very showy, bright rose-purple with a yellow or orange streak down the centre of the lip; pedicel and ovary 1.6–2 cm long. **Sepals** narrowly elliptic or oblong-elliptic, subacute, 4–5 cm long, 1.1–1.6 cm wide. **Petals** reflexed, oblanceolate, obtuse, 4–4.3 cm long, 1.4–1.9 cm wide. **Lip** deeply cucullate, broadly flabellate and obscurely 3-lobed when flattened, emarginate, 3.9–4 cm long, 5–6 cm wide; callus of 4–5 lines of long hairs from base almost to the apex. **Column** clavate, 2.5–2.7 cm long, notched on each side at the apex.
DISTRIBUTION   China: probably Yunnan only; habitat unknown.
HISTORY   This spectacular species was described in 1988 in *Die Orchideen* by P. Cribb and H. Pfennig based on cultivated material thought to come from S.W. China. It is allied to *P. hookeriana* but has much larger, more

brightly coloured flowers and a callus with fewer lines of hairs.

Pleione bulbocodioides (Franch.) Rolfe
[Colour Plate]
Small terrestrial or lithophytic plants. **Pseudobulbs** conical to pyriform, 2–2.6 cm long, 1.2–2 cm wide, unifoliate, green. **Leaf** developing after the inflorescence, narrowly elliptic-lanceolate, acute to acuminate, 10–20 cm long, 2–3 cm wide. **Inflorescence** 1-flowered, erect, up to 20 cm long; peduncle 6–16 cm long; bract elliptic-obovate, rounded or obtuse, 2.9–4 cm long. **Flower** showy, with rose-purple to pink sepals and petals and a rose-purple lip spotted with dark purple and with white callus ridges. **Dorsal sepal** oblanceolate, obtuse, 3.4–4.5 cm long, 0.5–0.8 cm wide; **lateral sepals** obliquely narrowly elliptic, obtuse to subacute, 3.3–4.4 cm long, 0.6–1 cm wide. **Petals** obliquely oblanceolate, acute or subacute, 3.7–4.6 cm long, 0.4–0.7 cm wide. **Lip** obscurely 3-lobed, obovate, emarginate, 3.2–4.5 cm long, 2.5–3.5 cm wide, the margins lacerate; callus of 4–5 erose lamellae, the central one subquadrate. **Column** 2.7–3.6 cm long.
DISTRIBUTION   China: Kansu, Sichuan and Yunnan east to Hubei; in deep leaf litter in open *Pinus/Rhododendron* woodland and rocky places, 900–3600 m.
HISTORY   A widespread and variable species allied to *Pleione formosana* but with smaller more deeply coloured flowers and a somewhat different callus. It was first described by Franchet in 1888 as *Coelogyne bulbocodioides* in *Nouvelles Archives du Muséum d'Histoire Naturelle de Paris* (p. 84). Rolfe transferred it to *Pleione* in 1903 in the *Orchid Review* (p. 291).
SYNONYMS   include *Coelogyne bulbocodioides* Franch.; *C. delavayi* Rolfe; *C. henryi* Rolfe; *P. fargesii* Gagnep.; *Pleione delavayi* (Rolfe) Rolfe
CLOSELY RELATED SPECIES   *Pleione limprichtii* Schltr., from W. Sichuan, is closely allied and may be merely a variety of *P. bulbocodioides* [Colour Plate]. It differs in having a more or less elliptic lip with 2 jaggedly denticulate lamellae. *P. speciosa* Ames & Schltr., from Sichuan, Kweichow and Hubei, is also closely allied but has a larger brightly coloured rose-purple flower with blood-red blotches and 2 finely toothed parallel lamellae on the lip.

Pleione formosana Hayata [Colour Plate]
Small terrestrial or lithophytic plants. **Pesudobulbs** compressed ovoid to ovoid-conical, 1.3–3 cm long, 1.7–3.7 cm in diameter, unifoliate, green to dull purple. **Leaf** erect to arcuate, oblanceolate to elliptic, acuminate, 10–25 cm long, 3–5 cm wide, shortly petiolate. **Inflorescence** produced with the new growth, 1- or

rarely 2-flowered; peduncle 7–12 cm long; bract linear-lanceolate to obovate, 2.4–4.3 cm long. **Flower** large, showy, weakly fragrant, with pink or rarely white sepals and petals and a pink or white lip marked with brown to purple spots and yellow callus ridges; pedicel and ovary 1.5–2.5 cm long. **Sepals** narrowly elliptic-oblanceolate, acute or subacute, 4.2–5.7 cm long, 0.9–1.5 cm wide. **Petals** spreading, linear-oblanceolate, acute or subacute, 4.2–6 cm long, 1–1.5 cm wide. **Lip** obscurely 3-lobed, cornet-shaped, 4–5.5 cm long, 3.2–4.6 cm wide, with lacerate apical margins; callus of 2–5 interrupted lamellae with erose magins and obscurely dentate at the apex. **Column** 2.8–3.6 cm long.
DISTRIBUTION   Taiwan and possibly adjacent China; in shaded places in the mountains.
HISTORY   Originally described by Hayata in 1911 in the *Journal of the College of Science, Tokyo* (p. 326) based on a collection by Mori from Nano in Taiwan.
SYNONYMS   *Pleione pricei* Rolfe; *P. hui* Schltr.

Pleione forrestii Schltr. [Colour Plate]
A lithophytic herb. **Pseudobulbs** conical-pyriform, 2.8 cm long, 2.5 cm broad. **Leaves** narrowly elliptic-lanceolate, 15 cm long, 1.5–4 cm broad, acute. **Inflorescence** 7–10 cm high, appearing when leaves absent; bracts larger than ovary. **Flowers** erect, 5.5 cm across, yellow to orange; lip blotched red or red-brown; column yellow. **Sepals** lanceolate, 3–4.5 cm long, 0.7–1 cm broad, subobtuse. **Petals** oblanceolate, 3.6–4.4 cm long, 0.7–0.9 cm broad, subobtuse. **Lip** obscurely 3-lobed, rotund, 3.4–3.7 cm long, 2.7–3.1 cm broad, emarginate; side lobes short, rounded; mid-lobe broadly reniform, margins lacerate; disc bearing about 6 undulate irregular lamellae. **Column** curvate, 2.6–3.5 cm long.
DISTRIBUTION   China (Yunnan) and N. Burma; growing on moss-covered rocks and cliffs, 2400–3100 m altitude.
HISTORY   This beautiful yellow-flowered species was first collected by George Forrest in the Tali Range in Yunnan and was subsequently named after him by Rudolf Schlechter in the *Notes of the Royal Botanic Garden, Edinburgh* (p. 106) in 1912.

P. forrestii is quite distinctive in the genus being the only species with predominantly yellow flowers.

Pleione hookeriana (Lindl.) B.S. Williams
[Colour Plate]
An epiphytic or lithophytic herb. **Pseudobulbs** conical, 1–3 cm long, 0.5–1.5 cm in diameter, 1-leafed at apex. **Leaf** persistent, elliptic-lanceolate, 5–21 cm long, 1–4.6 cm broad, acute, tapering gradually at base. **Inflores-**

cence up to 12 cm high, appearing with young leaves; bracts tubular, obliquely truncate, obtuse. **Flowers** up to 6 cm across; sepals and petals pink; lip white to pink, with a central band of yellow lamellae, heavily brown- to purple-spotted, apex often pink or purple; column white. **Dorsal sepal** elliptic-oblong to oblanceolate, obtuse, 2.5–3.2 cm long, 0.7–1.2 cm broad; **lateral sepals** obscurely falcate, oblong, acute. **Petals** spreading, oblanceolate, 2.5–3.3 cm long, 0.3–0.7 cm broad. **Lip** obscurely 3-lobed, reniform, 2.2–4 cm long, 2.5–4 cm broad, margins ciliate; side lobes rounded, erect over column; mid-lobe emarginate at apex; disc with 6–7 barbate lamellae on lip. **Column** 1.5–2.2 cm long; apex winged.
DISTRIBUTION India (Assam, Sikkim), Nepal, Bhutan, Burma, S.W. China, Thailand and Laos; 2200–4200 m altitude.
HISTORY Sir Joseph Hooker collected this species near Darjeeling and John Lindley named it *Coelogyne hookeriana* after him in 1854 *Folia Orchidacea* (*Coelogyne*: p. 14). In 1885, B.S. Williams in the *Orchid Growers' Manual* (p. 548) transferred it to the genus *Pleione*.
SYNONYMS *Coelogyne hookeriana* Lindl.; *Pleione laotica* A.F.G.Kerr
CLOSELY RELATED SPECIES See *P. humilis*.

Pleione humilis (J.E. Smith) D. Don
An epiphytic or lithophytic herb. **Pseudobulbs** ovoid-conical, 2–6 cm long, 0.8–2 cm broad, 1-leafed at apex. **Leaf** oblanceolate, up to 26 cm long, 4.5 cm broad, subacute. **Inflorescence** very short, appearing before the leaves; scape clothed in greenish sheaths. **Flowers** erect or nodding, up to 8.5 cm across, white; lip heavily spotted with dark purple or yellow-orange; column white, spotted purple towards apex. **Sepals** narrowly oblong to oblanceolate, 3.3–4.5 cm long, 0.7–1.3 cm broad, subacute. **Petals** narrowly oblanceolate, 3.5–4.6 cm long, 0.5–0.7 cm broad, obtuse. **Lip** obscurely 3-lobed, elliptic, 3–4.4 cm long, 2.5–3 cm broad, margins lacerate or long-dentate; side lobes curved up over column; mid-lobe spreading, margins slightly recurved; lamellae on lip 6–7, barbate, **Column** apex irregular.
DISTRIBUTION India (Sikkim), Nepal and Burma; growing in thick moss, 1100–3200 m altitude.
HISTORY Originally collected in Nepal by F. Buchanan-Hamilton and described as *Epidendrum humilis* by J.E. Smith (1806) in *Exotic Botany* (p. 75, t. 98). With *P. praecox* it was transferred first to *Coelogyne* by John Lindley and, in 1825, to *Pleione* by D. Don in his *Prodromus Florae Nepalensis* (p. 37).
SYNONYMS *Coelogyne humilis* (J.E. Smith) Lindl.; *Pleione diantha* Schltr.

CLOSELY RELATED SPECIES *P. humilis* is allied to *P. hookeriana* but differs in that the flowers are produced when the pseudobulbs are leafless and the lip is larger and elliptic rather than reniform. From *P. bulbocodioides*, it differs in having 6–7 barbate keels on the lip.

Pleione maculata (Lindl.) Lindl.
[Colour Plate]
Pseudobulbs clustered, shortly cylindrical to conical, 1–3 cm long, 1–2 cm in diameter, marked with green and maroon covered with small white warts, 2-leaved at apex, abruptly contracted into a beak. **Leaves** elliptic-lanceolate to oblanceolate, up to 26 cm long, 3 cm broad, acute. **Inflorescence** 5–8 cm high, borne from base of leafless pseudobulbs, autumn-flowering; basal sheaths of peduncle not warty. **Flowers** up to 6 cm across; sepals and petals creamy-white; lip purple-lined at the base and on side lobes, white above with dark purple blotches on margins of mid-lobe, lamellae white at base, yellow towards apex. **Sepals** narrowly oblong-lanceolate, 3–4 cm long, 0.7–0.9 cm broad, acute. **Petals** narrowly lanceolate, 3–4.2 cm long, 0.6–0.8 cm broad, acute. **Lip** 3-lobed, oblong, 2–3.5 cm long, 2–2.5 cm broad; side lobes obscure, truncate, curved over column; mid-lobe margins undulate-erose; lamellae 5–7, extending onto apex of lip, each divided, somewhat crenulate. **Column** slender, clavate, 1.7–2 cm long, erose-dentate at apex.
DISTRIBUTION India (Assam, Sikkim), Bhutan, Burma and Thailand.
HISTORY Originally described by John Lindley in 1830 in *Genera and Species of Orchidaceous Plants* (p. 43) as *Coelogyne maculata*, based on a collection by N. Wallich from Pundua in India. Lindley transferred it in 1851 to the genus *Pleione* in J. Paxton's *Flower Garden* (p. 5, t. 39).
SYNONYMS *Coelogyne maculata* Lindl.; *Pleione diphylla* Lindl.; *Gymnostylis candida* Wall. ex Pfitz.
CLOSELY RELATED SPECIES Allied to *P. praecox* but with smaller flowers in which the keels extend to the apex of the lip and the basal sheath of the inflorescences are not warty.

Pleione praecox (J.E. Smith) D. Don
[Colour Plate]
An epiphytic or lithophytic herb. **Pseudobulbs** shortly cylindrical, 1.5–3 cm long, 1–1.5 cm broad, maroon, covered with greenish warts, abruptly contracted into a beak at apex, often covered by net-like veins of old basal sheath, 2-leaved at apex. **Leaves** narrowly elliptic-lanceolate, 15–26 cm long, 3–6 cm broad, acute. **Inflorescence** up to 13 cm high, from base of leafless pseudobulbs, autumn-flowering; basal sheaths of peduncle warty. **Flowers** up to

8 cm across, white to purplish-pink; lateral sepals sometimes with a brownish central longitudinal stripe on outer side; lip white with purple stripes at base and purple blotches on apical margins, lamellae white at base, yellow towards apex; column greenish-white, the anther-cap yellow. **Sepals** narrowly oblong-lanceolate, 4.5–7 cm long, 0.9–1.2 cm across, acute. **Petals** slightly falcate, narrowly lanceolate, 4–7 cm long, 0.7 cm across, acute. **Lip** oblong, 3-lobed, 4–5 cm long, 3 cm broad; side lobes obscure, erect over column; mid-lobe emarginate, margins spreading dentate-lacerate; disc bearing 5 papillate keels onto base of mid-lobe. **Column** slender, curved in apical half, 3.5–4.5 cm long, apex irregularly lobed.
DISTRIBUTION S.W. China, India (Assam, Sikkim), Nepal, N. Thailand and Burma; growing on mossy branches or mossy rocks, 1500–3400 m altitude.
HISTORY This species was first collected in Nepal by Dr Francis Buchanan-Hamilton and was described by J.E. Smith in *Exotic Botany* (p. 73, t. 97) in 1806 as *Epidendrum praecox*. Subsequently, it was transferred by John Lindley to the genus *Coelogyne* and later, in 1825, by D. Don to *Pleione* in his *Prodromus Florae Nepalensis* (p. 37).
SYNONYMS *Epidendrum praecox* J.E. Smith; *Coelogyne praecox* (J.E. Smith) Lindl.; *C. wallichiana* Lindl.; *Pleione reichenbachiana* (T. Moore & Veitch) B.S. Williams; *P. concolor* Hort.; *Coelogyne reichenbachiana* T. Moore & Veitch
CLOSELY RELATED SPECIES See *P. maculata*.

Pleurothallis R. Br.
Subfamily Epidendroideae
Tribe Epidendreae
Subtribe Pleurothallidinae

Small to medium-sized epiphytic or lithophytic herbs with tufted stems from a creeping rhizome. Stems ramicaul, erect, short, jointed, mostly 1-leafed. **Leaves** fleshy to coriaceous, erect to spreading, sessile or petiolate. **Inflorescence** apical, short to very long, racemose, fasciculate or 1-flowered. **Flowers** small, occasionally secund. **Sepals** ± subequal, spreading or ringent, ± connate; lateral sepals connate at base to completely united to apex, ± forming a short mentum with the column-foot. **Petals** smaller than the sepals. **Lip** small, simple to 3-lobed, mostly clawed. **Column** ± winged, foot mostly distinct; pollinia 2, waxy, pyriform to sphaerical, lacking a stipe, rostellum well-developed.
DISTRIBUTION One of the largest genera in the Orchidaceae with about 900 species con-

fined to the tropical Americas but commonest in montane regions.

DERIVATION OF NAME From the Greek *pleuron* (rib) and *thallos* (short, branch) in allusion to the many rib-like stems which arise in tufts in many species.

TAXONOMY Robert Brown described *Pleurothallis* in the 2nd edition of W. Aiton's *Hortus Kewensis* (p. 211) in 1813. Because of their small-sized flowers and great diversity, the species of *Pleurothallis* have remained relatively poorly known and little studied. Newly introduced plants are often very difficult or impossible to name as many species are poorly defined or undescribed.

Recently, C. Luer has begun the monumental task of monographing the genus in a series of articles in the journal *Selbyana*. Here, each species dealt with has been fully described and illustrated and although only a few parts have so far been produced, many new species have already been described.

Pleurothallis is allied to *Masdevallia* but differs in having much smaller flowers which lack the characteristic sepaline tube of the latter.

The division of the genus most often used until recently was that proposed by E. Pfitzer in A. Engler and K.A. Prantl's *Die Natürlichen Pflanzenfamilien* (1897), but P. Allen in the *Flora of Panama* (1949) states that it 'is wholly artificial and quite impossible to use'. Fortunately, Luer (1986) in the third volume of his monumental *Icones Pleurothallidinarum* has produced an infrageneric classification of the genus which he has divided into 27 subgenera and 25 sections.

TYPE SPECIES *P. ruscifolius* (Jacq.) R. Br.
SYNONYMS *Kraenzlinella* O. Ktze.
CULTURE Compost A or mounted. Temp. Winter min. 12–15°C. Although such a large genus, most *Pleurothallis* species may be grown under similar conditions. Most grow well in pots or pans, while creeping species may be better grown on slabs of fern-fibre or cork. During active growth, good shade and humidity are needed, with plenty of water at the roots, but when the new leaves are fully formed less water should be given without the plants ever remaining dry.

Pleurothallis bivalvis **Lindl.** [Colour Plate]
A medium-sized tufted, epiphytic plant. **Stems** long, terete, erect, up to 20 cm long, with 2 grey or brown appressed tubular sheaths. **Leaf** ovate, cordate at base, acuminate at the apex, coriaceous, up to 16 cm long, 5 cm broad. **Inflorescence** very short, bearing a succession of 1–4 flowers at a time from a brown basal sheath. **Flowers** with light greeny-yellow or brownish-yellow sepals; petals maroon; lip red

or maroon with a white base; column orange, flushed with maroon. **Dorsal sepal** elliptic-ovate, subacute, 1.9 cm long, 1.1 cm broad; **lateral sepals** united, obtuse, 1.6 cm long, 1 cm broad. **Petals** falcate, linear, margins ciliate, 1.2 cm long, 0.1 cm broad. **Lip** fleshy, ovate-elliptic, subobtuse, margins minutely denticulate, 1.1 cm long, 0.6 cm broad; disc with a round glossy area at the base. **Column** truncate, 0.2 cm long; foot papillose.
DISTRIBUTION Colombia and Venezuela.
HISTORY Discovered in the forests of the Savanna of Chiquara in Mérida Province of Venezuela by Jean Linden and described by John Lindley in 1846 in *Orchidaceae Lindenianae* (p. 2).
SYNONYM *Humboldtia bivalvis* (Lindl.) O.Ktze.

Pleurothallis ciliaris **(Lindl.) L.O. Williams**
A small, caespitose epiphytic plant, 5–14 cm high. **Stems** slender, fractiflex, 3–8.5 cm long, 1-leafed at apex, concealed by lepanthoid sheaths; sheaths ciliate along costae and apical margins. **Leaf** coriaceous, oblong-elliptic, lanceolate or linear, acute or subacute, 2–6.5 cm long, 0.35–1.3 cm broad, purplish-green. **Inflorescences** several, fasciculate, few-flowered, racemose, up to 2.5 cm long. **Flowers** yellow-green to purplish-red, spotted purplish-red. **Dorsal sepal** oblong-elliptic, subacute, ciliate, 0.4 cm long, 0.2 cm broad; **lateral sepals** united into a suborbicular lamina, recurved above, margins ciliate, 0.35 cm long, 0.2–0.3 cm broad. **Petals** cuneate to oblong-quadrate, rounded above, margins irregularly dentate-ciliate, 0.15 cm long, 0.05 cm broad. **Lip** arcuate, oblong-spathulate, rounded at apex, with a small mammillate auricle on each side at base, ciliate, 0.2 cm long, 0.1 cm broad; disc with a linear callus on basal third, forked in front. **Column** slender, recurved, 0.2 cm long.
DISTRIBUTION Mexico to Costa Rica; in forests and coffee plantations up to 1800 m altitude.
HISTORY Described by John Lindley in 1838 as *Specklinia ciliaris* in the *Botanical Register* (misc. p. 31) based on a plant imported from Mexico by Messrs Loddiges. L.O. Williams transferred it to the genus *Pleurothallis* in 1942 in *Caldasia* (p. 14).

P. ciliaris is one of the *Lepanthes*-like species with ciliate margins to the trumpet-shaped sheaths on its stem. It is readily recognised, however, by its pubescent, purplish red-spotted flowers with petals which are lacerate towards the apex, a pubescent lip and a lacerate column-apex.
SYNONYMS *Specklinia ciliaris* Lindl.; *Pleurothallis gnomonifera* Ames; *P. brevis* Schltr.

Pleurothallis crenata **Lindl.**
A small repent or caespitose plant, up to 15 cm tall. **Stems** up to 1 cm long, 1-leafed at apex. **Leaf** broadly to narrowly oblanceolate, acute or obtuse, 4.5–13 cm long, 1–2.7 cm broad, petiolate below. **Inflorescence** ± half as long as the leaves, 1- to several-flowered; peduncle and rhachis terete. **Flowers** dull yellow, spotted with purple; petals and lip purple, bordered with purple spots on a yellow background; column white. **Sepals** ± spreading, lanceolate, acute, 1.1–1.8 cm long, 0.15–0.35 cm broad, minutely papilliferous within, keeled or winged dorsally; lateral sepals connate to middle. **Petals** oblong-lanceolate, somewhat pandurate, acute, 0.4–0.45 cm long, 0.15–0.2 cm broad. **Lip** oblong-lanceolate, obtuse or subacute; sides erect and fleshy; disc densely papillose-verrucose. 0.45–0.5 cm long, 0.15–0.2 cm broad.
DISTRIBUTION Costa Rica, Mexico and Panama.
HISTORY *P. crenata* was described by John Lindley in the *Gardeners' Chronicle* (p. 207) in 1846 based on a collection from Mexico introduced by Messrs Loddiges.
SYNONYMS *Masdevallia aperta* Kraenzl.: *Pleurothallis hunterana* Schltr.: *P. hamata* Ames; *P. aperta* (Kraenzl.) Ames

Pleurothallis endotrachys **Rchb.f.**
[Colour Plate]
A medium-sized epiphytic plant. **Stems** clustered, short, stout, sulcate, 1–2 cm long, 1-leafed at apex. **Leaf** fleshy, oblanceolate, obtuse or subacute and tridenticulate at apex, 6–22 cm long, 1.4–3 cm broad. **Inflorescence** erect, racemose, few- to many-flowered, 12–35 cm long; peduncle ancipitous, winged; rhachis fractiflex; bracts conduplicate, 0.5–1 cm long. **Flowers** fleshy, red or orange-red, produced singly and successively. **Dorsal sepal** ovate-lanceolate, subacute, 1.6–2 cm long, 0.45–0.6 cm broad; **lateral sepals** oblanceolate, subacute, united in basal half to form a shallow mentum; all sepals papillate-rugulose on inner surface. **Petals** small, narrowly oblong, rounded, papillate within, 0.5 cm long, 0.1 cm broad. **Lip** arcuate, fleshy, oblong, subacute, 0.5–0.6 cm long, 0.2 cm broad; with a longitudinal lamella towards each margin. **Column** arcuate, dilated and denticulately-winged above; foot 0.3 cm long.
DISTRIBUTION Mexico to Panama, Colombia and Venezuela: growing on the trunks of large trees in cloud forests, 1300–2500 m in altitude.
HISTORY *P. endotrachys* was described in 1876 by H.G. Reichenbach in *Linnaea* (p. 95) based on a plant collected in Costa Rica by A. R. Endres.

Pleurothallis glandulosa Ames [Colour Plate]

A small, densely-tufted, epiphytic plant, 2–5 cm tall. **Stems** very obscure, up to 0.5 cm long, 1-leafed at apex. **Leaf** erect, coriaceous, narrowly linear or linear-oblanceolate, obtuse, 2–4 cm long, 0.1–0.3 cm broad. **Inflorescence** 1- or 2-flowered, 1.5–4.5 cm long; peduncle filiform, glandular-pubescent; bracts scarious, apiculate, papillose on outer surface, 0.3 cm long. **Flowers** reddish-yellow or greenish-yellow; sepals with glandular-papillose margins. **Dorsal sepal** elliptic or narrowly lanceolate, acute or subacute, 0.4–0.8 cm long, 0.15–0.3 cm broad; **lateral sepals** united in basal half, oblong-lanceolate, 0.4–0.8 cm long, 0.2 cm broad. **Petals** obovate, oblique, anterior margins dilated above, mucronate at apex, 0.2–0.3 cm long, 0.2 cm broad. **Lip** shortly clawed. arcuate, linear-oblong or lanceolate, cordate at base, rounded or obtuse at the ciliate apex. 0.2–0.4 cm long, 0.1–0.2 cm broad, basal teeth suberect; disc glandular. **Column** slender, 3-toothed at apex; 0.3 cm long.

DISTRIBUTION Mexico to Panama; widespread but local in forests, up to 1000 m altitude.

HISTORY *P. glandulosa* was described by Oakes Ames in 1923 in his *Schedulae Orchidianae* (p. 60) based on a plant collected by C.W. Powell in the Juna Grande range in Panama.

SYNONYM *Pleurothallis vittariaefolia* Schltr.

Pleurothallis grobyi Batem. ex Lindl.
[Colour Plate]

A small, tufted epiphytic plant, 3–15 cm high. **Stems** very short, 0.6 cm long, 1-leafed at apex. **Leaf** coriaceous, obovate, elliptic-oblong or oblanceolate, obtuse or retuse at apex, conspicuously marginate, 2–7 cm long, 0.3–1.1 cm broad, ± purple below. **Inflorescence** solitary, laxly few-flowered, 2.5–15 cm long; peduncle filiform, purple, ± fractiflex. **Flowers** variable, pale green or yellow marked with red-purple. **Dorsal sepal** ovate-oblong or oblong-lanceolate, acuminate, concave, 0.3–1 cm long, 0.15–0.3 cm broad; **lateral sepals** united to form a concave ovate-elliptic bidentate lamina, 0.3–1.1 cm long, up to 0.6 cm broad. **Petals** obovate to lanceolate, acute or obtuse, 0.1–0.25 cm long, 0.1 cm broad. **Lip** linear-ligulate or oblong, rounded or obtuse at apex, canaliculate, 0.2–0.3 cm long, 0.1 cm broad; disc lightly keeled on side nerves. **Column** slightly winged towards apex, tridentate at apex, 0.3 cm long.

DISTRIBUTION W. Indies, Mexico, Central and S. America; a common species of dense forests, usually at low altitudes but up to 1500 m altitude.

HISTORY Imported from Demerara (now Georgetown), Guyana by James Bateman who named it in honour of Lord Grey of Groby, a keen and skilled orchid grower. It was described by John Lindley in 1835 in the *Botanical Register* (t. 1797), the illustration being drawn from a plant cultivated by Messrs Loddiges of Hackney, London.

SYNONYMS *Pleurothallis marginata* Lindl.; *P. choconiana* S. Wats.; *P. picta* Lindl.

Pleurothallis lanceana Lodd.

A small, tufted epiphytic plant. **Stems** short, sulcate, 1-leafed at apex. **Leaf** fleshy, rigid, oblong-elliptic, obtuse, 9 cm long, 3 cm broad. **Inflorescences** 1–3 in succession, longer than the leaves, racemose, many-flowered. **Flowers** with mustard-yellow sepals, flecked with purple on the dorsal sepal; petals golden-yellow, flushed pink; lip yellowish-brown, spotted with maroon. **Dorsal sepal** linear, acute, thickened in apical half, 1 cm long, 0.15 cm broad; **lateral sepals** united almost to apex, acute, lamina concave, 1 cm long, 0.5 cm broad, pubescent. **Petals** ovate, acute, margins lacerate, 0.3 cm long. **Lip** fleshy, shortly clawed, elliptic, rounded, 0.3 cm long, 0.2 cm broad, coarsely papillate all over. **Column** slender, arcuate, 0.2 cm long.

DISTRIBUTION Guatemala, Costa Rica, tropical S. America and Trinidad: in cloud forest at about 1500–2000 m altitude.

HISTORY Described and illustrated in Loddiges *Botanical Cabinet* (t. 1767) in 1831 based on a plant sent from Surinam in 1831 by J. Lance after whom it was named.

P. lanceana is distinguished by its fleshy leaf and petiole, and by its densely many-flowered inflorescence in which the flowers have united lateral sepals, a clavate dorsal sepal and petals with lacerate margins.

SYNONYMS *Pleurothallis ciliata* Knowles & Westcott; *P. plumosa* Lindl.; *P. crassiflora* Focke; *P. minax* Rchb.f.; *P. huebneri* Schltr.; *Humboldtia ciliata* (Knowles & Westcott) O. Ktze.

Pleurothallis loranthophylla Rchb.f.
[Colour Plate]

A tufted epiphytic plant. **Stems** erect, terete, up to 10 cm long, 1-leafed at apex. **Leaf** oblong-elliptic, suberect, coriaceous, tridenticulate at apex, up to 10 cm long, 3.5 cm broad. **Inflorescence** axillary, 1 to several, racemose, laxly several-flowered, subtended by a large, compressed sheath. **Flowers** pale brown, flushed with maroon and ± lightly spotted with maroon; lip often flushed with bright maroon. **Dorsal sepal** lanceolate, acute, 0.8–1.1 cm long, 0.2 cm broad; **lateral sepals** connate to

the apex, minutely bidentate at apex, 0.8–1 cm long, 0.4 cm broad. **Petals** lanceolate, 0.6–0.8 cm long, 0.15–0.2 cm broad, with a narrowly drawn-out apical half. **Lip** ovate, acute, slightly narrowed in centre, 0.45–0.6 cm long, 0.3 cm broad. **Column** curved, short, terete.

DISTRIBUTION Colombia and Venezuela, south to Bolivia.

HISTORY Originally described by H.G. Reichenbach in 1852 in the *Botanische Zeitung* (p. 674) based on a plant of unknown provenance.

SYNONYMS *Rhynchopera punctata* Karst.; *Pleurothallis subpellucida* Klotzsch; *P. intermedia* Schltr.; *P. punctata* (Karst.) Schltr.; *P. spathata* Schltr.

Pleurothallis octomerioides Lindl.
[Colour Plate]

A medium-sized epiphytic plant. **Stems** 0.1–1 cm apart on a creeping stout rhizome, terete, 12–15 cm long, 1-leafed above, covered by 3 or 4 tubular scabrous sheaths. **Leaf** narrowly elliptic, acute, coriaceous, 12 cm long, 2 cm broad. **Inflorescence** fasciculate, few- to many-flowered; bracts tubular, ciliate, 0.3 cm long. **Flowers** fleshy; sepals and petals pale yellow; lip red-purple; anther red or yellow. **Sepals** spreading, narrowly obovate, obtuse, 0.6–0.7 cm long, 0.2 cm broad; lateral sepals slightly oblique, joined at base to form a shallow mentum. **Petals** narrowly oblong-elliptic, subacute, 0.6 cm long, 0.15 cm broad. **Lip** fleshy, oblong, shortly clawed, rounded in front, papillate, 0.3 cm long, 0.1 cm broad, marginal crests verrucose. **Column** short, winged, toothed at the apex, 0.15 cm long; foot very short.

DISTRIBUTION Mexico to Panama.

HISTORY *P. octomerioides* was described by John Lindley in 1836 in the *Companion to the Botanical Magazine* (p. 354), being named for its resemblance to species in the genus *Octomeria*. It was first collected by John Henchman in Mexico and was cultivated by J. Willmore of Oldford, England whose plants provided Lindley with a description of the species.

P. octomerioides resembles some of the larger *Octomeria* species with its fasciculate inflorescences at the base of a large complanate leaf, but it has characteristically pleurothalloid yellow flowers with a reddish-purple lip which has a central longitudinal groove.

SYNONYMS *Humboldtia octomerioides* (Lindl.) O. Ktze.; *Pleurothallis octomeriae* Schltr.; *P. cerea* Ames

Pleurothallis phalangifera (Presl) Rchb.f.
[Colour Plate]

A medium-sized to large epiphytic plant. **Stems** slender, terete, 12–47 cm long, covered in basal part by 2 or 3 spotted tubular sheaths, 1-leafed. **Leaf** elliptic-ovate, apiculate, tridenticulate at the apex, coriaceous, rounded at base, 11–17 cm long, 4–7.5 cm broad. **Inflorescences** 1–3, racemose, laxly few-flowered, 15–25 cm long, subtended by a compressed sheath, up to 3 cm long. **Flowers** large in genus, spidery, purple. **Dorsal sepal** ovate, long-attenuate above, 3.6 cm long, 0.7 cm broad; **lateral sepals** united to the apex, ovate, long-acuminate, 3.2–3.6 cm long, 0.5–0.9 cm broad. **Petals** oblong-lanceolate, long-attenuate, margins erose, 3.1–3.4 cm long, 0.2–0.3 cm broad. **Lip** 3-lobed, deflexed in the middle, 0.5 cm long, 0.3 cm broad; side lobes rounded, erect: mid-lobe oblong, shortly apiculate; disc excavated near the middle. **Column** stout, 0.4 cm long, with a short foot.

DISTRIBUTION Venezuela and Colombia to Peru.

HISTORY Discovered in the mountains near Huanuco in Peru by Thaddaeus Haenke and described in 1827 in *Reliquiae Haenkeanae* (p. 104) by K.B. Presl as *Acronia phalangifera*. The species was transferred to *Pleurothallis* by H.G. Reichenbach in 1864 in *Walpers, Annales Botanices* (p. 168).

SYNONYMS *Acronia phalangifera* Presl; *Pleurothallis mathewsii* Lindl.; *P. bogotensis* Lindl.: *Humboldtia mathewsii* (Lindl.) O. Ktze.

Pleurothallis phyllocardia Rchb.f.

A medium-sized epiphytic plant. **Stems** slender, terete, clustered, purplish, 10–27 cm long, covered in basal half with 2–3 loose, tubular, brown sheaths. **Leaf** coriaceous, cordate, acuminate, deflexed, somewhat concave, 5–16 cm long, 3–7 cm broad. **Inflorescence** fasciculate, subtended by an erect compressed sheath. **Flowers** produced singly and successively, deflexed, purple. **Dorsal sepal** oblong-ovate, acute, margins revolute, 1.1–1.4 cm long, 0.6–0.8 cm broad; **lateral sepals** connate, lamina similar to dorsal sepal. **Petals** spreading, linear, acute, margins minutely denticulate, 0.7–1 cm long, 0.2 cm broad. **Lip** ± cordate-subtriangular, fleshy, papillose 0.35 cm long and broad; disc with 2 smooth concave areas. **Column** stout, 1 cm long, 2 cm broad; foot very short.

DISTRIBUTION Costa Rica and Panama; 1300–2500 m altitude.

HISTORY Collected for the first time in Costa Rica by H. Wendland and described by H.G. Reichenbach in 1866 in *Beiträge zu einer Orchideenkunde Zentral-Amerika's* (p. 97).

SYNONYM *Pleurothallis triangulabia* C. Schweinf.

Pleurothallis quadrifida (La Llave & Lex.) Lindl. [Colour Plate]

A medium-sized epiphytic plant, 12–60 cm tall.

Stems erect, terete, 4–18 cm long, 1-leafed at apex. **Leaf** coriaceous, linear to oblong-elliptic or oblanceolate, retuse and obtuse at the apex, usually marginate, up to 17 cm long, 0.3 cm broad. **Inflorescence** solitary, racemose, laxly many-flowered, up to 45 cm long; peduncle slender, subtended by a compressed sheath. **Flowers** nodding, fragrant, translucent, yellow or yellow-green, rarely cleistogamous. **Dorsal sepal** concave, ovate-oblong to elliptic-lanceolate, shortly acuminate or subacute, recurved at the apex, 0.6–1.2 cm long, 0.3–0.35 cm broad; **lateral sepals** united, lamina elliptic, bidentate, concave, 0.5–1.2 cm long, 0.35–0.55 cm broad. **Petals** shortly clawed, oblong-lanceolate, subacute, 0.5–1.1 cm long, 0.2–0.4 cm broad. **Lip** shortly clawed, arcuate, oblong-pandurate, canaliculate in basal half with erect, crenulate margins, up to 0.6 cm long, 0.3 cm broad; basal part fleshy; apical part thin-textured. **Column** short, irregularly dentate at apex, 0.2–0.4 cm long.

DISTRIBUTION W. Indies, Mexico south to Panama; common in forests up to 1500 m altitude.

HISTORY Discovered by P. La Llave and J. Lexarza in Mexico on the way to Jesus del Monte near Vallisolet and described by them in 1825 as *Dendrobium quadrifidum* in their *Novorum Vegetabilium Descriptiones* (p. 40). John Lindley transferred this species to *Pleurothallis* in 1840 in the *Botanical Register* (misc. p. 70). This species is still often cultivated under the name *P. ghiesbrechtiana* A.Rich. & Galeotti

SYNONYMS *Pleurothallis incompta* Rchb.f.; *P. longissima* Lindl.; *P. ghiesbrechtiana* A.Rich. & Galeotti; *Dendrobium quadrifidum* La Llave & Lex.

Pleurothallis secunda Poepp. & Endl.

A medium-sized to large, very variable, epiphytic or terrestrial plant. **Stems** caespitose, terete, slender to stout, 7–80 cm long, concealed in the basal part by 2–4 tubular sheaths. **Leaf** erect, elliptic or oblong, acute to shortly acuminate, coriaceous, 9–30 cm long, 2–13 cm broad. **Inflorescences** 1–5, pendent, racemose, 2- to 9-flowered, up to 20 cm long; bracts tubular, 0.5 cm long. **Flowers** non-resupinate; sepals translucent yellow-green, lateral sepals striped with purple; petals red or yellow. **Dorsal sepal** lanceolate, acute, 0.9–1.6 cm long, 0.3–0.5 cm broad; **lateral sepals** connate to apex; lamina concave, ovate, acuminate, 1–1.6 cm long, 0.7–1.2 cm broad. **Petals** fleshy, lanceolate, acuminate, porrect, 0.8–1.5 cm long, 0.2–0.3 cm broad. **Lip** suborbicular to transversely crescentic, apiculate, margins erose, 0.25–0.4 cm long, 0.25–0.45 cm broad; disc bearing a subconical callus on either side. **Column** short,

0.2 cm long, 0.15 cm broad.

DISTRIBUTION Venezuela and Colombia to Peru; 600–1900 m altitude.

HISTORY Originally collected by E.F. Poeppig near Cuchero in Peru and described by him and S.L. Endlicher in 1836 in their *Nova Genera et Species Plantarum* (p. 49, t. 85). The specific epithet was given by them in the mistaken impression that the flowers were secundly arranged in the inflorescence. This very variable species has been described several times subsequently under different names.

SYNONYMS *Pleurothallis lindenii* Lindl.; *Humboldtia lindenii* (Lindl.) O. Ktze.; *H. secunda* (Poepp. & Endl.) O. Ktze.; *Pleurothallis araguensis* Ames; *P. subreniformis* Schltr.; *P. pendula* Schltr.; *P. nutans* Schltr.

Pleurothallis segoviensis Rchb.f.

A small epiphytic plant, up to 22 cm tall. **Stems** caespitose, slender, concealed by scarious appressed sheaths, 1.5–5 cm long, 1-leafed at apex. **Leaf** erect, oblong-ligulate, obtuse and retuse at apex, coriaceous, 5–13 cm long, 0.5–1.4 cm broad. **Inflorescence** solitary, laxly few- to many-flowered, up to 17 cm long; peduncle filiform; bracts tubular, acuminate, 0.5 cm long. **Flowers** variable in colour, yellow-green marked with brown, to purplish-red. **Sepals** united at base, 0.5–1 cm long, 0.15–0.4 cm broad; dorsal sepal lanceolate, acute or apiculate; lateral sepals united to form an elliptic lamina, bidentate at apex, ± pilose on inner surface. **Petals** oblique, oblong, obtuse or apiculate, 0.2–0.35 cm long, 0.1–0.2 cm broad. **Lip** shortly clawed, glabrous, 3-lobed, arcuate-decurved, 0.25–0.4 cm long, 0.25 cm broad; side lobes erect, porrect, obliquely oblong; mid-lobe oblong, rounded at the apex; calli 2, mammillate, with 2 keels running on to centre of disc from side lobes. **Column** with a short foot, curved, clavate, 0.3 cm long.

DISTRIBUTION Mexico to Panama; common in dense forests and open woodlands to 2000 m altitude.

HISTORY Discovered by A.S. Oersted at Segovia and described by H.G. Reichenbach in 1855 in *Bonplandia* (p. 223).

P. segoviensis is distinguished by its inflorescence which is longer than the leaf and by its flowers in which the lip is 3-lobed with large side lobes parallel to the mid-lobe.

SYNONYMS *Pleurothallis wercklei* Schltr.: *P. amethystina* Ames

Pleurothallis tuerkheimii Schltr. [Colour Plate]

A medium-sized epiphytic plant, 15–70 cm high. **Stems** stout, terete, erect, up to 40 cm long, 1-leafed at apex, covered by 2 deep brown, glossy sheaths. **Leaf** oval, oblong-elliptic or lanceolate, obtuse, coriaceous, 4–25 cm long, 2–7.5 cm broad. **Inflorescence** racemose, laxly many-flowered, longer than the leaves, up to 35 cm long, subtended by a large compressed sheath. **Flowers** reddish-brown and white, papillose; petals white. **Dorsal sepal** lanceolate, acuminate, 1.3–2.5 cm long, 0.4–0.7 cm broad; **lateral sepals** united almost to apex, elliptic-oblong, concave, 1.3–2.7 cm long, 0.5–0.9 cm broad, acuminate. **Petals** oblong-obovate, rounded and cucullate at apex, 0.5–1 cm long, 0.3–0.4 cm broad. **Lip** shortly clawed, fleshy, linear-lanceolate, subacute to acuminate, margins reflexed, auriculate at the base, 0.5–1 cm long, 0.3 cm broad; callus on disc bilamellate, papillose. **Column** short, 4-toothed at apex, 0.4 cm long.

DISTRIBUTION Mexico to Panama; 1300–2600 m elevation.

HISTORY One of the many new species discovered in 1907 near Coban in Guatemala by H. von Tuerkheim and named after him by R. Schlechter in 1912 in *Fedde, Repertorium Specierum Novarum* (p. 292).

Pleurothallis uniflora Lindl

A very small, tufted epiphytic herb, up to 7 cm tall. **Stems** very short, covered in grey sheaths. **Leaf** erect, oblanceolate or narrowly elliptic, subacute, relatively thin-textured, up to 7.2 cm long, 1.2 cm broad. **Inflorescence** ± equal to leaf in length, mostly 1-flowered, up to 4.5 cm long. **Flowers** opening in succession, bright orange. **Sepals** elliptic-oblong obtuse, 0.65 cm long, 0.3 cm broad; lateral sepals connate for basal two-thirds. **Petals** obliquely obovate, obtuse, 0.25 cm long, 0.15 cm broad. **Lip** oblong-subrhombic, rounded in front, fleshy in the middle, papillate all over, 0.25 cm long, 0.15 cm broad. **Column** terete, 0.2 cm long.

DISTRIBUTION Brazil, Guyana, Surinam and Venezuela.

HISTORY Discovered in Brazil by M.E. Descourtilz and described by John Lindley in 1836 in Hooker's *Companion to the Botanical Magazine* (p. 355).

P. uniflora is rather distinctive, mostly bearing a single bright orange flower on a long scape ± equal in length to the leaf. The column bears 2 porrect acute stelidia.

SYNONYMS *Epidendrum marginatum* L.C. Rich.; *Pleurothallis striata* Focke; *Humboldtia striata* (Focke) O. Ktze.; *H. uniflora* (Lindl.) O. Ktze.; *Pleurothallis marginata* (L.C. Rich.) Cogn.

Plocoglottis Blume
Subfamily Epidendroideae
Tribe Arethuseae
Subtribe Bletiinae

Medium-sized terrestrial herbs with a short creeping rhizome. **Pesudobulbs** usually clustered, erect, cylindrical-tapering, unifoliate at apex. **Leaf** erect, plicate, longly petiolate. **Inflorescence** basal, erect, unbranched, laxly few-flowered, racemose; bracts small, persistent. **Flowers** borne in succession, yellow marked with red or purple. **Dorsal sepal** and petals subsimilar but the petals narrower, free, spreading; **lateral sepals** joined at the base to the column-foot, otherwise free and spreading. **Lip** convex, entire, fleshy, short, joined to the sides and tip of the column-foot to form a short sac at the base, attached by an elastic joint so that the lip will flip up when touched. **Column** rather short, with a short foot; pollinia 4, waxy.

DISTRIBUTION A genus of perhaps 40 species widespread from the Andaman Islands, Thailand and Indo-China to New Guinea and the Solomon Islands.

DERIVATION OF NAME From the Greek *ploke* (binding together) and *glotta* (tongue), in reference to the attachment of the lip-base to the column-foot.

TAXONOMY Described by C.L. Blume in 1825 in his *Bijdragen* (p. 381), *Plocoglottis* is a genus with a distinctive pollination mechanism whereby the pollinator, a bee, touches the lip which springs up to push the bee onto the pollinia thereby removing them on its back.

TYPE SPECIES *P. javanica* Bl.

CULTURE Temp. Winter min. 15°C. Grow in pots or pans in a terrestrial mix such as is used for *Spathoglottis*. Give shaded, humid conditions and water well while growing, with less given when growth is complete.

Plocoglottis acuminata Bl.
[Colour Plate]

A medium-sized to large terrestrial plant with a stout creeping rhizome. **Pseudobulbs** cylindrical, several-noded, 5–8 cm long, 0.3–0.7 cm in diameter, unifoliate at apex. **Leaf** erect, elliptic to ovate, acuminate, 20–40 cm long, 5.5–10 cm wide, longly petiolate; petiole slender, 5–14 cm long. **Inflorescence** erect, lateral from the lower nodes of the pseudobulb, laxly to densely few- to many-flowered, up to 50 cm long; peduncle and rhachis terete, densely shortly pubescent; bracts lanceolate, acuminate, 6–10 mm long. **Flowers** yellow with red spots on the sepals and petals; pedicel and ovary 12–17 mm long, shortly pubescent. **Sepals** spreading, lanceolate, acuminate, 18–22 mm long, 3–4 mm wide; **lateral sepals** slightly falcate and back-to-back. **Petals** slightly oblique, lanceolate, acuminate, 15–17 mm long, 3 mm wide. **Lip** strongly deflexed, recurved, convex, subquadrate, shortly apiculate, 7–10 mm long and wide. **Column** erect, 4–5 mm long.

DISTRIBUTION Java, Sumatra and Borneo; in rain forest at low elevations below 500 m.

HISTORY Described by C.L. Blume in *Museum Botanicum Lugduno-Batavum* (p. 46) based on a collection from Java by Korthals.

CLOSELY RELATED SPECIES *Plocoglottis javanica* Bl. is similar but has shorter broader sepals and petals; *P. lowii* has blunt sepals with swollen areas on the laterals which are rather twisted.

Podangis Schltr.
Subfamily Epidendroideae
Tribe Vandeae
Subtribe Aerangidinae

Small epiphytic plants with a very short stem. **Leaves** bilaterally flattened, fleshy, iridiform, arranged in a fan on the stem. **Inflorescences** much shorter than the leaves, densely many-flowered. **Flowers** hyaline, white with a green anther, long-pedicellate. **Sepals** and **petals** similar, concave, free. **Lip** entire, concave, ecallose, with a long spur; spur longer than lip, with a broad mouth, swollen at the obscurely 2-lobed apex, nearly straight. **Column** very short; pollinia 2, on separate stipites; viscidium common.

DISTRIBUTION A single species in W. and C. Africa.

DERIVATION OF NAME From the Greek *podos* (foot) and *angos* (vessel) in reference to the foot-like spur of the lip.

TAXONOMY *Podangis* was established by R. Schlechter in 1918 in *Beihefte zum Botanischen Zentralblatt* (p. 82) based on *Listrostachys dactyloceras* Rchb.f.

It is a monotypic genus allied to *Bolusiella*, having bilaterally compressed, iridiform leaves borne in a fan, but the flowers are much larger and quite distinct in structure. Although the flower somewhat resembles those of some species of *Diaphananthe*, being hyaline, the fine structure of its column and pollinating apparatus as well as the spur are quite different. The flower is also quite distinct in general form and structure from those of *Aerangis* species.

TYPE SPECIES *Listrostachys dactyloceras* Rchb.f. [= *Podangis dactyloceras* (Rchb.f) Schltr.].

CULTURE Compost A. Temp. Winter min. 12–15°C. These small plants are probably best mounted on a block of cork or fern-fibre. They

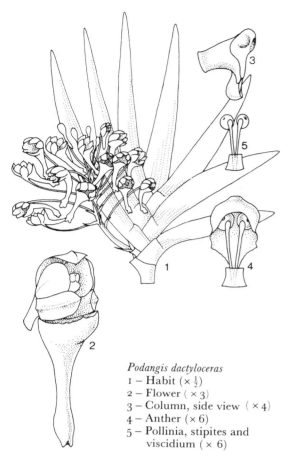

Podangis dactyloceras
1 – Habit (×½)
2 – Flower (×3)
3 – Column, side view (×4)
4 – Anther (×6)
5 – Pollinia, stipites and
    viscidium (×6)

require humid and fairly shady conditions and should be watered carefully throughout the year, allowing the roots to become dry between waterings.

Podangis dactyloceras (Rchb. f.) Schltr.
[Colour Plate]

A small epiphytic plant with a short stem, up to 11 cm long but usually much shorter, leafy at the apex. **Leaves** 4–8, distichous, ± falcate, bilaterally compressed, acute, fleshy, 4–16 cm long, 0.5–1.2 cm broad. **Inflorescences** axillary, up to 6 cm long, including the flowers, several-flowered, subumbellate. **Flowers** ± campanulate, translucent, pearl-white with a green anther-cap. **Sepals** and **petals** ± elliptic, obtuse, 0.3–0.5 cm long, 0.3–0.5 cm broad. **Lip** ± orbicular, concave, 0.6 cm long, spurred at base; spur 1.1–1.4 cm long, broad at the mouth, constricted in the middle and swollen and slightly 2-lobed at the apex. **Column** very short; pollinia attached by 2 linear stipites to a single circular viscidium.

DISTRIBUTION W. Africa from Sierra Leone to Cameroon, south to Angola and also in Uganda and Tanzania; in rain forest, 750–1950 m altitude.

HISTORY F.M. Welwitsch collected the type specimen at Pungo Adongo in Angola and it was described as *Listrostachys dactyloceras* by H.G. Reichenbach in 1865 in the journal *Flora* (p. 190).

Rudolf Schlechter transferred it to *Podangis* in 1918 in *Beihefte zum Botanischen Zentralblatt* (p. 82).

SYNONYM *Listrostachys dactyloceras* Rchb.f.

Polycycnis Rchb.f.
Subfamily Epidendroideae
Tribe Gongoreae
Subtribe Stanhopeinae

Medium-sized epiphytic plants. **Stems** very short, sheathed, 1-leafed, soon developing into a fleshy pseudobulb. **Leaf** large, lanceolate-elliptic, petiolate, plicate. **Inflorescence** lateral, basal, erect, distantly few-sheathed below, laxly racemose, several- to many-flowered. **Flowers** medium-sized to rather large. **Sepals** subequal, free, spreading. **Petals** similar to sepals but smaller. **Lip** fixed to the base of the column, spreading, 3-lobed; side lobes narrow; mid-lobe rhombic-ovate to lanceolate, acute to acuminate, entire or obscurely 3-lobed. **Column** elongate, slender, arcuate, somewhat clavate above, footless; pollinia 2, cylindric.

DISTRIBUTION A genus of about seven species extending from Panama to Costa Rica to Colombia, Guyana and Peru.

DERIVATION OF NAME From the Greek *polys* (many) and *kyknos* (swan), in allusion to the fancied resemblance of the flowers to small swans.

TAXONOMY A genus established by H.G. Reichenbach in 1855 in *Bonplandia* (p. 218). It differs from *Cycnoches* in having hermaphrodite flowers which are smaller and lack a fleshy lip. Vegetatively, it is close to *Gongora* but lacks the complex fleshy lip of that genus.

TYPE SPECIES *P. muscifera* (Lindl.) Rchb.f.

CULTURE Compost A. Temp. Winter min. 12–15°C. As most of the species have hanging inflorescences, these plants are probably best grown in baskets, although *P. vittata* is an exception and may be grown in a pan. Conditions similar to those given to *Stanhopea* species are suitable and the plants require ample water while growing. Much less should be given when the pseudobulbs have finished growing.

Polycycnis barbata (Lindl.) Rchb.f.
[Colour Plate]

An epiphytic herb. **Pseudobulbs** ovoid, sulcate, 2.5–4.5 cm long, 1.8–2.5 cm in diameter, 1-leafed at apex. **Leaf** elliptic-lanceolate, plicate, acute or acuminate, suberect, 25–40 cm long, 4–10 cm broad. **Inflorescences** basal,

arcuate to pendent, racemose, 28–32 cm long, laxly many-flowered; axis minutely pubescent. **Flowers** medium-sized; sepals and petals pale translucent yellow, spotted with red; lip white, spotted with red; column green, anther purple. **Dorsal sepal** lanceolate, acuminate, 1.7–2.5 cm long, 0.6–0.8 cm broad; **lateral sepals** obliquely lanceolate, connate at the base, acuminate, 1.8–2.4 cm long, 0.6–0.8 cm broad. **Petals** narrowly oblanceolate, 1.8–2.4 cm long, 0.3 cm broad. **Lip** complex, shortly clawed, auriculate at the base of the lamina, 3-lobed, adnate to the column at the base; side lobes rounded, erect; mid-lobe ovate, apiculate, long-pubescent; callus central, fleshy, porrect, pubescent. **Column** slender, arcuate, clavate, 1.8–2.2 cm long.

DISTRIBUTION Costa Rica, Panama, Colombia, Venezuela and Brazil.

HISTORY Originally described in 1849 as *Cycnoches barbatum* by John Lindley in the *Journal of the Horticultural Society of London* (p. 268) from a plant introduced into cultivation from Colombia by Jean Linden. H.G. Reichenbach transferred it in 1855 to the genus *Polycycnis* in *Bonplandia* (p. 218).

SYNONYMS *Cycnoches barbatum* Lindl.; *Polycycnis gratiosa* Endres & Rchb.f.

Polycycnis muscifera (Lindl.) Rchb.f.
[Colour Plate]

A medium-sized epiphytic plant. **Pseudobulbs** pyriform-cylindric, 5–6 cm long, 1-leafed at apex, clothed with evanescent sheaths below. **Leaf** petiolate, elliptic, acute, up to 37 cm long, 12 cm broad, plicate; petiole sulcate, 10 cm long. **Inflorescence** lateral, suberect to arcuate, racemose, laxly to densely many-flowered, up to 60 cm long; peduncle up to 30 cm long, pubescent. **Flowers** with spreading or reflexed segments, membranaceous, pale buff-coloured, densely spotted brown, pubescent on outer surface. **Sepals** oblong-lanceolate, acute, up to 2 cm long, 0.5 cm broad; lateral sepals oblique. **Petals** linear-oblanceolate, somewhat S-shaped, acute, 2.2 cm long, 0.3 cm broad. **Lip** deeply 3-lobed, with a definite hypochile, up to 1.7 cm long; hypochile with a pair of linear-falcate suberect horns at the base, dilated above into a pair of erect, lanceolate side lobes; epichile large, hastate or ovate, acuminate or acute at the apex; disc with a pubescent semi-elliptic ridge. **Column** very slender, arcuate, winged at the apex, 2 cm or more long.

DISTRIBUTION Colombia to Peru.

HISTORY Discovered by Jean Linden in Colombia and introduced into cultivation by Messrs Rollisson. It was described by John Lindley as *Cycnoches musciferum* in his and Paxton's *Flower Garden* (p. 28, fig. 248) in 1852–53. This species was transferred in 1855 to the

genus *Polycycnis* by H.G. Reichenbach in *Bon-plandia* (p. 218).
SYNONYM   *Cycnoches musciferum* Lindl.

Polyradicion Garay
Subfamily Epidendroideae
Tribe Vandeae
Subtribe Angraecinae

Small epiphytes lacking leaves but with many elongate chorophyllous roots emerging from a short stem. **Inflorescences** spreading-arcuate, 1- to few-flowered. **Flowers** large for the plant, white. **Sepals** and **petals** free, subsimilar, lanceolate. **Lip** 3-lobed, the mid-lobe larger than the side lobes and with 2 long divergent tails, with a slender broad-mouthed spur at the base. **Column** short, fleshy; pollinia 2, waxy, each attached by a simple stipe to a viscidium; rostellum deeply emarginate.

DISTRIBUTION   A genus of some five species in the W. Indies and S. Florida.
DERIVATION OF NAME   From the Greek *poly* (many) and *radicion* (root).
TAXONOMY   Leslie Garay established the genus *Polyradicion* in 1969 in the *Journal of the Arnold Arboretum* (p. 467) for the species previously known as *Polyrrhiza lindenii*. The generic name *Polyrrhiza* is a synonym of *Dendrophylax* Rchb.f., an allied but distinct genus.
TYPE SPECIES   *P. lindenii* (Lindl.) Garay
CULTURE   Temp. Winter min. 12°C. Grows best mounted on slabs and watered carefully throughout the year. The species grow well in conditions suitable for cattleyas.

Polyradicion lindenii (Lindl.) Garay
A small leafless epiphyte with a short stem; roots up to 50 cm long, 3–5 mm broad, somewhat compressed, unbranched, green with white streaks. **Inflorescences** 1 or 2, 1- to 10-flowered, up to 25 cm long; bracts scarious, lanceolate, 4 mm long. **Flowers** produced in succession, white; pedicel and ovary 2.5–3 cm long. **Sepals** spreading widely, lanceolate, acute, 2–2.5 cm long, 5–6 mm wide, white suffused with green. **Petals** similar, 2–2.1 cm long, 4.5 mm wide. **Lip** 3-lobed; the side lobes obliquely triangular, acuminate, 1.5–1.8 cm across; the mid-lobe obtriangular, with 2 lateral linear-tapering twisted spreading tails, 4–6.5 cm long; spur tapering-filiform from a conical mouth, up to 12 cm long. **Column** 2 mm long. 5 mm wide; pollinia orange.
DISTRIBUTION   S. Florida, the Bahamas and Cuba; in swamp forest.
HISTORY   The popular name of this dainty and striking orchid is the Frog or Ghost orchid, the former from its distinctive lip. John Lindley described it first as *Angraecum lindenii* in 1846 in

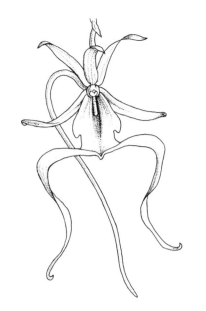

Polyradicion lindenii (× $\frac{2}{3}$)

the *Gardeners' Chronicle* (p. 135) based on a collection made in 1844 by Jean Linden in the dense forests of Sagua and Nimanima in Cuba. Leslie Garay transferred it to the present genus in 1969 in the *Journal of the Arnold Arboretum* (p. 467). It is probably best known under the name *Polyrrhiza lindenii* (Lindl.) Pfitzer.
SYNONYMS   *Angraecum lindenii* Lindl.; *Aeranthus lindenii* (Lindl.) Rchb.f.; *Dendrophylax lindenii* (Lindl.) Benth.; *Polyrrhiza lindenii* (Lindl.) Pfitzer

Polystachya Hooker
Subfamily Epidendroideae
Tribe Polystachyeae

Small to large epiphytic, lithophytic or rarely terrestrial herbs. **Stems** caulescent or pseudobulbous, sometimes compressed, 1- to several-leaved, clustered or at intervals from a short rhizome. **Leaves** erect to spreading, coriaceous, fleshy or thin-textured. **Inflorescence** racemose or paniculate, rarely 1-flowered; branches ± secund. **Flowers** small, rarely showy, white, green, yellow, purple or pink. **Dorsal sepal** free; **lateral sepals** larger, united to the column-foot to form a more or less prominent mentum. **Petals** smaller than the sepals, free. **Lip** entire to 3-lobed, mostly uppermost in the flower, ± callose, often pubescent. **Column** mostly short; pollinia 4, globose or ellipsoid; stipe 1, short, ± cucullate above; viscidium 1, ovate to elliptic.
DISTRIBUTION   A large genus of about 150 species mostly confined to Africa but with

several species in the tropical Americas, Asia and Madagascar.
DERIVATION OF NAME   From the Greek *poly* (many) and *stachys* (ear of grain or spike), referring to either the resemblance of the inflorescences of some species to an ear of grain or possibly to the tufted stems of some species.
TAXONOMY   Sir William Hooker established the genus *Polystachya* in 1825 in his *Exotic Flora* (t. 103). It was last revised in 1926 by F. Kraenzlin in *Fedde, Repertorium Specierum Novarum, Beihefte*. Since that time much of Africa has been better collected and many new species have been discovered, notably in E. and S. Central Africa. In addition, many of the species described prior to Kraenzlin's account are now better understood and his treatment of the genus is largely out of date. In particular, the limits of many of his sections, such as *Grandiflorae*, need revision. The majority of species are to be found in tropical Africa. An account of the W. African species is given by V.S. Summerhayes (1968) in the *Flora of West Tropical Africa;* the E. African species are dealt with by P. Cribb (1984) in the *Flora of Tropical East Africa*.

Polystachya may possibly be confused with *Bulbophyllum* and with *Stolzia* Schltr., a small African genus of about 10 species. From the former, *Polystachya* differs in having a terminal inflorescence and pseudobulbs generally of 2 or more internodes; whilst from the latter it differs in having 2 or 4 rather than 8 pollinia and also in its 1- to several-noded pseudobulbs.

The generic name *Polystachya* has been conserved over *Dendrorkis* Thou. (1809), an earlier name for the genus.
TYPE SPECIES   *P. luteola* Hooker nom. illeg. [= *P. minuta* (Aubl.) Hooker, syn. *Epidendrum minutum* Aubl.].
CULTURE   Compost A. Temp. Winter min. 12–15°C. *Polystachya* species need to be kept warmer or cooler according to their origins. All of them require humid, shady conditions while growing and plenty of water at the roots. Those species having prominent pseudobulbs, such as *P. paniculata*, should be given little water when growth is complete but smaller plants from higher altitudes, such as *P. vulcanica*, must never become very dry.

Polystachya affinis Lindl. [Colour Plate]
A suberect to pendent epiphytic plant, up to 59 cm high. **Pseudobulbs** rotund, compressed, ± appressed to the substrate, conspicuously 1-noded, 1–4.8 cm in diameter, 2- or rarely 3-leaved at apex. **Leaves** petiolate, oblanceolate, oblong-oblanceolate or oblong-elliptic, 9–28 cm long, 2.6–6 cm broad, acute, subacute or shortly acuminate; petiole articulated at or above middle, subcylindrical, 5–14 cm long. **In-**

florescence erect, or suberect or arcuate, racemose or paniculate, laxly many-flowered, 6–40 cm long; peduncle ± covered with imbricating, scarious, acute sheaths; rhachis terete, densely pubescent; branches few, 3–11 cm long, suberect; bracts ovate-lanceolate, long-acuminate, 0.6–1.4 cm long, densely pubescent. **Flowers** whitish, yellow or mustard yellow, ± marked with brown or red, densely pubescent on outer surface. **Dorsal sepal** elliptic-lanceolate to oblong elliptic, 0.65–0.7 cm long, 0.27–0.4 cm broad, rounded at apex; **lateral sepals** obliquely ovate-triangular, 0.65–0.8 cm long, 0.45–0.6 cm broad, subacute, forming with the column-foot a conical mentum, 0.43–0.58 cm high. **Petals** oblanceolate to oblong, 0.57–0.65 cm long, 0.12–0.22 cm broad, subacute to truncate at the apex. **Lip** obscurely 3-lobed in middle, 0.63–0.73 cm long, 0.47–0.57 cm broad; side lobes narrowly oblong; mid-lobe oblong-ovate, subacute to rounded at apex, 0.22–0.28 cm long, 0.26–0.36 cm broad; disc puberulent, with a central fleshy ridge to the middle of the lip. **Column** short, stout, 0.1 cm long.

DISTRIBUTION W. Africa, Zaïre, Angola and Uganda; in rain and riverine forests, 500–1350 m altitude.

HISTORY Discovered by G. Don in Sierra Leone and cultivated by the Horticultural Society of London. John Lindley described *P. affinis* in 1830 in his *Genera and Species of Orchidaceous Plants* (p. 73).

It is a distinct species easily recognised by its prostrate, compressed pseudobulbs.

Polystachya bifida Lindl. [Colour Plate]

A medium-sized epiphytic herb. **Stems** clustered, slender, up to 40 cm high, up to 8-leaved. **Leaves** distichous, linear, obtusely unequally 2-lobed above, apiculate, up to 13 cm long, 1 cm broad. **Inflorescence** racemose 7–8 cm long, few- to many-flowered, glabrous; bracts minutely triangular, acute. **Flowers** pale rose-pink. **Dorsal sepal** minute, broadly ovate, obtuse, 0.28 cm long and broad; **lateral sepals** larger, triangular, obtuse, 0.6–0.8 cm long, 0.65 cm broad; mentum conical, rounded at apex, up to 0.6 cm high. **Petals** oblanceolate, subacute, 0.28 cm long, 0.1 cm broad. **Lip** 3-lobed in the apical half, 0.75 cm long, 0.3 cm broad; side lobes erect, porrect, subacute in front; mid-lobe oblong, emarginate; disc farinaceous at base; callus central, porrect, fleshy. **Column** short, stout, 0.1 cm long.

DISTRIBUTION Cameroon, Macias Nguema and São Tomé.

HISTORY Discovered in 1860 on Fernando Póo (now Macias Nguema) by Gustav Mann, *P. bifida* was described in 1862 in the *Journal of the Linnean Society* (p. 129) by John Lindley.

SYNONYM *Polystachya farinosa* Kraenzl.

Polystachya caloglossa Rchb.f.

An erect or rarely pendulous epiphytic plant, up to 50 cm high. **Stems** terete, clustered, 5–40 cm long, 0.2–0.7 cm in diameter, 4- to 5-leaved in apical half. **Leaves** obovate or oblanceolate. obtuse, margins undulate, 6–17 cm long, 1.3–4.8 cm broad, dark green, ± purple below. **Inflorescence** racemose or paniculate. 4–12 cm long, up to 5-branched, several-flowered; peduncle compressed; branches short, up to 3.5 cm long; bracts ovate, imbricate, up to 0.5 cm long. **Flowers** open successively, fleshy, yellow, apricot or reddish-green, pubescent on outer surface. **Dorsal sepal** narrowly oblong, apiculate, 0.8–1.1 cm long, 0.4 cm broad; **lateral sepals** obliquely triangular, acute, 1–1.3 cm long, 0.8 cm broad, forming a broadly conical mentum 0.75 cm high. **Petals** oblanceolate, obtuse, 0.9 cm long, 0.4 cm broad. **Lip** shortly clawed, obscurely 3-lobed in middle, 0.9–1.1 cm long, 1–1.2 cm broad; side lobes incurved-erect, rounded; mid-lobe broadly ovate, acute; disc with a porrect callus in middle. **Column** stout, 0.2 cm long.

DISTRIBUTION Cameroon, Macias Nguema, Zaïre and Uganda; up to 1500 m elevation.

HISTORY Discovered by Gustav Mann on Cameroon Mt in 1867 and described by H.G. Reichenbach in *Otia Botanica Hamburgensia* (p. 111) in 1881.

Polystachya concreta (Jacq.) Garay & Sweet [Colour Plate]

A small to medium-sized epiphytic plant. **Stem** short, up to 5 cm long, 3- to 5-leaved. **Leaves** oblong-lanceolate to oblanceolate, acute, 8–30 cm long, 1–5.7 cm broad. **Inflorescence** erect, up to 45 cm long, paniculate, many-flowered; peduncle and rhachis covered with pale, scarious sheaths; branches 12–15, secund. **Flowers** greenish-yellow, pink or dull red, with a white lip, fleshy. **Dorsal sepal** ovate, 0.25 cm long; **lateral sepals** obliquely triangular or ovate-triangular, 0.35 cm long; mentum ovoid, obtuse. **Petals** linear, acute, 0.25–0.35 cm long, 0.1 cm broad. **Lip** cuneate, obovate, obscurely 3-lobed, 0.35–0.5 cm long, 0.25–0.4 cm broad; side lobes small, acute, tooth-like; mid-lobe transversely oblong, margin crenulate, apex retuse; disc furfuraceous-farinose. **Column** fleshy, very short.

DISTRIBUTION Florida, Guyana, Surinam, Brazil and the W. Indies, tropical Africa and Asia.

HISTORY N.J. Jacquin discovered this species on the W. Indian island of Martinique and described it in s11760 in *Enumeratio Systematica Plantarum* (p. 30) as *Epidendrum concretum*. However, Jacquin's name was ignored by later botanists who took up the O. Swartz name *Cranchis luteola* which Sir William Hooker trans-

ferred to *Polystachya* in 1824 in his *Exotic Plants*. In 1974, L. Garay and H. Sweet in the *Flora of the Lesser Antilles* (p. 178) dispensed with the name *Polystachya flavescens* as an illegitimate name under the *Code of Botanical Nomenclature* and have transferred Jacquin's name *Epidendrum concretum* to the genus *Polystachya* as *P. concreta*.

In the same year Garay and Sweet in *Orquideologia* (p. 206) have shown that the distribution of *P. concreta* is pantropical and many names have been reduced to synonyms, including several currently in common use such as *P. tessellata* Lindl., *P. modesta* Rchb.f. and *P. flavescens* (Blume) J.J. Smith.

SYNONYMS include *Cranichis luteola* Sw.; *Polystachya luteola* (Sw.) Hooker; *P. minuta* Britton; *Dendrobium polystachyum* Sw., *Dendrorchis minuta* O. Ktze.; *Polystachya tessellata* Lindl.; *P. modesta* Rchb.f.; *P. mauritiana* Sprengel

CLOSELY RELATED SPECIES See *P. odorata*.

Polystachya cultriformis (Thou.) Sprengel [Colour Plate]

A small, erect epiphytic or lithophytic plant. **Pseudobulbs** narrowly conical-cylindrical, 4–10 cm long, up to 1 cm broad, 1-leafed at apex. **Leaf** erect or suberect, coriaceous, oblong, oblanceolate or elliptic, auriculate at base, 7–36 cm long, up to 5.5 cm broad. **Inflorescence** erect, paniculate, as long or longer than the leaf, many-flowered; bracts small, triangular, acute, up to 0.5 cm long. **Flowers** very variable in colour, white, pink or yellow, or yellow-green. **Dorsal sepal** ovate, apiculate, 0.4–0.8 cm long, 0.2–0.4 cm broad; **lateral sepals** obliquely triangular, apiculate, 0.25–0.6 cm long, 0.5–0.8 cm broad, forming with the column-foot an ovoid conical mentum 0.7 cm high. **Petals** linear to spathulate, acute or obtuse, 0.35–0.75 cm long, 0.1–0.25 cm broad. **Lip** 3-lobed, strongly recurved in middle, 0.4–0.8 cm long, 0.2–0.6 cm broad; side lobes rounded; mid-lobe ovate-triangular, acute; callus central. **Column** semiterete.

DISTRIBUTION Tropical Africa, Madagascar and the Mascarene Islands.

HISTORY Discovered on Mauritius by Aubert du Petit Thouars and figured by him in *Orchidées des Iles Australes de l'Afrique* (t. 87) in 1822 as *Dendrobium cultiforme*. Kurt Sprengel transferred it to *Polystachya* in 1826 in *Systema Vegetabilium* (p. 742).

SYNONYMS *Polystachya gerrardii* Harv.; *P. kirkii* Rolfe; *Dendrobium cultriforme* Thou.; *Polystachya cultrata* Lindl.; *P. monophylla* Schltr.; *P. lujae* De Wild.; *P. appendiculata* Kraenzl.

CLOSELY RELATED SPECIES Closely allied to *Polystachya bicarinata* Rendle which, however, has much larger bracts and prominently erosely-keeled lateral sepals.

Polystachya fallax Kraenzl. [Colour Plate]
A small epiphytic plant. **Pseudobulbs** conical-fusiform, erect, borne at intervals on an ascending rhizome, 6 cm long, 1 cm broad, 1-leafed at apex. **Leaf** erect, ligulate-lanceolate, rounded at apex, up to 12 cm long, 1 cm broad. **Inflorescence** erect, shorter than the leaf, up to about 7-flowered, subtended by a scarious sheath. **Flowers** white with a yellow callus and purple anther-cap. **Dorsal sepal** ovate-lanceolate, acuminate, up to 1.1 cm long, 0.3 cm broad; **lateral sepals** narrowly obliquely triangular, acuminate, up to 1.4 cm long, 0.7 cm broad. **Petals** linear-lanceolate, acute, 0.8 cm long, 0.2 cm broad. **Lip** 3-lobed in middle, strongly recurved in middle, up to 1.2 cm long, 0.6 cm broad; side lobes rounded; mid-lobe linear-lanceolate, acuminate; callus fleshy, in centre of lip. **Column** short, 0.2 cm long.
DISTRIBUTION W. Uganda and E. Zaïre; 1350–1600 m altitude.
HISTORY Discovered by Dawe on the Mpanga River in W. Uganda in 1905 and described by F. Kraenzlin in 1926 in the *Kew Bulletin* (p. 292).
CLOSELY RELATED SPECIES Not unlike a small form of *P. virginea* but distinguished by its narrower sepals and lip and the purple anther-cap.

Polystachya odorata Lindl. [Colour Plate]
An erect, epiphytic or rarely lithophytic plant, up to 40 cm high. **Pseudobulbs** subglobose to narrowly cylindrical, 2–4.5 cm long, 0.6–1.5 cm in diameter, 4- to 8-leaved. **Leaves** oblanceolate to narrowly oblong-elliptic, rounded to subacute, 13–26 cm long, 2.8–4.2 cm broad. **Inflorescence** erect, paniculate, equal to or longer than the leaves, 10–30 cm long, many-flowered; branches spreading, pubescent; bracts ovate-lanceolate, acuminate, 0.4 cm long. **Flowers** fragrant, pubescent on outer surface, white or pale green, flushed or striped red or purple on sepals; lip white, mid-lobe ± marked with pink, callus yellow, **Sepals** ovate, apiculate, 0.5–0.8 cm long, 0.2–0.6 cm broad; lateral sepals forming a conical mentum 0.4–0.5 cm high. **Petals** oblanceolate, oblique, rounded or obtuse, 0.5 cm long, 0.15 cm broad. **Lip** recurved, 3-lobed in the middle, 0.8 cm long, 0.6 cm broad; side lobes erect, falcately oblong, subacute; mid-lobe suborbicular, emarginate; disc puberulent; callus elliptical, fleshy. **Column** 0.2 cm long
DISTRIBUTION Ghana, Macias Nguema south to Angola and east to Kenya and Tanzania; 750–1350 m altitude, in riverine or rain forest.

HISTORY Discovered by Gustav Mann on Fernando Póo (now Macias Nguema) in 1860 and described by John Lindley in 1862 in the *Journal of the Linnean Society* (p. 130).
SYNONYM *Polystachya rufinula* Rchb.f.
CLOSELY RELATED SPECIES *P. concreta* is allied but has a secund inflorescence and smaller flowers.

Polystachya paniculata (Sw.) Rolfe [Colour Plate]
A medium to quite large epiphytic herb, up to 40 cm tall. **Pseudobulbs** cylindric-compressed to fusiform-compressed, 4- to 6-noded, up to 12 cm long, 2.2 cm broad, 4- to 5-leaved. **Leaves** coriaceous, suberect, narrowly oblong, rounded and unequally 2-lobed at apex, up to 25 cm long, 3.5 cm broad, articulated to a compressed leaf-sheath below. **Inflorescence** erect, up to 22 cm long, paniculate, densely many-flowered, up to 10-branched; peduncle enclosed at base by 2 compressed sheaths; bracts minute, triangular, acuminate. **Flowers** small, orange-red or rarely yellow. **Sepals** lanceolate, acute, 0.3–0.37 cm long, 0.12 cm broad. **Petals** linear, 0.25–0.3 cm long. **Lip** entire, ovate, acute, 0.25–0.3 cm long, 0.15–0.2 cm broad, recurved and callose at base. **Column** very short, fleshy, 0.1 cm long.
DISTRIBUTION Sierra Leone across to Zaïre and Uganda; 400–1950 m.
HISTORY One of the prettiest *Polystachya* species, *P. paniculata* was originally described in 1805 by O. Swartz as *Dendrobium paniculatum* in *Schrader, Neues Journal* (p. 97) based on an A. Afzelius collection from Sierra Leone. R.A. Rolfe transferred it in 1897 to its present genus in the *Flora of Tropical Africa* (p. 113).
SYNONYM *Dendrobium paniculatum* Sw.

Polystachya pubescens (Lindl.) Rchb.f. [Colour Plate]
A small epiphytic or occasionally lithophytic plant. **Pseudobulbs** clustered, narrowly conical-pyriform, 2–3 cm long, 1–1.5 cm broad at the base, 2- or 3-leaved at apex. **Leaves** ligulate, spreading, unequally 2-lobed at apex, 5–10 cm long, 1–2.3 cm broad, articulate to a short sheathing base below. **Inflorescence** erect, racemose, much longer than the leaves, 7–11 cm long, 7- to 12-flowered. **Flowers** sulphur-yellow, lined with red-brown on base of segments. **Dorsal sepal**, elliptic, subacute, 0.8 cm long, 0.3 cm broad; **lateral sepals** spreading, oblong, subacute, 1–1.1 cm long, 0.4 cm broad. **Petals** spathulate, 0.8 cm long, 0.35 cm broad. **Lip** 3-lobed in middle, densely covered with long white hairs on upper surface, 0.6–0.7 cm long, 0.4–0.6 cm broad; side lobes falcate, suberect; mid-lobe ovate, acute. **Column** short.

DISTRIBUTION S. Africa (from Cape Province to the Transvaal) and Swaziland ; up to 1000 m elevation.
HISTORY Described by John Lindley in 1836 as *Epiphora pubescens* in Sir William Hooker's *Companion to the Botanical Magazine* (p. 201). H.G. Reichenbach transferred it to the genus *Polystachya* in 1864 in *Walpers, Annales Botanices* (p. 643).
SYNONYMS *Polystachya lindleyana* Harv.; *Epiphora pubescens* Lindl.; *Lissochilus sylvaticus* Eckl. ex Sonder
CLOSELY RELATED SPECIES Easily confused with its allies *Polystachya zambesiaca* Rolfe and *P. sandersonii* Harv., but readily distinguished when in flower by its flower colour and the shaggy pubescence of the lip.

Polystachya stricta Rolfe
An erect epiphytic plant, 13–35 cm high. **Stems** clustered, terete, covered with loose tubular sheaths, 9–24 cm long, 3–5 cm in diameter, 3- to 6-leaved. **Leaves** well separated, suberect or spreading, ligulate to narrowly elliptic, acute, 10–23 cm long, 1.2–2 cm broad. **Inflorescence** erect but often recurved in apical half, many-branched, 9–31 cm long; peduncle terete, covered with scarious acute sheaths; rhachis pubescent, ± covered with scarious sheaths; branches secund, recurved, up to 4 cm long. **Flowers** pubescent on outer surface, cream to greenish-yellow; lip lined with red or brown on side lobes; ovary densely pubescent. **Dorsal sepal** oblong-lanceolate, subacute, up to 1 cm long, 0.35 cm broad; **lateral sepals** obliquely triangular-lanceolate, up to 1.1 cm long, 0.65 cm broad; forming with the column-foot a conical mentum up to 0.6 cm long. **Petals** oblanceolate, subacute, up to 0.8 cm long, 0.25 cm broad. **Lip** shortly clawed, 3-lobed in the middle, 0.7–1 cm long, 0.7 cm broad, pubescent all over; side lobes obliquely triangular, erect; mid-lobe ovate, recurved, acute; disc with central fleshy keel. **Column** broad, 0.2 cm long.
DISTRIBUTION Nigeria, Cameroon, Zaïre, Uganda, Tanzania and Kenya; in open woodlands or riverine forest, 900–1900 m altitude.
HISTORY Discovered in E. Africa, probably in Kenya, early this century and flowered in cultivation by R. Lynch in 1903. Robert Rolfe described it in 1909 in the *Kew Bulletin* (p. 63).
CLOSELY RELATED SPECIES Very closely related to *Polystachya albescens* Ridley and *P. bennettiana* Rchb.f.

Polystachya tenuissima Kraenzl.
A small epiphytic herb, up to 20 cm high. **Stems** clustered, erect, slender, 1–6 cm long, 0.1–0.2 cm broad, 1-leafed at apex. **Leaf** linear, suberect or erect, fleshy, retuse at apex, 2–14

cm long, 0.2–0.7 cm broad. **Inflorescence** mostly longer than the leaf, paniculate, 3–16 cm long, up to 40-flowered; branches secund. **Flowers** yellow or yellow-green; column and side lobes of lip tinged purple. **Dorsal sepal** elliptic, shortly apiculate, up to 0.3 cm long, 0.2 cm broad; **lateral sepals** obliquely triangular, 0.45 cm long, 0.6 cm broad, forming with the column-foot a cylindrical mentum, obscurely 2-lobed at the apex. **Petals** oblong-lanceolate or linear, subacute, 0.3 cm long, 0.1 cm broad. **Lip** fleshy, strongly recurved, clased, 3-lobed in apical third, 0.3–0.7 cm long, 0.2–0.4 cm broad; side lobes oblong, porrect; mid-lobe rounded-subquadrate, glandular-pubescent; callus obscure, fleshy. **Column** very short.

DISTRIBUTION W. Africa, Zaïre, Uganda and Kenya; 300–2300 m altitude.

HISTORY Discovered in Cameroon at Yaoundé by Zenker and described by F. Kraenzlin in Engler's *Botanische Jahrbücher* (p. 250) in 1894.

SYNONYMS *Polystachya inconspicua* Rendle; *P. ashantensis* Kraenzl.

Polystachya transvaalensis Schltr.
An epiphytic herb up to 50 cm tall. **Stem** slender, not swollen, completely covered by tubular leaf bases, several-leaved in upper half. **Leaves** distichous, oblong, obtuse or rounded at apex, 5–13 cm long, 0.7–2 cm wide. **Inflorescence** shorter than the leaves, simple or up to 3-branched, laxly several-flowered; peduncle and rhachis sparsely pubescent or glabrous; bracts ovate, acute, recurved, 0.3–0.7 cm long. **Flowers** non-resupinate, cream to greenish or yellowish and flushed with purple or brown, the petals and lip creamy or whitish green, the latter veined with purple. **Dorsal sepal** ovate, acute, 5–8 mm long, 2.5–4 mm wide; **lateral sepals** obliquely triangular, acute, 8–11 mm long; 6–9.5 mm wide, forming an obliquely conical, 5.5–6 mm long mentum with the column-foot. **Petals** subspathulate, obtuse, 5–6.5 mm long, 1–2 mm wide. **Lip** 3-lobed in apical half, 6.5–10.5 mm long, 6–8 mm wide; side lobes erect, rounded, obscure; mid-lobe, broadly triangular, obtuse to subacute, 2.5 mm long, 3.5 mm wide. Column 2.5 mm long, with a 5–6 mm long foot.

DISTRIBUTION Uganda and Kenya south to South Africa; in upland rain forest and moss forest, 1200–2900 m.

HISTORY This well-known species was first collected near Barberton in the Transvaal by Culver and was described by Rudolf Schlechter in 1895 in Engler's *Botanische Jahrbucher* (p. 28). It is commonly confused with *Polystachya albescens* Ridl. widespread in tropical Africa, but that always has longer acute leaves, imbricate bracts and flowers with an obviously 3-lobed

lip with well-marked sinuses between the lobes. SYNONYMS *Polystachya nigrescens* Rendle; *P. rendlei* Rolfe; *P. natalensis* Rolfe

Polystachya virginea Summerh.
[Colour Plate]
A medium-sized epiphytic plant, up to 40 cm high. **Pseudobulbs** erect, emitted from an ascending rhizome, narrowly cylindrical to fusiform, somewhat compressed, up to 15 cm long, 0.5–1 cm across, 1-leafed at apex. **Leaf** oblong-ligulate. erect, rounded at apex, 10–27 cm long. 1–3.6 cm broad. **Inflorescence** erect, shorter than the leaf, up to 10-flowered; peduncle terete, subtended by an inflated papery sheath; bracts small, triangular, 0.25 cm long. **Flowers** showy, pure white. **Dorsal sepal** lanceolate, acute or subacute, 0.8–1 cm long, 0.5 cm broad; **lateral sepals** obliquely triangular, shortly acuminate, 1.5 cm long, 0.85–1.1 cm broad; forming with the column-foot a mentum 0.8–1 cm long. **Petals** obliquely oblanceolate, subacute, 0.8–1 cm long, 0.3–0.4 cm broad. **Lip** 3-lobed in middle, 1.3 cm long, 0.9–1 cm broad; side lobes rounded; mid-lobe triangular; callus fleshy, central. **Column** fleshy, 0.3 cm long.

DISTRIBUTION Uganda, Zaïre and Burundi; 2000–2600 m altitude.

HISTORY Discovered in the Ruwenzori Mts of W. Uganda in 1936 by W. Eggeling and sent by him to V. Summerhayes who described it in the *Botanical Museum Leaflets of Harvard University* (p. 290) in 1942.

CLOSELY RELATED SPECIES Allied to *Polystachya doggettii* Rendle & Rolfe, which may be distinguished by its pale lemon flowers and uninflated basal cataphyll to the inflorescence.

Also allied to *P. fallax* but readily recognised by its much larger size and larger flowers with broader triangular lateral sepals.

Polystachya vulcanica Kraenzl. [Colour Plate]
A small, tufted epiphytic plant. **Stems** very slender, narrowly cylindrical, up to 6 cm long, 0.1 cm in diameter, 1-leafed at apex. **Leaf** cylindrical, terete, sulcate, 5–11 cm long, 1.5–2 cm in diameter. **Inflorescences** mostly shorter than the leaf, several-flowered but flowers produced 1 at a time, up to 8 cm long; bracts triangular, acute, 0.3 cm long. **Flowers** large for size of plant, white or pale rose, marked with purple; lip and anther-cap rich purple. **Dorsal sepal** ovate-elliptic, shortly apiculate, concave, up to 0.7 cm long, 0.35 cm broad; **lateral sepals** obliquely triangular, shortly apiculate, 0.8 cm long, 0.8 cm broad; mentum conical, up to 0.6 cm high. **Petals** spathulate, obtuse, 0.6 cm long, 0.2 cm broad. **Lip** fleshy, obscurely 3-lobed. 0.9 cm long, 0.6 cm broad; side lobes obliquely triangular; mid-lobe

oblong, emarginate, obscurely apiculate behind; callus fleshy, somewhat obscure, in centre of lip. **Column** short, fleshy, 0.2 cm long.

DISTRIBUTION E. Zaïre and W. Uganda: 1800–2200 in altitude.

HISTORY Discovered in E. Zaïre to the north of Lake Kivu in 1908 by Kässner and described by F. Kraenzlin in 1923 in *Vierteljahrschrift der Naturforschenden Gesellschaft in Zürich* (p. 422).

CLOSELY RELATED SPECIES Closely allied to *Polystachya aconitiflora* Summerh. which has shorter linear leaves and smaller flowers.

Ponera Lindl.
Subfamily Epidendroideae
Tribe Epidendreae
Subtribe Laeliinae

Small epiphytes or lithophytes with creeping rhizomes and cane-like leafy stems. **Leaves** 6 or more, distichous, flat. **Inflorescences** lateral, short, 1-flowered or sessile to subsessile racemes, often glomerate, few-flowered. **Flowers** small. **Sepals** subsimilar; **dorsal sepal** free; **lateral sepals** attached to the column-foot to form a mentum. **Petals** decurrent on the column. **Lip** arcuate-recurved, bilobed at the apex, attached at the base to the column-foot. **Column** short, thick, lacking wings, with a foot; pollinia 4, hard, laterally compressed, with caudicles.

DISTRIBUTION Some seven species mostly from Mexico and Central America but with a single species extending south to Ecuador.

DERIVATION OF NAME From the Greek *poneros* (miserable) in apt allusion to the rather insignificant flowers and habit of the genus.

TAXONOMY *Ponera* was described by John Lindley in 1831 in his *Genera and Species of Orchidaceous Plants* (p. 113). It is related to *Scaphyglottis* and *Hexisea*.

TYPE SPECIES *Ponera juncifolia* Lindl.

CULTURE Temp. Winter min. 12°C. Probably best grown as rather untidy pot plants in epiphyte mix. Give moderate shade and humidity with water throughout the year.

Ponera striata Lindl.
A pendent or descending tufted epiphyte with slender stems, 30–80 cm long, and leafy in the apical part, covered by verrucose leaf sheaths. **Leaves** distichous, linear-lanceolate, tapering to an obliquely bilobed apex, 6–20 cm long, 0.4–0.9 cm wide. **Flowers** sessile, solitary or 2- to 4-fasciculate, terminal or produced opposite the leaf axils after the leaves have fallen, subtended by several conspicuous bracts; bracts suborbicular-ovate to oblong, 2–5 mm long, verrucose. **Flowers** with pale green sepals and

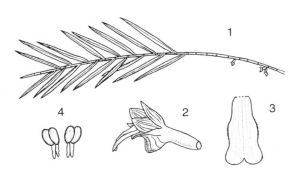

Ponera striata
1 – Habit (× ⅙)
2 – Flower (× 1)
3 – Lip (× 2)
4 – Pollinarium (× 11)

petals with lavender or red-brown stripes; lip white with several lavender stripes. **Dorsal sepal** ovate to oblong-elliptic, acute to obtuse, 5–7 mm long, 2–4 mm wide; **lateral sepals** obliquely triangular, acute, 6–8 mm long, 4–6 mm wide; mentum prominent. **Petals** elliptic-oblong to oval, rounded or obtuse. 5–7 mm long, 2–4 mm wide. **Lip** arcuate-recurved, oblong-cuneate to pandurate, bilobed at apex, 6.5–10 mm long, 3–5.5 mm wide, fleshy and channelled in lower third, thin above, with a transverse callus in the middle. **Column** stout, up to 5 mm long, with a 3.5–4 mm long foot.

DISTRIBUTION Mexico to Costa Rica, Venezuela and Brazil, in a variety of habitats from open woodland and dense rain forest, up to 3000 m.

HISTORY This rather dull species was originally described by John Lindley in 1843 in the *Botanical Register* (misc. p. 18) based on a collection by George Ure Skinner from Guatemala.

Ponerorchis Rchb.f.

Subfamily Orchidoideae
Tribe Orchideae
Subtribe Orchidinae

Small terrestrial or rarely epiphytic plants with ellipsoid to ovoid, tomentose tubers (root-stem tuberoids) and slender erect stems. **Leaves** 1 to several, borne along the stem, linear to oblong, acute to acuminate, sometimes grass-like. **Inflorescence** terminal, racemose, laxly to densely 2- to many-flowered. **Flowers** often showy and large for size of plant, white to pink and usually marked with purple especially on the lip. **Dorsal sepal** and **petals** adnate, forming a hood over the column; **lateral sepals** free, falcate, spreading to suberect. **Lip** deflexed, 3-lobed, with spreading lobes, spurred at the

base, lacking a callus; spur cylindrical, elongate. **Column** erect; pollinia 2, clavate, sectile, mealy, each attached by a caudicle to a small linear viscidium.

DISTRIBUTION A small genus of perhaps 10 species in Japan and Taiwan.

DERIVATION OF NAME From the Greek *poneros* (miserable) and *orchis* (orchid), in allusion to the small size of these orchids.

HISTORY H.G. Reichenbach established *Ponerorchis* in 1852 in the journal *Linnaea* (p. 227). It is closely allied to *Gymnadenia* but differs in its diminutive size, lack of palmate tubers, and in having fewer relatively large flowers in a laxer inflorescence.

TYPE SPECIES *P. graminifolia* Rchb.f.

CULTURE Temp. Winter min. 10°C. Grows well in a mix of fine bark, peat and perlite, but after flowering the growths die down, and little water is then needed. Give shady and humid conditions for growth, and repot when dormant.

Ponerorchis graminifolia Rchb.f.
[Colour Plate]

A dwarf terrestrial or rarely epiphytic plant with a slender purplish stem 5–25 cm tall. **Leaves** grass-like, suberect-arcuate, linear-tapering, acuminate, 1.5–14 cm long, 0.2–0.9 cm wide. **Inflorescence** 2- to 10-flowered; rhachis 1.5–4.5 cm long; bracts 4–20 mm long. **Flowers** secund, white to pink with purple markings on the lip; pedicel and ovary 1–1.4 cm long. **Dorsal sepal** hooded, oblong-elliptic, obtuse, 4–5.5 mm long, 2 mm wide, adnate to the petals; **lateral sepals** spreading or erect, falcate-lanceolate, acute or subacute, 6–8 mm long, 2.5–3.5 mm wide. **Petals** falcate-lanceolate, acute, 4–5 mm long, 2 mm wide. **Lip** deflexed or porrect, 3-lobed, the lobes subequal, 7–9 mm long, 10–11 mm wide; spur cylindrical, curving above ovary, incurved in apical part, 13–15 mm long. **Column** 3–4 mm long.

DISTRIBUTION Japan only; in mountains above 500 m.

HISTORY H.G. Reichenbach described this pretty species in 1852 in the journal *Linnaea* (p. 75). It is very popular in cultivation in Japan where colour variants are collected, the more unusual ones being greatly prized.

SYNONYM *Gymnadenia graminifolia* (Rchb.f.) Schltr.

Ponthieva R. Br.

Subfamily Spiranthoideae
Tribe Cranichideae
Subtribe Cranichidinae

Small terrestrial herbs with fleshy fibrous roots. **Leaves** in a basal rosette, sessile to long-petiolate. **Inflorescence** racemose, laxly densely few- to many-flowered; peduncle pubescent. **Flowers** small, non-resupinate. **Dorsal sepal** and petals ± adherent at the apex; **lateral sepals** free or united at the base. **Petals** attached to the column at base, asymmetric. **Lip** uppermost in flower, adnate to the column at the base, clawed, abruptly dilated above. **Column** short; pollinia 2, powdery-granular.

DISTRIBUTION About 25 species from southern USA, Mexico and the W. Indies, south to Chile.

DERIVATION OF NAME Named in honour of Henri de Ponthieu, a merchant in the French W. Indies who sent plants to Sir Joseph Banks in 1778.

TAXONOMY *Ponthieva* was described by Robert Brown in 1813 in the 2nd edition of W. Aiton's *Hortus Kewensis* (p. 199). It is allied to *Cranichis* but is distinguished by the petals (and occasionally the lip) being inserted on the column.

TYPE SPECIES *P. glandulosa* R. Br [= *P. racemosa* (Walter) Mohr.].

CULTURE Compost C. Temp. Winter min. 12–15°C. While growing, *Ponthieva* species should be given shady, moist conditions. After flowering, less water is required but the plants should never become very dry as they lack the ability to store water.

Ponthieva maculata Lindl. [Colour Plate]

An attractive epiphytic or occasionally terrestrial plant, up to 30 cm high. **Leaves** basal, sessile or petiolate, ovate-lanceolate to oblanceolate, acute or shortly acuminate, 7–28 cm long, 15–5 cm broad. **Inflorescence** erect, racemose, laxly several-flowered; bracts elliptic-lanceolate, concave, acuminate, 1–2 cm long. **Flowers** quite showy, non-resupinate, glandular-pubescent on sepals; dorsal sepal and petals bronze-coloured or yellow, striped with brown or maroon; lateral sepals white, spotted green or dull maroon; lip dark red to greenish-red, marked with white or creamy-white. **Sepals** elliptic, elliptic-lanceolate or orbicular, acute, 0.9–1.6 cm long, up to 0.8 cm broad. **Petals** shortly clawed, ovate-elliptic, oblique, obtuse, 0.7–1.2 cm long, 0.2–0.3 cm broad. **Lip** small, fleshy, obovate, concave, 0.2–0.4 cm long, 0.3 cm broad, fleshy and sulcate at base. **Column** clavate, 0.4 cm long.

DISTRIBUTION Mexico south to Venezuela and Ecuador; in forests up to 2500 m altitude.

HISTORY *P. maculata* was discovered by Theodore Hartweg at Bogotá in Colombia and was described in 1845 by Lindley in the *Annals and Magazine of Natural History* (15: p. 385).

SYNONYMS *Ponthieva formosa* Schltr.; *P. brenesii* Schltr.

Porphyroglottis Ridley
Subfamily Epidendroideae
Tribe Cymibidieae
Subtribe Cyrtopodiinae

Large epiphytic plants with clustered stems. **Stems** elongate, many-noded, cylindrical, pseudobulbous, leafy, resembling those of *Grammatophyllum speciosum*. **Leaves** distichous, linear-lanceolate, spreading, subcoriaceous, grass-like, with sheathing imbricate bases. **Inflorescences** lateral, suberect, elongate, lengthening slowly, simple or 1-branched, laxly few- to several-flowered. **Flowers** small, somewhat insect-like. **Sepals** and **petals** subsimilar, free, strongly reflexed. **Lip** hinged at the base to the column-foot, very mobile, convex, bee-like, lacking a spur. **Column** elongate, arcuate, slender, with 2 prominent lateral wings and a short foot; pollinia 2, ovoid-subsphaerical, slightly cleft, attached by flattened stipes to a large circular viscidium.

DISTRIBUTION A monotypic genus found in Borneo and Johore in Malaya.

DERIVATION OF NAME From the Greek *porphyra* (purple) and *glotta* (tongue), in reference to the lip of the type species.

TAXONOMY This extraordinary genus was established by Henry Ridley in 1896 in the *Journal of the Linnean Society* (p. 290). It is closely allied to *Grammatophyllum* and it closely resembles a small *G. speciosum* in habit. However, its flowers are quite different, much smaller and with a bee-like lip. Holttum (1964) in his *Orchids of Malaya* suggests that its lip mimics the body of a bee and that the flowers are pollinated by carpenter bees.

TYPE SPECIES *P. maxwelliae* Ridley

CULTURE Temp. Winter min. 18°C. Grow as for *Grammatophyllum* in a pot or basket. Give moderate shade and humidity with plenty of water while growing and much less when growth is complete.

Porphyroglottis maxwelliae Ridley
A large epiphyte with clustered, erect, cylindrical, leafy stems up to 2 m long. **Leaves** ascending, distichous, linear, acuminate, 25–35 cm long, 0.6–1 cm wide, articulated to a sheathing base. **Inflorescences** lateral, erect to erect-arcuate, simple or 1-branched, up to 150 cm long, laxly few-flowered; peduncle and rhachis slender, dull pink; bracts ovate, 1–2 mm long. **Flowers** borne in succession, 2–3 open at a time, the sepals and petals dull pink, the lip glossy maroon with a yellowish apex; pedicel and ovary 2–2.5 cm long, dull pink. **Sepals** and **petals** reflexed strongly, elliptic-oblong, obtuse, 2–2.4 cm long, 0.6–0.8 cm wide. **Lip** mobile, strongly convex, obovate, truncate, 1.5 cm long, 0.6–0.9 cm wide, pubescent especially at apex and base, attached by a strap-like hinge to the column-foot; callus of obscure ridges at base of lip. **Column** slender, arcuate, 1.5 cm long, bearing 2 lateral porrect wings in the middle; foot 0.4–0.5 cm long.

DISTRIBUTION Borneo and S. Malaya; at low altitudes, often on *Tristania* trees.

HISTORY Originally described in 1896 by Henry Ridley in the *Journal of the Linnean Society*

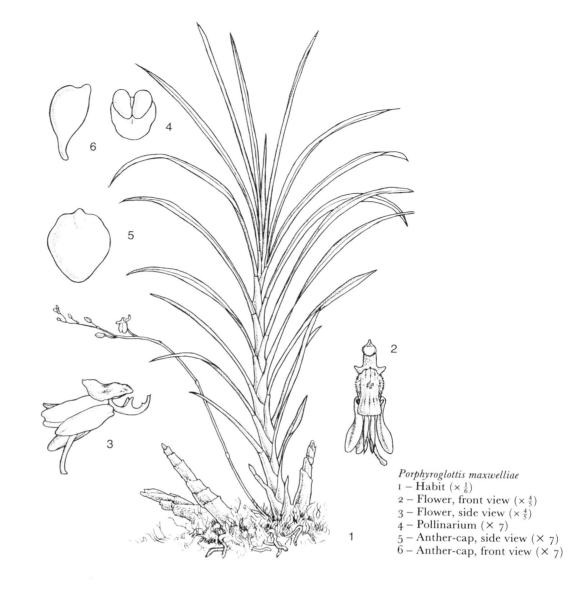

Porphyroglottis maxwelliae
1 – Habit ($\times \frac{1}{6}$)
2 – Flower, front view ($\times \frac{4}{5}$)
3 – Flower, side view ($\times \frac{4}{5}$)
4 – Pollinarium ($\times 7$)
5 – Anther-cap, side view ($\times 7$)
6 – Anther-cap, front view ($\times 7$)

(p. 290), based on a collection discovered in 1890 near Kuching in Sarawak by Mrs Maxwell who flowered it in her garden there.

Porroglossum Schltr.
Subfamily Epidendroideae
Tribe Epidendreae
Subfamilly Pleurothallidinae

Small to medium-sized epiphytic or lithophytic plants with short to long rhizomes and short unifoliate aerial stems (ramicauls) that are not swollen and are enclosed in 2–3 imbricate sheaths. **Leaf** erect, coriaceous, smooth to verrucose, petiolate. **Inflorescence** racemose, few- to several-flowered, usually dense; peduncle smooth to long-pubescent (mossy); bracts thin, tubular. **Flowers** resupinate or non-resupinate, small; ovary verrucose or papillate.

Sepals membranous to fleshy, smooth to verrucose or pubescent, connate to the middle to form a sepaline cup, with the tips usually attenuate and tail-like or clavate. **Petals** small, cartilagenous, oblong, often clavate at the tips. **Lip** sensitive, spathulate, obtriangular or obovate, with a longitudinal callus or a short transverse callus at the base. **Column** short, semiterete, with a long curved free foot; pollinia 2, pyriform, attached to a common viscidium.

DISTRIBUTION A genus of some 27 species from Venezuela and Colombia south to Peru and Bolivia. Fifteen species are known from Ecuador which seems to be the centre of diversity of the genus; mostly epiphytes of montane cloud forest.

HISTORY The genus *Porroglossum* is a segregate and close ally of *Masdevallia* distinguished by its sensitive lip of distinctive shape. The lip is important in the pollination mechanism of the genus. Rudolf Schlechter established *Porroglossum* in 1920 in *Fedde, Repertorium Specierum Novarum, Beihefte* (vol. 7: p. 82) based on his *P. colombianum.*

The genus has recently been monographed by Carlyle Luer (1987) in *Icones Pleurothallidinarum* (vol. 4: pp. 25–90 and vol. 5: pp. 108–111).
TYPE SPECIES *P. colombianum* Schltr.
CULTURE Temp. Winter min. 12°C. Cultivate as for many other pleurothallids. The species prefer shady, humid conditions without marked dry periods.

Porroglossum echidna (Rchb.f.) Garay

A small, tufted epiphytic to lithophytic plant. **Leaves** elliptic-oblong, petiolate, erect, coriaceous, 5–14 cm long, 1.5–4 cm broad, minutely tridentate at apex, dull green, tinged with purple. **Inflorescence** erect, much longer than the leaves, with several flowers borne in succession; peduncle terete, 10–20 cm long, bearing 2–3 pale green sheaths, covered with long mossy hairs. **Flowers** urceolate, with spreading sepals; sepals pale yellow, lined with purple and with darker yellow tails; petals yellow, striped brown in centre; callus bright yellow spotted red; column pale green with brown apex; perianth-tube with a distinct saccate mentum below. **Dorsal sepal** triangular-oblong, 0.5–0.7 cm long; tail reflexed, subclavate, 2–2.5 cm long; **lateral sepals** united for basal 0.8 cm, triangular-oblong, 0.5–0.75 cm long; with slender reflexed tails 2.5 cm long; clavate at apex. **Petals** linear, curved, angled on upper margin, apex rounded and thickened, 0.4 cm long. **Lip** sensitive, clawed, spathulate, cochleate above, apiculate, 0.8 cm long; lamina velvety within, margin set with stiff hairs; callus cushion-like and rounded. **Column** short.
DISTRIBUTION Colombia; growing on

trunks of small trees or on volcanic rocks, up to 3200 m altitude.
HISTORY This strange miniature was discovered by E. Shuttleworth when collecting for Mr Bull in the Cordillera Central in Tolima, Colombia. H.G. Reichenbach described it in 1855 in *Bonplandia* (p. 69), naming it for the spiky hairs on the peduncle-sheaths which fancifully resemble the coat of the Australian echidna, a hedgehog-like animal. L. Garay (1953), in *Svensk Botanisk Tidskrift* (p. 201), removed this species from *Masdevallia* and, placed it in the genus *Porroglossum* Schltr.
SYNONYMS *Masdevallia echidna* Rchb.f.
CLOSELY RELATED SPECIES *Porroglossum muscosum* (Rchb.f.) Schltr. [Colour Plate], from Venezuela, Colombia and Ecuador, differs in having shorter, less clavate tails to the sepals, shorter hairs on the lip margins, and shorter hairs on the peduncle.

Porroglossum muscosum (Rchb.f.) Schltr.
[Colour Plate]
A medium-sized epiphyte or lithophyte with 1–4 cm long erect stems. **Leaf** erect, thickly coriaceous, oblanceolate, acute, 4–15 cm long, 1–1.8 cm wide, the petiole 1–4 cm long. **Inflorescence** erect, 8–26 cm long, densely successively few-flowered at the apex; peduncle densely long-hairy; bracts tubular, imbricate, 5–7 mm long. **Flowers** with green, light brown or tan sepals with darker veins, the petals off-white to tan with a purple mid-vein, and the lip white suffused with purple; ovary verrucose, 5–6 mm long. **Dorsal sepal** obovate, 7–8 mm long, 5–6 mm wide, with a 10–20 mm long apical tail; the **lateral sepals** connate in the basal half and with the column-foot, obliquely ovate, 7–8 mm long, with 10–20 mm long deflexed tails. **Petals** obliquely lanceolate, acuminate, 4–5 mm long, 1–1.5 mm wide. **Lip** obovate from a slender geniculate claw, 4–5.5 mm long, 3.5–4 mm wide, pubescent, ciliate at apex; callus a longitudinal ridge in basal half of lip, **Column** terete, 2.5 mm long; column-foot 4–6 mm long.
DISTRIBUTION W. Venezuela, Colombia and Ecuador; montane forests from 1600–2700 m.
TAXONOMY H.G. Reichenbach described this charming little orchid in 1875 in the *Gardeners' Chronicle* (ser. 2, 3: p. 460), as *Masdevallia muscosa*, based on a collection by Shuttleworth from Frontino in the Department of Antioquia in Columbia. Rudolf Schlechter transferred it to the present genus in 1920 in *Fedde, Repertorium Specierum Novarum, Beihefte* (vol. 7: p. 83).
SYNONYMS *Masdevallia muscosa* Rchb.f.; *M. xipheres* Rchb.f.; *Scaphosepalum xipheres* (Rchb.f.) Schltr.; *Porroglossum xipheres* (Rchb.f.) Garay

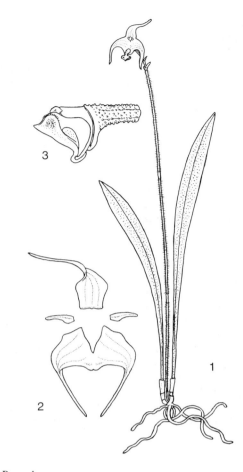

Porroglossum muscosum
1 – Habit ($\times \frac{1}{2}$)
2 – Sepals and petals ($\times 1\frac{1}{2}$)
3 – Lip, column and ovary, side view ($\times 2\frac{1}{2}$)

CLOSELY RELATED SPECIES *P. echidna* (Rchb.f.) Garay from N.E. Colombia, has a similarly hairy flower stalk but possesses a more markedly campanulate flower with longer tails to the sepals.

Prescottia Lindl.
Subfamily Spiranthoideae
Tribe Cranichideae
Subtribe Cranichidinae

Small to medium-sized terrestrial plants with short rhizomes and fasciculate fleshy elongate roots. **Leaves** conduplicate, suberect or erect, elliptic-lanceolate to cordate, petiolate or sessile. **Inflorescence** erect, terminal, simple, densely few- to many-flowered; peduncle covered by membranous sheaths. **Flowers** small, non-resupinate, globose. **Sepals** united to the petals at the base. **Petals** smaller than the sepals, linear, frequently revolute. **Lip** deeply concave, entire or obscurely 3-lobed, enveloping the column, ecallose, lacking a spur. **Column** short and thick; rostellum blunt; anther dorsal, equalling rostellum; pollinia 4, mealy, lacking caudicles.

DISTRIBUTION A genus of about 35 species; widespread in tropical Central and S. America, the W. Indies and Florida.

DERIVATION OF NAME Commemorating John Prescott, an English merchant in St Petersburg, Russia, and also an amateur botanist and friend of John Lindley.

TAXONOMY This genus was named by John Lindley in the second volume of W. Hooker's *Exotic Botany* (t. 115).

Prescottia is a distinctive genus related to *Cranichis* but it is easily recognised by its spike of small globose non-resupinate flowers.

TYPE SPECIES *P. plantaginifolia* Lindl. [Colour Plate]

CULTURE Temp. Winter min. 15°C. Grow in well-drained terrestrial mix containing peat, bark, leaf-mould and perlite. Water well while growing but, after the leaves die down, keep much drier as the roots will rot easily. Give shady conditions to protect the leaves.

Prescottia plantaginifolia Lindl.
[Colour Plate]

A terrestrial plant, 35–85 cm tall. **Leaves** in a basal rosette, suberect-spreading, oblong, oblanceolate or ovate-lanceolate, acute, 7–35 cm long, 1.8–4 cm wide, bluish-green. **Inflorescence** densely many-flowered in a cylindrical spike; peduncle bearing several sterile bracts; bracts lanceolate, acuminate, 3–9 mm long. **Flowers** non-resupinate, small, green with a darker lip and white column; ovary 4–5 mm long. **Dorsal sepal** oblong, obtuse, 1.5–2 mm long; lateral sepals jointed at the gibbous base, linear, obtuse, 1.5–2 mm long. **Petals** thin-textured, linear, obtuse, 1.5–2 mm long. **Lip** deeply concave-subsphaerical, with a narrow slit-like mouth, 2–2.5 mm long. **Column** very short, 1 mm long.

DISTRIBUTION E. Brazil.

HABITAT In grassland and scrub, up to 500 m.

HISTORY John Forbes, a plant collector for the Horticultural Society of London, collected the type material near Rio de Janeiro in Brazil and it flowered in the Society's garden at Chiswick in 1822. It was described by Lindley in Hooker's *Exotic Botany* (t. 115) in the same year. The plate calls the species *P. plantaginea*, while the text and index refer to *P. plantaginifolia*. It is quite clear that the latter name was the one intended by Lindley for the plant he called the 'plantain-leaved prescottia'.

Prescottia stachyodes (Sw.) Lindl.

A slender to stout glabrous plant 40–95 cm tall. **Leaves** basal, ovate to elliptic-oblong, acuminate, slightly asymmetric at the base, 7–22 cm long, 3.5–16 cm wide, mottled light and dark green; petiole slender up to 25 cm long. **Inflorescence** erect, densely many-flowered; peduncle reddish-brown, covered by membranous sheaths; spike cylindric; bracts lanceolate, acuminate, 7–20 mm long. **Flowers** small, globose, green with reddish-brown on the sepals and petals; pedicel and ovary 4–5 mm long. **Sepals** oblong, obtuse, 3–3.5 mm long, 1 mm wide. **Petals** linear, subacute, 3–3.5 m long, 0.5 mm wide. **Lip** shortly clawed, subcircular, obtuse, deeply concave, 4–5 mm long, 3–4 mm wide, with a backward-pointing auricle each side of the claw. **Column** 2 mm long.

DISTRIBUTION W. Indies, Central and S. America from Mexico to Brazil; in montane and lower montane cloud forest.

HISTORY Olof Swartz (1799) described this species as *Cranichis stachyodes* in his *Flora Indiae Occidentalis* (p. 1427). It was transferred to *Prescottia* by John Lindley in the *Botanical Register* (sub t. 1916) in 1836.

SYNONYMS *Cranichis stachyodes* Sw.; *Prescottia colorans* Lindl.

Promenaea Lindl.

Subfamily Epidendroideae
Tribe Maxillarieae
Subtribe Zygopetalinae

Small to medium-sized epiphytic plants. **Pseudobulbs** distinct, fleshy, ovoid, compressed, 1- to 3-leaved, borne on a very short rhizome. **Leaves** small, membranaceous, slightly plicate-venose. **Inflorescence** 1-flowered and often shorter than the leaves. **Flowers** medium-sized, ± showy. **Sepals** and **petals** subsimilar, free, spreading; lateral sepals obliquely inserted on the short column-foot, forming a short mentum. **Lip** articulated to the apex of the column-foot, distinctly 3-lobed; side lobes narrow, erect, enclosing the column; mid-lobe spreading; disc with fleshy, transverse-lobed or tuberculate cristae. **Column** fleshy, slightly incurved, semiterete, wingless, with a short foot at the base; pollinia 4, waxy, obovoid, compressed, unequal, sessile on viscidium.

DISTRIBUTION A small genus of about 15 species in Brazil.

DERIVATION OF NAME Promencia was a priestess of Dodona mentioned by Herodotus.

TAXONOMY This genus was described by John Lindley in 1843 in the *Botanical Register* (misc. p. 13). *Promenaea* is allied to *Huntleya* and *Warscewiczella* but differs in being small plants having distinct naked pseudobulbs and herbaceous leaves.

Rudolf Schlechter revised the genus in *Notizblatt des Botanischen Gartens, Berlin* (1921) accepting 14 species in the genus and giving a key for their identification. More recently, G. Pabst and F. Dungs in *Orchidaceae Brasilienses* (1977) have conveniently divided the genus into three groups as follows:

1. *P. rollisonii* alliance – flowers in which the calli on the disc of the lip reach the side lobes.
2. *P. xanthina* alliance – the calli of the lip do not reach the side lobes; flowers yellow.
3. *P. stapelioides* alliance – the calli of the lip do not reach the side lobes; flowers brown-violet.

TYPE SPECIES Several species were cited by Lindley when he described *Promenaea*.

CULTURE Compost A. Temp. Winter min. 12–15°C. *Promenaea* species are best grown in small pans under humid and fairly shady conditions. While growing, they should not become dry but it is important to avoid getting water on the young growths as they readily rot. When the pseudobulbs are fully formed much less water is needed so long as shrivelling is avoided.

Promenaea xanthina (Lindl.) Lindl.
[Colour Plate]

A small epiphytic plant with short branching stems and fleshy leaves. **Pseudobulbs** densely tufted, erect, broadly ovoid, compressed, obscurely 4-angled, up to 2 cm long, 1.5 cm broad, 2-leaved at apex, subtended by 1 or 2 leaf-bearing sheaths. **Leaves** narrowly oblanceolate, acute, up to 7 cm long, 1–1.5 cm broad. **Inflorescence** basal, spreading, up to 10 cm long, 1- or rarely 2-flowered. **Flowers** showy, bright yellow with dull reddish blotches on the lip base and side lobes and the column. **Sepals** narrowly oblong-lanceolate to ovate-lanceolate, acute, 2 cm long, 0.8–1 cm broad. **Petals** narrowly ovate, acute, slightly shorter than the sepals. **Lip** 3-lobed, oblong, obtuse or rounded at the apex, 1.5 cm long, 1.2 cm broad; side lobes oblong-subfalcate, erect; mid-lobe broadly obovate-suborbicular; callus with a prominent 3-lobed crest, the mid-lobe with a fleshy prominence and a denticulate apex. **Column** clavate, arcuate, with a short foot, 1.5–1.7 cm long in all.

DISTRIBUTION Brazil.

HISTORY Discovered in 1837 by George Gardner in the Organ Mts near Rio de Janeiro at about 1700 m and first described by John Lindley as *Maxillaria xanthina* in the *Botanical Register* (sub t. 17) in 1839. He later transferred it to his new genus *Promenaea* in the *Botanical Register* (misc. p. 13) in 1843.

Psychilis Raf.
Subfamily Epidendroideae
Tribe Epidendreae
Subtribe Laeliinae

Epiphytic or lithophytic plants with short stout creeping rhizomes completely enclosed by imbricate scarious sheaths. **Stems** erect or ascending, clustered, pseudobulbous, several-noded, up to 6-leaved at the apex, enclosed when young by scarious sheaths. **Leaves** coriaceous, with entire to erose or denticulate margins. **Inflorescences** terminal, capitate, with several racemes, produced one or two at a time at the apex of an elongate slender peduncle; peduncle enclosed by appressed, imbricate chartaceous sheaths. **Flowers** several produced in succession, usually pink or purple; pedicel and ovary slender. **Sepals** and **petals** subsimilar, free, spreading or reflexed. **Lip** 3-lobed, clawed and adnate to the column at the base, with a callus beneath the column and a canaliculate callus on the mid-lobe; side lobes basally adnate to the column; mid-lobe entire to bilobed. **Column** fleshy, lacking auricles or wings; pollinia 4, equal, compressed, waxy, connected by a caudicle.

DISTRIBUTION A genus of some 15 species endemic to the W. Indies.
DERIVATION OF NAME From the Greek *psyche* (butterfly) and *cheilos* (lip), in allusion to the large free brightly coloured lip which fancifully resembles a butterfly.
HISTORY This is a segregate genus of *Epidendrum* that was established by the eccentric American botanist C.S. Rafinesque in 1838 in the fourth volume of his *Flora Telluriana* (p. 40). However, Rafinesque's work has been largely ignored and it is only as recently as 1988 that *Psychilis* has been resurrected by Ruben Sauleda in *Phytologia* (p. 3), where a key to the species and a full treatment of the genus is provided.

Psychilis is most closely allied to *Encyclia*, in which several species have been included by various authors. It differs, however, both vegetatively and florally. The pseudobulbs are fusiform and several-noded, while the inflorescence is very distinctive, with its elongate peduncle topped by several racemes. The flowers also differ in having the bases of the side lobes of the lip fused to the column and the lip has a distinctive callus structure.
TYPE SPECIES *Epidendrum bifidum* Aublet
CULTURE Temp. Winter min. 15°C. Grow as for *Broughtonia*.

Psychilis bifida (Aublet) Sauleda
An epiphyte with slender pyriform to cylindrical pseudobulbs, up to 10 cm long, 2.5 cm in diameter. **Leaves** linear-lanceolate, acute or subacute, 15–24 cm long, 1–1.8 cm wide, with entire margins. **Inflorescence** up to 150 cm long; peduncle erect; racemes erect, several, up to 18 cm long, up to 25-flowered; bracts ovate, acute, 1 mm long. **Flowers** pale rose-carmine; pedicel and ovary 2–2.5 cm long. **Dorsal sepal** obovate to oblanceolate, subacute, 1.3–1.5 cm long, 0.5 cm wide; **lateral sepals** elliptic, obtuse, mucronate, 1.4–1.5 cm long, 0.7 cm long. **Petals** oblanceolate, acute, 1.2–1.3 cm long, 0.3 cm wide. **Lip** 3-lobed, 2–2.4 cm long and wide; side lobes ovate, obtuse, erect embracing column; mid-lobe reniform, emarginate, with a cordate canaliculate callus. **Column** 1–1.2 cm long.
DISTRIBUTION Hispaniola: N. Haiti only. In xeric coastal areas.
HISTORY This attractive species was first described as *Epidendrum bifidum* by Aublet in 1775 in *Histoire des Plantes de Guiane* (p. 824). Sauleda transferred it to the present genus in 1988 in *Phytologia* (p. 8).
SYNONYMS *Epidendrum bifidum* Aublet; *E. papilionaceum* Vahl; *Encyclia bifida* (Aublet) Britton & Wilson; *Epidendrum eckmanii* Urban
CLOSELY RELATED SPECIES *P. atropurpurea* (Willd.) Sauleda, also from Haiti, is often confused with this species but it differs in having maroon sepals and petals and a lip which is flabellate in outline and has an elliptic callus.

Psychilis atropurpurea
Flower (× 1)

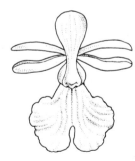

Psychilis bifida
Flower (× 1)

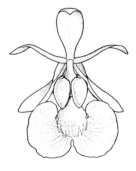

Psychopsiella Lueckel & Braem
Subfamily Epidendroideae
Tribe Oncidieae

Dwarf epiphytic herbs with an ascending rhizome. Pseudobulbs small, obovoid, bilaterally flattened on the substrate, unifoliate at the apex. **Leaf** coriaceous, elliptic, obtuse, mottled with dull green and red. **Inflorescence** erect to arcuate, much longer than the leaf, up to 3-flowered; peduncle slender, wiry. **Flowers** large for plant, showy. **Sepals** spreading, free, subsimilar. **Petals** larger than the sepals, free, spreading. **Lip** dependent, 3-lobed, the side lobes much smaller than the mid-lobe, with a fleshy ridged basal callus, saccate at the base. **Column** erect, with bilobed lacerate wings; pollinia 2, sulcate, ovoid, attached by a triangular stipe to a lunate viscidium.
DISTRIBUTION A monotypic genus from Brazil and Venezuela.
DERIVATION OF NAME The diminutive of *Psychopsis*, an allied genus of larger orchids.
TAXONOMY *Psychopsiella* was established recently in *Die Orchidee* (p. 7) by E. Lueckel and G. Braem (1982) for *Oncidium limminghei*, a species that occupied an isolated position in *Oncidium* because of its unusual habit, leaves marked rather like those of *Psychopsis*, and the bilobed lacerate column-wings. It is undoubtedly allied to *Psychopsis* but the habit and flower are very different.
TYPE SPECIES *Oncidium limminghei* E. Morr. ex Lindl.
CULTURE Temp. Winter min. 15°C. Grow mounted, as for *Psychopsis*, and water carefully throughout the year, but less when not actively growing.

Psychopsiella limminghei (E. Morr. ex Lindl.) Lueckel & Braem [Colour Plate]
A dwarf epiphyte with a creeping ascending bilaterally compressed obovoid pseudobulb, 1–2 cm long, 0.8–1.5 cm wide, prostrate upon the substrate. **Leaf** elliptic, obtuse, held close to the substrate, 2.5–3.5 cm long, 1.5–3 cm wide, mottled with dull green and red. **Inflorescence** erect, 1- to 3-flowered, up to 15 cm long; peduncle slender, wiry; bracts lanceolate, acute, 2–3 mm long. **Flowers** showy, with dark red-brown sepals and petals, the latter with faint yellow banding, and a yellow lip spotted with orange-brown. **Sepals** obovate, obtuse, 13–15 mm long, 8–9 mm wide. **Petals** oblong-obovate, truncate, 15–17 mm long, 8–9 mm wide. **Lip** 3-lobed, up to 20 mm long and wide; side lobes spreading-suberect, oblong, rounded at the apex; mid-lobe narrowly clawed, reniform above, with a broad sinus; callus 3-ridged, the central one longer than the outer

ones. **Column** erect, 8–9 mm long, the lateral wings bilobed, lacerate.

DISTRIBUTION   Brazil and Venezuela.

HISTORY   The type collection of this dainty orchid was imported from Caracas in Venezuela by Edward Morren and was described by John Lindley in *Folia Orchidacea Oncidium* (p. 56) in 1855. E. Lueckel and G. Braem made it the type of their new genus *Psychopsiella* in 1982 in the journal *Die Orchidee* (p. 7).

SYNONYM   *Oncidium limminghei* E. Morr. ex Lindl.

Psychopsis Raf.
Subfamily Epidendroideae
Tribe Oncidieae

Medium-sized epiphytic plants with 1-noded unifoliate bilaterally flattened pseudobulbs subtended by distichous sheaths. **Leaves** coriaceous, sometimes attractively mottled with red. **Inflorescences** erect, elongate, basal. **Flowers** large, showy, produced in succession at the apex of the peduncle. **Dorsal sepal** and **petals** free, linear-spathulate, erect; **lateral sepals** broader, petaloid. **Lip** large, with a basal callus, at right angles or more to the column. **Column** erect, short, fleshy, winged, lacking a foot; pollinia 2, hard, attached by a stipe to a viscidium.

DISTRIBUTION   A small but distinctive genus of four or five species distributed from Costa Rica to Peru.

DERIVATION OF NAME   From the Greek *psyche* (butterfly) and *opsis* (resembling), describing the attractive variegated flowers which are striking and similar to some tropical butterfly species.

TAXONOMY   The American botanist C.S. Rafinesque described this genus in 1836 in the fourth volume of his *Flora Telluriana* (p. 40). The genus had been considered a synonym of *Oncidium* until very recently when in 1982 it was revived by E. Lueckel and G. Braem in *Die Orchidee* (pp. 1–7). Most recent authors have followed the trend to split up the larger genera and *Psychopsis* has been quite widely accepted.

TYPE SPECIES   *Psychopsis picta* Raf. (= *Psychopsis papilio* (Lindl.) H.G. Jones)

CULTURE   Temp. Winter min. 15°C. Grow either mounted or in pots under conditions of moderate shade and humidity. Water well when growing but keep drier when growth is complete.

Psychopsis krameriana (Rchb.f.) H.G. Jones
[Colour Plate]
An epiphyte with small subsphaerical bilaterally compressed pseudobulbs, 1.5–2 cm in diameter, mottled dark green and purple, uni-

foliate at apex. **Leaf** oblong to oblong-elliptic, subacute, 10–30 cm long, 3.5–6 cm wide, purple-spotted beneath. **Inflorescence** erect, producing 1-2 flowers at a time, up to 75 cm long; peduncle terete, with swollen nodes; bracts ovate-triangular, 1–1.5 cm long. **Flowers** large, up to 10 cm or more tall, 8 cm across; dorsal sepal and petals brick-red below, purple above with yellow margins; lateral sepals yellow with brick-red spots; lip yellow with a brick red submarginal area and base; column green with a yellow anther spotted with purple; pedicel and ovary 1.5–2.2 cm long. **Dorsal sepal** erect, linear-spathulate, acute, 5–7.5 cm long, 0.3–0.5 cm wide, undulate and recurved on the margins; **lateral sepals** deflexed, shortly clawed, obliquely ovate, acute, 4 cm long, 1.2–2.4 cm wide, with undulate margins. **Petals** suberect, falcate, linear-spathulate, acute, 6.5–7.2 cm long, 0.4–0.9 cm wide, with undulate and recurved margins. **Lip** pendent, 3-lobed, 3–4.5 cm long, 2.3–4.2 cm wide; side lobes small, subquadrate, with an erose front margin; mid-lobe shortly clawed, reniform, bilobulate, with crisped-undulate margins; callus fleshy obscurely 3-lobed in front with mid-lobe much exceeding the side lobes. **Column** erect, with reniform wings, antenna-like and gland-tipped above and fimbriate or erose below.

DISTRIBUTION   Costa Rica and Panama to Ecuador and Peru; 200–1000 m.

HISTORY   H.G. Reichenbach described this strange orchid as *Oncidium kramerianum* in 1855 in Otto and Dietrich's *Allgemeine Gartenzeitung* (p. 9). It was transferred to *Psychopsis* by H.G. Jones in 1975 in the Russian journal *Novosti Sistematiki Vysshikh Rastenii* (p. 141).

Albino forms in which the red-brown markings are replaced by yellow ones are occasionally seen in cultivation.

SYNONYMS   *Oncidium kramerianum* Rchb.f.; *O. papilio* var. *kramerianum* (Rchb.f.) Lindl.; *O. nodosum* Morren; *O. papilioniforme* Regel

CLOSELY RELATED SPECIES   Similar to *Psychopsis papilio* which lacks the swollen nodes on the terete peduncle and has differently shaped column wings; and to *P. sanderae* (Rolfe) Lueckel & Braem from Peru which has remarkably developed glandular fimbriate wings to the column and a lip with a purple-spotted margin rather than a purple band around it.

Psychopsis papilio (Lindl.) H.G. Jones
[Colour Plate]
An epiphytic plant up to 1 m tall. **Pseudobulbs** clustered, sphaerical, bilaterally compressed, 3–5 cm in diameter, brown, wrinkled, unifoliate. **Leaf** oblong to oblong-elliptic, obtuse, up to 21 cm long, 5.7 cm wide, dark green mottled with dark red or purple. **Inflorescence** erect, up to 1 m long, producing

a single flower at a time; peduncle terete at base but bilaterally compressed above; bracts triangular, 5–7 mm long. **Flowers** large, showy, up to 10 cm tall; sepals purple; petals yellow blotched with orange-brown; lip yellow spotted red-brown on the side lobes and with a red-brown marginal band; callus white with purple spots; pedicel and ovary 1.3–2.2 cm long. **Dorsal sepal** and **petals** erect or suberect, linear-spathulate, acute, 6–9 cm long, 0.5–0.6 cm wide, with undulate and reflexed margins; **lateral sepals** spreading-deflexed, falcate, lanceolate, 4.5–5 cm long, 2 cm wide, with undulate-crispate margins. **Lip** dependent, 3-lobed, 4 cm long, 3.5 cm wide; side lobes small, rounded; mid-lobe broadly clawed, orbicular, emarginate, with erose margins; callus of erect ridges on a fleshy plate, the mid-ridge longer than the lateral ones. **Column** erect, 7 mm long, with fimbriate wings and an antenna-like projection on either side of the anther.

DISTRIBUTION   Trinidad, Venezuela, Colombia, Ecuador and Peru; a widespread species in lower montane forests.

HISTORY   This remarkable and well-known orchid was originally described by John Lindley as *Oncidium papilio* in 1825 in the *Botanical Register* (t. 910), having been introduced the previous year from Trinidad by Sir Ralph Woodford, the Governor of the island.

It was placed in *Psychopsis* by H.G. Jones in the *Journal of the Barbados Museum Historical Society* (p. 32) in 1975. It is still widely grown under its previous name.

SYNONYMS   *Oncidium papilio* Lindl.; *Psychopsis picta* Raf.

CLOSELY RELATED SPECIES   Very close to *P. kramerianum* but distinguished by its bilaterally compressed peduncle which also lacks swollen nodes, and by details of the flower.

Psygmorchis Dodson & Dressler
Subfamily Epidendroideae
Tribe Oncidieae

Dwarf epiphytes lacking pseudobulbs and with a very short stem. **Leaves** distichous in a fan, bilaterally flattened, succulent. **Inflorescences** lateral, 1-flowered. **Flowers** large for plant, resembling an *Oncidium*. **Dorsal sepal** and **petals** free; **lateral sepals** partially united. **Lip** large, 4-lobed, at right angles to the column, with a basal callus. **Column** winged, short; anther triangular; pollinia 2, hard, laterally attached to a long narrow stipe which is broadest distally or in the middle and folded over; viscidium 1.

DISTRIBUTION   A small genus of four or

five species in Central and S. America south to Brazil and Bolivia.

DERIVATION OF NAME   From the Greek *psygma*, (fan) and *orchis* in reference to the characteristic habit of the plant.

TAXONOMY   The genus *Psygmorchis* is a segregate of *Oncidium* that was established by Calaway Dodson and Robert Dressler in 1972 in the journal *Phytologia* (vol. 24, p. 288). It is notable for its distinctive habit, the plants lacking pseudobulbs and having iridiform leaves, the condensed inflorescence producing one flower at a time, the triangular anther, and the distinctive pollinarium.

TYPE SPECIES   *Epidendrum pusillum* L.

CULTURE   Temp.   Winter   min.   15°C. Another genus of twig epiphytes which should be grown mounted in moderate shade and humidity. Water throughout the year but allow to dry quickly between waterings.

Psygmorchis pusilla (L.) **Dodson & Dressler**

A dwarf epiphyte with clustered very short stems, 3–5 mm long. **Leaves** arranged in a fan, bilaterally compressed, conduplicate, oblong-lanceolate to oblong-elliptic in side view, acute, 4–7 cm long, 0.5–1.2 cm wide. **Inflorescences** axillary, erect or spreading, 1- to 6-flowered, up to 6 cm long; peduncle bilaterally compressed; bracts ovate, 2–3 mm long. **Flowers** large for size of plant, 1.5 cm across, 2.5–3 cm high; sepals and petals yellow with some red bars at the base; lip yellow marked with red-brown at the base and on the callus; pedicel and ovary 5–8 mm long. **Dorsal sepal** concave, obovate-elliptic, obtuse, 5 mm long, 2 mm wide; **lateral sepals** similar but united at the base, acute, keeled behind. **Petals** spreading, oblong-ovate, obtuse, 8 mm long, 4 mm wide, with slightly erose and crinkled margins. **Lip** spreading, 3-lobed, 1.3–2 cm long and wide; side lobes spreading, clawed, obovate, rounded, much smaller than the mid-lobe; mid-lobe broadly clawed, 4-lobulate; lobules rounded, the middle two larger than the outer ones; callus of 3 raised plates, the basal one square, the middle one rounded and the apical one broader towards the apex, all minutely papillate on the margins. **Column** erect, 3 mm long, enclosed within the dorsal sepal; wings large, with toothed margins.

DISTRIBUTION   Mexico south to Brazil and Bolivia, also in Trinidad; in forest and plantations of coffee; 100–800 m.

HISTORY   Originally described by Linnaeus in 1763 in the 2nd edition of *Species Plantarum* (p. 1352) as *Epidendrum pusillum*. H.G. Reichenbach transferred it to *Oncidium* in 1863 in *Walpers, Annales Botanices* (p. 716) and it is still commonly grown under that name. More recently, in 1972, Calaway Dodson and Robert

Dressler included it in their new genus *Psygmorchis* in the journal *Phytologia* (p. 288).

SYNONYMS   *Epidendrum pusillum* L.: *Oncidium pusillum* (L.) Rchb.f.; *O. iridifolium* H.B.K.

CLOSELY RELATED SPECIES   It is closely allied to *Psygmorchis pumilio* (Reichb.f.) Dodson & Dressler (syn. *Oncidium pumilio* Reichb.f.) [Colour Pate] and to *P. glossomystax* (Reichb.f.) Dodson & Dressler which differ in having a fringed 4-lobed callus, and column-wings with undulate margins. In *P. glossomystax* the lip is as long as broad and is spotted, while in *P. pumilio* the lip is longer than broad and pure yellow.

Pterostylis **R. Br.**

Subfamily Orchidoideae
Tribe Diurideae
Subtribe Pterostylidinae

Small to medium-sized, solitary or colony-forming, terrestrial herbs with subterranean tubers. **Leaves** usually in a basal rosette or borne along the stem, the rosette either at the base of the flowering shoot or on a separate sterile shoot. **Inflorescences** 1- to few-flowered, erect. **Flowers** erect to nutant, somewhat tubular. **Dorsal sepal** hooded, forming a galea with the adnate petals; **lateral sepals** fused in basal part, erect, with short to long apical tails. **Lip** more or less hidden in flower, more or less entire, linear to ovate, hinged to the column-foot by an elastic strap, often with a penicellate appendage at the base of the lip. **Column** slender, with 2 wings at the apex; pollinia 4, mealy.

DISTRIBUTION   Some 120 species, the majority in Australia with about 17 species endemic in New Zealand and outliers in New Caledonia, Vanuatu and New Guinea.

DERIVATION OF NAME   The name derives from the Greek *pteron* (wing) and *stylis* (column), referring to the prominent broad columnar wings found in all species of the genus.

TAXONOMY   Robert Brown established the genus *Pterostylis* in 1810 in his *Prodromus Florae Novae Hollandiae* (p. 326), the seminal work on Australian plants.

Pterostylis is the largest genus of Australasian terrestrial orchids and some species are difficult for the amateur to distinguish. However, an excellent account of the Australian species can be found in D. Jones's (1988) *Native Orchids of Australia*, together with details of their cultivation.

Popularly called 'Greenhoods' in Australia and New Zealand, the colonial species are generally excellent subjects for cultivation, multiplying freely in the right conditions.

TYPE SPECIES   *P. curta* R. Br.

CULTURE   Temp.   Winter min. 5–10°C. Mix

as for *Diuris*. Some species multiply rapidly and need repotting regularly.

Pterostylis baptistii **Fitzg.** [Colour Plate]

A large colony-forming terrestrial, 20–40 cm tall. **Leaves** 5–8 in a basal rosette, ovate to oblong, obtuse, up to 8 cm long, 2.5 cm wide, with wavy or crisped margins, shortly petiolate. **Inflorescence** 1-flowered. **Flower** 5–6 cm tall, white with green and brown veins and brown tips to the dorsal sepal and petals; lip red-brown. **Dorsal sepal** erect and concave at the base, curving forwards towards the acute apex, 5–6 cm long; **lateral sepals** united in basal third, upcurved in apical half above galea, 4–4.5 cm long. **Petals** very broad with crinkled margins. **Lip** erect, oblong-ligulate, suddenly constricted and deflexed at the apex, 1.8–2.5 cm long, 4 mm wide. **Column** a little shorter than the lip, only slightly incurved; upper wings filiform, 2–3 mm long.

DISTRIBUTION   Australia, N. Queensland to Victoria, in dense high-rainfall forest and near swamps.

HISTORY   *P. baptistii* is the largest-flowered species in the genus and it is perhaps surprising that it was not described until 1875 by Fizgerald in the first volume of his *Australian Orchids* (t. 2). He named it after John Baptist who discovered it at Hen and Chickens' Bay near Sydney where it was growing in a *Melaleuca* swamp. It is a vigorous plant in cultivation.

Pterostylis curta **R. Br.** [Colour Plate]

A medium-sized colony-forming terrestrial plant, 10–30 cm tall. **Leaves** 2–6 in a basal rosette, ovate to oblong, 5–10 cm long, 2–3 cm wide, with crisped margins, distinctly stalked. **Inflorescence** 1-flowered. **Flower** 2–3.5 cm tall, green with a red-brown lip. **Dorsal sepal** concave, acute, curving forwards at apex; **lateral sepals** united in basal half, tails spreading, erect above the galea, 2–2.5 cm long. **Petals** as long as the dorsal sepal, obtuse. **Lip** shortly clawed, linear-ligulate, twisted towards the obtuse apex, 1.5–2 cm long, 4–5 mm wide, with a central fleshy ridge. **Column** erect; wings with upper lobes short, erect, subulate.

DISTRIBUTION   S.E. Queensland to southern S. Australia and Tasmania, common in open forests especially near streams.

HISTORY   Robert Brown discovered *P. curta* near Port Jackson (now Sydney) and described it in 1810 in his *Prodromus Florae Novae Hollandiae* (p. 326).

Rangaeris (Schltr.) Summerh.

Subfamily Epidendroideae
Tribe Vandeae
Subtribe Aerangidinae

Small to medium-sized epiphytic plants. **Stems** short to elongate, leafy. Leaves distichous, coriaceous, ligulate or oblanceolate, acute, obtuse or unequally 2-lobed at apex. **Inflorescence** racemose, suberect or spreading-arcuate, sublaxly many-flowered. **Flowers** small to fairly large, often stellate, white or yellowish. **Sepals** and **petals** spreading, lanceolate to ovate, rarely 3-lobed at the base; spur narrow-cylindrical, often very long. **Column** short to long; pollinia 2, globose or ellipsoidal; viscidium 1 or 2, elliptic; stipites 2, linear or oblanceolate.

DISTRIBUTION A small genus of six species widespread in tropical Africa with one species reaching S. Africa.

DERIVATION OF NAME *Rangaeris* is allied to *Aerangis* and the name is meant to be an anagram of the latter.

TAXONOMY V.S. Summerhayes described this genus in the *Kew Bulletin* (p. 227) in 1936 for some aberrant species which Schlechter had placed originally in the section *Rangaeris* of the genus *Aerangis*. Species of *Rangaeris* differ from *Aerangis* species in possessing a viscidium bearing 2 stipites rather than a single one.

TYPE SPECIES *R. muscicola* (Rchb.f.) Summerh.

CULTURE Compost A or mounted. Temp. Winter min. 12–15°C. As for *Diaphananthe* and *Tridactyle*.

Rangaeris muscicola (Rchb.f.) Summerh.
[Colour Plate]
A small epiphytic plant. **Stem** short, stout, 2.5–6 cm long, 0.8–1 cm in diameter, sheathed in pale red-brown leaf-bases, 6- to 8-leaves. **Roots** stout, grey-brown, 0.5–0.8 cm in diameter. **Leaves** distichous, arranged in a fan-shape, conduplicate, fleshy, ligulate, unequally 2-lobed at apex, 7–20 cm long, 1–2 cm broad. **Inflorescence** racemose, borne in axils of leaves, spreading-suberect, 7–22 cm long, 5- to 12-flowered; peduncle green, terete; bracts ovate, acute, sheathing, dark brown. **Flowers** sweetly scented, white, fading to pale orange. **Sepals** narrowly elliptic-lanceolate, spreading, acute, 0.7–1.2 cm long, 0.3–0.4 cm broad. **Petals** spreading, falcate-lanceolate, acute, 0.65–1 cm long, 0.3 cm broad. **Lip** entire, decurved, ovate-lanceolate, acute, 0.7–1 cm long, 0.6 cm broad; spur pendulous, 5.5–9.5 cm long, twisted slightly. **Column** erect, 0.3 cm long.

DISTRIBUTION Tropical and S. Africa; in forest and woodland, 110–2200 m.

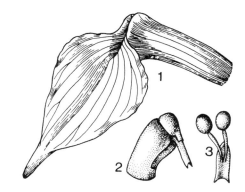

Rangaeris muscicola
1 – Lip and base of spur (× 5)
2 – Column, side view (× 5)
3 – Pollinia, stipites and viscidium (× 8)

HISTORY Discovered at Pungo Andongo by Dr F.M. Welwitsch, this species was described in 1865 by H.G. Reichenbach as *Aeranthus muscicola* in *Flora* (p. 190). It was subsequently transferred to the genus *Listrostachys* by R.A. Rolfe in 1897 in the *Flora of Tropical Africa* (p. 158) and later by V.S. Summerhayes to *Rangaeris* in 1936 in the *Flora of West Tropical Africa* (p. 450).

SYNONYMS *Aeranthus muscicola* Rchb.f.; *Angraecum batesii* (Rolfe) Schltr.; *Listrostachys muscicola* (Rchb.f.) Rolfe

Renanthera Lour.

Subfamily Epidendroideae
Tribe Vandeae
Subtribe Sarcanthinae

Large epiphytic plants with long monopodial stems, often very long. **Leaves** very leathery, often oblong, unequally 2-lobed at apex. **Inflorescences** paniculate, many-flowered, often very long. **Flowers** showy, flat, predominantly red, yellow and orange. **Dorsal sepal** and **petals** similar, spreading; lateral sepals larger, subparallel. **Lip** very much smaller than the other segments, 3-lobed, spurred or saccate at the base; side lobes erect; mid-lobe ligulate, reflexed; callus lamellate. **Column** short, stout; pollinia 4, in 2 pairs, kidney-shaped, unequal; stipe 1, linear; viscidium elliptic.

DISTRIBUTION About 15 species in S.E. Asia across to the Philippines.

DERIVATION OF NAME From the Latin *renes* (kidneys) and the Greek *anthera* (anther), in allusion to the kidney-shaped pollinia of the type species.

TAXONOMY Juan Loureiro established this genus in 1790 in the *Flora Cochinchinensis* (p. 521).

The structure of the column, and especially the pollinary apparatus of *Renanthera* indicates the close affinity of this genus with *Vanda* and *Aerides*, to one or other of which most species were first referred. However, the form of the perianth in *Renanthera* is very different and, in particular, the lateral sepals are usually longer than the other segments and are parallel or nearly so.

TYPE SPECIES *R. coccinea* Lour.

CULTURE Compost A. Temp. Winter min. 15°C. As for *Vanda*, except that the tall-growing species such as *R. coccinea* require some support.

Renanthera imschootiana Rolfe
[Colour Plate]
A scrambling liana-like plant with a long stem about 0.5 cm thick. **Leaves** linear, truncately rounded, 2-lobed at apex, 6–11 cm long, 1.5–1.8 cm broad. **Inflorescence** racemose or paniculate, laxly many-flowered; bracts semi-orbicular, 0.2 cm long. **Flowers** 1–2 cm apart, 3–4 cm across; sepals orange or red, yellow at base; petals yellow, spotted with red; lip and column red. **Dorsal sepal** linear to oblance-olate, obtuse or acute, 1.8–2.2 cm long, 0.4–0.5 cm broad; **lateral sepals** clawed, oblong, slightly undulate on the lower margins, slightly papillose within, 2.5–3.7 cm long, 1.6 cm broad. **Petals** similar to dorsal sepal but slightly shorter, 1.2 cm long. **Lip** 3-lobed, 0.6 cm long; side lobes lanceolate, acute, with a small auricle at the base, 0.2 cm long; mid-lobe elliptic, concave, spreading or pendent, 0.2 cm long; callus tuberculate at base; spur 0.4 cm long. **Column** truncate, papillose, 0.3 cm long.

DISTRIBUTION India (Assam), Burma and Indo-China.

HISTORY Imported by Messrs Sander & Co. of St Albans. A plant grown by M.A. van Imschoot of Gand (Ghent) in Belgium was described by R.A. Rolfe in 1891 in the *Kew Bulletin* (p. 200).

Renanthera matutina (Blume) Lindl.
[Colour Plate]
A scrambling, liana-like plant, up to about 1 m tall. **Stem** stout, climbing or hanging, 30–90 cm long, leafy. **Leaves** 2–3 cm, distant, oblong or somewhat lorate, fleshy, stiff, 5–20 cm long, 1.2–1.6 cm broad. **Inflorescence** erect, 60–90 cm long, laxly many-flowered; branches long, spreading; bracts ovate, reflexed. **Flowers** 2.5–5 cm across: sepals and petals light crimson, spotted with red; lip orange-yellow and white, spotted with red, mid-lobe red-brown. **Sepals** subsimilar, free, 1.5–2.5 cm long, 0.4–0.6 cm broad in the middle. **Petals** nearly straight, linear, obtuse, up to 2.3 cm long, 0.3 cm broad. **Lip** 3-lobed, very small, 0.7 cm long, 0.8 cm broad; side lobes short, broad, margins revo-

lute; mid-lobe ligulate, revolute; calli 2, basal on mid-lobe: spur large, cylindric, obtuse, somewhat recurved, o.3 cm long. **Column** nearly o.5 cm long; stipe linear, acuminate; viscidium small.

DISTRIBUTION   Malaya, Java and Sumatra.

HISTORY   Discovered by C.L. Blume in Java on Mt Salak and described by him as *Aerides matutinum* in *Bijdragen* (p. 366) in 1825. John Lindley transferred it to *Renanthera* in 1833 in his *Genera and Species of Orchidaceous Plants* (p. 218).

SYNONYMS   *Renanthera micrantha* Blume; *Saccolabium reflexum* Lindl.; *Aerides matutinum* Blume; *A. angustifolia* Hooker f.

Renanthera monachica Ames [Colour Plate]

An erect epiphytic herb, 50 or more cm high. **Leaves** distichous, approximate, ligulate, unequally and obtusely 2-lobed at apex, coriaeous, 5.5–13 cm long, 1–1.5 cm broad. **Inflorescence** axillary, suberect, simple, laxly racemose, 18.5 cm long; bracts tubular, about o.2 cm long. **Flowers** ± 2.5 cm across, yellow, spotted with red. **Dorsal sepal** narrowly lanceolate, acute, 1.5 cm long, o.3 cm broad; **lateral sepals** clawed, lanceolate. with an unciform process near the apex, 3 cm long, o.6 cm broad. **Petals** subfalcate, attenuate below, acuminate, 1.2 cm long, o.4 cm broad. **Lip** very small, fleshy, saccate, 3-lobed; side lobes triangular to acute; mid-lobe oblong, rounded, obtuse at the apex, 2.5 cm long, o.1 cm broad; saccate base obtuse, cylindric, o.15 cm long. **Column** fleshy, o.4 cm long, minutely puberulous, with a ring of hairs at the apex.

DISTRIBUTION   The Philippines (Luzon).

HISTORY First collected by H.M. Curran in the Province of Zambales on Luzon and described by Oakes Ames in 1915 in vol. 5 of *Orchidaceae* (p. 224).

CLOSELY RELATED SPECIES   Allied to *Renanthera angustifolia* Hooker f. but distinguished by its differently-shaped petals and sepals; unbranched inflorescence; the entire apex of the column; and the hook-like process just below the apex of each lateral sepal.

Renanthera storiei Rchb.f. [Colour Plate]

Stem stout, 20–30 cm long, 1–1.4 cm in diameter. **Leaves** broad, distichous, oblong, 10–20 cm or more long, about 3.5 cm broad, coriaceous, retuse and 2-lobed at apex. **Inflorescence** opposite the leaves, horizontal, paniculate, many-flowered; peduncle woody; branches several, long, all nearly in 1 plane. **Flowers** 4–4.5 cm across, deep red; dorsal sepal and petals orange somewhat mottled; lateral sepals rose-purple, spotted crimson; lip red with yellow side lobes striped with red; callus

and base of mid-lobe white. **Dorsal sepal** narrowly oblanceolate, 2.2–2.8 cm long, o.3–o.5 cm broad; **lateral sepals** clawed, oblong, undulate, 2.7–3.5 cm long, 1.2–1.4 cm broad. **Petals** cuneate-ligulate, obtuse, margins crisped-undulate, 2.2–2.7 cm long, o.6–o.7 cm broad. **Lip** 3-lobed, 1.2–1.4 cm long, 1–1.7 cm broad; side lobes triangular, acute; mid-lobe ligulate, obtuse, porrect, with 2 quadrate lamellae in the mouth of the conical spur.

DISTRIBUTION   The Philippines.

HISTORY   H.G. Reichenbach described this showy species in the *Gardeners' Chronicle* (n.s. 14: p. 296) of 1880 based on a plant cultivated by Stuart Low. This species in named in honour of James G. Storie who was the first to flower it in cultivation.

SYNONYM   *Vanda storiei* (Rchb.f.) Rchb.f.

CLOSELY RELATED SPECIES   Similar to *Renanthera coccinea* Lour. but with rather shorter flowers, broader sepals and petals and a larger lip which has side lobes with an acute rather than retuse upper margin.

Renantherella Ridl.

Subfamily Epidendroideae
Tribe Vandeae
Subtribe Sarcanthinae

Small to medium-sized epiphytic plants with erect to pendent monopodial leafy stems. **Leaves** fleshy-coriaceous, distichous, linear-tapering, acute or acuminate, channelled on upper side, articulated to persistent sheathing bases. **Inflorescences** lateral, simple, racemose, laxly few- to several-flowered; bracts small. **Flowers** relatively small but pretty, fleshy, non-resupinate. **Sepals** and **petals** spreading, free, subsimilar, the laterals strongly incurved. **Lip** small, 3-lobed, with a low fleshy bilobed callus, shortly spurred at the base. **Column** slender, elongate, with a short foot; pollinia 4, of two sizes in appressed pairs, attached by an oblanceolate stipe to broadly elliptic viscidium.

DISTRIBUTION   A small genus of one or possibly two species from peninsular Thailand, Malaya and Borneo.

DERIVATION OF NAME   The diminutive of *Renanthera*, a closely allied orchid genus.

TAXONOMY   *Renantherella* was established by Henry Ridley in 1896 in the *Journal of the Linnean Society* (p. 354) as a segregate genus of *Renanthera*. Its recognition is still disputed but it differs in its linear-tapering leaves, the non-resupinate flowers, and the elongate slender column. We have followed Seidenfaden (1988) in *Opera Botanica* (p. 64) in accepting this genus.

TYPE SPECIES   *R. histrionica* (Rchb.f.) Ridl.

CULTURE   Temp. Winter min. 15°C. Probably best grown mounted under conditions of moderate shade and humidity. Water when in active growth and give less when growth slows or ceases.

Renantherella histrionica (Rchb.f.) Ridl.

A suberect to pendent epiphyte. **Stems** elongate, leafy, slightly zigzag, occasionally branching, 15–50 cm long, 3 mm in diameter. **Leaves** fleshy, linear, acuminate, channelled on upper surface, 6–11 cm long, 4–7 mm wide. **Inflorescences** horizontal, 5–12 cm long, laxly 3- to 10-flowered; rhachis zigzag; bracts triangular, 2 mm long. **Flowers** non-resupinate, lemon-yellow spotted with crimson-maroon on the sepals and petals, the lip yellow spotted with crimson; pedicel and ovary 9–10 mm long. **Sepals** and **petals** recurved. **Dorsal sepal** oblanceolate, obtuse, 13–14 mm long, 2–4 mm wide; **lateral sepals** incurved-falcate, spathulate, rounded, 9–11 mm long, 2–3 mm wide. **Petals** linear-spathulate, acute to obtuse, 9–11 mm long, 2.5 mm wide. **Lip** 3-lobed, 4 mm long, 5 mm wide when flattened; side lobes erect, oblong, rounded; mid-lobe deflexed, ovate-elliptic, obtuse, callus fleshy, 2-lobed, between the side lobes; spur pendent, conical-cylindric, 3 mm long **Column** slender, incurved, 7–8 mm long; foot obscure.

DISTRIBUTION   Peninsular Thailand, Malaya and Borneo; lowland and mangrove forests; up to 300 m.

HISTORY   The type collection from Malaya was flowered by John Day of Tottenham who sent flowers to H.G. Reichenbach. Reichenbach described it as *Renanthera histrionica* in 1878 in the *Gardeners' Chronicle* (n.s. vol. 10: p. 74). It was transferred to *Renantherella* by Ridley in 1896 in the *Journal of the Linnean Society* (p. 355).

Var. *auyongii* (Christensen) Senghas [Colour Plate] from Sarawak differs in its longer 5 mm long spur, and golden flowers spotted with wine-red.

SYNONYM   *Renanthera histrionica* Rchb.f.

Restrepia H.B.K.

Subfamily Epidendroideae
Tribe Epidendreae
Subtribe Pleurothallidinae

Small epiphytic or rarely lithophytic herbs with tufted 1-leafed, short stems (ramicauls). **Leaf** coriaceous, conduplicate, suberect or erect. **Inflorescences** 1- to several, terminal, 1-flowered; peduncle elongated; bract sheathing. **Flower** fairly large for size of plant, narrow, pale green to yellow, ± suffused, spotted or striped crimson or purple. **Dorsal sepal** linear-lanceolate, attenuate with a slightly swollen apex; **lateral sepals** ± connate, often to the apex, cucullate below. **Petals** similar to dorsal sepal but smaller. **Lip** much smaller than the sepals, oblong to ± 3-lobed, bilobulate in front. **Column** slender, arcuate, dilated towards apex; pollinia 4.

DISTRIBUTION Some 30 or so species from Mexico south to N. Argentina.

DERIVATION OF NAME Named in honour of Sr. José E. Restrepo 'who first investigated the geography and Natural History of the Antioquian Andes' in Colombia.

TAXONOMY *Restrepia* was first described in F.H.A. von Humboldt, A. Bonpland and C.S. Kunth's *Nova Genera et Species Plantarum* (p. 366) in 1815.

It is closely allied to *Pleurothallis* and has been included in that large genus by some botanists in the past. However, most now keep *Restrepia* as distinct from *Pleurothallis*, the former being distinguished by the characteristic club-shaped extensions of the dorsal sepal and petals; the more or less united lateral sepals which lack any club-shaped extensions; and the elongated peduncle bearing a single terminal flower. For their size many *Restrepia* species are quite showy and are generally much prettier than *Pleurothallis* species.

R. Schlechter revised the genus in 1918 in *Fedde, Repertorium Specierum Novarum* where he divided the 21 species known up to that time into three sections: *Pleurothallopsis*, *(Eu) Restrepia* and *Archaetochilus*. At the same time he removed 14 species previously included in *Restrepia* to his new genus *Barbosella*.

TYPE SPECIES *R. antennifera* H.B.K.

CULTURE Compost A. Temp. Winter min. 10–13°C. As for small *Pleurothallis* species. *Restrepia* species grow well in small pots under humid, shady conditons. They should never remain dry for very long and usually flower more than once annually.

Restrepia antennifera H.B.K.

A small, tufted epiphytic plant. **Stems** erect, up to 10 cm long, covered by 3 or 4 purple-spotted sheathing bracts. **Leaf** erect or erect-spreading, ovate or elliptic, obtuse or rounded, coriaceous, 5–5.5 cm long, 2.5–3 cm broad. **Inflorescence** axillary, 1-flowered; peduncle terete, slender. **Flower** large for plant, translucent, white to pale yellow-brown striped with dark purple; tails of sepals greenish; lip pale brown, spotted maroon; column creamy-brown at apex, white below. **Dorsal sepal** narrowly ovate below, long-caudate above, 2–3 cm long, 0.3 cm broad, tail swollen in apical half; **lateral sepals** united almost to the apex, narrowly elliptic, subacute, 2.3 cm long, 0.6 cm broad. **Petals** like dorsal sepal but smaller, porrect. **Lip** 3-lobed at base, 1 cm long, 0.3 cm broad; side lobes setose,

suberect; mid-lobe oblong-pandurate, papillose. **Column** clavate-arcuate, 0.5 cm long.

DISTRIBUTION Venezuela, Colombia and Ecuador.

HISTORY Collected for the first time by F.H.A. von Humboldt and A. Bonpland and described by them and C.S. Kunth in 1815 in *Nova Genera et Species Plantarum* (p. 367).

SYNONYM *Pleurothallis ospinae* R.E. Schultes

Restrepia elegans Karst. [Colour Plate]

A small epiphytic plant, up to 8 cm high. **Stems** clustered, erect, about 4–6 cm long, covered by tubular, acute, white sheaths. **Leaf** elliptic, obtuse, coriaceous, suberect, margins lightly recurved, up to 6 cm long, 4 cm broad. **Inflorescence** axillary, erect-spreading, 1-flowered; peduncle long, terete, slender, up to 4 cm long; bract white, amplexicaul. **Flower** narrow; dorsal sepal and petals translucent, white, lined with maroon; lateral sepals orange-brown, spotted maroon; lip pale brown, spotted with maroon; column pale green, flushed with pink. **Dorsal sepal** erect, lanceolate, long-attenuate, 2.5 cm long, 0.3 cm broad at base, apex slender, clavate; **lateral sepals** united to just below apex, saccate at base, 2.4 cm long, 0.9 cm broad. **Petals** similar to dorsal sepal but smaller and porrect. **Lip** fleshy, 3-lobed at base, flexuous, truncate at apex, 1.1 cm long, 0.5 cm broad; side lobes erect, porrect, falcate-

Restrepia antennifera

1 – Flower (× 1)
2 – Ovary, bract and column, side view (× 3⅓)
   a bract, b ovary, c column, e lip
3 – Anther-cap (× 4⅓)
4 – Pollinia and viscidium (× 4⅓)
   d viscidium

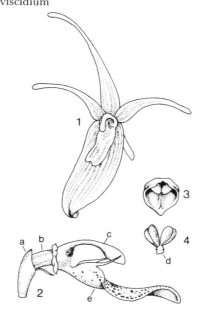

lanceolate, acuminate; mid-lobe oblong-oblanceolate, slightly restricted just above the base, verrucose. **Column** slender, arcuate, clavate, 0.5 cm long.

DISTRIBUTION Venezuela.

HISTORY Originally described in 1847 by Karsten in the *Allgemeine Gartenzeitung* (p. 202) from a plant collected in Venezuela and flowered in Berlin.

SYNONYM *Restrepia punctulata* Lindl.

Restrepia maculata Lindl. [Colour Plate]

A small, erect, tufted epiphytic or rarely lithophytic plant. **Stems** erect, terete, clothed by 3–4 compressed sheaths, 1–15 cm long, 1-leafed at apex. **Leaf** elliptic or ovate-elliptic, obtuse, coriaceous, rigid, up to 8 cm long, 3 cm broad, carinate. **Inflorescence** held behind the leaf, 1-flowered, axillary; peduncle long, slender, up to 7 cm long. **Flower** narrow, up to 5 cm long; dorsal sepal and petals whitish, lined with pink to purple and with a pink-purple apex; lateral sepals orange-brown, spotted dark maroon; lip light brown, spotted with pink-purple; column pale cream with a maroon spot on ventral surface at the base. **Dorsal sepal** lanceolate, up to 2.5 cm long, 0.3 cm broad, long-attenuate and clavate above; **lateral sepals** connate to apex or just below apex, elliptic-oblong, ± bidentate, up to 2.5 cm long, 1 cm broad. **Petals** similar to dorsal sepal but smaller, up to 1.3 cm long, 0.1 cm broad. **Lip** 3-lobed, fleshy, up to 1 cm long, 0.4 cm broad, papillose-verrucose in apical half, concave at base; side lobes curved forwards, aristate; mid-lobe oblong-subpandurate, truncate, much longer than side lobes. **Column** arcuate, slender, dilated slightly towards apex.

DISTRIBUTION Colombia. Ecuador and Venezuela; 2400–3900 m.

HISTORY Described in 1846 by John Lindley in *Orchidaceae Lindenianae* (p. 4) based on plants collected by Jean Linden in Colombia. Linden collected it growing both epiphytically near Salto de Tequendama in Bogotá Province and also growing on the ground at a higher altitude on the Paramo of Portachuela in Mérida Province. The species may prove to be conspecific with *R. guttulata* Lindl.

SYNONYMS *Restrepia pardina* Lemaire; *R. leopardina* Hort.

Restrepiella Garay & Dunsterv.

Subfamily Epidendroideae
Tribe Epidendreae
Subtribe Pleurothallidinae

Small to medium-sized epiphytes with short creeping rhizomes and stout, clustered, well-developed, erect stems each bearing a single leaf at the apex and covered in the middle by a large tubular sheath. **Leaf** erect, coriaceous. **Inflorescences** successive, axillary, single-flowered. **Flowers** fleshy, small. **Sepals** pubescent, larger than the other floral parts, the lateral sepals more or less fused. **Petals** small, entire, ciliate. **Lip** fleshy, very small, entire, with 2 longitudinal ridge-like calli. **Column** porrect, semiterete, with a long foot; pollinia 4, pyriform.

DISTRIBUTION A monotypic genus from tropical Central America.

DERIVATION OF NAME From the resemblance of the species to *Restrepia*, an allied genus of orchids.

HISTORY *Restrepiella* was established in 1966 by Garay and Dunsterville in the fourth volume of their *Venezuelan Orchids Illustrated* (p. 226). It differs from *Restrepia* in lacking the hair-like appendages on the lip and in having a mobile lip; and from *Pleurothallis* in having 4 rather than 2 pollinia.

TYPE SPECIES *Pleurothallis ophiocephala* Lindl. [= *Restrepiella ophiocephala* (Lindl.) Garay & Dunsterv.].

Restrepiella ophiocephala (Lindl.) Garay & Dunsterv.

A medium-sized epiphyte with clustered erect stems, 8–23 cm long, bearing a large 3–8 cm long sheath in the middle. **Leaf** erect, oblong to oblong-lanceolate obtuse or rounded at the apex, 8–18 cm long, 1.2–4.3 cm wide; petiole 1–2 cm long. **Inflorescences** fasciculate, produced successively, 1-flowered, subtended by large papery bracts. **Flowers** purple, 1.4–2 cm long, pubescent on outer surface. **Dorsal sepal** elliptic, rounded, 1.4–2 cm long, fused at the base to the lateral sepals; **lateral sepals** fused almost to the apex, the synsepalum cucullate at the base, obtusely bilobed at the apex, 1.5–2 cm long, 0.8–0.9 cm wide. **Petals** elliptic, obtuse or rounded, 0.45–0.55 cm long, 0.2 cm wide, ciliate. **Lip** fleshy, porrect, ovate-elliptic, rounded in front; callus of 2 low linear longitudinal ridges, 0.3–0.4 cm long, 0.15 cm wide. **Column** 0.3–0.4 cm long; foot 0.2–0.3 cm long.

DISTRIBUTION Mexico, Belize, Guatemala, El Salvador and Costa Rica; in riverine forest at low altitude.

HISTORY Originally described by John Lindley as *Pleurothallis ophiocephala* in the *Botanical Register* (misc. p. 34) in 1838 based on collections of Mexican origin sent him by Messrs Loddiges of Hackney and Mr Barker of Birmingham. It was transferred as the type of their new genus by Garay & Dunsterville in the fourth volume of *Venezuelan Orchids Illustrated* (p. 266) in 1966.

SYNONYM *Pleurothallis ophiocephala* Lindl.

Rhyncholaelia Schltr.

Subfamily Epidendroideae
Tribe Epidendreae
Subtribe Laeliinae

Medium-sized epiphytic herbs with short stout creeping rhizomes. **Pseudobulbs** elongate, clavate, compressed, unifoliate, covered when young by whitish chartaceous sheaths. **Leaf** erect, coriaceous-fleshy, elliptic or oblong-elliptic, obtuse. **Inflorescence** terminal, axillary, 1-flowered; peduncle stout, subtended by a large compressed sheath, short. **Flower** large, fleshy, showy, the sepals olive-green or yellow-green, the petals and lip cream or greenish-white, fragrant; pedicel and ovary elongate. **Sepals** subsimilar, spreading, free. **Petals** broader than the sepals and thinner-textured,

Restrepiella ophiocephala
1 – Habit (× 1)
2 – Sepals and petals (× 2)
3 – Column and lip, side view (× 5)
4 – Pollinia (× 15)

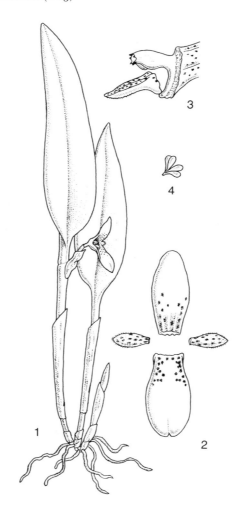

with entire or erose-fimbriate margins. **Lip** large, obscurely 3-lobed, funnel-shaped, with entire or fimbriate margins, with a callus in the basal half. **Column** elongate, clavate, stout; rostellum triangular; pollinia 8, 4 in each cell of the anther, waxy, ovoid.

DISTRIBUTION Two species only in Mexico, Guatemala, Honduras and Belize.

DERIVATION OF NAME From the Greek *rhynchos* (snout) and *Laelia*, the name of a closely allied orchid genus, given because the rostrate fruit distinguishes this genus from *Laelia*.

TAXONOMY Rudolf Schlechter established this genus in 1918 in *Beihefte zum Botanisches Zentralblatt* (Abt 2: p. 477). It is closely allied to both *Brassavola* and *Laelia* and the species have at various times been included in one or the other of these genera. It differs from the former in its broader flat leaves and much larger flowers; and from the latter in its distinctive beaked fruit and greenish or whitish flowers.

For orchid hybrid registration purposes this genus is considered synonymous with *Brassavola*.

TYPE SPECIES *R. glauca* (Lindl.) Schltr.

CULTURE Temp. Winter min. 15°C. Grow under light *Cattleya*-type conditions either in pans, or mounted, but with a more pronounced dry period when growth is complete.

Rhyncholaelia digbyana (Lindl.) Schltr
[Colour Plate]

An epiphytic plant, often found in large colonies. **Pseudobulbs** elongated, clavate, jointed, compressed, up to 15 cm long, 1-leafed at apex. **Leaf** suberect, elliptic, fleshy-coriaceous, glaucous, up to 20 cm long, 5.5 cm broad, obtuse at apex. **Inflorescence** 1-flowered, subtended by a large sheath, up to 13 cm long. **Flower** large, showy, very fragrant; sepals and petals pale yellowish-green; lip white or creamy-white with a greenish hue. **Sepals** oblong-ligulate to elliptic-lanceolate, up to 10 cm long, 2.5 cm broad, obtuse. **Petals** obliquely elliptic-oblanceolate, up to 9 cm long, 3 cm broad, obtuse. **Lip** obscurely 3-lobed, very large, emarginate at apex, 7.5 cm long, 8 cm broad when spread; side lobes erect at base forming a tube over the column; mid-lobe margin and front margin of side lobes deeply lacerate-fimbriate; disc bearing several short, fleshy lamellae. **Column** stout, semicylindrical, up to 3.5 cm long.

DISTRIBUTION Mexico and Belize.

HISTORY Introduced into cultivation from Honduras by Mrs McDonald who gave a plant to Edward St Vincent Digby of Minterne in Dorsetshire, England. Digby flowered it in 1845 and John Lindley described it in his honour the following year in the *Botanical Register* (t. 53) as *Brassavola digbyana*. George Bentham later transferred it to the genus *Laelia* and in 1918 Rudolf Schlechter placed it in the genus *Ryncholaelia*.

SYNONYMS *Brassavola digbyana* Lindl.; *Laelia digbyana* (Lindl.) Benth.; *Bletia digbyana* (Lindl.) Rchb.f.

Ryncholaelia glauca (Lindl.) Schltr.
[Colour Plate]

A terrestrial or epiphytic plant, up to 30 cm tall. **Pseudobulbs** short, oblong-fusiform, slightly compressed, 2–9 cm long, 1-leafed at apex. **Leaf** erect, oblong-elliptic, coriaceous, glaucous, 6–12 cm long, 2.5–3.5 cm broad, obtuse at apex. **Inflorescence** erect, 1-flowered, subtended by a large tubular sheath somewhat inflated in the middle, up to 10 cm long. **Flower** showy, fragrant, suberect, later becoming nodding; sepals and petals pale green, white or lavender; lip white or creamy with a purple triangular mark at the base and ± purple stripes in throat. **Sepals** linear, subobtuse or subacuminate, 5.5–6.5 cm long, 1–1.5 cm broad. **Petals** linear or oblong-oblanceolate, obtuse to subacute, margins slightly undulate, 5–6.3 cm long, 1.3–2.2 cm broad. **Lip** ± 3-lobed, 5–5.5 cm long, 4 cm across when spread; side lobes rounded, erect at base, forming a tube around the column, spreading and undulate on front margins; midlobe transversely oblong-subquadrate, spread out, margins slightly undulate. **Column** short, stout, clavate, ± 5-toothed at the apex, 0.6–1 cm long.

DISTRIBUTION Mexico, Guatemala and Honduras: rare in open montane forests up to 1500 m altitude.

HISTORY Originally found near Xalapa in Mexico by John Henchman and introduced into cultivation by Deschamps. Later it was also collected by the indefatigable Th. Hartweg near Veracruz in Mexico and sent to John Lindley who described it in 1839 in the *Botanical Register* (misc. no. 67) as *Brassavola glauca*.

Since that time it has been transferred to the genera *Bletia* and *Laelia* and, finally, by Rudolf Schlechter in 1918 in the *Beihefte zum Botanischen Zentralblatt* (p. 477), to the genus *Ryncholaelia*.

SYNONYMS *Brassavola glauca* Lindl.; *Laelia glauca* (Lindl.) Benth.; *Bletia glauca* (Lindl.) Rchb.f.

Rhynchostylis Blume
Subfamily Epidendroideae
Tribe Vandeae
Subtribe Sarcanthinae

Epiphytic monopodial plants with short, stout, leafy stems, lacking pseudobulbs. **Leaves** distichous. very thick, linear, channelled, unequally 2-lobed and toothed at the apex. **Inflorescence** erect, drooping or arcuate, densely few- to many-flowered. **Flowers** showy, mainly white. marked with pink, bluish or purple. **Sepals** and broader **petals** spreading, contracted at the base. **Lip** adnate to base of column-foot, deeply saccate or with a backward-pointing, bilaterally-flattened spur and with a porrect, unlobed or slightly 3-lobed lamina. **Column** short, stout; foot present but often obscure; pollinia 2, subglobose, cleft, on a long slender stipe slightly widened at the apex only; viscidium small; rostellum and anther long-pointed.

DISTRIBUTION About six species in India, Malaya, Indonesia and the Philippines.

DERIVATION OF NAME From the Greek *rhynchos* (beak) and *stylis* (column), in reference to the beaked column of the flowers of the type species.

TAXONOMY *Rhynchostylis* was described by C.L. Blume in 1825 in *Bijdragen* (p. 286). This small genus vegetatively resembles *Aerides* and also has rather similar inflorescences of closely-packed flowers, but its stem is shorter and its leaves thicker. The lip is not sharply delimited from the column-foot as in *Aerides*, the spur points backwards and the lip is only slightly lobed. When not in flower the pale lines on the leaves serve to distinguish it from *Aerides*.

Some botanists include all the species of *Rhynchostylis* in *Saccolabium* whilst R. Schlechter included *R. violacea* and *R. gigantea* (Lindl.) Ridley in his genus *Anota*. However, these species do not lack a column-foot as he stated, the column-foot is merely greatly reduced. R. Holttum reviewed the genus in the *Orchid Journal* (1953) and discussed in detail its affinities. In his account he recognises four species in the genus and provides a key for their identification.

TYPE SPECIES *R. retusa* (L.) Blume
CULTURE Compost A. Temp. Winter min. 15°C. As for *Aerides* or *Vanda*. The plants require high humidity, moderate shade and plenty of water while growing with less water when the roots become inactive. They are best grown in hanging baskets so that the numerous aerial roots can hang freely.

Rhynchostylis gigantea (Lindl.) Ridley
[Colour Plate]

Stem stout, 15–20 cm long, 2 cm in diameter. **Roots** stout, 1.2–1.8 cm in diameter. **Leaves** imbricating at the base, linear, very thick, channelled, apical lobes acute, 15–35 cm long, 3.7–7.5 cm broad, striped pale and darker green. **Inflorescences** 2–4, with a very short, stout peduncle; raceme cylindric, densely many-flowered, pendulous, 20–35 cm long; bracts ovate-triangular. **Flowers** 2.5–3.1 cm across, fragrant, white ± with a few purple spots all over, to dark violet; lip white with bright purple terminal lobes. **Sepals** elliptic-oblong, obtuse or rounded, 1.5–1.7 cm long, 0.8–1 cm broad. **Petals** similar to the sepals, 1.5 cm long, 0.6 cm broad. **Lip** 3-lobed at apex, cuneate, fleshy, slightly pubescent, 1.4 cm long, 0.8 cm broad; disc with 2 pubescent ridges descending into the spur; spur short, inflated, backward-pointing. **Column** 2 mm long, with an indistinct foot.

DISTRIBUTION Burma, Indo-China and Thailand.

HISTORY Discovered by Dr N. Wallich near Prome, Burma and described by John Lindley in 1833 in *Genera and Species of Orchidaceous Plants* (p. 221) as *Saccolabium giganteum*. Ridley transferred it to *Rhynchostylis* in 1896 in the *Journal of the Linnean Society* (p. 356).

Pure white and pure rose-purple-flowered forms are known.

SYNONYMS include *Saccolabium giganteum* Lindl.; *Vanda densiflora* Lindl.

Rhynchostylis retusa (L.) Blume
[Colour Plate]

A very variable epiphytic herb. **Stem** stout, repent, up to 12-leaved, fairly short, up to 1 cm broad. **Leaves** curved, fleshy, ligulate, deeply channelled, keeled, praemorse or retuse at apex, 15–50 cm long, 1.6–5 cm broad. **Inflorescences** drooping, racemose, densely many-flowered, 10–45 cm long. **Flowers** 1.2–1.8 cm across; sepals and petals white, spotted with pink or violet; lip purple above, white at base; spur pale mauve. **Dorsal sepal** oblong, acute, 1.2 cm long, 0.7 cm broad; **lateral sepals** gibbously orbicular-ovate, obtuse or apiculate, up to 1 cm broad. **Petals** elliptic, obtuse, 1.2 cm long, 0.6 cm broad. **Lip** concave, 1.2 cm long, 0.8 cm broad; epichile variable in size, cuneiform, entire or emarginate at the apex; disc flat or obscurely canaliculate; spur saccate, longer than the limb of the lip, 0.8 cm long. **Column** with an indistinct foot.

DISTRIBUTION India, Burma, Sri Lanka to Malaya, Indo-China and the Philippines.

HISTORY Originally described in 1753 as *Epidendrum retusum* by Carl von Linné in *Species Plantarum* (p. 953), based on Rheede's drawing of an Indian plant, but transferred by C.L. Blume to *Rhynchostylis* in 1825 in his *Bijdragen* (p. 286). It was introduced from Java in 1838–39 by Messrs Loddiges but John Lindley recorded its earlier cultivation under the name *Sarcanthus guttatus* when he saw a plant which had been cultivated at Kew in Sir Joseph Banks's library.

SYNONYMS include *Rhynchostylis praemorsa* Blume; *R. guttata* Rchb.f.; *R. garwalica* Rchb.f.;

Saccolabium guttatum Lindl.; *S. praemorsum* Lindl.; *S. rheedii* Wight; *S. retusum* (L.) Lemaire; *S. heathii* Hort.; *S. blumei* Lindl.; *S. garwalicum* Lindl.; *Sarcanthus guttatus* Lindl.; *Aerides guttatum* Roxb.; *A. retusum* (L.) Sw.; *A. spicatum* D. Don; *A. praemorsum* Willd.; *Limodorum retusum* Sw.; *Epidendrum retusum* L.

Robiquetia Gaud.
Subfamily Epidendroideae
Tribe Vandeae
Subtribe Sarcanthinae

Epiphytic herbs with usually pendulous short or long stems. **Leaves** distichous, oblique, oblong or narrowly elliptic. **Inflorescences** racemose, conical or cylindrical, moderately long, usually pendulous, many-flowered. **Flowers** small. **Sepals** and **petals** free; dorsal sepal cucullate over column. **Lip** immovably joined to column, 3-lobed, spurred below; side lobes small, ± fleshily thickened, ± joined to column on posterior margin; mid-lobe small, tapering or linear, fleshy, concave, often with a ridge at the base; spur rather long, ± cylindrical, often bent and flattened, aseptate, ecallose but sometimes thickened on back wall. Column footless, short, ± bent backwards at top; pollinia 2, round, ± cleft; stipe 1, dilated above; viscidium small.

DISTRIBUTION A genus of some 30–40 species widespread from S.E. Asia, Indonesia, the Philippines, Australia and the Pacific Islands.
DERIVATION OF NAME Named in honour of a French chemist, Pierre Robiquet, who discovered, amongst other chemicals, caffeine and morphine.
TAXONOMY *Robiquetia* was established by Charles Gaudichaud in 1826 in Louis de Freycinet's *Voyage sur l'Uranie et la Physicienne* (p. 426, t. 34). *Robiquetia* is distinguished from other monopodial sarcanthoid orchid genera by its bottle-brush-like, racemose inflorescence and flowers in which the lip has an entire mid-lobe and is spurred, but the spur lacks appendages within.
TYPE SPECIES *R. ascendens* Gaud.
CULTURE Compost A or mounted. Temp. Winter min. 12–15°C. *Robiquetia* species may be grown in pans or mounted on slabs of cork-bark etc. They require good humidity and moderate shade with plenty of water while growing and less when growth is complete.

Robiquetia spathulata (Blume) J.J. Smith
[Colour Plate]
A medium-sized epiphytic plant. **Stem** hanging, up to 50 cm long, nodes 2–3 cm apart.

Leaves twisted at the base so that the blades lie in 1 plane, obovate-oblong, 12–20 cm long, 4–5 cm broad, unequally 2-lobed at apex. **Inflorescences** pendulous, up to 25 cm long, densely many-flowered; bracts narrow, reflexed, up to 0.5 cm long. **Flowers** small; sepals and petals yellow, heavily marked red-brown on side lobes and mid-lobe and spotted red-brown on spur; column white. **Dorsal sepal** concave, elliptic, obtuse, 0.5 cm long, 0.35 cm broad; **lateral sepals** falcate, elliptic, obtuse or rounded, 0.65 cm long, 0.4 cm broad. **Petals** obovate, obtuse, 0.4 cm long, 0.4 cm broad; side lobes erect, oblong-subquadrate; mid-lobe porrect, ovate or triangular, apiculate, thickened and narrowed at the apex; spur broad at the mouth, dilated and truncate at the apex, 0.5 cm long, with a fleshy callus on the ventral inner side towards the apex. **Column** short, stout, 0.25 cm long.

DISTRIBUTION Burma, Thailand, Malaya, Indonesia across to the Philippines; commonly in lowland riverine forest.
HISTORY Described originally in 1825 as *Cleisostoma spathulatum* by C. Blume in his *Bijdragen* (p. 364), based on his own collection from Pantjar in Java. J.J. Smith transferred it to *Robiquetia* in 1912 in *Natuurkundig Tijdschrift voor Nederlandsch-Indië* (p. 114).
SYNONYMS *Cleisostoma spathulatum* Blume; *C. spicatum* Lindl; *Saccolabium densiflorum* Lindl.

Rodriguezia Ruiz & Pavon
Subfamily Epidendroideae
Tribe Oncidieae

Epiphytic plants with elongated rhizomes. **Pseudobulbs** short, ovoid, compressed, distant or approximate, usually covered by leaf-bearing sheaths, 1- or 2-leaved at apex. **Leaves** coriaceous. **Inflorescences** lateral, 1 to several, few- to many-flowered, racemose. **Flowers** medium-sized to large, ± showy. **Dorsal sepal** and **petals** similar; **lateral sepals** variously connate, ± gibbose. **Lip** clawed, ± shortly connate to the column-base, produced into a short spur at the base; lamina obovate; disc ± cristate. **Column** slender, lacking a foot, apically dilated and winged; pollinia 2, waxy, attached by a narrow stipe to a small viscidium.

DISTRIBUTION About 35 species or less in the American tropics and most numerous in Brazil.
DERIVATION OF NAME Dedicated to the Spanish botanist and royal apothecary Don Manuel Rodriguez.
TAXONOMY *Rodriguezia* was established by H. Ruiz and José Pavon in 1794 in *Prodromus Florae Peruvianae et Chilensis* (p. 115, t. 25). It is

allied to *Ionopsis* and *Trichocentrum*, differing from the former in having a spurred, saccate or appendaged base to the lip and from the latter in having connate lateral sepals.

R. Schlechter reviewed the generic limits of *Rodriguezia* in *Fedde, Repertorium Specierum Novarum* (1919–20) and provided a key to separate *Rodriguezia* from *Rodrigueziella* and *Capanemia*. The Brazilian species have been treated in six groups by G. Pabst and F. Dungs in their *Orchidaceae Brasilienses* (1977) as follows:

1. *R. maculata* alliance – lip lacking a spur; rhizome short.
2. *R. decora* alliance – as group 1 but rhizome up to 30 cm long.
3. *R. lanceolata* alliance – lip with a spur; flowers small, lip up to 1.5 cm long.
4. *R. bracteata* alliance – lip with a spur; flowers larger, lip more than 2 cm long and with 2–4 keels.
5. *R. candida* alliance – as group 4 but lip with 0.8–10 keels; spur 0.2–0.4 cm long.
6. *R. leeana* – as group 5 but lip with a spur 0.8–1 cm long.

No attempt has been made by the authors formally to recognise these groupings and they may not reflect the true affinities of the species but are merely useful in subdividing the genus for identification purposes.
TYPE SPECIES *R. lanceolata* Ruiz & Pavon (lectotype).
SYNONYMS *Burlingtonia* Lindl.; *Physanthera* Steud.
CULTURE Compost A. Temp. Winter min. 12–15°C. Apart from *R. decora*, which is best mounted on a slab of fern-fibre or cork, *Rodriguezia* species should be grown in small pans. They all require humid conditions under moderate shade. Water may be freely given while the plants are growing, but much less is needed at other times.

Rodriguezia batemannii Poepp. & Endl.
A very variable, small to medium-sized herb with a creeping, simple or branching rhizome. **Pseudobulbs** distant, cylindric, compressed, 3–5 cm long, 1-leafed at apex, ± concealed by 1-3 pairs of distichous, leaf-bearing conduplicate sheaths. **Leaves** oblong to linear, acute or apiculate, thickly coriaceous, 7–35 cm long, 3 cm broad. **Inflorescences** axillary, flexuous or pendent, shorter than the leaves, racemose, laxly few- to many-flowered. **Flowers** variable in size and colour, white, white and yellow or lilac, ± spotted with lilac. **Dorsal sepal** oblong-lanceolate or narrowly elliptic, acute, 1.6–2.5 cm long, 0.8–1.2 cm broad; **lateral sepals** connate, deeply concave, oblong-lanceolate, bidentate at the apex, 2–3 cm long. **Petals** obliquely elliptic-lanceolate, rounded to acute at the apex, up to 2.5 cm long. **Lip**

simple, cuneate-obovate, emarginate, 1.8–3.5 cm long, 0.9–2.2 cm broad, produced at the base into a short, fleshy horn; disc with a pair of fleshy lamellae curving onto the lateral dilations. **Column** slender, ± pubescent, clavate. 0.8–1.1 cm long, auriculate above.

DISTRIBUTION   Peru.

HISTORY   Discovered at Yumaguas Mission in Maynas Province of Peru by E.F. Poeppig and described by him and S.L. Endlicher in their *Nova Genera ac Species* (p. 41, t. 70) in 1836.

SYNONYMS   *Burlingtonia rubescens* Lindl.; *Burlingtonia batemannii* Cogn.; *Rodriguezia candida* Rchb.f. var. *batemannii* Hort.

Rodriguezia candida **Lindl.** [Colour Plate]

A medium-sized epiphytic plant with a repent or scandent habit. **Pseudobulbs** ovoid-ellipsoid, strongly compressed, ridged down the middle, approximate on the rigid rhizome, up to 3 cm long, 1.3 cm broad, 1-leafed at apex, subtended by 2–3 leaf-bearing sheaths. **Leaves** oblong to elliptic-oblong, ± unequally, obtusely 2-lobed at apex, spreading, rigid-coriaceous, 9–15 cm long, 2–3 cm broad. **Inflorescence** arcuate to pendent, racemose, few-flowered. **Flowers** showy, large; sepals, petals and column white; lip white with a clear yellow disc. **Dorsal sepal** obovate, rounded or obtuse and concave at the apex, 3 cm long, 1.3 cm broad; **lateral sepals** united to the apex; lamina abruptly curved in the basal part, deeply concave and unspreadable, bifid at the apex, 3 cm long. **Petals** obliquely obovate, truncate and ± emarginate at the apex, 3.3 cm long, 1.7 cm broad, mid-nerve dorsally thickened in basal half. **Lip** clawed, obovate-oblong above, deeply emarginate, 5.4 cm long, 2.7 cm broad; claw margins rigid, involute; callus fleshy, a raised broad ridge in the basal part of the lamina. **Column** slender, dilated and auriculate at the apex, 2 cm long.

DISTRIBUTION   Brazil, Guyana and Venezuela.

HISTORY   Introduced from Demerara (now Georgetown) by James Bateman who flowered it at Knypersley, England, in April 1835. It was described by John Lindley in 1837 in the *Botanical Register* (sub t. 1927). The Schomburgk brothers found it shortly afterwards near the Demerara River in Guyana.

SYNONYM   *Burlingtonia candida* (Lindl.) Lindl.

Rodriguezia decora **(Lemaire) Rchb.f.**
[Colour Plate]

A small epiphytic plant with a slender, scandent, jointed rhizome. **Pseudobulbs** produced at intervals of about 12 cm or more on the rhizome, ovoid, compressed, 2.5 cm long, 1-leafed at apex and base on 1 side. **Leaves** linear-oblong, acute, about 15 cm long. **Inflorescences** from axils of basal leaves, erect, 30–40 cm long, racemose, 5- to 15-flowered; bracts small, membranaceous, sheathing. **Flowers** 3.5 cm long; sepals and petals white, spotted with brown; lip white; column with purple apical horns. **Dorsal sepal** elliptic-oblong, 1.2 cm long, 0.4 cm broad; **lateral sepals** narrowly oblong, connate to above the middle, apiculate, 1.5 cm long. **Petals** elliptic-oblong, slightly concave, obliquely shortly acuminate, 1.4 cm long, 0.6 cm broad. **Lip** broadly clawed, suborbicular and bilobulate above, 2.5–2.8 cm long, 1.1–1.4 cm broad; callus with 5 raised lines; spur 0.2 cm long, obtuse. **Column** terete, prolonged at apex into 2 erect, hairy horns and 2 smaller paler ones.

DISTRIBUTION   Brazil.

HISTORY   First collected by J. Libon for J. de Jonghe in São Paulo State of S. Brazil and described by C. Lemaire as *Burlingtonia decora* in *Le Jardin Fleuriste* (misc. 96) in 1852. H.G. Reichenbach transferred it to the genus *Rodriguezia* later the same year in the *Botanische Zeitung* (p. 771). It was first flowered in cultivation by Jacob Makoy of Liège in May 1851.

SYNONYMS   *Burlington decora* Lemaire; *B. amoena* Planchon

Rodriguezia lanceolata **Ruiz & Pavon**
[Colour Plate]

An erect epiphytic herb. **Pseudobulbs** oblong-elliptic, compressed, 2–3.5 cm long, 1–1.6 cm across, 1-leafed at apex, almost covered by conduplicate, imbricate leaf-sheaths. **Leaves** coriaceous or rather fleshy, linear-ligulate to elliptic-oblong, subacute to obtuse, 7–24 cm long, 1–3.5 cm broad. **Inflorescences** 1–6, erect or arcuate, racemose, 15–38 cm long, many-flowered. **Flowers** fairly small, pink to rose-red. **Dorsal sepal** ovate, concave, minutely apiculate or subacute, 0.9–1.2 cm long, 0.5–0.6 cm broad; lateral sepals connate to the apex, gibbous at the base, 1–1.5 cm long, 0.6 cm broad. **Petals** obovate, acute or apiculate, 0.9–1.2 cm long, 0.6 cm broad. **Lip** obscurely clawed, entire; the biauriculate claw adnate to the base of the column and produced into a short spur below; lamina oblong-obovate, with undulate margins, 1.2–1.5 cm long, 0.5–0.7 cm broad, apex deeply emarginate; callus fleshy, prominent, bicarinate. **Column** sub-cylindric, with a dilated apex, bidentate ventrally at the apex.

DISTRIBUTION   Panama, Colombia, Ecuador, Peru, Venezuela, Guyana, Surinam and Trinidad.

HISTORY   Originally collected at Pozuzo, Peru by J. Pavon and described by Ruiz and Pavon in their *Systema Vegetabilium Florae Peruviana et Chilensis* (p. 219) in 1798. This species is commonly found in cultivation under the later name *R. secunda* H.B.K.

SYNONYMS   *Pleurothallis coccinea* Hooker; *Rodriguezia lanceolata* Lodd.; *R. secunda* H.B.K.

Rodrigueziella **O. Ktze.**
Subfamily Epidendroideae
Tribe Oncidieae

Small epiphytic herbs. **Pseudobulbs** leafy at apex, ovoid-conical, clustered. **Leaves** sub-erect, linear-lanceolate to narrowly elliptic-lanceolate, acuminate. **Inflorescences** ascending to arcuate, racemose, laxly many-flowered. **Flowers** small, spreading or drooping; bracts often conspicuous. **Sepals** and **petals** free, subsimilar. **Lip** reflexed, ± entire, with 2 basal, ± pubescent calli. **Column** short, semiterete; pollinia 2 ovoid-pyriform; stipe ovate; viscidium minute.

DISTRIBUTION   About five species in Brazil.

DERIVATION OF NAME   Dedicated to Dr João Barbosa Rodrigues, the author of *Orchidearum Novarum* (1877–82) where many new species and genera of Brazilian orchids were described.

TAXONOMY   Established by O. Kuntze in 1891 in his *Revisio Genera Plantarum* (p. 649) to replace the name *Theodorea* Barb. Rodr. (1877) which had already been used for a genus *Theodorea* Cassini (1818) in the Compositae.

Rodrigueziella is closely allied to *Gomesa* being distinguished by its much more obvious rostellum and often recurved column which does not widen apically.

TYPE SPECIES   *Theodorea gomezoides* Barb. Rodr. [= *Rodrigueziella gomezoides* (Barb. Rodr.) O. Ktze.].

CULTURE   Compost A. Temp. Winter min. 12–15°C. As for *Gomesa*. These small plants may be grown in pots or mounted on pieces of cork or fern-fibre. They need good humidity and moderate shade with plenty of water while growing and less when growth is complete.

Rodrigueziella gomezoides **(Barb. Rodr.) O. Ktze.** [Colour Plate]

A small epiphytic plant. **Pseudobulbs** elongate, compressed, semitranslucent, 2-leaved. **Leaves** linear-lanceolate, acuminate, 7–15 cm long, 0.6–1.3 cm broad. **Inflorescence** a little shorter than the leaves, spreading-arcuate, 8–15 cm long, laxly many-flowered; bracts longer than the ovary, lanceolate, acuminate. **Flowers** pendulous; sepals and petals yellow-green with a brown base; lip white with a yellow or orange callus. **Sepals** free, linear-lanceolate, acuminate, 0.9–1.1 cm long, 0.2 cm broad. **Petals** similar to the sepals but smaller. **Lip** clawed, lanceolate, acuminate, abruptly reflexed, 0.7–0.9 cm long, 0.3 cm broad; callus in reflexed part, bicristate, sulcate, pubescent, with fimbriate margins. **Column** short, erect, dentate at the base, 0.3 cm long.

DISTRIBUTION   E. Brazil.

HISTORY   Discovered in the forests of the Serra dos Poços in Minas Gerais State and also at S. João da Boa Vista in São Paulo State by J. Barbosa Rodrigues and described by him in 1877 in his *Genera et Species Orchidearum Novarum* (p. 144) as *Theodorea gomezoides*. The specific epithet refers to the flower colour of the species which is similar to that found in *Gomesa* species. Indeed, A. Cogniaux included it in the genus *Gomesa* in Martius's *Flora Brasiliensis* as *Gomesa theodorea*.

O. Kuntze transferred the species to *Rodrigueziella* in 1891 in his *Revisio Genera Plantarum* (p. 649).

SYNONYMS   *Gomesa theodorea* Cogn.; *Theodorea gomezoides* Barb. Rodr.

Rossioglossum (Schltr.) Garay & Kennedy

Subfamily Epidenroideae
Tribe Oncidieae

Medium-sized to large epiphytic plants with a short rhizome. **Pseudobulbs** approximate, ovoid, 2-leaved. **Leaves** large, broadly elliptic, petiolate. **Inflorescences** lateral, longly pedunculate, laxly racemose above; bracts linear, very short. **Flowers** large, showy, mainly yellow, marked with red-brown; perianth segments spreading widely. **Sepals** and **petals** subsimilar or with petals broader. **Lip** free, pandurate, deflexed, forming with the column a right-angle; side lobes auriculate; mid-lobe much larger; callus basal, fleshy, several-lobed. **Column** erect, slightly arcuate; outgrowths on each side of stigmatic cavity linear and falcate-incurved, canaliculate or produced into a plate below the stigma; rostellum short; pollinia 2; stipe narrowly triangular; viscidium small.

DISTRIBUTION   A small genus of six species in Central America from Mexico south to Panama.

DERIVATION OF NAME   Named in honour of John Ross who collected orchids in Mexico between 1830 and 1840.

TAXONOMY   This genus was originally considered by R. Schlechter in *Orchis* (1916) to be a section of the large genus *Odontoglossum*. However, in 1976, L. Garay and G. Kennedy in the *Orchid Digest* (p. 142) decided that the species of this section did not conform with the generic description of *Odontoglossum* and they

therefore raised Schlechter's section to generic rank as *Rossioglossum*. *Rossioglossum* may be readily distinguished from *Odontoglossum* by its free (rather than partly adnate) lip which forms a right-angle with the column; the auriculate basal lobes of the lip; the distinctive callus; and the basal structure of the column.

TYPE SPECIES   *R. grande* (Lindl.) Garay & Kennedy [syn. *Odontoglossum grande* Lindl.].

SYNONYMS   *Odontoglossum sect. Rossioglossum* Schltr.; *O.* sect. *Grandia* Pfitz.; *O.* sect. *Rossiorchis* O. Ktze.

CULTURE   As for larger *Oncidium* species.

Rossioglossum grande (Lindl.) Garay & Kennedy [Colour Plate]

A coarse epiphytic plant, up to 40 cm tall, with a short rhizome. **Pseudobulbs** clustered, ovoid or orbicular, compressed, ancipitous, 4–10 cm long, 3–6 cm across, 1- to 3-leaved at apex, glaucous. **Leaves** elliptic or lanceolate, coriaceous, glaucous, 10–40 cm long, 3–6.5 cm broad, acute. **Inflorescence** up to 30 cm long, 4- to 8-flowered; bracts lanceolate, appressed, scarious, 3.5–4.5 cm long. **Flowers** showy, large; sepals yellow, barred and flecked red-brown; petals yellow, red-brown in basal half with yellow margins; lip cream, flecked red-brown. **Sepals** lanceolate, 5.5–8.5 cm long, 1–2 cm broad, acute or acuminate, margins undulate. **Petals** oblong-elliptic to oblanceolate, 5–8 cm long, 1.8–3.2 cm broad, acute or obtuse, margins undulate. **Lip** sessile, pandurate, unequally 3-lobed, 2.5–4.3 cm long; side lobes basal, auriculate, 0.5 cm long; mid-lobe shortly clawed, suborbicular-quadrate, emarginate, 2–3.7 cm broad; disc with a fleshy quadrate 2-lobed callus between side lobes. **Column** puberulent, with a convex incurved wing on each side at apex, 1–1.5 cm long.

DISTRIBUTION   Guatemala and Mexico; uncommon in forests up to 2700 m altitude.

HISTORY   Discovered by George Ure Skinner near Guatemala City and described as *Odontoglossum grande* by John Lindley in the *Botanical Register* (misc. p. 47) in 1840. L. Garay and G. Kennedy transferred it to the genus *Rossioglossum* in the *Orchid Digest* (p. 142) in 1976.

SYNONYM   *Odontoglossum grande* Lindl.

CLOSELY RELATED SPECIES   *R. grande* is often confused with *R. williamsianum* but it may be distinguished by its larger flowers and rounded column-wings.

Rossioglossum insleayi (Barker ex Lindl.) Garay & Kennedy [Colour Plate]

Pseudobulbs ovoid, compressed, 7.5–10 cm long, 2- or 3-leaved at apex. **Leaves** oblong-elliptic, 10–12.5 cm long. **Inflorescence** erect, up to 30 cm long, 5- to 10-flowered. **Flowers** up to 9 cm across; sepals and petals dull yel-

low, barred and blotched with red-brown; lip yellow, barred red on claw of mid-lobe and spotted red around the margins; callus yellow, spotted red. **Sepals** narrowly oblong-elliptic, apiculate. **Petals** slightly falcate, narrowly oblong-oblanceolate, obtuse, margins recurved. **Lip** 3-lobed; side lobes auriculate, upcurved; mid-lobe narrowly clawed, flabellate-spathulate, margins undulate; callus between side lobes fleshy, obscurely 2-lobed at front. **Column** erect, short, with apical, incurving filamentous horns.

DISTRIBUTION   Mexico.

HISTORY   Discovered in 1838 or 1839 by John Ross who sent living plants of it to George Barker of Birmingham. Barker flowered it successfully and sent a specimen to John Lindley who described it as *Oncidium insleayi* in 1840 in the *Botanical Register* (misc. no. 21), naming it at the owner's suggestion after Mr Insleay who was Barker's head gardener. Little was heard of this species after this until 1866 when it was reintroduced by Messrs Low & Co. with a better understanding of its cultural requirement. This introduction met with greater success than the earlier ones. The intermediate nature of *O. insleayi* is emphasised by the fact that Lindley transferred it from *Oncidium* to *Odontoglossum* in 1852 in *Folia Orchidacea* and in 1976 L. Garay and G. Kennedy transferred it to the new genus *Rossioglossum* in the *Orchid Digest* (p. 142).

SYNONYMS   *Oncidium insleayi* Barker ex Lindl.; *Odontoglossum insleayi* (Barker ex Lindl.) Lindl.

Rossioglossum schlieperianum (Rchb.f.) Garay & Kennedy [Colour Plate]

Pseudobulbs ovoid, compressed, 7.5–10 cm long, 2- to 3-leaved at apex. **Leaves** elliptic-oblong, 10–12.5 cm long. **Inflorescence** erect, 2- to 8-flowered, up to 25 cm tall. **Flowers** large, showy, 7–8 cm across; sepals and petals yellow or greenish-yellow, barred with red-brown in basal half; lip similarly coloured, callus bright yellow, marked with red. **Sepals** lanceolate to elliptic-lanceolate, margins incurved, slightly acute. **Petals** oblong-elliptic, margins slightly undulate, acute or subacute. **Lip** obscurely 3-lobed, oblong-pandurate to spathulate, emarginate; side lobes auriculate, erect; mid-lobe oblong-spathulate, side margins recurved, obtuse at apex. **Column** erect, short, with filamentous, incurving horns at apex.

DISTRIBUTION   Costa Rica and Panama.

HISTORY   First introduced from Central America in 1856 when it appeared amongst a miscellaneous group of orchids up for sale at Stevens' Sale Rooms. Subsequently, it was re-collected in Costa Rica by H. Wendland of Herrenhausen, Germany. Although first described by John Lindley as a variety of *Odonto-*

glossum insleayi, it was given specific rank by H.G. Reichenbach in 1865 in the *Gardeners' Chronicle* (p. 1082). Reichenbach named it in honour of Herr Schlieper of Elberfeld who was amongst the first to flower it in cultivation. In 1976 L. Garay and G. Kennedy transferred this species to the genus *Rossioglossum* in the *Orchid Digest* (p. 143).

SYNONYMS *Odontoglossum schlieperianum* Rchb.f.; *O. warscewiczii* Bridges; *O. insleayi* var. *macranthum* Lindl.; *O. lawrenceanum* Hort.

Rossioglossum williamsianum (Rchb.f.) Garay & Kennedy [Colour Plate]

An epiphytic plant, up to 60 cm tall. **Pseudobulbs** oblong-ellipsoid, compressed, 9–10 cm long, 4–5 cm broad, 1- or 2-leaved at apex. **Leaves** elliptic, coriaceous, 40 cm long, 7–8 cm broad, subacute or obtuse, shortly petiolate. **Inflorescence** erect, up to 60 cm long, 6- to 8-flowered; bracts spathaceous, 2–2.5 cm long, subacuminate. **Flowers** showy; sepals yellow, barred with red-brown; petals yellow in apical half and on margins below, brown below; lip yellow, spotted with brown, callus spotted orange; column yellow. **Sepals** elliptic-lanceolate, margins undulate, 4–5.2 cm long, 1–2 cm broad, apex acute and recurved; lateral sepals oblique, united for basal 0.5 cm. **Petals** shortly clawed, oblong-elliptic above, 3.3–5 cm long, 1.8–2.8 cm broad, apiculate or rounded. **Lip** sessile, broadly pandurate, 2.5–3.5 cm long, 1.7–2.7 cm broad; side lobes small, subquadrate, revolute, 0.5 cm long; mid-lobe clawed, suborbicular-obovate, emarginate; callus on claw, fleshy, 2-lobed, with 2 additional blunt teeth at base. **Column** stout, 1–1.3 cm long. ± pubescent; wings uncinate.

DISTRIBUTION Guatemala, Costa Rica and Honduras; rare in rain forests up to 1000 m altitude.

HISTORY Described by H.G. Reichenbach as *Odontoglossum williamsianum* in the *Gardeners' Chronicle* (s. 3, 34: p. 134) in 1890 but in 1976 transferred by L. Garay and G. Kennedy to the genus *Rossioglossum* in the *Orchid Digest* (p. 143).

SYNONYMS *Odontoglossum williamsianum* Rchb.f.; *O. grande* var. *williamsiamum* Rchb.f.

CLOSELY RELATED SPECIES Distinguished from *R. grande* by its uncinate column-wings; longer inflorescence; smaller flowers; and shorter, broadly-rounded petals.

Rudolfiella Hoehne
Subfamily Epidendroideae
Tribe Maxillarieae
Subtribe Zygopetalinae

Small to medium-sized epiphytic herbs. **Pseudobulbs** ovoid or almost circular, flattened with a terminal, plicate, petiolate leaf. **Inflorescence** lateral, very lax, several-flowered, simple. **Flowers** ± showy, with spreading or somewhat incurved tepals. **Sepals** and **petals** free; lateral sepals attached at base to column-foot to form a rectangular mentum. **Lip** markedly 3-lobed with a narrow basal claw and a central fleshy callus; mid-lobe strongly thickened towards the base. **Column** lacking wings, somewhat arcuate, with a conspicuous foot; pollinia 4, waxy; stipites 2, oblong, short; viscidium 1.

DISTRIBUTION About five species in tropical S. America and Panama.

DERIVATION OF NAME The genus is dedicated to Dr Rudolf Schlechter (1872–1925), the eminent German orchid taxonomist.

TAXONOMY *Rudolfiella* was established by F.C. Hoehne in *Arquivos de Botánicos do Estado de São Paulo* (p. 14) in 1944. The genus is included by some authors such as L. Garay and G.C.K. Dunsterville in *Venezuelan Orchids Illustrated*, vol. 1 (1959) in *Bifrenaria* but most recent accounts, such as G. Pabst and F. Dungs in *Orchidaceae Brasilienses*, vol. 2 (1977), have kept these genera apart. They distinguish *Rudolfiella* from *Bifrenaria* by its flattened pseudobulbs; flowers with a rectangular mentum; and the deeply 3-lobed lip with its small raised callus between the side lobes.

TYPE SPECIES *R. aurantiaca* (Lindl.) Hoehne

CULTURE Compost A. Temp. Winter min. 12–16°C. During growth, species should be given warm, humid conditions and moderate shade, with plenty of water at the roots. When the pseudobulbs are fully formed, the plants require less warmth and much less water.

Rudolfiella aurantiaca (Lindl.) Hoehne [Colour Plate]

A medium-sized epiphytic herb. **Pseudobulbs** clustered, ovoid-orbicular, compressed, obscurely 4-angled, 5 cm long, 4 cm broad, 1-leafed at apex. **Leaf** petiolate, suberect, oblong-cuneate, acute, 10–20 cm long; 3–5 cm broad. **Inflorescence** up to 30 cm long, laxly up to about 15-flowered. **Flowers** showy, orange or yellow-orange, spotted with brown. **Sepals** oblong-ovate, acute to obtuse, 1.2–1.3 cm long, 0.4–0.6 cm broad. **Lip** long-clawed, 3-lobed in the middle, 1.2–1.5 cm long; side lobes erect,

obovate-arcuate; mid-lobe transversely oblong, minutely apiculate, 0.8 cm broad; callus pubescent below, 3-lobed at apex. **Column** slightly pubescent, 0.8–0.9 cm long.

DISTRIBUTION Guyana, Venezuela and Trinidad.

HISTORY This species was originally described by John Lindley in 1836 in the *Botanical Register* (t. 1875) as *Bifrenaria aurantiaca* from a plant collected in Demerara (now Georgetown), Guyana which flowered in October 1835 in the collection of the Duke of Devonshire at Chiswick, London. It was transferred by F.C. Hoehne to the present genus in 1944 in the *Archivos de Botánicos do Estado de São Paulo* (p. 14).

SYNONYMS *Lindleyella aurantiaca* (Lindl.) Schltr.; *Bifrenaria aurantiaca* Lindl.

Sarcochilus R. Br.
Subfamily Epidendroideae
Tribe Vandeae
Subtribe Sarcanthinae

Epiphytic or lithophytic plants with short stems, usually horizontal or ascending. **Leaves** 2-ranked, often spreading and drooping, unequally 2-lobed at apex. **Inflorescence** few- to many-flowered, racemose or spicate. **Flowers** showy, fragrant, moderately short-lived, usually wide opening, facing all ways or 2-ranked, opening 1 at a time or a few together. **Sepals** and **petals** free, subsimilar; lateral sepals ± joined to the column-foot for a short distance. **Lip** hinged to the apex of the column-foot, shallowly saccate, 3-lobed; side lobes large, usually narrow, erect, curved; mid-lobe small and fleshy, ± 3-lobed; basal sac almost filled by a callus attached along mid-line of sac, ± continuing the line of the column-foot. **Column** short or fairly short; foot mostly well-developed, joined to lateral sepals; pollinia 4 in 2 pairs; stipe rather short; viscidium small, circular or elliptic.

DISTRIBUTION About 16 species mainly confined to N. and E. Australia and New Caledonia.

DERIVATION OF NAME From the Greek *sarx* (flesh) and *cheilos* (lip), in allusion to the fleshy lip of the type species.

TAXONOMY *Sarcochilus* was established in 1810 by Robert Brown in his *Prodromus* (p. 332) based on a single Australian species *S. falcatus*. It is closely allied to several other Asiatic sarcanthoid genera including *Gastrochilus* D. Don, *Pteroceras* Hassk. and *Thrixspermum* Lour. but it is characterised by having 4 (rather than 2) pollinia in 2 pairs on a stipe which is not greatly elongated; a long column-foot in part joined to the lateral sepals and with the lip distinctly joined to it; a rather shallowly saccate lip which is almost filled by a callus attached along the mid-line of the sac; and by the large side lobes and small fleshy mid-lobe of the lip.

Historically the genus has been the cause of great confusion and at various times has been taken to include *Chiloschista* Lindl., *Gunnia* Lindl., *Dendrocolla* Blume, *Ornitharium* Rchb.f., *Grosourdya* Rchb.f., *Cylindrochilus* Thio., *Micropera* Lindl., and *Camarotis* Lindl., whilst *Sarcochilus* itself was considered a synonym of *Thrixspermum* Lour. by H.G. Reichenbach in *Xenia Orchidacea* (1867).

Several botanists, notably J.J. Smith and R. Schlechter, have attempted to reduce *Sarcochilus* to a more natural genus and their attempts have been summarised and established by R. Holttum in the *Kew Bulletin* (1960). There he indicated that his earlier treatment of *Sarcochilus* in the *Orchids of Malaya* (1957) was unsatisfactory as the Asian and Indonesian species differ markedly from the Australian species. In his opinion *Sarcochilus* is almost entirely an Australian genus and he refers the extra-Australian species to *Pteroceras* Hassk. A. Dockrill follows this treatment in *Australian Indigenous Orchids* (1969). The most recent accounts of the genus are by D. Jones (1988) in *Native Orchids of Australia* and M. Clements (1989) in his *Catalogue of Australian Orchidaceae* and their treatments of the genus are followed here.

TYPE SPECIES *S. falcatus* R. Br.
SYNONYM *Gunnia* Lindl.
CULTURE Compost A. Temp. Winter min. 12–15°C. Those species with an erect habit of growth are best grown in pans or baskets, while more pendent species would be better on slabs of fern-fibre or cork. All species should be given conditions of high humidity and moderate shade while growing but water needs to be carefully given when growth is complete.

Sarcochilus fitzgeraldii F. Muell.
[Colour Plate]
An epiphytic or lithophytic herb. **Stem** rather long, somewhat branched, 0.5–0.6 cm in diameter, covered by fibres of old leaf-bases below and bearing a tuft of leaves at apex. **Roots** numerous, long, green, adventitious. **Leaves** thin-textured and drooping, narrowly oblong-ligulate to ligulate, 6–16 cm long, 1 cm broad, acute, rich dark green. **Inflorescences** horizontal to pendent or rarely erect, up to 22 cm long, 4- to 6-flowered; peduncle slender, terete; rhachis somewhat zigzag; bracts ± spreading, triangular, acute, 0.2–0.5 cm long. **Flowers** spreading; sepals and petals white, pink or rarely pale crimson, barred with darker pink or red in lower half; lip streaked with red or crimson inside, with a yellow or orange callus and mid-lobe and a yellow spur. **Sepals** oblanceolate-spathulate, obtuse, 1.2–1.7 cm

long, 0.6–0.7 cm broad. **Petals** oblanceolate, obtuse, 1.2–1.7 cm long, 0.5 cm broad. **Lip** distinctly but unequally 3-lobed, 0.5 cm long; side lobes erect, somewhat falcate-elliptic; mid-lobe smaller, ± truncate; disc with a large callus, 2-lobed in front; spur formed by base of lip and column-foot, conical. **Column** short, 0.2–0.25 cm long, flattened on front and bent forwards; foot as long as the column.
DISTRIBUTION Australia (Queensland and New South Wales); in deep moist ravine-like valleys of the coastal region and eastern slopes of the Dividing Range.
HISTORY Discovered by R.D. Fitzgerald in 1870 at Naroo Falls on the Bellingen River in N. New South Wales and named in 1870 after its discoverer by Baron Ferdinand von Mueller in *Fragmenta Phytographiae Australiae* (p. 115).
CLOSELY RELATED SPECIES See *S. hartmannii*.

Sarcochilus hartmannii F. Muell.
[Colour Plate]
A very variable, medium-sized lithophytic or less commonly epiphytic plant. **Stems** numerous, rather stout, erect, 5–10 cm long, 6- to 8-leaved. **Leaves** thick, fleshy, oblong-lanceolate, falcate, acute or obliquely emarginate, 10–18 cm long, 1.5–2 cm broad **Inflorescences** erect, stout, longer than the leaves, up to 16-flowered. **Flowers** 1–3.5 cm across, white with crimson spots or blotches in the centre of the perianth, rarely flowers wholly white or wholly crimson; pedicels up to 2 cm long, finely spotted with red. **Sepals** and **petals** ovate, obovate or oblong-elliptic, rounded, 0.8–1.6 cm long, 0.3–0.8 cm broad; petals slightly narrower than sepals. **Lip** small, 3-lobed; side lobes ovate to subquadrate, rounded at apex; mid-lobe very short, obtuse, erect, with a large bifid callus on the disc; spur subconical, fleshy, 0.1–0.2 cm long. **Column** 0.1–0.2 cm long; foot almost at right-angles, 0.15–0.3 cm long.
DISTRIBUTION Australia (New South Wales and Queensland); up to 1000 m on exposed cliffs, etc. near to the sea.
HISTORY Described in 1874 by Baron F. von Mueller in *Fragmenta Phytographiae Australiae* (p. 248) based on a collection by C.H. Hartmann from near Toowoomba in Queensland.
SYNONYM *Sarcochilus rubicentrum* Fitzg.
CLOSELY RELATED SPECIES Allied to *S. fitzgeraldii* which has a similar habit, but distinguished by its thicker more sickle-shaped leaves and by its smaller lip with a subconical spur.

Sarcoglottis Presl
Subfamily Spiranthoideae
Tribe Cranichideae
Subtribe Spiranthinae

Terrestrial herbs, glabrous or often pubescent. **Roots** fleshy, tuberous. **Leaves** rosulate, often variegated, ± petiolate, often absent at time of flowering. **Inflorescence** erect, spicate, laxly few- to several-flowered. **Flowers** small to medium-sized, rarely showy, often glandular pubescent on outer surface, mostly green, white or yellow, ± erect, not secund. **Dorsal sepal** and **petals** connivent, forming a hood over the column; **lateral sepals** deflexed, often longly decurrent onto the ovary at the base. **Lip** sessile or distinctly clawed, often narrow, concave, enclosing the column below, lacking calli or lamellae at the base. **Column** terete, ± decurrent at the base; anther ovate or oblong, sessile or stipitate; pollinia powdery-granular, produced into a short caudicle; rostellum bidentate.
DISTRIBUTION A large genus of about 50 species widespread in Central and S. America and the W. Indies.
DERIVATION OF NAME From the Greek *sarx* (flesh) and *glotta* (tongue), being descriptive of the fleshy lip of the type species.
TAXONOMY *Sarcoglottis* was established by K.B. Presl in 1827 in *Reliquiae Haenkeanae* (p. 95, t. 15) based on a species collected by Thaddeus Haenke in Peru. *Sarcoglottis* is closely allied to *Spiranthes* and has been considered congeneric with the latter by many authors. However, we have followed here R. Schlechter who, in *Beihefte zum Botanischen Zentralblatt* (1920), retained *Sarcoglottis* as a distinct genus.

Sarcoglottis is distinguished from other allied S. American genera by its lack of a mentum, the nectary being parallel with and inseparable from the ovary; and from *Spiranthes* by the non-spiral inflorescence and characters of the anther and rostellum.
TYPE SPECIES *S. speciosa* Presl
CULTURE Compost C. Temp. Winter min. 12–15°C. As for *Pelexia*. The plants need rather larger pans and may benefit from bed culture due to their habit of forming clumps.

Sarcoglottis acaulis (J.E. Smith) Schltr.
A large, rather variable terrestrial herb with a basal rosette of leaves. **Leaves** obovate-elliptic, acute to subacute, up to 30 cm long, 6 cm broad, velvety green above, ± marked with white, duller green below. **Inflorescence** erect, up to 75 cm long, racemose, 5- to 10- (or more)-flowered; peduncle, rhachis and ovary pubescent; bracts erect, lanceolate, acute, as long or longer than the ovary, up to 6 cm long.

Flowers erect; sepals green; petals and lip white with green venation. **Dorsal sepal** lanceolate, acute, porrect, 3 cm long, 0.5 cm broad; **lateral sepals** recurved, falcate, lanceolate, acute, 4 cm long, 0.6 cm broad, connate in basal half and enclosing lip base. **Petals** adnate to the dorsal sepal, oblanceolate, obtuse or retuse, 2.5 cm long, 0.4 cm broad. **Lip** oblanceolate, slightly contracted below apex then dilated above, reflexed at apex, glandular pubescent at base, margins incurved around column, 3.8 cm long, 1 cm broad. **Column** straight, with an acute rostellum, 1.5 cm long.
DISTRIBUTION Widespread in the American tropics from Mexico south to Argentina.
HISTORY Originally described in 1806 by J.E. Smith as *Neottia acaulis* in his *Exotic Botany* (p. 91, t. 105) from a plant flowered in cultivation by Mr Evans of Stepney, London who received it from Trinidad.

R. Schlechter transferred it to *Sarcoglottis* in 1919 in *Fedde, Repertorium Specierum Novarum, Beihefte* (p. 53).
SYNONYMS *Neottia acaulis* J.E. Smith; *N. picta* R. Br.; *Sarcoglottis speciosa* Presl; *S. picta* (R. Br.) Lindl.; *Spiranthes picta* (R. Br.) Lindl.; *S. acaulis* (J.E. Smith) Cogn.; *S. speciosa* (Presl) Lindl.

Sarcoglottis sceptrodes (Rchb.f.) Schltr.
[Colour Plate]
A terrestrial plant with a basal rosette of leaves and several fasciculate swollen elongate roots. **Leaves** several, spreading, elliptic, acute or subacute, up to 25 cm long, 7 cm wide. **Inflorescence** erect, apical, up to 70 cm long, spicate, subdensely to laxly 2- to 15-flowered; peduncle terete, pubescent, bearing several sheaths along its length; bracts lanceolate, 2–5.5 cm long. **Flowers** ascending, not opening widely, yellow-green with a pale green lip with darker veins; ovary as long as or longer than the bracts, pubescent. **Dorsal sepal** somewhat sigmoid in side view, linear, rounded at the apex, 2.5–3.5 cm long, 0.4–0.5 cm broad, pubescent on outer surface; **lateral sepals** shortly clawed, oblong, shortly apiculate, 2.9–3.5 cm long, 0.6–0.8 cm wide, with undulate margins, pubescent without. **Petals** hyaline, adnate to the dorsal sepal, spathulate, obtuse, 2–3 cm long, 0.4–0.5 cm wide. **Lip** pandurate-spathulate, obtuse, 3.5–4 cm long, 1–1.1 cm broad, the apical lobe broadly ovate, with 2 retrorse filaments at the base, pubescent at the base. **Column** short, c. 2 cm long.
DISTRIBUTION El Salvador, Nicaragua and Panama. This plant is terrrestrial in lowland forests.
HISTORY H.G. Reichenbach originally described this species as *Spiranthes sceptrodes* in 1855 in the journal *Bonplandia* (p. 214), based

on a collection from Nicaragua by Oersted. It was transferred to *Sarcoglottis* by Rudolf Schlechter (1920) in *Beihefte zum Botanisches Zentralblatt* (p. 421).

It is often confused in the literature with *S. acaulis* but differs in having straighter broader lateral sepals and petals and longly petiolate, unspotted leaves.
SYNONYM *Spiranthes sceptrodes* Rchb.f.

Satyrium Sw.
Subfamily Orchidoideae
Tribe Diseae
Subtribe Disinae

Terrestrial herbs with leafy unbranched stems arising from rounded tubers. In some species the foliage arises on separate sterile shoots. **Inflorescence** terminal, racemose or spicate, few- to many-flowered. **Flowers** non-resupinate, often showy, white, green, yellow, pink, red or purple. **Petals** and **sepals** small, subsimilar, mostly fused in basal part. **Lip** hooded, bearing 2 short to long spurs at back. **Column** erect, long, inside the hooded lip; terminal lobe forming the stigma, cushion-like or hooded; anther-loculi hanging, with a 3-lobed rostellum between them; viscidia 2, attached by caudicles to the pollinia.
DISTRIBUTION About 100 species mainly in S. Africa but also widespread in the rest of tropical Africa, mostly growing in wet grassland areas. Five species occur in Madagascar and two in Asia.
DERIVATION OF NAME In the Greek herbals of Dioscorides and Pliny *satyrion* refers to the man orchid *(Aceras anthropophorum)*. The Satyri were sylvan demigods in Greek mythology noted especially for their lasciviousness, and the name was applied to the man orchid possibly because of the presumed aphrodisiac properties possessed by the plant's tubers.
TAXONOMY *Satyrium* was established by O. Swartz in *Kungliga Svenska Vetenskapsakademiens Avhandlingar, Stockholm* (p. 214) in 1800 and it has been conserved over the earlier *Satyrium* L. (1753).

Satyrium has been monographed twice by F. Kraenzlin in his *Orchidacearum Genera et Species* (1901) and by R. Schlechter in A. Engler's *Botanische Jahrbücher* in the same year. Kraenzlin treated 79 species in three sections, two of which, *Aviceps* and *Satyridium*, contained but a single species and had previously been treated as distinct genera. The other 77 species he divided into seven subsections in section *(Eu) Satyrium*. Schlechter's account covered fewer species, some 63 in all, and divided these into seven sections accepting sections *Aviceps* and

Satyridium but raising some of Kraenzlin's subsections to sectional rank.

In subsequent accounts, such as that of V.S. Summerhayes in the *Flora of Tropical East Africa* (1968) where some 37 species are described in full, Schlechter's treatment of the genus is followed. The following features are most useful in the identification of *Satyrium* species; the position and number of the leaves and whether distinct fertile and sterile shoots are produced; the shape and size of the hooded lip and the spurs; and features of the column such as the position of the anther, rostellum shape and column length. The South African species are covered by J. Stewart et al. (1982) in *Wild Orchids of Southern Africa*.
TYPE SPECIES *Orchis bicornis* L. [= *Satyrium bicorne* L. Thunb.] typ. cons.
SYNONYMS *Satyridium* Lindl.; *Aviceps* Lindl.

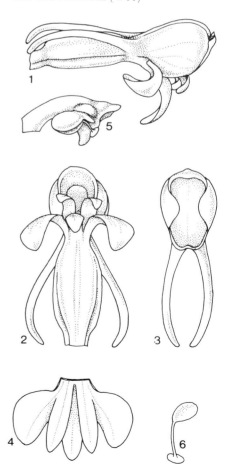

Satyrium nepalense
1 – Flower, side view (× 3)
2 – Flower from below (× 3)
3 – Lip and spurs (× 3)
4 – Sepals and petals (× 4)
5 – Column, side view (× 6)
6 – Pollinium and viscidium (× 11)

507

CULTURE Compost C. Temp. Min. 12–15°C while growing, 8–10°C while resting. *Satyrium* species may be grown in pans and, while growing, require ample water. Most require moderate shade. After flowering, when the stems and leaves have died back, the plants require a cool, dry resting period until new growth begins.

Satyrium nepalense D. Don

A medium-sized erect, terrestrial herb, 15–75 cm high. **Stem** fairly stout, sheathed above. **Leaves** few, oblong to linear-oblong, acute, rather fleshy, sheathing at base, 10–25 cm long, 5–10 cm broad. **Inflorescence** spicate, 2.5–15 cm long, densely many-flowered; bracts larger than the flowers, oblong to lanceolate, erect spreading or recurved. **Flowers** white to deep pink, fragrant. **Sepals** linear-oblong, obtuse, spreading and recurved, to 0.7 cm long, 0.15 cm broad. **Petals** similar to sepals but narrower. **Lip** superior, broadly oblong, concave, strongly keeled on the back, 0.7 cm long, 1 cm broad; spurs 2, variable in length, about 0.8–1.2 cm long. **Column** enclosed within the lip, terete and contracted at the base; anther broad, with clavate pollinia, short caudicles and orbicular glands.

DISTRIBUTION Widespread in India, Sri Lanka, the Himalayas and Burma; mostly from 1200–2000 m but often found up to 4000 m in the Himalayas.

HISTORY First collected by Dr N. Wallich at Gosaingsthan in Nepal, *S. nepalense* was described in 1825 by D. Don in his *Prodromus Florae Nepalensis* (p. 26).

SYNONYMS *Satyrium perrottetianum* A. Rich.; *S. albiflorum* A. Rich.; *S. pallidum* A. Rich.

Scaphosepalum Pfitz.

Subfamily Epidendroideae
Tribe Epidendreae
Subtribe Pleurothallidinae

Creeping or tufted epiphytic herbs. **Secondary stems** (ramicauls) short, bearing scarious sheaths, 1-leafed at apex. **Leaves** coriaceous, erect. **Inflorescences** lateral, from the base of the secondary stems, erect to spreading, racemose, laxly few- to many-flowered. **Flowers** non-resupinate, small. **Sepals** spreading, narrow, caudate at the apex; lateral sepals united in basal part or almost to apex, forming a concave lamina with a fleshy callus on each towards apex. **Petals** smaller than the sepals. **Lip** 3-lobed, uppermost, small; disc lamellate. **Column** incurved, dilated and emarginate or winged above, with a short foot below; pollinia 2, waxy, narrowly ovoid, compressed.

DISTRIBUTION A small genus of about 30

species confined to the tropical Americas from S. Mexico to Bolivia.

DERIVATION OF NAME From the Greek *skaphe* (bowl) and the Latin *sepalum* (sepal), as the sepals are connate to form a single concave lamina.

TAXONOMY *Scaphosepalum* was established in 1888 by E. Pfitzer in A. Engler and K.A. Prantl's, *Die Natürlichen Pflanzenfamilien* (2(6): p. 135). The only genus of the Pleurothallidinae with a lateral inflorescence, *Scaphosepalum* is allied to *Masdevallia*, *Pleurothallis* and *Lepanthes*.

F. Kraenzlin first revised the genus in 1925 in *Fedde, Repertorium Spicierum Novarum, Beihefte* where 23 species are described and keyed out. The most recent and recommended monograph is that of C. Luer (1988) in the fifth volume of *Icones Pleurothallidinarum* where a key is given to the 30 accepted species, each being described and illustrated in detail.

TYPE SPECIES *S. ochthodes* (Rchb.f.) Pfitz.
CULTURE Compost A. Temp. Winter min. 10–12°C. As for *Pleurothallis*, except for species such as *S. punctatum* which have downward-growing inflorescences. These plants need to be grown in small open baskets. Most species have the useful property of flowering throughout the year. At no time should the plants become dry.

Scaphosepalum verrucosum (Rchb.f.) Pfitzer
[Colour Plate]

A small epiphyte or lithophyte with short clustered stems 1–3.5 cm long. **Leaves** petiolate, spathulate-oblong, acutely tridentate at the apex, 5–15 cm long, 1.5–3 cm wide, sometimes suffused with purple, the petiole 1.5–4 cm long. **Inflorescences** erect, racemose, laxly many-

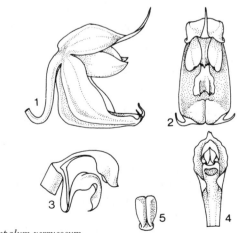

Scaphosepalum verrucosum
1 – Flower, side view (× 3)
2 – Flower, front view (× 3)
3 – Column and lip, side view (× 4)
4 – Column from below (× 6)
5 – Pollinia and viscidium (× 11)

flowered, 20–50 cm long; peduncle and rhachis minutely verrucose; bracts obconical, multipustulate, 3–4 mm long. **Flowers** non-resupinate, fleshy, yellow or yellow-green lined and marked with red-brown or purple; pedicel verrucose, 4–12 mm long, articulated to the subverrucose 4 mm long ovary. **Dorsal sepal** porrect, concave, lanceolate, attenuate at the fleshy apex, 6–8 mm long, 3–4 mm wide; **lateral sepals** united in basal two-thirds, elliptic, with spreading slender apicules, 6–7 mm long, 5–6 mm wide, each with a fleshy cushion in the apical half within. **Petals** obliquely oblong-elliptic, obtuse, 3–4 mm long, 1.5 mm wide, translucent. **Lip** reflexed in the middle, subpandurate, obtuse, 3–4 mm long, 1.5–2 mm wide, with 2 longitudinal serrate ridges in middle of lip, the apical margins denticulate. **Column** 3–4 mm long, broadly winged above the middle; foot thick, 2 mm long.

DISTRIBUTION Colombia; in oak forests and on roadside banks, 2400–3500 m.

HISTORY H.G. Reichenbach described this species in 1849 as *Masdevallia verrucosa* in the journal *Linnaea* (p. 819) based on a collection of Schlim from near La Baja in Santander Department of Colombia. Pfitzer transferred it to the present genus in 1888 in Engler's *Die Natürlichen Pflanzenfamilien* (2(6): p. 139). This species is often seen in cultivation under the later name *Scaphosepalum ochthodes*.

SYNONYMS *Masdevallia verrucosa* Rchb.f.; *M. ochthodes* Rchb.f.; *Pleurothallis verrucosa* (Rchb.f.) Rchb.f.; *Humboldtia verrucosa* (Rchb.f.) Kuntze; *H. ochthodes* (Rchb.f.) Kuntze

CLOSELY RELATED SPECIES One of the most spectacular species in the genus is *S. swertifolium* (Rchb.f.) Rolfe from Colombia and Ecuador. It is readily distinguished by the spreading apical tails of the lateral sepals giving the flower a spread of up to 8 cm.

Scaphyglottis Poepp. & Endl.

Subfamily Epidendroideae
Tribe Epidendreae
Subtribe Laeliinae

Small epiphytic or lithophytic plants. **Stems** clustered or creeping, indurated or pseudobulbous, simple or branching or fasciculate, 1- to several-leaved at apex. **Leaves** thin-textured and grass-like to fleshy-coriaceous. **Inflorescence** terminal or at nodes on stem, racemose or fasciculate. **Flowers** small. **Sepals** erect and spreading; lateral sepals united to column-foot to form a short mentum. **Petals** similar but smaller than the sepals. **Lip** entire, 3-lobed or emarginate, ± recurved. **Column** short, broadly winged to wingless, produced into a foot at the base; anther with 4 or 6, waxy, compressed pollinia.

DISTRIBUTION   About 40 species from the American tropics.

DERIVATION OF NAME   From the Greek *skaphe* (bowl) and *glotta* (tongue), alluding to the concave shape of the lip.

TAXONOMY   *Scaphyglottis* was established by E.F. Poeppig and S.L. Endlicher in 1835 in *Nova Genera ac Species Plantarum* (p. 58). P. Allen in *Flora of Panama* (1949) states that 'The original generic description of *Scaphyglottis* obviously applies more to *Scaphyglottis parviflora* Poepp. & Endl. than any of the other component species. Of the species described in the original publication, most are *Maxillaria*, and the generic description applies best to these species which belong to the genus *Maxillaria*.'

The genus *Scaphyglottis* as understood today, is allied to *Laelia*, *Epidendrum* and their allies but differs in having a distinct column-foot. Some authorities place it closer to *Ponera* and *Isochilus* from which it differs in lacking distichously-arranged leaves and in occasionally having 6 pollinia.

Many species in the genus are poorly known and specific limits of others are poorly defined.

TYPE SPECIES   *S. graminifolia* Poepp. & Endl.

CULTURE   Compost A. Temp. Winter min. 12–15°C. These plants grow well in pots or pans, and soon form tangled clumps. They require conditions of moderate shade and humidity with plenty of water while growing. When the new pseudobulbs are fully grown, less water should be given.

Scaphyglottis amethystina (Rchb.f.) Schltr
[Colour Plate]

A small epiphytic plant, 10–35 cm long. **Stems** pseudobulbous, short, erect or ascending, tufted, ± branching, rooted at the nodes, curved, 2-leaved at apex, up to 12 cm long, 1 cm broad. **Leaves** linear, suberect, obliquely 2-lobed at apex, 2.5–12.5 cm long, 0.5–1.2 cm broad. **Inflorescence** fasciculate at the apex of each pseudobulb, several- to many-flowered. **Flowers** white or lilac. **Sepals** oblong-elliptic, acute to subacute, concave, 0.5–0.8 cm long, 0.1–0.2 cm broad; lateral sepals joined below to form a prominent mentum. **Petals** linear, acute, falcate, 0.5–0.6 cm long, 0.1 cm broad. **Lip** flabellate-cuneate, deeply 3-lobed above, 0.6–0.8 cm long, 0.4–0.5 cm broad; side lobes ovate, obtuse; mid-lobe similar but acute. **Column** slender, with a prominent foot, auriculate on each side near apex, 0.5–0.7 cm long.

DISTRIBUTION   Guatemala to Costa Rica and Panama; in forests or open woodlands, up to 300 m altitude.

HISTORY   Originally described by H.G.

Reichenbach as *Ponera amethystina* in 1869 in Saunders' *Refugium Botanicum* (t. 93) from a collection made by George Ure Skinner at Santa Fé de Veraguas in Guatemala and sent by him to W. Wilson Saunders. R. Schlechter transferred it to the genus *Scaphyglottis* in 1918 in *Beihefte zum Botanischen Zentralblatt* (p. 456).

SYNONYM   *Ponera amethystina* Rchb.f.

Scaphyglottis prolifera (Rchb.f.) Cogn.

A medium-sized epiphytic plant. **Stems** numerous, fasciculate, dichotomously branching, erect or ascending, articulated, fusiform below, cylindrical above, 10–20 cm long, 0.2–0.3 cm in diameter, 2-leaved at apex. **Leaves** spreading, subopposite, coriaceous, linear-ligulate, obtuse or emarginate at apex, 2–4 cm long, 0.3–0.5 cm broad, pale green. **Flowers** geminate or fasciculate, more or less spreading, pale yellow. **Sepals** erect, narrowly oblong-subspathulate, acute, 0.5 cm long, 0.15 cm broad; mentum somewhat obscure. **Petals** narrowly linear-subspathulate, obtuse, 0.5 cm long, 0.1 cm broad. **Lip** entire, oblong-spathulate, long-attenuate below, rounded and slightly retuse at the apex, 0.5 cm long, 0.25 cm broad. **Column** slender, erect, straight or slightly incurved, 0.4 cm long.

DISTRIBUTION   Brazil, Venezuela, Guyana and Surinam.

HISTORY   Described originally in 1787 by Olof Swartz as *Epidendrum proliferum* in his *Prodromus* (p. 124) of W. Indian orchids. Robert Brown described it as *Isochilus prolifer* in 1813 in the 2nd edition of W. Aiton's *Hortus Kewensis* from a plant introduced in 1793 from the W. Indies by Edward Elcock. A. Cogniaux transferred it to *Scaphyglottis* in 1898 in Martius's *Flora Brasiliensis* (3, 5: p. 15).

SYNONYMS   *Isochilus prolifer* R. Br.; *Ponera prolifera* (R. Br.) Rchb.f.

Scelochilus Klotzsch
Subfamily Epidendroideae
Tribe Oncidieae

Small epiphytes with clustered 1-noded unifoliate pseudobulbs subtended by imbricate distichous sheaths. **Leaves** coriaceous. **Inflorescences** axillary from the basal sheaths, 1- to few-flowered, often pendent. **Flowers** small. **Dorsal sepal** and **petals** free, erect around the column; **lateral sepals** often more or less connate, produced at the base to form a prominent spur-like mentum. **Lip** with a narrow claw, entire or obscurely 3-lobed, spathulate, with a complex callus and with 2 basal horns inserted into the mentum, the side margins sometimes denticulate. **Column** with a foot; pollinia 2,

hard, attached by a short to long stipe to a small viscidium.

DISTRIBUTION   A genus of perhaps 25 species distributed from Mexico to Brazil and Bolivia.

DERIVATION OF NAME   From the Greek *skelos* (leg) and *chilos* (lip), probably in allusion to the 2 basal horn-like structures on the margin of the lip.

TAXONOMY   Klotzsch established this genus in 1841 in Otto and Dietrich's *Allgemeine Gartenzeitung* (p. 261). It is closely allied to *Comparettia*, *Ionopsis* and *Rodriguezia*, differing in details of the lip and column structure.

TYPE SPECIES   *S. ottonis* Klotzsch

CULTURE   Temp. Winter min. 12°C. Probably best grown mounted and hanging under conditions of moderate shade and humidity. Allow to dry out between waterings.

Scelochilus ottonis Klotzsch

A small epiphyte with clustered, cylindrical, dark green, unifoliate pseudobulbs, 1–1.5 cm long, 3–4 mm in diameter, covered by distichous, imbricate, ovate, conduplicate sheaths when young. **Leaves** oblong or oblong-elliptic, acute, 8–14 cm long, 2.5–4 cm wide. **Inflorescence** basal, axillary, laxly 4- to 12-flowered,

Scelochilus ottonis
1 – Habit ($\times \frac{3}{4}$)
2 – Dorsal sepal ($\times 1\frac{1}{2}$)
3 – Petal ($\times 1\frac{1}{2}$)
4 – Lip ($\times 2$)
5 – Column and lip, side view ($\times 2$)

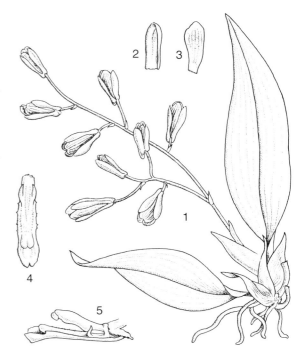

9–30 cm long; peduncle terete; bracts triangular, appressed, 1 mm long. **Flowers** bright yellow with red venation on the petals and lip and greenish-yellow callus ridges; pedicel and ovary 4–5 mm long. **Dorsal sepal** oblong-elliptic, rounded at the apex, concave, 12–13 mm long, 5 mm wide; **lateral sepals** united almost to the apex, 15–16 mm long, 5–6 mm wide, the free tips subacute; mentum conical-saccate, 1 mm long. **Petals** falcate, obovate, rounded, 13–14 mm long, 5–6 mm wide. **Lip** spathulate, 14–16 mm long, 4 mm wide; callus of 2 recurved fleshy horns at the base, and 2 pubescent fleshy rounded ridges coalescing and roundly bilobed in front. **Column** cream, 7–8 mm long.

DISTRIBUTION Venzuela; endemic in montane mist forest.

HISTORY Klotzsch described this species in 1841 in the journal *Allgemeine Gartenzeitung* (p. 261).

Schlimmia Planch. & Linden

Subfamily Epidendroideae
Tribe Gongoreae
Subtribe Stanhopeinae

Epiphytes with clustered, ovoid, unifoliate pseudobulbs subtended by imbricate, distichous sheaths. **Leaf** plicate, heavily veined, petiolate. **Inflorescences** pendent, few-flowered, basal. **Flowers** bell-shaped, medium-sized. **Dorsal sepal** and **petals** free, hooded over column; **lateral sepals** united to form a saccate mentum. **Lip** small, bipartite with a broad hypochile and a small cordiform epichile. **Column** short, winged; pollinia 2, hard, attached by a slender stipe to a small round viscidium.

DISTRIBUTION A small genus of about five species from the N. Andes.

DERIVATION OF NAME Named in honour of Louis Schlim who collected orchids in Colombia and Venezuela with N. Funck for the nursery of J. Linden. Schlim was Linden's cousin.

TAXONOMY The genus was established by the Belgians Planchon and Jean Linden in 1852 in Paxton's short-lived journal, the *Flower Garden* (p. 115).

TYPE SPECIES *S. jasminodora* Planch. & Linden

CULTURE Temp. Winter min. 12°C. Grow in a basket under shady, humid conditions. Water carefully throughout the year, with less given after growth is finished.

Schlimmia alpina Rchb.f. & Warsc.

A medium-sized epiphyte. **Pseudobulbs** ovoid or elongate-ovoid, up to 5 cm long, 1.5 cm in diameter, slightly wrinkled, 1-leafed at the apex, subtended by several sheaths at the base. **Leaf** erect, elliptic, acute, 20–30 cm long, 5–10 cm wide; petiole short. **Inflorescence** pendent, 3- to 5-flowered, up to 15 cm long; peduncle purple; bracts inflated, c. 1 cm long. **Flowers** fleshy, white to pale greeny-cream, spotted pale pink at the base, with yellow swellings at the base of the lip, spicily scented; pedicel and ovary 12–14 mm long, furfuraceous. **Dorsal sepal** oblong-elliptic, obtuse, 2.2–2.5 cm long, 8–10 mm wide; **lateral sepals** obliquely oblong-ovate, obtuse, 2.2–2.5 cm long, 1.3–1.5 cm wide, forming with the column-foot a saccate 1–1.2 cm long mentum. **Petals** falcate-oblanceolate, obtuse, 2 cm long, 0.4 cm wide. **Lip** 8 mm long, 4 mm wide; hypochile subquadrate, trifid in front, with 2 fleshy yellow swellings; epichile ovate, apiculate. **Column** clavate, pale green, papillate beneath, c. 1 cm long.

DISTRIBUTION Venezuela, Colombia and Ecuador; rain forest, 1500–3000 m.

HISTORY H.G. Reichenbach and Warscewicz first described this species in 1854 in *Bonplandia* (p. 98) based on a Warscewicz collection from Colombia.

CLOSELY RELATED SPECIES Allied to *S. jasminodora* Planch. & Linden but that differs in having an entire hypochile to the lip; and to *S. trifida* [Colour Plate] in having subquadrate but not dolabriform wings to the column.

Schoenorchis Blume

Subfamily Epidendroideae
Tribe Vandeae
Subtribe Sarcanthinae

Epiphytic herbs with erect or pendulous stems, often only branching or rooting at the base. **Leaves** very narrow to narrow. **Inflorescences** simple or branching, erect or horizontal, bearing many small flowers. **Sepals** and **petals** subsimilar, scarcely spreading. **Lip** 3-lobed, spurred, ± with a fleshy callus or swelling at the entrance to the spur on the side away from the column; side lobes erect, low, rounded; mid-lobe straight, fleshy, often angled, contracted at the base; spur cylindric or ellipsoid, incurved or porrect, sometimes septate. **Column** short; anther with a long beak abruptly upcurved from its base; rostellum of 2 long slender erect arms; pollinia 4, united in 2 sphaerical bodies attached to a long slender viscidium.

DISTRIBUTION Some 10 species from the Himalayas to New Guinea.

DERIVATION OF NAME From the Greek *schoenos* (reed or rush) and *orchis* (orchid), in allusion to the narrow rush-like leaves.

TAXONOMY *Schoenorchis* was established by C. Blume in 1825 in his *Bijdragen* (p. 361). It is allied to other Asiatic vandaceous orchids such as *Phalaenopsis* and *Gastrochilus* but the plants are usually tiny and have a quite characteristic flower structure, particularly in rostellum and anther shape. An account of the genus in cultivation is given by E. Christensen (1985) in the *American Orchid Society Bulletin* (p. 851). Seidenfaden (1988) in *Opera Botanica* (p. 66) discusses eight species from Thailand and neighbouring countries.

TYPE SPECIES *S. juncifolia* Blume

CULTURE Compost A or mounted. These small plants are probably best grown mounted on slabs of fern-fibre or cork so that their stems may climb or hang as required. They all need humid and moderately shady conditions with plenty of water while growing and less at other times.

Schoenorchis gemmata (Lindl.) J.J. Smith
[Colour Plate]

A pendulous or drooping epiphytic herb. **Stems** curved, rooting at the base, terete, 15–30 cm or more long, leafy throughout. **Leaves** linear-terete, unequally 2- or 3-toothed at apex, fleshy, sheathing at base, curved, channelled, 5–10 cm long, 0.3–0.6 cm broad. **Inflorescences** suberect to drooping, longer than the leaves, paniculate, axillary, laxly many-flowered; bracts small, acute. **Flowers** minute, 0.3–0.4 cm long; sepals white or purple with white apices; petals purple; lip white with purple on spur and side lobes. **Sepals** ovate-oblong, acute, 0.15–0.2 cm long, 0.1 cm broad. **Petals** obovate, obtuse, 0.12 cm long, 0.07 cm broad. **Lip** fleshy, obscurely 3-lobed at base, up to 0.2 cm long, 0.15 cm broad; side lobes rounded, erect; mid-lobe obovate, obtuse or rounded, very fleshy; spur straight, swollen towards apex, 0.2 cm long. **Column** very short, fleshy.

DISTRIBUTION N. India, Himalayas, Burma, S. China, Thailand and Indo-China; 600–1600 m altitude, fairly common.

HISTORY Originally described by John Lindley in the *Botanical Register* (misc. p. 50) in 1838 as *Saccolabium gemmatum* based on a plant collected by J. Gibson in the Khasia Hills in 1837 which flowered for the Duke of Devonshire at Chatsworth, England in May of the following year. J.J. Smith transferred it in 1912 to *Schoenorchis* in *Natuurkundig Tijdschrift voor Nederlandsch Indië* (p. 100).

SYNONYM *Saccolabium gemmatum* Lindl.

Schomburgkia Lindl.
Subfamily Epidendroideae
Tribe Epidendreae
Subtribe Laeliinae

Medium-sized to large epiphytic or lithophytic plant. **Pseudobulbs** large, subcylindric-fusiform, often hollow with age, 2- or 3-leaved at apex. **Leaves** spreading, leathery, mostly oblong or linear-oblong. **Inflorescences** erect, very long or long, laxly racemose or paniculate, 10- to many-flowered; peduncle slender, many-jointed, each with a conspicuous sheath. **Flowers** medium-sized to large, showy long-pedicellate. **Sepals** and **petals** free, subsimilar, ± undulated. **Lip** 3-lobed; side lobes erect on either side of the column but not enveloping it; mid-lobe spreading. **Column** porrect, curved, fairly short; pollinia 8 in 2 groups of 4.

DISTRIBUTION   About 12 species in tropical N. America, the W. Indies and northern S. America.

DERIVATION OF NAME   Named in honour of Sir Richard Schomburgk (1811–91) who explored and collected extensively in British Guiana (now Guyana) with his brother Robert. In 1865 he became Director of the Adelaide Botanic Garden in Australia.

TAXONOMY   This genus was established by John Lindley in *Sertum Orchidacearum* (tt. 10, 13) stating it was allied to *Epidendrum* from which it is distinguished by its 'large spathaceous bracts, by its membranous labellum adhering to the column only at the base, and having below the middle a distinctly marked prominence, which corresponds with an impression on the under side, and by its having eight pollinia.'

R. Schlechter revised *Schomburgkia* in *Orchis* (1913) and established two sections:

1. sect. *Schomburgkia* where the pseudobulbs are fusiform, the leaves long and narrow and the inflorescence simple with long pendulous bracts.
2. sect. *Chaunoschomburgkia* with conical or cylindrical pseudobulbs, short broad leaves, a branched inflorescence and reduced bracts.

The species of the former section are mainly S. American, whilst in the latter the species are mainly from Central America and the W. Indies.

R.A. Rolfe raised sect. *Chaunoschomburgkia* to generic rank as *Myrmecophila* in the *Orchid Review* (1917) and we follow this here. Conversely, several authorities have followed L.O. Williams who treated *Schomburgkia* as a section of *Laelia* in the *Botanical Museum Leaflets of Harvard University* (1941). H.G. Jones in *Taxon* (1973) has reviewed the sectional limits of *Schomburgkia* and argues for the retention of it as distinct from *Laelia* on the grounds that L.O. Williams emphasised the similarities of these genera whilst overlooking their differences. *Schomburgkia* species may be fairly easily distinguished from *Laelia* species by their undulate petals and sepals and by the open lip which does not enfold the column as in the latter genus.

TYPE SPECIES   *S. crispa* Lindl.

CULTURE   Compost A. Temp. Winter min. 12–15°C. As for *Cattleya*. The *Schomburgkia* species fall into two groups: those like *S. tibicinis* with hollow pseudobulbs here treated as *Myrmecophila* and those related to *S. undulata*, with fusiform pseudobulbs. Both groups should be given good light and plenty of water while growing, but *S. tibicinis* and its allies need a longer dry period when the pseudobulbs are complete. All species should be repotted as infrequently as possible.

Schomburgkia crispa Lindl. [Colour Plate]
See under *Schomburgkia gloriosa*.

Schomburgkia gloriosa Rchb.f
A large epiphytic plant with a creeping rhizome. **Pseudobulbs** 3–5 cm apart, clavate, terete below, lightly compressed and grooved above, up to 30 cm long, 5 cm in diameter, 4- to 6-noded, 2- or 3-leaved at apex. **Leaves** narrowly oblong, obtuse, coriaceous, up to 32 cm long, 6 cm broad, carinate. **Inflorescence** terminal, erect, up to 75 or more cm long, with a dense terminal raceme, 8- to 15-flowered; bracts deflexed, linear-lanceolate, acuminate, up to 6 cm long, 1.2 cm broad. **Flowers** large, showy; sepals and petals light honey-brown, ± tinged with purple with dark brown nerves; lip white with light yellow-brown margins and mid-lobe to pink with pinkish-brown margins and mid-lobe; column white at base, yellow

Schomburgkia gloriosa
1 – Flower (× ⅘)
2 – Lip (× ⅘)
3 – Pollinia (× 6)

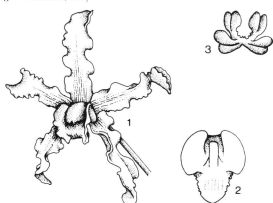

and pink above, spotted red beneath. **Sepals** and **petals** narrowly oblong, obtuse or shortly apiculate, margins undulate-crisped, 3.5–4 cm long, 1–1.2 cm broad. **Lip** 3-lobed in the middle, up to 2 cm long, 1.8 cm broad; side lobes narrowly elliptic, erect; mid-lobe reflexed, ovate-elliptic, obtuse, bearing 3 raised ridges in centre; disc with a hollow swelling below the column. **Column** 1.8 cm long.

DISTRIBUTION   Venezuela, Guyana and Surinam.

HISTORY   Described by H.G. Reichenbach in 1860 in the *Hamburger Gartenzeitung* (p. 178) based on a specimen cultivated by Messrs Booth. A plant mistakenly named as *S. crispa* sent to Mr Marryat by R. Schomburgk from Demerara (now Georgetown) had been earlier figured in the *Botanical Register* (t. 23) in 1844 by John Lindley.

SYNONYMS   *Bletia gloriosa* (Rchb.f.) Rchb.f.; *Laelia gloriosa* (Rchb.f.) L.O. Williams; *Schomburgkia crispa* auct.

CLOSELY RELATED SPECIES   Similar to *Schomburgkia crispa* Lindl. [Colour Plate] which differs in its lip shape and column structure, the lip having a shorter mid-lobe separated from the side lobes by deep sinuses and the column having broader wings.

Schomburgkia superbiens (Lindl.) Rolfe
[Colour Plate]
A large, stout epiphytic or terrestrial plant up to 3.5 m tall. **Pseudobulbs** elongated, oblong-fusiform, slightly compressed, up to 3 m long, 3.5 cm in diameter, furrowed, 1- to 2-leaved at apex. **Leaves** oblong or oblong-lanceolate, obtuse or acute, very leathery, up to 30 cm long, 6.5 cm broad. **Inflorescence** simple, many-flowered, racemose; peduncle up to 80 cm long or more, 1 cm in diameter; bracts large, lanceolate, acuminate, brown and spotted, up to 12 cm long. **Flowers** showy, large, purple, variegated with yellow; pedicel and ovary up to 8 cm long. **Sepals** linear-oblong to narrowly lanceolate, obtuse or acute, sometimes undulate, 5–7 cm long, 1–1.5 cm broad. **Petals** spreading, narrowly oblong to narrowly oblanceolate, rounded to acute, 4.5 cm long, 1.2–1.8 cm broad. **Lip** free, 3-lobed above the middle, arcuate-decurved, margins convolute, enfolding the column, 4–5.5 cm long, 2.8–3.5 cm broad; side lobes short, oblong, rounded at the crisped apex; mid-lobe larger, broadly obovate to obcordate, emarginate, up to 2 cm broad; disc yellowish, with 5–6 prominent, crisped and serrate lamellae. **Column** elongate, arcuate, clavate, 2.5–3 cm long.

DISTRIBUTION   Mexico, Guatemala and Honduras; uncommon in open or rain forests, up to 2000 m altitude.

HISTORY   Discovered by George Ure Skin-

ner in Guatemala and described as *Laelia superbiens* by John Lindley in the *Botanical Register* (misc. p. 46) in 1840. R.A. Rolfe transferred it to *Schomburgkia* in 1917 in the *Orchid Review* (p. 49).
SYNONYMS *Cattleya superbiens* (Lindl.) Beer; *Laelia superbiens* Lindl.

Schomburgkia undulata Lindl. [Colour Plate]
A large epiphytic plant. **Pseudobulbs** fusiform, tapering at the base, sulcate, shiny, up to 25 cm long, 5 cm broad, 2-leaved at apex. **Leaves** oblong-ligulate, coriaceous, rigid, up to 30 cm long, 5 cm broad. **Inflorescence** erect, racemose, subumbellate, laxly about 20-flowered, up to 1.5 cm long; bracts tubular and dependent. **Flowers** showy; sepals and petals rich shiny maroon; lip bright rose-purple, ± white in the centre; column white, flushed lavender; pedicel very long. **Sepals** and **petals** oblong-narrowly elliptic, rounded at the apex, margins undulate-crisped, 3.2–3.5 cm long, 1–1.3 cm broad. **Lip** 3-lobed in the basal half, porrect, 2.5–2.7 cm long, 1.7–2 cm broad; side lobes erect, rounded in front; mid-lobe oblong, decurved in apical half, minutely apiculate; disc bearing 3–5 parallel lamellae onto middle of mid-lobe. **Column** short, stout, 1.6 cm long.
DISTRIBUTION Trinidad and Venezuela.
HISTORY Collected by Jean Linden at La Guayra and sent to Rucker. It was described by John Lindley in 1844 in the *Botanical Register* (sub t. 23, misc. no. 21).
SYNONYMS *Cattleya undulata* (Lindl.) Beer; *Bletia undulata* (Lindl.) Rchb.f.; *Laelia undulata* (Lindl.) L.O. Williams

---

Scuticaria Lindl.
Subfamily Epidendroideae
Tribe Maxillarieae
Subtribe Maxillariinae

Medium-sized epiphytic plants with a very short, 1-leafed stems. **Leaf** long, fleshy, subterete or terete, sulcate, contiguous with the stem. **Inflorescence** lateral, often 1-flowered. **Flowers** large or medium-sized, showy. **Sepals** and **petals** free, subsimilar, erect-spreading; lateral sepals adnate to the column-foot forming a prominent mentum. **Lip** sessile, attached to the apex of the column-foot, articulated, broad, concave, deeply 3-lobed; side lobes large, erect; mid-lobe smaller. **Column** erect, fleshy, semiterete, wingless, produced at the base into a foot; pollinia 4, ovoid, waxy; stipites very short or obsolete, attached to transversely squamiform viscidia.
DISTRIBUTION A small genus of five species only in Brazil, Guyana and Venezuela.
DERIVATION OF NAME From the Latin

scutica (lash), referring to the pendent whip-like leaves.
TAXONOMY *Scuticaria* was first described by John Lindley in 1843 in the *Botanical Register* (misc. no. 14). It is allied to *Maxillaria* being distinguished by its subterete or terete leaves.
TYPE SPECIES *S. steelii* (Hooker) Lindl.
CULTURE Compost A. Temp. Winter min. 15°C. Because of their pendent growth habit, *Scuticaria* species are best mounted on slabs of fern-fibre or cork, or may be grown in a shallow tilted basket. They require plenty of water and moderate shade while growing and a drier period after flowering.

Scuticaria hadwenii (Lindl.) Hooker
[Colour Plate]
A medium-sized, epiphytic plant. **Stems** very short, knotty, swollen at the base, ash-brown. **Leaves** cylindric, narrowly sulcate above, acute, 22–45 cm long, 0.5–0.7 cm thick, deep green, deflexed. **Inflorescence** ascending or deflexed, 4–5 cm long, 1- or 2-flowered, sheathed at the base by brownish, acute, scale-like bracts. **Flowers** nodding, 6–7.5 cm long; sepals and petals fleshy, chestnut-brown, paler towards the apex sometimes broken into blotches on a yellowish-green background; lip pale yellow, blotched and spotted light brown, with a white margin spotted with light rose; column spotted with purple and white at the apex. **Sepals** spreading, oblong, acute, 4–4.5 cm long, 1.2–1.5 cm broad. **Petals** similar to sepals. **Lip** broadly obovate or suborbicular, concave, downy within, 3–3.5 cm long, 2.5–3 cm broad; callus an oblong plate, tridentate in front, swollen at the base. **Column** incurved, obscurely clavate, slightly puberulent, 1.5 cm long.
DISTRIBUTION Brazil and Guyana.
HISTORY Introduced from Rio de Janeiro by Isaac Hadwen of Liverpool, England in whose collection it flowered in 1851. He sent it to the Royal Botanic Gardens at Kew and John Lindley named it in his honour as *Bifrenaria hadwenii* in his and Paxton's *Flower Garden* (p. 67). Sir William Hooker transferred it to the genus *Scuticaria* in Curtis's *Botanical Magazine* (sub. t. 4629) in 1852.
SYNONYM *Bifrenaria hadwenii* Lindl.

Scuticaria steelii (Hooker) Lindl.
[Colour Plate]
A large, slender, epiphytic plant. **Pseudobulbs** proximate, small, fusiform-pyriform, several-noded, up to 3 cm long, 1 cm in diameter, concealed by close-fitting grey bracts, 1-leafed at apex. **Leaf** arcuate-pendent, terete, slender, longitudinally grooved above, up to 145 cm long, 0.6 cm in diameter. **Inflorescence** basal, a very short raceme, 1- to 3-flowered. **Flowers** large, showy; sepals and petals fleshy, pale greenish-yellow, marked with chocolate-

maroon spots; lip pale greenish-white, striped with reddish-chocolate brown, callus yellow; column off-white, lined with pinkish-purple. **Dorsal sepal** narrowly elliptic, acute, somewhat hooded, 4.2 cm long, 1.5 cm broad; **lateral sepals** obliquely oblong-elliptic, subacute, 3.2 cm long, 2 cm broad, forming with the column-foot a distinct mentum, 1.5 cm long. **Petals** obliquely narrowly elliptic, subacute, 3.8 cm long, 1.2 cm broad. **Lip** 3-lobed in the apical half, thick and rigid in the centre, 3.2 cm long, 4 cm broad; side lobes erect-incurved, semicircular; mid-lobe smaller than side lobes, transversely oblong, emarginate; callus transverse, 5-pointed, finely pubescent above. **Column** semiterete, curved slightly at the apex, 2.2 cm long.
DISTRIBUTION Brazil, Guyana, Surinam, French Guiana and Venezuela.
HISTORY Originally described in the genus *Maxillaria* by Sir William Hooker in 1837 in the *Botanical Magazine* (t. 3573) from a plant collected in the previous year in Demerara (now Georgetown) by Matthew Steele and flowered by John Moss at Otterspool, near Liverpool, England. John Lindley transferred it to *Scuticaria* in the *Botanical Register* (misc. no. 14) in 1843.
SYNONYMS *Maxillaria steelii* Hooker; *M. flabellifera* Lindl.; *Scuticaria keyseriana* Hort.

Sedirea (Linden & Rchb.f.) Garay & Sweet
Subfamily Epidendroideae
Tribe Vandeae
Subtribe Sarcanthinae

Small monopodial epiphytic plants with very short leafy stems covered by leaf bases and fleshy flexuous roots. **Leaves** coriaceous, distichous, articulated to a sheathing leaf base. **Inflorescences** axillary, erect to arcuate-pendent, laxly few- to 12-flowered; peduncle terete. **Flowers** fleshy, showy. **Sepals** subsimilar, free, spreading; **lateral sepals** decurrent on the column-foot. **Petals** subsimilar to sepals. **Lip** very fleshy, obscurely 3-lobed at base, spurred at base, articulated to the column-foot; mid-lobe strongly clawed. **Column** elongate, arcuate; rostellum prominent, triangular, recurved; pollinia 2, deeply cleft; stipe oblong; viscidium triangular-ovate.
DISTRIBUTION A monotypic genus from Korea, Japan and the Ryukyu Islands.
DERIVATION OF NAME An anagram of the generic name *Aerides*.
TAXONOMY *Sedirea* is, as its name suggests, a segregate genus of the well-known *Aerides*. It was established by Garay and Sweet in 1974 in their *Orchids of the Southern Ryukyu*

Islands (p. 149) to accommodate the aberrant *Aerides japonica*. *Sedirea* differs from *Aerides* in having an elongate column with a short foot, and a lip which is not continuous with the column-foot but articulate with it.

TYPE SPECIES *Aerides japonica* Linden & Rchb.f.

CULTURE Temp. Winter min. 12°C. Grow as *Phalaenopsis*, either in pots of epiphyte mix or mounted.

Sedirea japonica (Linden & Rchb.f.) Garay & Sweet [Colour Plate]

An epiphyte with a very short stem. **Leaves** 5–8, narrowly elliptic to strap-shaped, obtuse at obscurely bilobed apex, 8–15 cm long, 2–3 cm wide. **Inflorescences** 1 to several, 2- to 12-flowered; peduncle terete, green; bracts ovate or elliptic, cucullate, obtuse, 6–10 mm long. **Flowers** fleshy, 2.5 cm across; dorsal sepal and petals whitish; lateral sepals white with transverse pale purple bars in basal half; lip whitish with pink spots and a yellow central stripe; spur yellowish; pedicel and ovary 1.5–2 cm long. **Dorsal sepal** obovate, obtuse, concave or with reflexed margins, 13–15 mm long, 4–5 mm wide; **lateral sepals** deflexed, oblong-elliptic, obtuse, 13–15 mm long, 5 mm wide. **Petals** elliptic, obtuse, somewhat porrect, 13–15 mm long, 4–5 mm wide. **Lip** obscurely 3-lobed, 1.5–2 cm long, 1 cm wide; side lobes incurved, subquadrate to triangular, very small; mid-lobe spathulate, rounded at apex, with an undulate-crisped margin; spur strongly incurved, narrowly conical. **Column** elongate, 1 cm long, incurved in apical half; foot short.

DISTRIBUTION Korea, S. Japan and the Ryukyu Islands.

HISTORY Originally described as *Aerides japonica* by H.G. Reichenbach in 1863 in the *Hamburger Gartenzeitung* (p. 210). Garay and Sweet made it the type of their new genus *Sedirea* in 1974 in their *Orchids of the Southern Ryukyu Islands* (p. 149).

SYNONYM *Aerides japonica* Linden & Rchb.f.

Seidenfadenia Garay
Subfamily Epidendroideae
Tribe Vandeae
Subtribe Sarcanthinae

Epiphytic plants with a very short leafy stem covered by sheathing leaf bases. **Leaves** articulate, semiterete, elongate. **Inflorescences** axillary, shorter than the leaves, unbranched, laxly to densely many-flowered. **Flowers** attractive. **Sepals** and **petals** free, spreading, subequal. **Lip** attached to the base of the column, lobed; side lobes minute, horn-like; mid-lobe promin-ent, flat; spur bilaterally compressed, semilunate in side view, parallel to lip mid-lobe, ecallose. **Column** short, fleshy, dilated at the base to form an obscure foot; dilated at apex; rostellum erect, bidentate, an elevated keel running across the clinandrium and projecting above the column at the apex; pollinia 2; stipe elongate, linear-spathulate; viscidium prominent.

DISTRIBUTION A monotypic genus in Burma and Thailand only.

DERIVATION OF NAME Named in honour of the eminent Danish orchid taxonomist and diplomat Dr Gunnar Seidenfaden, co-author of *Orchids of Thailand* and the author of a series of definitive accounts of the orchid genera of Thailand in the journals *Dansk Botanisk Arkiv* (1975–80) and *Opera Botanica* (1982–8).

TAXONOMY *Seidenfadenia* was established by Leslie Garay in 1972 in the *Botanical Museum Leaflets of Harvard University* (p. 203) as a segre-gate genus of *Aerides*. It is readily distinguished from *Aerides* by its unique column structure in which the crest-shaped rostellum projects across the clinandrium and protrudes dorsally on the column. Garay comments that in the adnation of the column and in the pollinia *Seidenfadenia* is more reminiscent of *Rhynchostylis* than of *Aerides*.

TYPE SPECIES *Aerides mitrata* Rchb.f.

CULTURE Temp. Winter min. 15°C. Prefer to have their roots exposed, so best grown mounted and watered daily during growth. A dry, dormant period with brighter light and cooler nights should follow.

Seidenfadenia mitrata (Rchb.f.) Garay [Colour Plate]

A pendent epiphyte with a short stem up to 12.5 cm long. **Leaves** pendent, semiterete, grooved on upper surface, acuminate, 10–90 cm long, 2–5 mm wide. **Inflorescences** 6–25 cm long, horizontal-ascending to erect, 10- to many-flowered; peduncle terete, 1.5–2 mm in diameter; bracts triangular-ovate, 2 mm long. **Flowers** fragrant; sepals and petals white tinted with mauve and with mauve tips; lip mauve; pedicel and ovary 1.5–1.7 cm long. **Dorsal sepal** narrowly elliptic, obtuse or rounded, 8–9 mm long, 3.5–4 mm wide; **lateral sepals** obovate, obtuse or rounded, 8–10 mm long, 4–4.5 mm wide. **Petals** obovate-elliptic, rounded, 7 mm long, 4 mm wide. **Lip** obscurely 3-lobed, oblong-flabellate, emargin-ate, 7–9 mm long, 4–5 mm wide, slightly con-duplicate at the apex; spur ellipsoidal in side view, recurved below lip, 4–5 mm long, bilateral-ly compressed. **Column** 4 mm long.

DISTRIBUTION Burma and Thailand only; 100–800 m.

HISTORY The type material from Burma was flowered by John Day of Tottenham in England in 1864 and was described in the same year by Reichenbach in the *Botanische Zeitung* (p. 415) as *Aerides mitrata*. Garay transferred it to his new genus *Seidenfadenia* in 1972 in the *Botanical Museum Leaflets of Harvard University* (p. 204).

SYNONYM *Aerides mitrata* Rchb.f.

Selenipedium Rchb.f.
Subfamily Cypripedioideae

Tall pubescent terrestrial plants with leafy, often branching stems. **Leaves** plicate, thinly chartaceous, narrow, convolute when young. **Inflorescences** terminal and/or lateral, race-mose, many-flowered. **Flowers** small to medium-sized, resupinate. **Sepals** spreading; lateral sepals connate almost to the apex. **Petals** narrow, free. **Lip** sessile, inflated, slipper-shaped. **Column** short, terete; stamens 2, stipitate; stigma papillose.

DISTRIBUTION Five species from Trinidad and Costa Rica south to Colombia and Brazil.

DERIVATION OF NAME From the Greek *selene* (crescent or the moon) and *pedilon* (san-dal) referring to the deeply saccate lip.

TAXONOMY *Selenipedium* was described in 1854 by H.G. Reichenbach in *Bonplandia* (p. 116). *Phragmipedium*, which differs in having larger flowers with a 4–6 cm long lip, short stems and conduplicate leaves, and *Selenipedium* are the two tropical American genera of the subfamily Cypripedioideae. For further details of the subfamily see the discussion under *Paphiopedilum*.

TYPE SPECIES *S. chica* Rchb.f.

CULTURE Compost B. Temp. Winter min. 10–12°C. *Selenipedium* species are difficult to accommodate on account of their height, poten-tially of several metres. In general they should be grown as *Sobralia* species, never becoming very dry and with moderate shade from sum-mer sun.

Selenipedium palmifolium (Lindl.) Rchb.f.

An erect terrestrial plant, up to 2 m tall. **Stem** terete, rather sparingly branched above; bran-ches densely and coarsely glandular-hairy. **Leaves** narrowly oblong to narrowly elliptic, glabrous above, sparsely pubescent below, 11–22 cm long, 2–6 cm broad, acute. **Inflores-cence** up to 20 cm long; bracts broadly lanceolate, up to 2 cm long, glandular-hairy. **Flowers** up to 4 cm long, yellow with purple spots on a paler yellow lip. **Dorsal sepal** elliptic-ovate, up to 1.8 cm long, 0.8 cm broad, acute, ciliate; **lateral sepals** shorter but broad-er, connate, apex bidentate and ciliate. **Petals** linear, up to 1.9 cm long, acute, margins wavy.

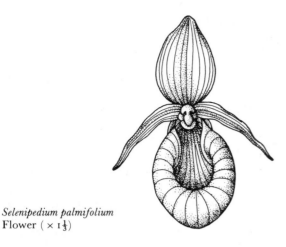

Selenipedium palmifolium
Flower (× 1⅓)

Lip broadly ellipsoidal, slipper-shaped, margins incurved, mouth circular to elliptic.
DISTRIBUTION Guyana, Venezuela, Brazil and Trinidad.
HISTORY Originally placed in 1840 by John Lindley in his *Genera and Species of Orchidaceous Plants* (p. 527) in the genus *Cypripedium*, this species was transferred by H.G. Reichenbach in 1854 to the genus *Selenipedium* in *Xenia Orchidacea* (p. 5, t. 2). For a key to the generic separation of these two genera see the notes under *Paphiopedilum*.
SYNONYM *Cypripedium palmifolium* Lindl.

Serapias L.
Subfamily Orchidoideae
Tribe Orchideae
Subtribe Orchidiinae

Small to medium-sized terrestrial plants, often forming colonies, with leafy stems and perennating by ovoid or sphaerical root-stem tuberoids. **Leaves** fleshy, lanceolate. **Inflorescences** terminal on leafy stems, laxly to densely few- to many-flowered; bracts often overtopping flowers, grey to purplish. **Flowers** yellow, pink or purple. **Sepals** and **petals** free, subsimilar, connivent. **Lip** 3-lobed with a 1- or 2-lobed callus between the side lobes; side lobes erect, hidden within sepals and petals; mid-lobe tongue-shaped, elongate, pendent, pubescent near the base. **Column** erect, with 2 parallel anther loculi; pollinia 2, mealy, with caudicles.
DISTRIBUTION A small genus of about six or seven species in the Mediterranean region of Europe, N. Africa and the Middle East.
DERIVATION OF NAME An ancient name for European orchids derived from Serapias, an Egyptian god known for his licentious following, an allusion no doubt to the supposed aphrodisiac qualities of the tubers of these orchids.

TAXONOMY The species of *Serapias* can be difficult to name and they are usually distinguished by features of the lip shape and callus structure. The European species are well covered in most guides to European orchids such as that of K.P. Buttler, *Orchideen* (1986). The recent revision of *Serapias* by Baumann and Kunkele (1989) in *A.H.O. Mitteilungsblatt* (pp. 701–946) is, in our view, unworkable. They have recognised 17 species and three subspecies, many differing in very minor features. These are probably best treated as varieties.
TYPE SPECIES *S. lingua* L.
CULTURE Temp. Winter min. 5°C. As for *Barlia*.

Serapias lingua L.
A colony-forming small terrestrial, 10–35 cm tall, stoloniferous. **Leaves** 4–8, linear-lanceolate, acuminate, 5–13 cm long, 0.8–1.3 cm wide. **Inflorescence** laxly 2- to 8-flowered; bracts 1.5–3.5 cm long. **Flowers** horizontal to the rhachis; sepals and petals greyish-purple, with darker purple veins; lip yellow flushed more or less with purple on lobes, the callus maroon; ovary 0.8–1.5 cm long. **Dorsal sepal** lanceolate, acuminate, 15–25 cm long, 4.5–6 mm wide; **lateral sepals** similar but slightly oblique. **Petals** ovate-lanceolate at the base, abruptly long-acuminate above, 13–18 mm long, 3–4.5 mm wide. **Lip** 3-lobed, 22–29 mm long, 14–16 mm wide; side lobes oblong, rounded in front, erect; mid-lobe pendent, ovate, acute, 13–19 mm long; callus a single, raised, dark purple, longitudinally grooved boss. **Column** 7–9 mm long.
DISTRIBUTION Mediterranean Europe, from France and Portugal to the Greek Islands, and N.W. Africa, in damp meadows, dune slacks, fields and marshes, up to 1200 m.
HISTORY *Serapias lingua* has been known since ancient times but it was first given a binomial by Linnaeus in 1753 in the 1st edition of his *Species Plantarum* (p. 950).
SYNONYMS *S. oxyglottis* Willd.; *S. stenopetala* Maire & Steph.; *S. excavata* Schltr.; *S. mauretanica* Schltr.
CLOSELY RELATED SPECIES. All of the other species have 2 rounded calli at the base of the lip. *S. neglecta* De Not. [Colour Plate], from Italy and S. France, has the largest flowers with a lip mid-lobe up to 2.8 cm long and 1.6 cm wide; *S. vomeracea* (Burm.f.) Briq., widespread in the Mediterranean region, is a tall plant up to 60 cm high, and has a lanceolate blood-red lip mid-lobe, up to 2.8 cm long but only 0.8–1.3 cm wide.

Sievekingia Rchb.f.
Subfamily Epidendroideae
Tribe Gongoreae
Subtribe Stanhopeinae

Epiphytic or lithophytic plants with clustered ovoid 1-noded pseudobulbs with a single apical leaf, or rarely 2, and surrounded by imbricate basal sheaths. **Leaves** plicate, heavily veined, petiolate. **Inflorescences** pendent, short to elongate, densely few- to many-flowered at the apex, basal. **Flowers** medium-sized. **Sepals** and **petals** subequal, free, spreading. **Lip** simple or 3-lobed with an entire or a lacerate-fimbriate margin, rhombic to ovate or obovate; callus basal, fimbriate or with erect lamellae. **Column** subarcuate, clavate or broadly winged; pollinia 2, hard, attached by an elongate stipe to a round viscidium.
DISTRIBUTION A genus of some 10 species from the tropical Americas from Costa Rica to Bolivia.
DERIVATION OF NAME This genus commemorates Herr Dr Sieveking, Burgomeister of Hamburg, where Reichenbach lived at the time.
TAXONOMY Reichenbach described this genus in 1871 in of this *Beiträge zur systematischen Pflanzenkunde* (p. 3).
The genus can be divided into those species with an entire margin to the lip and those in which the lip is fimbriate-lacerate. A synopsis of the genus has been given by Rudolf Jenny in *Die Orchideen* (pp. 73–80) in 1986.
The monotypic genus *Soteranthus* Lehm. ex Jenny (*Die Orchidee* 37(2): 73) is closely allied to *Sievekingii* and its single species, *S. shepheardii* (Rolfe) Jenny from Colombia, was previously included there. However, it differs in having an erect inflorescence, non-resupinate flowers, with an entire lip with a small hairy callus near the base, and a column that is distally winged.
TYPE SPECIES *S. suavis* Rchb.f.
CULTURE Temp. Winter min. 15°C. Grow in baskets as *Stanhopea* and *Schlimmia*. The small plants should not be allowed to become too dry at any time.

Sievekingia peruviana Rolfe ex C. Schweinfurth [Colour Plate]
A medium-sized epiphyte with clustered, ovoid, unifoliate pseudobulbs, up to 3.5 cm long. **Leaf** longly petiolate, oblong-elliptic to elliptic, acute, 12–22 cm long, 3.5–6 cm wide; petiole up to 6 cm long. **Inflorescence** pendent; peduncle about 4–5 cm long, subdensely several-flowered; bracts lanceolate, acute, 0.8–1.2 cm long. **Flowers** with creamy sepals, yellow petals and a yellow lip, the sepals lepidote on the outside; pedicel and ovary 1.9–2.5 cm

long. **Dorsal sepal** lanceolate, acuminate, 1.6–2 cm long, 0.4–0.5 cm wide; **lateral sepals** similar but broader, 0.7–0.9 cm wide. **Petals** porrect, oblanceolate, acute, 1.6–2 cm long, 0.3–0.45 cm wide. **Lip** concave, entire, triangular when flattened, acute, 1.3–1.5 cm long and wide; sides erect; callus of several tapering fleshy protuberances at the base and a fleshy bilobed porrect flap in front. **Column** clavate, 1.1–1.2 cm long.

DISTRIBUTION Peru only; in lower montane forest at 1200–1500 m.

HISTORY The type was collected in the Chanchamayo Valley of Junin Province in Peru by Schunke and was described in the *American Orchid Society Bulletin* (p. 176) in 1943 by Charles Schweinfurth who used a name given to it by Robert Rolfe in the *Orchid Review* (p. 310) in 1910. Unfortunately, Rolfe did not validly describe it at the time.

Sievekingia reichenbachiana **Lehm. ex Rolfe**

A small epiphyte or lithophyte with a creeping elongate rhizome bearing ovoid, unifoliate pseudobulbs, 3–3.5 cm long, 1–1.2 cm in diameter, covered by distichous, scarious, lanceolate, finely spotted sheaths. **Leaves** erect, oblanceolate, 15–30 cm long, 2.5–3.5 cm wide,

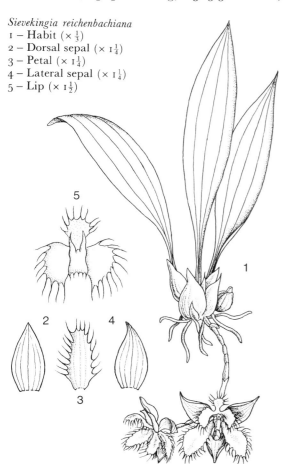

Sievekingia reichenbachiana
1 – Habit (× ⅓)
2 – Dorsal sepal (× 1¼)
3 – Petal (× 1¼)
4 – Lateral sepal (× 1¼)
5 – Lip (× 1½)

with a long slender petiole. **Inflorescences** pendent, rather densely 3- to 9-flowered, 5–10 cm long; bracts elliptic-lanceolate, acute or acuminate, 8–13 mm long, green spotted with purple. **Flowers** non-resupinate, with yellow petals, purple-spotted at the base, pale yellow sepals and a yellow, purple-spotted lip; pedicel and ovary 1.5–3.3 cm long. **Dorsal sepal** lanceolate, acuminate or acute, 13–19 mm long, 4–5 mm wide; **lateral sepals** lanceolate, acuminate, 15–21 mm long, 5–7 mm wide. **Petals** elliptic-lanceolate, deeply lacerate on all the margins, 14–19 mm long, 5 mm wide. **Lip** 3-lobed, with longly lacerate margins, 9–11 mm long, 8–9 mm wide; side lobes falcate-elliptic; mid-lobe linear-oblong; callus lacerate at the base and with 2 slender prongs in front. **Column** slender, clavate, 11–15 mm long.

DISTRIBUTION Colombia and Ecuador; in lower montane rain forest, 200–900 m.

HISTORY F.C. Lehmann collected the type material in the foothills of the Andes near Guayaquil in Ecuador and named it as *Gorgoglossum reichenbachiana* in his field notes. However, it was left to Robert Rolfe formally to describe this species as *Sievekingia reichenbachiana* in 1898 in Curtis's *Botanical Magazine* (t. 7576).

Sigmatostalix **Rchb.f.**

Subfamily Epidendroideae
Tribe Oncidieae

Small epiphytic herbs with short rhizomes. **Pseudobulbs** small, ancipitous, 1- or 2-leaved, usually subtended by 2 or more leaves. **Leaves** subcoriaceous to coriaceous. **Inflorescence** lateral, from base of pseudobulb, subtended by a leaf, racemose, usually longer than the leaves. **Flowers** small, often on short fasciculate branches that are concealed by several bracts. **Sepals** and **petals** similar, subequal, spreading or reflexed, free or with the lateral sepals somewhat connate at the base. **Lip** sessile or with a long claw, entire or variously lobed, often complex. **Column** slender, elongated, slightly dilated towards the apex; pollinia 2, waxy.

DISTRIBUTION Some 20 or more species confined to the American tropics from Mexico to Brazil.

DERIVATION OF NAME From the Greek *sigma* (C-shaped) and *stalix* (stake), probably in allusion to the slender arcuate column.

TAXONOMY H.G. Reichenbach described *Sigmatostalix* in the *Botanische Zeitung* (p. 769) in 1852.

Sigmatostalix is allied to *Leochilus* but differs in that the anther is not produced in front into a membranaceous appendage longer than the locule. From *Oncidium* and *Odontoglossum* it may

be distinguished by its ± elongated and slender column which is mostly not 2-winged above.

The genus has been revised by R. Schlechter in *Fedde, Repertorium Specierum Novarum* (1918) and by F. Kraenzlin in A. Engler's *Das Pflanzenreich* (1923). Schlechter included nine species in the genus but separated seven species with a sessile lip which had previously been included in *Sigmatostalix* to form two new genera: *Petalocentrum* with two species and *Roezliella* with five species. Kraenzlin accepted the former as distinct but reunited the latter with *Sigmatostalix*. In all he described 23 species in four sections divided on their lip structure plus a further three obscure species. Kraenzlin also considered the Brazilian *Ornithophora* congeneric with *Sigmatostalix* but recent accounts have resurrected *Ornithophora* (e.g. G. Pabst and F. Dungs in *Orchidaceae Brasilienses*, 1977).

TYPE SPECIES *S. graminea* (Poepp. & Endl.) Rchb.f.

SYNONYM *Roezliella* Schltr.

CULTURE Compost A. Temp. Winter min. 10–12°C. *Sigmatostalix* species grow well in small pots or pans under humid, shady conditions. A little less water should be given when growth is complete but the plants must never become very dry.

Sigmatostalix bicallosa **Garay**

[Colour Plate]

A medium-sized, slender, erect plant, up to 30 cm high. **Pseudobulbs** narrowly ovoid, 2.5–3 cm long, 1-leafed at apex, subtended by 2 distichous leaf-bearing sheaths below. **Leaf** linear-lanceolate, apiculate, 8–12 cm long, 0.6–0.7 cm broad. **Inflorescence** lateral, erect, racemose, distantly many-flowered. **Flowers** large in genus, membranaceous. **Sepals** narrowly elliptic-lanceolate, acuminate, 1 cm long, 0.2 cm broad. **Petals** obliquely oblong-lanceolate, acuminate, 1 cm long, 0.2 cm broad. **Lip** narrowly longly clawed, with a cordate-reniform lamina, acuminate, front margins ciliolate, 0.8 cm long, 0.8 cm broad; calli 2 at base of mid-lobe, semirhombic. **Column** erect, very slender, abruptly inflexed and dilated near the apex, about 1 cm long.

DISTRIBUTION Peru.

HISTORY First collected when found growing epiphytically on coffee trees in April 1905 on the Rio Branco in Peru by E. Koehler and described in 1951 by L. Garay in the *Arquivos do Jardim Botánico do Rio de Janeiro* (p. 57, t. 2).

CLOSELY RELATED SPECIES Allied to *Sigmatostalix crescentilabia* Schweinf. and *S. picta* Rchb.f. but differs from both in having 2 calli on the lip which are not connected directly with the claw. The lip is also fine papillose and ciliolate around the margins in the basal two-thirds.

Sigmatostalix graminea (Poepp. & Endl.) Rchb.f.

A small epiphytic plant with a short, creeping, branched rhizome. **Pseudobulbs** numerous, approximate, very small, cylindric-ellipsoid, compressed, 0.7–1.2 cm long, 1-leafed at apex, with several imbricating, leaf-bearing sheaths below. **Leaf** small, linear, acute or subobtuse, arcuate-recurved, 3–5 cm long, 0.2 cm broad. **Inflorescence** basal, equalling the leaves, erect or spreading, 3–6 cm long, laxly few-flowered, racemose. **Flowers** very small, membranaceous, pale yellow, spotted purple. **Sepals** oblong or elliptic-lanceolate, acute, concave, 0.25 cm long, 0.1 cm broad. **Petals** lanceolate, acute, 0.25 cm long, 0.1 cm broad. **Lip** shortly and broadly clawed, ovate-subquadrate, retuse, truncate at base, 0.3 cm long and 0.3 cm broad; disc excavated at base, centrally ridged through the middle. **Column** very slender, clavate, 0.15 cm long, rounded-auriculate above; rostellum short-triangular, minutely bidentate.

DISTRIBUTION   Peru and Brazil.

HISTORY   Discovered at Cuchero in Peru by E.F. Poeppig and S.L. Endlicher and described by them as *Specklinia graminea* in their *Nova Genera ac Species Plantarum* (p. 51, t. 89) in 1836. H.G. Reichenbach transferred it to the new genus *Sigmatostalix* as the type species in 1852 in the *Botanische Zeitung* (p. 769).

SYNONYM   *Specklinia graminea* Poepp. & Endl.

Sigmatostalix guatemalensis Schltr.

A small, tufted epiphytic plant, 10–34 cm high. **Pseudobulbs** ellipsoid or ovoid, compressed, 1.5–4 cm long, 0.7–1.8 cm across, 1-leafed at apex, subtended by leaf-bearing sheaths. **Leaf** erect-spreading, elliptic-lanceolate or ligulate, obtuse to subacute, subcoriaceous, up to 13 cm long, 0.8–1.7 cm broad. **Inflorescence** erect or suberect, racemose, laxly several-flowered. **Flowers** with greenish-yellow petals and sepals; lip yellow, ± marked with red-brown. **Sepals** and **petals** subsimilar, reflexed, lanceolate, acute to obtuse, 0.65–0.9 cm long, 0.15–0.25 cm broad. **Lip** with a short fleshy claw, sagittate-ovate above, 0.6–1 cm long, 0.6 cm broad; lamina auriculate at base, truncate or apiculate at apex; callus small, suberect, blunt or notched at apex. **Column** slender, arcuate, 0.6–0.7 cm long.

DISTRIBUTION   Mexico to Panama; in humid forests up to 1700 m altitude.

HISTORY   H. von Tuerkheim discovered *S. guatemalensis* at Cobán in the Department of Alta Verapaz, Guatemala and it was described by R. Schlechter in 1911 in *Fedde, Repertorium Specierum Novarum* (p. 253).

Smitinandia Holtt.
Subfamily Epidendroideae
Tribe Vandeae
Subtribe Sarcanthinae

Small epiphytic herbs with elongate monopodial leafy stems. **Leaves** distichous, coriaceous, conduplicate, flat, unequally bilobed at the apex, articulated to persistent leaf sheaths. **Inflorescences** lateral, emerging through the leaf sheaths, simple, densely many-flowered. **Flowers** small. **Sepals** and **petals** free, subsimilar. **Lip** 3-lobed, with a distinct spur lacking inner ornamentation but with the mouth almost closed by a high fleshy transverse wall at the base of the lip. **Column** short, cylindrical, somewhat broadened at the base but lacking a foot; rostellum short; pollinia 4 in 2 compressed pairs, attached by a rather short obovate stipe to an ovate or cordate viscidium.

DISTRIBUTION   A small genus of three species in S.E. Asia across to Sulawesi.

DERIVATION OF NAME   Named in honour of Tem Smitinand, joint author of *Orchids of Thailand* (1959–65) and former Director of the Royal Thailand Department of Forestry.

TAXONOMY   *Smitinandia* was established by R.E. Holttum in 1969 in the *Gardens Bulletin of the Singapore Botanic Gardens* (p. 105). It is allied to *Sarcanthus* but differs in its lip shape and the wall-like callus that blocks the mouth of the spur.

TYPE SPECIES   *S. micrantha* (Lindl.) Holtt.

CULTURE   Temp. Winter min. 12–15°C. Grow either in pots or mounted under conditions of moderate shade and humidity. Water well while growing but keep drier at other times, generally in winter.

Smitinandia micrantha (Lindl.) Holtt.

A pendent epiphyte with an elongate 10–25 cm long stem ascending in the apical part. **Leaves** linear, unequally obtusely bilobed at the apex, 6–11 cm long, 1.1–2.1 cm wide. **Inflorescences** simple, shorter or longer than the leaves, 7–17 cm long, densely many-flowered, with the flowers spirally arranged; peduncle and rhachis thick; bracts triangular, acute, 1 mm long. **Flowers** small, the sepals and petals white, the lip marked with violet; pedicel and ovary 1–1.5 mm long. **Dorsal sepal** ovate, subacute, 2.5 mm long, 1.5 mm wide; **lateral sepals** broadly oblong-ovate, obtuse, 2.5–3 mm long, 2–2.5 mm wide. **Petals** oblanceolate-oblong, obtuse, erose on the margins, 2–2.5 mm long, 1 mm wide. **Lip** 3-lobed, 3.5–4 mm long, 3–3.5 mm wide; side lobes erect; mid-lobe oblong-ovate to obovate, blunt, with erose margins; spur shortly conical, rounded at the apex, 2 mm long. **Column** fleshy, 1 mm long.

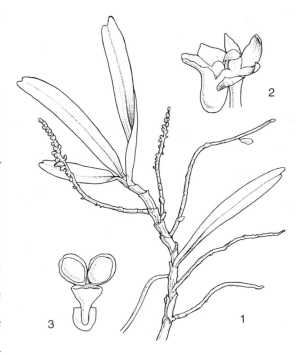

Smitinandia micrantha
1 – Habit ($\times \frac{1}{2}$)
2 – Flower ($\times 3\frac{1}{2}$)
3 – Pollinarium ($\times 21$)

DISTRIBUTION   N.W. Himalayas across to Laos and south to Malaya and Borneo; in lowland and lower montane forest, up to 1300 m.

HISTORY   Nathaniel Wallich collected the type specimen in Nepal and it was described by John Lindley in 1833 as *Saccolabium micranthum* in his *Genera and Species of Orchidaceous Plants* (p. 220). R.E. Holttum transferred it to the present genus in 1969 in the *Gardens Bulletin of the Singapore Botanic Gardens* (p. 106).

SYNONYMS   *Saccolabium micranthum* Lindl.; *S. fissum* Ridley; *Gastrochilus parviflorus* Kuntze; *Cleisostoma micranthum* (Lindl.) King & Pantling; *C. poilanei* Gagn.; *C. tixieri* Guill.; *Uncifera albiflora* Guill.; *Ascocentrum micranthum* (Lindl.) Holtt.; *Pomatocalpa poilanei* (Gagn.) Tang & Wang

Sobennikoffia Schltr.
Subfamily Epidendroideae
Tribe Sarcanthinae
Subtribe Angraecinae

Robust epiphytic, lithophytic or terrestrial erect monopodial plants with short to long leafy stems. **Leaves** distichous, coriaceous, linear-ligulate, unequally bilobed at the apex, conduplicate, articulated to a stout sheathing base.

Inflorescences lateral, axillary, as long as or longer than the leaves, spreading to suberect. **Flowers** large, showy, white with a green mark on the lip and a greenish spur. **Sepals** and **petals** spreading, free, lanceolate, acute or acuminate. **Lip** much larger than the other segments, porrect, 3-lobed in apical part, with a linear longitudinal narrow callus, spurred at the base; mid-lobe narrow, much narrower than the side lobes; spur tapering from a broad mouth, upcurved in the apical half. **Column** short, fleshy, lacking a foot; pollinia 2, ovoid, each attached by a caudicle to a hyaline viscidium.

DISTRIBUTION A small genus of three species from Madagascar.

DERIVATION OF NAME Named by Rudolf Schlechter for his wife whose maiden name was Alexandra Sobennikoff.

TAXONOMY *Sobennikoffia* is closely allied to *Angraecum* but readily distinguished by its flowers which have a distinctive prominently 3-lobed lip. It was established by Rudolf Schlechter in 1925 in *Fedde, Repertorium Specierum Novarum* (p. 361).

TYPE SPECIES *S. fournieriana* (Kraenzl.) Schltr. and *S. robusta* (Schltr) Schltr.

CULTURE Compost A. Temp. Winter min. 15°C. As for *Oeoniella*. These plants require humid conditions under moderate shade and should be well watered while in active growth. When growth is completed, they may be kept somewhat drier.

Sobennikoffia humbertiana H. Perr.

A medium-sized lithophytic plant. **Stem** 15–20 cm long, 1–1.2 cm broad, about 7-leaved towards apex. **Leaves** distichous, ligulate, obtusely and unequally 2-lobed at apex, 9–20 cm long, 1.8–2.2 cm broad. **Inflorescence** erect, longer than the leaves, axillary, 5- to 8-flowered; peduncle 9–11 cm long; bracts obtuse, very broad, 0.6 cm long. **Flowers** white, turning yellowish with age. **Dorsal sepal** elliptic-lanceolate, attenuate, 2.5 cm long, 0.6 cm broad; **lateral sepals** curved, narrow. **Petals** ovate-lanceolate, 2 cm long, 0.7 cm broad. **Lip** oblong, 3-lobed in the apical half, 3–3.2 cm long; side lobes small, obtuse, shorter than the mid-lobe; mid-lobe linear-lanceolate, acuminate, 1–1.2 cm long; disc with 3 ridges, the middle one bifid at the apex; spur attenuate-curvate, with a broad mouth, 1.8–2.5 cm long. **Column** thick, 0.3 cm long, auriculate; rostellum mid-lobe small, cylindric, 0.6 cm long.

DISTRIBUTION Central and S. Central Madagascar: in dry forests, 400–1200 m altitude.

HISTORY Discovered by H. Humbert on Mt Vohipolaka, and in the Andranomiforitra

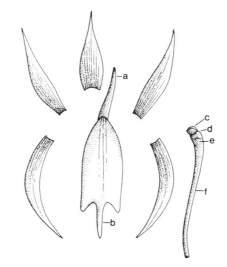

Sobennikoffia humbertiana
Floral dissection (×1)
a – Spur
b – Lip
c – Anther
d – Column
e – Ovary
f – Pedicel

and Manambolo Valleys in Central Madagascar and described by H. Perrier de la Bâthie in 1938 in *Notulae Systematicae* (p. 134).

Sobennikoffia robusta (Schltr.) Schltr.
[Colour Plate]

A medium-sized terrestrial or, less commonly, epiphytic or lithophytic plant up to 40 cm tall with a stout stem up to 15 mm in diameter; roots numerous, 5–6 mm in diameter, white with green tips. **Leaves** linear-loriform, unequally bluntly bilobed at the apex, 25–38 cm long, 2.5–3.5 cm wide, conduplicate, attached to distichous, imbricate leaf bases. **Inflorescences** as long as or longer than the leaves, 12- to 17-flowered; peduncle stout, 3 mm in diameter; bracts elliptic, obtuse, 3–5 mm long. **Flowers** large, white with a green base to the lip and a greenish spur, turning yellow with age; pedicel and ovary c. 3 cm long. **Sepals** lanceolate, acuminate, recurved at the tip, 2.5–4 cm long, 1–1.4 cm wide. **Petals** similar but shorter, to 3.5 cm long, 1.3 cm wide. **Lip** concave, 3-lobed, 2.4–4.5 cm long, up to 2.5 cm wide; side lobes oblong, suberect, subacute in front; mid-lobe narrowly lanceolate, acuminate, up to 1.5 cm long; spur tapering to apex, upcurved in apical half above the ovary, 2.8–4.5 cm long. **Column** 3–5 mm long, with 2 apical broad auricles.

DISTRIBUTION W. Madagascar, usually growing at the foot of shrubs in seasonally dry woodland.

HISTORY This attractive orchid was discovered by H. Perrier de la Bâthie at Manongarivo in W. Madagascar and was described

as *Oeonia robusta* by Rudolf Schlechter in 1913 in the *Annales du Muséum Colonial, Marseille* (p. 41). Schlechter transferred it to his new genus *Sobennikoffia* in 1925 in *Fedde, Repertorium Specierum Novarum* (p. 362).

SYNONYMS *Oeonia robusta* Schltr.; *Angraecum robustum* (Schltr.) Schltr.

CLOSELY RELATED SPECIES *S. humbertiana* H. Perr. from Central and S.C. Madagascar is similar to *S. robusta* but differs in having smaller flowers in which the sepals generally reach only 2.5 cm long, a shorter spur up to 2.5 cm long, and obtuse or rounded side lobes to the lip.

Sobralia Ruiz & Pavon

Subfamily Epidendroideae
Tribe Arethuseae
Subtribe Sobraliinae

Terrestrial or epiphytic herbs with reedy, short to very long stems. **Leaves** cauline, strongly nerved, coriaceous, articulated to tubular leaf-sheaths. **Flowers** mostly large, showy, often short-lived in a short terminal raceme. **Sepals** and **petals** free, subsimilar. **Lip** tubular below, spreading above, entire or 3-lobed, adnate to column at base; disc smooth or crested with calli. **Column** elongate, 3-lobed at the apex; pollinia 8, granulose.

DISTRIBUTION About 35 species, confined to the tropics of Mexico and Central and S. America.

DERIVATION OF NAME Named in honour of the Spanish physician and botanist Dr Francisco Sobral, a friend of the authors.

TAXONOMY *Sobralia* was described by H. Ruiz and J. Pavon in 1794 in *Prodromus Florae Peruvianae et Chilensis* (p. 120, t. 26). It is allied to *Elleanthus* but differs in having mostly larger flowers in which the base of the lip is neither saccate nor gibbous and lacks prominent calli.

TYPE SPECIES *S. dichotoma* Ruiz & Pavon

SYNONYMS *Fregea* Rchb.f.; *Lindsayella* Ames & Schweinf.

CULTURE Compost A. Temp. Winter min. 12–15°C. All *Sobralia* species grow and flower in suitably sized pots or tubs but the larger-growing species such as *S. macrantha*, are better planted out in well-drained beds. The plants require plenty of water and moderate shade while growing but less water should be given when they are not in active growth.

Sobralia candida (Poepp. & Endl.) Rchb.f.

A large, slender, terrestrial or epiphytic herb, up to 90 cm tall. **Stems** clustered, leafy above, covered by elongate, tubular sheaths. **Leaves** 3–6, distant, narrowly lanceolate to lanceolate, long-acuminate, up to 22 cm long, 3 cm broad, largest in the middle. **Inflorescence** terminal, 1-flowered, or 1 flower at a time, arcuate-recurved; bracts numerous, appressed, imbricate. **Flower** membranaceous, white or creamy-white; lip snow-white or salmon, mottled with pink. **Sepals** lanceolate, acute, 2.5–3 cm long, 0.5–0.6 cm broad. **Petals** similar, narrowly elliptic-lanceolate. **Lip** oblong-elliptic or elliptic when spread, acute or apiculate, constricted or obscurely 3-lobed above, 2.5–3 cm long 1–1.4 cm broad. **Column** dilated above, winged towards apex, 1.4–2 cm long.

DISTRIBUTION   Peru and Venezuela.
HISTORY   Discovered growing on tree trunks by E.F. Poeppig near Pampayacu and Cuchero in Peru and described by him and S.L. Endlicher in 1836 in their *Nova Genera ac Species Plantarum* (p. 56, t. 94) as *Cyathoglottis candida*. H.G. Reichenbach transferred it to the genus *Sobralia* in 1853 in *Flore des Serres* (p. 247).

S. *candida* is readily distinguished by its long, narrowly lanceolate leaves and by its flower which is predominantly white and spotted red near the apex of the lip which has a low, longitudinal, 5-ridged callus.
SYNONYM   *Cyathoglottis candida* Poepp. & Endl.

Sobralia cattleya Rchb.f.

A large, caespitose terrestrial plant. **Stems** stout, erect or arcuate, leafy, over 2 m tall. **Leaves** plicate, narrowly elliptic-lanceolate, acuminate, up to 30 cm long, 7 cm broad. **Inflorescences** from the axils of the uppermost 4 leaves, shortly paniculate, 5- to 12-flowered: peduncle and rhachis stout, slightly angled in cross-section; bracts small; green. **Flowers** large, showy, scented; sepals white or creamy with rose-pink or pinkish-brown margins, apex white; petals maroony-pink or pinkish-brown within, white on outer surface; lip white at the base, maroon-purple above with a white margin, keels yellow or yellow-brown; column white. **Sepals** oblong-elliptic, subacute, 5–5.5 cm long, 1.3 cm broad; lateral sepals falcate. **Petals** oblong-oblanceolate, obtuse, margins undulate-crisped, up to 4.6 cm long, 1.3 cm broad. **Lip** obscurely 3-lobed, ovate-circular when spread out, 4.5 cm long, 5 cm broad; side lobes erect around the column; mid-lobe broadly oblong, emarginate, margins undulate-crenulate; disc with 3 longitudinal keels, fimbriate in front, running to the apex and shorter keels on either side. **Column** clavate, 2.6 cm long.

DISTRIBUTION   Venezuela and Colombia.
HISTORY   Collected in Colombia by J. Carder and E. Shuttleworth who sent living plants to W. Bull. H.G. Reichenbach described it in 1877 in the *Gardeners' Chronicle* (n.s. 7: p. 72).

S. *cattleya* is a most distinctive species, readily identified by its lateral, many-flowered inflorescences and whitish-pink flowers with a maroon lip and low, yellow central ridges.

Sobralia dichotoma Ruiz & Pavon
[Colour Plate]
A very tall, robust and variable plant, up to 6 m high. **Stems** stout, caespitose, leafy, often growing in dense thickets. **Leaves** narrowly lanceolate to ovate-lanceolate, long-acuminate, rigid, chartaceous, up to 35 cm long, 8.5 cm broad. **Inflorescences** lateral, racemose, laxly few- to many-flowered, arcuate or spreading. **Flowers** somewhat fleshy, white on outside, violet, pale rose or deep red within, fragrant. **Sepals** oblong-oblanceolate to elliptic-oblong, acute and mucronate, up to 6 cm long, 1.4 cm broad. **Petals** oblong-spathulate to elliptic-oblong, margins ± crisped, slightly broader than the sepals. **Lip** involute below, spreading above, ovate-subquadrate when spread, subentire to obscurely 3-lobed, 6.5 cm long; mid-lobe bilobulate; disc bearing numerous narrow keels, central ones lacerate towards the apex, forming a prominent central tuft. **Column** clavate, half the length of the lip.

DISTRIBUTION   Colombia, Peru and Bolivia; 750–2800 m altitude
HISTORY   Discovered by José Pavon growing in abundance in hot, rocky places in open woodland near Muña, Pozuzo and Chinchao in Peru and described by him and H. Ruiz in their *Systema Naturae* (p. 232) in 1798.
SYNONYMS   *Cattleya dichotoma* (Ruiz & Pavon) Beer; *Sobralia mandonii* Rchb.f.

Sobralia leucoxantha Rchb.f. [Colour Plate]
See under *Sobralia macrantha*.

Sobralia macrantha Lindl. [Colour Plate]
A very large terrestrial or very rarely epiphytic plant, up to or over 2 m tall. **Stems** terete, clustered, leafy throughout. **Leaves** narrowly to broadly lanceolate, long-acuminate, spreading, rigid, 13–30 cm long, 2–7.5 cm broad. **Inflorescence** terminal, 1-flowered, subtended by a large foliaceous bract. **Flower** large, showy, rose-purple; lip white inside tube, tinged yellow in centre. **Sepals** linear-oblong, acute to subacute, recurved, 8–10 cm long, 1.5–2.6 cm broad. **Petals** oblong-obovate, rounded and shortly mucronate at apex, margins undulate-crisped in apical half, 6.5–9 cm long, 2.3–4 cm broad. **Lip** oblong-obovate when spread out, tubular in basal half, rotund and deeply 2-lobed in apical half, margins undulate-crisped, 8–11 cm long, 7 cm broad. **Column** slender, clavate, 3–3.5 cm long.
DISTRIBUTION   Mexico to Costa Rica; growing commonly in leaf mould on rocks or in

sandy soils by streams, up to 3400 m altitude.
HISTORY   S. *macrantha* was described by John Lindley in 1836 in *Sertum Orchidacearum* (sub t. 29) from plants discovered near Oaxaca in Mexico by Count Karwinsky and later near the Hacienda de la Laguna by C.J. Schiede.
CLOSELY RELATED SPECIES   *Sobralia leucoxantha* Rchb.f [Colour Plate] from Costa Rica and Panama is allied to S. *macrantha* but has smaller, distinctly-coloured flowers with a column which is much larger in relation to the lip.

Solenidium Lindl.
Subfamily Epidenroideae
Tribe Oncidieae

Medium-sized epiphytic plants with a short but prominent rhizome. **Pseudobulbs** approximate, bilaterally compressed, ± sulcate, 2-leaved at apex. **Leaves** relatively thin-textured, flexuose. **Inflorescence** lateral from the immature, developing pseudobulbs, erect, laxly racemose, often many-flowered. **Flowers** medium-sized, not very showy. **Sepals** and **petals** free, spreading. **Lip** adnate to column-foot and at right-angles to it, clawed; disc callose. **Column** erect or somewhat arcuate, thinly alate with a pair of rounded arms below the stigma, with a short, obliquely descending foot; pollinia 2, ovoid, on a narrow oblanceolate stipe; viscidium prominent, one-third the length of the stipe.

DISTRIBUTION   One or two species in Venezuela, Colombia, Brazil and possibly Peru.
DERIVATION OF NAME   From the Greek *solenidion* (small canal), in allusion to the supposed channelled claw of the lip. Unfortunately, this observation was based on a badly folded and pressed flower.
TAXONOMY   *Solenidium* was established by John Lindley in 1846 in his *Orchidaceae Lindenianae* (p. 15). It is superficially similar to some species of *Oncidium* but is considered by H. Sweet in *Orquideologia* (1973) to be more closely allied to *Leochilus*, sharing with it the pair of brachiae under the stigma and similar pollinia. From *Oncidium* it differs in its narrowly stalked, wartless lip and 3-lobed anther-bed; its pollinia which are bent down upon their stipe; the wingless column which has a thin, membranous border; and the peculiar lip callus. Sweet is also of the opinion that the genus is monotypic, but G. Pabst and F. Dungs in *Orchidaceae Brasilienses* (1977) include the type species and S. *lunatum* (Lindl.) Kraenzl. in the genus.
TYPE SPECIES   S. *racemosum* Lindl.
CULTURE   Compost A. Temp. Winter min. 12–15°C. *Solenidium* species should be grown

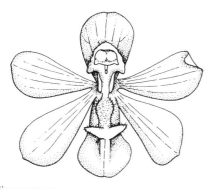

Solenidium racemosum
Flower (× 2)

under moderate shade and given plenty of water after flowering when the new growths develop. After the pseudobulbs have fully formed less water is required but shrivelling should be avoided.

Solenidium racemosum Lindl. [Colour Plate]
A small to medium-sized epiphytic herb with a stout creeping rhizome. **Pseudobulbs** cylindric, bilaterally compressed, up to 6 cm long. 2.5 cm broad, 2-leaved at apex. **Leaves** ligulate, acuminate, up to 30 cm long, 2.2. cm broad. **Inflorescence** suberect, from the base of the new growth, racemose, up to 35 cm long, up to 40-flowered; bracts lanceolate, acute, 0.4 cm long. **Flowers** small; sepals and petals yellow, heavily marked with chestnut-brown; lip similarly coloured with a large white callus. **Sepals** and **petals** obovate, truncate or slightly emarginate, 1.1–1.4 cm long, 0.5–0.6 cm broad. **Lip** obovate, slightly emarginate, entire, 1.4 cm long, 0.5 cm broad; callus pubescent, oblong below, bilobulate above, apical lobules erect. **Column** short, 0.5 cm long, apex dentate, with 2 basal cushions.
DISTRIBUTION Colombia and Venezuela; above 500 m.
HISTORY Discovered by J. Linden in 1842 near Pamplona in Colombia and about five years later by H.C. Funck and Louis Schlim in the same region. John Lindley described it in 1846 in *Orchidaceae Lindenianae* (p. 15).
SYNONYM *Oncidium racemosum* (Lindl.) Rchb.f.

Sophronitella Schltr.
Subfamily Epidendroideae
Tribe Epidendreae
Subtribe Laeliinae

Small epiphytic plants with a slender creeping rhizome. **Pseudobulbs** ovoid, fluted, in parallel

lines, covered with white sheaths, 1-leafed at apex. **Leaves** linear, sulcate, keeled below. **Inflorescences** shorter than the leaves, 1- to 2-flowered. **Flowers** large for plant, violet-magenta, with a paler centre. **Sepals** and **petals** spreading, similar, oblong-lanceolate, up to 1.4 cm long. **Lip** oblong or obovate, subacute, broader than the other segments, with an obscurely 2-lobed, fleshy, basal callus. **Column** short, stout, with an oblong, falcate, truncate arm on each side at the sides of the stigmatic cavity.
DISTRIBUTION A single species in E. Brazil.
DERIVATION OF NAME *Sophronitella* is the diminutive of *Sophronitis*, a related genus of S. American orchids. *Sophronitis* is derived from the Greek word *sophronia* (chaste or modest), in allusion to the small, relatively inconspicuous habit.
TAXONOMY *Sophronitella* was first described by Rudolf Schlechter in 1925 in *Fedde, Repertorium Specierum Novarum, Beihefte* (p. 76). It is distinguished from *Sophronitis* by its flower colour; its deflexed oblong or obovate lip which does not enfold the column at its base; its obscure basal callus; the elongate anther-cap; and the short, winged column.
TYPE SPECIES *S. violacea* (Lindl.) Schltr.
CULTURE Compost A. Temp. Winter min. 12–15°C. As for *Sophronitis*. The plants may be mounted or grown in small pans. They require humid, shady conditions and should be carefully watered throughout the year.

Sophronitella violacea (Lindl.) Schltr.
[Colour Plate]
A small epiphytic plant with a creeping, slender rhizome. **Pseudobulbs** densely clustered, robust, oblong-fusiform or narrowly ovoid, 1- or 2-noded at the base, 1.5–3 cm long, 0.3–0.8 cm broad 1- leafed at apex. **Leaf** more or less spreading, fleshy-coriaceous, linear, conduplicate, abruptly acute and minutely apiculate, 4–7 cm long, 0.3–0.5 cm broad. **Inflorescence** erect, 1- to 2-flowered; bracts ovate, acute, 0.4–0.9 cm long. **Flowers** showy, fleshy, purple-violet. **Sepals** oblong-lanceolate, acute, 2 cm long, 0.3–0.4 cm broad. **Petals** oblong, acute, 2 cm long, 0.4–0.5 cm broad. **Lip** submembranaceous, connate to the column at the base, entire, narrowly obovate, abruptly acute, 1.7 cm long, 0.6 cm broad; disc gibbous at the base. **Column** erect, straight, clavate, 0.5–0.6 cm long; terminal wings fleshy, obtuse, falcate.
DISTRIBUTION E. Brazil.
HISTORY Discovered by George Gardner in the Organ Mts near Rio de Janeiro, it was described by John Lindley as *Sophronitis violacea* in the *Botanical Register* (misc. no. 18) in 1840. Rudolf Schlechter transferred it to the new

genus *Sophronitella* in 1925 in *Fedde, Repertorium Specierum Novarum* (p. 76).
SYNONYMS *Sophronitis violacea* Lindl.; *Cattleya violacea* (Lindl.) Beer

Sophronitis Lindl.
Subfamily Epidendroideae
Tribe Epidendreae
Subtribe Laeliinae

A genus of dwarf epiphytic or lithophytic plants. **Pseudobulbs** clustered on the rhizome, each bearing a solitary leaf. **Leaf** coriaceous, suberect or erect. **Inflorescence** terminal, 1- or rarely 2- (or more-) flowered. **Flowers** showy, mostly scarlet, purple or orange-red with yellow on the lip, large for size of plant. **Sepals** elliptic, spreading subsimilar. **Petals** broader, spreading. **Lip** much smaller than other segments, erect, sessile at base of column or shortly adnate to it, entire or 3-lobed, enfolding the column below. **Column** thick, short, with a subpetaloid wing on each side of the stigmatic cavity; pollinia 8 in 2 series of 4.
DISTRIBUTION A small genus of about seven species confined to E. Brazil and Paraguay.
DERIVATION ON NAME Diminutive of *Sophronia*, another genus of South American orchids. The Greek word *sophronia* means modest and is applicable to *S. cernua* but scarcely to *S. coccinea*.
TAXONOMY *Sophronitis* was described by John Lindley in 1828 in the *Botanical Register* (t. 1129). It is allied to *Epidendrum* and *Laelia*, being similar to the latter in having 8 pollinia but differing in the erect lip which is sessile at the base of the column, or is shortly adnate to it, and in having a moderately thick column with a subpetaloid wing on each side of the stigmatic cavity.

The recent articles of J.A. Fowlie in the *Orchid Digest* (1972, 1977) have greatly clarified the specific limits in the genus and both articles are well illustrated by colour photographs of most of the known species in the genus.

Sophronitis species (in particular, *S. coccinea*) have been used extensively in hybridisation programmes to introduce their vivid scarlet coloration into larger-flowered forms. They hybridise readily with the allied genera *Laelia*, *Cattleya*, *Schomburgkia*, *Epidendrum* and *Brassavola* and many remarkable scarlet- and red-flowered hybrids have resulted in the hybrid genera such as *Sophrolaelia* and *Epiphronitis*.
TYPE SPECIES *S. cernua* Lindl.
CULTURE Compost A. Temp. Winter min. 10–12°C. These dwarf plants may be grown

mounted on pieces of fern-fibre or cork or in shallow pans. They require humid conditions under moderate shade and should never become very dry. However, water must be very carefully given during the winter months.

Sophronitis cernua Lindl. [Colour Plate]

A small epiphytic or lithophytic plant with a robust, creeping, somewhat branched rhizome. **Psedobulbs** densely clustered, subcylindric or ovoid, 2- to 3-noded at the base, 1–2 cm long. 0.5–1.2 cm thick, 1-leafed at apex. **Leaf** small, ± spreading, thickly coriaceous, broadly ovate or elliptic-ovate, obtuse or minutely apiculate, 2–2.5 cm long, 1.2–1.8 cm broad, glossy dark green above, purple below. **Inflorescence** erect or somewhat spreading 2–5 cm long, 2- to 5-flowered. **Flowers** rich cinnabar-red, white or yellow at the base of the lip, fleshy. **Sepals** ovate-oblong, acute, 1.2 cm long, 0.5 cm broad. **Petals** narrowly ovate-rhomboid, obtuse or minutely apiculate, 1–1.2 cm long, 0.5–0.6 cm broad. **Lip** connate at the base to the column, broadly triangular-ovate, abruptly acute at the apex, 0.8–1 cm long, 0.6–0.7 cm broad; disc excavate at the base and transversely cristate. **Column** erect, clavate, biauriculate above, tridenticulate at the apex, 0.5 cm long.

DISTRIBUTION   E. Brazil.

HISTORY   Discovered growing epiphytically near Botofogo, 3 miles from Rio de Janeiro by William Harrison who sent it to his sister-in-law, Mrs Arnold Harrison of Aigburgh, near Liverpool, England. She flowered it in December 1826 and it was described in 1828 by John Lindley in the *Botanical Register* (t.1129).

SYNONYMS   *Sophronitis modesta* Lindl.; *S. hoffmannseggii* Rchb.f.; *S. isopetala* Hoffmannsegg; *S. nutans* Hoffmansegg; *Cattleya cernua* (Lindl.) Beer; *Epidendrum humile* Vell.

Sophronitis coccinea (Lindl.) Rchb.f [Colour Plate]

A small epiphytic or lithophytic plant with a creeping, elongate, branching rhizome. **Pseudobulbs** clustered, erect or ascending, terete, fusiform or oblong-ovoid, 1- or 2-noded below, 1.5–4 cm long, 0.2–0.6 cm in diameter, 1-leafed at apex. **Leaf** erect-spreading, fleshy-coriaceous, oblong-elliptic or narrowly ovate, obtuse or acute, 3–6 cm long, 1–2.5 cm broad. **Inflorescence** erect or somewhat spreading, 1-flowered, 3–6 cm long. **Flowers** very showy, fleshy, scarlet-red with a yellow base to the lip; column often pale purple. **Sepals** spreading, broadly oblong, 1.7–2.2 cm long, 0.7–1 cm broad. **Petals** ovate-rotund, obtuse, 2–3 cm long and broad. **Lip** connate to column at base, broadly ovate-triangular, distinctly 3-lobed, 1.3–2 cm long, 1.5–2.2 cm broad; side lobes erect, broadly triangular-rotund, obtuse; mid-

lobe oblong-triangular, obtuse, concave; disc transversely cristate at the base. **Column** clavate, slightly 2-lobed at the apex, 0.6–0.9 cm long.

DISTRIBUTION   E. Brazil.

HISTORY   Originally described as *Cattleya coccinea* by John Lindley in 1836 in the *Botanical Register* (sub t. 1919) from a plant collected by M.E. Descourtilz in the mountains which separate Bananal from Ilha Grande. H.G. Reichenbach transferred it to the genus *Sophronitis* in 1864 in *Walpers, Annales Botanices* (p. 465). The plant is still often grown under the later synonym *S. grandiflora*, which Lindley described in 1838 in *Sertum Orchidacearum* (t. 5).

Several varieties are or have been in cultivation, including var. *aurantiaca* with orange flowers and var. *purpurea* with purple flowers.

SYNONYMS   *Cattleya coccinea* Lindl.; *Sophronitis grandiflora* Lindl.; *Cattleya grandiflora* (Lindl.) Beer; *Sophronitis militaris* Rchb.f.

Spathoglottis Blume
Subfamily Epidendroideae
Tribe Arethuseae
Subtribe Bletiinae

Terrestrial herbs with fibrous, epiphytic-type roots. **Pseudobulbs** conic-ovoid, covered with scarious sheaths. **Leaves** 1–2, elongate-lanceolate, plicate, sheathing at the base. **Inflorescence** lateral, erect, stout, racemose and many-flowered above. **Flowers** pedicellate, showy. **Sepals** and **petals** erect-spreading; petals broader than sepals. **Lip** 3-lobed at base, with a depressed pubescent callus between the side lobes; limb erect, linear or spathulate. **Column** erect-incurved, dilated above; pollinia 8, 4 in each cell, clavate, floury: stigma apical under rostellum.

DISTRIBUTION   About 40 species in India. S.E. Asia, China, Indonesia. New Guinea, Australia and the Pacific Islands.

DERIVATION OF NAME   From the Greek *spathe* (spathe) and *glotta* (tongue), alluding to the unusually broad mid-lobe of the lip.

TAXONOMY   C.L. Blume described *Spathoglottis* in 1825 in his *Bijdragen* (p. 400). It is widely distributed in E. Asia and adjacent islands, with the largest number of species being recorded from New Guinea. A few species of *Spathoglottis*, such as the Malayan *S. affinis* de Vries, are deciduous, losing their leaves in the dry season, and flowering when almost leafless.

S. plicata in pink-, purple- or white-flowered forms is widely cultivated as are several other species. Indeed, the former has often escaped from cultivation and has been mistakenly recorded as a wild plant in both E. and W. Africa.

R. Holttum in the *Orchids of Malaya* (1964) has described and keyed out 13 species. being all the known native species of Malaya, Indonesia and the Philippines.

Spathoglottis is allied to *Ipsea* Lindl. and *Pachystoma* Blume but may be distinguished from them on account of the column not being produced at the base.

TYPE SPECIES   *S. plicata* Blume

CULTURE   Compost B. Temp. Winter min. 12°C. During growth, *Spathoglottis* species should be given plenty of water and moderate shade. When the pseudobulbs are fully formed much less water is required until the new shoots appear.

Spathoglottis petri Rchb.f. [Colour Plate]

A terrestrial herb up to 70 cm tall. **Pseudobulbs** ovoid, 1–2.5 cm in diameter, several-leaved. **Leaves** plicate, suberect, lanceolate or linear-lanceolate, 30–70 cm long, 2.5–8 cm wide. **Inflorescence** erect, up to 70 cm long, densely 6- to 20-flowered at the apex; peduncle stout, terete; bracts cucullate, elliptic, obtuse, 1–1.8 cm long, pink or purple. **Flowers** magenta, permanganate purple or rarely pinkish-purple; pedicel and ovary 3–4 cm long. **Sepals** elliptic-ovate, 1.6–1.8 cm long, 0.7–1 cm wide. **Petals** similar but smaller. **Lip** 3-lobed 1.3–1.6 cm long and wide; side lobes erect, elliptic, rounded in front; mid-lobe shortly clawed, transversely elliptic-oblong in front, obtuse, 0.8–1 cm long; callus a hairy mound at the base of the mid-lobe. **Column** arcuate, 1–1.2 cm long.

DISTRIBUTION   Vanuatu and New Caledonia only; on open slopes and in grassland, up to 800 m.

HISTORY   This vividly coloured orchid was discovered by Peter Veitch in Vanuatu. H.G. Reichenbach named it after him in 1877 in the *Gardeners' Chronicle* (ser. 2, 8: p. 392).

Spathoglottis plicata Blume [Colour Plate]

A terrestrial herb, up to 1 m or more tall, but mostly shorter with a short leafy pseudobulb, up to 7 cm long, 5 cm in diameter. **Leaves** numerous, linear-lanceolate, acuminate, plicate, 30–120 cm long, 2–7 cm broad; petiole dilated at base, 10–15 cm long. **Inflorescence** lateral, 15–95 cm long, distantly several-flowered; raceme puberulous: bracts lanceolate, acuminate, 1.5–2.2 cm long. **Flowers** 2.5 cm across, lilac, rose-coloured or purple; callus yellow. **Dorsal sepal** elliptic, apiculate, 1.2 cm long, 0.6 cm broad; **lateral sepals** similar but somewhat falcate, 1.3 cm long, 0.7 cm broad. **Petals** elliptic-ovate, obtusely acuminate, 1.5 cm long, 0.8 cm broad. **Lip** 3-lobed, 1.7 cm long, 1.4 cm broad; side lobes oblong-obovate, basal, 0.7 cm long, obtuse to subtruncate; mid-lobe longly clawed, cuneate, 1 cm long, 0.6 cm broad; callus on the claw of the mid-lobe, sparsely villose, cordate. **Column** 1.2 cm long, clavate, winged.

DISTRIBUTION India, S.E. Asia, Indonesia, New Guinea to the Philippines.

HISTORY Discovered in the E. Indies by C.L. Blume and described in 1825 by him in *Bijdragen* (p. 401) with the note that it is found in woody places.

SYNONYMS include *Bletia angustata* Gagn.; *Spathoglottis lilacina* Griff.

Spiranthes L.C. Rich.
Subfamily Spiranthoideae
Tribe Cranichideae
Subtribe Spiranthinae

Small to medium-sized terrestrial herbs with fleshy swollen tuberous roots. **Leaves** several in a basal rosette, convolute, conduplicate, thin-textured to fleshy, lanceolate to oblanceolate, non-articulate. **Inflorescence** erect, terminal, densely many-flowered, spicate. **Flowers** resupinate, usually arranged in a tight spiral, small, white, green, yellow or pink, not opening widely. **Dorsal sepal** porrect, free but adnate to the 2 petals to form a hood over the column; **lateral sepals** free, spreading, enclosing the base of the lip. **Lip** porrect, longer than the other segments, enveloping the column at the base, often recurved at the apex, rarely lobed, saccate or not at the base and with 2 glands inside; nectary adnate to the ovary. **Column** erect; pollinia 2, deeply cleft, mealy, attached to a terminal viscidium; rostellum apical, elongate.

DISTRIBUTION A genus of perhaps 50 species, the majority in the Americas, but with a few species in Europe and Asia, one species extending to the Pacific Islands and Australia.

DERIVATION OF NAME From the Greek *speira* (coil) and *anthe* (flower), in allusion to the spiral inflorescence of the type species.

TAXONOMY *Spiranthes* was established by the French botanist L.C. Richard in 1818 in *Mémoires du Musée d'Histoire Naturelle, Paris* (p. 59).

It has been interpreted in two quite different ways by taxonomists over the past century. In its strict sense it includes those species lacking a spur or mentum and with a spiralled inflorescence. In the broader sense, *Spiranthes* has been used to include all of the tropical American Spiranthinae. We consider this latter view simplistic and have broadly followed the treatments of Schlechter (1920) in *Beihefte zum Botanisches Zentralblatt* (p. 317) and Garay (1976) in

Botanical Museum Leaflets of Harvard University (pp. 277–425) here.

TYPE SPECIES *S. autumnalis* L.C. Rich. (= *S. spiralis* (L.) Chevall.).

CULTURE Temp. Winter min. 5–15°C. depending on origin of plant. Temperate species may be grown in the same conditions as *Anacamptis*, while the more tropical species can be grown like *Prescottia*.

Spiranthes cernua (L.) L.C. Rich.
[Colour Plate]
A colony-forming terrestrial, at times almost aquatic plant, up to 50 cm tall. **Leaves** 3–6, linear-oblanceolate, acute, 5–20 cm long, 0.5–2 cm wide. **Inflorescence** cylindrical, 30–50 cm tall, with the flowers arranged spirally in 2–4 ranks; peduncle bearing leafy sterile bracts; bracts lanceolate, acuminate, 5–15 mm long, green. **Flowers** not opening widely, white with a greenish-yellow mark on the lip, usually fragrant; ovary 10 mm long. **Dorsal sepal** oblong-lanceolate, obtuse to subacute, 6–11.5 mm long, 2–3 mm wide; **lateral sepals** lanceolate, subacute, 6–11.5 mm long, 1.5–3 mm wide. Petals lanceolate-falcate, acute, 6–11 mm long, 2–3 mm wide. **Lip** subpandurate to oblong-ovate, obtuse, recurved towards the apex, 6–10 mm long, 3–6 mm wide, with 2 basal backward-pointing fleshy pubescent tubercles, with an erose apical margin. **Column** 3–5 mm long, green.

DISTRIBUTION Widespread in E and central N. America from N. Florida to Canada; growing on the wet margins of streams and lakes, and in meadows and wet woods.

HISTORY Linnaeus described this handsome orchid as *Ophrys cernua* in 1753 in the 1st edition of his *Species Plantarum* (p. 946). L. C. Richard transferred it to *Spiranthes* in 1818 in *Mémoires du Muséum d'Histoire Naturelle, Paris* (p. 59).

SYNONYMS include *Ophrys cernua* L.; *Limodorum autumnale* Walter; *Spiranthes constricta* (Small) K. Schumann

Spiranthes sinensis (Pers.) Ames
A terrestrial plant 15–45 cm tall, with cylindrical hairy roots. **Leaves** 3–5, in a basal rosette, oblong-elliptic to linear-lanceolate, acute, 5–16 cm long, 0.4–1 cm wide, glossy dark green. **Inflorescence** densely many-flowered, with the flowers arranged in a spiral; peduncle bearing 2–3 distant sheaths, glandular hairy; bracts lanceolate, acuminate, 4–8 mm long, glandular hairy. **Flowers** spreading, pink with a white lip or white; ovary 5–6 mm long, glandular. **Dorsal sepal** oblong-lanceolate, acute, 4–5 mm long, 2 mm wide; **lateral sepals** oblong-ovate, obtuse, 4–5 mm long, 2–2.5 mm wide; all sepals glandular on the outside. **Pet-**

als oblong-obovate, obtuse, 4–5 mm long, 2 mm wide. **Lip** concave, obovate, obtuse, 4.5–6 mm long, 3 mm wide, with an erose-undulate apical margin, with 2 large glands enclosed within the base. **Column** 2–3 mm long.

DISTRIBUTION Widespread from E. Russia throughout Asia to the Malay Archipelago, Australia and the S.W. Pacific Islands; in grassy places, roadsides and waste places, up to 2000 m.

HISTORY Originally described as *Neottia sinensis* by C.H. Persoon (1807) in his *Synopsis Plantarum* (p. 511) based on a Chinese plant collected by J. Loureiro. It was transferred to the present genus by Oakes Ames in the second volume of his *Orchidaceae* (p. 53) in 1908.

This is a weedy species that is self-pollinating in much of its range. In cultivation it will seed freely in a greenhouse frequently appearing as a weed in other pots.

SYNONYMS include *Neottia sinensis* Pers.; *Spiranthes australis* (R. Br.) Lindl.; *S. neocaledonica* Schltr.

Sphyrarhynchus Mansf.
Subfamily Epidendroideae
Tribe Vandeae
Subtribe Aerangidinae

Dwarf epiphytic plants with very short leafy stems. **Leaves** distichous, linear-elliptic, coriaceous. **Inflorescences** axillary, few-flowered, shorter than the leaves. **Flowers** large for size of plant, white. **Sepals** and **petals** subsimilar, elliptic-lanceolate, acute. **Lip** spurred, lamina ovate-elliptic, concave; spur pendent, clavate. **Column** very short; rostellum short, porrect, hammer-shaped in front; pollinia 2, subglobose; stipites 2, filiform; viscidium 1, oblong.

DISTRIBUTION One or possibly two species in Tanzania.

DERIVATION OF NAME From the Greek *sphyra* (hammer) and *rhynchos* (beak), in allusion to the hammer-shaped dilation of the rostellum.

TAXONOMY *Sphyrarhynchus* was established by R. Mansfield in 1935 in *Notizblatt des Botanischen Gartens, Berlin-Dahlem* (p. 706). It very much resembles a small *Aerangis* in habit but is easily recognised by its very short inflorescences, its clavate spur and its very distinctive rostellum.

TYPE SPECIES *S. schliebenii* Mansf.

CULTURE Probably best mounted. Temp. Winter min. 10–12°C, rising to 25–30°C during the day. These small plants are best established on a piece of cork or tree-fern fibre. Moderately shaded, humid conditions are required, and water should be carefully given throughout the year.

Sphyrarhynchus schliebenii Mansf.

[Colour Plate]

A tiny epiphytic plant. **Stem** very short. **Roots** flattened onto substrate, greenish-grey. **Leaves** elliptic or oblong-elliptic, up to 3.5 cm long, 0.5 cm broad, unequally 2-lobed at apex. **Inflorescence** spreading or pendulous, 2- to 7-flowered or more, up to 3 cm long; peduncle slender, with several short black sheathing bracts. **Flowers** large for the size of the plant, white, with a bright green central mark on the lip. **Sepals** narrowly oblong-elliptic, acute, reflexed somewhat, 1–1.4 cm long, 0.3–0.4 cm broad. **Petals** narrowly oblong, acute, 0.9–1.4 cm long, 0.3–0.4 cm broad. **Lip** entire, reflexed, ligulate, acute, 0.4–0.6 cm long, 0.2–0.35 cm broad; spur clavate, 0.6 cm long. **Column** with a hammer-like rostellum, 0.15 cm long.

DISTRIBUTION   N. and Central Tanzania; in montane forest, 900–1600 m.

HISTORY   Discovered by H.J. Schlieben in the Uluguru Mts of E. Central Tanzania in 1935 and described as the type species of a new genus by R. Mansfield in 1935 in *Notizblatt des Botanischen Gartens, Berlin-Dahlem* (p. 706).

Stanhopea Hooker

Subfamily Epidendroideae
Tribe Gongoreae
Subtribe Stanhopeinae

Medium-sized to large epiphytic, lithophytic or terrestrial plants. **Pseudobulbs** small, 1-leafed. **Leaf** large, plicate, with a slender, sulcate petiole. **Inflorescence** lateral, pendent, racemose, 1- to several-flowered; bracts large, chartaceous. **Flowers** ephemeral, large, showy, fleshy, strongly scented. **Sepals** and **petals** subsimilar, free, spreading to reflexed. **Lip** complex, fleshily-thickened; hypochile calceiform or globose; mesochile, if present, entire or divided, often 2-horned; epichile articulated to mesochile, entire or 3-lobed. **Column** long, erect, ± arcuate, wingless to broadly winged above; pollinia 2 waxy.

DISTRIBUTION   About 25 species widely distributed in the American tropics.

DERIVATION OF NAME   In honour of the Rt Hon. Philip Henry Stanhope who was president of the London Medico-Botanical Society from 1829 to 1837.

TAXONOMY   Sir William Hooker described *Stanhopea* in 1829 in the *Botanical Magazine* (tt. 2948, 2949). The flowers are often very variable in colour within a single species. Many species have been described based on flower colour differences which are now not considered sufficient to justify specific recognition. In all, about 100 specific names have now been reduced to about 25 valid species. The most useful characters for taxonomic purposes have proven to be the features of the tripartite lip.

Stanhopea is allied to *Coryanthes* but lacks the saccate epichile of the lip of that genus. C. Dodson and Frymire have discussed aspects of the biology and taxonomy of *Stanhopea* in the *Annals of the Missouri Botanic Garden* (1961). Their studies have been subsequently extended in two articles by Dodson in *Selbyana* (1975), where several critical species have been discussed and their status elucidated. The pollination biology of *Stanhopea* is discussed in some detail also by L. van der Pijl and Dodson in *Orchid Flowers* (1966).

TYPE SPECIES   *S. insignis* Hooker
CULTURE   Compost A. Temp. Winter min. 12–15°C. Min. 15°C while growing. As their inflorescences grow downwards or sideways beneath the pseudobulbs, *Stanhopea* species must be grown in open baskets with gaps in the bottom. While growing, the plants need high humidity, plenty of water at the roots and moderate shade – enough to prevent scorching. When the pseudobulbs are mature, much less water is required and the plants should also be kept cooler. The flowers appear mostly in summer.

Stanhopea ecornuta Lemaire [Colour Plate]

An epiphytic plant. **Pseudobulbs** clustered, ovoid, sulcate, up to 6 cm long, 3 cm in diameter, subtended by scarious sheaths, 1-leafed at apex. **Leaves** oblong-elliptic or broadly elliptic, acute or subacuminate, membranaceous, petiolate, 35–40 cm long, 8–18 cm broad; petiole slender, sulcate, up to 12 cm long. **Inflorescence** pendulous, 1- to 3-flowered;

Stanhopea lips and column (All × ⅔)
After Dodson (1975)
a Lips from above, b Columns, side view
1 – *S. graveolens*
2 – *S. hernandezii*
3 – *S. tigrina*
4 – *S. jenischiana*
5 – *S. oculata*
6 – *S. ecornuta*
7 – *S. wardii*

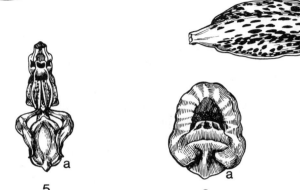

peduncle up to 12 cm long, bearing several scarious, lepidote sheaths. **Flowers** large, fleshy; sepals and petals creamy-white; petals spotted with purple towards base; lip yellow, orange-yellow at the base and inside; column yellow. **Dorsal sepal** oblong-subquadrate, almost truncate, convex, 4.5–5.5 cm long, 2.7–3 cm broad; **lateral sepals** ovate or ovate-elliptic, obtuse, oblique, concave below, 5–6.3 cm long, 3.8 cm broad. **Petals** obliquely elliptic, convex, obtuse, 3.8–4 cm long, 2.2–2.5 cm broad. **Lip** simple, lacking any horns, calceolate, compressed, obtuse, thick, fleshy, 3.8–4.5 cm long, 3 cm broad, with several swellings on inner base and on apical margin. **Column** 2 cm long.

DISTRIBUTION Guatemala, Honduras, Nicaragua and Costa Rica; in forests up to 1200 m altitude.

HISTORY Collected by J. Warscewicz in Central America and sent to the van Houtte garden in Belgium where it flowered in July 1846. C. Lemaire described it the same year in *Flore des Serres* (t. 181).

Stanhopea graveolens Lindl. [Colour Plate]
An epiphytic or lithophytic plant. **Pseudobulbs** ovoid-conical to rhomboidal, sulcate, somewhat compressed, 5–7 cm long, up to 4 cm across, 1-leafed at apex. **Leaf** elliptic-lanceolate to broadly obovate-elliptic, abruptly acute, petiolate, 20–50 cm long, 8–17 cm broad; petiole slender, sulcate, up to 15 cm long. **Inflorescence** pendent, 3- to 9-flowered; peduncle bearing several scarious, lepidote sheaths. **Flowers** showy, unpleasantly scented; sepals and petals greenish or creamy-white, spotted with maroon dots; lip yellow-orange at base with a maroon spot on either side, creamy-white above. **Sepals** ovate-elliptic to oblong-ovate, obtuse, rounded or acute, concave, 4.8–6.5 cm long, 2.6–4.5 cm broad; lateral sepals joined for basal 1 cm. **Petals** recurved, elliptic-lanceolate, acute to acuminate, margins undulate-crisped, 4.5–5.5 cm long, 1.3–2.3 cm broad. **Lip** up to 5.5 cm long, 3 cm broad; hypochile short, saccate angled or toothed at base, thickened and sulcate above; mesochile with a pair of arcuate, porrect, acuminate horns, 3–3.5 cm long; epichile ovate to subrotund, acute or revolute. **Column** arcuate, broadly winged above, 4–5 cm long.

DISTRIBUTION Mexico, Guatemala and Honduras; in forests up to 2700 m altitude.

HISTORY *S. graveolens* was described by John Lindley in 1840 in the *Botanical Register* (misc. no. 125). Lindley thought that his plant came from Peru and later gave the same name to Brazilian plants with the same unpleasant odour. However, C. Dodson has shown in *Selbyana* (1975) that *S. graveolens* is, in fact, con-

fined to Mexico and Guatemala, where it has often been mistakenly named as *S. wardii* Lodd. ex Lindl.

CLOSELY RELATED SPECIES *S. wardii* is closely allied but has smaller flowers with a smaller lip and shorter, chunkier horns on the lip mesochile.

Stanhopea hernandezii (Kunth) Schltr.
[Colour Plate]
An epiphytic or rarely lithophytic plant. **Pseudobulbs** obliquely ovoid-conical, 6 cm long, 3 cm broad, subtended by scarious sheaths, 1-leafed at apex. **Leaf** oblong to elliptic-lanceolate, acuminate, petiolate, 20–30 cm long, 5–6.5 cm broad; petiole slender-sulcate, 10 cm long. **Inflorescence** lateral, 2- to 3-flowered; peduncle stout, covered by membranaceous, lepidote sheaths. **Flowers** large, fragrant; sepals and petals pale yellow or yellowish-orange, spotted with red-brown blotches; lip creamy-white, marked with dark purple; column white, spotted crimson. **Sepals** ovate-oblong to ovate-elliptic, obtuse or rounded at apex, 5.5–6.5 cm long, 2.5–3.8 cm broad. **Petals** oblong-lanceolate, recurved, acute, 4–5 cm long, 1.5–2 cm broad. **Lip** very fleshy: hypochile subrotund-globose, with a warty inner surface, 2.5 cm long, 3 cm broad; mesochile with 2 incurved horns, arising from a broad fleshy tubercle, 2.5 cm long; epichile ovate, somewhat canaliculate, ± tridentate at apex, 2.5 cm long, 1.5 cm broad. **Column** ± narrowly winged, 4–5.5 cm long.

DISTRIBUTION Mexico and Guatemala: a rare plant in forests up to 1900 m altitude.

HISTORY First described as *Anguloa hernandezii* by C.S. Kunth in 1822 in the first volume of his *Synopsis Plantarum* (p. 332). This name was based on *Coatzonte Coxoahitl*, an Aztec name published in the previous century by Francesco Hernandez in his *Thesauro*. Rudolf Schlechter transferred it to *Stanhopea* in *Beihefte zum Botanisches Zentralblatt* (2: p. 490) in 1918.

This striking orchid is better known under the later name *Stanhopea devoniensis*, described by John Lindley in 1838 in his *Sertum Orchidacearum* (t. 1), based on a plant that flowered in the Duke of Devonshire's collection at Chatsworth.

SYNONYMS *Anguloa hernandezii* Kunth; *Stanhopea devoniansis* Lindl.

Stanhopea oculata (Lodd.) Lindl.
[Colour Plate]
An epiphytic or terrestrial plant. **Pseudobulbs** obliquely ovoid, 3.5–6.5 cm long, 1-leafed at apex. **Leaf** elliptic or broadly lanceolate, acute or acuminate, petiolate, 30–45 cm long, 3–14 cm broad; petiole slender, sulcate, up to 12 cm long. **Inflorescence** up to 25 cm long, pendu-

lous, 5- to 8-flowered; peduncle bearing several clasping, distichous inflated sheaths. **Flowers** showy, fragrant, variable in colour; yellow or white, spotted red-purple; lip with a large red-purple spot on each side at base and many smaller spots on rest of lip. **Sepals** elliptic to ovate, concave, acute to obtuse, 5.5–7 cm long, 2.5–5 cm broad. **Petals** oblong-lanceolate, acute, margins crisped-undulate, 5–5.5 cm long, 1–2 cm broad. **Lip** very fleshy, up to 6.5 cm long; hypochile concave, thickened and sulcate in front, 3.5 cm long, 1.5 cm broad; mesochile with 2 falcate porrect horns curving over epichile, 3 cm long; epichile ovate-elliptic, acute, 2–3.2 cm long, 1.5–3.2. cm broad. **Column** arcuate, broadly winged in apical half, 5–6 cm long.

DISTRIBUTION Mexico, Guatemala, Belize and Honduras.

HISTORY Introduced into cultivation by Messrs Loddiges and described by them in the *Botanical Cabinet* (t. 1764) as *Ceratochilus oculatus* in 1832. John Lindley transferred it to the genus *Stanhopea* in the same year in his *Genera and Species of Orchidaceous Plants* (p. 158).

SYNONYMS *Ceratochilus oculatus* Lodd.; *Stanhopea cymbiformis* Rchb.f.; *S. bucephalus* Lindl.; *S. guttata* Lindl.

Stanhopea platyceras Rchb.f. [Colour Plate]
A large epiphytic plant. **Pseudobulbs** ovoid-pyriform, up to 6.5 cm long, 3 cm broad, 1-leafed at apex. **Leaf** elliptic, acute, arcuate above, petiolate, 25–40 cm long, 7–12 cm broad; petiole up to 10 cm long. **Inflorescence** pendulous, 2-flowered; bracts oblong-ovate, obtuse, 4–5 cm long. **Flowers** large, pendulous; sepals and petals cream to yellow, marked with small purple spots or rings; lip cream with a large purple spot on each side of hypochile which is purple-suffused, all of lip spotted with purple; column greenish-cream, spotted dark purple. **Sepals** reflexed, oblong to oblong-ovate, obtuse, margins reflexed, up to 8.5 cm long, 3–5 cm broad. **Petals** oblong, obtuse, reflexed, up to 7.5 cm long, 2.2 cm broad. margins undulate. **Lip** complex, very fleshy, up to 7.5 cm long, 2.5 cm broad; hypochile deeply saccate, longer than the rest of lip; mesochile with 2 short fleshy porrect horns, lying over the epichile; epichile ovate, subacute **Column** arcuate, winged for apical two-thirds, up to 6.5 cm long.

DISTRIBUTION Colombia.

HISTORY Introduced from Colombia by Messrs H. Low & Co. who sold a plant to John Day of Tottenham, London for whom it flowered late in 1867. H.G. Reichenbach described it in the *Gardeners' Chronicle* (p. 27) in 1868.

Stanhopea tigrina Batem. [Colour Plate]

A large epiphytic plant. **Pseudobulbs** clustered, ovoid or ovoid-conical, longitudinally many-grooved ± corrugate, 4–6 cm long, 2.5–4 cm in diameter, covered at first by many membranaceous long-acuminate sheaths. **Leaves** erect or erect-spreading, petiolate, coriaceous, oblong, acute, 20–35 cm long, 5–10 cm broad; petiole robust, canaliculate, 6–15 cm long. **Inflorescence** deflexed or pendulous, 6–15 cm long, 2- to 4-flowered. **Flowers** large, showy, fragrant; sepals and petals pale or dark yellow, heavily spotted reddish-purple; lip with a golden-yellow hypochile, spotted on each side maroon-purple, an ivory-white mesochile, spotted purple on the lateral horns and an ivory-white epichile also often purple-spotted. **Sepals** reflexed, membranaceous, ovate-oblong or narrowly ovate, acute, 7–8 cm long, 3.5–5 cm broad; lateral sepals connate below. **Petals** ± reflexed, linear-ligulate, acute, margins revolute and undulate, 7–7.5 cm long, 1.2–1.5 cm broad. **Lip** erect, complex, 7–7.5 cm long; hypochile semiglobose, somewhat carinate, with several radiating glandulose lamellae within; mesochile 2-horned; epichile ovate, unequally tridentate at the apex. **Column** broadly semi-oblong, winged, 7–8 cm long.

DISTRIBUTION   Mexico.

HISTORY   Described by James Bateman in 1837 in his monumental *Orchidaceae of Mexico and Guatemala* (t. 7) from a plant collected in Mexico near Xalapa by John Henchman.

SYNONYM   *Stanhopea expansa* P.N. Don

CLOSELY RELATED SPECIES   See *S. devoniensis*.

Stanhopea wardii Lindl.

A large epiphytic plant. **Pseudobulbs** ovoid, somewhat compressed, dark green, up to 6 cm long. **Leaves** plicate, elliptic, petiolate, dark green, up to 30 cm long, 12 cm broad. **Inflorescences** pendent, 8- to 10-flowered; bracts thin-textured. **Flowers** large, grotesque, strongly scented; petals and sepals pale yellow, ± orange at the base, finely spotted purple; lip orange with 2 maroon eyes in basal part, creamy-green above; column very pale green. **Sepals** subsimilar, concave, elliptic, obtuse, margins recurved, 5.5–5.7 cm long, 3.5 cm broad. **Petals** lanceolate, acute, recurved, margins crisped-undulate, 4.8 cm long, 1.5 cm broad. **Lip** complex; hypochile (basal part) fleshy, concave; mesochile bearing 2 sharply pointed, curved horns, 3 cm long; epichile fleshy, broadly ovate, subacute, 2.4 cm long, 3 cm broad. **Column** arcuate winged, 4 cm long.

DISTRIBUTION   Venezuela to Peru and in Central America, north to Nicaragua.

HISTORY   Sent to Messrs Loddiges from La Guayra, Venezuela by Ward after whom it was named. John Lindley described it and had it figured in 1838 in *Sertum Orchidacearum* (t. 20).

SYNONYMS   *Stanhopea aurea* Lindl.; *S. venusta* Lindl.; *S. amoena* Klotzsch

CLOSELY RELATED SPECIES   See *S. graveolens*.

Staurochilus Ridl. ex Pfitzer

Subfamily Epidendroideae
Tribe Vandeae
Subtribe Sarcanthinae

Medium-sized to large epiphytic monopodial plants with short to elongate leafy stems covered by persistent sheathing leaf bases. **Leaves** coriaceous, spreading, linear-ligulate, unequally bilobed at the apex, articulated at the base. **Inflorescences** lateral, simple or branched, few- to many-flowered. **Flowers** small to medium-sized, more or less flat, fleshy. **Sepals** and **petals** similar or subsimilar, free, spreading. **Lip** very fleshy, 3- to 5-lobed, with or without a spur at the base, usually pubescent on the upper surface; spur with a prominent flap-like ligule on the upper side at the mouth of the spur. **Column** short, fleshy; rostellum short, pendent; pollinia 4 in 2 unequal pairs; stipe oblong to oblanceolate; viscidium horseshoe-shaped to cordate.

DISTRIBUTION   A genus of some 12–14 species, widespread from the E. Himalayas to the Philippines and Borneo.

DERIVATION OF NAME   From the Greek *stauros* (cross) and *chilos* (lip), in reference to the cruciform lip of the type species.

TAXONOMY   *Staurochilus* was first suggested by Henry Ridley in 1896 in the *Journal of the Linnean Society* (p. 350) but was not validated until Pfitzer described it in Engler's *Pflanzenreich* (p. 16) in 1900. It is closely related to *Trichoglottis* but can readily be distinguished by its elongated inflorescences of 3 or more flowers. Species of *Staurochilus* are still found in cultivation and in nursery catalogues under *Trichoglottis*.

TYPE SPECIES   *S. fasciatus* (Rchb.f.) Ridley

CULTURE   Temp. Winter min. 12–15°C. May be grown mounted or in baskets under moderate shade and humidity. Water while growing but keep drier at other times.

Staurochilus fasciatus (Rchb.f.) Ridley
[Colour Plate]

A large epiphyte with an elongate stem, up to 30 cm or more long, 6–8 mm in diameter. **Leaves** oblong-ligulate, unequally roundly bilobed at the apex, 7.5–16 cm long, 1.5–2.4 cm wide. **Inflorescences** simple, longer than the leaves, suberect, 11–19 cm long, 2- to 6-flowered; rhachis flattened, somewhat zigzag; bracts small, triangular-ovate, subacute, 6–8 mm long. **Flowers** with yellow sepals and petals marked with transverse brown bands and spots, the lip white with greenish-yellow tips and a few reddish-brown spots; pedicel and ovary 1.3–2.6 cm long. **Dorsal sepal** oblong-obovate, acute or shortly acuminate, 2.3–2.9 cm long, 0.9–1.1 cm wide; **lateral sepals** dependent, obliquely oblong-elliptic, apiculate, 2.4–3.2 cm long, 0.8–1 cm wide. **Petals** slightly falcate, oblanceolate, shortly apiculate or obtuse, 2.6–3.1 cm long, 0.6–1 cm wide. **Lip** bipartite, cruciform, 1.5–2 cm long, 1.2–1.5 cm wide, lacking a spur; hypochile with erect narrowly oblong side lobes; the epichile tripartite, lanceolate, acute side lobes spreading at right-angles to the lip, 6–7 mm long, the mid-lobe fleshily thickened, lanceolate, acute, pubescent. **Column** fleshy, 0.6–0.8 cm long, with 2 acuminate apical stelidia.

DISTRIBUTION   Thailand, Laos, Vietnam and Malaya to Borneo and the Philippines; lowland and lower montane forest, up to 1000 m.

HISTORY   H.G. Reichenbach originally described this orchid in 1872 as *Trichoglottis fasciata* in the journal *Flora* (p. 137), based on a collection probably from the Malay peninsula. It was transferred to the present genus by Ridley in 1896 in the *Journal of the Linnean Society* (p. 350).

SYNONYMS   *Trichoglottis fasciata* Rchb.f.; *Stauropsis fasciata* (Rchb.f.) Bentham; *Vandopsis leytensis* Ames

Staurochilus dawsonianus (Rchb.f.) Schltr.

An erect epiphyte with an elongate monopodial unbranched stem, up to 30 cm long, 5–6 mm in diameter. **Leaves** narrow, linear, unequally obtusely bilobed at the apex, 5–18 cm long, 1.5–2.3 cm wide. **Inflorescences** erect or suberect, simple or few-branched, laxly many-flowered, up to 70 cm long; branches 5–18 cm long, somewhat zigzag; bracts elliptic-ovate, acute, 5–7 mm long. **Flowers** fleshy, stellate, the sepals and petals creamy, pale green or pale yellow with transverse bands and spots of red, the lip yellow marked with red; pedicel and ovary 0.7–1.7 cm long. **Sepals** and **petals** similar, spathulate, shortly apiculate, 1.4–1.9 cm long, 4–5 mm wide. **Lip** 5-lobed, 6–8 mm long, 6–8 mm wide when spread, saccate at the base, pubescent within and with a basal fleshy callus; the basal lobes falcately upcurved, 3 mm long; the apical part 3-lobed, the lateral lobes spathulate and upcurved, the middle one oblong and emarginate, 2 mm long. **Column** short, fleshy, 3–4 mm long, with 2 apical fleshy hairy short stelidia.

DISTRIBUTION   Burma, Thailand and

Laos; lowland and lower montane forest up to 1000 m.

HISTORY   Charles Parish, that indefatigable collector of Burmese orchids, collected the type at Moulmein and it was described by H.G. Reichenbach as *Cleisostoma dawsoniana* in the *Gardeners' Chronicle* (p. 815) in 1868. Rudolf Schlechter transferred it to the present genus in 1915 in *Die Orchideen* (p. 577).

SYNONYMS   *Cleisostoma dawsoniana* Rchb.f.; *Trichoglottis dawsonianus* (Rchb.f.) Rchb.f.; *T. multiloba* Guill.

Stelis Sw.
Subfamily Epidendroideae
Tribe Epidendreae
Subtribe Pleurothallidinae

Small, tufted epiphytic or lithophytic herbs, with a horizontal creeping rhizome (primary stem). **Secondary stems** erect, 1-leafed. **Leaf** fleshy or coriaceous, suberect, subsessile or petiolate. **Inflorescence** axillary, 1 to many, racemose, slender. **Flowers** minute to small, numerous. **Sepals** ± subequal, ± connate, mostly spreading, the most prominent segments of the flower. **Petals** and **lip** minute, fleshy, surrounding the column. **Column** short, thickened above; rostellum ligulate; anther terminal; pollinia 2, waxy, pyriform, lacking a stipe.

DISTRIBUTION   About 200 species in the tropics of America from Mexico and the W. Indies south to Bolivia and Brazil.

DERIVATION OF NAME   From the Greek *stelis* (little pillar), a word used by the Ancient Greeks for the mistletoe which, like *Stelis* species, grows on trees.

TAXONOMY   *Stelis* was described by O. Swartz in *Schrader, Journal für die Botanik* (p. 239) in 1799. The small flowers and minute petals, lip and column make specific determinations in this genus exceedingly difficult. Indeed, as with *Pleurothallis*, the genus has been by-passed by botanists and horticulturalists as the species are of little horticultural merit. It is, therefore, not unlikely that many species remain to be described or, on the other hand, that many have been described more than once.

Stelis is allied to *Pleurothallis* but differs in having distinctly connate sepals, and petals and a lip which are similar and minute and are often broader than long.

The first attempt to subdivide the genus was made by John Lindley in *Folia Orchidacea* (1858) who recognised three sections, (*Eu*) *Stelis*, *Dialissa* and *Labiatae* each with several subdivisions. H.G. Reichenbach in *Walpers, Annales Botanices* (1864) recognised but two sections, uniting the latter two of Lindley's in sect. *Dis-*

epaleae. L. Garay in the *Canadian Journal of Botany* (1956) reviewed the previous attempts to treat *Stelis* at the subgeneric level and concluded that the previous groupings were largely unnatural and they were no longer useful, particularly in the light of the many new species described subsequent to Reichenbach's work. Garay divided the genus into three subgenera: *Stelis* with all sepals similar; *Inaequales* with ringent flowers having dissimilar sepals and the lateral sepals shortly connate; and *Dialissa* with dissimilar sepals in which the dorsal and lateral sepals are connate for over half their lengths. Subgenus *Stelis* is further subdivided into three sections on lip shape; subgenus *Inaequales* is divided into two sections on the degree of connation of the lateral sepals; whilst subgenus *Dialissa* is not subdivided. We have not followed Garay (1979) in his subsequent treatment of *Stelis* in the *Botanical Museum Leaflets of Harvard University* (pp. 167–259) in which he splits off *Apatostelis* as a separate genus.

TYPE SPECIES   *S. ophioglossoides* (Jacq.) Sw. [= *Epidendrum ophioglossoides* Jacq.] typ. cons.

SYNONYM   *Humboldtia* Ruiz & Pavon non Vahl.; *Apatostelis* Garay

CULTURE   Compost A. Temp. Winter min. 12–15 °C. Below 26 °C. in summer if possible. As for *Pleurothallis*. The plants should never be very dry and should be kept in a humid atmosphere. They mostly form compact clumps and all newly-completed growths may be expected to produce an inflorescence. Good shade is required in warm weather.

Stelis aprica Lindl.
A small, tufted epiphytic herb. **Stems** erect, straight or slightly flexuose, 3–5 cm long, terete. **Leaf** erect, coriaceous, linear-oblong or slightly spathulate, obtuse, 5–8 cm long, 0.5–0.7 cm broad, reddish-green. **Inflorescence** solitary, racemose, many-flowered almost to the base, 5–12 cm long, subtended by a rigid basal sheath; bracts erect-spreading, distichous, broadly ovate, very acute to obtuse, tubular below. **Flowers** minute, secund, spreading, greenish-yellow. **Sepals** glabrous, erect-spreading, connate below, elliptic-ovate, obtuse, membranaceous, 0.2–0.22 cm long, 0.2 cm broad. **Petals** concave, minute. **Lip** fleshly, subquadrate, obtuse at apex, pubescent at base.

DISTRIBUTION   Panama to Brazil and Venezuela.

HISTORY   First collected by R.B. Hinds in Santa Catarina State of Brazil and described by John Lindley in 1836 in Hooker's *Companion to the Botanical Magazine* (p. 353).

S. aprica is recognised by its very slender, elongate inflorescences bearing many minute flowers scarcely 0.3 cm across. The lip of each flower is subquadrate and obtuse.

SYNONYM   *Stelis herzogii* Schltr.

Stelis argentata Lindl. [Colour Plate]
A very small to small epiphytic herb with clustered stems. **Stems** very short, covered by sheaths, 1-leafed at apex. **Leaf** erect, oblanceolate, shortly petiolate, rounded or roundly 2-lobed at apex, up to 10 cm long, 2.5 cm broad. **Inflorescence** terminal, erect, racemose, laxly many-flowered, up to 20 cm long; rhachis glabrous, pale green suffused with maroon; bracts small, pale green. **Flowers** flat, greenish to pale pink-purple, darker brown-purple on outer surfaces, about 0.8 cm across; column pale brown, anther cream. **Sepals** spreading, connate towards base, subsimilar, ovate-cordate, obtuse, 0.55 cm long, 0.5 cm broad. **Petals** very much smaller than sepals, fleshy with white crystalline intrusions, truncate and lunate in front view, 0.15 cm long, 0.08 cm broad. **Lip** similar to petals, transversely oblong, fleshy, with a short, erect apicule in front. **Column** short, stout, porrect, 0.08 cm long.

DISTRIBUTION   Widespread in the tropical Americas from Mexico south to Brazil.

HISTORY   Originally described by John Lindley in 1842 in the *Botanical Register* (misc. p. 64) based on a specimen collected by R. Schomburgk in Guyana.

SYNONYMS   *Stelis heylindiana* Focke: *S. endresii* Rchb.f.; *S. littoralis* Barb. Rodr.; *S. yauaperyensis*, Barb. Rodr.; *S. parvibracteata* Ames; *S. huebneri* Schltr.

Stelis fragrans Schltr.
A small epiphytic herb, 10–12 cm high, with a very short rhizome. **Stems** slender, 1-leafed, 2.5–3 cm long. **Leaf** erect, oblanceolate-ligulate, subacute, petiolate, 4.5–6 cm long, 0.5–0.7 cm broad. **Inflorescence** racemose, erect, longer than the leaf, laxly 8- to 15-flowered; bracts ovate-cucullate, cuspidate-apiculate. **Flowers** greyish, suffused with rose.

Stelis argentata
1 – Flower (× 4)
2 – Column and lip, side view (× 13)
3 – Column, petals and lip, front view (× 11)

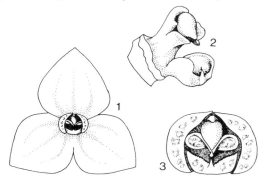

Sepals broadly ovate-rhombic, obtuse, margins and inner surface minutely papillose-ciliolate, 3-nerved, 0.4 cm long; lateral sepals oblique. **Petals** obliquely reniform, subtruncate, fleshy, minute, glabrous. **Lip** hemispherical, obtuse, with a linear depression almost to the apex, similar in size to the petals. **Column** short, truncate.

DISTRIBUTION Brazil.

HISTORY Discovered at Paraná by P. Dusen who sent plants to Berlin where they flowered in the Botanical Garden in March 1918. Rudolf Schlechter described it in the same year in *Notizblatt des Botanischen Gartens, Berlin* (p. 209).

S. fragrans is recognised by its sepals which have ciliate margins and by its semicircular lip which is longitudinally sulcate.

Stelis ophioglossoides (Jacq.) Sw.

Plants small, tufted. **Stems** erect or ascending, up to 7 cm long. **Leaf** thinly coriaceous, elongate-oblong or elliptic-oblong, 4–10 cm long, 0.6–1.6 cm broad, tridentate at apex, petiolate. **Inflorescence** usually solitary, densely many-flowered, up to 16 cm long, much longer than the leaves, enclosed at the base in a short sheath. **Flowers** very small, yellowish-green, ± purple-spotted. **Dorsal sepal** deltoid-ovate, concave, 0.3 cm long and broad; **lateral sepals** similar to dorsal sepal, joined to each other and dorsal sepal for half their length. **Petals** minute, triangular-obovate, 0.06 cm long, 0.1 cm broad. **Lip** fleshy, apex rounded or subtruncate, 0.06 cm long and broad.

DISTRIBUTION Widely distributed in the W. Indies.

HISTORY One of the first American orchids known to science. N.J. Jacquin collected and described it in 1760 as *Epidendrum ophioglossoides* in his *Enumeratio Systematica Plantarum.* (p. 29). It was transferred to the genus *Stelis* (of which it is the type species) by O. Swartz in 1799 in *Schrader, Journal für die Botanik* (p. 239).

SYNONYMS *Epidendrum ophioglossoides* Jacq.; *E. trigoniflorum* Sw.; *Dendrobium ophioglossoides* (Jacq.) Sw.

Stenia Lindl.
Subfamily Epidendroideae
Tribe Maxillarieae
Subtribe Zygopetalinae

Small to medium-sized epiphytic plants with a short stem. **Pseudobulbs** clustered, 1- to 3-leaved. **Leaves** 1–3, rigid-chartaceous. **Flowers** large, showy, lemon-yellow, ± brown-spotted on the lip. **Sepals** and **petals** spreading, subequal; lateral sepals adnate to the column-base. **Lip** fleshy, 3-lobed, concave-subsaccate; side

lobes small, entire; mid-lobe entire, much larger; callus transverse, cristate. **Column** elongate, ± pubescent; pollinia 4 in 2 pairs, linear-cylindrical.

DISTRIBUTION Eight species from Central and northern S. America.

DERIVATION OF NAME From the Greek *stenos* (narrow), referring to the slender pollinia characteristic of the genus.

TAXONOMY *Stenia* was first described by John Lindley in 1837 in the *Botanical Register* (sub t. 1991) where he distinguished it from *Maxillaria* by its non-articulated lip and very narrow pollinia. However, it is far more closely related to *Bollea*, *Huntleya* and *Chondrorhyncha* from which it is distinguished by its elongate semiterete column and markedly unequal pollinia which are linear-oblong in side view.

TYPE SPECIES *S. pallida* Lindl.

CULTURE Compost A. Winter min. 15°C. As for *Chondrorhyncha*, *Pescatorea*, etc. Shady, humid conditions are required and the compost should never become very dry.

Stenia guttata Rchb.f. [Colour Plate]

A small epiphytic plant. **Pseudobulbs** small, clustered, 1- to 3-leaved at apex, covered with spathaceous sheaths. **Leaves** obovate, oblong or elliptic, acute, up to 13 cm long, 3.5 cm broad. **Inflorescences** lateral, very short, recurved or prostrate, 1-flowered. **Flower** large, membranaceous, straw-coloured to bright yellow-green, spotted dark purple. **Dorsal sepal** oblong-ovate, subacute, 2–2.6 cm long, 0.6–0.8 cm broad; **lateral sepals** obliquely lanceolate-ovate, subacute, larger than the dorsal sepal. **Petals** similar to the dorsal sepal. **Lip** deeply concave or saccate at the base, fleshy, obscurely 3-lobed; side lobes indistinct, semi-orbicular, 1.5–1.7 cm long; mid-lobe ovate-triangular; disc with a transverse crest of 7 teeth. **Column** obscurely angled on each side.

DISTRIBUTION Peru; 800–2100 m altitude.

HISTORY Discovered in Peru by W. Davis who collected for Messrs Veitch and described by H.G. Reichenbach in 1880 in the *Gardeners' Chronicle* (n.s. 14: p. 134).

Stenoglottis Lindl.
Subfamily Orchidoideae
Tribe Orchideae
Subtribe Orchidinae

Terrestrial or epiphytic herbs with short stems and fleshy or tuber-like roots. **Leaves** in a basal rosette or tuft, numerous. **Inflorescences** erect, many-flowered in an elongate raceme, bearing a few scattered sheaths along the scape; bracts small, shorter than the ovary. **Flowers** usually

pink with darker spots or white. **Sepals** united for a short distance to the column and lip, otherwise free; lateral sepals obliquely spreading later. **Petals** often a little broader than the sepals, oblique, erect. **Lip** spurless or with a short spur, united to column, wedge-shaped, 3- to 5-lobed in upper part, longer than tepals. **Column** very short and broad; anther loculi parallel, canals absent; caudicles of pollinia short; viscida naked; stigmas club-shaped; rostellum very short.

DISTRIBUTION Four species in E. Central and S. Africa.

DERIVATION OF NAME From the Greek *stenos* (narrow) and *glotta* (tongue), descriptive of the tongue-like free part of the lip.

TAXONOMY *Stenoglottis* was described by John Lindley in 1836 in Hooker's *Companion to the Botanical Magazine* (p. 209). It is allied to *Holothrix* Lindl. and to *Habenaria* but is distinct from the former in having sessile stigmas and from the latter in having a lip more or less united to the column.

F. Kraenzlin who revised the genus in his *Orchidacearum Genera et Species* (1901) considered the genus to be monotypic. More recently authorities, such as V.S. Summerhayes in the *Flora of Tropical East Africa* (1968), consider that the variability in the material allows two or three species to be recognised. However, in the most recent account of the genus in the *Kew Magazine* (pp. 9–22) J. Stewart (1989) has recognised four species and has provided a key to their identification.

TYPE SPECIES *S. fimbriata* Lindl.

CULTURE Compost C. Temp. Winter min. 10–12°C. *Stenoglottis* species should be given moist, shady conditions while growing. During and after flowering the leaves will tend to die back and the plants should then be given little water until new growth commences.

Stenoglottis fimbriata Lindl.

An erect terrestrial, epiphytic or lithophytic herb, 10–35 cm high. **Tubers** several, oblong, fleshy. **Leaves** 6–16, in a basal rosette, oblong or lanceolate, acute, margins undulate, usually maroon-spotted, 2.5–11 cm long, 1.2–2 cm broad. **Inflorescence** erect, scaberulous, up to 21 cm long, many-flowered. **Flowers** secund, pink or purple, spotted darker purple on lip; column white. **Dorsal sepal** ovate, obtuse or subacute, 0.5 cm long, 0.2 cm broad; **lateral sepals** falcate-oblong, obtuse. **Petals** curved forward to form a hood over the column. **Lip** oblong-obovate in outline, 3-lobed in apical half, 0.9 cm long, 0.3 cm broad; lobes linear-lanceolate, acute. **Column** short.

DISTRIBUTION Widespread in Africa from Tanzania to S. Africa (Cape Province).

HISTORY *S. fimbriata* is the type species of

its genus and was discovered between Omsamwubo and Omsamcabe in Cape Province in S. Africa by J.F. Drége. It was described by John Lindley in Hooker's *Companion to the Botanical Magazine* (p. 210) in 1836.

SYNONYM *Stenoglottis zambesiaca* Rolfe

CLOSELY RELATED SPECIES *S. fimbriata* is closely allied to the larger *S. longifolia* but differs in having a 3-lobed lip.

Stenoglottis longifolia Hooker f.[Colour Plate]
A small terrestrial, lithophytic or epiphytic plant. **Leaves** numerous, arranged in a dense rosette, ensiform or linear-oblong, acuminate and recurved at the apex, margins undulate, 7.5–18 cm long, 0.8–2.5 cm broad. **Inflorescences** erect, 22–50 cm long, covered with linear-lanceolate sheaths below, racemose; bracts lanceolate, acuminate, 0.8–1.2 cm long. **Flowers** pink, light purple or rarely white, spotted dark purple on the lip. **Sepals** broadly ovate, subobtuse, 0.8 cm long. **Petals** ovate, subacute, erose or minutely denticulate, smaller than the sepals. **Lip** linear-oblong, 5-fid or 5-partite, 0.8–1.2 cm long. **Column** short, broad.

DISTRIBUTION S. Africa.

HISTORY *S. longifolia* was sent to the Royal Botanic Gardens of Kew by J. Medley Wood, Curator of the Durban Botanic Gardens in Natal. It first flowered at Kew in September 1889 and was described by Sir Joseph Hooker in 1891 in the *Botanical Magazine* (t. 7186). Hooker noted its great similarity to *S. fimbriata* but considered it sufficiently distinct to be considered a good species rather than a variety of that species.

CLOSELY RELATED SPECIES See *S. fimbriata*.

Stenorrhynchus L.C. Rich.

Subfamily Spiranthoideae
Tribe Cranichideae
Subtribe Spiranthinae

Small to large terrestrial herbs, glabrous or often pubescent. **Roots** often fleshy, fasciculate. **Stems** leafy or leafless. **Leaves,** when present, oblong to lanceolate, sessile or petiolate, often in a rosette but reduced to sheaths above. **Inflorescence** erect, racemose. **Flowers** small to fairly large, drab to showy; bracts mostly lanceolate. **Sepals** free, subsimilar; dorsal sepal erect, forming a hood with the petals; lateral sepals erect or spreading, obliquely attached to the apex of the ovary, forming at the base a saccate mentum. **Lip** sessile or distinctly clawed, often narrow, concave; enveloping and adhering to the sides of the column below; apex spreading, entire or 3-lobed; disc ± hairy. **Column** terete, decurrent at base; rostellum bidentate, shorter or longer than anther; pollinia granular-powdery, produced into a short caudicle in front.

DISTRIBUTION A large genus of probably more than 60 species widespread in Central and both tropical and temperate S. America and the W. Indies.

DERIVATION OF NAME From the Greek *stenos* (narrow) and *rhynchos* (snout), after the typically narrow rostellum.

TAXONOMY This genus was established by L.C. Richard in 1818 as *Stenorrhynchus* in the *Mémoires du Muséum d'Histoire Naturelle, Paris* (p. 59). Subsequently, it has often been incorporated in *Spiranthes* by various authorities but we have followed here the treatment of both A. Cogniaux in Martius's *Flora Brasiliensis* (1893) and R. Schlechter in *Beihefte zum Botanischen Zentralblatt* (1920).

Stenorrhynchus may be distinguished from *Spiranthes* by its non-spiral inflorescence, by characters of the rostellum and by its distinct, prominent mentum formed by the oblique bases of the lateral sepals and the decurrent base of the column.

TYPE SPECIES *S. speciosus* (Gmelin) L.C. Rich.

SYNONYMS *Stenorrhychium* Rchb.f.; *Stenorrhynchos* Sprengel

CULTURE Compost C. Winter min. 12–15°C. As for *Pelexia*.

Stenorrhynchus lanceolatus (Aubl.) L.C. Rich. [Colour Plate]
A very variable terrestrial plant, 35–90 cm tall. **Leaves** basal, appearing after flowering, oblong-elliptic to oblong-lanceolate, acute or obtuse, 10–40 cm long, 2.5–5 cm broad. **Inflorescence** erect, densely many-flowered; peduncle glandular-pubescent; bracts narrowly lanceolate, acuminate, spotted with red resinous dots. **Flowers** variable, showy, spreading-suberect, greenish-white to brick-red or crimson. **Sepals** lanceolate, acuminate, 1.4–3 cm long, 0.35–0.7 cm broad; lateral sepals elongated at base to form a short mentum. **Petals** lanceolate, falcate, acute or acuminate, 1.3–2 cm long, 0.6 cm broad. **Lip** sessile, entire, obovate-lanceolate, acuminate, 1.5–2.5 cm long, 0.5–8 cm broad, saccate near the middle, convolute below the middle; calli linear, flat, submarginal; disc and margins pubescent. **Column** 1 cm long.

DISTRIBUTION Florida, the W. Indies and Mexico, south to northern S. America; in grasslands, drier forest and pine woodlands, up to 1500 m altitude.

HISTORY Discovered in Martinique by C. Plumier who described it in 1759 as *Helleborine purpurea asphodeli radice*, a pre-Linnaean polynomial. Aublet gave Plumier's species the binomial *Limodorum lanceolatum* in 1775 in *Histoire des Plantes de la Guiane Française* (p. 821). L. C. Richard transferred it to *Stenorrhynchus* in 1818 in *Mémoires du Muséum d'Histoire Naturelle, Paris* (p. 59) and Leon later transferred it to *Spiranthes* in 1946 in *Contribuciones Ocasionales del Museo de Historia Naturel del Colegio de la Salle*. Although this latter name is still used, we have followed R. Schlechter's treatment of Spiranthinae here in accepting Richard's name.

SYNONYMS *Limodorum lanceolatum* Aubl.; *Satyrium orchioides* Sw.; *Stenorrhynchus guatemalensis* Schltr.; *Spiranthes orchioides* (Sw.) A. Rich.; *Stenorrhynchus orchioides* (Sw.) Sprengel; *Neottia aphylla* Hooker

Stenorrhynchus speciosus (Gmelin) L.C. Rich.
An epiphytic, or less commonly terrestrial or lithophytic plant, 10–50 cm high. **Leaves** basal, sessile or shortly petiolate, ovate-orbicular to oblanceolate, acute or acuminate, 4–20 cm long, 2–6 cm broad, green ± silver-spotted. **Inflorescence** erect, showy, with few to many flowers in a dense spike; bracts longer than the flowers, lanceolate, acuminate, red, 2.5–4 cm long. **Flowers** bright red to purplish-red. **Sepals** lanceolate, acuminate, margins involute and recurved near apex, 1.3–1.6 cm long, 0.4 cm broad. **Petals** similar to sepals, slightly narrower. **Lip** sessile, cuneate-lanceolate, shallowly 3–lobed in middle, acute to apiculate at apex, 1.2–1.5 cm long, 0.5–0.6 cm broad; side lobes broadly rounded; mid-lobe oblong with involute margins; disc pubescent in basal part with 2 flat, fleshy calli on each side at base. **Column** stout, densely pubescent beneath, 0.5–0.7 cm long.

DISTRIBUTION Mexico south to northern S. America and the W. Indies; in forests, thickets and on open plains, up to 3000 m altitude.

HISTORY Originally collected in the W. Indies by N.J. Jacquin and described in 1791 in the 13th edition of Linnaeus's *Systema Naturae* (p. 59) by J.F. Gmelin as *Serapias speciosa*. L.C. Richard transferred it to *Stenorrhynchus* in 1818 in *Mémoires du Muséum d'Histoire Naturelle, Paris* (p. 59). Although A. Richard later transferred it to *Spiranthes*, we have followed here R. Schlechter in *Beihefte zum Botanischen Zentralblatt* in accepting *Stenorrhynchus* as distinct from *Spiranthes*.

S. speciosus is readily recognised by its bright red to purple-red flowers, which are overtopped by long, reddish bracts, and because it flowers when the basal leaves are still present.

SYNONYMS *Serapias speciosa* Gmelin; *Spiranthes speciosus* (Gmelin) A. Rich.

Stolzia Schltr.

Subfamily Epidendroideae
Tribe Epidendreae
Subtribe Eriinae

Dwarf epiphytic or rarely lithophytic herbs with short to elongate rhizomes, often forming mats. **Pseudobulbs** ovoid, fusiform or clavate, often dorso-ventrally flattened or oblique, 1- or 2-leaved at the apex. **Leaves** fleshy or thinly coriaceous, spreading to erect, ligulate or obovate. **Inflorescences** terminal or rarely lateral, 1- to several-flowered. **Flowers** small, not opening widely. **Dorsal sepal** lanceolate; **lateral sepals** larger and more or less connate in the basal part, forming a distinct mentum with the column-foot. **Petals** small, free. **Lip** enclosed within the lateral sepals, fleshy, entire, often papillose. **Column** very short, fleshy, with a distinct incurved foot; pollinia 8, clavate or pyriform.

DISTRIBUTION A small genus of about 15 species in tropical Africa.

DERIVATION OF NAME Named in honour of Adolf Stolz, a German missionary and plant collector based at Tukuyu in S.W. Tanzania.

TAXONOMY Rudolf Schlechter established this genus in 1915 in Engler's *Botanische Jahrbücher* (p. 564). It is allied to the smaller species of *Eria* and *Porpax* from Asia and these relationships need further investigation.

The E. African species are covered by P. Cribb (1984) in the second part of the *Flora of Tropical East Africa* (Orchidaceae) (p. 325).

TYPE SPECIES *S. nyassana* Schltr.

CULTURE Temp. Winter min. 12°C. Grow mounted or in pans of epiphyte mix under shaded, humid conditions. Water well while growing but give less at other times.

Stolzia repens (Rolfe) Summerh.

[Colour Plate]

A creeping mat-forming epiphyte with rhizomatous asymmetric bifoliate pseudobulbs, up to 3 cm long, 0.3–0.4 cm in diameter. **Leaves** fleshy, circular to elliptic or obovate, rounded at the apex, 0.5–1.4 cm long, 0.3–0.8 cm wide. **Inflorescence** 1-flowered; peduncle very short. **Flower** sessile, not opening widely, emerging between the leaves, yellow to brown, striped with red on the sepals. **Dorsal sepal** oblong-ligulate, acute, 5–7 mm long, 2–3 mm wide; **lateral sepals** obliquely lanceolate, acuminate, 5–7 mm long, 3–4 mm wide. **Petals** lanceolate, acute, 4–5 mm long, 1–2 mm wide, erose. **Lip** fleshy, elliptic, obtuse, 2 mm long, 1 mm wide, erose on margins. **Column** 0.7 mm long.

DISTRIBUTION Tropical Africa from Gha-

Stolzia repens
1 – Habit (× 2)
2 – Flower with petal, lateral sepal and lip removed (× 3)
3 – Lip (× 5)
4 – Pollinia (× 24)

na across to Uganda and Kenya and south to Zimbabwe; 900–2200 m.

HISTORY Originally collected by E. Brown in Uganda and described as *Polystachya repens* by Robert Rolfe in 1912 in the *Kew Bulletin* (p. 132). It was transferred to the present genus by Victor Summerhayes in 1953 in the same journal (p. 141).

It is the commonest and most widespread species in the genus.

SYNONYM *Polystachya repens* Rolfe

Summerhayesia Cribb

Subfamily Epidendroideae
Tribe Vandeae
Subtribe Aerangidinae

Small to medium-sized epiphytic monopodial herbs with short leafy stems and aerial roots. **Leaves** distichous, coriaceous, linear, unequally bilobed at the apex, conduplicate. **Inflorescences** lateral, axillary racemose, laxly few- to several-flowered, usually longer than the leaves; bracts prominent. **Flowers** substellate, white, resupinate or non-resupinate. **Sepals** and **petals** free, subsimilar, spreading; lateral sepals shortly connate at the base. **Lip** porrect to deflexed, entire, cucullate, lacking a callus but with a slender elongate pendent cylindrical spur. **Column** short, fleshy, lacking a foot; rostellum obscurely 3-lobed, the mid-lobe taper-

ing, porrect; pollinia 2, waxy, ovoid, attached by a linear stipe to a slipper-shaped viscidium.

DISTRIBUTION A small genus of two species in W. and S. – Central tropical Africa.

DERIVATION OF NAME Named for Victor Summerhayes (1892–1974), Curator of the Kew Orchid Herbarium from 1926 until 1968 and an expert on African orchids.

TAXONOMY *Summerhayesia* is a segregate of *Aerangis* established by Phillip Cribb in the *Kew Bulletin* (p. 184) in 1977. It differs from *Aerangis* in having parallel-sided conduplicate leaves and flowers in which the lateral sepals are shortly connate at the base, the pollinia are deeply cleft, and the viscidium is distinctly slipper-shaped rather than flat.

TYPE SPECIES *S. laurentii* (De Wild.) Cribb

CULTURE Temp. Winter min. 12–15°C. Probably best grown as a mounted epiphyte under conditions of moderate shade and high humidity, although some specimens would suit small baskets. Water well while growing and less at other times.

Summerhayesia laurentii (De Wild.) Cribb

An epiphyte with a short stem, up to 18 cm long. **Leaves** conduplicate, arcuate, linear, unequally roundly bilobed at the apex, 11–19 cm long, 0.5–0.9 cm wide, articulated to stout persistent leaf bases. **Inflorescences** ascending to arcuate, laxly up to 20-flowered, 15–48 cm long; peduncle slender, terete, up to 19 cm long; rhachis somewhat fractiflex; bracts ovate, amplexicaul, 1.5–2 mm long. **Flowers** non-resupinate, white or cream shading to greenish on the spur; pedicel and ovary 1–1.3 cm long. **Dorsal sepal** elliptic, obtuse, 6–8 mm long, 3.4–4.5 mm wide; **lateral sepals** obliquely oblong-elliptic, obtuse, 6.5–9 mm long, 3–5 mm wide. **Petals** oblong, obtuse, 5.3–8 mm long, 2–3 mm wide. **Lip** uppermost in flower, upcurved, ovate, rounded or obtuse, 5–8.5 mm long, 3.5–6 mm wide; spur slender, cylindrical, 6–8 mm long. **Column** 1.5–2.5 mm long.

DISTRIBUTION Liberia, Ghana, Ivory Coast and Zaïre; in rain forest up to 800 m.

HISTORY This species was first collected in Zaïre by L.M. Laurent and was named in his honour as *Angraecum laurentii* by E. De Wildeman in *Notices des Plantes Utiliséés de Congo* (p. 322) in 1904. It was transferred to the present genus by P. Cribb in the *Kew Bulletin* (p. 185) in 1977.

SYNONYMS *Angraecum laurentii* De Wild; *Aerangis laurentii* (De Wlld.) Schltr.

CLOSELY RELATED SPECIES *Summerhayesia zambesiaca* Cribb, from Zimbabwe, Malawi and Zambia, has shorter, broader leaves and larger flowers in which the spur reaches 20 cm long.

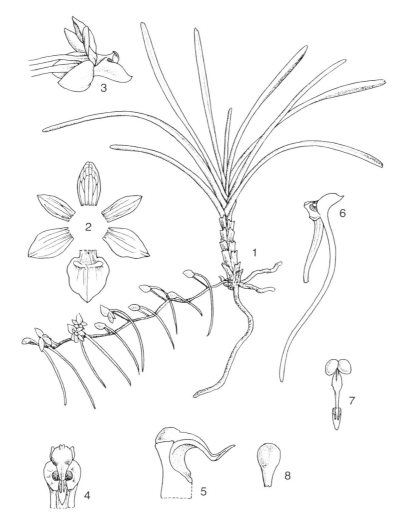

Summerhayesia laurentii
1 – Habit ($\times \frac{1}{3}$)
2 – Sepals, petals and lip ($\times 1\frac{1}{2}$)
3 – Flower, side view ($\times 1$)
4 – Column, side view ($\times 2\frac{1}{2}$)
5 – Column, side view ($\times 4\frac{1}{2}$)
6 – Column, lip and spur, side
    view ($\times 1$)
7 – Pollinarium ($\times 4\frac{1}{2}$)
8 – Anther-cap ($\times 4\frac{1}{2}$)

Sunipia J.E. Smith

Subfamily Epidendroideae
Tribe Epidendreae
Subtribe Sunipiinae

Small to medium-sized epiphytic plants with stout creeping rhizomes. **Pseudobulbs** more or less well spaced on rhizome, obovoid, unifoliate. **Leaf** coriaceous, erect or suberect, oblanceolate to oblong or elliptic, obtuse. **Inflorescence** basal, erect, short or long, laxly to densely 1- to many-flowered, racemose; peduncle and rhachis terete, slender; bracts distichous, usually prominent. **Flowers** distichous, small to medium-sized, usually not very showy. **Sepals** subsimilar; dorsal sepal free; lateral sepals free or variously connate. **Petals** much smaller than the sepals, entire or lacerate on the margins. **Lip** fleshy at apex, entire, often papillose, ecallose or with an obscure fleshy callus. **Column** short, fleshy, lacking a foot; anther-cap unmovable, persistent; pollinia 4 in 2 pairs, each pair attached by a linear stipe to separate small viscidia or to a single small viscidium.

DISTRIBUTION   A genus of about 18 species from India, Burma and Thailand across to Taiwan.

DERIVATION OF NAME   Apparently from a vernacular name in Nepal.

TAXONOMY   The name *Sunipia* was first published by J.E. Smith in *Rees' Cyclopaedia* (34, Art Stelis, nn. 11, 13) in 1816 as a *nomen nudum*, but was taken up by John Lindley in 1833 in his *Genera and Species of Orchidaceous Plants* (p. 179). It has been considered by some authors to be congeneric with *Bulbophyllum* which the species indeed superficially resembles in both habit and flowers. However, the column structure of *Sunipia* is quite distinct with each pair of pollinia attached by a linear stipe to a viscidium.

The genus was revised by Seidenfaden (1969) under the synonymous generic name *Ione* in *Dansk Botanisk Tidsskrift* (p. 205) and he has recently updated that account in 1986 in *Opera Botanica* (p. 171). His discussion of the affinities of the genus is recommended and he also provides a key to the 13 Thailand species.

TYPE SPECIES   *S. scariosa* Lindl.; *S. bicolor* Lindl.

SYNONYM   *Ione* Lindl.

CULTURE   Temp. Winter min. 12°C. Grow mounted or in pans of epiphyte mix under moderate shade and humidity. Water well while growing and keep drier when growth is complete.

Sunipia cirrhata (Lindl.) P.F. Hunt

[Colour Plate]

A medium-sized epiphyte with an elongate creeping rhizome. **Pseudobulbs** ovoid, 2.5–3.5 cm long, 1–1.5 cm in diameter. **Leaf** erect, oblong to oblanceolate, obtuse, 9–16 cm long, 2–3 cm wide, shortly petiolate. **Inflorescence** erect, 15–40 cm long, laxly 4- to 8-flowered; peduncle and rhachis slender; bracts papery, distichous, suberect, lanceolate, acute, 1.9–2.5 cm long. **Flowers** pendent, off-white with purple veins on the sepals and petals and with a rich purple lip; pedicel and ovary arcuate, 1–1.6 cm long. **Dorsal sepal** lanceolate, acuminate, 2–2.4 cm long, 0.3–0.5 cm wide; **lateral sepals** similar but united almost to the apex, 2–2.6 cm long. **Petals** oblique, broadly ovate, obtuse, 0.4–0.5 cm long, 0.5 cm wide, with erose margins. **Lip** pendent, lanceolate, acuminate, 1.5–2 cm long, 0.6–0.7 cm wide, shortly 2-ridged at the base. **Column** 0.3 cm long.

DISTRIBUTION   Nepal, N.E. India, Sikkim and Bhutan to Burma and Yunnan; 1600–1850 m.

HISTORY   Originally described as *Ione cirrhata* by John Lindley in 1853 in *Folia Orchidacea Sunipia* (p. 3) based on a collection by J.D. Hooker from Sikkim. It was transferred to *Sunipia* by P.F. Hunt in 1971 in the *Kew Bulletin* (p. 184).

SYNONYMS   *Ione cirrhata* Lindl.; *I. paleacea* Lindl.; *Bulbophyllum paleaceum* (Lindl.) Hook.f.; *Sunipia paleacea* (Lindl.) P.F. Hunt

Symphyglossum Schltr.

Subfamily Epidendroideae
Tribe Oncidieae

Small or medium-sized epiphytic herbs. **Pseudobulbs** proximate, ovoid, 2-leaved at apex, subtended by 1 to several distichous leaves. **Leaves** linear, suberect. **Inflorescence** at apex or young shoot, arcuate, simple or few-branched, laxly many-flowered; bracts triangular, appressed, much shorter than the pedicel and ovary. **Flowers** ± showy, crimson or rose-purple to yellow-brown or pale green. **Sepals** oblong or oblanceolate; lateral sepals joined in basal half rarely to middle. **Petals** broader than the sepals, adnate to column below. **Lip** entire, clawed, reflexed above; callus of 2 or 3 subparallel ridges to middle of lip. **Column** semiterete, dilated slightly above; rostellum suberect, bidentate; pollinia 2, pyriform; stipe linear-ligulate; viscidium oblong-linear, retrorse.

DISTRIBUTION   About six species in Venezuela, Colombia, Ecuador and Peru.

DERIVATION OF NAME   From the Greek *symphium* (to grow together) and *glossa* (tongue), referring to the lip, which is strongly adnate to the column.

TAXONOMY   This genus was established by R. Schlechter in 1919 in *Orchis* (p. 90). Although closely related to *Cochlioda*, *Symphyglossum* is kept distinct by virtue of its partially connate rather than free lateral sepals; its petals which are adnate to the column below; its simple rather than 3-lobed lip; and its simple stigmatic orifice (there being 2 separate ones in *Cochlioda*).

TYPE SPECIES   *S. sanguineum* (Rchb.f.) Schltr.

CULTURE   Compost A. Temp. Winter min. 12°C. As for *Cochlioda* and most *Odontoglossum* species.

Symphyglossum sanguineum (Rchb.f.) Schltr. [Colour Plate]

An epiphytic plant. **Pseudobulbs** oval-oblong, compressed, 3.5–5 cm long, 2-leaved at apex, sometimes transversely mottled with brown. **Leaves** linear, acute, 18–22 cm long, 1–1.5 cm broad. **Inflorescences** drooping, racemose, rarely branched near the base, 40–50 cm long, laxly many-flowered. **Flowers** 2.5 cm across, rose-pink; lip paler, callus white; column white. **Dorsal sepal** concave, narrowly elliptic, subacute, 1.1 cm long, 0.5 cm broad; **lateral sepals** connate to beyond the middle. **Petals** elliptic-oblong, apiculate, 1.1 cm long, 0.4 cm broad. **Lip** clawed, with a reflexed, ovate, acute lamina, 1 cm long; claw adnate to column; callus of 2 raised triangular plates adnate to the column behind. **Column** short, terete.

DISTRIBUTION   Ecuador.

HISTORY   Professor W. Jameson discovered this species near Quito in the Ecuadorian Andes where it was also found in 1851 by J. Warscewicz. It was not introduced into cultivation until 1866 when Messrs Backhouse of York, England received plants from Ecuador. H.G. Reichenbach described it in 1861 in *Walpers, Annales Botanices* (p. 858) as *Mesospinidium sanguineum*. George Bentham transferred it in 1883 in his and Hooker's *Genera Plantarum* (p. 560) to *Cochlioda* but Rudolf Schlechter placed it in his new genus *Symphyglossum* in 1919 in *Orchis* (p. 90).

SYNONYMS   *Mesospinidium cochliodum* Rchb.f.; *Cochlioda sanguinea* (Rchb.f.) Benth.

Tainia Blume
Subfamily Epidendroideae
Tribe Arethuseae
Subtribe Bletiinae

Terrestrial herbs with distinct rhizomes. **Pseudobulbs** or sterile shoots ovoid to subcylindric, covered by scarious sheaths, 1-leafed at apex. **Leaf** erect, plicate, distinctly petiolate. **Inflorescence** erect, usually laxly racemose. **Flowers** rather showy. **Sepals** and **petals** ± similar, spreading. **Lip** fixed to column-foot, erect, with a ± gibbous base or a short spur, 3-lobed; callus of 1 to 5 longitudinal ridges. **Column** rather slender, somewhat arcuate, ± with a foot, winged on each side; pollinia 8, 4 in each cell of anther, ± compressed; stigma beneath rostellum.

DISTRIBUTION   25 or 50 species in India, China, S.E. Asia and Indonesia.

DERIVATION OF NAME   From the Greek *tainia* (fillet), possibly in reference to the long narrow leaf with its long petiole, or to the elevated keels on the lip.

TAXONOMY   *Tainia* was described by C.L. Blume in 1825 in *Bijdragen* (p. 354). It is related to *Nephelaphyllum* and *Chrysoglossum*, differing from the former in having the lip lowermost in the flower and non-variegated leaves and from the latter in having 8 rather than 2 pollinia. *T. wrayana* (Hooker f.) J.J. Smith resembles *Nephelaphyllum* in having non-pleated leaves but otherwise its flowers are quite distinct. It has been placed in a distinct genus, *Mischobulbum*, by some authorities.

J.J. Smith in the *Bulletin du Jardin Botanique de Buitenzorg* (1919) discussed the subgeneric division of *Tainia* and included *Mischobulbum* as one of four sections in the genus, the others being (*Eu*) *Tainia* including *T. speciosa*; *Ascotainia* including *T. hookeriana* King & Pantling and *T. viridifusca* Lindl.; and *Mitopetalum* including *T. khasiana* Hooker f. Of these *Mischobulbum* is now considered to be a distinct genus.

Seidenfaden (1986) has recently revised the seven species from Thailand and adjacent regions in *Opera Botanica* (p. 27).

TYPE SPECIES   *T. speciosa* Blume

SYNONYMS   *Mitopetalum* Bl.; *Ania* Lindl.

CULTURE   Compost B or C. Temp. Min. 12–15°C while growing, 15–18°C while flowering. The plants generally flower after the leaves have dropped and from then until the new growths appear, very little water is required. During growth, shady humid conditions are required and plenty of water should be given until the leaves begin to die back. In those

species which have large ovoid pseudobulbs they frequently grow partially beneath the ground.

Tainia hookeriana King & Pantling
[Colour Plate]

A terrestrial herb with a short rhizome. **Pseudobulbs** closely spaced, ovoid, ± obtusely ribbed, up to 7.5 cm high, 6 cm in diameter, bluish or grey-green, 1-leafed at apex. **Leaf** with a long, thin petiole, up to 27 cm long; lamina lanceolate or elliptic-lanceolate, acute, plicate, 25–50 cm long, 4–10 cm broad. **Inflorescence** arising from the base of the pseudobulb, up to 90 cm long, laxly 10- to 25-flowered; bracts narrowly lanceolate, acuminate, 1–1.5 cm long. **Flowers** ascending; sepals and petals yellow, closely striped with brown; lip white, tinged yellow with fine reddish spots around the keels in front, spur, brownish. **Sepals** and **petals** subsimilar, lanceolate, acuminate, 1.7–2.5 cm long, 0.3–0.5 cm broad. **Lip** cuneate below, 3-lobed above the middle, 1.2–1.5 cm long and broad, united at the base with the column-foot to form an obtuse incurved spur, 0.3–0.4 cm long; side lobes suberect, rounded at the apex; mid-lobe transversely elliptic-circular, shortly acuminate; disc furnished with 3 smooth keels which are lowest at the base. **Column** semiterete, slightly incurved, 0.8–1 cm long; foot 0.3 cm long.

DISTRIBUTION   N.E. India, Sikkim, N. Thailand, S. China and Laos; in montane forest to 1200 m.

HISTORY   First recorded in 1896 from the Teesta valley in Sikkim where it grows between 300 and 750 m in forested areas, it was described in 1896 by Sir George King and R. Pantling in the *Journal of the Asiatic Society of Bengal* (pt. 2: p. 336).

SYNONYM   *Ania hookeriana* (King & Pantling) Tang & Wang; *Ascotainia hookeriana* (King & Pantling) Ridley; *Tainia siamensis* (Rolfe ex Downie) Seid. & Smitin.

CLOSELY RELATED SPECIES   *T. hookeriana* is allied to *Tainia viridifusca* Hooker, which differs in having unstriped tepals and a narrower lip with 2 extra keels on the mid-lobe.

Telipogon H.B.K.
Subfamily Epidendroideae
Tribe Maxillarieae
Subtribe Telipogoninae

Small to medium-sized epiphytic or terrestrial herbs with a creeping rhizome or decumbent lower part of the stem. **Stems** short to well-developed, ± branching above. **Leaves** few to many, distichous, mostly narrow, coriaceous or fleshy. **Inflorescences** terminal, erect, racemose, 1- to several-flowered. **Flowers** medium to large and showy, rarely small. **Sepals** subequal, free, spreading, narrow. **Petals** much larger than the sepals, mostly prominently veined and reticulated. **Lip** similar to the petals, often broader, simple, sessile. **Column** short, footless, wingless, hispid or long-setose; anther erect; pollinia 4, fixed to the slightly dilated apex of a linear stipe.

DISTRIBUTION Widely distributed and fairly frequent in Costa Rica and northern S. America, south to Bolivia; about 60 species.

DERIVATION OF NAME From the Greek *telos* (end) and *pogon* (beard), descriptive of the hairy apex of the column.

TAXONOMY *Telipogon* was described for the first time in 1815 in F.H.A. von Humboldt, A. Bonpland and C.S. Kunth's *Nova Genera et Species Plantarum* (p. 335, t. 75). The stiff hairs on the column are the distinctive feature of this genus which F. Kraenzlin revised in 1919 in the *Annalen des Naturhistorischen Museums in Wien*. He divided the genus into two sections: *Brevicaules* in which the stems are short and the peduncle is compressed; and *Caulescentes* where the stems are elongate and the peduncle is terete.

C. Dodson (1987) has revised the Costa Rican species in the journal *Orquideologia* (pp. 3–137).

TYPE SPECIES *T. angustifolius* H.B.K. [= *T. nervosus* (L.) Druce].

SYNONYMS *Telopogon* Mutis; *Thelypogon* Sprengel

CULTURE Compost A. Temp. Winter min. 10°C. Summer max. below 24°C. These difficult plants should be grown in small pots under conditions of high humidity and heavy shade. They should be kept evenly moist throughout the year.

Telipogon bruchmuelleri Rchb.f.

A small epiphytic plant, up to 8 cm high. **Stem** very short, several-leaved. **Leaves** distichous, oblong or narrowly elliptic, acute, up to 6 cm long, 1.5 cm broad, light green, articulated below to conduplicate leaf-bases. **Inflorescence** terminal, erect, racemose, 1- or 2-flowered; peduncle up to 8 cm long, winged; bracts ovate, sharply angular. **Flowers** large for plant, showy; sepals bright yellow-green; petals light yellow-green, grading to pinkish-maroon at base; lip light yellow-green, veined with pink, callus maroon and covered with rich maroon hairs; column brown. **Sepals** subsimilar, narrowly elliptic-lanceolate, acute, 1.5–2 cm long, 0.5–0.6 cm broad. **Petals** elliptic, acute, obscurely clawed, 1.6–2.2 cm long, 0.8–1.1 cm broad. **Lip** almost circular, apiculate, 1.4–1.9 cm long, 1.4–2.2 cm broad; basal callus flat, broadly ovate, pubescent. **Column** short, stout,

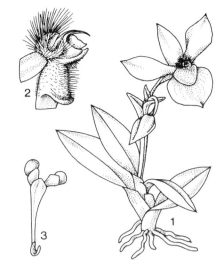

Telipogon bruchmuelleri
1 – Habit (× ¾)
2 – Column, side view (× 2)
3 – Pollinia, stipe and viscidium (× 4)
 (After Garay and Dunsterville, 1965)

covered with long hairs; rostellum porrect, pointed.

DISTRIBUTION Nicaragua south to Colombia and Venezuela; in montane forest at about 2000–2300 m.

HISTORY First collected by Albert Bruchmüller at Ocaña, Colombia and described by H.G. Reichenbach in his honour in 1877 in *Linnaea* (p. 28).

SYNONYMS *Telipogon wallisii* Rchb.f.; *T. biolleyi* Schltr.; *T. schmidtchenii* Rchb.f.; *T. endresianum* Kraenzl.

Telipogon nervosus (L.) Druce

A small to medium-sized (or rarely larger) terrestrial herb with suberect or sometimes scrambling and entwining stems, mostly 20–40 (rarely to 150) cm long. **Leaves** distichous, fleshy and fairly rigid, narrowly elliptic, acute, spreading, 2 cm long, 1.2 cm broad, basal sheath compressed. **Inflorescences** lateral or terminal, axillary, erect, racemose, laxly several-flowered, up to 28 cm long. **Flowers** large; sepals pale green; petals and lip greenish-yellow lined with brown or purple; column purple-maroon. **Sepals** ovate, acuminate, 1 cm long, 0.5 cm broad. **Petals** broadly ovate, acute to apiculate, 1.4 cm long, 1.2 cm broad. **Lip** broadly ovate or transversely elliptic, apiculate, with a fleshy pubescent rim at the base, 1.4 cm long, 1.7 cm broad. **Column** short, stout, fleshy, with fine hairs on apical part and a crest of long erect hairs on the top concealing the anther.

DISTRIBUTION Colombia, Venezuela and Ecuador; mostly above 2500 m in cloud forest.

HISTORY Originally described as *Tradescantia nervosa* by Linnaeus in *Mantissa Plantarum* (p. 223) in 1767. G.C. Druce transferred it in 1916 to *Telipogon* in the *Reports of the Botanical Exchange Club of the British Isles* (p. 650).

SYNONYMS *Tradescantia nervosa* L.; *Telipogon angustifolius* H.B.K.; *T. hoppii* Schltr.; *T. steyermarkii* Foldats

Telipogon papilio Rchb.f. & Warsc.

A small epiphytic plant with a short stem and long, fibrous, glabrous roots. **Leaves** several, congested, oblanceolate, apiculate, articulated to a leaf-base below, 3.5–6 cm long, 1.2–1.7 cm broad. **Inflorescence** erect, shorter or slightly longer than the leaves, 4–17 cm long, racemose, 1- to 7-flowered; peduncle subterete to narrowly 2-winged and angulate. **Flowers** orange-yellow or primrose-yellow, lined with red nerves; pedicel and ovary narrowly 3-winged. **Dorsal sepal** ovate-lanceolate, acuminate, concave, dorsally carinate, up to 1.8 cm long, 0.7 cm broad; **lateral sepals** shorter, oblique but otherwise similar. **Petals** broadly rhombic-obovate, oblique, acute, 13- to 15-veined, 1.9 cm long, 1.8 cm broad. **Lip** transversely suborbicular-ovate, minutely apiculate at the rounded and plicate apex, about 25-veined, 1.9 cm long, 2.5 cm broad. **Column** very stout, surrounded by a tuft of numerous, long bristles.

DISTRIBUTION Peru; epiphytic in forest up to 2700 m.

HISTORY Discovered in Peru by J. Warscewicz and described by him and H.G. Reichenbach in 1854 in *Bonplandia* (p. 101).

T. papilio is readily recognised by its very short stem, 1- to 7-flowered inflorescence and large flowers with 13- to 15-veined petals and a lip with about 25 veins.

Tetramicra Lindl.

Subfamily Epidendroideae
Tribe Epidendreae
Subtribe Laeliinae

Epiphytic rhizomatous herbs with short, erect, non-pseudobulbous, leafy stems. **Leaves** fleshy-coriaceous, semiterete, bilaterally compressed to triquetrous. **Inflorescence** terminal, racemose, laxly few- to several-flowered. **Flowers** often showy. **Sepals** and **petals** free, subsimilar, spreading. **Lip** forming a gibbous nectary with the base of the column, larger than the sepals and petals, 3-lobed; callus of low raised ridges on central veins. **Column** erect, distinctly winged and with a tridentate clinandrium, extended at the base to form a gibbous nectary; pollinia 8, of 2 sizes, connected by 4 caudicles.

DISTRIBUTION   A small genus of about 10 species in the W. Indies and Florida.

DERIVATION OF NAME   From the Greek *tetra* (four) and *mikros* (small), referring to the 4-locular anther.

TAXONOMY   *Tetramicra* was established by John Lindley in 1831 in his *Genera and Species of Orchidaceous Plants* (p. 119). It is allied to *Epidendrum* but differs in having 8 pollinia and a distinctive habit.

TYPE SPECIES   *T. rigida* (Willd.) Lindl.

CULTURE   Temp. Winter min. 15°C. Grow in pans of epiphyte mix under conditions of moderate shade and humidity. Water carefully throughout the year, giving less when growth is complete.

Tetramicra canaliculata (Aublet) Urban

Epiphytic plants up to 72 cm tall with a creeping wiry rhizome enclosed by imbricate papery sheaths. Stems erect, well-spaced, rather short, up to 2 cm long. **Leaves** 2 to 5, distichous, fleshy, semiterete, linear-subulate, acute, channelled above, 5–18 cm long, 0.3–0.5 cm wide.

Tetramicra canaliculata
1 – Habit ($\times \frac{3}{4}$)
2 – Inflorescence ($\times \frac{3}{4}$)
3 – Flower ($\times 1\frac{1}{2}$)

Inflorescence up to 70 cm long, laxly up to 8-flowered; peduncle slender, remotely several-sheathed; bracts ovate, acute, 2–3 mm long. **Flowers** showy, the sepals and petals greenish with a red or brownish suffusion, the lip rose-pink with a yellow central line; pedicel and ovary 2 cm long. **Sepals** reflexed-spreading, oblong-lanceolate, acute to obtuse, 9–10 mm long, 3–4 mm wide. **Petals** lanceolate to oblanceolate, acute, 10 mm long, 2.5 mm wide. **Lip** flat, deeply 3-lobed, 15–16 mm long, 21–22 mm wide; side lobes spreading, obliquely elliptic, rounded, 10 mm long, 7–8 mm wide; mid-lobe obovate-elliptic, obtuse or rounded, 10 mm long, 15–16 mm wide. **Column** 5 mm long, strongly winged on each side.

DISTRIBUTION   Florida, the Greater and Lesser Antilles; in scrub at low elevation.

HISTORY   This was one of the first W. Indian orchids to be collected. Aublet described this pretty orchid in 1775 as *Limodorum canaliculatum* in his *Histoire des Plantes de la Guiane Française* (p. 821), based on the name *Helleborine foliis rigidis angustis et canaliculatis* from Plumier's *Catalogus Plantarum Americanarum* (p. 9) of 1703. Alfred Cogniaux transferred it to the present genus in 1918 in *Fedde, Repertorium Specierum Novarum* (p. 306).

SYNONYMS   include *Limodorum canaliculatum* Aubl.; *Cymbidium rigidum* Willd.; *Tetramicra rigida* (Willd.) Lindl.; *Cyrtopodium elegans* Hamilt.; *Tetramicra elegans* (Hamilt.) Cogn.

Teuscheria Garay
Subfamily Epidendroideae
Tribe Maxillarieae
Subtribe Bifrenariinae

Epiphytes with clustered ovoid pseudobulbs with a single apical leaf and surrounded by chartaceous sheaths. **Leaf** plicate, convolute, lanceolate to elliptic, semicoriaceous. **Inflorescences** 1-flowered, basal, erect or pendent. **Flowers** medium-sized, resupinate or not. **Dorsal sepal** and **petals** free; **lateral sepals** connate, forming a spur-like conical mentum. **Lip** 3-lobed, attached to the apex of the column-foot, with a spur at the base extending into the sepaline mentum; callus low, smooth or farinose. **Column** short, fleshy, with an elongate foot; pollinia 4, hard, waxy, superimposed, attached to a long wide viscidium but lacking a stipe.

DISTRIBUTION   Six species distributed from Costa Rica to Peru.

DERIVATION OF NAME   Named for the Canadian botanist and orchid grower Henry Teuscher.

TAXONOMY   The genus was described by Leslie Garay in 1958 in the *American Orchid Society Bulletin* (p. 820). The most recent account of the genus is that of Dressler in 1972 in *Orquideologia* (p. 6) in which he provides a key to the known species. *Teuscheria* is allied to *Bifrenaria*.

TYPE SPECIES   *T. cornucopia* Garay

CULTURE   Temp. Winter min. 12°C. Best grown mounted to allow the pendent flowers to develop. Needs moderate shade and good humidity with careful watering throughout the year.

Teuscheria wageneri (Rchb.f.) Garay
[Colour Plate]

An epiphyte with clustered, ovoid pseudobulbs, 1–1.5 cm long, unifoliate, covered by the fibrous remains of sheaths. **Leaf** erect or suberect, oblanceolate, acuminate, 20–35 cm long, 2–2.7 cm wide. **Inflorescence** pendent, 1-flowered; peduncle lax, slender, terete, dark maroon; bracts elliptic, acute, 3–4 mm long. **Flower** hangs upside-down, fleshy, lasting 1 day; sepals and petals bronze with a light maroon tinge; lip white with a pink tinge near margins and pale peach in the throat; callus covered with a golden farina; pedicel and ovary 0.6–0.8 cm long. **Dorsal sepal** narrowly elliptic, obtuse, 1.7–2 cm long, 6–7 mm wide; **lateral sepals** united at the base for a quarter of their length to form a spur-like tube, obliquely oblong-elliptic, obtuse, 22–25 mm long, 7–8 mm wide. **Petals** oblanceolate, acute, 17–18 mm long, 4–5 mm wide. **Lip** uppermost in flower, 3-lobed in the apical part, 20–22 mm long, 17–18 mm wide, narrowly clawed; side lobes obliquely oblong, rounded and erose in front; mid-lobe transversely elliptic, obtuse and erose in front; callus fleshy, 3-ridged in basal half of lip, farinose. **Column** pale green with a maroon flush on back, 6 mm long; foot 5–6 mm long.

DISTRIBUTION   Venezuela only.

HISTORY   Discovered in Venezuela by the orchid collector Wagener and described by Reichenbach as *Bifrenaria wageneri* in 1854 in *Bonplandia* (p. 17). It was transferred to *Teuscheria* by Leslie Garay in 1967 in the *Botanical Museum Leaflets of Harvard University* (p. 256).

SYNONYMS   *Bifrenaria wageneri* Rchb.f.; *Teuscheria venezuelana* Garay

Thecopus Seidenf.
Subfamily Epidendroideae
Tribe Cymbidieae
Subtribe Thecostelinae

Medium-sized epiphytic plants with 1-noded unifoliate pseudobulbs. **Leaves** somewhat coriaceous. **Inflorescences** basal, racemose, few flowered; bracts small. **Flowers** fleshy, medium-sized or small. **Dorsal sepal** free, concave, hooded over column; **lateral sepals** similar, united at base to the column-foot. **Petals** similar but narrower. **Lip** articulated to the apex of the column-foot, clawed at base, 3-lobed, strongly recurved, with a callus. **Column** slender, arcuate, with a tubular nectariferous column-foot, winged on each side at the apex; pollinia 4, appressed in 2 unequal pairs; stipe elongate-tapering; viscidium small.

DISTRIBUTION A small genus of perhaps two or three species in S.E. Asia from Thailand to Borneo.

DERIVATION OF NAME From the Greek *theke* (box) and *pous* (foot), in reference to the shape of the base of the column.

TAXONOMY *Thecopus* was established by Gunnar Seidenfaden in 1983 in the journal *Opera Botanica* (p. 101). It is a segregate genus of *Thecostele* and he distinguishes it from *Thecopus* on account of its 4 pollinia borne on a slender stipe and an obscure viscidium and the lack of any sigmoid bending at the base of the column.

TYPE SPECIES *T. maingayi* (Hook.f.) Seidenf.

CULTURE As for *Thecostele*.

Thecopus maingayi (Hook.f.) Seidenf.

[Colour Plate]

An epiphytic plant with clustered pseudobulbs, 1.5–4 cm long, 2–2.5 cm wide, flattened. **Leaf** oblong, obtuse, 8–17 cm long, 2–3.6 cm wide, shortly petiolate. **Inflorescences** pendent, 10–35 cm long, 8- to 19-flowered; bracts triangular, acute, 2 mm long. **Flowers** fleshy, with green sepals and petals spotted with dark maroon and a white lip marked with purple, 2.5 cm across; pedicel and ovary 20 mm long. **Dorsal sepal** elliptic-ovate, acute, 13–20 mm long, 5–8 mm wide; **lateral sepals** obliquely ovate, acute, 13–20 mm long, 7–12 mm wide. **Petals** oblanceolate-falcate, acute, 14–18 mm long, 4–5.5 mm wide. **Lip** shortly narrowly clawed, strongly recurved and 3-lobed in the middle, 7–8 mm long, 6 mm wide; side lobes erect, elliptic, rounded in front; mid-lobe ovate, acute or subacute, papillose, 7 mm long, 7 mm wide; callus 2-ridged in the basal part of the lip; basal nectary 7 mm long. **Column** 7–9 mm long, apical wings pendent-porrect; foot 5 mm long.

DISTRIBUTION Thailand, Malaya and Borneo; in lowland and lower montane forest.

HISTORY J.D. Hooker first named this orchid in 1890 in his *Flora of British India* (6: p. 20) as *Thecostele maingayi*, based on a collection made in 1867 by A.C. Maingay at Malacca in peninsular Malaya. It remained so until 1983

when Gunnar Seidenfaden made it the type of his new genus *Thecopus*.

SYNONYMS *Thecostele maingayi* Hook.f.; *T. quinquefida* Hook.f.

Thecostele Rchb.f.
Subfamily Epidendroideae
Tribe Cymbidieae
Subtribe Thecostelinae

Small to medium-sized epiphytic plants. **Pseudobulbs** present, ellipsoid to ovoid, unifoliate. **Leaves** thinly coriaceous. **Inflorescences** pendent, racemose, laxly few- to many-flowered; bracts small. **Flowers** small, fleshy. **Sepals** subsimilar, spreading, free. **Petals** narrower but similarly coloured. **Lip** 3-lobed, deflexed, the side lobes smaller than the mid-lobe, with a basal pubescent fleshy callus, articulated to the apex of the column-foot. **Column** complex, replicate, somewhat sigmoid, recurved abruptly in basal part, arcuate and slender above, the basal part with a tubular short nectary, the apical part with 2 pendent linear wings; pollinia 2, deeply cleft, stipes short, broad, oblong; viscidium semicircular, broad.

DISTRIBUTION A monotypic genus widespread in S.E. Asia from N.E. India, Burma and Thailand south to Java, Borneo and the Philippines.

DERIVATION OF NAME From the Greek *theke* (box) and *stele* (column), in allusion to the strange shape of the base of the column.

TAXONOMY *Thecostele* was established by H.G. Reichenbach in 1857 in the journal *Bonplandia* (p. 37) and has been considered by most authorities to include the species now separated in *Thecopus*. However, the distinctive column and pollinarium of *Thecostele alata* convinced Seidenfaden (1983) in *Opera Botanica* to remove those species lacking a sigmoid column and with 4 pollinia to his new genus *Thecopus*.

Both genera are allied to *Acriopsis* which differs in having the lateral sepals forming a synsepalum and has 4 distinctive pyriform pollinia on a slender stipe.

TYPE SPECIES *T. zollingeri* Rchb.f. (= *T. alata* (Roxb.) Par. & Rchb.f.).

CULTURE Temp. Winter min. 15°C. May be grown mounted or in pots of epiphyte mix under conditions of moderate shade and humidity. Water well while growing but much less when growth is complete.

Thecostele alata (Roxb.) Par. & Rchb.f.
[Colour Plate]

A small or medium-sized epiphyte with clustered ovoid or ellipsoidal compressed unifoliate pseudobulbs, 3.5–6 cm long, 1.5–3 cm wide.

Leaves arcuate, linear-lanceolate to elliptic-obovate, acute, 13–37 cm long, 2.5–5.5 cm wide, with a grooved stalk, 1.5–3.5 cm long. **Inflorescences** pendent, laxly 20- to 40-flowered, 15–50 cm long; peduncle and rhachis slender, flexuous; bracts small, elliptic-lanceolate, acute, somewhat recurved, 2 mm long. **Flowers** lasting 2–3 days, with sepals and petals yellow at the base, white in the middle, light purple at the tips and with a few irregular purple or crimson spots, the lip white marked with purple on the mid-lobe; pedicel and ovary 4–5 mm long. **Dorsal sepal** concave, elliptic-ovate, acute, 7–8 mm long, 3–4 mm wide; **lateral sepals** ovate, acute, 6–7 mm long, 4–5 mm wide. **Petals** linear, obtuse, 7–8 mm long, 1 mm wide. **Lip** 3-lobed in basal half, clawed at base, recurved at the apex of the claw, 4–5 mm long, 3–3.5 mm wide; side lobes erect-porrect, elliptic, rounded in front, 2 mm long; mid-lobe broadly obovate, obtuse or truncate, papillose all over; callus a raised pubescent mound between the side lobes. **Column** 5–6 mm long, arcuate, with 2 apical porrect linear 2 mm long wings; basal nectary 3 mm long.

DISTRIBUTION Widespread from N.E. India, Burma and Thailand across to the Philippines and south to Java and Borneo; epiphyte in lowland and lower montane forest up to 1500 m.

HISTORY William Roxburgh described this pretty little orchid in 1814 in his *Hortus Bengalensis* (p. 63) as *Cymbidium alatum*. Charles Parish and H.G. Reichenbach transferred it to the present genus in the *Transactions of the Linnean Society* (pp. 135, 144) in 1874.

SYNONYMS include *Cymbidium alatum* Roxb.; *Thecostele zollingeri* Rchb.f.; *T. maculosa* Ridl.; *T. wrayi* (Hook.f.) Rolfe; *T. elmeri* (Ames) Ames; *T. poilanei* Gagnep.

Thelymitra J. & G. Forst.
Subfamily Orchidoideae
Tribe Diurideae
Subtribe Diuridinae

Small to large terrestrial often colony-forming herbs growing from fleshy elongated underground tubers (root-stem tuberoids). **Leaf** solitary, basal, erect, linear to lanceolate, formed before flowering commences. **Inflorescence** erect, laxly few- to many-flowered, simple; peduncle terete, bearing several sheaths along its length. **Flowers** almost regular, resupinate, showy, flat or campanulate, blue, yellow, red or rarely variegated. **Sepals** and **petals** subsimilar, free, spreading or incurved. **Lip** similar to the other segments, simple, lacking a spur and callus. **Column** erect, terete, bearing 2 apical tufted to entire appendages; pollinia 4, mealy, with a terminal viscidium; stigma entire.

DISTRIBUTION A predominantly Australian genus of some 45 species with a few species in New Zealand, and a single species extending to New Guinea, the Philippines and Java.

DERIVATION OF NAME From the Greek *thelys* (female) and *mitra* (headband), referring to the often ornate apical ornamentation of the column.

TAXONOMY These are commonly called Sun Orchids in Australia from the habit of most species of opening their flowers only when the sun is shining. The genus was established by J. & G. Forster, the botanists who accompanied Capt. Cook on his second voyage to Australia, in 1776 in their *Characteres Generum Plantarum* (p. 97).

Thelymitra is a distinct genus characterised by its almost regular flower, petaloid lip and column with apical often complex appendages. The flowers successfully mimic those of native Iridaceae and Liliaceae. *Thelymitra* is allied to the Australian genera *Calochilus* and *Diuris*.

Although many of the species have showy flowers, most are difficult to grow and seldom persist long in cultivation. Those that are more amenable do not usually multiply freely vegetatively but will occasionally do so if seed is sprinkled on the surface of the soil around an established plant.

TYPE SPECIES *T. longifolia* J. & G. Forst.
CULTURE As for *Acianthus*.

Thelymitra antennifera (Lindl.) Hook.f.
[Colour Plate]

A small terrestrial up to 25 cm tall, forming dense colonies. **Leaf** linear, acute, channelled, 5–12 cm long, 2–3 mm wide, dark green, often reddish at the base. **Inflorescence** 1- to 3-flowered, up to 25 cm tall; peduncle wiry; bracts obovate, obtuse, 7–10 mm long. **Flowers** fragrant, smelling of lemon, pale to primrose yellow, the outer surface of the sepals longitudinally flushed with red, the column appendages deep maroon; pedicel and ovary longer than the bracts. **Sepals** and **petals** narrowly elliptic to obovate, obtuse, 1.5–2 cm long, 4–6 mm wide. **Lip** narrowly oblong, obtuse or rounded at the apex, 1.6–2 cm long, 5–6 mm wide. **Column** 5–6 mm long, yellow with an orange anther, with entire maroon apical appendages, notched at the apex.

DISTRIBUTION Australia (Victoria, S. Australia, Tasmania and W. Australia); in coastal heathland, scrub and woodland.

HISTORY This is one of the easier species of *Thelymitra* to grow and one of the few yellow-flowered species. It was described by John Lindley in 1839 as *Macdonaldia antennifera* in the

Botanical Register (Swan River Suppl.: p. 50, t. 9) based on a collection from the Swan River by Drummond. J.D. Hooker transferred it to the present genus in 1858 in his *Flora Tasmaniae* (2: p. 4, t. 101A).

SYNONYM *Macdonaldia antennifera* Lindl.

Thelymitra variegata (Lindl.) Muell.
[Colour Plate]

A terrestrial up to 40 cm tall. **Leaf** erect or spirally twisted, linear to lanceolate, acute, occasionally lobed at the base, 5–10 cm long, 5–10 mm wide. **Inflorescence** erect, 2- to 4-flowered; peduncle slender, wiry; bracts lanceolate, acute, 5–7 mm long. **Flowers** stellate, 3.5–4 cm across, very showy, iridescent yellow, red and purple with black spots; pedicel and ovary longer than the bracts. **Sepals** ovate-lanceolate, acute, 2.5–3 cm long, 7–10 mm wide. **Petals** similar but narrower. **Lip** lanceolate, acute or acuminate, 2.5–2.9 cm long, 5–8 mm wide. **Column** erect, 5–6 mm long, with 2 apical ovoid yellow appendages.

DISTRIBUTION Australia: endemic to coastal south-western W. Australia.

HISTORY This is one of the most spectacular of all terrestrial orchids that fully deserves its colloquial name of 'Queen of Sheba Orchid'. It was first described by John Lindley in 1840 as *Macdonaldia variegata* in the *Botanical Register* (Swan River Suppl.: p. 50) based on a Drummond collection from the Swan River. Baron Ferdinand von Mueller transferred it to *Thelymitra* in 1865 in his *Fragmentae* (5: p. 97).

SYNONYM *Macdonaldia variegata* Lindl.

Thrixspermum Lour.
Subfamily Epidendroideae
Tribe Vandeae
Subtribe Sarcanthinae

Small to medium-sized, epiphytic or lithophytic plants either with short stems or with elongate climbing or scrambling leafy stems. **Leaves** coriaceous, distichous, articulated to sheathing leaf bases. **Inflorescences** axillary, short or long, with the flowers produced in 2 rows or 1 at a time on a congested rhachis; bracts small to large, either distichous or spirally arranged. **Flowers** short-lived, usually facing upwards. **Sepals** and **petals** free, similar, either long and slender or short and broad, lateral sepals oblique at base. **Lip** immovably attached to the column-foot, 3-lobed, saccate at the base, with a fleshy, often hairy or glandular, tongue-like callus on the front wall of the sac. **Column** short, with a broad distinct foot; pollinia 4, unequal, in 2 pairs, on a short broad stipe.

DISTRIBUTION A genus of perhaps 100 species widely distributed from the Himalayas

and India to the Philippines and the tropical islands of the S.W. Pacific.

DERIVATION OF NAME From the Greek *thrix* (hair) and *spermum* (seed), an allusion to hair-like seeds.

HISTORY Juan Loureiro established this genus as early as 1790 in his *Flora Cochinchinensis* (p. 520). A discussion of its chequered history, together with an account of 15 Thai species, is given by Seidenfaden (1988) in *Opera Botanica* (p. 148).

The species fall conveniently into two sections; the typical has elongate stems and inflorescences of distichously arranged bracts bearing spidery flowers; while, in section *Dendrocolla*, the stems are short and the flowers more rounded and appearing 1 at a time on a dense spiral rhachis.

TYPE SPECIES *T. centipeda* Lour.
SYNONYMS *Dendrocolla* Bl.; *Orcidice* Rchb.f.
CULTURE Temp. Winter min. 12–15°C. The species are usually grown mounted and watered or sprayed daily, hanging in a moderately shaded and humid atmosphere. Flowers short-lived but attractive.

Thrixspermum centipeda Lour. [Colour Plate]

An epiphyte with an elongate stem up to 15 cm long. **Leaves** distichous, fleshy, linear-oblanceolate, unequally obtusely bilobed at the apex, 5–12 cm long, 1–2 cm wide, sometimes purple-spotted when young, articulated to 1 cm long leaf sheaths at the base. **Inflorescences** axillary, 10–25 cm long; peduncle 4–8 cm long, terete; rhachis flattened; bracts distichous, ovate, obtuse, bilaterally flattened, 7–10 mm long. **Flowers** spidery, with pale yellow sepals and petals and a white lip spotted with orange or purple in the basal part; pedicel and ovary 7–10 mm long. **Sepals** linear-lanceolate, acuminate, the laterals oblique at the base, 3–3.5 cm long, 3–4 mm wide. **Petals** similar but slightly smaller. **Lip** 3-lobed in the basal half, saccate at the base, 8–10 mm long and wide; side lobes pointing forwards, erect, rounded; mid-lobe very fleshy, oblong-elliptic, rounded in front; callus a short forward-pointing flap in the middle of the lip. **Column** 3 mm long; foot short and broad.

DISTRIBUTION Widespread from the Himalayas throughout S.E. Asia and the Malay Archipelago to New Guinea, Australia and the Pacific Islands; in lowland and lower montane forest, up to 1500 m.

HISTORY Juan Loureiro described this orchid in 1790 in his *Flora Cochinchinensis* (p. 520) based on his own collection from near Hue in Vietnam. However, it is far better known as *T. arachnites* (Bl.) Rchb.f., a later synonym.

SYNONYMS include *Dendrocolla arachnites* Bl.; *Thrixspermum arachnites* (Bl.) Rchb.f.: *T. ser-*

raeformis (Lindl.) Rchb.f.; *T. platystachys* (Bail.) Schltr.

Thunia Rchb.f.
Subfamily Epidendroideae
Tribe Arethuseae
Subtribe Thuniinae

Medium-sized to large terrestrial plants lacking pseudobulbs. **Stems** clustered, erect, biennial, covered with sheaths below and leafy above. **Leaves** distichous, glaucous below, spaced along the stem. **Inflorescences** terminal, drooping, on young leafy shoots, racemose, 5- to 9(or more)-flowered; bracts large, spathaceous, persistent. **Flowers** short-lived, large, showy, mostly white or amethyst-purple, with yellow on the lip. **Sepals** and **petals** free, subsimilar. **Lip** entire, fringed on front margin, traversed by 5–7 fringed or entire lamellae, spurred at base; spur short, obtuse. **Column** 2-winged, slender, semiterete at the apex; pollinia 4, each bipartite.

DISTRIBUTION Less than half-a-dozen species in India, China and S.E. Asia.
DERIVATION OF NAME Named in honour of Count von Thun Hohenstein of Tetschin.
TAXONOMY *Thunia* was described in 1852 by H.G. Reichenbach in the *Botanische Zeitung* (p. 764). It may be distinguished from *Phaius* by its lack of pseudobulbs; by its biennial, slightly nodose stems which are covered by leafy sheaths below gradually passing to true leaves above; the terminal inflorescence; and the persistent bracts. The species from Thailand and adjacent regions have recently been revised by Seidenfaden (1986) in *Opera Botanica* (p. 10).

TYPE SPECIES *T. alba* (Lindl.) Rchb.f.
CULTURE Compost B. Temp. Winter min. 12°C, higher while growing. *Thunia* canes should be repotted when the new growths appear and placed in a warm, moist and moderately shady house. Water should be withheld until the shoots are about 15–20 cm high when the roots will be growing well. During growth and until the leaves yellow and fall, water should be freely given, but when the canes are bare, they must remain cool and completely dry until the new shoots appear in the spring.

Thunia marshalliana Reichb.f. [Colour Plate]
An erect terrestrial herb, 75–130 cm long. **Stems** robust, jointed, covered with leafy sheaths below, leafy above. **Leaves** oblong-lanceolate, acuminate, 15–20 cm long, pale green, glaucous below, with a pale mid-nerve. **Inflorescence** terminal, drooping, racemose, 5- to 9(or more)-flowered on short white pedicels, sheathed by a white, cucullate bract, 4 cm long. **Flowers** large, showy; sepals and petals white; lip white with a rich yellow apical half and fringed ridges of orange-yellow, spur yellowish. **Sepals** and **petals** similar, oblong-lanceolate, acute, 6.5–7.5 cm long, 1.3–1.6 cm broad. **Lip** elliptic-oblong, anterior margin fringed and undulate, 5.5 cm long, 4.3 cm broad; disc with several long-fringed deeply dissected lamellae particularly in apical half; spur 1 cm long, somewhat bifid at apex. **Column** short, stout, with dilated apical wings, 2.3 cm long.
DISTRIBUTION Burma, Thailand and S. China.
HISTORY Discovered at Moulmein, Burma and described by H.G. Reichenbach in 1877 in *Linnaea* (p. 65) based on a plant cultivated by W. Bull. Var. *ionophlebia* Rchb.f. has a yellowish central area to the lip and the side areas are streaked with purple.
CLOSELY RELATED SPECIES Allied to the slightly smaller-flowered and less showy *Thunia alba* Rchb.f. which has a narrow lip lined with paler yellow lamellae. Seidenfaden (1986) in *Opera Botanica* (p. 14) considers these to be conspecific. *Thunia bensoniae* Hooker f. is also closely allied differing mainly in the rich violet-purple coloration of its flowers.

Ticoglossum R. Lucas Rodrigues ex Halbinger
Subfamily Epidendroideae
Tribe Oncidieae

Small epiphytic plants with short rhizomes. **Pseudobulbs** appressed, ancipitous, circular to ovoid, unifoliate, subtended by several basal sheaths. **Leaves** conduplicate, elliptic-lanceolate, acute, petiolate. **Inflorescences** axillary from basal sheaths, erect or spreading, few-flowered, more or less as long as the leaves; bracts ovate, appressed. **Flowers** showy, large. **Sepals** sessile, free, elliptic to ovate, keeled on back. **Petals** similar to sepals, clawed. **Lip** with a short claw, at an angle of 50–65° to the column; callus on claw yellow with red spots, with retrorse trichomes at back. **Column** short, straight, lacking wings or auricles but with a pair of small protuberances alongside the stigma; pollinia 2, conical-reniform, grooved, attached to the sides of a triangular conduplicate stipe.
DISTRIBUTION A small genus of two species from Costa Rica and Panama.
DERIVATION OF NAME A name derived from the Costa Rican slang word *tico*, used as an affectionate name for a Costa Rican, and the Greek *glossa* (tongue). The name reflects the relationship of this genus to *Odontoglossum*.
TAXONOMY This is a segregate genus of *Odontoglossum* that was established by Federico Halbinger in 1983 in *Orquidea* (*Mex.*) (p. 4). It differs from *Odontoglossum* in its characteristic callus structure and the wingless column.
TYPE SPECIES *Odontoglossum oerstedii* Rchb.f.

Thunia alba (left)
Thunia bensoniae (middle)
Thunia marshalliana (right)
1 – Lip, side view (× $\frac{2}{3}$)
2 – Lip, flattened, from above (× $\frac{2}{3}$)
3 – Column, spur and ovary, from below (× $\frac{2}{3}$)

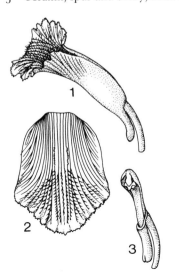
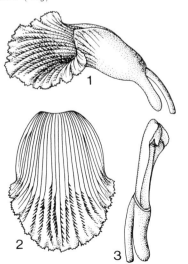
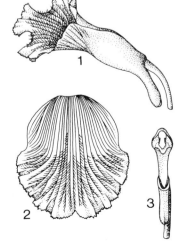

CULTURE Temp. Winter min. 12°C. Grow in conditions similar to *Odontoglossum*.

Ticoglossum krameri (Rchb.f.) Halbinger
[Colour Plate]

An epiphyte up to 25 cm tall. **Pseudobulbs** discoid, very compressed, ancipitous, up to 5 cm across, subtended by 5 or 6 basal bracts, unifoliate at the apex. **Leaf** elliptic-oblong to oblong-lanceolate, acute, 12–25 cm long, 3.5–4.3 cm wide, shortly petiolate, pale green. **Inflorescences** erect, basal, 16–21 cm long, 2- to 3-flowered; bracts lanceolate, acute, up to 1.2 cm long. **Flowers** showy, 4–5 cm across, pink or lilac-pink with a yellow callus spotted with red and with a brown or orange band in front; pedicel and ovary longer than the bracts. **Sepals** elliptic to obovate-elliptic, acute or apiculate, 1.7–2.1 cm long, 0.8–1 cm wide. **Petals** oblong-elliptic or obovate, apiculate or obtuse, 1.8–2 cm long, 0.8–0.9 cm wide. **Lip** shortly clawed, the apical lamina deflexed, broadly ovate-orbicular, emarginate, 1.7–1.9 cm long, 1.4 cm wide; callus on claw of lip fleshy, complex, hairy at base. **Column** fleshy, up to 8 mm long.

DISTRIBUTION Endemic to Costa Rica, on both the Atlantic and Pacific sides of the central Cordillera; in lower montane forest, 600–1200 m.

HISTORY First collected in Costa Rica by Kramer, one of the collectors sent out by Messrs Veitch, and described as *Odontoglossum krameri* by H.G. Reichenbach in 1868 in the *Gardeners' Chronicle* (p. 98). Halbinger transferred it to *Ticoglossum* in the journal *Orquidea* (p. 4) in 1983.

The albino variety, var. *album* R. Lucas Rodr., differs in having ellipsoid pseudobulbs and in its flower colour. It is commoner on the north-facing slopes of the Cordillera where the typical variety is absent.

SYNONYM *Odontoglossum krameri* Rchb.f.
CLOSELY RELATED SPECIES *T. oerstedii* (Rchb.f) Halbinger [Colour Plate], from Costa Rica and Panama, differs in having much slenderer petioles, 2–3 mm wide, and a bright yellow spot on the disc in front of the callus of the more rhombic lip.

Tolumnia Raf.
Subfamily Epidendroideae
Tribe Oncidieae

Small epiphytic herbs with more or less elongate creeping or scandent rhizomes. **Stems** more or less remote, very short, leafy; roots emerging below each growth. **Leaves** imbricate, distichous, fleshy to coriaceous, bilaterally flattened (equitant), channelled on upper surface. **Inflorescences** usually much exceeding the leaves, racemose to paniculate. **Flowers** flat, usually showy, large for the size of the plant. **Sepals** and **petals** subsimilar, the petals often slightly larger. **Lip** much larger than the other segments, deflexed, 3-lobed, with a more or less complex fleshy callus at the base, lacking a spur; side lobes usually smaller than the entire to bilobulate mid-lobe. **Column** erect, with a prominent wing either side of the stigma; pollinia 2, ovoid, cleft, attached by a long slender stipe to a small viscidium.

DISTRIBUTION A genus of possibly 31 species widespread in the W. Indies.

DERIVATION OF NAME Named probably for Tolumnius, a Rutulian mentioned by Virgil (fide Schultes and Pease, 1963).

TAXONOMY The genus *Tolumnia* was established by C.S. Rafinesque in his *Flora Telluriana* (p. 101) in 1836. However, it was not taken up until 1986 when G. Braem resurrected it in *Die Orchideen* (p. 55) for the group popularly called 'equitant' or 'variegata' oncidiums. He was able to do this because of a ruling by the International Committee for Spermatophyta in *Taxon* (p. 661) in the previous year that the type of the genus *Oncidium* was *O. altissimum* (Jacq.) Sw. and not *O. variegatum* (Sw.) Sw. as had been suggested by some authors. *O. variegatum* and its allies are rather distinct from other oncidiums in their habit, pollinarium, breeding behaviour and chromosome numbers. In nature, the specific delimitation of some species causes immense problems because of hybridisation in habitats that have been much changed by the influence of man. Some of the recognised species, such as *T. lucayana* (Nash) Braem, are undoubtedly hybrid complexes.

A discussion of the taxonomy and photographs of the flowers of many species are given by Withner (1980) in the *Orchid Digest* (pp. 84–94).

In cultivation and for hybrid registration purposes they are still generally referred to *Oncidium*.

TYPE SPECIES *Tolumnia pulchella* (Hook.) Raf.
SYNONYMS *Xaritonia* Raf.; *Oncidium* sect. *Equitantia* Lindl.; *Oncidium* sect. *Oncidium* sensu Garay & Stacy

CULTURE Temp. Winter min. 15°C. Must be mounted on a twig or small branch and hung under minimal shade but protected from scorching. Mist lightly daily as they are intolerant of excessive moisture.

Tolumnia calochila (Cogn.) Braem
A small epiphyte with a slender creeping rhizome and very short erect stems. **Leaves** 1–3, linear-aciculate, acuminate, 3–7 cm long, 0.1–0.2 cm wide. **Inflorescence** spreading, laxly

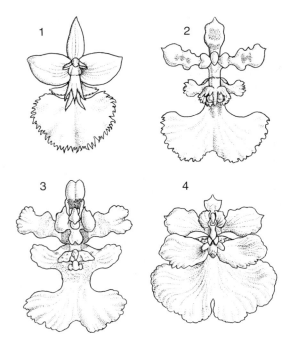

Tolumnia
Flowers (× 1½)
1 – *calochila*
2 – *lucayana*
3 – *variegata*
4 – *pulchella*

1- to 2-flowered, 3–8 cm long; peduncle very slender, wiry; bracts lanceolate, acuminate 2 mm long. Flowers bright yellow with yellow-green sepals and petals; pedicel and ovary 7–9 mm long. **Dorsal sepal** lanceolate, acuminate, 6–9 mm long, 2–2.5 mm wide; **lateral sepals** fused almost to the tip, lanceolate, acute, 7–9 mm long, 2–3 mm wide. **Petals** ovate-lanceolate, 9–11 mm long, 4–5 mm wide. **Lip** 3-lobed at the base, obtuse to acuminate, 14–16 mm long, 10–14 mm wide; lateral lobes auriculate, spreading; mid-lobe broadly ovate, with a lacerate or erose margin; callus of 4 fleshy prongs. **Column** erect, 4–4.5 cm long, with rounded wings.

DISTRIBUTION Hispaniola, the Cayman Islands and perhaps on an island off the E. coast of Cuba; in dry shrub up to 1500 m.

HISTORY Originally described by Alfred Cogniaux in Urban's *Symbolae Antillanae* (p. 660) in 1910. G. Braem transferred it to the present genus in 1986 in *Die Orchideen* (p. 58).

SYNONYM *Oncidium calochilum* Cogn.

Tolumnia pulchella (Hook.) Raf.
Medium-sized epiphytes with clustered short leafy stems. **Leaves** fleshy, distichous, equitant, lanceolate, falcate, acute, 6–12 cm long, 0.6–1.1 cm wide. **Inflorescences** up to 50 cm long,

branching, densely many-flowered; peduncle terete, up to 40 cm long; bracts lanceolate, acuminate, 3–4 mm long. **Flowers** very showy, flat, the sepals and petals off-white to purple, sometimes spotted, the lip pale rose-pink to rich purple with a yellow and white callus spotted finely with red; pedicel and ovary 12–19 cm long. **Dorsal sepal** elliptic-oblanceolate, acute, 6–8 mm long, 2–2.5 mm wide; **lateral sepals** fused almost to the apex, bifid at the tip, 8–11 mm long, 2.5–3 mm wide. **Petals** spreading, obovate, obtuse, 6–7.5 mm long, 5–7 mm wide. **Lip** 3-lobed at the base, dependent, 14–20 mm long, and wide; callus of 3 fleshy ridges in the basal part of the lip. **Column** 3–4 mm long, with obliquely ovate, falcate erect wings.

DISTRIBUTION Jamaica; on slender tree trunks in forest, 600–1000 m.

HISTORY Sir William Hooker described this attractive species as *Oncidium pulchellum* in Curtis's *Botanical Magazine* (t. 2773) based on a collection by D. Bancroft from Jamaica. It was moved to *Tolumnia* by C.S. Rafinesque in *Flora Telluriana* (p. 101) in 1836.

SYNONYM *Oncidium pulchellum* Hook.

Tolumnia variegata (Sw.) Braem

A creeping epiphyte with a slender ascending rhizome. **Leaves** 4–10, distichous, equitant, linear to elliptic-lanceolate, falcate, acute to acuminate, 2.5–14 cm long, 0.3–0.8 cm wide, serrulate. **Inflorescences** 15–80 cm long, simple or with 1- to few-branches, laxly few-flowered; branches suberect, each 4- to 5-flowered; bracts lanceolate, acute, 2–3.5 mm long. **Flowers** white or pink marked with red spotting on the lower two-thirds of the sepals and petals and around the lip-callus, the callus yellow. **Dorsal sepal** obovate-elliptic, obtuse, 4–5 mm long, 2 mm wide; **lateral sepals** united almost to the apex, spathulate, 4–5 mm long, 2–3 mm wide. **Petals** spreading-ascending, obovate, obtuse, 7–9 mm long, 4–6 mm wide. **Lip** 3-lobed at the base, 10–15 mm long, 13–20 mm wide; side lobes auriculate, spreading; mid-lobe reniform with a broad sinus; callus of 3 short spreading ridges at base of lip. **Column** erect, 4 mm long, with obliquely ovate, falcate wings.

DISTRIBUTION Cuba, Hispaniola, Puerto Rico; usually in xerophytic shrub and woods, sea level to 700 m.

HISTORY Olof Swartz described this species as *Epidendrum variegatum* in 1788 in his *Prodromus Descriptionem Vegetabilum* (p. 122). It was transferred to *Tolumnia* by G. Braem in 1986 in *Die Orchideen* (p. 59).

It is a very variable species and hybridises with allied species in nature thereby causing taxonomic confusion.

SYNONYM *Epidendrum variegatum* Sw.; *Oncidium variegatum* (Sw.) Sw.

Trevoria Lehmann
Subfamily Epidendroideae
Tribe Gongoreae
Subtribe Stanhopeinae

Epiphytes with ovoid or cylindrical clustered, 1-noded pseudobulbs, 1- or 2-leaved at the apex. **Leaves** coriaceous or thin-textured, plicate, petiolate, articulated at the base. **Inflorescences** pendent, basal, few-flowered. **Flowers** large, fleshy, campanulate, resupinate or not. **Dorsal sepal** and **petals** free; **lateral sepals** united at the base to the column-foot. **Lip** tripartite, with the hypochile unlobed, concave, cucullate, with a fleshy plate-shaped callus, the mesochile concave, fleshy, with a callus that sometimes has a free apex, and with the ovate epichile rigidly attached to it. **Column** short, fleshy, slightly dilated above, with a short foot;

Trevoria chloris
1 – Habit ($\times \frac{1}{2}$)
2 – Inflorescence ($\times \frac{1}{2}$)
3 – Column and lip ($\times$ 1)
4 – Pollinarium ($\times$ 2)

pollinia 2, hard, sulcate, attached by an oblanceolate stipe to the viscidium.

DISTRIBUTION A small genus of five species distributed from Nicaragua and Costa Rica to Bolivia.

DERIVATION OF NAME Named in honour of Sir Trevor Lawrence (1831–1914), one-time president of the Royal Horticultural Society and a well-known orchid grower of the Victorian era.

TAXONOMY *Trevoria* was established by Consul Lehmann, the German consul to New Grenada (now Colombia), in 1897 in the *Gardeners' Chronicle* (ser. 3, 21: 345).

TYPE SPECIES *T. chloris* Lehmann

SYNONYM *Endresiella* Schltr.

CULTURE Temp. Winter min. 10–12°C. Grow as for *Stanhopea*.

Trevoria chloris Lehmann

An epiphyte with clustered ovoid or longly pyriform, unifoliate pseudobulbs, up to 9 cm long, 0.8–1.5 cm wide. **Leaves** oblong-elliptic, acute or acuminate, 25–40 cm long, 5–10 cm wide, shortly petiolate. **Inflorescences** pendulous, laxly 3- to 4-flowered, up to 20 cm long; peduncle terete, green; bracts glumaceous, lanceolate, acuminate, up to 3.5 cm long. **Flowers** showy, non-resupinate, c. 10 cm across, green with a white disc to the lip, lepidote on the outside; pedicel and ovary up to 3 cm long. **Dorsal sepal** narrowly ovate-lanceolate, acuminate, 4–5 cm long, 1–1.5 cm wide; **lateral sepals** obliquely ovate-lanceolate, acuminate, strongly concave, 4–5 cm long, 2–3 cm wide. **Petals** falcate, linear, acuminate, 5–6 cm long, 0.6–0.8 cm wide, twisted. **Lip** uppermost in the flower, 5–6 cm long, 0.4 cm wide; hypochile strongly concave, subglobose, fleshily keeled in the middle, free and truncate at the apex; mesochile bilobed in front; epichile linear-hastate, acuminate. **Column** fleshy, 0.7–0.8 cm long.

DISTRIBUTION Colombia; 1000–1700 m.

HISTORY *T. chloris* was discovered by Consul F.C. Lehmann in Colombia and was described by him in the *Gardeners' Chronicle* (ser. 3, 21: 346) in 1897. The plant which figured in the *Botanical Magazine* (t. 7805) under this name is the closely allied *T. lehmannii* which differs in having broader petals and a broader lip in which the mid-lobe is ovate and acute.

Trias Lindl.
Subfamily Epidendroideae
Tribe Epidendreae
Subtribe Bulbophyllinae

Dwarf or small epiphytic herbs with short creeping rhizomes. **Pseudobulbs** ovoid, obliquely ovoid or sphaerical, often dorsoventrally compressed, unifoliate, smooth or rugulose. **Leaf** erect to spreading, fleshy-coriaceous, elliptic to oblong, sessile. **Inflorescences** 1 to few, 1-flowered, usually shorter than the leaf, basal; peduncle obscure or very short; bracts tubular. **Flowers** often large for plant, triangular; pedicel and ovary elongate. **Sepals** subsimilar, large, ovate to oblong-ovate; lateral sepals oblique, attached at the base to the column-foot to form a broad mentum. **Petals** much smaller than the sepals, lying adjacent to the column. **Lip** entire or obscurely 3-lobed, fleshy, recurved, ecallose; side lobes auriculate if present. **Column** short, with an elongate incurved foot; anther-cap with an entire or bilobed apical protrusion; pollinia 4, pyriform flattened to reniform, in 2 unequal pairs.

DISTRIBUTION A genus of perhaps 10 species centred on Thailand but extending east to Laos and west to the Indian peninsula.

DERIVATION OF NAME From the Greek *trias* (three) and descriptive of the triangular flower.

TAXONOMY *Trias* was described by John Lindley in 1830 in his *Genera and Species of Orchidaceous Plants* (p. 60). It is closely allied to *Bulbophyllum* and has been included in the latter by some authors as a section. It differs, however, in having a more or less triangular flower with prominent sepals and much smaller almost hidden petals and lip, and the distinctive prolonged and often bifid anther-cap.

The genus has been most recently revised by Seidenfaden (1976) in *Dansk Botanisk Tidsskrift*.

TYPE SPECIES *T. oblonga* Lindl.; *T. ovata* Lindl.

CULTURE Temp. Winter min. 15°C. These are small creeping plants which may be grown mounted or alternatively in pans. They require high humidity with plenty of water while growing and a drier period when growth is complete.

Trias picta (Par. & Rchb.f.) Hemsl.

A dwarf epiphyte with a short creeping rhizome. **Pseudobulbs** ovoid-sphaerical, 1–1.4 cm in diameter, borne 0.5–1.5 cm apart. **Leaf** very fleshy, oblong-elliptic, abruptly acuminate, 5–6 cm long, 0.7–1.6 cm wide. **Inflorescence** 2–2.5 cm long; bract tubular, 4–5 mm long. **Flower** triangular, yellow spotted with purple or purple-flushed; pedicel and ovary up to 1.5 cm long. **Sepals** ovate-triangular to oblong-ovate, subacute to obtuse, 8–10 mm long, 6–7 mm wide; mentum 4–5 mm long. **Petals** elliptic or obovate, rounded or emarginate, 3.5–4 mm long, 3 mm wide. **Lip** recurved, obovate, rounded in front, very obscurely 3-lobed, 4 mm long, 2 mm wide, rugulose above. **Column** 2 mm long; foot 3–4 mm long.

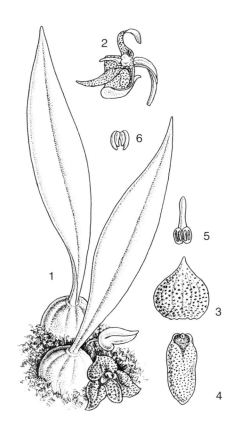

Trias picta
1 – Habit ($\times \frac{3}{4}$)
2 – Flower, side view ($\times 1\frac{3}{4}$)
3 – Dorsal sepal ($\times 1\frac{3}{4}$)
4 – Lip ($\times$ 3)
5 – Anther-cap ($\times 4\frac{1}{2}$)
6 – Pollinia ($\times$ 9)

DISTRIBUTION Burma and Thailand.

TAXONOMY The type collection was made by Charles Parish at Mergui and was described by him and H.G. Reichenbach in 1974 in the *Transactions of the Linnean Society* (p. 150) as *Bulbophyllum pictum*. Hemsley transferred it to *Trias* in 1882 in the *Gardeners' Chronicle* (n. s. 18: p. 427).

SYNONYM *Bulbophyllum pictum* Par. & Rchb.f.

Trichocentrum Poepp. & Endl.
Subfamily Epidendroideae
Tribe Oncidieae

Epiphytic plants with short rhizomes. **Pseudobulbs** minute, 1-leafed. **Leaf** small, coriaceous. **Inflorescence** 1- to 3-flowered. **Sepals** and **petals** similar, free, spreading. **Lip** suberect, simple or obscurely 3-lobed, with a slender or gibbous spur. **Column** short, stout, adnate almost to apex with the lip, auriculate or winged above, lacking a foot; pollinia 2, waxy, sulcate.

DISTRIBUTION Less than 12 species native to the American tropics.

DERIVATION OF NAME From the Greek *tricho* (hair) and *kentron* (spur), alluding to the very slender and long spur characteristic of the flowers of many species in the genus.

TAXONOMY E.F. Poeppig and S.L. Endlicher described *Trichocentrum* in 1838 in *Nova Genera ac Species Plantarum* (p. 11, t. 115).

In *Trichocentrum* the lateral sepals are free, the base of the lip is deeply saccate or forms a single spur and the inflorescence is 1- to 3-flowered. All these features serve to distinguish it from the somewhat allied *Comparettia* and *Ionopsis*.

TYPE SPECIES *T. pulchrum* Poepp. & Endl.

CULTURE Compost A. Winter min. 12–15 C. *Trichocentrum* species may be grown in small pots or mounted on slabs of fern-fibre or cork. They require humid and shady conditions and should never become very dry.

Trichocentrum albococcineum Linden

A small epiphytic plant, up to 10 cm or so high. **Pseudobulbs** small, clustered, ovoid, 1-leafed at apex. **Leaf** elliptic, acute, sessile, fleshy, 7.7–9 cm long, 2.5–4 cm broad. **Inflorescence** lateral, 1-flowered. **Flower** variable, rather large; segments spreading, brown within, tinged reddish inside, paler outside; lip lamina purple or white, with 2 large purple blotches at the base, with a white claw lined with purple. **Dorsal sepal** oblong-obovate, acute, 2 cm long, 0.9 cm broad; **lateral sepals** obliquely oblong-elliptic, subacute. **Petals** oblong-oblanceolate, 1.8 cm broad, acute. **Lip** adnate to the column at the base, with a broad cuneate claw and a subquadrate-pandurate lamina, 2.5 cm long, 2.2 cm broad; spur short, conical curved, 1.2 cm long. **Column** very short, stout, 0.5 cm long; wings apical, large, porrect, decurved, triangular-lanceolate.

DISTRIBUTION Brazil and Peru.

HISTORY Introduced into cultivation by G. Wallis from the Rio Negro and described by Jean Linden in 1865 in *La Belgique Horticole* (p. 103). It first flowered in cultivation in the collections of W. Saunders of Reigate and J. Bateman of Biddulph Grange, England.

T. albococcineum is readily identified by its rather small, distinctively coloured flowers.

SYNONYMS *Trichocentrum amazonicum* Barb. Rodr.; *T. albopurpureum* Linden & Rchb.f.

Trichocentrum tigrinum Linden & Rchb.f.
[Colour Plate]
A small epiphytic plant with a very short stem. **Leaves** narrowly oblong-elliptic, suberect or

spreading-arcuate, obtuse, coriaceous, 6–12 cm long, 2–3 cm broad, dark green, spotted dull crimson. **Inflorescences** pendulous to sub-erect-spreading, up to 15 cm long, 1- or 2-flowered; bracts lanceolate, acute, 1–1.3 cm long. **Flowers** large, showy; sepals and petals spreading, greyish-green, spotted or mottled with purplish-brown; lip white with pinkish-purple on either side towards the base and a yellow callus; column white, spotted purple. **Sepals** narrowly oblong-elliptic, acute, 3–3.6 cm long, 0.8–1.2 cm broad, margins slightly recurved. **Petals** narrowly oblong-oblanceolate, acute, 3–3.5 cm long, 0.8 cm broad, margins slightly recurved. **Lip** deflexed, at right-angles to the column, cuneate-flabellate, marginate, 4–4.5 cm long, 3–4.5 cm broad; callus of 5 ridges, the 2 outer ones half the length of the others and horn-like in front, the rest lamellate, raised and acute in front. **Column** erect, 0.8 cm long, with a lacerate wing on each side of the column.

DISTRIBUTION Central America (?) and Ecuador.

HISTORY Discovered by Richard Pfau in 1869 when collecting for Jean Linden. It was said to be from Central America and was described the same year by Linden and H.G. Reichenbach in the *Gardeners' Chronicle* (p. 892).

Trichoceros H.B.K.
Subfamily Epidendroideae
Tribe Maxillarieae
Subtribe Telipogoninae

Small to medium-sized scrambling terrestrial, lithophytic or epiphytic herbs with more or less elongate rhizomes bearing short pseudobulbs, 1-leafed at the apex but subtended by 2 to several leaves. **Leaves** distichous, imbricate, sheathing the pseudobulb, small, fleshy to coriaceous, unjointed. **Inflorescence** lateral, 1 or 2 from the base of the pseudobulb, simple, racemose, usually longer than the leaves, laxly few- to several-flowered. **Flowers** small to medium-sized, with spreading segments. **Sepals** subsimilar, subequal, free. **Petals** similar. **Lip** usually 3-lobed or rarely entire; side lobes spreading or erect, commonly narrow and retrorse; mid-lobe much larger, usually more or less ovate. **Column** very short and stout, lacking wings or a foot, with a fimbriate clinandrium, often dorsally longly setose; pollinia 4, hard, attached by a spathulate stipe to a hooked viscidium.

DISTRIBUTION A small genus of about five species in Andean S. America from Colombia south to Bolivia.

DERIVATION OF NAME From the Greek *thrix, tricho* (hair) and *keras* (horn), in allusion to the hairy antenniform process on each side of the column.

TAXONOMY This close ally of *Telipogon* was described by Humboldt, Bonpland and Kunth in 1815 in *Nova Genera et Species Plantarum* (p. 337, t. 76). It differs from *Telipogon* in having distinct pseudobulbs, lateral, basal inflorescences and a 3-lobed lip.

It is pollinated through pseudocopulation by bristly tachinid flies.

TYPE SPECIES *Epidendrum antenniferum* H.B.K.
CULTURE Temp. Winter min. 10–12°C. Rambling plants which may be grown on poles, or in shallow pans in an epiphyte mix. Grow under moderate shade and humidity and water throughout the year.

Trichoceros antennifer (H.&B.) H.B.K.
[Colour Plate]
A scrambling terrestrial or lithophytic plant with a more or less elongate, ascending, sometimes branching rhizome covered by evanescent sheaths; roots stout, 3 mm in diameter, emerging beneath each pseudobulb. **Pseudobulbs** remote, small, ellipsoidal to broadly cylindrical, 0.6–1.5 cm long, unifoliate at apex, enclosed by 2 to several leaf bases. **Leaves** coriaceous, distichous, imbricate, ovate to elliptic-oblong, acute or acuminate, 4–7 cm long, 0.6–2 cm wide. **Inflorescences** basal, lateral, much longer than the leaves, 10–35 cm long; peduncle up to 25 cm long; bracts ovate to ovate-lanceolate, acuminate, 5–8 mm long. **Flowers** produced in succession, flat, bee-like, greenish or yellowish with a maroon flush on the sepals and petals and with a reddish-maroon lip; pedicel and ovary 2–2.6 cm long. **Sepals** elliptic, acute or acuminate, 10–12 mm long, 6–7 mm wide. **Petals** clawed, elliptic or ovate, acute, 10–12 mm long, 4–5 mm wide. **Lip** 3-lobed at the base, 8–9 mm long; side lobes linear, 9–10 mm long, ciliate; mid-lobe ovate, obtuse to shortly apiculate. **Column** 4–5 mm long, densely bristly.

DISTRIBUTION Colombia to Bolivia; on steep mossy slopes in mist forest, 1800–3000 m.
HISTORY Originally described as *Epidendrum antenniferum* by Humboldt and Bonpland in 1816 in their *Plantae aequinoctiales* (p. 98). It was transferred to *Trichoceros* in 1816 by them and Kunth in *Nova Genera et Species Plantarum* (p. 338).
SYNONYMS *Epidendrum antenniferum* H.& B.; *Trichoceros parviflorus* H.B.K.; *T. armillatus* Rchb.f.; *T. muscifera* Kraenzl.

Trichoglottis Blume
Subfamily Epidendroideae
Tribe Vandeae
Subtribe Sarcanthinae

Epiphytic herbs with long, climbing or hanging, leafy, monopodial stems. **Leaves** narrow, distichous, coriaceous. **Inflorescences** axillary, sessile or pedunculate, racemose, 1- to 2-flowered. **Flowers** small, rather fleshy, rarely showy. **Sepals** and **petals** free, rather fleshy, spreading; lateral sepals adnate to the very short column-foot. **Lip** firmly united to the base of the column, fleshy and mostly partly hairy, ± 3-lobed, with a distinct basal sac or spur; side lobes erect, often decurrent on lamina of mid-lobe as keels; mid-lobe simple or 3-lobed, porrect; spur not septate, with a tongue-shaped, ± hairy lamella protruding from the back wall of the spur just below the column. **Column** short, auriculate; column-foot very short; clinandrium truncate; pollinia 4, unequal, united into 2 pairs on a narrow stipe with a small viscidium.

DISTRIBUTION About 60 species widespread in E. Asia, Malaysia, the Philippines, Melanesia and adjacent islands.
DERIVATION OF NAME From the Greek *thrix* (hair) and *glotta* (tongue), referring to the often pubescent dactylate process in the throat of the lip.
TAXONOMY C. Blume described this genus in 1825 in his *Bijdragen* (p. 359). Its characteristic features are the tongue-shaped lamella at the back of the spur, the auricles on the column and the usually 3-lobed mid-lobe to the lip.

The genus approaches *Acampe* through *T. misera* (Ridley) Holttum which has the typical tongue but lacks the column-wings of *Trichoglottis*. The larger-flowered species approach *Vandopsis* in structure whilst the smaller species approach *Cleisostoma*. *Pomatocalpa* is also allied but has a tongue at a deeper level in the spur. Undoubtedly, the interrelations between these genera need further study.

This genus is particularly well represented in the Philippines which boasts some 16 species.
TYPE SPECIES *T. retusa* Blume
CULTURE Compost A. Temp. Winter min. 15°C. As for *Vanda*. The climbing species need some support. Others hang downwards and might be better grown in baskets or mounted. The plants should be given moderate shade and good humidity, with plenty of water while growing.

Trichoglottis philippinensis Lindl.
[Colour Plate]
A tall epiphytic plant with elongated, branching, white roots produced along the stem.

Stem erect, stout, up to 90 cm long, 0.5 cm broad, leafy towards apex. **Leaves** distichous, at 2 cm intervals, coriaceous, oblong to oblong-ovate, retuse, mucronate, carinate, 3–6 cm long, 1.5–3 cm broad. **Inflorescences** axillary, 1-flowered. **Flowers** 3 cm across, fleshy, fragrant, greenish-brown outside, brownish or rich maroon within; lip rose-purple with white central hairs and yellow at the base; column predominantly white. **Dorsal sepal** oblong, acute, 1.5 cm long, 0.6 cm broad; **lateral sepals** lanceolate, acute, 1.5–1.8 cm long, 0.8 cm broad, apex abruptly curved. **Petals** linear-spathulate, obtuse or subacute, 1.6 cm long, 0.45 cm broad. **Lip** united with column at base, cruciform, villose on upper surface, 1.6–1.9 cm long; side lobes near the apex, narrowly triangular, acute; apex of lip bilaterally flattened with a vertical acute plate, strongly angled ventrally; disc with a round triangular lobule near the base on each side and a ligulate hairy appendage in the shallow saccate base. **Column** short, stout.

DISTRIBUTION The Philippines (Luzon, Mindanao and Negros); not uncommon from sea level to 300 m altitude.

HISTORY Described by John Lindley in 1845 in the *Annals and Magazine of Natural History* (p. 386).

SYNONYMS *Stauropsis philippinensis* (Lindl.) Rchb.f.

Trichopilia Lindl.

Subfamily Epidendroideae
Tribe Oncidieae

Small to medium-sized, epiphytic plants with a short creeping rhizome. **Pseudobulbs** small, clustered, 1-leafed, orbicular-ancipitous to slender-caulescent. **Leaf** suberect, coriaceous. **Inflorescence** basal, 1- to few-flowered. **Flowers** large and showy. **Sepals** and **petals** similar, spreading, narrow, ± twisted or contorted. **Lip** ± 3-lobed, fused to base of column, tubular-involute below, spreading above. **Column** slender, clavate, erect, 2-winged or bidentate above; pollinia 2, waxy; stipe broadly triangular.

DISTRIBUTION About 30 species in the tropics of Central and S. America.

DERIVATION OF NAME From the Greek *tricho* (hair) and *pilos* (felt), alluding to the ciliate or fimbriate margins of the clinandrium.

TAXONOMY John Lindley described *Trichopilia* in the 2nd edition of *Introduction to Natural History* (p. 446) in 1836.

It is one of a number of allied genera in the tribe Oncidieae which are characterised by some degree of fusion between the lip and column. This complex is bicentric with each of the genera *Aspasia* and *Trichopilia* forming the focus of a distinct group of genera that have probably evolved in parallel to each other (L. Garay in *Orquideologia*, 1972). The *Aspasia* alliance is characterised by the slender, linear-oblanceolate stipe of the pollinia while the *Trichopilia* alliance is distinguished by the broadly triangular stipe of the pollinia.

Trichopilia as originally established by Lindley was a well-defined genus but has subsequently been enlarged by some authors by the addition of elements such as *Leucohyle* Klotzsch, *Oliveriana* Rchb.f. and *Helcia* Lindl. Recently, several species formerly included in *Trichopilia* have been removed into *Cischweinfia* by R. Dressler and N. Williams and into *Neoescobaria* by L. Garay. All of the above-mentioned genera are now considered distinct, thus reducing the size of *Trichopilia*. *Leucohyle* and *Cischweinfia* are now considered to be closer to *Aspasia* than to *Trichopilia*.

From *Helcia*, *Oliveriana* and *Neoescobaria*, *Trichopilia* may be distinguished by the base or claw of the lip being centrally fused to the column through a keel-like connective and by the basal part of the lip tightly enveloping the column to form an infundibuliform throat.

TYPE SPECIES *T. tortilis* Lindl.

SYNONYM *Pilumna* Lindl.

CULTURE Compost A. Temp. Winter min. 12–15°C. These plants grow well in pans and baskets. They should have moderate shade and require careful watering while growing. After the pseudobulbs are fully grown, the plants should be kept nearly dry and somewhat cooler.

Trichopilia fragrans (Lindl.) Rchb.f.
[Colour Plate]
A medium-sized epiphytic or lithophytic plant. **Pseudobulbs** clustered, almost ligulate, very lightly compressed, up to 12 cm long, 3 cm broad, 1-leafed at apex. **Leaf** oblong-ligulate, subacute, erect or suberect, mid-nerve sulcate above, up to 26 cm long, 6 cm broad. **Inflorescence** basal, pendent, racemose, laxly few-flowered; bracts pale green, spotted dark brown. **Flowers** large; sepals and petals light green; lip white with a central pale yellow or orange stripe in the basal third; column white. **Sepals** and **petals** somewhat reflexed, narrowly linear-lanceolate, acute, margins undulate, 3.4–3.7 cm long, 0.6–0.7 cm broad. **Lip** oblong-elliptic, shortly clawed, emarginate, 3 cm long, 2.2 cm broad, basal margins upturned around the column, apical half spreading, margins erose-undulate; callus a thin ridge in the basal half. **Column** winged at the apex, dorsal apical margin erose-dentate.

DISTRIBUTION The W. Indies, Venezuela and Colombia to Bolivia; up to 2500 m.

HISTORY Originally described as *Pilumna fragrans* by John Lindley in 1844 in the *Botanical Register* (misc. no. 74) from a plant collected by Theodore Hartweg near Popayan. H.G. Reichenbach transferred it to the genus *Trichopilia* in 1858 in the *Hamburger Gartenzeitung* (p. 229).

SYNONYMS *Pilumna fragrans* Lindl.; *Trichopilia candida* Linden ex Lindl.; *Pilumna wagneri* Rchb.f.; *Trichopilia wagneri* (Rchb.f) Rchb.f.; *T. lehmannii* Regel

Trichopilia laxa (Lindl.) Rchb.f.
[Colour Plate]
A large epiphytic plant, up to 42 cm high, with ovoid, compressed, 1-leafed pseudobulbs. **Leaf** oblong, subacute, coriaceous, 16–30 cm long, 3.5–5 cm broad, margins often recurved. **Inflorescence** basal, lax or pendulous, racemose, 4- to 7-flowered, up to 26 cm long; rhachis terete, pale pinky-green; bracts green, spotted maroon. **Flowers** with pale green to pinkish-maroon sepals and petals and a pale green lip with a white base: column pale green, white at apex; anther white. **Sepals** and **petals** narrowly linear-elliptic, subacute, 2.5–3.6 cm long, 0.4–0.5 cm broad. **Lip** shortly clawed below, subquadrate above, emarginate, basal half of lip tubular-involute, appressed to column, deflexed-recurved above, 1.5–2.6 cm long, 0.8–1.4 cm broad; callus linear, in basal part of lip. **Column** slender, clavate, up to 1.3 cm long.

DISTRIBUTION Venezuela, Colombia and Peru; in rain forests, 1200–1800 m altitude.

HISTORY Discovered in woods at Timbio near Popayan by Theodore Hartweg. John Lindley described this species as *Pilumna laxa* in 1844 in the *Botanical Register* (misc. no. 74). H. G. Reichenbach transferred it to *Trichopilia* in 1858 in the *Hamburger Gartenzeitung* (p. 229).

SYNONYMS *Pilumna laxa* Lindl.; *P. reichenheimiana* Klotzsch

Trichopilia marginata Henfr. [Colour Plate]
An erect epiphytic plant. **Pseudobulbs** approximate, linear, strongly compressed-ancipitous, 6–14 cm long, 1–2.5 cm across, 1-leafed at apex, enveloped at the base by several, imbricate, papery, conspicuously maculate sheaths. **Leaf** elliptic-lanceolate to lanceolate, acute to acuminate, coriaceous, 12–30 cm long, 3–5.3 cm broad, conduplicate at the base into a short petiole. **Inflorescences** basal, shortly arcuate or pendent, 2- or 3-flowered. **Flowers** large, showy, variable in colour; sepals and petals mostly reddish with paler margins; lip usually white on outer surface, deep rose-red within, reflexed margins white. **Sepals** subsimilar, spreading, lanceolate to oblanceolate, acute, margins undulate, 4.5–6 cm long, 0.6–1 cm broad. **Petals** similar to the sepals. **Lip**

tubular at base, 3-lobed, obovate when spread, 5–8 cm long, 4–5 cm broad, adnate to column at the base; side lobes rounded and convolute; mid-lobe deeply emarginate, margins undulate; disc lacking a prominent keel. **Column** terete, margins projecting, obscurely 3-lobed and fimbriate at the apex.

DISTRIBUTION Guatemala south to Colombia; 1000–1500 m.

HISTORY First collected by J. Warscewicz in 1849 on the slopes of the Chiriqui Volcano in Panama and described by Arthur Henfrey in 1851 in the *Gardeners' Magazine of Botany* (p. 185).

Several well-marked colour forms of this species are known: var. *alba* Rchb.f. lacks any red markings; var. *lepida* Veitch has larger flowers than the type, with sepals and petals blotched rose-pink and with broad white margins; var. *olivacea* Rchb.f. has olive-green sepals and petals.

SYNONYMS *Trichopilia coccinea* Warsc.; *T. crispa* Lindl.; *T. lepida* Hort.

CLOSELY RELATED SPECIES This large, showy species is closely allied to *T. tortilis* from Mexico and Guatemala and according to P.H. Allen in the *Flora of Panama* (1949) may prove to be a robust variety of that species.

Trichopilia suavis Lindl. & Paxt.
[Colour Plate]

An erect epiphytic herb. **Pseudobulbs** approximate, fleshy, oblong-ovoid, elliptic or suborbicular, compressed, 3.5–8 cm long, 2.5–6 cm across, 1-leafed at apex, subtended at the base by several, papery, imbricate bracts. **Leaf** elliptic-lanceolate, acute, coriaceous, 10–40 cm long, 3.5–8 cm broad, with a conduplicate petiole. **Inflorescence** basal, short, arcuate or pendulous, 2- to 5-flowered. **Flowers** large, attractive, fragrant; sepals and petals white or creamy-white, spotted pale rose or red; lip white or creamy-white, heavily spotted rose-pink, with yellow or orange markings on the throat (rarely blotched red). **Sepals** subsimilar, free, spreading, lanceolate, acute, margins undulate, 3–5.5 cm long, 0.6–1 cm broad. **Petals** similar to the sepals. **Lip** tubular, 3-lobed, obovate when spread, 4.5–6.5 cm broad, 3–5 cm broad; side lobes rounded, convolute, anterior margins usually crisped undulate; mid-lobe retuse or emarginate, margins crisped and reflexed; disc keeled. **Column** elongate, apex fimbriate and 4-lobed.

DISTRIBUTION Costa Rica to Colombia.

HISTORY This attractive species was discovered by J. Warscewicz in 1848 in Costa Rica and it was described in 1850 by John Lindley and J. Paxton in their *Flower Garden* (p. 44). The most showy forms of this species are found on the Chiriqui Volcano in Panama where they grow in low mossy woods between 1100 and 1700 m altitude.

SYNONYM *Trichopilia kienastiana* Rchb.f.

Trichopilia tortilis Lindl. [Colour Plate]

A tufted epiphytic plant, up to 30 cm or more high. **Pseudobulbs** narrowly ovoid to oblong-cylindrical, ± covered by sheaths, 4–12 cm long, 1.3–2 cm across, 1-leafed at apex. **Leaf** suberect, elliptic-lanceolate to oblanceolate, acute or shortly acuminate, coriaceous, 9–22 cm long, 2.3–4.8 cm broad. **Inflorescence** lateral, 5–10 cm long, 1- to 2-flowered; peduncle slender; bracts tubular, scarious, up to 2.5 cm long. **Flowers** large, showy, fragrant; sepals and petals brownish-purple to pale lavender with yellow or greenish margins; lip white or yellowish-white with a yellow throat spotted with crimson or brown; column greenish-white. **Sepals** and **petals** spreading, linear, acute, conspicuously twisted and contorted, 5–8 cm long, 1 cm broad. **Lip** large, tubular below, enveloping column, 3-lobed above, broadly ovate, 4.8–6.5 cm long, 3.8–4.5 cm broad; disc bifoveate at base of column. **Column** slender, clavate, 3-lobed at apex, 2 cm long.

DISTRIBUTION Mexico, Guatemala, Honduras and El Salvador; in rain forests up to 1500 m altitude.

HISTORY Introduced into cultivation from Mexico by George Barker of Springfield near Birmingham and described by John Lindley in 1836 in *Natural System of Botany*, 2nd edition (p. 446).

CLOSELY RELATED SPECIES See *T. marginata*.

Trichotosia Bl.
Subfamily Epidendroideae
Tribe Epidendreae
Subtribe Eariinae

Small to large very hairy epiphytic plants. **Stems** elongate, cane-like, leafy and caespitose or creeping, hairy and branching with each growth 2–3-leaved. **Leaves** bristly-hairy, distichous on elongate stems, fleshy, lanceolate to obovate. **Inflorescences** terminal or lateral, 1- to many-flowered, simple; peduncle and bracts hairy, often densely so. **Flowers** not opening widely, hairy on the outside of the sepals. **Dorsal sepal** and **petals** free; **lateral sepals** obliquely triangular-ovate, united to the column-foot to form a distinct chin-like mentum. **Petals** narrower than the sepals, ciliate to pubescent. **Lip** entire to 3-lobed, lacking a spur, with a callus. **Column** short, fleshy, with a distinct foot; pollinia 8, clavate.

DISTRIBUTION A genus of some 40–50 species widespread from the Himalayas to the S.W. Pacific Islands.

DERIVATION OF NAME From the Greek *tricho* (hair) and *glotta* (tongue), an allusion to the hairy lip of the type species.

TAXONOMY *Trichotosia* was established by Carl Blume in 1825 in his *Bijdragen* (p. 359). For almost a century afterwards it was included as a section of *Eria* but most recent authorities have treated it as a separate genus. This is probably reasonable because *Eria*, as presently understood, is paraphyletic and several of its sections will undoubtedly be raised to generic rank in the future.

Trichotosia can be easily distinguished from *Eria* by its hairy habit and flowers.

TYPE SPECIES *T. ferox* Bl.

CULTURE Temp. Winter min. 12–15°C. Smaller pendent and creeping plants grow well when mounted, but larger ones are better managed in pots of epiphyte mix. With fine roots like many of the *Eria* alliance, they should not be allowed to become too dry, and otherwise require conditions of moderate shade and humidity.

Trichotosia dasyphylla (Par. & Rchb.f.) Kraenzl.

A dwarf hairy epiphyte forming dense mats, with an elongate creeping fleshy rhizome, up to several cm long, 2- or 3-leaved at the apex of each growth. **Leaves** subcircular or elliptic to obovate-elliptic, obtuse, 0.5–1.5 cm long, 0.3–1 cm wide, bluish-green, very hairy on both surfaces. **Inflorescence** terminal, very short, 1-flowered; peduncle terete, 1–2 mm long, hairy; bract ovate, acute, 1–1.5 mm long, hairy. **Flowers** hairy on outside, greenish-yellow or yellow, with a purple mark on the lip; pedicel and ovary 2 mm long, hairy. **Dorsal sepal** ovate, acute, 2.5–3 mm long, 2.5 mm wide; **lateral sepals** obliquely triangular, subacute, 3–4 mm long, 3–4 mm wide; mentum conical, 3–4 mm long. **Petals** oblong, obtuse, 3 mm long, 1 mm wide, ciliate. **Lip** entire, oblong-elliptic, rounded or obtuse at the apex, 4.5 mm long, 3 mm wide, with 2 fleshy rounded calli at the base. **Column** 1.5 mm long.

DISTRIBUTION Nepal and Sikkim across to S. China, Laos and Vietnam; in montane forest, 600–1800 m.

HISTORY Charles Parish discovered this tiny orchid in the Henzai basin in Burma and described it with H.G. Reichenbach, as *Eria dasyphylla*, in 1874 in the *Transactions of the Linnean Society* (p. 147). Fritz Kraenzlin transferred it to *Trichotosia* in 1911 in Engler's *Pflanzenreich* (50: 138).

SYNONYMS *Eria dasyphylla* Par. & Rchb.f.; *E. evrardii* Gagnep.; *Pinalia dasyphylla* (Par. & Rchb.f.) O. Kuntze

Trichotosia ferox Bl. [Colour Plate]

A large epiphyte or lithophyte with elongate cylindrical very hairy pendulous leafy stems up to 200 cm long, the hairs stiff and up to 5 mm long. **Leaves** lanceolate, acuminate, 10–20 cm long, 2–5 cm wide, very hairy, articulated to hairy sheathing bases. **Inflorescences** emerging opposite the leaves, zigzag, laxly few-flowered, up to 10 cm long; peduncle and rhachis slender, hairy; bracts elliptic, obtuse, 10–15 mm long. **Flowers** very hairy on outer surface; pedicel and ovary 4–8 mm long. **Dorsal sepal** ovate, acute, 8–10 mm long, 5–6 mm wide; **lateral sepals** very obliquely ovate, sub-acute, 8–11 mm long, 7–9 mm wide; mentum subcylindrical, 7–8 mm long. **Petals** obovate, obtuse, 5–8 mm long, 2–3 mm wide. **Lip** 3-lobed in the apical half, 7–9 mm long, 5–7 mm wide; side lobes erect, obliquely oblong, rounded in front; mid-lobe transversely oblong-elliptic, emarginate; callus of 3 verrucose lines in centre of lip. **Column** 2 mm long.

DISTRIBUTION S. Thailand, Malaya and Sumatra to Borneo and Lombok; in exposed places in montane forest, 700–1600 m.

HISTORY The type collection of this impressive orchid was collected on Mt Salak in Java by Carl Blume and was described by him in his *Bijdragen* (p. 342).

SYNONYMS *Eria ferox* (Bl.) Bl.; *Pinalia ferox* (Bl.) O. Kuntze; *Eria virescens* Schltr.; *E. pyrrhotricha* Ridl.; *Trichotosia pyrrhotricha* (Ridl.) Ridl.

Tridactyle Schltr.

Subfamily Epidendroideae
Tribe Vandeae
Subtribe Aerangidinae

Small to medium-sized epiphytic or rarely lithophytic herb. **Stems** short to long, erect to pendulous, leafy throughout, ± branching. **Leaves** distichous, mostly linear or narrowly oblong, unequally 2-lobed or dentate at apex. **Inflorescences** lateral, very short to long. **Flowers** small, distichously arranged, white, yellow, green, ochre or brown. **Sepals** and **petals** free, spreading or recurved. **Lip** deflexed, entire to 3-lobed, auriculate at the base; side lobes often spreading, digitate or fimbriate; spur short to long, often clavate-inflated. **Column** short, fleshy; pollinia 2, ovoid or subglobose; stipe 1, entire or bifid at apex; viscidium 1, orbicular to elliptic.

DISTRIBUTION About 45 species in tropical Africa to S. Africa.

DERIVATION OF NAME From the Greek *tri* (three or thrice) and *daktylos* (finger), descriptive of the 3-lobed lip.

TAXONOMY Many species of *Tridactyle* were originally described in the genus *Angraecum* but this genus became unwieldy and those species which were unrelated to the typical *Angraecum* species were removed and placed in new genera. R. Schlechter established the genus *Tridactyle* in 1914 in *Die Orchideen* (p. 601) based on *Angraecum bicaudatum* Lindl. [= *T. bicaudata* (Lindl.) Schltr.] and included 16 further species previously referred to other genera (mainly *Angraecum* and *Listrostachys*). A further 18 species have since been added to the genus by V.S. Summerhayes and R. Mansfeld.

The genus has most recently been revised by V.S. Summerhayes in the *Kew Bulletin* (1948) where two sections are recognised as follows:

1. sect. *Tridactyle* with erect or hanging stems; a lip lobulate or auriculate at the base; a stipe longer than the pollinia; a small viscidium; and a beak-like rostellum. All species bar one are placed in this section. Summerhayes divided the section into eight groups of species on the length of their inflorescences.

2. sect. *Scandentes* has slender scandent stems; an exauriculate lip; a stipe shorter than the pollinia; and a large viscidium. It includes a solitary species, *T. wakefieldii* (Rolfe) Summerh., which vegetatively closely resembles *Solenangis* Schltr, and *Dinklageella* Mansf.

P. Cribb and J. Stewart (1985) in the *Kew Bulletin* transferred *T. wakefieldii* to the genus *Solenangis*. The 27 E. African species are described and keyed out in the *Flora of Tropical East Africa Orchidaceae* pt. 3 (p. 605) by P. Cribb.

TYPE SPECIES *T. bicaudata* (Lindl.) Schltr.
CULTURE Compost A. Temp. Winter min. 12–15°C. Small plants tend to grow erect but older and larger specimens become pendulous so should be grown in hanging baskets or pots. While growing they require good humidity and shade with plenty of water. Less water should be given when growth is complete.

Tridactyle bicaudata (Lindl.) Schltr.
[Colour Plate]

An epiphytic, lithophytic or rarely terrestrial plant, growing in large, straggly clumps. **Stems** slender, upright to semipendulous, leafy in apical half, up to 40 cm long, 0.7 cm in diameter. **Roots** somewhat verrucose. **Leaves** 8–14, distichous, ligulate, spreading, unequally, roundly 2-lobed at apex, 6–12 cm long, 1–1.5 cm broad, articulated at the base to persistent leaf-sheaths. **Inflorescences** spreading, from stem below lowermost leaves, 6–7 cm long, 8- to 16-flowered. **Flowers** alternate on rhachis, buff turning to orange with age, 0.9–2 cm across; segments spreading widely; anther-cap red-brown. **Sepals** lanceolate, or ovate-oblong, acute, 0.5–0.7 cm long, 0.2 cm broad. **Petals** linear-lanceolate, acute, 0.5 cm long, 0.15 cm broad. **Lip** 3-lobed in apical half, auriculate at base, 0.8 cm long, 0.4 cm broad; side lobes linear, spreading, fimbriate at apex; mid-lobe narrowly triangular, acute; spur cylindrical, 1.4 cm long. **Column** very short.

DISTRIBUTION Tropical Africa and S. Africa to Cape Province; sea level to 2500 m altitude.

HISTORY Discovered in S. Africa by J.F. Drége near the Zwartkops River and described by John Lindley in 1837 in Hooker's *Companion to the Botanical Magazine* (p. 205) as *Angraecum bicaudatum*. R. Schlechter transferred it to *Tridactyle* in 1914 in *Die Orchideen* (p. 602). V.S. Summerhayes later designated this species as the type of the genus *Tridactyle*.

SYNONYMS *Angraecum bicaudatum* Lindl.; *Listrostachys fimbriata* Rendle; *L. cirrhosa* Kraenzl.; *L. bicaudata* (Lindl.) Finet; *Tridactyle fimbriata* (Rendle) Schltr.; *Angraecum laciniatum* Kraenzl.; *Tridactyle polyschista* Schltr. ex Mansf.

CLOSELY RELATED SPECIES *Tridactyle tridactylites* (Rolfe) Schltr., also widespread in tropical Africa, is closely related but lacks the fimbriate side lobes to the lip.

Tridactyle gentilii (De Wild.) Schltr.
[Colour Plate]

An epiphyte with a long stem, 30–85 cm long. **Leaves** linear, unequally bilobed at the apex, 10–21 cm long, 0.8–2.1 cm wide, articulated to 1–1.8 cm long sheaths. **Inflorescences** 7- to 15-flowered, 3.5–15 cm long; bracts amplexicaul, 1.5–2 mm long. **Flowers** white, fragrant, large in genus. **Dorsal sepal** oblong, obtuse, 7–9 mm long, 3–5 mm wide; **lateral sepals** obliquely ovate, acute, 8.5–9 mm long, 3–4.5 mm wide. **Petals** linear-lanceolate, acute, 7–9 mm long, 1.5–2 mm wide. **Lip** auriculate at base, 3-lobed in the middle, 9–10 mm long, 13–16 mm wide; side lobes spreading, lacerate at the apex; mid-lobe triangular, 3–4 mm long; spur

Tridactyle tridactylites
1 – Lip and base of spur (× 4)
2 – Column, side view (× 6)
3 – Pollinia, stipe and viscidium (× 6)

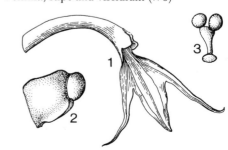

incurved, slenderly cylindric, 4.5–6.5 cm long. **Column** 2–3 mm long.

DISTRIBUTION Ghana, Nigeria, Cameroon, Zaïre, Uganda, Tanzania, Zambia and S. Africa; in swampy and montane forest; up to 1800 m altitude.

HISTORY Originally collected at Lomami in Zaïre by Gentil and described in 1903 by the Belgian botanist E. de Wildeman as *Angraecum gentilii* in *Notices des Plantes Utilisés de la Congo* (p. 140). Rudolf Schlechter transferred it to *Tridactyle* in 1918 in *Beihefte zum Botanisches Zentralblatt* (p. 145).

SYNONYM *Angraecum gentilii* de Wild.

Trigonidium Lindl.

Subfamily Epidendroideae
Tribe Maxillarieae
Subtribe Maxillariinae

Small to medium-sized epiphytic or lithophytic herbs with a short to elongate rhizome. **Pseudobulbs** cylindric to ovoid, 1- or 2-leaved at the apex, subtended by several imbricate sheaths. **Leaves** coriaceous, erect or suberect, linear, oblong or oblanceolate. **Inflorescences** erect, lateral, basal, 1-flowered, usually as long as or longer than the leaves; peduncle elongate, bearing several sheaths. **Flowers** somewhat tubular below, suberect to spreading. **Sepals** subequal, free, the showiest segments of the flower. **Petals** small, commonly somewhat swollen near the apex. **Lip** more or less 3-lobed, lacking a spur, ecallose or with a linear callus in the basal part. **Column** short, semiterete, lacking wings and a foot; anther terminal, operculate; pollinia 4, waxy; viscidium triangular.

DISTRIBUTION A small genus of about a dozen species from Mexico through S. America to Brazil and Peru.

DERIVATION OF NAME The diminutive of the Greek *trigonos* (3-cornered) from the triangular nature of the sepals, stigma and viscidium.

TAXONOMY John Lindley established this genus in 1837 in the *Botanical Register* (t. 1923). It is related to *Maxillaria* being distinguished by its cupulate flower in which the large sepals hide the smaller petals and lip.

TYPE SPECIES *T. obtusum* Lindl.

CULTURE Temp. Winter min. 12–15°C. Grow in pots or pans of epiphyte mix, as for *Maxillaria*. Do not allow the plants to remain dry for long periods because this would lead to shrivelling of the pseudobulbs.

Trigonidium egertonianum Batem. ex Lindl.
[Colour Plate]

An epiphyte or lithophyte with clustered, ovoid to ellipsoid, compressed, bifoliate pseudobulbs, 4–9 cm long, 2–3.5 cm across. **Leaves** linear-oblanceolate, acute to obtuse, 2–60 cm long, 1–3 cm wide. **Inflorescences** erect, 15–35 cm long, 1-flowered; peduncle slender, wiry; bracts tubular-inflated, 3–4.5 cm long. **Flowers** cupulate, yellow-green to greenish, with conspicuous red-brown veins, the lip green marked with purple; pedicel and ovary 4–5.5 cm long. **Sepals** suborbicular-obovate to oblong-elliptic, rounded to subacute, 2.7–4.2 cm long, 1–2 cm wide. **Petals** narrowly clawed, elliptic-lanceolate, acute to obtuse, 1.4–2.1 cm long, 0.4–0.7 cm wide. **Lip** suberect, 3-lobed, 0.8–1 cm long, 0.5–0.6 cm wide; side lobes thin, semielliptic, obtuse; mid-lobe short, fleshy-verrucose, sulcate, deflexed-recurved; callus linear-clavate. **Column** 0.7 cm long, puberulent.

DISTRIBUTION Mexico to Panama and Colombia; a common and widespread species in lowland forest from sea level to 1000 m.

HISTORY John Lindley described this species in 1838 in the *Botanical Register* (misc. p. 73) based on a George Ure-Skinner collection from Honduras.

SYNONYM *T. seemanii* Rchb.f.

Trisetella Luer

Subfamily Epidendroideae
Tribe Epidendreae
Subtribe Pleurothallidinae

Dwarf epiphytes with clustered, erect, abbreviated, unifoliate stems (ramicauls) on short creeping rhizomes. **Leaf** erect, coriaceous, narrowly elliptic. **Inflorescences** erect, a succession of flowers in a congested raceme. **Flowers** small; pedicel separated from the ovary by a distinct joint. **Sepals** with tails at the apex; laterals united to form a synsepalum. **Petals** tiny, membranous. **Lip** small, sagittate or cordate at the base, longitudinally callose, with the basal lobes pointing backward, hinged at the base to the column-foot. **Column** elongate, with a wedge-shaped foot; pollinia 2, hard.

DISTRIBUTION A small genus of about 20 species from the tropics of Central and S. America.

DERIVATION OF NAME From the diminutive of the Latin *trisetus* meaning three hairs, in allusion to the tails of the sepals

TAXONOMY *Masdevallia* sect. *Triaristellae* Rchb.f. was first raised to generic level as *Triaristella* by Brieger in 1976 in the 3rd edition of Schlechter's *Die Orchideen* (p. 449). Unfor-

tunately, he failed to observe the rules of nomenclature by omitting the basionym reference. Luer subsequently pointed out that *Triaristella* cannot be used as a generic name because of Malyavkina's genus of the same name which was established in 1949. He therefore coined the name *Trisetella* for the orchid genus in the journal *Phytologia* (p. 57) in 1980. *Trisetella* is a segregate of *Masdevallia* and is distinguished by its distinctive lip structure and column-foot.

The genus has recently been monographed by Carlyle Luer (1989) in *Icones Pleurothallidinarum* (vol. 6: pp. 69–123).

TYPE SPECIES *Masdevallia triaristella* Rchb.f.

SYNONYMS *Masdevallia* sect. *Triaristellae* Rchb.f.; *Triaristella* Brieg. ex Luer; *Triaristellina* Rauschert

CULTURE Temp. Winter min. 11–15°C. May be grown in small pots in a fine epiphyte mix or mounted. Requires high humidity and even moisture throughout the year, with moderate shade.

Trisetella triaristella (Rchb.f) Luer

A dwarf epiphyte often forming clumps; roots slender. **Stems** erect, slender, 3–5 mm long, covered by 2–3 tubular sheaths. **Leaves** erect, coriaceous, semiterete, linear or narrowly elliptic, acute, sulcate, 2.5–5 cm long, 2–2.5 mm wide. **Inflorescence** erect, 4–9 cm long; peduncle slender, wiry; rhachis congested, 2- to 5-flowered; bracts 3–4 mm long. **Flowers** borne in succession, the dorsal sepal yellow-orange suffused with purple, the lateral sepals and lip purple, the petals translucent yellow, suffused with purple; pedicel and ovary 6–9 mm long. **Dorsal sepal** broadly ovate, 3.5–4.5 mm long, 4–8 mm wide, with a slender erect apical yellow or purple 18–27 mm long tail; **lateral sepals** united almost to apex to form an ovate concave lamina, 14–19 mm long, 6–8 mm wide, bearing a slender spreading 16–21 mm long tail on each side towards the apex. **Petals** elliptic, obtuse and obscurely trilobed at the apex, 2.5–3.5 mm long, 1.5 mm wide. **Lip** oblong, rounded in front, 3.5–4 mm long, 1.2–2 mm wide, with 2 longitudinal shallow ridges in the basal two-thirds. **Column** 3–3.5 mm long; foot 1.5 mm long.

DISTRIBUTION Costa Rica, Panama, Colombia and Ecuador; 600–1700 m in lower montane and montane forest.

HISTORY Endres sent this small orchid to Messrs Veitch from Costa Rica. Veitch sent it to H.G. Reichenbach who described it as *Masdevallia triaristella* in the *Gardeners' Chronicle* (n.s. 6: p. 226) in 1876. Luer (1980) transferred it to *Trisetella* in the journal *Phytologia* (p. 58).

SYNONYMS *Masdevallia triaristella* (Rchb.f.)

Luer; *Triaristella reichenbachii* Brieger; *Triaristellina triaristella* (Rchb.f.) Rauschert

Trudelia Garay

Subfamily Epidendroideae
Tribe Vandeae
Subtribe Sarcanthinae

Monopodial epiphytes with short to long stems. **Leaves** coriaceous, distichous, spreading to arcuate, conduplicate, linear, unequally erosely bilobed at the apex, articulated at the base to imbricate sheathing leaf bases. **Inflorescences** lateral, axillary, few-flowered. **Flowers** small to medium-sized, fleshy. **Sepals** and **petals** free, ringent to subspreading, subsimilar. **Lip** continuous with the base of the column, excavate at base, usually lacking a spur, porrect. **Column** short, fleshy, tumid in front at base, lacking a foot; rostellum short; pollinia 2, subglobose; stipe broadly subtriangular; viscidium large, elliptic.

DISTRIBUTION A genus of five species from the Himalayas across to Vietnam.

DERIVATION OF NAME Named in honour of Niklaus Trudel of Meilen, Switzerland, an orchid grower and natural history photographer.

TAXONOMY *Trudelia* is a segregate genus of *Vanda* established in 1986 by Leslie Garay in the *Orchid Digest* (p. 73). He distinguished it from *Vanda* because of its *Luisia*-like flowers in which the sepals and petals are ringent, and the lip usually spurless and firmly attached to the column base. In habit it is quite unlike *Luisia* despite the superficial similarity of their flowers.

TYPE SPECIES *Luisia alpina* Lindl. (= *Trudelia alpina* (Lindl.) Garay)

CULTURE Temp. Winter min. 12°C. Grow in baskets or mounted under conditions of moderate shade and humidity. Give plenty of water while growing and less when growth is complete.

Trudelia alpina (Lindl.) Garay [Colour Plate]
A small epiphyte with terete stems, 10–18 cm long, 0.5 cm in diameter. **Leaves** broadly linear, unequally bilobed at the apex, 5–16 cm long, 1–1.4 cm wide. **Inflorescences** much shorter than the leaves, 1- to 3-flowered; bracts triangular, obtuse, 2–3 mm long. **Flowers** small, the sepals and petals green or yellow-green, the lip green with a whitish base and striped with purplish-brown on the apical lamina; pedicel and ovary longer than the bracts. **Sepals** elliptic to incurved, elliptic-ovate, obtuse, 1–1.3 cm long, 0.5 cm wide. **Petals** obovate, obtuse, 1–1.2 cm long, 0.4 cm wide. **Lip** deeply saccate at the base, the apical lamina ovate, obtuse, 1–1.2 cm long, 0.6–0.8 cm wide. **Column** short, fleshy, 5 mm long.

DISTRIBUTION N. India, Sikkim and Bhutan; in montane forest, 1000–1700 m.

HISTORY Discovered in 1836 at Nungklow in the Khasia Hills by J. Gibson and sent by him to the Duke of Devonshire at Chatsworth where it flowered in the following year. Lindley described it as *Luisia alpina* in 1838 in the *Botanical Register* (misc. no. 101). Leslie Garay made it the type of his new genus *Trudelia* in 1986 in the *Orchid Digest* (p. 76).

SYNONYMS *Luisia alpina* Lindl.; *Vanda alpina* (Lindl.) Lindl.

CLOSELY RELATED SPECIES *T. griffithii* (Lindl.) Garay from Bhutan is similar in habit and flower size but differs in having a longer lip with recurved margins.

Trudelia cristata (Lindl.) Senghas
[Colour Plate]
A medium-sized epiphyte with a stout stem, 7.5–15 cm long. **Leaves** coriaceous, recurved, truncately tridentate at the apex, 7.5–12.5 cm long, 1.2–1.8 cm wide. **Inflorescence** equalling or shorter than the leaves, 2- to 6-flowered; bracts very short, broad. **Flowers** 3.7–5 cm across, the sepals and petals yellow or green, the lip golden or white, striped with purple or red-brown; pedicel and ovary 1.5–3 cm long. **Sepals** incurved, spathulate-oblong, obtuse, 2–2.5 cm long, 0.5–0.6 cm wide. **Petals** incurved, linear-narrowly elliptic, obtuse or rounded, 1.8–2 cm long, 0.4 cm wide. **Lip** very fleshy, 3-lobed at the base, up to 2 cm long, 1.4 cm wide; side lobes erect, small, broadly triangular; mid-lobe oblong-tapering, truncate, with a rugulose upper surface with 2 slender elongate processes on the apical margin and a shorter mucro in the apical sinus; base saccate, conical, 6 mm long. **Column** 6 mm long.

DISTRIBUTION N. India, Nepal, Sikkim, Bhutan and Bangladesh; montane forest, 600–2000 m.

HISTORY Dr Nathaniel Wallich discovered this well-known orchid in Nepal in 1818 and sent plants of it to the Royal Botanic Gardens, Kew. William Griffith collected it in Bhutan, as did J.F. Cathcart in Sikkim, before it was eventually described by John Lindley as *Vanda cristata* in 1834 in his *Genera and Species of Orchidaceous Plants* (p. 216). Karlheinz Senghas transferred it to the present genus in 1988 in the 3rd edition of Schlechter's *Die Orchideen* (Bd. 19/20: 1210).

SYNONYM *Vanda cristata* Lindl.

Trudelia pumila (Hook.f.) Senghas
A small epiphyte with a stout short arcuate-ascending stem, 5–20 cm long. **Leaves** arcuate, ligulate, unequally tridentate at the apex, 8–24 cm long, 1.2–2 cm wide. **Inflorescences** axillary, erect, about as long as the leaves, 1- to 3-flowered; bracts elliptic-ovate, obtuse, 3–4 mm long. **Flowers** small, fragrant, 5–6.2 cm across, the sepals and petals cream to yellow, the lip pale streaked with purple, the column white; pedicel and ovary 2–2.5 cm long. **Sepals** oblanceolate, obtuse or subacute, 2.2–3 cm long, 0.6–0.8 cm wide. **Petals** linear, acute, 1.5–2.8 cm long, 0.3 cm wide. **Lip** 3-lobed and saccate at base, 1.8–2.3 cm long, up to 1.6 cm wide; side lobes short, triangular; apical lobe broadly ovate, concave, shortly acuminate; spur obconical, as long as the mid-lobe. **Column** short, stout, 4–5 mm long.

DISTRIBUTION N. India, Burma, Thailand, Laos and Vietnam; about 500–1100 m.

HISTORY Described in 1891 by Sir Joseph Hooker in his *Flora of British India—Orchideae* (p. 53) as *Vanda pumila* based on Lindley's *V. cristata* var. B. The type specimen was collected by J.F. Cathcart in Sikkim and his illustration of it is in the Kew Herbarium. K. Senghas transferred it to the present genus in 1988 in the 3rd edition of Schlechter's *Die Orchideen* (Bd. 19/20: p. 1211).

SYNONYM *Vanda pumila* Hook.f.

Vanda Jones

Subfamily Epidendroideae
Tribe Vandeae
Subtribe Sarcanthinae

Small to large epiphytic or lithophytic plants with short, leafy, monopodial stems. **Leaves** distichous, flat and keeled on reverse or terete. **Inflorescences** axillary, erect or suberect, racemose, laxly few- to many-flowered. **Flowers** mostly showy, often large. **Sepals** and **petals** free, subsimilar, spreading, often distinctly clawed. **Lip** adnate to base of column, spurred, 3-lobed; side lobes erect; mid-lobe porrect; spur conical, obtuse, naked within. **Column** short, cylindric, lacking a foot; anther terminal, 2-celled; pollinia 2 and cleft or 4, on a short, broad, subquadrate stipe with a large viscidium (gland).

DISTRIBUTION 30–40 species widespread in tropical Asia from India east to S.E. Asia, Indo-China, New Guinea, Australia and the Philippines to Taiwan and the adjacent islands.

DERIVATION OF NAME From the Sanskrit word referring to the plant now known as *Vanda tessellata* from Bengal and India.

TAXONOMY The genus *Vanda* was established by Sir W. Jones in 1795 in *Asiatic Researches* (p. 302). The floral structure of *Vanda* is simple compared with that of most orchids in the subtribe Sarcanthinae. The spur is relatively small and lacks a callus or septum, the lobes of the lip are simple in shape, lacking high keels, but the mid-lobe usually has low keels and 2 small humps at the base. Greatly reduced in size, the flowers of *Vanda* would most nearly resemble those of *Ascocentrum,* especially *A. micranthum,* but it is convenient to exclude that species from *Vanda.*

Most *Vanda* species have fairly long, flat, broad, terete leaves and long climbing stems.

A further fine species originally described in this genus is *Euanthe sanderiana.* Schlechter removed it from *Vanda* on account of its quite distinct lip structure and his treatment is followed here.

More recently, Garay (1986) in the *Orchid Digest* (p. 73) has removed a small group of species allied to *Vanda alpina* to the genus *Trudelia.* They differ in having ringent sepals and petals and a spurless lip which is firmly attached to the base of the column.

In the *Orchids of Malaya* (1964), Holttum describes and gives a key to 22 species of the genus including all of the horticulturally important species.

TYPE SPECIES *V. roxburghii* R.Br. [= *V. tessellata* (Roxb.) G. Don].

CULTURE Compost A. Temp. Mostly winter min. 15°C. *V. coerulea,* winter min. 12°C. As in the case of many monopodial orchids, *Vanda* species produce numerous aerial roots, so should be grown in baskets or large pots. Tropical species from higher altitudes such as *V. coerulea* require similar conditions during growth; but a cooler, dry period when growth is complete.

Vanda amesiana Rchb.f.

An erect lithophytic plant with stout roots. **Stems** short, stout, up to 8.5 cm long. **Roots** very thick in proportion to the plant, numerous. **Leaves** fleshy, rigid, semiterete, grooved, tapering from the base to the acute apex, 17–30 cm long. **Inflorescences** ascending, longer than the leaves, racemose or rarely paniculate, many-flowered. **Flowers** fragrant, 3.7 cm across; sepals and petals white with a delicate flush of pale rose-purple; lip side lobes white tinged with rose, mid-lobe amethyst-purple. ± white on the margins; column white, stained with purple. **Sepals** and **petals** subsimilar, elliptic-oblong, obtuse, about 1.6 cm long, 0.9 cm broad. **Lip** 3-lobed, up to 1.8 cm long, 1.8 cm broad in front; side lobes small, subquadrate, rounded above; mid-lobe broadly clawed, transversely oblong, emarginate, reflexed at the sides, traversed by 3 thickened, longitudinal, central lines; spur saccate, compressed.

DISTRIBUTION Burma, Kampuchea, Laos, China and possibly Thailand; between 1200 and 1600 m altitude, on rocks in full sun.

HISTORY Introduced into cultivation from the Shan States by Stuart Low of Messrs H. Low & Co. H.G. Reichenbach named it in 1887 in the *Gardeners' Chronicle* (s. 3, 1: p. 764) in honour of F.L. Ames of Massachusetts, USA.

Vanda coerulea Lindl. [Colour Plate]

A medium-sized epiphytic plant. **Stems** very stout, 75–150 cm long. **Leaves** coriaceous, ligulate, distichous, 7.5–25 cm long, 2–2.9 cm broad, obliquely truncate and toothed at the apex. **Inflorescences** erect or suberect, 20–60 cm long, laxly 6- to 15-flowered; peduncle elongate. **Flowers** 7–10 cm across; pale to fairly deep blue, ± tessellated; lip darker blue than other segments; column white above with a violet stain below the stigma. **Dorsal sepal** spathulate-obovate, clawed, 3.8–4.4 cm long, 2.2–2.6 cm broad; **lateral sepals** similar to but larger than the dorsal, about 5.5 cm long, 2.6 cm broad; **Petals** clawed, broadly obovate, 3.8–5.3 cm long, up to 3 cm broad; claw slightly twisted. **Lip** linear-oblong; 3-lobed, 1.5 cm long, 0.6 cm broad; side lobes small, acute; mid-lobe with 2 thickened ridges terminating in a bituberculate apex; spur conical, 0.8 cm long, obtuse. **Column** 0.4 cm long.

DISTRIBUTION India (Assam), Burma and Thailand; between 800 and 1700 m altitude, growing on stunted trees in exposed situations.

HISTORY Discovered in 1837 by William Griffith growing on oaks at an altitude of 1250 m in the Khasia and Jyntea Hills. John Lindley described it in 1847 in the *Botanical Register* (sub t. 30) and in the same year in his *Folia Orchidacea* from a dried specimen collected by Griffith. Sir Joseph Hooker and Dr T. Thomson rediscovered it in the Khasia Hills in 1850 but it was introduced into cultivation by Messrs Veitch & Sons whose collector, Thomas Lobb, sent a large consignment of specimens to them in the same year.

Vanda coerulescens Griff. [Colour Plate]

An epiphytic plant. **Stem** terete, about 10 cm long. **Leaves** ligulate, channelled above, keeled below, 2-lobed at apex, 12.5–20 cm long, 1.8 cm broad, apices spiny. **Inflorescences** suberect or drooping, much longer than the leaves, many-flowered, 50 cm or more long. **Flowers** 2.5–3.5 cm across; sepals and petals pale blue or pale lilac; lip deeper lilac or blue; column blue, anther yellowish. **Sepals** and **petals** obovate-spathulate, 1.4–1.6 cm long, 0.6 cm broad. **Lip** 3-lobed, 1.2 cm long or more, 0.7 cm broad: side lobes small, oblong; mid-lobe obovate, emarginate, margins reflexed above, with 2 somewhat thickened ridges above; spur short, 0.7 cm long, incurved slightly.

DISTRIBUTION N.E. India, S. China, Burma and Thailand; between 300 and 800 m altitude.

HISTORY Discovered near Bhamo in Upper Burma by William Griffith in April 1837 and described by him in his *Notulae* (p. 352) in 1851 Nothing more was seen of this species until 30 years after its discovery when General Benson rediscovered it in the Arracan Mts west of Prome. The following year he sent living material to Messrs Veitch & Sons and it flowered for the first time in their Chelsea nursery, London in February 1869.

Vanda lamellata Lindl.

Stem short, about 15 cm long. **Leaves** narrow, recurved, obliquely bidentate at apex, strongly keeled below, 30–42 cm long 1.2–1.8 cm broad. **Inflorescences** erect or suberect, as long as the leaves, many-flowered. **Flowers** 2.5–5 cm across, light yellow, blotched with chestnut-brown; side lobes of lip white; column pale violet. **Sepals** and **petals** oblong or spathulate, obtuse, about 1.8 cm long, 0.9 cm broad; lateral sepals broadest, falcate. **Lip** 3-lobed, 1.3 cm long, 0.8 cm broad; side lobes auriculate, rounded, erect; mid-lobe oblong-retuse, traversed longitudinally by 2 raised plates that are broadest in the middle and 2 tubercles just below the apex; spur conical, 0.6 cm long.

DISTRIBUTION The Philippines and N. Borneo.

HISTORY Introduced into cultivation by Messrs Loddiges whose collector. Hugh Cuming, sent them plants from Manila in 1838. John Lindley described it the same year in the *Botanical Register* (misc. no. 125).

Var. *boxallii* Rchb.f. with longer, narrower leaves and more brightly coloured flowers with a rose-purple mid-lobe to the lip was introduced into cultivation in 1879 from near Manila by Messrs Low & Co.

Vanda stangeana Rchb.f. [Colour Plate]

Stem erect, stout. **Leaves** distichous, ligulate, unequally 2-lobed above, spreading-recurved, about 15 cm long, 2 cm broad. **Inflorescences** erect or suberect, almost as long as leaves, laxly several-flowered. **Flowers** with sepals and petals golden-green, tessellated chestnut-brown; lip white, ochre in front with a streak of red dots on each side of spur; column white. **Dorsal sepal** cuneate-obovate, obtuse, 2.8 cm long, 2 cm broad; **lateral sepals** similar to the dorsal but larger. **Petals** obovate, narrowly clawed, 2.8 cm long, 2 cm broad, margins undulate. **Lip** auriculate; lamina gradually narrowed from a broad, semicordate base, bilobulate at the apex with a pair of small calli in the spur mouth, 2.2 cm long, 1.4 cm broad; auricules semiovate, divergent. **Column** short, stout.

DISTRIBUTION   India (Assam) and Nepal.

HISTORY   Introduced into cultivation from Assam by Consul Schiller and described by H. G. Reichenbach in 1858 in the *Botanische Zeitung* (p. 351) who named it after Schiller's head gardener F. Stange.

Vanda tessellata (Roxb.) G. Don

Stems climbing, 30–60 cm long. **Leaves** linear, narrow, conduplicate, tridentate at apex, 15–20 cm long, 1.2–1.8 cm broad. **Inflorescences** suberect, 15–25 cm long, 6- to 10-flowered. **Flowers** 3.7–5 cm across; sepals and petals yellowish-green or bluish, tessellated with brown, outer surface and margins white; lip violet with a white margin; column white. **Sepals** and **petals** subsimilar, clawed, obovate or elliptic-oblong, undulate, 2.2–3 cm long, 1.2–2 cm broad. **Lip** 3-lobed, 1.3–1.9 cm long, 0.8–1.2 cm broad; side lobes small, lanceolate, acute; mid-lobe panduriform, convex; apex dilated, fleshy, truncate, bilobulate; spur conical, obtuse, 0.7 cm long. **Column** short, 0.6 cm long.

DISTRIBUTION   India, Sri Lanka, Burma and Malaya.

HISTORY   Originally described and illustrated in 1795 as *Epidendrum tessellatum* by William Roxburgh in his *Plants of the Coast of Coromandel* (p. 34) based on a collection from the Circar Mts. O. Swartz transferred it to *Cymbidium* in 1799 but George Don, realising its true affinity, transferred it to *Vanda* in Loudon's *Hortus Britannicus* (p. 372) in 1830. *V. tessellata* is the type species of the genus since Robert Brown based the genus on *V. roxburghii* R. Br., which is a later synonym. Under this later synonym Sir Joseph Banks flowered it at Springrove, Isleworth, England for the first time in 1819.

SYNONYMS   *Vanda tesselloides* (Roxb.) Rchb.f.; *Cymbidium tess018elloides* Roxb.; *C. tessellatum* (Roxb.) Sw.; *Epidendrum tessellatum* Roxb.; *Aerides tessellatum* (Roxb.) Wight; *Vanda roxburghii* R. Br.

Vanda tricolor Lindl.

[Colour Plate]

A large, erect, lithophytic, epiphytic or terrestrial plant. **Stems** erect, 50–100 cm long, 1.4 cm thick. **Leaves** curved, ligulate, imbricate, unequally 2-lobed at apex, 37–45 cm long, 3–4 cm broad. **Inflorescences** ascending or spreading, shorter than leaves, 7- to 10 (or more)-flowered. **Flowers** large, showy, fragrant, 5–7.5 cm across, variable in colour; sepals and petals commonly light yellow, densely spotted bright red-brown, white on outer surface; lip whitish below, streaked with red-brown, bright

magenta-purple above, spur white. **Sepals** and **petals** subsimilar, clawed, obovate-oblong to orbicular-obovate, undulate, fleshy, 2–3 cm long, up to 2.2 cm broad, petals twisted at base. **Lip** 3-lobed, up to 2.5 cm long, 1.8 cm broad; side lobes subquadrate, incurved; mid-lobe subpanduriform, deeply emarginate, convex and 3-ridged above; spur short, compressed, 0.9 cm long. **Column** short, much swollen on each side at the base.

DISTRIBUTION   Java.

HISTORY   Originally collected in Java in 1846 by Thomas Lobb for Messrs Veitch & Sons and probably at about the same time or a little earlier by Dr C. Blume (who described it in 1848 as *V. suaveolens*). However, it was first described by John Lindley in 1847 in the *Botanical Register* (sub t. 59).

Many varieties of this showy and variable species have been described. Two of the best known are var. *planilabris* Lindl., which has a flatter rose or magenta-purple lip, and var. *suavis* (Lindl.) Veitch [syn. *V. suavis* Lindl.] which has a white background to the sepals and petals with few red-purple spots and a purple lip. This latter was introduced into cultivation by T. Lobb from Java where it grows with the typical variety, often on the stems of sugar palms.

SYNONYMS   *Vanda suaveolens* Blume; *V. suavis* Lindl.

Vandopsis Pfitz.

Subfamily Epidendroideae
Tribe Vandeae
Subtribe Sarcanthinae

Stout, erect plants with long stems of short internodes. Leaves strap-shaped, usually very fleshy. **Inflorescence** stout, simple, erect or curved, many-flowered. **Flowers** large, fleshy, showy. **Sepals** and **petals** subequal, widely spreading. **Lip** attached to base of column by the side lobes; side lobes small, joined to a fleshy flap which arches over the basal keel of the mid-lobe; mid-lobe fleshy, long, bilaterally flattened, keeled, with keel interrupted near the base, glabrous. **Column** short, with a projection in front at its base; pollinia 4, flat, almost equal, in 2 pairs; stipe short, broad, thin, with recurving edges; viscidium broad.

DISTRIBUTION   About eight species in S.E. Asia, S. China, the Philippines and New Guinea.

DERIVATION OF NAME   This genus was named for its resemblance to the genus *Vanda*, *opsis* being the Greek for 'resembles'.

TAXONOMY   *Vandopsis* was described in 1889 by E. Pfitzer in A. Engler and K.A. Prantl's *Die Natürlichen Pflanzenfamilien* (2, 6:

210). It is allied to *Arachnis* and to *Trichoglottis*. The flap joining the side lobes across the base is in the same position as the tongue in *Trichoglottis*, differing only in its shape. *V. undulata* from Burma has a long climbing stem, very like *Arachnis*, and a long-stalked inflorescence of a few white flowers flushed with pink.

TYPE SPECIES   *V. lissochiloides* (Gaud.) Pfitz.

CULTURE   Compost A. Temp. Winter min. 15°C. As for *Vanda*, but many of the species are more robust, so reach their full potential when grown in well-drained beds rather than pots or baskets. The small species grow well with the tropical *Vanda* species, and should be well watered at all times.

Vandopsis lissochiloides (Gaud.) Pfitz.

[Colour Plate]

A very large lithophytic or terrestrial plant with an elongate leafy stem. **Leaves** distichous, sword-shaped, coriaceous, 30–43 cm long, 2–3 cm broad, unequally, roundly 2-lobed at apex, imbricate at the base. **Inflorescences** up to 2 m high, or more, lateral, subterminal, many-flowered. **Flowers** showy, 5–6 cm across; sepals and petals yellow with red-purple blotches on the inside, greenish-yellow on outside; lip red with yellow base and side lobes; column yellow with red spots on dorsal side and a red blotch on each side. **Sepals** and **petals** oblong-obovate, obtuse, 2.6–3.5 cm long, 1–1.5 cm broad. **Lip** oblong, hooked at the apex, canaliculate, saccate at the base, with 2 small ascending lobes at the base on both sides, 1.5 cm long. **Column** stout, 0.4 cm long.

DISTRIBUTION   Thailand to Indonesia and the Philippines; growing on margins of evergreen jungle in shade.

HISTORY   Originally described by Charles Gaudichaud-Beaupré in 1829 in Louis de Freycinet's *Voyage sur l'Uranie et la Physicienne* (p. 424) as *Fieldia lissochiloides* based on a specimen collected in the Moluccas on the island of Rawak. E. Pfitzer transferred it in 1889 to his new genus *Vandopsis* as the type species in A. Engler and K.A. Prantl's *Die Natürlichen Pflanzenfamilien* (2, 6: 210).

SYNONYMS   *Fieldia lissochiloides* (Gaud.) Lindl.; *Stauropsis lissochiloides* (Gaud.) Pfitz.; *Vanda batemanii* Lindl.

CLOSELY RELATED SPECIES   *V. gigantea* (Lindl.) Pfitz., widespread in S.E. Asia, differs in its epiphytic habit, shorter inflorescences up to 40 cm long, and lip which has a yellow or white epichile.

Vanilla Miller

Subfamily Epidendroideae
Tribe Gastrodieae
Subtribe Vanillinae

Climbing or scrambling monopodial herbs with scandent, branching, often vine-like stems, bearing a leaf and root at each node. **Roots** adventitious. **Leaves** large or rarely scale-like, alternate, fleshy, leathery, chartaceous or membranous. **Inflorescence** racemose or spicate, axillary or subterminal, short. **Flowers** large, ephemeral, showy; segments free, spreading or ringent. **Lip** with a distinct claw adnate to column, ± involute at base, entire or 3-lobed above. **Column** slender, long, often pubescent below; anther incumbent; pollen powdery or granular. **Fruit** a fleshy pod, long-cylindric, often not dehiscing.

DISTRIBUTION About 60 species or more, widespread throughout the tropics.

DERIVATION OF NAME From the Spanish *vanilla* (small pod), referring to the long, slender vanilla pods.

TAXONOMY *Vanilla* was first described by Philip Miller in the 4th edition of the *Gardener's Dictionary* in 1754 although the name is often ascribed to O. Swartz who described it in 1799 in *Nova Acta Regiae Societatis Scientiarum Upsaliensis* (p. 66, t. 5)

One of the few orchids of commercial use (other than for their flowers) is the vanilla orchid (*Vanilla planifolia* G. Jackson). This plant is widely cultivated for vanilla flavouring which is extracted from the long fleshy pods. *V. planifolia* is a native of the American tropics where it grows as a climber in wet forest up to 600 m in altitude.

In its climbing habit *Vanilla* is comparable with *Vanda* and its allies, but it is at once distinguished by the adventitious roots, borne at each node opposite the leaf. These roots are the main supporting organs and do not grow very long. Those near the ground grow downwards and branch freely when they reach the leaf litter. Of the terrestrial orchids only *Vanilla* and *Galeola* have developed the climbing monopodial habit so well developed in the vandaceous orchids.

The taxonomy of *Vanilla* has been greatly hindered by the short-lived flowers of most species. R.A. Rolfe revised the genus in the *Journal of the Linnean Society, Botany* (1896) accepting 52 species of which 16 were newly described. He divided the genus into two sections: *Foliosae* in which the plants are leafy, and *Aphyllae* where the leaves are absent or reduced to scales. The most recent monograph is that of R. Portères (1954) in *Encyclopédie Biologique* (vol. 46) published by Editions Paul Lechevalier in Paris.

TYPE SPECIES *Epidendrum vanilla* L. [= *Vanilla mexicana* Miller].

CULTURE Compost B or C. Temp. Winter min. 15–18°C. Since they produce very long stems, *Vanilla* species need plenty of support. The rooted end may be placed in a pot or else planted in a well-drained bed, and the growing shoot should be trained up a support, and then along wires. Numerous nodal roots are produced and these will either hang free or grow over nearby objects. The plants require high humidity at all times and shade from summer sun – the leafless species needing rather less shade. Most species flower only when the plants have become very large.

Vanilla phalaenopsis Rchb.f. ex van Houtte
[Colour Plate]

A creeping, glabrous, apparently leafless, terrestrial or scrambling plant of indeterminate length, with short roots arising at the nodes. **Stem** internodes up to 15 cm long, 1.5 cm in diameter, succulent, terete but with a shallow groove on each side, dull greenish, with numerous vestigial scale-leaves, up to 2 cm long, 1 cm broad arising at each node. **Inflorescences** racemose, terminal or subterminal to axillary, unbranched, up to 35 cm long, up to 35-flowered; bracts triangular, acute, up to 1.5 cm long, 0.6 cm broad, pink when young. **Flowers** erect when young, deflexed with age, pure white with an apricot to salmon-pink throat to the lip. **Sepals** lanceolate-oblong, subobtuse, apiculate, up to 8 cm long, 2.5 cm broad. **Petals** elliptic-oblong to ovate, apiculate, up to 8 cm long, 3.8 cm broad. **Lip** entire, obtuse, apiculate, margins undulate, up to 8 cm long, 4.5 cm broad; margins of basal 2 cm adnate to sides of column; disc with 2 laciniate, undulate crests in basal half and a central shorter crest. **Column** up to 2.5 cm long.

DISTRIBUTION The Seychelles.

HISTORY *V. phalaenopsis* was described in 1867 by L.B. van Houtte in *Flore des Serres* (p. 97), (t. 1769–1770) based on an unpublished description and name given by H.G. Reichenbach. The type specimen was introduced from the Seychelles Islands by M. Bernard.

CLOSELY RELATED SPECIES This species is very closely allied to *Vanilla roscheri* Rchb.f. from E. Africa and to *Vanilla madagascariensis* Rolfe from Madagascar, both leafless species with white flowers with an apricot-coloured throat to the lip. Further study may show these to be conspecific with *V. phalaenopsis*.

Vanilla planifolia G. Jackson [Colour Plate]

A scandent liana-like plant with long, vine-like, fleshy stems bearing leaves at intervals along length. **Leaves** numerous, fleshy, elliptic-oblong or ovate-elliptic, acute or subacuminate, up to 20 cm long, 5 cm broad. **Inflorescence** axillary, subsessile, racemose, several-flowered, up to 5 cm long; bracts broadly ovate-triangular, acute, up to 0.7 cm long. **Flowers** produced in succession, pale green to yellowish-green, showy, ringent. **Sepals** and **petals** subsimilar, linear-oblong to narrowly ovate, obtuse or acute, up to 6 cm long. **Lip** narrowly clawed, tubular, cuneate-obtriangular when spread out, up to 4 cm long, truncate in front; terminal lobule emarginate; disc bearing longitudinal verrucose or papillose lines along the veins, with a central tuft of retrorse hairs. **Column** slender, slightly arcuate above, up to 4 cm long. **Pod** fleshy, up to 15 cm long.

DISTRIBUTION Native to Central America and the W. Indies but widely cultivated throughout the tropics to provide commercial vanilla essence.

HISTORY Originally described by G. Jackson in 1808 in Andrews' *Botanical Repository* (t. 538) from a plant introduced into England by the Marquis of Blandford and flowered in the collection of the Rt Hon. Charles Greville.

V. planifolia is one of the fleshy-leaved species and may be recognised by its yellow-green flowers with a ventrally-pubescent column and a lip bearing a central retrose callus of many denticulate projections and an apical papillate callus.

SYNONYMS *Myrobroma fragrans* Salisb.; *Vanilla fragrans* (Salisb.) Ames

Vanilla pompona Schiede

A scrambling plant. **Stems** fleshy, stout, branched, terete, each internode 5–13 cm long, 1.5 cm in diameter. **Leaves** thickly coriaceous, ovate-oblong to narrowly elliptic, 10–30 cm long, 4–10 cm broad, acute. **Inflorescence** axillary, up to about 8-flowered, up to 15 cm long. **Flowers** large, fleshy, greenish-yellow or yellow, up to about 9 cm long. **Sepals** narrowly oblanceolate, up to 8.5 cm long, 1.5 cm broad, obtuse. **Petals** similar to sepals but slightly smaller. **Lip** adnate to column for half its length, obscurely 3-lobed, obovate-oblong, up to 9 cm long; sides curved up and around column-apex, 4.5 cm broad; disc with thickened veins with a central area of back-pointing scales. **Column** arcuate, hairy below, 6–7 cm long.

DISTRIBUTION From Mexico south into tropical S. America and the W. Indies.

HISTORY Described in 1829 by C.J. Schiede in *Linnaea* (p. 573) and several times subsequently under other names by various authors.

SYNONYMS *Vanilla grandiflora* Lindl.; *V. surinamensis* Rchb.f.

Warmingia Rchb.f.
Subfamily Epidendroideae
Tribe Oncidieae

Small epiphytic herbs with very short, 1-leafed, pseudobulbous stems. **Leaf** flat, coriaceous, oblong or narrowly-oblong. **Inflorescence** axillary, from the base of the pseudobulb, nodding or pendulous, racemose, laxly or densely few-flowered. **Flowers** white, somewhat hyaline, fairly small. **Sepals** and **petals** subsimilar, free, spreading; petals with denticulate margins. **Lip** continuous with the base of the column, sessile, spreading, 3-lobed; side lobes short, broad, dentate; mid-lobe narrow, elongated; disc ± shortly bicallose. **Column** erect, free, semiterete, lacking a foot or wings; pollinia 2, waxy, subglobose, attached to a short, triangular stipe and a small subrotund viscidium.

DISTRIBUTION About two species in Brazil.

DERIVATION OF NAME Named in honour of Prof. Eugenius Warming, the founder of the science of plant ecology, who did most of his early work in tropical Brazil and discovered the type species.

TAXONOMY *Warmingia* was described by H.G. Reichenbach in 1881 in *Otia Botanica Hamburgensia* (p. 87). It is allied to *Macradenia* and to *Notylia*, being distinguished from the former by its divaricate side lobes to the lip which do not enclose the column; its long narrow mid-lobe; and by its pollinia which are affixed at the apex of a long dilated stipe. From *Notylia* it may be recognised by its sessile, rather than clawed, deeply 3-lobed lip.

TYPE SPECIES *W. eugenii* Rchb.f.

CULTURE Compost A. Temp. Winter min. 12–15°C. These plants may be grown in small pans under conditions of good humidity and moderate shade. They should be carefully watered throughout the year but especially when the new growths are developing.

Warmingia eugenii Rchb.f. [Colour Plate]
A small epiphytic herb, up to 20 cm high. **Pseudobulbs** small, tufted, conical or cylindrical, 1–2 cm high, 0.4 cm in diameter, 1-leafed at apex. **Leaf** somewhat coriaceous, narrowly oblong-elliptic, obtuse, 10 cm long, 2.5 cm broad; petiole short, 0.9 cm long, grooved above. **Inflorescence** racemose, pendent, up to 12 cm long, up to 30-flowered; bracts lanceolate, brown with age. **Flowers** pendent, translucent, white; lip-callus deep yellow. **Sepals** narrowly lanceolate, acute, 1.3–1.5 cm long, 0.3 cm broad. **Petals** lanceolate, acuminate, with erosely dentate margins, 1.4 cm long, 0.4 cm broad. **Lip** 3-lobed near the base, 1.1 cm long, 0.6 cm broad; side lobes rounded,

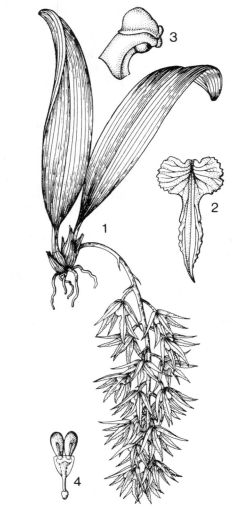

Warmingia eugenii
1   Habit ($\times \frac{1}{2}$)
2 – Lip ($\times 2\frac{1}{2}$)
3 – Column, side view ($\times 5\frac{1}{2}$)
4 – Pollinia, stipe and viscidium ($\times 8$)

irregularly dentate; mid-lobe oblanceolate, acuminate, margins serrate; callus basal, 2-lobed, centrally sulcate. **Column** subcylindric, 0.3 cm long, expanded and 2-lobed at the apex.

DISTRIBUTION E. Brazil; in forests.

HISTORY Discovered at Lagoa Santa in Minas Gerais State in Brazil by Eugenius Warming and named by H.G. Reichenbach in 1881 in *Otia Botanica Hamburgensia* (p. 87) in honour of its discoverer who is also widely regarded as the founder of the science of ecology.

SYNONYM *Warmingia loefgrenii* Cogn.

Warrea Lindl.
Subfamily Epidendroideae
Tribe Maxillarieae
Subtribe Zygopetalinae

Medium-sized to large terrestrial plants with several-noded ellipsoid or ovoid pseudobulbs enclosed by leaf sheaths, several leaved. **Leaves** distichous, plicate, usually lanceolate-elliptic, with prominent veins. **Inflorescences** erect, lateral, from the base of the immature pseudobulb, laxly few- to several-flowered. **Flowers** medium-sized to large, showy. **Dorsal sepal** and **petals** similar, free; **lateral sepals** similar but united at the base to form a mentum with the column-foot. **Lip** attached to the column-foot, entire or 3-lobed, with a basal callus of 3–5 united lamellae joined to the column-foot. **Column** rather long, semiterete, clavate, wingless; rostellum beaked; pollinia 4, hard, in 2 pairs, joined by a short stipe to the viscidium.

DISTRIBUTION A genus of some seven species distributed from Guatemala south to Brazil.

DERIVATION OF NAME Named in honour of Frederick Warre who collected orchids in Brazil in 1829 and sent them to John Lindley for identification.

TAXONOMY The genus *Warrea* was established by Lindley in the *Botanical Register* (misc. p. 14) in 1843 as a segregate genus from *Maxillaria*.

TYPE SPECIES *Warrea tricolor* Lindl.

CULTURE Temp. Winter min. 12–15°C, depending on the species. Grow under conditions of moderate shade and humidity in an open terrestrial compost, such as that used for *Phaius*. Water well while in growth but give much less when growth is complete.

Warrea warreana (Lodd. ex Lindl.) C. Schweinf. [Colour Plate]
A large terrestrial plant up to 100 cm tall with an abbreviated rhizome; pseudobulbs elongate, ovoid to ellipsoid, several-noded, 4–12 cm long. **Leaves** 3 to 5, erect, elliptic-lanceolate, acuminate, 30–60 cm long, 4–10 cm wide, imbricate at the base. **Inflorescence** up to 10- or more-flowered, up to 100 cm long; peduncle terete, stout, adorned with several remote tubular sheaths. **Flowers** large, globose, fleshy, white or yellowish-white with a large purple spot on the lip; pedicel and ovary longer than the bracts. **Sepals** broadly spreading, oblong to ovate-elliptic, obtuse or subacute, 3–3.5 cm long, 2–2.5 cm wide; the laterals oblique at the base. **Petals** ovate, acute, slightly smaller than the sepals. **Lip** subsessile, entire, obovate, obtuse or emarginate, 2.2–3.5 cm long, 1.8–3.2 cm wide, with incurved sides, with verrucose

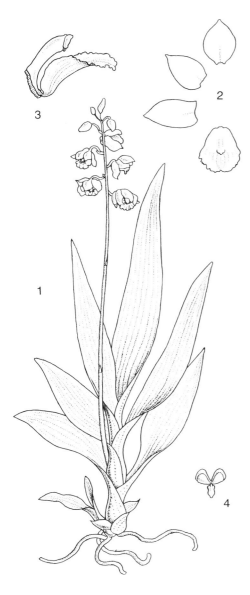

Warrea warreana
1 – Habit ($\times \frac{1}{6}$)
2 – Dorsal sepal, petal, lateral
   sepal and lip ($\times \frac{1}{2}$)
3 – Column and lip, side view ($\times \frac{3}{4}$)
4 – Pollinarium ($\times 1\frac{3}{4}$)

lines on the disc; callus trilamellate. **Column** arcuate, lacking wings, 2–2.5 cm long.
DISTRIBUTION Venezuela and Colombia to Peru and Brazil; growing in lower montane forest and scrub and in montane cloud forests, 800–200 m.
HISTORY John Lindley originally described this species in his *Genera and Species of Orchidaceous Plants* (p. 148) as *Maxillaria warreana* based on a specimen collected by Warre in Brazil. Charles Schweinfurth transferred it to

the present genus in 1955 in the *Botanical Museum Leaflets of Harvard University* (p. 55).
SYNONYMS *Maxillaria warreana* Lodd. ex Lindl.; *Warrea tricolor* Lindl.

Warreella Schltr.
Subfamily Epidendroideae
Tribe Maxillarieae
Subfamily Zygopetalinae

Large or medium-sized terrestrial plants with clustered several-noded pseudobulbs, covered by leaf bases, several-leaved. **Leaves** plicate, suberect, articulated at the base. **Inflorescence** erect, few- to many-flowered. **Flowers** medium-sized, resupinate, blue. **Sepals** and **petals** free, spreading. **Lip** slightly 3-lobed, with a 3- to 5- ridged callus. **Column** semiterete; pollinia 4, hard, superimposed in 2 pairs, attached to the viscidium by a very short stipe.
DISTRIBUTION A small genus of two species only from montane Colombia and Venezuela.
DERIVATION OF NAME The generic name is the diminutive of *Warrea*.
TAXONOMY A segregate genus of *Warrea* which was established by Rudolf Schlechter in the first edition of *Die Orchideen* (p. 424) in 1914.
TYPE SPECIES *Warrea cyanea* Lindl.
CULTURE Temp. Winter min. 12°C. Cultivation as for *Warrea*.

Warreella cyanea (Lindl.) Schltr.
A medium-sized to large terrestrial plant. **Pseudobulbs** ellipsoid, several-noded, 4–5 cm long, 1.5–2 cm in diameter, covered by imbricate, distichous leaf-bases. **Leaves** 5–9, erect-arcuate, plicate, lanceolate to elliptic-lanceolate, acuminate, 22–45 cm long, 2.2–4.5 cm wide. **Inflorescence** erect, axillary, basal, unbranched, laxly 5- to 9-flowered; peduncle reddish-green with pale brown sheaths; bracts linear to ovate, acute, 4–10 mm long. **Flowers** spreading, white with a pale pink or violet flush on the sepals and petals, the lip white with a pinkish-purple or violet flush, the column white; pedicel and ovary 12–20 mm long. **Dorsal sepal** elliptic-ovate, obtuse, 9–13 mm long, 4 mm wide; **lateral sepals** oblanceolate, subacute, 9–14 mm long, 4–5 mm wide. **Petals** narrowly elliptic, acute, 8–9 mm long, 3–4 mm wide. **Lip** obscurely 3-lobed, obovate, apiculate, 9–10 mm long, 7–8 mm wide; callus in the basal half of the lip, fleshy, 5-ridged. **Column** 6–7 mm long.
DISTRIBUTION Colombia and Venezuela; in forest at 1600–2200 m.
HISTORY Originally described as *Warrea cyanea* by John Lindley in 1844 in the *Botanical*

Warreella cyanea
1 – Habit ($\times \frac{1}{3}$)
2 – Sepals, petals and lip ($\times 1$)

Register (misc. p. 2). It was transferred to *Warreella* by Rudolf Schlechter in 1914 in his *Die Orchideen* (p. 425).
SYNONYMS *Warrea cyanea* Lindl.; *W. cinerea* Benth.; *Aganisia cyanea* (Lindl.) Veitch; *Warrea medellinensis* Kraenzl.; *Warreella medellinensis* (Kraenzl.) Garay

Xylobium Lindl.
Subfamily Epidendroideae
Tribe Maxillarieae
Subtribe Zygopetalinae

Epiphytic or rarely terrestrial, caespitose or rarely rhizomatous herbs. **Pseudobulbs** approximate, 1- or 2-leaved. **Leaves** large, plicate, often petiolate. **Inflorescence** lateral, pedunculate, racemose above, laxly to densely

4- to 30-flowered. **Flowers** rarely conspicuous, with spreading segments. **Sepals** free, ± spreading; lateral sepals decurrent on column-foot. **Petals** similar to dorsal sepal but smaller. **Lip** adnate to column-foot, entire or lobed, parallel to face of column, distinctly callose. **Column** erect, cylindric, with a distinct foot; pollinia 4, in 2 pairs on a transverse scale-like viscidium: stigmas confluent under rostellar plate.

DISTRIBUTION About 30 species in the American tropics.

DERIVATION OF NAME From the Greek *xylon* (long) and *bios* (life), referring to the usual epiphytic habit of *Xylobium* species.

TAXONOMY This genus, allied to *Maxillaria*, was described by John Lindley in the *Botanical Register* (sub t. 897) in 1825. It differs from *Maxillaria* in having plicate leaves and several-flowered inflorescences.

The genus was revised by R. Schlechter in *Orchis* (1913) where he recognised some 24 species, most of which had been described in the genus *Maxillaria*.

TYPE SPECIES *Dendrobium squalens* Lindl. [= *X. variegatum* (Ruiz & Pavon) Garay & Dunsterville].

CULTURE Compost A. Temp. Winter min. 15°C. *Xylobium* species grow well in pots under moderate shade. While growing they should be well watered but when the pseudobulbs are fully formed an almost-dry rest is required. The inflorescences are often very short with the flowers in a tight cluster at the base of the pseudobulbs.

Xylobium leontoglossum (Rchb.f.) Rolfe
[Colour Plate]

A large epiphytic plant, up to 90 cm high. **Pseudobulbs** clustered, ovoid, slightly grooved when old, 5–9 cm long, 1-leafed at apex. **Leaf** plicate, petiolate, suberect, elliptic, acute, 30–90 cm or more long, 3–11 cm broad, nerves keeled; petiole stout, terete, up to 30 cm long. **Inflorescence** basal, ± erect or arcuate-spreading, racemose, densely up to 30-flowered; bracts small, maroon, 0.2 cm long. **Flowers** creamy-white to golden-yellow, spotted and veined pale red, flushed maroon on outer surface; lip white or pale yellow, papillae tipped pink; column white, anther cream. **Sepals** oblong-lancolate, acute, 1.4–2.7 cm long, 0.9–1.2 cm broad; lateral sepals, forming a short mentum with the column-foot. **Petals** narrowly oblong-oblanceolate, acute, 1.2–2.5 cm long, 0.7 cm broad. **Lip** obscurely 3-lobed in the middle, 1.3–2 cm long, 0.6–1.1 cm broad; side lobes erect, front margin erose; mid-lobe oblong to suborbicular, appearing sulcate with age, rounded at the apex, fleshy, densely papillose-verrucose; callus obscurely oblong. **Column** short.

DISTRIBUTION Colombia, Ecuador, Peru and Venezuela; in mist forests up to about 2000 m altitude.

HISTORY Originally described by H.G. Reichenbach in 1855 in *Bonplandia* (p. 67) as *Maxillaria leontoglossa* from a specimen collected by H. Wagener at San Pedro, Ocaña in Colombia. R. A. Rolfe transferred it to the genus *Xylobium* in 1889 in the *Gardeners' Chronicle* (s. 3, 5: p. 485).

SYNONYMS *Maxillaria leontoglossa* Rchb.f.; *Xylobium gracile* Schltr.

Xylobium variegatum (Ruiz & Pavon) Garay & Dunsterville [Colour Plate]

A medium-sized epiphytic plant. **Pseudobulbs** ovoid, up to 8 cm long, 4.5 cm broad, bright green when young, 2 (rarely 3)-leaved at apex. **Leaves** oblong-elliptic, shortly petiolate, strongly ribbed, acute, up to 50 cm long, 9 cm broad. **Inflorescence** basal, racemose, densely many-flowered; bracts small, maroon-green. **Flowers** small; sepals and petals flesh-pink, ± flushed with maroon; lip flesh-pink, flushed maroon, grading to dark maroon at the apex; callus off-white; column white, anther yellow-brown. **Sepals** lanceolate, acute, 2.6 cm long, 0.7–0.9 cm broad; lateral sepals falcate, forming a short conical mentum. **Petals** obliquely lanceolate, acute, 2 cm long, 0.5 cm broad. **Lip** obscurely 3-lobed in the apical half, somewhat arcuate, 1.5 cm long, 0.8 cm broad; side lobes erect, erose in front; mid-lobe oblong, truncate, longitudinally crenately ridged; callus central, fleshy. **Column** 0.5 cm long.

DISTRIBUTION Costa Rica, Colombia and Venezuela south to Bolivia and Brazil.

HISTORY Originally described as *Maxillaria variegata* by H. Ruiz and J. Pavon in *Systema Vegetabilium Florae Peruvianae et Chilensis* (p. 222) in 1798 from a plant collected by them at Muña in Peru. Until 1961 this species has been better known as *Xylobium squalens* or *X. scabrilingue* when L. Garay and G.C.K. Dunsterville in *Venezuelan Orchids Illustrated*, vol. 2 (p. 342) showed that these were later synonyms of the Ruiz and Pavon name which they thus transferred to the genus *Xylobium*.

SYNONYMS include *Maxillaria variegata* Ruiz & Pavon; *M. squalens* (Lindl.) Hooker; *M. scabrilinguis* Lindl.; *Xylobium squalens* (Lindl.) Lindl.; *X. scabrilingue* (Lindl.) Schltr.; *X. carnosum* Schltr.

Ypsilopus Summerh.
Subfamily Epidendroideae
Tribe Vandeae
Subtribe Aerangidinae

Small, epiphytic, erect or pendent plants with short clustered or solitary leafy stems; roots elongate, slender to relatively stout. **Leaves** distichous, often arranged in a fan, flat to iridiform, linear to linear-oblong, acute or unequally bilobed at the apex. **Inflorescences** 1 to several, axillary, 1- to several-flowered, racemose, usually shorter than the leaves. **Flowers** stellate, white or pale green. **Sepals** and **petals** free, spreading, subsimilar, scabrid on outer surface and ovary. **Lip** entire or obscurely 3-lobed, lanceolate to obovate, ecallose, with a slender, elongate, cylindrical, incurved spur. **Column** short, semiterete, lacking a foot; rostellum pendent-recurved, bilobed, elongate; pollinia 2, ovoid, attached by a Y-shaped stipe to a small viscidium.

DISTRIBUTION A small genus of four species in tropical E. and S. Central Africa.

DERIVATION OF NAME From the Greek *ypsilon* (the letter Y) and *pous* (foot), from the Y-shaped stipe of the pollinarium.

TAXONOMY The genus was established by Victor Summerhayes in the *Kew Bulletin* (p. 439) in 1949 to accommodate two species previously referred to *Mystacidium* but which lacked the latter's characteristic habit and column. It is probably more closely related to *Tridactyle* but differs in its rostellum and stipe and in the lack of fleshy auricles at the base of the lip.

TYPE SPECIES *Y. longifolius* (Kraenzl.) Summerh.

CULTURE Temp. Winter min. 12°C. Grow as a mounted epiphyte under conditions of moderate shade and high humidity. Some, but not all, species are pendent. Water well while growing and less at other times.

Ypsilopus longifolius (Kraenzl.) Summerh.

A pendent epiphyte with a short leafy stem up to 6 cm long. **Leaves** 4–several, conduplicate, borne in a fan, linear, obtuse, 3–15 cm long, 0.3–0.6 cm wide, imbricate at the base. **Inflorescence** spreading to suberect, 5–20 cm long, laxly 4- to 12-flowered; rhachis somewhat fractiflex, slender; bracts triangular, acute, 1.5–2 mm long. **Flowers** white, stellate; pedicel and ovary scabrid, 0.9–1.2 cm long. **Sepals** and **petals** oblong-lanceolate, acute or acuminate, 5–7 mm long, 1.5–3 mm wide. **Lip** obscurely 3-lobed, subrhombic to lanceolate, acute, 5–6.5 mm long, 2.5–3 mm wide; spur slender, pendent, cylindrical, 3.5–5.3 cm long. **Column** 2 mm long.

DISTRIBUTION Kenya and N. Tanzania; on tree trunks in montane forest, 1450–2400 m.

HISTORY This orchid was first collected on the slopes of Mt Kenya by von Hoehnel and was described in 1893 by Fritz Kraenzlin as *Mystacidium longifolium* in Engler's *Botanische Jahrbücher* (p. 57). It was transferred to the present genus by Victor Summerhayes in 1949 in the *Kew Bulletin* (p. 440).

SYNONYMS *Mystacidium longifolium* Kraenzl.; *Listrostachys graminifolia* Kraenzl.; *Aerangis graminifolia* (Kraenzl.) Schltr.; *Ypsilopus graminifolius* (Kraenzl.) Summerh.

CLOSELY RELATED SPECIES *Ypsilopus erectus* (Cribb) Cribb & J. Stewart from S. – Central Africa has similar flowers to *Y. longifolius* but differs in its erect habit and broader shorter leaves.

Zeuxine Lindl.
Subfamily Spiranthoideae
Tribe Erythrodeae
Subtribe Goodyerinae

Small to medium-sized terrestrial herbs with a creeping fleshy rhizome, rooting at the nodes, and short remote erect leafy stems. **Leaves** fleshy, broad and petiolate to linear. **Inflorescence** terminal, laxly to densely few- to many-flowered. **Flowers** usually small, resupinate, tubular or subcampanulate, often glandular hairy on outer surface. **Dorsal sepal** erect; **lateral sepals** spreading. **Petals** smaller than the sepals, usually hyaline, adnate to the dorsal sepal to form a hood over the column. **Lip** more or less adnate to the base and sides of the column, tripartite, the basal part saccate and enclosing 2 glands, the middle linear, claw-like, the upper part a transversely oblong to reniform lamina. **Column** porrect, short, lacking wings or keels; rostellum elongate, bifid at apex; pollinia 2, deeply divided, granular, on a linear stalk attached to a small gland.

DISTRIBUTION About 70 species in the tropics and subtropics of the Old World, with a single species introduced into N. America.

DERIVATION OF NAME From the Greek *zeuxis* (yoking), referring to the partial union of the column and lip and possibly to the pollinial fusion.

TAXONOMY *Zeuxine* was described by John Lindley in 1826 in the Appendix (no. 18) to his *Collectanea Botanica*. It is allied to *Hetaeria* but differs in its resupinate flowers.

TYPE SPECIES *Pterygodium sulcatum* Roxb.

CULTURE Temp. Winter min. 12–15°C. *Zeuxine strateumatica* tends to grow in open grassland and should be given a compost similar to that for *Acianthus*. Most of the other species are forest dwellers and would benefit from a higher proportion of leaf mould and more shade. Water well when in growth and keep much drier when dormant.

Zeuxine strateumatica (L.) Schltr.
[Colour Plate]

A small terrestrial with a creeping fleshy rhizome and erect, leafy, pale brown stems, 5–21 cm long. **Leaves** suberect to erect, conduplicate, linear-tapering, acute, 2–6.5 cm long, 3–6 mm wide, pinkish-buff, sheathing at the base. **Inflorescence** terminal, densely 2- to many-flowered in a cylindrical spike, 1.5–4.5 cm long; bracts lanceolate, acuminate, 4–14 mm long, papery, reddish-brown. **Flowers** white with a yellow lip, about 5.5–6 mm long; ovary 6–7 mm long. **Dorsal sepal** cucullate, oblong-lanceolate, acute, 5–6 mm long, 3 mm wide; **lateral sepals** oblong, obtuse, 5–5.5 mm long, 2–3 mm wide. **Petals** adnate to the dorsal sepal to form a hood, hyaline, obliquely ovate, acute, 5–6 mm long, 3–4 mm wide. **Lip** arcuate-recurved, tripartite, 4 mm long, 3 mm wide, papillate, saccate at base and connate to the column, the mesochile oblong, the epichile transversely oblong-reniform. **Column** 2.6 mm long, papillate.

DISTRIBUTION Widespread throughout

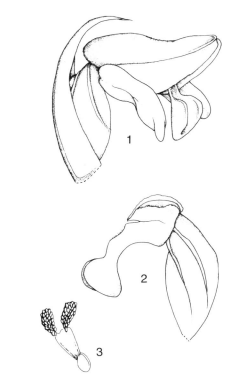

Zeuxine strateumatica
1 – Flower (× 6)
2 – Lip, column and ovary (× 6)
3 – Pollinia (× 10)

Asia from Afghanistan to Japan and Taiwan, also introduced into South-eastern N. America and S. Africa; common in grassland.

HISTORY Originally described by Linnaeus as *Orchis strateumatica* in *Species Plantarum* (p. 943) in 1753. Rudolf Schlechter transferred it to *Zeuxine* in 1911 in Engler's *Botanische Jahrbücher* (p. 394). In Florida it has become a common roadside weed in the Everglades.

SYNONYMS *Orchis strateumatica* L.; *Zeuxine sulcata* Lindl.; *Spiranthes strateumatica* (L.) Lindl.; *Zeuxine rupicola* Fuk.

Zootrophion Luer
Subfamily Epidendroideae
Tribe Epidendreae
Subtribe Pleurothallidinae

Small epiphytic plants lacking pseudobulbs but with well-developed erect 1-leafed stems (ramicauls), enclosed by inflated compressed sheaths and arising from a short or rarely a long rhizome. **Leaf** erect, coriaceous. **Inflorescence** axillary, 1-flowered. **Flowers** campanulate; pedicel separated from the ovary by a joint. **Sepals** connate at the apex. **Petals** small, enclosed within the sepals. **Lip** similarly enclosed, small, hinged to the column-foot. **Column** elongate, with a stout foot; pollinia 2, hard.

DISTRIBUTION A small genus of about 11 species distributed throughout tropical Central and S. America and Jamaica.

DERIVATION OF NAME From the Greek *zootrophion* (menagerie), in allusion to the similarity of the flowers to animal heads.

TAXONOMY *Zootrophion* was established in 1982 by Carlyle Luer in the journal *Selbyana* (p. 80) to accommodate those species previously referred to *Cryptophoranthus* but unrelated to the type species *C. fenestratus* Barb. Rodr. from Brazil. The latter is considered by Luer to be a species of *Pleurothallus* sect. *Acianthera*.

TYPE SPECIES *Specklinia atropurpurea* Lindl. (= *Zootrophion atropurpureum* (Lindl.) Luer).

CULTURE Temp. Winter min. 12–15°C. May be grown mounted or in small, well-drained pots under shady, humid conditions. Water carefully throughout the year.

Zootrophion atropurpureum (Lindl.) Luer
[Colour Plate]

A small creeping epiphyte or rarely a terrestrial, 7.5–15 cm tall, with a creeping rhizome. **Stems** erect, short, 3–5 cm long, covered with scarious inflated sheaths, unifoliate. **Leaf** coriaceous, erect, obovate-elliptic, subobtuse, 3–9 cm long, 1.5–3 cm wide, shortly petiolate. **Inflorescences** 1-flowered, much shorter than the leaf, solitary or clustered in the leaf axil; bracts 3–5 mm long. **Flowers** somewhat tubular, geniculate at the apex of the ovary, deep purple; pedicel c. 6 mm long; ovary erosely winged. **Sepals** oblong-ovate, connate except for an elliptic aperture between the dorsal and lateral sepals on each side, 13–15 mm long, 5 mm wide. **Petals** enclosed within the sepals, oblong, truncate, 4 mm long, 2 mm wide. **Lip** enclosed within the sepals, hastate, 4–5 mm long, 1–1.5 mm wide, the side lobes folded in front and with a small erect acute auricle at the base. **Column** erect, 2 mm long, produced into a distinct foot at the base.

DISTRIBUTION Jamaica, Cuba, Hispaniola, Colombia, Ecuador, Peru and Bolivia; on trees, logs and banks in montane forest, up to 1300 m.

HISTORY Lindley described this species in 1836 in the *Botanical Register* (sub t. 1797), as *Specklinia atropurpurea*, based on a plant introduced into cultivation from Jamaica and flowered at the Liverpool Botanic Garden. It has been known until recently as *Cryptophoranthus atropurpureus* but Luer (1983) recently transferred it to his new genus *Zootrophion* in *Selbyana* (p. 80).

SYNONYMS *Specklinia atropurpurea* Lindl.; *Pleurothallis atropurpureus* (Lindl.) Lindl.; *Cryptophoranthus atropurpureus* (Lindl.) Rolfe; *Masdevallia fenestrata* Lindl. ex Hook.; *C. alvaroi* Garay

CLOSELY RELATED SPECIES *Z. dayanum* (Rchb. f.) Luer, from Colombia, Ecuador, Peru and Bolivia, is a much larger plant up to 20 cm tall with longer, broader leaves, up to 13.5 cm long and 7.5 cm wide. Its flowers are also larger, 3–4 cm long, and yellow heavily spotted with deep purple. *Zootrophion hypodiscus* Reichb.f.) Luer (syn. *Cryptophoranthus hypodiscus* (Reichb.f.) Rolfe), from Panama, Colombia and Ecuador, is similar to *Z. atropurpureum* but differs in having wider sepaline windows, an erosely keeled ovary and sepals and smaller acute sidelobes to the lip.

Zygopetalum Hooker
Subfamily Epidendroideae
Tribe Maxillarieae
Subtribe Zygopetalinae

Medium-sized epiphytic plants. **Pseudobulbs** short, stout, 2- to several-leaved at apex. **Leaves** distichous, membranaceous to rigid, plicate-venose, elongate. **Inflorescence** 1 to several, lateral, 1- to several-flowered. **Flowers** small to large, mostly showy. **Sepals** and **petals** subsimilar, free or shortly connate at the base; lateral sepals inserted on the column-foot. **Lip** sessile, spreading, 3-lobed; side lobes small and spreading or large and erect; mid-lobe spreading, ovate to orbicular-obovate; disc bearing an entire or lobed fleshy callus or transversely crested. **Column** incurved, ± shortly winged at the apex; foot short; pollinia 4.

DISTRIBUTION About 40 species mostly in tropical S. America, Brazil, Paraguay, Argentina, Peru and Bolivia.

DERIVATION OF NAME From the Greek *zygon* (yoke) and *petalon* (petal or sepal), alluding to the thickened callus at the base of the lip which appears to hold together (or yoke) the petals.

TAXONOMY Sir William Hooker described *Zygopetalum* in 1827 in the *Botanical Magazine* (t. 2748). *Zygopetalum* is distinguished from *Lycaste* and *Xylobium* by its inflorescence which arises in the axils of the lower leaf-sheaths and by its lip which is usually provided with a transverse callus or a transverse flabellate crest. H.G. Reichenbach in *Walpers, Annales Botanices* (1864) treated *Pescatorea, Huntleya, Chondrorhyncha, Bollea, Kefersteinia, Pescatoria* and *Warscewiczella* as sections of *Zygopetalum*. This situation has never been universally accepted and the recent tendency has been to recognise some as valid genera and to reduce others to synonymy. Most genera when examined critically are found to be more or less arbitrary segregations, and should be recognised as being mostly artificial, albeit useful.

The whole *Zygopetalum* alliance of genera has recently been reviewed by L. Garay in *Orquidcologia* (1973). There, several species have been removed from *Zygopetalum* and have been placed in the allied genera *Mendoncella* A.D. Hawkes and *Neogardneria* Garay. In addition, *Acacallis, Aganisia, Batemannia, Koellensteinia, Paradisanthus, Pabstia* and *Zygosepalum* are all recognised as distinct genera. *Zygopetalum* is therefore left as a more natural and homogeneous genus, all the species having more or less large flowers without prominent side lobes to the lip and with the disc of the lip more or less cuneate and porrectly spreading in front. Moreover, Garay has elucidated the affinities of *Zygopetalum* and the closely allied genera mentioned above with the *Chrondrorhyncha* alliance of genera, the latter differing in lacking pseudobulbs or, if such are present, then they are minute and leafless or bear a terminal bract-like appendage.

TYPE SPECIES *Z. mackaii* Hooker
CULTURE Compost A. Temp. Winter min. 12° C. *Zygopetalum* species produce many thick roots so should be grown in good-sized pots. They require humid conditions under moderate shade with plenty of water while growing and less after the new pseudobulbs are fully formed.

Zygopetalum crinitum **Lodd.** [Colour Plate]
A medium-sized epiphytic plant. **Pseudobulbs** clustered, ovoid or ovoid-oblong, compressed, lightly sulcate, 4–7 cm long, 2–4 cm thick, shiny dark green, 3- to 5-leaved at apex. **Leaves** coriaceous, narrowly lanceolate or linear-lanceolate, acute or shortly acuminate, long-attenuate below, 25–40 cm long, 2–5 cm broad. **Inflorescence** erect, 30–50 cm long, 3- to 7-flowered above. **Flowers** showy, fragrant, spreading or slightly nodding; sepals and petals greenish or yellowish-green, densely spotted with chestnut-brown; lip white, lined along nerves with purple or red; column white or yellow, lined with red. **Sepals** fleshy, oblong, acute, 3.3–4 cm long, 1–1.4 cm broad. **Petals** narrowly oblong, acute, 3.3–4 cm long, 1–1.2 cm broad. **Lip** spreading, shortly unguiculate, obovate, cuneate below, front margin undulate-crisped, subrotund and slightly emarginate at the apex, 3–4 cm long, 2.5–3.5 cm broad, veins puberulous, with tufts of long hairs along length; callus horseshoe-shaped, fleshy, slightly striate, deeply sulcate to the middle. **Column** clavate, densely villose below, narrowly 2-winged above, 1.6–2 cm long.
DISTRIBUTION E. Brazil.

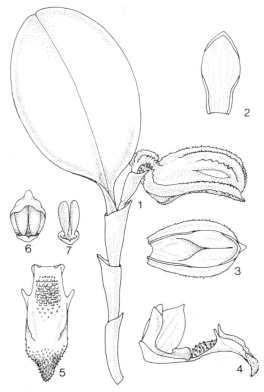

Zootrophion hypodiscus
1 – Habit (× 2)
2 – Dorsal sepal (× 2)
3 – Lateral sepals (× 2)
4 – Column, petal and lip, side view (× 4)
5 – Lip (× 6)
6 – Anther (× 6)
7 – Pollinia and viscidium (× 6)

HISTORY Discovered by Frederic Warre in Brazil, who sent plants to Messrs Loddiges of Hackney, London. They first flowered it in August 1829 and it was described and figured in their *Botanical Cabinet* (t. 1687) the following year.

SYNONYMS include *Zygopetalum mackaii* Hooker var. *crinitum* Lindl.; *Z. stenochilum* Lodd.; *Z. pubescens* Hoffmannsegg; *Z. microtos* Hoffmannsegg

Zygopetalum intermedium Lindl.
[Colour Plate]

A large terrestrial plant. **Pseudobulbs** clustered, ovoid-conical, 4–8 cm long, 3- to 5-leaved at apex. **Leaves** oblong or elliptic-lanceolate, acute or acuminate, plicate, 17–50 cm long, 2–6 cm broad. **Inflorescences** lateral, racemose, longer than the leaves, laxly 3- to 5-flowered, up to about 40 cm long; bracts prominent, equalling the pedicel and ovary. **Flowers** large, showy, variable; sepals and petals green, heavily blotched with crimson; lip white, heavily lined with purple. **Sepals** oblong-lanceolate, acute or subacute, 3–3.5 cm long, 1 cm broad. **Petals** similar to the sepals. **Lip** broadly obovate in outline, 3-lobed at the base, about 3.5 cm long, 3 cm broad; side lobes auriculate; mid-lobe large, cuneate-obovate to obcordate, retuse at the apex, margins undulate; callus basal, fleshy, 2-lobed, plurisulcate. **Column** short, stout, dilated and winged, about 1.3 cm long.

DISTRIBUTION Peru, Bolivia and Brazil.
HISTORY Introduced into cultivation in Europe by Messrs Loddiges and described by John Lindley in the *Botanical Register* (misc. p. 9) in 1844. Lindley states that *Z. intermedium* 'is perhaps the finest of the genus'.
SYNONYMS *Eulophia mackaiana* Lindl.; *Zygopetalum mackaii* Paxt. non Hooker; *Z. bolivianum* Schltr.
CLOSELY RELATED SPECIES Distinguished from *Zygopetalum mackaii* Hooker by its downy lip.

Zygosepalum (Reichb.f.) Reichb.f.
Subfamily Epidendroideae
Tribe Maxillarieae
Subtribe Zygopetalinae

Medium-sized epiphytes with bifoliate pseudobulbs borne on a short stout rhizome. **Leaves** plicate. **Inflorescences** erect or spreading, few-flowered. **Flowers** medium-sized to large, fleshy, often showy. **Dorsal sepal** and **petals** free, subsimilar, spreading; **lateral sepals** similar but basally connate. **Lip** lacking prominent sidelobes, deflexed; disc more or less cuneate, spreading; callus a grooved crest. **Column** cla-

vate, winged at apex, with a short foot; pollinia 4, on a broad oblong stipe; anther-cap with an elongate apical process.

DISTRIBUTION A small genus of about five species in tropical S. America.
DERIVATION OF NAME From the Greek *zygon* (yoke) and the Latin *sepalum* (sepal), referring to the connate base of the lateral sepals.
TAXONOMY *Zygosepalum* was originally established by H.G. Reichenbach in 1858 in *Nederlandisch Kruidkundig Archief*, Leiden (p. 330) as a segregate of *Zygopetalum*.

The genus is closely related to *Mendoncella* but differs in having petals and lateral sepals that are not decurrent on the column-foot, and an anther with a long subulate fleshy process at the apex. The latter also distinguishes it from *Zygopetalum*.
TYPE SPECIES *Z. kegelii* Rchb.f. (lectotype).
SYNONYM *Menadenium* Raf. ex Cogn.
CULTURE Temp. Winter min. 12–15°C. Since the pseudobulbs are separated by lengths of creeping rhizome, these plants can be mounted on a slab or branch. They require moderate shade and good humidity, without a marked dry season.

Zygosepalum labiosum (L.C. Rich.) Garay
[Colour Plate]

An epiphyte with a creeping ascending stout rhizome. **Pseudobulbs** ovoid-ellipsoidal, 4–5 cm long, 1.5–2 cm wide, 2- to 3-leaved at the apex, covered by imbricate distichous sheaths at base, some leaf-bearing. **Leaves** suberect-arcuate, oblanceolate, acute, 16–25 cm long, 2–5 cm wide, shortly petiolate. **Inflorescences** erect, 1- to 3-flowered, 11–21 cm long; peduncle terete, 1–3 mm in diameter; bracts lanceolate, acuminate, 2.8–5 cm long. **Flowers** fleshy; sepals greenish suffused with maroon in the centre or pale olive-green; petals similar, pale violet at the base; lip white with violet radiating veins from a violet callus; pedicel and ovary 2.5–3 cm. long. **Dorsal sepal** lanceolate, acuminate, 4.5–5 cm long, 1.5 cm wide; **lateral sepals** falcate, lanceolate, acuminate, 4.5–5 cm long, 1.3 cm wide. **Petals** lanceolate, acuminate, 4.5–4.7 cm long, 1.3 cm wide. **Lip** deflexed, shortly clawed, broadly ovate, acuminate, 3.1–4 cm long, 2.7–4 cm wide; callus a lunate raised 3-ridged rim around apex of claw. **Column** incurved, 3–3.5 cm long, erose and with 2 semicircular pendent wings at apex.
DISTRIBUTION The Guyanas, Venezuela and Brazil; up to 300 m.
HISTORY The French botanist L.C. Richard described this species as *Epidendrum labiosum* in 1792 in *Acta Societatis Historia Natura, Paris* (p. 112). Leslie Garay transferred it to the present genus in 1967 in *Orquideologia* (vol. 1 (3): p. 2).

SYNONYMS *Epidendrum labiosum* L.C. Rich.; *Zygopetalum rostratum* Hook.; *Menadenium rostratum* (Hook.) Raf.; *M. labiosum* (L.C. Rich.) Cogn.; *Zygosepalum rostratum* (Hook.) Rchb.f.

Zygosepalum lindeniae (Rolfe) Garay & Dunsterville [Colour Plate]

A creeping, ascending epiphyte with an elongate, woody rhizome almost covered in brown sheaths and roots. **Pseudobulbs** borne 5–10 cm apart on the rhizome, ellipsoidal, bilaterally compressed, longitudinally grooved, 5–6 cm long, 2.7–3 cm wide, unifoliate at the apex, subtended by several imbricate leaf-bearing sheaths. **Leaves** narrowly elliptic-oblanceolate, acute, 20–30 cm long, 3–4.5 cm wide, shiny green. **Inflorescence** axillary from the basal sheaths, up to 15 cm long, laxly 2- to few-flowered; peduncle slender, arcuate; bracts up to 2.5 cm long, white. **Flowers** with sepals and petals white at the base, greenish above with reddish veins; lip white with red veins and flushed red on side lobes; pedicel and ovary 2–3 cm long. **Sepals** and **petals** spreading, subsimilar, lanceolate, acuminate, 4–4.5 cm long, 0.7–1 cm wide. **Lip** deflexed, spreading, obscurely 3-lobed, broadly ovate-cordate, apiculate, 3–3.3 cm long, 3.1–3.5 cm wide; callus at base of lip, raised, fleshy, lunate, several-ribbed. **Column** arcuate, c. 2 cm long, with 2 apical semicircular pendent wings, erose at the apex.

DISTRIBUTION Venezuela only; in rain forest.
HISTORY Originally discovered by M. Bungeroth in Venezuela and sent by him to Jean Linden in Brussels. It was described in 1891 by Robert Rolfe as *Zygopetalum lindeniae* in *Lindenia* (vol. 6; p. 73, t. 275) and named after Mme Lucien Linden. Leslie Garay and Dunsterville transferred it to *Zygosepalum* in the third volume of *Venezuelan Orchids Illustrated* (p. 336).
SYNONYMS *Zygopetalum lindeniae* Rolfe; *Menadenium lindeniae* (Rolfe) Cogn.

Zygostates Lindl.
Subfamily Epidendroideae
Tribe Maxillarieae
Subtribe Ornithocephalinae

Dwarf epiphytic herbs with very short erect to pendent leafy non-pseudobulbous stems covered by persistent leaf bases. **Leaves** coriaceous, linear-oblong to elliptic-oblong, blunt, articulated to persistent imbricate compressed sheathing bases. **Inflorescences** erect to pendent, racemose, laxly few- to many-flowered; bracts small. **Flowers** membranaceous, white to greenish-yellow, translucent, delicate, opening widely. **Sepals** free, spreading or recurved, similar. **Petals** spreading, broader than the sepals, with entire or toothed margins. **Lip** entire, similar to petals, with entire or dentate margins with a basal fleshy callus, lacking a spur. **Column** slender, elongate, with 2 clavate basal staminodes; rostellum elongate, sigmoid-pendent; anther elongate; pollinia 4, waxy, attached by a slender sigmoid stipe to a small viscidium.

DISTRIBUTION   A small genus of perhaps a dozen species centred on Brazil but with a single species each in Argentina and Paraguay.

DERIVATION OF NAME   From the Greek *zygostates* (balance or scales), from the balance-like look of the clavate staminodes either side of the base of the column.

TAXONOMY   *Zygostates* was described by John Lindley in 1837 in the *Botanical Register* (sub t. 1927). It resembles *Ornithocephalus* but differs in its distinctive column with 2 prominent staminodes and an elongate sigmoid rostellum.

TYPE SPECIES   *Z. lunata* Lindl.; *Z. cornuta* Lindl.

CULTURE   Temp. Winter min. 12°C. Compact plants suited to pot culture in an epiphyte compost. Conditions need to be shady and humid without being allowed to dry out.

Zygostates lunata Lindl.

A dwarf epiphyte with a very short stem up to 1 cm long; roots fibrous. **Leaves** linear to oblong-elliptic, obtuse, 4.5–11 cm long, 0.7–1 cm wide, articulated at the base to persistent imbricate sheaths, up to 1 cm long. **Inflorescences** pendent, 8–17 cm long, laxly up to 30-

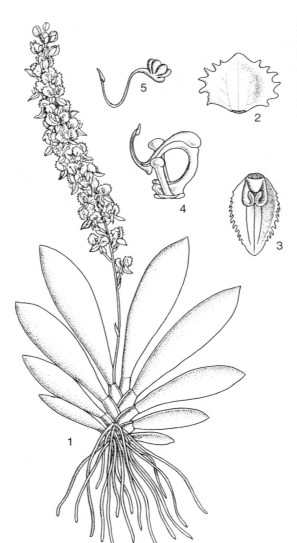

flowered; peduncle and rhachis very slender; bracts linear-lanceolate, acuminate, 3–4.5 mm long. **Flowers** membranaceous, the sepals white, the petals and lip greenish-yellow; pedicel and ovary 0.8–1.4 cm long. **Sepals** elliptic, subacute, 3–4 mm long, 2 mm wide. **Petals** obovate-flabellate, shortly clawed, 4–5 mm long, 5–6 mm wide, with denticulate or erose margins. **Lip** ovate, acute, 5–6 mm long, 3 mm wide, with denticulate margins; callus fleshy, basal, 3-lobed in front, the outer lobe spreading. **Column** slender, geniculate, 5 mm long including the rostellum.

DISTRIBUTION   E. Brazil only; Paraná, Rio de Janeiro and Minas Gerais States, in montane forests in mist zone.

HISTORY   This delicate little orchid was first collected by Martius near the town of Mariana in Minas Gerais, Brazil, and by Descourtilz in the Banabal district. It was described by John Lindley in the *Botanical Register* (sub t. 1927) in 1837.

SYNONYM   *Ornithocephalus navicularis* Barb. Rodr.

Zygostates lunata
1 – Habit ($\times \frac{3}{4}$)
2 – Petal ($\times 4\frac{1}{2}$)
3 – Lip ($\times 4\frac{1}{2}$)
4 – Column, side view ($\times 6\frac{1}{2}$)
5 – Pollinarium ($\times 8$)

Selected Biographical Notes

Alexander, H.G. (1875–1972) was born at Bath, Somerset, England. In 1897 he was appointed orchid foreman at Blenheim Palace and in 1899 took charge of Sir George Holford's magnificent collection at Westonbirt, Gloucestershire. His main interest lay in hybridising *Cymbidium*, and the white-flowered *Cymbidium* Alexanderi is named after him. On Sir George's death, Alexander then took over the collection and ran it for many years on a commercial basis.

Ames, Oakes (1874–1950) was born at North Easton in Massachusetts, USA. His long association with Harvard University began in 1895 as a student and lasted over 50 years during which time he was successively lecturer in botany, supervisor of the Arnold Arboretum, supervisor of the biological laboratories, Chairman of the Council of the Botanical Collections and Director of the Botanical Museum. He also, in 1941, donated his orchid herbarium of 64,000 specimens to Harvard University and this collection forms the basis of the famous Oakes Ames Orchid Herbarium. His interest in orchids was lifelong and was stimulated by his numerous expeditions, particularly to the Philippines. He subsidised there the collection of herbarium specimens of orchids under the direction of Dr E.D. Merrill who was then Director of the Bureau of Science and this led to his account of the Orchidaceae in Merrill's *Enumeration of Philippine Flowering Plants*. He later collaborated with Dr E. Quisumbing on a series of articles on Philippines orchids in the *Philippine Journal of Science* (1931–37). Other major botanical works on orchids by Oakes Ames were *Orchidaceae* in 7 volumes (1905–22) and *Schedulae Orchidianae* (1922–30). Much of his orchid work was ably illustrated by his artist wife Blanche Ames. Throughout his life Ames had a great influence on orchid taxonomy not least through his friendship and correspondence with his contemporary workers in Europe such as R.A. Rolfe, R. Schlechter and V.S. Summerhayes. The genera *Amesia* Nelson & Macbride; *Oakes-Amesia* Schweinf. & P.H. Allen and *Amesiella* Garay are named after him. Herbarium specimens at the Oakes Ames Herbarium, Harvard University, USA.

Barbosa Rodrigues, João (1842–1909) was born in Minas Gerais State in Brazil. He was one of the first native-born Brazilian plant taxonomists and the first to interest himself in orchids (his other main interest being the palms). His *Genera et Species Orchidearum Novarum* (1877–82) in 2 volumes was written in preparation of the account of the Orchidaceae for Martius's *Flora Brasiliensis* which was eventually written by A. Cogniaux. He also drew and coloured illustrations of many Brazilian orchids but these were never published. The originals are now at the Jardim Botânico, Rio de Janeiro and the Oakes Ames Herbarium and copies of all of them are at Kew. The genera *Barbosa* Becc., *Barbosella* Schltr. and *Rodrigueziella* O. Ktze. were named in his honour.
Herbarium specimens have not been located and may have been destroyed.

Banks, Sir Joseph (1743–1820) was born in London on 13 February 1743 and grew to be the leading scientist of his day. He was greatly influenced by and made his name when he accompanied Captain Cook on the voyage of the *Endeavour* (1768–71) to Australia where he acted as botanist. He was President of the Royal Society from 1778 until 1820 and was responsible for establishing the international role of the Royal Botanic Gardens at Kew. He was among the first to successfully grow tropical orchids and recommended the use of hanging baskets for their cultivation.
Herbarium at the British Museum.

Bateman, James (1811–97) was born at Bury in Lancashire, England. During his lifetime Bateman amassed a large living collection of tropical plants especially orchids and even employed T. Colley to collect orchids for him in British Guiana. His great love and enthusiasm for orchids is reflected in his several publications including the massive masterpiece *Orchidaceae of Mexico and Guatemala* (1837–43), a work on an unsurpassed scale, and several others including the *Monograph of Odontoglossum* (1864–74) and *Second Century of Orchidaceous Plants* (1867).

Throughout his life, Bateman was a patron and friend of most of the leading orchid authorities and is commemorated in the genus *Batemannia* Lindl.
Herbarium specimens at Kew.

Beccari, Odoardo (1843–1920) was born in Florence. In 1865 he left for Borneo where his three years of adventure were recorded in his *Wanderings in the Forests of the Far East* (1904). Later visits took him to Ethiopia, New Guinea and the Moluccas. He is commemorated by *Bulbophyllum beccarii* Rchb.f., *Coelogyne beccarii* Rchb.f. and *Dendrobium odoardii* Kraenzl. His herbarium collections are at Florence.

Bentham, George (1800–84) was born at Stoke, Plymouth in Devonshire, England. He was the nephew of Jeremy Bentham and became one of the leading taxonomists of his day and a great friend and collaborator of Joseph Hooker. His orchid work formed only a small part of his enormous output but was of major significance because he wrote the *Orchidaceae* for his and Joseph Hooker's *Genera Plantarum* (1862–83). Bentham was wealthy in his own right and worked for many years at the Royal Botanic Gardens where he was largely self-financed. He is commemorated by two orchid genera *Benthamia* Lindl. and *Neobenthamia* Rolfe.
Herbarium specimens at Kew.

Blume, Carl Ludwig (1796–1862) was born at Braunschweig, Germany and was one of several Germans employed by the Dutch in the East Indies. He arrived in Java in 1817 and worked there until 1826; from 1822 onwards as Director of the Buitenzorg (now Bogor) Botanic Garden. His interest in orchids developed rapidly and in 1825 he produced *Tabellen en Platen voor de Javaansche Orchideeën* which provided the first information to the outside world of this rich orchid flora. Further orchid species and genera were described the same year in his most influential work *Bijdragen tot der Flora van Nederlandsch Indië*. Ill-health forced Blume to leave Java the following year but he continued his work in Holland and was appointed Director of the State Herbarium (Rijksherbarium) at Leiden in 1829. Amongst his later works on orchids, the most important were *Rumphia* (1835–48) in which he reorganised G.E. Rumph's pre-Linnaean work and gave Lin-

naean binomials to all the species, and *Flora Javae et Insularum adjacentium* (1858) in which many orchids were described and beautifully illustrated. The genus *Blumea* Candolle was named in his honour.
Herbarium specimens at Leiden, Bogor (Java), Paris.

Bolus, Harry (1834–1911) Bolus's name is inextricably linked with South African botany, but he was born at Oxted in England and arrived in the Cape at the age of sixteen. During his life he collected plants extensively in South Africa and was the author of works of many families of plants other than orchids. His major works include *Icones Orchidearum Austro-Africanarum Extra-Tropicarum* (1888–1913) in 3 volumes. In 1902 he founded the Chair of Botany at South Africa College. He is commemorated by three genera named in his honour: *Bolusia* Benth.; *Neobolusia* Schltr. and *Bolusanthus* Harms.

Bonpland, Aimé-Jacques-Alexandre (1773–1858) was born at La Rochelle in France. He is best known for being the loyal companion of Alexander von Humboldt on his South American expedition. He wrote little during his life and returned to South America where he eventually died. The genera *Bonplandia* Willd., and *Bonplandia* Cav. were named after him.
Herbarium specimens at Paris and Berlin (destroyed).

Boxall, William (1884–1910) was one of the most widely travelled of all the orchid collectors. Initially employed by Messrs Veitch of Chelsea in the 1860s he later became a foreman with Hugh Low & Co. of Clapton. His orchid collecting for that firm took him to Burma, the Philippines, Borneo, Java, Brazil and Central America. Among the several orchids named after him are *Dendrobium boxallii* and *Paphiopedilum boxallii*.

Brown, Robert (1773–1858) was born at Montrose in Scotland on 21 December 1773. He initially studied medicine before joining Flinder's Australian Expedition (1801–5) as botanist. From 1810 to 1825 he was librarian to Sir Joseph Banks and in 1827 was made the first Keeper of Botany at the British Museum (Natural History). From 1849 to 1853 he was President of the Royal Society. His botanical works are extensive and by no means confined to orchids. His publication *Prodromus Florae Novae Hollandiae* (1810) was the first major work on Australian plants, many of which, including orchids, he described for the first time.
Herbarium specimens at Edinburgh and British Museum.

Burbidge, Frederick William Thomas (1847–1905) was born at Wymswold, Leicestershire, England. He trained as a gardener at Kew from 1868 to 1870 and was on the staff of the *Garden* magazine until 1877. He joined the staff of Messrs Veitch & Sons in that year and went for two years to Borneo to collect for them. From 1879 until his death he was the Curator of the Trinity College Gardens in Dublin. He was author in 1874 of *Cool Orchids and How to Grow Them*. The genus *Burbidgea* was named after him by J.D. Hooker.
Herbarium specimens at Kew and British Museum.

Burke, David (1854–97) was born in Kent, England. As a young man he entered the service of Messrs Veitch of Chelsea as a gardener and was sent with Charles Curtis in 1880 to Borneo to collect orchids and other plants of horticultural merit. He later collected in Guyana, the Philippines, New Guinea, Burma, Colombia and the Moluccas.
Herbarium specimens at Kew.

Cattley, William (1788–1835) was a merchant and benefactor of horticulture. He was John Lindley's first patron and Lindley's *Collectanea Botanica* was written for Cattley. His business interests were in East Anglia, London and St Petersburg. John Prescott, after whom Lindley named *Prescottia* was a cousin and ran the St Petersburg firm.
Cattley is commemorated by *Cattleya* Lindl.

Cavendish, William George Spencer, 6th Duke of Devonshire (1790–1858) was born in Paris. He became one of the greatest patrons of horticulture of his day and was President of the Horticultural Society of London from 1838 to his death in 1858. Perhaps his major achievement was his part in establishing the Royal Botanic Gardens at Kew as a national botanical garden. He employed Joseph Paxton to manage his celebrated garden at Chatsworth in Derbyshire where the finest orchids were grown. *Oncidium cavendishianum* and *Stanhopea devoniensis* are named in his honour.

Charlesworth, Joseph (1851–1920) is most noted for his famous orchid nursery which he set up with E. Shuttleworth at Haywards Heath, Sussex, England in 1908. Earlier, in 1889, he had collected plants in the Andes. He is commemorated by the beautiful slipper orchid *Paphiopedilum charlesworthii*.

Clemens, Joseph (1862–1936) was born at St Just in Cornwall. He collected plants in the Philippines between 1905 and 1929; in Borneo in 1915, 1916, 1929–32; Java in 1933; and in New Guinea in 1935–6 where he died in the field. His wife, Mary Strong Clemens (1873–1968), collected with him for much of his time in the Far East and continued, following his death. Their Bornean collections, in particular, are amongst the most important and numerous to have been made. Many orchids have been named in their honour, including the genus *Neoclemensia* Ames & Schweinf.

Cogniaux, Celestin-Alfred (1841–1916) was born at Robechies, south of Hainault in Belgium. His early botanical studies were made on cryptogams and in 1872 he became Conservator of the Brussels Botanic Garden. Cogniaux published many works on families as diverse as Cucurbitaceae and Melastomataceae but he is best remembered in the orchid world for his contribution of the Orchidaceae for Martius's *Flora Brasiliensis* (1893–1906). This work is still a standard reference for those interested in South American orchids. Just before and after his retirement in 1901 he collaborated with A. Goossens in writing the *Dictionnaire Iconographique des Orchidées* (1896–1907). He also wrote articles for *Lindenia* and the *Journal des Orchides*. His second major contribution to orchid taxonomy following *Flora Brasiliensis* was, however, the Orchidaceae for the 6th volume of I. Urban's *Symbolae Antillanae* (1910) in which over 500 species of West Indian orchids in 96 genera were described. Cogniaux is commemorated by the genus *Cogniauxiocharis* and by many species named in his honour such as *Maxillaria cogniauxiana* and *Miltonia cogniauxiana*.
Herbarium specimens at Brussels, New York, Liège, Utrecht.

Colman, Sir Jeremiah (1859–1942) was born and lived at Gatton Park, Reigate in Surrey, England. He was head of the famous mustard firm Colman & Sons and had probably one of the largest private orchid collections in the country. He was the author of *Hybridisation of Orchids* (1932).

Correll, Donovan Stewart (1908–83) was born at Wilson, North Carolina, USA. For several years he worked with Oakes Ames at Harvard University and was the author of *Native Orchids of North America* (1950), *Orchids of Guatemala* (1952–58) with Oakes Ames, and *The Genus Epidendrum in the United States and Middle America* (1936) with Ames and C. Schweinfurth. Herbarium specimens at Oakes Ames Herbarium, Harvard.

Cuming, Hugh (1791–1865) was born at West Alvington, Devonshire, England on 14 February 1791. He is best known for his expedition to the Philippines from 1836 to 1840 where he

pioneered the shipping to England of living orchids from Manila. His plant collecting began much earlier for in 1827–28 he visited, in his self-built yacht *Discoverer*, Juan Fernandez, Easter Island, Tahiti, Pitcairn. His second voyage (1828–30) took him along the west coast of South America. He is commemorated in the Philippine genus *Cumingia* Vidal in the Bombacaceae.
Herbarium specimens at Kew, Oxford and the British Museum.

Curtis, Charles (1853–1928) Born at Barnstaple in Devonshire, England, Curtis was one of Messrs Veitch & Sons' collectors from 1878 to 1884 in Madagascar, Mauritius, Borneo, Sumatra, Java, the Moluccas and later in the Malay Peninsula. He held the position of Superintendant of the Penang Botanic Gardens from 1884 to 1903, assisting H.N. Ridley in his early rubber introduction experiments there.
Herbarium specimens at Kew, British Museum, Kuala Lumpur, Penang, and Singapore.

Darwin, Charles (1809–82) Darwin is not only the best known of all biologists but was throughout his life an inspiration and friend to many of his fellow scientists amongst whom were numbered John Lindley and both Joseph and William Hooker. He was born at Shrewsbury, Shropshire, England and in 1831 joined the research vessel H.M.S. *Beagle* on its passage to South America, the Pacific Islands and Australia. He returned in 1836 with the raw material for a lifetime's work including his revolutionary ideas on plant and animal evolution which were so lucidly expounded in the *Origin of Species* (1859). His *The Various Contrivances by which British and Foreign Orchids are Fertilised* (1862) has seldom been equalled as a piece of astute observational research and most of the ideas outlined there are still valid today. Indeed, the work not only began the study of orchid pollination biology but stimulated research into the pollination biology of flowering plants in general.
Herbarium specimens from *Beagle* expedition at Cambridge.

Davis, Walter (1847–1930) was born at Amport, Hampshire, England and trained as a gardener on the estates of the Marquis of Winchester and Lady Herbert. He joined the staff of Messrs Veitch at Chelsea in 1870 and was sent by them to South America in 1873 to collect plants, and especially orchids. He eventually became Secretary to the Geological and the Royal Geographical Societies. He is commemorated by the orchid *Masdevallia davisii*.

Day, John (1824–88) was born in London and lived for much of his life in North London at Tottenham. He was an amateur grower of some repute and in 1881 his collection sold for the then astonishing sum of £1000. He travelled widely in India, Ceylon, Malaya, Brazil and Jamaica. His widely acclaimed 'orchid scrapbooks' consisting of hundreds of watercolour paintings of orchids which flowered in his and other collections are at Kew. Their importance to taxonomy lies in the fact that Day was a friend of H.G. Reichenbach and many of the orchids painted by Day were later described by Reichenbach in the *Gardeners' Chronicle*.

Dominy, John (1816–91) will be forever remembered as the horticulturalist who produced the first artificial hybrid orchid, *Calanthe Dominyi* in 1856. He was born at Gittisham, Devonshire, England and worked for Messrs Veitch at Exeter and later at Chelsea from 1834–80. He is also commemorated in *Cypripedium* [*Paphiopedilum*] *Dominianum*.

Don, David (1799–1841) was author of *Prodromus Florae Nepalensis* (1825) in which many of the showiest Himalayan orchids were first described. He was born in Forfarshire in Scotland and eventually became the Professor of Botany at King's College, Cambridge (1836–41).
Herbarium specimens at British Museum and at Brussels.

Don, George (1798–1856) was the elder brother of David Don and was also born in Forfarshire. He was foreman of the Chelsea Physic Garden from 1816–21 and collected plants for the Horticultural Society of London in Brazil, the West Indies, São Tomé and Sierra Leone.
Herbarium specimens at British Museum, Kew and Cambridge.

Drake, Miss S. (flourished in 1830s and 1840s) was probably a relative of John Lindley. She contributed illustrations of a high quality to many works including Lindley's *Sertum Orchidacearum*, Bateman's *Orchidaceae of Mexico and Guatemala* and over 1100 plates for the *Botanical Register*. Lindley named the genus *Drakea* in her honour.

Dunsterville, Galfrid Charles Kenneth (1905–88) was born in England and received his education at the University of Birmingham. His name will, however, forever be linked with Venezuela where he spent the last 40 or more years of his life. With his wife, Nora, he collected orchids throughout the country, particularly following his retirement from Shell (Venezuela) which he had managed. He painted and drew Venezuelan orchids, initially as a hobby, but latterly to illustrate his articles in the *American Orchid Society Bulletin* and for his and Leslie Garay's six-volume epic *Venezuelan Orchids Illustrated* (1959–76). He is commemorated by the orchid genera *Dunstervillea* Garay and *Stalkya* Garay. His herbarium specimens are at Harvard, Kew and the American Orchid Society.

Du Petit-Thouars, Aubert (1758–1831) was born at Saint-Martin-de-la-Place, Anjou in France. He was one of the first botanists to visit and study the unique floras of Madagascar and the Mascarene Islands. His main orchid publications, *Orchideanum Africanum Genera* (1804) and *Histoire Particulière des Plantes Orchidées ...* (1822) are of particular interest to taxonomists as they contain the earliest descriptions of Madagascan and Mascarene orchids. Furthermore, these works are of considerable significance as they contain his alternative system to the Linnaean one for naming orchids. This has been discussed in some detail by Friis and Rasmussen in *Taxon* (1975).
Herbarium specimens at Paris, Berlin (destroyed) and a few at Kew.

Fitch, Walter Hood (1817–92) was born in Glasgow, Scotland. For over forty years from 1834 he was the botanical artist for Curtis's *Botanical Magazine* drawing over 2700 plates, for much of that time based at the Royal Botanic Gardens, Kew. He is still generally accepted as probably the best botanical artist and his speed of work has never been surpassed. In all some 10,000 of his drawings have been published.

Fitzgerald, Robert David (1830–92) was born at Tralee, County Kerry in Ireland. He emigrated to Australia in 1856 and from 1864 devoted himself to the study of Australian orchids, regularly corresponding at this time with Charles Darwin. His beautiful *Australian Orchids* (1875–94) in two volumes is still a standard reference work.
Herbarium specimens at Melbourne and the British Museum.

Forstermann, Ignatz F. (1854–95) was born at Koblenz in Germany. From 1880 to 1886 he collected plants for Messrs Sander and Sons of St Albans, and afterwards became manager of their branch in Summit, New Jersey, USA. He travelled extensively for them in the Far East collecting in India, Burma, the Malay Archipelago and the Philippines. He rediscovered *Paphiopedilum fairrieanum* in Assam and discovered *P. sanderianum* in Borneo. *Coelogyne foerstermannii* is named in his honour.

Garay, Leslie A. (1924–) was born in Hungary but emigrated shortly after the last war to Canada and subsequently to the USA where he was appointed Curator of the Oakes Ames Herbarium, succeeding Charles Schweinfurth in the post. He has written extensively and authoritatively on tropical American and South East Asian orchids. His major orchid floristic publications are *Venezuelan Orchids Illustrated*, vols 1–6 (1959–76) with G.C.K. Dunsterville; *The Orchids of the Southern Ryukyu Islands* (1974) and the *Flora of Lesser Antilles—Orchidaceae* (1974) both with H. Sweet. He has also contributed many revisions of orchid genera including *Oncidium* and a survey of the vandoid genera. His ideas on orchid evolution and classification have been influential.
Herbarium specimens at Oakes Ames Herbarium, Harvard.

Gardner, George (1812–49) was born in Glasgow, Scotland. He collected orchids in Brazil between 1836 and 1841 and then spent the rest of his life in Ceylon where he died. He is commemorated by *Oncidium gardneri*.

Gibson, John (1815–75) was born at Eton Hall, Cheshire, England. He was gardener to the Duke of Devonshire at Chatsworth House in Derbyshire and was sent by him to India in 1835 to collect orchids and *Amherstia nobilis*. He later moved to London where he became Superintendent of several of the large London Parks. He is commemorated by the orchid *Cymbidium gibsonii*.

Griffith, William (1810–45) was born at Ham, Surrey and went to Madras in India in 1832 as assistant surgeon. He accompanied Dr N. Wallich to Assam in 1835–36 and later travelled alone in Bhutan, Afghanistan and Malaya collecting plants. In 1842 he succeeded Wallich as the Superintendant of the Calcutta Botanic Gardens but died only three years later at Malacca in Malaya.
Herbarium specimens at Kew.

Harrison, Richard (flourished 1820s) grew a large collection of Brazilian orchids at Aigburgh near Liverpool. The plants were mostly sent to him by his brothers, William and Henry, from Rio de Janeiro where they were resident at that time.

Hartweg, Carl Theodore (1812–71) was born at Karlsruhr in Germany. He was employed from 1836 onwards as a collector for the Horticultural Society of London and travelled widely up until 1854 collecting plants in Mexico, Guatemala, Ecuador, Jamaica, Madeira and Peru. John Lindley named the genus *Hartwegia* in his honour.
Herbarium specimens at Kew.

Hoehne, Frederico Carlos (1882–1959) born at Juan de Fora in Minas Gerais State, Brazil. As with so many other orchid taxonomists he began his career as a horticulturist at the Rio de Janeiro Botanical Garden. However, he soon became interested in taxonomy and ended his career as Director of the São Paulo Botanical Institute. Hoehne's main aim was to bring Martius's *Flora Brasiliensis* up to date with the production of a new *Flora Brasilica*. This was never completed, but about half of the Brazilian orchids were covered in four volumes (1940–58) which included excellent illustrations and descriptions. A condensed version was also published as *Iconografia de Orquídeas Brasileiras* (1949) for the enthusiastic amateur.
Herbarium specimens at São Paulo.

Holford, Sir George Lindsay (1861–1926) was born at Westonbirt in Gloucestershire, England and lived there for his entire life. He developed there the famous arboretum which his father had started but he is best known in orchid circles for the celebrated orchid collection that he assembled and which was latterly looked after by H.G. Alexander.

Holttum, Richard Eric (1896–1990) was a British botanist, educated at Cambridge. He went to Singapore in 1922 as Assistant Director of the Botanic Garden and three years later became Director. He did much to establish the Garden as a major centre for botanical research in South East Asia. He took a taxonomic and horticultural interest in a wide range of plants but particularly in ferns and orchids. His account of the *Orchids of Malaya* (3rd edition, 1964) for the *Flora of Malaya* is still the standard text on the subject. He also established in Singapore the foundations of the flourishing trade in cut flowers of hybrid vandaceous orchids through his early orchid hybridisation and seed-growing successes. He became the first Professor of Botany at Singapore University after World War 2. He continued to work on orchid and fern taxonomy at Kew on his return to England.
Herbarium specimens at Singapore and Kew.

Hooker, Sir Joseph Dalton (1817–1911) was born at Halesworth in Suffolk, England and was destined to outshine even his famous father, William, as a botanist. His early botanical career took him as naturalist and surgeon to the Antarctic, New Zealand and southernmost South America on board H.M.S. *Erebus* (1839–43) and this was followed in 1847 by four years of plant collecting in Sikkim and Nepal. On this latter expedition he undoubtedly gained his love and deep knowledge of Indian orchids although his collecting then is best known for his introduction to Europe of many of the most spectacular *Rhododendron* species. In 1865 after ten years as Deputy Director at Kew he succeeded as Director upon the death of his father. His output throughout his long life was prodigious and his scope was immense. He was author of books on plant geography, several floras, travel books and monographs. He was a great friend of Charles Darwin who constantly sought his opinions on matters concerning plants and plant geography. His major orchid contributions were *Genera Plantarum* (1883) with George Bentham and *Flora of British India, Orchideae* (1890). The latter is still the standard text on Indian orchids. For many years Sir Joseph Hooker also wrote the orchid accounts for Curtis's *Botanical Magazine*. He is commemorated in the genus *Sirhookera* O. Ktze.
Herbarium specimens at Kew.

Hooker, Sir William Jackson (1785–1865) was born at Norwich, Norfolk, England and was amongst the most influential botanists of his time. If for nothing else he will be remembered for being the first Director of the Royal Botanic Gardens at Kew (1841–65) which he succeeded in establishing as one of the foremost institutes studying all aspects of botany. Earlier, he had made his name as Professor of Botany at Glasgow University. His knowledge of plants was as prodigious as his output of botanical works. His major orchid work was *A Century of Orchidaceous Plants* (1849), a compilation of some of his many accounts (from 1826 onwards) of orchids in the *Botanical Magazine*, the illustrations for which he drew himself.
Herbarium specimens at Kew.

Jacquin, Nikolaus Joseph (1727–1817) was born in Leiden, Holland. On the advice of van Sweeten he was appointed Supervisor of the Schönbrunn Palace Gardens which under his care became the most famous and most beautiful of their time. In 1763 he was appointed Professor of Chemistry at Chemnitz near Dresden but five years later he returned to Vienna as Professor of Botany and Chemistry as well as Director of the University Gardens. He was greatly influenced by Linnaeus and worked in the immediate post-Linnaean period. He was a prolific author and described and named many new species of plant including some of the first tropical American orchids. His most significant works for orchid taxonomy are *Enumeratio Systematica Plantarum* (1760), *Enumeratio Stirpium Plerarumque* (1762) and *Selectarum Stirpium*

Americanarum Historia (1763 and 1780–81) all of which dealt with West Indian plants.
Herbarium at British Museum, but additional specimens may be found at Oxford, Vienna, Uppsala, etc.

Kraenzlin, Fritz Wilhelm Ludwig (1847–1934) was born at Magdeburg. He was a prolific author on orchid taxonomy throughout the periods dominated by H.G. Reichenbach, R.A. Rolfe, E. Pfitzer and R. Schlechter and he outlived them all. However, his taxonomical work was never of the same standard as that achieved by his illustrious contemporaries. He published several weighty volumes on orchids including *Orchidacearum Genera et Species*, vols I and II(1) (1887–1904) but the following volumes were never completed; *Monographie der Gattungen Masdevallia* (1925); several genera in A. Engler's *Das Pflanzenreich* (1907–23) and *Monographie der Gattung Polystachya* (1926).
Herbarium specimens at Berlin (but are now mostly destroyed) and Kew.

Kuntze, Carl Ernst Otto (1843–1907) was born at Leipzig in Germany. He was a merchant and a botanist who travelled widely in Malaya, Turkestan, South America and Africa. He is best remembered for his encyclopaedic work.

Lawrence, Sir James John Trevor (1831–1913) was born at London. He was President of the Royal Horticultural Society from 1885–1913 and had a large private collection of orchids at Burford near Dorking in Surrey. F.C. Lehmann named the genus *Trevoria* in his honour.
Herbarium specimens at Kew.

Linden, Jean (1817–98) was born in Luxembourg but whilst still a youth moved to Belgium and gained his education at the University in Brussels. In 1836 in the company of H.C. Funck and Ghiesbrecht he went to Brazil on a scientific expedition for the Belgian Government. He collected widely in Eastern Brazil in the States of Rio de Janeiro, Minas Gerais, Espíritu Santo and São Paulo. In 1837 he was again in the New World collecting plants in Cuba and the following year he visited the Mexican highlands and Yucatán. From Mexico he travelled south to Guatemala and, later on, collected in the USA, Venezuela and Colombia. In each area, he sought out the higher mountains for the cooler growing orchid species and discovered near Bogotá the exquisite orchid *Odontoglossum crispum*. This expedition was financed by Mr Rucker of Wandsworth and the Rev. J.C. Clowes of Manchester and they were honoured by his discovery of *Anguloa ruckeri* and *A. clowesii*.

After ten years of collecting, Linden returned to Europe and shortly afterwards established with his son Lucien his famous Ghent nursery which later moved to Brussels. Linden's firm was the most successful in Continental Europe and he financed a succession of profitable expeditions to South America to search for new species. Several orchids are named in his honour including *Odontoglossum lindenii*, *Phragmipedium lindenii* and *Maxillaria lindenii*. His contributions to orchid literature included *Lindenia* and *Illustration Horticole*.
Herbarium specimens at Kew and Brussels.

Lindley, John (1799–1865) was born near Norwich, England on 5 February 1799. His contribution to botany in general and to the study of orchids in particular was immense, Early in his career he became acquainted with Sir William Hooker and in 1818 he went to London to be assistant librarian to Sir Joseph Banks. This led to his recommendation to William Cattley as editor for the latter's *Collectanea Botanica* (1821), an enumeration of the many fine plants in Cattley's collection.

A short period as Garden Assistant Secretary to the Horticultural Society led to his appointment in 1826 as Assistant Secretary for the Society at both Chiswick and London. In 1841, with a number of others including Joseph Paxton, he founded and became editor of the *Gardeners' Chronicle* which was quickly to become the most prodigious and influential horticultural journal of the century.

Lindley's connections with many of the best known amateur and professional horticulturists undoubtedly led to his interest and considerable study of orchids. His *Genera and Species of Orchidaceous Plants* (1830–40) was a landmark in the study of orchids, for here Lindley proposed the first substantial classification of the family. Other important orchid works by him are *Folia Orchidacea* (1852–59), *Sertum Orchidacearum* (1837–42) and *Illustrations of Orchidaceous Plants* (1830–38) with F. Bauer.
Herbarium at Kew (orchids only).

Linné, Carl von (Linnaeus) (1707–78) was born near Stenbroholt in the province of Småland in Sweden. He is acepted as being the father of modern biology for his work in providing both botany and zoology with universal binomial nomenclature which has been followed by all biologists ever since. For botanists, his critical work is the 1st edition of *Species Plantarum* (1753) and this work is used as the base work for priority of scientific plant names. In this work, 69 species of orchid were described in eight genera: *Cypripedium, Epidendrum, Limodorum, Liparis, Ophrys, Orchis, Habenaria* and *Serapias*.

Herbarium specimens at the Linnean Society in London, Oxford and Stockholm.

Lobb, William (1809–64) the elder brother of Thomas (1820–1894), William Lobb was born at Perranar-worthal in Cornwall, England. He was also employed by Messrs Veitch & Sons and collected for them from 1840 to 1848 in Brazil, Chile, Patagonia, Peru, Ecuador, and Colombia and from 1849 to 1857 in California and Oregon.
Herbarium specimens at British Museum and Kew.

Lockhart, David (?–1846) was born in Cumberland, England. He trained as a gardener at Kew and was assistant to C. Smith on the latter's Congo expedition in 1816. In 1818 he became the first Superintendant of the Trinidad Botanic Garden, a position he held until his death. He sent many plants back to Kew, many of which were living and were studied by Lindley, Darwin, and W. Hooker. The genus *Lockhartia* was named after him by W. Hooker.
Herbarium specimens at Kew.

Loddiges, Conrad (1739–86) founded the famous nursery at Hackney in London which bore his name. This firm did much to popularise the cultivation of tropical epiphytic orchids due to the success of their cultivation methods and also to the constant supply of novelties sent to them by their collectors in the tropics. George Loddiges (1784–1846), the son of Conrad Loddiges, was also active in the firm and was responsible for the influential *Botanical Cabinet* (1817–34), drawing most of the plates himself.
Herbarium specimens at Kew.

Low, Sir Hugh (1824–1905) was born at Clapton, London the eldest son of Hugh Low (1793–1863) who founded the famous nursery of that name at Clapton. He entered the Diplomatic Service and went to Borneo in 1844, where in 1851 he ascended Mt Kinabalu, the highest peak in Borneo. From 1877 to 1889 he was resident in Perak, Malaya and throughout his foreign service sent back plants, especially orchids, to Kew. He is commemorated by the slipper orchid *Paphiopedilum lowii* amongst others.
Herbarium specimens at Kew.

Low, Stuart Henry (1826–90) was born at Clapton, the second son of Hugh Low. He followed his father with the nursery business and took over the business upon the latter's death. With his son, also Stuart Henry (1863–1962), he specialised in orchids, moving to Bush Hill Park Nursery, Enfield in 1882.
Herbarium specimens at Kew and Vienna.

Micholitz, Wilhelm (1854–1932) was born in Saxony in Germany but at an early age entered the employment of Messrs Sander & Sons of St Albans as a plant collector. Thus began a love-hate relationship which endured until the beginning of the 20th century. His travels were extensive, including expeditions to the Philippines (1884–85), the Moluccas (1891), New Guinea and Sumatra (1891–92), Burma (1900?) and South America (1900). His major discoveries were all in the Far East including the spectacular Philippine orchid *Vanda (Euanthe) sanderiana*, named after his employer, *Dendrobium phalaenopsis* var. *schroederae* in New Guinea and many others named after their discoverer such as *Aerides micholitzii*, *Phalaenopsis micholitzii*, *Bulbophyllum micholitzii* and *Coelogyne micholitzii*.
Herbarium specimens at Kew.

Millar, Andrée Norma (1916–) was born in Paris. From 1949 until 1982 she lived in New Guinea. From 1956 until 1971 she worked in the Lae Botanic Garden, latterly as Curator. She then transferred to Port Moresby where she created and became the first Director of the University Botanical Garden. She has collected widely in Papua New Guinea and her collections are at Lae, Kew, Leiden, Sydney and many other herbaria. *Dendrobium andreemillari* Reeve is named for her.

Mociño, Jose Mariano (1757–1820) was born at Temascaltepec in Mexico. He accompanied M. Sessé on the first botanical exploration of Mexico from 1787 to 1804. For futher details see Sessé.

Moore, Sir Frederick William (1857–1950), the son of David Moore (1807–79) was born in Dublin and after training at van Houtte's nursery in Ghent, and at Leiden, he became Curator of the Trinity College Botanical Garden in 1877. He succeeded his eminent father as Director of the Glasnevin Botanical Garden in 1879 where he established a fine collection of neotropical orchids. *Neomoorea* Rolfe is named in his honour.

Mueller, Sir Ferdinand Jakob Heinrich (1825–96) was born at Rostock and emigrated at the age of twenty-two to Australia. In 1852 he was appointed Government Botanist in Victoria and, in 1855, Director of the Melbourne Botanic Garden. He collected widely in Australia and described many new species including many orchids. Several of his new orchid descriptions appear in *Fragmenta Phytographiae Australiae*, 12 vols (1858–82).
Herbarium specimens at Melbourne.

Parish, Rev. Charles Samuel Pollock (1822–97) was born in Calcutta and after being ordained in England became Chaplain to the forces at Moulmein in Burma in 1852. In the next 25 years he collected extensively orchids and ferns, drawing them and sending living plants to England. H.G. Reichenbach named several orchids after him including *Paphiopedilum parishii* and *Dendrobium parishii*, whilst Sir Joseph Hooker named the genus *Parishia* in his honour.
Herbarium specimens at the Taunton Museum, Somerset. Drawings at Kew.

Pavon, José (1754–1844) was a Spanish explorer and botanist who travelled to South America with H. Ruiz and J. Dombey in 1778 and collected extensively in Peru and Chile for the next ten years. For further details see under Ruiz.

Paxton, Sir Joseph (1803–65) was born at Milton Bryant, in Bedfordshire, England. In 1823 he became gardener at the Chiswick garden of the Horticultural Society of London and in 1826 was appointed head gardener to the Duke of Devonshire at Chatsworth where he achieved the first blooming of the water lily *Victoria amazonica*. He was best known as the editor of Paxton's *Magazine of Botany* (1834–49), Paxton's *Flower Garden* (1850–53) written with John Lindley, and as one of the founders of the *Gardeners' Chronicle* in 1841. Lindley named the genus *Paxtonia* in his honour.
Herbarium specimens at Kew.

Pfitzer, Ernst Hugo Heinrich (1846–1906) was born at Konigsberg in East Prussia. In 1872 he was appointed Professor of Botany and Director of the Heidelburg Botanic Garden. Pfitzer's interest in orchids developed from his studies on the orchid collection in the Botanic Gardens there. His main interests lay in developing a new system of classification for the Orchidaceae which was outlined for the first time in the *Gardeners' Chronicle* (1880). His system differed from earlier attempts in placing emphasis upon vegetative as well as floral morphology as a basis for classification in the family. Several books on orchid morphology followed, including the influential *Grundzüge einer vergleichenden Morphologie der Orchideen* (1882), *Morphologische Studien über die Orchidblüthe* (1886) and *Entwurf einer natürlichen Anordnung der Orchideen* (1887) leading to his account of the family in Engler & Prantl, *Die Natürlichen Pflanzenfamilien* (1889). Pfitzer also did much of the early work on the generic delimitation of slipper orchids.

Poeppig, Eduard Friedrich (1798–1868) was born at Plauen in Saxony. He collected plants, including many orchids, in Chile, Peru, Ecuador and Brazil from 1827–72. With his co-author S.L. Endlicher, he described many of his discoveries in *Nova genera ac species plantarum* ... (1833–35) in four volumes.
Herbarium specimens at Vienna, Leningrad, Berlin (destroyed), Leipzig, British Museum, Brussels, and Goettingen.

Reichenbach, Heinrich Gustav (Reichenbach filius) (1823–89) probably described more orchid species than any other botanist. He was born in Leipzig, Germany, the son of H.G.L. Reichenbach, author of *Icones Florae Germanicae et Helveticae*. From the age of eighteen, he developed a passionate interest in orchids and published prolifically on the subject in an era when orchids were pouring into Europe from the tropics of the world. Many of his new species were published in the *Gardeners' Chronicle* founded by John Lindley who fostered the young Reichenbach's interest in orchids. His major orchid publications were *Xenia Orchidacea* in three volumes (1858–1900) the last volume being finished by F. Kraenzlin, *Otia botanica Hamburgensia*, two parts (1878–81) and *Orchides* in *Walpers, Annales Botanices Systematicae* (vol. 6) in 1864. Despite his great achievements during his lifetime, Reichenbach probably put orchid taxonomy back many years by a strange clause in his will whereby his herbarium, which had previously been thought destined for Kew, was to remain untouched and unconsulted for 25 years after his death. Thereby many orchids were redescribed which already bore Reichenbach names.

The genus *Reichenbachianthus* and the species *Kefersteinia reichenbachiana*, *Masdevallia reichenbachiana* and *Sievekingia reichenbachiana* were all named in his honour.
Herbarium specimens at Vienna.

Reinwardt, Caspar George Carl (1773–1854) was born at Luettringhausen in Germany. He entered the service of the Dutch East India Co. and in 1817 became the first Director of the Buitenzorg (now Bogor) Botanical Garden in Java. His herbarium collections are in Leiden.

Ridley, Henry Nicholas (1855–1956) was born at West Herling, Norfolk, England. In 1880 he became Assistant at the British Museum (Natural History) and from 1888 until 1911 was the Director of the Singapore Botanic Garden. He is best remembered for helping to introduce rubber in Malaya. He worked extensively on the Malayan flora including the orchids and wrote *The Orchideae and Apostasiaceae of the Malay Peninsula* (1896) and the Orchids

for the *Flora of the Malay Peninsula* (1924). Two genera *Ridleyella* Schltr. and *Ridleyinda* O. Ktze. are named in his honour.
Herbarium specimens at Singapore, Kew, and British Museum.

Roebelen, Carl (1855–1927) was a Swiss who collected orchids for Messrs Sander and later for Ravensway. He visited the Philippines in 1879 and is credited with the discovery and introduction of *Euanthe* (*Vanda*) *sanderiana*. *Paphiopedilum roebelenii* was named in his honour.

Roezl, Benedict (1823–85) has been described as 'perhaps the most intrepid orchid collector who ever lived'. Born in Prague, at the age of thirteen he entered the service of the Court of Tun at Tötschen, Bavaria as a gardener. He worked in many of the finest gardens in Europe until, in 1854, he could restrain his enthusiasm no longer and travelled via New Orleans to Mexico. There he started his own nursery but in 1868 lost his arm in an accident with a machine he had invented for removing the fibres from hemp and raffia. His collecting career in the employ of Messrs Sander & Co. took him all over the New World from Washington in the north to Bolivia in the south. His discoveries included 800 species of tree and herb new to science and several orchids are named in his honour, notably *Miltoniopsis roezlii*, *Masdevallia roezlii* and *Bletia roezlii*.
Herbarium specimens at Kew and Vienna.

Rolfe, Robert Allen (1855–1921) was born at Ruddington, Nottinghamshire, in England. From 1880 onwards he was employed in the Kew herbarium working for much of that time on orchid taxonomy. In 1893 he founded the *Orchid Review* which he edited until 1920. His major works on orchids were Orchidaceae for *Flora of Tropical Africa* (1897) and for *Flora Capensis* (1913), and the *Orchid Stud Book* (1909) with C.C. Hurst.
Herbarium specimens at Kew.

Ruiz Lopez, Hipolito (1754–1815) was born at Belorado in Spain. With his companions, Dr José Pavon and Dr José Dombey, he arrived in Peru in 1778 and they remained in South America for the next ten years, collecting plants mainly in the Andes from Huánuco in the north to Huancayo and Lima in the south, and later in Chile from Aconcagua south to Aranco and Malleco. The first results of their expeditions, including many new orchids, were published in *Prodromus Florae Peruvianae et Chilensis* (1794). This was followed in 1798 by *Systema Vegetabilium Florae Peruvianae et Chilensis* and by their *Flora Peruviana et Chilensis* (1778–1802) in

four volumes which includes descriptions and illustrations of their new species. Herbarium specimens at Madrid, British Museum, Oxford, Geneva and Washington.

Rumphius, Georg Everard (1628–1702) was born in Germany at either Wetterau or Muenzenberg. In 1652 he enlisted in the service of the Dutch and arrived in Java in the following year. In 1662 he was appointed Merchant in Ambon in the Moluccas and began to collect plants there, the first to be collected from the Spice Islands. He produced a manuscript for his *Herbarium Amboinense* and this has formed the basis for botanical research in the Malay Archipelago, notably by C.L. Blume. Sadly, Rumphius went blind in 1670 and never saw his completed work. Parts of his herbarium are at Florence and Vienna.

Sander, Henry Frederick Conrad (1847–1920) was born at Bremen in Germany and emigrated to England in 1865. He established the famous orchid nursery of F. Sander at St Albans in 1881 and subsequently also established nurseries in New Jersey and at Bruges. Sander specialised in orchid species and was supplied by numerous collectors whom he sent to both the New and Old World tropics, probably the best known of these being W. Micholitz who collected in the Far East for him. Sander will probably best be remembered for his folio work *Reichenbachia* (1886–94) written in honour of his friend H.G. Reichenbach.
Herbarium specimens at Kew and Vienna.

Schiller, Consul formed an orchid collection at Hamburg which was one of the most important in Europe. Many plants flowered by him were sent to H.G. Reichenbach for determination and if, as was often the case, they were new then Reichenbach described them. The beautiful *Cattleya schilleriana* is named in his honour. Upon his death the collection was acquired by the Hamburg Botanic Garden where it was destroyed during World War 2.
Herbarium specimens at Vienna.

Schlechter, Friedrich Richard Rudolf (1872–1925) has probably been the most influential orchid taxonomist since John Lindley. He was born in Berlin and after an apprenticeship as a horticulturalist, left Europe for Africa in 1891. Thus began his botanical and plant collecting career which took him to South Africa, Mozambique, Cameroon and Togo in Africa (1895–98), New Guinea (1901–02 and 1907–1909), New Caledonia (1902–03) and also to Sumatra, Java, Sulawesi, Borneo and the Bismark Archipelago. He was a prolific author and described hundreds of new orchid

species. Amongst his most important floristic accounts are *Die Orchidaceen von Deutsch-Neu-Guinea* (1911–14) including 1450 (1102 new) species in 116 genera; many articles on tropical American orchids in *Fedde*, *Repertorium* and in *Fedde*, *Repertorium*, *Beihefte* and *Orchidaceae Stolzianae* (1915) on East African orchids. In addition he contributed many generic revisions to the journal *Orchis* and wrote the standard horticultural work *Die Orchideen* (1914–15).

Schlechter died at the age of fifty-three and his carefully amassed herbarium was tragically destroyed in World War 2 in Berlin. Duplicates of his collection exist at several institutes notably at Oakes Ames Herbarium, Harvard, Paris, Brussels, Bogor, and at Kew.

One of Schlechter's most influential works, *Das System der Orchidaceen* (1926) was published posthumously and consisted of his classification of the family. It was quickly accepted by other botanists and remained for many years the most widely used system. Even today it is still used, albeit in a modified form, for arranging the orchid herbarium at several institutions, most notably at Kew.

Schlechter had many orchids named after him including the genera *Rudolfiella* Hoehne and *Schlechterella* Hoehne and several species such as *Epidendrum schlechterianum* and *Goodyera schlechteri*.

Schomburgk, Sir Robert Herman (1804–65) was born at Freiburg. He is best remembered as the discoverer of the water lily, *Victoria amazonica*, in British Guiana (Guyana). He travelled extensively in the West Indies, Guyana (with his brother Moritz Richard), Santa Domingo and Siam (Thailand) collecting plants. Lindley named the orchid genus *Schomburgkia* in his honour.
Herbarium specimens at British Museum and Kew.

Schomburgk, Sir Moritz Richard (1811–91) was born at Fribault in Saxony. In 1840 he joined his brother, Robert, in Guyana where they climbed Mt Roraima (the Lost World of Sir Arthur Conan-Doyle). In 1865 he was appointed Director of the Adelaide Botanic Garden.
Herbarium specimens at Kew.

Seden, John (1840–1921) was born at Dedham in Essex, England and became gardener to Messrs Veitch & Sons at Chelsea in 1861. There he was taught by John Dominy to grow and hybridise orchids and eventually took over this work when Dominy retired.

Seidenfaden, Gunnar (1908–) was born at Varde in Denmark and is an authority on the

orchids of Thailand and S.E. Asia. He was co-author of *Orchids of Thailand* (1959–64) with Tem Smitinand. His recent series *Orchid Genera in Thailand* (1975–88) covers the orchids of Thailand and surrounding countries in greater detail. He is also the author of *Contributions to a Revision of the Orchid Flora of Cambodia, Laos, and Vietnam* (1974). As a diplomat and botanist he has travelled widely in Greenland, Thailand, the New World, and the Far East.
Herbarium specimens at Copenhagen and the Royal Forest Herbarium, Bangkok.

Sessé y Lacasta, Martin de (?–1809). Little is known of the early life of Martin Sessé, but in 1787 he led the first botanical expedition to Mexico for King Carlos III of Spain. His companion in Mexico was José Mociño and they explored Mexico's rich flora together until 1804 when they returned to Spain. They discovered many new species of plants and the results of their labours were published in *Plantae Novae Hispaniae* (1887–90) and in *Flora Mexicana* (1891–97).
Herbarium specimens at Madrid, Geneva, British Museum, Kew, New York, Missouri, and Chicago.

Skinner, George Ure (1804–67) was born at Newcastle-upon-Tyne in Northumberland, England. A merchant, he went to Guatemala in 1831 where he resided for most of his life until his untimely death in 1867. He collected orchids for James Bateman and also sent plants to Sir William Hooker, discovering many of the showiest Central American orchid species. Several of these were named after him, such as *Lycaste skinneri, Cattleya skinneri, Odontoglossum uro-skinneri* etc. His collections formed the basis of James Bateman's monumental work *The Orchidaceae of Mexico and Guatemala* (1837–43).
Herbarium specimens at Kew.

Smith, Johann Jacob (1867–1947) Our knowledge of Indonesian orchids rests largely upon the work of two botanists, firstly, C. Blume and subsequently J.J. Smith. The latter was born in Antwerp in Belgium and trained as a horticulturist first in Amsterdam and later at Kew and Brussels. In 1891, he went to the Dutch East Indies as an agronomist. However his botanical instincts quickly surfaced and he began to work at the Buitenzorg Botanic Gardens in Java where he remained for the next 33 years. He travelled widely in the East Indies, Malaya and in Dutch New Guinea (now West Irian) and the results of his orchid studies were published mostly in the *Bulletin du Jardin Botanique de Buitenzorg*. These include orchid accounts of Java, Sumatra, Malaya, Amboina and other islands, mostly copiously illustrated by line drawings of the flowers. His major contribution to the study of New Guinea orchids was published in a series of six volumes between 1909 and 1934 in *Résultats de l'expédition scientifique Néerlandaise à la Nouvelle-Guinée*. Together with Schlechter's work it constitutes almost the sum total of our knowledge of that remarkable orchid flora.
Herbarium specimens at Bogor (Java) and Leiden.

Summerhayes, Victor Samuel (1897–1974) was born at Street in Somerset. He was in charge of the orchid herbarium at Kew from 1924 to 1964, succeeding R.A. Rolfe. His main work as an orchid taxonomist was concentrated upon African orchids and he wrote the Orchidaceae for the *Flora of West Tropical Africa* (1936, revised 1968). He was also an expert on European orchids and wrote *The Wild Orchids of Britain* (1951, revised 1968). He is commemorated by the African orchid genus *Summerhayesia* Cribb.
Herbarium specimens at Kew.

Swartz, Olof (1760–1818) like Linnaeus, was a Swede. He was born at Nordköping and was educated at Uppsala where he was a student of Linnaeus' son. He left Sweden in 1783 for North America where he spent a year and then moved on to Jamaica, Santo Domingo, the West Indies and the northern shores of South America, returning to Europe in 1786. His major works on orchids include *Prodromus Descriptionem Vegetabilium in Indiam Occidentalem* (1778), a description of West Indian plants including seven genera of orchids, and *Florae Indiae Occidentales* (1797–1806) where 27 species of orchid in 13 genera were recognized. These two form the basis of our knowledge of American tropical orchids. Another seminal work of his on orchid morphology was *Orchidernes Slägter ach Arter Upstallde* published in *Kungliga Vetenskaps akademiens Avhandlingar* (1800).
Herbarium specimens at Uppsala and Stockholm

Thomson, Thomas (1817–78) was born at Glasgow where he later became a pupil of W.J. Hooker. In 1849 he joined J.D. Hooker on a Himalayan expedition collecting many orchids. From 1854 to 1861 he was the Superintendent of the Calcutta Botanic Garden and during this period he collected plants in Kashmir.
Herbarium specimens at Kew, British Museum and Oxford.

Veitch, Sir Harry James (1840–1924) was born at Exeter, Devonshire in England, the youngest son of James Veitch (1815–69) who founded the Veitch nursery at Exeter. He acquired, in 1865, a partnership in the firm which had moved to Chelsea 12 years earlier. *Masdevallia harryana* was named in his honour by H.G. Reichenbach.

Veitch, James Herbert (1868–1907) was the son of J.J. Veitch and was born at Chelsea. He travelled widely, collecting plants for the firm in Japan, India, Australia, etc. and was the author of *Hortus Veitchii* (1906) amongst other works.
Herbarium specimens at Kew.

Veitch, John Gould (1835–70) was born at Exeter, the second son of James Veitch (1815–69). He visited Japan, China and the Philippines in 1860, Australia and the Pacific in 1864 collecting plants for Messrs Veitch & Sons. *Dendrobium gouldii* Rchb.f. was named in his honour.
Herbarium specimens at Kew.

Wallich, Nathaniel (1786–1854) was born in Copenhagen where he studied medicine and also botany under Vahl. He went as surgeon to the Danish settlement at Serampore, India in 1807 and entered the service of the East India Company in 1813. He was Superintendent of the Calcutta Botanic Garden from 1815 to 1841 and during this time travelled and collected in Nepal amassing a large collection of herbarium specimens. These formed the basis of his *Tentamen Florae Napalensis Illustratae* (1824) and *Plantae Asiaticae Rariores* (1830–32). His *Catalogue* of Nepalese plants was never published but his herbarium specimens and catalogue names of orchids were used extensively by John Lindley in *Genera and Species of Orchidaceous Plants* (1830–40).
Herbarium specimens at Kew.

Wallis, Gustav (1830–78) was born at Lüneburg near Hanover. After an early horticultural training at Detmold and Munich, he was sent to South Brazil to start a horticultural establishment which by 1858 had collapsed through bankruptcy. Luckily he was then offered a post as a plant collector by Jean Linden who sent him to Brazil, where he hazardously ascended the Amazon to its source. In 1870, Messrs Veitch & Sons commissioned him to explore the Philippines for them to look for *Phalaenopsis* species. In 1872 he returned to Colombia where he collected many valuable orchids for Veitch. He remained in the New World tropics until his death in Ecuador in 1878.

Many of his discoveries are named in his honour including *Epidendrum wallisii, E. pseudo-wallisii, Masdevallia wallisii*, and many others.
Herbarium specimens at Kew and Vienna.

Warner, Robert (?1814–96), was the author of *Select Orchidaceous Plants* (1862–91) and, with B.S. Williams, of the *Orchid Album* in 11 volumes (1832–97). *Cattleya warneri* was named by T. Moore in his honour.

Warscewicz, Josef Ritter von Rawicz (1812–66) was born at Wilno in Lithuania. He left his homeland in the first Polish revolution and from 1840 to 1844 was an assistant in the Berlin Botanical Garden. In December 1844, having finished his studies in Berlin, he left for Guatemala where he collected large quantities of orchids and other plants for the nurseryman L.B. van Houtte of Ghent who was his sponsor. For the first time the botanical gardens in Germany at Hamburg, Berlin and Erfurt and in Switzerland at Zürich received directly seeds, tubers and living plants which previously had been received only via England and it opened a new era of horticulture in those countries. Warscewicz spent several years collecting in the mountains from Guatemala south to Panama discovering *en route* the spectacular *Cattleya dowiana*. In 1849, he collected in Colombia but the following year returned to Europe to recover from yellow fever. Back in Berlin in 1850 he met and assisted H.G. Reichenbach. However, in 1851 he returned to orchid collecting and for the next three years travelled profitably and widely in Ecuador, Peru and Bolivia. A second yellow-fever attack forced him to return to Europe in 1853 where he accepted the post of Supervisor in the Cracow Botanic Garden in Poland.

Many orchids which he discovered were named after him including species of *Miltonia*, *Sobralia*, *Brassia*, *Epidendrum*, *Mesospinidium*, *Oncidium*, and *Stanhopea*. Reichenbach also named the genus *Warscewiczella* after him.
Herbarium specimens at Kew and Vienna. His own herbarium at Berlin is now destroyed.

Welwitsch, Friedrich Martin Joseph (1806–72) was born at Maria-Saal near Klagenfurt in Austria. After qualifying in medicine in Vienna he went to Lisbon in 1839 and eventually became Director of the Botanic Gardens there. In 1852 he went to Angola where he stayed collecting plants until 1861. The remarkable Namibian gymnosperm *Welwitschia* is named in his honour. He also collected there many new species of orchid some of which H.G. Reichenbach named in his honour, e.g. *Eulophia welwitschii* and *Habenaria welwitschii*.
Herbarium specimens at Kew, British Museum, Lisbon and Vienna.

Wight, R. (1796–1872) was born at Milton in East Lothian, Scotland. He studied medicine at Edinburgh and in 1819 went to India as assistant surgeon to the East India Company. In 1826 he became Superintendent of the Madras Botanic Garden. Amongst his many works on Indian botany are *Icones Plantarum Indiae Orientalis* (1840–53) in six volumes and *Prodromus Florae Peninsulae Orientalis* (with G. Arnott) (1834). Wallich named the genus *Wightia* in his honour.
Herbarium specimens at Kew.

Williams, Benjamin Samuel (1824–90) was born at Hoddesdon in Hertfordshire, England. He was gardener to Robert Warner at Hoddesdon and in 1854 founded a nursery with Robert Parker at Holloway, moving eventually to the Victoria and Paradise Nurseries, Upper Holloway. He is best known as the author of *The Orchidgrowers' Manual* (1852) whose popularity and influence may be judged by the fact that it has gone to 7 editions. With R. Warner he was co-author of the *Orchid Album* (1882–97) in 11 volumes and also contributed to R. Warner's *Select Orchidaceous Plants* (1862–97). *Dendrobium williamsianum* was named by H.G. Reichenbach in his honour.

Withner, Carl (1918–) was born at Indianapolis, Indiana and was educated at the Universities of Illinois and Yale. He trained as a plant physiologist and has written extensively on both orchid physiology and taxonomy. For 30 years he lectured at Brooklyn College in New York and is currently a Research Associate of the Biology Dept. of Western Washington University. He has specialised in the taxonomy of neotropical orchids and is the author of two influential compendia on orchid science.

Selected Bibliography

1. General

ARDITTI, J. (1977) *Orchid Biology. Reviews and Perspectives.* Cornell U.P., Ithaca & London.

ARDITTI, J. (1982) *Orchid Biology. Reviews and Perspectives II.* Cornell U.P., Ithaca & London.

ARDITTI, J. (1984) *Orchid Biology. Reviews and Perspectives III.* Cornell U.P., Ithaca & London.

ARDITTI, J. (1987) *Orchid Biology. Reviews and Perspectives IV.* Cornell U.P., Ithaca & London.

BATEMAN, J. (1874) *A Monograph of Odontoglossum.* L. Reeve & Co., London.

BAUER, F. & LINDLEY, J. (1830–38) *Illustrations of Orchidaceous Plants.* J. Ridgeway & Sons, London.

BERNARD, N.L. (1909) L'évolution dans la symbiose. In *Annales des Sciences Naturelles, Botanique:* 1–96.

BENTHAM, G. & HOOKER, J. (1883) Orchideae. In *Genera Plantarum* 3: L. Reeve & Co., London.

BLUME, C.L. (1858) *Collection des Orchidées.* Sulpke, Amsterdam.

BURGEFF, H. (1936) *Die Samenkeimung der Orchideen.* G. Fischer, Jena.

BURGEFF, H. (1959) Mycorrhiza of Orchids. In C. Withner ed. *The Orchids. A Scientific Study:* 361–96. Ronald, New York.

COGNIAUX, A. & GOOSSENS, A. (1896) *Dictionnaire Iconographique des Orchidées.* Brussels.

CRIBB, P., J. GREATWOOD & P.F. HUNT eds. (1985) *Handbook of Orchid Nomenclature,* 3rd ed. International Orchid Commission, London.

CURTIS, J.T. (1939) The relation of the specificity of orchid mycorrhizal fungi to the problem of symbiosis. In *American Journal of Botany* 26: 390–398.

DARWIN, C. (1862) *On the Various Contrivances by which British and Foreign Orchids are Fertilised by Insects.* J. Murray, London.

DRESSLER, R. (1974) Classification of the orchid family. In *Proceedings of the 7th World Orchid Conference:* 259–78. Medellin, Colombia.

DRESSLER, R. (1981) *The Orchids. Natural History and Classification.* Harvard U.P., Cambridge, Mass., USA.

DRESSLER, R. (1983) Classification of the Orchidaceae and their probable origin. In *Telopea* 2(4): 413–24.

GARAY, L. (1960) On the origin of the Orchidaceae. In *Botanical Museum Leaflets of Harvard University* 19(3): 57–96.

GARAY, L. (1972) On the origin of the Orchidaceae 2. In *Journal of the Arnold Arboretum* 52: 202–15.

HAGSATER, E. (1976) Can there be a different view of orchids and their conservation? In *American Orchid Society Bulletin* 45: 18–21.

HARLEY, J.L. (1959) *The Biology of Mycorrhiza.* Leonard Hill, London.

HARLEY, J.L. & SMITH, S. (1983) *Mycorrhizal symbiosis.* Academic Press, London.

HAWKES, A.D. (1965) *Encyclopaedia of Cultivated Orchids.* Faber, London.

HOFMANN, M. (1975) Eine Statistik kultivierter Orchideen. In *Die Orchideen* 26: 30–33.

HUNT, P.F. (1968) Conservation of orchids. In *Orchid Review* 76: 320–27.

INTERNATIONAL UNION FOR THE CONSERVATION OF NATURE (1973) *Convention on International Trade in Endangered Species of Wild Fauna and Flora.* Morges, Switzerland.

JEFFREY, C. (1968) *Plant Taxonomy.* Churchill, London.

JEFFREY, C. (1973) *Biological Nomenclature.* E. Arnold, London.

JOHANSON, D. (1974) The ecology of vascular epiphytes in West Africa. In *Acta Phytogeographia Suecica* 59: 1–129.

KNUDSEN, L. (1922) Non-symbiotic germination of orchid seeds. In *Botanical Gazette* 75: 1–25.

KNUDSEN, L. (1930) Flower production by orchids grown non-symbiotically. In *New Phytologist* 32: 192–99.

LINDEN, J. (1860) *Pescatorea.* Gand (Ghent.)

LINDEN, J. (1885–1901) *Lindenia.* Gand. (Ghent.)

LINDLEY, J. (1830–40) *Genera and Species of Orchidaceus Plants.* J. Ridgway & Sons, London.

LINDLEY, J. (1837–42) *Sertum Orchidacearum.* J. Ridgway & Sons, London.

LINDLEY, J. (1853) *The Vegetable Kingdom,* 3rd. ed.

LINDLEY, J. (1852–59) *Folia Orchidacea.* J. Matthews, London.

MELVILLE, R. (1970) *Red Data Book, vol. 5. Angiospermae.* I.U.C.N., Morges, Switzerland.

MOREL, G.M. (1974) Clonal multiplication of orchids. In C. Withner ed., *The Orchids. Scientific Studies:* 169–222. Wiley-Interscience, New York.

PROCTER, M. & YEO, P. (1973) *The Pollination of Flowers.* New Naturalist, Collins, London.

REICHENBACH, H.G. (1854–1900) *Xenia Orchidacea,* 3 vols. A. Brockhaus, Leipzig.

REICHENBACH, H.G. (1861–64) Orchides. In *Walpers, Annales Botanices* 6.

REINEKKA, M.A. (1972) *A History of the Orchid.* Univ. of Miami Press, Florida.

ROLFE, R. & HURST, C. (1909) *Orchid Stud Book.* F. Leslie & Co., Kew.

SANDER, F. (1888–94) *Reichenbachia.* St Albans.

SANDER, F. (1901) *Sander's Orchid Guide.* St Albans.

SANDER, F. (1906) *Sander's List of Orchid Hybrids.* St Albans.

SANFORD, W.W. (1974) The ecology of orchids. In C. WITHNER ed. *The Orchids. Scientific Studies:* 1–100. Wiley-Interscience, New York.

SCHLECHTER, R. (1962) Das System der Orchideen. In *Notizblatt des Botanischen Gartens und Museums, Berlin* 9: 563–91.

SCHLECHTER, R. (1927) *Die Orchideen,* 2nd ed. Parey, Berlin.

SCHULTES, R.E. & PEASE, A.S. (1963) *Generic Names of Orchids.* Academic Press, New York & London.

SCHWEINFURTH, C. (1959) The classification of orchids. In C. Withner ed., *The Orchids. A Scientific Survey:* 15–43. Ronald, New York.

SHEEHAN, T. & M. (1979) *Orchid Genera Illustrated.* Van Nostrand Reinhold, New York.

SPRUNGER, S. & P. CRIBB (1986) *Orchids from Curtis's Botanical Magazine.* C.U.P., Cambridge.

SUMMERHAYES, V.S. (1968) *The Wild Orchids of Britain,* 2nd ed. New Naturalist, Collins, London.

VAN DER PIJL, L. & DODSON, C. (1966) *Orchid Flowers – their Pollination and Evolution.*

VEITCH, H.J. (1887–94) *A Manual of Orchidaceous Plants*. Veitch & Sons, London.

WARNER, R. (1862–78) *Select Orchidaceous Plants*. Lovell Reeve & Co., London.

WARNER, R. & WILLIAMS, B.S. (1882–97) *The Orchid Album*. B.S. Williams, London.

WITHNER, C. (1959) *The Orchids. A Scientific Study*. Ronald, New York.

WITHNER, C. (1974) *The Orchids. Scientific Studies*. Wiley-Interscience, New York.

WITHNER, C. (1977) Threatened and endangered species of orchids. In G.T. PRANCE & T.S. ELIAS eds., *Extinction is Forever*: 314–22. New York Botanical Garden.

2. *Horticulture*

CRIBB, P.J. & BAILES, C. (1989) *Hardy Orchids*. C. Helm, London.

FAST, G. ed. (1980) *Orchideenkultur*. Ulmer, Stuttgart.

NORTHEN, R. (1990) *Home Orchid Growing*, 3rd. ed. Van Nostrand, New York.

RICHARDS, H., WOOTTON, R. & DATODI, R. (1988) *Cultivation of Australian Native Orchids*, 2nd ed. Australasian Native Orchid Soc., Melbourne.

RICHTER, W. (1965) *The Orchid World*. Studio Vista, London.

RITTERSHAUSEN, B. & W. (1985) *Orchid Growing Illustrated*. Blandford, Poole, Dorset.

WILLIAMS, B. ed. (1980) *Orchids for Everyone*. Salamander, London.

WILLIAMS, B.S. & H. (1894). *The Orchid Grower's Manual*, 7th ed. B.S. Williams, London.

3. *Regional*

Europe and the Middle East

A.H.O. Baden Württenburg Mitteilungsblatt (1969 onwards). Many articles on European orchids.

BAUMANN, H. & KUENKELE, S. (1982) *Die wildwachsenden Orchideen Europas*. Kosmos, W. Keller, Frankfurt.

BUTTLER, K.P. (1986) *Orchideen*. Steinbachs Naturfuehrer, Mosaik, Muenchen.

CAMUS, E.G. (1908) *Monographie des Orchidées*. Lechevalier, Paris.

DANESCH, O. & E. (1962–73) *Orchideen Europas*, 3 vols. Hallweg, Berne & Stuttgart.

DANESCH, O. & E. (1977) *Tiroler Orchideen*. Athesia, Bozen.

DANESCH, O. & E. (1984) *Les orchidées de Suisse*. Silva, Zurich.

DAVIES, P. & J. & HUXLEY, A. (1983) *Wild Orchids of Britain and Europe*. Chatto & Windus, London.

Die Orchideen (1949 – present) Many articles on European and Middle Eastern orchids.

KELLER, G. & SCHLECHTER, R. (1925–43). Monographie und Iconographie der orchideen Europas und des Mittelmeergebietes. *Fedde, Repertorium, Sonderbeheit A*, 1–45.

GODFREY, M.J. (1933) *British Orchidaceae*. Cambridge U.P., England.

LANDWEHR, J. (1977) *Wilde orchideen van Europa*, 2 vols. Natuurmonumenten, Netherlands.

LANG, D. (1989) *Orchids of Britain*, 2nd ed. Oxford U.P.

MOORE, D. & SOÓ, R. (1980) Orchidaceae. In V. HEYWOOD et al. eds. *Flora Europea* 5. Cambridge U.P.

NELSON, E. (1962) *Gestaltwandel und Artbildung Erortert am Beispiel der Orchidaceen Europas un der Mittelmeerlaender Insbesondere der Gattung Ophrys*. E. Nelson, Chernex-Montreux.

NELSON, E. (1968) *Monographie und Ikonographie der Orchidaceen – Gattung* Serapias, Aceras, Loroglossum, Barlia. E. Nelson, Chernex-Montreux.

NELSON, E. (1976) *Monographie und Ikonographie der Orchidaceen – Gattung* Dactylorhiza. E. Nelson, Chernex-Montreux.

NELSON, E. & FISCHER, H. (1931) *Die Orchideen Deutschlands und der angrenzenden Gebiete*. Frisch, Berlin.

REICHENBACH, H.G. (1851) Orchideae. In *Flora Germanica Recensitae*. Hofmeister, Leipzig.

RENZ, J. (1978) Orchidaceae. In K.H. RECHINGER ed. *Flora Iranica*. Graz, Austria.

RENZ, J. & TAUBENHEIM, G. (1984) Orchidaceae. In DAVIES, P. ed. *Flora of Turkey* 8: 450–626.

SUMMERHAYES, V.S. (1968) *Wild Orchids of Britain*, 2nd. ed. New Naturalist, Collins, London.

SUNDERMANN, H. (1980) *Europaische und Mediterrane Orchideen*, 3rd. ed. Bruecke, Hannover.

Japan, China, Taiwan and Central Asia

Acta Phytotaxonomica Sinica (1951–onwards) Many articles on Chinese orchids by Tang, Wang, Chen, Tsi, Liu, Feng et al.

BARRETTO, G. & YOUNGE SAYE, J.L. (1980) *Orchids of Hong Kong*. Govt. Printer, Hong Kong.

CHOW CHENG (1987) *Formosan Orchids* Taichung, Taiwan.

GARAY, L. & SWEET, H. (1974) *Orchids of the Southern Ryukyu Islands*. Harvard U.P., Cambridge, Mass.

HASHIMOTO, T. (1981) *Japanese Indigenous Orchids in Colour* (in Japanese). Kiyoshi Kanda, Japan.

HU, S.Y. (1971–75). The Orchidaceae of China. In *Quarterly Journal of the Taiwan Museum*.

HU, S.Y. (1977) *The genera of the Orchidaceae in Hong Kong*. Chinese U.P., Hong Kong.

KRAENZLIN, F. (1931) Orchidaceae Sibiriae enumeratio. In *Fedde, Repertorium, Beihefte* 65.

LIN, T.P. (1975, 1977, 1983) *Native Orchids of Taiwan*, 3 vols. Taipei, Taiwan. R.O.C. & Southern Materials Center Inc., Taipei.

MAEKWA, F. (1971) *The Wild Orchids of Japan in Colour* (in Japanese). Tokyo.

SCHLECHTER, R. (1919) Orchideologiae Sino-Japonicae prodromus. In *Fedde, Repertorium, Beihefte* 4.

Pakistan, India and Burma

DUTHIE, J.F. (1906) The Orchids of the North-Western Himalaya. In *Annals of the Royal Botanic Garden, Calcutta* 9.

GRANT, B. (1895) *The Orchids of Burma*. Rangoon.

HEGDE, S.N. (1984) *Orchids of Arunchal Pradesh*. Forest Dept., Itanagar.

HOOKER, J.D. (1890) Orchideae. In *Flora of British India* 5. L. Reeve & Co., London.

JOSEPH, J. (1987) *Orchids of Nilgiris*. Bot. Survey India, Calcutta.

KATAKI, S.K. (1986) *Orchids of Meghalaya*. Forest Dept., Shillong.

KING, G. & PANTLING, R. (1898) The orchids of the Sikkim-Himalaya. In *Annals of the Royal Botanic Garden, Calcutta* 8.

PRADHAN, U.C. (1976–79) *Indian orchids: Guide to Identification and Culture*, 2 vols. U. Pradhan, Kalimpong.

RENZ, J. (1984) Orchidaceae. In NASIR, E. & ALI, S.I. eds. *Flora of Pakistan* no. 164: 1–63.

SEIDENFADEN, G. (1983) Orchidaceae. In MATHEW, K.M. ed. *Flora of Tamilnadu Carnatic*: 1550–1611.

South East Asia and Indonesia

AMES, O. & SCHWEINFURTH, C. (1920) The Orchids of Mount Kinabalu, British North Borneo. In O. AMES, *Orchidaceae* 6. Merrymount Press, Boston.

BACKER, C.A. & BACKHUISEN VAN DEN BRINK, R.C. (1960) Orchidaceae. In C.A. BACKER ed. *Flora of Java* 3: 215–451.

COMBER, J.B. (1990). *Orchids of Java*. R.B.G. Kew.

CRIBB, P.J. (1987) *The genus Paphiopedilum*. Collingridge, London.

DU PUY, D. & CRIBB, P.J. (1988). *The genus Cymbidium*. C. Helm, London.

GAGNEPAIN, F. & GUILLAUMIN, A. (1932) Orchidacees. In *Flore Générale de L'Indo-Chine* 2. Masson, Paris.

HOLTTUM, R.E. (1964) Orchids of Malaya, 3rd ed. In *A Revised Flora of Malaya*. Government Printer, Singapore.

SCHLECHTER, R. (1934) Blütenanalysen neuer Orchideen IV. Indische und malesische Orchideen. In *Fedde, Repertorium, Beihefte* 74.

SEIDENFADEN, G. (1975a) *Contributions to a Revi-*

sion of the Orchid Flora of Cambodia, Laos and Vietnam, 1. A Preliminary Enumeration. Fredensborg, Denmark.

SEIDENFADEN, G. (1975b) Orchid Genera in Thailand I–III. In *Dansk Botanisk Arkiv* 29 (2–4): 5–94.

SEIDENFADEN, G. (1976) Orchid Genera in Thailand IV. *Loc. cit.* 31(2): 5–105.

SEIDENFADEN, G. (1977) Orchid Genera in Thailand V. *Loc. cit.* 31(3): 5–149.

SEIDENFADEN, G. (1978a) Orchid Genera in Thailand VI. *Loc. cit.* 32(2): 5–195.

SEIDENFADEN, G. (1978b) Orchid Genera in Thailand VII. *Loc. cit.* 33(1): 5–94.

SEIDENFADEN, G. (1979) Orchid Genera in Thailand VIII. *Loc. cit.* 33(3): 5–228.

SEIDENFADEN, G. (1980) Orchid Genera in Thailand IX. *Loc. cit.* 34(1): 5–104.

SEIDENFADEN, G. (1982) Orchid Genera in Thailand X. In *Opera Botanica* 62: 7–157.

SEIDENFADEN, G. (1983) Orchid Genera in Thailand XI. *Loc. cit.* 72: 5–124.

SEIDENFADEN, G. (1985) Orchid Genera in Thailand XII. *Loc. cit.* 83: 5–295.

SEIDENFADEN, G. (1986) Orchid Genera in Thailand XIII. *Loc. cit.* 89: 5–216.

SEIDENFADEN, G. (1988) Orchid Genera in Thailand XIV. *Loc. cit.* 95: 5–398.

SMITH, J.J. (1903) *Icones Bogorienses — Orchidees.* E.J. Brill, Leiden.

SMITH, J.J. (1905a) *Die Orchideen von Ambon.* Landsdrukkerij, Batavia.

SMITH, J.J. (1905b) Die Orchideen von Java. In *Flora von Buitenzorg* 6.

SMITH, J.J. (1907–24) Die Orchideen von Java 1–8. In *Bulletin du Département de L'Agriculture aux Indes Néerlandaises* and in *Bulletin du Jardin Botanique de Buitenzorg.*

SMITH, J.J. (1928a) Orchidaceae Buruenses. In *Bulletin du Jardin Botanique de Buitenzorg* 9.

SMITH, J.J. (1928b) Orchidaceae Seranenses. *Loc. cit.* 10.

SMITH, J.J. (1930–38) Icones Orchidacearum Malayensium, 1–2. *Loc. cit.* 11.

SMITH, J.J. (1931) On a Collection of Orchidaceae from Central Borneo. *Loc. cit.* 11.

SMITH, J.J. (1933) Enumeration of the Orchidaceae of Sumatra and neighbouring islands. In *Fedde, Repertorium* 32.

SWEET, H. (1980) *The genus Phalaenopsis.* Orchid Digest, Los Angeles.

The Philippines

AMES, O. (1909) Notes on Philippine Orchids. In *The Philippine Journal of Science* 4.

AMES, O. (1905–22) *Orchidaceae* 1–3 & 5–7. Several articles on Philippine orchids.

AMES, O. (1922–30) *Schedulae Orchidinae.* Several new species of Philippine orchids described.

AMES, O. (1925) Enumeration of Philippine Apostasiaceae and Orchidaceae. In E. MER-RILL, *Enumeration of Philippine Flowering Plants.* Manila, Philippines.

AMES, O. & QUISUMBING, E. (1931–36) New and noteworthy Philippine Orchids, 1–6. In *The Philippine Journal of Science* 44–59.

Philippine Orchid Review (1948–59) Many articles on native orchids.

QUISUMBING, E. (1981) *The Complete Writings of Eduardo A. Quisumbing on Philippine Orchids,* 2 vols. ed. by H. Valmayor, E. Lopez Foundation Inc., Manila.

VALMAYOR, H. (1987) *Orchidiana Philippiniana,* 2 vols. E. Lopez Foundation Inc., Manila.

New Guinea

MILLAR, A. (1978) *Orchids of Papua-New Guinea.* Australian National U.P., Canberra.

SCHLECHTER, R. (1914, 1928) Die Orchidaceen von Deutsch-Neu-Guinea. In *Fedde, Repertorium, Beihefte* 1 & 21.

SCHLECHTER, R. (1982) *The Orchidaceae of German New Guinea,* ed. by D. Blaxell. Australian Orchid Foundation, Melbourne.

SMITH, J.J. (1909-34) Die Orchidaceen von Niederlandisch-Neu-Guinea. In *Résultats de l'Expédition Scientifique Néerlandaises à la Nouvelle Guinée.* E. J. Brill, Leiden.

VAN BODEGOM, J. (1973) *Enige Orchideen van West Nieuw Guinea.* Enschede, Netherlands.

Australia

CLEMENTS, M.A. (1989) Catalogue of Australian Orchidaceae. In *Australian Orchid Research* 1: 1–160.

DOCKRILL, A.W. (1969) *Australian Indigenous Orchids I. The Epiphytes: Tropical Terrestrial Species.* Halstead Press, Sydney.

FIRTH, M.J. (1965) *Native Orchids of Tasmania.* C.L. Richmond, Devonport, Tasmania.

FITZGERALD, R.D. (1875–94) *Orchids of Australia,* 2 vols. Sydney.

HOFFMAN, N. & BROWN, A. (1984) *Orchids of South-west Australia.* Univ. of Western Australia Press, Perth.

JONES, D. (1988) *Native Orchids of Australia.* Reed Books, Sydney.

NICHOLLS, W.H. (1969) *Orchids of Australia.* T. Nelson, Melbourne.

Orchadian (1963–present) Journal of Australasian Native Orchid Society containing many articles on native species.

The Pacific Islands

GUILLAUMIN, A. (1948) Orchidacees. In *Flore analytique et synoptique de la Nouvelle Calédonie.* Paris.

HALLÉ, N. (1977) Orchidacées, In *Flore de la Nouvelle-Calédonie et Dépendences* 8. Muséum National d'Histoire Naturelle, Paris.

HUNT, P.F. (1969) Orchids of the Solomon Islands. In *Philosophical Transactions of the Royal Society of London* 255.

JOHNS, J. & MOLLOY, B. (1983) *Native Orchids of New Zealand.* Reed Books, Wellington.

KORES, P.J. (1989) A precursory study of Fijian orchids. In *Allertonia* 5: 1–222.

KRAENZLIN, F. (1929) Neu-Caledonische Orchideen. In *Vierteljahreschrift der Naturforschen den Gesellschaft, Zurich* 74.

LEWIS, B. & CRIBB, P.J. (1989) *Orchids of Vanuatu.* Royal Botanic Gardens, Kew.

LEWIS, B. & CRIBB, P.J. (1991) *Orchids of the Solomon Islands and Bougainville.* R.B.G. Kew.

MOORE, L.B. & EDGAR, E. (1970) Orchidaceae. In *Flora of New Zealand* 2. Wellington.

PARHAM, J.W. (1972) Orchidaceae. In *Flora Vitiensis.* Suva, Fiji.

SEEMAN, B. (1865–73) Orchideae. In *Flora Vitiensis.* L. Reeve, London.

Tropical Africa

CRIBB, P.J. (1984) Orchidaceae pt. 2. In R. POLHILL ed. *Flora of Tropical East Africa.* Balkema, Rotterdam.

CRIBB, P.J. (1989) Orchidaceae pt. 3. In R. Polhill ed. *Flora of Tropical East Africa.* Balkema, Rotterdam.

GEERINCK, D. (1984) Orchidaceae pt. 1. In P. BAMPS ed. *Flore d'Afrique Centrale.* Jardin Botanique National de Belgique, Brussels.

LA CROIX, I., E. & T., HUTSON, J.A. & JOHNSTON-STEWART, N. (1983) *Malawi Orchids 1. Epiphytic Orchids.* National Fauna Pres. Soc., Blantyre, Malawi.

MORRIS, B. (1970) *Epiphytic Orchids of Malawi.* The Society of Malawi, Blantyre.

PIERS, F. (1968) *Orchids of East Africa,* 2nd ed. Cramer, Lehre.

ROLFE, R.A. (1897) Orchidaceae. In *Flora of Tropical Africa* 7. L. Reeve & Co., London.

SCHLECHTER, R. (1915) Orchidaceae Stolzianae. In *Engler, Botanische Jahrbücher.*

SCHLECHTER, R. (1918) Versuch einer natürlichen Neuordnung der afrikanischen angraekoiden Orchidaceen. In *Beihefte zum Botanischen Zentralblatt* 36 (2).

STEWART, J. (1974) Orchidaceae. In A. AGNEW, *Upland Kenya Wild Flowers.* Oxford Univ. Press.

STEWART, J. & CAMPBELL, R. (1970) *Orchids of Tropical Africa.* W.H. Allen, London.

SUMMERHAYES, V.S. (1936–68) Several papers on African orchids in *Kew Bulletin* and in *Botanical Museum Leaflets of Harvard University.*

SUMMERHAYES, V.S. (1968a) Orchidaceae. In HEPPER, F. ed. *Flora of West Tropical Africa* ed. 2. Crown Agents, London.

SUMMERHAYES, V.S. (1968b) Orchidaceae pt. 1. In *Flora of Tropical East Africa.* Crown Agents, London.

WILLIAMSON, G. (1977) *The Orchids of South-Central Africa.* Dent, London.

South Africa

BOLUS, H. (1893–1913) *Icones Orchidearum Austro-Africanarum.* Weldon & Wesley, London.

HARRISON, E.R. (1972) *Epiphytic Orchids of Southern Africa.* Durban.

KRAENZLIN, F. (1898) *Orchidacearum genera et species* 1. I. Mayer & Mueller, Berlin.

ROLFE, R.A. (1913) Orchidaceae. In W. THISELTON-DYER ed., *Flora Capensis.* L. Reeve & Sons, London.

SCHELPE, E.A. (1966) *An Introduction to South African Orchids.* MacDonald, London.

SCHLECHTER, R. (1924) Contributions to South African orchidology. In *Annals of the Transvaal Museum* 10.

South African Orchid Journal (1970–present). Numerous articles on native orchids.

STEWART, J., LINDER, H.P., SCHELPE, E.A. & HALL, A.V. (1982) *Wild Orchids of Southern Africa.* Macmillan, Johannesburg.

Madagascar and adjacent islands

Adansonia (1960–present) Many articles on Malagasy orchids.

CADET, J. (1989). *Les Orchidées de la Réunion.* Nouvelle Impr. Dionysienne, Réunion.

HILLERMAN, F. & HOLST, A. (1986). *An Introduction to the Cultivated Angraecoid Orchids of Madagascar.* Timber Press, Portland, Oregon.

PERRIER DE LA BÂTHIE, H. (1939–41) Orchidacées. In *Flore de Madagascar.* Tananarive.

RICHARD, A. (1828) *Orchidées des Iles de France et Bourbon.* Paris.

SCHLECHTER, R. (1913) Orchidacéae de Madagascar – Orchidacéae Perrieranae Madagascarienses. In *Annales du Musée Colonial de Marseille* ser. 3, 1: 5–59.

THOUARS, A. DU PETIT (1822) *Orchidées des Iles Australes de l'Afrique.* Paris.

North America

American Orchid Society Bulletin (1932–present) Many articles on native species.

CASE, F. (1987) *Orchids of the Western Great Lakes,* 2nd ed. Cranbrook Inst Science Bull. 48.

CORRELL, D.S. (1950) *Native Orchids of North America.* Stanford U.P., California.

LUER, C. (1972) *The Native Orchids of Florida.* New York B.G., New York.

LUER, C. (1975) *The Native Orchids of the United States and Canada.* New York B.G., New York.

Central America

AMES, O. & CORRELL, D.S. (1952–53) *Orchids of Guatemala,* 2 vols. plus suppl. In *Fieldiana* 26(1, 2) & 31(7).

BATEMAN, J. (1837–43) *Orchidaceae of Mexico and Guatemala.*

HAMER, F. (1974). *Las orquideas de El Salvador,* 2 vols. Min. de Educación, San Salvador.

HAMER, F. (1981) *Orchids of El Salvador* vol. 3. Marie Selby B.G., Sarasota, Florida.

HAMER, F. (1982–84) Orchids of Nicaragua, 4 vols. In *Icones Plantarum Tropicarum* 7–9, 11, 12. Marie Selby B.G., Sarasota, Florida.

HAMER, F. (1989) Orchids of Central America A – L. In *Selbyana* 10, Supplement.

Orchid Digest (1937–present) Many articles on Central American orchids.

Orquidea (Mexico) (1971–present) Many relevant articles especially on Mexican orchids.

RODRIGUES CABALLERO, R.L., EMILIA MORA, D., EUGENIA BARAHONA, M. & WILLIAMS, N.H. (1986) *Orquideas de Costa Rica.* Univ. de Costa Rica.

SCHLECHTER, R. (1922–23) Beiträge zur Orchideenkunde von Zentralamerika. In *Fedde, Repertorium Specierum Novarum, Beihefte* 17: 4–95. & 19: 3–307.

WILLIAMS, L.O. (1951) The Orchidaceae of Mexico. In *Ceiba* 2: 1–321.

WILLIAMS, L.O. (1956) An Enumeration of the Orchidaceae of Central America. In *Ceiba* 5: 1–256.

WILLIAMS, L.O. & ALLEN, P.H. (1946–49). Orchidaceae. In R.E. WOODSON & R.W. SCHERY eds. *Flora of Panama.* Missouri Botanical Garden (a new edition (1980) with an updated checklist by R.L. Dressler has been published).

The West Indies

ACUNA GALE, J. (1938) *Catalogo descriptivo de las orquideas Cubanas.* Estacion Experimental Agronomica Boletim 60.

COGNIAUX, C.A. (1909–10) Orchidaceae. In I. Urban, *Symbolae Antillanae* 6.

FAWCETT, W. & RENDLE, A.B. (1910) Orchidaceae. In *Flora of Jamaica* 1. British Museum, London.

GARAY, L. & SWEET, H. (1974) Orchidaceae. In R. HOWARD ed. *Flora of the Lesser Antilles.* Arnold Arboretum, Jamaica Plain, Mass.

SCHULTES, R.E. (1960) *Native Orchids of Trinidad.* Pergamon Press, Oxford.

South America

American Orchid Society Bulletin (1932–present) Many articles on South America orchids.

BARBOSA RODRIGUES, J. (1877–81) *Genera et species orchidearum novarum.* Fleiuss, Rio de Janeiro.

Bradea (1969–present). Many articles on orchids particularly by G. Pabst.

COGNIAUX, C.A. (1893–1906) Orchidaceae, 3 vols. In Martius, *Flora Brasiliensis.* Leipzig.

CORREA, M.N. (1970) Orchidaceae. In *Flora Patagonica* 8.

DODSON, C.A. & P.M. (1980–84) Orchids of Ecuador. In *Icones Plantarum Tropicarum* 1–5, 10. Marie Selby B.G., Sarasota, Florida.

DODSON C.H. & BENNETT, D.E. (1989) Orchids of Peru, 2 fasc. *Icones Plantarum Tropicanum* ser. 2, 1 & 2.

DODSON C.H. & VASQUEZ, R. CH. (1989) Orchids of Bolivia, 2 fasc. In *Icones Plantarum Tropicanum* ser. 2, 3 & 4.

DODSON C.H. & P.M. DE (1989) Orchids of Ecuador, 2 fasc. *I.P.T.* ser. 2, 5 & 6.

DUNSTERVILLE, G.C.K. (1987) *Venezuelan Orchids.* E. Armitano, Caracas.

DUNSTERVILLE, G.C.K. & GARAY, L. (1959–76) *Venezuelan Orchids Illustrated,* 6 vols. André Deutsch, London.

DUNSTERVILLE, G.C.K. & GARAY, L. (1979) *Orchids of Venezuela. An Illustrated Field Guide,* 3 vols. Botanical Museum, Harvard Univ., Cambridge, Mass.

FOLDATS, E. (1969–70) Orchidaceae. In *Flora de Venezuela* 1–5. Inst. Botanico, Caracas.

GARAY, L. (1978) Orchidaceae 1. In G. HARLING & B. SPARRE eds. *Flora of Ecuador.* Univ. Goteborg, Sweden.

HOEHNE, F.C. (1940–53) Orchidaceas. In *Flora Brasilica.* São Paulo.

HOEHNE, F.C. (1949) *Iconographia de Orchidaceas do Brasil.* São Paulo.

LEMÉE, A. (1955) Orchidacées. In *Flore de la Guyane française:* 368–470. Paris.

NAKAO, I. et al. eds. (1983) *Native Orchids of Brazil.* Ass. Orquidofila de São Paulo.

Orchid Digest (1937 – present) Many articles on South American orchids.

Orquidea (1938–73) Many articles on Brazilian orchids.

Orquideologia (1966–present) Many articles on Colombian orchids.

ORTIZ VALDIVIESCO, P. (1976). *Orquideas de Colombia.* Univ. Javeriana, Bogotá.

ORTIZ V., P., MARTINEZ M., A. & MISAS U., G. (1980) *Orquideas ornamentales de Colombia.* CARLOS VALENCIA Ed., Bogota.

PABST, G. & DUNGS, F. (1975–77) *Orchidaceae Brasilienses,* 2 vols. Brücke Verlag, Hildesheim.

SCHLECHTER, R. (1919-29) Several lengthy articles on South American orchids in *Fedde, Repertorium Specierum Novarum, Beihefte.*

SCHLECHTER, R. & HOEHNE, F.C. (1921–22) Contribuições ao Conhecimento das Orquidáceas do Brasil. In *Anexos das Memorias do Instituto de Butantan* and *Arquivos de Botanico do Estado de São Paulo.*

SCHWEINFURTH, C. (1958, 1961, 1970) Orchids of Peru, 2 vols and suppl. In *Fieldiana* 30 & 33.

VASQUEZ CHAVEZ, R. & C.H. DODSON (1982) Orchids of Bolivia. In *Icones Plantarum Tropicarum* 6. MARIE SELBY B.G., Sarasota, Florida.

WERKHOVEN, M.C.M. (1986) *Orchids of Suriname.* Vaco, Paramaribo.

WILLIAMS, L.O. (1980) Las Orquideas del Noroeste Argentino. In *Lilloa* 4.

Glossary

ACRANTHOUS: applied to a sympodium with a main axis of annual portions of successive axes, each beginning with scale-leaves, and ending with an inflorescence.

ACULEATE: prickle-shaped.

ACUMEN: a tapering point.

ACUMINATE: having a gradually tapering point.

ACUTE: distinctly and sharply pointed, but not drawn out.

ADNATE: with one organ united to another.

ADVENTITIOUS: applied to roots which do not arise from the radicle or its subdivisions, but from a node on the stem, etc.

AMPLEXICAUL: clasping the stem.

ANASTOMOSE: when one vein unites with another, the connection forming a reticulation.

ANGULATE: more or less angular.

ANTHER: that part of the stamen in which the pollen is produced.

ANTHESIS: that period between the opening of the bud and the withering of the stigma or stamens.

ANTICOUS: the fore-part, i.e. that most remote or turned away from the axis.

ANTROSE: turned backwards, directed upwards.

APHYLLOUS: without leaves.

APICAL (inflorescence): borne at the top of the stem or pseudobulb.

APICULATE: furnished with a short and sharp, but not stiff, point.

APICULE: a short and sharp, but not stiff, point.

APPLANATE: flattened out or horizontally expanded.

APPRESSED: lying flat for the whole length of the organ.

ARCUATE: curved like a bow.

ARISTATE: awned.

AURICLE: a small lobe or ear.

AXILLARY (inflorescence): borne in the axil, i.e. the junction between petiole and stem.

BASAL (inflorescence): at the base of an organ or part such as the stem or pseudobulb.

BIFID: divided into 2 shallow segments, usually at the apex.

BIFURCATE: forked.

BRACT: a frequently leaf-like organ (often very reduced or absent) bearing a flower, inflorescence or partial inflorescence in its axil.

BULLATE: blistered or puckered.

BURSICLE: The pouch-like expansion of the stigma into which the caudicle of the pollinarium is inserted.

CADUCOUS: falling off early.

CAESPITOSE: tufted.

CALCEIFORM or CALCEOLATE: slipper-shaped.

CALLUS: a thickened area on the labellum.

CAMPANULATE or CAMPANULIFORM: bell-shaped.

CANALICULATE: channelled, with a longitudinal groove.

CAPILLARY (spur): slender, hair-like.

CAPITATE: like a pin-head, or knols.

CARINATE: keeled.

CATAPHYLL: the early leaf-forms of a plant or shoot, as cotyledons, bud-scales, rhizome-scales, etc.

CAUDATE: tailed.

CAUDICLE: the lower stalk-like part of a pollinium, attaching the pollen-masses to the sticky disc or viscidium.

CAULESCENT: becoming stalked, where the stalk is clearly apparent.

CAULINE: borne on the stem.

CERACEOUS or CEREOUS: waxy.

CHAFFY: furnished with small membranous scales.

CHARTACEOUS: papery.

CILIATE: fringed with hairs.

CLAVATE: club-shaped, thickened towards the apex.

CLAW: the conspicuously narrowed and attenuate base of an organ.

CLINANDRIUM: the anther-bed, that part of the column in which the anther is concealed.

COCHLEATE: shell-shaped.

COLUMN: an advanced structure composed of a continuation of the flower-stalk, together with the upper part of the female reproductive organ (pistil) and the lower part of the male reproductive organ (stamen).

COMPLANATE: flattened, compressed.

CONDUPLICATE: folded face to face.

CONNATE: united, congenitally or subsequently.

CONNIVENT: coming into contact or converging.

CORDATE: heart-shaped.

CORIACEOUS: leathery.

COROLLA: the inner whorl of the flower.

CORYMBOSE (inflorescence): ± flat-topped.

CRENATE: scalloped, toothed with crenatures.

CRENULATE: crenate, but the toothing themselves small.

CRISPATE: curled.

CRISTATE: crested.

CUCULLATE: hooded or hood-shaped.

CUNEATE or CUNEIFORM: wedge-shaped.

CUSPIDATE: tipped with a sharp, rigid point.

CYMBIFORM: boat-shaped.

CYMOSE: a broad divaricately branched inflorescence, of determinate or centrifugal type.

DECURRENT: running down, as when leaves are prolonged beyond their insertion, and thus run down the stem.

DEFLEXED: bent outwards.

DENTATE: toothed.

DENTICULATE: minutely toothed.

DIAPHANOUS: permitting the light to shine through.

DISC: the face of any organ.

DISTICHOUS: leaves or flowers borne in spikelets alternating in 2 opposite ranks.

DIVARICATE: extremely divergent.

ECHINATE: prickly.

ELLIPTIC: ellipse-shaped, oblong with regularly rounded ends.

EMARGINATE: notched, usually at the apex.

ENSIFORM: sword-shaped.

ENTIRE: simple and with smooth margins.

EPICHILE: the terminal part of the lip when it is distant from the basal portion.

EPIPHYTE: a plant growing on another plant, but not parasitic.

EROSE: bitten or gnawed.

EXSERT: protrude beyond.

FALCATE: sickle-shaped.

FARINOSE: mealy.

FASCICLE: a small bunch or bundle.

FASCICULATE: clustered or bundled.

FIBRILLAE: small fibres.

FILIFORM: thread-like.

FIMBRIATE: fringed.

FLABELLATE: fan-shaped.

FLEXUOSE: bent alternately in opposite directions.

FORCIPATE: forked like pincers.

FRACTIFLEX: zigzag.

FURFURACEOUS: scurfy, having soft scales.

FUSIFORM: spindle-shaped.

GALEATE: helmet-shaped.
GEMINATE: paired.
GENICULATE: abruptly bent like a knee-joint.
GIBBOUS: pouched, more convex in one place than another.
GLABROUS: hairless.
GLAUCOUS: covered with a bluish-grey or sea-green bloom.
GLOBOSE: ± spherical.
GYROSE: curved backward and forward in turn.

HAMATE: hooked at the tip.
HASTATE: spear-or halbert-shaped, with the basal lobes turned outward.
HETERANTHOUS: an apical inflorescence produced on a separate shoot which does not develop to produce a pseudobulb and leaves.
HIPPOCREPIFORM: horseshoe-shaped.
HIRSUTE: hairy.
HISPID: bristly.
HYALINE: colourless or translucent.
HYPOCHILE: the basal portion of the lip.
HYSTERANTHOUS: used of an apical inflorescence produced after the pseudobulbs and leaves have developed.

IMBRICATE: overlapping.
INCUMBENT: lying on or against.
INFLORESCENCE: the disposition of the flowers on the floral axis or the flowers, bracts and floral axis in toto.

LABELLUM: a lip, used here for the enlarged, often highly modified abaxial petal of the orchid flower.
LACERATE: torn, or irregularly cleft.
LACINIATE: deeply slashed into narrow divisions.
LAMELLA: a membrane or septum.
LANCEOLATE: narrow, tapering to each end, lance-shaped.
LATERAL (inflorescence): borne on or near the side of pseudobulb or stem, usually in the axils of the bracts or leaves.
LAXLY: loose, distant.
LIGULATE or LINGUIFORM: tongue or strap-shaped.
LIGULE: a tongue-like outgrowth.
LINEAR: at least 12 times longer than broad, with the sides ± parallel.
LIP: a modified abaxial petal, the labellum.
LITHOPHYTIC: growing upon stones and rocks.
LORATE: thong- or strap-shaped.
LUNATE: half-moon-shaped.

MAMMILLATE: teat-shaped.
MENTUM: a chin-like projection formed by the sepals and extended column-foot.
MESOCHILE: the intermediate portion of the lip when divided into three portions.

MONOPODIAL: growth which continues from a terminal bud from season to season.
MUCRO: a sharp terminal point.
MUCRONATE: possessing a mucro.
MULTICOSTATE: many-ribbed.
MURICATE: rough, with short and hard tubercular excrescences.
MYCORRHIZAL: of roots having a symbiotic relationship with certain fungi.

NAVICULAR: boat-shaped.
NERVOSE: prominently nerved.
NODE: that part of a stem which normally has a leaf or a whorl of leaves.
NON-RESUPINATE: of a flower that is not turned upside down.

OBCUNEATE: inversely wedge-shaped.
OBLANCEOLATE: tapering towards the base more than towards the apex.
OBLONG: much longer than broad, with nearly parallel sides.
OBOVATE: inversely ovate.
OBSCURE: dark or dingy in tint; uncertain in affinity or distinctiveness; hidden.
OBTUSE: blunt or rounded at the apex.
OVATE: egg-shaped, broader at the base.

PALEACEOUS: chaffy.
PANDURATE: fiddle-shaped.
PANICLE: a much-branched inflorescence.
PAPILLOSE: covered with soft superficial glands or protuberances, i.e. papillae.
PAPYRACEOUS: papery.
PECTINATE: combed.
PEDICEL: the stalk of a single flower in an inflorescence.
PEDUNCLE: the stalk bearing an inflorescence or solitary flower.
PELLUCID: wholly or partially transparent.
PELTATE: disc-shaped, the stalk arising from the under-surface.
PENDENT: hanging.
PERIANTH: the outer, sterile whorls of a flower, often differentiated into calyx and corolla.
PILOSE: softly hairy.
PLICATE: folded in many pleats.
PLURICOSTATE: many ribbed.
PLURISULCATE: many grooved or furrowed.
POLLINARIUM: the male reproductive system of an orchid.
POLLINIA: pollen-masses.
PORATE: set with pores.
PORRECT: directed outward and forward.
PRAEMORSE: bitten off at the apex.
PROTERANTHOUS: of an apical inflorescence produced before the pseudobulbs and leaves on the same shoot.
PROTOCORM: the embryo before primary differentiation is complete.
PSEUDOBULB: a swollen aerial stem.

PUBERULENT: slightly hairy.
PUBESCENT: softly hairy or downy.
PYRIFORM: pear-shaped.

QUADRATE: four-cornered, square.

RACEME: a single, elongate, indeterminate inflorescence with pedicellate flowers.
RECLINATE: turned or bent downward.
RECURVED: curved backward or downward.
REFLEXED: abruptly bent or turned downward or backward.
RENIFORM: kidney-shaped.
REPENT: prostrate and rooting.
RESUPINATE: upside-down, or apparently so.
RETICULATE: netted.
RETRORSE: directed backward or downward.
RETUSE: shallowly notched at a rounded apex.
REVOLUTE: rolled back from the margin.
RHACHIS: the axis of an inflorescence or compound leaf.
RHIZOME: underground stem bearing scale leaves and adventitious roots.
ROSTELLUM: the often beak-like sterile third stigma lying between the functional stigmas and stamen.
ROSTRATE: beaked.
ROSULATE: in rosettes.
ROTUND: rounded in outline.
RUGOSE: wrinkled.
RUGULOSE: somewhat wrinkled.
RUPICOLOUS: growing on or amongst rocks.

SACCATE: with a conspicuous hollow swelling.
SAGITTATE: arrow-head-shaped.
SAPROPHYTE: a plant which obtains its food materials by absorption of complex organic chemicals from the soil; often without chlorophyll.
SCANDENT: climbing.
SCAPE: a leafless peduncle arising directly from a rosette of basal leaves.
SCARIOUS: thin, dry and membranous.
SCORPIOID: a coiled, determinate inflorescence.
SECUND: directed to one side only.
SEPTATE: divided by partitions.
SEPTUM: a partition.
SERRATE: with sharp, ± regular teeth, like a saw.
SESSILE: not stalked.
SETACEOUS: thread- or bristle-like.
SETOSE: bristly.
SINUATE: with a deep wavy margin.
SPATHACEOUS: bearing a spathe.
SPATHE: a large bract sheathing an inflorescence.
SPATHULATE: oblong and attenuated at the base, like a spatula.
SPICATE: like a spike, disposed in a spike.

SPUR: a long, usually nectar-containing, tubular projection of a perianth-segment, commonly the lip.

STAMINODE: a sterile stamen, often modified in shape and size.

STELIDIA: column teeth.

STELLATE: star-shaped.

STIGMA: the receptive part(s) of the gynoecium, i.e. female sex organs, on which the pollen germinates.

STIPE (pl. STIPITES): the stalk-like support of an organ, e.g. pollinium.

STRIGOSE: beset with sharp-pointed appressed straight and stiff hairs or bristles; hispid.

SUBCYLINDRIC: half cylindric.

SUBEQUITANT (leaves): half folded sharply inwards from the midrib.

SUBSPREADING: half or somewhat having a gradually outward direction.

SUBQUADRATE: half square, somewhat square.

SUBSIMILAR: somewhat similar.

SUBULATE: awl-shaped.

SUBTEND: to extend under, or be opposite to.

SULCATE: grooved or furrowed.

SUPERPOSED: one above the other.

SYMPODIAL: growth in which each new shoot is determinate and terminates in a potential inflorescence or solitary flower.

SYNANTHOUS: when pseudobulb, leaves and apical inflorescence are produced together.

SYNSEPALUM: two sepals united together, e.g. in *Paphiopedilum*.

TERETE: circular in transverse section, cylindric and usually tapering.

TESSELLATE: chequered.

TRIDENTATE: three-toothed.

TRIFID: three-cleft.

TRIQUETROUS: three-edged.

TRULLATE: trowel-shaped.

TRUNCATE: ending abruptly, as though broken off.

TUBER: a thickened and short subterranean branch, beset with buds or 'eyes'.

UMBEL: a usually flat-topped inflorescence in which the pedicels arise from the same point on the peduncle.

UNCIFORM: hook-shaped.

UNCINATE: hooked.

UNDULATE: waved.

UNGUICULATE: contracted at the base into a claw.

VALVATE: margins of sepals or petals not overlapping.

VELAMEN: a parchment-like sheath or layer of spiral-coated air-cells on the root which may act as protective insulation.

VENOSE: having veins.

VENTRICOSE: swollen or inflated on one side.

VERRUCOSE: warty.

VISCIDIUM: a sticky disc or plate joined to the pollinium, enabling it to adhere to an insect's body during cross-fertilisation.

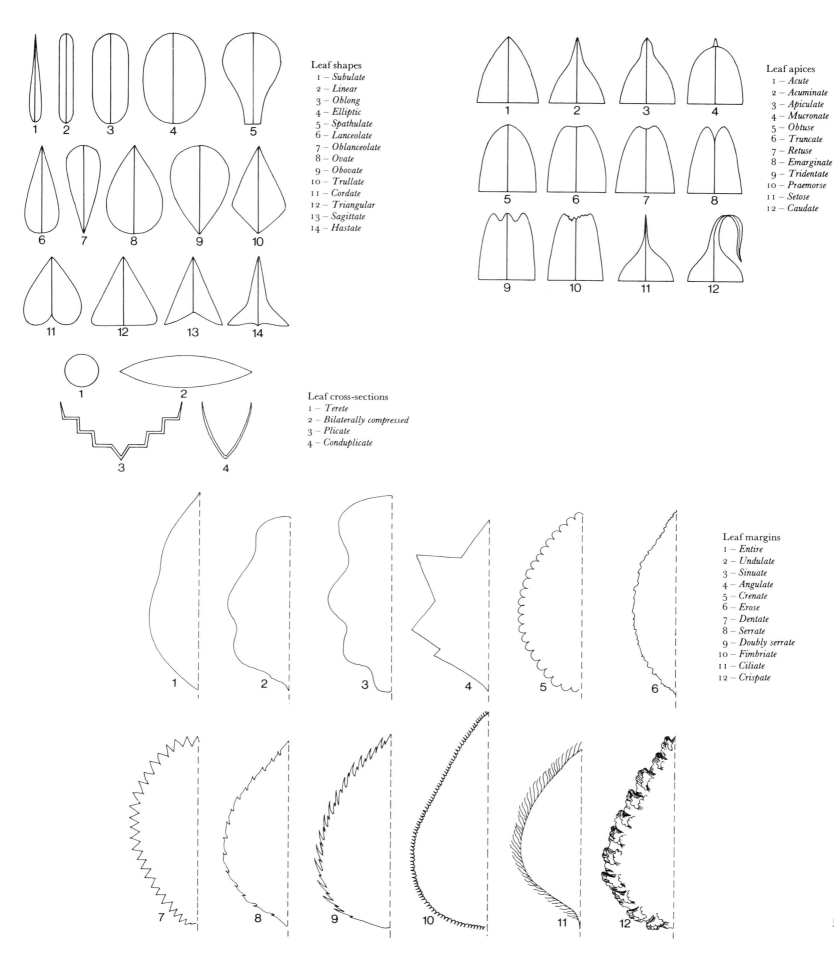

Leaf shapes
1 – *Subulate*
2 – *Linear*
3 – *Oblong*
4 – *Elliptic*
5 – *Spathulate*
6 – *Lanceolate*
7 – *Oblanceolate*
8 – *Ovate*
9 – *Obovate*
10 – *Trullate*
11 – *Cordate*
12 – *Triangular*
13 – *Sagittate*
14 – *Hastate*

Leaf apices
1 – *Acute*
2 – *Acuminate*
3 – *Apiculate*
4 – *Mucronate*
5 – *Obtuse*
6 – *Truncate*
7 – *Retuse*
8 – *Emarginate*
9 – *Tridentate*
10 – *Praemorse*
11 – *Setose*
12 – *Caudate*

Leaf cross-sections
1 – *Terete*
2 – *Bilaterally compressed*
3 – *Plicate*
4 – *Conduplicate*

Leaf margins
1 – *Entire*
2 – *Undulate*
3 – *Sinuate*
4 – *Angulate*
5 – *Crenate*
6 – *Erose*
7 – *Dentate*
8 – *Serrate*
9 – *Doubly serrate*
10 – *Fimbriate*
11 – *Ciliate*
12 – *Crispate*

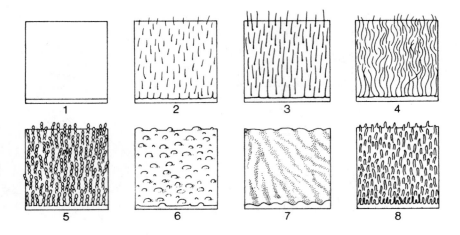

Surface textures (all much magnified)
1 – *Glabrous*
2 – *Pilose*
3 – *Hirsute*
4 – *Woolly*
5 – *Farinose*
6 – *Verrucose*
7 – *Rugulose*
8 – *Papillose*

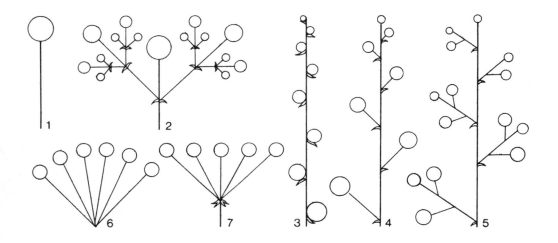

Inflorescence types
1 – *Single-flowered*
2 – *Cymose*
3 – *Spicate*
4 – *Racemose*
5 – *Paniculate*
6 – *Fasciculate*
7 – *Umbellate*

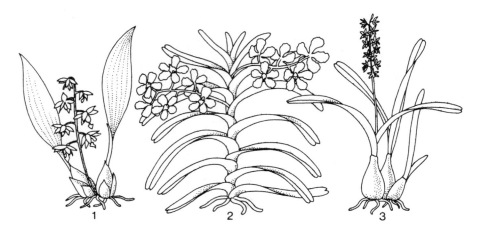

Inflorescence position
1 – Basal, *Houlletia*
2 – Axillary, *Vanda*
3 – Apical, *Encyclia*

Index of Synonyms

pentandra **Dilochia wallichii**
wallichii **Dilochia wallichii**
Asarca dasypogon **Chloraea crispa**
pogonata **Chloraea crispa**
Ascocentrum hendersonianum **Dyakia hendersoniana**
micranthum **Smitinandia micrantha**
Ascotainia hookeriana **Tainia hookeriana**
Aviceps **Satyrium**

Barombia **Aerangis**
gracillima **Aerangis gracillima**
Bartholina pectinata **Bartholina burmanniana**
Batemannia burtii **Huntleya meleagris**
fimbriata **Mendoncella fimbriata**
grandiflora **Mendoncella grandiflora**
meleagris **Huntleya meleagris**
peruviana **Batemannia colleyi**
petronia **Batemannia colleyi**
yauaperyensis **Batemannia colleyi**
Bathiea perrieri **Neobathiea perrieri**
Beclardia elata **Cryptopus elatus**
Bifrenaria aurantiaca **Rudolfiella aurantiaca**
hadwenii **Scuticaria hadwenii**
wageneri **Teuscheria wageneri**
Birchea teretifolia **Luisia birchea**
Blephariglottis **Platanthera**
psycodes **Platanthera psycodes**
Bletia albida **Laelia albida**
anceps **Laelia anceps**
angustata **Spathoglottis plicata**
autumnalis **Laelia anceps**
capitata **Elleanthus capitatus**
cinnabarina **Laelia cinnabarina**
crispa **Laelia crispa**
digbyana **Rhyncholaelia digbyana**
gebina **Bletilla striata**
glauca **Rhyncholaelia glauca**
gloriosa **Schomburgkia gloriosa**
longipes **Laelia longipes**
lundii **Laelia lundii**
pumila **Laelia pumila**
rodriguesii **Bletia catenulata**
sanguinea **Bletia catenulata**
sherrattiana **Bletia catenulata**
tuberculosa **Phaius tuberculosus**
undulata **Schomburgkia undulata**
watsonii **Bletia catenulata**
Bletia graminifolia **Arundina graminifolia**
Bletia striata **Bletilla striata**
Bollea pulvinaris **Bollea coelestis**
wendlandiana **Cochleanthes aromatica**
Bolusiella imbricata **Bolusiella maudiae**
Brachtia verruculifera **Brachtia andina**
Brassavola chacoensis **Brassavola cebolleta**
cuspidata **Brassavola cucullata**
digbyana **Rhyncholaelia digbyana**
fragans **Brassavola tuberculata**
gibbiana **Brassavola tuberculata**
glauca **Rhyncholaelia glauca**
perrinii **Brassavola tuberculata**
rhopalorrhachis **Brassavola nodosa**
venosa **Brassavola nodosa**
Brassia angusta **Brassia lawrenceana**
aristata **Brassia verrucosa**
brachiata **Brassia verrucosa**
cinnabarina **Ada aurantiaca**
cinnamomea **Ada keiliana**

cochleata **Brassia lawrenceana**
coryandra **Brassia verrucosa**
glumacea **Ada glumacea**
guttata **Brassia maculata**
havanensis **Ada keiliana**
imbricata **Ada glumacea**
keiliana **Ada keiliana**
lawrenceana **Brassia arcuigera**
lewisii **Brassia caudata**
longiloba **Brassia verrucosa**
longissima **Brassia arcuigera**
oestlundiana **Lemboglossum maculatum**
ophioglossoides **Brassia verrucosa**
wrayae **Brassia maculata**
Bromheadia palustris **Bromheadia finlaysoniana**
sylvestris **Bromheadia finlaysoniana**
Broughtonia **Otochilus**
coccinea **Broughtonia sanguinea**
domingensis **Laeliopsis domingensis**
grandiflora **Maxillaria grandiflora**
lilacina **Cattleyopsis lindenii**
Bulbophyllum breviscapum **Bulbophyllum lasiochilum**
careyanum **Bulbophyllum crassipes**
clavigerum **Bulbophyllum longiflorum**
godseffianum **Bulbophyllum dearei**
leptorhachis **Bulbophyllum falcatum**
lichenastrum **Dendrobium lichenastrum**
occidentale **Encyclia polybulbon**
paleaceum **Sunipia cirrhata**
pictum **Trias picta**
pumilum **Genyorchis pumila**
taylori **Cadetia taylori**
Burlingtonia amoena **Rodriguezia decora**
batemannii **Rodriguezia batemannii**
candida **Rodriguezia candida**
decora **Rodriguezia decora**
rubescens **Rodriguezia batemannii**

Caladenia macrophylla **Caladenia menziesii**
Calanthe amamiana **Calanthe discolor**
corymbosa **Calanthe sylvatica**
cosma **Calanthe triplicata**
curculigodes **Calanthe pulchra**
furcata **Calanthe triplicata**
hosseusiana **Calanthe cardiglossa**
lurida **Calanthe discolor**
natalensis **Calanthe sylvatica**
perrottielii **Calanthe triplicata**
phajoides **Calanthe angustifolia**
succedoanea **Calanthe cardiglossa**
sumatrana **Calanthe ceciliae**
tokunoshimensis **Calanthe discolor**
veratrifolia **Calanthe triplicata**
volkensii **Calanthe sylvatica**
warpurii **Calanthe sylvatica**
wrayi **Calanthe ceciliae**
Callista aemula **Dendrobium aemulum**
aggregata **Dendrobium lindleyi**
amabilis **Dendrobium hercoglossum**
beckleri **Dendrobium schoeninum**
gracilicaulis **Dendrobium gracilicaule**
hercoglossa **Dendrobium hercoglossum**
kingiana **Dendrobium jonesii**
linguiformis **Dendrobium linguiforme**
rigida **Dendrobium rigidum**
smillieae **Dendrobium smillieae**
striolata **Dendrobium striolatum**

Calopogon pulchellus **Calopogon tuberosus**
Calypso borealis **Calypso bulbosa**
japonica **Dactylostalix ringens**
occidentalis **Calypso bulbosa**
Camaridium **Maxillaria**
Campylocentrum panamense **Campylocentrum micranthum**
peniculus **Campylocentrum micranthum**
Capanemia juergensenii **Capanemia superflua**
uliginosa **Capanemia superflua**
Catasetum baraguinianum **Catasetum saccatum**
bungerothii **Catasetum pileatum**
ciliatum **Catasetum discolor**
claesianum **Catasetum discolor**
claveringii **Catasetum macrocarpum**
cogniauxii **Catasetum fimbriatum**
crinitum **Catasetum barbatum**
cruciatum **Catas tum saccatum**
eburneum **Dressleria dilecta**
floribundum **Catasetum macrocarpum**
gardneri **Catasetum discolor**
garnettianum **Catasetum barbatum**
heteranthum **Catasetum gnomus**
histrio **Catasetum saccatum**
incurvum **Catasetum saccatum**
linguiferum **Catasetum macrocarpum**
macrocarpum **Catasetum barbatum**
maculatum **Catasetum integerrimum**
oerstedii **Catasetum maculatum**
ornithorrhynchum **Catasetum fimbriatum**
pflanzii **Catasetum fimbriatum**
polydactylon **Catasetum barbatum**
proboscideum **Catasetum barbatum**
roseo-album **Catasetum discolor**
russellianum **Clowesia russelliana**
secundum **Catasetum saccatum**
sodiroi **Catasetum platyglossum**
spinosum **Catasetum barbatum**
stupendum **Catasetum saccatum**
suave **Dressleria dilecta**
tricolor **Catasetum macrocarpum**
tridentatum **Catasetum macrocarpum**
wredeanum **Catasetum fimbriatum**
Cattleya amabilis **Cattleya intermedia**
amethystina **Cattleya intermedia**
autumnalis **Cattleya bowringiana**
bogotensis **Cattleya trianaei**
brysiana **Laelia purpurata**
bulbosa **Cattleya walkeriana**
casperiana **Laelia purpurata**
cernua **Sophronitis cernua**
citrina **Encyclia citrina**
coccinea **Sophronitis coccinea**
crispa **Laelia crispa**
dichotoma **Sobralia dichotoma**
domingensis **Laeliopsis domingensis**
eliator **Cattleya guttata**
flavida **Cattleya luteola**
fulva **Cattleya forbesii**
gigas **Cattleya warscewiczii**
grandiflora **Sophronitis coccinea**
guttata **Cattleya leopoldii**
insopetala **Cattleya forbesii**
lemoniana **Cattleya labiata**
lutea **Laelia fulva**
marginata **Laelia pumila**
maritima **Cattleya intermedia**

mcmorlandii **Cattleya eldorado**
meyeri **Cattleya luteola**
ovata **Cattleya intermedia**
patinii **Cattleya deckeri**
pauper **Cattleya forbesii**
pinelii **Laelia pumila**
pumila **Laelia pumila**
quadricolor **Cattleya trianaei**
skinneri **Cattleya bowringiana, Cattleya deckeri**
sulphurea **Cattleya luteola**
superbiens **Schomburgkia superbiens**
tigrina **Cattleya guttata**
vestalis **Cattleya forbesii**
violacea **Sophronitella violacea**
virginalis **Cattleya eldorado**
Cattleyopsis delicatula **Cattleyopsis lindenii**
Caucaea obscura **Caucaea radiata**
Centrosis aubertii **Calanthe sylvatica**
sylvatica **Calanthe sylvatica**
Cephalangraecum **Ancistrorhynchus**
Cephalantheropsis longipes **Cephalantheropsis gracilis**
Ceratochilus oculatus **Stanhopea oculata**
Ceratostylis latipetala **Ceratostylis retisquama**
rubra **Ceratostylis retisquama**
Chaetocephala **Myoxanthus**
Chelonanthera **Pholidota**
speciosa **Coelogyne speciosa**
sulphurea **Chelonistele sulphurea**
Chelonistele cuneata **Chelonistele sulphurea**
perakensis **Chelonistele sulphurea**
pusilla **Chelonistele sulphurea**
Chloidia **Corymborkis**
Chloraea dasypogon **Chloraea crispa**
pogonata **Chloraea crispa**
Chondrorhyncha aromatica **Cochleanthes aromatica**
discolor **Cochleanthes discolor**
lojae **Kefersteinia lojae**
Chrysocycnis trigonidii **Chrysocycnis schlimii**
Chysis aurea **Chysis bractescens**
Cirrhaea loddigesii **Cirrhaea dependens**
tristis **Cirrhaea dependens**
viridipurpurea **Cirrhaea dependens**
warreana **Cirrhaea dependens**
Cirrhopetalum **Bulbophyllum**
breviscapum **Bulbophyllum lasiochilum**
longiflorum **Bulbophyllum longiflorum**
longissimum **Bulbophyllum longissimum**
mastersianum **Bulbophyllum mastersianum**
medusae **Bulbophyllum medusae**
ornatissimum **Bulbophyllum ornatissimum**
roxburghii **Bulbophyllum roxburghii**
thouarsii **Bulbophyllum longiflorum**
umbellatum **Bulbophyllum longiflorum**
Cleisostoma dawsoniana **Staurochilus dawsonianus**
cryptochilum **Ascoglossum calopterum**
micranthum **Smitinandia micrantha**
poilanei **Smitinandia micrantha**
spathulatum **Robiquetia spathulata**
spicatum **Robiquetia spathulata**
tixieri **Smitinandia micrantha**
Clynhymenia **Cryptarrhena**
pallidiflora **Cryptarrhena lunata**
Cochleanthes trinitatis **Chaubardia surinamensis**
Cochlioda sanguinea **Symphyglossum sanguineum**
Coelandria smillieae **Dendrobium smillieae**
Coelia baueriana **Coelia triptera**

bella **Bothriochilus bellus**
glacialis **Coelia triptera**
Coelogyne beyrodtiana **Chelonistele sulphurea**
brunnea **Coelogyne fuscescens**
bulbocodioides **Pleione bulbocodioides**
convallariae **Pholidota convallariae**
coronaria **Eria coronaria**
dayana **Coelogyne massangeana**
decipiens **Chelonistele sulphurea**
delavayi **Pleione bulbocodioides**
densiflora **Coelogyne massangeana**
henryi **Pleione bulbocodioides**
hookeriana **Pleione hookeriana**
huettneriana **Coelogyne lactea**
humilis **Pleione humilis**
laotica **Coelogyne fimbriata**
leungiana **Coelogyne fimbriata**
maculata **Pleione maculata**
ochracea **Coelogyne nitida**
porrecta **Otochilus porrectus**
praecox **Pleione praecox**
reichenbachiana **Pleione praecox**
tomentosa **Coelogyne massangeana**
tripicatula **Coelogyne ovalis**
wallichiana **Pleione praecox**
Colax aromaticus **Lycaste aromatica**
jugosus **Pabstia jugosa**
Comparettia rosea **Comparettia falcata**
Cordyla discolor **Nervilia plicata**
Corybas dilatatus **Corybas diemenicus**
Corymbis disticha **Corymborkis veratrifolia**
veratrifolia **Corymborkis veratrifolia**
Corymborchis assamica **Corymborkis veratrifolia**
rhytidocarpa **Corymborkis veratrifolia**
Corysanthes **Corybas**
diemenica **Corybas diemenicus**
dilatatus **Corybas diemenicus**
Cranichis bradei **Cranichis muscosa**
luteola **Polystachya concreta**
stachyodes **Prescottia plantaginifolia**
Cremastra triloba **Cremastra appendiculata**
wallichiana **Cremastra appendiculata**
Crinonia **Pholidota**
Crybe **Bletia**
Cryptarrhena brasiliensis **Cryptarrhena lunata**
kegelii **Cryptarrhena lunata**
unguiculata **Cryptarrhena lunata**
Cryptochilus luteus **Cryptarrhena sanguineus**
Cryptophoranthus alvaroi **Zootrophion atropurpureum**
atropurpureus **Zootrophion atropurpureum**
Cryptosaccus scriptus **Leochilus scriptus**
Cryptostylis longifolia **Cryptostylis subulata**
stenochila **Cryptostylis arachnites**
Cyathoglottis candida **Sobralia candida**
Cyclopogon ovafolium **Cyclopogon elatus**
Cycnoches barbatum **Polycycnis barbata**
cucullata **Cycnoches loddigesii**
lindleyi **Lueddemannia pescatorei**
pescatorei **Lueddemannia pescatorei**
Cymbidiella humblotii **Cymbidiella falcigera**
rhodochila **Cymbidiella pardalina**
Cymbidium alatum **Thecostele alata**
albuciflorum **Cymbidium madidum**
aloifolium **Cymbidium finlaysonianum**
amabile **Phalaenopsis amabilis**
andersonii **Cyrtopodium andersonii**
appendiculatum **Cremastra appendiculata**

aspidistrifolium **Cymbidium lancifolium**
bambusifolium **Arundina graminifolia**
crassifolium **Cymbidium aloifolium**
crispatum **Laelia crispata**
dependens **Cirrhaea dependens**
erectum **Cymbidium aloifolium**
gibsonii **Cymbidium lancifolium**
giganteum **Cymbidium lowianum**
gomphocarpum **Cymbidium suave**
grandiflorum **Cymbidium hookerianum**
hillii **Cymbidium canaliculatum**
humblotti **Cymbidiella falcigera**
hyacinthinum **Bletilla striata**
iridifolium **Cymbidium madidum**
javanicum **Cymbidium lancifolium**
leai **Cymbidium madidum**
mannii **Cymbidium aloifolium**
moschatum **Dendrobium moschatum**
papuanum **Cymbidium lancifolium**
pumilum **Cymbidium floribundum**
queenianum **Cymbidium madidum**
rhodochilum **Cymbidiella pardalina**
rigidum **Tetramicra canaliculata**
sikkimense **Cymbidium devonianum**
sparkesii **Cymbidium canaliculatum**
syringodorum **Cymbidium eburneum**
tenuifolium **Luisia teretifolia**
tessellatum **Vanda tessellata**
tesselloides **Vanda tessellata**
tripterum **Coelia triptera**
triste **Luisia teretifolia**
umbellatum **Bulbophyllum longiflorum**
violaceum **Cattleya violacea**
Cymbiglossum **Lemboglossum**
Cynorkis purpurascens **Cynorkis lowiana**
Cypripedium appletonianum **Paphiopedilum appletonianum**
argus **Paphiopedilum argus**
assurgens **Cypripedium calceolus**
aureum **Cypripedium calceolus**
barbatum **Paphiopedilum barbatum**
bellatulum **Paphiopedilum bellatulum**
bulbosum **Calypso bulbosa**
bullenianum **Paphiopedilum bullenianum**
callosum **Paphiopedilum callosum**
caricinum **Phragmipedium caricinum**
caudatum **Phragmipedium caudatum**
chamberlainianum **Paphiopedilum victoriaregina**
charlesworthii **Paphiopedilum charlesworthii**
ciliolare **Paphiopedilum ciliolare**
concolor **Paphiopedilum concolor**
druryi **Paphiopedilum druryi**
exul **Paphiopedilum exul**
fairrieanum **Paphiopedilum fairrieanum**
flavescens **Cypripedium calceolus**
furcatum **Cypripedium calceolus**
glanduliferum **Paphiopedilum glanduliferum**
godefroyae **Paphiopedilum godefroyae**
haynaldianum **Paphiopedilum haynaldianum**
hirsutum **Cypripedium reginae**
hirsutissimum **Paphiopedilum hirsutissimum**
humboldtii **Phragmipedium caudatum**
humile **Cypripedium reginae**
insigne **Paphiopedilum insigne**
lawrenceanum **Paphiopedilum lawrenceanum**
lowii **Paphiopedilum lowii**
luteum **Cypripedium calceolus**

mastersianum **Paphiopedilum mastersianum**
niveum **Paphiopedilum niveum**
palmifolium **Selenipedium palmifolium**
parishii **Paphiopedilum parishii**
parviflorum **Cypripedium calceolus**
praestans **Paphiopedilum glanduliferum**
pubescens **Cypripedium calceolus**
rothschildianum **Paphiopedilum rothschildianum**
schlimii **Phragmipedium schlimii**
schomburgkianum **Phragmipedium klotzscheanum**
spicerianum **Paphiopedilum spicerianum**
stonei **Paphiopedilum stonei**
superbiens **Paphiopedilum superbiens**
tonsum **Paphiopedilum tonsum**
venustum **Paphiopedilum venustum**
villosum **Paphiopedilum villosum**
warscewizianum **Phragmipedium caudatum**
Cyrotopera **Eulophia**
gigantea **Eulophia speciosa**
Cyrtochilum bictoniense **Lemboglossum bictoniense**
citrinum **Oncidium concolor**
flexuosum **Oncidium cimiciferum**
stellatum **Miltonia flavescens**
Cyrtoglottis **Mormolyca**
Cyrtopodium elegans **Tetramicra canaliculata**

Dactylorchis **Dactylorhiza**
Dendrobium acrobaticum **Dendrobium capillipes**
aggregatum **Dendrobium lindleyi**
alboviride **Dendrobium scabrilingue**
amoenum **Dendrobium aphyllum**
andersonii **Dendrobium draconis**
atractodes **Dendrobium heterocarpum**
aureum **Dendrobium heterocarpum**
beckleri **Dendrobium schoeninum**
boxallii **Dendrobium gratiosissimum**
brachycarpum **Aerangis brachycarpa**
braianense **Dendrobium capillipes**
brisbanense **Dendrobium gracilicaule**
bullerianum **Dendrobium gratiosissimum**
bursigerum **Dendrobium secundum**
calceolaria **Dendrobium moschatum**
cariniferum **Dendrobium williamsonii**
catenatum **Dendrobium moniliforme**
cebolleta **Oncidium cebolleta**
ciliatum **Dendrobium delacourii**
coeleste **Dendrobium victoriae-reginae**
coelogyne **Epigeneium coelogyne**
comatum **Flickingeria comata**
crassinode **Dendrobium pendulum**
cultriforme **Polystachya cultriformis**
cupreum **Dendrobium moschatum**
cymbidioides **Epigeneium cymbidioides**
dalhousieanum **Dendrobium pulchellum**
densiflorum **Dendrobium farmeri**
elongatum **Dendrobium gracilicaule**
fellowsii **Dendrobium gracilicaule**
flexuosum **Dendrobium longicornu**
foelschei **Dendrobium canaliculatum**
fredianum **Dendrobium longicornu**
fusiform **Dendrobium jonesii**
fusiforme **Dendrobium jonesii**
galactanthum **Dendrobium scabrilingue**
grandiflorum **Maxillaria grandiflora**
hanburyanum **Dendrobium lituiflorum**
harrisoniae **Bifrenaria harrisoniae**
hedyosmum **Dendrobium scabrilingue**
henshallii **Dendrobium transparens**

heterostigma **Dendrobium secundum**
hillii **Dendrobium speciosum**
hirsutum **Dendrobium longicornu**
hispidum **Cadetia taylori**
hollrungii **Dendrobium smillieae**
imthurnii **Dendrobium gouldii**
infundibulum **Dendrobium formosum**
jamesianum **Dendrobium infundibulum**
japonicum **Dendrobium moniliforme**
javanicum **Eria javanica**
johansoniae **Dendrobium johnsoniae**
lawanum **Dendrobium crepidatum**
leopardinum **Bulbophyllum leopardinum**
leucorhodum **Dendrobium anosmum**
lindleyanum **Dendrobium nobile**
macfarlanei **Dendrobium johnsoniae**
macranthum **Dendrobium anosmum**
macrophyllum **Dendrobium anosmum**
margaritaceum **Dendrobium christyanum**
marginatum **Epigeneium cymbidioides**
melanophthalmum **Dendrobium pendulum**
micranthum **Dendrobium aloefolium**
milliganii **Dendrobium striolatum**
monile **Dendrobium moniliforme**
monodon **Dendrobium johnsoniae**
moulmeinense **Dendrobium dixanthum**
niveum **Dendrobium johnsoniae**
nobile **Dendrobium primulinum**
ophioglossoides **Stelis ophioglossoides**
ostrinoglossum **Dendrobium lasianthera**
paniculatum **Polystachya paniculata**
paxtonii **Dendrobium chrysanthum**
phalaenopsis **Dendrobium bigibbum**
pierardii **Dendrobium aphyllum**
polystachya **Polystachya concreta**
pubescens **Eria pubescens**
pulchellum **Dendrobium loddigesii**
pumilum **Genyorchis pumila**
pungentifolium **Dendrobium pugioniforme**
quadrifidum **Pleurothallis quadrifida**
rhombeum **Dendrobium heterocarpum**
ruppianum **Dendrobium jonesii**
sanguineum **Broughtonia sanguinea**
schroederi **Dendrobium densiflorum**
scortechinii **Dendrobium anosmum**
seidelianum **Dendrobium loddigesii**
sophronites **Dendrobium cuthbertsonii**
suavissimum **Dendrobium chrysotoxum**
superbum **Dendrobium anosmum**
tattonianum **Dendrobium canaliculatum**
taylori **Cadetia taylori**
teres **Papilionanthe teres**
teretifolium **Dendrobium striolatum**
thysanochilum **Flickingeria comata**
tigrinum **Dendrobium spectabile**
topaziacum **Dendrobium bullenianum**
tosaense **Dendrobium stricklandianum**
undulatum **Dendrobium discolor**
uniflos **Cadetia taylori**
utricularioides **Ionopsis utricularioides**
velutinum **Dendrobium trigonopus**
vexans **Dendrobium hercoglossum**
wardianum **Dendrobium pendulum**
Dendrochilum **Platyclinis**
saccolabium **Acoridium saccolabium**
Dendrocolla **Thrixspermum**
arachnites **Thrixspermum centipeda**
Dendrophylax lindenii **Polyradicion lindenii**

Dendrorchis minuta **Polystachya concreta**
Desmotrichum comatum **Flickingeria comata**
cymbidioides **Epigeneium cymbidioides**
triflorum **Epigeneium cymbidioides**
Diacrium **Caularthron**
bicornutum **Caularthron bicornutum**
Dicrypta **Maxillaria**
iridifolia **Maxillaria valenzuelana**
longifolia **Maxillaria tarumaensis**
Dilochia pentandra **Dilochia wallichii**
Dimerandra stenopetala **Dimerandra emarginata**
Dinema paleacea **Nidema boothii**
polybulbon **Encyclia polybulbon**
Diothonea gratissima **Diothonea lloensis**
Dipera capensis **Disperis capensis**
tenera **Disperis capensis**
Dipodium pandanum **Dipodium pictum**
Disa barelli **Disa uniflora**
grandiflora **Disa uniflora**
Doritis wightii **Kingidium decumbens**
Dracula ubanquia **Dracula vampira**
Dressleria eburnea **Dressleria dilecta**
suavis **Dressleria dilecta**
Duboisia reymondii **Myoxanthus reymondii**
Duboisreymondia pulpiguera **Myoxanthus reymondii**

Earina brousmichei **Earina valida**
samoensium **Earina valida**
Eckardia **Peristeria**
Elleanthus cephalotus **Elleanthus capitatus**
Encheiridion **Microcoelia**
Encyclia bifida **Psychilis bifida**
brachycolumna **Hagsatera brachycolumna**
deamii **Encyclia livida**
doeringii **Encyclia cordigera**
guttata **Encyclia maculosa**
latro **Encyclia bulbosa**
nemoralis **Encyclia adenocaula**
Endresiella **Trevoria**
Ephemerantha comata **Flickingeria comata**
Ephippium **Bulbophyllum**
Epidendrum aberrans **Oerstedella centropetala**
acuminatum **Encyclia baculus**
adenocaulon **Encyclia adenocaula**
adolphii **Oerstedella centropetala**
aloifolium **Cymbidium aloifolium**
amabile **Phalaenopsis amabilis**
amazonicum **Epidendrum coronatum**
antenniferum **Trichoceros antennifer**
articulatum **Encyclia livida**
atropurpureum **Encyclia cordigera**
aurantiacum **Cattleya aurantiaca**
auritum **Nidema boothii**
avicula **Lanium avicula**
baculus **Encyclia baculus**
belizense **Encyclia belizensis**
beyrodtianum **Encyclia baculus**
bicornutum **Caularthron bicornutum**
bifidum **Psychilis bifida**
boothii **Nidema boothii**
brachycolumna **Hagsatera brachycolumna**
brassavolae **Encyclia brassavolae**
brevicaule **Epidendrum schlechterianum**
broughtonioides **Domingoa hymenodes**
bulbosum **Encyclia bulbosa**
caespitosum **Encyclia pygmaea**
calamarium **Encyclia calamaria**

calanthum **Epidendrum ibaguense**
capense **Mystacidium capense**
caudatum **Brassia caudata**
cearense **Epidendrum anceps**
centropetalum **Oerstedella centropetala**
chacaoense **Encyclia chacaoensis**
ciliare **Epidendrum oerstedii**
citrinum **Encyclia citrina**
cochleatum **Encyclia cochleata**
compositum **Epidendrum coronatum**
condylochilum **Encyclia livida**
congestoides **Epidendrum schlechterianum**
coriaceum **Encyclia vespa**
costaricense **Epidendrum oerstedii**
cucullatum **Brassavola cucullata**
dasytaenia **Encyclia livida**
deamii **Encyclia livida**
decipiens **Epidendrum ibaguense**
densiflorum **Epidendrum paniculatum**
dickinsonianum **Encyclia guatemalensis**
discolor **Epidendrum schlechterianum**
eckmanii **Psychilis bifida**
endressii **Oerstedella centropetala**
floribundum **Epidendrum paniculatum**
flosaëris **Arachnis flosaëris**
fragrans **Encyclia baculus**
fulgens **Epidendrum ibaguense**
galeottianum **Epidendrum anceps**
gnomus **Epidendrum porpax**
guatemalensis **Encyclia guatemalensis**
guttatum **Encyclia maculosa**
haematochilum **Domingoa hymenodes**
hanburyi **Encyclia hanburyi**
henricii **Encyclia livida**
hoffmanii **Encyclia chacaoensis**
humile **Sophronitis cernua**
hymenodes **Domingoa hymenodes**
imetrophyllum **Epidendrum imatophyllum**
inversum **Encyclia bulbosa**
ionophlebium **Encyclia chacaoensis**
labiosum **Zygosepalum labiosum**
laeve **Epidendrum paniculatum**
lamellatum **Dimerandra emarginata**
latilabre **Epidendrum difforme**
leopardinum **Encyclia vespa**
leprosum **Oerstedella centropetala**
ligulatum **Oncidium pumilum**
lindleyanum **Barkeria lindleyana**
lineare **Isochilus linearis**
lividum **Encyclia livida**
lorifolium **Epidendrum imatophyllum**
luteolum **Cattleya luteola**
macrochilum **Encyclia cordigera**
maculosum **Encyclia maculosa**
madrense **Encyclia chacaoensis**
marginatum **Pleurothallis uniflora**
matthewsii **Epidendrum porpax**
maximum **Cattleya maxima**
moschatum **Dendrobium moschatum**
moyobambae **Epidendrum coronatum**
musciferum **Epidendrum anceps**
nemorale **Encyclia adenocaula**
nocturnum **Epidendrum latifolium**
nodosum **Brassavola nodosa**
ochraceum **Encyclia ochracea**
ophioglossoides **Stelis ophioglossoides**
pachycarpum **Encyclia chacaoensis**

paleaceum **Nidema boothii**
palpigeneum **Epidendrum imatophyllum**
papilionaceum **Psychilis bifida**
paranthicum **Epidanthus paranthicus**
parviflorum **Encyclia ochracea**
pentotis **Encyclia baculus**
piliferum **Epidendrum paniculatum**
polybulbon **Encyclia polybulbon**
polystachys **Oeniella polystachys**
porphyrophyllum **Epidendrum porpax**
praecox **Pleione praecox**
punctatum **Cyrtopodium punctatum**
pusillum **Psygmorchis pusilla**
pygmaeum **Encyclia pygmaea**
radiatum **Encyclia radiata**
radicans **Epidendrum ibaguense**
raniferum **Epidendrum cristatum**
rhabdobulbon **Encyclia vespa**
sanguineum **Broughtonia sanguinea**
selligerum **Encyclia selligera**
skinneri **Barkeria skinneri**
stenopetalum **Dimerandra emarginata**
subpatens **Epidendrum coronatum**
superbum **Cattleya violacea**
tessellatum **Encyclia livida**
tibicinis **Myrmecophila tibicinis**
tigrinum **Encyclia vespa**
trigoniflorum **Stelis ophioglossoides**
tripterum **Coelia triptera**
triste **Encyclia ochracea**
tuberosum **Bletilla striata**
umbellatum **Epidendrum difforme**
umlauftii **Epidendrum oerstedii**
uniflorum **Encyclia pygmaea**
utricularioides **Ionopsis utricularioides**
vagans **Encyclia vagans**
variegatum **Encyclia vespa**
verrucosum **Encyclia adenocaula**
violaceum **Cattleya violacea**
virens **Encyclia belizensis**
viridipurpureum **Epidendrum anceps**
vitellinum **Encyclia vitellina**
volucre **Oeonia volucris**
walkerianum **Cattleya walkeriana**
wallisii **Oerstedella wallisii**
Epidorchis calceolus **Angraecum calceolus**
Epidorchis volucris **Oeonia volucris**
Epipactis americana **Epipactis gigantea**
Epiphora pubescens **Polystachya pubescens**
Eria convallarioides **Eria spicata**
 cylindropoda **Eria coronaria**
 dasyphylla **Trichotosia dasyphylla**
 evrardii **Trichotosia dasyphylla**
 ferox **Trichotosia ferox**
 flava **Eria pubescens**
 fordii **Eria carinata**
 fragrans **Eria javanica**
 laniceps **Eria pubescens**
 pseudostellata **Eria javanica**
 pyrrhotricha **Trichotosia ferox**
 rosea **Eria carinata**
 rugosa **Eria javanica**
 stellata **Eria javanica**
 suavis **Eria coronaria**
 vaginata **Eria javanica**
 virescens **Trichotosia ferox**
Eriopsis fuerstenbergii **Eriopsis biloba**

 rutidobulbon **Eriopsis biloba**
 schomburgkii **Eriopsis biloba**
Erycina major **Erycina echinata**
Esmeralda bella **Esmeralda clarkei**
 sanderiana **Euanthe sanderiana**
Eucnemis **Govenia**
Eulophia bierleri **Oeceoclades saundersiana**
 caffra **Eulophia petersii**
 cordylinophylla **Oeceoclades cordylinophylla**
 krebsii **Eulophia streptopetala**
 ledienii **Oeceoclades maculata**
 lokobensis **Oeceoclades cordylinophylla**
 lurida **Graphorkis lurida**
 mackaiana **Zygopetalum intermedium**
 maculata **Oeceoclades maculata**
 mildbraedii **Oeceoclades saundersiana**
 murrayana **Neoescobaria brevis**
 paivaeana **Eulophia streptopetala**
 saundersiana **Oeceoclades saundersiana**
 schimperiana **Eulophia petersii**
Eulophidium **Oeceoclades**
 angustifolium **Oeceoclades angustifolia**
 lokobense **Oeceoclades cordylinophylla**
 maculatum **Oeceoclades maculata**
 nyassanum **Oeceoclades maculata**
 roseovariegatum **Oeceoclades roseovariegata**
 saundersianum **Oeceoclades saundersiana**
 warneckianum **Oeceoclades maculata**
Eulophiopsis **Graphorkis**
 lurida **Graphorkis lurida**
Evelyna capitata **Elleanthus capitatus**
 longibracteata **Elleanthus longibracteatus**

Fernandezia **Lockhartia**
 acuta **Lockhartia acuta**
 lunifera **Lockhartia lunifera**
 robusta **Lockhartia oerstedii**
Fieldia lissochiloides **Vandopsis lissochiloides**
Finetia falcata **Neofinetia falcata**
Fissipes hirsuta **Cypripedium reginae**
Fregea **Sobralia**

Galeandra petersii **Eulophia petersii**
Galeottia **Mendoncella**
 grandiflora **Mendoncella grandiflora**
Gastrochilus miniatus **Ascocentrum miniatum**
 parviflorus **Smitinandia micrantha**
 tuberculosus **Phaius tuberculosa**
Geodorum neocaledonicum **Geodorum purpureum**
 pacificum **Geodorum purpureum**
 pictum **Geodorum purpureum, Oeceoclades maculata**
Ghiesbrechtia **Calanthe**
Gomesa erectiflora **Caucaea radiata**
 theodorea **Rodrigueziella gomezoides**
Gomphostylis **Coelogyne**
Gongora atropurpurea **Gongora quinquenervis**
 macrantha **Coryanthes macrantha**
 maculata **Gongora quinquenervis**
 nigrita **Gongora quinquenervis**
 retrorsa **Gongora quinquenervis**
 viridifusca **Cirrhaea dependens**
Goodyera discolor **Ludisia discolor**
Govenia boliviensis **Govenia utriculata**
 ernestii **Govenia utriculata**
 gardneri **Govenia utriculata**
 sodiroi **Govenia utriculata**

Grammangis falcigera **Cymbidiella falcigera**
  pardalina **Cymbidiella pardalina**
Grammatophyllum ellisii **Grammangis ellisii**
  finlaysonianum **Bromheadia finlaysoniana**
Graphorkis maculata **Oeceoclades maculata**
  saundersiana **Oeceoclades saundersiana**
Gunnia **Sarcochilus**
Gussonia globulosa **Microcoelia globulosa**
Gymnadenia gracillima **Gymnadenia conopsea**
  graminifolia **Ponerorchis graminifolia**
  helferi **Brachycorythis helferi**
  ornithis **Gymnadenia conopsea**
  pseudoconopsea **Gymnadenia conopsea**
  transsilvanica **Gymnadenia conopsea**
Gymnostylis candida **Pleione maculata**
Gyrostachys ovafolia **Cyclopogon elatus**

Habenaria helferi **Brachycorythis helferi**
  militaris **Habenaria rhodocheila**
  pusilla **Habenaria rhodocheila**
  xanthocheila **Habenaria rhodocheila**
Haemaria discolor **Ludisia discolor**
Hartwegia purpurea **Nageliella purpurea**
Helleborine gigantea **Epipactus gigantea**
  palustris **Epipactus palustris**
Hemihabenaria radiata **Habenaria radiata**
Heterotaxis **Maxillaria**
Hoehneella **Chaubardia**
  santos-nevesii **Chaubardia surinamensis**
  trinitatis **Chaubardia surinamensis**
Holcoglossum falcatum **Neofinetia falcata**
Hologyne **Coelogyne**
Hormidium pygmaeum **Encyclia pygmaea**
  uniflorum **Encyclia pygmaea**
Humboldia **Stelis**
Humboldtia bivalvis **Pleurothallis secunda**
  ciliata **Pleurothallis lanceana**
  endotrachys **Pleurothallis endotrachys**
  mathewsii **Pleurothallis phalangifera**
  lindenii **Pleurothallis secunda**
  octomerioides **Pleurothallis octomerioides**
  secunda **Pleurothallis secunda**
  striata **Pleurothallis uniflora**
  uniflora **Pleurothallis uniflora**
  verrucosa **Scaphosepalum verrucosum**
Huntleya albo-fulva **Huntleya meleagris**
  burtii **Huntleya meleagris**
  cerina **Pescatorea cerina**
Hysteria **Corymborkis**
  veratrifolia **Corymborkis veratrifolia**

Ione **Sunipia**
  cirrhata **Sunipia cirrhata**
  paleacea **Sunipia cirrhata**
Ionopsis paniculata **Ionopsis utricularioides**
Iridorchis gigantea **Cymbidium iridioides**
Isochilus proliferum **Scaphyglottis prolifera**

Jimensia striata **Bletilla striata**

Katherinea **Epigeneium**
  coelogyne **Epigeneium coelogyne**
Kingiella **Kingidium**
  decumbens **Kingidium decumbens**
Kochiophyton **Acacallis**
  coerulens **Acacallis cyanea**
  coerulens **Acacallis cyanea**
  negrense **Acacallis cyanea**

Kraenzlinella **Pleurothallis**
  platyrachys **Pleurothallis endotrachys**

Laelia acuminata **Laelia rubescens**
  digbyana **Rhyncholaelia digbyana**
  fulva **Laelia flava**
  glauca **Rhyncholaelia glauca**
  gloriosa **Schomburgkia gloriosa**
  lindenii **Cattleyopsis lindenii**
  monophylla **Neocogniauxia monophylla**
  peduncularis **Laelia rubescens**
  regnelli **Laelia lundii**
  reichenbachiana **Laelia lundii**
  rupestris **Laelia crispata**
  tenebrosa **Laelia grandis**
  tereticaulis **Laelia crispata**
  tibicinis **Myrmecophila tibicinis**
  undulata **Schomburgkia undulata**
  wetmorei **Laelia xanthina**
Latouria spectabilis **Dendrobium spectabile**
  lehmannianus **Caucaea radiata**
  pulchellus **Oncidium waluewa**
  radiatus **Caucaea radiata**
Lepanthes micrantha **Lepanthes lindleyana**
  secunda **Lepanthopsis floripecten**
Lepanthopsis secunda **Lepanthopsis floripecten**
Leptoceras menziesii **Caladenia menziesii**
  oblonga **Caladenia menziesii**
Leucohyle dasyandra **Cischweinfia dasyandra**
Lichterveldia **Cuitlauzina**
  lindleyi **Cuitlauzina pendula**
Limatodes mishmensis **Phaius mishmensis**
Limodorum autumnale **Spiranthes cernua**
  bidens **Diaphananthe bidens**
  canaliculatum **Tetramicra canaliculata**
  cucullatum **Eulophia cucullata**
  eburneum **Angraecum eburneum**
  flosaëris **Arachnis flosaëris**
  giganteum **Epipactis gigantea**
  graminifolium **Arundina graminifolia**
  incarvilliae **Phaius tankervilleae**
  lanceolatum **Stenorrhynchus lanceolatus**
  longicorne **Mystacidium capense**
  luridum **Graphorkis lurida**
  maculatum **Oeceoclades maculata**
  pulchellum **Calopogon tuberosus**
  striatum **Bletilla striata**
  tankervilleae **Phaius tankervilleae**
  tuberculosum **Phaius tuberculosus**
  tuberosum **Calopogon tuberosus**
  utriculatum **Govenia utriculata**
  veratrifolium **Calanthe triplicata**
Lindleyella **Bifrenaria**
  aurantiaca **Rudolfiella aurantiaca**
Linsayella **Sobralia**
Liparis boothii **Liparis viridiflora**
  longipes **Liparis viridiflora**
  neglecta **Liparis bowkeri**
  pendula **Liparis viridiflora**
  pleistantha **Liparis viridiflora**
  spathulata **Liparis viridiflora**
  triloba **Liparis viridiflora**
Lissochilus **Eulophia**
  arenarius **Eulophia cucullata**
  barombensis **Oeceoclades saundersiana**
  cordylinophyllus **Oeceoclades cordylinophylla**
  krebsii **Eulophia streptopetala**

lokobensis **Oeceoclades cordylinophylla**
  speciosus **Eulophia speciosa**
  streptopetalus **Eulophia streptopetala**
  sylvaticus **Polystachya pubescens**
Listrostachys bicaudata **Tridactyle bicaudata**
  cephalotes **Ancistrorhynchus cephalotes**
  chailluana **Cyrtorchis chailluana**
  cirrhosa **Tridactyle bicaudata**
  dactyloceras **Podangis dactyloceras**
  fimbriata **Tridactyle bicaudata**
  graminifolia **Ypsilopus longifolius**
  imbricata **Bolusiella maudiae**
  iridifolia **Bolusiella iridifolia**
  jenischiana **Listrostachys pertusa**
  muscicola **Rangaeris muscicola**
  mystacioides **Diaphananthe bidens**
  odoratissima **Chamaeangis odoratissima**
  pellucida **Diaphananthe pellucidum**
  sedenii **Cyrtorchis arcuata**
  whitei **Cyrtorchis arcuata**
Lockhartia pallida **Lockhartia acuta**
  chiriquensis **Lockhartia micrantha**
  lankesteri **Lockhartia micrantha**
  robusta **Lockhartia oerstedii**
  verrucosa **Lockhartia oerstedii**
Loroglossum **Himantoglossum**
Ludisia furetii **Ludisia discolor**
Lueddemannia sanderiana **Lacaena bicolor**
  wallisii **Neomoorea wallisii**
Luisia alpina **Trudelia alpina**
  burmanica **Luisia teretifolia**
  platyglossa **Luisia teretifolia**
  zeylandica **Luisia teretifolia**
Lycaste balsamea **Lycaste cruenta**
  candida **Lycaste brevispatha**
  colleyi **Batemannia colleyi**
  cristata **Paphinia cristata**
  gigantea **Lycaste longipetala**
  grandiflora **Maxillaria grandiflora**
  harrisoniae **Bifrenaria harrisoniae**
  jugosa **Pabstia jugosa**
  lawrenceana **Lycaste brevispatha**
  leuco-flavescens **Lycaste leucantha**
  suaveolens **Lycaste aromatica**
  virginalis **Lycaste skinneri**
Lycomormium elatum **Lycomormium squalidium**

Macdonaldia antennifera **Thelymitra antennifera**
  variegata **Thelymitra variegata**
Macradenia modesta **Macradenia brassavolae**
Macrochilus fryanus **Miltonia spectabilis**
Macroclinium **Notylia**
Macroplectrum calceolus **Angraecum calceolus**
  leonis **Angraecum leonis**
  ochraceum **Angraecum ochraceum**
  sesquipedale **Angraecum sesquipedale**
Macrostomium aloefolium **Dendrobium aloefolium**
Malaxis caudata **Brassia caudata**
  iridifolia **Oberonia iridifolia**
  subulata **Cryptostylis subulata**
Marsupiaria iridifolia **Maxillaria valenzuelana**
  valenzuelana **Maxillaria valenzuelana**
Masdevallia **Dracula**
  acrochordonia **Masdevallia trochilus**
  aequiloba **Masdevallia civilis**
  albida **Masdevallia infracta**
  aperta **Pleurothallis crenata**

backhouseana **Dracula chimaera**
bella **Dracula bella**
biflora **Masdevallia caloptera**
bruchmuelleri **Masdevallia coriacea**
candida **Masdevallia tovarensis**
chimaera **Dracula chimaera**
echidna **Porroglossum echidna**
ellipes **Masdevallia civilis**
ephippium **Masdevallia trochilus**
erythrochaete **Dracula erythrochaete**
fenestrata **Zootrophion atropurpureum**
fragrans **Masdevallia civilis**
galeottiana **Masdevallia floribunda**
guatemalensis **Dryadella simula**
haematostica **Masdevallia civilis**
klabochorum **Masdevallia caudata**
leontoglossa **Masdevallia civilis**
lilliputana **Dryadella lilliputana**
lindenii **Masdevallia coccinea**
linearifolia **Dryadella simula**
longicaudata **Masdevallia infracta**
ludibunda **Masdevallia estradae**
macroglossa **Masdevallia civilis**
muscosa **Porroglossum muscosum**
myriostigma **Masdevallia floribunda**
normanii **Masdevallia reichenbachiana**
ochthodes **Scaphosepalum verrucosum**
porcellipes **Masdevallia civilis**
shuttleworthii **Masdevallia caudata**
simula **Dryadella simula**
sodiroi **Dracula sodiroi**
sulphurea **Masdevallia civilis**
triaristella **Trisetella triaristella**
vampira **Dracula vampira**
verrucosa **Scaphosepalum verrucosum**
wallisii **Dracula chimaera**
xipheres **Porroglossum muscosum**
Masterallia platyrhachis **Pleurothallis endotrachys**
Maxillaria acutifolia **Maxillaria rufescens**
amparoana **Maxillaria ringens**
aromatica **Lycaste aromatica**
articulata **Maxillaria rufescens**
atrata **Maxillaria cucullata**
atropurpurea **Bifrenaria atropurpurea**
angustifolia **Maxillaria variabilis**
boothii **Nidema boothii**
brevispatha **Lycaste brevispatha**
colleyi **Batemannia colleyi**
coriacea **Maxillaria desvauxiana**
cristata **Paphinia cristata**
cruenta **Lycaste cruenta**
deppei **Lycaste deppei**
dichroma **Maxillaria elegantula**
eburnea **Maxillaria grandiflora**
flabellifera **Scuticaria steelii**
fuscata **Maxillaria picta**
galeata **Gongora galeata**
gigantea **Lycaste longipetala**
gracilifolia **Maxillaria tenuifolia**
graminea **Koellensteinia graminea**
harrisoniae **Bifrenaria harrisoniae**
hatschbachii **Maxillaria mosenii**
houtteana **Maxillaria curtipes**
iridifolia **Maxillaria valenzuelana**
jugosa **Pabstia jugosa**
kreysigii **Maxillaria picta**
lactea **Maxillaria ringens**

lehmannii **Maxillaria grandiflora**
leontoglossa **Xylobium leontoglossum**
leucantha **Lycaste leucantha**
leucocheila **Maxillaria picta**
lindeniana **Maxillaria meleagris**
longifolia **Maxillaria tarumaensis**
longipetala **Lycaste longipetala**
luteograndiflora **Maxillaria luteoalba**
maclaei **Maxillaria uncata**
obscura **Maxillaria cucullata**
pertusa **Maxillaria lepidota**
picta **Maxillaria consanguinea**
praestans **Maxillaria cucullata**
pubilabia **Maxillaria ringens**
punctata **Maxillaria gracilis**
punctostriata **Maxillaria meleagris**
queirogana **Maxillaria gracilis**
rhombea **Maxillaria cucullata**
rousseauae **Maxillaria ringens**
rubrofusca **Maxillaria nigrescens**
rugosa **Maxillaria rufescens**
rupestris **Maxillaria picta**
saxicola **Maxillaria lepidota**
scabrilinguis **Xylobium variegatum**
serolina **Maxillaria consanguinea**
skinneri **Lycaste skinneri**
squalens **Xylobium variegatum**
steelei **Scuticaria steelii**
striatella **Maxillaria uncata**
tuerckheimii **Maxillaria ringens**
vanillodora **Maxillaria rufescens**
variegata **Xylobium variegatum**
virginalis **Lycaste skinneri**
warreana **Warrea warreana**
xanthina **Promenaea xanthina**
yzabalana **Maxillaria ringens**
Mediocalcar bifolium **Maxillaria alpinum**
Megaclinium **Bulbophyllum**
endotrachys **Bulbophyllum falcatum**
falcatum **Bulbophyllum falcatum**
Meiracyllium gemma **Meiracyllium wendlandii**
Menadenia **Maxillaria**
Menadenium labiosum **Zygosepalum labiosum**
lindeniae **Zygosepalum lindeniae**
rostratum **Zygosepalum labiosum**
Mesopinidium aurantiacum **Ada aurantiaca**
Mesopinidium roseum **Cochlioda rosea**
radiatum **Caucaea radiata**
Mesuspinidium cochliodum **Symphyglossum sanguineum**
Microcoelia guyoniana **Microcoelia globulosa**
Microstylis **Malaxis**
calophylla **Malaxis calophylla**
humilis **Encyclia pygmaea**
scottii **Malaxis calophylla**
Miltonia candida **Anneliesia candida**
endresii **Miltoniopsis warscewiczii**
phalaenopsis **Miltoniopsis phalaenopsis**
roezlii **Miltoniopsis roezlii**
superba **Miltoniopsis warscewiczii**
vexillaria **Miltoniopsis vexillaria**
warswewiczii **Miltonioides warszewiczii**
Mitopetalum **Tainia**
Monachanthus **Catasetum**
discolor **Catasetum discolor**
viridis **Catasetum macrocarpum**
Monixus polystachys **Oeniella polystachys**

Moorea **Neomoorea**
Mormodes histrio **Mormodes warscewiczii**
macranthum **Mormodes colossus**
pardina **Mormodes maculatum**
wendlandii **Mormodes colossus**
Mormolyca lineolata **Mormolyca ringens**
Morrea irrorata **Neomoorea wallisii**
Myanthus **Catasetum**
barbatus **Catasetum barbatum**
fimbriatus **Catasetum fimbriatum**
spinosus **Catasetum barbatum**
Myoda rufescens **Ludisia discolor**
Myrobroma fragrans **Vanilla planifolia**
Mystacidium calceolus **Angraecum calceolus**
infundibulare **Angraecum infundibulare**
leonis **Angraecum leonis**
longifolium **Ysilopus longifolius**
ochraceum **Angraecum ochraceum**
sesquipedale **Angraecum sesquipedale**

Nanodes discolor **Epidendrum schlechterianum**
matthewsii **Epidendrum porpax**
medusae **Epidendrum medusae**
Neippergia **Acineta**
chrysantha **Acineta chrysantha**
Neogardneria binotii **Neoescobaria brevis**
Neolehmannia porpax **Epidendrum porpax**
Neomoorea irrorata **Neomoorea wallisii**
Neottia acaulis **Sarcoglottis acaulis**
aphylla **Stenorrhynchus lanceolatus**
minor **Cyclopogon elatus**
picta **Sarcoglottis acaulis**
sinensis **Spiranthes sinensis**
Nervilia discolor **Nervilia plicata**
velutina **Nervilia plicata**
Nipponorchis falcata **Neofinetia falcata**
Notylia albida **Notylia barkeri**
bernoullii **Notylia barkeri**
bipartita **Notylia barkeri**
guatemalensis **Notylia barkeri**
trisepala **Notylia barkeri**

Octadesmia monophylla **Neocogniauxia monophylla**
Octomeria arcuata **Octomeria grandiflora**
pubescens **Eria pubescens**
robusta **Octomeria grandiflora**
ruthiana **Octomeria grandiflora**
spicata **Eria spicata**
surinamensis **Oberonia iridifolia**
Odontochilus **Anoectochilus**
Odontoglossum alexandrae **Odontoglossum crispum**
asperum **Lemboglossum rossii**
bictoniense **Lemboglossum bictoniense**
bluntii **Odontoglossum crispum**
boddaertianum **Odontoglossum constrictum**
brevifolium **Otoglossum brevifolium**
cariniferum **Oncidium carniferum**
caulescens **Lemboglossum rossii**
cervantesii **Lemboglossum cervantesii**
chaetostroma **Odontoglossum hallii**
citrosum **Cuitlauzina pendula**
cordatum **Lemboglossum cordatum**
crispulum **Gomesa crispa**
gloriosum **Odontoglossum odoratum**
grande **Rossioglossum grande**
hastilabium **Oncidium hastilabium**
hookeri **Lemboglossum cordatum**

hrubyanum **Odontoglossum cirrhosum**
hystrix **Odontoglossum luteopurpureum**
humeanum **Lemboglossum rossii**
insleayi **Rossioglossum insleayi**
krameri **Ticoglossum krameri**
lawrenceanum **Rossioglossum schlieperianum**
liliflorum **Odontoglossum ramosissimum**
londesboroughianum **Mesoglossum**
   londesboroughianum
lueddemannii **Lemboglossum cordatum**
maculatum **Lemboglossum maculatum**
membranaceum **Lemboglossum cervartesii**
pendulum **Cuitlauzina pendula**
phalaenopsis **Miltoniopsis phalaenopsis**
recurvum **Gomesa recurva**
retusum **Cyrtochilum retusum**
roezlii **Miltoniopsis roezlii**
roseum **Cochlioda rosea**
rossii **Lemboglossum rossii**
sanderianum **Odontoglossum constrictum**
schlieperianum **Rossioglossum schlieperianum**
triumphans **Odontoglossum spectatissimum**
uroskinneri **Lemboglossum uroskinneri**
vexillarium **Miltoniopsis vexillaria**
victor **Odontoglossum hallii**
warneri **Mexicoa ghiesbrechtiana**
warnerianum **Lemboglossum rossii**
warscewiczianum **Miltoniopsis warscewiczii**
warscewiczii **Miltoniopsis warscewiczii**
weltonii **Miltonioides warszewiczii**
youngii **Lemboglossum rossii**
Oeceoclades falcata **Neofinetia falcata**
Oeonia aubertii **Oeonia volucris**
  humblotii **Oeonia volucris**
  polystachya **Oeoniella polystachys**
  robusta **Sobennikoffia robusta**
Oncidium acrobotryum **Oncidium harrisonianum**
  aurosum **Oncidium excavatum**
  bernoullianum **Oncidium ampliatum**
  bicornutum **Oncidium pubes**
  brassia **Brassia maculata**
  brenesii **Oncidium obryzatum**
  brunleesianum **Baptistonia echinata**
  bryolophotum **Oncidium heteranthum**
  calochilum **Tolumnia calochila**
  candidum **Palumbina candida, Anneliesia candida**
  caudatum **Brassia caudata**
  cervantesii **Lemboglossum cervantesii**
  cinnabarinum **Ada aurantiaca**
  citrosmum **Cuitlauzina pendula**
  cirrhosum **Odontoglossum cirrhosum**
  crispum **Oncidium forbesii**
  cruentum **Oncidium reflexum**
  cucullatum **Oncidium dayanum**
  delumbe **Oncidium ansiferum**
  dentatum **Oncidium micropogon**
  digitatum **Oncidium leucochilum**
  echinatum **Erycina echinata**
  emarginatum **Dimerandra emarginata**
  falcipetalum **Cyrtochilum falcipetalum**
  flabelliferum **Oncidium gardneri**
  flavescens **Miltonia flavescens**
  flexuosum **Oncidium cimiciferum**
  forbesio-dasytele **Oncidium gardneri**
  fulgens **Oncidium obryzatum**
  fuscatum **Miltonioides warszewiczii**
  galeottianum **Cuitlauzina pendula**

guiesbrechtianum **Mexicoa ghiesbrechtianum**
ghillanyi **Oncidium spilopterum**
glumaceum **Ada glumacea**
graciliforme **Oncidium obryzatum**
henekenii **Hispaniella henekenii**
imbricatum **Ada glumacea**
insleayi **Rossioglossum insleayi**
ionops **Oncidium heteranthum**
iridifolium **Psygmorchis pusilla**
janeirense **Oncidium longipes**
keilianum **Ada keiliana**
kramerianum **Psychopsis krameriana**
kymatoides **Oncidium carthagenense**
lankesteri **Oncidium ansiferum**
lawrenceanum **Brassia lawrenceana**
limminghei **Psychopsiella limminghei**
loxense **Cyrtochilum loxense**
macranthum **Cyrtochilum macranthum**
massangei **Oncidium sphacelatum**
megalous **Oncidium heteranthum**
micranthum **Cyrtopodium andersonii**
micropogon **Oncidium ansiferum**
modosum **Psychopsis krameriana**
monoceras **Oncidium longicornu**
naranjense **Oncidium ansiferum**
obryzatoides **Oncidium obryzatum**
pachyphyllum **Oncidium cavendishianum**
pallidum **Oncidium harrisonianum**
pantherinum **Oncidium harrisonianum**
papilio **Psychopsis papilio**
papilioniforme **Psychopsis krameriana**
pelicanum **Oncidium reflexum**
phalaenopsis **Oncidium dayanum**
praetextum **Oncidium gardneri**
pulchellum **Tolumnia pulchella**
pusillum **Psygmorchis pusilla**
racemosum **Solenidium racemosum**
ramosissimum **Odontoglossum ramosissimum**
regnellii **Miltonia regnellii**
retusum **Cyrtochilum retusum**
rigbyanum **Oncidium sarcodes**
saint-legerianum **Oncidium spilopterum**
scansor **Oncidium globuliferum**
suave **Oncidium reflexum**
superbiens **Cyrtochilum superbiens**
superfluum **Capanemia superflua**
unguiculatum **Oncidium tigrinum; Oncidium**
  concolor
unicorne **Oncidium longicornu**
varians **Oncidium obryzatum**
variegatum **Tolumnia variegata**
verrucosum **Brassia verrucosa**
vexillarium **Oncidium bifolium**
warneri **Mexicoa ghiesbrechtiana**
weltonii **Miltonioides warszewiczii**
werklei **Oncidium globuliferum**
Onkeripus **Maxillaria**
Ophrys cernua **Spiranthes cernua**
  scolopax **Ophrys vernixia**
  speculum **Ophrys vernixia**
Orchis burmanniana **Bartholina burmanniana**
  conopsea **Gymnadenia conopsea**
  falcata **Neofinetia falcata**
  foliosa **Dactylorhiza foliosa**
  hircinum **Himantoglossum hircinum**
  manderensis **Dactylorhiza foliosa**
  pectinata **Bartholina burmanniana**

psycodes **Platanthera psycodes**
pyramidalis **Anacamptis pyramidalis**
strateumatica **Zeuxine strateumatica**
triplicata **Calanthe triplicata**
Orcidice **Thrixspermum**
Ornithidium densum **Maxillaria densa**
  sophronitis **Maxillaria sophronitis**
Ornithocephalus navicularis **Zygostates lunata**
Ornithochilus eublepharon **Ornithochilus difformis**
  fuscus **Ornithochilus difformis**
Ornithophora quadricolor **Ornithophora radicans**
Otochilus latifolius **Otochilus porrectus**

Pachystoma speciosum **Ipsea speciosa**
Paphiopedilum braemii **Paphiopedilum tonsum**
  caudatum **Phragmipedium caudatum**
  chamberlainianum **Paphiopedilum victoriaregina**
  klotzscheanum **Phragmipedium klotzscheanum**
  laevigatum **Paphiopedilum philippinense**
  leucochilum **Paphiopedilum godefroyae**
  roebelinii **Paphiopedilum philippinense**
  topperi **Paphiopedilum kolopakingii**
  wolterianum **Paphiopedilum appletonianum**
Pecteilis radiata **Habenaria radiata**
Pedilonum secundum **Dendrobium secundum**
Pentulops **Maxillaria**
Peramium giganteum **Epipactis gigantea**
Pergamena **Dactylostalix**
  uniflora **Dactylostalix ringens**
Peristeria humboldtii **Acineta superba**
  longiscapa **Lacaena bicolor**
  fuscata **Lycomormium squalidum**
Petronia regia **Batemannia colleyi**
Phaius bicolor **Phaius tankervilleae**
  crinita **Phaius mishmensis**
  gracilis **Cephalantheropsis gracilis**
  grandifolius **Phaius tankervilleae**
  roseus **Phaius mishmensis**
  wallichii **Phaius tankervilleae**
  warpurii **Phaius tuberculosus**
Phalaenopsis antennifera **Doritis pulcherrima**
  acutifolia **Phalaenopsis sumatrana**
  boxallii **Phalaenopsis manii**
  decumbens **Kingidium decumbens**
  deliciosa **Kingidium decumbens**
  esmeralda **Doritis pulcherrima**
  foerstermannii **Phalaenopsis pallens**
  gloriosa **Phalaenopsis amabilis**
  grandiflora **Phalaenopsis amabilis**
  hebe **Kingidium decumbens**
  laycockii **Paraphalaenopsis laycockii**
  proboscidioides **Phalaenopsis lowii**
  pulcherrima **Doritis pulcherrima**
  rimestadiana **Phalaenopsis amabilis**
  riteiwanensis **Phalaenopsis equestris**
  schilleriana **Phalaenopsis stuartiana**
  stauroglottis **Phalaenopsis equestris**
  wightii **Kingidium decumbens**
  zebrina **Phalaenopsis sumatrana**
Pholidota fragrans **Pholidota convallariae**
Phragmipedium ecuadorense **Phragmipedium carcinum**
  hartwegii **Phragmipedium longifolium**
  hincksianum **Phragmipedium longifolium**
  roezlii **Phragmipedium longifolium**
  warscewiczianum **Phragmipedium caudatum**
Phyllompax halferi **Brachycorythis helferi**
Phyllorchis dearei **Bulbophyllum dearei**

medusae **Bulbophyllum medusae**
ornatissimum **Bulbophyllum ornatissimum**
Physosiphon guatemalensis **Physosiphon tubatus**
Pilumna **Trichopilia**
 fragrans **Trichopilia fragrans**
 laxa **Trichopilia laxa**
 reichenheimiana **Trichopilia laxa**
Pinalia dasyphylla **Trichotosia dasyphylla**
 ferox **Trichotosia ferox**
Plantanthera cristata **Platanthera psycodes**
 incisa **Platanthera psycodes**
 helferi **Brachycorythis helferi**
 radiata **Habenaria radiata**
Platyclinis cobbiana **Dendrochilum cobbianum**
 filiformis **Dendrochilum filiforme**
 longifolia **Dendrochilum longifolium**
Pleione concolor **Pleione praecox**
 delavayi **Pleione bulbocodioides**
 diantha **Pleione humilis**
 diphylla **Pleione maculata**
 fargesii **Pleione bulbocodioides**
 hui **Pleione formosana**
 laotica **Pleione hookeriana**
 pricei **Pleione formosana**
 reichenbachiana **Pleione praecox**
Pleurothallis amethystina **Pleurothallis segoviensis**
 aperta **Pleurothallis crenata**
 araguensis **Pleurothallis secunda**
 atropurpurens **Zootrophion atropurpureum**
 bogotensis **Pleurothallis phalangifera**
 cerea **Pleurothallis octomerioides**
 choconiana **Pleurothallis grobyi**
 ciliata **Pleurothallis lanceana**
 coccinea **Rodriguezia lanceolata**
 crassifolia **Pleurothallis lanceana**
 floripecten **Lepanthopsis floripecten**
 gheisbrechtiana **Pleurothallis quadrifida**
 gnomonifera **Pleurothallis ciliaris**
 hamata **Pleurothallis crenata**
 huebneri **Pleurothallis lanceana**
 hunterana **Pleurothallis crenata**
 incompta **Pleurothallis quadrifida**
 intermedia **Pleurothallis loranthophylla**
 lindenii **Pleurothallis secunda**
 longissima **Pleurothallis quadrifida**
 marginata **Pleurothallis grobyi**
 mathewsii **Pleurothallis phalangifera**
 minax **Pleurothallis lanceana**
 nutans **Pleurothallis secunda**
 octomerioides **Pleurothallis octomerioides**
 ospinae **Restrepia antennifera**
 pendula **Pleurothallis secunda**
 pertusa **Dresslerella pertusa**
 pfavii **Pleurothallis endotrachys**
 picta **Pleurothallis grobyi**
 platyrhachis **Pleurothallis endotrachys**
 plumosa **Pleurothallis lanceana**
 purpurea **Bulbophyllum careyarum**
 reymondii **Myoxanthus reymondii**
 spathata **Pleurothallis loranthophylla**
 striata **Pleurothallis uniflora**
 subpellucida **Pleurothallis loranthophylla**
 subreniformis **Pleurothallis secunda**
 triangulabia **Pleurothallis phyllocardia**
 tubatus **Physosiphon tubatus**
 unilateralis **Lepanthopsis floripecten**
 verrucosa **Scaphosepalum verrucosum**

vittariaefolia **Pleurothallis glandulosa**
 wrecklei **Pleurothallis segoviensis**
Pogonia discolor **Nervilia plicata**
 rosea **Cleistes rosea**
Polychilos cornucervi **Phalaenopsis cornucervi**
Polycycnis gratiosa **Polycycnis barbata**
Polyrrhiza lindenii **Polyradicion lindenii**
Polystachya appendiculata **Polystachya cultriformis**
 ashantensis **Polystachya tenuissima**
 bulbophylloides **Genyorchis pumila**
 cultrata **Polystachya cultriformis**
 farinosa **Polystachya bifida**
 gerrardii **Polystachya cultriformis**
 inconspicua **Polystachya tenuissima**
 kirkii **Polystachya cultriformis**
 lindleyana **Polystachya pubescens**
 luteola **Polystachya concreta**
 mauritiana **Polystachya concreta**
 minuta **Polystachya concreta**
 modesta **Polystachya concreta**
 monophylla **Polystachya cultriformis**
 repens **Stolzia repens**
 rufinula **Polystachya odorata**
 tessellata **Polystachya concreta**
Pomatocalpa poilanei **Smitinandia micrantha**
Ponera amethystina **Scaphyglottis amethystina**
 prolifera **Scaphyglottis prolifera**
Ponthieva formosa **Ponthieva maculata**
Porroglossum xipheres **Porroglossum muscosum**
Preptanthe rubens **Calanthe rubens**
Prescottia colorans **Prescottia plantaginifolia**
Pseuderiopsis schomburgkii **Eriopsis biloba**
Pseudopidendrum spectabile **Epidendrum pseudepidendrum**
Psittacoglossum **Maxillaria**
Psychopsis picta **Psychopsis papilio**
Ptilocnema **Pholidota**
Ptychogyne **Coelogyne**

Quekettia micromera **Capanemia micromera**

Regnellia purpurea **Bletia catenulata**
Renanthera arachnitis **Arachnis flosaëris**
 flosaëris **Arachnis flosaëris**
 histrionica **Renantherella histrionica**
 lowii **Dimorphorchis lowii**
 micrantha **Renanthera matutina**
 sulingii **Armodorum sulingii**
Restrepia leopardina **Restrepia maculata**
 pandina **Restrepia maculata**
 punctulata **Restrepia elegans**
Reymondia **Myoxanthus**
Rhaphidorhynchus fastuosus **Aerangis fastuosa**
Rhipidoglossum **Diaphananthe**
Rhynchopera puncata **Pleurothallis loranthophylla**
Rhynchostelis **Leochilus**
Rhynchostylis garwalica **Rhynchostylis retusa**
 guttata **Rhynchostylis retusa**
 praemorsa **Rhynchostylis retusa**
Rödriguezia anomala **Capanemia superflua**
 candida **Rodriguezia candida**
 crispa **Gomesa crispa**
 obscura **Caucaea radiata**
 recurva **Gomesa recurva**
 secunda **Rodriguezia lanceolata**
Rynchanthera **Corymborkis**
 paniculata **Corymborkis veratrifolia**

Sacanthus pallidus **Cleisostoma racemiferum**
 tricolor **Cleisostoma racemiferum**
Saccolabium acutifolium **Gastrochilus acutifolius**
 ampullaceum **Ascocentrum ampullaceum**
 bellinum **Gastrochilus bellinus**
 calopterum **Ascoglossum calopterum**
 carinatum **Acampe papillosa**
 curvifolium **Ascocentrum curvifolium**
 dasypogon **Gastrochilus dasypogon**
 densiflorum **Robiquetia spathulata**
 denticulatum **Gastrochilus acutifolius**
 filiforme **Cleisostoma filiforme**
 fissum **Smitinandia micrantha**
 gemmatum **Schoenorchis gemmata**
 giganteum **Rhynchostylis gigantea**
 guttatum **Rhynchostylis retusa**
 hendersonianum **Dyakia hendersonianum**
 micranthum **Smitinandia micrantha**
 miniatum **Ascocentrum miniatum**
 papillosum **Acampe papillosa**
 purpureum **Ascoglossum calopterum**
 racemiferum **Cleisostoma racemiferum**
 reflexum **Renanthera matutina**
 rubrum **Ascocentrum curvifolium**
 schleinitzianum **Ascoglossum calopterum**
 speciosum **Aerides jarckiana**
Sacroglottis elata **Cyclopogon elatus**
 picta **Sarcoglottis acaulis**
Sacropodium **Epigeneium**
 acuminatum **Epigeneium acuminatum**
 coelogyne **Epigeneium coelogyne**
 dearii **Bulbophyllum dearei**
Sarcanthus **Cleisostoma**
 filiformis **Cleisostoma filiforme**
 insectifer **Pelatantheria insectifera**
 racemifer **Cleisostoma racemiferum**
 scortechinii **Cleisostoma scortechinii**
Sarcochilus rubicentrum **Sarcochilus hartmannii**
 difformis **Ornithochilus difformis**
 obtusus **Camarotis obtusa**
Sarcopodium leopardinum **Bulbophyllum leopardinum**
Sarcorhynchus **Diaphananthe**
Sarochilus luniferus **Chiloschista lunifera**
Satyrium albiflorum **Satyrium nepalense**
 archioides **Stenorrhynchus lanceolatus**
 elatum **Cyclopogon elatus**
 giganteum **Eulophia speciosa**
 grandiflorum **Disa uniflora**
 hiricinum **Himantoglossum hircinum**
 pallidum **Satyrium nepalense**
 perrottetianum **Satyrium nepalense**
Scaphosepalum xipheres **Porroglossum muscosum**
Scaphyglottis fusiformis **Hexadesmia fusiformis**
Schomburgkia brysiana **Myrmecophila brysiana**
 crispa **Schomburgkia gloriosa**
 tibicinis **Myrmecophila tibicinis**
Scuticaria keyseriana **Scuticaria steelii**
Selenipedium longifolium **Phragmipedium longifolium**
 sargentianum **Phragmipedium sargentianum**
 schlimii **Phragmipedium schlimii**
 schomburgkianum **Phragmipedium klotzscheanum**
Serapias excavata **Serapias lingua**
 gigantea **Epipactis gigantea**
 mauretanica **Serapias lingua**
 oxyglottis **Serapias lingua**
 palustris **Epipactis palustris**

speciosa **Stenorrhynchus speciosus**
stenopetala **Serapias lingua**
Serrastylis modesta **Macradenia brassavolae**
Sigmatostalix radicans **Ornithophora radicans**
Sobralia mandonii **Sobralia dichotoma**
Sophronitis hoffmannseggii **Sophronitis cernua**
isopetala **Sophronitis cernua**
militaris **Sophronitis coccinea**
modesta **Sophronitis cernua**
nutans **Sophronitis cernua**
violacea **Sophronitella violacea**
Spathoglottis lilacina **Spathoglottis plicata**
Specklinia atropurpurea **Zootrophion atropurpureum**
ciliaris **Pleurothallis ciliaris**
graminea **Sigmatostalix graminea**
Spiranthes acaulis **Sarcoglottis acaulis**
australis **Spiranthes sinensis**
constricta **Spiranthes cernua**
elata **Cyclopogon elatus**
maculata **Pelexia maculata**
neocaledonica **Spiranthes sinensis**
orchioides **Stenorrhynchus lanceolatus**
picta **Sarcoglottis acaulis**
preslii **Cyclopogon elatus**
sceptrodes **Sarcoglottis sceptrodes**
speciosa **Sarcoglottis acaulis**
speciosus **Stenorrhynchus speciosus**
strateumatica **Zeuxine strateumatica**
variegata **Cyclopogon elatus**
Stanhopea aurea **Stanhopea wardii**
bucephalus **Stanhopea oculata**
devoniana **Stanhopea hernandezii**
expansa **Stanhopea tigrina**
guttata **Stanhopea oculata**
rodigasiana **Embreea rodigasiana**
symbiformis **Stanhopea oculata**
venusta **Stanhopea wardii**
Stauritis violacea **Phalaenopsis violacea**
Stauroglottis equestris **Phalaenopsis equestris**
Stauropsis fasciata **Staurochilus fasciatus**
lissochiloides **Vandopsis lissochiloides**
parishii **Hygrochilus parishii**
philippinensis **Trichoglottis philippinensis**
Stelis endresii **Stelis argentata**
herzogii **Stelis aprica**
heylindiana **Stelis argentata**
huebneri **Stelis argentata**
littalis **Stelis argentata**
parvibracteata **Stelis argentata**
tubatus **Physosiphon tubatus**
yauaperyensis **Stelis argentata**
Stenocoryne **Bifrenaria**
Stenoglottis zambesiaca **Stenoglottis fimbriata**
Stenorrhychium **Stenorrhynchus**
Stenorrhynchus guatemalensis **Stenorrhynchus lanceolatus**
orchioides **Stenorrhynchus lanceolatus**
Sunipia paleacea **Sunipia cirrhata**
Synadena amabilis **Phalaenopsis amabilis**

Tainia cordifolia **Mischobulbum cordifolium**
siamensis **Tainia hookeriana**
Telipogon angustifolius **Telipogon nervosus**
biolleyi **Telipogon bruchmuelleri**
endresianum **Telipogon bruchmuelleri**
hoppii **Telipogon nervosus**
schmidtchenii **Telipogon bruchmuelleri**

steyermarkii **Telipogon nervosus**
wallisii **Telipogon bruchmuelleri**
Telopogon **Telipogon**
Tetramicra bicolor **Leptotes bicolor**
elegans **Tetramicra canaliculata**
rigida **Tetramicra canaliculata**
Tetrapeltis **Otochilus**
fragrans **Otochilus porrectus**
Teuscheria venezuelana **Teuscheria wageneri**
Thecostele elmeri **Thecostele alata**
maculosa **Thecostele alata**
maingayi **Thecopus maingayi**
poilanei **Thecostele alata**
quinquefida **Thecopus maingayi**
wrayi **Thecostele alata**
zollingeri **Thecostele alata**
Thelypogon **Telipogon**
Theodorea gomezoides **Rodrigueziella gomezoides**
Thonealdsenia speciosa **Chysis bractescens**
Thrixspermum arachnites **Thrixspermum centipeda**
luniferum **Chiloschista lunifera**
platystachys **Thrixspermum centipeda**
serraeformis **Thrixspermum centipeda**
Todaroa **Campylocentrum**
Tradescantia nervosa **Telipogon nervosus**
Triaristella reichenbachii **Trisetella triaristella**
Triaristellina triaristella **Trisetella triaristella**
Tribrachia purpurea **Bulbophyllum careyanum**
Trichocentrum albopurpureum **Trichocentrum albococcineum**
amazonicum **Trichocentrum albo-coccineum**
Trichoceros armillatus **Trichoceros antennifer**
muscifera **Trichoceros antennifer**
parviflorus **Trichoceros antennifer**
Trichoglottis dawsonianus **Staurochilus dawsonianus**
difformis **Ornithochilus difformis**
fasciata **Staurochilus fasciatus**
multiloba **Staurochilus dawsonianus**
pallens **Phalaenopsis pallens**
Trichopilia candida **Trichopilia fragrans**
coccinea **Trichopilia marginata**
crispa **Trichopilia marginata**
dasyandra **Cischweinfia dasyandra**
kienastiana **Trichopilia suavis**
lehmannii **Trichopilia fragrans**
lepida **Trichopilia marginata**
subulata **Leucohyle subulata**
wagneri **Trichopilia fragrans**
Trichosma suavis **Eria coronaria**
Trichotosia pyrrhotricha **Trichotosia ferox**
Tridachne **Notylia**
Tridactyle fimbriata **Tridactyle bicaudata**
Trigonanthe **Dryadella**
Trigonidium monophyllum **Neocogniauxia monophylla**
ringens **Mormolyca ringens**
seemanii **Trigonidium egertonianum**
Tropianthus **Aspasia**

Uncifera albiflora **Smitinandia micrantha**
Uropedium lindenii = **Pragmipedium lindenii**

Vanda alpina **Trudelia alpina**
amesiana **Holcoglossum amesianum**
batemanii **Vandopsis lissochiloides**
cristata **Trudelia cristata**
densiflora **Rhynchostylis gigantea**
hookeriana **Papilionanthe hookerianum**
kimballiana **Holcoglossum kimballianum**

longifolia **Acampe rigida**
lowii **Dimorphorchis lowii**
multiflora **Acampe rigida**
parishii **Hygrochilus parishii**
pumila **Trudelia pumila**
roxburghii **Vanda tessellata**
sanderiana **Euanthe sanderiana**
storiei **Renanthera storiei**
suaveolens **Vanda tricolor**
suavis **Vanda tricolor**
sulingii **Armodorum sulingii**
teres **Papilionanthe teres**
tesselloides **Vanda tessellata**
Vandopsis leytensis **Staurochilus fasciatus**
lowii **Dimorphorchis lowii**
parishii **Hygrochilus parishii**
Vanilla fragrans **Vanilla planifolia**
grandiflora **Vanilla pompona**
surinamensis **Vanilla pompona**

Wailesia picta **Dipodium pictum**
Waluewa pulchella **Oncidium waluewa**
Warmingia loefgrenii **Warmingia eugenii**
Warrea cinerea **Warreella cyanea**
cyanea **Warreella cyanea**
discolor **Cochleanthes discolor**
medellinensis **Warreella cyanea**
tricolor **Warrea warreana**
Warscewiczella **Chondrorhyncha**
aromatica **Cochleanthes aromatica**
discolor **Cochleanthes discolor**
wendlandii **Cochleanthes aromatica**

Xaritonia **Tolumnia**
Xiphosium acuminatum **Eria carinata**
Xylobium carnosum **Xylobium variegatum**
scabrilingue **Xylobium variegatum**
squalens **Xylobium variegatum**
gracile **Xylobium leontoglossum**

Ypsilopus graminifolius **Ypsilopus longifolius**

Zeuxine rupicola **Zeuxine strateumatica**
sulcata **Zeuxine strateumatica**
Zosterostylis arachnites **Cryptostylis arachnites**
Zygoglossum **Bulbophyllum**
Zygopetalum africanum **Lemboglossum bictoniense**
aromaticum **Cochleanthes aromatica**
binottii **Neoescobaria brevis**
bolivianum **Zygopetalum intermedium**
burtii **Huntleya meleagris**
cerinum **Pescatorea cerina**
coeleste **Bollea coelestis**
discolor **Cochleanthes discolor**
gramineum **Kefersteinia graminea**
grandiflorum **Mendoncella grandiflora**
jugosum **Pabstia jugosa**
lindeniae **Zygosepalum lindeniae**
microtos **Zygopetalum crinitum**
murrayanum **Neoescobaria brevis**
pubescens **Zygopetalum crinitum**
rhombilabium **Huntleya heteroclita**
rostratum **Zygosepalum labiosum**
stenochilum **Zygopetalum crinitum**
trinitatis **Chaubardia surinamensis**
wendlandii **Cochleanthes aromatica**
xanthinum **Promenaea xanthina**
Zygosepalum rostratum **Zygosepalum labiosum**

Index of Related Species

This index is made up of those species mentioned only in the Closely Related Species sections of the text. All the species described in full are arranged in Part II of the book in alphabetical order.